CAPITAL MARKETS
AND INSTITUTIONS:

A GLOBAL VIEW

CAPITAL MARKETS AND INSTITUTIONS:

A GLOBAL VIEW

LINDA ALLEN

Baruch College, City University of New York

WILEY

JOHN WILEY & SONS, INC.

NEW YORK • CHICHESTER • WEINHEIM • BRISBANE • SINGAPORE • TORONTO

Cover Art	Telegraph Colour Library/FPG International
Acquisitons Editor	Whitney Blake
Marketing Managers	Karen Allman, Wendy Goldner
Production Manager	Charlotte Hyland
Text Designer	Lynn Rogan
Cover Designer	Madelyn Lesure
Assistant Manufacturing Manager	Mark Cirillo
Outside Production Manager	Suzanne Ingrao
Illustration Coordinator	Anna Melhorne

This book was set in Adobe Garamond, and printed and bound by Donnelley/Willard. The cover was printed by Phoenix Color.

Recognizing the importance of preserving what has been written, it is a policy of John Wiley & Sons, Inc. to have books of enduring value published in the United States printed on acid-free paper, and we exert our best efforts to that end.

ISBN: 0-471-130494
Printed in the United States of America
10 9 8 7 6 5 4 3 2 1

Linda Allen is a Professor of Finance at Baruch College of the City University of New York. Professor Allen received her Ph.D. from New York University in 1984 and has taught both undergraduate and graduate level courses in finance, investments, financial intermediation, and capital markets. She has served as a Research Fellow at the Salomon Center for the Study of Financial Institutions at NYU, as well as conducted executive education programs at financial institutions in New York and abroad. She is an Associate Editor of the *Journal of Banking and Finance* and on the Board of Advisors of *The Financier*. She has a published widely, with articles appearing in such journals as the *Journal of Business*, the *Journal of Money, Credit, and Banking*, the *Journal of Financial and Quantitative Analysis*, the *Journal of Banking and Finance*, the *Journal of International Business Studies*, and the *Journal of Futures of Markets*.

PREFACE

When I was growing up, my mother used to tell my brother, sister, and me the bedtime story of the "Grasshopper and the Ant" in French. Unfortunately, none of us understood French, which is why the story accomplished its short term goal of putting us all to sleep. When I had children, I followed in the family tradition and searched around for an equally incomprehensible bedtime story to tell my own sons. Not speaking French, I started telling my sons about the principles of finance. My stories turned out to be as incomprehensible as my mother's and accomplished the same short term goal!

This book is an attempt to make finance less incomprehensible. The stories of finance deal with people making decisions that they believe to be in their own self-interest; sort of like the grasshopper's decision to play, while the ant worked all day. In the fable, the grasshopper and the ant have different attitudes toward risk and the timing of cash flows. These two basic concepts—risk and the timing of cash flows—are the motivating forces that drive all financial innovation undertaken by financial intermediaries. In this book, we examine how financial institutions provide risk shifting and cash flow timing services to their customers using financial markets.

This book seeks to integrate financial markets with financial institutions. We take the approach that one cannot understand financial markets without understanding the financial institutions that shape them. Financial institutions both: (1) provide access to standardized financial instruments traded on global financial markets; and (2) offer customized services tailored to the risk and cash management goals of commercial, consumer, and institutional clients.

The paradigm guiding this book is that while the financial institution provides the laboratory to develop techniques to manage the risk exposure of the positions of both the institution and its customers, financial markets disseminate these techniques by trading financial securities. Financial institutions innovate financial products to manage risk and to adjust the timing of cash flows. Once successful, financial innovations are then standardized and disseminated via financial markets.

In the finance literature, the word innovation often connotes an unanticipated perturbation of a financial market. In the context of this book, the word refers to a financial invention. These two meanings are not incongruous since new financial products typically are engineered to respond to a perceived change in some aspect of financial market volatility. It is this concept of financial innovation in response to either market-driven or regulatory changes in the financial environment that is the focus of the view of financial intermediation expounded in this book. Since this process is global in scope, international examples are ubiquitous throughout the text. For example, the chapter on central banks describes and compares the U.S. Federal Reserve, the Bundesbank, the Bank of Japan, and the Bank of England, as well as the IMF, the BIS, and the World Bank.

Although we cover some rather advanced concepts in finance, each topic begins with a common sense, intuitive description of the relevant basic financial principle. We introduce each financial market with a historical description of the forces that led to the market's development. Thus, the range of possible academic applications is quite broad—from a basic investments survey course to an advanced elective in financial markets and institutions, and the level is appropriate for either BBA or MBA courses. The end of chapter questions are highly quantitative in order to encourage the student to replicate the analytics in each chapter. Since the entire book, as well as all Ancillary Materials, is written by a single author, the material speaks with a single voice—within each chapter, across chapters, in the Test Bank, and in the Instructor's Manual. PowerPoint presentations and a computerized test bank are also available.

How to Use the Book

The book is divided roughly into two parts. The first (consisting of Chapters 1-9) is the "tools" section in which the reader develops the analytical tools needed in the second part of the book (Chapters 10-21), which consists of a comprehensive survey of financial market instruments. The twelve market chapters (Chapters 10-21) are free standing and can be used as independent modules to adjust coverage as desired.

At the end of each topic grouping, a short checklist, called a *Border Crossing*, supplies the reader with concepts that will be necessary to proceed further. The border crossings also state where each topic can be found so that the reader can refer back to the appropriate pages for a refresher before resuming the journey. Within each chapter, a *Checkpoint* list of questions tests the reader's mastery of the material. Readers can self test their understanding of the material by using the *Checkpoints* interspersed throughout each chapter. New terms are presented in bold face and defined in the margin, as well as tabulated in the index and glossary at the end of the text.

The book's modular format offers maximum flexibility. There are four clearly delineated, free standing sections in most chapters that can be used to fine tune the coverage of each topic (for example, more or less quantitative; more or less institutional).

* *Practitioner's Primer.* For highly quantitative BBA or MBA courses, these sections add institutional detail to the basic coverage.

* *Calculation Complications.* For highly quantitative BBA or MBA courses, these sections add more mathematical rigor to the basic coverage.

* *Case Study.* For those who use the case study method, the case studies are simulations of realistic situations constructed to illustrate the chapter's concepts.

* *Timely Topics.* Feature real world applications of the concepts using newspaper accounts of recent financial events.

Acknowledgments

My heartfelt gratitude goes to Dina Naples for her excellent research assistance. Powerpoint transparencies were prepared by Dina Naples and Ahmet Karagozoglu. I'd also like to thank many friends and colleagues who acted as reviewers and advisors: Robert Eisenbeis (Federal Reserve Bank of Atlanta), Elyas Elyasiani (Temple University), Mark Flannery (University of Florida), Jennifer Foo (Stetson University), Donald Fraser (Texas A & M), Erika Gilbert (Illinois State University), Lawrence Goldberg (University of Miami), Diana Hancock (Board of Governors, Federal Reserve), Chris Hessel (Baruch College–CUNY), George Kanatas (Rice University), Gary Koppenhaver (Iowa State University), Steve Malin (Federal Reserve Bank of New York), Loretta Mester (Federal Reserve Bank of Philadelphia), Anoop Rai (Hofstra University), Ajay Samat (Western Michigan University), Tony Saunders (New York University), Lemma Senbert (University of Maryland), and Ingo Walter (New York University).

CONTENTS

➤ Chapter 8   Computing Foreign Exchange Rates and Risk Exposure   241

CAPITAL MARKETS AND INSTITUTIONS:

A GLOBAL VIEW

CHAPTER 1

FINANCE AND YOU

"If there's no money in poetry, neither is there poetry in money."—Robert Graves, speech at London School of Economics, Dec. 6, 1963, in *Mammon and Black Goddess* (1965), p. 3.

Learning Objectives

- To examine the two goals of all financial activity: cash flow transfers across time and risk transfer.

- To distinguish between Funds Deficit and Funds Surplus Units.

- To derive the efficient frontier in order to maximize return for any possible level of risk.

➤ Introduction

You use finance in ways you probably don't realize. In fact, if you are currently reading this book as an academic assignment, then you can be considered an investor. By pursuing your education, you are accepting a subsistence standard of living with the expectation that you will earn a higher salary upon graduation. In other words, you are shifting some of your current potential income into the future so as to increase your lifetime standard of living. We therefore say that you are investing in **human capital**, the knowledge and expertise that makes you a more productive worker.

human capital: knowledge and expertise that makes a person a more productive worker.

You might also be borrowing against that investment in human capital. If you have a student loan to finance your education, then you are shifting some of that higher future income that you expect into the present. So you can invest and borrow at the same time. When you *invest*, you transfer current cash flows to the future; when you *borrow*, you transfer future cash flows to the present. These cash flow transfers across time are one of the two primary goals of all financial activity and what we mean when we refer to **intertemporal cash flow shifting**.

intertemporal cash flow shifting: cash flow transfers across time.

The second major goal of financial activity is risk transfer. Risk is uncertainty about future outcomes. Although some of us have more tolerance for risk than others, no one likes it. Financial activity allows us to reduce the overall level of risk as well as to transfer some unavoidable risk to those who are most willing to bear it. Although you may not know it, you also are a consumer of these risk transfer services. If you have an auto insurance policy, you can choose the level of your **deductible** or **copayment**. This is the amount of loss that is uninsured. If you have greater tolerance for risk, then you will have a higher deductible. If, on the other hand,

deductible or copayment: the amount of loss that is uninsured.

1

you are more risk averse, then you will be willing to pay for additional insurance to protect yourself against possible loss and your insurance policy will have a lower deductible amount.

These two goals, intertemporal cash flow shifting and risk transfer, are the building blocks of finance, driving all financial market activity as well as the role of financial intermediaries in those markets. And it all begins with you and with your desire to control your lifetime series of cash flows and risk exposures. We will analyze all of the financial activities covered in this book in terms of these financial objectives. Let's begin with intertemporal cash flow shifting services.

Checkpoint

✓

1. How does your status as a student change your human capital?

2. How can we determine an individual's attitude toward risk by examining his or her insurance investments?

➤ Intertemporal Cash Flow Shifting

In finance, as in life, timing is everything, but in finance, as opposed to life, we don't have to accept the tyranny of time. We can control time, or at least the timing of cash flows, using financial activity. Thus, whenever you make a financial decision, you must consider its repercussions through time. We all have a certain financial starting point, called an initial **endowment**. Let's see how you can control financial time.

endowment: a financial starting point.

A Student's Problem

Consider the case of a typical student—you, for instance. There are only two dates of concern to you: time period 0 before graduation and a nebulous time period 1 after graduation. Figure 1.1 shows your income before and after graduation. The curves in the figure are **indifference curves**, each of which depicts the income combinations that keep you at a constant level of satisfaction. Currently, before graduation, your income level from a part time job is $5,000. After graduation, you expect to earn $50,000. Thus, your initial endowment is equal to current spending of $5,000 and future annual spending levels of $50,000. This initial endowment (point O) gives you a certain level of satisfaction as represented by the indifference curve I_0. Clearly, you will be happier as either your current or future income increases. Higher levels of income enable you to achieve higher levels of satisfaction, as denoted by the higher indifference curves I_1, I_2, I_3, such that $I_0 < I_1 < I_2 < I_3$. Is there a way to increase your level of satisfaction and move to higher indifference curves? The answer is yes.

indifference curve: a curve depicting the income combinations that maintain a constant level of satisfaction.

Suppose your current employer offers you an opportunity to increase your level of satisfaction. Your employer offers you an immediate $10,000 raise if you agree to work for him after graduation at an annual salary of $39,000. Is this a good deal? Let's first examine the terms of the deal. Your employer is offering to shift forward in time an amount equal to $10,000 per year in exchange for a payment in the future of $11,000 (your $50,000 expected future income minus $39,000, the amount you will have to accept if you take the deal). You can view this as a loan of $10,000 with a future payment (say, next year) of $11,000. The rate of interest on the loan is $\frac{\$1,000}{10,000}$ = 10%.

budget line: a line showing all possible combinations of current and future cash flows.

Figure 1.2 shows a **budget line** through your initial endowment point O. The budget line shows all possible combinations of current and future cash flows, and denotes the tradeoff between current and future income. You can shift future income into the present by borrowing at the cost of a 10% rate of interest, denoted r. The slope of the budget line reflects that cost r and is equal to $-(1 + r)$. We draw the budget line through the initial endowment point to show all possible combinations available to you. You may stay at your initial endowment

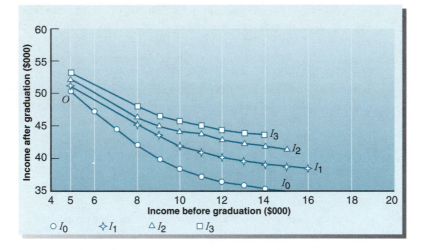

Figure 1.1   Indifference curves

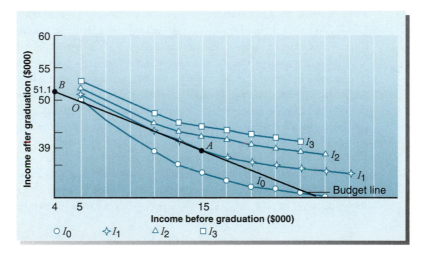

Figure 1.2   Indifference curves and the budget line

point. Alternatively, you may *save* some money, which would reduce your current spending and increase your future spending. So if you decide to save $1,000, your current spending will decline to $4,000 and your future income will increase to $51,100 = $50,000 + $1,000(1 + .10) (point B in Figure 1.2). If, on the other hand, you want to increase your current spending, then you may borrow against future income (point A in Figure 1.2). You borrow $11,000 from future income in order to receive $10,000 today. Thus, borrowing is shown as sliding down along the budget line, and investing appears as shifts up along the budget line.

But *is* your employer's offer a good deal? To answer that question we must look at your indifference curves to determine your personal preferences. Since higher indifference curves mean that you are happier, any policy that enables you to jump up to a higher indifference curve is desirable. Figure 1.2 shows that by borrowing against your future income, you can increase your satisfaction to the level represented by indifference curve I_1. So this is a good deal for you, and you should accept your employer's offer. Another way of stating this is that the benefit you derive from receiving an additional $10,000 in current cash flows exceeds the 10% cost of interest. Your **rate of time preference**—the value to you of accelerating the timing of future cash flows—exceeds 10%. Your rate of time preference is shown in the slope of your indifference curves. Each of us has a different rate of time preference. Misers, for example, tend to have lower rates than do those who live for today. When faced with the same interest rate of 10%, misers will be savers (since their rates of time preference will be lower than 10%) and the "now generation" will be borrowers (since their rates of time preference will be higher than 10%).

Point A in Figure 1.2 gives you the greatest satisfaction possible, given your initial endowment and a constant rate of interest on borrowing (and investing) of 10%. We can see that because the budget line is tangent to the indifference curve I_1. This is the highest indifference curve you can reach and still remain within the limitations of your budget as imposed by your initial endowment. You are still better off at point A than at your initial point, but can you do even better? Again, the answer is yes.

Suppose your employer comes to you with another proposition. He is concerned that you might still leave after graduation, in violation of your agreement. So, he offers you a stake in his business. If he makes you a part-owner, then he feels you will certainly devote all of your talents and energies to his business. He suggests that if you invest $4,000 in the business, you will receive a 5% stake in all of the business's profits. With expected future profits of $100,000, you can expect to earn $5,000 after graduation, for a 25% average rate of return on your investment ($\frac{\$5,000-4,000}{4,000} = .25$). Indeed, your employer offers you an entire schedule of possible investment levels with expected future outcomes (see Figure 1.3). Whereas the budget line is a straight line, with its slope equal to the constant interest rate, this is a concave curve. This is because real investments in business opportunities generally are subject to the **law of diminishing returns**. After some point, the more you invest, the less each additional investment dollar earns. Thus, the rate of return on investments is not a constant interest rate. The schedule of investment returns subject to the law of diminishing returns is the investment **production possibilities frontier**.

Is this a good deal for you? Again, the answer is yes. Figure 1.3 shows that the investment production possibilities frontier enables you to reach an even higher indifference curve, I_2, for an additional increase in your level of satisfaction. Point C, which represents a current spending level of $11,000 ($15,000 minus your $4,000 investment in the business) and a

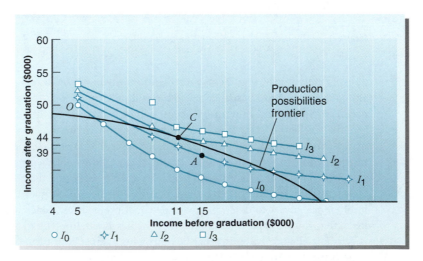

Figure 1.3   Indifference curves and the production possibilities frontier

future spending level of $44,000 ($39,000 plus your expected profits of $5,000), is tangent to indifference curve I_2.

But you can do even better than this by combining your real investment with a financial investment. That is, we can bring together Figures 1.2 and 1.3 to achieve the highest level of satisfaction possible. Figure 1.4 shows how you can make your employer a counteroffer that will maximize your satisfaction level.

First, choose the appropriate amount of investment in the business. Since you can earn 10% by simply lending money along the budget line, you will keep investing in the business until the rate of return on any additional investment equals 10%. This is the point of tangency between the budget line and the investment production possibilities frontier. Figure 1.4 shows that this point of tangency is point D with current income of $7,000 and future income of $48,500, which represents a $4,000 decline in current income from point C. This decline occurs because you are investing another $4,000 ($11,000 – $7,000) in the business for a total investment of $8,000. In keeping with the law of diminishing returns, you do not earn the same return on the $8,000 investment as you did on the first $4,000 investment. Your second $4,000 is expected to generate a return of $4,500 for a total return on your $8,000 investment in the business of $9,500 ($5,000 on the first $4,000 investment and $4,500 on the second $4,000 investment). That gives you a future income level of $48,500 after graduation ($39,000 plus $9,500).

To achieve these increases in your well-being, you have depended on your employer's suggestions. In practice, it is the role of financial intermediaries in financial markets to offer these types of opportunities. Financial intermediaries provide information and execute the transaction at low cost. Indeed, you can use a financial intermediary to improve your level of satisfaction even more, above indifference curve I_2, by borrowing, say $2,000, against some of that $48,500 future income at the rate of 10%. This increases your current income from $7,000 to $9,000, but it reduces your future income by $2,200—$2,000(1 + .10)—for a future spending level of $46,300 ($48,500 minus $2,200). This brings you to point E which is tangent to the higher indifference curve I_3. You have a plan that can maximize your satisfaction by shifting the timing of your cash flows.

Recall how far you have come from your initial endowment of $5,000 today and $50,000 after graduation that placed you on the lowest indifference curve I_0. You have borrowed a total

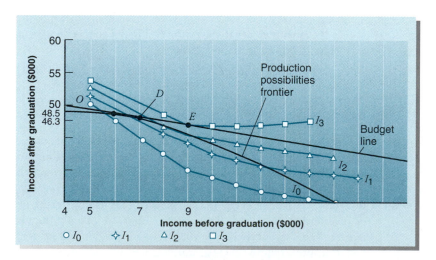

Figure 1.4   Intertemporal cash flow shifting in debt and equity markets

of $12,000 ($10,000 from your employer and $2,000 from financial intermediaries). Out of this amount, you invested $8,000 in a business. The net impact of these two actions on your current income is to increase your current spending level over your initial endowment by $4,000 ($12,000 minus $8,000) for a total income before graduation of $9,000 ($5,000 + $4,000).

What will happen after graduation? You will repay all loans at a rate of 10% for a total payment of $13,200, which is $12,000(1 + .10). However, you expect to receive a $9,500 return on your investment in the business, for a net future income of $46,300 ($50,000 initial endowment minus $13,200 plus $9,500). You've managed to increase your satisfaction both by better allocating cash flows over time and by building an investment nestegg.

Checkpoint

1. How can you reach higher and higher indifference curves? Why do you try to do so?
2. Why does the slope of your indifference curve equal your rate of time preference?
3. Why is the budget line a straight line, whereas the investment production possibilities frontier is a concave curve?

Funds Deficit and Surplus Units

In solving their intertemporal cashflow problems, some people tend to be net borrowers and others tend to be net lenders. Access to financial markets makes everyone better off, for it allows them to alter the timing of their cash flows from their initial endowment levels. Financial markets operate by facilitating this exchange between **Funds Deficit Units** and **Funds Surplus Units**. Funds Deficit Units are those individuals, corporations, and governments that spend more than they currently earn. In contrast, Funds Surplus Units are entities that spend less than they currently earn. In our example, you are a Funds Deficit Unit when it comes to the debt market, but a Funds Surplus Unit when it comes to your equity investment in the business. Funds Surplus and Deficit Units have a symbiotic relationship since they each make the other's goals possible.

> **Funds Deficit Units:** individuals, corporations, and governments that spend more than they currently earn.
> **Funds Surplus Units:** entities that spend less than they currently earn.

None of the financial activities in our examples thus far carries any risk in our example. Of course, in reality you would be exposed to a considerable amount of risk in the business returns as well as in your future earning capacity. Let's examine how you can use finance to manage your risk exposure.

Checkpoint

1. If everyone were satisfied with their initial endowment, would there be Funds Surplus Units and Funds Deficit Units?
2. How do Funds Surplus Units and Funds Deficit Units work together?

➤ Managing Risk

The many choices available to you in the world of finance are causes for both celebration and chagrin. On one hand, the more choices you have, the more opportunities you have to fulfill your personal goals. On the other, choosing becomes that much more difficult. Figure 1.5 illustrates this dilemma. Suppose that you considered every possible investment alternative in the world. Each point in Figure 1.5 represents another investment, or **portfolio**, a combination of investments in individual securities. There are literally thousands of such points, each representing another choice for your financial position. We summarize each portfolio with two descriptive statistics: (1) the expected rate of return or yield on the portfolio; and (2) the risk or uncertainty of future return on the portfolio. How can you choose from among these thousands of points of financial light?

> **portfolio:** a combination of investments in individual securities.

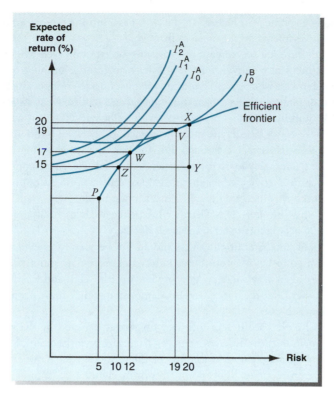

Figure 1.5 The efficient frontier without a risk free asset

The Efficient Frontier

Along with all other investors, you like to receive return, but you do not like risk. This simple observation enables us to simplify your financial investment problem. Consider two points Y and Z in Figure 1.5. Both represent investments that offer an expected annual return of 15%. But the risk level of investment Z is 10, whereas investment Y is exposed to double that amount of risk.[1] Since you, along with the rest of us, do not like risk, you will always prefer investment Z to investment Y. When one investment is always preferred to another, we say that investment Z *dominates* investment Y.

Similarly, consider investments Y and X. Both portfolios have the same amount of risk, but investment X offers a 20% expected annual rate of return, while the return on investment Y is only 15%. Again, it should be clear that investment X will dominate investment Y because everyone always prefers more return to less return, holding risk exposure constant. No rational investor will ever invest in portfolio Y when portfolios Z and X are available. We can eliminate this point from the list of investment candidates.

efficient frontier: the set of all portfolios that are not dominated by any other feasible portfolio.

Applying this reasoning to all possible portfolios shown in Figure 1.5 allows us to trace out a curve, containing all possible candidates for investment, which is called the **efficient frontier**. This is the set of all portfolios that are not dominated by any other feasible portfolio. Put another way, the efficient frontier contains all investments that maximize return for any given level of risk and, equivalently, minimize risk for any given level of return. This is the curve

---

[1] We do not discuss the scale used to measure risk and expected return until Chapter 9. At this point, it is sufficient to consider the risk and return measures as ordinal rankings where higher numbers denote more risk exposure and higher return.

beginning at point P in Figure 1.5. Point P has a unique interpretation; it is the least risky of all risky investments on the efficient frontier.

We still have not solved your investment problem, however. We may have narrowed down the investment alternatives, but we still have an infinite number of choices on the efficient frontier. How do we choose? Here again we must turn to your personal preferences as illustrated by the indifference curves shown in Figure 1.5. As before, we draw each indifference curve to show all combinations that provide you with a single level of satisfaction. Higher indifference curves ($I_2 > I_1 > I_0$) denote greater satisfaction. But the indifference curves look different from those in Figures 1.1 through 1.4, for now we are choosing combinations of risk and return that stabilize your satisfaction level. Earlier, we chose combinations of current and future income that yielded a constant level of satisfaction. As opposed to current and future income, both of which are desirable, risk is undesirable. Thus, satisfaction increases as return increases and risk *decreases*. That is why higher levels of indifference curves contain higher levels of expected return and lower levels of risk.

The booming gambling business should not be viewed as evidence that people like risk. When you go to Las Vegas or buy a lottery ticket, you are purchasing entertainment, as well as risking only a very small portion of your wealth. Demand for insurance and for financial products that offer insurance benefits demonstrates that most people are risk averse in their day-to-day activities.

Each of us has a different tolerance for risk as denoted by the tradeoff between risk and return shown in the indifference curves. To maximize satisfaction, we try to get to the highest indifference curve possible by finding the point of tangency between the efficient frontier and the indifference curves. This point, shown in Figure 1.5, is point W, which represents the portfolio that maximizes investor A's satisfaction. Investor A is willing to take on a risk level of 12 in order to earn an expected rate of return of 17%. In contrast, investor B has more tolerance for risk than investor A. This is demonstrated by investor B's flatter indifference curves which require a smaller increase in expected return to compensate for additional risk. This leads investor B to choose the riskier efficient portfolio V that offers an expected return of 19% with a risk level of 19. If both investors begin with identical initial endowments that offer expected returns of 18% and risk levels of 15, then investor A will shift some risk to investor B in exchange for a 1% deduction in expected return. This will enable both investors to reach their preferred portfolios W and V.

The slope of the indifference curves therefore tells us about the individual's attitude toward risk. A flatter indifference curve denotes a less risk averse individual since that person requires a smaller increase in return as compensation for additional risk. A steeper indifference curve denotes a very risk averse individual, since that person will demand a high premium in order to be willing to take on additional levels of risk.

Checkpoint

✓

1. Contrast the shape of indifference curves between risk and return with the shape of indifference curves between current and future income.
2. What does the slope of the indifference curve between risk and return tell us?
3. What is the efficient frontier? What is an efficient portfolio?

The Risk Free Rate

Up until this point, we have considered the investors' choices in a world in which all investments had some risk exposure. Indeed, the least risky alternative, point P, still had a risk level equal to 5. In reality, however, investors can choose between risky portfolios along the

risk free: an investment that contains no risk at all.

efficient frontier and a **risk free** investment that contains no risk at all. The best example of a risk free investment is the three month U.S. Treasury bill. Because it is an obligation of the U.S. federal government, the Treasury bill presents no default risk exposure. If you hold it until maturity, you are guaranteed a certain rate of interest that is paid up front in the form of a discount from its face value. The Treasury bill's short time to maturity and the very active international market make it possible to obtain its fair market value at any point in time with very little transactions cost. Although Treasury bill returns are exposed to the risks of inflation and interest rate fluctuations, we will use the three month Treasury bill rate as our proxy for the risk free rate. Figure 1.6 shows a hypothetical risk free rate of 6% as point R_F.

How does the existence of a risk free investment improve our investment choices? As with any new alternative, the addition of a new financial asset to our analysis expands our investment opportunities. Indeed, now we have the additional choice of investing in combinations of the risk free asset and any of the risky efficient portfolios. If we draw a line through the risk free rate that is tangent to the efficient frontier, both investors can obtain a new, higher level of satisfaction. The line touches the efficient frontier at risky portfolio M. This line represents investment alternatives that dominate the efficient frontier. Let's see why. Every point on the line (except point M) lies above and to the left of the points on the efficient frontier. But that is the direction of higher and higher indifference curves since it represents higher expected returns and lower levels of risk. Every point on the line dominates every point on the efficient frontier except point M, which lies on both. Thus, our *new* efficient frontier is the line containing the risk free rate and point M.

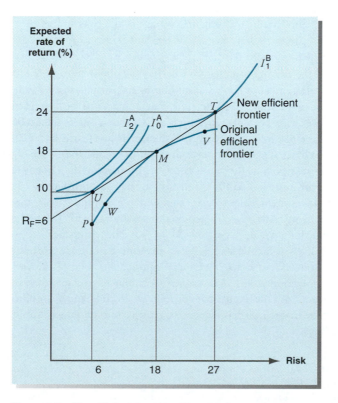

Figure 1.6   The efficient frontier with a risk free market

How can investors obtain the higher levels of satisfaction on the new efficient frontier line? To answer that question, note that the line simply represents combinations of two components: the risk free asset and portfolio M. The investor can obtain either point R_F or M by investing 100% of her money either in the risk free asset or in the risky asset M. But the investor can achieve any point between R_F and M by simply varying the amount invested in each asset. Midway between points R_F and M is represented by a 50% investment in the risk free asset and a 50% investment in the risky asset M. Three-quarters of the way toward point M is represented by a 25% investment in the risk free asset and a 75% investment in the risky asset M. All points along the line segment $R_F M$ are traced out by varying the proportion invested in the risk free asset from 100% (point R_F) to 0% (point M).

What about the points on the line to the right of M? These, too, are simply portfolio combinations of the risk free asset and the risky asset M. However, these points are traced out by increasing the amount of your investment in asset M over 100%. How can you invest more money than you have? The answer is simple: by borrowing. The points on the line to the right of point M can be reached by borrowing, at the risk free rate, in order to raise additional funds that are invested in risky portfolio M. As the proportion of your portfolio invested in M increases and the proportion invested in the risk free asset decreases (indeed, becomes negative when you borrow at the risk free rate), both the risk exposure and expected return of the portfolio increase.

Again, the choice of optimal investment portfolio depends on investor preferences. We find the investor's optimal portfolio by choosing the indifference curve tangent to the new higher efficient frontier line. The more risk averse investor A maximizes satisfaction by choosing point U, which consists of one-third of investor A's portfolio invested in the risky asset M and two-thirds in the risk free U.S. Treasury bills. What is the expected risk and return of this portfolio? Simply take the weighted average of the risks and returns of the components in the portfolio.[2] Since the risk free rate is 6% and portfolio M offers an expected return of 18%, the expected return on portfolio U is $\frac{2}{3}(6\%) + \frac{1}{3}(18\%) = 10\%$. Because the risk on point M is 18 and the risk free asset has no risk, the risk of portfolio U is $\frac{2}{3}(0) + \frac{1}{3}(18) = 6$.

In contrast, investor B takes on additional risk in exchange for additional return. Finding the highest possible indifference curve, I_1^B, that is tangent to the new efficient frontier yields optimal portfolio T. Fifty percent of investor B's original investment stake is borrowed at a rate of interest equal to the risk free rate.[3] Suppose, then, that investor B had $100,000 to invest. Optimal portfolio choice suggests that investor B **sell short** $50,000 (50% of $100,000) of the risk free asset. Short sales entail the sale of assets that the investor does not own. This raises an additional $50,000 for a total of $150,000 that is invested in portfolio M. Short sales are expressed as negative investment, since securities are sold to raise funds. The proportion invested in the risk free asset by investor B is $-.50$ (representing a short sale of 50% of the portfolio value), whereas the proportion invested in portfolio M is 1.50. Thus, investor B's expected return from portfolio T is $-.50(6\%) + 1.50(18\%) = 24\%$. Investor B's optimal portfolio T earns a much higher expected rate of return than investor A's optimal portfolio U. However, investor B is taking on considerably more risk than investor A. Portfolio T's risk exposure is: $-.50(0) + 1.50(18) = 27$ as compared with the risk of 6 for portfolio U. Both U and T are efficient choices of investment alternatives that represent different risk/return combinations available to investors with different preferences.

sell short: the sale of assets that the investor does not own.

---

[2] Since there is no interaction between returns on point M and the risk free asset, portfolio U's risk is computed as the simple average.

[3] This can be viewed as a short sale of the risk free asset. In reality, individual investors cannot borrow at the risk free rate, and the solution would depend on the rate of interest charged to investors who borrow to finance their investment portfolios.

Note that the building blocks of both optimal portfolios U and T, and indeed all efficient choices along the new efficient frontier line, are simply two assets: the risk free asset and the risky portfolio M. We have eliminated all other candidates (points P, W, V, etc.) from our investment alternatives. We need only to vary the relative proportions invested in the risk free asset and portfolio M to achieve the highest possible levels of satisfaction.

This limitation to one single risky efficient portfolio as the basis for all investment decisions is called the *Single Fund Theorem*. Point M can be thought of as a broad portfolio consisting of all risky financial securities available in the market. Individual investors can choose their own optimal levels of risk and return by varying their relative holdings of U.S. Treasury bills and this market portfolio.[4] Investors A and B have a symbiotic relationship. Investor A buys the risk free assets sold by investor B to finance portfolio T.

More risk averse investors will hold less of the risky market portfolio and more of the risk free asset, whereas less risk averse investors will do the opposite. Their choices will balance out for an average level of risk in the economy equal to the market portfolio. However, individuals can benefit by either increasing or decreasing their personal risk exposures as their preferences dictate. The risk shifting opportunities made available by financial markets make all investors better off.

Checkpoint

1. How does the existence of a risk free asset alter the efficient frontier?
2. How can you trace out points along the new efficient frontier line?
3. How can you increase the expected rate of return on your portfolio over the risk free rate?
4. How can you increase the expected rate of return on your portfolio over the return on the market portfolio?

Synthesizing Cash Flow Timing and Risk Shifting

Most risk shifting activities contain some element of altering the timing of cash flows and vice versa. For example, risk reducing activities, such as buying insurance, can be viewed as shifting cash flows to time periods in which adverse events occur (for example, when you have a car accident). You pay your insurance premiums during uneventful time periods in order to shift some cash flows (insurance claims payments) into the time periods in which you need them. Indeed, when one breaks down most financial products into their component parts, at the heart is an insurance contract that is being packaged and sold to customers.

Because all transactions contain elements of both cash flow timing and risk shifting, the distinction between them is somewhat artificial. You can consider financial transactions to be on a spectrum of purely intertemporal cash flow transfer (for example, investment in a risk free asset) to purely risk shifting transactions (for example, purchase of a lottery ticket). Most transactions fall somewhere in between these two extremes.[5] We will use this dichotomy throughout the book in order to discuss the goals of different securities transactions. Most transactions are motivated by the pursuit of either intertemporal cash flow shifting services or risk management services. It is the financial intermediaries (FIs), both public and private, that provide these services. We turn to a description of private FIs in our next chapter.

---

[4] If individuals cannot borrow at the risk free rate and must instead pay a higher rate of interest on their investment loans, then a Two-Fund Theorem results in which there are two efficient risky portfolios and the risk free asset that make up all portfolio choices.

[5] F. Allen and D. Gale (in "A Welfare Comparison of the German and U.S. Financial Systems," Wharton Working Paper 94-12, 1994) describe intergenerational risk sharing, which consists of smoothing fluctuations in returns across time. This entails both intertemporal cash flows and cross-sectional risk shifting.

Summary

In this chapter, we demonstrated the use of finance to shift both the timing of cash flows and the investor's risk exposure. Individuals pursuing their own self-interest can maximize their personal satisfaction by choosing optimal combinations of current and future income as well as optimal combinations of risk and return.

Those individuals that prefer to accelerate future expected income levels into the present are called Funds Deficit Units, whereas individuals that prefer to defer some current income for future use are Funds Surplus Units. These two units have a symbiotic relationship since each makes the other's goals possible.

Similarly, investors can choose their optimal efficient portfolios by trading off risk and expected return. Those investors who want additional return take more risk than those investors who are more risk averse. The symbiotic relationship between these investors stems from the willingness of more risk averse investors to buy the low risk assets sold by less risk averse investors.

Questions

1. Use the following investment schedule to draw a production possibilities frontier. (Be sure to calculate the future income for each level of current investment.)

Initial Investment	Expected Rate of Return	Initial Investment	Expected Rate of Return
First $1,000	25%	Sixth $1,000	14%
Second $1,000	22%	Seventh $1,000	13%
Third $1,000	20%	Eighth $1,000	11%
Fourth $1,000	18%	Ninth $1,000	7%
Fifth $1,000	15%	Tenth $1,000	5%

2a. Draw a budget line if the rate of interest on borrowing and lending is 15%.
2b. Contrast the shape of the budget line with that of the production possibilities frontier.

3a. Using the production possibilities frontier in question 1 and the budget line in question 2, what is the optimal level of real investment? Explain.
3b. If the initial endowment is current income of $100,000 and future income of $10,000, describe how you can improve the timing of cash flows. Currently, is the investor a Funds Surplus or a Funds Deficit Unit?
3c. Use your answer to part a to show the investor's choice of current and future income levels.

4. Use the following indifference curve to determine the investor's solution to the intertemporal cash flow problem in questions 1 through 4.
Satisfaction levels are constant for the following income combinations:

Current Income	Future Income
$50,000	$68,500
$75,000	$38,500
$85,000	$27,000

Use the following information to answer questions 5–10.

Risk Level	Efficient Frontier Return	Investor A Return	Investor B Return
1	8.0%	8.1%	9.75%
2	9.3	9.9	10.9
3	10.5	10.5	11.5
4	11.9	12.3	12.2
5	12.5	13.5	13.0
6	13.3	14.75	13.3
7	14.15	16.0	14.75

5a. Use the data to draw the efficient frontier.

5b. What determines each point on the efficient frontier? Why is the efficient frontier efficient?

5c. How does the efficient frontier constrain the investment choices of investors A and B?

6a. Use the information about investor A's and B's preferences to draw their indifference curves.

6b. Contrast the two investor's attitudes towards risk. Which investor is less risk averse? Explain your answer.

6c. How does the investor's attitude toward risk affect the investor's choice of a preferred portfolio from the efficient frontier?

6d. Describe investor A's optimal portfolio. Describe investor B's optimal portfolio.

7a. How does the introduction of a risk free asset earning 7.5% change the efficient frontier in question 5?

7b. The introduction of a risk free asset makes the following risk/return combinations feasible:

Risk	Return	Risk	Return
1	8.6%	5	13.0%
2	9.7	6	14.1
3	10.8	7	15.2
4	11.9		

Plot these risk/return combinations. How does their feasibility affect the efficient frontier?

7c. Describe the efficient frontier with the existence of a risk free asset. How is the new efficient frontier constructed?

7d. To what portfolio does the Single Fund Theorem apply in this example? How is it determined?

8a. Use the following indifference curves to determine investor A's and B's optimal portfolios, using the new efficient frontier in question 7.

Risk	Investor A	Investor B	Risk	Investor A	Investor B
1	8.6%	9.95%	5	13.6%	13.2%
2	10.0	11.1	6	14.9	14.5
3	10.9	11.7	7	16.1	15.2
4	12.4	12.5			

8b. Compare these indifference curves to the indifference curves in question 5. Which indifference curve offers each investor greater satisfaction?

8c. Use the indifference curves to determine each investor's optimal portfolio. What investments are chosen by each investor? (Be sure to show the proportion invested in each financial security.)

8d. Contrast the optimal portfolios in part c to the optimal portfolios in question 6. How does the introduction of a risk free asset affect the level of investor satisfaction?

9a. How does the introduction of a risk free asset affect each investor's risk exposure? (Illustrate using the scenario in question 8.)

9b. How does the introduction of a risk free asset affect the overall level of risk in the economy?

10. *Challenge Question*: What is the equation of the new efficient frontier in question 9? What is the tradeoff between risk and return along the new efficient frontier?

CHAPTER 2

PRIVATE FINANCIAL INTERMEDIARIES (FIs)

"And all these financiers, all the little gnomes in Zurich and the other financial centres about whom we keep hearing..." Harold Wilson, *Hansard*, Nov. 12, 1956, vol. 578.

Learning Objectives

- To describe private FIs.
- To study the role of FIs in our daily lives.
- To see how FIs act as financial matchmakers, bringing together the two sides of a financial transaction.
- To examine the technologies used by FIs to intermediate between these parties and to illustrate the technologies using evidence from FIs in 12 countries.

➤ Introduction

Financial intermediaries (FIs) are the professionals that guide us through our risk shifting and cash flow timing transactions in financial markets. As private, for-profit companies, they sell their expertise about financial opportunities. If you are a Funds Deficit Unit seeking sources of financing, chances are you will turn to some type of FI. If you are interested in reducing the risk of your financial activities, a FI can help you. It is the go-between that links a Funds Surplus Unit with a Funds Deficit Unit. The Funds Surplus Unit provides the money in exchange for the promise of a future investment return. The FI then is simply the matchmaker connecting those with excess funds or risk with those who want to take on additional funds or risk. Since both parties to the transaction often do not know one another, it is the FI that intermediates between them. The only product that the FI has to sell is information—information about the other side of the transaction. Private FIs can be viewed as private libraries of financial information about risk shifting and cash flow timing opportunities.

We need FIs to guide us through financial markets because the markets have become more complex and global, and so have become less accessible to the average individual, corporation, or government. If you were limited to financial transactions with only those you came in contact with on a regular basis, you would miss many potential opportunities. By casting a wide, indeed global net, the FI has information on a broad range of opportunities. The FI sells this information to its clients so that they can make more intelligent financial decisions.

Table 2.1a

A Typical Auto Manufacturing Firm ($ million)

Cash	$ 1		Accounts payable	$ 5
Accounts receivable	$ 7		Short term debt	$10
Auto inventories	$ 8		Long term debt	$10
Plant and equipment	$24		Equity	$25
Buildings and land	$10			
Total assets	$50		Total liabilities and net worth	$50

Table 2.1b

A Typical Commercial Bank ($ million)

Cash	$ 5		Deposits	$35
Financial securities	$14		Long term debt	$10
Loans	$30		Equity	$ 5
Buildings and land	$ 1			
Total assets	$50		Total liabilities and net worth	$50

➤ What Are Private FIs?

Defining private FIs is a little like defining pornography: they may be difficult to describe, but you know them when you see them! If you were asked to list companies that you would consider FIs, you would include the names of commercial banks, savings banks, thrift institutions, insurance companies, mutual funds, investment banks, and securities firms. What do all of these disparate firms have in common that makes them all FIs? To answer that question, we will examine the balance sheets, shown in Tables 2.1a and b, of two $50 million companies. One is a typical auto manufacturing company, and the other is a typical commercial bank.

Beginning with an examination of the two firms' liabilities and net worth, we find mostly financial obligations (both debt and equity) on their balance sheets. However, when examining the asset side of the balance sheets, we see that, although the auto manufacturing firm has real assets such as inventories and plant and equipment, the bank's assets are almost entirely financial. This is typical for all financial firms. Their balance sheets contain very few real, physical assets. Thus, we define **private FIs** as profit-seeking firms whose assets are predominantly financial.[1] Accordingly, all of the financial companies that you placed on your list are FIs.

private FIs: profit-seeking firms whose assets are predominantly financial.

Checkpoint

1. What distinguishes FIs from nonfinancial firms?
2. How does the structure of FIs enable them to provide cash flow timing and risk shifting services to their customers?

How Do Private FIs Intermediate in Financial Markets?

The primary difference between financial and nonfinancial firms is the predominance of financial assets on the balance sheets of FIs. How do all those financial assets get onto the balance sheets of private FIs? Just as automobile inventories are generated in the normal course of the auto company's business, so are financial assets for FIs. The normal course of business for a FI is to intermediate between Surplus Units and Deficit Units. How does the process of intermediation translate into a balance sheet replete with financial assets? The answer depends

---

[1] Throughout the book, we use the term *private FIs* to distinguish FIs motivated by profit from public FIs motivated by governmental policy goals. This definition applies even if the government owns the private FI, as long as its policies are determined chiefly by the profit motive.

on the intermediation technology used by the FI. The two intermediation technologies are (1) the broker/dealer approach and (2) asset transformation.

Broker/Dealer Operations   How does the broker/dealer approach to financial intermediation determine the makeup of the FI's balance sheet? First, let's consider broker operations. If the FI acted purely as a **broker**, bringing together buyers and sellers without acting as a principal in the transaction, then we would not expect to see *any* financial assets on the FI's balance sheet. The FI would simply connect the buyer and seller so that they could transfer the financial assets between themselves without the assets ever having to move through the FI. The broker technology is a form of financial intermediation, but it typically goes hand in hand with the dealer approach. A **dealer** makes a market in a financial security, thereby participating as a principal in the financial transaction.

Why do broker and dealer operations often go together? Suppose that a client wants to sell a thinly traded foreign stock. The FI, in its capacity as broker, searches for buyers but can find none offering fair market value. To satisfy the customer (and make some money as well), the FI may offer to buy the stock for its own account. If the offer is accepted, the trade is executed, with the FI as a principal (the buyer in this case) to the transaction. The stock is placed in the FI's inventory and appears on the balance sheet as a financial asset until it is subsequently sold, perhaps in response to another customer's order to buy.

The existence of a dealer operation often enhances the FI's ability to provide brokerage and other financial services. For example, in an **underwriting**, the FI brings to market a newly issued financial security. In doing so, the FI is required to provide assistance in pricing and structuring the financial aspects, registering and doing all the legal work for the security, as well as ultimately distributing the financial security. If the FI has a dealer operation, then some portion of the new issue may be absorbed into the FI's securities inventories. The security issuer is often reassured that the FI will do its best to ensure that the new issue is a success since it knows that the FI itself has an investment in the new issue.

Since broker/dealers facilitate the transfer of marketable securities between Deficit and Surplus Units, we would expect their balance sheets to contain mostly marketable financial securities. Marketable securities are transferred either over organized securities exchanges or directly via negotiations between buyers and sellers. In either case, the FI acts as the go-between to complete the transaction.

Asset Transformation   In a broker/dealer operation, the FI is a conduit for the issuer or seller to reach potential buyers. The FI itself is *transparent* inasmuch as the buyer can see through the FI to the original issuer of the security. The transparency of the FI is necessary for the buyer to be able to evaluate the risk/return characteristics of the financial security since the security's cash flows are ultimately paid by the issuer, not by the FI. However, the broker/dealer technology is not the only available approach to financial intermediation. If the FI in some way guarantees or alters the security's cash flows, then sometimes the buyer need not know the identity of the seller or the issuer. Indeed, the FI can place itself in between the buyer and seller by altering the characteristics of the financial security. The financial security that comes into the FI is therefore not the same as the financial security that goes out. In this case, the FI is *opaque*, for the buyer knows nothing about the original seller and the seller knows nothing about the original buyer. Both parties deal individually with the FI and need only to evaluate the risk characteristics of the FI itself. This approach to financial intermediation is called **asset transformation** because the FI creates new financial securities by selling financial securities that are different from the financial securities that it buys.

Opaque FIs that use asset transformation to intermediate between Funds Surplus Units and Funds Deficit Units borrow funds by issuing one financial security and invest those funds by

broker: a FI that brings together buyers and sellers without acting as a principal in the transaction.

dealer: a FI that makes a market in a financial security, thereby participating as a principal in the financial transaction.

underwriting: the process whereby the FI brings to market a newly issued financial security.

asset transformation: the FI's creation of new financial securities by selling financial securities that are different from the financial securities it buys.

purchasing another financial security. The two financial securities can differ by the timing of their cash flows or by their risk exposures. Figure 2.1 shows how typical FIs utilize both approaches to financial intermediation. The three FIs in the top half of the figure (brokers, dealers, and underwriters) are transparent FIs that specialize in broker/dealer operations, whereas the three FIs in the bottom half of the figure (mutual funds, banks, and insurance companies) are opaque FIs that specialize in asset transformation. Funds Deficit Units raise needed funds by issuing financial securities to the different types of FIs. The FIs, using both the broker/dealer and asset transformation technologies, sell financial securities to Funds Surplus Units to raise the funds that are passed along to the Funds Deficit Units.

Brokers, dealers, and underwriters/investment banks all sell the same financial securities to Funds Surplus Units that they purchase from Funds Deficit Units. Their entire function is to facilitate the transfer of financial securities from one party to another. They may accomplish this function by simply identifying buyers and sellers (as in a broker operation), by placing themselves in the middle of the transaction (as in the dealer operation), or by advising the issuer how best to structure the security (as in underwriting).

Asset transformers, on the other hand, alter the financial securities that they purchase from Funds Deficit Units. For example, banks purchase loans from borrowers (Funds Deficit Units), which they ultimately sell to Funds Surplus Units in the completely different form of deposits. This is considered asset transformation because the risk/return and timing of cash flows on the loans are quite different from those of the deposits. Similarly, insurance companies raise

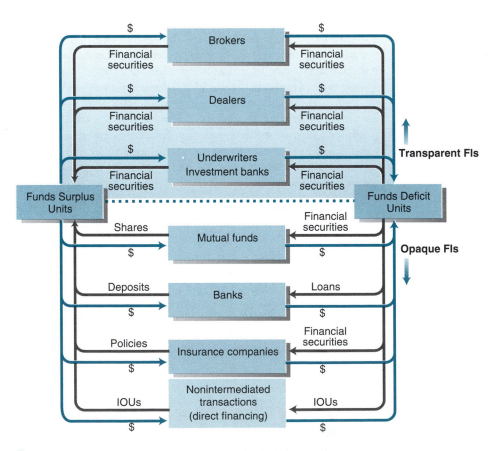

Figure 2.1

funds by selling policies but invest those funds by purchasing financial securities. Mutual funds can be viewed as *translucent* because, although they are asset transformers, Funds Surplus Units can see through them to identify the Funds Deficit Units. Thus, the mutual fund constructs a portfolio of financial securities that it resells to Funds Surplus Units in the form of mutual fund shares. Although the mutual fund share is a new financial security, its value is entirely determined by the value of the underlying financial securities in the mutual fund's portfolio. The mutual fund does not signficantly transform the risk or cash flow timing of the original securities, although it does provide the benefits of portfolio diversification to Funds Surplus Units.

A Continuum of Intermediation Technologies   Both Funds Deficit Units and Funds Surplus Units evaluate the entire range of FIs before entering into financial transactions. Thus, the six types of FIs shown in Figure 2.1 compete with one another. Indeed, the Deficit and Surplus Units compare the costs of transacting with the different types of FIs. In general, the cost of a financial transaction using the broker/dealer technology is lower than that of asset transformation. Asset transforming, opaque FIs provide additional services that broker/dealers do not. The additional transactions costs are, therefore, compensation for risk shifting and for the cash flow timing services provided by asset transformers.

Although we have presented the intermediation technologies as separate and distinct, most financial transactions have elements of both the broker/dealer and asset transformation approaches. Indeed, there is a continuum of intermediation technologies, with the broker/dealer and asset transformation approaches representing the two polar extremes. Part of the life cycle of a financial instrument is its journey through the continuum of intermediation technologies. A new type of financial security is often developed by an opaque financial intermediary that transforms existing financial securities into a new financial product with unique risk/return characteristics. If the new product is successful, other opaque FIs will imitate the innovator and many of these financial securities will be issued. When enough of these new financial securities are issued, the supply is sufficient to support the activities of transparent FIs who facilitate their exchange. A new financial market has come into being. Throughout this book, we illustrate this evolutionary approach to security design using recently innovated financial instruments, as well as some well-established instruments.

Sometimes the same financial security can be transferred using the broker/dealer and the asset transformation technologies simultaneously. Loans can be viewed as both asset transformations and broker/dealer operations. Traditional loans originated by banks are funded with bank deposits and other sources of funds that are clearly asset transformations. However, loan **securitization** uses the broker/dealer technology. Securitization is the packaging of nontraded financial securities into a newly created tradable financial security. These newly created securities are traded with the assistance of broker/dealers who bring together buyers and sellers and make markets. With the explosive growth of securitization, financial transactions that were formerly the exclusive domain of asset transformers (in this case, bank loans) are now performed by all types of FIs.

If all financial transactions passed through the continuum of intermediation technologies, then FIs would be foolish to specialize in only one approach to intermediation. Because opaque, translucent, and transparent FIs all compete to provide financial services to Deficit and Surplus Units, the lines of distinction among the six types of FIs shown in Figure 2.1 become blurred. Because all FIs, whatever their names or company charters, offer different ranges of intermediation services, we utilize a *functional*, rather than a legal, classification scheme to describe FIs throughout the world. *Timely Topics 2.1* shows how this functional approach to financial intermediation has permeated the thinking of U.S. bank regulators.

securitization: the packaging of nontraded financial securities into a newly created tradable financial security.

TIMELY TOPICS 2.1

FINANCIAL INNOVATIONS AND THE SUPERVISION OF FINANCIAL INSTITUTIONS

[I]t is increasingly difficult to distinguish the core functions of banking from the core functions of other financial intermediaries. Each of the various "types" of financial firms increasingly engages in activities traditionally the province of the others. And each of these types of financial business has as its core functions the measurement, acceptance, and management of risk.

Examples abound that demonstrate this blurring of distinctions. For instance, the economics of a typical loan syndication, including the types of risk, do not differ essentially from the economics of a best-efforts securities underwriting. . . . Except for differences imposed by law or regulation, it is difficult to identify substantive differences between a guaranteed investment contract provided by an insurance company, and a bank investment contract provided by a bank.

My list could go on. It is sufficient to say that, in my judgment, a strong case can be made that the evolution of financial technology has changed forever our ability to place financial functions in neat little boxes. . . . [A]ttempts to pigeonhole financial functions into narrowly defined roles traditionally ascribed to a particular type of financial institution would severely curtail some of the risk reduction benefits of consolidated risk management, and could reduce the overall effectiveness of firm-wide management. Enlightened functional regulation must strive to avoid such results. . . .

In conclusion, the forces shaping our banking and financial system are fundamental and on-going. Through it all, the core functions of banks and bank supervisors remain unchanged. In addition, while blurring of traditional distinctions between the institutional forms of financial intermediation makes repeal of the Glass–Steagall Act [that separates commercial from investment banking in the U.S.] ever more natural, nonstop innovation raises new challenges for both the public and private sectors.

Source: A. Greenspan, Press Release, May 1995.

Checkpoint

1. Contrast the broker/dealer and asset transformation technologies of financial intermediation.
2. Why would you expect the transactions cost of asset transformation to exceed that of broker/dealer operations?
3. Why can't broker/dealers be opaque or translucent?
4. Why must asset transformers be opaque or translucent?

➤ A Functional Classification of FIs

The legal definition of a commercial bank versus a thrift institution versus an insurance company differs from country to country as the legal system changes. Deficit and Surplus Units around the world are not concerned with legal definitions, however. They demand efficient financial intermediation services and are unconcerned about the legal identity of the FI providing those services. If you could finance your mortgage at either a bank or a mortgage broker or an

universal banking: the offering of a wide range of financial services, such as banking, insurance, securities trading, and underwriting, in one financial supermarket.

insurance company, you would investigate all three FIs and choose the best deal. Indeed, most countries (with the glaring exception of the United States) allow **universal banking**, which is the offering of a wide range of financial services, such as banking, insurance, securities trading, and underwriting, in one financial supermarket. Rather than describing the world's private FIs by legal definition, we therefore use a functional definition based on the two approaches to financial intermediation. We use our two intermediation technologies to classify the FIs into (1) broker/dealers and (2) asset transformers. The same company will usually perform both tasks. Thus, we classify each intermediation activity into one of the two categories in order to create a composite of an average broker/dealer, which can then be compared to the composite of an average asset transformer. We do this for 396 FIs from 12 countries (the United States, Canada, Germany, the United Kingdom, France, Japan, Switzerland, Spain, Italy, Sweden, Australia, and Hong Kong) using an international financial database (Standard & Poor's GLOBAL Vantage).

Summarizing the Balance Sheets of Private FIs

financial leverage: firm indebtedness as measured by the ratio of either total debt to total assets or total debt to total equity.

Table 2.2 shows that the average FI had total assets of over $60 million in 1994. The most striking aspect of the summary of the FIs' balance sheets is their high amount of **financial leverage**—that is, firm indebtedness as measured by the ratio of either total debt to total assets or total debt to total equity. In 1994 the debt to assets ratio averaged 94.6%, and the

Table 2.2

Descriptive Statistics: Private FIs from 12 Countries (End of Fiscal Year 1994)[a]

Description	Global Average ($000)	Total Assets (%)
Summarizing Private FIs' Balance Sheets		
1. Total assets	60,036	100
2. Total liabilities	56,782	94.6
3. Shareholders equity	3,113	5.2
Off-Balance Sheet Contingencies		
4. Total off-balance sheet items	158,966	229
4a. Letters of credit	315	0.5
4b. Guarantees	3,873	5.6
4c. Loan commitments	7,779	11.2
4d. Foreign currency commitments	46,443	66.9
4e. Forward/futures contracts	50,686	73.0
4f. Interest rate swaps	45,859	66.1
4g. Other off-balance sheet items	3,948	5.7
4h. Convertible debt	63	0.1
Summarizing Private FIs' Income Statements		
5. Net income	236	0.4
6. Revenue	5,326	8.9
7. Total expenses	4,954	8.3
8. Interest expenses	2,070	3.4

[a]The data are averaged over all 396 FIs reporting these items. The end of the fiscal year is March 31 in Japan; October 31 in Canada; and December 31 in the rest of the countries. The balance sheets were evaluated as of the last day of the country's fiscal year. Data are provided in local currencies, which are converted to U.S. dollar values using the exchange rate prevailing on the last day of the fiscal year. All data are presented for year-end 1994. Only the largest 300 banks report data for off-balance sheet items.

Source: Standard & Poor's GLOBAL Vantage database.

Table
2.3

International Comparisons and Descriptive Statistics: Private FIs from 12 Countries (End of Fiscal Year 1994)[a]

	USA		Canada		Germany		U.K.		France		Japan	
	$000	%	$000	%	$000	%	$000	%	$000	%	$000	%
No. of FIs	99		27		31		40		31		57	
Summarizing Private FIs' Balance Sheets												
1.	48,654		26,827		88,336		53,483		52,223		153,582	
2.	44,995	92.5	25,073	93.5	85,139	96.4	50,671	94.7	49,352	94.5	147,104	95.8
3.	3,619	7.4	1,522	5.7	3,014	3.4	2,664	5.0	2,274	4.4	6,409	4.2
Off-Balance Sheet Contingencies												
4.	259,383	453	138,037	384	14,292	13.0	334,337	436	371,799	573	39,616	22.7
4a.	443	0.8	173	0.5	690	0.6	511	0.7	0	0	48	0
4b.	8,034	14.0	1,455	4.0	4,193	3.8	3,728	4.9	6,579	10.1	649	0.4
4c.	15,964	27.9	13,390	37.2	9,363	8.5	9,243	12.0	7,329	11.3	541	0.3
4d.	69,595	122	43,334	121	1	0	108,196	141	100,053	154	9,521	5.4
4e.	73,301	128	24,574	68.3	0	0	119,077	155	110,703	17	17,239	9.9
4f.	86,912	152	25,074	69.7	0	0	92,837	121	141,429	218	11,253	6.4
4g.	5,120	8.9	29,986	83.4	46	0	704	0.9	5,654	8.7	103	0.1
4h.	14	0	52	0.1	0	0	40	0	51	0.1	262	0.2
Summarizing Private FIs' Income Statements												
5.	482	1.0	159	0.6	165	0.2	441	0.8	54	0.1	49	0
6.	5,430	11.2	2,557	9.5	8,728	9.9	5,312	9.9	6,436	12.3	8,987	5.9
7.	4,725	9.7	2,286	8.5	8,395	9.5	4,722	8.8	6,241	12.0	8,757	5.7
8.	1,343	2.8	820	3.1	3,821	4.3	1,592	3.0	2,357	4.5	5,008	3.3

[a]The data are averaged over all 396 FIs reporting these items. % are percentages of total assets. Item numbers in the first column are defined in Table 2.2.

Source: Standard & Poor's GLOBAL Vantage database.

debt to equity ratio was over 18. In a nonfinancial firm, these levels of leverage would be a signal of impending bankruptcy. For FIs, however, a high amount of leverage is normal because the FIs' function is to intermediate between Funds Deficit Units and Funds Surplus Units. To accomplish this intermediation, the FI must borrow from Funds Surplus Units in order to lend to Funds Deficit Units. By definition, this requires a high amount of leverage.[2]

When examining the FIs by country (see Table 2.3), we see that most countries' FIs exhibit the same high degree of financial leverage. FIs in 11 out of the 12 countries show average leverage ratios exceeding 90%, with resulting equity levels below 10% of assets. The one exception is Hong Kong, with its abnormally low average leverage of 75.5% and equity of 23.9% of total assets. This reflects the recent rapid growth of FIs in Hong Kong as well as uncertainty about the future as the 1997 deadline for absorption into China approaches. *Timely Topics 2.2* describes some of the upheavals in the Hong Kong market.

---

[2] However, it is not financially prudent for FIs to take on unlimited amounts of leverage. In Chapter 5, we see how regulators impose limitations on the amount of financial leverage by imposing minimum capital requirements.

Switzerland		Spain		Italy		Sweden		Australia		Hong Kong	
$000	%	$000	%	$000	%	$000	%	$000	%	$000	%
34		12		36		15		9		5	
36,496		35,990		14,631		14,046		37,737		14,049	
34,021	93.2	33,874	94.1	13,633	93.2	13,078	93.1	34,836	92.3	10,604	75.5
2,392	6.6	1,778	4.9	900	6.2	952	6.8	2,874	7.6	3,353	23.9
191,608	424	43,611	112	16,690	43.4	22,669	161	200,123	420	1,138	8.1
600	1.4	36	0.1	73	0.4	249	1.8	627	1.3	108	0.8
2,289	5.3	1,884	4.8	1,632	9.8	848	6.0	1,913	4.0	925	6.6
2,873	6.6	5,273	13.5	375	2.3	451	3.2	10,147	21.3	0	0
58,889	136	17,635	45.1	3,675	22.0	11,795	84.0	90,195	189	27	0.2
100,070	231	70,236	26.2	1,248	7.5	4,544	32.4	60,295	126	0	0
17,561	40.6	7,728	19.8	0	0	4,684	33.3	36,534	76.6	0	0
1,265	2.9	805	2.1	174	1.0	20	0.1	413	0.9	0	0
5	0	13	0	66	0.4	79	0.6	0	0	79	5.6
158	0.4	204	0.6	−6	−0.1	92	0.7	382	1.0	332	2.4
3,801	10.4	3,448	9.6	1,613	11.0	1,910	13.6	3,292	8.7	931	6.6
3,662	10.0	3,198	8.9	1,584	10.8	1,825	13.0	2,774	7.4	588	4.2
1,154	3.2	1,868	5.2	843	5.8	807	5.7	1,241	3.3	379	2.7

TIMELY TOPICS 2.2

INSIDE THE WORLD'S MOST PROFITABLE BANK: THE HONGKONG AND SHANGHAI BANKING CORPORATION

If money talks, then the local currency here says it all. Four out of every five bills in Hong Kong bear the image of the erector set-style headquarters of the Hongkong and Shanghai Bank, the most powerful financial presence in this British colony and by far, the most visible and influential bank in Asia.

Besides minting Hong Kong dollars, the bank has spent much of the last century swaggering through China and across Asia. It has supported trading throughout the region for more than a century. . . . And it has grown spectacularly in the last decade, benefiting from the rapid advance of Asia's economies and using its Asian profits to pay for the bank's moves into the Middle East, Europe, and North America. . . .

The Hong Kong bank's London-based parent company, known as HSBC Holdings Plc. is quite simply "the most profitable bank in the world," observes Karen Udovenya, a vice president with Morgan Stanley Asia.

But today, the financial juggernaut may be losing momentum. Throughout its Asian stronghold, the Hong Kong bank faces a growing crop of newly aggressive rivals—banks from the United States, other Asian countries, even mainland China. In Hong Kong, the bank has the uncertainty of what, if any, changes the Communist landlords will make in the colony's vibrant capitalist economy. . . .

Though it has offices in 65 countries, the bank still earns two thirds of its profits in tiny Hong Kong. . . . What's more, the bank's staid culture—an old boy network dominated by Englishmen and Scots—is under assault. Evolved from the bank's colonial heritage, it worked well when banking profits depended on long standing relationships with clients, government connections and limited competition. But competition is much more open today, as banks are increasingly becoming fast-paced traders in the global money markets. . . .

The bank certainly does not want to see change in Hong Kong. It is one of the coziest banking environments on earth, especially for the Hongkong and Shanghai Bank. Because the bank's parent also owns 61.48 percent of its next largest competitor in Hong Kong, the Hang Seng Bank Ltd., it jointly controls 365 bank branches in Hong Kong, and enjoys 60 percent of the market as measured by deposits, analysts estimate.

And the market is a banker's dream of high profit margins and low taxes. Corporate taxes here are just 16.5 percent, and deposit accounts yield less than the rate of inflation, largely because of a government-sanctioned banking cartel. That means that banks can get away with charging 7 or 8 percent interest on funds that only cost them 1 or 2 percent.

Still, there is no guarantee that the bank's lucrative arrangement will continue. And the political uncertainty of China taking over the colony may be less a threat than the changes in local banking that are being wrought by market forces. . . . Hong Kong's effective negative interest rates are already pinching deposit growth, chasing funds into the stock market and into real estate [and explaining Hong Kong's relatively low leverage ratios, shown in Table 2.3]. An easing of growth in the bank's high-margin business of deposit-taking and lending comes at a time when the Hongkong and Shanghai Bank's earnings from foreign exchange and bond trading operations are down.

Source: E. Gargan, *New York Times*, August 21, 1994, Section 3, page 1.6.

Off-Balance Sheet Activity

off-balance sheet items: contingencies that, under certain circumstances, may eventually become balance sheet items, but since they require no current cash flows, do not appear on the balance sheet.

We are accustomed to evaluating companies by studying their balance sheets, and in the remainder of this chapter we will examine the FIs' balance sheets in depth. First, however, it is important to remember that some very significant activities do not appear on the balance sheet. These **off-balance sheet items** are contingencies that, under certain circumstances, may eventually become balance sheet items, but since they require no current cash flows, do not appear on the balance sheet. Table 2.2 demonstrates that the total of these off-balance sheet items is more than double (229%) the FIs' total balance sheet assets. There is a shadow balance sheet of possible claims and commitments that bind the FI.

The off-balance sheet activity of FIs is growing rapidly as FIs recognize the opportunities that these contingent securities provide for risk shifting and cash flow timing services.[3] Table 2.2 shows that the largest components of off-balance sheet items are foreign currency commitments (averaging 66.9% of total assets), forward/futures contracts (averaging 73.0% of total assets), and interest rate swaps (averaging 66.1% of total assets). These securities are examples of **derivatives**, so-named because their value is derived from the value of other financial securities. For example, the value of foreign currency commitments depends on exchange rates, and the values of both forward/futures and interest rate swaps are determined by the price of each contract's underlying security.

derivatives: securities whose value is derived from the value of other financial securities.

Not all FIs around the world have embraced these derivatives. Table 2.3 shows that FIs in Germany, Japan, Italy, and Hong Kong have been slow to participate in these markets. The most active participants are FIs in France (with total off-balance sheet activity averaging 573% of total assets), the United States (453% of total assets), the United Kingdom (436% of total assets), Switzerland (424% of total assets), and Australia (420% of total assets).

Summarizing the Income Statements of Private FIs

The average FI earned a rate of return on assets of 0.4% in 1994 (Table 2.2). Revenue averaged 8.9% and total expenses 8.3% of total assets. Interest expenses averaged 3.4%, leaving noninterest expenses of 4.9% of total assets. Financial intermediation is a high-overhead, low-profit margin enterprise.

FI profitability varied considerably around the world. Table 2.3 shows that the most profitable FIs in 1994 were to be found in Hong Kong (with a return on assets of 2.4%), with the United States, Australia, and the United Kingdom distant followers at profitability rates of 1.0%, 1.0%, and 0.8%, respectively. The least profitable FIs were in Italy (with an average net loss of 0.1% of assets), Japan (0% return on assets), France (0.1%), and Germany (0.2%). The poor financial performance of these countries reflects the economic upheavals they have experienced in recent years, ranging from the bursting of the speculative land price bubble in Japan to the unification of East and West Germany to political instability in Italy.

Interest expenses tended to be in the range of 2% to 4% of total assets in all countries except in Spain, Italy, and Sweden where interest expenses were higher. Hong Kong and the United States had significantly lower levels of interest expenses (2.7% and 2.8%, respectively). Subtracting interest expenses (item 8) from total expenses (item 7) to derive noninterest expenses shows that the world's most efficient (with the lowest noninterest costs) FIs were in Hong Kong and Japan (with noninterest expenses of 1.5% and 2.4% of assets, respectively). The most inefficient FIs had the highest noninterest expenses (7.5%, 7.3%, 6.9%, and 6.8% of assets, respectively), and these were in France, Sweden, the United States, Switzerland, and the United Kingdom.

Sources of Funds

The interest expenses of FIs represent the cost of borrowing from Funds Surplus Units in order to lend to Funds Deficit Units. Table 2.4 divides the funds sources into two groups of FI liabilities, based on the intermediation technology used. The broker/dealer sources of funds are market-based, whereas the asset transformer sources are more dependent on the FI's customer relationships.

The largest source of funds available to broker/dealers is long term debt, which accounts for an average of 60.8% of the total. However, pure brokerage operations do not appear on the balance sheet. Thus, a transaction in which the FI buys a security from one client in order to simultaneously resell it to another will not be included on the balance sheet since the FI never takes delivery of the security.

FIs also rely on other FIs to finance their portfolios. The first two categories (interbank deposits and Federal Funds and commercial paper) consist mostly of one FI lending to

---

[3] We describe each of these instruments at length in the derivatives section of this book.

FIs' Sources of Funds (End of Fiscal Year 1994)[a]

Liability Description	Global Average ($000)	Total Assets (%)
Broker/Dealers		
1. Interbank deposits	4,791	34.8
2. Federal funds and commercial paper	577	4.2
3. Long term debt	8,383	60.8
4. Foreign exchange liabilities	36	0.3
5. Total market sources of funds	13,788	100
Asset Transformers		
6. Insurance policy reserves	5,330	13.4
7. Bank deposits	27,041	68.0
8. Reinsurance liabilities	44	0.1
9. Other borrowings	6,696	16.9
10. Reserves	626	1.6
11. Total customer sources of funds	39,738	100

[a]The data are averaged over all 396 FIs reporting these items.

Source: Standard & Poor's GLOBAL Vantage database.

International Comparisons: FIs' Sources of Funds (End of Fiscal Year 1994)[a]

Liability Description	USA $000	%	Canada $000	%	Germany $000	%	U.K. $000	%	France $000	%	Japan $000	%
No. of FIs	99		27		31		40		31		57	
Broker/Dealers												
1.	66	0.8	2,338	71.2	21,446	46.8	6,640	59.5	10,997	48.4	14	0.1
2.	2,138	27.2	4	0.1	0	0	64	0.6	35	0.2	89	0.5
3.	5,647	71.9	941	28.7	24,342	53.2	4,453	39.9	11,712	51.5	19,219	98.4
4.	0	0	0	0	0	0	0	0	0	0	201	1.0
5.	7,851		3,282		45,788		11,157		22,744		19,523	
Asset Transformers												
6.	6,957	20.4	2,684	12.6	10,009	25.1	9,403	25.5	8,835	35.9	3,108	2.7
7.	16,674	48.9	15,857	74.3	25,783	64.6	24,687	67.0	7,828	31.8	93,382	81.1
8.	37	0.1	0	0	108	0.3	4	0	104	0.4	62	0.1
9.	10,323	30.3	2,787	13.1	2,799	7.0	1,930	5.2	7,116	28.9	16,922	14.7
10.	129	0.4	16	0.1	1,231	3.1	822	2.2	746	3.0	1,716	1.5
11.	34,120		21,343		39,930		36,846		24,628		115,190	

[a]Percents are of total assets. Item numbers in the first column are defined in Table 2.4.

Source: Standard & Poor's GLOBAL Vantage database.

another. Together, they comprise an average of 39% of the total sources of funds available to broker/dealers. The activity of the inter-FI market varies considerably from country to country (see Table 2.5). The market is most active in Canada, the United Kingdom, Switzerland, Spain, and Italy since, in these countries, FIs rely on other FIs for considerably more than half of their market sources of funds. In contrast, long term debt is the most important source of funds for FIs in the United States, Germany, France, Japan, Sweden, Hong Kong, and Australia.

The largest source of funds available to asset transformers are bank deposits, representing an average of 68% of the global total for 1994 (see Table 2.4). Bank deposits as a fraction of total sources available to asset transformers are smallest in France (31.8% of the total, shown in Table 2.5). This reflects the continuing decline in the French banking industry as it loses market share to other, nonbank types of FIs.

Total insurance and reinsurance liabilities comprise an average of 13.5% of asset transformer sources of funds (see Table 2.4). The most active insurance market is found in France, comprising an average of 36.3% of total funds raised by asset transforming FIs. Reserves, which can be viewed as past profits retained to finance future activities, comprise only 1.6% of the FIs' sources of funds in 1994 (see Table 2.4). The low level of reserves (which is observed in each of the 12 countries) is the result of historically low average default rates on loans and other FI investments. However, Table 2.5 shows that Italian FIs hold the highest level of reserves (3.7% of total assets).

Broker/Dealer Uses of Funds

The receipt of financing from Funds Surplus Units is only half of the financial intermediation picture; the other half is the transfer of cash to Funds Deficit Units in order to finance investment projects. This is what is meant by the "use" of the FIs' funds. Tables 2.6 and 2.7 examine how broker/dealers around the world use their funds.

Switzerland		Spain		Italy		Sweden		Australia		Hong Kong	
$000	%	$000	%	$000	%	$000	%	$000	%	$000	%
34		12		36		15		9		5	
7,099	65.6	7,925	85.0	4,829	72.6	1,520	23.5	2,706	43.3	168	21.0
0	0	0	0	10	0.1	81	1.3	214	3.4	0	0
3,729	34.4	1,400	15.0	1,743	26.2	4,872	75.3	3,323	53.2	633	79.0
0	0	0	0	74	1.1	0	0	0	0	0	0
10,828		9,325		6,655		6,474		6,242		801	
4,635	20.8	405	1.7	269	4.1	1,145	19.1	499	1.8	0	0
15,735	70.6	17,151	71.4	5,089	76.9	4,134	73.2	21,525	78.7	9,227	96.9
79	0.4	15	0.1	10	0.2	15	0.3	0	0	0	0
1,274	5.7	5,978	24.9	1,001	15.1	325	5.4	4,821	17.6	152	1.6
559	2.5	465	1.9	247	3.7	123	2.1	493	1.8	144	1.5
22,282		24,015		6,616		5,997		27,338		9,523	

Table 2.6

FIs' Investment Portfolios: Broker/Dealer Operations Use of FIs' Funds to Finance Funds Deficit Units (End of Fiscal Year 1994)[a]

Asset Description	Global Average ($000)	Total Assets (%)
1. Cash	3,364	25.9
2. Short term securities	2,233	17.2
Trading/Dealing Securities		
3. Government securities	836	6.4
4. Corporate debt securities	321	2.5
5. Corporate equity securities	139	1.1
6. Money market securities	74	0.6
7. Securities' inventories	27	0.2
8. Securities in custody	185	1.4
9. Other trading/dealing securities	189	1.5

[a]The data are averaged over all 396 FIs reporting these items. The end of the fiscal year is March 31 in Japan; day of the country's fiscal year. Data are provided in local currencies, which are converted to U.S. dollar values

Source: Standard & Poor's GLOBAL Vantage database.

Table 2.7

International Comparisons FIs' Investment Portfolios Broker/Dealer Operations—Use of FIs' Funds to Finance Funds Deficit Units (End of Fiscal Year 1994)[a]

Asset	USA $000	%	Canada $000	%	Germany $000	%	U.K. $000	%	France $000	%	Japan ($000)	%
No. of FIs	99		28		31		40		31		56	
1.	1,747	12.7	368	12.3	1,990	13.7	1,534	17.7	1,374	15.1	16,374	44.0
2.	3,545	25.8	518	17.3	1,049	7.2	1,577	18.2	1,470	16.2	4,777	12.8
Trading/Dealing Securities												
3.	1,832	13.3	179	6.0	0	0	584	6.7	474	5.2	447	1.2
4.	492	3.6	0	0	0	0	489	5.7	1,258	13.9	13	0
5.	256	1.9	0	0	0	0	147	1.7	303	3.3	5	0
6.	39	0.3	0	0	0	0	279	3.2	176	1.9	0	0
7.	28	0.2	6	0.2	0	0	10	0.1	50	0.5	1	0
8.	650	4.7	7	0.2	0	0	1	0	0	0	154	0.4
9.	573	4.2	0	0	0	0	1	0	0	0	2	0
Investment Securities												
10.	3,235	23.5	1,281	42.8	3,676	25.3	1,683	19.4	646	7.1	3,991	10.7
11.	702	5.1	224	7.5	6,254	43.1	1,280	14.8	1,791	19.7	2,370	6.4
12.	107	0.8	257	8.6	319	2.2	190	2.2	187	2.1	4,818	12.9
13.	84	0.6	121	4.0	673	4.6	810	9.4	1,009	11.1	151	0.4
14.	13	0.1	24	0.8	0	0	76	0.9	298	3.3	0	0
15.	461	3.4	10	0.3	541	3.7	0	0	44	0.5	3,241	8.7
16.	0	0	0	0	0	0	0	0	0	0	896	2.4
17.	13,764		2,996		14,502		8,659		9,080		37,239	

[a]Percents are of total assets. Item numbers in the first column are defined in Table 2.6.

Source: Standard & Poor's GLOBAL Vantage database.

Asset Description	Global Average ($000)	Total Assets (%)
Investment Securities		
10. Government securities	2,133	16.4
11. Corporate debt securities	1,487	11.5
12. Corporate equity securities	802	6.2
13. Real estate assets	342	2.6
14. Investment property	68	0.5
15. Other securities held		
in investment accounts	640	4.9
16. Foreign exchange assets	133	1.0
17. Total investments	12,971	100

October 31 in Canada; and December 31 in the rest of the countries. The balance sheets were evaluated as of the last using the exchange rate prevailing on the last day of the fiscal year. All data are presented for year-end 1994.

Switzerland		Spain		Italy		Sweden		Australia		Hong Kong	
$000	%	$000	%	$000	%	$000	%	$000	%	$000	%
34		12		36		15		9		5	
779	14.4	986	9.9	414	15.3	140	6.2	547	14.8	461	7.3
1,224	22.6	1,076	32.2	130	4.8	91	4.0	449	12.1	3,602	57.1
978	18.0	0	2.1	974	36.0	97	4.3	1,040	28.1	0	0
206	3.8	142	1.4	204	7.5	206	9.1	0	0	0	0
378	7.0	14	0.1	22	0.8	15	0.7	0	0	0	0
0	0	0	0	93	3.4	295	13.1	110	3.0	0	0
0	0	0	0	27	1.0	102	4.5	21	0.6	592	9.4
0	0	0	0	0	0	0	0	0	0	0	0
440	8.1	0	0	75	2.8	16	0.7	0	0	0	0
212	3.9	3,771	16.8	399	14.8	264	11.7	1,239	33.4	0	0
338	6.2	3,407	34.0	187	6.9	603	26.7	0	0	0	0
67	1.2	302	3.0	2	0	0	0	0	0	0	0
744	13.7	72	0.7	55	2.0	40	1.8	78	2.1	0	0
0	0	0	0	7	0.2	148	6.6	221	6.0	1,649	26.2
61	1.1	−26	−.3	47	1.7	240	10.6	0	0	0	0
0	0	0	0	68	2.5	0	0	0	0	0	0
5,428		10,011		2,702		2,257		3,705		6,304	

Table 2.8

FIs' Investment Securities: Asset Transformation Use of FIs' Funds to Finance Funds Deficit Units (End of Fiscal Year 1994)[a]

Asset Description	Global Average ($000)	Total Assets (%)
1. Total Loans	20,364	71.9
1a. Loans to governments	331	1.2
1b. Loans to banks	4,111	14.5
1c. Insurance company investment loans	590	2.1
1d. Consumer loans	1,787	6.3
1e. Commercial loans	3,153	11.1
1f. Mortgages	9,643	34.0
1g. Lease loans	389	1.4
1h. Other loans	688	2.4
2. Insurance company investments	4,309	15.2
3. Reinsurance	267	0.9
4. Accounts receivable	1,276	4.5
5. Permanent investment	372	1.3
6. Fixed assets	695	2.5
7. Customers' acceptances	924	3.3
8. Intangibles	132	0.5
9. Total	28,339	100

[a]The data are averaged over all 396 FIs reporting these items. Total loans are computed by adding all loan categories (items 1a through 1h) and then subtracting the reserves for credit losses and unearned income (not shown in table).

Source: Standard & Poor's GLOBAL Vantage database.

Table 2.9

International Comparisons FIs' Investment Securities: Asset Transformation Use of FIs' Funds to Finance Funds Deficit Units (End of Fiscal Year 1994)[a]

	USA		Canada		Germany		U.K.		France	
	$000	%	$000	%	$000	%	$000	%	$000	%
No. of FIs	99		28		31		40		31	
1.	19,556	66.9	16,671	82.8	34,773	76.5	22,490	68.3	11,607	45.2
1a.	0	0	0	0	3,581	7.9	3	0	0	0
1b.	609	2.1	1,420	7.0	18,692	41.1	6,416	19.5	5,655	22.0
1c.	743	2.5	973	4.8	1,121	2.5	414	1.3	8	0
1d.	4,187	14.3	2,292	11.4	0	0	2,025	6.2	573	2.2
1e.	5,459	18.7	5,514	27.4	372	0.8	4,253	12.9	704	2.7
1f.	8,449	28.9	5,808	28.8	11,006	24.2	7,740	23.5	1,218	4.7
1g.	312	1.1	10	0.1	0	0	1,023	3.1	1,651	6.4
1h.	348	1.2	952	4.7	1	0	1,147	3.5	2,489	9.7
2.	5,641	19.3	1,864	9.3	7,783	17.1	8,387	25.5	6,794	26.5
3.	651	2.2	34	0.2	238	0.5	176	0.5	342	1.3
4.	2,177	7.4	355	1.8	496	1.1	828	2.5	4,748	18.5
5.	63	0.2	176	0.9	1,362	3.0	174	0.7	1,397	5.4
6.	697	2.4	262	1.3	757	1.7	784	2.4	543	2.1
7.	114	0.4	733	3.6	0	0	0	0	0	0
8.	320	1.1	47	0.2	70	0.2	77	0.2	251	1.0
9.	29,220		20,142		45,480		32,917		25,682	

[a]The data are averaged over all 396 FIs reporting these items. Total loans are computed by adding all loan Percents are of total assets. Item numbers in the first column are defined in Table 2.8.
Source: Standard & Poor's GLOBAL Vantage database.

liquidity: the ability to
sell a financial security at
its fair market value at any
point in time.

The broker/dealer's primary function is to provide **liquidity** to financial markets. A market's liquidity increases as the volume of transactions increases because liquidity measures the ability to sell a financial security at its fair market value at any point in time. It is therefore not surprising that the broker/dealer's largest category of investments is in the short term securities and cash category, representing 17.2% and 25.9% of the total, respectively, as shown in Table 2.6.

The next major category of investments for broker/dealers in 1994 was government securities which were held for either trading or investment purposes. Table 2.6 shows that all government securities holdings comprise 22.8% (6.4% in trading/dealing and 16.4% in investment securities) of the FIs' total investments. The size of the FIs' holdings of government securities reflects the development of the government bond market. Most developed are the markets in the United States, Canada, Italy, and Australia since each of these countries FIs' holds significant portions of their portfolios in the form of government securities. This is evidence of customer interest in transactions using either foreign or domestic government securities.

Asset Transformer Uses of Funds

Asset transformers are not limited to investing in marketable securities and may instead engineer new financial assets with distinctive risk/return characteristics. The terms of the financial contract are negotiated by the FI and the Funds Deficit Unit. Tables 2.8 and 2.9 show the picture for 1994.

In 1994 loans averaged $20,364,000 comprised an average of 71.9% of the total investments of asset transforming FIs (see Table 2.8). The largest category of loans was mortgages, representing 34% of total investments. A distant second was the category of loans to banks, accounting for 14.5% of total assets, with commercial loans just behind at 11.1%. Loans

Japan		Switzerland		Spain		Italy		Sweden		Australia		Hong Kong	
$000	%	$000	%	$000	%	$000	%	$000	%	$000	%	$000	%
57		34		12		36		15		9		5	
39,351	80.3	16,316	76.6	13,076	82.2	3,326	67.4	777	66.9	20,679	76.1	1,592	58.2
0	0	142	0.7	583	3.7	0	0	0	0	216	0.8	0	0
1,074	2.2	6,138	28.8	6,288	39.5	2,696	54.6	921	30.9	2,463	9.1	1,600	58.6
854	1.7	863	4.1	11	0.1	6	0.1	70	2.4	25	0.1	0	0
1,380	2.8	0	0	1,988	12.5	0	0	0	0	3,285	12.1	0	0
5,050	10.3	0	0	1,711	10.8	0	0	0	0	4,913	18.1	0	0
31,050	63.4	7,617	35.8	1,540	9.7	446	9.0	7	0.2	6,343	23.3	0	0
0	0	68	0.3	504	3.2	177	3.6	51	1.7	1,746	6.4	4	0.2
39	0.1	1,488	7.0	1,004	6.3	0	0	0	0	2,695	9.9	0	0
2,710	5.5	3,443	16.2	268	1.7	163	3.3	958	32.2	389	1.4	0	0
113	0.2	165	0.8	47	0.3	10	0.2	133	4.5	28	0.1	0	0
414	0.9	476	2.2	695	4.4	689	13.9	211	7.1	809	3.0	219	8.0
38	0.1	213	1.0	904	5.7	346	7.0	488	16.4	19	0.1	240	8.8
1,143	2.3	680	3.2	833	5.2	360	7.3	343	11.5	765	2.8	679	24.9
5,198	10.6	0	0	0	0	0	0	0	0	4,296	15.8	0	0
10	0	6	0	91	0.6	45	0.9	67	2.3	193	0.7	3	0.1
48,978		21,299		15,915		4,939		2,978		27,176		2,733	

categories (items 1a through 1h) and then subtracting the reserves for credit losses and unearned income (not shown in table).

dominate assets of FIs in all countries except France, where total loans represent only 45.2% of the total of asset transformers' assets (see Table 2.9).

Insurance company investments represent a substantial portion of total asset-transformer portfolios with an average of 15.2% of the total in 1994 shown in Table 2.8. However, the importance of the insurance industry varied considerably from country to country. Their assets were most substantial in France, Sweden and the United Kingdom, where they each comprised more than 25% of total asset transformer investments (see Table 2.9).

Asset transformation portfolios are significantly larger than those belonging to broker/dealers. In 1994 asset transformation assets averaged $28,339,000. Table 2.6 shows that broker/dealer assets averaged only $12,971,000. This is not surprising given the differences in the intermediation technology. Broker/dealers take positions in the financial securities that they trade for short periods of time only. Their goal is to turn over their inventory as rapidly as possible so as to reduce costs and maximize revenues. In contrast, asset transformers often hold the financial securities that they create in their dealings with Funds Deficit Units. Why don't the asset transformers sell these financial securities? Sometimes they do, as in the case of asset securitization. However, sometimes they cannot receive the fair market value of the security.

The fair market value of any security is determined by the present value of its future cash flows. In the case of asset transformation, the FI has the most information about the security's fair market value. Without this information, outsiders cannot evaluate the security and therefore will be unwilling to buy it. Moreover, since the FI's information superiority is well known, buyers may interpret the FI's willingness to sell as a signal that the security is a lemon. FIs may have incentives to sell their lemons and keep their gems. Indeed, FIs could actually *create* securities that they know are lemons with the intent of selling them to uninformed Funds Surplus Units. This **moral hazard** problem occurs because one party has an incentive to shift risk onto an uninformed other party. Moral hazard problems may occur whenever there are **information asymmetries**—that is, one side is more informed than the other. To defend themselves, all buyers consider all securities placed for sale as lemons and reduce their valuation. The buyers' concerns are self-fulfilling prophecies since the FIs will only place lemons on the market. To prevent this possibility, the FI avoids the market entirely and may hold large amounts of these difficult-to-evaluate, asset-transformer securities in its portfolio.

moral hazard: a problem that occurs when one party has an incentive to shift risk onto an uninformed other party.

information asymmetries: a situation in which one side is more informed than the other.

Checkpoint

1. Why is the financial leverage of FIs so high?
2. Compare the level of off-balance sheet items with the level of on-balance sheet assets.
3. What are the most important sources of funds for broker/dealers? asset transformers?
4. What are the most important uses of funds for broker/dealers? asset transformers?

➤ Summary

Private FIs are profit-seeking firms whose assets are predominantly financial. FIs provide both risk shifting and timing of cash flow services to their customers. Risk shifting services entail the creation of a competitive market that allows customers to alter their risk exposures to their desired levels. The timing of cash flow services entails the transfer of funds from Funds Surplus Units to Funds Deficit Units. Funds Surplus Units receive the promise of an investment re-turn, whereas Funds Deficit Units receive the financing for their investment projects.

FIs use two technologies to perform their intermediation function. They can act as either (1) broker/dealers or (2) asset transformers. Broker/dealers transfer the financial securities they receive from Funds Deficit Units in unaltered form to the Funds Surplus Units. Asset transformation, on the other hand, allows the FI to change the risk/return characteristics of the financial securities it receives from Funds Deficit Units before transferring them to Funds Surplus Units. Each side therefore deals individually with the FI and need not know the identity of the other party. We say that the asset-transforming FI is opaque when Funds Surplus Units cannot see through the FI to the Funds Deficit Units that receive their investment financing. Broker/dealers are transparent because the Funds Surplus Units must evaluate the securities of the Funds Deficit Units in order to determine whether to make an investment. Translucent FIs transform the financial assets issued by Funds Deficit Units into different, but still identifiable, obligations of the FI.

Using the distinction between broker/dealers and asset transformers, we examined FIs in 12 countries (the United States, Canada, Germany, the United Kingdom, France, Japan, Switzerland, Spain, Italy, Sweden, Australia, and Hong Kong) and found that financial intermediation is a highly leveraged, low profit margin, high-overhead business. The portfolios of asset transformers are significantly larger than those of broker/dealers.

➤ Questions

1. State whether the following activities are performed by (i) broker/dealers or (ii) asset transformers.
   a. Exchange of Deutschemark for French francs.
   b. Distribution of newly issued stock.
   c. Purchase of newly issued stock for inventory, to be held until buyers can be found.
   d. Extension of a mortgage to a new home buyer.
   e. Extension of a second mortgage to a homeowner to finance home remodeling.
   f. Sales of an auto insurance policy.
   g. Sales of a life insurance policy.
   h. Sales of property/casualty insurance policies.

2. Use Tables 2.2 and 2.3 to answer the following, basing your answers on absolute dollar amounts:
   a. Which countries' FIs have average asset size that exceed the global average? Which are less than the global average?
   b. Which countries' FIs have average off-balance sheet contingencies that exceed the global average? Which are less than the global average?
   c. Which countries' FIs have average net income that exceeds the global average? Which are less than the global average?

3. Use relative values (as a percentage of total asset size) and Tables 2.2 and 2.3 to answer the following:
   a. Which countries' FIs have average off-balance sheet contingencies that exceed the global average? Which are less than the global average?
   b. Which countries' FIs have average net income that exceeds the global average? Which are less than the global average?
   c. Compare your answers to parts (a) and (b) to your answers to question 2.

4. How does an increase in financial leverage increase the value of the FI? How does it decrease the value? Which effect prevails?

5. Describe the relationship between financial leverage and shareholders equity.

6. Use Tables 2.4 and 2.5 to answer the following:
   a. Which country has the most (least) interbank deposits, in both absolute and relative terms?
   b. Which country has the most (least) Federal Funds and commercial paper, in both absolute and relative terms?
   c. Which country has the most (least) long term debt, in both absolute and relative terms?
   d. Which country has the most (least) foreign exchange liabilities, in both absolute and relative terms?

e. Which country has the most (least) insurance policy reserves, in both absolute and relative terms?

f. Which country has the most (least) bank deposits, in both absolute and relative terms?

g. Which country has the most (least) reinsurance liabilities, in both absolute and relative terms?

h. Which country has the most (least) reserves, in both absolute and relative terms?

7. Why is the average size of broker/dealer operations smaller than that of asset transformers?

8. Use Tables 2.6 and 2.7 to answer the following:

a. Which countries' FIs are most active in the government securities markets? Which are least active? Distinguish between trading and investment activity.

b. Which countries' FIs are most active in the corporate debt markets? Which are least active? Distinguish between trading and investment activity.

c. Which countries' FIs are most active in the corporate equity markets? Which are least active? Distinguish between trading and investment activity.

9. Describe the pros and cons of holding cash and short term securities. Use the description of the banking environment in Hong Kong from Timely Topics 2.2 to explain the existence of large cash and short term securities holdings by the FIs in Hong Kong.

10. Use Tables 2.8 and 2.9 to compare the importance of different loan categories by size across countries. Be sure to use both absolute and relative rankings.

11. How would you describe the size of FIs' fixed assets? How can you explain this?

CHAPTER 3

THE WORLD'S CENTRAL BANKS AND REGULATORY AUTHORITIES

"Who believed that the bank was mightier than the sword, And that an umbrella might pacify barbarians abroad" William Plomer, *The Dorking Thigh* (1945) "Father and Son"

Learning Objectives

- To learn why governments set up public FIs.

- To obtain an overview of the three major goals of public FIs: (1) supervising the safety and soundness of private FIs and setting public disclosure requirements; (2) managing the level of aggregate economic activity; and (3) maintaining the payments system.

- To compare some of the most important public FIs in the world: the U.S. Federal Reserve System, the Bank of England, the Bundesbank of Germany, the Bank of Japan, the Bank for International Settlements, the World Bank, and the IMF.

➤ Introduction

In the last two chapters, we described several types of private FIs. In this chapter, we examine public or governmental FIs, which may be national, regional, or global in scope. Whereas private FIs are guided by the profit motive and so are designed to maximize the value of the firm to shareholders and other stakeholders, public FIs are operated to benefit the public and so they undertake policies that maximize society's welfare. Public FIs are not limited to profit-making activities[1] and may undertake unprofitable projects (such as intervening in foreign currency markets to support the value of the local currency) if these are judged to have beneficial public impacts.

➤ Policy Goals of Public FIs

Efficient operation of financial markets is too important to a free market economy to leave its management entirely to the private sector. Private FIs monitor the unobstructed free flow of financial transactions through the global economy. But who is to monitor the FIs themselves?

---

[1] The Federal Reserve System in the United States typically earns positive net income, part of which is transferred to the U.S. Treasury in the form of interest on Federal Reserve notes. In 1994 the Fed paid $20.47 billion to the U.S. Treasury.

shareholders: owners of common stock; the owners of a corporation.

stakeholders: any party who benefits from the success of the company, for example, shareholders, bondholders, creditors, managers, and employees.

negative externalities: result whereby individual actions impose costs on society not paid for by the person initiating the action.

positive externality: result whereby individuals whose actions benefit society are not compensated for them.

aggregate level of economic activity: the economy's use of scarce resources to produce goods and services.

gross domestic product GDP: the sum total of the economy's production of goods and services.

The answer, in part, is the **shareholders**, the owners of the corporation, and other **stakeholders**, any party who benefits from the success of the FI, all of whom have an incentive to monitor the FIs' actions so as to protect their own private investments. Sometimes, however, these private stakeholders need help monitoring the activities of their private FIs. The public FI then acts as an objective third party, helping to improve both the efficiency and availability of financial intermediation services.

This is only part of the public FIs' function. Because interruption of private FIs' activities can be disruptive to the macroeconomy, potential **negative externalities** exist that can be avoided only through coordinated action. Coordination by public FIs is required because externalities arise when individuals do not consider relevant factors external to their private decision-making process. Negative externalities arise when individual actions impose costs on society not paid for by the person initiating the action. For example, the failure to charge a price for the use of publicly owned resources, such as clean air, leads individuals to underestimate the cost of pollution, thereby creating a negative externality since the polluter does not take into consideration the costs to society of his actions. Alternatively, individuals underestimate the value of education since they do not consider the **positive externality** of the improved quality of social decision making resulting from a more educated voting populace. Positive externalities arise when the individuals whose actions benefit society are not compensated for them.

Public FIs coordinate action and monitor the financial health of the private FIs that are so crucial to the efficient operation of capitalist economies. A well-functioning system of financial intermediation raises the **aggregate level of economic activity**, mobilizing the economy's scarce resources to produce the goods and services that comprise the economy's **gross domestic product GDP**.

Private FIs are subject to considerable scrutiny and supervision by public FIs. At any point in time, various regulatory agencies can stress different goals, some of which overlap and others of which are in conflict with one another. These goals can be divided into three broad categories:

- To supervise the safety and soundness of private FIs and set public disclosure requirements (see Chapter 5).
- To manage aggregate economic activity (see Chapter 4).
- To maintain the payments system (see Chapter 6).

The three goals are sometimes mutually reinforcing as described in this quotation:

> Monetary policy is implemented through the depository operated payment system and is enriched by the flow of real time financial intelligence that is generated in the process of supervising and regulating depository institutions and participating in the payment system. In the long run, a sound payment system depends on sound [monetary] policy [and maintenance of price stability]. . . .[E]ach of these three activities is necessary to the full effectiveness of the other and, hence, to the central bank's ability to fulfill its mission at the highest possible level.[2]

Access to an efficient means of transferring money (as in maintenance of the payments system) enhances the central bank's ability to control the money supply and conduct monetary policy (as in management of aggregate economic activity). Information gathered in the course of supervising the banking system (as in supervision of private FIs) provides guidelines that are valuable to formulating that monetary policy (management of aggregate economic activity). Success in one of the goals brings success in the others.

Conversely, the three roles of public FIs are sometimes mutually exclusive. For example, providing credit to troubled banks may conform with the central bank's role in monitoring the safety of the banking industry, but it may also conflict with the conduct of monetary policy.

---

[2] Edward Kelley, Jr., "A Businessman Looks at the Fed—Up Close," Speech before the National Economists Club, June 8, 1993.

Supervision of Private FIs

safety and soundness: the maximum allowed risk taking behavior permitted for regulated private FIs.

public disclosure: the release of publicly available information about FI performance and risk exposure.

Private FIs receive significantly more regulatory attention than do nonfinancial companies. The focus of supervision is on monitoring the FI's **safety and soundness** and facilitating **public disclosure** in order to protect small investors and promote the efficiency of financial intermediation. Safety and soundness sets the maximum allowed risk taking behavior permitted for regulated private FIs. It is often more a focus of bank regulation, whereas public disclosure, the release of publicly available information about FI performance and risk exposure, tends to be a higher priority for regulators of firms with securities activities. But the intended results of all supervisory activities are the same—investor protection, the integrity and operational efficiency of financial markets, and systemic stability.

Safety and Soundness

FIs can perform their functions of financial intermediation and innovation only if they retain the confidence of their clientele. Many financial products offered by FIs are simply obligations or promises committing the FI to future activities if certain contingencies occur. These **commitments**, or promises, will be credible only if the FI is **solvent** at the time that the commitment is exercised or performed. The FI is solvent if its net worth—the value of assets minus liabilities—is nonnegative. Thus, customers have incentives to limit the FI's risk taking activities, so as to enhance the value of its commitments. Since it would be too costly for each customer to monitor each FI individually, the public FI monitors private FIs on behalf of their customers. Supervision is designed to ensure that all FIs meet minimum standards of safety and soundness. The macroeconomy is then guaranteed a certain level of financial intermediation services to support aggregate levels of economic activity.

commitments: promises that are exercised when the party who made the promise is required to carry out the promised activities.

solvent: having net worth—the value of assets minus liabilities—that is nonnegative.

capital: the investment made by shareholders and other long term stakeholders in the FI.

The public FIs' major tool ensuring safety and soundness is **capital** regulation. Capital is the investment made by shareholders and other long term stakeholders in the FI. An important feature of most FIs, as noted in Chapter 2, is their high degree of financial leverage. FIs are typically financed with large amounts of debt and relatively small amounts of capital. Capital regulation mandates minimum required capital levels. If this capital requirement is set too low, then shareholders and other FI decision makers have little of their own money invested in the FI. Thus, if the FI undertakes excessively risky activities, they have very little of their own money to lose; conversely, if these risky ventures succeed, the payoff to the FI's stakeholders is very large. It's as if the shareholders get to say to bondholders and other stakeholders, "Heads, I win, tails you lose"! The shareholders have incentives to invest in riskier propositions. This moral hazard problem can be mitigated somewhat if shareholders are required to contribute higher levels of capital. Then shareholders will have an incentive to prevent the FI from engaging in excessively risky policies since they will have their own money at stake.

demand deposits: checking accounts.

bank run: behavior that occurs when depositors rush to withdraw their funds when they suspect the bank has a liquidity problem.

reserves: liquid assets in the form of bank vault cash as well as bank demand deposits held at the central bank.

Capital acts as a cushion to absorb losses without triggering the FI's insolvency. Insolvency occurs when the market value of a FI's liabilities exceeds the market value of its assets. However, even solvent FIs may have liquidity problems if assets cannot easily be sold for prices that reflect the assets' true market value. Many FIs, such as banks, issue highly liquid liabilities, such as **demand deposits** (checking accounts), and invest the proceeds in relatively illiquid assets, such as loans. If the bank experiences an unexpectedly large deposit drain, it may have insufficient cash on hand to meet withdrawal demands and may be forced to liquidate its assets at a loss (or at a high transaction cost). Depositors have an incentive to withdraw their money precipitously if they even suspect that the bank has a liquidity problem. This behavior, called a **bank run**, occurs because depositors are served on a first-come, first-served basis. The first depositors who withdraw their funds are paid in full, and nothing is left over for depositors who wait.

Public FIs require banks to hold minimum levels of liquid assets, called **reserves**, that can be used to meet the bank's liquidity needs. These reserves are held in the form of vault cash as well

reserve requirement: the minimum level of reserves required as a cushion against the liquidation of bank deposits.

as bank demand deposits at the central bank. In the United States, the **reserve requirement** on demand deposits is currently set at 10%. Thus, banks need hold only a small fraction, 10%, of their demand deposit liabilities in the form of liquid assets to meet the withdrawal demands of depositors. This **fractional reserve system of banking** allows banks to be highly profitable, since 90% of their deposits can be invested in interest-earning assets, but it is also subject to liquidity risk. Even essentially solvent FIs may become insolvent as a result of losses caused by early liquidation of assets in the wake of a bank run.

fractional reserve system of banking: the requirement that banks need hold only a small fraction of their deposit liabilities in the form of liquid assets available to meet the withdrawal demands of depositors.

Another way of reducing the risk of loss is to require that the private FI be well diversified. The FI can reduce its variance of returns by holding a portfolio of imperfectly correlated assets. To obtain the risk reducing benefits of diversification, the British Banking Act of 1987 requires that any one transaction that risks losing more than 10% of a bank's capital has to be reported to the Bank of England, with prior notification required if a transaction exposes the bank to the risk of losing over 25% of its capital. In the United States, national banks are prohibited from extending to any one borrower credit that exceeds 15% of the bank's capital.

Although the role of public FIs is to oversee and limit the private FIs' risk exposures, they are not alone in this quest. The public relies on the disclosure of accurate and timely financial information in order to pursue a similar goal.

Public Disclosure

Financial markets operate on the fuel of information; without information, market participants cannot evaluate financial products. Since most financial products entail future cash flows, the financial condition of the FI offering the product is critical to the product's valuation. By enhancing the disclosure of necessary information to the general public, the public FIs enable stakeholders to assist regulators in monitoring the safety and soundness of FIs. This process, called **market discipline**, entails scrutiny by stockholders and other stakeholders based on financial information disclosed about the FI.

market discipline: scrutiny by stockholders and other stakeholders based on financial information disclosed about the FI.

publicly held corporations: firms that issue stock that is publicly traded on an organized exchange or over the counter.

To help the market monitor the FIs, public FIs require private FIs to disclose detailed financial statements at regular intervals (weekly, monthly, quarterly or annually). In the United States, all **publicly held corporations** must file 10-Q forms that contain balance sheet and income statement data. Publicly held corporations are firms that issue stock that is publicly traded on an organized exchange or over the counter. All banks in the United States (publicly or privately held) must provide detailed financial **Call Reports** on a quarterly basis. Call reports contain balance sheet and income statement data, as well as off-balance sheet activity such as swaps, futures, and options transactions, all of which are contingent assets and liabilities. Swaps, futures, and options are not shown on the balance sheet because they require no principal cash flows upon their initiation. They are contingencies since future cash flows are required only if certain future events occur. Shareholders and other stakeholders analyze FIs' public financial statements. FIs with healthy financial statements attract shareholders, with resulting increases in their stock prices, whereas the opposite occurs for FIs with shaky financials.

Call Reports: quarterly balance sheet and income statements that must be submitted to federal regulators of all depository FIs in the United States.

generally accepted accounting principles (GAAP): the rules of financial reporting required of all companies.

book value accounting methods: methods that value assets and liabilities on the basis of historical acquisition costs.

market value accounting methods: methods that evaluate assets and liabilities at their current market prices.

The United States has the strictest disclosure requirements in the developed world. The purpose of disclosure is to give market participants an early warning of potential problems. However, even the most detailed financial reports can obscure rather than illuminate because **generally accepted accounting principles (GAAP)**, the rules of financial reporting required of all companies, often utilize **book value accounting methods**. Book value accounting values assets and liabilities on the basis of historical, acquisition cost as opposed to current market values required by **market value accounting methods**. Market value accounting evaluates assets and liabilities at their current market prices. For example, a property that has a book value (based on its acquisition price) of $10 million, but can be sold for only $2 million (perhaps because toxic wastes were subsequently discovered on the property), from a book value accounting viewpoint, would be represented on the financial statement as an asset worth $10 million although its true worth is only $2 million. This inflates the value of the firm's assets, perhaps overstating the firm's value and understating the firm's liquidity risk and insolvency risk exposures.

Indeed, the use of GAAP (and even more lenient accounting practices) delayed detection of the problems at U.S. thrift institutions in the early 1980s. From a book value perspective, many of the thrifts were technically solvent. However, the market value of their assets was a mere fraction of their stated book value, because of interest rate increases and credit risk problems. The shortcomings of GAAP financial statements were exacerbated by even more lenient **regulatory accounting principles (RAP)**, which are the financial reporting methods required of regulated firms such as thrifts and banks. Public FIs responsible for regulating thrifts found themselves unable to take action against financially nonviable institutions that were solvent "on the books." White (1991) shows how prevalent this problem was. At the height of the thrift crisis in the United States in 1987, the RAP method detected only 52% of those thrifts that were insolvent on a GAAP basis. These RAP-insolvent thrifts represented only 28% of the assets of all technically insolvent thrifts by GAAP standards. Even this understates the true extent of the obfuscation since many more thrifts were market value insolvent than were considered technically insolvent according to GAAP.

Accurate financial data that are disclosed to the public in a timely fashion enhance the market's ability to monitor FI activities. Public FIs also receive detailed financial statements from private FIs (usually at quarterly intervals), which are later made public. Regulators use these financial reports to monitor the FIs' capital levels as well as their overall financial condition. To augment their oversight abilities, regulatory authorities obtain private information about the safety and soundness of FIs by means of on-site bank examinations. Smaller FIs are examined periodically (on an annual or biannual basis), while larger FIs are continually under scrutiny by regulators. On-site examinations investigate the FI's **CAMEL rating**, a bank rating scheme based on a scale of 1 (best) to 5; CAMEL is an acronym for *C*apital adequacy, *A*sset quality, *M*anagerial ability, *E*arnings, and *L*iquidity. Typically, the results of on-site examinations are for the internal use of the regulatory authority only. This conflicts with the disclosure goal, however, for if an FI fails an on-site examination (by receiving a CAMEL rating of 4 or 5 on the five-point scale), the bank is put on a problem bank list, but this information is not typically disclosed to the general public. In January 1995 the Fed adopted a similar performance rating system for foreign banks in the United States called ROCA (an acronmym for *R*isk management, *O*perational controls, *C*ompliance, and *A*sset quality).

Depository FIs are not the only institutions that must comply with disclosure requirements. Underwriters of newly issued financial securities must also undergo strict disclosure procedures in the United States. Indeed, fulfilling the information requirements is so time consuming that 36.7% of all debt offerings priced in 1994 were **shelf registrations** in accord with Rule 415 implemented by the SEC in 1983; this rule allows the SEC to preapprove a security for later sale.[3] Shelf registration allows the issuing firm to provide the SEC with all required information during the initial registration process prior to sale of the securities. Then the securities can be expeditiously sold, without providing additional information, at any time during the two years after registration.

regulatory accounting principles (RAP): financial reporting methods required of regulated firms such as thrifts and banks.

CAMEL rating: a bank rating scheme based on a scale of 1 (best) to 5.

shelf registration: the SEC's preapproval of a security for later sale.

---

[3] In 1994 a total of 1,181 debt issues were shelf registered for a total amount of $191.92 billion, as compared with 2,148 nonshelf issues raising $330.587 billion in debt. These figures understate the relative importance of Rule 415 since the 2,148 nonshelf debt issues include a large number of government agency issues. Universal shelf registration, approved in October 1992, allows issuers to file one shelf registration statement that can be applied to different types of securities. This gives the issuer flexibility to adjust the mix of debt and equity in the public offering in response to market conditions.

contagion: a condition that develops if a troubled bank's illiquidity could bring about subsequent financial distress at other FIs.

London gold fixing: the official gold price setting.

Improving the quality of data provided in financial reports makes possible more effective scrutiny of FIs by both regulators and market participants. However, monitoring will take place only if regulators and market participants have the incentive to do so. Creditors and shareholders have little or no incentive to monitor FIs' financial conditions if the government provides them with either de facto or de jure guarantees against default. For instance, if the government offers a guarantee that it will bail out any FI that becomes insolvent, then there will be no need for the public to evaluate the FIs' risk taking behavior. Public FIs in many countries have, at times, extended such a guarantee to large FIs. Governments often consider large FIs "too big to fail" (TBTF) because of their importance to other FIs, the integrity of the payments mechanism, and overall economic conditions. **Contagion** occurs if a troubled bank's illiquidity could produce subsequent financial distress at other FIs. Concern about contagion effects is the motivation behind rescuing TBTF banks. For example, because of its prominence in the international gold bullion and commodity markets, the Bank of England fully supported Johnson Matthey Bankers Ltd. when it experienced financial problems in 1984. Johnson Matthey was a member of the **London gold fixing**, the official gold price setting, and had gold deposits that could be withdrawn at short notice. There was concern that this withdrawal could prompt other withdrawals of liquid funds by gold market members, thereby causing an international liquidity crisis. As a result, the Bank of England "bailed out" Johnson Matthey with injections of funds to meet its liabilities.

Public FIs prioritize their goals differently at different points in time. In 1982 U.S. bank regulators chose to allow the Penn Square National Bank to fail (as a signal of market discipline), but in 1984 Continental Illinois National Bank and in 1991 the Bank of New England were both considered TBTF. In 1983 the German Bundesbank organized a rescue of Schroder, Munchmeyer, Hengst, and Company. Other examples of FIs considered to be TBTF occurred in Canada in 1985 with the Canadian Commercial and Northland Bank of Calgary and in France in 1988 with the Al Saudi Banque.

The pendulum in regulatory policy may be swinging away from the practice of TBTF. In allowing the venerable investment bank Barings PLC to fail in February 1995, the Bank of England reasserted the importance of market discipline by refusing to write a "blank check" to cover the company's trading losses (estimated to be over $1 billion, thereby wiping out the firm's capital of $750 million). In the United States, passage of the Federal Deposit Insurance Corporation Improvement Act, FDICIA of 1991 has limited regulators' ability to bail out banks considered to be TBTF. The policy of "prompt corrective action" is applied across the board to banks of all sizes, thereby limiting the flexibility of public FIs to deviate from strictly defined standards of safety and soundness.

Checkpoint

✓

1. What are the goals of public FIs? Why can't these goals be accomplished by private FIs?

2. What role does capital regulation play in promoting the safety and soundness of FIs?

3. What role does the on-site bank examination play in promoting the safety and soundness of FIs?

4. What role does disclosure play in promoting the safety and soundness of FIs?

5. How does the FDICIA of 1991 enhance the public FI's control over bank safety and soundness?

6. Contrast GAAP, RAP, and market value accounting. Which is the most useful for disclosure purposes?

7. What does "too big to fail" mean? What problems does the policy hope to remedy? What problems does the policy create?

Managing the Level of Aggregate Economic Activity

Central bankers are major players in the macroeconomic policy arena. Whether the economy is sluggish with unemployment high, or overheated with inflation high, or some combination of the two conditions, the central banker is often called upon to deliver some monetary medicine. **Monetary policy** is the manipulation of **monetary aggregates** (the supply of money) or interest rates so as to achieve the macroeconomic policy objectives of full employment and stable prices. An easy money policy stimulates the economy, because credit availability increases and interest rates decrease, thereby encouraging investment and purchases of consumer durable goods, which in turn increase employment. A tight money policy slows down an overheated economy by reducing credit availability, raising interest rates, and thereby dampening consumption and investment activities and reducing general price inflation.

The central bank utilizes the banking system as a conduit for its monetary policy. Thus, its role as regulator of the banking system enhances the central bank's ability to fulfill its monetary policy mission. The central bank can pursue a tight (or easy) money policy with some combination of the following three tools of monetary policy: (1) raising (lowering) the **discount rate**, the interest rate charged to banks for borrowing from the central bank; (2) raising (lowering) the reserve requirement; or (3) selling (buying) government securities, a process called **open market operations**. By impacting the supply of money, each of these tools affects the level of interest rates, the price of money.

Manipulation of interest rates and monetary aggregates is not the only monetary policy vehicle available to public FIs attempting to adjust the level of aggregate economic activity. Several regulatory authorities (for example, the Japanese Ministry of Finance and Ministry of International Trade and Industry) have pursued industrial policy to target specific industries for subsidies and other government benefits. Moreover, regulators provide backup sources of liquidity and guarantees to encourage production and real investment in targeted sectors of the economy. In **newly industrialized countries (NICs)**, such as the "Asian Tigers," and **less developed countries (LDCs)**, liquidity provided by public FIs may take the form of investment in infrastructure and public utilities to improve both the standard of living and productive capacity.

Public FIs provide liquidity to financial markets in both formal and informal ways. Formally, most central banks throughout the world act as **lenders of last resort**. In that capacity, the central bank extends credit directly to private FIs that cannot borrow on private capital markets. The central bank can provide loans in the form of either **adjustment credit** or **extended credit**. Adjustment credit consists of short term, often overnight, loans available to banks experiencing unanticipated or seasonal liquidity problems. As a general rule, adjustment credit is available only to those smaller FIs without access to international money markets. On the other hand, extended credit is granted to banks experiencing prolonged liquidity and solvency problems if it is determined that the troubled bank's problems could become contagious to the entire financial system.

Central banks also provide liquidity to financial markets in informal ways. On Black Monday, October 19, 1987, in the wake of a record 508.32-point drop, or a loss of 23% of its opening value, in the Dow Jones Industrial Average on the New York Stock Exchange, Alan Greenspan, chairman of the Board of Governors of the Federal Reserve Bank, publicly announced the Fed's intention to provide backup liquidity to banks that supported the credit needs of securities dealers. He privately applied **moral suasion**, or informal discussions to convince banks to fill credit requests from other FIs. These prudent injections of liquidity and the Fed's verbal assurances calmed the financial markets on Tuesday, October 20, and reversed the slide in international financial markets.

monetary policy: the manipulation of monetary aggregates or interest rates so as to achieve the macroeconomic policy objectives of full employment and stable prices.

monetary aggregates: the supply of money.

discount rate: the interest rate charged to banks for borrowing from the central bank.

open market operations: the central bank's buying and selling of government securities to implement monetary policy.

newly industrialized countries (NICs): also known as the Asian Tigers, such as Taiwan, South Korea, and Singapore.

less developed countries (LDCs): less developed (nonindustrialized) countries in Africa, Asia, and Latin America.

lender of last resort: role of a central bank when it lends to private FIs that cannot borrow on private capital markets.

adjustment credit: short term, often overnight, loans available to banks experiencing unanticipated or seasonal liquidity problems.

extended credit: credit granted to banks experiencing prolonged liquidity and solvency problems.

moral suasion: informal discussions used by central banks and other public FIs to convince private FIs to follow certain policies.

Checkpoint

1. List the three major tools of monetary policy.
2. List the two major goals of monetary policy.
3. How can public FIs impact the aggregate level of economic activity without manipulating the money supply or interest rates?

➤ Maintaining the Payments System

payments system: the means of making payment for transactions.

For firms to be able to engage in commercial and financial business transactions, an inviolate **payments system** must be intact to handle monetary transfers. The payments system is the means of making payment for transactions. The services provided by public FIs often tend to be related to maintaining the integrity and efficiency of the payments mechanism: the system of money and near-money used to make transactions. As characterized in a speech by Fed Board member, Edward Kelley, Jr.: "Our payment system. . . is a vast and complex public utility, analogous to our electrical power grid, that moves mind-boggling quantities of funds around the country and the world in settlement of financial obligations."

electronic funds transfer network: a computerized system of payment for transactions.

Fedwire: an electronic payment network that allow the transfer of cash and securities.

immediately available funds: funds in reserve accounts at Federal Reserve Banks that are available for immediate transfer.

book-entry securities: the names of all security owners recorded in a computerized database.

systemic risk: the risk of default resulting from a breakdown in the global payments mechanism.

Maintenance of the payments system includes the check-clearing activities of the Federal Reserve Bank which ensure the prompt transfer of funds by check. In the modern era of electronic communications, **electronic funds transfer networks**, computerized payment systems, are even more important components of the payments system. The Federal Reserve Bank maintains the **Fedwire**, an electronic payments network that enables participants to transfer **immediately available funds**, which are funds in reserve accounts at Federal Reserve banks, and **book-entry securities** instantaneously. Normal turnover in foreign exchange markets alone approximates $1 trillion a day. In 1994 daily Fedwire activity averaged $841 billion for a total annual volume of $211 trillion.

Development of new financial products to manage risk has generated a web of financial interrelationships that traverse national borders. International payments networks link FIs across the world. A financial crisis in one country may be transmitted throughout the world economy, exposing global financial markets to **systemic risk**, the risk of default resulting from a breakdown in the global payments mechanism. Public FIs, both individually and in cooperation with one another, must accept responsibility for the stability of the world financial system. Avoidance of "financial meltdown" adds an international component to any public FI's responsibilities. Connected by payments criss-crossing the globe, each public FI must assure the integrity of its own mechanism to process transactions denominated in the home currency. However, since the viability of each country's payments system depends on its ability to collect payments from foreigners, there is a need for international cooperation and coordination to set standards and react to crises. (For a discussion of international central bank coordination, see *Timely Topics 3.1*.)

TIMELY TOPICS 3.1

GLOBAL BANKING AND CENTRAL BANK COORDINATION

"When the oil crisis came upon us in October 1973, and stock markets in all the capitals of the OECD countries collapsed like nine pins, that was one moment of truth. The world, all of a sudden, was seen and felt as one interdependent world."—Lee Kuan Yew, Prime Minister of Singapore, October 5, 1978.[4]

[4] Anthony Sampson, *The Money Lenders: Bankers and a World in Turmoil* (New York: Viking Press, 1981), p. 129.

It took financial crises in major banking sectors throughout the world—the 1973 "lifeboat" rescue operation in the United Kingdom, the 1974 failure of Franklin Bank in the United States, the 1974 failure of Bankhaus I.D. Herstatt in Germany, and the 1991 BCCI scandal—to convince central bankers how interdependent the world's banks had become. In September 1974, there were 11 countries (the United States, Japan, France, Germany, Italy, Spain, Portugal, the United Kingdom, Belgium, the Netherlands, and Luxembourg) signing the Basel Concordat, in which each central bank pledged to support its own country's troubled banks so as to prevent international financial crises. The countries' chief banking supervisors (the Committee on Banking Regulation and Supervisory Practices, also known as the Cooke Committee after its first chairman) meet three times a year in Basel, Switzerland, to maintain international channels of communication among central bankers.

Recognition of interdependence across national financial markets has led the European Community (EC) to pursue a policy of consolidation of regulations. "The commission's approach to creating a community–wide market for financial services is based on three principles: harmonization of essential prudential requirements, mutual recognition by the supervisory authorities of all member states, and wherever possible, supervision and control by the home country's authorities" (*Bulletin of the European Community*, February 1989, p. 15). The EC's First Banking Directive requires member nations to establish authorization procedures for banking firms. The Consolidated Supervision Directive obligates supervisory authorities to monitor bank performance on a consolidated basis, including the performance of the home office as well as any and all foreign subsidiaries.

Cooperation among public FIs enhances their supervisory authority over global depository institutions with international operations. For example, in the United States when the Bank of New England became insolvent in 1990, the Federal Reserve coordinated policy with the Bank of England in order to unwind the bank's foreign exchange transactions. Unwinding the rogue Bank of Credit and Commerce International (BCCI) in 1991 took the cooperation of public FIs from the 70 countries in which BCCI had business dealings.

The world's central bankers are not drawn together solely by financial crises. Regular meetings of national regulators are sponsored by the major international public FIs: the Bank for International Settlements (BIS), the International Monetary Fund (IMF), and the World Bank. For example, the BIS hosts regular meetings of the governors of the world's central banks. Close cooperation among public FIs is evidenced by international policies regarding the supervision of private FIs, enhancement of financial efficiency, and protection against global systemic risk.

Checkpoint

✓

1. What is an electronic payments network? List examples.
2. Why is it so important to maintain an efficient payments network? How does this goal complement the other two goals of public FIs? How does this goal conflict with the other two goals of public FIs?
3. Why is it important to coordinate the policies of national public FIs? How is this coordination accomplished?

➤ National Central Banks

The mix of public policy objectives that make up any particular public FI's agenda at any particular point in time varies across the world. We now examine how major national, regional, and international public FIs fulfill their public policy responsibilities.

The U.S. Federal Reserve System

Historically, Americans have been very suspicious of any centralized financial authority, fearing its potential for abuse of power. This may explain the long delay in establishing a central bank in the United States. The Federal Reserve System was not established until 1913 (following two earlier short-lived experiments with national banking authorities: the First and Second Banks of the United States) and is best characterized by its decentralized structure.

The United States is divided into 12 Federal Reserve districts (see Figure 3.1), each with its own Federal Reserve Bank. These regional banks perform most of the system's operations, clearing checks, distributing currency, making discount loans to individual banks, conducting bank examinations, and providing banking services to the U.S. Treasury. The Federal Reserve regional banks are private corporations owned by the member banks headquartered in their region or district. Member banks in each district elect six of the nine directors of their district bank, with the Board selecting the remaining three. The member banks are required to contribute a portion of their Reserve Bank's capital and annually receive a fixed dividend payment out of the Federal Reserve's net income. The balance of the Federal Reserve's profits is turned over to the Treasury.

Membership in the Federal Reserve System is voluntary. As of December 31, 1994, there were 4,115 member banks in the Federal Reserve System as opposed to 6,327 nonmember banks. Only about 40% of the banks in the United States are members of the Federal Reserve System, but they control almost three quarters of all loans and investments in the banking system. Prior to 1980, Federal Reserve membership was on the decline since nonmember banks were not required to comply with reserve requirements. In response to that trend, the Depository Institutions Deregulatory and Monetary Control Act (DIDMCA) of 1980 extended reserve requirements to all member and nonmember banks.

The Board of Governors of the Federal Reserve System, located in Washington, D.C., is responsible for determining the policies implemented by the Federal Reserve banks. The president of the United States, in consultation with the Senate, appoints the seven members of the Board of Governors to staggered 14 year terms. To further insulate the Fed from short term

*Alaska and Hawaii are also under the jurisdiction of the Federal Reserve Bank of San Francisco

‡The Washington, D.C. office is the headquarters of the Board of Governor of the Federal Reserve System

Figure 3.1   The Federal Reserve System

political pressures, governors once appointed can be removed only for official misconduct.[5] The chairperson, sometimes referred to as the second most powerful person in the United States, is appointed to a four year term.

equity margin requirements: the percentage of a stock price that must be paid for in cash as opposed to borrowings using the stock as collateral.

The Board of Governors sets reserve requirements and **equity margin requirements** (the percentage of a stock price that must be paid for in cash as opposed to borrowings using the stock as collateral), and it reviews and determines discount rates. The discount rate is an important tool of monetary policy. However, the most important tool of monetary policy, open market operations, is controlled by the Federal Open Market Committee (FOMC), established in the Banking Act of 1935 and made up of the seven members of the Board of Governors, four of the Reserve Bank presidents (who each serve one year on a rotating basis), and the president of the Federal Reserve Bank of New York as permanent vice chair. The FOMC influences the money supply by buying or selling Treasury securities. Traditionally, FOMC meetings have been highly secretive. However, in February 1994, in response to congressional hearings regarding lack of disclosure, the Fed undertook a policy of publicly announcing the FOMC's monetary policy actions on the day they were implemented. (See *Timely Topics 3.2* for a discussion of central banks and political independence.)

The Fed's major function is to conduct monetary policy. This was not always its role, however. For decades, the Fed and the Treasury fought over who should control monetary policy. The Treasury, as manager of the federal government's budget, sought to pursue monetary policy objectives that would keep interest rates low so as to reduce the Treasury's borrowing costs. The Treasury Accord of 1951 finally resolved this dispute and granted the Fed independent control over monetary policy. The Fed's monetary policy goals are to promote full employment while maintaining price and exchange rate stability. Sometimes these goals conflict. Since October 1979, the Fed's primary monetary policy objective has been to maintain price stability.[6]

bank holding company: a parent company that owns a controlling interest in at least one subsidiary bank.

The Fed is also responsible for supervising the banking activities of all its member banks as well as all **bank holding companies**. A bank holding company is a parent company that owns a controlling interest in at least one subsidiary bank. Since the largest banks in the United States are either members of the Federal Reserve System or organized on a bank holding company basis, or both, the Fed has direct supervisory responsibilities over the bulk of U.S. banking assets. The Fed discharges its supervisory duties by performing on-site bank examinations, as well as by analyzing the quarterly financial data regularly reported in the Call Reports. Because of the large number of private FIs in the United States, federal regulators rely heavily on reports and compliance with formalized regulations to oversee banking activity. This is in contrast with other countries' central banks (the German Bundesbank, the Bank of England, and the Bank of Japan), which rely much more heavily on personal interviews and informal consultations between bank managers and central bank representatives. Supervision of the banking system also provides the Fed with information about the condition of banks and the overall economy that aids in the conduct of monetary policy.

TIMELY TOPICS 3.2

CENTRAL BANKS AND POLITICAL INDEPENDENCE

Central bankers must often undertake politically unpopular policies that have short term costs but long term economic benefits. It is the long time horizon of central

[5] However, Miller and Velz (1992) find evidence of an impact of presidential policies on the Fed's conduct of monetary policy.

[6] However, Hardouvelis and Barnhart show that the Fed gained credibility as an inflation fighter only gradually after announcement of its monetary policy goals. See Hardouvelis and Barnhart, (1989).

bankers that is most critical to successful administration of the nation's money supply. As Alan Greenspan stated in his congressional testimony on October 13, 1993:

The lure of short-run gains from gunning the economy can loom large in the context of an election cycle, but the process of reaching for such gains can have costly consequences for the nation's economic performance and standards of living over the longer term. The temptation is to step on the monetary accelerator, or at least avoid the monetary brake, until after the next election. Giving in to such temptations is likely to impart an inflationary bias to the economy and could lead to instability.

As Greenspan makes eminently clear, the central banker's focus extends beyond the next election deadline. In the United States, each governor of the Federal Reserve System is appointed to a 14 year term. To keep the Fed as apolitical as possible, only two governors' terms expire during any four year presidential term. Moreover, the Fed maintains its independence by financing its own operations with interest income on its portfolio of government securities. Since the Fed is not dependent on congressional appropriations, it is less likely to be subject to political pressure.

Historically, some central bankers have been more politically independent than others. Yasushi Mieno, who served as the plainspoken governor of the Bank of Japan from 1989 to 1995, earned a reputation as an unpopular inflation disciplinarian by raising the discount rate from 2.5% when he took office to a record 6% less than two years later. These actions were undertaken to puncture the "bubble economy" of the 1980s, in which speculative activity sent land prices in Japan to astronomical, unsustainable levels. At the peak of the bubble, the land beneath the Imperial Palace in central Tokyo was said to be worth more than all the real estate in California. Mieno's tight money policy successfully reduced the availability of financing to fuel speculative real estate activity. In contrast, in May 1994, when the Bundesbank significantly reduced two key interest rates, there were accusations that Hans Tietmeyer, the president of Germany's central bank, was accommodating the election strategies of Chancellor Helmut Kohl who was facing a tough reelection campaign. "Tietmeyer's background is clearly more political than his predecessors'," said Gert von der Linde, the retired chief economist of Donaldson, Lufkin and Jenrette. Alan Greenspan, the chairman of the Federal Reserve Board, has also been accused, at times, of undertaking policies for political, as opposed to economic, reasons.

Despite such criticisms, the Fed and the Bundesbank are the most independent central banks in the world. In contrast, the Bank of England is required to implement the monetary and economic policy objectives of the elected government:

In Britain, the Chancellor of the Exchequer and the Prime Minister, both elected officials, enjoy decisive authority over the policies of the Bank of England. In the United States the Federal Reserve System is subject to Congressional review and its Chairman regularly sits before House and Senate committees on Capitol Hill and must submit a biannual report of its books to Congress. The Bundesbank is comparatively unconstrained by such constitutional arrangements, and pursues its policies formally independent of the elected officials of the West German government and the Federal Assembly, the Bundestag.[7]

Table TT.1 examines the legal statutes and stated policies of 17 countries, ranking central bank independence using four different statistical models. Although there are some disagreements among the four classification schemes shown, the most independent central banks are in Germany and Switzerland, with a higher score indicating greater central bank independence in all four classifications.

---

[7] Ellen Kennedy, *The Bundesbank: Germany's Central Bank in the International Monetary System* (New York: Council on Foreign Relations Press, 1991).

Table TT.1	Summary of Measures of Central Bank Independence			
Country	Bade–Parkin[a]	Grill 1991[a]	A-S 1993[a]	Cukierman 1992[a]
All country avg.	2.179	2.221	2.529	0.388
Australia	1	3	2	0.30
Austria	NA	1	3	0.57
Belgium	2	2	2	0.19
Canada	2	3	2.5	0.46
Denmark	2	3	2.5	0.47
France	2	2	2	0.28
Germany	4	4	4	0.66
Greece	NA	1	1	0.52
Ireland	NA	2	2	0.45
Italy	1.5	2	1.75	0.25
Japan	3	2	2.5	0.18
Netherlands	2	3	2.5	0.42
New Zealand	1	1	1	0.26
Spain	1	2	1.5	0.12
Switzerland	4	4	4	0.64
United Kingdom	4	2	2	0.32
United States	3	4	3.5	0.51

[a]For each of the four statistical classification methods, the higher the number, the greater the measure of central bank independence.

Source: A. Posen, "Central Bank Independence and Disinflationary Credibility: A Missing Link?" Federal Reserve Bank of New York, *Staff Reports*, No. 1, May 1995.

In the United States, the Congress has perennially discussed making the Federal Reserve more accountable to the political arm of government. The Full Employment and Balanced Growth Act of 1978 (also known as the Humphrey-Hawkins Act) requires the chair of the Federal Reserve Board to make semiannual reports to Congress on monetary policy. Six weeks following each meeting date, the minutes of the Federal Open Market Committee (FOMC) meetings are published. In 1993 the Committee on Banking, Finance and Urban Affairs of the U.S. House of Representatives considered legislation (the Federal Reserve System Accountability Act of 1993) that would require full disclosure of the content of FOMC meetings. This threat was successfully repelled by the Fed's February 1994 decision to publicly announce its monetary policy actions. David Mullins, vice chair of the Board of Governors of the Fed, in his congressional testimony on October 19, 1993, summed up the Fed's position: "I believe a substantial degree of confidentiality is necessary to ensure the effectiveness of this deliberative process [of monetary policy decision making]. . . . [P]roposed substantial changes in disclosure of FOMC deliberations would threaten the quality of monetary policy decisions, and. . . not serve the public interest."

William McDonough, president of the Federal Reserve Bank of New York, summarizes the Fed's position when he states:

Central banks that are both powerful and autonomous, yet at the same time responsive to the needs and wishes of their people, are fundamental to the economic development and political stability of all countries. . . . Ultimately the only way central banks can achieve their goals is if their integrity is without question and people have confidence in the policies they pursue. At the end of the day, it is public confidence that is a central bank's most precious commodity in a democracy.[8]

---

[8] W. McDonough, "An Independent Central Bank in a Democratic Country: The Federal Reserve Experiment," Federal Reserve of New York *Quarterly Review* (Spring 1994): 1–6.

The Bank of England

Next to Sweden, the United Kingdom has the oldest central bank in the world. Established in 1694 in London, the Bank of England was owned by private shareholders until 1946, when the government bought all its stock. The Bank of England is responsible for the implementation of monetary policy, foreign exchange operations, and supervision of the British financial system. In addition, it controls the printing of bank notes. The Bank of England is divided into two departments: the Banking Department and the Issue Department. The Banking Department monitors the activities of FIs in the United Kingdom. The Issue Department implements the country's monetary policy. In contrast to other central banks, the Bank of England's autonomy, particularly in the conduct of monetary policy, is limited by its accountability to elected officials of government. The Chancellor of the Exchequer announces the government's monetary policy goals in the form of a letter to the Treasury. The Bank of England implements the policies required to achieve those goals and publishes an independent assessment of their outcomes on a quarterly basis.

The Bank of England historically undertook a *laissez-faire* attitude toward bank supervision in the United Kingdom. Authority was administered informally through the tradition-bound old boy network that characterized the British banking system. Bank of England officials frequently interact with FI executives. Indeed, the Bank of England has, at times, managed the accounts of several *corporate* (non-FI) customers in order to get familiar with the FIs' clients as well as with the FIs themselves. Whereas the U.S. Fed relies largely on formal rules and regulations, the Bank of England relies on an informal style of control.

> How did the Bank of England manage without so many rules? By the "eyebrow policy." If they did not like what you were doing, they would do the equivalent of raising their eyebrows. They would ring up and ask, "Would you like to come over for a cup of tea?" Such invitations were generally not good news. The rule of thumb for most banks was that they should get a cup-of-tea invitation about once a year. If they got it more often, they were probably doing something they should not be doing; if they did not get an invitation once a year, they were not showing enough independence.[9]

price bubble: speculative excess that drives prices far above their fundamental values.

This system was challenged during the 1973 banking crisis emanating from a speculative property **price bubble** (speculative excess that drives prices far above their fundamental values) that, when burst, left many newly formed banks insolvent. The then governor of the Bank of England, Lord Gordon Richardson, orchestrated a "lifeboat" rescue operation to bail out 26 secondary banks, an operation that was funded by the Big Four U.K. and Scottish clearing banks (Barclays, Lloyds, Midland, and NatWest) at a cost of US$3 billion. The tradition-bound and centralized structure of British banking enabled the Bank of England to quickly mobilize the banks to participate in the rescue effort. Securities firms and pension funds took enormous losses when property prices fell precipitously, but most of the banks were bailed out.

This harrowing experience induced the Bank of England to reorder its priorities and focus on bank supervision by devising new banking laws and restraints. In 1979 a banking act was passed that for the first time made it illegal to take deposits in the United Kingdom without prior authorization from the Bank of England. Moreover, FIs were required to register as "licensed deposit takers," participating in the newly introduced compulsory deposit insurance program.

Universal banking is permitted in the United Kingdom, allowing FIs to engage in a broad range of financial and commercial activities, such as banking, insurance, securities trading, and underwriting. Nonbanking activities are conducted by wholly owned subsidiaries of the parent bank corporation. The Bank of England, together with the Building Society Commission as

---

[9] Dennis Weatherstone, "Change and the Art of Monetary Policy," in D. Colander and D. Daane, eds., *The Art of Monetary Policy* (Armonk, N.Y.: M. E. Sharpe, 1994), p. 35.

well as the Department of Trade and Industry,[10] must therefore monitor the entire range of the FIs' banking as well as nonbanking financial activities.

Eurocurrencies: currency deposits held in banks outside the country of the currency's origin.

The United Kingdom plays host to a wide array of international FIs in large part because of London's prominent position in the Eurocurrency markets. **Eurocurrencies** are currency deposits held in banks outside the country of the currency's origin; for example, Eurodollars are U.S. dollar-denominated deposits held in banks outside of the United States. As of December 31, 1992, overseas banks held 58.6% of all loans booked in the United Kingdom, with 27.4% of all sterling-denominated loans.[11] The Bank of England, in its capacity as supervisor of the banks, considers discussions with bank managers to be a significant component of the bank regulatory process. Interviews are held at least once a year with the managers of foreign banks located in the United Kingdom. For instance, in 1991–1992, over 3,500 interviews were held. These meetings take three forms: (1) *nonroutine* to discuss specific issues; (2) *routine, prudential* to discuss the FI's performance; and (3) *routine, trilateral* attended by the Bank of England, the managers of the FI, and the FI's reporting accountants to conduct a bank examination.

Despite passage of several formal regulations governing FIs (such as the 1979 and 1987 Banking acts), the Bank of England continues to rely primarily on informal surveillance and prudential oversight as opposed to legislative regulatory powers in order to supervise private FIs. David Llewellyn states that "[t]he regulation of banks and other sectors of the financial sector has traditionally been informal, based upon self-regulatory principles and reliant substantially on the moral suasion of the Bank of England."[12] If British regulations played a role in the evolution of FIs, it was to speed up the competitive changes already inspired by market forces. For example, the 1986 Building Societies Act, which broadened the powers of building societies (formerly limited to financing mortgages), broke the securities cartel on the London Stock Exchange and led to the Big Bang restructuring that (1) eliminated fixed commissions for securities trading; (2) removed restrictions on ownership of brokers and dealers on the London Stock Exchange, thereby allowing banks to acquire securities firms; and (3) merged the domestic and Eurobond markets. In revolutionizing the regulation of British FIs and securities markets, however, the Bank of England was merely following market realities. The London Stock Exchange (LSE) had steadily been losing market share to foreign markets. Stock exchange firms were undercapitalized as a result of the requirement that LSE member firms had to be partnerships, with outside (nonmember) ownership limited to 29.9% of the firm's capital. The Big Bang regulations simply validated new practices that would have occurred anyway as a competitive response to the changing international environment.

That changing environment also strained the informal oversight capabilities on which the Bank of England relies so heavily. On July 5, 1991, after the Bank of Commerce and Credit International (BCCI) amassed losses totaling more than $5 billion, the Bank of England, leading the regulators of 60 other nations, seized BCCI's assets and finally closed the bank. At the time, the bank had $20 billion in deposits with 1.2 million depositors spread over 70 countries. In 1991 New York Attorney General Robert Morgenthau asserted in his indictment of BCCI that "the corporate structure of BCCI was set up to evade international and national banking laws so that its corrupt practices would be unsupervised and remain undiscovered" (Attorney

---

[10] Overall FI safety and soundness is monitored by the Bank of England for banks, the Building Society Commission for building societies, also called thrifts, and the Department of Trade and Industry for insurance companies. However, individual financial products and functions are monitored by the Securities and Investments Board, the Personal Investment Authority, and the Investment Management Regulatory Organisation.

[11] In contrast, nondomestic banks held 17.9% of all loans in Germany and 35.4% of all commercial loans in the United States. See *Banking in a Global Economy: Economic Benefits to the U.S. from the Activities of International Banks*, Institute of International Bankers, September 1993.

[12] David Llewellyn, "Universal Banking and the Public Interest: A British Perspective," Conference on Universal Banking, New York University Salomon Center, February 23–24, 1995.

Table
3.1

Central Bank Balance Sheet (1994)

Assets	Japan (% Assets)[a]	Germany (% Assets)[b]	England (% Assets)[c]	U.S. (% Assets)[d]
Gold	0.44	3.84		2.53
Cash (including SDRs)	0.65	2.83	0.02	1.91
Loans to FIs	9.05	61.07	20.65	0.05
Government securities	77.09	3.33	43.51	86.69
Treasury bills purchased	10.55			40.60
Short term	33.50			35.42
Long term	33.04			10.67
Foreign assets (Other securities in UK)	5.25	17.55	31.75	5.04
Agency deposits (EMS Funds in Germany)	6.35	8.90		
Money in custody in government accounts	0.01	0.76		
Checks & bills in process of collection	0.04	0	1.50	1.19
Accrued interest	0.26	0.03	0.47	1.90
Deferred payments	0.45			0.24
Bank premises	0.37	1.00	1.50	0.36
Other assets	0.04	0.68	0.59	0.08
	(bil. yen)	(DM mil)	(mil. sterling)	(mil. dollars)
Total assets (in local currency)	48,550.5	356,483	25,874.1	436,896

[a]Year ending 3/31/95.   [c]Year ending 2/28/95.
[b]Year ending 12/31/94.   [d]Year ending 12/31/94.

General's Office News Release, July 29, 1991). The BCCI experience spurred an initiative by international bank regulators to coordinate the supervisory activities of national authorities and to promote cooperation through regular meetings of bank supervisors (see *Timely Topics 3.1*).

The Bundesbank of Germany

The Bundesbank is probably the most conservatively managed central bank in the world. Its first priority is to maintain price stability. Accordingly, growth-enhancing policies are scrutinized for their impact on price inflation. The Bundesbank has a strong social mandate to pursue price stability because of the Germans' memories of the 1923 **hyperinflation**, a very rapid and extreme increase in the general level of prices. The value of a U.S. dollar, 4.2 marks in 1914, rose to 4 billion marks in 1923. Because of the fear of inflation, the Bundesbank Law of 1957 granted the central bank independent powers unmatched by those in any other country. The law explicitly states that the central bank "shall be independent of instructions from the federal government." The Bundesbank is designated as "protector of the currency" and is largely free of the political pressures imposed by elected officials. Indeed, some describe the Bundesbank as an autonomous "fourth branch of the government." Although the Bundesbank is required to coordinate its monetary policies with the economic policies of the government, in disputes the Bundesbank invariably prevails.

The Bundesbank's unquestionable domestic authority in Germany is mitigated somewhat by international challenges to its power. The importance of foreign trade to the German economy and the Deutschemark's role as a second **reserve currency** require the Bundesbank to actively monitor **exchange rate** movements for their impact on domestic monetary aggregates. A reserve currency is used throughout the world as the basis for international trade and settlement of accounts between national central banks as well as for management of their domestic currencies. The U.S. dollar is the world's principal reserve currency. The importance of foreign currency

hyperinflation: a very rapid and extreme increase in the general level of prices.

reserve currency: currency used throughout the world as the basis for international trade and settlement of accounts.

exchange rate: the price of one currency in terms of another.

U.S. (% Assets)[d]	England (% Assets)[c]	Germany (% Assets)[b]	Japan (% Assets)[a]	**Liabilities and Net Worth**
87.32	69.80	66.25	78.53	Banknotes
7.05	6.61	15.76	8.20	Private FI deposits
		0.06	1.51	Government deposits (domestic)
1.64		0.01	0.82	Treasury deposit
		0.05	0.70	Other accounts
0.06	5.44	5.20		Foreign deposits
0.18	13.12	0.20	0.03	Other deposits
0.88		0.55	0.01	Unearned interest
		1.69	0.01	Liabilities from security operations
1.02		0.77	0.01	Deferred receipts
0.15	1.14	0.15	3.76	Other liabilities
0.03			2.71	Allowances and accrued liabilities
		0.20	2.68	Allowance for losses
		0.77	0	Accrued taxes
		2.04	0.03	Other accrued liab.
98.31	96.11	93.65	94.78	Total liabilities
0.84	0.06	0.08	0.0002	Capital
		3.15	2.20	Legal reserve
0.84	0.88	0.08	1.80	General reserve (surplus)
0	2.96	3.05	1.22	Annual net income (undistributed)
1.69	3.89	6.36	5.22	Total capital

operations to the Bundesbank is seen in Table 3.1. In 1994 Bundesbank assets to support foreign activities accounted for more than 26% of total assets (the sum of foreign assets of 17.55% plus agency deposits of 8.9%), a number far in excess of that of other central banks, with the exception of the United Kingdom. The Bundesbank's freedom of operations, therefore, is limited by Germany's international obligations regarding exchange rate stabilization.

The unelected officials of the Bundesbank wield enormous economic power. The Bundesbank is structured regionally so as to diffuse power, along the lines of the U.S. Federal Reserve System, thereby encompassing nine geographically dispersed main office banks that maintain branch offices in provincial cities (see Figure 3.2).[13] The main office of the Bundesbank is located in Frankfurt. The main policy-making body is the Central Bank Council (CBC), which includes the Länder central bank presidents, the Bundesbank president and vice president, and up to eight members of the Frankfurt Directorate of the Bundesbank, who are appointed by Germany's president. The CBC meets every two weeks to decide monetary policy using its four instruments:

1. The discount rate—for loans made by the Bundesbank directly to banks.
2. The *Lombard rate*—the rate on overnight (and short term) bank deposits.
3. Open market operations—the purchase or sale of government securities.
4. Minimum bank reserve policy—the required level of liquid reserves held by banks to support deposits.

---

[13] Prior to the Fourth Act amending the Deutsche Bundesbank Act effective November 1, 1992, there were 11 Länder (state) central bank offices, one in each of the western Länder, including Berlin, Breman, and Hamburg. After the unification of East and West Germany in July 1990, the number of regional offices was consolidated, with each office's purview expanded.

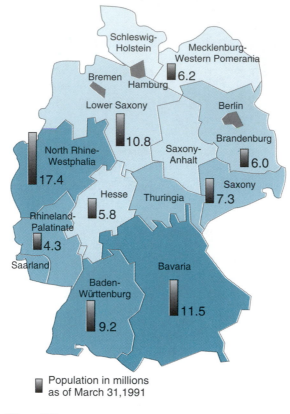

Population in millions
as of March 31, 1991

Figure 3.2

Like the Fed in the United States, the Bundesbank does not directly control most interest rates, although it wields a great deal of influence over both long and short term interest rates as well as exchange rates through its control of the money supply.

The Credit Law of 1961 delegated banking supervision in Germany to the federal Credit Regulatory Agency (CRA), an autonomous body within the Ministry of Economics. The CRA is required by law to impose liquidity requirements that are approved by the Bundesbank and to support Bundesbank monetary policy in its supervision of the banking system. Bank supervision is accomplished through strong prudential supervision as opposed to formal statutory programs. The *Sparkassen* (German savings banks), controlling over 60% of total banking volume, are publicly owned. Private banking firms are required to communicate with German central bank representatives on a regular basis.

Although the CRA is independent, it is required to seek the opinion of the Bundesbank in the event of a banking crisis. The Bundesbank also plays an important role in administering the safety and soundness of the German banking system in its capacity as lender of last resort. The importance of this function is seen in Table 3.1. The largest category of assets, representing 61.07% of Bundesbank assets, is "Loans to FIs."

German bank supervisory practices became considerably stricter in the wake of the 1974 failure of Bankhaus I.D. Herstatt, one of the largest private banks in Germany. As a result of reckless speculation in foreign currencies, Herstatt's 1974 liabilities were US$840 million against assets of US$380 million. Many U.S. and British banks were liability holders (for example, US$10 million owed to British merchant bank Hill Samuel, US$10 million to Citibank, US$13 million to J.P. Morgan, US$12 million to Manufacturer's Hanover, and US$5 million to Bank of America). To avert an international banking crisis, the Bundesbank quickly organized a consortium to pay back most of the money owed to Herstatt's creditors.

As a result of the 1974 Bankhaus Herstatt failure, the CRA expanded its supervisory powers and amended its bank closure rules. In the event of financial distress, the CRA may declare a moratorium and (1) ban receipts and payments by the troubled bank; (2) order the bank to be closed to customer business; (3) replace the bank's management; and (4) negotiate a depositor compensation plan. The CRA can revoke the bank's license if there is a loss in one accounting year amounting to 50% of the bank's equity capital. This early closure policy, predating the policy of prompt corrective action in the United States, is designed to prevent depositor losses by closing the bank before it becomes technically insolvent.

Despite the challenges posed by the July 1990 monetary, economic and social union with the former German Democratic Republic (East Germany), the Bundesbank's basic mandate is unaltered. As reiterated in the 1992 amendment to the Bundesbank Act: "[T]he independence of the Bundesbank from instructions on the part of the government. . . and the priority of safeguarding the currency over any general economic tasks, remains unchanged. . . [and] forms the best prerequisite for ensuring price stability."[14]

The Bank of Japan

The Bank of Japan acts as a banker to the government. The close relationship between the government and the Bank of Japan is shown in Table 3.1 by the preponderance of government securities in the Bank of Japan's balance sheet, representing 77.09% of the central bank's assets in the year ending March 31, 1995. Government activity is also a major source of revenue for the Bank of Japan since fees are charged for issuing the government's checks and for holding its deposits of foreign currencies. Thus, the central bank intermediates between the government and the private sector. Together with another branch of the government, the Ministry of Finance, the Bank of Japan closely administers the lending activities of Japanese banks both at home and abroad. Much of this control takes the form of verbal directives through the "administrative guidance" provided by the Ministry of Finance or the "window guidance" used by the Bank of Japan to control the amount of credit offered by the banks. Bankers meet monthly with central bank officials at the "Second Wednesday Club" at the Bankers' Association in Tokyo. Because of this active level of interaction between public and private FIs in Japan, a system of trust, as opposed to exhaustive disclosure requirements such as those required in the United States, is used to monitor the financial condition of private FIs. However, a series of crises in the 1990s have led to a questioning of this policy of trust. The discovery in 1995 of a $1.1 billion trading loss scandal at Daiwa Bank Ltd. and the 1995–1996 bailout of the troubled Japanese credit unions have proded the Finance Ministry to expand its formal oversight of private FIs.

The influence of the Bank of Japan and the Ministry of Finance (MoF) on the financial system is pervasive and affects the entire Japanese economy. The MoF collects taxes, writes national budgets, regulates Japan's FIs and disburses funds. Despite widespread dissatisfaction with the MoF's handling of the Japanese economy, a 1996 attempt to break up this concentration of financial power failed. The outcome of this initiative was a change in the Bank of Japan's charter to give it more independence from the MoF.

Bank of Japan and MoF policy is transmitted to the nonfinancial sector via the *keiretsu* (literally, "business affiliations"), which are cohesive groups of companies centered around each group's commercial (city) bank. The stability of each keiretsu is enhanced by reciprocal shareholding among its members. These business empires parallel the *zaibatsu* business conglomerates, which had a bank at their core and built the industrial-military machine of prewar

---

[14] *Monthly Report of the Deutsche Bundesbank*, August 1992, p. 53.

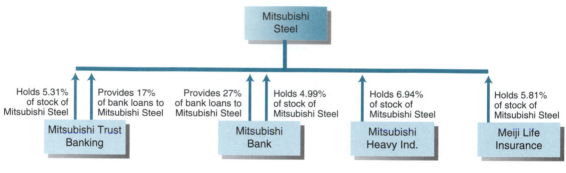

Figure 3.3

main bank system: a relationship form of banking whereby close bank–firm ties are fostered by interlocking directorates and cross holdings of shares.

Japan. After World War II, the *zaibatsu* were disbanded, but they soon reformed around the "big four" banks—Fuji, Sumitomo, Sanwa, and Mitsubishi. Currently, there are six large *keiretsu* in Japan: Mitsubishi, Mitsui, Sumitomo, Fuyo, Sanwa, and DKB. Their "main banks" are Mitsubishi Bank, Sakura Bank, Sumitomo Bank, Fuji Bank, Sanwa Bank, and Daiichi Kangyo Bank respectively. Fuji's keiretsu (called the Fuyo group) include Nissan Motors, Marubeni Trading Corporation, Canon Cameras, Hitachi, and the Yasuda insurance companies; by the 1980s they accounted for nearly 10% of Japan's GNP. Figure 3.3 shows the relationship among some of the companies that form the Mitsubishi Group. The keiretsu companies shown in the figure hold a total of 23.05% of Mitsubishi Steel's stock and provide 44% of Mitsubishi Steel's bank financing. This is typical of the **main bank system** of Japan. The main bank system is a relationship form of banking whereby close bank–firm ties are fostered by interlocking directorates and cross holdings of shares.

The Ministry of Finance and the Bank of Japan work closely to set fiscal and monetary policy. However, it is the Ministry of Finance that supervises the banking system, collects taxes and customs duties, controls foreign exchange, and influences investment policy both in Japan and abroad. The Banking Bureau in the MoF oversees the activities of the banking sector, whereas the Securities Bureau regulates the brokerage industry. Banks, though subject to regulations different from those applicable to securities firms and other FIs, are allowed to enter into the securities business, but they cannot provide insurance. Thus, Japan does not permit universal banking as in Germany and the United Kingdom. Table 3.2 compares the availability of universal banking in the United States, the United Kingdom, Germany, and Japan.

Comparing the Major Central Banks

Table 3.1 highlights the similarities and differences among the world's four major central banks: the Federal Reserve System, the Bank of Japan, the German Bundesbank, and the Bank of England.

Similarities in Assets   For each of the four central banks, holdings of gold bullion represent significantly less than 5% of total assets. This shows that rather than transferring gold bullion when one country's net balance of payments requires payment to another country, the public FIs use the world's primary reserve currency, the U.S. dollar. Central banks need not hold large amounts of gold as reserves backing their country's foreign trade and international investment activities. Instead, they hold interest-earning securities (either domestic or foreign government securities). Holdings of domestic and foreign government securities represented 86.69% of the Fed's 1994 assets; 77.09% of the Bank of Japan's assets; and 43.51% of the Bank of England's assets, with the only exception that of the 3.32% government security holdings of the Bundesbank in 1994 (Table 3.1). These securities holdings provide interest income that

Table 3.2

Services of Commercial Banks by Country[a]

Financial Service	U.S.	U.K.	Germany	Japan
Insurance				
Brokerage	N*	Y	Y	N
Underwriting	N	Y	Y	N
Equities				
Brokerage	Y	Y	Y	Y*
Underwriting	N	Y*	Y	Y*
Investment	N	Y	Y	Y
Other underwriting				
Government debt	Y	Y*	Y	Y*
Private debt	N	Y*	Y	Y*
Mutual funds				
Brokerage	N	Y	Y	N
Management	N	Y	Y	N
Real estate				
Brokerage	N*	Y	Y	N
Investment	N	Y	Y	N
Other brokerage				
Government debt	Y	Y	Y	Y
Private debt	Y	Y	Y	Y

[a]N = NO; N* = NO with exceptions; Y = YES; Y* = YES but must be in a subsidiary separate from the bank.

Source: Yung Chul Park, Dong Won Kim, and Kyung Suh Park, "Transition to Universal Banking: The Korean Experience", New York University Salomon Center Conference on Universal Banking, February 23–24, 1995.

finances the operations of the central bank. As is true for all FIs, most of the asset entries on the public FIs' balance sheets are financial securities, with less than 2% of total assets made up of real investment in bank premises.

Similarities in Liabilities   A striking feature of all central bank liabilities is the relatively small amount of bank reserves (FI deposits) as a fraction of total assets. FI deposits are less than 10% of each of the public FI's assets in all countries except Germany, where the proportion in 1994 was 15.76%. This is far less than the proportion of **banknotes** (domestic currency), which exceeded 65% in all countries. The proportions of banknotes and FI deposits to central bank assets were 87.32% and 7.05% in the U.S., 69.8% and 6.61% in the U.K., 66.25% and 15.76% in Germany, and 78.53% and 8.2% in Japan.

banknotes: domestic currency

The small quantities of bank reserves, in the form of private FI deposits, in the balance sheets of public FIs are misleading. Despite their small quantities, bank reserves are called **high-powered money** because of their multiplicative power in fueling banking activity. The trend in recent years has been toward lower and lower levels of bank reserves, demonstrating the ability of global FIs to utilize their reserve base more efficiently. Reserve requirements in the United States comprise less than 10% of bank liabilities and less than 5% in Japan and Germany. Banks are therefore able to invest more than 90% of their deposit funds in interest-earning financial securities. This is the source of both the profitability of financial intermediation and the power of the banking industry to create money.

high-powered money: bank reserves.

Despite the close relationship between the central bank and the government, the proportion of government deposits to central bank assets is extremely low for all countries: 0.06% in Germany, 1.51% in Japan, and 1.64% in the United States. Public FIs are similar to private FIs in their high degree of financial leverage. The leverage ratios for each of the four central banks exceed 93%, with the U.S. Fed exhibiting the highest leverage (or equivalently the lowest capital ratio) of 98.31% and the Bundesbank the least leverage at 93.65%.

Differences in Assets   Differences among the major central banks are also apparent from Table 3.1. Discount window loans to FIs are practically nonexistent in the United States (at 0.05% of 1994 assets at the Fed), but quite significant in Japan and England (at 9.05% and 20.65% of assets, respectively). Even the higher levels of lending to FIs in Japan and England are small, however, when compared to those in Germany. The exceptionally high 61.07% of assets lent to German domestic credit institutions reflects the regulatory structure of German FIs. Germany allows FIs to conduct their securities activities under the same corporate structure as their banking activities. As we saw in Table 3.2, this universal banking environment differs from that of the United States and Japan, in which banks are prohibited from commercial and many securities activities, as well as that of the United Kingdom, in which the FI's non-banking securities activities must be segmented into separately incorporated subdivisions of the bank. Thus, when the German Bundesbank performs open market operations in the course of conducting monetary policy, this is shown on the Bundesbank's balance sheet as lending to domestic credit institutions. When this is excluded, the portion of Bundesbank lending to German FIs falls to 20% (not shown on Table 3.1), which is still a significant amount of central bank lending to banks.

The relatively high levels of central bank lending to FIs in Germany, the United Kingdom, and Japan reflect the residue of troubled banks in those countries. In Japan, the bursting of the speculative property bubble in 1991 reduced the value of real estate collateral held against bank loans and precipitated a wave of loan defaults.[15] In Germany, the monetary costs of unification of East and West Germany proved more costly than anticipated, and in 1994 British banks were still struggling to make their way out of an extended recession. The Fed is more critical of bank requests for discount window credit. Moreover, the securities markets are much more highly developed in the U.S. and the U.K., providing private FIs with a substitute source of financing in lieu of central bank borrowing.

The dominance of domestic government securities in the asset portfolios of the U.S. Fed can be contrasted with the positions of other central banks. Because of the importance of the U.S. dollar as a reserve currency, the Banks of Japan and England, as well as the Bundesbank, hold significant quantities of U.S. government securities (entered on their balance sheets as "foreign assets"). As we will see in our flow of funds analysis in Tables 3.3a and 3.3b, international public FIs have been important sources of funds to finance the U.S. government's growing national debt fueled by annual federal budget deficits. In the 1970s the dominant international investors in U.S. government securities were Arab nations flush with oil money. As oil prices dropped, the Arabs were largely replaced in the 1980s by Japanese investors. As the Japanese economy sagged in the 1990s, the source of funds shifted to international public FIs. The central banks of India, Malaysia, Taiwan, Brazil, Mexico, and Chile doubled their holdings of U.S. Treasury securities to $70 billion in 1993.

Differences in Liabilities   The importance of the foreign sector in the United Kingdom and Germany can be seen in the relatively high proportions of foreign deposits (5.44% and 5.2% of assets, respectively) as opposed to only 0.06% in the United States (Table 3.1). Despite their focus on maximizing social welfare, the size of undistributed annual net income shows that the central banks are quite profitable. In the year ending March 31, 1995, the Bank of Japan generated 1.2% of its assets in earnings, the Bank of England 2.96%, and the Bundesbank 3.05%. All of the Fed's profits, accounting for more than 4.7% of assets in 1994, are distributed to the Treasury and are not reflected in Table 3.1.

---

[15] In 1991 Japanese bankruptcies rose 74.3% from the level a year earlier, and the Japanese stock market's Nikkei average lost two-thirds of its value.

Table 3.3a

The International Flow of Funds for the United States 1994 QIV–1995 QI (US$ billion)[a]

Sector	Sources Net Borrowing 1995 QI	Uses Net Lending 1995 QI	Net Flow of Funds Sources – Uses 1995 QI	Quarterly Change in Flow of Funds Change in Net Borr. 95QI – 94QIV	Quarterly Change in Flow of Funds Change in Net Lending 95QI – 94QIV
Households	324.4	148.3	+176.1	−82.0	−212.0
Nonfinancial business	302.4	7.1	+295.3	+168.6	−31.6
State and local government	−56.2	−189.2	+133.0	+16.4	−28.7
U.S. government	271.8	−13.0	+284.8	+115.4	+11.7
Foreign	64.3	260.1	−195.8	+31.4	+52.0
Private FIs	315.3	1,008.8	−693.5	−206.6	+252.0
Total	1,222.0[b]	1,222.1[b]	0	+43.2[b]	43.4[b]

[a]Quarterly data are annualized using a seasonal adjustment. Excludes mutual funds and corporate equities totaling $49.6 billion in 1995 QI.

[b]Differences due to rounding.

Source: *Federal Reserve Bulletin* (January 1996): Tables 1.57 and 1.58.

Table 3.3b

Financial Securities Flows in the United States Behind the International Flow of Funds 1994 QIV and 1995 QI[a]

Sector/Instrument	Net Borrowing 1995 QI	Change in Net Borrowing (US$b) 1994QIV – 1995QI
U.S. Government	271.8	+115.4[b]
Treasury securities	273.0	+110.9
Agency issues & mortgages	−1.2	+4.5
Private Domestic Nonfinancial Sectors	570.6	+103.1[b]
Tax-exempt debt instruments	−57.4	+0.5
Corporate bonds	41.4	+38.7
Mortgages	241.1	+49.8
Other (consumer, bank loans, commercial paper)	345.5	14.0
Foreign	64.3	+31.4[b]
Bonds	13.5	−14.2
Other (bank loans, commercial paper, U.S. govt. loans)	50.9	+45.7
Financial Sector	315.3	−206.6[b]
U.S. government-related	125.4	−177.0
Corporate bonds	150.3	+59.1
Other (mortgages, bank loans, thrift loans)	39.6	−88.6
Total	1,222.0	+43.3[b]

[a]Quarterly data are annualized using a seasonal adjustment. Excludes mutual funds and corporate equities totaling $49.6 billion in 1995 QI.

[b]Differences due to rounding.

Source: *Federal Reserve Bulletin* (January 1996): Tables 1.57 and 1.58.

The balance sheets of Table 3.1 are illuminating snapshots of the public FIs' financial picture *at a single point in time*. Also revealing is the flow of funds, over time, among the individuals and governments represented by the world's public FIs; our next topic of discussion.

Checkpoint

✓

1. Contrast the structure of the four national central banks: the Fed, the Bundesbank, the Bank of England, and the Bank of Japan. How does each of these central banks conduct (a) monetary policy, (b) FI supervision, and (c) maintenance of the payments system?

2. What are the major public policy objectives of each of the central banks? How do they perform these functions?

3. What are the most important assets and liabilities for each of the four national central banks? How do these positions emanate from the banks' pursuit of their public policy goals?

The International Flow of Funds

Global financial intermediation requires interactions among the public and private FIs. To best observe the give and take of global financial transactions among public FIs, we use a flow of funds approach that examines the sources and uses of funds during the course of the entire year's transactions. Funds are obtained through the sale of financial assets and net borrowings. Uses of funds include lending and the purchase of financial assets. Here we concentrate on the financial flows through the U.S. economy.

Table 3.3a shows the U.S. flow of funds by economic sector for the first quarter (QI) of 1995. Sources represent net borrowings, while uses are net lending activities. Households, business firms, and the government were net borrowers in the United States during 1995. The household sector borrowed $324.4 billion and lent out $148.3 billion, for a net inflow of funds of $176.1 billion. The largest inflows of funds were into the business and federal government sectors, at $295.3 billion and $284.8 billion, respectively, although all government sectors combined consumed a total of $417.8 billion ($133.0 plus $284.8 billion) of all funds in the U.S. economy during the first quarter of 1995. Net lending was provided by foreigners and private FIs, at $195.8 billion and $693.5 billion, respectively, demonstrating the role of FIs in financing economic activity.

The financial transactions behind the flow of funds shown in Table 3.3a are presented in Table 3.3b. In the first quarter of 1995, the U.S. government financed the federal budget deficit by issuing $273.0 billion in Treasury securities. In contrast, the total mortgages outstanding in the private nonfinancial sector was $241.1 billion. Corporate bonds in all sectors totaled $191.7 billion ($41.4 plus $150.3 billion).

Table 3.3a shows the quarterly change in the flow of funds from 1994 QIV until 1995 QI. Because of sluggishness in household incomes during 1994–1995, households reduced their net lending by $212 billion. However, the expanding economy during this period is reflected in the $168.6 billion increase in net business borrowing. During this period, the financial sector experienced a $206.6 billion decrease in net borrowing, in conjunction with a $252 billion increase in net lending. The impact of these quarterly changes on financial instruments can be seen in Table 3.3b. During the period, the financial sector decreased its net borrowings by $206.6 billion. The $59.1 billion increase in corporate bond issues is consistent with a shift toward securitization, since corporate bonds often replace bank loans as debt instruments that are traded as securities on financial markets. The continuing absorption of funds by the government and business sectors is revealed by the $115.4 billion and $103.1 billion increases in net borrowings for each of these sectors, respectively. The largest increase in private domestic nonfinancial borrowings occurred in the mortgage sector, with an increase of $49.8 billion.

Thus far, we have focused on the central banks of four major industrialized nations. We now broaden our international survey to include offshore banking, regional development banks, and international public FIs.

Offshore Banking

Offshore operations allow companies to access international capital markets with a minimum of taxes and regulations. Tax havens such as the Cayman Islands, the Isle of Man, and the Netherlands Antilles offer a complete menu of financial services that can be accessed with complete anonymity. More than any other political reality, it is the existence of these unregulated tax havens that constrains the regulatory activities of central banks. If national regulatory restrictions become too binding, then financial market participants will take their business elsewhere. The globalization of financial markets makes it convenient to do business anywhere in the world.

The allure of offshore business locales is their secrecy. As many as 11,000 companies are registered in Grand Cayman, although only 10,000 people live there. No one, not even the registrar, knows who owns these companies. Banks establish an offshore presence to service these companies. This presence need not be an expensive bank branch. Most foreign banks conduct their offshore banking business with a brass plate, a secretary, a telex machine, and access to an electronic payment system, such as Fedwire. By 1980, $90 billion in deposits were held by banks in the Bahamas alone. This represented almost 10% of the world's supply of Eurodollars.

➤ International Public FIs

Public FIs such as central banks are creations of their home country's laws and customs. With their focus primarily *intra*national, even coordinated central bank activities cannot manage today's *inter*national financial markets. International public FIs cross national boundaries to regulate global financial markets and monitor the activities of international private FIs.

Regional Development Banks

Regional development banks intermediate between developed and developing countries. They are funded by large capital commitments and loans from developed countries such as the United States, Japan, and Switzerland. These funds are then lent out at low rates of interest to developing countries and used to finance basic projects investing in the country's infrastructure.

The largest regional development bank is the Inter-American Development Bank headquartered in Washington, D.C. Funds are contributed by developed countries in the Western Hemisphere and used to finance projects in Latin American countries. The Asian Development Bank was set up in 1966 and headquartered in the Philippines to foster economic growth in Asia and the Pacific region. The smallest regional development bank is the African Development Bank, located in Abidjan in the Ivory Coast. The European Investment Bank provides funds for local projects in Western Europe, such as the Channel Tunnel, or Chunnel, project connecting England and France. In 1990 the European Bank for Reconstruction and Development was established to aid the emerging economies of Eastern Europe.

The Bank for International Settlements

The Bank for International Settlements (BIS) can be viewed as the central bankers' central bank. In proposing its establishment in 1930, Shepard Morgan of Chase Manhattan Bank envisioned it as "a positive agency of collaboration between central banks . . . to further central bank solidarity." The bank would be a cooperative venture "rid . . . of political entanglements," able to help "relieve credit dislocation, to build a bridge between countries overstocked with capital and those understocked with it."[16] The BIS facilitates the international transfer of funds between central banks by maintaining accounts for all major central banks. For instance, the BIS was empowered to manage Germany's payments of World War I reparations. Payments are cleared using a book-entry system in much the same way as checks are cleared within a national banking system.

The BIS also acts as a lender of last resort, providing funds to central banks around the world to meet sudden financial crises. These loans are undertaken to stabilize the international financial system and are often in the form of short term **bridge loans**—short maturity loans offered by FIs as a stopgap measure until permanent financing can be arranged. In this capacity, the BIS works closely with the World Bank and the International Monetary Fund.

bridge loans: short maturity loans offered by FIs as a stopgap measure until permanent financing can be arranged.

The BIS is headquartered in Basel, Switzerland. Shares in the bank are owned by the central banks of most European countries, as well as Australia, Canada, Japan, and South Africa (see Table 3.4). When the BIS was founded, the U.S. Federal Reserve was allocated a continuous seat on its Board of Directors as well as an allocation of shares. However, since the United States viewed the BIS as a European institution that allowed the participation of Eastern bloc countries during the Cold War period,[17] it was not until September 1994 that the Fed assumed its seat on the Board of Directors. At that time, the Fed was not required to purchase shares of the BIS, but as of June 1995 it has been entitled to vote the shares that were originally allocated to the United States in 1930.

Central banks own 84% of the BIS's outstanding shares, and the remainder are held by private shareholders who receive annual dividends but have no voting rights. Annual profits for the financial year 1993–1994 were $268 million, of which $80 million was distributed as dividends and the remainder added to the BIS's reserves, which totaled $3.4 billion as of March 31, 1994. As of that date, 96% of BIS liabilities took the form of deposits by central banks, with the remainder deposits by international public FIs. These deposits used to be in the form of gold rather than currency, although as of March 1994, the proportion of gold deposits had declined to 7%. The BIS's financial reserves have been used as the clearing agent for innovative financial securities.

The World Bank and the International Monetary Fund

John Maynard Keynes was the intellectual mentor of the International Monetary Fund and the World Bank. In 1941 Keynes, convinced of the need for global cooperation, called for "financial disarmament . . . [in the form of an] International Clearing Union to generalise the essential prinicple of banking as it is exhibited within any closed system."[18] He envisioned a world central bank (which he called Bancor) issuing its own banknotes and intermediating between developed and developing nations. Bancor resources would be used to finance basic development projects, stabilize commodity prices, and smooth trade cycles.

The international banking organizations that were actually established were considerably less ambitious than those envisioned by Keynes. In 1944 the Bretton Woods Conference established both the International Monetary Fund (IMF) and the World Bank as specialized agencies of the United Nations. The newly formed IMF was limited to redistributing the funds

---

[16] Shepard Morgan, "Constructive Functions of the International Bank," *Foreign Affairs*, July 9, 1931, pp. 583, 588.

[17] Active participation in the BIS was less important for the United States since it did not receive any payments of war reparations. Moreover, following the establishment of the International Monetary Fund and the World Bank, a perceived conflict arose among the international public FIs, and so, until recently, the U.S. role in the BIS had been dormant.

[18] John Maynard Keynes, *Collected Writings of J. M. Keynes*, Vol. 25 (London: Macmillan, 1980), p. 195.

Table 3.4

Member Central Banks of the Bank for International Settlements[a]

Country	Central Bank
Australia	Reserve Bank of Australia
Austria	Austrian National Bank
Belgium	National Bank of Belgium
Bulgaria	Bulgarian National Bank
Canada	Bank of Canada
Czech Republic	Czech National Bank
Denmark	National Bank of Denmark
Estonia	Bank of Estonia
Finland	Bank of Finland
France	Bank of France
Germany	German Bundesbank
Greece	Bank of Greece
Hungary	National Bank of Hungary
Iceland	Central Bank of Iceland
Ireland	Central Bank of Ireland
Italy	Bank of Italy
Japan	Bank of Japan
Latvia	Bank of Latvia
Lithuania	Bank of Lithuania
Netherlands	The Netherlands Bank
Norway	Central Bank of Norway
Poland	National Bank of Poland
Portugal	Bank of Portugal
Romania	National Bank of Romania
Slovakia	National Bank of Slovakia
South Africa	South African Reserve Bank
Spain	Bank of Spain
Sweden	Bank of Sweden
Switzerland	Swiss National Bank
Turkey	Central Bank of the Republic of Turkey
United Kingdom	Bank of England
United States	Federal Reserve System
Yugoslavia	National Bank of Yugoslavia[b]

[a]The State Bank of Albania was a member for many years, but withdrew its membership in 1977. Russia and the other former Soviet republics have never been members.

[b]The membership of the central bank of the former state of Yugoslavia is currently suspended, pending a final determination of the legal status of the Yugoslav issue of the BIS's shares.

Source: Charles Seigman, "The Bank for International Settlements and the Federal Reserve," *Federal Reserve Bulletin* (October 1994): 900–906.

contributed by its members (called quotas), as opposed to Keynes's vision of an IMF with the power to create credit by issuing its own banknotes. Moreover, IMF loans were restricted to loans for the purpose of offsetting short term fluctuations in the borrowing country's exchange rates. The World Bank was given the power to borrow funds from international capital markets, but its lending was restricted to less risky, specific projects.

As of 1995, the IMF had 178 member countries. Membership in the IMF is required for membership in the World Bank (officially known as the International Bank for Reconstruction and Development). The World Bank receives funds from wealthy member countries and then re-lends them at favorable rates to needy countries. The World Bank focuses on financially prudent developmental lending. In 1948 its first development loan was extended to Chile and was conditioned on Chile's making payments on previously defaulted debts. In 1960, to engage in more charitable lending, the World Bank established the International Development Association (IDA), which offered "soft loans" requiring interest of only 0.75% per year that could be repaid over 50 years. IDA's funds came from 19 of the world's richest countries, with a commitment that the funds would be "replenished" every three years. Recently, many World Bank governors called for an increase in the Tenth Replenishment of IDA funds to better meet the "urgent needs of developing members." Thus, the World Bank's focus is on aid for the development of Third World countries. In contrast, the IMF's mandate is to uphold financial discipline, coordinate economic policies, and stabilize exchange rates so as to enhance international trade.

Both the IMF and the World Bank were originally capitalized by contributions of the wealthy member nations. The IMF began operating in 1947 with a fund of $9 billion in gold and currency, a third of which was contributed by the United States. In 1969 the IMF created a type of reserve assets called **Special Drawing Rights (SDRs)**, which act as the IMF's unit of account. Special Drawing Rights are IMF reserve assets consisting of a basket of five international currencies with a value equal to the weighted average of the currencies' values. SDRs represent interest-bearing IMF securities backed by the quotas contributed by member countries. In 1993 the IMF controlled assets that amounted to almost 155 billion SDRs, out of which almost SDR 139 billion were quota currencies. SDR interest rates are calculated each Friday as a weighted average of money market interest rates in the five countries whose currencies make up the SDR.

Special Drawing Rights (SDRs): IMF reserve assets consisting of a basket of five international currencies that act as the IMF's unit of account.

The five currencies currently included in the SDR are the U.S. dollar, the Deutschemark, the Japanese yen, the French franc, and the pound sterling (see Table 3.5). The composition of the SDR currency basket (columns 2 and 3 in the table) is determined by the IMF at periodic intervals. The values shown in the table were effective as of January 1, 1996, with the value of each unit of the SDR in terms of the U.S. dollar calculated using February 16, 1996 exchange rates. The number of units of each currency in the SDR basket (column 3) is divided by the exchange rate (column 4) to determine the U.S. dollar equivalent of each component of the SDR. This is summed up to equal a value of US$1.472184 per SDR, or inversely, each U.S. dollar equals 0.67926 SDRs. A private market has evolved in an array of SDR-denominated financial instruments.

In contrast to the IMF, the World Bank has been allowed to expand its assets permanently beyond its capital base by accessing international money and capital markets. On the World Bank's fiftieth anniversary, in 1994, its president, Lewis Preston, stated the Bank's five basic challenges:

Table 3.5

SDR Valuation Basket, as of January 1, 1996

Currency (1)	Pct. Weight (2)	Currency Amount (3)	Exchange Rate (4)	U.S. Dollar Equivalent (5)
U.S. dollar	39	0.582	1.0	0.582
Deutschemark	21	0.446	1.4553	0.306466
Japanese yen	18	27.2	105.20	0.258555
French franc	11	0.813	5.01090	0.162246
Pound sterling	11	0.105	0.6445	0.162917
Total	SDR 1 =			US$1.472184

Source: International Monetary Fund *Survey*, October 9, 1995. All exchange rates are as of February 16, 1996, and are expressed in terms of foreign currency units per U.S. dollar.

1. Promoting broad-based economic growth that benefits the poor.

2. Encouraging human development programs that support education, nutrition, family planning, and the role of women. Human resource development projects accounted for 17% of all World Bank loans in 1994 as opposed to only 5% in the 1980s.

3. Protecting the environment and considering the environmental impact of development projects. In the 1980s there were only three environmentalists out of a staff of 11,000, while in 1994 there were 200.

4. Stimulating the private sector. As of 1994, the World Bank had financed more than 400 privatizations.

5. Reorienting governments to become more efficient and more cooperative with the private sector, particularly in formerly communist nations.

Both the IMF and the World Bank channel private funds into public projects in developing countries, thereby engaging in international financial intermediation. An example of the role of the global FIs in intermediating international capital flows occurred after the oil crises of 1974 and 1979. In 1981, in response to international political pressure, Saudi Arabia increased its quota contribution to the IMF. These petrodollars from OPEC (Organization of Petroleum Exporting Countries) were recycled to Third World nations in the form of IMF loans.

Each country's IMF quota, which reflects the relative size of the member country's economy, determines the member's voting power (one vote for each SDR 100,000 of its quota plus 250 basic votes), as well as the member's access to the IMF's financial resources. Each member must pay about 25% of its quota in SDRs or in other countries' currencies, with the balance in its own currency. IMF lending to member nations is linked to the size of the quota contribution as well as the country's financial needs. In 1993, 38% of total IMF new lending took the form

reserve tranche: IMF lending tied to members' quotas.

of automatic **reserve tranche** lending tied to members' quotas. This policy has been criticized because it favors large, industrialized nations at the expense of smaller, developing nations that are in greater need of the loans. Indeed, some lending programs designed to provide relief to troubled countries have set such strict conditions that only richer countries qualify. For instance, the IMF lending facility established in the wake of the oil crisis to assist oil-importing countries was too harsh for developing countries and ultimately granted loans only to Britain and Italy. *Timely Topics 3.3* discusses criticisms of the IMF and the World Bank and evaluates their future in a world of private FIs.

The IMF concentrates on providing advice and temporary funds to countries with economic difficulties, with emphasis on exchange rate stabilization. To be eligible for World Bank loans, a country must signal its willingness to resolve its long range structural problems by adopting an IMF plan of economic action. Failure to implement the IMF economic stabilization plan may result in a cutback in the availability of funds from both the IMF and the World Bank as well as from private international FIs. The 1982 debt crisis in less developed countries (LDCs) illustrates this role of the IMF in international finance. When many sovereign countries defaulted on their debts to the private banking community, the IMF issued billions of dollars of "stabilization loans." IMF member countries were called upon to increase their contributions by an average of 50% (in the United States an $8.4 billion additional contribution) to accommodate the IMF's increased lending activity. Granting of these loans was contingent upon the borrower's entry into an IMF program designed to enforce good financial behavior. By 1983 dozens of countries (as opposed to one or two in a normal year) were participating in some IMF economic stabilization program.

The LDC debt crisis illustrates the complementarity in the roles of public FIs and private FIs. We have seen that the IMF, the BIS, and the World Bank, as well as regional and national public FIs, were active lenders to developing countries, recycling funds obtained from developed nations. However, all their activities combined represented only a fraction of the lending to LDCs during the 1970s and 1980s. Private FIs (international banks) were active partners with public FIs in providing intermediation services to LDCs. In 1982 developing countries in Latin America, Africa, and Asia owed over $600 billion to international private FIs. Creating this amount of credit requires coordination between private banks and central banking authorities.

Timely Topics 3.3

An International Public FI: Solution or Problem?

The role of the United States in the world is at a crossroads. With the end of the Cold War, the triumph of market-based democracy is more than ever within reach. Unfortunately, just when we are so near to victory, some are tempted prematurely to declare the battle won. In the international financial realm, such thinking takes the form of calls to let free markets alone do the work of spreading democracy, anchoring strategic stability, and carrying beleaguered societies in sensitive regions to prosperity. . . .

It is true private capital markets have attained a depth and breadth unimagined even a few years ago. They can now deliver investments with greater speed and greater efficiency to many regions of the globe. Nonetheless, to leap from there to the idea that capital markets can do all the work of development, or that the international FIs should be privatized, betrays a misunderstanding of what markets can accomplish. Markets last year directed 80% of private capital flows to developing countries to just 12 nations. Markets alone will not educate children on the edge of starvation or provide clean water to shantytowns. Both public and market involvement are needed to redesign a tax code, build bridges, or finance the enormous variety of public goods that provide the foundation for modern capitalism.

Critics of international FIs argue that they either duplicate work that private banks could do—by offering "parasitic" loans at discount to market rates—or waste U.S. tax-payer money by taking on projects that private financiers would never support, because the returns are inadequate. But the whole point of public institutions is that they try to make investments that pay a high social return, where the benefits to all in a society exceed what any one investor can collect. . . .

It has never been more in our strategic and economic interest to induce the kinds of policy changes needed to set market wheels in motion. Lending conditioned on such policy reform is precisely what the international FIs have focused on in recent years. From India to Mexico to Poland, some 75 countries have received $35 billion in World Bank loans from 1981 to 1993 that were directly conditioned on trade and investment liberalization. . . .

We and other donors to the development banks contribute only a relatively small amount of money as paid-in capital; the rest is a pledge that, in 50 years, has never been called. This financial structure, coupled with the banks' solid loan portfolios and recourse to financial markets, means that for every dollar of U.S. paid-in capital, the Inter-American Development Bank has lent $40, the Asian Development Bank has lent $80, and the World Bank has lent $135. . . .

The growth of private finance cannot replace the [public FIs'] work. Nonetheless, the development of private capital markets can and should lead the [international public FIs] to focus their energies on what they do best. If a private construction company cannot ensure government performance of investment guarantees, a World Bank cross guarantee can do so. Risk guarantees and co-financing with the private sector, as well as a still greater emphasis on conditional lending, all harness the international FIs' enormous comparative advantages in contract enforcement and policy design.

Source: L. Summers, "An IFI Question: Are Multilaterals the Solution...," *Wall Street Journal*, October 12, 1995, p. A22.

A half-century after it was founded, the best that can be said of the International Monetary Fund is that it has managed to preserve itself as a free-standing global bureaucracy. The most charitable estimation of its record of service has to recognize that it has failed in its assigned role as guardian of the international economy.

As it meets with its benefactors this week in Washington, D.C., for its annual celebration of itself, the agency is struggling more than ever to put a good face on this dismal record. Its complicity in promoting the financial crisis in Mexico a year ago would have destroyed an institution of even minimal public accountability. The IMF, though, is a creature of the world's elite ruling classes, which gives it an almost unlimited capacity to survive financial crises of its own making. . . .

The banks, which had made what appeared to be solid loans to governments in Asia, Africa, and Latin America, found them going sour in the environment of global inflation and less-than-pristine Third World accounting standards. Collecting on debts from sovereign governments was a distasteful business for a private bank. The IMF thus became the collection agent, its primary job. If Zaire, for example, can't meet its hard currency obligations to the Western banks, the IMF will step in with public funds, collected from the taxpayers of its member nations, of course including ours. On the condition that it undergo a regimen of austerity, Zaire will get the cash and pay its bankers in New York, London, or wherever.

The IMF has had a great record of success in collecting debts. Alas, the governments it doctors rarely survive the austerity programs. These almost always require a currency devaluation to drive down the real wages of the workers, to make their exports competitive. Tax increases are also routinely prescribed to balance the budget. When Dr. IMF makes a house call to treat the sniffles, pneumonia soon follows. . . .

Probably the worst of the IMF doctorings was the advice it gave to Yugoslavia in 1987, urging upon it the "shock therapy" that it later sold to the Soviet Union, beginning with a devaluation of the dinar. As the economy contracted from the shock, government revenues plummeted, and the IMF pressured Belgrade into tax hikes to balance the budget, sending the dinar into another downward spiral. By 1989, Croatia and Slovenia, the two richest provinces of the Yugoslav federation, objected to being drained of resources by the poorer provinces, and with the help of Germany, persuaded the Bush administration to recognize their secession. The rest is bloody history. . . .

[The IMF] primarily needs a change of philosophy about the way the world works, a theory that would enable it to really do what it is supposed to do: Diagnose economic illness in its early stages and bring the patient to a cure.

Source: J. Wanniski, ". . . Or Part of the Problem?," *Wall Street Journal*, October 12, 1995, p. A22.

Checkpoint

1. What is the function of international and regional public FIs? What role do they play that is not performed by national central banks?

2. Distinguish between the Bank for International Settlements, the International Monetary Fund, and the World Bank.

3. How do private FIs and public FIs work together?

Summary

Public FIs perform many of the same intermediation functions as do private FIs. However, they differ from private FIs in that their goals are to pursue public policies that maximize society's economic welfare. The policy objectives of public FIs are (1) supervision of private FIs, (2) management of aggregate economic activity, and (3) maintenance of the payments system.

The supervisory tasks of public FIs require policies to monitor the safety and soundness of private FIs. Public FIs accomplish this function through capital, reserve, and disclosure requirements. Public FIs limit the risk exposure of private FIs by restricting their activities, as well as by eliciting the public's monitoring assistance, via market discipline.

Public FIs manage aggregate economic activity by pursuing the monetary policy goals of full employment and stable prices. Monetary policy is conducted by influencing interest rates and the money supply using the central bank's three major tools: setting reserve requirements, setting the discount rate, and conducting open market operations. Open market operations, the buying and selling of government securities to affect the supply of high-powered money, is the most commonly used tool of monetary policy. The central bank can also influence private FIs' behavior by moral suasion—that is, verbal guidance used to induce private FIs to undertake desirable policies.

An efficiently operating market economy must have a reliable system of monetary transmission called the payments system, to finalize financial transactions. In the past, this objective was largely accomplished using the check-clearing system. However, the electronic funds transfer network is becoming an increasingly large component of the monetary transfer system, particularly for global transactions. The U.S. Federal Reserve System maintains one such electronic funds transfer network, the Fedwire. Liquidity must be maintained by public FIs to preserve confidence in these payments systems.

The role of public FIs in managing the externalities associated with private market transactions is demonstrated by our international survey of public FIs. *National* public FIs are central banks such as the Federal Reserve System (U.S.), the Bank of England (U.K.), the Bundesbank (Germany), and the Bank of Japan (Japan). *Regional* public FIs are the Inter-American Development Bank, the Asian Development Bank, the African Development Bank, the European Investment Bank, and the European Bank for Reconstruction and Development. *International* Public FIs include the World Bank, the International Monetary Fund, and the Bank for International Settlements.

References

Allen, L. "Bank Capital and Deposit Insurance Regulations," in C. Stone and A. Zissu, eds., *Global Risk Based Capital Regulations: Capital Adequacy*. Burr Ridge, Ill.: Irwin, 1994.

Federal Reserve Bank of New York. "Capital Adequacy Guideline for U.S. Government Securities Dealers." May 20, 1985.

Hardouvelis, G. A., and S. W. Barnhart. "The Evolution of Federal Reserve Credibility: 1978–1984." *Review of Economics and Statistics* (1989): 385–393.

Kennedy, E. *The Bundesbank: Germany's Central Bank in the International Monetary System*. New York: Council on Foreign Relations Press, 1991.

Llewellyn, D. "Universal Banking and the Public Interest: A British Perspective." Conference on Universal Banking, New York University Salomon Center, February 23–24, 1995.

McDonough, W. "An Independent Central Bank in a Democratic Country: The Federal Reserve Experiment." Federal Reserve of New York *Quarterly Review* (Spring 1994): 1–6.

Miller, S., and O. Velz. "Do United States Presidential Administrations Influence Monetary Policy?" *Journal of Policy Modeling*, 14, no. 2 (1992): 221–226.

Morgan, S. "Constructive Functions of the International Bank." *Foreign Affairs*, July 9, 1931.

Park, Yung Chul, Dong Won Kim, and Kyung Suh Park. "Transition to Universal Banking: The Korean Experience." New York University Salomon Center Conference on Universal Banking, February 23–24, 1995.

Sampson, A. *The Money Lenders: Bankers and a World in Turmoil*. New York: Viking Press, 1981.

Saunders, A., and I. Walter. *Universal Banking in the United States*. New York: Oxford University Press, 1994.

Seigman, Charles. "The Bank for International Settlements and the Federal Reserve." *Federal Reserve Bulletin* (October 1994): 900–906.

Weatherstone, D. "Change and the Art of Monetary Policy." In D. Colander and D. Duane, eds., *The Art of Monetary Policy*. Armonk, N.Y.: M. E. Sharpe, 1994.

White, L. *The S&L Debacle*. New York: Oxford University Press, 1991.

Wright, R., and Gunter P. *The Second Wave: Japan's Assault on Financial Services*. New York: St. Martin's Press, 1987.

➤ Questions

1. How do the three major functional responsibilities of public FIs complement one another? How do they contradict one another?

2. Contrast the U.S. Federal Reserve System, the German Bundesbank, the Bank of England, and the Bank of Japan, with regard to
   a. political independence.
   b. priorities of monetary policy.
   c. method of supervision of private FIs.
   d. intervention in financial markets.

3. How is the role of the BIS similar to that of the IMF and the World Bank? How is it different?

4. What are the limitations on the power of the world's major public FIs? Who controls global financial markets?

5. Use the following quotes from the *Wall Street Journal* to calculate the U.S. dollar value of the SDR:
   British pound (in U.S. dollars): 1.5275
   Japanese yen (per U.S. dollar): 98.90
   German mark (per U.S. dollar): 1.598
   French franc (per U.S. dollar): 5.46

6. Use the following currency cross rates in the same issue of the *Wall Street Journal* to calculate the yen value of the SDR. All exchange rates are stated per Japanese yen.
   British pound sterling: .00662
   U.S. dollar: .01011
   German mark: .01616
   French franc: .05526

7. *Challenge Question:* How do exchange rate fluctuations affect (a) the value of the SDR? (b) IMF transactions with its member countries? (c) transactions between national public FIs?

8. Use Tables A and B to analyze the U.S. economy's flow of funds.

9. Use the balance sheets in Table C for the world's four major central banks to analyze the similarities and differences of their assets and liabilities.

International Flows of Funds for the United States

Sector	Sources ($b)	Uses ($b)	Net Borrowing ($b)	Quarterly Change ($b)
Households	189	105.2	83.8	–18.2
Business firms	40.4	–7.4	47.8	–58
Private FIs	255.4	664.2	–408.8	4.9
Governments	331.5	–23.9	355.4	105.2
Foreign	21.2	99.4	–78.2	–34.1
Total	837.5	837.5	0	53.5

Central Bank Balance Sheets

Assets	Japan (% Assets)[a]	Germany (% Assets)[b]	England (% Assets)[c]	U.S. (% Assets)[d]
Gold bullion	0.31	3.37		2.73
Cash (incl. SDRs)	1.37	2.60	0.02	2.09
Loans to FIs	13.63	63.49	20.48	0.11
Bills purchased	23.81		3.81	
Government securities	46.99	3.31	27.35	85.66
Short term	28.91			42.62
Long term (Loans)	18.08			43.04
Foreign assets (Other securities in UK)	6.42	15.88	44.69	5.75
Agency deposits (EMS funds in Germany)	6.52	8.92		
Money in custody in government accounts	0.01	0.11		
Checks and bills in process of collection	0.09	0.73	1.47	1.17
Accrued interest and others	0.23	0.12	0.38	
Deferred payments	0.21			
Bank premises	0.42	0.84	1.48	0.26
Other assets	0.0004	0.62	0.31	2.23
	(bil. yen)	(DM mil)	(mil. sterling)	(mil. dollars)
Total assets (in local currency)	45754.3	405566.9	24975.31	405013

[a]Year ending 3/31/93.   [c]Year ending 2/28/93.

[b]Year ending 12/31/93.   [d]Year ending 3/31/94.

Table B

Financial Securities Flows in the U.S. Behind the International Flow of Funds[a]

Sector/Instrument	Quarterly Change in Net Borrowing ($b)	
U.S. Government Securities		+42.3
Treasury securities	+41.9	
Agency issues	+0.3	
Private Domestic Nonfinancial Sectors		−168.4
Tax-exempt debt	−19.7	
Corporate bonds	+33.6	
Mortgages	−53.7	
Other(consumer credit, bank loans)	−128.6	
Foreign Net Borrowing		−11.7
Bonds	+22.5	
Other	−34.2	
Financial Sector		+84.5
U.S. government-related	+47.3	
Corporate bonds	+30.1	
Thrift borrowing	+15.0	
Other Private Borrowing (mortgages, bank loans)	−8.1	
Total Quarterly Change		−53.3[a]

[a]Table B shows a decrease of $53.3 billion in quarterly securities issues, resulting from the $53.5 billion net increase in the quarterly inflow of funds into the economy shown in Table A. The difference is due to rounding.

U.S. (% Assets)[d]	England (% Assets)[c]	Germany (% Assets)[b]	Japan (% Assets)[a]	Liabilities
85.80	67.95	55.32	76.05	Banknotes
8.82	6.24	18.09	7.11	FI deposits
	9.37	3.33	5.42	Government deposits (domestic)
1.53		3.21	3.96	Treasury deposit
0.08		0.12	1.46	Other accounts
0.11	10.17	5.44		Foreign deposits
	1.48	0.19	0.73	Other deposits
			0.04	Unearned interest
		6.46	0.01	Liabilities from securities operations
1.04	0.15	0.71	0.03	Deferred receipts
0.66		0.14	0.05	Other liabilities
			4.62	Allowances and accrued liabilities
		0.12	4.57	Allowance for losses
	0.90	0.66	0.01	Accrued taxes
		2.13	0.04	Other accrued liabilities
98.04	96.26	92.41	94.06	Total liabilities
0.85	0.06	0.07	0.0002	Capital
	3.68	2.63	1.98	Legal reserve
0.84		0.07	1.84	General reserve
0.27				Special reserve
		4.64	2.13	Annual net income
1.96	3.74	7.42	5.94	Total capital
405013	24975.31	405566.9	45754.3	Total assets (in local currency)

BORDER CROSSING I:
CHAPTERS 1–3

Before proceeding, make sure that you understand the following concepts:

1. The definition of Funds Deficit and Funds Surplus Units. (Ch. 1, p. 6)

2. The role of financial markets in shifting cash flows across time. (Ch. 1, p. 2–6)

3. How an efficient frontier enables investors to choose the appropriate levels of risk and return. (Ch. 1, p. 7–11)

4. The difference between private and public FIs. (Ch. 3, p. 35–36)

5. Goals of private FIs. (Ch. 2, p. 15)

6. Goals of public FIs. (Ch. 3, p. 35)

7. The difference between broker/dealer and asset transformation technologies of financial intermediation. (Ch. 2, p. 16–19)

8. The role of regulation in a world of positive and negative externalities. (Ch. 3, p. 36

9. The similarities and differences among the world's top central banks: the U.S. Federal Reserve System, the German Bundesbank, the Bank of Japan, and the Bank of England. (Ch. 3, p. 43–58)

10. The role of international public FIs, such as the International Monetary Fund (IMF), the Bank for International Settlements (BIS), and the World Bank. (Ch. 3, p. 59–64)

CHAPTER 4

MONETARY POLICY

"Money doesn't talk, it swears." Bob Dylan, *It's Alright Ma* (1965 song).

Learning Objectives

- To learn how money is created.

- To learn about the central bank's conduct of monetary policy.

- To examine how the activities of the central bank and other players (such as private FIs, international public FIs, individuals, and businesses) affect the supply of money.

- To study monetary policymaking, observing the difficult tasks of (1) interpreting the often mixed signals about macroeconomic conditions, (2) choosing among various fiscal or monetary policy targets, (3) devising a policy goal that will neither overshoot nor undershoot the desired target, and (4) assessing the results of policy actions.

➤ Introduction

In Chapter 3, we found that one of the major functions of public FIs is to conduct monetary policy. This function stems from the objectives of public FIs as maximizers of social welfare. Society benefits if the level of economic activity grows at a steady rate so as to increase its citizens' standard of living. Public FIs intervene if the rate of economic growth is either deficient or excessive. If deficient, the economy suffers from chronic unemployment of resources and depressed levels of economic activity; if excessive, the economy suffers from unrealistic expectations that ultimately result in general price inflation. The goal of public FIs is to monitor the condition of the economy so as to steer a course between the two perils of unemployment and inflation. This task is complicated by the need to move preemptively and take actions today that will take effect in the future. The outcome of the central bank's monetary policy initiatives is determined, in large part, by the actions of private FIs operating in global financial markets. Accordingly, successful monetary policy requires extensive coordination and cooperation between public and private FIs.

➤ What Is Money?

You can't write monetary policy without money. What is money? If you answered "the cash in your pocket," you would be partially correct. If you added in your checking account balance, then you would still be partially correct. The definition of money is what you want it to be. No, you can't *define* yourself an extra million or so. But you can choose the definition of money that best suits the problem at hand. Sometimes we prefer to use a very narrow definition of money; at other times a broader definition is more useful. *Timely Topics 4.1* describes some recent innovations in a basic component of all definitions of money—cash.

TIMELY TOPICS 4.1

seignorage: the profit earned on currency issuance because the sum of the production costs and the intrinsic value (cost) of materials in the banknotes is less than their transaction value.

WHAT IS CASH?

Cash is legal tender issued by each country's central bank and is universally accepted as payment in transactions. In the United States, the Treasury issues currency notes through the Fed. Issuance of currency is a very profitable transaction for central governments because of **seignorage**—the profit earned on currency issuance because the sum of the production costs and the intrinsic value (cost) of materials in the banknotes is less than their transaction value. To protect their profits, central governments throughout the world are very serious about protecting the integrity of their currency

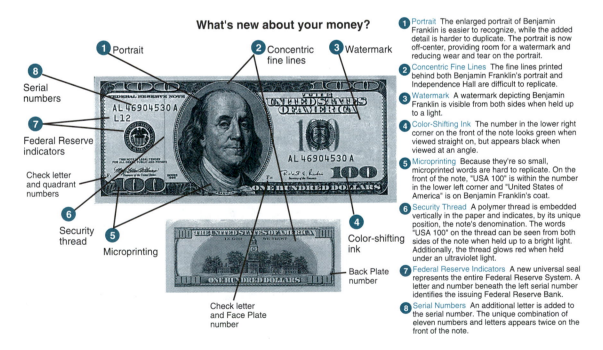

What's new about your money?

1. Portrait
2. Concentric fine lines
3. Watermark
8. Serial numbers
7. Federal Reserve indicators
Check letter and quadrant numbers
6. Security thread
5. Microprinting
Check letter and Face Plate number
Color-shifting ink
Back Plate number

1. **Portrait** The enlarged portrait of Benjamin Franklin is easier to recognize, while the added detail is harder to duplicate. The portrait is now off-center, providing room for a watermark and reducing wear and tear on the portrait.

2. **Concentric Fine Lines** The fine lines printed behind both Benjamin Franklin's portrait and Independence Hall are difficult to replicate.

3. **Watermark** A watermark depicting Benjamin Franklin is visible from both sides when held up to a light.

4. **Color-Shifting Ink** The number in the lower right corner on the front of the note looks green when viewed straight on, but appears black when viewed at an angle.

5. **Microprinting** Because they're so small, microprinted words are hard to replicate. On the front of the note, "USA 100" is within the number in the lower left corner and "United States of America" is on Benjamin Franklin's coat.

6. **Security Thread** A polymer thread is embedded vertically in the paper and indicates, by its unique position, the note's denomination. The words "USA 100" on the thread can be seen from both sides of the note when held up to a bright light. Additionally, the thread glows red when held under an ultraviolet light.

7. **Federal Reserve Indicators** A new universal seal represents the entire Federal Reserve System. A letter and number beneath the left serial number identifies the issuing Federal Reserve Bank.

8. **Serial Numbers** An additional letter is added to the serial number. The unique combination of eleven numbers and letters appears twice on the front of the note.

Figure 4.1

from counterfeiting. In 1996 the U.S. Treasury issued newly designed currency notes that have several new security features:

1. A security thread interwoven into the bills' fibers that will be located in different spots for different denomination bills.

2. A watermark image of the individual portrayed on the note.

3. A larger, more detailed portrait moved to the left so that both the watermark and the portrait will be used to authenticate the bill.

4. Variable-color ink, whose color will shift with the angle of viewing.

5. Infrared fibers and new magnetic patterns for improved mechanical verification.

The changes to the $100 bill are shown in Figure TT.1. However, even before the introduction of these security features, the U.S. currency had very low levels of counterfeiting activity in the United States—on the order of $25 million per year, or only 10 cents per capita.

The essential characteristic that makes something "money-like" is its liquidity. The more liquid an asset is, the higher its degree of "moneyness." In Chapter 2, we defined liquidity as a measure of the ability to sell an asset at its fair market value at any time. Any transaction costs incurred during the sale of the asset are deducted from the proceeds of its sale, thereby reducing the seller's receipts below the asset's true market value. The higher the transaction costs, the lower the net proceeds received by the seller upon liquidation, and the less liquid is the asset. Transaction costs include any commissions, fees, brokerage charges, legal costs, cost of time and inconvenience, plus the difference between the asset's true value and its sales (liquidation) price. If you have to accept "fire sale" prices to liquidate an asset, then the asset is relatively illiquid since its liquidation cost includes the price discount necessary to sell the asset expeditiously. Liquidation costs also include the value of your time standing in a bank line to withdraw your savings from your savings account, or the brokerage fee on the sale of stock, or an attorney's fees for the sale of property. **Transaction accounts** (such as demand deposits and negotiable order of withdrawal, or NOW, accounts) are the most liquid assets, next to cash, because withdrawals can be made with transferable instruments such as checks. Assets with higher transaction costs are less liquid and are placed closer to the right-hand side of the liquidity spectrum shown in Figure 4.1.

transaction account: a deposit against which the account holder is permitted to make an unlimited number of withdrawals using negotiable or transferable instruments such as checks.

In general, short term money market instruments (such as Treasury bills, repurchase agreements, or bankers acceptances) tend to be more liquid than medium term notes, which tend to be more liquid than long term notes. This is because the longer the asset's maturity, the more times it can be resold prior to its maturity. This causes longer maturity assets to have higher expected transaction costs of liquidation, and therefore lower levels of liquidity than equivalent shorter maturity assets. Alternatively, the shorter the maturity, the lower expected liquidation costs and, therefore, the more liquid the security. All else being equal, the greater the liquidity, the lower the security's risk-adjusted required rate of return.

Since liquidity is a spectrum, money can be defined as the most liquid asset on the line up until a certain point. The cutoff point is at the discretion of the person writing the definition. A very narrow definition of money would use a cutoff point close to the left-hand side of the liquidity spectrum. Broader definitions of money entail moving the cutoff point progressively to the right.

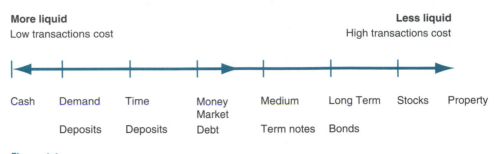

The liquidity spectrum

More liquid
Low transactions cost

Less liquid
High transactions cost

Cash   Demand   Time   Money   Medium   Long Term   Stocks   Property
                          Market
        Deposits Deposits Debt   Term notes Bonds

Figure 4.1

Checkpoint

1. What characteristics make an asset liquid?

2. List all the costs that are included in liquidation costs.

3. How is the liquidity spectrum used to define money?

How Does the Fed Define Money?

money supply: the amount of money in circulation.

The Fed uses four different definitions of money to measure the **money supply**, the amount of money in circulation. M1 is the narrowest definition (the cutoff point is closest to the left side of the liquidity spectrum), and L is the broadest definition. Table 4.1 shows these four definitions using the Fed's money supply statistics for 1995 expressed as monthly averages.

M1 consists of

- currency (Federal Reserve banknotes) in circulation (outside of the U.S. Treasury and bank vaults).

Table 4.1

Money Stock Statistics (U.S. dollar billions)[a]

Date		M1	M2	M3	L
1995	Jan.	1149.0	3628.9	4326.9	5309.6
	Feb.	1147.3	3624.6	4336.7	5349.5
	Mar.	1147.9	3632.2	4359.9	5392.5
	Apr.	1149.7	3645.4	4382.0	5421.1
	May	1143.0	3661.9	4409.7	5451.8
	June	1143.9	3698.1	4455.2	5491.8
	July	1145.0	3717.3	4486.3	5546.8
	Aug.	1143.4	3743.1	4516.9	5584.2
	Sep.	1139.8	3756.8	4533.8	5624.4
	Oct.	1129.9	3753.8	4546.2	5645.2
	Nov.	1126.5	3759.5	4548.2	5646.6
	Dec.	1122.9	3777.5	4561.2	NA

[a]These statistics are available on both a seasonally adjusted and an unadjusted basis. Figures shown here are seasonally adjusted.

Source: Federal Reserve Statistical Release H.6, Table 1, January 18, 1996.

- plus nonbank and nongovernmental demand deposits (checking accounts) at all commercial banks, credit unions, and thrift institutions.

float: the increase in bank reserves resulting from delays in check clearing.

- less cash items in the process of collection and the Federal Reserve **float**.
- plus travelers checks.
- plus other checkable deposits (such as NOW accounts).

The Federal Reserve float is the increase in bank reserves resulting from delays in check clearing. That is, the bank receiving the check credits the account of the check depositor before the checkwriter's bank has a chance to debit the account of the check issuer. The float acts like an interest-free loan from the banking system to the public and represents a temporary increase in the balance of funds immediately available for use by the public.

M2 consists of M1

- plus savings and time deposits in amounts of less than $100,000.
- plus money market deposit accounts (MMDAs).
- plus balances in money market mutual funds (except for IRA and Keogh plan balances).
- plus overnight repurchase agreements issued by all commercial banks.
- plus overnight Eurodollars issued to U.S. residents by foreign branches of U.S. banks.

repurchase agreements: fully collateralized loans where the collateral consists of marketable securities.

M2 excludes all accounts owned by banks or other FIs, the U.S. government, foreign governments, or foreign commercial banks. Thus, it represents private sector, non-FI holdings of liquid assets. As we will see in Chapter 11, **repurchase agreements** are fully collateralized loans in which the collateral consists of marketable securities, such that the securities are sold and then repurchased at a later date.

M3 consists of M2

- plus time deposits with balances exceeding $100,000.
- plus term repurchase agreements.
- plus term Eurodollars issued to U.S. residents by foreign branches of U.S. banks.
- plus all term Eurodollars in banking offices in the United Kingdom and Canada.
- plus all balances in money market mutual funds held by FIs.

L consists of M3

- plus nonbank public holdings of U.S. savings bonds.
- plus nonbank public holdings of short term Treasury securities.
- plus commercial paper.
- plus bankers acceptances.

commercial paper: short term (fewer than 270 days to maturity when issued) unsecured debt instruments.

- less money market holdings of the above assets.

Commercial paper holdings are short term (fewer than 270 days to maturity when issued) unsecured debt instruments (see Chapter 14). **Bankers acceptances** are short term liabilities issued by banks, often in conjunction with letters of credit supporting international trade (see Chapter 13).

bankers acceptances: short term liabilities issued by banks, often in conjunction with letters of credit supporting international trade.

What determines the amount of money in circulation? The supply of money is impacted by both the private and the public sector. It is the result of an interaction of decisions by private FIs, public FIs, nonfinancial businesses, and individuals.

Checkpoint

✓

1. What is the difference between M1 and M2?

2. What is the difference between M2 and M3?

3. What is the difference between M3 and L?

➤ The Role of the Private Sector in Determining the Money Supply

The money supply figures in Table 4.1 are the consequence of millions of individual decisions by households, businesses, and private FIs. Households and nonfinancial businesses must decide in what form to hold their assets. Should they hold assets evenly distributed across the liquidity spectrum of Figure 4.1, or should they keep most of their assets in more liquid, more money-like investments? The demand for money is determined by the public's willingness to hold liquid assets in the form of money.

The Private Sector's Demand for Money

Individuals and businesses hold money for *transactions purposes*. Suppose that you have a tuition payment due this week. Chances are that you will increase the liquidity of your asset portfolio in order to be able to meet your financial obligation. If all of your assets were in very illiquid investments, then it would be costly for you to liquidate your holdings so as to be able to pay your tuition.

Individuals and businesses also hold money for *speculative purposes*. Access to readily available funds is often necessary to take advantage of an extraordinary sale or an unanticipated business opportunity. Rapid liquidation of illiquid assets may prove so costly that the speculative opportunity is no longer worthwhile.

Liquidity, though beneficial for both transactions and speculative purposes, is also costly. If you hold all of your assets in their most liquid form, cash, then you give up potential earnings from investing your assets in less liquid, interest-bearing securities. Since, all else being equal, the more liquid the asset, the lower its required rate of return, greater liquidity entails an **opportunity cost**, measured as the foregone return on alternative investments. Individuals and businesses will determine their money holdings by weighing the benefits of liquidity against the opportunity cost. The greater the optimal level of liquidity, the more money-like the assets in private portfolios.

opportunity cost: the foregone return on alternative investments.

The optimal level of money holdings has changed over time, as the costs and benefits of liquidity have changed. The opportunity cost of liquidity increases when interest rates are high, thereby reducing optimal money holdings. The benefits of liquidity decrease when the economy is stagnant since both speculative and transactions demand for money decrease, thereby reducing optimal money holdings. If individuals and businesses choose to hold less money, all else being equal, then that money has to work harder to pay for goods and services. Each dollar will be respent more frequently since money balances are reduced to the bare minimum. As people spend their money faster, we say that the velocity of money is increasing. The **velocity of money** is a measure of the rate of monetary turnover, the number of times that the average dollar is respent in the course of the year. Currently, the value of velocity of M1 (M2) is almost 6 (1.75) in the United States; that is, each dollar's worth of cash and demand deposits is respent an average of six times a year. Velocity levels in the 20 to 50 range have been observed in countries suffering from very high levels of inflation. Figure 4.2*a* shows

velocity of money: the measure of the rate of monetary turnover, the number of times that the average dollar is respent in the course of the year.

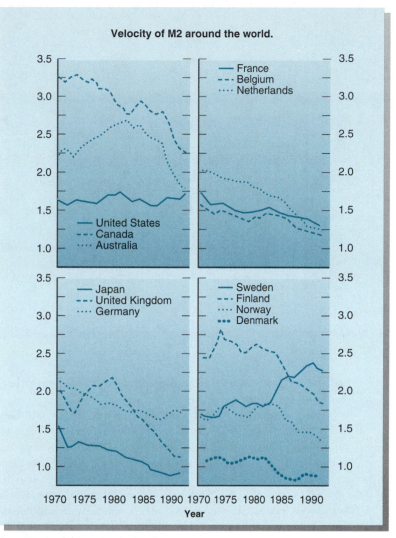

Velocity of M2 around the world.

Source: National data and author's estimates.

Figure 4.2a

that velocity varies across countries. As Figure 4.2*b* shows, velocity is closely related to the opportunity cost of holding money; as the opportunity cost increases (as in the inflationary late 1970s to early 1980s), the velocity increases, and as the opportunity cost decreases (following the December 1982 introduction of NOW accounts), velocity decreases, although this relationship has changed in the early 1990s.

We have focused on individuals' and businesses' desires to hold money balances. However, demand is only half of the story. We now must examine the banking system's role in supplying money.

Private FIs' Supply of Money: The Banks' Role

The narrowest definition of the money supply, M1, includes currency and checking accounts held by individuals and businesses in the private sector. Banks also hold currency (vault cash)

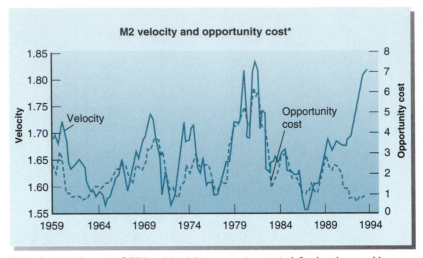

M2 velocity and opportunity cost*

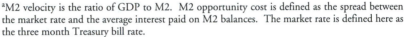

[a]M2 velocity is the ratio of GDP to M2. M2 opportunity cost is defined as the spread between the market rate and the average interest paid on M2 balances. The market rate is defined here as the three month Treasury bill rate.

Source: Board of Governors of the Federal Reserve System.

Figure 4.2b

and checking accounts (demand deposits at the Fed). But the banking system's holdings of vault cash and demand deposits are not included in the definition of the money supply. This is because these balances do not enter the money supply until they are transferred to either individuals or businesses. When these balances are still in the possession of the banks, they are called bank **reserves**. Total bank reserves consist of the sum of vault cash and demand deposits at the central bank. During the biweekly period ending November 8, 1995, U.S. banks held an average of $41.123 billion in vault cash and $19.332 billion in demand deposits at the Fed, for total reserves of $56.179 billion. Since only banks that are members of the Federal Reserve System can hold reserve accounts at the Fed, nonmember banks maintain reserve accounts with member banks who process nonmembers' reserves on their behalf. Reserve accounts at the Fed pay no interest.

reserves: bank holdings of vault cash and demand deposits at the central bank.

Banks hold reserves for the same reasons that individuals and businesses hold money. Immediately available reserves are the most liquid assets on the banks' balance sheets. These assets can be liquidated at low transactions cost when banks must either make transactions or take advantage of business opportunities. Bank payment transactions stem from depositors' requests for withdrawal of their funds, whereas bank speculative payments stem from potential borrowers' requests for loans. If a bank is to satisfy the demands of both its depositors and potential borrowers, then it must have access to immediately available funds. These funds are the bank's reserves.

Bank reserves enter the money supply when they are paid out to the public. Thus, the quantity of bank reserves is directly related to the size of the money supply. However, bank reserves are only a small fraction of even the narrowest definition of the money supply. Comparing the November 1995 bank reserves total of $56.179 billion against a value of M1 of $1,126.5 billion, total bank reserves represented only 5% of M1, 1.5% of M2, and less than 1% of L. This relationship between bank reserves and the money supply is the result of a fractional reserve system of banking. Banks need hold only a small fraction of their deposit liabilities in the form of reserves because at any one point in time only a small fraction of depositors withdraw money from their accounts. The portion of bank assets held in the form of liquid reserves depends on the bank's expectations of deposit withdrawals (transactions demand for money) and loan demand (speculative demand for money). When banks determine their expected demand for reserves for both transactions and speculative purposes, they weigh these benefits of liquidity against the opportunity cost. The bank's opportunity cost is the interest that could have been earned if the reserves were instead invested in interest-bearing instruments.

The level of reserves held by banks is not entirely left to their discretion. Central banks set reserve requirements that establish *minimum* levels of required reserves. In other words, a bank can exceed these regulatory minimums. Any reserves over the reserve requirement are **excess reserves** or **free reserves**. The November 1995 reserves of $56.179 billion were $1.05 billion above the reserve requirement of $55.129 billion. The reserve requirement is stated in the form of a **reserve ratio**, which is the minimum required fraction of reserves for each type of bank deposit. In the United States, the reserve ratio for each bank's first $52 million of demand deposits is currently 3%, with a 10% reserve requirement for any additional demand deposits.[1] Currently, the reserve ratios on time deposits and Eurocurrency liabilities are set at zero. Reserves must be held by commercial banks, mutual savings banks, savings and loan associations, credit unions, agencies and branches of foreign banks, and **Edge Act corporations**—separately incorporated bank subsidiaries that specialize in international transactions.

excess reserves or **free reserves:** reserves over the reserve requirement.

reserve ratio: the minimum required fraction of reserves for each type of bank deposit.

Edge Act corporations: separately incorporated bank subsidiaries that specialize in international transactions.

Checkpoint

1. Why do individuals hold money? What are the benefits and the opportunity costs?
2. Why do banks hold reserves? What are the benefits and the opportunity costs?
3. What is the velocity of money? How is it affected by the levels of interest rates and inflation?
4. In what form do banks hold reserves?
5. What determines the level of required reserves?

➤ Calculating Reserve Requirements

Reserve requirements represent a fraction of the deposit liabilities held by the bank and are calculated in a two-step process. Step 1 consists of totaling the deposit balances in the bank at the close of each business day. Since deposit balances fluctuate each day, the daily deposit amounts are averaged over a prespecified **reserve computation period** to obtain an average daily deposit balance. Step 2 consists of applying the reserve ratio to the average daily deposit amount so as to calculate the average daily reserve requirement. Average daily reserves over the **reserve maintenance period** must not be less than this average daily reserve requirement.

reserve computation period: period over which reserves are calculated.

reserve maintenance period: period over which actual reserves have to meet or exceed the required reserve target.

Prior to February 1984, the Fed utilized a *lagged reserve accounting period* (LRA) under which all amounts (both deposit balances and reserves) were averaged over a seven day period. The reserve computation period began two weeks prior to the beginning of the reserve maintenance period. In this way, the bank had perfect information about its daily average reserve requirement during the entire reserve maintenance period.

LRA allowed banks to meet their reserve requirements exactly with little or no excess reserves. As Figure 4.3 shows, before 1984 almost no relationship existed between changes in bank reserves and the supply of money. Concern about bank liquidity and the efficacy of monetary policy led the Fed to switch to *contemporaneous reserve accounting* (CRA) in February 1984. Since 1984, there has been a close and stable relationship between bank reserves and demand

---

[1] Moreover, the first $4.3 million of demand deposits are exempt from all reserve requirements.

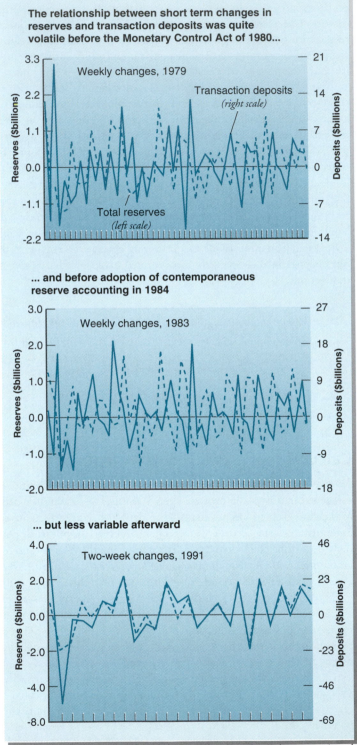

The relationship between short term changes in reserves and transaction deposits was quite volatile before the Monetary Control Act of 1980...

Weekly changes, 1979

Transaction deposits *(right scale)*

Total reserves *(left scale)*

... and before adoption of contemporaneous reserve accounting in 1984

Weekly changes, 1983

... but less variable afterward

Two-week changes, 1991

All data are in billions of dollars, not seasonally adjusted.   Scaling approximately reflects each year's average ratio of transaction deposits to total reserves.

Source: Federal Reserve Bank of Chicago, *Modern Money Mechanics,* February 1994 p. 37

Figure 4.3

deposits (see bottom graph of Figure 4.3), thereby allowing the Fed to conduct monetary policy more effectively. Under CRA, both the reserve computation period and the reserve maintenance periods were extended from 7 to 14 days. The two time periods overlap for 12 of their 14 days. The two week reserve computation period begins on a Tuesday, and the two week reserve maintenance period begins two days later on the following Thursday. This means that the last two days of the reserve maintenance period (Tuesday and Wednesday) occur after the end of the reserve computation period. Thus, the bank knows its reserve requirements exactly on the last two days of the reserve maintenance period, but not before. Because banks are uncertain about their exact reserve requirement for most of the reserve maintenance period, it is prudent to hold excess reserves to keep the bank from paying a penalty rate on reserve deficiencies, which equals a rate that is two percentage points above the discount rate.

Suppose that you had to compute the reserve requirements of a $1.3 billion U.S. bank under CRA. Let's examine the two-step process.

Step 1: Calculating Deposit Balances   At the close of business each day, the bank's computers generate a record of all transactions posted to customers' demand deposits during the day. Daily totals of checking account balances are:

Date	Mon. 2/5	Tues. 2/6	Wed. 2/7	Thurs. 2/8	Fri. 2/9
Deposit amt. ($m)	469	483	437	512	405
Date	Mon. 2/12	Tues. 2/13	Wed. 2/14	Thurs. 2/15	Fri. 2/16
Deposit amt. ($m)	491	504	477	502	426
Date	Mon. 2/19	Tues. 2/20	Wed. 2/21	Thurs. 2/22	Fri. 2/23
Deposit amt. ($m)	511	498	427	438	416

The 14 day reserve computation period begins on Tuesday, 2/6, and ends on Monday, 2/19. This period contains two weekends, 2/10–2/11 and 2/17–2/18. Since bank balances are generally not posted on Saturdays and Sundays, each Friday balance is used three times. This lends extra weight to the Friday closing figures. A bank can reduce its two week average daily deposit balance (and therefore its reserve requirement) by transferring deposits to an offshore affiliate on Fridays and returning them on Mondays. If each Friday $10 million were shifted in this *weekend game*, then the sum of daily deposit balances would decline by $40 million, calculated as –$60 million (two Fridays times three days times $10 million) + $20 million (two Mondays times $10 million), for a decline of $\frac{$40}{14}$ = $2.857 million in the bank's average daily deposit balance over the 14 day reserve computation period.

Using the deposit balances shown above, average daily deposits over the reserve computation period 2/6–2/19 are

$$\frac{1}{14}(483 + 437 + 512 + 3(405) + 491 + 504 + 477 + 502 + 3(426) + 511) = \$457.857 \text{ million}$$

Our hypothetical bank has an average daily deposit balance of $457.857 million over the two week reserve computation period. Reserves must be held against this deposit base. What is the level of the bank's required reserves?

Step 2: Calculating the Bank's Reserves   The reserve requirement is calculated as a fraction of the bank's deposit base. For our hypothetical bank, using a reserve ratio of 3% for the first $47.7 million of deposits and 10% for all deposits above $52 million,[2] we find that the average daily reserve requirement is

$$(3\% \times \$47.7) + [10\% \times (\$457.857 - \$52)] = \$1.4 + \$40.6 = \$42 \text{ million}$$

This is the bank's daily minimum level of required reserves. The bank does not have to meet this reserve requirement each day of the reserve maintenance period, but its average daily reserves must not be less than $42 million. How does the bank compute its average daily level of reserves?

---

[2] The $52 million cutoff for a 3% reserve requirement less the exemption of $4.3 million.

The bank must meet its reserve requirement over a prespecified 14 day reserve maintenance period. This period begins two days after the start of the reserve computation period and ends two days after the reserve computation period ends. For our hypothetical bank, the reserve maintenance period begins on Thursday, 2/8, and ends on Wednesday, 2/21. To complete Step 2, we must calculate the bank's reserve levels over this 14 day period, noting again that Friday balances are counted three times and used in place of Saturday and Sunday computations.

Let's first consider demand deposits at the Fed. At the close of business each day, the bank's computers generate the bank's balances at the Fed. Suppose that the 14 day record of reserve account balances at our hypothetical bank was as follows:

Date	Mon. 2/5	Tues. 2/6	Wed. 2/7	Thurs. 2/8	Fri. 2/9
Deposit amt. ($m)	39	43	33	21	45
Date	Mon. 2/12	Tues. 2/13	Wed. 2/14	Thurs. 2/15	Fri. 2/16
Deposit amt. ($m)	21	34	27	32	36
Date	Mon. 2/19	Tues. 2/20	Wed. 2/21	Thurs. 2/22	Fri. 2/23
Deposit amt. ($m)	21	29	27	33	41

Average daily balances in the bank's reserve account at the Fed over the reserve maintenance period 2/8–2/21 are

$$\tfrac{1}{14}(21 + 3(45) + 21 + 34 + 27 + 32 + 3(36) + 21 + 29 + 27) = \$32.5 \text{ million}$$

The second component of reserves is vault cash. Since vault cash must be laboriously counted, CRA uses the average level of vault cash in the bank over the two week period prior to the beginning of the reserve computation period. For our example, then, the 14 day average daily amount of vault cash would be computed over the period 1/23–2/5. Suppose that the 14 day record of vault cash balances at our hypothetical bank was as follows:

Date	Mon. 1/22	Tues. 1/23	Wed. 1/24	Thurs. 1/25	Fri. 1/26
Deposit amt. ($m)	9	13	7	12	15
Date	Mon. 1/29	Tues. 1/30	Wed. 1/31	Thurs. 2/1	Fri. 2/2
Deposit amt. ($m)	11	7	11	12	6
Date	Mon. 2/5	Tues. 2/6	Wed. 2/7	Thurs. 2/8	Fri. 2/9
Deposit amt. ($m)	11	2	7	8	11

Average daily holdings of vault cash over the period 1/23–2/5 are

$$\tfrac{1}{14}(13 + 7 + 12 + 3(15) + 11 + 7 + 11 + 12 + 3(6) + 11) = \$10.5 \text{ million}$$

Completing Step 2, to compute the bank's reserve holdings, we must add the average daily balances at the Fed to average daily holdings of vault cash, so that:

Average daily reserves over the reserve maintenance period
= Average daily demand deposits at the Fed plus average daily holdings of vault cash.

For our hypothetical bank, average daily reserves are

$$\$32.5 \text{ million} + \$10.5 \text{ million} = \$43 \text{ million}.$$

Our hypothetical bank has met its reserve requirements since its average daily reserves of $43 million exceed its average daily reserve requirement of $42 million. During the period 2/8–2/21, the bank has average daily excess reserves of $43 – $42 = $1 million for a two week total of $14 million in excess reserves.

An excess or deficiency of up to 4% of required reserves can be carried forward to the next reserve maintenance period only. Since 4% of our hypothetical bank's reserves is 4% × $42 =

$1.7 million, the bank can have a reserve deficiency next period of up to $1.7 million. If the bank has excess reserves next period, then it loses this carryforward. If the bank is short reserves during the next reserve maintenance period, it can utilize up to $1.7 million in average daily reserves to make up the deficiency. The bank can therefore carry forward its excess reserves of $1 million to be used to satisfy next-period reserve requirements.[3]

Why do banks hold excess reserves if they are costly and are not needed to satisfy reserve requirements? They try their hardest not to do so. It is the job of traders on the banks' money market trading desks to satisfy the banks' reserve requirements without either undershooting the target (resulting in a reserve deficiency) or overshooting the target (resulting in excess reserves). This may sound easy, but its practice is complicated by the problem of imperfect information.

What Do We Know and When Do We Know It?

Federal Funds: unsecured, interbank loans of immediately available funds.

cleared transactions: transactions that have been settled.

The bank's **Federal Funds** traders are responsible for managing the bank's reserve position. Federal Funds are unsecured, interbank loans of immediately available funds and are important components of bank reserves since they are deposited directly into the bank's reserve account at the Fed. The bank's reserve position fluctuates constantly throughout the day as transactions are **cleared**, or settled, causing reserve adjustments. Reserve balances turn over many times in the average day.[4] If our hypothetical bank's Federal Funds traders wanted to hit the required reserve target exactly, so as to minimize the bank's opportunity cost of reserves, they would have to know the bank's average daily deposit balance over the reserve computation period. When would they receive this information? Not until the end of the reserve computation period, on February 19! That would leave only two days, February 20 and February 21, to buy up sufficient Federal Funds to meet the bank's reserve requirement. If the bank held only vault cash and no reserve balances for the first 12 days of the reserve maintenance period, the bank's Federal Funds traders would have to buy reserves amounting to $31.5 million daily to meet the $42 million daily reserve requirement over the 14 day period, totaling $441 million, or an average of $220.5 million each day on Tuesday, February 20, and on Wednesday, February 21. It would be extremely costly, and perhaps even impossible, for one bank to buy this amount of Federal Funds in such a short time period. In practice, the bank's Federal Funds traders try to estimate the bank's reserve requirements during the course of the two week reserve maintenance period. They are likely to hold some amount of excess reserves as a cushion against errors in their forecast of the bank's reserve requirements.

The forecast of the bank's reserve requirements is actually a forecast of the aggregate daily balances of the bank's demand deposit liabilities. The bank will examine seasonal factors such as the increase in cash balances from the payment of Social Security benefits on the third of every month. However, forecasts can be wrong, and the last Wednesday of each reserve maintenance period (February 21 in our example) is always a busy day on the Federal Funds market, as traders scurry to adjust their positions and meet their reserve requirements before the markets close. In fact, Federal Funds rates tend to be higher and more volatile on the last Wednesday of the reserve maintenance period than on any other of the 14 days.[5]

---

[3] If, however, the bank held $2 million in excess reserves, then it would lose $300,000 in daily excess reserves (i.e., $2 million minus the carryforward allowance of $1.7 million equals $300,000). In this case, the hypothetical bank gets no credit for these excess reserves, even though it forfeited interest-earning potential to hold these liquid assets.

[4] For a discussion, see Ann-Marie Meulendyke, "Reserve Requirements and the Discount Window in Recent Decades," Federal Reserve Bank of New York *Quarterly Review* (Autumn 1992): 25–43.

[5] Federal Funds rates are also volatile on Fridays because of the triple counting of Friday closing balances. Griffiths and Winters (1995) find that Federal Funds rate volatility increases significantly on the second Wednesday of each settlement period and on each Friday. They find evidence of increased lending pressure on Fridays and increased borrowing pressure on settlement Wednesdays. (See Chapter 10.)

Checkpoint

✓

1. How long is the reserve computation period under lagged reserve accounting (LRA)? under contemporaneous reserve accounting (CRA)?

2. How long is the reserve maintenance period under LRA? under CRA?

3. What is the primary difference between LRA and CRA?

4. What is the most important determinant of the level of bank reserve requirements?

5. What is a bank's desired level of excess reserves? Why is it more difficult to keep excess reserves around zero under CRA than under LRA?

➤ The Relationship Between Reserves and the Money Supply

We have seen how banks hold required reserves as well as excess reserves. These reserves constitute only a fraction of deposit balances. Deposits are a major component of the supply of money. How much money can a banking system with a given level of reserves create? We can answer this question by simply inverting the calculations we performed in Step 2 of the required reserve computations. If required reserves are only 10% of demand deposits, then banks need hold only 10 cents of each marginal dollar of deposits as reserves. The remaining 90 cents on each dollar of deposits can be lent out or invested in securities. Indeed, the bank generates profits by investing the 90 cents per dollar of deposits in interest-earning investments. The balance sheet for our hypothetical $1.3 billion bank might look like this:

No–Name Bank, Inc. ($ million)

Vault cash	10.5	Demand deposits	457.857
Demand deposits at Fed	32.5	Time deposits	725
Securities	330	Capital	117.143
Loans	927		
Total	1,300	Total	1,300

As in this example, the bank's reserves totaling $43 million consist of $10.5 million vault cash and $32.5 million reserve balances at the Fed. Since required reserves are only on average $42 million daily, the bank has excess reserves of $1 million. These excess reserves earn no interest for the bank. What would happen to the supply of money if the bank decided to lend out its excess reserves?

Suppose the bank decided to lend the $1 million to a company called Bright Idea, Inc. to purchase a fleet of trucks. Upon granting the loan, the bank receives a loan promissory note from Bright Idea, Inc. for $1 million plus interest. The bank provides the company with a demand deposit with a $1 million balance. As shown in Table 4.2a representing balance sheet *changes*, No-Name Bank's balance sheet shows an additional $1 million loan asset (for total loans of $928 million) and an additional $1 million demand deposit liability (for total deposits of $458.857 million).

Bright Idea pays for the truck fleet by writing a check drawn on its checking account at No-Name Bank. The check clears through the bank's reserve account at the Federal Reserve Bank. The truck retailer, Trucks R Us, banks with Detroit AutoBank, Inc. Bright Idea pays Trucks R Us $1 million. To clear this transaction, No-Name pays Detroit AutoBank $1 million on behalf of its customers. Changes to No-Name Bank's balance sheet are shown in Table 4.2b.

Table 4.2a	**Changes to No–Name Bank's Balance Sheet:** **Lends $1 million to Bright Idea, Inc.**

Assets	Liabilities
Loans +$1m	Demand deposits: Bright Idea, Inc. +$1m

Table 4.2b	**Changes to No–Name Bank's Balance Sheet:** **Pays $1 million to Detroit AutoBank**

Assets	Liabilities
Reserves −$1m	Demand deposits: Bright Idea, Inc. +$1m
Loans +$1m	−$1m

No-Name Bank's balance sheet reflects a $1 million decline in reserves to a total amount of $42 million from $43 million. No-Name Bank's reserves are exactly equal to its required reserves. We say that No-Name Bank is "fully loaned up" since its excess reserves are equal to zero. The impact of the transaction for No-Name Bank is to transform $1 million of noninterest-bearing reserves into a $1 million interest-earning loan asset.

What is happening at Detroit AutoBank? The balance sheet changes are shown in Table 4.2c. If Detroit AutoBank formerly was fully loaned up, then this transaction creates excess reserves. This is because the bank's required reserves increase by the reserve ratio (10%) of the increase in demand deposits ($1 million), or an increase in reserve requirements of $100,000. However, reserves have increased by $1 million, leaving Detroit AutoBank with excess reserves of $900,000 which can be lent out, used to purchase securities, or held as excess reserves. Suppose that Detroit AutoBank decides to lend the $900,000 to General Motors, Inc. for the purchase of computer workstations. This transaction is shown on Detroit AutoBank's balance sheet in Table 4.2d.

If the aggregate money supply was measured at this stage in the process, then the value of M1 would show an increase of $1.9 million in newly created demand deposits. No-Name Bank's decision to lend out its $1 million excess reserves had almost a twofold impact on the money supply, but, of course, the process is not yet done. GM spends the $900,000 on computer equipment, causing the cash flows shown in Table 4.2e.

Table 4.2c	**Changes to Detroit AutoBank's Balance Sheet:** **Receives $1 million on Behalf of Trucks R Us**

Assets	Liabilities
Reserves +$1m	Demand deposits: Trucks R Us +$1m

Table 4.2d	**Changes to Detroit AutoBank's Balance Sheet:** **Lends $900,000 to GM**

Assets	Liabilities
Reserves +$1m	Demand deposits: Trucks R Us +$1m
Loans +$.9m	Demand deposits: GM +$.9m

Table 4.2e

Changes to Detroit AutoBank's Balance Sheet: Pays $900,000 to Silicon Valley Bank

Assets		Liabilities	
Reserves	+$1m	Demand Deposits: Trucks R Us	+$1m
	−$.9m	Demand deposits: GM	+$.9m
Loan to GM	+$.9m		−$.9m

Table 4.2f

Changes to Silicon Valley Bank's Balance Sheet: Receives $900,000 from Detroit AutoBank

Assets		Liabilities	
Reserves	+$.9m	Demand deposits: Micro Tech	+$.9m

GM's check for $900,000 is cleared through the Fed, resulting in the $900,000 reduction in Detroit AutoBank's reserve account balances. Then GM's demand deposit balance is reduced by $900,000. The $900,000 check is cleared at Silicon Valley Bank by the computer company, Micro Tech, Inc. The impact on Silicon Valley Bank's balance sheet is shown in Table 4.2f.

Since reserve requirements are only 10% of the increase in demand deposits, required reserves increase by $90,000 (10% × $900,000), and Silicon Valley Bank's excess reserves increase by $810,000 ($900,000 − $90,000). Silicon Valley Bank can either lend out its excess reserves, or buy securities, or hold additional excess reserves. If Silicon Valley Bank does anything except hold the entire $810,000 as excess reserves, then the expansionary process will continue. Silicon Valley Bank puts the newly received excess reserves back into circulation either by its lending activities or by purchasing securities. These funds ultimately find their way into the banking system in the form of deposits, thereby increasing the size of the money supply. This process continues until excess reserves are no longer created. The amount of money created in each step of the process will naturally diminish since the amount of excess reserves is automatically decreased in each round owing to the leakage of required reserves. Each time the money is relent, 10% must be taken off the top for reserve requirements, thereby diminishing the amount of money that is available to fuel further rounds. This money-creation process therefore converges to a limit:

Maximum Amount of Newly Created Deposits (ΔM) =
Initial Increase in Bank Reserves in Circulation (ΔR)/Reserve Ratio (RR)

$$\Delta M = \frac{\Delta R}{RR}$$

For this example, the initial increase in bank reserves in circulation (the decision by No-Name Bank to utilize its excess reserves) was $1 million. The reserve ratio is 10% for a tenfold ultimate maximum increase in the money supply to $10 million. The inverse of the reserve ratio ($\frac{1}{RR}$) is called the **money multiplier**, and it tells us the upper bound on the money-creation powers of the banking system. This upper bound is reached only if, at each stage of the process, each bank passes along all of its windfall increase in excess reserves. If Silicon Valley Bank chooses not to lend its excess reserves of $810,000, new deposits will total only $1.9 million (the total of new deposits in Tables 4.2d and 4.2f) as opposed to the maximum attainable level of $10 million.

money multiplier: the inverse of the reserve ratio ($\frac{1}{RR}$), which tells us the upper bound on the money creation powers of the banking system.

In our example, No-Name Bank decided spontaneously to lend out its excess reserves. This began the entire process of money creation, which could be either sustained or curtailed by the actions of other banks in the banking system. Any change in the level of bank reserves will start the process. It would go in the opposite direction if excess reserves were decreased. The sum of all bank reserves in the system is called the **monetary base**, or **high-powered money**. It is not hard to see why it is called high-powered. With a reserve ratio of 10%, any increase (decrease) in the monetary base results in a maximum tenfold increase (decrease) in the supply of money in circulation. The supply of money is increased by injecting high-powered money into the system; the supply of money is decreased by draining high-powered money from the system.

monetary base or **high-powered money:** the sum of all bank reserves in the system.

Checkpoint

1. What is the money multiplier and how is it calculated?

2. How do banks create money?

3. What is the monetary base? What is its role in money creation?

Determining the Level of Bank Reserves

We have seen how private FIs can impact the supply of money by altering their desired levels of excess reserves. Banks' decisions to exchange their noninterest-bearing excess reserves for interest-earning, less liquid assets (such as loans) represent a downward shift in their willingness to hold "money." The decrease in the banks' willingness to hold liquid reserves resulted in an increase in their lending activity, which increased the money supply by the multiple of the money multiplier.

Similarly, if individuals and businesses decide to shift some of their noninterest-bearing, liquid assets into less liquid, interest-earning assets, then this will represent a reduction in their willingness to hold money. As can be seen in Table 4.3, a decrease in demand deposits (reduction in the demand for money) results in a decrease in reserve balances, which fuels a multiplied decrease in the money supply.

When individuals increase their holdings of currency, they withdraw deposits from the banking system, thereby reducing bank reserves. Rather than resulting in a fractional decrease in the bank reserves, this currency leakage reduces the level of bank reserves on a one for one basis: a $1 increase in currency uses up $1 of bank reserves since the entire $1 is drawn from vault cash. If the $1 is not replaced (deposited in another bank somewhere), then this represents a $1 decrease in total bank reserves. Thus, when a depositor cashes a $100 check written on Bank A, both deposits and vault cash reserves decline $100.

With a 10% reserve ratio, the cash withdrawal results in a $90 reserve deficiency (if the bank was formerly fully loaned up) and requires the bank to reduce its deposits by an additional $900. The result is a tenfold reduction in the money supply. Of course, if that currency is spent and the recipient deposits the cash into his checking account, then the money reenters the banking system, reserves are increased on a dollar for dollar basis, and the supply of money returns to its original level.

The demand for currency varies according to seasonal factors. Typically, then, the Fed uses its policy tools to offset the powerful impact of changes in private-sector currency holdings on the aggregate supply of money. Although the Fed has the greatest impact on the level of bank reserves, *Practitioner's Primer 4.1* shows how other players (such as the Treasury and foreign central banks) affect the money supply.

Table 4.3

Factors Changing Reserve Balances—Independent and Policy Actions

Factor	Change in Federal Reserve Liabilities	Change in Money Supply
Individual and Business Private Actions		
Increase in demand deposits	↑	↑
Decrease in demand deposits	↓	↓
Increase in currency holdings	↓	↓
Decrease in currency holdings	↑	↑
Treasury, FI, and Foreign Actions		
Increase in Treasury deposits in Fed	↑	↓
Transfer from Treasury account at Fed to TT&L account	↓	↑
Treasury Gold purchases[a]	↓	↑
Treasury Gold sales[a]	↑	↓
Sales of U.S. dollars	↑	↓
Purchases of U.S. dollars	↓	↑
Increase in Treasury expenditures	no change	↑
Decrease in Treasury expenditures	no change	↓
Increase in foreign deposits at Fed	↑	↓
Decrease in foreign deposits at Fed	↓	↑
Increase in service-related balances	↓	↓
Decrease in service-related balances	↑	↑
Federal Reserve Actions		
Monetary Policy Actions		
Purchase of Securities	↑	↑
Sales of Securities	↓	↓
Loans to private FIs	↑	↑
Repayment of Loans by private FIs	↓	↓
Increase in reserve requirements	no change[a]	↓
Decrease in reserve requirements	no change[a]	↑
Nonmonetary Policy Actions		
Increase in float	↑	↑
Decrease in float	↓	↓

[a]Effect on excess reserves. Total reserves are unchanged. If reserve changes are in the form of vault cash, Federal Reserve accounts are not affected.

Source: Federal Reserve Bank of Chicago, *Money Market Mechanics*, February 1994, p. 15.

PRACTITIONER'S PRIMER 4.1

NONMONETARY POLICY FACTORS DETERMINING BANK RESERVES

Treasury Tax and Loan (TT&L) note accounts: interest-bearing deposits issued to the Treasury by private banks.

Who are the other players whose actions determine the level of reserves? The Treasury's activities impact the level of reserve balances. The Treasury keeps part of its operating cash balances on deposit with banks in interest-bearing **Treasury Tax and Loan (TT&L) note accounts**, which are interest-bearing deposits issued to the Treasury by private banks and are protected from bank default by government securities collateral. Prior to the authorization of TT&L accounts, the Treasury kept all of its cash balances in its reserve accounts at the Fed. Currently, only the portion of the Treasury's balances that are most actively used to make disbursements are kept on deposit at Federal Reserve banks.

Funds are regularly transferred from the TT&L accounts at the banks into the Treasury's Fed account to finance Treasury expenditures. Because Treasury deposits at the Fed are not considered to be in circulation until they are paid out (or transferred to TT&L accounts), they are not included in any definition of the money supply. Any activity that increases Treasury deposit balances at the Fed takes reserves out of circulation and reduces the overall level of bank reserves. Conversely, any activity that induces the Treasury to pay out balances (such as gold purchases or increased government spending) reduces the Treasury's money holdings and increases the money in circulation. For example, suppose that the Treasury's payment for a $500 hammer is in the form of a check that is cleared by Bank B through the Fed. Table PP.1 shows the resulting increase in bank reserves. The $500 increase in bank reserves can be multiplied tenfold (assuming a 10% reserve ratio) into a $5,000 increase in the money supply.

Table PP.1

Treasury Disbursements Increase Bank Reserves

Bank B		Federal Reserve	
Reserves +$500m	Deposits +$500m	Bank B Reserves	+$500m
		Treasury deposits	−$500m

The normal business activities of private FIs can also affect the level of bank reserves in the economy. We will see in Chapter 6 how important the payments system is to the daily operations of private FIs. The Fed is a vital part of the payments mechanism engaging in check clearing, Fedwire transactions, securities settlement, and safeguarding. Prior to 1980, the Fed provided these services free of charge to Federal Reserve members. The Depository Institutions Deregulatory and Monetary Contral Act (DIDMCA) of 1980 mandated that the Fed expand the availability of these services to nonmember banks and price them appropriately. Banks may pay for these services by depositing **earnings credits** with the Fed. These are bank reserves that can be used to pay for Fed services but cannot be used to satisfy reserve requirements. Since these reserves cannot be lent out, increases in service-related balances (such as earnings credits) reduce reserves in the banking system (see Table 4.3), thereby reducing the money supply.

earnings credits: bank reserves that can be used to pay for Fed services but cannot be used to satisfy reserve requirements.

International transactions by public FIs also impact the domestic level of bank reserves. The Fed acts as the agent for foreign currency transactions of both the U.S. Treasury and foreign central banks. In addition, the Fed intervenes in currency markets to adjust exchange rates. This **exchange rate intervention** is performed either using the Fed's own account or the Treasury's Exchange Stabilization Fund (ESF), a specially designated account that finances currency interventions by the U.S. Treasury. What is the impact on U.S. bank reserves of both forms of intervention? Sales of dollars (to lower the dollar exchange rate) add to reserves, whereas purchases of dollars (to prop up the dollar) drain reserves. This is because the Fed uses the international banking system as the vehicle for foreign currency interventions. When selling dollars, the Fed induces U.S. banks to sell their foreign currency holdings in exchange for dollar reserves at the Fed. When buying dollars, the Fed induces foreign commercial banks to sell their dollar-denominated deposits at U.S. banks in exchange for reserves at foreign central banks.

exchange rate intervention: the Fed's intervention in currency markets to adjust exchange rates.

dollar-denominated deposit: deposit of U.S. dollars in either a U.S. bank or a foreign bank in the United States.

Suppose that the Fed wanted to support the dollar by buying $100 million of U.S. dollars on international currency markets. The Fed does not buy $100 million in currency, but instead buys a $100 million **dollar-denominated deposit** held by a foreign bank, say, the British bank Barclays, at a U.S. bank (say, Citibank, as in Table PP.2). The Fed pays for these deposits by transferring $100 million from the Fed's account at the Bank of England to the reserve account of Barclays. Foreign currency interventions (whether on the Fed's own account or through the Treasury's ESF) always are cleared through central bank accounts. In this transaction, U.S. dollar reserves decrease by $100 million, and foreign currency reserves increase by $100 million in foreign currency. Thus, the money supply decreases in the United States but increases in the foreign country (England in this example).

Table PP.2

Fed Purchases of U.S. Dollars Decrease Bank Reserves

Citibank (US$ million)[a]		
Reserves −$100	Deposits: Barclays −$100

Barclays (US$ million)[b]	
Deposits at Citibank −$100	
Reserves (UK) +$100	

Federal Reserve (US$ million)[c]	
Deposits at Bank of England −$100	Citibank Reserves −$100

Bank of England (US$ million)	
	Deposits: Fed −$100
	Reserves (UK) +$100

[a]Fed purchases of U.S. dollars decrease bank reserves. [b]The foreign bank receives local currency reserves (UK) in exchange for a U.S. dollar-denominated deposit. [c]U.S. bank reserves decrease. [d]The Fed pays for the U.S. dollars out of its account at the foreign central bank.

When the Fed undertakes a foreign currency intervention, either on its own account or on behalf of the Treasury's ESF, the level of U.S. dollar bank reserves changes. The impact of various foreign currency interventions on bank reserves is shown in Table PP.3. The monetary impact of the foreign exchange (FX) intervention on the level of U.S. bank reserves can be negated by the Fed's offsetting actions. An offsetting transaction is shown in Table PP.3 as ESF intervention financed through Treasury TT&L accounts.

Table PP.4 examines the impact of a Fed purchase of dollars on behalf of ESF that is financed using Treasury securities. In our example, the Fed purchases $100 million of dollar deposits held at a U.S. bank, say, Bankers Trust, by a German bank, say, Deutschebank. This purchase is paid for out of ESF's foreign currency account held at the German central bank shown on the German central bank's balance sheet. In exchange for the dollar-denominated deposit, Deutschebank receives an increase in its foreign currency (DM) reserves. These transactions are shown on the balance sheets of both the German central bank and Deutschebank. ESF has exchanged $100 million in Deutschemark-denominated deposits at the German central bank for a $100 million dollar-denominated deposit at the Fed.

Thus far (the unshaded transactions in Table PP.4), U.S. bank reserves have declined by $100 million since $100 million have been transferred out of the banking system into the

Table PP.3

Federal Reserve Foreign Currency Interventions

Fed Pays with	To Buy	Impact on Fed Portfolio	Δ US Bank Reserves
Sell Dollars: Buy Foreign Currency (FX) Deposits Using Dollars			
Direct Intervention by the Fed			
$ reserves held by a U.S. bank at Fed	Foreign currency deposit of U.S. bank at for. bank	Inc. in Fed FX-deposit at foreign central bank	↑
Fed Intervention on Behalf of ESF			
$ deposits held by ESF at Fed	Foreign currency deposit of U.S. bank at for. bank	Inc. in ESF's FX-deposit at foreign central bank	↑
ESF Intervention Financed Through the Treasury's Tax & Loan Accounts			
TT&L accounts	Foreign currency deposit of U.S. bank at for. bank	Dec. in TT&Ls held at U.S. banks = inc. in ESF deposit at Fed	No change
Buy Dollars: Buy U.S. $-Denominated Deposits Using Foreign Currency			
Direct Intervention by the Fed			
Fed FX deposit at foreign central bank	$-deposit of foreign comml. bank at U.S. bank	Dec. in Fed FX-deposit at foreign central bank	↓
Fed Intervention on Behalf of ESF			
ESF FX deposit at foreign central bank	$-deposit of foreign bank at U.S. bank	Inc. in ESF's $-denominated deposit at the Fed	↓
ESF Intervention Financed Through the Treasury's Tax & Loan Accounts			
TT&L accounts, Treasury securities	$-deposit of foreign comml. bank at U.S. bank	Inc. in TT&L at US bank = dec. in ESF deposit at Fed	No change

Treasury's ESF account (not counted in the monetary base). The increase in the balance of the ESF's deposits at the Fed permits a transfer into the Treasury's interest-bearing tax and loan note accounts (TT&Ls) at another U.S. bank, Bank of America. Bank of America receives a credit to its reserve account at the Fed in payment for the increase in the Treasury's balance in its TT&L note account, shown as the shaded transaction in Table PP.4.

The Fed transfers reserves from the ESF's account to Bank of America's account. The decrease in U.S. bank reserves resulting from the foreign currency intervention is reversed with an offsetting, equal increase in U.S. bank reserves (shown as the shaded transactions in Table PP.4). There is no contraction in bank reserves from this foreign currency intervention to buy dollars. Since the ESF's accounts are independent of the Treasury, the transfer of reserves from the ESF to the Treasury's tax and loan accounts is paid for by the transfer of U.S. government securities from the Treasury to ESF.

The end result is a $100 million decrease in Bankers Trust reserve deposits at the Fed as well as a $100 million increase in Bank of America reserve deposits at the Fed. Since the monetary base is the total of all U.S. bank reserves at the Fed, the ultimate impact on total bank reserves is zero.

We have seen how foreign currency interventions initiated by the Federal Reserve affect U.S. bank reserves. However, foreign central banks also initiate foreign currency interventions. Most foreign central banks maintain deposits at the Fed to facilitate their dollar-denominated transactions. The sum total of these deposits averaged $231 million in 1991, ranging from $178 million to $319 million on a weekly average basis.

<table>
<tr><td rowspan="8">**Table PP.4**</td><td colspan="2">**Fed Purchase of U.S.$ on Behalf of the ESF Financed by Treasury Securities**</td></tr>
</table>

Fed Purchase of U.S.$ on Behalf of the ESF Financed by Treasury Securities

Bankers Trust (US$ million)[a]

Reserves	−$100	Deposits Deutschebank	−$100

Deutschebank (US$ million)[b]

Deposits at BT	−$100		
Reserves (DM)	+$100		

Fed (US$ million)[c]

		Bankers Trust Reserves	−$100
		Deposits: ESF	+$100
			−$100
		Bank of America Reserves	+$100

German Central Bank (US$ million)[d]

		ESF DM Deposits	−$100
		Deutschebank Reserves	+$100

ESF (US$ million)[e]

Deposits at German central bank	−$100		
Deposits at Fed	+$100		
	−$100		
Treasury securities	+$100		

Bank of America (US$ million)[f]

Reserves	+$100	TT&L account	+$100

US Treasury[g]

TT&L account at Bank of America	+$100	Securities issued to ESF	+$100

[a]The Fed purchases a U.S. dollar-denominated deposit held by Deutschebank at Bankers Trust. [b]The foreign commercial bank receives local currency reserves (Deutschemark) in exchange for the U.S. dollar-denominated deposit at Bankers Trust. [c]The Fed purchases U.S. dollar-denominated deposits from Deutschebank by selling ESF's Deutschemark deposits. ESF's dollar-denominated balances are transferred to the Treasury's TT&L account held at Bank of America. [d]The Fed pays for the U.S. dollars out of ESF's account at the German central bank. [e]ESF sells a Deutschemark-denominated deposit held at the German central bank in order to buy U.S. dollars. These dollars are then used to buy Treasury securities from the U.S. Treasury. [f]The ESF transfers its balance into the Treasury's TT&L account at Bank of America. [g]Treasury securities are transferred to ESF in exchange for TT&L account balances.

These balances are used to finance foreign exchange interventions, purchases of U.S. government securities, and international transactions.

Suppose that the Bank of England wants to prop up the British pound sterling by purchasing sterling in exchange for U.S. dollars. The Bank of England will sell $100 million of U.S. dollars and purchase $100 million of sterling. The Bank of England accomplishes this transaction by purchasing a pound-denominated deposit owned by a U.S. bank, Chase, held at a British bank, Nat West. The impact on the British bank's balance sheet, shown in Table PP.5, is to reduce deposits and reserves.

Several mechanical, nonmonetary policy actions by the Federal Reserve, shown in the bottom of Table 4.3, also have an effect on the level of bank reserves in the system. The first of these is changes in Federal Reserve float or items in process of collection. As we saw earlier in this chapter, checks are cleared through bank reserve accounts at the Fed. Sometimes there is a time lag between the date that the depositing bank's reserve account is credited and the date that the paying bank's reserve account is debited. Because of technological advances, this time lag has been reduced in recent years to under two business days under most circumstances. During that time lag, however, the level of total reserves in the banking system increases. That is, Bank A's depositor deposits a check for $100,000 on Monday morning. Bank A sends that check on Monday to the regional Federal Reserve Bank. At the close of business on Monday, Bank A receives a credit of $100,000 to its reserve account. If the check was drawn on another bank, say Bank B, within the same regional district, then on Monday Bank B's reserve account is debited $100,000 and there is no change in total bank reserves. However, if Bank B is in another regional Federal Reserve district, then it may take a day or two for the check to be physically transferred to the appropriate regional Federal Reserve Bank. That means that Bank B's reserve account will not be debited until Tuesday or Wednesday. During this time period, from Monday until Tuesday or Wednesday, Bank A has received a reserve credit of $100,000 which has not been offset by a debit to Bank B's reserve account of $100,000. Temporarily, total bank reserves have increased by $100,000, thereby enabling the money supply to increase.

Since this expansion in the money supply is both temporary and unintended, the DIDMCA of 1980 mandated the Fed to put into practice technology to control the float. As can be seen in Figure PP.1, the level of float was dramatically decreased in the period following passage of the DIDMCA of 1980. However, unexpected weather-related or processing problems still create unpredictable fluctuations in the level of reserve float. We have seen that many players can alter the level of bank reserves. Their actions either increase or decrease the money supply. But that is not why they undertake these actions. The impact on the money supply is often an unintended and

Table PP.5

Bank of England Sale of U.S. $ in Support of Sterling

Chase (US$ million)[a]

Reserves(U.S.)	+$100		
£-denominated deposits	−$100		

Nat West (US$ million)[b]

Reserves (UK)	−$100	Chase's Deposit	−$100

Federal Reserve (US$ million)[c]

		Bank of England Deposits	−$100
		Reserves: Chase	+$100

Bank of England (US$ million)[d]

Deposits at Fed	−$100	Reserves: Nat West	−$100

[a]Chase receives $100 million in bank reserves from the Fed in exchange for its £-denominated deposit at Nat West. [b]Chase transfers its £-denominated deposit out of Nat West by selling to the Bank of England. [c]The Fed transfers the U.S. dollars from the account of the Bank of England to Chase. U.S. dollar reserves increase by $100 million. [d]The Bank of England pays for Chase's £-denominated deposit by transferring U.S. dollars to the Fed.

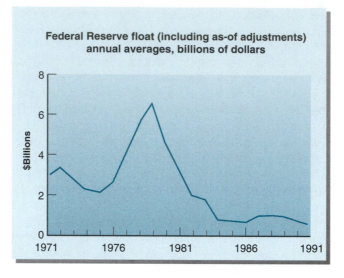

Figure PP.1

unrecognized corollary of their actions. The Fed, or the national central bank, however, undertakes policies *designed* to alter the level of bank reserves. This is what we mean by monetary policy. Indeed, the Fed will often undertake reserve-altering activities to offset independent changes in bank reserves resulting from foreign bank, Treasury, or private FIs' activities.

Checkpoint

1. Describe how the following players' activities affect the level of U.S. bank reserves: the banking system, individuals and businesses, foreign central banks, the Treasury, the Federal Reserve Bank.

2. What is the impact of Fed dollar purchases on U.S. bank reserves? of Fed dollar sales? of foreign central bank dollar purchases? of foreign central bank dollar sales?

3. What is the float? How does it affect the level of bank reserves?

➤ The Implementation of Monetary Policy

The central bank is the major player impacting the level of bank reserves in the system. One of the central bank's principal functions is to conduct monetary policy, and it does so by altering the level of bank reserves. The impact of the Federal Reserve's actions on the level of bank reserves is shown in boldface in Table 4.3. The Fed's three major monetary policy tools are as follows:

discount window loans:
loans by the central bank to depository institutions.

1. *Discount window lending.* Direct loans to depository institutions, requiring marketable securities as collateral, are called **discount window loans**. Banks' repayments of loans to the Fed result in a decrease in reserve balances and in the Fed's loan assets (see Table 4.3).

2. *Reserve requirements.* The Fed sets the reserve ratio. By increasing reserve requirements, the Fed changes excess reserves into required reserves, thereby decreasing loanable reserves and reducing the potential supply of money.

3. *Open market operations.* By far the most important of the three tools, open market operations consist of the purchase or sale of securities. The purchase of securities

Table 4.4

Borrowings of Depository FIs from the Fed, December 1992–October 1995, (Monthly Averages, U.S. $ millions)

Date	Seasonal Credit	Extended Credit	Adjustment Credit	Total	Pct. Adjustment
Dec. 1992	18	1	105	124	84.7
Dec. 1993	31	0	51	82	62.2
Dec. 1994	100	0	109	209	52.2
Apr. 1995	82	0	29	111	26.1
June 1995	172	0	100	272	36.8
July 1995	231	0	140	371	37.7
Aug. 1995	258	0	27	285	9.5
Sept. 1995	252	0	26	278	9.4
Oct. 1995	199	0	46	245	18.8

Source: Federal Reserve Bulletin (January 1996): Table 1.12. All columns are reported except Adjusment Credit and Pct. Adjustment, which have been computed.

Table 4.5

Discount Window Borrowing

U.S. Bank H ($ million)			
Before the Discount Window Loan			
Reserve account at the Fed	$9m	Deposits	$100m
Securities	$21m	Capital	$10m
Loans	$80m		
After the Discount Window Loan			
Reserves from discount window	+$1m	Borrowings from Fed	+$1m

Federal Reserve Bank ($ million)			
Loans to Bank H	+$1m	Reserves: Bank H	+$1m

injects high-powered money into circulation (see Table 4.3), thereby increasing bank reserves as well as increasing the Fed's holdings of marketable securities.

Discount Window Lending

Since passage of the DIDMCA of 1980, access to the discount window has been expanded to all banks, no longer being limited only to member banks holding deposits that require reserves. Table 4.4 shows the amount of each type of discount window loan (extended credit, adjustment credit, and seasonal credit)[6] offered during the period 1992–1995.

Suppose that a bank approaches the discount window for adjustment credit of $1 million. The Fed will first ascertain that the bank has exhausted all other market sources of funds. If the bank has not overused the discount window in the past and if the bank's loan request is for approved purposes (such as an unanticipated, temporary reserve shortfall), then the loan is granted. In exchange for marketable securities (to be held by the Fed as collateral against the discount window loan), the bank receives reserves. The bank in Table 4.5 has a reserve requirement of $10 million using a reserve requirement of 10%. However, the bank has only

---

[6] As we saw in Chapter 3, adjustment credit is short term credit to meet a temporary need for funds. Seasonal credit is extended to smaller institutions experiencing cash outflows related to seasonal fluctuations. Extended credit is provided to a troubled FI experiencing prolonged liquidity pressures.

$9 million in reserves and therefore has a reserve deficiency of $1 million. It can sell $1 million from its loan or securities portfolio, but if, say, market interest rates are at relatively high levels, the liquidation transactions cost will be high.[7] If the reserve shortfall is expected to be shortlived, then the bank does not have to sell relatively illiquid assets but can instead obtain a discount window loan of $1 million.

The discount window loan directly *increases* the aggregate level of bank reserves, whereas repayment of the loan directly *decreases* the aggregate level of bank reserves. To obtain this loan, the bank must transfer to the Fed more than $1 million of securities as collateral. The value of the collateral is *discounted* (hence the name "discount window") at the discount rate. The following securities are acceptable forms of collateral: U.S. government securities (valued at 100% of their market value); state municipal securities (valued at 90% of their par value); county municipal bonds (valued at 80% of their market value); and commercial customer notes and residential real estate loans (accepted at between 50% and 100% of their face value).[8]

Suppose that the discount rate was 4.5% per annum. The discount rate is a simple interest rate based on the assumption of a 365 day year. Thus, the discount rate for a short term loan is calculated using the daily rate: 4.5%/365 = 0.0123%. Suppose that the bank in our example requests a $1 million discount window loan for a period of seven days. The market value of the securities offered as collateral must be sufficient to repay both principal and interest on the discount window loan. Thus,

$$\text{Securities Collateral} = \text{Loan Principal} \times (1 + \text{Discount Rate})$$

$$\$1,000,863 = \$1 \text{ million} \left(1 + \frac{.045(7)}{365}\right)$$

How does the Fed use the discount window as a monetary policy tool? By either raising or lowering the discount rate, the Fed could either discourage or encourage discount window borrowing. This is clearly demonstrated by the discounting process. If instead of a discount rate of 4.5%, the discount rate was 9%, then the securities collateral required for the same discount window loan would be

$$\$1,001,726 \text{ million} = \$1 \text{ million} \left(1 + \frac{.09(7)}{365}\right)$$

for an increase in required collateral of $863 per $1 million discount window loan.

The cost to the bank of borrowing at the discount window is not limited to the interest cost as measured by the discount rate. The Fed may interpret repeated, temporary liquidity crises as a sign of mismanagement or financial problems at the borrowing bank. Since the Fed combines its role as bank supervisor with that of monetary policymaker, excessive discount window borrowing could be interpreted as an early warning signal of potential insolvency and could trigger additional monitoring activity by Fed bank supervisors. As a result, banks view discount window borrowing only as a last resort. This is reflected in declines in the volume of discount window borrowing since 1987.[9] Indeed, Table 4.4 shows that most discount window borrowing is for routine seasonal adjustments, particularly through the summer months, although the fraction of adjustment credit out of total borrowing varies from 9.4% to 86.7%.

Discount window borrowing has long been a relatively minor component of monetary policy in the United States. Contributing to that trend was the passage of the FDICIA of 1991, which

---

[7] K. Hamdani and S. Peristiani (1991) show that bank discount window borrowing tends to increase when the spread between the Fed Funds rate and the discount rate increases.

[8] The Fed evaluates collateral more leniently (that is, at a higher percentage valuation) for problem banks.

[9] One of the justifications for an increase from 2% to 4% in reserve requirements' carryforward provision in September 1992 was to make it possible for banks to lend to each other in times of tight credit, since banks with reserve deficiencies were unwilling to utilize the discount window as a lender of last resort.

made the Fed liable for certain losses to the deposit insurance fund if discount window lending to an undercapitalized bank delayed the bank's closure. In December 1994 stringent rules were adopted which stated that if a "nonviable, undercapitalized" bank has continued its operations by borrowing at the discount window 60 out of 120 days, the Fed is liable for the bank's losses during that time. The goal of this regulation is to prevent the Fed from using the discount window to prop up troubled banks for long periods. In recent years, other countries (e.g., France and Japan)[10] have also deemphasized the role of the discount window in the conduct of their monetary policies.

Reserve Requirements

Prior to the passage of the DIDMCA of 1980, only member banks of the Federal Reserve System were required to hold reserves against their deposits. In part because of the high cost of this requirement (the reserve ratio against demand deposits was 16.5%), the number of banks choosing to be members of the Federal Reserve System steadily declined during the 1970s. This decline was reversed with the passage of the DIDMCA of 1980, which required all banks to hold reserves and which lowered the reserve ratio required against demand deposits to 12%. In December 1990, the reserve requirements against nonpersonal time deposits and Eurocurrency liabilities were lowered from 3% to zero. Effective in April 1992, the reserve requirement on demand deposits was again lowered to 10%.

Changes in reserve requirements have a powerful impact on the economy's supply of money. When reserve requirements are lowered, required reserves are transformed into excess reserves, which can be lent out, fueling a multiplied increase in the money supply. In addition, the size of the money multiplier increases, thereby expanding the money-creating power of the banking system. Let's examine, in Table 4.6, the impact of the decrease in the reserve ratio from 12% to 10% at a $10 billion bank. Suppose the bank is fully loaned up at the old reserve ratio. Against its demand deposits of $9 billion, Bank I holds $1.08 billion of required reserves. With the decline in the reserve ratio, $180 million of required reserves become excess reserves (0.12 × $9 billion − 0.10 × $9 billion = $180 million) and can be either spent or relent. The maximum attainable increase in the money supply from the decline in the reserve ratio is $1.8 billion ($180 million × 10) for Bank I alone, a process repeated at each bank. The money multiplier increases from $\frac{1}{0.12}$ = 8.33 to $\frac{1}{0.10}$ = 10. The overall impact is to drastically expand the available supply of money. Because of its overwhelming effect on the supply of money, reserve requirement changes are used sparingly as a monetary policy tool. Indeed, when changes in the reserve requirement are mandated for reasons other than monetary policy goals (as in the reduction from 16.5% to 12% mandated by DIDMCA of 1980), the Fed often undertakes open market operations to absorb some of the impact of the reserve requirement changes.

Table
4.6

Decrease in Reserve Requirements

U.S. Bank ($ billion)			
At a Reserve Ratio of 12%			
Reserve account at the Fed	$1.08b	Demand deposits	$9b
Securities	$2b	Capital	$1b
Loans	$6.92b		
After the Change to a Reserve Ratio of 10%			
Required reserves	−$.18b		
Excess reserves	+$.18b		

---

[10] See Jacques Melitz (1990).

Open Market Operations

The most effective tool of reserve management available to the Fed is open market operations: the sale or purchase of U.S. government securities. The Federal Open Market Committee (FOMC) can conduct open market operations in three ways:

1.   *Outright transactions*. Since security ownership is permanently transferred, the impact on reserves is permanent. For outright purchases (sales) of securities, reserves are permanently increased (decreased).

2.   *Maturing securities*. As securities held by the Fed mature, they are exchanged for new securities from the Treasury. If the Fed decides to exchange the maturing securities dollar for dollar, then there is no impact on bank reserves. However, if the Fed decides to buy fewer securities from the Treasury than those that mature, then bank reserves will fall permanently. For instance, if the Fed exchanges only $75 million out of $100 million of maturing Treasury securities in its portfolio, then the Treasury will have to pay the Fed the balance of $25 million for the maturing securities that were not exchanged. This will reduce the balances in the TT&L note accounts by $25 million, thereby permanently reducing bank reserves by $25 million. If the Fed instead decided to buy $110 million of Treasury securities for its portfolio, then the Fed would permanently inject $10 million of additional reserves into the banking system.

3.   *Temporary transactions*. The most commonly used method to execute open market operations is the repurchase agreement (RP). When the Fed executes a RP, it buys securities from dealers in the market who agree to buy them back at some later date. A **system repurchase agreement (RP)** has a term of between 1 day and 15 days. A **customer RP** usually matures the next business day and is of smaller magnitude than the system RP. Both system and customer RPs temporarily inject reserves into the system. When the Fed wants to temporarily drain reserves from the system, the FOMC conducts a **matched sale purchase (MSP)** in which the Fed sells securities to dealers who agree to sell them back at a later date. **System MSPs** typically are larger and longer in duration (with a term of up to 15 days) than are **customer MSPs**, which usually mature the next day.

system repurchase agreement (RP): a repurchase agreement with a term of between 1 day and 15 days.

customer RP: a repurchase agreement that usually matures the next business day and is of smaller magnitude than the system RP.

matched sale purchase (MSP): the Fed's sale of securities to dealers who agree to sell them back at a later date.

system MSPs: a matched sale purchase with a term of up to 15 days.

customer MSPs: a MSP that usually matures the next business day and is of smaller magnitude than the system RP.

tight money policy: monetary policy transactions to cool off an overheated economy by decreasing the level of bank reserves: (1) increase discount rate; and/or (2) increase reserve requirements; and/or (3) sell securities (MSPs) on open market operations.

Temporary transactions are particularly useful when the Fed is offsetting the unintended consequences of other players' actions on bank reserves. For instance, we have seen the impact on bank reserves of a temporary increase in the public's demand for currency, or from changes in Treasury disbursements, or from weather-related fluctuations in the float, or from foreign currency interventions. The Fed may choose to offset the effect each of these events has on bank reserves. Temporary open market transactions are the most effective tool, negating the impact of short term episodes on bank reserves. It is also less expensive for the Fed to adjust the level of bank reserves using RPs and MSPs as opposed to outright purchases or sales of Treasury securities.

Even in the conduct of monetary policy, temporary transactions are the open market operation tool of choice. If the Fed wants to stimulate the economy by pursuing an easy money policy, it can inject reserves into the banking system with the goal of increasing the money supply. Suppose, however, that shortly after this policy goal is formulated and implemented, new information is received that casts some doubt on the desirability of pursuing an easy money policy. If outright transactions were used originally in the injection of bank reserves, the Fed would then have to undertake an opposite **tight money policy** transaction to drain reserves from the banking system. This may confuse the market and communicate unintended signals about future Fed policy actions. On the other hand, if temporary transactions were used initially to accomplish the easy money policy, they would automatically reverse themselves, thereby freeing the Fed from having to undertake any offsetting transactions.

Conducting Open Market Operations   Each day, around 11:15 A.M., the manager of the Open Market Function trading desk at the Federal Reserve Bank of New York in New York City places a conference call (referred to as "the call") to the director of the Division of Monetary Affairs at the Board of Governors and one of the four Reserve Bank presidents outside of New York serving on the FOMC. The call usually lasts around 15 to 20 minutes. The desk manager reports on the condition of the market and states the desk's daily program, or the proposed open market operation for the day. If approved,[11] the trading desk in New York implements the daily program of open market operations.

The first step in implementing the daily program of open market operations is the **go-around**—the process of obtaining market quotations for open market transactions to implement the Fed's daily program. At around 11:40 A.M., each day, the Fed traders call a number of the **primary government securities dealers** to obtain price quotes for the transactions on the daily program. The primary government securities dealers are the 37 firms, listed in Table 4.7, that have been preapproved for trading with the Fed. They commit themselves to be ready to rapidly quote a price on any government security bid by the Fed during the go-around. Within 10 minutes, the trading desk has quotes on rates and quantities for a variety of securities transactions. Within a half hour, the Fed traders identify the most attractive bids for temporary transactions and notify all dealers of the bids that are accepted or rejected. It is the trading desk's responsibility to quickly implement the Fed's daily program so as to shorten the **announcement time**, the time period between the beginning of the go-around and the execution of the orders. Since outright transactions are more complicated because of the permanent transfer of ownership, the time required for execution of purchases or sales of Treasury securities is longer than for temporary transactions such as RPs and MSPs. This is another drawback of the use of outright, as opposed to temporary, transactions to conduct open market operations. The Fed tries to keep the announcement period as short as possible since market participants follow the Fed's activities closely (see discussion of Fedwatching later in this chapter). The Fed's intentions are not made clear until the orders are executed. The announcement period, then, is a time of great speculation and uncertainty about the Fed's upcoming transactions. As market participants trade on their hunches, prices and interest rates fluctuate. Since the Fed tries to accomplish its monetary policy goals with a minimum amount of upheaval to financial markets, it tries to minimize these fluctuations by reducing the length of the announcement period.

How do temporary open market transactions alter the level of bank reserves? Let's consider how system RPs create reserves. All temporary transactions are cleared through the account of the Federal Reserve Bank of New York, whereas permanent transactions are cleared through the System Open Market Account and divided among the 12 Federal Reserve banks at the end of each business day. Suppose that the trading desk initiated a five day system RP of $1.5 billion. That is, the Fed agrees to buy Treasury securities with a market value exceeding $1.5 billion[12] from a government securities dealer who agrees to repurchase these securities at the end of five days. Table 4.8 shows how this transaction is cleared. The Federal Reserve Bank of New York wires $1.5 billion to the government security dealer's bank, which then credits the dealer's account. Total bank reserves are increased by $1.5 billion, thereby temporarily increasing the money supply by $15 billion ($1.5 billion times the money multiplier of 10). At the end of five days, the RP is reversed (essentially identical to a MSP), and the Fed sells the securities back to the government security dealer. At that date, $1.5 billion of reserves are drained from the system unless the Fed conducts an additional RP to continue to inject reserves into the banking system.

go-around: the process of obtaining market quotations for open market transactions to implement the Fed's daily program.

primary government security dealers: 37 firms preapproved for trading with the Fed.

announcement time: the time period between the beginning of the go-around and the execution of the orders.

---

[11] Although the chairman of the Board of Governors does not typically sit in on the call, he is kept fully informed and can call for a consultation of the full FOMC, if desired.

[12] In Chapter 11, we discuss why the market value of the securities collateral exceeds the RP face value of $1.5 billion.

The Primary Government Securities Dealers, as of January 1995

BA Securities, Inc.
Barclays de Zoete Wedd Securities Inc.
Bear, Stearns & Co., Inc.
BT Securities Corporation
Chase Securities Inc.
CIBC Woody Gundy Securities Corp.
Citicorp Securities, Inc.
CS First Boston Corporation
Daiwa Securities America Inc.
Dean Witter Reynolds Inc.
Deutsche Bank Securities Corporation
Dillon, Read & Co. Inc.
Donaldson, Lufkin & Jenrette Securities Corporation
Eastbridge Capital Inc.
First Chicago Capital Markets, Inc.
Fuji Securities Inc.
Goldman, Sachs & Co.
Greenwich Capital Markets, Inc.
HSBC Securities, Inc.
Aubrey G. Lanston & Co., Inc.
Lehman Government Securities, Inc.
Merrill Lynch Government Securities Inc.
J.P. Morgan Securities, Inc.
Morgan Stanley & Co. Incorporated
NationsBanc Capital Markets, Inc.
Nesbitt Burns Securities Inc.
The Nikko Securities Co. International, Inc.
Nomura Securities International, Inc.
Paine Webber Incorporated
Prudential Securities Incorporated
Salomon Brothers Inc.
Sanwa Securities (USA) Co., L.P.
Smith Barney Inc.
UBS Securities Inc.
S.B.C. Warburg & Co., Inc.
Yamaichi International (America), Inc.
Zions First National Bank

Source: Market Reports Division, Federal Reserve Bank of New York.

Open Market Operations: $1.5 billion RPs

Bank J ($ billion)			
Reserve Account at the Fed	+$1.5b	Dealer's Deposits	+$1.5b

Federal Reserve Bank of New York ($ billion)			
System RPs	+$1.5b	Bank J's Deposits	+$1.5b

We have seen how the central bank can use its monetary policy tools to impact the level of bank reserves. But this ability appears far removed from the goals of public FIs that we stated in Chapter 3. If the goal of public FIs is to maximize society's welfare, how does the manipulation of bank reserves help accomplish that goal? What is the connection between bank reserves, the supply of money, and economic welfare? That is the topic we turn to now.

Checkpoint

✓

1. What are the three tools of monetary policy? Which is used most frequently?

2. Discuss how the Fed could increase the level of bank reserves using each of its three tools of monetary policy.

3. Discuss how the Fed could decrease the level of bank reserves using each of its three tools of monetary policy.

4. Why are temporary transactions used more frequently than outright transactions in open market operations?

▶ The Conduct of Monetary Policy: A Case Study

Although the central bank bears ultimate responsibility for the country's supply of money, it must take into account the actions of individuals, private FIs, other businesses, and foreign central banks since their actions also affect the country's supply of money. The central bank's monetary policy, then, is a combination of intentional intervention to accomplish public policy goals as well as "unintentional" intervention to offset the uncoordinated actions of other players affecting money supply. Volatility in the level of bank reserves can destabilize the economy since unintentional money supply adjustments impact the level of macroeconomic activity. The Fed can use open market operations to smooth out the daily fluctuations in the level of nonborrowed reserves. Let's examine a day in the life of the U.S. Fed to see how a daily stabilization adjustment in bank reserves was actually determined.

Table 4.9 follows the Fed's analysis of reserve adjustments by starting with an enumeration of the routine, nonmonetary policy factors that absorb bank reserves. These factors reduce the availability of reserves for lending and money creation. For example, during the month of October 1995, the Treasury estimated an increase of $562 million in the amount of currency in circulation. As we saw in Table 4.3, the impact of an increase in the public's holdings of currency reduces the level of bank reserves, thereby reducing the money supply if not subsequently neutralized. The Fed must decide whether to counteract or enhance the tightening effect of this nonmonetary policy-oriented reduction in bank reserves.

The Fed can counterbalance the impact by increasing bank reserves using its monetary policy tools. We see evidence of this activity in the reserve-producing factors using monetary policy tools shown at the bottom of Table 4.9. By offsetting the expansionary tendency in the monetary sector, the Fed reduced bank reserves by a net daily average of $394 million during the month of October 1995. With a money multiplier of about 10, this would mean a $3.94 billion net reduction in the money supply.

The Impact of Monetary Interventions on Interest Rates

The interaction of all the above monetary interventions by the major players in the money market is shown in Figure 4.4. On the demand side, individuals and businesses demand money for transactions and speculative purposes, foreign public FIs demand money to clear international transactions, and domestic governments demand money to make payments for goods and services. On the supply side, the central bank uses monetary policy to administer the level of bank reserves. The banking system expands those reserves into a supply of money.

The demand schedule is pictured as downward sloping since as the level of interest rates increases, the opportunity costs of holding money, as opposed to interest-earning assets, in-

Table 4.9

Factors Affecting the Level of Bank Reserves (Average Daily Balances for the Month of October 1995, $ million)

	10/95 Totals	Change from 9/95–10/95
Reserve Absorbing Factors		
Currency in circulation	411,565	+562
Treasury cash holdings	315	-7
Treasury deposits with Fed banks	5,384	-1,466
Foreign deposits with Fed banks	179	0
FIs' deposits for service-related adjustments	4,874	+186
Other deposits with Fed banks	386	+38
Other Fed liabilities and capital	12,938	+762
Total factors absorbing bank reserves	435,641	+75
Reserve supplying factors using nonmonetary policy tools		
Gold stock	11,051	-1
Special Drawing Rights	10,168	-198
Treasury currency outstanding	23,799	+78
Float	537	+129
Other Fed assets	32,425	+535
Total nonmonetary policy factors producing reserves	77,980	+543
Reserve Producing Factors Using Monetary Policy Tools		
Discount window loans: Adjustment credit	45	+17
Discount window loans: Seasonal credit	204	-50
Discount window loans: Extended credit	0	0
Open market operations: Outright transactions	373,777	-223
Open market operations: Temporary transactions	3,706	-606
Total monetary policy factors producing reserves	377,732	-862
Total factors producing bank reserves	455,712	-319
Net impact on bank reserves	20,070	-394

Source: Federal Reserve Bulletin, (January, 1996): Table 1.11.

crease. As the cost of liquidity increases, businesses, individuals, and public FIs reconfigure their portfolios so that they hold relatively less money and relatively more illiquid assets.

The supply schedule is pictured as upward sloping because of the pro-cyclical activities of the banking sector. As interest rates increase, the returns to bank lending and investing increase. This induces the banks to economize on their holdings of excess reserves. We saw in Tables 4.2 that a spontaneous reduction in excess reserves held by the banking system increases the money supply through the money multiplier. Unless offset by central bank monetary policy (which is depicted as shifts in the entire supply schedule), increases in interest rates result in expansionary increases in the quantity of money supplied.

Table 4.9 presents the factors affecting reserves during a fairly typical month, October 1995. The column showing totals demonstrates that bank reserves are quite small when compared to currency in circulation, with daily averages of $20.07 billion versus $411.565 billion. Moreover, outright purchases of Treasury securities by the Fed amount to $373.777 billion, far exceeding the $3.706 billion volume of temporary transactions using repurchase agreements. However, it is temporary transactions that the Fed uses most actively to conduct its monetary policy. Most of the Fed's monetary policy during October 1995 was conducted using temporary open market transactions, decreasing reserves by $606 million. During the month of October 1995, the demand for reserves increased a total of $75 million, while the supply of reserves increased

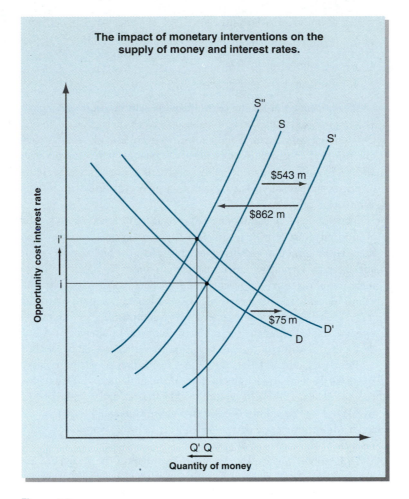

The impact of monetary interventions on the supply of money and interest rates.

Figure 4.4

$543 million over the levels prevailing during September 1995. This is shown in Figure 4.4 as the $75 million upward shift in demand to D' and the $543 million upward shift in supply to S'. During October 1995, the Fed responded by draining reserves by a total of $862 million, shown by the decrease in supply to S'', resulting in a net decrease in bank reserves of $394 billion. Thus, the Fed conducted a tight money policy in October 1995, circumventing the market factors that would have increased the money supply, and increasing interest rates to i'.

We have demonstrated the impact of the major players (the central bank, private FIs, individuals, businesses, foreigners) on bank reserves and, by extension, on the supply of money and the level of interest rates. But the goal of public FIs is to pursue policies to make society better off. How does control over the supply of money and the level of interest rates fit into the public FI's social welfare goals?

➤ The Goals of Monetary Policy

Because of the connection between the supply of money and the level of economic activity, central banks are charged with the mandate to pursue policies that

1. Promote price stability.

2. Encourage full employment of resources.

3. Stabilize exchange rates.

4. Enhance economic growth.

It is not practical for the central bank to address all of these goals simultaneously, and so, as we saw in Chapter 3, central banks prioritize their goals. The priorities are determined by the national culture (for example, for the Bundesbank, price stability is always the number one priority) and by current events. For instance, when the persistent economic recession of 1990–1992 resulted in undesirably high levels of unemployment in the United States, the Fed's priorities shifted somewhat away from a preoccupation with inflation and toward measured stimulation of the economy.

The public FI, in conducting a discretionary monetary policy, must carefully tread a middle ground: it must provide a sufficient supply of money to fuel economic activity, but not an excessive amount that gets dissipated in the form of higher prices. The central bank uses **target variables** to formulate and implement its monetary policy. Target variables are empirical measures of macroeconomic conditions that are used as monetary policy goals. Many different economic indicators can serve as target variables. At any point in time, the Fed chooses the target variables that are most relevant to accomplishing its monetary policy. The choice of the target variable reveals the central bank's monetary policy priority at any point in time. Table 4.10 presents a brief history of recent target variables used by the Fed.

Prior to October 1979, the FOMC issued very narrow ranges to define the acceptable range for Federal Funds rates. Often, if the rate was as little as 5 **basis points** above (below) the desire range, the Fed would quickly step in and visibly add (drain) reserves using RPs (MSPs). The Fed's policy of micromanaging even small fluctuations in the Fed Funds rate led to an administered rate that provided little information to the market about the availability of reserves or the supply of money.

In October 1979 newly appointed chairman of the Board of Governors Paul Volcker, in a highly unusual and secretive Saturday meeting of the FOMC, dramatically changed the focus of Fed monetary policy targets. In an effort to communicate a new resolve in the fight against inflation, the FOMC began to target M1 directly. Federal Funds rates were allowed to fluctuate according to market forces, and, as Figure 4.5 shows, Federal Funds rates increased drastically during this period in terms of both levels and volatility.

How did the FOMC control M1 directly? We have seen that the central bank has control over the level of bank reserves but that other players (such as the banking system, foreign central banks, individuals, and businesses) are instrumental in transforming bank reserves into money. To formulate a target for M1, the FOMC reverses the process of money creation, based on the level of bank reserves. Total reserves consist of borrowed reserves (obtained at the discount window) plus nonborrowed reserves. The FOMC derives its target nonborrowed reserve level by subtracting the amount of discount window loans granted. If actual nonborrowed reserves are more (less) than the target, then the FOMC drains (adds) reserves using MSPs (RPs).

target variables: empirical measures of macroeconomic conditions that are used as monetary policy goals.

basis point: one hundredth of one percentage point.

Table 4.10

A History of Fed Monetary Policy Target Variables

Prior to October 1979: The Federal Funds rate
October 1979–October 1982: M1 and nonborrowed reserves
October 1982–1985: Borrowed reserves and M2, M3, and L
1985–1988: U.S. dollar exchange rates, M2, M3, and L
1988–February 1994: The Fed Funds rate and nonfinancial debt
February 1994–present: The Fed Funds rate, inflation rates, and
the percent deviation of real GDP from a target

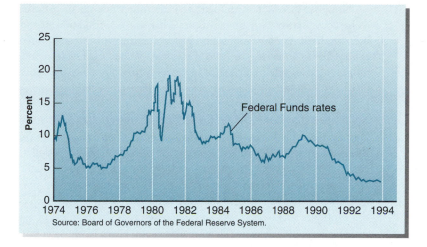

Source: Board of Governors of the Federal Reserve System.

Figure 4.5

The 1979–1982 period was a period of rapid deregulation of the banking industry. Interest rate ceilings (Regulation Q limitations on deposit rates) were gradually lifted, and new interest-bearing transactions accounts (NOW accounts and money market deposit accounts, MMDAs) were introduced. These changes altered the demand for money and made M1 a less reliable measure of the supply of money. With the inclusion of popular NOW accounts and MMDAs in the definition of M1, the growth of M1 was far higher than could be explained by an increase in the level of economic activity. The usefulness of M1 as a monetary policy target variable was at an end.

In December 1982 the FOMC responded by replacing the narrow M1 definition of money with the broader (M2, M3, and L) definitions. Instead of computing the appropriate level of total and nonborrowed reserves needed to generate a particular level of M2 or M3, the FOMC decided to target borrowed reserves directly. Whenever M2, M3, or L levels fell below (exceeded) their targets, the Fed drained (added) nonborrowed reserves. The idea was that the reduced (increased) availability of nonborrowed reserves would induce banks to increase (decrease) their level of discount window borrowing. However, the banking system was to enter a period of reregulation during this time period. The savings and loan debacle as well as the impact of the LDC debt crisis shook the financial foundations of the U.S. banking industry. Cries of regulatory **forbearance** (laxity in monitoring the activities of troubled banks) made regulators more stringent in enforcing safety and soundness regulations. Banks and regulators alike frowned on discount window borrowing as a signal of imprudent or ineffective financial management. Consequently, banks chose to contract their lending activities rather than present themselves at the discount window. Reductions in the volume of discount window borrowing over this period reduced the effectiveness of the borrowed reserves target as a tool of monetary policy.

Concern about the growing U.S. federal budget deficit as well as the international trade deficit led to the next change in policy targets. In September 1985 the ministers from the **G–5 countries** (the United States, Germany, Japan, France, and England) issued the Plaza Accord, which committed their countries to presenting a unified front on both trade and the "grossly overvalued" U.S. dollar. They agreed on an "orderly appreciation" in their currencies, which resulted in a 4% devaluation of the U.S. dollar in one day.[13]

forbearance: laxity in monitoring the activities of troubled banks.

G–5 countries: the United States, Germany, Japan, France, and England.

---

[13] Foreign exchange rates in this book will always be stated in terms of number of US$ per unit of foreign currency. Thus, when we say that the Deutschemark has appreciated (the U.S. dollar depreciated), we will see that the foreign exchange rate went up from, say, $0.55 per DM to $0.58 per DM since holders of Deutschemarks received more U.S. dollars for each DM.

The Plaza Accord constrained the Fed's independence since domestic monetary policy had to be coordinated with foreign central banks. Coordination of monetary policy among the industrialized nations' public FIs creates the threat of *imported inflation* by requiring that the central banks intervene to keep the values of their currencies within agreed-upon bands, or ranges. A relatively high rate of inflation in the United States reduces the purchasing power of the U.S. dollar, in terms of goods, services, and other currencies. Hence, if the inflation rate is significantly higher in the United States than in Germany or Japan, then, all else being equal, the value of the U.S. dollar will fall relative to the Deutschemark and the Japanese yen. If the dollar falls to the bottom of the agreed-upon range, then public FIs must coordinate their intervention to prop up the exchange rate of the U.S. dollar in terms of the stronger currencies. As we have seen, this is done by selling Deutschemarks or Japanese yen to buy U.S. dollar-denominated deposits. The impact of this intervention is to increase bank reserves in Germany and Japan (and decrease bank reserves in the United States), thereby increasing the supply of Deutschemarks and Japanese yen. The increase in the domestic money supply in Germany and Japan tends to fuel price increases in those countries, thereby "importing" the higher U.S. inflation rate. As a result, Germany and Japan, in particular, put increasing pressure on the U.S. Fed to undertake strict monetary policies to reduce the U.S. inflation rate.

The good intentions of coordination and international cooperation were abandoned in the face of an increasingly severe recession in the United States. The tight money policy required by international currency markets to stabilize the dollar exchange rate became increasingly inconsistent with the domestic policy goals of full employment and economic growth. German and Japanese pressure to fight inflation in the United States took a back seat to growing concerns about a **credit crunch**, which is a reduction in the overall availability of credit even for prudent investments resulting from a policy that limits the banks' willingness to lend at any interest rate. This led to the Fed's decision in 1992 to utilize nonfinancial debt as a monetary policy target. To encourage lending and finance investment and consumption, an increasingly accommodative monetary policy was implemented, leading to a reduction in interest rate levels as shown in Figure 4.5.

credit crunch: reduction in the overall availability of credit even for prudent investments.

With increasing signs of an economic recovery, the Fed changed policy gears in February 1994. Fourth-quarter 1993 GDP growth rates were estimated to be 5.9% (later revised to 7.5%), and the Fed reoriented its priorities toward a concern about inflation. The Fed announced its intentions to drain reserves so as to orchestrate a series of Federal Funds interest rate hikes, each ranging from 25 to 50 basis points, thereby causing a rapid increase in yields, thereby signalling a shift once again toward interest rate targeting. During this period, the Fed orchestrated a remarkably *soft landing* by emerging from a persistent recession without igniting inflation. Concerns about sluggishness in the economy's productivity growth rate (another target variable) have encouraged the Fed to permit a slight loosening of its monetary policy, with the goal of encouraging economic activity.

Fedwatching: a preoccupation of market participants as each one tries to guess the upcoming Fed positions.

Discerning the shifts in the Fed's monetary policy, called **Fedwatching**, is a preoccupation of market participants as each one tries to guess upcoming Fed positions. Analysts believe that Fedwatching is the Fed's strongest monetary policy tool.[14] By shaping expectations, either directly by using moral suasion or indirectly through Fedwatchers' analyses, the Fed's desired outcomes can become self-fulfilling. Moral suasion can take the form of an informal directive issued by central bank officials to the top management of private FIs, with the goal of influencing their behavior. Moreover, if the market's Fedwatchers expect the Fed's goal is a tighter monetary policy, thereby raising interest rates as the supply of money is reduced, traders and FIs will be reluctant to bet against the Fed. They may therefore sell long term bondholdings in anticipation

---

[14] In particular, J. Boschen and L. Mills (1995) find that monetary policy directly impacts the Fed Funds rate only in the very short run, whereas nonpolicy sources have a larger impact on market rates.

of the price decline in the event that the Fed pursues a more restrictive monetary policy. This sales pressure reduces prices and raises rates, making expectations a self-fulfilling prophecy.

The role of monetary policy in improving society's economic welfare depends on the coordinated actions of the world's central banks and other public FIs as well as those of individual households and businesses. We have seen how the Fed sometimes uses its tools of monetary policy to further its goals of price stability and economic growth. At other times, the Fed must undertake mechanical adjustments to offset the unintended consequences of other players' activities. Fed policies must be flexible enough to adjust to changes in the overall market and regulatory environment. Public FIs both conform to and shape the regulatory environment.

Checkpoint

1. What are the four goals of monetary policy?
2. List five monetary policy targets used by the Fed over the past 20 years. How and when were they used?
3. What is Fedwatching? How is it used as a monetary policy tool?
4. What is moral suasion? How is it used as a monetary policy tool?

➤ Summary

A nation's money supply consists of its most liquid assets. Liquidity is measured by calculating the transaction costs that must be paid in order to expeditiously transform an asset into cash. The lower the transaction costs, the more liquid the asset. Since liquidity is a spectrum, money can be defined very narrowly (consisting of only cash and demand deposits) or more broadly (including less and less liquid assets such as time deposits). The size of the nation's money supply is determined by the actions of individuals, businesses, foreigners, and public FIs as well as the nation's central bank. The banking system has a dominant role to play in determining the size of the money supply. This is because a fractional reserve system of banking enables banks to create money by lending and investing most of the funds they receive as deposits. Only a small fraction (say 10%) need be held idle as reserves. The remainder (90%) is available to finance economic activity. The minimum fraction that must be held idle in the form of reserves, the required reserves ratio, is determined by the central bank.

The central bank manages the nation's money supply. This responsibility takes two forms.

1. *Mechanical adjustments.* The central bank undertakes corrective adjustments to offset the unintended consequences of transactions by FIs, individuals, businesses, foreigners, and public FIs on the money supply.

2. *Monetary policy.* The central bank manipulates the money supply to pursue its monetary policy goals of

- Price stability
- Full employment
- Exchange rate stability
- Enhanced economic growth

Central banks adjust the money supply by adjusting the level of bank reserves using

1. Open market operations: the buying and selling of government securities to the public.

2. Discount window lending: the lending of reserves to banks as lender of last resort.

3. Reserve requirements: the required levels of vault cash and demand deposits at the central bank (reserves) that must be held to back up bank deposits.

A fourth, informal tool of monetary policy is moral suasion, which is the forming of expectations by convincing major market and opinion makers to follow the central bank's desired course of action.

Depending on the conduct of monetary policy, the actions of the central bank may affect interest rates, exchange rates, gross domestic product (GDP), and the rate of price inflation. Over time, the focus of monetary policy changes with the goals of the central bank as well as with the condition of the economy. One of the greatest challenges for the monetary policymaker is to acquire timely information about the impact of the money supply on macroeconomic conditions. Central bankers typically focus on several target variables both to diagnose economic conditions and to fine tune their responses in order to accomplish their monetary policy goals. The identity of these target variables in the United States has at times varied from the Federal Funds rate to M1, M2, M3 aggregates to the level of nonfinancial debt to the long term Treasury bond rate. Monetary policy is a dynamic process requiring constant monitoring and intervention.

► References

Boschen, J., and L. Mills. "The Relation Between Narrative and Money Market Indicators of Monetary Policy." *Economic Inquiry* (January 1995): 24–44.

Clark, Todd. "Cross-Country Evidence on Long Run Growth and Inflation." Working Paper RWP 93–05, Federal Reserve Bank of Kansas City, May 1993.

Colander, David, and Dewey Daane, eds. *The Art of Monetary Policy*. Armonk, N.Y.: M. E. Sharpe, 1994.

Cosimano, Thomas, and Dennis Jansen. "Federal Reserve Policy, 1975–1985: An Empirical Analysis." *Journal of Macroeconomics*, 10, No. 1 (Winter 1988): 27–47.

Englander, A. S. "Optimal Monetary Policy Design: Rules versus Discretion Again." Federal Reserve Bank of New York *Quarterly Review* (Winter 1991): 65–79.

Federal Reserve Bank of Chicago. *Modern Money Mechanics: A Workbook on Bank Reserves and Deposit Expansion*. February 1994.

Griffiths, M. D., and D. B. Winters. "Day-of-the-Week Effects in Federal Funds Rates: Further Empirical Findings." *Journal of Banking and Finance* 19, No. 7 (October 1995): 1265–1284.

Hallman, J., R. Porter, and D. Small. "M2 Per Unit of Potential GNP as an Anchor for the Price Level." Staff Study No. 157, 1989, Federal Reserve Board of Governors, Washington, D.C.

Hamdani, K., and S. Peristiani. "A Disaggregate Analysis of Discount Window Borrowing." Federal Reserve Bank of New York *Quarterly Review* (Summer 1991): 52–62.

Hoon, Hian Teck, and Edmund Phelps. "Macroeconomic Shocks in a Dynamized Model of the Natural Rate of Unemployment." *American Economic Review* (September 1992): 889–900.

Jones, David. "Monetary Policy as Viewed by a Money Market Participant." in D. Colander and D. Daane, eds. *The Art of Monetary Policy*. Arnonk, N.Y.: M. E. Sharpe, 1994.

Melitz, J. "Financial Deregulation in France." *European Economic Review*, 34 (1990): 394–402.

Meulendyke, Ann-Marie. "Reserve Requirements and the Discount Window in Recent Decades." Federal Reserve Bank of New York *Quarterly Review* (Autumn 1992): 25–43.

Meulendyke, Ann-Marie. *U.S. Monetary Policy and Financial Markets*. Federal Reserve Bank of New York, 1989.

Meulendyke, Ann-Marie. "A Review of Federal Reserve Policy Targets and Operating Guides in Recent Decades." Federal Reserve Bank of New York *Quarterly Review* (Autumn 1988): 6–17.

Pecchenino, R. A., and, Robert Rasche. "*P** Type Models: Evaluation and Forecasts." *International Journal of Forecasting* 6 (October 1990): 421–440.

Peristiani, Stavros. "An Empirical Investigation of the Determinants of Discount Window Borrowing: A Disaggregate Analysis." *Journal of Banking and Finance* 18 (1994): 183–197.

Peristiani, Stavros. "The Model Structure of Discount Window Borrowing." *Journal of Money, Credit, and Banking* 23 (February 1991): 1313–1334.

Sbordone, A., and K. Kuttner. "Does Inflation Reduce Productivity?" Federal Reserve Bank of Chicago *Economic Perspectives* (1994): 2–14.

Shapiro, Carl, and Joseph Stiglitz. "Equilibrium Unemployment as a Discipline Device." *American Economic Review* (June 1984): 433–444.

Smyth, J. "Inflation and Growth." *Journal of Macroeconomics* 16, No. 2 (Spring 1994): 261–270.

Weiner, Stuart. "Challenges to the Natural Rate Framework." Federal Reserve Bank of Kansas City *Economic Review* (Second Quarter 1995): 19–25.

➤ Questions

1. Enumerate the liquidation transaction costs for (a) Treasury bills; (b) Treasury bonds; (c) 100 shares of stock in a blue chip company; (d) 10 shares of stock in a blue chip company; and (e) 500 shares of stock in a startup company trading over the counter. Rank the securities in terms of liquidity.

2. Place the following financial assets on a liquidity spectrum:
   a. Cash.
   b. Municipal notes (5 year maturity).
   c. Zero-coupon Treasury notes (7 year maturity).
   d. Deed to a vacant lot.
   e. One year certificate of deposit.
   f. Common stock.
   g. Perpetual preferred stock.
   h. Corporate bonds (7 year maturity).
   i. 91 day Treasury bills.

3a. Use the following information to compute the bank's required reserves and excess reserves.

Daily Demand Deposit Balances

Date	Mon.2/5	Tues.2/6	Wed.2/7	Thurs.2/8	Fri.2/9
Deposit amt.($m)	265	300	295	319	211
Date	Mon.2/12	Tues.2/13	Wed.2/14	Thurs.2/15	Fri.2/16
Deposit amt.($m)	291	304	297	332	276
Date	Mon.2/19	Tues.2/20	Wed.2/21	Thurs.2/22	Fri.2/23
Deposit amt.($m)	321	296	325	348	402

Daily Balances at the Federal Reserve Bank

Date	Mon.2/5	Tues.2/6	Wed.2/7	Thurs.2/8	Fri.2/9
Deposit amt.($m)	19	23	19	23	36
Date	Mon.2/12	Tues.2/13	Wed.2/14	Thurs.2/15	Fri.2/16
Deposit amt.($m)	19	27	35	21	36
Date	Mon.2/19	Tues.2/20	Wed.2/21	Thurs.2/22	Fri.2/23
Deposit amt.($m)	11	16	29	29	31

Daily Holdings of Vault Cash

Date	Mon.1/22	Tues.1/23	Wed.1/24	Thurs.1/25	Fri.1/26
Deposit amt.($m)	5	21	5	10	11
Date	Mon.1/29	Tues.1/30	Wed.1/31	Thurs.2/1	Fri.2/2
Deposit amt.($m)	18	16	18	19	8
Date	Mon.2/5	Tues.2/6	Wed.2/7	Thurs.2/8	Fri.2/9
Deposit amt.($m)	15	7	8	9	23

3b. Use a 10% reserve ratio to calculate the increase in the money supply if the bank lends out all of its excess reserves.

4a. Compute the banking system's excess reserves if the economy's monetary base is $250 million, currency in circulation is $110 million, demand deposits total $1,200 million, and the reserve ratio is 10%.

4b. What would be the impact on the money supply if all banks simultaneously decided to lend out 25% of their existing excess reserves and 100% of any future excess reserves.

4c. Compute the impact on the money supply if banks decided as a rule to lend out 25% of all excess reserves: either existing or newly received.

4d. Contrast your answers to parts b and c.

5a. Why might the Federal Reserve decide to sell dollars in a foreign currency intervention?

5b. Show all of the balance sheet transactions associated with a $100 million sale of dollars by the Fed.

5c. Show all of the balance sheet transactions associated with a $100 million sale of dollars by the Fed on behalf of the Treasury's Exchange Stabilization Fund.

5d. Show all of the balance sheet transactions associated with a $100 million sale of dollars by the Fed on behalf of the Treasury's Exchange Stabilization Fund financed with Treasury tax and loan note accounts.

6. Clear a $1 billion 10 day MSP. Be sure to show the impact on the Fed's balance sheet and on bank reserves. What happens at the end of 10 days?

7. Use the following table to analyze the Fed's monetary adjustment policy. How did the Fed utilize open market operations to offset the impact of private decisions on the money supply?

Factors Affecting the Level of Bank Reserves

Average Daily Balances for the Week Ending July 28
($ millions)

Reserve Absorbing Factors	
Currency in circulation	+ 36,881
Treasury cash holdings	− 51
Treasury deposits with Fed banks	− 62
Foreign deposits with Fed banks	− 71
FIs' deposits for service-related adjustments	− 562
Other deposits with Fed banks	− 23
Other Fed liabilities & capital	+ 1,474
Total Factors Absorbing Bank Reserves	+ 37,586
Reserve Producing Factors Using Nonmonetary Policy Tools	
Gold stock	− 5
Special drawing rights	0
Treasury currency outstanding	+ 832
Float	+ 29
Other Fed assets	+ 1,175
Reserve Producing Factors Using Monetary Policy Tools:	
Discount window loans: Adjustment credit	+ 27
Discount window loans: Seasonal credit	+ 181
Discount window loans: Extended credit	0
Open market operations: Outright transactions	+ 34,384
Open market operations: Temporary transactions	0
Total Factors Producing Bank Reserves	+ 36,624
Net Impact on Bank Reserves	− 962

Source: Federal Reserve Table H.4.1 dated July 28, 1994.

8. Why are temporary transactions used to conduct open market operations? Compare the use of temporary transactions to outright transactions in the conduct of monetary policy.

9. List two target variables used by the Fed to conduct monetary policy in recent years. How does the Fed utilize its monetary policy tools to affect the target variables?

10. Calculate the collateral required for the following discount window loans:
   a. An overnight loan of $100 million at a discount rate of 5.25% p.a.
   b. A 14 day loan of $2.5 million at a discount rate of 6.5% p.a.
   c. A 45 day loan of $0.5 million at a discount rate of 3.15% p.a.

CHAPTER 5

REGULATORY POLICY

Dateline: Moscow, August 4, 1994: "The collapse of the MMM [Company's] investment pyramid has focused attention on the worst aspects of Russia's new and poorly regulated stock markets."

Dateline: Shanghai, August 4, 1994: "On the Shanghai exchange, the index of so-called A shares, available only to Chinese buyers, was above the 10,000 level in February 1993. By the end of last month, it had fallen more than 80 percent to 1,744.01."

Learning Objectives

- To learn how public FIs use regulations to promote the safety and soundness of private FIs.
- To understand the use of regulation to promote full and accurate disclosure.
- To examine the impact of regulation on financial market structure.

➤ Introduction

Many noncapitalist societies believe that free markets mean markets free of *any* government involvement. Perhaps because of their history of Big Government, the people often fearlessly embrace this improbable promise, requiring neither safeguards nor assurances. In many emerging countries, therefore, free markets have provided the opportunity for unscrupulous entrepreneurs to "freely" help themselves to the life savings of their unsophisticated compatriots. These countries have rushed to adopt the outward trappings of capitalism without first building the legal and economic foundations that provide the market's infrastructure.

Markets without rules and regulations foster inefficient and counterproductive distributions of scarce resources. Public FIs use regulations to create an environment in which safe, prudent, and efficient private FIs provide their clients with all the necessary information they need to make their own decisions based on their own personal risk and timing preferences. Private FIs respond to the incentives created by regulatory policy. Regulations can accomplish their goals of enhancing financial performance only if they are well designed and compatible with private incentives. If not, they create distortions that are exploited by private FIs.

➤ Safety and Soundness Regulation

In Chapter 3 we observed that supervision of private FIs is one of the three major policy tasks of public FIs. Supervision is critical to the efficient operation of free markets. In the course of arranging financing, structuring investments, and managing risk on behalf of their clients, private FIs typically offer guarantees or agree to undertake certain obligations. These commitments are simply promises obligating the FI to future activities if certain contingencies occur. Since financial transactions focus on the redistribution of cash flows over time, the FI's customers must be convinced that the FI is not in imminent danger of collapse. Regulators, in their role as supervisors of private FIs, commit themselves to a policy of monitoring and of validating the FI's financial solvency to market participants. Public assurances of FI safety induce small, unsophisticated customers to trust the FI with their life savings. The role of public FIs is to ensure that this trust is not misplaced.

Safety and soundness regulation not only protects the consumer but, more important, also promotes general economic prosperity, which depends on the existence of stable, efficient FIs. As we saw in Chapter 4, public FIs use monetary policy to steer the economy toward economic growth with price stability. Another tool they have in this quest is the regulation of private FIs.

Public FIs supervise private FIs through both a direct and an indirect approach. In the *direct approach*, the regulator itself monitors the activities of the private FI on behalf of the FI's customers and clients so as to ensure the FI's safety and soundness. In the *indirect approach*, the regulator requires the private FI to disclose sufficient information so as to enable market participants themselves (for example, the FI's customers and clients) to monitor the private FI's activities.

The Safety Net: An International Comparison

safety net: government benefits provided directly to private FIs to guarantee their financial viability.

Private FIs in general, and banks in particular, generate positive externalities that promote the efficient operation of capitalist economies. To ensure their financial integrity, public FIs provide them with a **safety net** that is not available to nonfinancial private firms. The safety net consists of special government benefits provided directly to private FIs to guarantee their financial viability. In most capitalist countries, the safety net revolves around three privileges: (1) access to the lender of last resort (see discussion of the discount window in Chapter 4); (2) deposit insurance guarantees; and (3) explicit or implicit promises of governmental subsidies in the event of insolvency. Of course, public FIs choose the level of generosity of the safety net provided to private FIs based on the amount of control required. For example, the extremely generous safety net traditionally available to Japanese banks allowed them to engage in speculative activity, with the result that, as of June 1995, the top 21 banks had delinquent loans amounting to 50 trillion yen ($590 billion), or one-eighth of Japan's GDP.

"The mere presence of a safety net implies something of a covenant between those institutions that are beneficiaries of the safety net and the society at large. Under the terms of that covenant, the affected institutions agree to conduct their affairs in a safe and impartial manner."[1]

G–7 countries: Germany, France, Japan, the U.K., Italy, Canada, the U.S.

Table 5.1 summarizes the governmental safety nets in the **G–7 countries**: Germany, France, Japan, the United Kingdom, Italy, Canada, and the United States. Four countries (Japan, the United Kingdom, Canada, and the U.S.) have formal deposit insurance programs that protect depositors from losses in the event of bank failure. The extensiveness of these programs varies from country to country, with the provisions of the U.S. program being the most generous. In return for the benefits of the safety net, the FIs must comply with an extensive array of regulations, thereby making FIs the most highly regulated of private firms.

---

[1] Corrigan (1991), p. 7.

The Role of Capital   Capital requirements are designed to ensure that FIs operate in ways that are financially prudent and fiscally sound. How do they accomplish this role? All firms—financial and nonfinancial—have always issued equity capital as a cushion against financial insolvency. But the level of bank capital in the United States has steadily declined over time (see Figure 5.1). In part, this is a response to the increasing generosity of the governmental safety net. As the safety net expands, the private FI needs to hold lower amounts of capital as self-insurance against insolvency. To limit this decline, minimum capital requirements have become a mainstay of safety and soundness regulation in recent years.

equity capital: funds raised through the FI's sale of both common and preferred stock.

Equity capital consists of the funds raised through the FI's sale of both common and preferred stock. These securities are considered capital because they are residual claims on the FI's assets and are therefore paid only after all other claims are fully satisfied. In contrast, holders of securities with **seniority** are the first to receive payment according to the securities' contractual obligations. Those securities with **subordinated** status are junior claims that receive their contractually obligated payments only after all senior claims are fully paid. Creditors and other stakeholders with seniority prefer that FIs issue large amounts of equity capital because

seniority: status whereby holders of securities are the first to receive payment according to the securities' contractual obligations.

1.   Equity capital acts as a cushion against losses to creditors in the event of insolvency.

2.   Equity capital prevents insolvency by absorbing unanticipated losses.

3.   Equity capital provides the FI with funds to finance long term investment.

subordinated: status whereby holders of securities receive their contractually obligated payments only after all senior claims are fully paid.

4.   By increasing the shareholders' investment in the FI, equity capital decreases the shareholders' propensity to engage in risky activities that may lead to default. Since this lowers the FI's default risk exposure, the FI's cost of funds declines.

Shareholders prefer to economize on the amount of capital issued by the FI because

1.   Equity capital is the FI's most expensive source of funds.

2.   Equity capital requirements limit the FI's rate of growth of assets.

3.   By reducing the FI's leverage, equity capital requirements limit the FI's profitability.

There is an inherent conflict here since shareholders prefer less capital and creditors prefer more. By setting minimum capital requirements, regulators require that the FI's shareholders hold more capital than they would choose to if they were unregulated. Regulators side with creditors because bank creditors consist mostly of depositors. Protection of depositors and other small investors is a policy goal of public FIs. As we saw in Chapter 4, depositors play a critical role in the conduct of monetary policy; they also are important in the payments mechanism. Because of these two roles, public FIs are committed to their protection. Regulators also identify with the FI's creditors because the regulators are themselves creditors of the FI. Depositors lend money to the bank in exchange for the bank's issuance of a deposit liability drawn on the bank (a checking or savings account). Public FIs are creditors of the bank in their roles as (1) the lender of last resort, (2) the administrator of deposit insurance, and (3) the financier in the event of bailouts of insolvent FIs.

We have already seen the central bank's function as lender of last resort in the form of discount window loans made to troubled banks. The public FI is the lender of last resort because discount window loans are approved only after all alternative market sources of funds are exhausted. The central bank lends to these troubled FIs in order to pursue its public policy goals. Although discount window loans are fully backed by securities collateral, the Federal Deposit Insurance Corporation Improvement Act (FDICIA) of 1991 requires the Fed to place limitations on access to discount window credit for **undercapitalized** insured depository FIs with insufficient amounts of equity capital. The Act defines these FIs to be those with risk based capital levels below 8 percent.

undercapitalized: FIs with insufficient amounts of equity capital.

**Table
5.1**

Government Safety Nets in G–7 Countries

	Germany	France	Japan
Deposit Protection Method			
Date established	1966[a]	1980	1971
Govt. administered or private	Private	Private	Govt. and private
Voluntary or compulsory	Voluntary	Voluntary	Compulsory for some
Funding method	Contributions from members	Loss-sharing agreement[b]	Insurance premiums
Level of contributions	Annual premiums = 0.06% of deposits	Regressive scale based on deposits up to FR 30 billion	Annual premium = 0.132% of insured deposits
Coverage Offered			
Basic protection[c]	Up to 30% of liable capital[d] per depositor	Up to 400,000 francs $63,000 per deposit	10 million yen $74,000 per depositor
Deposits in foreign currency	Yes	No	No
Interbank deposits	No	No	No
Branches of foreign banks	Yes	Yes	No
Branches in other countries	Yes	No	No
Prudential Supervision and Industry Structure			
Number of banks	4,400 commercial (incl. 1,200 small banks)	<500 banks	<500 banks
Reporting requirements	Monthly return and balance sheet data[e]	Balance sheet data, incl. nonbanks	Periodic financial reports
On-site exams conducted by	Qualified outside auditors	High-ranking senior bank regulators	Bank regulators
Ownership	Private commercial Public savings[f]	68% publicly owned	Private ties to MoF
Universal banking	Yes (insurance through subsidiaries)	Yes (insurance through subsidiaries)	No
Unofficial too big to fail?	Yes, e.g., Schroder Munchmeyer, Hengst & Co. in 1983	Yes, e.g., Al Saudi Banque in 1988 and during 1990s financial crisis	Yes, mortgage banks and large banks

[a] Does not include German savings banks and cooperative societies, which are covered by different deposit protection schemes.

[b] Under Section 52, the Bank of France can assess the banking community for funds needed to rescue a failing bank. If this is depositors. However, since the resources available are insufficient to offer protection to depositors of large banks, the loss-sharing

[c] All dollar amounts are based on 1989 end-of-year exchange rates.

[d] Liable capital is defined as the paid-up endowment capital and the reserves.

[e] German bank reporting regulations allow banks to obscure loan loss and hidden reserves by granting them considerable leeway in bank's Board of Management) and passed on to the Bundesaufsichtsamt (the Federal Banking Supervisory Office) and the Bundesbank

[f] A depository institution must have a minimum of DM 6 million in capital to obtain a banking license.

[g] Fund target is 4,000 billion lire.

[h] The Bank of England Act of 1949 (Schedule 9) permitted banks to make transfers to or from reserves before disclosing annual profits, the hidden reserve privilege are the members of the British Merchant Bank Association as well as other banks that apply for the privilege, Banco Urquijo Hispano Americano Ltd.

[i] The Bank of Italy's resolve to impose market discipline is currently being tested in the case of Cassa di Prato Savings Bank which was

[j] Formal regulatory oversight procedures are to be implemented as part of the ongoing reform of the system of Canadian banking

Source: L. Allen. "Deposit Insurance and Bank Capital Regulation." In A. Stone and C. Zissu, eds., *Global Risk Based Capital Regulations.*

United Kingdom	Italy	Canada	United States
1979	1987	1967	1934
Government	Private	Government	Government
Compulsory	Voluntary	Compulsory	Voluntary
Routine and special contributions	Callable commitments	Insurance premiums	Insurance premiums
$10,000 + special assessments if fund<$3 million ≤ 0.3% of domestic deposits	Up to 1% of total deposits and 0.5% of members' customers' deposits[g]	Annual premium of 0.1% of insured deposits	Annual premium of 0.23% of total domestic deposits (see Table 5.4)
75% of first $20,000 ($33,000) per depositor	100% of first 200 million lire ($146,000) 80% of next 800 million lire ($584,000) per deposit	C$60,000 (US$50,000) per depositor	$100,000 per deposit
No	Yes	No	Yes
No	No	Yes	Yes
No	Yes	Not available	Yes
No	Only if host country doesn't cover	No	No
500	1,000 but majority of assets held by top 25 banks	<500 banks	12,800 commercial banks (1990)
Monthly balance sheet and income statement[h]	Data on bank ratios and liquidity levels	Not available[j]	Quarterly balance sheet and income statement
Outside auditors	Bank regulators	Bank regulators[j]	Bank regulators
Private, licensed by Bank of England as per Banking Act of 1979	Not available	Federally and provincially chartered	National and state charters
Yes (through subsidiaries)	Yes	Yes	No
Yes, e.g., Johnson Matthey Bankers, 1984	No, e.g., Banco Ambrosiano in 1982[i]	es, e.g., 1985, Canadian Commercial and Northland Bank of Calgary	Yes, e.g., Bank of New England in 1991

unsuccessful, the governor can let the bank fail and ask the banking system to activate the loss-sharing agreement which is designed to protect small arrangement is prorated so that smaller banks pay a larger percentage of their deposit base than do larger banks.

netting these items off of (sometimes arbitrarily chosen) asset and liability accounts. However, in a confidential report made to the Vorstand (the (Central Bank), auditors are required to report in detail on the bank's loan loss and hidden reserves.

thereby allowing banks to maintain hidden reserves. Most banks decided to forgo this privilege as far back as 1969. Banks that still make use of with the most recent (before 1981) privileges granted to Henry Ansbacher and Company, Ltd., Robert Fleming and Company, Ltd., and

taken over by the Bank of Italy because it incurred 1.297 billion lire in bad debts.

supervision.

Vol. I. Burr Ridge, Ill: Irwin, 1994.

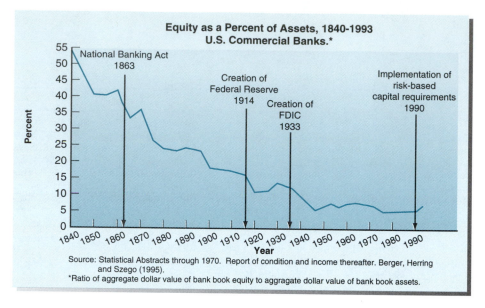

Figure 5.1

Public FIs become creditors when insured banks fail. Then the deposit insurer tries to recoup its costs from sales of the bank's assets. Since this often takes some time, the deposit insurer becomes another of the bank's creditors during this time interval.

How Does Capital Protect the FI's Creditors?   Equity capital serves as a cushion against insolvency in the following way. Consider two banks with identical asset portfolios: Shake E. Bank, Inc. and Rock Solid Bancorp. Both banks are holding identical asset portfolios with market values of $120 million. However, Rock Solid Bancorp has utilized more equity and less debt to finance its asset portfolio than has Shake E. Bank, Inc. Shake E. Bank's **leverage ratio**, the proportion of debt to equity, is $\frac{115}{5} = 23$, whereas Rock Solid's leverage ratio is only $\frac{90}{30} = 3$.

> **leverage ratio:** the proportion of debt to equity.

Shake E. Bank, Inc. ($million)			
Reserves	10	Deposits	80
Bonds	50	Debt	35
Loans	60	Equity	5

Rock Solid Bancorp. ($million)			
Reserves	10	Deposits	70
Bonds	50	Debt	20
Loans	60	Equity	30

Suppose that both banks experience unexpected defaults on 10% of their loan portfolios. The **loan writeoffs** (losses resulting from defaults on loans that the bank does not expect to collect from borrowers) amount to $6 million. Who bears these losses? As in any other business, it is the owners who both receive the profits and bear the losses from the business's operations. In a corporate enterprise, the owners are the equityholders. We record corporate profits on the balance sheet as a credit to the equity capital account. Conversely, we record corporate losses on the balance sheet as a debit to the equity capital account.

> **loan writeoffs:** losses resulting from defaults on loans that the bank does not expect to collect from borrowers.

Shake E. Bank, Inc. ($million)			
Reserves	10	Deposits	80
Bonds	50	Debt	35
Loans	54	Equity	-1

Rock Solid Bancorp. ($million)			
Reserves	10	Deposits	70
Bonds	50	Debt	20
Loans	54	Equity	24

Recording the $6 million loss reduces Rock Solid Bancorp's equity capital from $30 million to $24 million. But, booking the $6 million loss reduces Shake E. Bank's capital from $5 million to −$1 million! A negative capital position denotes that the FI is insolvent; its liabilities are worth more than its assets. Rock Solid Bancorp had a sufficient capital cushion to absorb the loan losses without throwing the bank into insolvency, but Shake E. Bank did not. Even if all of Shake E. Bank's assets are sold, only $114 million out of the bank's $115 million worth of debts can be paid. Creditors with claims worth $1 million will lose their money. In contrast, Rock Solid Bancorp's creditors are paid in full. This shows how the creditors of the better capitalized bank are protected from unanticipated losses.

Setting Bank Capital Requirements   In the tug-of-war over bank capital, creditors and public FIs pull in the direction of higher capital levels, whereas equityholders pull in the direction of lower levels of capital. During the 1960s and 1970s, public FIs used informal methods to encourage banks to issue more equity. However, as the banking systems' capital levels continued to fall (as shown in Figure 5.1 for the United States), regulators began to impose formal capital requirements that mandated minimum capital levels. Typically, these capital requirements took the form of **capital–asset ratios**, the minimum acceptable percentage of total assets that must be held in the form of equity capital. Capital–asset ratios are used to calculate capital requirements in much the same way that reserve ratios are used to compute reserve requirements. If the capital requirement is 5.5%, the two banks in our example would be required to hold at least 5.5% × $120 million = $6.6 million in capital. Before the loan losses, Rock Solid Bancorp is in compliance with this hypothetical capital requirement, whereas Shake E. Bank Inc. has a capital deficiency. To comply with the 5.5% capital requirement, Shake E. Bank must issue $1.6 million additional capital. How is this done?

> **capital–asset ratio:** the minimum acceptable percentage of total assets that must be held in the form of equity capital.

What Is Bank Capital?   Private FIs may sell newly issued equity securities in order to raise capital. Thus far, we have concentrated only on the equity capital contributed by common stockholders and preferred stockholders. However, regulations permit a broader definition of capital.

Bank capital is divided into three classes: *Tier 1*, *Tier 2*, and *Tier 3* (see Table 5.2). Tier 1 capital is a higher form of capital than Tier 2, which is higher than Tier 3. What does this mean? Capital is meant to act as a cushion to protect creditors' claims against the FI. This protection arises because holders of capital securities have only **residual claims** against the FI's earnings. Residual claims are capital securities that receive cash flows only after all other claimants (creditors and public FIs) are fully paid. The feature that makes a security "capital-like" is its place in the priority of payment line. The lower down in the payment priority, the more subordinated is the security's claim and the more it is like capital. Thus, common stock is the purest form of capital (Tier 1) since equityholders are the very last in line to receive payments.

> **residual claims:** capital securities that receive cash flows only after all other claimants (creditors and public FIs) are fully paid.

Other securities with claims that are slightly more senior than common stock can also be considered capital. The definition of capital is analogous to the definition of money inasmuch as both depend on the choice of a cutoff point along a spectrum. Just as we discussed the liquidity spectrum in Figure 4.1, Figure 5.2 illustrates a capital spectrum, and Table 5.2 shows the formal definitions of Tier 1, Tier 2, and Tier 3 capital. Tier 1 capital includes common stock and its close substitutes, whereas Tier 2 capital includes other subordinated securities which upon the FI's insolvency automatically convert into either common stock or perpetual preferred stock. Tier 3 includes subordinated and unsecured debt that is sufficiently liquid and accessible to absorb losses.[2]

What determines the amount of Tier 1, Tier 2, and Tier 3 capital issued by FIs? We have seen that because capital is expensive, FIs prefer to economize on their capital holdings. Tier 1 capital

---

[2] In 1992 and 1996 regulators expanded the list of securities that were acceptable as capital in order to stem a decline in the FIs' capital levels during the 1980s and to encourage FIs to access broader capital markets.

Table 5.2

paid–in surplus: the funds received in excess of par value when a firm sells stock; often generated by stock dividends.

earned surplus: past retained earnings (net profits after taxes that are not paid out in the form of dividends).

goodwill: the difference between the purchase price and the book value of acquired assets.

cumulative perpetual preferred stock: preferred stock with dividends that are deferred and accumulated to be paid at some later date, if they cannot be paid on their due date.

noncumulative perpetual preferred stock: the same as cumulative perpetual preferred stock, but the dividends do not accumulate.

perpetual preferred stock: preferred stock with an infinite time to maturity.

mandatory convertible debt: a debt issue that obligates the issuer to exchange the debt for either common or preferred stock.

Definitions of Tier 1, Tier 2, and Tier 3 Capital

Tier 1 capital consists of

- common stockholders' equity comprising common stock, **paid-in surplus** (the funds received in excess of par value when a firm sells stock), and **earned surplus** (past retained earnings, which are net profits after taxes that are not paid out in the form of dividends), excluding **goodwill** (the difference between the purchase price and the book value of acquired assets).
- plus minority interests in the equity accounts of consolidated subsidiaries.
- plus **cumulative** or **noncumulative perpetual maturity preferred stock**. Cumulative perpetual preferred stock carries a stipulation that if preferred stock dividends cannot be paid on their due date, they are deferred and accumulated to be paid at some later date when and if the company returns to profitability and there are sufficient cash flows after satisfying all obligations to creditors. For noncumulative preferred stock, if a dividend is missed, it is not accumulated and made up at some later date. **Perpetual preferred stock** (both cumulative and noncumulative) has an infinite time to maturity. To qualify as Tier 1 capital, the issuer must be able to defer or eliminate payment of predetermined dividends.[a] Dividends must be predetermined and independent of any changes in the issuer's credit risk exposure.

Tier 2 capital consists of

- cumulative perpetual preferred stock when not eligible for Tier 1;
- plus long term preferred stock with an original maturity of 20 years or more;
- plus perpetual preferred stock with a dividend that may fluctuate with changes in the issuer's credit risk exposure;
- plus perpetual subordinated debt;
- plus **mandatory convertible debt**, which is a debt issue that obligates the issuer to exchange the debt for either common or preferred stock;
- plus subordinated debt with an average life exceeding five years at the date of issue (with the subordinated debt required to be unsecured and junior to the claims of depositors and general creditors);
- plus allowances for loan and lease losses (up to 1.25% of risk weighed assets).

Tier 3 capital consists of

- subordinated debt with maturities of five years or less, subject to the following conditions: (1) it should have an original maturity of at least two years and will be limited to 250% of the bank's Tier 1 capital; and (2) it is subject to a "lock-in" provision, which stipulates that neither interest nor principal may be paid if such payment reduces the bank's overall capital below required levels.

[a]Both cumulative and noncumulative perpetual preferred qualify as Tier 1 capital for bank holding companies, whereas banks and thrifts can only include noncumulative perpetual preferred stock. The amount of cumulative preferred that can be included in the bank holding company's Tier 1 capital is limited to 25% of total Tier 1 capital. Any remainder can be counted as Tier 2 capital.

The capital spectrum

Highest priority liability   Lowest priority
Most senior claim   Residual claimant

Insured deposits Uninsured deposits Short term debt Long term debt Preferred stock Common stock
Debt   Tier 3 capital   Tier 2 capital   Tier 1 capital

Figure 5.2

is more expensive than Tier 2 because Tier 1 securities' cash flows are riskier than those of Tier 2 securities. The additional risk premium in Tier 1 capital required rates of return compensates securities holders for taking up the last position in the priority of payment line. Tier 1 capital is also more costly for FIs than Tier 2 capital because dividend payments are not tax deductible, whereas interest payments on the debt component of Tier 2 capital are tax deductible.

For these reasons, FIs' shareholders prefer less capital to more and prefer Tier 2 or 3 capital to Tier 1. However, creditors and public FIs prefer more capital to less and prefer Tier 1 capital to Tier 2 or 3. Thus, public FIs must force adequate capital positions on FIs by imposing Tier 1, Tier 2, and Tier 3 capital levels. Current international capital requirements set Tier 1 and Tier 2 capital ratios each at a minimum of 4% for a total capital requirement of 8%.[3] If the private FI does not meet these minimum standards, then regulators will force it to raise more capital by issuing additional subordinated debt and equity securities.

Checkpoint

1. Why do creditors and public FIs want banks to hold equity capital?
2. Why do banks try to economize on their equity capital holdings?
3. How does bank capital protect creditors and public FIs?
4. What features make some securities "capital-like"?
5. What is included in Tier 1 capital? Tier 2 capital? Tier 3 capital?

The Basel Risk Adjusted Capital Requirements   Capital–asset regulations set the minimum required capital position as a fraction of the FI's total assets. Thus, both Shake E. Bank and Rock Solid Bancorp had a minimum capital requirement of $6.6 million in our example using a 5.5% capital-assets ratio. We have seen that if Shake E. Bank had complied with this capital requirement, then it would have had a cushion sufficient to absorb the 10% in loan losses that both banks experienced. If Shake E. Bank is to live up to its name, however, it is reasonable to expect its asset portfolio also to be riskier than Rock Solid Bancorp's. Suppose that, because of lax lending and credit approval practices, Shake E. Bank experiences a loan default rate of 20% as opposed to only 5% for the more prudently managed Rock Solid Bancorp. Loan writeoffs at Shake E. Bank are 20% × $60 = $12 million, while they are only 5% × $60 = $3 million at Rock Solid. After posting these losses, the balance sheets are as follows:

Shake E. Bank, Inc. ($million)				Rock Solid Bancorp. ($million)			
Reserves	10	Deposits	80	Reserves	10	Deposits	70
Bonds	50	Debt	35	Bonds	50	Debt	20
Loans	48	Equity	−7	Loans	57	Equity	27

Under these circumstances, even the 5.5% capital–assets requirement of $6.6 million is insufficient to protect the creditors of riskier Shake E. Bank, Inc. This highlights the major shortcoming of simple capital–assets requirements. Since no adjustment is made for risk, the same capital requirements apply to risky, speculative activities as to prudently managed, low-risk FI portfolios.

In recent years, capital regulation has been refined to reflect the risk of the FI's activities. That is, FIs that undertake riskier ventures are required to hold larger amounts of capital than are equal-sized safer FIs. These risk based capital regulations have been applied to FIs throughout the world. For banks, the *Basel capital requirements* were fully implemented as

---

[3] Countries differ as to the degree that they permit banks to use Tier 3 capital to satisfy Tier 2 capital requirements. We thus discuss all capital requirements in terms of Tier 1 and 2 only.

of December 31, 1992. These regulations emanated from an agreement, the Basel Accord, reached in July 1988 by the major industrial countries (the United States, the United Kingdom, Japan, France, Germany, Italy, Belgium, Canada, Luxembourg, the Netherlands, Sweden, and Switzerland) participating in the Basel Committee on Banking Supervision and subsequently adopted throughout the world.

Risk based capital requirements are structured so that riskier assets require higher levels of capital. Risk based capital regulations dictate the methodology used to measure the risk exposure of each asset in the FI's portfolio, setting a different capital requirement for each risk level. The Basel regulations measure risk by delineating four asset risk categories on the basis of **credit risk** exposure. Credit risk measures the extent to which unanticipated defaults on assets impact a FI's market value and profitability. The first, lowest risk category, with no credit risk, is the 0% risk weight, which consists of cash and obligations of any of the Organization for Economic Cooperation and Development (OECD) governments of developed countries. No capital need be held to back up this safest class of assets. The second, 20% risk weight category consists of local, nonfederal government obligations, bank-backed securities, claims on regional public FIs, and items in process of collection. Banks must hold capital levels totaling 1.6% (20% × 8%) of the amount of assets in this risk category. The third, 50% risk weight category consists of mortgage loans and requires a 4% (50% × 8%) total capital ratio against the quantity of mortgages in the bank's portfolio. The fourth, 100% risk weight category includes all other assets, such as loans. The full 8% capital requirement is levied against these assets.

Capital requirements are levied against off-balance sheet items using a two-stage method. First, the off-balance sheet item is classified using one of four risk conversion factors—0%, 20%, 50%, and 100%. The greater the probability that the off-balance sheet contingency will be realized, the greater the risk conversion factor percentage. Second, the value of the off-balance sheet item is classified into risk weight categories on the basis of credit risk exposure. Thus, in order to determine the risk adjusted amount, the value of any off-balance sheet item is multiplied by two factors: (1) the risk weight classification; and (2) the risk conversion factor. For example, five year loan guarantees to a municipality would have (1) a 20% risk weight and (2) a 100% risk conversion factor for a total capital requirement of 8% × 100% × 20% = 1.6%.

Consider Rock Solid Bancorp's asset portfolio (prior to the loan writeoffs) as an example of how Basel capital requirements are calculated. Assume that the bank has no off-balance sheet activities.

credit risk: the extent to which unanticipated defaults on assets impact a FI's market value and profitability.

Rock Solid Bancorp

Asset Account	Amt. ($mil.)	Tier 1 + 2 Capital	Capital Req. ($mil.)
0% risk weight category			
Reserves	$10m	8% × 0% = 0%	$0m
20% risk weight category			
Municipal bonds	$50m	8% × 20% = 1.6%	$0.8m
50% risk weight category			
Mortgage loans	$30m	8% × 50% = 4%	$1.2m
100% risk weight category			
Other loans	$30m	8% × 100% = 8%	$2.4m
Total	$120m		$4.4m

Rock Solid Bancorp's total capital requirement would be $4.4 million, reflecting the FI's relatively low level of credit risk exposure. On the other hand, Shake E. Bank's riskier asset portfolio (including an assumed $185 million equivalent value of off-balance sheet items) would imply a significantly higher Basel capital requirement, as shown below.

Shake E. Bank, Inc.

Asset Account	Amt.($mil.)	Tier1 + 2 Capital	Capital Req.($mil.)
0% risk weight category			
Reserves	$10m	8% × 0% = 0%	$0m
20% risk weight category			
Municipal bonds	$50m	8% × 20% = 1.6%	$0.8m
Guarantees 100% risk conversion	$25m	8% × 20% × 100% = 1.6%	$0.4m
50% risk weight category			
Mortgage loans	$10m	8% × 50% = 4%	$0.4m
100% risk weight category			
Other loans	$50m	8% × 100% = 8%	$4m
Off-balance sheet commitments: 50% risk conversion factor	$160m	8% × 100% × 50% = 4%	$6.4m
Totals			
On-balance sheet	$120m		$5.2m
Off-balance sheet	$185m		$6.8m

Shake E. Bank's capital requirement against its $120 million asset portfolio is $5.2 million. Since Shake E. Bank's assets are riskier than Rock Solid Bancorp's, its capital requirement is higher, even though both banks have asset portfolios of the same size. In addition, Shake E. Bank has $185 million in off-balance sheet guarantees and commitments (shaded in the above table) that require an additional $6.8 million capital for a total capital requirement of $12 million. Compliance with this risk adjusted capital requirement would enable Shake E. Bank to withstand the 20% loan writeoffs in its loan portfolio without jeopardizing the claims of creditors.

Table 5.3 shows the Tier 1 plus Tier 2 capital requirements for selected bank activities. Before entering into any particular transaction, the bank calculates its costs in terms of the transaction's capital requirement. For example, the cost of extending a $10 million commercial loan (100% risk weight) will include the cost of holding an 8% total capital requirement in the amount of $800,000 (8% × $10 million). In contrast, a $10 million residential mortgage (50% risk weight) requires only a 4% total capital requirement of $400,000 (8% × 50% × $10 million). A six month $10 million loan commitment (0% risk conversion factor) would require no capital, whereas a $10 million commercial letter of credit (20% risk weight, 100% risk conversion factor) would require a $160,000 increase in capital (8% × 20% × 100% × $10 million). Ten million dollars in 100% risk weighted interest rate contracts (such as swaps, futures, or options contracts whose values depend on interest rate fluctuations) will have no potential future exposure if the time until maturity is less than one year and a $2,000 (0.02% × $10 million) capital requirement if the time until maturity is one to five years. At a 12% risk adjusted market cost of capital, the annual costs of the above transactions are: $96,000 (0.12 × $800,000) for the commercial loan; $48,000 (0.12 × $400,000) for the mortgage; $19,200 (0.12 × $160,000) for the commercial letter of credit; and $240 (0.12 × $2,000) for the one to five year interest rate off-balance sheet contract. To compensate the FI for these costs, an asset in the 100% risk class would have to earn twice as much as an asset in the 50 risk class.

Basel capital requirements have been criticized because they focus exclusively on bank credit risk exposure. The four risk weight categories, as well as the classification of off-balance sheet items, are determined by each asset's credit risk exposure. The greater the asset's credit risk, the higher its risk weight. However, this focus on credit risk neglects other important sources of risk. Over $150 billion in S&L losses in the United States during the 1980s can be blamed on the FIs' excessive exposures to unanticipated changes in interest rates, or **interest rate risk**. The impact of unanticipated exchange rate fluctuations, or

interest rate risk: the impact of unanticipated changes in interest rates on the FI's market value and profitability.

Table 5.3

Capital Requirements for Selected Bank Activities

On-Balance Sheet Item	Tier 1 + 2 Ratio	Off-Balance Sheet Item	Tier 1 + 2 Ratio
0% Risk Weight		**0% Conversion Factor**	
Cash; OECD govt. securities	0%	Loan commitments <1 yr.	Risk weight × 0%
20% Risk Weight		**20% Conversion Factor**	
General obligation municipals	1.6%	Commercial letters of credit	Risk weight × 1.6%
Interbank claims and repos	1.6%	Bankers acceptances	Risk weight × 1.6%
Some mortgage-backed securities	1.6%		
50% Risk Weight		**50% Conversion Factor**	
Revenue munis	4%	Standby letters of credit	Risk weight × 4%
1–4 family home mortgages	4%	Commercial loan commitments >1 yr.	Risk weight × 4%
100% Risk Weight		**100% Conversion Factor**	
Commercial loans	8%	Direct credit substitutes to businesses	Risk weight × 8%
Interest rate and foreign exchange contracts			
(Off-balance sheet potentional future exposure)[a]			
<1 yr. interest rate[b]	Risk weight × 0%	<1 yr. exchange rate[b]	Risk weight × 0.04%
1–5 yr. interest rate	Risk weight × 0.02%	1–5 yr. exchange rate	Risk weight × 0.20%
≥5 yr. interest rate	Risk weight × 0.06%	≥5 yr. exchange rate	Risk weight × 0.30%

[a] An additional capital charge for possible loss resulting from the off-balance sheet contract's mark-to-market value is called current exposure. Risk weights and risk conversion factors are not applied to off-balance sheet contracts.

[b] We do not list the capital charges for off-balance sheet contracts linked to equity, precious metals, and other commodities.

foreign exchange rate risk: the impact of unanticipated exchange rate fluctuations on the FI's market value and profitability.

foreign exchange rate risk, is also omitted from the Basel capital regulations.[4] Other short-comings of the Basel Accord are (1) their use of book values, rather than market values; (2) the ad hoc nature of the risk weights and conversion factors; and (3) the failure to take into account correlations between and within risk classifications. These shortcomings have led to a distortion of bank risk taking incentives, implicitly rewarding interest rate and exchange rate risk while penalizing credit risk.[5] See *Timely Topics 5.1* for an illustration of some portfolio-distorting implications of this policy.

Timely Topics 5.1

Thank Basel for Credit Crunch

Say what you may about bankers, they tend to be rational human beings. Tell them they have to maintain 8% capital against business and consumer loans—and no capital or materially less capital against government bonds or single-family mortgage loans—and most bankers will put much of their money in the assets that require little or no capital. Who can blame them? Make a business loan and you have to maintain 8% capital against it, plus you run the risk of a default (or an adverse classification of the loan by the regulators, even in the absence of a default), which will require

---

[4] As of January 1996, banks are required to hold Tier 3 capital to cover market risk exposure, as calculated from in-house bank models, such as the value at risk model presented in Chapter 9.

[5] Allen, Jagtiani, and Landskroner (1996) show that U.S. banks responded to these incentives in the wake of the 1992 implementation of the Basel Accords by increasing their interest rate risk and decreasing their credit risk exposures.

a write-down of the loan. Invest in a government bond and you will never need to write it down or maintain capital against it.... Since the new capital rules went into effect in March 1989, U.S. bank holdings of government bonds have increased 68% and their holdings of real-estate loans (primarily single-family loans) have increased 27%.... While commercial and industrial loans at banks fell by some $30 billion during this period, non-financial corporate bonds outstanding in the U.S. increased by some $200 billion.... The bank customers that tend to suffer the most are consumers and small businesses that have nowhere else to turn for credit.... They represent roughly half of our gross domestic product.... In addition to distorting credit flows, the risk based capital rules may be creating a potentially serious safety and soundness problem. Because the new rules do not require capital to be held against government bonds, many banks are building up significant interest rate risk.... The interest rate mismatch could cause serious problems for at least some banks should interest rates begin to climb.

Source: Richard Breeden and William Isaac, reprinted from the *Wall Street Journal*, November 4, 1992.

Checkpoint

1. How do Basel capital requirements measure risk?
2. What assets are included in the 0% risk weight category? the 20% risk weight category? the 50% risk weight category? the 100% risk weight category?
3. What are the shortcomings of the Basel capital requirements as currently implemented?

Risk Adjusted Capital Requirements for Insurance Companies   Risk based capital requirements for life–health insurance companies were adopted in December 1992 by the National Association of Insurance Commissioners (NAIC) in the United States. A property-liability insurer risk based capital formula was adopted in December 1993 and became effective in 1994. The NAIC risk based capital requirements use four major risk classifications:

1. Underwriting risk for losses incurred on insurance policies that exceed premiums collected. This loss reserve requirement, calculated using loss ratios for the worst year over the past 10 years, is the most significant component of risk based capital, amounting to half of total industry capital requirements.
2. Asset risk determined by the credit risk and price risk of the insurance company's asset portfolio.[6] This represents approximately 20% of property-liability insurer risk based capital requirements.
3. Credit risk on reinsurance and other receivables, accounting for approximately 5% of capital requirements.
4. Off-balance sheet risk, which includes a measure of growth risk.

The risk based capital requirement is calculated by summing each of the four risk components and then deducting a covariance adjustment that reflects the effects of diversification. Capital requirements are used to dictate regulatory action. Thus, the lower the insurer's risk based capital levels, the more intervention on the part of the insurance commissioner. Intervention ranges from requiring the insurance company to submit an explanation and a plan for correcting deficiencies to forced liquidation and seizure.

---

[6] As in Basel capital requirements, interest rate risk is ignored.

Risk Adjusted Capital Requirements for Securities Firms   Securities firms must also comply with risk adjusted capital requirements. Their capital regulations differ from those of banks and insurance companies, however, in that *all* risk exposures (credit, interest rate, and exchange rate risks) are considered in levying capital requirements. Securities firms that are regulated by the Securities and Exchange Commission (SEC) must comply with the Uniform Net Capital Rule for Brokers and Dealers (Rule 15c3–1) that specifies the minimum required ratio of liquid capital to risk exposure. Liquid capital is defined as the net capital held as **haircuts** on securities. The haircut is a capital charge since it is the fraction of a broker/dealer's securities portfolio that cannot be traded but must instead be held as capital to act as a cushion against loss. The size of the haircut on a security is set equal to the estimate of the transaction's risk exposure. Risk is defined as potential price volatility and potential credit losses on the dealer's transactions. The greater the risk exposure and the less the security's marketability, the higher the required haircut.

> **haircut:** the fraction of a broker/dealer's securities portfolio that cannot be traded but must instead be held as capital to act as a cushion against loss.

Suppose that Secure Securities, Inc.'s inventory includes a $1 million face value 20 year, 8% coupon U.S. Treasury bond selling at par. Assume that it is highly likely that interest rates may increase by 50 basis points. If interest rates increase, the bond's price will decline. The haircut is the expected price decline. What is the haircut for this security?

Since the bond sold at par, the yield to maturity before the interest rate increase was equal to the coupon rate of 8% paid, as for all U.S. Treasury notes and bonds, at semiannual intervals. Repricing the 20 year U.S. Treasury bond at an interest rate of 8.50% yields a price of $952,306.81.[7] The haircut is set equal to the potential price decline of $1 million − $952,306.81 = $47,693.19.

The Uniform Net Capital Rule for securities firms requires that all securities be sorted into product groups. The product groups (or "haircut families") are governments, corporates, futures, municipals, convertibles, preferred stock, common stock, money markets, agencies, risk arbitrage, and options. Within each family, the securities are grouped by risk exposure into maturity timebands, marketability levels, default ratings, and so on. The percentage of capital required (the haircut rate) varies from 0% to 100%, depending on the risk characteristics of the securities group. However, the broker/dealer's total capital requirement is not simply equal to the sum of all haircuts on all individual transactions as is true for banks and insurance companies. Haircut charges can be significantly decreased by **hedging** specific securities holdings. Hedging is the process of investing in two sets of securities whose values move in opposite directions, thereby reducing the overall risk of the portfolio.

> **hedging:** The process of investing in two sets of securities whose values move in opposite directions, thereby reducing the overall risk of the portfolio.

If the FI's risk exposure from holding one security is offset by its holdings of another security, then the FI need not hold capital against each of the individual securities. Thus, the capital requirement is determined on a net capital basis to be a function of the residual risk left over after the offsetting impact of holding both securities is considered. The capital requirements of securities firms are computed on a net capital basis, whereas those of other financial firms are computed on an aggregate capital basis.[8] The FI's capital requirement on an aggregate capital basis is equal to the sum of all capital requirements on each of the firm's securities holdings.

---

[7] Quick refresher on bond valuation: this U.S. Treasury bond pays FV = $1 million principal plus N = 40 semiannual payments, each equaling $.08/2 = .04 \times$ $1 million face value, or PMT = $40,000. The present value (PV) of these cash flows using the i = 8.5% p.a. yield is

$$PV = \sum_{t=1}^{N} \frac{PMT}{(1 + \frac{i}{2})^t} + \frac{FV}{(1 + \frac{i}{2})^N} =$$

$$\sum_{t=1}^{40} \frac{\$40,000}{(1 + \frac{.085}{2})^t} + \frac{\$1 \text{million}}{(1 + \frac{.085}{2})^{40}} = \$952,306.81$$

[8] The Basel capital requirements allow netting for the calculation of the current exposure of off-balance sheet contracts only.

Since a net capital requirement considers the interaction among securities holdings, all else being equal, moving from an aggregate capital to a net capital requirement reduces the FI's required level of capital.

Suppose that Secure Securities, Inc. had a portfolio of securities with the market values shown on the following balance sheet:

Secure Securities, Inc. ($ million)

Assets		Liabilities	
6.5% p.a. 4 yr. T-notes, par value $15, semiannual coupon	12	4.75% p.a. 1 yr. notes, par value $25, annual coupon	25
12% p.a. 30 yr. CMOs, par value $60, monthly coupon	55	8% p.a. 2 yr. bonds, par value $40, annual coupon	42

If all interest rates are expected to increase by 30 basis points, then what is the haircut on each security?

1. The U.S. Treasury note asset earns a yield to maturity of 13.08% p.a. If interest rates increase 30 basis points to 13.38%, the asset's price falls from $12 million to $11,881,449.04 for a loss of $118,550.96.

2. The nonamortizing collateralized mortgage obligations (CMOs) earn a yield to maturity of 13.115%. If interest rates increase 30 basis points to 13.415%, then the asset's price falls from $55 million to $53,786,926.97 for a loss of $1,213,073.03.

3. The one year note liability selling at par pays a yield of 4.75% p.a. If interest rates increase 30 basis points to 5.05%, the value of this liability falls from $25 million to $24,928,605.43 for an equity gain of $71,394.57.

4. The two year debt liability pays a yield of 5.3% p.a. If interest rates increase 30 basis points to 5.6%, then the liability's price falls from $42 million to $41,769,972.45 for a gain of $230,027.55.

Totaling the gains (decreases in the market values of the FI's liabilities): $301,422.12.

Totaling the losses (decreases in the market values of the FI's assets): $1,331,623.99

Secure Securities' net loss is $1,030,201.87. This would be the required haircut on a net capital basis if all interest rates were expected to increase by the same 30 basis points.

Checkpoint

1. Contrast capital-asset ratios against risk adjusted capital regulations.

2. What is a haircut?

3. Compare capital regulations computed on the basis of net capital as opposed to aggregate capital.

Deposit Insurance and Capital Regulation

Capital acts as a cushion to absorb losses without triggering the insolvency of the FI. To promote capital adequacy, we have seen that public FIs require minimum levels of capital holdings. But since by definition total assets must equal the sum of debt plus equity capital, the setting of minimum capital requirements is equivalent to setting maximum debt levels. Capital requirements then simultaneously set limitations on the FI's potential leverage or indebtedness. As we have seen, however, some debt can be included in Tier 2 capital. Therefore, we may ask whether we can limit and encourage indebtedness at the same time.

We must draw a distinction between secured and unsecured debt. To be included in Tier 2 capital, the debt must be unsecured and subordinated to the claims of other creditors. Who are these other creditors and how are their claims secured? For depository FIs, these other creditors are depositors, and their deposit liabilities are secured by the FI's asset portfolio. In addition, many countries offer depositors additional protection in the form of deposit insurance against FI defaults on deposit liabilities. If a bank does fail, then public FIs like the FDIC in the United States are required to make full payment to holders of insured deposits. In exchange for these payments, the FDIC receives a senior claim on the bank's assets. That is, the FDIC must be compensated for its payments to insured depositors before equityholders and subordinated debtholders can be paid. Thus, these capital claims are subordinated to the claim of the deposit insurer. When we say that capital requirements limit the FI's potential leverage, we are referring to limitations on the FI's access to liabilities insured by public FI guarantees. So there is no contradiction between regulations that simultaneously limit indebtedness (e.g., by limiting access to insured deposits)[9] and encourage the issuance of subordinated debt (that counts toward the FI's capital requirement).

The United States, Canada, the United Kingdom, and Japan all have government deposit insurance programs (see Table 5.1). The U.S. deposit insurance program is the most generous with basic protection up to $100,000 per *deposit*, with a limitation on the number of accounts any one individual can have at a single bank. Coverage in Japan is capped at US$74,000 per depositor; in Canada at US$50,000 (Canadian $60,000) per depositor; and in the United Kingdom at 75% of the first US$33,000 per depositor. There is a tradeoff between the generosity of basic coverage and the market discipline that limits the banks' risk taking behavior. The more generous the deposit insurance plan, the less likely that bank runs will occur, but the more likely that banks will become insolvent because of incentives to engage in excessive bank risk taking. The bank's shareholders maximize the value of deposit insurance by increasing the bank's risk exposure, whereas depositors have no incentive to monitor the activities of shareholders since their deposits are insured by the government. This incentive conflict was a primary cause of the thrift debacle in the United States during the late 1980s, which resulted in a $500 billion bailout of the savings and loan industry.[10]

As a result of this expensive lesson, the Federal Deposit Insurance Improvement Act of 1991 mandated that, as of 1994, a risk adjusted deposit insurance premium schedule (see Table 5.4) be put in place in the United States. Deposit insurance premiums vary from a minimum of zero for low-risk, well-capitalized banks to a maximum of 27 cents per $100 of deposits for high-risk, undercapitalized banks.[11]

Checkpoint

1. What characteristics of debt make it eligible to be considered as Tier 2 capital?

2. What is a bank run? Why is it disruptive to the efficient operation of the economy? How does government-provided deposit insurance prevent bank runs?

3. How does a fixed deposit insurance premium create unintended negative consequences?

4. How does the FDIC Improvement Act of 1991 propose to remedy some of the problems associated with deposit insurance in the United States?

---

[9] In the prompt corrective action provisions of the FDICIA of 1991 (see Table 5.5), the first mandatory penalty imposed on adequately capitalized banks is the prohibition of access to brokered deposits that carry deposit insurance.

[10] For an in-depth discussion of deposit insurance and the thrift crisis in the United States, see White (1991).

[11] However, in 1995 the deposit insurance premium paid by banks was set equal to zero because the surplus in the bank insurance fund was sufficient to pay out any claims.

Table 5.4

Risk Adjusted Deposit Insurance Premiums: United States, 1996
(cents per $100 of deposits)

Capital Classifications	Tier 1	Tier2	Total	Healthy	Supervisory Concern	Substantial Supervisory Concern
Deposit Insurance Premiums for Banks (27-cent rate spread)						
Well capitalized	>6%	>5%	>10%	0[a]	3	17
Pct. of banks in each group*				92%	5.2%	1.3%
Adequately capitalized	>4%	>4%	>8%	3	10	24
Pct. of banks in each group				0.7%	0.2%	0.3%
< Adequately capitalized				10	24	27
Pct. of banks in each group				0.1%	0.04%	0.2%
Undercapitalized	<4%	<4%	<8%			
Significantly undercapitalized	<3%	<3%	<6%			
Critically undercapitalized	<2%					
Deposit Insurance Premiums for Thrifts (8-cent rate spread)						
Well capitalized				23	26	29
Pct. of thrifts in each group				86.1%	7.7%	1.4%
Adequately capitalized				26	29	30
Pct. of thrifts in each group				1.2%	1.7%	1.5%
Undercapitalized				29	30	31
Pct. of thrifts in each group				0.0%	0.0%	0.4%

[a] Subject to the statutory minimum of $2,000 per institution per year.

Source: FDIC Corporate Communications Office.

Early Intervention

Shareholders and public FIs are not the only ones threatened by troubled FIs; insolvent FIs also pose trouble for solvent FIs. Deposit insurance plus insolvency is a particularly lethal combination because insolvent, insured FIs can raise unlimited amounts of funds thanks to their access to the deep pockets of government deposit insurance. Indeed, the policy of forbearance by regulators, which delayed the closure of insolvent thrifts (dubbed "zombie thrifts" by Professor Ed Kane of Boston College), allowed them to bid up interest rates, thereby reducing the profitability of their solvent FI competitors. This phenomenon spread the thrift crisis by forcing marginally solvent S&Ls to pay higher and higher rates to raise funds, which caused them to incur losses and ultimately to become insolvent themselves.

The FDICIA of 1991 limits regulators' discretion as to when to close troubled FIs. It requires that troubled FIs be recognized long before they become insolvent. Programs are mandated to prevent these troubled FIs from destabilizing the industry. Termed *prompt corrective action*, these programs require regulators to follow the steps outlined in Table 5.5. For instance, within 90 days of detection, critically undercapitalized FIs, with tangible equity less than 2% of assets, must be placed in either **conservatorship** or **receivership**. A receivership is the condition of an insolvent FI over whom a receiver has been appointed for protection of its assets and for ultimate sale and distribution to creditors. A conservatorship is the condition of a FI over whom a conservator has been appointed to manage or liquidate the incompetently managed (not necessarily insolvent) FI. If prompt corrective action operates as intended, all other elements of the safety net are rendered moot, since troubled FIs will be closed before they reach insolvency.

Federal banking regulations permit the reallocation of corporate resources using the "source of strength" doctrine. In the event of bank insolvency, parent bank holding companies are required to "transfer" assets to subsidize the losses of their separately incorporated troubled subsidiaries. This is a departure from standard corporate law since the mandated capital infu-

conservatorship: the condition of a FI over whom a conservator has been appointed to manage or liquidate the incompetently managed (not necessarily insolvent) FI.

receivership: the condition of an insolvent FI over whom a receiver has been appointed for protection of its assets and for ultimate sale and distribution to creditors.

Table 5.5

Prompt Corrective Action in the FDICIA of 1991

Classification[a]	Mandatory Actions	Discretionary Actions
Well capitalized	No restrictions	
Adequately capitalized	Limit access to brokered CDs	
Undercapitalized	No dividends paid File capital restoration plan Restrict asset growth	Require additional capital Restrict interaffiliate transactions Restrict deposit rates
Significantly undercapitalized	Require additional capital Restrict interaffiliate transactions Restrict deposit rates and officers pay	Conservatorship if no plan submitted
Critically undercapitalized	Conservatorship within 90 days Suspend payments on subordinated debt	

[a] For definitions of the capitalization classification, see Table 5.4.

sions by the parent corporation "pierce the corporate veil" by requiring the parent corporation to transfer its assets to its subsidiary. In December 1991, when Bank One Corp. attempted to invest $65 million to buy insolvent Premier Bancorp, the Fed ruled that Banc One's entire capital base of $3.8 billion must be made available for possible future bailouts of Premier. Needless to say, Banc One found such terms unacceptable and chose not to buy Premier Bank.

Many of the regulations discussed thus far apply to depository institutions such as banks and thrifts. However, the FDICIA of 1991 also applies to FIs defined to include a securities broker or dealer, a depository institution, a **futures commission merchant**, or any other institution as determined by the Fed. A futures commission merchant is a FI that executes or clears any futures contract approved for trading on an organized exchange.

Insurance companies must also comply with regulations dictating minimum required levels of reserves against policy liabilities. These requirements are risk based. Insurance companies must file detailed Regulation 126 reports examining the risk exposure of the asset and liability portfolios under a number of different interest rate scenarios. However, well-capitalized FIs are exempt from filing these reports to the National Association of Insurance Commissioners. As Table 5.6 shows, this exemption is related to size. To be exempted, smaller insurance companies must have higher capital and reserves levels than do larger insurance companies. This concept illustrates the substitutability between safety and soundness regulation and public disclosure requirements. Since public disclosure is aimed at market participants who use the information to monitor the FIs' activities, the more actively the market oversees the FI, the less critical is direct safety and soundness monitoring by public FIs. The presumption is that larger insurance companies are more likely to be publicly traded and therefore more likely to be scrutinized by market participants than are smaller insurance companies. Therefore, regulators can concentrate much of their efforts on the companies that are smaller or riskier while allowing the market to discipline the more visible, larger FIs. But the financial health of the largest of these FIs is crucial to the unobstructed operation of financial markets. Their dominance and potential for disruption of financial markets justifies the most stringent reporting requirements for these largest FIs.

futures commission merchant: a FI that executes or clears any futures contract approved for trading on an organized exchange.

Checkpoint

1. What is prompt corrective action?
2. What is forbearance? How does it benefit the economy? How does it hurt the economy?
3. How do public FIs prioritize their monitoring activities using exemption from regulatory reporting requirements? Discuss this question using insurance companies' regulations.

Table 5.6

Exemptions from Insurance Company Regulatory Reporting Requirements

Asset Range	Capital/Assets	Liabilities/Assets	Noninvestment Grade Bonds/Capital
To Be Exempt from Regulation 126 Reporting Requirements:			
If assets < $20million	≥ 10%	< 30%	< 50%
If assets $20m–$100m	≥ 7%	< 40%	< 50%
If assets $100m–$500m	≥ 5%	<50%	< 50%
If assets > $500m	No exemption		

Credit Allocation and Regulation

Risk adjusted capital requirements and deposit insurance premiums ultimately reallocate FIs' portfolios away from riskier activities. Public FIs can also utilize specific regulations to reallocate portfolios in ways that are deemed to be financially sound and socially beneficial. One example is the prohibition against lending more than 10% of the bank's capital to any one borrower. Barings PLC collapsed in 1995 after a 233 year history of investment banking because it violated a Bank of England prohibition against devoting more than 25% of capital to one activity (in this case, a highly speculative futures position). FIs are required to follow a prudent approach to financial risk management by diversifying their asset portfolios.

Another example of a credit allocation regulation designed to induce prudent financial management is the Regulation O limitation on insider loans. Conflicts of interest created by loans to officers and directors of private FIs make such loans prone to default. Managerial fraud, often involving insider loans, was the number one cause of failure of U.S. thrifts during the S&L crisis of the 1980s. Insider loans and fraud at rogue international bank BCCI left the bank with only $1.16 billion in assets against liabilities of $10.64 billion when the Bank of England and other regulators closed it in 1991. Similarly, prohibitions against insider trading are designed to prevent abuses by securities firms.

Some regulations mandate credit reallocations specifically in order to achieve social policy goals, as opposed to inducing financially prudent FI behavior. Examples of regulations designed to induce socially desirable behavior are listed in Table 5.7. When successfully implemented, these regulations assist FIs in finding profitable markets that have been underserved. When

Table 5.7

Selected U.S. Legislation to Encourage Equal Access to Banking Services

1968 Housing and Urban Development Act
      FHA insurance extended to housing in older, declining urban areas.
1968 Fair Housing Act of the Civil Rights Act
      Prohibits discrimination in the sale, rental, financing, or marketing of housing.
1974 Equal Credit Opportunity Act
      Prohibits discrimination against credit applicants on the basis of
          age, race, color, religion, national origin, marital status.
1975 Home Mortgage Disclosure Act (HMDA)
      Requires that banks/thrifts disclose the race and region of all mortgage loans applicants.
1977 Community Reinvestment Act (CRA)
      Requires all banks and thrifts to serve the credit needs of their communities,
          specifically in low- and moderate-income areas.
1990 Truth in Lending Regulation Z
      By standardizing disclosure requirements, protects borrowers and depositors.
1994 Riegle Community Development, Credit Enhancement, and Regulatory Improvement Act
      Creates a small business-related security that is an investment-grade participation
          in a pool of small business loans. Creates a Community Development FIs Fund
          to encourage lending in distressed communities.

allowed to run amuck, the solvency of the very FIs most responsive to these regulations can be jeopardized, as pointed out in *Timely Topics 5.2*.

TIMELY TOPICS 5.2

GIVING DUE CREDIT WHERE CREDIT IS DUE

There have been deep-seated concerns for some time that certain segments of our society, particularly minority consumers and minority small business owners, have difficulty obtaining credit, difficulty that may not be justified by economic factors alone. This has had a major impact on the ability of minorities to build businesses, own homes, accumulate wealth, and generally, participate in our economy on an equal footing. It has been well publicized, for example, that Home Mortgage Disclosure Act (HMDA) data have documented patterns of comparatively low levels of mortgage lending in minority areas and higher loan denial rates for minorities than for whites. . . . [C]onstructive programs and activities fall into two basic categories: (1) those that I believe are simply extensions of ordinary business practices that institutions pursue as a matter of course, and (2) those that entail special initiatives, often in the form of public/private partnerships, which have been developed and refined over the last ten years.

Source: John LaWare, member of the Board of Governors of the Federal Reserve System, October 8, 1992.

If the Community Reinvestment Act (CRA) is perceived by banks as a tax or credit allocation, it will fail in the long run. Banks are not philanthropic institutions. . . . They are for-profit entities with obligations to their stockholders, and subject to a regulatory apparatus which protects their depositors from losses due to unsound practicies. . . . CRA must meet the test of the market if it is to provide the long term benefits of revitalization that we all desire. . . . We simply cannot as a nation tolerate unfair and illegal activity that puts some of our citizens at a disadvantage as they try to participate in the credit markets. We all know that the raw HMDA numbers are not a reliable gauge of whether discrimination is at work or to what degree. But the general story they tell cannot be encouraging to anyone, and is a strong signal that work needs to be done. . . . Free market capitalistic systems rooted in individual freedom cannot and should not abide such unjust behavior. To the extent that individual contributions to the market place are judged, and rewarded on any basis other than economic values, the system suffers and the nation's standard of living is impaired. We may never reach perfection in this regard, but we should never cease to persevere.

Source: Alan Greenspan, February 8, 1994.

Checkpoint

1.   Why do public FIs use credit allocation regulation?

2.   What is Regulation O and why was it passed?

3.   Describe three regulations designed to promote social policy goals rather than FI safety and soundness.

The Examination Process

bank examination: an on-site auditing of a depository FI to ascertain its financial condition and future prospects.

Public FIs could not verify the efficacy of their attempts at capital regulation, deposit insurance protection, and credit reallocation without some formal examination process. The **bank examination** consists of the on-site auditing of a depository FI to ascertain its financial condition and future prospects. The FDICIA of 1991 required regulators to set standards for prudent banking practices and early intervention procedures in the event of financial distress. Auditors and examiners were required to document the prudent and effective use of (1) internal controls, information systems, and internal audit systems; (2) loan documentation; (3) credit underwriting; (4) controls over interest rate risk exposure; (5) controls over asset growth; (6) controls over compensation, fees, and benefits; (7) specifying a maximum ratio of **classified**

classified assets: nonperforming assets that are not yielding the contractually obligated cash flows.

assets (nonperforming assets that are not yielding the contractually obligated cash flows) to capital; (8) computing the minimum earnings sufficient to absorb losses without impairing capital; and (9) setting a minimum ratio of market value to book value for publicly traded shares of FIs and holding companies.

Banks must pay for the cost of the examination in terms of examiner time, travel, and other expenses. The Foreign Bank Supervision Enhancement Act of 1991 (FBSEA) required the Board of Governors of the Federal Reserve System to charge foreign banks for the cost of examining their branches, agencies, and representative offices. In 1993 the total cost of examination of the U.S. offices of foreign banks was $11.7 million.

Public FIs use the results of on-site examinations to guide their regulatory intervention policies. However, the results are not made public even if they result in the bank's placement on a problem bank list. Indeed, the names of the FIs on this list are a most carefully guarded secret. Clearly, market participants would like to have access to this information. They attempt to compile their own "problem FI list" by analyzing publicly available information. It is the role of public FIs to assure that the private FI releases sufficient amounts of accurate and revealing information about its financial condition so as to enable the market to conduct its own analysis. This leads us to the indirect form of regulatory policy: disclosure requirements.

▶ Disclosure Requirements

Public FIs elicit the assistance of market participants in monitoring private FIs by requiring prompt and extensive public disclosure of information about the FI's financial condition. Thus, market participants who have a stake in the private FI can help public FIs supervise its activities. Indeed, the Reserve Bank of New Zealand does not examine its banks at all, but instead requires them to disclose detailed information about their operations to the public on a quarterly basis, thereby depending on market discipline to maintain bank safety and soundness.

Many depository FIs rely on insured deposits as an important source of funds. We have seen how the availability of deposit insurance and "too big to fail" protection erodes market discipline. Insured depositors have no incentive to evaluate the bank's performance and risk taking activities, since they know that their money is not at risk. In contrast, holders of subordinated debt and other uninsured obligations of the bank have a stake in monitoring its performance. Because they have more subordinated debtholders, nondepository FIs are typically subject to less direct supervision than are depository FIs. Instead, public FIs discharge their supervisory duties by requiring strict adherence to extensive disclosure requirements. By disseminating financial data, public FIs enable market participants to actively supervise the activities of private FIs. Disclosure requirements protect investors from FIs that make fraudulent or misleading claims. The United States has the strictest disclosure requirements in the world, dealing with regularly released financial statements as well as with news of events that may have an impact on financial markets and participants. The rulemaking board of the

Securities and Exchange Commission runs a Continuing Disclosure Information Pilot system that acts as an automated clearinghouse that transmits breaking financial information to its users.

All **public companies** in the United States with stock trading on the New York Stock Exchange, American Stock Exchange, Nasdaq, or over the counter must regularly file documents reporting

public companies: companies with stock traded on the New York Stock Exchange, American Stock Exchange, Nasdaq or over the counter.

1. Description of business, including SIC codes.

2. Financial statements.

3. The identity of the firm's auditors.

4. Any ongoing legal proceedings.

5. The names of directors and officers of the corporation.

6. Any material events or corporate changes.

7. Proposed offerings of securities.

8. Status of pension plans.

9. Location and character of principal properties.

10. Number of employees.

11. Number of shareholders.

12. Amount of stock options and compensation of top executives.

13. Exhibits, contracts, and all other material agreements.

This filing can be accomplished via the following reports: the annual 10-K; the annual N-SAR (the same as the 10-K but for investment companies); the annual 18-K; the annual 20-F; the quarterly 10-Q; the periodic 8-K (to be filed 15 days after unscheduled material events); the periodic 10-C (the same as the 8-K but for over-the-counter stocks); the quarterly 13-F; the annual proxy statement; and special reports triggered by corporate events such as tender offers, acquisitions, mergers, and public offerings. These reports are available in computer-readable format on the SEC's EDGAR (Electronic Data Gathering, Analysis, and Retrieval) system. Figure 5.3 provides an overview of the extensive public disclosure requirements in the United States.

In March 1995 the SEC and the Commodity Futures Trading Commission (CFTC) orchestrated an agreement with six securities firms to voluntarily disclose written statements describing their derivatives transactions. The securities firms agreed to report to the SEC and the CFTC (but not to the general public) information about their derivatives portfolios, listing their top 20 derivatives trading partners, as well as details regarding the FI's risk monitoring and risk management controls. FIs are expected to evaluate the impact on their derivatives portfolios of specified **core risk factors**. Rather than considering only the FI's risk exposure resulting from marginal market movements, core risk measures the impact on the FI's portfolio value of systemic shifts in market conditions. The specified core risk factors are:

core risk factors: the impact of systemic shifts in market conditions on the value of a portfolio.

1. *Interest rate risk*, as measured by specific shifts in the structure of current interest rates.

2. *Exchange rate risk*, as measured by specific shifts in the prices (relative to the U.S. dollar) and volatilities for the major currencies.

3. *Market risk*, as measured by changes in equity index values and volatilities.

In our earlier example using Secure Securities, Inc., we saw how we could evaluate the impact of interest rate risk by examining a parallel shift in interest rates. That is, we considered

Quick reference Chart to contents of SEC filings.

Report contents	18-K	19-K 20-K	10-Q	8-K	10-C	6-K	Proxy Statement	Prospectus	Registration Statements '34 Act F-10	Registration Statements '34 Act 8-A 8-B	Registration Statements '33 Act "S" Type	ARS	Listing Application	N-SAR
Auditor														
Name	A	A	■				■	A	A		A	A	■	A
Opinion	A	A	■						A			A		A
Changes				A			■							
Compensation laws														
Equity							F	F	A		F		■	■
Monetary								F	A		F		■	
Company information														
Nature of Business	A	A				F		A	A		A	■	■	
History	F	A						A			A	■		
Organization and Change	F	F		A	■	F	■	A		F	A	■		
Debt Structure	A					F	■	A	A		A	A		A
Depreciation & Other Schedules	A	A				F		A	A		A			
Dilution Factors	A	A		F		F		A	A		A	A		
Directors, Officers , Insiders	A	A		A		A		A	A		A	A		A
Identification	F	A				F	A	A	A		A	F		
Background	■	A				F	F	A	■		A	■		
Holdings	■	A		■			A	A	A		A			
Compensation	■	A		■			A	A	A		A			
Earnings Per Share	A	A	A			F			A			A		A
Financial Information														
Annual Audited	A	A		■					A			A		A
Interim Audited		A		■			■	■			■			
Interim Unaudited	■		A	■		F		F			F	F		
Foreign Operations	A			■			■	A	A		A	■	F	
Labor Contracts		■		■			■		F		F			
Legal Agreements	F	■		■					F		F			
Legal Counsel				■				A			A		■	
Loan Agreements	F		F	■			■		F		F			■
Plants and Properties	A	A		■				F	A		F	■		
Portfolio Operations	A	A		A		A		A	A		A	A		A
Content (Listing of Securities)														A
Management														A
Product-Line Breakout	A							A			A	■		
Securities Structure	A	A						A	A		A			
Subsidiaries	A	A					■	A	A		A	■	■	
Underwriting				■				A	A		A			
Unregistered Securities	■			■			■	F			F			
Block Movements	■			F			■		A				■	

Legend

A - *always included - included-if occured or significant*

F - *frequently included*

■ - *special circumstances only*

Tender Offer/Acquisition Reports	130	13 G	14D-1	14D-9	13E-3	13E-4
Name of Issuer (Subject Company)	A	A	A	A	A	A
Filing Person (or Company)	A	A	A	A	A	A
Amount of Shares Owned	A	A				
Percent of Class Outstanding	A	A				
Financial Statements of Bidders			F		F	F
Purpose of Tender Offer			A	A	A	A
Source and Amount of Funds	A		A		A	
Identity and Background Information			A	A	A	
Persons Retained, Employed or to be Compensated			A	A	A	A
Exhibits	F		F	F	F	F

Source: Disclosure, Inc.

Figure 5.3

a 30-basis-point increase in all yields. To estimate its core risk exposure, Secure Securities must calculate the impact of the three components of risk on its portfolio, using predetermined scenarios. These detailed computations about risk exposure are revealed to the SEC and CFTC and are not to be used to adjust capital requirements to reflect risk, as in the Basel capital requirements discussed earlier. Instead, both public and private FIs use the information as a vehicle for periodic, regular consultations between regulators and regulated management. This is similar to the longstanding traditions of public FIs in countries such as Japan, Germany, and the United Kingdom where (as we saw in Chapter 3) there is a close relationship between the managements of the public and private FIs. Traditionally, this has not been the case in the United States, perhaps because of its large number of private FIs. The voluntary derivatives policy is a step toward achieving greater integration of public and private FIs in the United States.

Market Value Accounting

Disclosure requires that financial statements be issued on a frequent, periodic basis, but these statements are useful only if they reveal an accurate and comprehensive view of the FI's financial condition. Accuracy in financial disclosure dictates marking the FI's balance sheet to market by using market values as opposed to book values. However, several objections have delayed implementation of market value accounting for all FIs.

1. *Liquidation value.* Market values are the selling prices upon liquidation of the FI's portfolio of securities. This may reflect artificially deflated "fire sale" values, particularly for relatively illiquid assets. To get a fair view of the true market value of a FI's assets, market prices of similar risk assets are often used.

2. *Volatility.* Since market values fluctuate, a shift to market value accounting would increase the volatility of FIs' earnings, suggesting that book value accounting understates the true volatility of the FI's earnings. The prices of financial securities are adjusted upon receipt of all new information about interest rates, default risks, liquidity risks, and so on. Revaluation of the FIs' securities portfolios reassesses their financial positions, creating instability in financial reporting. Of course, if this instability is an indication of true FI value, market participants would rather have this information than be lulled by a false sense of security engendered by an artificially stable book value balance sheet.

3. *Inability to measure market value for illiquid assets held to maturity.* Since some assets do not have secondary markets and are therefore held until maturity, their market value is neither measurable nor relevant. The FI expects to receive all required cash flows ultimately; thus, any paper profits or losses resulting from interest rate fluctuations are not relevant if the asset is held until maturity.

4. *Impact on capital levels.* Temporary changes in market values could cause a bank's capital to fall below required minimum levels, forcing regulators (under the prompt, corrective action regulations of the FDICIA of 1991) to close the bank precipitously.

In May 1993 the U.S. Financial Accounting Standards Board (FASB) issued Rule 115 (which took effect on December 15, 1993) requiring that fair or market values be utilized to evaluate certain assets held by FIs. FASB 115 applies to banks,[12] thrift institutions, finance companies, and insurance companies. Broker/dealer securities firms and investment companies must evaluate *all* of their investments at market values. Under FASB 115, the FI classifies each newly acquired asset as (1) held to maturity; (2) available for sale; or (3) trading. These

---

[12] Because of concern about capital adequacy, in November 1994, Federal bank regulators exempted banks from FASB 115 in their computation of compliance with minimum capital requirements.

classifications are based on the FI's intentions upon acquisition and must be reassessed in each financial report.

All debt securities that are not classified as held-to-maturity as well as all equity securities must be valued at their market values. The rule states that for equity, market values are obtained from "sales prices or bid-and-asked quotations... on a securities exchange registered with the SEC or in the over-the-counter market" or on "a foreign market... if that foreign market is of a breadth and scope comparable to one of the U.S. markets." For debt securities, market values are calculated for four maturity groupings: within one year; one to five years; five to ten years; and more than ten years to maturity. Debt securities classified as held-to-maturity may be carried as book values.

An example of market value accounting is shown using Table 5.8 for Infinite Life Insurance Company with a book value of assets of $190 million. First, the FI must classify its assets into the three categories. Assume that the one year Treasury note is considered a trading security; the Eurobonds are available for sale; and the 10 year corporate bond is to be held until maturity. Since it is held until maturity, the 10 year corporate bond is carried at book value. The Treasury note and the Eurobonds must be revalued at their market values.

The Treasury note is selling at a premium since its yield is only 6%, but the coupon is 7% p.a. (3.5% semiannually). Pricing the Treasury note at the 3% semiannual yield for a $15 million face value, we get

$$P = \sum_{t=1}^{2} \frac{(.035)(\$15m)}{1.03^t} + \frac{\$15m}{1.03^2} = \$15.144 \text{ million}$$

repricing date, or roll date: the day on which interest rates on floating rate instruments are recalculated using some specified current market interest rate.

floating rate instruments: debt instruments with coupon payments that vary with variations in some prespecified market interest rate.

If today is the **repricing date** on the Eurobonds, then they are priced at par since the coupon rate is reset to the market yield. The repricing date, or **roll date**, is the day on which interest rates on **floating rate instruments** are recalculated using some specified current market interest rate. Floating rate instruments, in contrast to fixed income securities, are debt instruments with coupon payments that vary with some prespecified market interest rate. The market value balance sheet is shown in Table 5.8a.

Suppose that the day after the balance sheets in Tables 5.8 and 5.8a are recorded, all interest rates increase by 75 basis points (0.75%). The valuation of the 10 year corporate bond is unaffected since it has been classified as held-to-maturity. The one year Treasury note must be revalued at a yield of $\frac{6.75\%}{2} = 3.375\%$ semiannually:

$$P = \sum_{t=1}^{2} \frac{(.035)(\$15m)}{1.03375^t} + \frac{\$15m}{1.03375^2} = \$15.036 \text{ million}$$

Table 5.8

Infinite Life Insurance Company[a]

Book Values ($million)			
1 yr. Treasury note, 7% p.a. yielding 6%	15	Net policy reserves	150
10 yr. corp. bond, 8% p.a. yielding 11% p.a.	105	5 yr. notes, LIBOR[b] + 1.5% repriced quarterly	20
1 yr. Eurobonds, LIBOR[b] + 3% repriced annually	70	Capital	20

[a] Treasury securities yield fixed coupon payments semiannually. The corporate bonds have fixed annual coupons.

[b] The London InterBank Offer Rate (LIBOR) is a market interest rate. In this example, the current LIBOR is 5.5%.

Table 5.8a

Infinite Life Insurance Company

FASB 115 Market Values ($million)

1 yr. Treasury note, 7% p.a. yielding 6%	15.144	Net policy reserves	150
10 yr. corp. bond, 8% p.a. yielding 11% p.a.	105	5 yr. notes, LIBOR + 1.5% repriced quarterly	20
1 yr. Eurobonds, LIBOR + 3% repriced annually	70	Capital	20
		Unrealized gains on trading securities	0.144

Table 5.8b

Infinite Life Insurance Company

FASB 115 Market Values After 75-Basis-Point Interest Rate Increase ($million)

1 yr. Treasury note, 7% p.a. yielding 6%	15.036	Net policy reserves	150
10 yr. corp. bond, 8% p.a. yielding 11% p.a.	105	5 yr. notes, LIBOR + 1.5% repriced quarterly	20
1 yr. Eurobonds, LIBOR + 3% repriced annually	69.519	Capital	20
		Unrealized gains on trading securities	+0.144
		Unrealized loss on Treasury note	−0.108
		Unrealized loss on Eurobonds	−0.481

for a net decline in value of $108,000. These unrealized holding losses are charged to the FI's capital account in Table 5.8b.

The Eurobonds must also be repriced since they are classified as available for sale. **LIBOR** (the London InterBank Offer Rate, which is an international money market interest rate) on the repricing date (a day before the interest rate increase) was 5.5%. Since the annual coupon on the Eurobonds is set at LIBOR plus 3%, its coupon rate is 8.5%, for an end-of-year payment of $70m(1.085) = $75.95 million. However, market yields increased by 75 basis points, raising the risk adjusted yield on the Eurobonds to 9.25%. Using this as a discount factor, we find that the price of the Eurobonds is

$$P = \frac{FV}{1 + r} = \frac{70(1.085)}{1.0925} = \$69.519m$$

for an unrealized holding loss of $481,000 ($69.519m − $70m) which is charged to the FI's capital account, and thereby bring Infinite Life's asset market value to $189.555 million, as shown in Table 5.8b.

Since assets classified as held-to-maturity[13] and all liabilities are not recorded at their market values, FASB 115 still does not require that FIs reveal their true market value. Reluctance to fairly value *all* securities (assets and liabilities) on the FIs' portfolios stems from the concern about injecting volatility into financial reports. FASB 115 represents a compromise that sidesteps some of the most difficult valuation problems, such as valuation of deposit liabilities and illiquid assets without secondary markets that are held-until-maturity. However, the practice of marking to market only a portion of the balance sheet may actually *inject* volatility into the FIs' financial reports. That is, if FIs have matched their asset and liability positions so as to protect themselves against risk exposure, then partial marking to market includes the effect of one side of the balance sheet without including the possibly offsetting other side of the balance sheet. Thus, although partial market-to-market accounting is a step in the right direction, the failure to implement *complete* market value accounting exacerbates some of the problems that most concern its opponents.

LIBOR: London InterBank Offer Rate, which is an international money market interest rate.

---

[13] If a security is transferred from the held-to-maturity category, the unrealized gain or loss is immediately charged to shareholders equity.

Table 5.9

Meeting U.S. Accounting Standards: The Number of SEC Registered Companies in Europe, by Country, 1995

Country	Number	Country	Number
United Kingdom	52	Ireland	6
Netherlands	10	Norway	3
France	8	Portugal	2
Spain	7	Denmark	2
Italy	7	Germany	1
Sweden	6		

Source: Wall Street Journal, March 15, 1995, p. C1.

hidden reserves: capital reserves held by FIs in Germany, Switzerland, the Netherlands, and the U.K. whose value is not revealed.

International Accounting Standards   As obscure as accounting procedures are in the United States, they are far more revealing than in the rest of the world.[14] Swiss and German accounting standards are notorious for their opaqueness, allowing Swiss and German FIs to hold large quantities of **hidden reserves** that are not revealed in financial statements. FIs in Germany, Switzerland, the Netherlands, and the U.K. are encouraged to create these inner capital reserves as protection against loan and trading losses without revealing their values. In order to access the U.S. capital market, these foreign companies must comply with SEC disclosure requirements which, among other things, prohibit hidden reserves. Table 5.9 shows the number of European companies that were in compliance as of 1995. The only German company included in the table was Daimler–Benz AG, which in 1993, so as to obtain a listing on the NYSE, issued two separate sets of accounts—one according to German standards and the other according to U.S. standards.

Although attempts have been made to standardize international accounting standards (most notably by the International Accounting Standards Committee, a private voluntary agency consisting of 109 professional accounting organizations in 80 countries), disagreements remain. Indeed, attempts to harmonize disclosure requirements and regulatory policy often become emeshed in political considerations, resulting in compromises that leave no party satisfied. Moreover, international agreements are particularly difficult to amend or update, as a result of the high cost of reaching consensus. *Timely Topics 5.3* describes the challenges in harmonizing international accounting standards.

TIMELY TOPICS 5.3

DO ALL ACCOUNTANTS SPEAK THE SAME LANGUAGE?

The major roadblock to foreign companies listing their overseas stock on U.S. exchanges has long been the difference between accounting standards in the U.S. and abroad. For decades, leading accounting theorists have advocated the harmonization of accounting principles worldwide to end the confusion and lack of comparability. But major foreign companies have resisted the move because they've felt that the tougher U.S. accounting rules would likely prevail in formulating global standards. . . .

The boards of the International Accounting Standards Committee, or IASC, which makes international rules, and the International Organization of Securities Commis-

---

[14] For a study of the information content of U.S. GAAP financial reports, see Amir, Harris, and Venuti (1993), pp. 230–275.

sions, have just agreed to develop accounting standards by mid-1999 for companies seeking stock lists in global markets to raise cross-border capital. And the Financial Accounting Standards Board, the chief rule-making body for U.S. accountants, has joined with standards setters in Canada, Mexico, and Chile to explore areas in which the four countries can harmonize their accounting standards.

Even the Securities and Exchange Commission, which has long fought to maintain tough U.S. accounting standards, is easing the barriers somewhat. Last year for the first time the SEC accepted three international accounting standards on cash flow data, the effects of hyperinflation, and business combinations for cross-border stock filings. Such filings are offered by foreign companies in more than one nation, including the U.S. . . .

But. . . the SEC. . . is adamant that U.S. accounting standards still won't be dropped. . . . Whatever the outcome, the stakes are enormous for both U.S. capital markets and the investment community. Big Board officials note that 55 million shares of nonregistered foreign stocks already trade in the U.S. over-the-counter. And they believe the U.S. stock market may lose world prominence to London and other European exchanges if foreign stocks aren't listed in New York. But financial analysts and accountants say that permitting foreign stocks to be listed here under non-U.S. accounting rules would only confuse and penalize U.S. investors. Currently, only 204 non-U.S.companies list on the New York Stock Exchange. To the Big Board, this seems like a pittance because there are 2,000 other major foreign companies out there that could qualify for listing. . . .

But some U.S. stock market analysts fear that these benefits wouldn't be worth the price, which is lack of comparable disclosure among U.S. and foreign stocks. . . . Accountants note, for example, that the U.S. annual report of Daimler–Benz, one of the few German companies to adhere to U.S. GAAP because it was forced to raise money here, shows a $1 billion annual loss. Under German accounting rules, Daimler reports a $100 million profit. In Japan, interest income is overstated, even when not received, and trading-account losses there can be hidden by shifting securities into an investment account—an accounting ploy forbidden in the U.S. . . .

Before any meaningful progress can be made in harmonization, international standard setters need a lot more resources and clout. Consider that IASC, which sets international standards, has only three or four full-time staff members, while the FASB has 45 staff members. And IASC has an annual budget of only $1.7 million compared with $15.8 million for FASB.

With such meager resources, IASC needs more money and staff to help cope with the sizable workload it has undertaken. If it cannot get this support from industry, government and accounting organizations, it will be difficult if not impossible to topple the long-standing Tower of Babel in accounting and produce a lingua franca to dispel the clouds over worldwide financial disclosure.

Source: L. Berton, Business World, *Wall Street Journal*, August 29, 1995, p. A.15.

Checkpoint

1.   What is market value accounting?

2.   Why are market values more useful than book values in disclosing FIs' financial conditions?

3.   What are the three categories of asset classifications under FASB 115? How are the assets in each category evaluated?

Disclosure and Market Discipline

An exception to the extensive regulatory scrutiny of FIs in the United States is the mutual fund industry. Mutual fund managers invest the proceeds of public sales of fund shares in portfolios that vary widely in terms of both composition and risk exposure. Although in 1994 there were more than 4,900 mutual funds in the United States controlling over $2 trillion in assets (nearly double the amount of assets in 1990 and 15 times the level of 1980), direct regulatory practices remain relatively lax. The SEC's division of mutual fund supervision has only 183 examiners (one examiner for about 27 funds) to directly supervise the funds, making it impossible to conduct annual on-site examinations for all of the funds. Large mutual funds are inspected, on average, once every two years, while smaller funds are inspected only once every four or five years and investment managers only once every 22 years. In March 1995, in order to improve efficiency, the SEC consolidated all of its inspections of brokerage firms, mutual funds, and other securities firms within a single SEC examination unit, so as to better mobilize the SEC's resources.

blue sky laws: laws that prohibit a FI from making misleading or false claims.

prospectus: a sales document that must be prepared before any financial security can be publicly sold.

Most mutual fund supervision takes the form of public disclosure requirements such as **blue sky laws** that prohibit FIs from making misleading or false claims in either their advertising or the sales document called the **prospectus**, which must be prepared before any financial security can be publicly sold. In March 1993 the SEC standardized reporting requirements in the prospectus. All mutual funds must provide (1) the name and background of the fund manager, (2) a chart comparing the fund's 10 year performance to a market average, and (3) an explanation of the fund manager's strategies and performance. Effective January 1995, the SEC amended disclosure rules to require that mutual funds release more information about directors' compensation and about the cost to investors if management fees are raised. However, if there is a material change in fund operations (e.g., departure of a key executive), there are no prompt disclosure requirements since the fund reports only twice a year to the SEC.

net asset value: the market value of the fund's portfolio divided by the number of shares outstanding.

This is not to suggest that the U.S. mutual fund industry is unsupervised—only that it is relatively unsupervised by public FIs and government agencies. To the contrary, the market disciplines mutual funds quite effectively by utilizing publicly available sources of information about the funds' **net asset value**. The net asset value is the market value of the fund's portfolio divided by the number of shares outstanding and is publicly reported in the financial press each and every business day. The transparency of mutual fund operations provides an opportunity for private monitors (such as Morningstar, Lipper Analytical Services, and CDA/Wiesenberger) to offer fund analysis services. The market is extremely sensitive to any hint of inaccuracy in the publicly released information about mutual fund values. When the world's largest mutual fund, Fidelity Investments, announced on June 18, 1994, that it had released incorrect pricing information for its funds on several occasions, the market was thrown into an uproar, prompting calls for stricter governmental regulations of mutual funds.

The investment companies have an interest in maintaining the regulatory status quo. Investment companies actively self-monitor in part to maintain their reputation for integrity and in part to avoid more intrusive regulation by public FIs. Following their pricing debacle, Fidelity announced in July 1994 that all employees' stock trades must be cleared through Fidelity's own discount brokerage subsidiary, stating that the change "will make it easier for us to modify and monitor our Code of Ethics in the future." As another example of the lengths that mutual funds go to avoid violating the public trust, BankAmerica Corporation injected its Pacific Horizon Prime money market fund with $17.4 million in capital during May 1994 in order to preserve its $1 net asset value, although BankAmerica was not required to do so.

➤ Market Structure

FIs are the target of an extensive amount of regulation; this can be viewed as either a blessing or a curse. We have seen how regulations constrain the activities of FIs, imposing burdensome capital constraints and reporting requirements. Nonetheless, regulations can also protect FIs. Deposit insurance and regulatory forbearance protect FIs from the harsh discipline of the market. Market forces dictate that inefficient firms be competed out of business. However, regulated firms, like FIs, are often shielded from competition. Regulation may shelter a market from competition from other similar FIs or from other types of financial and nonfinancial firms. For example, U.S. insurance companies are exempted from antitrust limitations by the McCarran–Ferguson Act of 1945, which grants ultimate regulatory authority to the states. Thus, regulation can affect the market's structure and the level of competition in the market for financial services.

Structure, Conduct, and Performance of FIs

The financial services industry has undergone dramatic changes in recent years. The United States had over 15,000 commercial banks in the early 1980s; by 1993 the number had declined to under 11,500. At the end of World War II, commercial banks extended almost 60% of all credit in the country; by 1993 that percentage had declined to 22%. U.S. and Japanese banks' market share has been eroded by competition from nonbank FIs such as insurance companies, finance companies, and broker/dealer securities firms. In contrast, in countries like Germany and the United Kingdom, the FIs' response to these competitive pressures has been to expand the FIs' offerings of financial services so as to create financial services supermarkets called universal banks.

Universal banks offer an array of banking and nonbanking financial products, such as insurance, underwriting, and market making, as well as nonfinancial services such as consulting, computer information services, and telecommunications. In contrast, this conglomeration of banking, nonbanking financial, and nonfinancial commercial activities is prohibited in the United States by the Glass-Steagall Act of 1933. Although market forces have eroded the effectiveness of these restrictions, there are still binding limitations on the activities of U.S. banks. For instance, thrift institutions are constrained under the **Qualified Thrift Lender Test** to hold at least 65% of their assets in mortgage-related securities.

Qualified Thrift Lender Test: restrictions on thrifts to hold at least 65% of their assets in mortgage-related securities.

Activity Restrictions in the United States   The Glass-Steagall Act of 1933 separates commercial banking (defined as deposit taking and commercial lending) from investment banking (defined as underwriting, brokerage, and money management). FIs with both commercial and investment banking functions prior to the passage of the Glass-Steagall Act were forced to split their commercial banking activities from their investment banking activities. In the early days of the Act, the FI was separated into two separate companies. For example, the powerhouse J. P. Morgan, Inc. was split into Morgan Guaranty and Morgan Stanley.

In time, however, FIs found ways to circumvent the restrictions of the Act. Bank holding companies were formulated, with the commercial bank representing one wholly owned subsidiary and the investment bank another. The legality of these structures was challenged time and again in the courts until in 1987 the Federal Reserve Board allowed commercial bank holding companies to establish separate nonbank **Section 20 subsidiaries**. Section 20 subsidiaries are investment banking subsidiaries of bank holding companies that can deal directly in activities that are "ineligible" from the standpoint of the Glass-Steagall Act of 1933, such as the underwriting of debt and equity. Section 20 subsidiaries' revenue from these "ineligible securities" could not exceed 10% of total gross revenues earned by the subsidiary. Since this 10% revenue limitation was subject to manipulation, as bank holding companies shifted revenue-producing eligible (i.e., commercial banking) activities into their Section 20 subsidiaries so as to increase the allowable ineligible activities, the Fed adopted an alternative asset-based 10% measure in August 1994. This limitation was raised to 25% in September 1996. Since 1984, Congress has intermittently considered legislation to effectively repeal the Glass-Steagall Act, without passage as of this date.

Section 20 subsidiaries: investment banking subsidiaries of bank holding companies that can deal directly in "ineligible activities."

International Comparisons   Universal banks in Germany, Austria, Switzerland, Spain, and Great Britain are characterized by the predominance of long term customer relationships and highly developed private information systems that give universal banks substantial market power. This means that many transactions take place *within* a single universal banking FI. In contrast, specialized banking in the United States and Japan requires that financial transactions often involve many different specialized FIs interacting in well-developed financial markets. Financial markets therefore tend to be more active in countries that prohibit universal banking.[15] They are less developed in universal banking countries because more transactions take place intrafirm as opposed to interfirm in specialized banking countries.

A useful exposition of this difference is shown in Table 5.10 depicting polar cases of FIs: a market-based system (denoted M), a bank-based system (denoted B), and a universal banking system (denoted UB). Typically, the market-based system, characteristic of the U.S. and, to a lesser extent, the U.K., is composed of open markets with considerable public disclosure requirements and a rapid rate of financial innovation. The table shows that regulation concentrates on ensuring market competitiveness as well as international accessibility.

The bank-based and universal banking systems of Germany, Austria, Switzerland, Spain, Japan, Scandinavia, and Italy are less competitive and more centrally controlled either by government or by the private FIs themselves. Since much information is private, financial markets (which rely on public disclosure) are less developed. In universal banking countries, the FIs dominate both financial and commercial sectors of the economy via their "voice" in corporate decisions. Universal banks are allowed to hold equity stakes in commercial concerns, and so they often control a large block of the corporation's stock, thereby granting the bank a voice in running the company. We saw in Chapter 3 that interlocking corporate directorships as well as shareholdings are an important characteristic of Japanese keiretsu, as well as the German **hausbank** (a single bank used to satisfy most business deposit and investment needs). In Germany, the three largest universal banks (Deutschebank, Dresdner Bank, and Commerzbank) have substantial holdings in the top German companies.[16] A 10% shareholding (known as a *paket*) entitles the German bank to a seat on the company's supervisory board. A shareholding of 25% or more (known as a *schachtel*) brings the German bank tax advantages and gives the bank the right to veto certain decisions such as the raising of capital by the commercial firm.

Table 5.11 compares the limitations on activities across five lines of business for banks in 11 countries, including the United States. Specialized banking exemplified by Glass-Steagall Act restrictions on U.S. banking activity (no matter how circumvented) may actually be counterproductive, especially if cost savings are to be obtained from allowing a single FI to perform related activities. If the goal of regulatory policy is to reduce the FIs' risk exposure, activity restrictions, by limiting bank activity diversification, may actually increase a bank's risk exposure. Concern about universal banking in the United States has revolved around three problems.

1. *Fear of reduced competitiveness in the market for financial services.*   Concentration of financial services in universal banks may increase the average size of the banking organization, thereby raising the spectre of monopolization. However, if entry into the financial services market is unencumbered by activity restrictions, the number of potential competitors may increase, resulting in greater market competition.

2. *Possibility of conflicts of interest.*   To prevent universal banks from showing preferential treatment to its own affiliates, universal banks are required to erect internal *Chinese walls*, like the Great Wall of China, also known as *firewalls*, to keep any private information

hausbank: a single bank used to satisfy most business deposit and investment needs.

---

[15] An exception is the United Kingdom, which has active financial markets and universal banking. This is perhaps a vestige of Britain's historic role in international trade and finance.

[16] As of 1990, the Deutschebank held 28% of the shares of Daimler Benz, 30% of Philipp Holzmann, and 23% of Sudzucker.

Table
5.10

Market versus Bank–Dominated Financial Institutions

Structure Countries	Role of Government	Central Bank Objectives	Openness	Information	Conflict of Interest	Conflict Resolution	Corporate Governance
M U.S. U.K.	Commitment to markets	Detailed micro regulation to ensure competitive conditions	Very open	High public disclosure requirements; rating agencies play a significant role.	Present, but criminal offense	Explicit contracts; court settlement	Through stock market and ownership control— "exit" is ultimate penalty.[a]
B Italy, Scandinavian countries (and many others)	Greater belief in government interventions	Competition of lesser concern; more direct intervention (credit controls)	Regulation provides protection from foreign competition.	More private information; markets less developed and less informative	Present; legal dispositions less severe	Implicit contracts; conflicts resolved in bilateral negotiations and monitoring	"Exit" and "voice" and banks monitor.[a]
UB Germany, Austria, Switzerland, Spain, and Japan	Same as (B)	Macro-economic goals dominate	No regulatory protection but systemic resistance to foreign penetration	Most developed private information system	Potentially most pronounced; legal dispositions less severe	Court settlement rare and marginal	"voice"[a] dominates; long term relationship and strong corporate control through holdings of debt and equity.

M = market-based; B = bank-dominated; UB = universal bank-dominated.

[a]"Exit" occurs through shareholders' sale of stock. "Voice" is the use of insiders' voting power to effect firm behavior.

Source: Steinherr and Huveneers (1994). pp. 274–275.

within segmented areas. In the U.K., banking and nonbanking functions are separated into different subsidiaries, whereas in Germany they are segmented into departments. Chinese walls prevent the improper transfer of private information across the lines of either separate subsidiaries or separate functional departments.

3. *Access to the government-provided bank safety net.* Governments provide subsidized services, such as deposit insurance and lender of last resort, to the banking system in order to protect its safety and soundness. If the universal bank's nonbanking activities generate losses, the safety and soundness of the universal bank may be impaired, perhaps requiring expensive government bailouts. To some extent, even nonuniversal bank countries already have safeguards against this problem. In the United States, Section 23A restrictions limit intercompany loans to any one affiliate to under 10% of capital,

Performance Returns to Scale	Returns to Scope	Competition	Innovation	Range	Risk	Internation-alization	Market Penetrability by Foreigners
M In market size	None	Through substitute products; absence of entry barriers	Strong product innovation; regulatory circumvention; openness	Deal-based short term performance	Greater volatility but higher liquidity (primary and secondary securitization	Easy	High contestability; exiting possible
B In firm size	Some	Restricted by lack of substitutes; barrier of entry through regulation and established distribution network	Strong process innovation, product innovation hampered by lack of developed securities markets and lesser competitive pressure	Short term horizon	Low-asset liquidity, stable deposit base, but low-activity diversification	More difficult and not of obvious interest as bank brand names are not doing well in foreign countries	Difficult; traditional distribution network provides protection—exiting rare
UB In firm and market size	Most	Lack of substitutes and strong relationships	As (B)	Long term relationship and performance	High-activity diversification; superior information and loan monitoring; mixture of liquid and illiquid assets	Most difficult as relationship banking builds on tradition	Most difficult as relationship banking most developed and backed by equity participations; economics of scale—exiting rare

with a total to all affiliates limited to less than 20% of capital. Section 23B requires that interaffiliate transactions be on the same terms and conditions as are transactions with nonaffiliated firms. These restrictions limit the possibility of contagion of financial distress from nonbanking subsidiary to bank subsidiary.

Checkpoint

1. What is universal banking?
2. Discuss the Glass-Steagall Act. How have FIs in the United States circumvented the Act?
3. What are Section 20 subsidiaries?
4. Contrast market-based with bank-based systems throughout the world.

Table 5.11

Permissible FI Activities: A Survey of 11 Countries

Country	Securities	Insurance	Real Estate	Bank Investments in Industrial Cos.	Industrial Firm Bank Holdings
Belgium	Unlimited; some activities through subsidiaries	Unlimited through subsidiaries	Generally limited to holding bank premises	Single shareholding may not exceed 10% of bank's own funds; may not exceed 35% of company's own funds.	Unlimited, but subject to previous approval of authorities.
Canada	Unlimited through subsidiaries	Unlimited through subsidiaries	Unlimited through subsidiaries	Permitted to hold up to 10% with aggregate shareholdings not to exceed 70% of bank's capital.	Permitted to hold up to 10% interests.
France	Unlimited	Unlimited, usually through subsidiaries	Unlimited	Permitted with regulatory approval of interests in excess of 10%.	Not prohibited, but rare.
Germany	Unlimited	Unlimited, but only through insurance subsidiaries	Permitted, subject to limits based on bank's capital; unlimited through subsidiaries.	Limited to 15% of bank's capital; in aggregate limited to 60% of bank's capital.	Permitted (subject to regulatory consent based on suitability of the shareholder).
Italy	Unlimited, but not permitted to operate directly on the stock exchange	Limited to 10% of own funds for each insurance company and 20% aggregate investment in insurance cos.	Generally limited to holding bank premises	Not permitted	Permitted up to 15% of shares of the bank, subject to approval of the Bank of Italy.
Japan	Permitted through subs except for equity brokerage; allowed to own more than 50% of a securities subsidiary	Not permitted	Generally limited to holding bank premises	Limited to holding 5% interests	Permitted, provided total investment does not exceed investing firm's capital or net assets.
Netherlands	Unlimited	Unlimited through subsidiaries	Unlimited	Subject to regulatory approval for voting shares in excess of 10%.	Subject to regulatory approval for voting shares in excess of 5%.
Sweden	Unlimited	Unlimited	Generally limited to holding bank premises	Limited	Not prohibited, but rare.
Switzerland	Unlimited	Unlimited through subsidiaries	Unlimited	Unlimited	Not prohibited, but rare.
United Kingdom	Unlimited usually through subsidiaries	Unlimited through subsidiaries	Unlimited	On approval of the Bank of England.	No prohibitions.
United States	Limited, through affiliates	Generally not permitted	Generally limited to holding bank premises	Can hold up to 5% of voting shares through a holding company.	Can make non-controlling investments up to 25% of voting shares.

Source: Thompson's International Banking Register, October 25, 1993, pp. 6–9. R Herring and R. Littan, *Financial Regulation in the Global Economy* 1995 Brookings Institute, Washington D.C. p. 168–169.

Geographic Restrictions   In keeping with Americans' concerns about overconcentration of financial power, the U.S. banking industry has been characterized by restrictions on interstate banking. The power of interstate banking restrictions has been steadily eroding, however, particularly with the formation of interstate banking pacts, which allow interstate banking activity within specified regions comprised of a limited number of contiguous states. With the passage of the Interstate Banking and Branching Efficiency Act of 1994, all interstate banking restrictions were lifted.[17] As of June 1, 1997, U.S. banks can consolidate their interstate activities into a single corporate entity, thereby permitting a full array of banking services across the nation.

To understand the importance of this legislation, it is important to understand the dual system of banking in the United States that has prevailed since the nineteenth century. To be eligible to issue insured deposits, a bank must obtain a charter, or permit, to conduct banking business. That charter may be issued by either the state in which the bank is headquartered or the federal government by the Office of the Comptroller of the Currency. Preservation of this duality and concern about the federal government's usurption of state powers led to the McFadden Act of 1927, which stated that all banks (whether federally or state chartered) must comply with their home state's regulations about branching.[18] Thus, the McFadden Act did not prohibit interstate banking but instead stated that it was permitted only if the home state allowed interstate banking. In this way, it created a patchwork of regulations that varied across states. The 1994 legislation should level the playing field and allow the consolidation of banking services, promoting greater efficiency of operation.

➤ Regulatory Burden

As you might imagine, complying with the many regulations imposed on FIs is not an inconsequential task. The Federal Financial Institutions Examination Council, an umbrella group of U.S. Federal bank regulators, in its 1992 study of regulatory burden found that, in 1991, the costs of complying with the extensive network of bank regulations ranged from about 6 to 14% of noninterest expenses, totaling between $7.5 and $17 billion.[19] The Independent Bankers Association of America estimated that the total costs of examinations and regulations equaled nearly 7% of the community banks' total pretax income in 1992, with the U.S. Office of Management and Budget estimating that compliance with Truth in Lending laws alone required 7.5 million labor hours.[20]

Both the increased costs associated with the proliferation of regulations and the increased complexity of the regulated FIs suggest that the future trend in supervision will be away from formal rulemaking. Instead public FIs will concentrate on developing supervisory procedures that can be applied to FIs on a case-by-case basis. In this way, only the relevant regulations need be applied to any particular FI. As William McDonough, former president of the Federal Reserve Bank of New York, states in his 1993 annual report,

> [M]arket surveillance would allow market participants leeway to conduct business without unnecessary restrictions but still be subject to scrutiny by supervisors. It would be

---

[17] The Interstate Banking and Branching Efficiency Act of 1994 permits bank holding companies to acquire banks anywhere in the United States. Limitations on de novo entry (the opening of new banks) remain, however. See McLaughlin (May 1995) for an analysis of the limited and delayed impact of past reforms in state interstate banking regulations.

[18] The home state is the state in which the bank is headquartered.

[19] This estimate includes the cost of deposit insurance premiums but excludes any measurement of the opportunity costs of reserve requirements or prohibited activities.

[20] See Shaffer (1995), pp. 15–29.

incumbent on market participants to develop codes of conduct, guidelines of sound practices, and other elements of self-regulation for their activities. . . . Firms demonstrating that they have the needed capital strength, internal controls, management information systems, and management experience would be subject to comparatively less oversight over the conduct of their activities than those lacking these strengths. . . . This implies a continuing role for periodic on-site examinations by examiners expert in the specific services provided to assess whether institutions are financially strong and operate in a safe and sound manner.

The success of this initiative depends on the efficacy of the on-site and off-site examination procedures in auditing and monitoring FI actions. Technological advances enable public FIs to follow the trails of transactions and therefore evaluate the effectiveness and risks associated with the operational procedures of private FIs. Technology has also fueled the exponential growth in international financial markets making it even more challenging to design accurate management information systems.

➤ The Regulatory Dialectic

Typically, regulations are written in response to a financial crisis, and often the regulations come too late. They are implemented at a point where they are no longer needed because the market has already expeditiously moved to address the source of the financial problem. For example, junk bond disclosure requirements for mutual funds were imposed *after* the market crashed. And we have prompt corrective action legislation *after* the leniency of thrift regulators allowed insolvent thrifts to remain in business and abuse the system. And we have derivatives disclosure requirements *after* the losses suffered during the 1994–1995 interest rate hike in the United States.

regulatory dialectic: a cyclical process of regulatory and market evolution.

This process of cyclical regulatory and market evolution has been called the **regulatory dialectic**. Regulatory policy is not static but is dynamic as it adjusts to changing market conditions. Moreover, markets change in response to incentives created by regulatory policy. FIs are particularly adept at innovating in order to avoid regulatory taxes and constraints. These market innovations create challenges for public FIs charged with protecting the safety and soundness of FIs. Regulatory policy reacts to these market innovations so as to adapt to the changing environment. This induces another round of market innovation as private FIs devise novel approaches to circumvent the new set of regulatory restrictions. **Regulatory arbitrage** occurs as private FIs search the world for the least restrictive regulatory environments in which to introduce their new products. This prompts a responsive round of regulatory revision. And the process continues.

regulatory arbitrage: private FIs' search for the least restrictive regulatory environments in which to introduce their new products.

Regulators invariably remain behind the market because they respond to market events with a time lag. When they do respond, it is in the form of a generalized, "one size fits all" regulation that is easily circumvented, thereby setting the groundwork for the next round in the continued process. To break the cycle, regulators have shifted their focus away from defining generalized rules, toward defining processes for self-monitoring by the private FIs. The goal of these processes is to align private FIs' incentives with regulatory policy goals.

Checkpoint

1. What is the McFadden Act of 1927?
2. What is a regional interstate banking pact?
3. What is the Interstate Banking and Branching Efficiency Act of 1994?
4. What is the regulatory burden? Why is it a cause for concern?
5. How costly is it for banks to comply with U.S. bank regulations?

➤ Summary

Public FIs use two approaches to supervise private FIs:

1. *Direct supervision.* Public FIs directly monitor the activities of private FIs by imposing regulations and auditing compliance.

2. *Indirect supervision.* Public FIs elicit the assistance of market participants in monitoring private FIs by requiring prompt and extensive public disclosure of information about the FI's financial condition. This enables market participants who have a stake in the FI to supervise its activities.

Direct supervision takes the form of explicit capital requirements, deposit insurance and closure regulations, and on-site examinations. Capital regulations require FIs to hold minimum levels of capital to act as a cushion against financial insolvency. In recent years, capital requirements have been risk adjusted. Thus, the riskier the FI's asset portfolio, the higher the required level of capital. Capital serves as a safeguard against financial insolvency, because it is made up of residual claims on the FI's assets that are subordinated to the claims of senior debtholders.

Indirect supervision takes the form of financial reporting requirements, voluntary compliance with industry standards, and self-regulatory programs. To improve the quality of information in financial statements, FIs must provide some information on market values, as opposed to book values, of their assets. To balance the public disclosure objective against the concern about excess volatility of financial statements, FIs can classify their assets into three categories: (1) held-to-maturity; (2) available for sale; and (3) trading. All securities not classified as held-to-maturity must be evaluated at their market values.

Public FI supervisory policies also alter the FIs' market environment. Credit reallocation programs subsidize activities that are deemed to have socially beneficial side effects and penalize those considered to be less desirable. Limitations on FI activities and geographic dispersion allow public FIs' greater control over relatively homogeneous institutions. However, this is often at a cost of inadequate diversification, resulting in the FIs' excessive risk exposure.

➤ References

Alexander, D., and S. Archer, eds. "An Overview of European Accounting." *The European Accounting Guide.* London: Academic Press, 1992.

Allen, L. "Bank Capital and Deposit Insurance Regulations." In A. Stone and C. Zissu, eds., *Global Risk Based Capital Regulations.* Vol. I. Burr Ridge, Ill.: Irwin, 1994.

Allen, L., J. Jagtiani, and Y. Landskroner. "Interest Rate Determination and Subsidies in International Bank Capital Regulations." *Journal of Economics and Business,* forthcoming 1997.

Amir, Harris, and Venuti. "A Comparison of Value-Relevance of U.S. versus Non-U.S. GAAP Accounting Measures Using Form 20-F Reconciliations." *Journal of Accounting Research,* 31 (Supplement 1993): 230–275.

Berger, A., R. Herring, and G. Szegö. "The Role of Capital in FIs." *Journal of Banking and Finance,* 19, No. 3–4, (June 1995): 393–430.

Bliss, R. "Risk Based Bank Capital: Issues and Solutions." Federal Reserve Bank of Atlanta *Economic Review* (Sept–Oct 1995): 32–40.

Calem, P. "The Community Reinvestment Act: Increased Attention and a New Policy Statement." Federal Reserve Bank of Philadelphia *Business Review* (July–August 1989): 3–16.

Corrigan, G. "Balancing Progressive Change and Caution in Reforming the Financial System." Federal Reserve Bank of New York *Quarterly Review* 16, No. 2 (Summer 1991): 1–12.

Cummins, J. D., S. E. Harrington, and R. Klein. "Insolvency Experience, Risk Based Capital, and Prompt Corrective Action in Property-Liability Insurance." The Wharton Financial Institutions Center Working Paper 95–06.

Larson, R., and S. Y. Kenny. "Raising Capital Overseas: International Accounting Standards May Facilitate the Process." *CPA Journal* 64, No. 9 (September 1994): 64–68.

McLaughlin, S. "The Impact of Interstate Banking and Branching Reform: Evidence from the States." *Current Issues in Economics and Finance* 1, No. 2 (May 1995).

Shaffer, S. "Marking Banks to Market." Federal Reserve Bank of Philadelphia *Business Review* (July–August 1992): 13–22.

Shaffer, S. "Rethinking Disclosure Requirements." Federal Reserve Bank of Philadelphia *Business Review* (May–June 1995): 15–29.

Steil, Benn. *International Financial Market Regulation.* Chichester: John Wiley & Sons, 1994.

Steinherr, A., and Ch. Huveneers. "On the Performance of Differently Regulated Financial Institutions: Some Empirical Evidence." *Journal of Banking and Finance* 18 (1994): 271–306.

White, Lawrence. *The S & L Debacle.* New York: Oxford University Press, 1991.

➤ Questions

1. Contrast the interests of FI shareholders with those of FI creditors in determining the FI's optimal capital level.

2. Consider the following two banks:

   Shake E. Bank, Inc. ($million)

Reserves	25	Deposits	400
T-bonds	105	Debt	55
Loans	350	Equity	25

   Rock Solid Bancorp. ($million)

Reserves	25	Deposits	400
T-bonds	105	Debt	30
Loans	350	Equity	50

   a. Calculate each bank's debt/equity leverage ratio.

   b. Which bank is in compliance with a 5.5% capital-assets requirement?

   c. Compute the impact on both banks' balance sheets of a 5% loan writeoff? 10% loan writeoff? Discuss the implications for the claims of creditors and equityholders.

3. Calculate Shake E. Bank's Basel capital requirements using the information provided in question 2 (assume that 50% of loans are mortgages) and the following data on off-balance sheet activities:
   20% risk weight category: $55 million
   50% risk weight category: $90 million
   100% risk weight category: $200 million

4. Calculate the haircut on the following securities if all interest rates are expected to increase by 25 basis points:

   a. $100,000 face value 2 year 5% coupon U.S. Treasury note selling at $101 per $100 face value.

   b. $50,000 face value 5 year 12% annual coupon corporate bond selling at $107.5 per $100 face value.

   c. $5 million face value 7 year quarterly 9% p.a. coupon municipal bond selling at $95 per $100 face value.

5. Suppose that Secure Securities, Inc. had a portfolio of securities with the market values shown on the following balance sheet:

Secure Securities, Inc. ($million)

Assets		Liabilities	

7% p.a. 10 yr. T-bonds
   Par value: $25, semiannual coupon
	$24	6% p.a. 2 yr. notes
		   Par value: $55, annual coupon
			$50

18% p.a. 15 yr. CMOs
   Par value: $70, monthly coupon
   100% amortizing (no future value)
	$66	9% p.a. 5 yr. bonds
		   Par value: $40, annual coupon
			$40

If all interest rates are expected to increase by 15 basis points, then what is the haircut on each security? What is Secure Securities' haircut on a net capital basis?

6. Use the Tier 1 capital requirements in Table 5.3 to calculate the minimum required Tier 1 + Tier 2 capital for the following transactions:
   a. $50 million in U.S. government securities.
   b. $35 million in general obligation municipal securities.
   c. $2.5 million in repos collateralized by U.S. Treasury securities.
   d. $12 million in revenue municipal securities.
   e. $250 million in residential mortgages.
   f. $550 million in commercial and industrial loans.
   g. $60 million in commercial loan commitments with less than one year until maturity.
   h. $60 million in commercial loan commitments with more than one year until maturity.
   i. $20 million in performance-related standby letters of credit issued to private customers.
   j. $75 million in direct credit substitutes issued to commercial customers.
   k. $70 million in interest rate contracts with less than one year until maturity.
   l. $70 million in interest rate contracts with two years until maturity.
   m. $70 million in exchange rate contracts with less than one year until maturity.
   n. $70 million in exchange rate contracts with four years until maturity.

7. How does regulation impact the evolution of global financial markets? Be sure to discuss how regulation both impedes and encourages financial innovation.

8. Describe the regulatory dialectic. Illustrate the concept using capital requirements.

9. Revalue the following book value balance sheet using
   a. FASB 115 if all assets are assumed to be available for sale.
   b. FASB 115 if all assets with maturities exceeding 10 years are assumed to be held-to-maturity.
   c. Market values only.
   d. Compare your answers to parts a-c.

Ye Ole FI ($thousand)

Assets		Liabilities	
1 yr. treasury note, Coupon = 4% p.a. semiannually, Yield = 3.8% p.a.	750	1 yr. CD, Coupon = 3% p.a. annually, Yield = 3.2% p.a.	925
5 yr. corporate note, Coupon = 5% p.a. annually, Yield = 5.75% p.a.	325	2 yr. note, Coupon = 4 % p.a. quarterly, Yield = 4.5% p.a.	65
15 yr. mortgage, Coupon = 8% p.a. monthly, Yield = 7.6% p.a. (100% amortizing)	250	10 yr. note, Coupon = 6% p.a. semiannually, Yield = 6.5% p.a.	335
Total assets	1,325	Total liabilities	1,325

10. Revalue Ye Ole FI's balance sheet in question 9 if all interest rates decrease 50 basis points using
    a. FASB 115 if all assets are assumed to be available for sale.
    b. FASB 115 if all assets with maturities exceeding 10 years are assumed to be held-to-maturity.
    c. Market values only.
    d. Compare your answers to parts a-c.

11a. Use FASB rule 115 to reevaluate the following book value balance sheet if all asset and liability market values decline by 10 percent.

Private FI ($million)

Trading securities	$100	Debt	375
Securities held until maturity	350	Equity	75

11b. If the private FI classifies half of its trading securities as "held until maturity," how does that impact the FI's market value? Reevaluate the balance sheet.

11c. Using standard financial analysis, reevaluate the private FI's original balance sheet.

CHAPTER 6

CLEARING AND SETTLEMENT OF TRANSACTIONS

"Never ask of money spent, where the spender thinks it went."—Robert Frost, *Further Range* (1936), "Hardship of Accounting".

Learning Objectives

- To learn how financial transactions are completed using both electronic and nonelectronic means of payment.

- To learn about new methods of electronic payment mechanisms that are very efficient at processing large-value transactions.

- To see how settlement risk affects financial market activity.

- To investigate systemic risk exposure when electronic payment systems allow any one default to pyramid through the entire system, resulting in a cascading of failures affecting FIs throughout the world.

➤ Introduction

counterparties: the participants who agree to enter into financial transactions.

settlement, or clearing: the counterparties' compliance with the terms of their financial agreement.

spot market transactions: transactions that are settled immediately, upon arrangement of the financial agreement.

forward market transactions: deferred settlement transactions.

When a central bank buys government securities from a private individual, or when a private FI lends money to a business, or when an importer transfers foreign currency from one FI to another—all of these activities are examples of financial transactions, agreements that entail the transfer of financial securities and/or cash from one party to another counterparty. **Counterparties** are the participants who agree to enter into financial transactions. **Settlement**, or **clearing**, is reached when the counterparties each comply with the terms of their financial agreement.[1] Settlement can take place immediately, upon arrangement of the financial agreement. Such transactions are called **spot market transactions**. For example, spot market equity transactions must be cleared within three days of the transaction date.

On the other hand, the financial agreement may call for settlement at some later point in time. Deferred settlement transactions are called **forward market transactions**. These transactions may call for settlement in a month, or a year, or five years into the future. Ultimately, however, all financial transactions must be cleared. Decades ago, when most financial transactions took place

---

[1] Technically, clearance is the determination of the cash and security flows required to complete a transaction, whereas settlement is the actual transfer of securities for cash. We use the terms *clearance* and *settlement* interchangeably to refer to the entire process.

between two local counterparties, settlement relied on paper-based, nonelectronic payment mechanisms such as cash, checks, and the transfer of physical security certificates. Today's large-value transactions on global financial markets demand the use of rapid, computerized electronic clearing systems.

➤ Electronic versus Nonelectronic Payment Systems

A payment system is the method utilized to complete, or settle, financial transactions. It can be as simple as the transfer of cash and as complex as international electronic networks. **Nonelectronic payment systems**, mostly paper-based, require the physical transfer of assets (either cash, checks, or securities). **Electronic payment systems** require no physical delivery and instead use accounts held at central banks to settle transactions. Since cash and securities are represented by accounting entries on the central bank's books, payment requests can be transmitted electronically, thereby eliminating the need to make physical transfers. Although we distinguish between electronic and nonelectronic payment systems, the lines of distinction will be blurred in the future when businesses adopt virtual monetary systems that clear over cyberspace. These developments, discussed in *Timely Topics 6.1*, are not considered here because we strictly segment transactions into those requiring some physical transfer (denoted nonelectronic payment) versus those that take place, from beginning to end, over a computer system (electronic payment).

nonelectronic payment systems: systems that require the physical transfer of assets (either cash, checks, or securities) to settle transactions.

electronic payment systems: systems that require no physical delivery and instead use accounts held at central banks to settle transactions.

TIMELY TOPICS 6.1

THE FUTURE OF MONEY

A raft of companies are developing their own forms of electronic money, known as E-cash. E-cash is money that moves along multiple channels largely outside the established network of banks, checks, and paper currency overseen by the Federal Reserve. These channels enable consumers and businesses to send money to each other more cheaply, conveniently, and quickly than through the banking system.

Some of the E-cash players are faceless, dubious outfits that exist in cyberspace and can be traced only to a post-office box in the physical world. But there are plenty of others, ranging from techno-savvy startups with names such as DigiCash and CyberCash to corporate icons including Microsoft, Xerox, and Visa. Citicorp is even developing what it calls the Electronic Monetary System, an entire infrastructure for using electronic money to be issued by Citi and other banks. . . .

With E-cash, you'll no longer need to carry a wad of bills in your pocket or fumble for exact change. Instead, you might carry a credit card size piece of plastic with an embedded microchip that you will "load" up with E-money you buy with traditional currency. Or, you might store your digital coins and dollars—downloaded over phone lines from your bank or other issuer of E-money—on your PC or in an electronic "wallet," a palm-size device used to store and transmit E-money.

This digital money will let you shop online, zapping money to a merchant over the Internet, or perhaps paying for a movie on demand over an interactive TV network. It also has the potential to replace cash and checks for everyday purchases—in stores, restaurants, or taxis that accept E-cash. Businesses could also keep a stash of E-cash on hand for buying office supplies or use it to transact directly with each other instead of going through banks and electronic funds transfers.

In many ways, E-cash, which can be backed by any currency or other asset, represents the biggest revolution in currency since gold replaced cowrie shells. . . . But the advent of E-cash raises all sorts of questions, most of which remain unanswered: Who should be allowed to issue E-cash, and who will regulate those issuers? How will taxes be applied in cyberspace, which transcends physical boundaries? Who will set the standards? How do you ensure that payments made over the Net will be secure? How will consumers be protected? How will regulators police money laundering and counterfeiting on private networks?   . . .The stakes are enormous. Seamus McMahon, a vice-president at Booz, Allen & Hamilton, sees as much as 20% of total household expenditures taking place on the I-way just 10 years from now. If any operation, whether Citicorp or a startup such as Mondex, gained control of a new medium for even part of these exchanges, it would have the opportunity to charge royalties for its use and earn interest on the E-money sitting in its accounts. Even a tiny charge, when applied to millions of transactions, would be hightly lucrative.

E-cash could also create a competitive free-for-all. Because the Internet knows no boundaries, a company offering E-money can gain direct access to millions of consumers and businesses—no matter what state or country they are in. . . . [S]ome regulators are beginning to explore the concept of E-money so they can set policies. . . . It's not a moment too soon. "There's no going back," says DataLiberty ['s co-founder Bill] Frezza. "The genie's out of the bottle. The Internet doesn't have an off switch." And no amount of wishing by regulators will change that.

Source: *Business Week*, June 12, 1995, pp. 66–78.

Table 6.1 shows the relative importance of electronic versus nonelectronic means of payment throughout the world. In all countries, with the exception of Canada, the *value* of electronic transactions far exceeded their *volume*. For example, although electronic transactions comprised only 3.2% of the total number of U.S. transactions in 1994, they accounted for 87.7% of their value.[2] The principal electronic payment systems for large-value[3] U.S. dollar payments are Fedwire and the Clearing House Interbank Payment System (CHIPS). The volumes of transactions are enormous. It takes Fedwire and CHIPS 2.5 days to process transactions that are the equivalent of the annual U.S. gross domestic product (GDP). Japan's payment system turns over Japan's GDP every three days, and it takes four days in the United Kingdom to transact Britain's entire annual GDP. Figure 6.1 shows the growth of payment systems relative to GNP in the U.S., Japan, and the U.K.

Although 85% of all checks deposited for collection are cleared overnight, electronic settlement has a speed advantage over nonelectronic settlement. However, the fixed costs of entering into an electronic payment network are considerable and may not be warranted for small, non-recurring payments. Moreover, slower movement of funds benefits the payor at the expense of the payee since a time lag exists between the time when the check is written and the time when the funds are transferred. This time lag creates the float, which can be considerable for nonelectronic payment systems but is practically nonexistent for electronic networks. The float essentially is an interest-free loan to the check writer, since it represents an amount of money

---

[2] The importance of checks and cash as methods of payment will be dramatically reduced even further if the "electronic purse" becomes widely used in routine transactions. The electronic purse, the size of a credit card, contains a stored value that can be transferred at an automated teller machines (ATM) or point-of-sale (POS) terminal. Funds can be deducted or added to the card. This technology would be an important part of the fabled "cashless society" that would result in a paperless financial system.

[3] In July 1994 the Fed defined a "large-value" transaction as one having a stated dollar value exceeding $500,000.

Table
6.1

Cashless Payment Systems: Electronic and Nonelectronic Payment Throughout the World, 1994[a]

| Country | Nonelectronic Payments (pct.) | | Electronic Payments (pct.) |
	Checks	Cards	Credit and Debit Transfers
Belgium (% of volume)	11.7	18.0	70.3
(% of value)	4.6	0.1	95.2
Canada (% of volume)	52.8	35.3	11.9
(% of value)	98.7	0.3	0.9
France (% of volume)	46.9	16.3	27.4
(% of value)	4.4	0.2	94.8
Germany (% of volume)	7.9	3.1	89.0
(% of value)	2.3	0.02	97.7
Italy (% of volume)	34.0	5.2	51.5
(% of value)	4.5	0.04	94.6
Netherlands (% of volume)	6.0	7.9	86.1
(% of value)	0.1	0.1	99.8
Sweden (% of volume)[b]	9.3	11.6	88.4
(% of value)	NA	1.0	99.0
Switzerland (% of volume)	2.6	16.2	81.2
(% of value)	0.1	NA	99.9
U.K. (% of volume)[c]	40.3	23.1	36.6
(% of value)	7.6[c,d]	0.2	92.3
U.S. (% of volume)	78.2	18.7	3.2
(% of value)	12.2	0.1	87.7

[a]Percent of total value and volume of transactions, excluding cash. Percentages may not sum to 100% because of other items. Figures for Japan are not available.

[b]Statistics for the volume and value for check payments in Sweden are shown for 1992.

[c]The total of check volume includes Town cheques.

[d]Electronic transfers include all large-value CHAPS transactions. CHAPS is the analog of CHIPS for pound sterling transactions.

Source: Bank for International Settlements, *Statistics on Payment Systems in the Group of Ten Countries* (December 1995): Basel.

that remains in limbo during the time period between the date a check is written and the date it is collected.[4]

During the time lag between check writing and funds transfer, the check writer has use of the funds without either relinquishing those funds or paying an interest charge for their use. As individuals economize on their money holdings (perhaps because of the high opportunity costs of holding money during times of high interest rates), the value of this interest-free loan increases, further encouraging the shift to electronic (float-free) payment systems from nonelectronic settlement. The size of the float is minimized for checks that are deposited in the same institution on which they were drawn. In 1992 these "on-us checks" constituted approximately 30% of all checks cleared in the United States.

During the end-of-year holiday season, the float averages over $1 billion each month. In Chapter 4, we saw that increases in the float increase the level of bank reserves and have the same impact as an expansionary monetary policy. The **non-Federal Reserve float** occurs from the time a check is written until the payee bank receives the credit. The **Federal Reserve float** occurs from the time the payee bank receives credit until the time the payor bank collects the payment. The longer these time periods, the larger the float. Figure 6.2 shows the seasonal variability of the float.

non-Federal Reserve float: the value of checks written but not yet credited to the payee bank.

Federal Reserve float: the value of checks written, credited to the payee bank, but not yet collected from the payor bank.

---

[4] In the United States, 16 % of all retail payments create float. By way of international comparison, the percentages for Canada are 14%; 5% for Britain; 3% for Japan; and 2% for Germany.

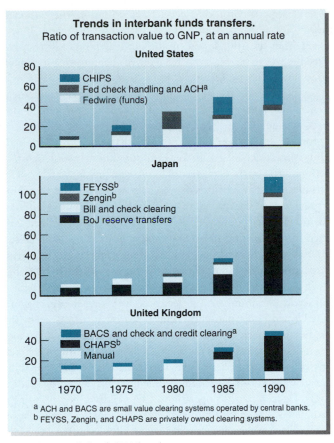

Source: Borio & de Bergh (1993), p.6.

Figure 6.1

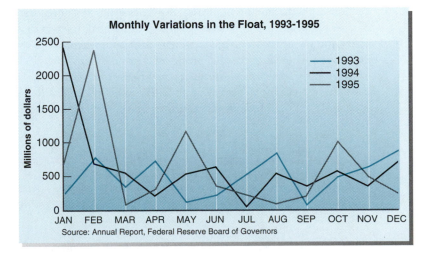

Figure 6.2

Check clearing is considered *non*electronic (despite the existence of an Electronic Check Clearing House Organization, ECCHO) because, no matter how much the operations are automated, they are still slowed by the need to physically transport checks from payor to payee, from payee to payee's bank, from payee's bank to clearinghouse, and from clearinghouse to payor's bank. This process was simplified on January 3, 1994, when **same-day settlement** regulations became effective in the United States. Same-day settlement enables the payee's bank to present local checks to the payor's bank directly for payment in same-day funds (adjustment to reserve accounts at the Fed) without waiting for the check to make its way through the entire process—from payee bank to Fed to payor bank. The Fed estimates that its total check collection volume declined 10% as a result of same-day settlement.

Check clearing can be expected to decrease further in March 1997 when the Treasury implements its Electronic Benefit Transfer program, which permits electronic payment of government benefits such as food stamps, Aid to Families with Dependent Children, and Supplemental Security Income. The Fed's noncash collection service has also declined as more and more bonds have converted from **bearer bonds** to **book-entry bonds**. Bearer interest coupon bonds carry periodic interest payments that are made upon presentation of coupons clipped from the bond by the bearer. Book-entry bonds are registered to a specific owner, so that ownership and any payments can be automatically transferred electronically. These developments may be expected to further increase the dominance of electronic over nonelectronic payment systems in the future.[5]

In the United States, nationwide check clearing is performed by the Federal Reserve System. But just because check clearing is considered a nonelectronic payment system does not mean that it is not automated. Computerized reading and sorting machines have increased the speed of check collection and processing. The Expedited Funds Availability Act of 1988 mandates funds availability within prespecified time intervals.[6] Improved technology has enhanced the efficiency of check-transfer operations. The FedNet is a network of Federal Reserve check processing sites that speed up interdistrict electronic communication. Specifically, it reduces the time required to clear checks across Federal Reserve districts by standardizing procedures. In 1992 the Fed processed 12 million items per month and charged per-item fees of approximately $0.022 per check.[7] Of that amount, about 1 million used an *extended magnetic ink character recognition (MICR) service*, which allows the check to be read electronically. This service reduces the number of paper checks transmitted between banks since only those checks that cannot be paid (say, because of insufficient funds) need to be returned to the paying bank. This innovation cuts down on the amount of physical deliveries required and reduces the size of the float.

As we saw in Chapter 4, check clearing utilizes bank reserves to make payments. How are electronic payment systems used to settle financial transactions? We will see how central banks and private FIs are juxtaposed in providing electronic clearing services. We examine three types of electronic payment mechanisms: (1) real-time gross settlement—electronic settlement processed by each country's central bank, for example, the Federal Reserve's Automated Clearing House (ACH)[8] and Fedwire; (2) netted settlement—electronic settlement processed by inter-

same-day settlement: settlement that enables the payee's bank to present local checks to the payor's bank directly for payment in same-day funds.

bearer bonds: bonds on which periodic interest payments are made upon presentation of a coupon clipped from the bond by the bearer.

book-entry bonds: bonds registered to a specific owner, so that ownership and any payments can be automatically transferred electronically.

---

[5] Despite longstanding predictions of a completely "paperless financial system," checks appear to be here to stay, as indicated by recent private investments in check-clearing technology designed to improve efficiency and prevent fraud. For example, in December 1994 the privately owned Funds Availability Notification System (FANS) went into effect to transmit bad-account information more rapidly to participating banks.

[6] Legal access to funds from deposits of local checks must be available within two business days and for out-of-district checks, within five days.

[7] Arend (1992), pp. 58–60.

[8] Technically, the ACH is not a real-time gross settlement system, since the Fed reserves the right to reverse transactions up to a day following the settlement day. However, since payments are typically transmitted one to two days prior to settlement date, the ACH functions as if it were a real-time gross settlement system, with funds available on the settlement date.

national consortiums of private FIs, for example, PAXS and CHIPS; and (3) message centers that send instructions for final settlement, for example, the Society for Worldwide Interbank Financial Communications (S.W.I.F.T.).

Checkpoint

1. What is the spot market? the forward market?
2. Describe the nonelectronic payment system.
3. Describe the electronic payment system.
4. Why have nonelectronic payments persisted despite advances in computer technology that make electronic payments more accessible?

Real-Time Gross Settlement: Central Bank Electronic Payment Systems

real-time gross settlement: final settlement of transactions as soon as they are received.

Payments systems that offer **real-time gross settlement** are usually owned and operated by central banks. The deep pockets of the central bank assure immediate, irrevocable settlement. Each transaction clears individually and immediately, hence, the terms *real time* (referring to settlement immediacy) and *gross settlement* (referring to the clearing of each individual transaction without dependence on the completion of any other transaction). Settlement takes place immediately in the form of adjustments to bank reserve accounts. Central bank electronic payment systems can deal with both small and large-sized transactions.

Small-Value Payments: The ACH

automated clearing house (ACH): a national network to process small-value payments.

The first publicly owned, **automated clearing house (ACH)** for small-value payments was founded by the Federal Reserve Bank of San Francisco in 1972. In 1978 it was expanded into a national network which, by 1994, was processing transactions for over 20,000 depository FIs. An estimated 30% of the U.S. labor force currently have their wages directly deposited into their bank accounts by ACH payment. There are two types of ACH transactions:

1. *Credit transfers.* Initiated by the payor; authorizes the transfer of funds to be credited into another account—for example, a household authorizing the payment of a monthly telephone bill. The Electronic Transfer Benefits program is another example of a credit ACH transaction. Over 85% of Social Security benefits are paid by ACH. All credit transfers are posted at the opening of the business day.

2. *Debit transfers.* Initiated by the payee; the payor preapproves periodic withdrawals from her account into the account of the payee—for example, a household authorizes the electric company to withdraw payment for the utility bill on an agreed-upon date each month. All debit transfers are posted at 11:00 A.M. eastern time.

Figure 6.3 shows the growth of ACH transaction volume for the period 1986–1992. In 1992, 2 billion payments were processed with a value of $7.8 trillion. Growth in the volume of ACH transactions has been predominantly in the areas of government payments and direct deposits of payroll. However, use of ACH to pay consumer bills and process corporate trade payments has been slow because of

1. The loss of freedom to delay bill payment associated with debit ACH transactions.

2. The need to have a record of payment such as a canceled check.

3. The large fixed costs that make the use of ACH costly for both payors and payees. Both counterparties must have a computer linkup with the bank.

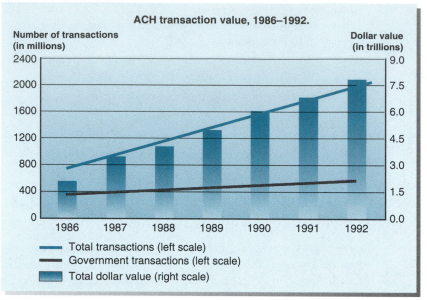

Source: McAndrews, (1994), p. 19.

Figure 6.3

4. The lack of a standardized computer format to transmit both invoice and payment information.

5. Access to bank deposit accounts necessary to utilize ACH.

Electronic Benefit Transfer (EBT) is a potential source of growth in the number of small-value electronic payment transactions. EBT allows recipients of government programs to access cash benefits from special accounts established by the government at designated FIs or retail establishments. These transfers can therefore be used even if the recipient does not have a bank account.

The average transaction dollar value on the ACH in 1991 was about $3,900. In 1991 the average transaction on a large-value payment system, Fedwire, was over $3 million. Given the large size of funds transfer and the repetitive nature of the transactions, electronic settlement is the norm in large-value payments.

Large-Value Payments: The Fedwire

In the United States, the Federal Reserve System operates a large-dollar value transfer system for both funds and financial securities called the Fedwire. The Fed guarantees settlement on all payments sent to receivers, even if the sender is subsequently found to be insolvent. The counterparties to the financial transaction must utilize banks to access the Fedwire. As of 1994, there were 11,000 participating banks with access to the Fedwire. Of these banks, more than 7,000 were on-line participants undertaking 99.5% of all Fedwire transactions. Table 6.2 shows that on average in 1994, 287,000 transactions were cleared daily with an average transaction value of $2.9 million. Total dollar value of transactions grew from $1.6 trillion on 1.7 million transactions in 1960 to $211 trillion on 72 million transactions in 1992. This volume will surely increase when, in 1997, Fedwire on-line services extend operating hours from 10 to 18

Electronic Benefit Transfer (EBT): an electronic payment system that allows recipients of government programs to access cash benefits from special accounts established by the government at designated FIs or retail establishments.

Electronic Payment Systems: Funds Transfer Activity, 1994

	Fedwire	CHIPS
Total participants	11,000	115
Daily average originations	287,000	182,000
Annual originations (million)	72.0	45.7
Average value/transfer (million)	$2.9	$6.5
Average value/day (billion)	$841	$1,178
Total annual dollar value (trillion)	$211	$296

Source: Federal Reserve Bank of New York.

Table 6.2

Settlement Transactions

Table 6.3

ABC Bank

Reserves at Fed	−$9,772,825.83	ABC's securities deposits	−9,772,825.83

XYZ Bank

Reserves at Fed	+$9,772,825.83	XYZ's securities deposits	+9,772,825.83

ABC Securities

U.S. Treasury securities	+$9,772,825.83	
Deposits at ABC Bank	−$9,772,825.83	

XYZ Securities

U.S. Treasury securities	−$9,772,825.83	
Deposits at XYZ Bank	+9,772,825.83	

hours a day—from 12:30 A.M. to 6:30 P.M. eastern time, five days a week. These extended operating hours are for cash settlement, not securities clearing operations.

Table 6.3 examines how the Fedwire might clear a transaction between two government securities dealers: ABC Securities, Inc. and XYZ Securities, Inc. ABC agrees to a spot market purchase of a $10 million five year U.S. Treasury bond from XYZ. The bond's coupon rate is 6%, paid semiannually, but the market yield on similar risk securities is a **bid** of 6.55% and an **asked yield** of 6.52%. The bid is the price offered by **market makers** to buy securities. The asked price is offered by market makers to sell securities. A market maker is a FI who stands ready to buy and sell securities upon demand. ABC and XYZ agree upon a yield of 6.54 %. The price of the U.S. Treasury bond is

bid: price offered by market makers to buy securities.

asked yield: price offered by market makers to sell securities.

market maker: a FI who stands ready to buy and sell securities upon demand.

$$P = \sum_{t=1}^{10} \frac{\$.3m}{1.0327^t} + \frac{\$10m}{1.0327^{10}} = \$9,772,825.83$$

XYZ must transfer the U.S. Treasury bond to ABC, and ABC must transfer $9,772,825.83 to XYZ. Since ABC is probably buying the security on behalf of a customer, it will subsequently need the bond for another spot or forward transaction with its own customer. To speed up the settlement of the transaction between ABC and XYZ, they utilize the Fedwire. They access Fedwire through their banks, ABC Bank and XYZ Bank. Cash clearing takes place utilizing the banks' reserve accounts at the regional Federal Reserve Bank.

Since all U.S. Treasury securities are currently issued as book-entry, there is no physical security certificate and the securities are transferred as accounting entries via message over Fedwire.

Table 6.4

A Comparison of Settlement Charges

Settlement Charges	Check-Clearing	ACH	Fedwire
Interregional transaction fee/item	$0.002 –$0.060	$0.015	$0.53
Account servicing fee (monthly)	0	$10	$65 (dial-up line)
			$700 (dedicated leased line)
Settlement entry to reserve account	0	1.50	$1.00

If this transaction was cleared nonelectronically, say, using checks and a physical delivery of the securities, then the outcome would be the same as shown in Table 6.3. However, whereas the entire nonelectronic clearing process could take up to a week, the Fedwire transaction clears within the hour. In 1993 the daily average value of transfers of securities across Fedwire was $580 billion.

Transaction costs are considerably higher for electronic settlement than for nonelectronic settlement. Table 6.4 shows the 1993 fee schedules for check clearing and settlement on Fedwire and on the Fed's ACH. Check clearing appears to be considerably less expensive than electronic settlement. However, the table enumerates out-of-pocket transaction costs only. It neglects the time value of money inherent in the float, and so it underestimates the true cost of nonelectronic settlement of financial transactions. For example, a five day delay in transfer of funds while the check clears hurts the payee (in our example, XYZ Securities) and benefits the payor (ABC Securities). For example, suppose that the short term money market rate is 5.90% p.a.;[9] then the cost of a five day, interest-free float is

$$\frac{9,772,825.83}{\left(1 + \frac{.059}{360}\right)^5} = \$9,764,821.48$$

When ABC Securities pays for the Treasury bond using a $9,772,825.83 check that will take five days to clear, the present value of the payment received by XYZ is $9,764,821.47. If XYZ accepts that check in payment for the hand-delivered securities, then XYZ is granting ABC an interest-free loan worth $8,004.36, the difference between the value of the Treasury bonds and the value of ABC's check. The interest cost of the float is more significant and the electronic settlement transaction costs are less relevant if

- The payment value is larger.
- The money market interest rate is higher.
- The check-clearing process is slower.

It is for these transactions that the opportunity cost of nonelectronic clearing is the highest.

The costs of electronic settlement depend on the efficiency of the payment system. Table 6.5 compares the efficiency of operation of national payment systems for 20 countries in 1994. The United States has the most efficient, least costly clearing mechanisms in the world, and Finland, Norway, and Spain have the least efficient systems.

The U.S. Fedwire is not the only real-time gross settlement electronic payment system in the world, but it is the oldest. Table 6.6 shows the status of payment systems administered by central banks throughout the world. Each of the 13 payment systems listed in the table is administered by the country's central bank to clear domestic currency transactions. Since all

---

[9] The Monetary Control Act of 1980 directs the Fed to price the Federal Reserve float at the Federal Funds interbank rate. In this example, the daily Federal Funds rate, using the Treasury's assumption of a 360 day year, is $\frac{5.9\%}{360} = 0.01639\%$.

Table 6.5

Electronic Settlement Efficiency Around the World, 1994[a]

Country	Efficiency Index	Country	Efficiency Index
Australia	94.8	Austria	87.4
Belgium	88.0	Canada	92.6
Denmark	94.3	Finland	77.0
France	92.8	Germany	91.1
Hong Kong	91.7	Italy	92.9
Japan	93.8	Netherlands	89.4
New Zealand	90.2	Norway	77.6
Singapore	88.5	Spain	77.8
Sweden	86.5	Switzerland	85.9
U.K.	86.4	U.S.	96.7

[a]Settlement efficiency is measured by Global Securities Consulting Services using a benchmark index with a maximum score of 100. The lower the score, the higher the effective operational costs of failed transactions in any given market.

Source: Giddy, Saunders, and Walter (1995), p. A –2.

transactions require a transfer of funds from the payor's FI to the payee's FI, some provision must be made for the cash flow debits and credits. Reserve accounts at the central bank are used to process cash flows in 10 of the countries (Germany, France, Ireland, Italy, the Netherlands, Poland, Switzerland, the U.K., the U.S., and Japan). In Belgium and Denmark, intraday loans (requiring collateral in Belgium but not in Denmark) are automatically extended during the course of the day's settlements. These loan balances must be repaid by the end of each day. In addition, private FIs with access to the electronic payment systems in France and the United States may obtain intraday loans without providing the collateral often required by central banks as protection against the FI's default risk on discount window loans.

Administrators of real-time gross settlement payment systems are exposed to considerable risks of default if either counterparty fails to settle the transaction. This is because all payments are irrevocable. **Settlement risk** is the risk that a counterparty is unable to make final payment. If that happens, the administrator of the payment system (the central bank) is forced to make the required cash payment immediately, but does not simultaneously receive the offsetting promised cash inflow. To eliminate settlement risk to the administrator of the payment system, banks would have to hold extremely large levels of reserves that could be used to fill payment requests as they come in. On a single day, November 21, 1985, a computer malfunction at the Bank of New York required $30 billion in loans and a $23.6 billion overnight discount window loan from the Fed to prevent a financial meltdown of the electronic payment system. Requiring banks to hold monetary balances of this magnitude would be very costly because of the opportunity costs of holding idle reserves.

How can real-time gross settlement electronic payment networks guarantee final settlement without requiring exorbitant levels of reserves? The administrator of the payment network (the central bank) can choose one of the two methods of settlement risk management listed in Table 6.6. In one method, the network's administrator automatically adjusts the timing of the payment orders so that payments from banks with insufficient balances are delayed until the FI's balance in its reserve accounts is increased. This approach, called queue management facilities in Table 6.6, is utilized in Switzerland, Belgium, Denmark, Germany, France, Italy, and Poland. However, this method compromises on the guarantee of immediacy in settlement activity.

Through the second method, the central bank allows private FIs to run negative balances (**daylight overdrafts**) during the course of the day, with the requirement that all account balances be made nonnegative at the end of the day. All countries except Switzerland and Japan allow intraday, daylight overdrafts. Now you can see why central banks, as opposed to

settlement risk: the risk that a counterparty is unable to make final payment.

daylight overdrafts: negative balances during the day but a nonnegative balance at day's end.

Table 6.6

Real-Time Gross Settlement Systems Throughout the World

	Belgium	Denmark	Germany	Greece	France	Ireland	Italy	Neth.	Poland	U.K.	Switz.	U.S.	Japan
Year of Initiation													
	1995	1985	1988	1996	1995	1995	1989	1985	1994	1995	1987	1982	1988
Liquidity Provisions													
Intraday use of required reserves[a]	N	N	Y	NA	Y	Y	Y	Y	Y	Y	Y	Y	Y
Intraday credit facilities requiring collateral	Y	N	Y	NA	Y	Y	Y	Y	Y	Y	N	N	NA
Intraday credit facilities that do not require collateral	N	Y	N	NA	Y	N	N	N	N	N	N	Y	N
Settlement Risk Management													
Queue management facilities	Y	Y	Y	NA	Y	NA	Y	N	Y	N	Y	N	N
Pricing of intraday overdrafts	N	N	N	NA	NA	NA	NA	N	N	NA	N	Y	N

[a] Y = yes; N = no; NA = not available.

Source: Tommaso Padoa–Schioppa, "Central Banking and Payment Systems in the European Community," in *Symposium Proceedings International Symposium on Banking and Payment Services*, (Washington, D.C.: Board of Governors of the Federal Reserve System, December 1994), p. 34.

consortiums of private FIs, operate real-time gross settlement payment systems. It takes the financial power of the central bank to guarantee the finality of payments by extending large overdraft loans whenever needed to clear transactions. During the course of the trading day, these overdrafts often reach peak levels that are twice as large as total reserve balances.[10]

At times, daylight overdrafts have been quite large, often several times larger than the bank's total capital. This is because daylight overdrafts represent interest-free loans from central banks to private FIs. The United States is the only country that currently levies penalties on daylight overdrafts to discourage their abuse. How did this policy evolve?

Daylight Overdrafts   The opportunity to time Fedwire transactions so as to obtain an interest-free loan proved to be a powerful inducement to private FIs, leading to an explosion in the size of daylight overdrafts during the 1980s and early 1990s. Daylight overdrafts occur when, during the course of the trading day, the sum of the FI's debits exceed the sum of the credits to the FI's reserve account. Since most payments are not made until the end of the day, FIs commonly have negative balances during the day.[11] By the close of the day, the private FIs have to raise the balances in their reserve accounts out of the red. But during the course of the trading day, the Fed places no limit on what amounts to interest-free intraday loans by the Fed

---

[10] A third method that could be used to control settlement risk to the payment system administrator is the outright prohibition of all transactions for which there are insufficient immediately available funds. This solution was rejected because it would significantly disrupt financial markets and undermine the effectiveness of electronic payment systems.

[11] On CHIPS, which has no restrictions against daylight overdrafts, more than 95% of all payments are made during the last three hours of operation. Prior to introducing daylight overdraft fees, over 80% of all daily payment value on Fedwire was entered after noon.

to private FIs. During 1993, peak overdrafts on Fedwire (maximum aggregate daylight overdrafts measured at the end of each minute during the operating day) averaged $128.5 billion per day, more than 25% of the system's average daily volume! This means that each day, the Fed has the potential to lose, on average, $128.5 billion on uncollateralized loans to banks. A Fed study suggests that more than 6,000 institutions incur daylight overdrafts at least once a month, but it was the 15 largest banks in the United States that accounted for 60% of daylight overdrafts.[12]

One reason the Fed is concerned about daylight overdrafts stems from monetary policy considerations. With no upper bound on the levels of daylight overdrafts, during the course of the day, private FIs can expand the money supply at will, possibly offsetting the monetary policy objectives of the central bank. But since all end-of-day balances must be positive, this effect is transitory. A more pressing reason for concern about daylight overdrafts is the potential for credit risk to the Fed, since the bank provides no collateral. The Fed guarantees every transaction that clears over Fedwire and is concerned about potential defaults by private FIs unable to clear their reserve account deficits by the close of the trading day. To make good on its Fedwire clearing guarantee, the Fed has to advance loans to all FIs with net deficits in their reserve accounts. But this rewards excessively aggressive risk taking on the part of the private FI and subsidizes those poorly managed FIs by granting them interest-free loans, a policy unlikely to encourage prudent financial management.

The Fed's first reaction to the problem of daylight overdraft came in 1986 when it established voluntary caps, or limits, on the size of daylight overdrafts. However, the six largest daylight overdraft offenders (each with per-minute overdrafts averaging more than $1 billion) did not decrease the number of their overdrafts significantly until fees were imposed in April 1994. As of April 14, 1994, a daily overdraft fee of 10 basis points was levied on each FI's average per-minute overdraft.[13] Between April 1994 and March 1995, average daylight overdrafts decreased by 48% to an aggregate peak of $70 billion.[14] Effective April 13, 1995, the daylight overdraft fee was increased to 15 basis points. As of December 1995, per-minute daylight overdrafts averaged $43 billion. The level of financial market activity did not decline in response to the imposition of daylight overdraft fees. Instead, FIs reduced their daylight overdrafts by scheduling their Fedwire transactions earlier in the day. The end-of-day surge in transactions that had created havoc (and extended closing time) on the Fedwire prior to April 1994 virtually disappeared after the imposition of fees.

During the period April 1994–April 1995, the Fed collected $18.5 million in daylight overdraft fees from a total of 280 FIs. Overdraft fees are quoted on a 360 day year basis assuming that the Fedwire operates 10 out of the 24 hours, that is, 600 minutes, in the day. The average daily overdraft is calculated by averaging each FI's per-minute overdrafts, calculated by summing the negative minute-end balances and dividing by 600 minutes in the operating day.

As an example, consider the intraday record of payments between ABC and XYZ Banks shown in Table 6.7. Suppose that the four transactions shown are minute-by-minute totals and that ABC Bank's initial reserve account balance is zero. We can calculate ABC Bank's average intraday overdraft for the first four minutes of the day. (Of course, in practice this is done for all 600 minutes of the 10-hour trading day.) During the first minute, ABC Bank receives a payment of $110 million for a positive reserve account balance of $110 million

[12] See Curran (1993), pp. 46–52.

[13] There is also a deductible amount equal to 10% of the bank's risk based capital. In addition, fees of less than $25 are waived.

[14] The pricing of daylight overdrafts should also encourage the development of a market mechanism for intraday credit similar to the one that exists in Japan, where banks can borrow from other banks between 9:00 A.M. and 1:00 P.M. for a cost of between 7 and 11 basis points (annual rate). This is similar to the evolution of the Federal Funds market as a response to the demand for interday reserve balances. (see Chapter 10).

Table 6.7

Daily Transactions Involving ABC Bank and XYZ Bank ($ millions)[a]

ABC Bank		XYZ Bank	
Customer A & Customer Z	+$110	Customer A & Customer Z	−$110
Customer B & Customer Y	− $60	Customer B & Customer Y	+$60
Customer C & Customer X	−$200	Customer C & Customer X	+$200
Customer D & Customer W	+$120	Customer D & Customer W	−$120
Net Total	− $30	Net Total	+$30

[a]Positive entries denote that the bank's customer is the payee in the transaction. Negative entries denote thatthe bank's customer is the payor in the transaction.

(or a zero overdraft) at the end of the first minute of activity. During the second minute, a $60 million debit reduces ABC's reserve balances to a still positive $50 million (still, a zero overdraft balance). During the third minute, a $200 million payment order causes the ABC Bank account to show a $150 million negative balance. This is the first minute that will be subject to overdraft charges. During the fourth minute, a credit of $120 million reduces the overdraft to $30 million. ABC Bank's average per-minute overdraft for the first four minutes of operation is $\frac{0+0+150+30}{4}$ = $45 million. If this were the average level of overdraft per minute for the entire day, then ABC Bank's *daily* overdraft fee would be

$$\left(\frac{.0015}{360}\right) (\$45 \text{ million}) = \$187.50$$

The Fed charges the bank once for the sum total of all daily overdraft fees over the two week reserve maintenance period (see Chapter 4).

Daylight overdraft fees are charged against negative reserve balances, with no credit given for positive reserve balances. Positive reserve balances are computed only at the end of the day in order to determine whether the bank has met its reserve requirement. As we saw in Chapter 4, reserve requirements are supposed to force banks to maintain sufficient levels of liquidity to be able to clear transactions. However, if the goal of real-time gross settlement systems with daylight overdraft charges is to encourage FIs to hold sufficient reserves to clear their daily payments, then *intraday* reserve balances should also be used to calculate reserve requirements. Otherwise, the introduction of daylight overdraft charges distorts FIs' incentives and increases the costs of clearing. Rather than sending out payments as fast as they can, with daylight overdraft charges, FIs will do the opposite and delay sending out payments so as to avoid daylight overdraft charges.[15] This may result in costly, idle balances during the day. When daylight overdrafts were free, FIs overutilized them and held too few reserves to clear daily transactions. Simple introduction of daylight overdraft fees threatens to induce FIs to hold too many reserves, thereby reducing payment turnover and increasing clearing costs. A proposal for a possible remedy, minute-by-minute reserve maintenance, is the focus of *Timely Topics 6.2*.

TIMELY TOPICS 6.2

MINUTE-BY-MINUTE RESERVE MAINTENANCE

Rather than charging for daylight overdrafts, the market system solution is to change Regulation D [setting reserve requirements] by specifying that reserve maintenance be

[15] Shortly after the introduction of daylight overdraft charges, major money center banks introduced "priority" Fedwire service to speed up those payments necessary to avoid daylight overdrafts.

calculated as an average of minute-by-minute reserve balances held throughout the 24 hour day. A minute of reserve holding would count whether Fedwire is open or closed. Imposing a charge on balances within the day without providing a credit for positive balances within the day is to suggest that the current reserve requirement tax is too low. A Federal Reserve accounting change would impart value for meeting reserve requirements during the day.

The objective is to foster an intraday Federal Funds market in which the Funds rate throughout the day would vary depending on supply and demand. With reserve balances having intraday value, arbitrage opportunites would connect the intraday funds market with markets for longer-dated instruments, hence generating a tendency for prices of these instruments to appreciate in value during the night and during the day. In general, the market for dollar-denominated instruments would become more attractive to international investors. . . . A revision of Regulation D reserve accounting would afford net intraday positive balance banks direct benefits. Then they could let their intraday net positive balances satisfy their reserve requirement. . . . Banks with intraday deficits would need to hold enough overnight balances to bring their time weighted average balance up to the maintenance period average requirement. . . . Intraday markets would tend to become fully integrated with longer-term markets and the value of money would become relevant to shorter time periods than 24 hours.

Source: Wayne Angell, "Payment and Settlement Systems Policies and Incentives: A Proposal for Defining the Property Rights of Daylight Reserve Holdings," *Symposium Proceedings*: *International Symposium on Banking and Payment Services*, Board of Governors of the Federal Reserve System, December 1994, pp. 120–121.

Checkpoint

✓

1. How are transactions cleared on Fedwire?

2. What is book-entry?

3. Why is electronic clearing more expensive than nonelectronic settlement?

4. What is the float? What determines the cost of the float?

5. What are daylight overdrafts?

6. Why is the Fed concerned about daylight overdrafts?

➤ Netted Settlement Using International Consortiums of Private FIs

Although public FIs maintain electronic payment networks to clear both small- and large-value transactions, the largest payment system in the world (in terms of volume) is operated not by a central bank but by a consortium of private FIs who are the payment system's shareholders.

The major difference between privately and publicly owned payment systems is the method of settlement. As we have seen, in real-time gross settlement, each transaction is immediately cleared independently of all other transactions; that is, each transaction results in an immediate transfer of funds equal to the amount of the transaction. Privately owned payment systems use a **netted settlement method**, which permits the transaction's counterparties to take advantage of offsetting transactions. That is, the transactions are not cleared until the end of the day. At the end of each trading day, all the day's transactions are tallied, and only one payment is actually transferred between each pair of counterparties. The party that owes the larger amount sends the counterparty an amount equal to the *difference* between the amount owed by both

netted settlement method: method whereby the parties take advantage of offsetting transactions by waiting until the end of the day to settle the entire day's payments.

counterparties. This reduces the costs of settlement since fewer transfers have to cross the electronic payment system.

Small-Value Payments: PAXS

In April 1994 the Visa Automated Clearing House and the New York and Arizona clearinghouse associations combined to offer nationwide electronic small-value settlement on a private sector payment system called PAXS.[16] If both counterparties belong to PAXS, then the transaction clears on PAXS. If either counterparty does not belong to PAXS, then the transaction is settled using the Fed's ACH.

PAXS utilizes a netted settlement method. To see how netting works, recall that Table 6.7 examines the day's transactions between two counterparties: ABC Bank and XYZ Bank. Under a real-time gross settlement system, funds transfers totaling $490 million take place during the course of the trading day. If these transactions were cleared using netted settlement, only the net amount of $30 million would need to change hands. That is, ABC owes XYZ $260 million whereas XYZ owes ABC $230 million. The difference, or net amount, is $260 minus $230 or $30 million. At the end of the day, ABC Bank simply pays XYZ Bank $30 million to settle all of the day's transactions.

Netting reduces the amount of reserves that banks must hold to clear their daily transactions. If the transactions in Table 6.7 were entered in the order in which they were received during the course of the day, after the third trade ABC Bank would be required to pay out to XYZ Bank $150 million in bank reserves under gross settlement. By the end of the day, however, under netting, ABC Bank would need transfer only $30 million in bank reserves. In July 1992, for the 10 largest users of ACH in the Third Federal Reserve district (Philadelphia), the average daily gross payments were $1.34 billion, but net payments were only $214 million, just 16% of gross payments. Netting reduces clearing costs by allowing FIs to hold reserves averaging $214 million rather than the full $1.34 billion.

point-of-sale (POS) systems: installed at retail establishments, that directly debit the amount of the purchase from an electronically accessed bank account.

Automatic Teller Machines (ATMs): systems that allow the electronic transfer of funds both within and between banks after normal banking hours.

check truncation: technological advance that allows a digital image of a check to be transmitted from the payee's bank to the payor's bank, thereby eliminating the need to transport the physical check.

Point-of-sale (POS) systems are another form of small-value netted settlement. In POS systems, which are often installed at grocery stores and gas stations, the customer's account is directly debited by the amount of the purchase. **Automatic Teller Machines (ATMs)** allow the electronic transfer of funds both within and between banks after normal banking hours. **Check truncation** is another technological advance that is a hybrid of check-clearing and electronic methods of payment. In check truncation, a digital image of the check is transmitted from the payee's bank to the payor's bank, thereby eliminating the need to transport the physical check. With technological improvements, this could enable small-value, nonrecurring payments to be settled both inexpensively and rapidly. These settlement methods are all netted, since transmittals are finalized at the end of the day.

Large-Value Payments: CHIPS

In 1975 the Clearing House Interbank Payment System (CHIPS) processed a mere 6 million U.S. dollar-denominated transactions for an annual dollar value of $11 trillion. By 1988 it had grown to an annual dollar value of $165 trillion volume, processing 34 million transactions and surpassing, for the first time, the Fedwire volume of that year of 56 million transactions valued at $161 trillion. As shown in Table 6.2, CHIPS has continued to grow from there, reaching a $296 trillion annual value on 45.7 million transactions in 1994, to make it the world's largest payment system. The private FIs' first choice of settlement network for dollar payments on foreign currency transactions is CHIPS.

---

[16] The counterpart of PAXS for nonfinancial businesses is EDI Banx, a payment system that allows nonfinancial companies to electronically transfer payments and remittance data to vendors and suppliers. EDI Banx was also inaugurated in April 1994 by a consortium of 13 banks, including Bank of America and Mellon Bank.

CHIPS is owned by the New York Clearing House Association, a consortium of 10 member banks (the Bank of New York, Chase Manhattan Bank, N.A., Citibank, N.A., Morgan Guaranty Trust Company of New York, Bankers Trust Company, Marine Midland Bank, U.S. Trust Company of New York, National Westminster Bank USA, European American Bank, and Republic National Bank of New York) with 115 bank participants. It began operation in 1971 in response to a financial market challenge. In the late 1960s interbank Eurodollar transactions had grown to significant levels. To clear these interbank transfers of funds, banks were forced to rely on physical delivery of official bank checks. At the end of each day, messengers would criss-cross the streets of Manhattan bearing these good-as-cash checks among the major money center banks. There had to be a better way! According to John Lee, the president of the New York Clearing House Association,

> [W]e had no intention of building a device that would attract national or international attention. We were simply engaged in problem solving.... The problem was the proliferation of international dollar payments which could not be processed speedily enough or accurately enough in paper form. The solution was an elemental application of computer and telecommunications technology. It was only later that we realized we had created a new kind of money—electronic money which could move with the speed of light and which carried with it none of money's age old infirmities. It could be tallied and posted quickly and accurately and finally it could be settled promptly on the books of the Federal Reserve Bank.[17]

In contrast to the real-time gross settlement during the course of the day on Fedwire, settlement on CHIPS occurs at the *close* of each day, at 4:30 P.M. eastern time. At that time, each of the 115 banks' transactions is tallied, and final, net balances are transferred across Fedwire and made available for use by 6 P.M. eastern time. The banks' reserve accounts at the Fed are altered by the net amount of their transactions only. For example, the transactions between ABC Bank and XYZ Bank, on behalf of their customers, would be netted against other transactions during the course of a day's trading. Only if, at the end of the day, ABC Bank owed more to XYZ Bank than it was owed would a debit (credit) be made to ABC's (XYZ's) reserve account at the Fed, and vice versa. This method of settlement conserves on the amount of reserves that the banks must hold for clearing purposes. Since reserves are adjusted only by net amounts, as opposed to transaction-by-transaction gross adjustments, and since banks tend to undertake offsetting transactions (as do most intermediaries), then the net effect on reserves at the end of each trading day is close to zero. Because no payments are finalized during the course of the trading day, there are no formal daylight overdrafts. However, there is another pressing problem: systemic risk exposure.

Systemic risk exposure, first described in Chapter 3, is the risk that the failure of one participant may trigger a chain reaction that may lead to the collapse of the entire system. Suppose that customer C in Table 6.7 defaults on the $200 million payment owed to customer X. The entire day's transactions must then be *unwound*, or recalculated, omitting the defaulting participant's trades. If, at the end of the day, customer C's transaction is removed from the grid in Table 6.7, then XYZ Bank goes from an end-of-day net cash inflow of $30 million to a net cash outflow of $170 million, due upon close of the trading day. If XYZ Bank does not have sufficient reserves to make the $170 million payment, then all of XYZ Bank's transactions for the day are canceled until the system can be brought into balance. This *unwinding* begins a chain reaction that affects ABC Bank as well as all other counterparties that has had transactions with XYZ Bank during the entire day. If XYZ Bank is active, then the ramifications of one customer's failure will be felt worldwide.

---

[17] Lee (1991), pp. 28–30.

In our example, in order to unwind the day's transactions, suppose that XYZ Bank begins the day with a zero reserve balance. When customer C defaults, the transactions between customers D and W and between customers B and Y must be canceled. If these customers utilize their cash balances to finance additional trades, then those trades will also be canceled—and so on. The domino effect is potentially devastating. For this reason, all transactions cleared on netted settlement systems must be considered tentative until finality is obtained upon close of business at the end of the day.

Private electronic payment networks have devoted considerable effort to reducing the problem of systemic risk. Public FIs also have a stake in reducing systemic risk exposure. The problem was addressed by the G-10 countries in the Lamfalussy Report,[18] which led to passage of Regulation EE in the United States, effective March 1994. The regulatory mechanisms to reduce systemic risk exposure take four forms:

1. *Controls on access.* Private FIs allowed to access electronic payment systems directly are required to comply with special minimum capital standards. CHIPS has an aggregate capital level of $3–$4 billion contributed by participants on the network. This capital acts as collateral to back up a FI's potential indebtedness from failed clearing transactions. However, since average intraday aggregate credit on CHIPS amounts to $20–$30 billion, this collateral is insufficient to cover the losses induced by the simultaneous failure of two or more members.

2. *Control of net exposure.* Caps on activity are prespecified for every pair of counterparties as well as for groups of counterparties. These caps act as limits on credit lines that the private FIs preapprove and that are used to provide financing to back up the clearing transactions. The **bilateral net credit limit** is a cap on exposure vis-à-vis each other FI on the network. The **multilateral net credit limit** is a cap on aggregate exposure to all other FIs on a network.[19]

3. *Settlement risk management.* Short of unwinding transactions, with the resulting impact on systemic liquidity, a failed transaction can be cleared against collateral. Along with loss-sharing rules that allocate the loss across FIs, these agreements can be used to prevent one customer's failure from becoming a global liquidity crisis. Each settlement system has installed mechanisms to ensure sufficient liquidity in the event that the single largest participant failed. Then when, in our example, customer C defaulted on his $200 million payment, the loss would be covered by all FIs on the network, on a pro-rated basis, instead of undoing an entire day's worth of activity as trades were canceled.

4. *Control of flow of transactions.* A system is implemented to monitor transactions and to reject or hold payments that exceed bilateral or multilateral net credit limits.

bilateral net credit limit: a cap on exposure vis-à-vis each other FI on the network.

multilateral net credit limit: a cap on aggregate exposure to all other FIs on a network.

Although these protective mechanisms do not eliminate systemic risk, they reduce its expected impact on the global financial system. In reality, FIs do not worry much about systemic risk when they transfer funds over CHIPS. The widespread perception in the market is that CHIPS is "too big to fail." If all of the protective mechanisms ever failed to prevent a system meltdown, private FIs would expect the Fed and other public FIs to step in and cover the system's losses. As one bank executive stated, "CHIPS cannot *not* settle because, if it were to fail to do so, it would destroy confidence in the money market internationally."[20] Market participants act as if the Fed provides a backup guarantee of payment finality on CHIPS. This

---

[18] See *Timely Topics 6.3* and the Bank for International Settlements, *Report of the Committee on Interbank Netting Schemes of the Central Banks of the Group of Ten Countries,* Basel, November 1990.

[19] Through January 1997, CHIPS is phasing in a 20% reduction in caps and an increase in collateral requirements to further reduce systemic risk exposure.

[20] Stigum (1990), p. 903.

leads to the problem of moral hazard since if participants believe that payments carry an implicit government guarantee, they will not take steps to reduce their private risk exposure.

TIMELY TOPICS 6.3

THE LAMFALUSSY GUIDELINES

Large-dollar multilateral netting systems can create a significant degree of credit and liquidity risk for their participants and also expose the U.S. payment system and financial markets to systemic risk. In the context of large-dollar multilateral netting systems, systemic risk is the risk that the inability of one institution within such a system, including a central counterparty if one exists, to meet its obligations when due will lead to the illiquidity or failure of other institutions, either within the particular system or in the financial markets as a whole.

Large-dollar multilateral netting systems may produce efficiencies in the clearance and settlement of payments and financial contracts. At the same time, multilateral netting may obscure, concentrate, and redistribute the credit and liquidity risks associated with clearance and settlement. . . .

Certain types of netting system rules may also create sizable systemic liquidity risks, if employed by systems that process large-value payments. . . . For example, privately operated payment systems that permit a system operator to unwind, recast, or otherwise reverse same-day funds transfers made by system participants, . . . [are *not*] satisfactory mechanism[s] for managing liquidity and settlement risks in large-dollar multilateral netting arrangements. . . .

The Federal Reserve's policy on privately operated large-dollar multilateral netting systems is designed to strike an appropriate balance between the requirements of market efficiency and payment system stability. A direct means of achieving this balance is to ensure that large-dollar multilateral netting systems are designed and operated so that the participants and service providers have both the incentives and the ability to manage the associated credit and liquidity risks. The Board's approach. . . to apply whether or not these systems operate domestically or in other countries. . . is:

1. Netting systems should have a well-founded legal basis under all relevant jurisdictions.

2. Netting system participants should have a clear understanding of the impact of the particular system on each of the financial risks affected by the netting process.

3. Multilateral netting systems should have clearly defined procedures for the management of credit risks and liquidity risks which specify the respective responsibilities of the netting provider and the participants. . . .

4. Multilateral netting systems should, at a minimum, be capable of ensuring the timely completion of daily settlements in the event of an inability to settle by the participant with the largest single net debit position.

5. Multilateral netting systems should have objective and publicly disclosed criteria for admission which permit fair and open access.

6. All netting systems should ensure the operational reliability of technical systems and the availability of backup facilities capable of completing daily processing requirements.

Source: Federal Reserve Press Release, Statement on the Report of the Committee on Interbank Netting Schemes (chaired by international banker Alexandre Lamfalussy), December 21, 1994.

Private versus Public Electronic Payment Systems

A payment system is successful if it processes financial transactions reliably and inexpensively, but sometimes these two goals are mutually exclusive. We have seen that real-time gross settlement is more reliable since payments are immediate and irrevocable. However, netted settlement is less expensive because it reduces the required amount of cash flows. Because the deep pockets of a central bank are required to ensure payment finality, most real-time gross settlement systems are owned and operated by public FIs. Privately owned payment networks often utilize netted settlement. We therefore contrast the advantages of publicly owned real-time gross settlement and privately owned netted settlement systems.

Advantages of the Publicly Owned Systems

1. Provide stability of the money supply, financial markets, and the banking system by controlling systemic risk.

2. Aid the central bank in its conduct of monetary policy since the administration of the payment system provides information about cash flows and float.

3. Can use the central bank's lender of last resort status to provide reserves to banks with shortfalls in reserves, which threaten to destabilize the payments mechanism.

4. Offer a mechanism to the central bank that can be used to rapidly enhance market liquidity in response to a financial crisis.

Advantages of the Privately Owned Systems

1. Reduce the cost of clearing financial transactions by economizing on cash flows, thereby reducing the required balances in noninterest-bearing reserve accounts needed to clear transactions.

2. Avoid moral hazard problems resulting from the central bank guarantee that insures all participants against settlement risk exposure (unless participants believe that the central bank implicitly guarantees all payments).

3. Encourage private FIs to devise protective mechanisms to reduce settlement risk exposure. These mechanisms include capital requirements, as well as bilateral and multilateral caps on net exposure.

Clearly, both real-time gross settlement and netted settlement are here to stay. The coexistence of both forms allows market participants to choose the procedure that best suits their purpose. For trades that do not require intraday finality, a netted settlement system is most efficient; when immediacy and finality are important, then real-time gross settlement systems will be used.

The Frontier   At the end of 1995, the German Bundesbank introduced a liquidity-saving gross settlement system that is a hybrid between gross and netted clearing networks. Dubbed EAF 2, it clears transactions in two phases. Phase 1 is a modified real-time gross settlement system, and phase 2 uses netted settlement. During phase 1, individual transactions are cleared *with finality* only if another offsetting transaction has been received during a predetermined 20-minute cycle. For example, if XYZ Bank transmits an order to pay ABC Bank DM100 million, this order can be cleared immediately if, within the 20-minute period, XYZ also receives a payment of DM100 million, say, from DEF Bank. If the transaction does not have

Table
6.8

Turnover Ratios on Electronic Payment Systems (US$ billions)

	SIC	Fedwire	CHIPS
Funds transfer payments	$68.5	$605.0	$635.0
Payment reserves			
Central bank reserves	2.7	37.6	0
Daylight overdrafts	0	59.0	44.9
Total	2.7	96.6	44.9
Turnover ratio	25.37	6.26	14.14

Source: Humphrey (1989), p. 25.

an offsetting match, it is held until the next 20-minute cycle and is given priority using a first-in, first-out basis. Phase 1 runs for about 4.75 hours and clears approximately 75% of the total volume of payments.

During the subsequent phase 2, netted settlement of the remaining payments takes place wherever possible. At the end of the day, FIs have a 45-minute period to cover their net debit balances using reserves. Thus, reserves do not sit idle all day in noninterest-bearing accounts, but are instead transmitted on an as-needed basis at the end of the day. No unwinding of transactions takes place if net debit balances remain uncovered, for all phase 1 transactions are considered final. Only those transactions in the final phase that cannot be covered will be removed from the grid and held over for clearing. This procedure achieves the best of both settlement worlds: final, close-to-immediate settlement, together with a reduction in the required level of reserves needed to clear transactions.

The German system is patterned after the Swiss Interbank Clearing (SIC) system that has already demonstrated its effectiveness. Since its inauguration in 1987, processing efficiency has improved dramatically, as measured by the reduced volume of reserves required to clear transactions. Before adoption of SIC, Swiss banks held $22.2 billion in payment reserves ($5.1 billion central bank reserves plus $17.1 billion in daylight overdrafts) in order to clear $61.6 billion in settlements for a turnover ratio (defined as settlements/reserves) of $\frac{61.6}{22.2}$ = 2.77. After the institution of SIC, $68.5 billion worth of payments could be cleared on only $2.7 billion of reserves with no daylight overdrafts, a turnover ratio of 25.37 ($\frac{68.5}{2.7}$)—almost a tenfold increase in reserve turnover (see Table 6.8). The Swiss system economizes on the banks' required reserves, when compared to Fedwire and CHIPS. Both CHIPS and Fedwire are far less efficient, with reserve turnover ratios of 14.14 ($\frac{635}{44.9}$) and 6.26 ($\frac{605}{96.6}$), respectively. The greater efficiency of the Swiss payment system is attained by matching payment inflows and outflows as much as possible.

Checkpoint

1. What is the difference between PAXS and ACH? between CHIPS and Fedwire?
2. Why are real-time gross settlement payment systems operated by central banks?
3. What risks are associated with netted settlement? How are these risks reduced?
4. Contrast real-time gross settlement with netted settlement. Which system is more efficient? Which system is safer?

➤ Cross–Border and Multicurrency Settlement

On any given day an average of $1 trillion worth of foreign currencies changes hands around the world. The bulk of these payments are processed on electronic payment systems. More than 80% of all transactions processed on electronic payment networks stem from foreign exchange transactions, and they present their own special challenges. Three problems that particularly complicate cross-border transactions are (1) asynchronous payments; (2) differences in national legal systems; and (3) the exponential increase in both global settlement risk and the cost of settlement resulting from multiple currencies.

The first challenge is asynchronous payments. Each side, or *leg*, of the foreign currency transaction must be cleared by a home currency clearing system. For example, a trade of U.S. dollars for Japanese yen will most likely be cleared on two payment systems: CHIPS for the dollar leg of the transaction and the Bank of Japan's BoJ-Net (a real-time gross settlement system) for the yen leg of the transaction. The two sides of this transaction cannot be cleared simultaneously, however, (see Figure 6.4). BoJ-Net closes at 6 A.M. Greenwich mean time (GMT), whereas CHIPS opens at 12 noon GMT. At no time of the day are both systems simultaneously open. If the yen side of the transaction clears at the end of the day in Japan, the counterparty must wait six hours for the dollar leg of the transaction to become finalized. This

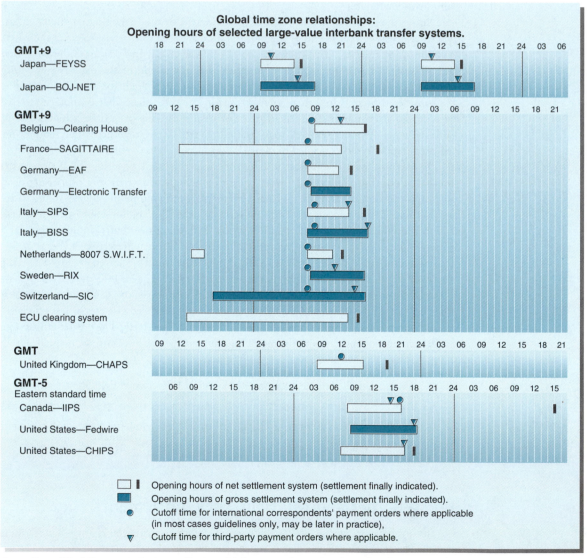

Source: Central Bank Payment & Settlement Services with Respect to Cross – Boarder and Multicurrency Transactions, BIS, September 1993.

Figure 6.4

exposes the yen trader to settlement risk if the yen are paid out irrevocably before the dollars are received with finality. Similarly, if the dollar side of the transaction clears at the end of the day in the United States, there is a three-hour wait for the opening of the BoJ-Net to clear the yen leg. This is referred to as **Herstatt risk** in memory of the 1974 crisis precipitated by the failure of German Herstatt Bank, which almost brought the international currency system to a halt (see Chapter 3). Herstatt risk is the risk associated with the fact that payment in one currency is finalized before the offsetting payment in another currency becomes final. As the world becomes more interconnected, problems in one currency are transmitted to other currencies. In 1974 it took intervention by the German Bundesbank to provide liquidity to world financial markets by settling the defaulted foreign currency trades on behalf of the bankrupt Herstatt Bank.

Herstatt risk: the risk associated with the fact that payment in one currency is finalized before the offsetting payment in another currency becomes final.

A response to nonsynchronous payments is to extend the length of the electronic payment systems' operating day. Fedwire's plan to open at 5:30 A.M. GMT (12:30 A.M. ET) as of 1997, coupled with the Bank of Japan's proposal to keep the BoJ-Net open an additional two hours in the afternoon, will create a 2.5-hour overlap during which both systems are operating (from 5:30 A.M. GMT until 8 A.M. GMT). This will permit simultaneous clearing of both legs of the U.S. dollar–yen foreign currency transaction.

A second difficulty associated with cross-border transactions stems from differences in legal systems in different countries. Property rights are not standardized throughout the world, and transfers may be challenged if national bankruptcy courts intervene. Some countries have highly developed laws governing contracts and business relations, whereas others (particularly the emerging Eastern bloc countries) have no legally defined private property rights whatever. A standardized international ownership and transfer law must be instituted to resolve this problem.

With regard to the third challenge, global settlement risk, each foreign currency transaction must be cleared on at least two domestic currency payment systems: one for each currency. During a systemic crisis, the central bank, as the ultimate guarantor of the domestic currency, may be forced to insure all counterparties against settlement risk. In the absence of a single domestic currency or a single local central bank, however, there is no ultimate protection against settlement risk. In the case of the U.S. dollar–yen foreign currency transaction, who would provide this backup liquidity, the Fed or the Bank of Japan? The central banks' potential for haggling about responsibility threatens the stability of the world payment system.[21]

Multilateral cross-border netting, by establishing a central clearinghouse to net all currency transactions for all counterparties, can reduce but not eliminate Herstatt risk. The Lamfalussy Report recommends the establishment of common agents to clear multicurrency settlements. As with electronic clearinghouses, these agents can be privately or publicly operated. In exchange for transactions fees, the private clearinghouses provide custodial services, offer credit lines, and monitor the system so as to ensure safe and efficient multicurrency clearing. Competition among private clearinghouses for this lucrative business has resulted in a low-cost, low-risk system that links world currency markets.

Many private FIs act as clearinghouses to provide these cross-border services, thereby creating a very profitable operation for some private FIs, such as J.P. Morgan's Euroclear. For example, securities settlements on two privately owned international electronic payment systems, Euroclear and Cedel (the Centrale de Livraison de Valeurs Mobilieres, meaning "securities clearing center") increased sixfold between 1988 and 1994. (See Table 6.9 for a comparison of these two clearinghouses.) Estimates of J.P. Morgan's annual earnings from Euroclear exceeded $250 million (or 16% of Morgan's total profit after taxes) in 1993. Euroclear and Cedel allow payment in over 25 different currencies, including the ECU.

---

[21] Since European unification in 1992, several central banks (the Bank of France, the Bank of England, and the Bank of Portugal) have introduced plans for collective backing of financial transactions, but these have not yet been formalized. Moreover, the Bank for International Settlements has been authorized to offer *temporary* lender of last resort services to back up ECU-denominated transactions only.

Characteristics of Euroclear and Cedel

	Euroclear	Cedel
Year founded	1968	1970
Location	Brussels, Belgium	Luxembourg
Ownership	Euroclear Clearance System S.C., a Belgium cooperative, operated by Morgan Guaranty	Over 100 banks and FIs
Fungibility	Fungible only (specific certificates of a security not attributed to any one participant)	Fungible or nonfungible (can attribute specific certificate numbers for specific transactions)
Settlement	Next day	If informed by 10 A.M., then same day; otherwise, next day
1992 turnover		
US$ securities (billion)	$2,178	$1,269
Other securities (billion)	$7,570	$3,475

Source: Jones and Fabozzi (1992), p. 20 and Perold (1995), p. 35.

Two multicurrency netting schemes currently under development are the Exchange Clearing House Organization (ECHO), designed by a group of European banks, and Multinet, sponsored by a consortium of U.S. and Canadian banks together with a subsidiary of the Options Clearing Corporation in Chicago. When private FIs act as the clearing agent, however, the question of ultimate responsibility in the event of global systemic settlement problems remains. If another major player like Herstatt Bank defaults on its international obligations, who will play the role of the Bundesbank and come to the rescue? This potential problem has led to calls for a centralized clearing system that has some central bank backing.[22]

Clearing using Multicurrency Payment Systems   Single currency transactions clear using either netted or real-time gross settlement. For multicurrency transactions, there are three possible settlement methods:

1. *Real-time gross settlement.* In gross settlement, used by Fedwire, each FI pays an amount for each transaction with each counterparty participating in the network.

2. *Bilateral netted settlement.* **Bilateral netting** requires a single end-of-day net settlement of the entire day's transactions in each currency between each pair of counterparties. If there are 50 FIs dealing in five different currencies, each FI makes 49 end-of-day net payments in each of the currencies, for a total of 245 (49 × 5) transfers for each FI. The total daily transfers for the entire system, using bilateral netting, is 12,250 (50 × 245).

3. *Multilateral netted settlement.* **Multilateral netting** tallies all of the day's transactions for each FI with all other FIs on the network. There is only a single end-of-day settlement in each currency for each FI, consisting of the FI's net transactions with the rest of the network. In our example, this is a total of five transfers in all currencies for each FI. Thus, multilateral netting requires only 250 daily transfers (50 × 5) rather than the 12,250 required using bilateral netting.

If each FI has transactions in all five currencies shown in Table 6.10 (the U.S. dollar, the British pound, the Canadian dollar, the Deutchemark, and the Japanese yen), there is a total of

bilateral netting: a settlement method that requires a single end-of-day net settlement of the entire day's transactions in each currency between each pair of counterparties.

multilateral netting: a settlement method that requires only a single end-of-day settlement in each currency for each FI consisting of the FI's net transactions with the rest of the network.

---

[22] See recommendations of the Bank for International Settlements, Committee on Payment and Settlement Systems of the central banks of the Group of Ten countries, *Central Bank Payment and Settlement Services with Respect to Cross-Border and Multicurrency Transactions* (September 1993).

Table 6.10

Daily Cross–Border Currency Transactions: Bilateral and Multilateral Netting[a]

Bilateral Netting	Receiving FI			
Paying FI: Currency	1	2	3	4
1:$		−100m	+500m	−1.1b
1:£		+275m	−25m	−800m
1:C$		+350m	−375m	+555m
1:DM		−125m	+89m	−650m
1:yen		+1.3b	−750m	+200m
2:$	+100m		−175m	+875m
2:£	−275m		+10m	−290m
2:C$	−350m		+220m	−1.5b
2:DM	+125m		−125m	+725m
2:yen	−1.3b		+300m	−950m
3:$	−500m	+175m		−325m
3:£	+25m	−10m		+680m
3:C$	+375m	−220m		−750m
3:DM	−89m	+125m		−450m
3:yen	+750m	−300m		+850m
4:$	+1.1b	−875m	+325m	
4:£	+800m	+290m	−680m	
4:C$	−555m	+1.5b	+750m	
4:DM	+650m	−725m	+450m	
4:yen	−200m	+950m	−850m	

Multilateral Netting	Paying FI			
Currency	1	2	3	4
$	−700m	+800m	−650m	+550m
£	−550m	−555m	+695m	+410m
C$	+530m	−1.63m	−595m	+1.695b
DM	−686m	+725m	−414m	+375m
yen	+750m	−1.95b	+1.3b	−100m

[a]Only the positive numbers represent outgoing payments from the FIs. The negative numbers represent receipts of payments by the FIs.

30 (six bilateral pairs of FIs—FI 12, 13, 14, 23, 24, 34— times five currencies) daily clearing transactions.[23] They are all listed as the positive entries in the table, which also shows that multilateral clearing reduces the required number of clearing transactions required. Rather than the 30 transactions required under bilateral netting, multilateral netting requires only 20 (four FIs times five currencies) clearing transactions in all five currencies for the four FIs in the network. For example, FI 2 owes US$100 million to FI 1, is owed US$175 million from FI 3, and owes US$875 million to FI 4, for a net U.S. dollar outflow of US$800 million, shown in the bottom of the table as a multilateral payment of +US$800m. Only the US$800 million actually crosses the multilateral electronic payment system. FI 2 gives up the rights to the three cash flows of +$100, −$175m, and +$875m and exchanges them for a single cash outflow of $800 million.

To whom is the US$800 million sent? To the clearinghouse. The clearinghouse accepts all payment requests (within certain limitations) and legally exchanges them for single end-of-day

---

[23] This assumes that each FI is willing to hold reserves in all five currencies. If, at the end of each day, each FI converted all reserves to its home currency, then the example collapses to the single currency case.

netting by novation:
legal replacement of one
net obligation for many
individual payment
requests transferred over
the network.

payments to be made to each FI, a process called **netting by novation**. The clearinghouse is legally liable for all payments, whether or not the counterparties have fulfilled their obligations. Netting by novation occurs when one relatively small net payment legally replaces the many individual payment requests transferred over the network. In effect, the clearinghouse legally offers its own guarantee of the myriad of individual payment requests in exchange for a single net payment to be to each FI.

The clearinghouse for exchange-traded futures and options operates in much the same manner. The payment system *guarantees* the prompt clearing of all accepted transactions, regardless of whether it receives all payments to which it is due. The 1992 International Swap Dealers Association (ISDA) Master Agreement governing international financial transactions contains a netting by novation clause. Moreover, a private consortium called FXNET allows counterparties to enter into bilateral netting agreements.

Multilateral netting exposes the clearinghouse payment system to large amounts of settlement risk. In the example presented in Table 6.10, the clearinghouse is legally required to make U.S. dollar-denominated payments to FIs 1 and 3 of $700 million and $650 million, respectively, whether or not it receives the $800 million from FI 2 or the $550 million from FI 4. This risk is resolved in the following ways. One international clearinghouse, Multinet, requires all participants to provide collateral equal to almost six times their average daily transactions. This covers six days of possible defaults, on average, therefore giving the clearinghouse time to draw down collateral as it covers the defaulting FI's debts. To further assure the creditworthiness of Multinet participants, members must have a minimum of US$1 billion in Tier 1 capital, a minimum Baa Moody's credit rating, supervision by a financial regulator, and an active trading presence, and they must provide quarterly financial statements demonstrating high operational standards. New members participate in bilateral netting only after they have demonstrated their stability.[24]

Checkpoint

1. What three problems are associated with the clearing of cross-border payments?

2. Contrast bilateral netted settlement and multilateral netted settlement. Which is more efficient? Which has more settlement risk exposure?

3. Why is multilateral settlement more important for cross-border transactions than for domestic payments?

European Union and International Settlement

Centralizing international payment systems into large multilateral hubs reduces the costs of clearing financial transactions globally. This is because large economies of scale and scope are achieved when centralized clearing systems offer full-service, global settlement services, ranging from pre-trade information flows to after-trade accounting. Centralized payment systems also create positive externalities once they reach a "critical mass" of membership. It is more efficient for FIs to belong to a single worldwide clearing system than to belong to many individual national systems. Indeed, if European financial market union is ever to become a reality, a centralized clearing system is a prerequisite.

Existing international settlement systems, such as Euroclear and Cedel, have failed to coalesce into this worldwide clearance hub in part because of opposition from local, domestic central

---

[24] Multinet's founding banks are The Bank of Montreal, Bank of Nova Scotia, Canadian Imperial Bank of Commerce, Chase Manhattan Bank, First National Bank of Chicago, National Bank of Canada, Royal Bank of Canada, and Toronto–Dominion Bank. Other participants are Citibank, Canada and Union Bank of Switzerland (Canada) as well as the Options Clearing Corporation and its wholly owned subsidiary, the International Clearing Systems, Inc.

banks and FIs that provide their own clearance services. Politicians claim that maintaining domestic settlement systems (and the jobs they generate) are in the "national interest." Legal, institutional, and regulatory differences across countries also create barriers to international harmonization. For instance, restrictions on access to national payment systems and exchange rate fluctuations hamper the adoption of a single currency (such as the ECU) that can be used to clear all trades in all currencies. Moreover, taxation differs across countries, as shown by the United Kingdom's 1.5% stamp tax on cross-border trades, as opposed to the 0.50% tax on domestic trades in U.K. equities. Until these barriers are lifted, the current disjointed system will remain, thereby hampering the development of a unified, liquid financial market in Europe.

Electronic Message Systems: S.W.I.F.T.

Electronic message systems can be used to exchange documents and transaction information expeditiously if the information is presented in a standardized format. Electronic data interchange (EDI) is an electronic format used in the United States to transmit payment information across payment systems. The Society for Worldwide Interbank Financial Telecommuniciations (S.W.I.F.T.) is an EDI message transmittal system privately owned by 1,900 member FIs worldwide. Bank Identifier Codes, a computer-readable address used to identify partners in financial transactions, have been assigned to approximately 25,000 FIs throughout the world. S.W.I.F.T. is not a settlement system but, rather a system to transmit private and confidential financial messages electronically. More than 2 million messages are transmitted each day, 28% of which are related to interbank payments; 14% are confirmations of foreign exchange deals; and 23% are account statements. S.W.I.F.T. messages are often used in lieu of telex messages, which require time-consuming manual entry of data, with the resulting possibility of error. By automating message transmittal, S.W.I.F.T. speeds processing and transmission and reduces the risk of loss from error in payment instructions. The controls and protective mechanisms built into the standardized S.W.I.F.T. message have encouraged FIs to utilize this system to confirm transactions that are subsequently cleared using CHIPS, Fedwire, or other payment systems.[25]

Figure 6.5 shows how a S.W.I.F.T. message can interface with a Fedwire transaction.[26] Translation of the message is provided in the description, whereas the text of the electronic message is shown in boldface. First Bronx NY receives a S.W.I.F.T. message from Black Forest Bank Munich (S.W.I.F.T. identifier BBFBKDEZZ) to pay Cowboy Trust, Dallas, for further credit to T. Edwards, account 123456 at the Rodeo Road Branch in Austin. The S.W.I.F.T. message indicates that Franz Mousse, doing business as Steak Palace, Maximillianstrasse 38, Munich, is paying T. Edwards US$34,000, US$10,000 on invoice TT33 for two cases of Texas T's Bar-B-Q sauce and US$24,000 as a franchise fee for the use of the Texas T's Secret Recipe. Black Forest Bank includes an instruction that states, "Pay immediately. Do not deduct any related fees from the transfer amount—charge fee separately." First Bronx prepares the Fedwire transmittal shown in boldface in Figure 6.5.

In a Federal Reserve Board policy statement of December 1992, FIs were encouraged to "include, where possible, complete information on the sender and recipient of large payment orders including those sent through Fedwire, CHIPS, and S.W.I.F.T." This initiative addresses the problem of *money laundering* of funds obtained through illegal activities. Since S.W.I.F.T. has pioneered the standardizing of messages containing a wide array of identifying information, it can comply with this policy initiative without hampering the efficiency of its operations.

---

[25] In 1993 CHIPS adopted the S.W.I.F.T. message format, making it possible for participants to send payments directly to and from CHIPS. This ease of operation further contributed to the shift in volume from Fedwire to CHIPS. As a competitive response, Fedwire will also adopt S.W.I.F.T. in late 1997.

[26] This example is taken from a Federal Reserve Press Release dated November 29, 1993, recommending that Fedwire adopt the S.W.I.F.T. message format.

Description	Tag	Elements
Type/subtype	[1510]	**1000**
IMAD	[1520]	**0712B9999999000001**
Amount	[2000]	**$34,000.00**
Sender DFI	[3100]	**029999999FIRST BRONX NY***
Sender reference	[3320]	**9999999999999999**
Receiver DFI	[3400]	**119999999COWBOYBANK***
Business function code	[3500]	**CTR**
Intermediary FI	[4000]	**F029999999FIRST BRONX NY***
Beneficiary FI	[4100]	**F119999999*COWBOYBANK** **RODEO ROAD BRANCH*** **AUSTIN***
Beneficiary	[4200]	**D123456*T. EDWARD***
Originator	[5000]	**DUNKNOWN*FRANZ MOUSSE*** **DBA STEAK PALACE*** **MAXIMILLIANSTRASSE 38*** **MUNICH, GERMANY***
Originator FI	[5100]	**BBFBKDEZZ*BLACKFOREST BK*** **MUNICH, GERMANY***
Originator to beneficiary info.	[6000]	**pay T. EDWARDS $34,000 US*** **$10,000 INV#TT33 2 CASES TEXAS T'S*** **BAR-B-Q SAUCE, $24,000 FRANCHISE FEE*** **FOR TEXAS T'S SECRET RECIPE***
FI to FI Receive FI information	[6100]	**PER BLACK FOREST BANK*** **PAY IMMEDIATELY. DO NOT DEDUCT ANY*** **RELATED FEES FROM THE TRANSFER*** **AMOUNT—CHARGE FEE SEPARATELY**

Figure 6.5   A S.W.I.F.T. message. A "tag" is the S.W.I.F.T. identifier code for each element.

➤ Clearing Securities Transactions

delivery-versus-payment:
the settlement method in which securities and cash change hands simultaneously.

Securities transactions are less risky if the securities and cash change hands simultaneously. This concept of **delivery-versus-payment** reduces the costs of transferring securities by enabling the safe and efficient clearing of securities transactions. This safety has been enhanced by the proliferation of book-entry securities held in FIs called **book-entry depositories**—specialized FIs that accept securities for safekeeping and maintain transferable accounts of those securities. Transfer of these securities is accomplished through electronic account entry as opposed to physical delivery with its accompanying verification, insurance, delivery, and storage costs.

book-entry depository: a specialized FI that accepts securities for safekeeping and maintains transferable accounts of those securities.

Figure 6.6 shows the rapid growth in the volume of book-entry securities over a 15 year span. All new U.S. Treasury securities are issued in book-entry form, as are many corporate stocks and bonds, municipal bonds, and securities issued by federal agencies. In 1990, 66% of all U.S. companies listed on the New York Stock Exchange, 43% of the shares listed on the American Stock Exchange, 87% of outstanding municipal bonds, and 77% of the corporate debt held on the New York Stock Exchange were held at the Depository Trust Company, the largest private book-entry depository. The Fed acts as a book-entry depository for 8,500 FIs, holding securities with a par value totaling over $3 trillion and processing an average of 47,000 securities transfers daily. Since 1989, all equities in France have been held in the form of electronic book-entries in the depository Sicovam, whereas the U.K.'s Talisman and Crest clearing systems are still paper-based (although Crest allows investors to choose electronic book-entry).

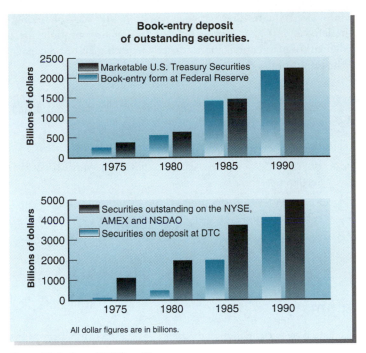

Book-entry deposit of outstanding securities.

Source: McAndrews (1992), p. 21.

Figure 6.6

U.S. government securities are cleared on the Fedwire book-entry securities transfer system using real-time gross settlement. Corporate stocks and bonds are typically cleared over private securities systems, using netted settlement. Two private book-entry depositories, the Participants Trust Company (for GNMA mortgage-backed securities and other agency securities) and the Depository Trust Company (for commercial paper and other corporate securities), have end-of-day multilateral netted settlement operated by a clearinghouse called the National Securities Clearing Corporation (NSCC). The NSCC clears trades between FIs by injecting itself into the middle of all trades using netting by novation. It is responsible for the delivery of securities (via book-entries to the Depository Trust Company's accounts) and thus guarantees both sides of the trade. All trades are netted multilaterally, so that each counterparty need transmit only one net amount to NSCC at the end of each day. In 1992 the Fed processed more than 12 million securities transfers across the Fedwire book-entry system, with total value of $140 trillion. In contrast, the NSCC cleared 140 million equity and bond transactions valued at $11 trillion. The DTC settled 83 million book-entry transactions, valued at $19 trillion, using next-day settlement, and an additional 1.9 million transactions, valued at $9.7 trillion, using same-day funds settlement.

All FIs in the United States have three days in which to clear their securities transactions, referred to as **T plus 3** or "trade plus three days." Before June 1, 1995, the counterparties had five days in which to clear any securities transaction in the United States.[27] Since three days is too short a time to allow for physical delivery, all stocks and corporate bonds traded in the United States are in the process of shifting to paperless, book-entry trading. The demands of securities traders for rapid settlement continue to increase. The Commodity Futures Trading

T plus 3: "trade plus three days," the time limitation allowed to settle securities transactions.

---

[27] Settlement cycles range from T + 20 in Italy to T + 2 in Germany, T + 3 in France, and T + 5 in the United Kingdom.

Commission requires that settlement prior to the start of trading via Fedwire transfers be completed by 10 A.M. eastern time. Clearing organizations are moving toward same-day settlement of margin obligations, thereby requiring end-of-day payment transfers determined by the results of the day's trading activity.

Checkpoint

1. What has hampered the development of a single centralized clearing system for all of Europe?
2. Is S.W.I.F.T. a payment system? Why or why not?
3. How can S.W.I.F.T. be used in conjunction with CHIPS to increase the efficiency of settlement?
4. How can S.W.I.F.T. be used in conjunction with Fedwire to increase the efficiency of settlement?
5. What is delivery-versus-payment? How does it affect settlement risk?
6. How does book-entry facilitate delivery-versus-payment?

➤ Summary

All financial transactions end up the same way—in an exchange of cash and financial instruments. The completion of any financial transaction is called settlement or clearing. Settlement can take place electronically or non-electronically, the latter requiring some form of physical delivery. The majority of financial transactions, in terms of number of payments, are cleared nonelectronically via some payment system such as checks. However, the vast majority of all financial transactions in terms of *value* of payments use some form of electronic settlement.

The two major forms of electronic settlement are real-time gross settlement and netted settlement. Real-time gross settlement entails immediate payment transfers for each individual transaction. Each transaction is independent of all others and is cleared immediately with finality. Most of these systems are operated by central banks, which can guarantee final payment even if one of the counterparties defaults. However, FIs participating in real-time gross settlement systems must hold large amounts of reserves, which are used to clear transactions.

Netted settlement systems are exposed to settlement risk because transactions are not finalized until the end of each day. At the close of the day, all payment orders are added up, and only the net amount is transmitted from the owing FI to the owed FI, thereby economizing on the required levels of reserve. If the owing FI cannot make payment, however, then the day's transactions are unwound; that is, all transactions involving the defaulting FI are removed from the payments grid, and net settlements are recomputed. This is done until all settlements can be paid. The default of a large FI could disrupt the entire global payment system. This is called systemic risk. Netted settlement systems require participants to pledge collateral and credit lines to reduce, but not eliminate, systemic risk exposure.

Cross-border transactions are subject to special problems because of asynchronous payments called Herstatt risk; differences across national legal systems; and global settlement risk. Multilateral netting enhances global market efficiency by reducing the number of payment transactions required to clear foreign currency trades. Electronic payment systems are used to transfer book-entry securities as well as currencies. Book-entry securities are not physically transferred; instead ownership changes are recorded on an electronic balance sheet.

➤ References

Arend, Mark. "Consolidation, Truncation Mark Fed Operations Strategy." *ABA Banking Journal* (August 1992): 58–60.

Board of Governors of the Federal Reserve System. *Symposium Proceedings International Symposium on Banking and Payment Services*. Washington, D.C.: December 1994.

Borio, C.E.V., and P. V. den Bergh. "The Nature and Management of Payment System Risks: An International Perspective." *BIS Economic Papers*, No. 36 (February 1993).

Committee on Payment and Settlement Systems of the Central Banks of the Group of Ten Countries, Bank for International Settlements. *Central Bank Payment and Settlement Services with Respect to Cross-Border and Multicurrency Transactions*. September 1993.

Curran, Frank. "Importance to Banks and Treasury Managers." *Journal of Cash Management* 13, No. 4 (July–August 1993): 46–52.

Emmons, W. "Why Are Americans Enamored With Float?" Federal Reserve Bank of St. Louis *Monetary Trends* (August 1996): 1.

Giddy, I., A. Saunders, and I. Walter. "Barriers to European Financial Market Integration: Clearance and Settlement of Equities," NYU Salomon Center, Working Paper, October 26, 1995.

Humphrey, David. "Market Responses to Pricing Fedwire Daylight Overdrafts." Federal Reserve Bank of Richmond *Economic Review* (May–June 1989): 23–34.

Jones, F., and F. Fabozzi. *The International Government Bond Markets*. Chicago: Probus Publishing Co., 1992.

Lee, John. "Corporate Electronic Payments: Where We've Been and Where We're Going." *The World of Banking* (November–December 1991): 28–30.

McAndrews, James. "The Automated Clearinghouse System: Moving Toward Electronic Payment." Federal Reserve Bank of Philadelphia *Business Review* (July–August 1994): 15–23.

McAndrews, J. "Where Has All the Paper Gone?" Book-Entry Delivery Against Payment Systems."

Perold, A. F. "The Payment System and Derivative Instruments." In D. B. Crane, K. A. Froot, S. P. Mason, et al. *The Global Financial System*. Boston: Harvard Business School Press, 1995, 33–79.

Pieptea, Dan. "Electronic Trading and Futures Market Efficiency." *International Journal of Technology Management, Special Issue on the Strategic Management of Information and Telecommunication Technology* 7, Nos. 6, 7, 8 471–477.

Richards, H. W. "Daylight Overdraft Fees and the Federal Reserve's Payment System Risk Policy." *Federal Reserve Bulletin* (December 1995): 1065–1077.

Roberds, William. "The Rise of Electronic Payment Networks and the Future Role of the Fed with Regard to Payment Finality." Federal Reserve Bank of Atlanta *Economic Review* 78, No. 2, (March–April 1993): 1–22.

Saunders, Anthony, and Lawrence White. *Technology and the Regulation of Financial Markets: Securities, Futures, and Banking*. Lexington, Mass.; Lexington Books, 1986.

Stigum, Marcia. *After the Trade: Dealer and Clearing Bank Operations in Money Market and Government Securities*. Homewood, Ill.: Dow Jones–Irwin, 1988.

Stigum, Marcia. *The Money Market*. 3rd ed. Homewood, Ill.: Dow Jones–Irwin, 1990.

VanHoose, David. "Bank Behavior, Interest Rate Determination, and Monetary Policy in a Financial System with an Intraday Federal Funds Market." *Journal of Banking and Finance* 15 (1991): 343–365.

VanHoose, David, and Gordon Sellon. "Daylight Overdrafts, Payment System Risk, and Public Policy." Federal Reserve Bank of Kansas City *Economic Review* (October 1989): 9–29.

Questions

1. Show how the following transaction would clear on the Fedwire. ABC agrees to a spot market purchase of a $5 million 10 year U.S. Treasury bond from XYZ. The bond's coupon rate is 8%, paid semiannually, but the market yield on similar risk securities is a bid of 8.05% and an asked yield of 7.99 %. ABC and XYZ agree on a yield of 8.04%.

2. Using the transaction in question 1, what is the cost of a 10 day float if money market rates are 7.5% p.a.?

3. Consider the following minute-by-minute intraday payment transactions between ABC Bank and XYZ Bank for the first five minutes of operation.

Daily Transactions Involving ABC Bank and XYZ Bank ($ millions)[a]

ABC Bank		XYZ Bank	
Customer A & Customer Z	−$560	Customer A & Customer Z	+$560
Customer B & Customer Y	−$95	Customer B & Customer Y	+$95
Customer C & Customer X	−$220	Customer C & Customer X	+$220
Customer D & Customer W	+$780	Customer D & Customer W	−$780
Customer E & Customer V	+$40	Customer E & Customer V	−$40
Net Total	−$55	Net Total	+$55

[a]Positive entries denote that the bank's customer is the payee in the transaction; negative entries denote that the bank's customer is the payor in the transaction.

a. Calculate the per-minute overdraft balance for ABC Bank's first five minutes of operation.
b. What is ABC Bank's average per-minute daylight overdraft balance?
c. Using your answer to part b, calculate ABC Bank's daily overdraft fee.
d. Calculate the minimum level of reserve account balances that would be necessary for ABC Bank to utilize gross settlement if daylight overdrafts were absolutely prohibited.
e. Calculate the minimum level of reserve account balances that would be necessary for ABC Bank to utilize net settlement over the first five minutes of trade.

4. Using the minute-by-minute intraday payment transactions in question 3:
a. Calculate the per-minute overdraft balance for XYZ Bank's first five minutes of operation.
b. What is XYZ Bank's average per-minute daylight overdraft balance?
c. Using your answer to part b, calculate XYZ Bank's daily overdraft fee.
d. Calculate the minimum level of reserve account balances that would be necessary for XYZ Bank to utilize gross settlement if daylight overdrafts were absolutely prohibited.
e. Calculate the minimum level of reserve account balances that would be necessary for XYZ Bank to utilize net settlement over the first five minutes of trade.

5. Use the table of bilateral netted foreign currency settlements on the following page to calculate the settlements required under multilateral netting.

6a. Suppose that Bank ABC transmitted a $75 million payment to Bank XYZ electronically on Fedwire. Both banks' starting positions are shown in the following table. Show the impact of the funds transfer. How are the banks' balance sheets affected? What are the banks' reserve positions?
6b. If at the end of the day Bank XYZ's depositor transmitted a $75 million payment to Bank ABC, what would be the impact on the banks' closing balance sheets? What are the banks' reserve positions?
6c. If at the end of the day Bank XYZ's depositor transmitted a $50 million payment to Bank ABC, what would be the impact on the banks' closing balance sheets? What are the banks' reserve positions?
6d. If at the end of the day Bank XYZ's depositor transmitted a $100 million payment to Bank ABC ($75 million to Bank ABC and $25 million to Bank ABC's depositor), what would be the impact on the banks' closing balance sheets? What are the banks' reserve positions?

Before Daily Fedwire Transactions Involving ABC Bank and XYC Bank

Bank ABC ($ millions)				Bank XYZ ($ millions)			
Reserves	$90	Deposits	$900	Reserves	$50	Deposits	$500
Loans	$900	Net worth	$90	Loans	$500	Net worth	$50

7. There are 11 FIs participating on the payment system. Use all three methods of settlement (gross, bilateral netted, and multilateral netted) to clear the following transactions. (Be sure to calculate the total number of transactions and the total volume of cash flows under each method of settlement.)
a. Each FI owes the other 10 FIs the gross daily amount of $10 million each.
b. Each FI has transactions with only two other FIs. It owes one of the FIs $10 million and the other FI $5 million per day. (*Hint*: Number each of the FIs 1, . . . , 11. Each FI transacts with

Daily Cross-Border Currency Transactions: Bilateral Netting

Bilateral Netting		Receiving FI		
Paying FI	1	2	3	4
1:$		−230m	−485m	+175m
1:£		+305m	+90m	+225m
1:C$		−400m	−310m	−50m
1:DM		+25m	−10m	+50m
1:yen		−2.1b	+925m	−775m
2:$	+230m		−75m	+875m
2:£	−305m		+10m	−290m
2:C$	+400m		−150m	−1.5b
2:DM	−25m		+105m	+725m
2:yen	+2.1b		−670m	−950m
3:$	+485m	+75m		+100m
3:£	−90m	−10m		+80m
3:C$	+310m	+150m		−150m
3:DM	+10m	−105m		−250m
3:yen	−925m	+670m		−400m
4:$	−175m	−875m	−100m	
4:£	−225m	+290m	−80m	
4:C$	+50m	+1.5b	+150m	
4:DM	−50m	−725m	−250m	
4:yen	+775m	+950m	+400m	

[a]Only the positive numbers represent outgoing payments from the FIs.
The negative numbers represent receipts of payments by the FIs.

the two contiguous FIs only (e.g., FI 2 deals with 1 and 3 only, etc.), and pays the FI with the lower number $5 million while receiving $10 million from the FI with the higher number. FI 1 deals with FIs 11 and 2.)

c. Each FI has transactions with only one other FI, to which it owes $10 million.

8a. Are credit cards considered an electronic or nonelectronic payment mechanism? Why?

8b. Are debit cards considered an electronic or nonelectronic payment mechanism? Why?

9. Consider the following daily transactions for the three FIs that make up an electronic payment system:

FI 1 pays FI 2 $105 million. FI 1 pays FI 3 $210 million.
FI 2 pays FI 1 $75 million. FI 2 pays FI 3 $15 million.
FI 3 pays FI 1 $10 million. FI 3 pays FI 2 $25 million.

Assume that FIs 2 and 3 start the day with a zero balance in their reserve accounts. FI 1 has a beginning balance of $230 million.

a. Clear the daily transactions using (i) gross settlement, (ii) bilateral netting, and (iii) multilateral netting.

b. What is the impact on payments if FI 3 cannot meet its obligations: (i) if the payment system is gross settled? (ii) if the payment system is netted bilaterally? (iii) if the payment system is netted multilaterally?

c. What is the impact on payments if FI 1 cannot meet its obligations: (i) if the payment system is gross settled? (ii) if the payment system is netted bilaterally? (iii) if the payment system is netted multilaterally?

d. How are the Lamfalussy Report recommendations reflected in your answers to parts b and c?

10.   Suppose that the day's dollar-denominated transactions between FIs 1 and 2 are: (i) $20 million paid to 1; (ii) $10 million paid to 2; (iii) $50 million paid to 1; (iv) $75 million paid to 1; (v) $25 million paid to 2; (vi) $60 million paid to 1; and (vii) $70 million paid to 2. List the day's clearing transactions using

a.   Real-time gross settlement

b.   Bilateral netting

c.   Multilateral netting.

BORDER CROSSING II:
CHAPTERS 4–6

Before proceeding, make sure that you understand the following concepts:

1. The definition of liquid, money assets. (Chapter 4, p. 75–77)

2. The conduct of monetary policy using (Chapter 4, p. 96–103)

   a. Open market operations
   b. Discount window borrowing
   c. Reserve requirements

3. The mechanics of reserve maintenance. (Chapter 4, p. 81–85)

4. The concept of safety and soundness. (Chapter 5, p. 116–135)

5. The tradeoff between safety and soundness and disclosure requirements. (Chapter 5, p. 135–143)

6. The regulatory dialectic. (Chapter 5, p. 150)

7. Real-time gross settlement. (Chapter 6, p. 161–168)

8. Bilateral and multilateral netting. (Chapter 6, p. 169–180)

CHAPTER 7

COMPUTING INTEREST RATES AND RISK EXPOSURE

For all participants—issuers, dealers, salespeople, and the investors—the money market reduces to a *numbers game.* . . . [T]hose who earn most are those who best understand how to figure odds and make other simple but important calculations.—M. Stigum (1981), p. 1.

Learning Objectives

- To learn to perform interest rate calculations.

- To compare different rate quotations to determine whether they are computed (1) on a simple interest or compounded basis; (2) on a 360 or 365 day year basis; or (3) for spot or forward delivery.

- To examine several models of interest rate fluctuations and calculate the impact on security valuation using duration and convexity measures.

➤ Introduction

Imprecise terminology and notation generate a lot of confusion in yield calculations. Etymologists in the finance profession suffer from a distinct lack of imagination, for they use the same words over and over again to connote different meanings. Words like *spot rate*, *basis*, and *discount* have multiple definitions that make their usage confusing. In this chapter, we formulate a vocabulary of terms that will help avoid this confusion.

Terminology is important because, in the shorthand of today's fast-moving financial markets, imprecise terms can lead to costly errors of judgment. Whether you are investing $1,000 or $10 million, you want to know the return on your investment. Interest rates communicate information about rates of return without reference to either the scale or the type of investment. Interest rates or yields can be useful tools to compare expected returns on alternative investment vehicles ex ante (before the investment is made), as well as ex post (after the fact) to measure performance. In the hands of unscrupulous securities salespersons, however, interest rates can also be tools of obfuscation. To protect yourself and to use interest yield quotations to your best advantage, you must understand how they are calculated. For example, which is the better investment: a U.S. Treasury bill with 73 days until maturity and a yield of 6.16%, or a bank certificate of deposit with the same maturity date and a compound yield of 6.25%? To compare the two investments, you must know exactly how each yield is computed.

In this chapter, we also divorce the method of yield calculation from specific financial instruments. That is, we can state the yield on the same zero coupon bond in either a *simple interest* format (assuming no compounding) or in a *compounded yield* format (assuming compounding at any desired interval). As an analogy, if the streetcorner vendor sells apples at $0.50 each, you may state that price equivalently as 50 pennies, 2 quarters, or one half dollar. The choice of unit of measure (pennies, quarter, or half dollars) does not affect the value of the apple. The same holds true for a financial security; we can state its rate of return using several different units of measure.

The two units of measure examined in this chapter are **simple interest** and **compound interest** yields.[1] Simple interest computes the rate of interest earned on principal without considering compounding. In contrast, compound interest computes the rate of interest earned on principal, assuming periodic compounding, that is, reinvestment of previously earned interest.

No matter what the frequency of the compounding or the time to maturity of the instrument, all interest rates are annualized and stated p.a. That is, periodic rates (semiannual, monthly, daily) must be converted to a yearly rate of return for purposes of comparison. This permits us to compare different securities with different investment time horizons, as well as varying cash flow payment schedules. All rates of return will be comparable if we are clear about the assumptions that determine the rates. Simple interest rates are annualized by merely taking intrayear payments and multiplying them by the number of payments per year in order to generate an annualized rate of return. Compound rates are annualized by assuming that intrayear payments are reinvested at some prevailing interest rate, so that the annualized rate of return includes reinvestment income as well as simple interest income. Compound yields always exceed simple interest yields, other things being equal, since they include the yield earned on the reinvestment of interest.

simple interest: the rate of interest earned on principal, assuming no compounding.

compound interest: the rate of interest earned on principal, assuming periodic compounding—that is, reinvestment of previously earned interest.

Computing Yields for Zero Coupon Instruments

All interest rates are rates of return, so that no matter how complex the calculation, it can be boiled down to an essential ratio:

$$\frac{\text{Cash Flows Received}}{\text{Initial Investment}}$$

Since zero coupon bonds have no interim cash flows, the numerator in the basic rate of return ratio is simply the difference between the face value minus the price paid for the zero coupon security. For example, a one year maturity, zero coupon security paying $1,000 at maturity and priced at $900 would yield a cash flow equal to $1,000 − $900 = $100. The simple interest rate of return is equal to the dollar discount cash flow as a fraction of the original investment, or equivalently: $\frac{F-P}{P} = \frac{1,000-900}{900} = 11.11\%$. For zero coupon instruments that do not mature in exactly one year, this simple interest rate must be annualized (on a 365 day year basis) by multiplying by $\frac{365}{t}$, where t is as defined in Table 7.1, to derive the formula for a simple interest rate on a pure discount instrument, denoted i, and shown in Table 7.1 as

$$i = \frac{F-P}{P}\left(\frac{365}{t}\right)$$

Let's examine this process using our introductory example, a 73 day U.S. Treasury bill (which is a zero coupon security), with a contractual rate of discount of $d = 6\%$ p.a. We will perform all calculations per $100 face value (denoted F), although the prices for any denomination are

[1] Simple interest yields are also called spot rates or discount yields or bond equivalent yields; compound yields are also called yields to maturity or effective yields.

Table 7.1

Summary of Interest Rate Calculations

Security Type	Contractual Cash Flows[a]	Annualized Effective Rates	
		Simple Interest	Compound Interest
Zero coupon	Rate of discount: d	$i = \dfrac{F-P}{P}\left(\dfrac{365}{t}\right)$	$i^* = \left(1 + \dfrac{F-P}{P}\right)^{365/t} - 1$
	$d = \dfrac{F-P}{F}\left(\dfrac{360}{t}\right)$	$i = \dfrac{365d}{360 - dt}$	$i^* = \left(1 + \dfrac{it}{365}\right)^{365/t} - 1$
Coupon bearing	Coupon rate: c	y such that $P = \left[\displaystyle\sum_{s=1}^{T}\dfrac{\frac{c}{n}F}{\left(1 + \frac{y}{n}\right)^s}\right] + \dfrac{F}{\left(1 + \frac{y}{n}\right)^T}$	$y^* = \left(1 + \dfrac{y}{n}\right)^n - 1$

Notation

- $F \equiv$ face value.
- $P \equiv$ price.
- $t \equiv$ time to maturity stated in days. $\frac{t}{365} \equiv$ time to maturity stated in years.
- $n \equiv$ number of coupon payments in each year.
- $c \equiv$ annualized coupon rate as a fraction of face value. The per period coupon rate is the per annum coupon rate, c, divided by n.
- $T \equiv$ number of payment periods until maturity.
- $d \equiv$ rate of discount on a zero coupon security. For most money market zero coupons (for example, U.S. Treasury bills), the rate of discount is calculated on the assumption of a 360 day year rather than a 365 day year. For these securities, $P = F(1 - \frac{dt}{360})$.
- $s \equiv$ period number.

[a]Both contractual rates (the coupon rate and the rate of discount) are used only to calculate cash flows, not as a measure of effective yield. The effective yields (simple and compounded interest) are annualized assuming that the year has 365 days. The simple interest yields, i, y are converted into compound interest yields, i^*, y^*. For any given financial security, $i < i^*$ and $y < y^*$ because of the yield-enhancing impact of compounding.

simply multiples of these amounts (that is, for $100,000 face value, multiply all numbers by 1,000, etc.). Figure 7.1a shows the cash flows at each date. In 73 days (the time to maturity, denoted t), the security will pay $100. What is its price (denoted P) today? The price of the zero coupon instrument can be derived from the definition of the rate of discount[2] which is

$$d = \frac{F-P}{F}\left(\frac{360}{t}\right)$$

---

[2] Note that the definition of the rate of discount differs from the general rate of return formulation because the denominator is the face value, F, not the initial price, P. Moreover, the rate is annualized on a 360 day, not a 365 day year, as defined by the U.S. Treasury. Thus, $d < i$.

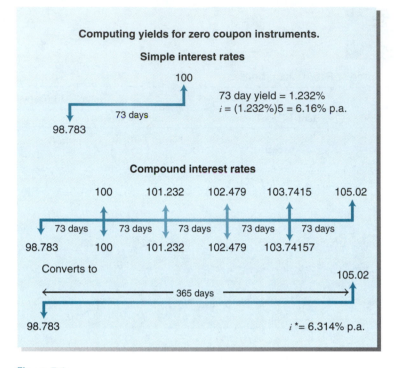

Figure 7.1a

Using algebraic manipulation to solve for P, we find that the price of a zero coupon instrument is

$$P = F\left(1 - \frac{dt}{360}\right)$$

The price of the 73 day U.S. Treasury bill in our example is

$$P = F\left(1 - \frac{dt}{360}\right) = 100\left(1 - \frac{.06(73)}{360}\right) = \$98.783$$

The cash flows earned over the 73 day holding period of this investment are $\$100 - \$98.783 = \$1.217$ per \$100 face value. This implies a 73 day rate of return of $\frac{\$1.217}{\$98.783} = 1.232\%$. To convert this 73 day rate of return to an annualized *simple* interest rate, we realize that over a 365 day year we can consecutively invest in five ($\frac{365}{73} = 5$) of these securities. The simple interest rate is $1.232\% \times 5 = 6.16\%$ or, equivalently:

$$i = \frac{F - P}{P}\left(\frac{365}{t}\right) = \frac{100 - 98.783}{98.783}\left(\frac{365}{73}\right) = 6.16\% \text{ p.a.}$$

Multiplying the 73 day yield by five is the simple interest method of calculating the annualized rate of return for this zero coupon security. But Figure 7.1a shows another way of annualizing the 1.232% 73 day yield. If upon maturity each 73 days all cash flows are used to purchase another, identical security, then the investor will gain the benefits of compound interest, which is the reinvestment of previously earned interest payments. At the end of the first 73 day investment period, a second 73 day, 6% p.a. discount security is purchased. Rather than investing only $98.783 in the second security, however, the investor has $100 to invest. Inverting the price formula on U.S. Treasury bills to solve for F, we find that the future value of this investment is

$$F = \frac{P}{\left(1 - \dfrac{dt}{360}\right)} = \frac{\$100}{\left(1 - \dfrac{.06(73)}{360}\right)} = \$101.232$$

After 73 days, this $101.232 is reinvested in a third, 73 day zero coupon security, yielding a future value of $102.479 ($101.232/$(1 - \frac{.06(73)}{360})$ = $102.479). This takes place five times until the entire year (365 days) is completed. With the help of compound interest, the face value of the fifth zero coupon security is $105.02. We have used five consecutive 73 day zeros to construct a one year, zero coupon security with no interim cash flows, a price of $98.783, and a face value of $105.02. This represents an annualized compound rate of interest of

$$i^* = \frac{F - P}{P} = \frac{105.02 - 98.783}{98.783} = 6.314\% \text{ p.a.}$$

This is equivalent to the compound yield obtained by applying the formula in Table 7.1 to the 73 day zero coupon instrument:

$$i^* = \left(1 + \frac{F - P}{P}\right)^{365/t} - 1 = \left(1 + \frac{100 - 98.783}{98.783}\right)^{365/73} - 1 = 6.314\% \text{ p.a.}$$

This formula states that if the zero coupon investment is rolled over $\frac{365}{t}$ times each year, then the compound yield, denoted i^*, is calculated using

$$i^* = \left(1 + \frac{F - P}{P}\right)^{365/t} - 1$$

If we rearrange the first simple interest equation in Table 7.1 to obtain

$$\frac{F - P}{P} = \frac{it}{365}$$

and substitute into our equation for i, we obtain another, equivalent formula for the compound yield on a pure discount bond, also shown in Table 7.1

$$i^* = \left(1 + \frac{it}{365}\right)^{365/t} - 1$$

For any zero coupon instrument, $d < i < i^*$. Thus, the 360 day discount yield, d, is less than the 365 day simple interest yield, i, which is less than the 365 day compounded yield, i^*. *Practitioner's Primer 7.1* examines an alternative calculation of i, using d.

Now we have the answer to the investment question posed in the introduction to this chapter. Surprisingly, the U.S. Treasury bill earning 6.16% p.a. is a *better* investment than the certificate of deposit earning a compound yield of 6.25% p.a. The U.S. Treasury bill earns 6.16% p.a. on a simple interest basis but 6.314% p.a. on a compound yield basis. Thus, the yield on the Treasury bill is more than 6 basis points higher than the yield on the certificate of deposit.

PRACTITIONER'S PRIMER 7.1

AN ALTERNATIVE CALCULATION OF SIMPLE INTEREST RATES FOR ZERO COUPONS

The rate of discount can be directly converted into a simple interest rate, i. Substituting the zero coupon price formula, $P = F(1 - \frac{dt}{360})$, into the simple interest formula in Table 7.1 yields

$$ i = \frac{F - F\left(1 - \dfrac{dt}{360}\right)}{F\left(1 - \dfrac{dt}{360}\right)} \left(\frac{365}{t}\right) $$

Simplifying results, we obtain the alternative formula, also shown in Table 7.1, that can be used to convert a rate of discount into a simple interest yield for a zero coupon instrument:

$$ i = \frac{365d}{360 - dt} $$

Similarly, the price of a zero coupon instrument using the simple interest yield i, rather than the discount yield d, can be derived from algebraic manipulation of the definition

$$ i = \frac{F - P}{P} \left(\frac{365}{t}\right) $$

to yield

$$ P = \frac{F}{\left(1 + \dfrac{it}{365}\right)} $$

Computing Yields for Coupon Bearing Instruments

Zero coupon instruments have no interim cash flows between the up-front price and the face value paid at maturity. In contrast, coupon bearing securities carry periodic interest payments. These periodic cash flows must be taken into consideration when calculating a rate of return. If the investor receives only one periodic coupon payment per year, then the annualized simple interest yield is the same as the annualized compound interest yield. If more than one periodic coupon payment is paid per year, however, then the computation of the yields depends on whether the coupons are reinvested (to obtain a compound yield) or not (to obtain a simple yield) during the course of the year.

Figure 7.1b illustrates the concept for a two year 8% p.a. coupon instrument that pays interest semiannually. Every six months, the investor receives a $4 coupon payment per $100 face value, which is spent rather than reinvested. The present value of the first coupon payment is $\frac{4}{1.04}$ = $3.846, assuming that interest rates are constant at 8% p.a., or 4% per half year, for the two year life of the bond. If we add the present values of all four cash flows (including the par value received at maturity), then we obtain a present value (price) of $100, or par value. The simple interest rate on the coupon bearing instrument, denoted y, is 8% p.a.

If, however, the investor chooses to reinvest each coupon payment, then we must calculate the interest earned on the reinvested coupons in order to determine the bond's total cash flows

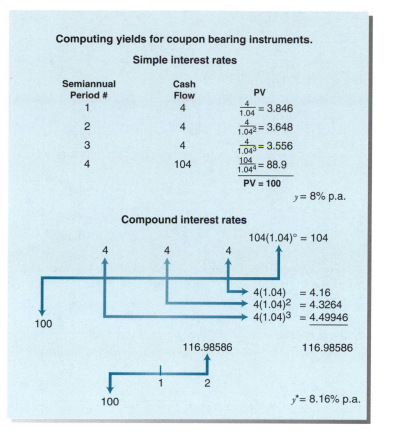

Figure 7.1*b*

and the compound interest rate. This is shown in the bottom panel of Figure 7.1*b*. The first coupon payment is not spent but instead is reinvested at a semiannual rate of 4% for 1.5 years (or three half years). At maturity of the two year bond, the value of that first coupon payment is $4(1.04)^3 = \$4.49946$ per \$100 face value. Adding the total value of reinvested coupons yields a future value of \$116.98586. We have constructed a two year, pure discount instrument that has a present value of \$100 and a future value of \$116.98586. Using our computations for zero coupon instruments (and 730 days in place of two years), we find that the compound yield is

$$ i^* = \left(1 + \frac{F - P}{P}\right)^{365/t} - 1 = \left(1 + \frac{116.98586 - 100}{100}\right)^{365/730} - 1 = 8.16\% \text{ p.a.} $$

We derive the compound yield formula for a coupon bearing instrument, denoted y^*, shown in Table 7.1, where for the two year semiannual coupon bond, $n = 2$ and $y = 8\%$ p.a., so that

$$ y^* = \left(1 + \frac{y}{n}\right)^n - 1 = \left(1 + \frac{.08}{2}\right)^2 - 1 = 8.16\% \text{ p.a.} $$

Simple interest rates are used to calculate prices for coupon bearing securities. For example, a 14 year bond[3] with a 15% p.a. semiannual coupon yielding an annualized simple interest yield, $y = 10\%$, is priced (per \$100 face value), using the formula in Table 7.1, as

---

[3] Note that the time to maturity, T, is always stated in terms of the number of coupon payments until maturity. In this example, therefore, $T = 28$ semiannual coupons.

$$P = \sum_{s=1}^{T} \frac{\frac{c}{n}F}{\left(1 + \frac{y}{n}\right)^s} + \frac{F}{\left(1 + \frac{y}{n}\right)^T}$$

$$P = \sum_{s=1}^{28} \frac{7.5}{\left(1 + \frac{.10}{2}\right)^s} + \frac{100}{\left(1 + \frac{.10}{2}\right)^{28}} = \$137.245$$

Using the formula in Table 7.1, we find that the compound yield is

$$y^* = \left(1 + \frac{y}{n}\right)^n - 1 =$$

$$\left(1 + \frac{.10}{2}\right)^2 - 1 = 10.25\%$$

The choice of interest rate has real economic consequences. For instance, if the compound yield was mistakenly used to price the semiannual coupon bond, then the price would be

$$P = \sum_{s=1}^{T} \frac{\frac{c}{n}F}{\left(1 + \frac{y^*}{n}\right)^s} + \frac{F}{\left(1 + \frac{y^*}{n}\right)^T}$$

$$P = \sum_{s=1}^{28} \frac{7.5}{\left(1 + \frac{.1025}{2}\right)^s} + \frac{100}{\left(1 + \frac{.1025}{2}\right)^{28}} = \$134.907$$

Use of the compound yield rather than the simple interest yield underprices the bond by \$2.338 per \$100 face value.

As with zero coupon instruments, compound yields always exceed simple interest yields, or using our notation, $y^* > y$. If the coupon bearing security sells at par (the price equals the security's face value), then the coupon rate equals the simple interest yield, or $c = y$. If the security sells at a premium (priced above par value), then $c > y$, and $c < y$ if it is selling at a discount (priced below par value). All rates can be stated in either the simple interest format or the compound format. Market convention and force of habit dictate which method is utilized for each financial instrument. *Practitioner's Primer 7.2* and *7.3* describe market convention with regard to daycount conventions and equivalent bond yields.

PRACTITIONER'S PRIMER 7.2

DAYCOUNT CONVENTIONS

We have seen how to make the interest yield of any investment appear larger simply by increasing the number of days that we assume make up a year. For example, the 365 day bond equivalent yield is always larger than the 360 day rate of discount. This is part of a broader calendar problem that each financial market must solve using "daycount conventions." The two related aspects of daycount conventions are (1) counting the number of days until maturity (or until the next coupon payment date); and (2) counting the number of days in a year. Practitioners in financial markets count the number of days until maturity in two ways: ACT and 30.[4]

ACT: the actual number of calendar days until maturity.

30: the number of days until maturity assuming 30 day months.

Thus, if today's date is February 20, during a nonleap year, and the maturity date is March 15, the actual number of calendar days until maturity using ACT is 23 days. But the number of calendar days using the 30 daycount convention is 25 days (10 days assumed to remain in a 30 day month of February plus 15 days in March).

The three possible assumptions for the number of days in a year are

365: 365 days in all years.

ACT: the actual calendar number of days in the year.

360: 12 month years, each month with 30 days, for a total of 360 days.

Of the six possible combinations of daycount conventions, the following four are used in financial markets:

ACT/365: Used in government bond markets in the U.K. and Japan. The number of days until maturity is calculated using ACT, assuming a 365 day year.

ACT/360: Used for U.S. Treasury bills. The number of days is calculated using ACT, with a 360 day year.

30/360: Used for U.S. federal agency debt, U.S. corporate debt, Eurobonds, German government bonds, and Dutch government bonds. The number of days until maturity is on a 30 basis, and the number of days in the year is assumed to be 360.

ACT/ACT: Used for U.S. Treasury notes and bonds, French government bonds, and Australian government bonds. The actual calendar time is used to calculate both the time until maturity and the number of days in the year.

PRACTITIONER'S PRIMER 7.3

equivalent bond yield:
the simple interest yield on a zero coupon bond restated as a simple interest yield on a coupon bearing security.

SEMIANNUAL COMPOUNDING AND EQUIVALENT BOND YIELDS

Our classification of yields as either simple or compound interest is designed to facilitate yield comparisons between zero coupon and coupon bearing instruments. When we restate the simple interest yield on a zero coupon bond as a simple interest yield on a coupon bearing security, we calculate the **equivalent bond yield**. To calculate the equivalent bond yield, the yield on the zero coupon security is adjusted to replicate the coupon payments on the coupon bearing bond. Since most coupon bearing securities pay interest semiannually, we will calculate the equivalent bond yield assuming semiannual interest payments. We consider two possible scenarios: (1) the time to maturity is less than 182 days; and (2) the time to maturity exceeds 182 days but is less than 365 days.

---

[4] Euromarkets and European domestic markets use a modified version of 30 called 30E, which differs slightly from 30 in some cases when the time until maturity is less than one calendar month.

Less than 182 days until maturity: If the time to maturity is less than 182 days, neither the coupon bearing instrument nor the zero coupon security carries coupon payments. The equivalent bond yield is merely the simple interest yield for a zero coupon instrument, $i = \frac{F-P}{P}\left(\frac{365}{t}\right)$. Consider a 90 day Treasury bill with a $1 million face value and a rate of discount of 7% p.a. Using the formula for a simple interest yield shown in Table 7.1, we obtain

$$i = \frac{365d}{360 - dt} = \frac{365(.07)}{360 - (.07)(90)} = 7.2236\% \text{ p.a.}$$

Now consider a $1 million face value, 15 year, 12% p.a. semiannual coupon Treasury bond, with 90 days left until maturity. That means that in 90 days the holder of the bond will receive the principal payment of $1 million plus the last semiannual coupon of $60,000, which is $\frac{.12}{2}$($1 milllion), for a total face value $F = $1.06 million. What price would you be willing to pay for the Treasury bond? The Treasury bond's yield must be equivalent to the Treasury bill's yield since their risk exposures are identical, such that

$$P = \frac{F}{1 + \dfrac{it}{365}} = \frac{1.06m}{1 + \dfrac{.072236(90)}{365}} = \$1,041,450$$

Alternatively, recognize that the Treasury bond with only 90 days until maturity is a zero coupon instrument. Using the price calculation for a U.S. Treasury bill earning a rate of discount of 7% p.a. with a face value of $1,060,000 yields

$$P = 1.06m\left(1 - \frac{.07(90)}{360}\right) = \$1,041,450$$

Between 182 and 365 days until maturity: If the zero coupon instrument has more than 182 days until maturity, then the equivalent bond yield, denoted i, is more complicated. The zero's discount interest, $F - P$, must be restated in terms of a coupon payment value and can be decomposed as follows:

$$F - P = \frac{i}{2}P + \frac{i}{365}\left(t - \frac{365}{2}\right)\left(1 + \frac{i}{2}\right)P$$

where[5] the first term on the right is the first half year's imputed coupon payment, and the second term on the right is the interest earned on the second coupon payment

---

[5] The equation for $F - P$ can be rewritten as

$$F = P\left(1 + \frac{i}{2}\right)\left(1 + \frac{it}{365} - \frac{i}{2}\right)$$

which states that the face value is equal to the price plus the imputed semiannual coupon compounded over the period of time from the coupon payment date until maturity (a period lasting $t - \frac{365}{2}$ days). To solve this equation, set the face value equal to 1, for simplicity, and restate as

$$P(1 + .5i)\left[1 + .5i\left(\frac{2t}{365} - 1\right)\right] = 1$$

Multiplying and simplifying results in

$$i^2\left(\frac{2t}{365} - 1\right) + i\frac{4t}{365} + 4\left(1 - \frac{1}{P}\right) = 0$$

Solving this quadratic equation yields the final expression for i given in the text.

accrued at the daily equivalent bond yield, $\frac{i}{365}$. Solving for i yields

$$i = \frac{\frac{-2t}{365} + 2\sqrt{\left(\frac{t}{365}\right)^2 - \left(\frac{2t}{365} - 1\right)\left(1 - \frac{1}{P}\right)}}{\frac{2t}{365} - 1}$$

Consider a $1 million face value, 270 day Treasury bill with a rate of discount of 5% p.a. The price is

$$P = \$1m\left(1 - \frac{.05(270)}{360}\right) = \$962,500 = \$.9625 \text{ per \$1 face value}$$

The equivalent bond yield is

$$i = \frac{\frac{-2(270)}{365} + 2\sqrt{\left(\frac{270}{365}\right)^2 - \left(\frac{2(270)}{365} - 1\right)\left(1 - \frac{1}{.9625}\right)}}{\frac{2(270)}{365} - 1} = 5.22\% \text{ p.a.}$$

We can construct two alternative 270 day Treasury investments that have the same yield of 5.22% p.a. Suppose that the coupon bearing Treasury was a $1 million face value 8% p.a. semiannual coupon Treasury bond maturing on December 20, 1998, and priced on March 25, 1998, at $1,019,771. Solving the coupon bond valuation formula in Table 7.1, we obtain a yield of 5.22% p.a. Alternatively, an investor could hold the 270 day Treasury bill (priced at $1,019,771 with a face value of $1,059,148) and earn the same yield of 5.22% p.a. Since the yields are the same, these two investments are equivalent, although one is a pure discount instrument whereas the other pays a coupon.

Practice Calculations

Table 7.2 shows some calculations of simple and compound interest rates for zero coupon and coupon bearing securities. In the top half, several zero coupon securities are evaluated. For example, the 4% rate of discount, 90 day maturity bill is priced at $0.99 per $1 face value. This price is calculated as

$$P = F\left(1 - \frac{dt}{360}\right) = \$1\left(1 - \frac{.04(90)}{360}\right) = \$0.99$$

To calculate the simple interest yield,

$$i = \frac{1 - 0.99}{0.99}\left(\frac{365}{90}\right) = 4.097\% \text{ p.a.}$$

Converting the simple interest yield to a compounded interest rate:

$$i^* = \left(1 + \frac{.0409652(90)}{365}\right)^{365/90} - 1 = 4.16\% \text{ p.a.}$$

Table 7.2

Calculations of Simple and Compound Interest Yields[a]

Zero Coupon	d	t	P	i	i^*
	4%	90	0.99	4.097%	4.16%
	4%	180	0.98	4.138%	4.18%
	5%	90	0.9875	5.134%	5.234%
	5%	180	0.975	5.199%	5.268%

Coupon Bearing	c	t	n	P	y	y^*
Semiannual coupon	4%	730	2	0.99	4.529%	4.58%
Semiannual coupon	4%	1,460	2	1.01	3.729%	3.763%
Semiannual coupon	5%	730	2	0.99	5.535%	5.612%
Semiannual coupon	5%	1,460	2	1.01	4.723%	4.778%

[a] Prices are stated per $1 face value. Prices of the zero coupon instruments are calculated (following the convention in most money markets) as $P = F(1 - \frac{dt}{360})$. The prices of the coupon bearing instruments are assumed to be obtained from market quotations.

In the bottom half of Table 7.2, the coupon bearing security is evaluated. For instance, the two year (730 day) maturity paying a 4% coupon rate p.a. compounded semiannually ($n = 2$) is priced at discount at $0.99 per $1 face value (obtained from a market quotation), thereby yielding more than 4%. Since coupons are paid semiannually, the per period coupon rate, $\frac{c}{n}$, is 4%/2 = 2%. The simple interest yield is the value of y that satisfies the equation

$$0.99 = \sum_{s=1}^{4} \frac{.02}{\left(1 + \frac{y}{2}\right)^s} + \frac{1}{\left(1 + \frac{y}{2}\right)^4}$$

The simple interest yield is $y = 4.52862\%$ p.a. Compounding semiannually:

$$y^* = \left(1 + \frac{.0452862}{2}\right)^2 - 1 = 4.58\% \text{ p.a.}$$

These four yields—i, i^*, y, y^*—are the building blocks of interest rate computations. Variations on these basics are shown in *Calculation Complications 7.1–7.3*. *Timely Topics 7.1* shows the interest rates that FIs must disclose in order to comply with Truth in Lending regulations.

CALCULATION COMPLICATIONS 7.1

ACCRUED INTEREST

That we must be precise about the timing of cash flows when calculating yields for coupon-bearing instruments is particularly true when coupons are paid twice a year as they are for semiannual coupon bonds. Since most years consist of 365 days, the number of days in each coupon period can range from 181 to 184 days. The differential length of each coupon period has not affected our calculations because

1.   The same yield, y, is utilized to discount all coupon payments. Later in this chapter, we will relax this assumption, thereby requiring the exact computation of the length of each coupon payment period.

2.   We have been concerned with examples of bonds with a *whole* number of coupon periods until maturity. That is, the bonds are priced only on coupon

payment (or issue) dates, so as to exclude the possibility of fractional coupon payment periods. This assumption is overly restrictive since we must price the securities on each possible **settlement date** whether or not it coincides with a coupon payment date. The settlement date is the date on which the transaction is cleared by completing the specified funds/securities transfers.[6]

Bond valuation *between* coupon payment dates requires the computation of **accrued interest**. In the United States, France, and Canada, all government bonds are sold "cum-coupon" (with coupons). So if the settlement date takes place one day prior to the next coupon payment date, the bond buyer receives the entire next day's coupon payment, representing six months worth of interest. But the seller has held the bond for almost the entire coupon payment period (less one day) and is therefore entitled to most of that interest payment. To compensate the seller for the loss of the next coupon, the buyer must pay the seller for the amount of interest already earned, or the accrued interest. The accrued interest is the interest due from the last coupon payment date until the settlement date. In some countries (Japan, Germany, the U.K., Australia), government bonds are sold without the next coupon if the next coupon payment date is close to the settlement date. For example, in Japan, if the settlement date falls within a 14 day period prior to the next coupon payment date, the next coupon is paid entirely to the bond seller. The *seller* must then pay the *buyer* for the accrued interest that the buyer earns from the settlement date until the next coupon payment date.

Let's examine how accrued interest is calculated for cum-coupon bonds. In Figure CC.1, B days denote the **basis**, which is the number of days in the current coupon payment period.[7] There are t_c days from today's settlement date until the next coupon payment date. (Note that in all of our previous examples, t_c equaled B since the dates were lined up so as to exclude fractional coupon periods.) The security seller has held the bond for $B - t_c$ days and must be compensated for that amount of accrued interest. That is, the bond seller is entitled to the fraction $(B - t_c)/B$ of the next coupon payment, whereas the bond buyer receives the remainder, t_c/B. Phrased another way, the bond buyer will earn a fraction, t_c/B, of the next coupon payment but not the already accrued interest portion, $(B - t_c)/B$. Thus, the accrued interest is $(cF/n)[(B - t_c)/B]$, where cF/n is the next coupon payment.

The cash bond price that the bond buyer actually pays consists of (1) the **flat price** (also known as the "clean price"), the quoted price of a coupon bearing security excluding accrued interest; and (2) the accrued interest. The sum of the flat price and any accrued interest is called the **full accrual price** (also known as the "dirty price"), the price actually paid on the settlement date.

Bond valuation between coupon payment dates entails four steps:

Step 1. Utilize the formula given in Table 7.1 to determine the price on the next coupon payment date, immediately following the payment of the next coupon.

Step 2. Add the next coupon payment to the value computed in Step 1.

---

settlement date: the date on which the transaction is cleared by completing the specified funds/securities transfers.

accrued interest: interest due from issue date or last coupon payment date until settlement date.

basis: the number of days in a coupon payment period.

flat price: the quoted price of a coupon bearing security excluding accrued interest.

full accrual price: the sum of the flat price and any accrued interest.

---

[6] The settlement date is usually the same day as the *value date*, the trade date on which the securities are priced. We will assume that the settlement date and value date fall on the same day.

[7] Counting the number of days in the basis, B, may seem simple, but even this is subject to market conventions and practices that differ across countries according to the daycount convention (see *Practitioner's Primer 7.2*). In France and Australia, and for U.S. Treasury securities, B is the number of actual calendar days between coupon payments. However, for U.S. Federal Agency bonds, Eurobonds, German government bonds, and U.S. corporate bonds, the number of days in the year is assumed to be equal to 360 and the basis evaluated using the assumption of a 30 day month. We will calculate B using the actual number of calendar days between coupon payments.

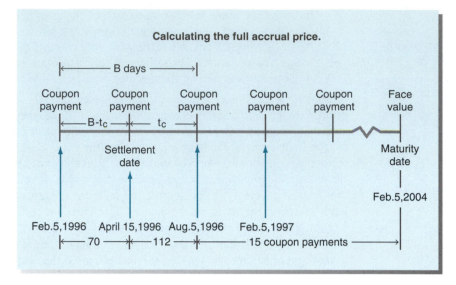

Calculating the full accrual price.

Figure CC.1

Step 3. Discount the value obtained in Step 2 (the value of the bond on the next coupon payment date) back at the simple interest yield, y, over the t_c days from settlement until the next coupon payment date. This yields the full accrual price.

Step 4. Deduct the accrued interest to obtain the flat price.

Applying these four steps to a semiannual coupon bond yields the following formula for the flat price, P_F is:

$$P_F = \frac{\displaystyle\sum_{s=1}^{T} \frac{0.5cF}{\left(1 + \frac{y}{2}\right)^{s-1}} + \frac{F}{\left(1 + \frac{y}{2}\right)^{T-1}}}{\left(1 + \frac{y}{2}\right)^{t_c/B}} - 0.5cF(1 - t_c/B) \tag{7.1}$$

where y is the annualized simple interest yield; T is the number of semiannual coupons payable between settlement date and maturity date; c is the annual coupon rate; $.5c$ is the semiannual coupon rate; F is the face value; t_c is the number of days between settlement date and the next coupon payment date; B is the total number of days in the current coupon period; and P_F is the bond's flat price. The first term on the right in equation (7.1), obtained by following steps 1, 2, and 3 only, is the total price including accrued interest. Thus, the formula for the full accrual price, P, of a semiannual coupon bond is

$$P = \frac{\displaystyle\sum_{s=1}^{T} \frac{0.5cF}{\left(1 + \frac{y}{2}\right)^{s-1}} + \frac{F}{\left(1 + \frac{y}{2}\right)^{T-1}}}{\left(1 + \frac{y}{2}\right)^{t_c/B}}$$

Equation (7.1) directly results from the four-step valuation process. The numerator of the first term on the right in this equation is the value of all future bond cash flows as of the next coupon payment date as obtained from Steps 1 and 2. The value of the entire first term is the Step 3 present value of the bond's future cash flows as of the settlement date. The final term, accrued interest, is subtracted in Step 4.

Using the dates in Figure CC.1, consider a 6.75% p.a. semiannual coupon bond yielding a simple interest return $y = 8.25\%$ p.a. As of April 15, 1996, there are $T = 16$ coupon payments remaining.

Step 1. At the close of business on August 5, 1996, there are 15 remaining coupon payments (excluding the payment on August 5, 1996) from the payment on February 5, 1997, until maturity on February 5, 2004. This is standard bond valuation since there is a complete 6 month period from August 5, 1996 until the "first" of 15 remaining coupon payments, beginning on February 5, 1997. The present value of these payments (per $100 of face value) is

$$P_{\text{Aug}5,96} = \sum_{s=1}^{15} \frac{6.75/2}{\left(1 + \frac{.0825}{2}\right)^s} + \frac{100}{\left(1 + \frac{.0825}{2}\right)^{15}} = \$91.7336242$$

Step 2. Adding the August 5, 1996 coupon payment of $\frac{6.75}{2} = \$3.375$ yields: $P_{\text{Aug}5,96} = \$95.1086242$.

Step 3. Discounting the value in step 2 back 112 days until settlement date on April 15, 1996, we obtain

$$P_{\text{Apr}15,96} = \frac{95.1086242}{\left(1 + \frac{.0825}{2}\right)^{112/182}} = \$92.7719774$$

This is the full accrual price that is actually paid on April 15, 1996.

Step 4. Deducting accrued interest to determine the bond's flat price, we get

$$P_F = \$92.7719774 - \frac{6.75}{2}\left(1 - \frac{112}{182}\right) = \$91.4739$$

CALCULATION COMPLICATIONS 7.2

360 VERSUS 365 DAY YEARS

Although we have chosen to state both simple and compound interest yields in terms of 365 day calendar years (366 in leap years), there are some financial instruments that quote rates under the assumption that there are only 360 days in each year (for example, repurchase agreements, negotiable certificates of deposits, corporate and municipal bonds). To convert a 365 day rate to a 360 day rate, simply multiply by $\frac{360}{365} = 0.9863$. If the 365 day simple interest rate is 10%, then the 360 day simple interest rate is

$$\frac{360}{365}(.10) = 9.863\%$$

This is a difference of almost 14 basis points. This yield (often referred to as a money market yield) is simply the uncompounded rate on a zero coupon instrument, assuming that there are 360 days in the year. This can also be expressed as

$$\left(\frac{F - P}{P}\right)\left(\frac{360}{t}\right)$$

To illustrate, consider a 192 day zero coupon security priced at $95 per $100 face value. Using the formula from Table 7.1, we find that the simple interest yield is

$$i = \left(\frac{F-P}{P} \right) \left(\frac{365}{t} \right) = \left(\frac{100-95}{95} \right) \left(\frac{365}{192} \right) = 10\% \text{ p.a.}$$

If the simple interest rate was instead quoted on a 360 day basis, then the yield would be[8]

$$\frac{F-P}{P} \left(\frac{360}{t} \right) = \frac{100-95}{95} \left(\frac{360}{192} \right) = 9.868\%$$

CALCULATION COMPLICATIONS 7.3

callable bonds: bonds with an embedded option that permits the issuer to redeem the bonds at par on a specified date prior to maturity.

YIELD TO CALL

The yield formulas in Table 7.1 assume that the bond is held until maturity, so that all contractual cash flows are received. However, there are **callable bonds** that may be retired prior to maturity. Callable bonds have an embedded option that permits the issuer to redeem the bonds at par on a specified date prior to maturity. The *yield to call* can be calculated for callable bonds, using the formulas in Table 7.1, except the call date is substituted for the maturity date.

As an example, consider a 14% p.a. semiannual coupon, U.S. Treasury bond maturing in 20 years but callable in 6 years, currently priced at $121 per $100 face value. Computing the simple interest yield, y, using 20 years (40 half years) until maturity results in a yield to maturity of 11.33% p.a. However, when the 6 year (12 half year) call period is used, the yield to call is only 9.35% p.a. Which yield is correct? We don't know. It depends on the likelihood that the bond will be called. If market rates are lower than 14% p.a. on the call date, then the U.S. Treasury can reduce its interest expenses by calling the 14% coupon bonds and replacing them with bonds that pay a lower rate of interest. Another way of stating this is that, if interest rates are below 14% on the call date, then the bond will be selling at a premium *above par*. But the call provision allows the Treasury to repurchase the bonds at par. It will therefore be advantageous for the Treasury to call the bonds when interest rates are lower than the coupon rate on the bonds. Since this will be disadvantageous for the bondholder, callable bonds typically are priced at a premium yield (lower price) as compared to noncallable bonds. We will measure this differential in chapter 16.

---

[8] The difference between 9.863% and 9.868% arises because of rounding errors. If we solve for the factor of proportionality, call it Z, converting the 365 day rate into a 360 day rate, then

$$\left(\frac{F-P}{P} \right) \left(\frac{360}{t} \right) = Z \left(\frac{F-P}{P} \right) \left(\frac{365}{t} \right)$$

Solving for Z yields the adjustment factor $\frac{360}{365}$ shown in the text.

TIMELY TOPICS 7.1

THE APR AND TRUTH IN LENDING

Compounding and discounting of intrayear cash flows are inevitable in financial decision making by investors, consumers, and businesses. . . . The common practice in consumer finance (home mortgage, auto loans, etc.) is to determine the monthly rate as one-twelfth of the annual rate. This annual rate should then be considered as the nominal annual rate or simply the APR, a household word in consumer finance. [The Truth in Lending] Code of the Federal Reserve states that, "The annual percentage rate(s) to be disclosed for the purpose of Sect. 226.7(d) shall be computed by multiplying each period's rate by the number of periods in a year." This approach of estimating the annual rate, although legal, understates the true (annual) cost of credit which, for monthly payments, effectively is

$$\text{APRE} = (1 + \text{APR}/12)^{12} - 1$$

Note that APRE $\geq$ APR. In addition, the shorter the payment intervals or the higher the APR, the greater the difference between APRE and APR. . . . The Truth in Lending Code of the Federal Reserve recommends the "actuarial method" to measure the true cost of credit, but defines the APR using the simple interest approach with no mention of annual effective [compound] rate (APRE). Thus, the code contradicts itself in the sense that its definition of APR ignores the actuarial method. Even worse, the code is biased against borrowers because lenders, by advertising the APR, understate the true annual cost of credit. For example, for 12% APR and monthly payments, the true annual cost is 12.68%. [A]t 12% APR, monthly payment on a $60,000 mortgage loan for 20 years will be $660.65 under the current practice. On the other hand, [if period rates are stated] using the geometric mean approach, that is,

$$ip = (1 + \text{APR})^{1/m} - 1$$

where m = number of payment periods in a year; ip = periodic rate, then the monthly rate is $ip = 1.12^{1/12} - 1 = 0.94888\%$. The mortgage payments will be $635.17. Over a 20 year period, the home buyer will be shortchanged by $6,115 on an uncompounded basis and by $23,435 on a monthly compounded basis!

Source: Shyam Bhandari, "Compounding/Discounting of Intrayear Cash Flows: Principles, Pedagogy, and Practices," in *Financial Practice and Education* (Spring 1991): 87–89.

Evaluating Equity

The valuation equations for coupon bearing securities, shown in Table 7.1, can also be used to evaluate preferred and common stock issues that pay dividends.[9] Since dividend payments are periodic cash flows, they take the place of the fixed coupon payments in the discounting formula. The time to maturity for equity, however, is not fixed, but is infinite, since the possible life span of the company is unlimited. If a dividend payment is paid n times each year and the dividend payment in each period s is denoted D_s, the price of the stock is calculated as the

---

[9] Nondividend paying common stocks are evaluated as zero coupon instruments.

present value of all future cash flows as follows:

$$P = \sum_{s=1}^{\infty} \frac{D_s}{\left(1 + \dfrac{y}{n}\right)^s}$$

preferred stock: an equity security that carries a predetermined constant dividend payment. **Preferred stock** is an equity security that carries a predetermined constant dividend payment, denoted D. Thus, the valuation expression for preferred stock is

$$P = \sum_{s=1}^{\infty} \frac{D}{\left(1 + \dfrac{y}{n}\right)^s} \equiv \frac{D}{y/n}$$

Applying this formula, if a share of preferred stock has a guaranteed quarterly dividend of $0.25 and an annual risk adjusted yield of 10%, we find that the preferred stock price is $\frac{0.25}{.10/4} = \$10$.

common stock: an equity share that does not have a fixed dividend yield   **Common stock** is an equity share that does not have a fixed dividend yield. Indeed, since common stockholders are the residual claimants on the firm's assets, any growth in asset value belongs to them in the form of both higher dividend payouts and capital gains (increase in stock price). Consider the common stock of a corporation with a 10% p.a. risk adjusted required rate of return and an expected end-of-year dividend of $0.35 per share of common stock. If the expected stock price on the dividend payment date is $5.15, the common stock price is just the present value of all future cash flows, or

$$P = \frac{\$0.35}{1.1} + \frac{\$5.15}{1.1} = \$5.00$$

The first term in the stock price expression is the present value of all dividend payments (one $0.35 payment expected at the end of this year) and the second term is the present value of the stock's sale price. Suppose, however, that the investor wants to hold the stock for two years. The price should then be the present value of all future dividends expected over the next two years plus the present value of the sale price upon the sale of the stock at the end of the investment period. Suppose that the second year's annual dividend payment is expected to be $.36 and the sale price at the end of the second year is forecast at $5.30. The current stock price is

$$P = \frac{\$.35}{1.1} + \frac{\$.36}{1.1^2} + \frac{\$5.30}{1.1^2} = \$5.00$$

Indeed, no matter how long the stock is held, the current stock price will be the same: $5.00. (Try it with an expected third year dividend of $0.37 and an end-of-third year price of $5.46.) Of course, this example is contrived. The dividend and sale price forecasts are not arbitrarily determined, but are based on the expectation of a constant 3% annual growth rate in the company's dividends and share price. This basic, and somewhat restrictive, assumption of the *constant dividend growth model* applies the discounting formula in Table 7.1 to stock price calculation only for mature firms with stable annual growth rates. In this case, the stock price can be expressed as

$$P_0 = \sum_{s=1}^{\infty} \frac{D\left(1 + \dfrac{g}{n}\right)^{s-1}}{\left(1 + \dfrac{y}{n}\right)^s} \equiv \frac{D_1}{\dfrac{y}{n} - \dfrac{g}{n}}$$

where g is the annualized growth rate of dividends and share prices, D_0 is the next expected dividend payment, n is the number of dividend payments per year, and y is the risk adjusted annualized required rate of return used to discount all cash flows. Applying this formula to our example, we obtain $P_0 = \frac{\$0.35}{.10-.03} = \$5.00$ current common stock price.

Checkpoint

✓

1. Distinguish between a simple interest yield and a compound interest yield.

2. Why is the compound interest yield for a particular security always higher than its simple interest yield?

3. In pricing zero coupon instruments on money markets, what is the assumption about the number of days in the year? For calculation of simple interest yields, what is the assumption about the number of days in the year? For calculation of compound yields, what is the assumption about the number of days in the year?

4. How frequently is interest compounded for calculation of compound interest yields on zero coupon securities?

5. Why is the calling of a bond disadvantageous for bond investors?

➤ Hidden Assumptions: The Role of the Yield Curve

Conversion of interest rates from simple interest format to compound interest format (see Tables 7.1 and 7.2) requires several assumptions about frequency of compounding and the annualizing convention. Although we have stated those assumptions, the most important assumption is not explicitly stated. It is an assumption about the reinvestment rate. The compound yield is an effective yield if and only if interest can be reinvested at the assumed reinvestment rate. We have assumed that the reinvestment rate is constant for the life of the security. That is, coupon payments on the two year 4% p.a. semiannual coupon note described in Table 7.2 can be reinvested at a 4.529% simple interest yield every six months for the next two years. Clearly, this is a drastic assumption about the stability of interest rates over time. It amounts to an assumption that the **yield curve** is both flat and constant. The yield curve is a graphical depiction of the current relationship between interest rates and time to maturity, holding all other factors (such as credit risk) constant. Yield curves are typically drawn using the yields on government securities with varying times to maturity. The range of yields for securities with varying maturities is called the **term structure of interest rates**. Figure 7.2 shows the Treasury yield curve that was in effect as of October 24, 1994.

Simple interest yields on zero coupon Treasury securities with different maturity dates are depicted on the yield curve. The full range of maturities, from short to long term, are obtained using Treasury bills (up to one year maturity) and, for longer maturities, actively traded Treasury **STRIPS** (Separate Trading of Registered Interest and Principal Securities), which are pure discount instruments constructed by detaching each individual coupon or principal payment from a Treasury note or bond (see discussion in the section entitled Linking the Pricing of Pure Discount and Coupon Instruments). Zero coupon instruments are used in drawing the yield curve in order to avoid the confounding effects of different coupon rates. Simple interest yields are used instead of compounded rates to avoid the reinvestment rate assumption that is built into the compound rate calculation. Several points on the yield curve are:

yield curve: a graphical depiction of the current relationship between interest rates and time to maturity, holding all other factors (such as credit risk) constant.

term structure of interest rates: the range of yields for securities with varying maturities.

STRIPS (Separate Trading of Registered Interest and Principal Securities): pure discount instruments constructed by detaching each individual coupon or principal payment from a Treasury note or bond.

The Term Structure of Interest Rates, October 24, 1994

Time to Maturity, t	Rate of Discount, d	Simple Interest Yield, i
85 days	5.00%	5.13%
176	5.46%	5.69%
274	5.67%	6.01%
358	5.85%	6.30%

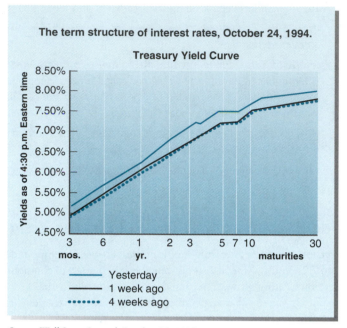

Source: Wall Street Journal, October 25, 1994.

Figure 7.2

What Determines the Shape of the Yield Curve?

The yield curve pictured in Figure 7.2 is upward sloping with a horizontal section in the 5 to 7 year maturity range. The shape of the yield curve is determined by three factors: market expectations; liquidity preference; and market segmentation.

The Expectations Hypothesis   The yield curve reflects the market's consensus expectations of future interest rates. Market participants act on their expectations. Thus, if borrowers expect interest rates to increase in the future, they will attempt to lock in today's lower spot rates for longer periods of time. The supply of longer term debt instruments will increase, lowering their price relative to the supply of shorter term debt and raising rates. Conversely, reluctance to issue shorter term debt will reduce the relative supply of shorter maturity debt instruments, thereby raising prices and lowering rates relative to longer maturities. The result will be an upward-sloping yield curve. Thus, the term structure will reveal the expectations-driven activities of investors who purchase and issue debt instruments of varying maturities.

Each investor will calculate the rate of return over an expected investment time horizon, but securities of different maturities can be used to construct any investment portfolio over any time period. The investor wants to maximize the **holding period yield**, the annualized rate of return over the expected investment time horizon, by choosing the investments with the appropriate maturities. Say the investor has a five year investment time horizon. A few possible investment alternatives are the purchase of a five year bond, five consecutive purchases of one year bonds, or a 25 year bond to be sold after five years. The investor will calculate the rates of return on each one of these alternative investments and choose the one that has the highest yield over the entire five year holding period.

If every other investor is performing the same analysis, however, using different investment time horizons tailored to each investor's circumstances, the per period yield will be equalized

holding period yield: the annualized rate of return over the expected investment time horizon.

across all holding periods in equilibrium, no matter what the composition of maturities used to achieve that yield. This is the **expectations hypothesis:** the per period yield is the same across securities, for all possible holding periods. If securities markets are efficient, then the equality of rates across all holding periods can be utilized to detect the market's expectations about forward rates, so that the yield curve's shape reflects market expectations. This implies that the yield curve can be decomposed into a series of forward rates that can be interpreted as expected future spot rates.

expectations hypothesis: the per period yield is the same across securities, for all possible holding periods.

Some Notation   The yield curve depicts spot rates, which are current interest rates for immediate delivery securities of varying maturities. Forward rates are the yields on securities with deferred delivery. Therefore, there are two relevant time periods: the time to maturity and the time to delivery. Here we introduce notation that clearly specifies these two time periods. Yields will be expressed as $_nR_t$, where n is the time to delivery, t is the number of periods between delivery and maturity, and R is the the choice of yield format (i, i^*, y, y^*). Periods for n and t can be stated in terms of days, months, or years. Thus, $n = 0$ for all spot rates since delivery takes place immediately. For example, the 90 day zero coupon security in Table 7.2 offers a simple interest yield denoted, using this notation, as $_0i_{90} = 4.097\%$ p.a. If delivery of this security were deferred for 180 days, then the forward rate (in simple interest format) would be denoted as $_{180}i_{90}$, with a compound interest rate of $_{180}i_{90}^*$. The maturity date of this forward transaction is 270 days from today: 180 days until delivery plus 90 days until maturity.

The Decomposition of the Yield Curve   Consider the term structure of October 24, 1994. The simple interest yield is 5.69% for a 176 day maturity Treasury security and 5.13% for an 85 day maturity. If the expectations hypothesis holds, over the 176 day holding period, the 5.69% yield must be equalized with the yield on two consecutive transactions: the purchase of the 85 day Treasury today followed by, on the date of the maturity of the 85 day Treasury security, the purchase of a 91 day Treasury security for a total holding period of 85 plus 91 equals 176 days. We know the yield on the first leg of this transaction: the spot rate on the 85 day Treasury security, or 5.13% (in simple interest format). If all 176 day holding period yields are equal, then we can solve for the 91 day *implied forward rate*—that is, the rate on the 91 day Treasury security that will be delivered in 85 days, denoted $_{85}i_{91}$.

Figure 7.3 shows the decomposition of the yield curve for the 176 day and 85 day spot yields. In the top transaction, the investor buys the 176 day bill, with a face value set at $1, for simplicity, for a price of[10]

$$P = \frac{F}{1 + \dfrac{_0i_{176}(176)}{365}} = \frac{1}{1 + \dfrac{.0569(176)}{365}} = \$0.973295959$$

If the expectations hypothesis holds, then this investment must be equivalent to the bottom transaction in Figure 7.3: the purchase of a spot 85 day bill followed by the purchase of a 91 day bill in 85 days. Setting the price of the 85 day bill equal to $0.973295959, we find that the face value, upon maturity, is $F = P(1 + \frac{it}{365}) = 0.973295959(1 + \frac{.0513(85)}{365}) = \$0.984923512$,

---

[10] This formula is obtained by rearranging the formula in Table 7.1 for a simple interest yield on a discount bond

$$_0i_t = \left(\frac{P-F}{P}\right)\left(\frac{365}{t}\right)$$

Solving for P, we obtain

$$P = \frac{F}{1 + \dfrac{_0i_t t}{365}}$$

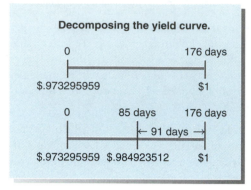

Figure 7.3

thereby yielding the 85 day spot yield of 5.13% p.a. This is immediately reinvested in a 91 day forward bill to mature 176 days from today at a face value of $1. The yield on that bill is

$$\frac{F-P}{P}\left(\frac{365}{t}\right) = \frac{1-0.984923512}{0.984923512}\left(\frac{365}{91}\right) = 6.14\%.$$

This yield is the implied forward rate on the 91 day bill to be delivered in 85 days, denoted $_{85}i_{91}$.

Restating this in a simplified formula, we obtain

Price of 176 day spot =   Price of 85 day spot ×   Price of 91 day implied forward

$$\frac{1}{1+\dfrac{_{0}i_{176}(176)}{365}} = \left(\frac{1}{1+\dfrac{_{0}i_{85}(85)}{365}}\right) \times \left(\frac{1}{1+\dfrac{_{85}i_{91}(91)}{365}}\right)$$

$$\frac{1}{1+\dfrac{.0569(176)}{365}} = \left(\frac{1}{1+\dfrac{.0513(85)}{365}}\right) \times \left(\frac{1}{1+\dfrac{_{85}i_{91}(91)}{365}}\right)$$

where $_{85}i_{91}$ denotes the implied forward rate.

The implied forward rate of 6.14% can be interpreted as the market's consensus that the expected spot rate on 91 day bills will be 6.14% in 85 days from today. Thus, the upward slope of the yield curve suggests that the market expects interest rates to rise in the future. The implied forward rate can be used as an estimate of how high rates are expected to rise.

This process can be repeated for other maturity pairs of spot interest rates. For instance, we can use the 85 day and 274 day spot rates of October 24 to solve for the implied forward rate, $_{85}i_{189} = 6.33\%$, on a 189 day maturity security to be delivered in 85 days. Similarly, using the 85 day and 358 day securities, we can show that the implied forward rate, $_{85}i_{273}$, on a 273 day maturity security to be delivered in 85 days is 6.59%. Plotting the implied forward rates (see 6.14%, 6.33%, and 6.59% in Figure 7.4) expected to prevail in 85 days, we obtain a **forward yield curve**, which graphically depicts the implied forward rates for different maturities on a specific date in the future. This can be used as a consensus estimate of expected future spot rates.

forward yield curve: a graph that depicts the implied forward rates for different maturities on a specific date in the future.

The implied forward rate is a forecast of expected future spot rates. If the expectations hypothesis holds, then the implied forward rate tells us the rate that investors expect to prevail

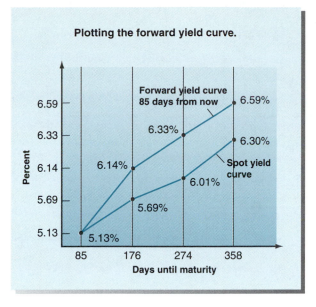

Plotting the forward yield curve.

Figure 7.4

on deferred delivery securities. This implied forward rate should be equal to the spot rate expected to prevail on the deferred delivery date.

Linking the Pricing of Pure Discount and Coupon Instruments   Thus far we have priced pure discount instruments as if they were entirely distinct and unconnected to coupon instruments. However, in August 1982 both Salomon Brothers and Merrill Lynch pioneered a new financial market when they recognized that fixed coupon instruments are just portfolios of zeros. By **stripping** the whole (the fixed coupon bond) into the sum of its parts, a series of pure discount instruments is constructed consisting of the principal and interest payments as separate stand-alone zero coupon securities). Merrill's TIGRS (Treasury Income Growth Receipts) and Salomon's CATS (Certificates of Accrual on Treasury Securities), followed in 1985 by the Treasury's STRIPS, are constructed by cutting Treasury bonds and notes into their component interest and principal payments. Since it is a simple matter to go from coupon instrument to the component discount instruments and back again,[11] some connection must exist between the yields of pure discount and fixed coupon instruments. The implied forward rate provides that link.

stripping: separating the whole (the fixed coupon bond) into the sum of its parts.

From Table 7.1, the pricing formula for a semiannual coupon fixed income security is

$$P = \sum_{s=1}^{T} \frac{\frac{c}{n}F}{\left(1 + \frac{y}{n}\right)^s} + \frac{F}{\left(1 + \frac{y}{n}\right)^T}$$

where P is the price, c is the annual coupon rate, F is the face value, T is the number of periods until maturity, n is the number of payment dates within each year, and y is the annualized (simple interest) yield to maturity. This assumes that each coupon payment, $\frac{c}{n}F$, is reinvested at a constant rate, $\frac{y}{n}$. As shown in Figure 7.5 for a two year Treasury note paying interest semiannually, the simple pricing formula assumes that each coupon payment is discounted at the same spot rate, $_0\left(\frac{y}{n}\right)_{365/n}$, where $n = 2$ and each basis period, t, is set equal to $365/2 = 182.5$ days. We know that this is inaccurate because

---

[11] Since 1985, any owner (whether a FI or an individual investor) can have the Treasury either strip or reassemble any Treasury bond or note issue using its component pieces, if the security is in book-entry (electronically recorded) format.

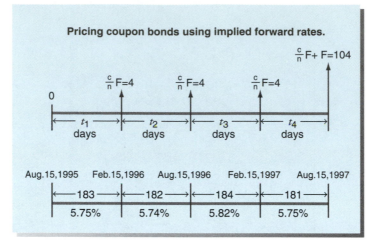

Figure 7.5

1.   The number of days in each basis period, t, is not equal to 182.5.   It equals 180 for corporate and municipal securities and varies between 181 and 184 for U.S. Treasury securities.

2.   The appropriate discount rate changes to reflect the changing yields that are expected to prevail in each semiannual period. That is, decomposition of the yield curve shows us that yields vary across maturity lengths and delivery dates.

Using Figure 7.5, we find that the two year semiannual coupon bond price equals

The first coupon payment, cF/n, discounted at the zero coupon simple interest yield $_0i_{t_1}$ for a period of t_1 days.

+ The second coupon payment, cF/n discounted at the zero coupon simple interest yield $_0i_{t_1+t_2}$ for a period of $t_1 + t_2$ days.

+ The third coupon payment, cF/n discounted at the zero coupon simple interest yield $_0i_{t_1+t_2+t_3}$ for a period of $t_1 + t_2 + t_3$ days.

+ The fourth coupon payment, cF/n, discounted at the zero coupon simple interest yield $_0i_{t_1+t_2+t_3+t_4}$ for a period of $t_1 + t_2 + t_3 + t_4$ days.

+ The principal payment, F, discounted at the zero coupon simple interest yield $_0i_{t_1+t_2+t_3+t_4}$ for a period of $t_1 + t_2 + t_3 + t_4$ days.

This can be written as

$$P = \frac{cF/n}{1 + \dfrac{_0i_{t_1}(t_1)}{365}} + \frac{cF/n}{1 + \dfrac{_0i_{t_1+t_2}(t_1 + t_2)}{365}} + \frac{cF/n}{1 + \dfrac{_0i_{t_1+t_2+t_3}(t_1 + t_2 + t_3)}{365}}$$

$$+ \frac{cF/n}{\dfrac{_0i_{t_1+t_2+t_3+t_4}(t_1 + t_2 + t_3 + t_4)}{365}} + \frac{F}{\dfrac{_0i_{t_1+t_2+t_3+t_4}(t_1 + t_2 + t_3 + t_4)}{365}} \qquad (7.2)$$

But the implied forward rate is defined as $_{t_1}i_{t_2}$, such that

$$\frac{1}{1 + \dfrac{_0i_{t_1+t_2}(t_1 + t_2)}{365}} = \left[\frac{1}{1 + \dfrac{_0i_{t_1}(t_1)}{365}}\right]\left[\frac{1}{1 + \dfrac{_{t_1}i_{t_2}(t_2)}{365}}\right] \tag{7.3}$$

Substituting equation (7.3) into equation (7.2) yields

$$P = \frac{cF/n}{1 + \dfrac{_0i_{t_1}(t_1)}{365}} + \frac{cF/n}{\left[1 + \dfrac{_0i_{t_1}(t_1)}{365}\right]\left[1 + \dfrac{_{t_1}i_{t_2}(t_2)}{365}\right]}$$

$$+ \frac{cF/n}{\left[1 + \dfrac{_0i_{t_1}(t_1)}{365}\right]\left[1 + \dfrac{_{t_1}i_{t_2}(t_2)}{365}\right]\left[1 + \dfrac{_{t_2}i_{t_3}(t_3)}{365}\right]}$$

$$\tag{7.4}$$

$$+ \frac{cF/n}{\left[1 + \dfrac{_0i_{t_1}(t_1)}{365}\right]\left[1 + \dfrac{_{t_1}i_{t_2}(t_2)}{365}\right]\left[1 + \dfrac{_{t_2}i_{t_3}(t_3)}{365}\right]\left[1 + \dfrac{_{t_3}i_{t_4}(t_4)}{365}\right]}$$

$$+ \frac{F}{\left[1 + \dfrac{_0i_{t_1}(t_1)}{365}\right]\left[1 + \dfrac{_{t_1}i_{t_2}(t_2)}{365}\right]\left[1 + \dfrac{_{t_2}i_{t_3}(t_3)}{365}\right]\left[1 + \dfrac{_{t_3}i_{t_4}(t_4)}{365}\right]}$$

Equation (7.4) shows that the simple interest yield to maturity on a coupon bearing instrument is the average of a series of implied forward rates obtained by decomposing the spot yield curve.

Let's use equation (7.4) to price a two year Treasury note paying an 8% p.a. semiannual coupon newly issued on August 15, 1995 if the spot yield curve is as follows:

Treasury STRIP Spot Yields as of August 15, 1995

Maturity Date	Days to Maturity	Simple Interest Yield, i
February 15, 1996	183	5.75% p.a.
August 15, 1996	365	5.83
February 15, 1997	549	5.94
August 15, 1997	730	6.02

Based on equation (7.2), the price, per $100 face value, of the two year 8% coupon Treasury note (with coupons received on February 15 and August 15 of each year until maturity) is

$$P = \frac{4}{1 + \dfrac{.0575(183)}{365}} + \frac{4}{1 + \dfrac{.0583(365)}{365}} + \frac{4}{1 + \dfrac{.0594(549)}{365}} + \frac{104}{1 + \dfrac{.0602(730)}{365}} = 104.163$$

Priced at $104.163 per $100 face value, this note yields a simple interest yield to maturity, y, of 5.766% p.a. The note's price and yield can also be expressed as the geometric mean of implied forward rates. Solving for implied forward rates as of August 15, 1995:

Treasury STRIP Implied Forward Yields as of August 15, 1995

Maturity Date	Days Until Delivery Date	Days to Maturity	Implied Forward Yield
February 15, 1996	0	183	5.75
August 15, 1996	183	182	5.74
February 15, 1997	365	184	5.82[a]
August 15, 1997	549	181	5.75

[a] To illustrate the calculations shown in this column, the implied forward rate for the 184 day STRIP to be delivered in one year (365 days), denoted $_{365}i_{184}$, is computed as follows:

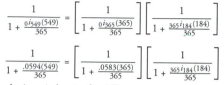

$$\cfrac{1}{1 + \frac{_0i_{549}(549)}{365}} = \left[\cfrac{1}{1 + \frac{_0i_{365}(365)}{365}}\right]\left[\cfrac{1}{1 + \frac{_{365}i_{184}(184)}{365}}\right]$$

$$\cfrac{1}{1 + \frac{.0594(549)}{365}} = \left[\cfrac{1}{1 + \frac{.0583(365)}{365}}\right]\left[\cfrac{1}{1 + \frac{_{365}i_{184}(184)}{365}}\right]$$

Since the number of days in the basis period varies for different coupon payment periods, the implied forward rates do not increase over time despite the rising spot yield curve.

Using the implied forward rates and equation (7.4), we can price the two year Treasury note as follows:

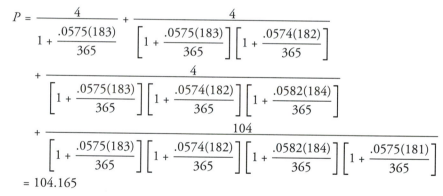

$$P = \cfrac{4}{1 + \frac{.0575(183)}{365}} + \cfrac{4}{\left[1 + \frac{.0575(183)}{365}\right]\left[1 + \frac{.0574(182)}{365}\right]}$$

$$+ \cfrac{4}{\left[1 + \frac{.0575(183)}{365}\right]\left[1 + \frac{.0574(182)}{365}\right]\left[1 + \frac{.0582(184)}{365}\right]}$$

$$+ \cfrac{104}{\left[1 + \frac{.0575(183)}{365}\right]\left[1 + \frac{.0574(182)}{365}\right]\left[1 + \frac{.0582(184)}{365}\right]\left[1 + \frac{.0575(181)}{365}\right]}$$

$$= 104.165$$

which is the same, except for rounding differences, as the answer we obtained using the series of spot rates in equation (7.2). This should come as no surprise, since the implied forward rates were derived from the spot rates.

Liquidity Preference   The implied forward rate is a good estimate of the expected future spot rate if and only if the expectations hypothesis holds.[12] For example, the expectations hypothesis holds if investors are indifferent between buying and holding the 176 day Treasury bill versus buying the 85 day Treasury bill and subsequently investing in the 91 day bill with a guaranteed rate of 6.14%. Even with a guarantee that interest rates will not change over the next 85 days, investors may prefer the second alternative (the 85 day and 91 day bills) to the first (the 176 day bill) if they have any uncertainty about their holding period. It is true that if the holding period is kept constant at 176 days, then the investment period yield is identical

---

[12] To be precise, the implied forward rate is an exact measure of expected future spot rates only if the *unbiased expectations* hypothesis holds. Cox, Ingersoll, and Ross (1981) show that this is not the case and that only the *local expectations hypothesis* holds in equilibrium, suggesting that returns are equalized only over short term spot investment horizons. Although some empirical studies reject the strict validity of the expectations hypothesis (see Jones and Roley 1983 and Mankiw and Miron 1986), Hardouvelis (1988) and Fama (1984) find evidence of some predictive power in forward rates.

for both alternatives. However, the investor faces the risk that the investment period itself may change. For instance, the investor may be forced to liquidate prematurely, say, 10 days after the initiation of the investment. Under the 176 day buy and hold investment, this would require the sale of a 166 day bill. Under the rollover strategy, this early liquidation would require the sale of a 75 day bill. The longer maturity 166 day bill has greater price volatility than does the shorter maturity 75 day bill.[13] This would lead the investor to prefer the shorter maturity bills so as to minimize price risk upon early liquidation.

liquidity preference: other things being equal, investors' preference of securities with shorter maturities.

term premium: the extra yield necessary to compensate investors for greater price risk upon liquidation.

This **liquidity preference** implies that longer maturity investments must offer a **term premium** to compensate investors for greater price risk upon liquidation. If investors prefer shorter term to longer term securities, then they exhibit liquidity preference. To induce investors to bear the price risk associated with longer term securities, they must receive an additional yield, called a term premium, that is added to the risk free rate. The existence of a positive term premium does not mean that yield curves will always be upward sloping; it just means that forward yield curves will shift upward by the amount of the term premium. This suggests that the implied forward rate is an overestimate of expected future spot rates. It is upwardly biased by the unidentified term premium. The term premium must be deducted from the implied forward rate before it can be utilized as a forecast of future interest rates. Unfortunately, the term premium is not constant over time. That makes it difficult to deduct from the implied forward rate since, as a general rule, the size of the term premium is unknown.[14]

Market Segmentation   You may have noticed the flat section of the yield curve in Figure 7.2 around the five to seven year maturity range; this may be explained by market segmentation. Certain maturity ranges are in great demand, either for regulatory reasons (restrictions on permissible maturity ranges) or for hedging purposes. The five to seven year maturity security is particularly useful in constructing hedges that match the maturity of a portfolio of mortgage-backed securities. The extraordinary demand for these maturities explains why investors are willing to accept lower relative yields than are obtainable on either four year or eight year maturities. This **market segmentation** introduces discontinuities into securities prices that cause yields to be unequal across all holding periods, thus violating the conditions of the expectations hypothesis. The use of the implied forward rate will be an inaccurate measure of expected future spot rates if market segmentation is distorting demand or supply of a particular maturity issue.

market segmentation: discontinuities in securities prices that cause yields to be unequal across all holding periods.

➤ Inflation/Deflation and Interest Rate Determination

In Chapter 4, we discussed how the supply and demand for money together determine the equilibrium level of interest rates. The tradeoff between the opportunity cost of holding liquid assets in the form of money on the one hand and the benefits of liquidity (in terms of transactions and speculative returns) on the other hand determines the real interest rate, or the time value of money. However, all of our calculations as well as quotations are in the form of nominal rates, which are stated in terms of the currency's current purchasing power.

The theory that relates nominal and real interest rates dates back to the Fisherian relationship, named for the monetary economist Irving Fisher. Simply stated, it is

---

[13] We will demonstrate this assertion at the end of this chapter using the concept of duration.

[14] If we assume that there are no arbitrage opportunities in the cash and futures U.S. Treasury bill market, then an estimate of the term structure can be obtained. Allen and Thurston (1988) use this methodology to derive estimates of term premiums that vary from an average of 4 basis points for 7 day maturities to 34 basis points for 90 day maturities.

$$(1 + r) = (1 + R)(1 + \pi) = 1 + R + \pi + R\pi$$

where r is the nominal rate, R is the real rate, and π is the expected rate of price inflation.[15] Thus, an anticipated rate of inflation of 5% p.a. will transform a real interest rate of 3% into a nominal rate of 8.15%. Either simple interest or compound interest rates can be transformed from nominal to real terms and vice versa. The nominal (real) simple interest yield on a zero coupon instrument would be denoted i (I). The nominal (real) simple interest yield on a coupon instrument would be denoted y (Y). Since the value of the last term, $R\pi$, is very small (unless the economy is suffering from very high rates of inflation), it is typically ignored, so that the nominal interest rate is equal to the sum of the real rate of interest plus the expected rate of inflation.

The nominal rate, r, is readily observable using market price quotations. A price index is used to measure the inflation rate, π. That leaves an unobservable last term, R, the real rate of interest. What is the real rate of interest? The real rate of interest, R, is a measure of the time value of money. It is a commonly stated rule of thumb that the real rate of interest is around 3% p.a., but studies show that this is not the case. Over the long run, the real rate of interest since the end of World War I has averaged around zero.[16] This should not be puzzling, for short term Treasury bills can be viewed as highly liquid "near money." Since money carries a zero real rate of return, it is not that surprising that close money substitutes, such as Treasury bills, do as well.

Over the short run, real interest rates demonstrate significant volatility over time. For example, during deflationary periods, such as the Great Depression when the Consumer Price Index in the United States fell by nearly 25%, the nominal rate fell as low as it could go—to zero, because if nominal rates were below zero, people would simply stash their savings in their mattresses. Applying the Fisherian equation under these circumstances implies a real rate of interest of +25% p.a. There have also been periods of time when real interest rates have been negative, particularly during periods of rapid economic growth when increases in nominal rates lag behind increases in prices.

Checkpoint

✓

1. If the expectations hypothesis holds, what can be deduced from the observation of a downward-sloping yield curve? an upward-sloping yield curve? a flat yield curve?

2. If investors display liquidity preference, what will be the shape of the yield curve if the market expects interest rates to remain unchanged at the same current level for all maturities?

3. How does the market segmentation hypothesis contradict the expectations hypothesis? the liquidity hypothesis?

➤ The Impact of Interest Rate Fluctuations on Security Prices

Measurement of interest rate levels is critical for the valuation of *all* financial securities: fixed income, equity, or derivatives. Each security's cash flows are discounted at some time value

---

[15] By specifying expected inflation rates, we use the ex ante, or anticipatory, version of the Fisherian relationship. An ex post version would utilize actual inflation rates. Fama in his classic 1975 study finds evidence of an ex post Fisher effect. However, Mishkin (1990) finds this evidence for longer maturities (9 to 12 months), but not for shorter maturities. Moreover, Barsky (1987) finds evidence of an ex post Fisher effect in the period since the beginning of the 1960s but not before. Chan (1994) finds evidence of a significant inflation risk premium in 3 month, 6 month, and 12 month interest rates during the 1959–1989 period, but observes it to be small in average size.

[16] See Ibbotson Associates (1992), p. 29, Exhibit 9, and also Ariel and Pohlman (1994).

of money to determine the security's present value price. When interest rates fluctuate, then security values are affected. In this section, we describe two concepts used to measure the impact of interest rate fluctuations on security prices: duration and convexity.

Duration

Whatever model we use to forecast future interest rates (for instance, the expectations hypothesis or liquidity preference models), we can be sure of one thing: unexpected interest rate movements. When interest rates move, all security prices are affected. Interest rate risk exposure, the impact of unanticipated changes in interest rates on securities prices, is measured by the security's price volatility. Earlier in this chapter, we measured a security's price risk using "time to maturity." The longer the time to maturity, the greater the security's price volatility. Although time to maturity is good as a rule of thumb, it is not a sufficiently accurate measure of price volatility. Imagine two securities with 10 years until maturity. One is a zero coupon bond selling at a deep discount, and the other is a 100% amortizing mortgage-backed security paying interest and principal monthly. Both have the same time to maturity. But do they have the same price volatility? The answer is no. The mortgage-backed securities are less subject to price volatility than the zero coupon bond, other things being equal.

Time to maturity neglects the impact of the timing of cash flows on the security's valuation. The mortgage-backed securities *self-liquidate* a little each month since interest and some principal are due. The zero coupon bond, however, has no interim cash flows to cushion the impact of interest rate fluctuations on its price. Thus, interest rate fluctuations cause the zero coupon bond prices to fluctuate more than the prices of the mortgage-backed securities.

To illustrate, let's suppose that the 10 year zero coupon bond is priced at $55 per $100 face value. The annual simple interest yield is 6.16% p.a. ($55 = $\frac{\$100}{1.0616^{10}}$). The mortgage-backed securities are priced at $55 per $100 face value and yield the same simple interest yield of 6.16% p.a., but they offer monthly payments of $0.615 per $100 face value:

$$\$55 = \sum_{s=1}^{120} \frac{\$0.615}{\left(1 + \frac{.0616}{12}\right)^s}$$

Assume that all interest yields increase by 20 basis points (.20%) to 6.36%. The mortgage-backed securities price falls to

$$P = \sum_{s=1}^{120} \frac{\$0.615}{\left(1 + \frac{.0636}{12}\right)^s} = \$54.50$$

The zero coupon bond's price falls to

$$P = \frac{\$100}{1.0636^{10}} = \$53.98$$

The percentage rate of price decline on the mortgage-backed securities is $\Delta P/P$ = (54.50 − 55)/55 = −.909%, whereas the percentage rate of price decline on the zero coupon bond is $\Delta P/P$ = (53.98 − 55)/55 = −1.85%. The price volatility of the zero coupon bond is more than twice that of the mortgage-backed securities, although both securities have the same time to maturity of 10 years.

We need a measure that is more precise than the time until maturity to serve as an indicator of a security's price volatility. One measure, named after a mathematician who worked for

Macaulay duration: the factor of proportionality that relates a given change in interest rates to an induced security price change.

the insurance industry, is the **Macaulay duration**—the factor of proportionality that relates a given change in interest rates to an induced security price change. That is

$$\frac{\Delta P}{P} \approx -D\frac{\Delta y}{1+y} \tag{7.5}$$

where $\Delta P \equiv$ the change in price and $P \equiv$ the original price, so that $\frac{\Delta P}{P}$ is the percentage change in price; $y \equiv$ the original interest yield; and $\Delta y \equiv$ the change in interest rates, so that $\frac{\Delta y}{1+y}$ is the percentage change in interest rates; and $D \equiv$ duration such that

$$D = \frac{\displaystyle\sum_{s=1}^{T} \frac{c_s s}{(1+y)^s}}{\displaystyle\sum_{s=1}^{T} \frac{c_s}{(1+y)^s}}$$

where $c_s \equiv$ the cash flow received in period s; and $T \equiv$ the number of periods until maturity. This formula is simply the first derivative of the security price with respect to yield, or, in discrete terms $\Delta P/\Delta y$, which measures the sensitivity of security prices to interest rate fluctuations.

Duration is measured in time periods, although we will see that duration can be either positive or negative. It can be interpreted as the length of time required to recoup the present value (denoted PV) of all future cash flows. Since zero coupon instruments have no interim cash flows, the investor must wait until maturity until any cash flows are received and the pure discount bond's duration always equals the time to maturity. The duration of coupon bearing bonds is always less than the time to maturity. Thus, duration is always less than or equal to the time until maturity.

The length of a bond's duration is shorter:

1. The higher the coupon payments.

2. The shorter the time to maturity.

3. The higher the yield, y.

The Inverse Relationship Between Duration and the Coupon Payment   To illustrate the first feature of duration, let's consider three different five year bonds, each yielding 7% p.a.: (a) a zero coupon bond; (b) a 3% annual coupon nonamortizing bond; and (c) a 10% annual coupon nonamortizing bond. The duration of the zero coupon bond is equal to the time to maturity, five years. The duration of the 3% coupon bond (per $100 face value) is

s	c_s	$PV(c_s)$ @ 7%	col. (1) × (3)
(1)	(2)	(3)	(4)
1	3	$\frac{3}{1.07} = 2.804$	2.804
2	3	$\frac{3}{1.07^2} = 2.62$	5.24
3	3	$\frac{3}{1.07^3} = 2.449$	7.347
4	3	$\frac{3}{1.07^4} = 2.289$	9.156
5	103	$\frac{103}{1.07^5} = 73.438$	367.19
Total		83.60	391.737
Duration =			$\frac{391.737}{83.60} = 4.686$ years

The duration of the 10% coupon bond (per $100 face value) is

s (1)	c_s (2)	$PV(c_s)$ @ 7% (3)	col. (1) × (3) (4)
1	10	$\frac{10}{1.07}$ = 9.346	9.346
2	10	$\frac{10}{1.07^2}$ = 8.734	17.468
3	10	$\frac{10}{1.07^3}$ = 8.163	24.489
4	10	$\frac{10}{1.07^4}$ = 7.629	30.516
5	110	$\frac{110}{1.07^5}$ = 78.428	392.14
Total		112.30	473.959
Duration =			$\frac{473.959}{112.30}$ = 4.22 years

The duration of the zero coupon bond is five years; the 3% coupon bond's duration is 4.686 years; and the 10% coupon bond's duration is 4.22 years. Thus, the higher the coupon, the shorter the bond's duration.

The Direct Relationship Between Time to Maturity and Duration   Consider two 5% p.a. coupon (paid semiannually) par value bonds, one with 2 years until maturity and the other with 20 years until maturity. Since duration measures the timing of cash flows, each coupon payment must be evaluated as it occurs. In this case, since coupons are received semiannually, the two year note has four payments as follows

s (1)	c_s (2)	$PV(c_s)$ @ 5% p.a. (3)	col. (1) × (3) (4)
1	2.5	$\frac{2.5}{1.025}$ = 2.439	2.439
2	2.5	$\frac{2.5}{1.025^2}$ = 2.38	4.759
3	2.5	$\frac{2.5}{1.025^3}$ = 2.321	6.964
4	102.5	$\frac{102.5}{1.025^4}$ = 92.86	371.44
Total		100	385.60
Duration =			$\frac{385.6}{100}$ = 3.856 half years = $\frac{3.856}{2}$ = 1.928 years[a]

[a] For discussion of duration with semiannual (or more frequent) compounding, see *Calculation Complications 7.4.*

The par value 20 year 5% p.a. semiannual coupon bond has a duration of 12.865 years. Although the longer the time to maturity, the longer the duration, the relationship is not linear. A linear relationship would imply that the 20 year bond had a duration that is ten times longer than the two year bond, that is, 1.928 years. Since the 20 year bond's duration is only 12.865 years, this suggests that duration increases with time to maturity *at a decreasing rate.*

The Inverse Relationship Between Duration and Yield   Let's consider two different five year 6% p.a. annual coupon bonds, one yielding 4% p.a. and the other 9% p.a. The duration of the 4% yield bond (per $100 face value) is

s	c_s	$PV(c_s)$ @ 4%	col. (1) × (3)
(1)	(2)	(3)	(4)
1	6	$\frac{6}{1.04}$ = 5.769	5.769
2	6	$\frac{6}{1.04^2}$ = 5.547	11.095
3	6	$\frac{6}{1.04^3}$ = 5.334	16.002
4	6	$\frac{6}{1.04^4}$ = 5.129	20.515
5	106	$\frac{106}{1.04^5}$ = 87.124	435.621
Total		108.90	489.002
Duration =			$\frac{489.002}{108.90}$ = 4.49 years

The duration of the 9% yield bond (per $100 face value) is

s	c_s	$PV(c_s)$ @ 9%	col. (1) × (3)
(1)	(2)	(3)	(4)
1	6	$\frac{6}{1.09}$ = 5.505	5.505
2	6	$\frac{6}{1.09^2}$ = 5.05	10.10
3	6	$\frac{6}{1.09^3}$ = 4.633	13.899
4	6	$\frac{6}{1.09^4}$ = 4.251	17.002
5	106	$\frac{106}{1.09^5}$ = 68.893	344.464
Total		88.331	390.97
Duration =			$\frac{390.97}{88.331}$ = 4.43 years

The duration of the 4% yielding bond's duration is 4.49 years; the 9% yielding bond's duration is 4.43 years. Thus, the higher the yield, the shorter the duration. In *Calculation Complications 7.4, 7.5, 7.6, 7.7,* and *7.8,* we examine special problems encountered when computing duration.

CALCULATION COMPLICATIONS 7.4

INTRAYEAR COMPOUNDING

In our examples, we have used securities with annual coupons. However, our duration (and convexity) formulas can handle semiannual, quarterly, monthly, or whatever frequency of payments. We simply use per-period yields in the discount factor, y/n where y is the annualized yield and n is the frequency of payment per year. Thus, we can generalize the duration expression, equation (7.5) to accommodate the frequency of coupon payments so that

$$\frac{\Delta P}{P} \approx -D \frac{\Delta y}{1 + \frac{y}{n}}$$

where

$$D = \frac{\sum\limits_{s=1}^{T} \dfrac{c_s s}{\left(1 + \dfrac{y}{n}\right)^s}}{\sum\limits_{s=1}^{T} \dfrac{c_s}{\left(1 + \dfrac{y}{n}\right)^s}}$$

Solving for D yields the duration in terms of number of periods. To express duration in years, simply divide by n, which is the number of periods in each year.[17]

As an example, consider a two year 6% p.a. semiannual coupon note yielding 7% p.a., calculating duration as follows:

s half yrs. (1)	c_s (2)	$PV(c_s)$ @ 3.5% per half year (3)	col. (1) $\times$ (3)
1	30	$\frac{30}{1.035}$ = 28.98551	28.98551
2	30	$\frac{30}{1.035^2}$ = 28.00532	56.01064
3	30	$\frac{30}{1.035^3}$ = 27.05828	81.17484
4	1030	$\frac{1030}{1.035^4}$ = 897.5855	3590.342
Total	Price	981.6346	3756.513

$$\text{Duration} = \frac{3756.513}{981.6346} = 3.826794 \text{ half years}$$
$$\frac{3.826794}{2} = 1.91 \text{ years}$$

Duration is 3.827 semiannual periods, or, dividing by n = 2, 1.91 years.

CALCULATION COMPLICATIONS 7.5

DURATION OF FLOATING RATE INSTRUMENTS

The duration of floating rate instruments is relevant given the issuance of securities such as adjustable rate mortgages and other floating rate notes. Floating rate instruments are debt securities with coupon payments that are not fixed, but instead fluctuate according to some predetermined formula indexed to some market rate of interest, for example, LIBOR (the London InterBank Offered Rate). The coupon rate and the time to maturity define the cash flows for a fixed income security. For floating rate securities, the cash flows are determined by the indexed rate of interest, the spread above (or below) that market rate, and the time until the next repricing date of the instrument. For example, suppose your 15 year home equity loan is repriced quarterly. On the last day of each quarter, your loan rate is adjusted according to a predetermined index formulation. If your 15 year home equity loan is indexed to, say, the 91 day U.S. Treasury bill rate plus 2.75%, then on each quarter-end date your loan rate is adjusted to reflect the day's Treasury bill rate plus 2.75%. If on that day the 91 day U.S. Treasury bill is

---

[17] Similarly, to annualize convexity, simply divide the per-period convexity value by n^2.

priced at a discount of \$97.5 per \$100 face value, then the simple interest yield is

$$i = \frac{100 - 97.5}{97.5} \left(\frac{365}{91} \right) = 10.285\%$$

Your annualized loan rate for the next 91 days would be 10.285% + 2.75% = 13.035%.

At repricing, the home equity loan is revalued since future interest payments are adjusted to reflect shifts in market interest rates. Because it is updated on the repricing date to reflect spot interest rates, the loan is identical to similar newly created home equity loans. The FI is indifferent between either selling the loan or holding the loan and collecting the future stream of cash flows. We can think of a floating rate loan as a fixed income security where the next cash flow is received on the next repricing date. That cash flow consists of a lump sum comprising the regular interest payment (using the reset rate of 13.035% of face value), plus the current price of a similar newly created home equity loan. This is equivalent to a zero coupon instrument with a time to maturity equal to the time until the next repricing. Since the duration of a zero coupon instrument equals its time to maturity, the duration of the floating rate instrument equals its time until the next repricing date. Thus, in our example, the duration of your 15 year home equity loan is 91 days.

CALCULATION COMPLICATIONS 7.6

DURATION OF PREFERRED STOCK PERPETUITIES

Preferred stock pays a fixed amount into perpetuity. Since it pays a fixed amount of dividends, it is like a bond without any maturity date. The price of a share of preferred stock that pays an annual dividend equal to C is equal to C/r, where r is the annual interest rate. The duration of preferred stock with a fixed dividend rate is

$$D = \frac{\displaystyle\sum_{s=1}^{\infty} \frac{sC}{(1+y)^s}}{\displaystyle\sum_{s=1}^{\infty} \frac{C}{(1+y)^s}} = \frac{1+y}{y}$$

Thus, if current yields are 5% p.a., the duration of an issue of preferred stock is $\frac{1.05}{.05}$ = 21 years.

CALCULATION COMPLICATIONS 7.7

YIELD CURVES ARE NOT FLAT

You may have noticed that the discount factor used to calculate Macaulay duration is constant for all cash flows. For example, consider a 10 year bond with a 5% p.a.

annual coupon selling at a par value of $1,000. We calculate the Macaulay duration as follows.

s (1)	c_s (2)	$PV(c_s)$ @ 5% (3)	col. (1) × (3) (4)
1	50	$\frac{50}{1.05}$ = 47.619	47.619
2	50	$\frac{50}{1.05^2}$ = 45.351	90.703
3	50	$\frac{50}{1.05^3}$ = 43.192	129.576
4	50	$\frac{50}{1.05^4}$ = 41.135	164.54
5	50	$\frac{50}{1.05^5}$ = 39.176	195.882
6	50	$\frac{50}{1.05^6}$ = 37.311	223.865
7	50	$\frac{50}{1.05^7}$ = 35.534	248.738
8	50	$\frac{50}{1.05^8}$ = 33.842	270.736
9	50	$\frac{50}{1.05^9}$ = 32.23	290.074
10	1,050	$\frac{1050}{1.05^{10}}$ = 644.609	6446.089
Total		1000	8107.821

$$\text{Duration} = \frac{8107.821}{1000} = 8.108 \text{ years}$$

This means that each cash flow, whether paid in 1 year or 10 years, is discounted at the same rate—5% p.a. But this assumes that the yield curve is constant for all maturities at the 5% rate. We have expended a considerable amount of effort to analyze the shape of the yield curve, and we have seen that it need not be flat. We can incorporate other shapes of the yield curve in the computation of duration by using the appropriate forward rates as discount factors for each cash flow. Here is one possibility using the upward-sloping yield curve shown in Figure CC.2.

s (1)	c_s (2)	$PV(c_s)$ @ varying yields (3)	col. (1) × (3) (4)
1	50	$\frac{50}{1.01}$ = 49.505	49.505
2	50	$\frac{50}{1.015^2}$ = 48.533	97.066
3	50	$\frac{50}{1.02^3}$ = 47.116	141.348
4	50	$\frac{50}{1.025^4}$ = 45.298	181.19
5	50	$\frac{50}{1.03^5}$ = 43.13	215.652
6	50	$\frac{50}{1.035^6}$ = 40.675	244.05
7	50	$\frac{50}{1.04^7}$ = 37.996	265.971
8	50	$\frac{50}{1.045^8}$ = 35.159	281.274
9	50	$\frac{50}{1.045^9}$ = 33.645	302.807
10	1,050	$\frac{1050}{1.05425^{10}}$ = 619.089	6190.892
Total		1000	7969.756

$$\text{Duration} = \frac{7969.756}{1000} = 7.97 \text{ years}$$

The bond is still selling at par with a yield to maturity of 5% p.a. However, each cash flow is discounted at the rate expected to prevail on the date that the cash flow is received. That is, the fifth $50 coupon payment is discounted at the five year forward rate of 3% p.a., whereas the ninth coupon payment is discounted at 4.5% p.a. The

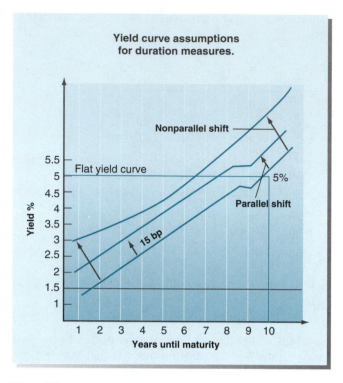

Figure CC.2

result is a lower value of duration (7.97 years as opposed to 8.108 years for Macaulay duration).

Why is it important to use a measure of duration that reflects the actual shape of the yield curve? To correctly gauge the impact of interest rate fluctuations on bond prices, the duration measure must reflect the actual reinvestment rates received at each point in time. Suppose that *all* interest rates increase by 15 basis points. This is shown as a parallel shift upward in the yield curve shown in Figure CC.2. If we use the Macaulay duration measure assuming a flat yield curve, we obtain

$$\Delta P \approx -8.108(\$1,000) \left(\frac{.0015}{1.05} \right) = -\$11.58$$

But if the correct yield curve is used to calculate duration, then the estimate of the price impact of the 15 basis point rate increase is

$$\Delta P \approx -7.97(\$1,000) \left(\frac{.0015}{1.05} \right) = -\$11.39$$

This estimate of the price change is closer to the exact solution than the one obtained using Macaulay duration. Using the exact solution to compute the impact of a 15 basis point parallel shift in the yield curve, we find that the new price is $988.84 for a price decline of $11.16 from $1,000 par value. The Macaulay duration approximation performs quite poorly when the yield curve is not flat.

CALCULATION COMPLICATIONS 7.8

NONPARALLEL SHIFTS IN THE YIELD CURVE

Calculation Complications 7.7 shows that when we account for the slope of the yield curve when computing duration, we obtain a measure of price sensitivity that is different from the Macaulay duration measure. We used this revised duration to evaluate the impact of an interest rate change on bond prices. We illustrated this using the example of a 15 basis point interest rate increase. That is, we assumed that each rate along the yield curve increased by the same amount—15 basis points. (This is shown in Figure CC.2 as a parallel shift in the yield curve.) But what impact would a nonparallel shift in the yield curve have on prices?

All forward rates need not change by the same amount. Expectations may cause a pivoting of the yield curve that adjusts its slope, instead of simply a parallel shifting in the yield curve. Figure CC.2 also illustrates such a nonparallel shift. Empirical evidence suggests that rates are most volatile at the very short and very long maturity extremes of the yield curve.[18] Therefore, in the figure, we assume that one year and two year forward rates each increase 100 basis points, while nine and ten year rates increase 50 and 7.5 basis points, respectively. The impact of this nonparallel shift in the yield curve is shown in the following table as a price decline of $9.00 for a new price of $991.

s (1)	c_s (2)	$PV(c_s)$ @ varying yields (3)
1	50	$\frac{50}{1.02} = 49.02$
2	50	$\frac{50}{1.025^2} = 47.591$
3	50	$\frac{50}{1.0215^3} = 46.909$
4	50	$\frac{50}{1.0265^4} = 45.033$
5	50	$\frac{50}{1.0315^5} = 42.818$
6	50	$\frac{50}{1.0365^6} = 40.323$
7	50	$\frac{50}{1.0415^7} = 37.614$
8	50	$\frac{50}{1.0465^8} = 34.758$
9	50	$\frac{50}{1.05^9} = 32.23$
10	1,050	$\frac{1050}{1.055^{10}} = 614.702$
Total Price		990.998

Clearly, this is only one interest rate scenario. Consideration of nonparallel shifts in the yield curve requires estimation of the price impact under numerous interest rate scenarios. Assuming only parallel shift in the yield curve greatly simplifies the analysis.

---

[18] For U.S. Treasury securities over the period December 1987–July 1992, weekly rate changes were decomposed into parallel shifts versus slope shifts. For 90 day maturities, parallel shifts explained 36% of the variation, while slope shifts explained an additional 15% of the weekly fluctuation in forward rates. For half year maturities, the figures were 64% and 9%, respectively. For one year, two year, and five year maturities, parallel shifts accounted, respectively, for 75%, 85%, and 82% of the variation, but slope shifts only 9%, 3%, and 2%, respectively. For 10 year and 20 year maturities, 37% and 39% of the rate fluctuations could be attributed to parallel shifts, while 42% and 44% appear to be slope shifts. See Duffie (1995).

1. What is the relationship between duration and time to maturity? coupon yield? yield to maturity?
2. Why is duration a better measure of price volatility than time to maturity?
3. What is the duration of a zero coupon instrument?

Convexity: The Nonlinear Relationship Between Prices and Interest Rates

Duration is a measure of price volatility. The higher the security's duration, the greater the impact on price of any given interest rate change. How accurately does duration measure price fluctuations?

The duration measure of price volatility is stated as an approximation, as we saw in equation (7.5):

$$\frac{\Delta P}{P} \approx -D \frac{\Delta y}{1 + y} \tag{7.5}$$

Let's see why. Consider the above example of the five year 10% p.a. annual coupon bond yielding 7% p.a. The current price is $112.30 per $100 face value. We can use the bond valuation formula (from Table 7.1) to solve for the exact price change given a change in interest yields:

$$P = \sum_{s=1}^{T} \frac{\frac{c}{n}F}{\left(1 + \frac{y}{n}\right)^{s}} + \frac{F}{\left(1 + \frac{y}{n}\right)^{T}}$$

$$\$112.30 = \sum_{s=1}^{5} \frac{10}{1.07^{s}} + \frac{100}{1.07^{5}}$$

where $n = 1$ (annual coupons), $y = 7\%$ p.a. before any interest rate fluctuations, $c = 10\%$, and F is set at $100.

Let's examine the impact of a series of interest rate changes on this bond's price. The yield declines as low as 5% (for a $\Delta y = -2\%$) and increases as high as 9% (for a $\Delta y = +2\%$). In Table 7.3, columns (2) and (3), the duration formula, $-D\frac{\Delta y}{1+y}$, and the bond's duration of 4.22 years are used to solve for the percentage price change as well as the new price implied by a shift in the bond's yield. This is contrasted with the exact solution presented in columns (4) and (5). The last column presents the discrepancy between the exact solution and the duration measurement. What is striking is that the discrepancy is always positive. That is, the exact

Table 7.3

The Accuracy of the Duration Approximation of Price Volatility

Δy (%)	Duration Measurement		Exact Measurement		Discrepancy ($)
	ΔP (%)	Price/$100F	ΔP (%)	Price/$100F	
−2	+7.89	$121.1581	+8.32	$121.6474	$ .4893
−1.5	+5.92	$118.9435	+6.16	$119.2163	$ .2728
−1	+3.94	$116.729	+4.05	$116.8495	$ .1205
−0.5	+1.97	$114.5145	+2.00	$114.5449	$ .0304
−0.25	+0.99	$113.4073	+0.99	$113.4153	$ .008
0	0	$112.30	0	$112.30	0
+0.25	−0.99	$111.1927	−0.89	$111.2995	$ .1068
+0.5	−1.97	$110.0855	−1.95	$110.1147	$ .0292
+1	−3.94	$107.871	−3.84	$107.9854	$ .1144
+1.5	−5.92	$105.6565	−5.69	$105.911	$ .2545
+2	−7.89	$103.4419	−7.49	$103.8897	$ .4478

price is always above the duration-approximated price. Table 7.3 also demonstrates that as the yield shift gets larger, the duration approximation gets less and less accurate as an estimate of the impact on the security's price.

This is because duration is a pessimistic approximation: it overestimates price declines and underestimates price increases. Duration approximation errors result from the assumed linear relationship between price changes and interest rate fluctuations. As shown in Figure 7.6, the graph of the duration formula is a downward-sloping straight line with a negative slope equal to the security's duration measure.

The exact valuation expression is not linear but is instead a polynomial of degree T. This curvature in the nonlinear price–yield relationship around some interest rate level is measured by **convexity**. The bond's convexity can be seen in Table 7.3. Using the exact valuations, if we find that interest yields decline 2% to 5%, then the bond's price increases by \$9.3474 per \$100 face value. However, if interest yields increase 2% to 9%, then the bond's price decreases by only \$8.4103 per \$100 face value. The price increases and decreases estimated by the duration approximation are the same at \$8.8581 per \$100 face value. By neglecting the convexity of the valuation expression, the duration approximation overstates price declines and understates price increases. Figure 7.6 shows the pessimism of the duration approximation for selected values from Table 7.3. To improve the accuracy of the duration approximation, we must measure convexity.

convexity: the degree of curvature of the price–yield relationship around some interest rate level.

Checkpoint

✓

1. What is the duration of a floating rate instrument?
2. How do you calculate the duration of equity?
3. What does the Macaulay duration measure assume about the yield curve?
4. Why is the duration measure only an approximation of the relationship between prices and yields?
5. Describe the estimation errors obtained when using Macaulay duration to approximate price volatility.

Measuring Convexity   Figure 7.6 shows that duration is the slope of the straight-line tangent to the price–yield valuation function. The security's price sensitivity to small yield changes is measured by the slope of a tangent line, which is equal to the first derivative of the function, denoted $\frac{dP}{dy}$.[19] Convexity measures the *rate* at which prices change in response to small yield changes, or the rate at which the slope of the price–yield function changes as yields shift. This rate of change is measured by the second derivative of the valuation function, denoted $\frac{d^2P}{dy^2}$. Differentiating the valuation function

$$P = \sum_{s=1}^{T} \frac{\frac{c}{n}F}{\left(1+\frac{y}{n}\right)^s} + \frac{F}{\left(1+\frac{y}{n}\right)^T}$$

results in

$$\frac{dP}{dy} = -\frac{\sum_{s=1}^{T} \frac{\frac{sc}{n}F}{\left(1+\frac{y}{n}\right)^s} + \frac{TF}{\left(1+\frac{y}{n}\right)^T}}{1+\frac{y}{n}} \tag{7.6}$$

[19] Duration is the first derivative of the price–yield relationship, or $\frac{\Delta P}{\Delta y}$ in discrete terms; convexity is the second derivative, or the rate of change in the price–yield relationship, which is $\frac{\Delta\left(\frac{\Delta P}{\Delta y}\right)}{\Delta y}$ in discrete terms.

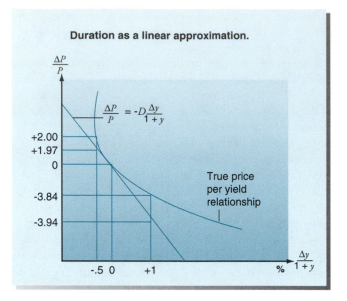

Figure 7.6

which is simply the numerator of Macaulay duration multiplied by -1. Equation (7.6) can be rewritten as

$$\frac{dp}{dy} = -DP \text{ or } D = -\frac{dP}{dy}\frac{1}{P}$$

which illustrates that duration is simply a price-adjusted first derivative of the security price with respect to yields. Taking the derivative of equation (7.6), we can approximate the curvature, or convexity, of the valuation function:

$$\frac{d^2P}{dy^2} = \frac{\displaystyle\sum_{s=1}^{T} \frac{s(s+1)\frac{c}{n}F}{\left(1+\frac{y}{n}\right)^s} + \frac{T(T+1)F}{\left(1+\frac{y}{n}\right)^T}}{\left(1+\frac{y}{n}\right)^2}$$

The measure of convexity is

$$CV = \left(\frac{1}{\left(1+\frac{y}{n}\right)^2 P}\right)\left(\sum_{s=1}^{T} \frac{s(s+1)\frac{c}{n}F}{\left(1+\frac{y}{n}\right)^s} + \frac{T(T+1)F}{\left(1+\frac{y}{n}\right)^T}\right) \qquad (7.7)$$

Convexity can be utilized to improve the accuracy of measurement of price fluctuations in equation (7.5) as follows:[20]

$$\frac{\Delta P}{P} \approx -D\frac{\Delta y}{1+\frac{y}{n}} + .5CV(\Delta y)^2 \qquad (7.8)$$

modified duration:
Macaulay duration divided by 1 plus the interest rate; that is $D^* \equiv D/\left(1+\frac{y}{n}\right)$.

This formula can be restated in simpler terms by defining **modified duration** as Macaulay duration divided by 1 plus the interest rate—that is, $D^* \equiv D/\left(1+\frac{y}{n}\right)$, where D^*, D are

---

[20] The convexity-adjusted price equation (7.8) is still an approximation, although it is a more accurate approximation than the duration-adjusted price equation (7.5). Equation (7.8) is a Taylor series expansion using the first and second derivatives (duration and convexity, respectively).

modified and Macaulay duration, respectively. Then the convexity-adjusted approximation of price fluctuations is

$$\frac{\Delta P}{P} \approx -D^*(\Delta y) + .5CV(\Delta y)^2$$

Calculate the convexity of the five year 10% p.a. annual coupon bond yielding 7%

$$CV = \left(\frac{1}{(1.07)^2 112.30}\right)\left(\sum_{s=1}^{5} \frac{s(s+1)10}{(1+.07)^s} + \frac{5(5+1)100}{(1+.07)^5}\right)$$

using the following spreadsheet

s	c_s	$PV(c_s)$ @ 7%	$(s)(s+1)PV(c_s)$
(1)	(2)	(3)	(4)
1	10	$\frac{10}{1.07^1}$ = 9.346	18.692
2	10	$\frac{10}{1.07^2}$ = 8.734	52.406
3	10	$\frac{10}{1.07^3}$ = 8.163	97.956
4	10	$\frac{10}{1.07^4}$ = 7.629	152.579
5	110	$\frac{110}{1.07^5}$ = 78.428	2352.854
Total		112.30	2674.5
Convexity =		$\frac{2674.5}{(1.07)^2 112.30}$ = 20.8 years	

In Table 7.4 we use the convexity adjustment to price the five year 10% p.a. annual coupon bond yielding 7% in Table 7.3. For example, if rates fall by 1.5%, equation (7.8) can be solved:

$$\frac{\Delta P}{112.30} \approx -\frac{4.22}{1.07}(-.015) + .5(20.8)(-.015)^2$$

$$\Delta P \approx \$6.9063$$

This estimate of the price fluctuation resulting from a 1.5% deline in interest rates is closer to the exact price change of $6.9163 than is the duration estimation that underestimates the price increase to be $6.6435.

The properties of convexity can be described just as we described those of duration. Convexity increases as

1. *Maturity increases.* The 10 year 5% p.a. annual coupon bond priced at a par value of $1,000 has a convexity of 37.5. A five year 5% p.a. annual coupon bond priced at a

Table 7.4

The Accuracy of the Duration Approximation of Price Volatility

	Duration Measurement		Convexity Measurement		Exact Measurement	
Δy (%)	ΔP (%)	Price/$100F	ΔP (%)	Price/$100F	ΔP (%)	Price/$100F
−2	+7.89	$121.1581	+8.31	$121.6321	+8.32	$121.6474
−1.5	+5.92	$118.9435	+6.15	$119.2063	+6.16	$119.2163
−1	+3.94	$116.729	+4.05	$116.8458	+4.05	$116.8495
−0.5	+1.97	$114.5145	+2.00	$114.5437	+2.00	$114.5449
−0.25	+0.99	$113.4073	+0.99	$113.4146	+0.99	$113.4153
0	0	$112.30	0	$112.30	0	$112.30
+0.25	−0.99	$111.1927	−0.89	$111.2000	− .89	$111.2005
+0.5	−1.97	$110.0855	−1.95	$110.1147	−1.95	$110.1147
+1	−3.94	$107.871	−3.84	$107.9878	−3.84	$107.9854
+1.5	−5.92	$105.6565	−5.69	$105.9193	−5.69	$105.911
+2	−7.89	$103.4419	−7.47	$103.9089	−7.49	$103.8897

par value of $1,000 has a convexity of 12, while a one year zero coupon bond yielding 5% has a convexity of only 0.91.

2. *Yields decrease.* Figure 7.6 shows that at relatively low rates, the price–yield relationship is steep, suggesting a relatively high duration. When rates start to increase (as we shift along the curved price–yield function), the duration declines rather rapidly. That is, the rate of change in the duration measure is large in the low-rate region. Since the rate of change of duration is the convexity, this states that at low rates, convexity tends to be high. In contrast, in the high rate region, the price–yield relationship is rather flat. That is, the slope (duration) does not change much as rates decline. This high rate region is the area of relatively low convexity. As an example, consider the 10 year 5% p.a. annual coupon bond priced at par with a convexity equal to 37.5. At lower yields, say 2% p.a., the convexity increases to 41.3. If the yield increases to 8% p.a., the convexity falls to 33.9 and, for a yield of 10% p.a., to 31.7.

3. *Coupon rates decrease, for a given yield and maturity.* The zero coupon bond has the highest convexity, since rate changes have a greater impact on prices, the lower the coupon payment. Using the 10 year 5% p.a. par value bond as comparison, we find that if the coupon rate is increased to 10% p.a., the convexity falls to 32, whereas if the coupon rate is decreased to 2.5% p.a., the convexity increases to 42.

4. *Coupon rates increase, for a given duration.* The 10 year 5% p.a. annual coupon par value bond has a duration of 8.108 years and convexity equal to 37.5. A zero coupon bond with a maturity of eight years has a duration of eight years but a convexity value of only 29.8.

Bond investors like convexity and are willing to pay a premium for bonds with higher levels of convexity. This is illustrated in Figure 7.7, which shows two bonds with the same durations and the same yields. If rates increase, the bond with greater convexity will experience a smaller price decline than the bond with less convexity. Alternatively, if rates decrease, the price of the

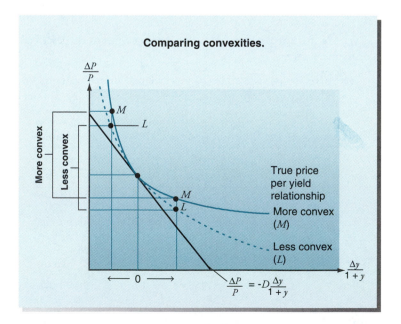

Figure 7.7

more convex bond will increase by more than the price of the less convex bond. It's a win–win situation!

Checkpoint

1. What does convexity measure?
2. How does the convexity approximation correct some of the estimation errors of the duration approximation?

Measuring the Interest Rate Risk of Portfolios of Financial Securities

Interest rate risk is a security's price volatility induced by changes in market yields. It is a basic tenet of finance that diversification reduces risk. By focusing only on individual securities, we are overestimating the interest rate risk exposure of a portfolio of financial securities. To correct this overestimation, we first consider the measurement of interest rate risk if all securities are on the same side of the balance sheet—that is, they are either all assets or all liabilities. Then we will consider the possibility that some securities are assets and some liabilities, thereby creating the possibility of risk reducing portfolio effects.

Interest Rate Risk Calculations for Portfolios of Either Assets OR Liabilities   As long as all securities are on the same side of the balance sheet (either all assets or all liabilities), interest rate risk can be measured using a weighted average of all securities' durations. That is, the duration of assets (liabilities) is D_A (D_L):

$$D_A = \sum_{i=1}^{N} \frac{MV_i}{MV_A} D_i$$

where there are a total of N assets (liabilities) in the portfolio with an aggregate value of MV_A (MV_L for liabilities). Each asset (liability) has a price equal to MV_i. Thus, each security's duration is weighted by the proportion of market value comprised by that security in the total portfolio.

Consider a portfolio consisting of two securities: (1) a one year zero coupon yielding 5% p.a. with a price of $1,000; and (2) a 10 year 5% p.a. annual coupon, priced at par at $1,000. We know that the duration of the zero is one year since it has no coupons. From *Calculation Complications 7.7* (the flat yield curve example), we know that the 10 year bond has a duration of 8.108 years. Using the weighted average of durations formula for this portfolio of assets valued at $2,000, we obtain

$$D_A = \frac{1000}{2000}(1) + \frac{1000}{2000}(8.108) = 4.55 \text{ years}$$

Contrast this portfolio with a $2,000 investment in a five year bond with a 5% p.a. annual coupon priced at a par value of $2,000. Computing duration, we obtain

s	c_s	$PV(c_s)$ @ 5%		col. (1) × (3)
(1)	(2)	(3)		(4)
1	50	$\frac{50}{1.05}$ =	47.619	47.619
2	50	$\frac{50}{1.05^2}$ =	45.351	90.703
3	50	$\frac{50}{1.05^3}$ =	43.192	129.576
4	50	$\frac{50}{1.05^4}$ =	41.135	164.54
5	1050	$\frac{1050}{1.05^5}$ =	822.703	4113.512
Total			1000	4545.951
Duration =				$\frac{4545.951}{1000}$ = 4.55 years

This bond has a duration of 4.55 years. Does this mean that the portfolio has the same interest rate risk exposure as does the single bond investment? Have we found a counterexample to the risk reducing benefits of portfolio diversification? The answer is no. The portfolio has less interest rate risk exposure than does the single bond investment. But this is not apparent when we examine the duration measures alone. To see this, we must examine the convexity of the portfolio versus the convexity of the five year bond.

Using the formula for convexity of a zero coupon instrument shown in *Calculation Complications 7.9*, we find that the convexity of the one year zero coupon is $\frac{1(2)}{(1.05)}$ = 1.90. The convexities of the ten and five year bonds, respectively, are 75 and 23.9. The convexity of a portfolio is the weighted average of the convexities of the securities comprising the portfolio. Thus, the convexity of the portfolio in our example is $\frac{1000}{2000}(1.9) + \frac{1000}{2000}(75)$ = 38.45. The portfolio has greater convexity (38.45) than does the five year (23.9) bond. Thus, even though the durations are identical, investors prefer the portfolio because of its greater convexity. This "barbell strategy" suggests that portfolio diversification benefits are alive and well, capable of reducing interest rate risk exposure.

CALCULATION COMPLICATIONS 7.9

CONVEXITY OF ZERO COUPON SECURITIES

Since the zero coupon security has a single cash flow equal to the face value, F, received at time T, the maturity date, we can solve for the zero's convexity by substituting F and T into equation (7.7) as follows:

$$CV = \frac{1}{P} \frac{T(T+1)F}{\left(1 + \frac{y}{n}\right)^{T+2}}$$

Simplifying (using the definition $P = F/\left(1 + \frac{y}{n}\right)^{T}$ for zero coupon instruments) yields convexity equal to

$$CV = \frac{T(T+1)}{\left(1 + \frac{y}{n}\right)^{2}}$$

Consider five year zero coupon Treasury STRIPS yielding 7% p.a. The current price is $\frac{100}{1.07^5}$ = $71.2987 per $100 face value. The convexity is $CV = \frac{5(6)}{(1.07)^2}$ = 26.20. If interest rates increase by 100 basis points to 8% p.a., we can use the duration and convexity approximations to calculate the price change:

$$\frac{\Delta P}{P} \approx -D \frac{\Delta y}{1 + \frac{y}{n}} + 0.5CV(\Delta y)^2$$

$$= -5 \frac{.01}{1.07} + 0.5(26.20)(.01)^2 = -0.04673 + 0.00131 = -0.04542$$

The duration approximation estimates a 4.673% drop in the price of the zero coupon bond. The convexity adjustment approximates a 4.542% drop in the zero's price. The exact solution is $P = \frac{100}{1.08^5}$ = $68.0582 per $100 face value for a price decline of $3.24, which represents 4.54% of the zero's market value. Thus, the convexity-adjusted approximation gives us the same result as the exact solution.

Interest Rate Risk Calculations for Portfolios of Assets AND Liabilities   FIs are distinguished from nonfinancial firms in that they carry financial securities on both sides of their balance sheets: assets and liabilities. If interest rates increase, the market values of the FI's assets will decline, creating the interest rate risk exposure that we measured using duration and convexity. However, if the FI holds financial liabilities, the same interest rate increase will simultaneously *decrease* the market values of its liabilities, thereby offsetting the impact of rate changes on the FI's assets and reducing the FI's interest rate risk exposure. To summarize the offsetting impact of interest rate risk of assets and liabilities, we examine the duration of equity, using a measure known as the **duration gap**. The duration gap is calculated as the difference between the durations of assets and liabilites. It is used to measure the impact of a given shift in interest rates on the market value of the entire portfolio.

duration gap: a measure of the duration of equity, computed as the difference between the durations of assets and liabilites.

The net impact of interest rate fluctuations on the entire balance sheet can be summarized by examining the impact on net worth. By definition, the market value of net worth (denoted E) is the difference between the market value of assets and the market value of liabilities. Thus, changes in the market value of net worth are defined as

$$\Delta E = \Delta A - \Delta L$$

If these changes in market values occur because of price fluctuations induced by interest rate changes, we can obtain an expression for ΔE. Using the duration approximation, we can express the market value of assets (liabilities) using equation (7.5), as

$$\frac{\Delta P_A}{P_A} \approx -D_A \frac{\Delta y_A}{1 + y_A}$$

$$\frac{\Delta P_L}{P_L} \approx -D_L \frac{\Delta y_L}{1 + y_L}$$

Simplifying notation so that the market value of assets, P_A, is expressed as A, and the market value of liabilities, P_L as L, and substituting into the definition of ΔE yields

$$\Delta E \approx -D_A(A) \frac{\Delta y_A}{1 + y_A} + D_L(L) \frac{\Delta y_L}{1 + y_L} \tag{7.9}$$

If we make the assumption that all interest rates change by the same amount (i.e., a parallel shift in the yield curve), then

$$\frac{\Delta y_A}{1 + y_A} = \frac{\Delta y_L}{1 + y_L} \equiv \frac{\Delta y}{1 + y}$$

By substituting this into equation (7.9) and simplifying, we obtain the following expression for the impact of rate changes on net worth:

$$\frac{\Delta E}{A} \approx -\left(D_A - \frac{L}{A}D_L\right)\frac{\Delta y}{1 + y}$$

In form, this looks a lot like equation (7.5). The term in parentheses is the duration of equity (call it the duration gap, such that $DG \equiv D_A - \frac{L}{A}D_L$), so that

$$\frac{\Delta E}{A} \approx -DG \frac{\Delta y}{1 + y} \tag{7.10}$$

Equation (7.10) allows us to directly compute the impact of a given rate change on the firm's net worth. If rates increase at a rate of .5% (that is, if $\frac{\Delta y}{1+y} = .005$), across the board for all rates, then a firm with a duration gap of +2 years will experience a 1% decline in net worth. A firm with a duration gap of +4 years will experience a 2% decline in net worth, while a firm with a duration gap of -3 years will see its net worth increase by 1.5%. Just as duration is the factor of proportionality relating interest rate changes to price changes, the duration gap is the factor of proportionality relating interest rate changes to fluctuations in the market value of net worth.

Calculating the duration gap simply requires putting together many of the tools we already have at our disposal. Consider the following portfolio consisting of two assets and one liability: (1) a one year zero coupon asset yielding 5% p.a. with a price of $1,000; (2) a 10 year 5% p.a. annual coupon asset, priced at par at $1,000; and (3) a 5 year 5% p.a. annual coupon liability, priced at par at $2,000. In the last section, we found that the durations of these securities are (1) 1 year, (2) 8.108 years, and (3) 4.55 years, respectively. The duration of assets is

$$D_A = \frac{1000}{2000}(1) + \frac{1000}{2000}(8.108) = 4.55 \text{ years}$$

The duration gap is

$$DG \equiv D_A - \frac{L}{A}D_L = 4.55 - \frac{2000}{2000}(4.55) = 0$$

If interest rates increase by 0.5% p.a., then the impact on net worth, which we obtain by substituting into equation (7.10), is

$$\frac{\Delta E}{A} \approx -DG\frac{\Delta y}{1+y}$$
$$\frac{\Delta E}{2000} \approx -(0)(.005) = 0$$

The rate change has no impact on net worth because the firm has attained **immunization** against interest rate changes. Immunization is the balancing of the duration of assets and liabilities to eliminate any interest rate risk exposure. Although each security in the portfolio has interest rate risk, when they are combined into the portfolio, their interest rate risk exposures offset each other, so that interest rate fluctuations have no impact on net worth.

If the duration gap is positive, then the duration of assets exceeds the duration of liabilities, and the market value of equity will fall when interest rates increase. We say that a positive duration gap exposes the investor to increases in interest rates. Alternatively, if the duration gap is negative, then the net worth declines when interest rates decline, thereby exposing the investor to interest rate decreases. The sign of the duration gap dictates the direction of the interest rate risk exposure. The size of the duration gap dictates the magnitude of the interest rate risk exposure, as measured by the induced shift in the market value of net worth.

Checkpoint

1. What is the barbell strategy?
2. What is the duration gap?
3. Describe two ways that portfolio diversification can be used to reduce interest rate risk exposure.
4. Describe the interest rate risk exposure of a positive duration gap; of a negative duration gap.

Summary

Calculations of both simple and compound interest rates for zero coupon and coupon bearing instruments permit conversion between the various rate computations, so that the yield on any security can be stated in a form that can be compared to other similar securities. The financial calculators so useful in performing these computations have built–in valuation functions that assume flat yield curves. In this chapter, we discuss the many factors determining the shape of the yield curve, as well as their implications for security valuation.

Interest rate levels are determined by expectations, attitudes toward risk, liquidity preference, market segmentation, and inflation rates. When fluctuations take place in any or all of these factors, then interest rates change. The impact of interest rate volatility on securities' prices creates interest rate risk exposure. Duration and convexity are used to measure the amount of interest rate risk exposure for both individual securities and portfolios of securities.

The relationship between security prices and rates is not linear. However, duration is a linear approximation that obtains close estimates of the price impact of small changes in yields. However, duration is a pessimistic approximation, since it overstates price declines and under-

states price increases. Convexity is a more accurate, nonlinear approximation of the relationship between yields and security prices. The greater a security's convexity, the greater its value, since greater convexity implies higher price increases when rates fall and lower price decreases when rates rise.

FIs hold portfolios of financial securities. We use the duration gap to measure the interest rate risk of a financial portfolio. The duration gap is the difference between the duration of assets and the leverage-adjusted duration of liabilities. If the duration gap is positive, interest rate increases (decreases) result in decreases (increases) in the market value of the portfolio. If the duration gap is negative, interest rate increases (decreases) result in increases (decreases) in the market value of the portfolio.

➤ References

Allen, L., and T. Thurston. "Cash-Futures Arbitrage and Forward-Futures Spreads in the Treasury Bill Market." *Journal of Futures Markets* 8, No. 5 (1988): 565–573.

Ariel, R., and Pohlman, "Factors Influencing the Level of Interest Rates." In J. Francis and A. Wolf, eds., *The Handbook of Interest Rate Risk Management.* Burr Ridge, Ill.: Irwin Professional Publishing, 1994.

Barsky, R. "The Fisher Hypothesis and the Forecastability and Persistence of Inflation." *Journal of Monetary Economics* 19 (1987): 3–24.

Chan, L. "Consumption, Inflation Risk, and Real Interest Rates: An Empirical Analysis." *Journal of Business* 67, No. 1 (1994): 69–96.

Cox, J., J. Ingersoll, and S. Ross. "A Re-examination of Traditional Hypotheses About the Term Structure of Interest Rates." *Journal of Finance* (September 1981): 769–799.

Duffie, Darrell. "Debt Management and Interest Rate Risk." In W. Beaver and G. Parker, eds., *Risk Management: Problems and Solutions.* New York: McGraw-Hill, 1995.

Fama, E. F. "The Information in the Term Structure." *Journal of Financial Economics* 13 (December 1984): 509–528.

Fama, E. F. "Short Term Interest Rates as Predictors of Inflation." *American Economic Review* 65 (1975): 269–282.

Hardouvelis, G. "The Predictive Power of the Term Structure During Recent Monetary Regimes." *Journal of Finance* 43, No. 2 (June 1988): 339–356.

Horvath, Philip. "A Pedagogic Note on Intra-Period Compounding and Discounting." *The Financial Review* 20 (February 1985): 116–118.

Ibbotson Associates. *Stocks, Bonds, Bills, and Inflation: 1992 Yearbook.* Chicago: 1992.

Jones, D., and V. Roley. "Rational Expectations and the Expectations Model of the Term Structure: A Test Using Weekly Data." *Journal of Monetary Economics* 12 (September 1983): 453–465.

Jones, F., and F. Fabozzi. *The International Government Bond Markets.* Chicago: Probus Publishing Co., 1992.

Logue, Dennis. *The WG&L Handbook of Financial Markets.* Cincinnati: Warren, Gorham & Lamont, 1995.

Mankiw, G., and J. Miron. "The Changing Behavior of the Term Structure of Interest Rates." *Quarterly Journal of Economics* 101 (May 1986): 211–228.

Mishkin, F. S. "What Does the Term Structure Tell Us About Future Inflation?" *Journal of Monetary Economics* 25 (1990): 77–95.

Stigum, Marcia. *Money Market Calculations: Yields, Break-Evens, and Arbitrage.* Homewood, Ill.: Dow Jones-Irwin, 1981.

Taylor, Richard. "The Valuation of Semiannual Bonds Between Interest Payment Dates." *The Financial Review* 23, No. 3 (August 1988): 365–368.

➤ Questions

1. Calculate the simple interest yields and compound interest rates for the following securities:
   a. A zero coupon security with 36 days until maturity and a rate of discount of 3.2%. (Use both conversion formulas to calculate the simple interest yield.)
   b. A zero coupon security with 150 days until maturity and a rate of discount of 6.5%. (Use both conversion formulas to calculate the simple interest yield.)
   c. A coupon bearing security paying a monthly coupon of 9% p.a. with seven years until maturity selling at a discount of $95 per $100 face value.
   d. A coupon bearing security paying a quarterly coupon of 7% p.a. with four years until maturity selling at a premium of $102 per $100 face value.

2. Use the following Treasury security quotations to draw the yield curve:

   • 92 days to maturity with a rate of discount of 5.04% p.a.

   • 190 days to maturity with a rate of discount of 5.51% p.a.

   • 270 days to maturity with a rate of discount of 5.73% p.a.

   • 375 days to maturity with a rate of discount of 5.93% p.a.

3. Use the term structure in question 2 to describe three expected future spot rates 92 days from today.

4a. Use the following yield curve to solve for implied forward rates.

   ### Treasury STRIP Spot Yields as of May 15, 1996

Maturity Date	Days to Maturity	Simple Interest Yield, i
November 15, 1996	184	5.25
May 15, 1997	365	5.39
November 15, 1997	549	5.47
May 15, 1998	730	5.72

4b. Use the yield curve and the implied forward rates to price a two year 6% p.a. Treasury note to be issued on May 15, 1996. (Use both methods.)

4c. What is the simple interest yield to maturity on the two year note in part (b)?

5. Calculate the duration of the following fixed income securities:
   a. An 18 month zero coupon bond yielding 5% p.a.
   b. An 18 month 2% p.a. quarterly coupon bond yielding 5% p.a.
   c. An 18 month 8% p.a. semiannual coupon bond yielding 5% p.a.

6. Calculate the price (both with and without accrued interest) of the following coupon bonds if settlement date is January 15, 1998:
   a. A 5.5% p.a. semiannual coupon bond yielding 4.80% p.a. that matures on March 15, 2007. The settlement date falls in the middle of the coupon payment period extending from September 3, 1997 (the last coupon payment or issue date) until March 3, 1998 (the next coupon payment date). There are 181 days in this coupon payment period and t_c = 47 days.
   b. An 8% p.a. semiannual coupon bond yielding 4% p.a. that matures on December 2, 1999. The settlement date falls in the middle of the coupon payment period extending from December 2,

1997 (the last coupon payment or issue date) until June 2, 1998 (the next coupon payment date). There are 182 days in this coupon payment period and t_c = 138 days.

  c. A 5% p.a. semiannual coupon bond yielding 6% p.a. that matures on August 10, 2010. The settlement date falls in the middle of the coupon payment period extending from August 10, 1997 (the last coupon payment or issue date) until February 10, 1998 (the next coupon payment date). There are 184 days in this coupon payment period and t_c = 26 days.

7. Complete the following table:

Zero Coupon Instruments						
	P per \$100 F	t days	d	Nominal i	π%	Real I
(a)	98.5	130	?	?	1.7%	?
(b)	?	271	8.30%	?	2.8%	?
Coupon Bearing Instruments						
	P per \$100 F	T periods	c	Nominal y	π%	Real Y
(c)	95	15	7%	?	4.4%	?
(d)	?	6	10%	9.55%	2.5%	?

8. Calculate the duration of the following fixed income instruments:
  a. A three year 4% p.a. annual coupon note yielding 6.2%.
  b. A one year 8% p.a. semiannual coupon note priced at \$101.5 per \$100 face value.
  c. A two year 6.25% p.a. annual coupon note priced at \$96.75 per \$100 face value.

9. Calculate the convexity of the following fixed income instruments:
  a. A three year 4% p.a. annual coupon note yielding 6.2%.
  b. A one year 8% p.a. semiannual coupon note priced at \$101.5 per \$100 face value.
  c. A two year 6.25% p.a. annual coupon note priced at \$96.75 per \$100 face value.

10. Use duration, convexity, and the bond valuation formula (from Table 7.1) to calculate the price impact of a 25 basis point increase in all interest rates for the three bonds in questions 8 and 9.

11. Calculate (i) the simple interest rate, (ii) the compound interest rate, and (iii) the future value of reinvested coupons for the bond in Figure 7.1*b* if
  a. The price is \$98.5 per \$100 face value.
  b. The price is \$103.75 per \$100 face value.

12. Compute the duration gap for the following portfolio of assets and liabilities. What general conclusions can you draw about interest rate risk exposure? What is the impact of a 10 basis point increase in interest rates on the market value of net worth?
Assets
  a. Five year 5% p.a. annual coupon bond priced at a par value of \$100,000.
  b. Ten year 5% p.a. annual coupon bond with a par value of \$50,000 and a yield of 8% p.a.
  c. Ten year 2.5% p.a. annual coupon bond with a par value of \$250,000 and a yield of 5% p.a.

Liabilities
  d. Two year zero coupon note with a par value of \$150,000 and a yield of 3% p.a.
  e. Five year 10% p.a. semiannual coupon bond with a par value of \$100,000 and a yield of 20% p.a.

13. Use the spot yield curve for August 15, 1995, shown on page 216 to calculate the forward yield curve on February 15, 1996 (183 days after August 15, 1995). Be sure to calculate $_{183}i_{182}$, $_{183}i_{366}$, and $_{183}i_{547}$.

14. Calculate the convexity for the semiannual coupon note in *Calculation Complications 7.4.*

15.   Additional practice using your calculator. State the bid/ask quotations for the following bonds:

a.   5 year, 8% p.a. semiannual coupon bond with a bid price of $95.75 per $100 face value and a bid/ask spread of $0.25.

b.   25 year, 12% p.a. quarterly coupon bond with an ask price of $107.50 per $100 face value and a bid/ask spread of $1.05.

c.   2 year, 6.75% p.a. annual coupon bond with an ask yield of 4.90% p.a. and a bid/ask spread of 3 basis points.

d.   6 year, 10% p.a. semiannual coupon bond with a bid yield of 5.75% p.a. and a bid/ask spread of 5 basis points.

CHAPTER 8

COMPUTING FOREIGN EXCHANGE RATES AND RISK EXPOSURE

"Go forth into a world that is not entirely composed of public-school men. . . but of men who are as various as the sands of the sea." EM Forster, *Abinger Harvest* (1936), "Notes on English Character."

Learning Objectives

- To learn about the quotation of foreign currency rates.
- To study the four parity relationships that theoretically determine the world's exchange rates.
- To examine the impact of deviations from parity relationships on exchange rate volatility.
- To learn to measure exchange rate volatility and currency risk exposure.

➤ Introduction

Nowhere is the globalization of financial markets more apparent than in international currency markets. As of April 1995, daily transactions taking place in round-the-clock global foreign exchange markets averaged $1.23 trillion worth of volume. This represents a 50% increase in daily volume over three years, implying a 14% increase in foreign exchange trading each year. More than half of this volume involved trade with a U.S. dollar component. Perhaps more than any other characteristic, this observation justifies the designation of the U.S. dollar as the world's primary reserve currency.

In addition to the U.S. dollar (denoted US$), the world's major currencies are the German mark (the Deutschemark, denoted DM), the Japanese yen (JY), the Swiss franc (SFr), and the British pound sterling (£). These currencies have assumed increasingly important roles in international financial markets. Indeed, the U.S. dollar's role as the world's reserve currency is being challenged by the Deutschemark (see Hakkio (1993), and *Timely Topics 8.1*). Other currencies include the Canadian dollar (C$), the Australian dollar (A$), and the European Monetary System's (EMS) currencies (the Belgian franc, the Danish krone, the Dutch guilder, the French franc, the Irish punt, the Italian lira, the Portuguese escudo, the Luxembourg franc, the Greek drachma, and the Spanish peseta).

TIMELY TOPICS 8.1

THE FUTURE OF THE U.S. DOLLAR

[T]he future of the [U.S.] dollar depends on which policies are pursued over the long term by the United States government and central bank. For in a very real sense, the international position of a currency is one of the most sensitive indicators of the efficacy of the policies being pursued.

The reason for this is that international currency markets are among the most competitive in the world. International contracts of all kinds can easily be written in any currency. The attractiveness of a currency for this purpose depends crucially on whether or not it is attractive as a medium of exchange. Open borders, liquid markets, and the absence of restrictions on capital movements are all essential to this attractiveness. The currency must also hold its purchasing power over the periods for which contracting parties may be concerned.

In the end, the value of a nation's currency depends on confidence in the decision making instituitions of the issuing country. Today, as the world approaches the celebration of a half century without a global conflagration, a number of countries have had the opportunity to develop sufficient international confidence in the stability of their instituitions to have their currencies play an international role. We in the United States cannot, therefore, assume that the international role of the dollar is unassailable. Unlike during the years immediately following the second world war, our institutions do not have a near-monopoly on global confidence. The position of the dollar in the world must no longer be taken for granted. It must be earned, it is not automatic. . . .

First, the United States government and central bank must run a credible long term anti-inflation policy. An international currency must be credible as a store of value as well as a medium of exchange. . . . [T]he political consensus against inflation is far weaker in [the U.S.] than in, say, Germany. . . .

A second constraint on policymakers seeking an international role for their currency is an obligation to keep their capital markets open and their currency readily convertible. I believe that a good portion of the decline in the international role of the British pound was the result of a series of experiments with exchange controls during the 1960s and 1970s. Convertibility is the sine qua non of internationalization of a currency. . . .

A third constraint on policy makers in countries with an international currency is the need to promote a generally free trade policy. While less obvious a threat to a currency's value than exchange or capital controls, an interventionist trade policy limits the domestic convertibility of a currency into goods and services. At the very least it creates artificial price differentials between the domestic and overseas use of the currency. . . .

In sum, . . . the price of maintaining an international currency is the pursuit of sound policies—ones which should be pursued in any event.

Source: Remarks by Lawrence Lindsey, Governor of the Federal Reserve System on May 25, 1994.

Not all currencies are dictated by national boundaries. In Chapter 3, we discussed the first international currency, special drawing rights (SDRs), which are market baskets of the world's five major currencies. Upon formation of the European Community in 1979, a new "European currency cocktail," the ECU, was created. Table 8.1 shows the composition of the ECU in terms of the currencies of the 12 EC countries. The German mark, the French franc, and the British pound jointly account for more than 60% of the ECU's value. The value of the ECU in terms of U.S. dollars fluctuates over time. The market value of the ECU in U.S. dollars is calculated using the exchange rates for each currency. Thus, the value of the ECU in January 1996 (using spot exchange rates in parentheses) is

$$ECU = DM0.6242(US\$0.6932) + FF1.332(US\$0.2030) + £0.08784(US\$1.5523)$$
$$+IL151.8(US\$0.0006341) + DG0.2198(US\$0.6194) + BF3.431(US\$0.0335)$$
$$+SP6.885(US\$0.008197) + DK0.1976(US\$0.1782) + IP0.008552(US\$1.5947)$$
$$+GD1.44(US\$0.004193) + PE1.393(US\$0.006632) = US\$1.307$$

Although planned for adoption in 1999 as the currency of a unified EC, it is not clear that the ECU will displace the national currencies of the European countries. Indeed, despite futuristic predictions of the ultimate emergence of a single world currency, there appear to be three distinct major currency blocs (or groups) in the world:

1. *The European bloc*, consisting of the EC, independent European currencies (such as the Swiss franc and the Scandinavian currencies), and the emerging Eastern European currencies. This bloc is currently dominated by the Deutschemark.

2. *The dollar bloc*, consisting of the North American and Caribbean currencies. This bloc is dominated by the U.S. dollar. Because the New Taiwan dollar, the South Korean won, the Singapore dollar, and the Hong Kong dollar all have been pegged to the U.S. dollar, these currencies are currently included in the dollar bloc.

3. *The yen bloc*, currently comprising only the Japanese yen. However, in recent years the "four Asian tigers"—South Korea, Taiwan, Malaysia, and Singapore—have moved away from the dollar bloc toward what might someday constitute an Asian yen bloc.

Daily volume exceeding $1 trillion translates into a lot of activity. Who trades in foreign currency markets?

Table 8.1

The Composition of the ECU (adopted September 20, 1989)[a]

Currency	Amount of Currency	Currency Weight (%)
Deutschemark	0.6242	30.1
French franc	1.332	19.0
British pound	0.08784	13.0
Italian lira	151.8	10.2
Dutch guilder	0.2198	9.4
Belgian franc	3.431	7.6
Spanish peseta	6.885	5.3
Danish krone	0.1976	2.4
Irish punt	0.008552	1.1
Greek drachma	1.44	0.8
Portuguese escudo	1.393	0.8

[a]The composition of the ECU basket is periodically adjusted by the European Monetary System to reflect changes in membership and the relative values of the component currencies. These adjustments are destabilizing (see Bessembinder, 1994); the Maastricht Treaty therefore froze the composition of the ECU at its September 20, 1989 levels.

Table 8.2

U.S. FIs' Currency Trading: Percentage Distribution of Monthly Gross Turnover

By Major Currency Pairs		By Type of Transaction			
Dollar–mark	34.25%	Financial Institutions		Average Size of Trade	
Dollar–yen	23.44	Spot	49.25%	FIs	$6 million
Dollar–sterling	9.19	Forward	7.09	Brokers	$7 million
Dollar–Swiss franc	7.84	Swaps	30.48	Spot: FIs	$4 million
Mark–yen	2.91	Options (OTC)	7.60	Spot: Brokers	$4 million
Dollar–French franc	2.71	Derivatives	5.58	Forward: FIs	$4 million
Sterling–mark	2.23	Brokers		Forward: Brokers	$23 million
Mark–Swiss franc	2.09	Spot	49.20	Swaps: FIs	$16 million
Dollar–Australian dollar	1.93	Forward	0.08	Swaps: Brokers	$32 million
Dollar–ECU	0.83	Swaps	37.68	Options: FIs	$14 million
Mark–French franc	0.58	Options (OTC)	12.31	Options: Brokers	$40 million
Sterling–yen	0.12	Other	0.73		
Other	11.87				

Source: "Summary of Results of the U.S. Foreign Exchange Market Turnover Survey," Conducted in April 1992 by the Federal Reserve Bank of New York.

1. Large multinational corporations and import/export firms engaging in international trade.

2. The central banks of various countries to conduct international operations and implement their monetary policies.

3. FIs which provide cash management and risk sharing services for their customers, as well as speculate on their own behalf.

Private FIs are needed to coordinate transactions in world currency markets. Table 8.2 shows the distribution of U.S. FIs' currency trading for 1992. Before we can examine the financial markets spawned by this volume of activity, we must understand the mechanics of exchange rate determination.

Table 8.3

Key Currency Cross Rates: Late New York Trading May 2, 1996

	U.S. Dollar	Pound	SFranc	Guilder	Peso
Canada	1.3625	2.0478	1.0953	0.79762	0.18240
France	5.1610	7.7570	4.1487	3.0213	0.69090
Germany	1.5285	2.2973	1.2287	0.89480	0.20462
Italy	1564.0	2350.7	1257.2	915.58	209.37
Japan	104.4	156.91	83.923	61.117	13.976
Mexico	7.4700	11.227	6.0048	4.3730	....
Netherlands	1.7082	2.5674	1.3732	....	0.22867
Switzerland	1.2440	1.8697	....	0.72825	0.16653
U.K.	0.66534	....	0.53484	0.38950	0.08907
U.S.	....	1.5030	0.80386	0.58541	0.13387

Source: Dow Jones Telerate Inc.

➤ **Definitions**

You may be aware of a distinction between the terms *currency rate* and *cross rate*. You might even have seen the Key Currency Cross Rates table in the *Wall Street Journal* (reproduced in Table 8.3) and thought that these were more exotic (or less important) versions of the exchange rates reported extensively in other parts of the newspaper. This is not the case. *All* exchange rates are really cross rates. **Foreign exchange rates** are the price of one currency in terms of another. When both currencies are nondomestic, then we have a **currency cross rate**. So, as with so many other concepts, the definition depends on your perspective. In Japan, the dollar-sterling exchange rate is a cross rate, while in the United States or the United Kingdom it is not.

We avoid this xenophobic distinction by treating all exchange rates as cross rates. Indeed, all exchange rates must be referred to in terms of both currencies being quoted. Thus, all exchange rates are hyphenated. The first currency named in the hyphenated exchange rate is the one being quoted, and the second currency denotes the currency of denomination. For example, a "mark-yen" exchange rate of 60 means that there are 60 yen to each Deutschemark. This allows us to use our intuition about price increases and decreases. When the mark-yen exchange rate increases to 61, there are 61 yen to each Deutschemark, and we can say that the mark has appreciated in terms of the Japanese yen. We can obtain one more yen for each Deutschemark at the new *higher* currency rate.

Since more than half of the world's foreign currency transactions utilize the global reserve currency, the U.S. dollar, we will standardize our treatment of exchange rates that involve the U.S. dollar. They will always take the form of "foreign currency-U.S. dollar" exchange rates; that is, the price of the foreign currency will always be denominated in terms of the U.S. dollar. Thus, we will always state exchange rates as, say, mark-dollar as opposed to dollar-mark. It should be clear that the dollar-mark exchange rate is simply the inverse of the mark-dollar exchange rate.

Reading the Cross-Rate Tables

In the *Wall Street Journal*'s Key Currency Cross Rates table for May 2, 1996 (see Table 8.3), the currencies listed in the top row across the table are the first currencies stated in our hyphenated exchange rate notation. The country names in the first column represent the second currency in the hyphenated exchange rate, or the currency of denomination. Thus, the number 2.0478 in the first row, second column of the table denotes the sterling-Canadian dollar exchange rate of C$2.0478 per British pound sterling. The number 303.04 in the fourth row, ninth

Yen	Lira	D-Mark	FFranc	CdnDlr
0.01305	0.00087	0.89140	0.26400	....
0.04943	0.00330	3.3765	....	3.7879
0.01464	0.00098	....	0.29616	1.1218
14.981	....	1023.2	303.04	1147.9
....	0.06675	68.302	20.229	76.624
0.07155	0.00478	4.8871	1.4474	5.4826
0.01636	0.00109	1.1176	0.33098	1.2537
0.01192	0.00080	0.81387	0.24104	0.91303
0.00637	0.00043	0.43529	0.12892	0.48832
0.00958	0.00064	0.65424	0.19376	0.73394

column of the table is the French franc-Italian lira exchange rate, denoting 303.04 Italian lira per French franc.

Notation and Terminology

Unfortunately, there is no standard practice used by all international currency markets. The Swiss franc, Japanese yen, and German mark all trade in terms of U.S. dollar-foreign currency; that is, the posted exchange rates for these three major money markets are dollar-Swiss franc, dollar-yen, and dollar-mark. In other words, if you obtained a price quote of 85 in the Japanese yen, you could obtain 85 yen per U.S. dollar. It is simple enough for us to convert this price quote into our standardized notational format. Simply take the inverse $(\frac{1}{85})$ to obtain the yen-dollar exchange rate of US$0.011765 per yen. Each Japanese yen costs 0.011765 U.S. dollars. Now you see why the market prefers to state prices in terms of the less cumbersome dollar-yen as opposed to yen-dollar. Under the dollar-yen price quotation system, however, we would show an *increase* in the Japanese yen against the dollar by a move in the exchange rate from 85 to 84! This counterintuitive decline in the price quotation refers to an appreciation in the currency's value because with a dollar-yen exchange rate of 84, we can obtain US$0.011905 per yen as opposed to only US$0.011765 when the dollar-yen was at 85. To avoid this confusion (and despite the extra number of decimal places in the price quotes), we will always state exchange rates in terms of U.S. dollars per foreign currency, that is, in foreign currency-U.S. dollar format. When you actually trade these currencies, however, you must be aware of the convention used in the particular market.

One advantage of the foreign currency-dollar format of exchange rate quotation is apparent in the interpretation of bid and asked prices. Currency brokers and dealers typically quote prices to buy or sell U.S. dollars. But a bid to buy dollars is equivalently a quote to sell foreign currency. Similarly, an offer to sell dollars is the same as a quote to buy foreign currency. Bid prices are lower than asked prices only if the foreign currency-dollar form of exchange quotation is used. If the dollar-mark quotation is 1.626–1.6313, which is the bid price and which is the asked price? Since the broker/dealer bids to buy Deutschemark, the bid price is DM 1.6313 per U.S. dollar since this is equivalent to US$0.613 per DM ($\frac{1}{1.6313}$ = 0.613). The offer price is 1.626 since this is equivalent to the *higher* US$0.615 per DM ($\frac{1}{1.626}$ = 0.615). The broker/dealer will offer to buy DM at US$0.613 per DM and to sell DM at US$0.615 per DM.

Another wrinkle in practitioner terminology occurs in the market for the British pound sterling and the Australian dollar. True to form, these countries are individualistic to a fault. Currency dealers who refer to "dollar-sterling" exchange rates are really quoting "sterling-dollar." When a trader quotes you a dollar-sterling exchange rate of 1.6, this means the exchange rate is US$1.60 per British pound sterling. That conforms with our notation as a "sterling-dollar" exchange rate, but you will never hear that terminology in the markets.

Checkpoint

✓

1.   What is the ECU?

2.   Who trades in foreign currency markets and why?

3.   Describe the three major currency blocs.

4.   What is a cross rate?

5.   How would you refer to an exchange rate that denominates the French franc in terms of Italian lira? the Deutschemark in terms of Japanese yen? the pound sterling in terms of U.S. dollars?

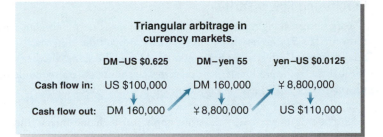

Figure 8.1

➤ Keeping Exchange Rates in Line: The Parity Relationships

Exchange rates are simply the price of one currency in terms of another. Since there is no limitation on how combinations of currencies can be quoted, all exchange rates must be internally consistent. Thus, if the mark-dollar is $0.0625 per DM and the yen-dollar is $0.0125 per JY, then the mark-yen exchange rate must be 50 JY per Deutschemark. That is, the mark-dollar exchange rate implies a dollar-mark price of DM 1.6 per US$, while the $0.0125 yen-dollar rate implies a dollar-yen price of JY 80 per U.S. dollar. Thus, DM 1.6 equals JY 80 or $\frac{80}{1.6}$ = JY 50 per per DM. If the mark-yen exchange rate was instead 55, then there would be an **arbitrage** opportunity since profit could be earned without requiring either risk or investment. You could risklessly profit by buying DM at the mark-dollar rate and selling them at the higher mark-yen rate so as to obtain the arbitrage profit on the yen-dollar exchange rate. How could this be done?

> **arbitrage:** an opportunity to earn profit that does not require either risk or investment.

Suppose that you invested US$100,000 in Deutschemarks.[1] At the current mark-dollar exchange rate of $0.625, you would receive 160,000 DM ($\frac{100,000}{0.625}$). Simultaneously, you would convert the Deutschemark into yen at the mispriced mark-yen exchange rate of 55. This would net 8.8 million yen (DM160,000 x 55). Now convert the yen back to U.S. dollars at the yen-dollar exchange rate of $0.0125 to obtain US$110,000 (8.8 million yen × $0.0125). The arbitrage profit is 800,000 yen, worth US$10,000. Without any risk, in no time at all, you have transformed US$100,000 into US$110,000. This "triangular arbitrage" is pictured in Figure 8.1. If such an arbitrage opportunity existed, the sophisticated traders in the currency markets would immediately exploit it. The spurt of additional volume in the mispriced DM-yen market would quickly reduce the price to 50, the point at which arbitrage opportunities no longer exist. Because of the liquidity and efficiency of major currency markets, such arbitrage opportunities are rare and fleeting.

In global equilibrium, arbitrage opportunities would not exist. All goods, services, and financial assets would be priced equally no matter how we chose to denominate that price—in U.S. dollars, Finnish markkas, Tunisian dinars, or Pakistani rupees. This observation can be formally stated in terms of four basic international parity relationships. When equating the prices of physical goods and services across countries, we obtain *purchasing power parity*. The relationship between nominal and real interest rates is dictated by the *international Fisherian relation*. The spot and forward exchange rates are linked by the *foreign exchange expectation expression*. Finally, when equating the rates of return on financial securities across countries, we obtain *interest rate parity*.

---

[1] In order to abstract from interest rate risk or market risk, throughout this chapter all investments are assumed to be free of any risk exposure except foreign exchange rate risk.

Purchasing Power Parity

purchasing power parity
(PPP): sale of identical
physical goods and
services for the same
price, whatever the
currency of denomination.

We are not speaking tongue in cheek when we say that purchasing power parity may best be illustrated by *The Economist*'s monthly publication of the "Big Mac Index." Given McDonald's quality control and standardization, a Big Mac is the same whether sold in Australia, Italy, or Zimbabwe. If the product is identical across all countries, so also should be its price. **Purchasing power parity (PPP)** asserts that identical physical goods and services sell for the same price, whatever the currency of denomination.

Purchasing power parity does not apply just to hamburgers. Indeed, it can be presented as the relationship between spot exchange rates and the price index, as measured by inflation rates. If $S_t^{JY,US}$, $S_{t+1}^{JY,US}$ are the spot exchange rates between the currencies of countries JY and US (stated as Japanese yen-US\$ exchange rates) at times t, and $t + 1$; and π_t^{JY}, π_t^{US} are the expected inflation rates in Japan and the United States, respectively, at time t, then:[2]

$$\frac{S_{t+1}^{JY,US}}{S_t^{JY,US}} = \frac{1 + \pi_t^{US}}{1 + \pi_t^{JY}}$$

If the yen-dollar exchange rates were \$0.0175 per yen at the beginning of the year and \$0.02 at the end of the year, we can say that the yen has appreciated against the U.S. dollar. Why would this happen? One reason is that, over the year, prices have increased at a faster rate in the United States than in Japan. This situation increases the value of the Japanese currency vis-à-vis the U.S. dollar. To achieve parity, more dollars are required to compensate for the dollar's reduced purchasing power. Let's see how this happens. Suppose that the annual inflation rate in the United States is 5% p.a. What is the Japanese inflation rate that is implied by PPP?

$$\frac{\$0.02}{\$0.0175} = \frac{1 + .05}{1 + \pi_t^{JY}}$$
$$\pi_t^{JY} = -8.125\% \text{ p.a.}$$

The annual Japanese inflation rate that is consistent with these exchange rates is a −8.125% p.a. rate of *decrease* in prices. The appreciation of the Japanese yen simply offsets the fact that, in our example, inflation rates are higher in the United States than in Japan.

Alternatively, if the inflation rate in Japan is expected to be 6.2%, using the PPP formula,[3] the spot exchange rate at time $t + 1$ is

$$\frac{S_{t+1}^{JY,US}}{\$0.0175} = \frac{1.05}{1.062}$$
$$S_{t+1}^{JY,US} = \$0.0173 \text{ per Japanese yen}$$

If the inflation rate in Japan is expected to be higher than the U.S. inflation rate, then the spot rate will fall from \$0.0175 per yen to \$0.0173 per yen, reflecting inflation's erosion of the yen's currency value.

PRACTITIONER'S PRIMER 8.1

APPROXIMATING THE PPP

The PPP relationship has a simpler presentation that, though not precise, is a good approximation. Since PPP expresses the fluctuations in spot exchange rates as a

---

[2] We illustrate the parity relationships using Japanese yen-U.S. dollar exchange rates, although they can be stated in terms of any two currencies j and k.

[3] A simplified form of PPP is shown in *Practitioner's Primer 8.1*.

function of differential inflation rates, we can restate it as

$$\frac{S_{t+1}^{JY,US}}{S_t^{JY,US}} - 1 \approx \pi_t^{US} - \pi_t^{JY}$$

When yen-dollar rates appreciate from \$0.0175 to \$0.02, then

$$\frac{\$0.02}{\$0.0175} - 1 = 0.143 \approx 0.05 - (-0.08125)$$

Alternatively, when yen-dollar rates depreciate from \$0.0175 to \$0.0173, then

$$\frac{\$0.0173}{\$0.0175} - 1 = -0.0114 \approx 0.05 - 0.062$$

International Fisherian Relation

Investment in a currency can be viewed as an investment in that country's money market. Thus, the yield on short term investments must reflect the value of the country's currency. An important consideration is the purchasing power of the currency. As we saw in Chapter 7, nominal interest rates comprise a real rate of interest plus expected inflation rates. This Fisherian relationship holds in each country. For any country, say Japan JY, domestic interest rates can be expressed as

$$1 + r_t^{JY} = (1 + R_t^{JY})(1 + \pi_t^{JY})$$

where r_t^{JY} is the nominal interest rate in currency JY at time t; R_t^{JY} is the real interest rate in currency JY at time t; and π_t^{JY} is the expected inflation rate in currency JY at time t. This Fisherian relation must hold internationally as well as domestically. Expressed as an international relationship, at any time t, the Fisherian relation between any two currencies, in this example the US\$ and the Japanese yen, is

$$\frac{1 + r_t^{JY}}{1 + r_t^{US}} = \frac{(1 + R_t^{JY})(1 + \pi_t^{JY})}{(1 + R_t^{US})(1 + \pi_t^{US})}$$

international Fisherian relation (IFR): relationship that dictates the association between nominal and real interest rates across countries.

If the expected inflation rate is 3% p.a. in Japan and 5% p.a. in the United States, and real interest rates are 1% p.a. in both countries, then nominal rates in Japan are $(1.01)(1.03) = 1.0403 - 1 = 4.03\%$ p.a. In the United States, nominal interest rates are $(1.01)(1.05) = 1.0605 - 1 = 6.05\%$ p.a. These rates would be consistent with international Fisherian relations. The **international Fisherian relation (IFR)** dictates the association between nominal and real interest rates across countries. A simplified form of the IFR is shown in *Practitioner's Primer 8.2*.

PRACTITIONER'S PRIMER 8.2

APPROXIMATING THE IFR

The more commonly used format of the domestic Fisherian relation is the approximation $1 + r \approx 1 + R + \pi$, which omits the cross-product term $R\pi$ (see Chapter 7). When interest and inflation rates are at relatively low levels, this approximation is very close to the exact solution. This approximation, together with the recognition that

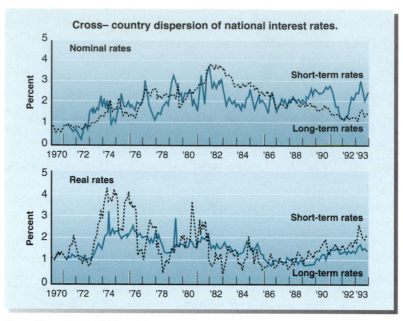

Source: Pigott (1993–1994), p. 28.

Figure 8.2

if international capital markets are efficient, then real interest rates will be the same throughout the world, produces a useful approximation of the international Fisherian relation:

$$r_t^{JY} - r_t^{US} \approx \pi_t^{JY} - \pi_t^{US}$$

International differentials in nominal interest rates can be approximated by international differentials in expected inflation rates. Thus, if expected inflation rates are 3% p.a. and 5% p.a. in Japan and the United States, respectively, then the differential between the countries' nominal interest rates is 2% p.a. as suggested by the exact solution, where 6.05% p.a. minus 4.03% p.a. is approximately equal to 2% p.a.

Note that this approximation makes use of the rule of thumb that real risk free interest rates are the same throughout the world. Figure 8.2 shows the dispersion in both short term and long term rates among the following countries: the United States, Canada, Germany, France, the United Kingdom, Japan, Italy, Belgium, and Switzerland. Although over the last 20 years the dispersion has been smaller among real rates than among nominal rates, Figure 8.2 shows that real rates are not equalized across countries. Hence, the practitioner's assumption that real rates are the same for all countries does not always hold in practice.[4]

The Foreign Exchange Expectation Expression

Thus far we have considered interest, exchange, and inflation rates at any point in time (either *t* or *t* + 1). However, one of the basic roles of financial markets is to allow us to move through time. We must therefore relate current exchange rates to future exchange rates. One way to

---

[4] Merrick and Saunders (1986) reject the hypothesis that real interest rates are equal in Belgium, Canada, France, Italy, Japan, Netherlands, Switzerland, the United Kingdom, the United States, and Germany.

accomplish this is to examine the relationship between spot rates (for immediate delivery) and forward rates (for deferred delivery). This concept is similar to the concept of forward interest rates discussed in Chapter 7. Just as you can lock in a forward interest rate, you can do the same for exchange rates. Purchasing (selling) a forward contract obligates you to take (make) delivery of one currency in exchange for another at a fixed, predetermined exchange rate at some prespecified date in the future.

Forward rates should be equal to expected future spot rates; that is, deviations between spot and forward rates are determined by expected shifts in spot rates over time. If everyone knew that exchange rates *never* changed, then forward rates would always equal current spot rates. Only if spot rates are expected to change in the future will forward rates deviate from current spot rates.

foreign exchange expectation expression (FEEE): the statement that forward exchange rates are equal to expected future spot rates.

The **foreign exchange expectation expression (FEEE)** states that forward exchange rates are equal to expected future spot rates. If $F_t^{JY,US}$ is the forward yen-dollar exchange rate at time t for end-of-year delivery[5] and if, as before, yen-dollar spot rates are expressed as $S_t^{JY,US}$ with $E_t(S_{t+1}^{JY,US})$ denoting the expectation at time t of period $t+1$ spot rates, then FEEE can be expressed as

$$\frac{F_t^{JY,US} - S_t^{JY,US}}{S_t^{JY,US}} = \frac{E_t(S_{t+1}^{JY,US}) - S_t^{JY,US}}{S_t^{JY,US}}$$

which simply reduces to $F_t^{JY,US} = E_t(S_{t+1}^{JY,US})$. If current spot rates are \$0.0175 per Japanese yen and are expected to increase to \$0.02, then $F_t^{JY,US}$ = \$0.02. If forward rates were only \$0.0195 and the market's consensus was that future spot exchange rates at the end of the year would be \$0.02, then there would be an arbitrage opportunity. To exploit this arbitrage opportunity, you could buy 100 million yen for delivery at the end of the year at the forward rate of \$0.0195. This would commit you to a payment of \$0.0195(100 million yen) = \$1.95 million. If your expectation is correct, the spot rate at the end of the year would be \$0.02, and you could simultaneously sell the 100 million yen for \$0.02(100 million yen) = \$2 million, for a \$50,000 profit (\$2 million minus \$1.95 million). Since this is a "no-money-down" transaction, everybody could, and would, perform the same arbitrage. But this would bid up the forward rates as demand for forward yen-dollar contracts increased, thereby bringing the forward rate into line with market expectations.

Interest Rate Parity

The first two parity relationships (PPP and IFR) have balanced interest, exchange, and inflation rates across countries. The third parity relationship (FEEE) links exchange rates across time periods. The **interest rate parity (IRP)** relationship balances interest rates across both countries and time periods by equating risk adjusted nominal rates of return on financial securities for different countries.

interest rate parity (IRP): relationship that equates risk adjusted nominal rates of return on financial securities for different countries.

Consider the following hypothetical interest rate opportunities. Nominal (simple) interest rates for one year maturity German government bonds are currently 4% p.a., whereas in Japan the analogous rate for Japanese government bonds is 2.5%. Moreover, assume that expected inflation in Germany is 2% p.a., whereas in Japan it is only 1.0%. Based on the international Fisherian relation, real interest rates in Germany are 2% p.a. but only 1.5% p.a. in Japan. Can you exploit this apparent arbitrage opportunity? Let's see if it is possible.

To take advantage of this apparent arbitrage opportunity, you would choose to borrow in Japan and lend in Germany, to pick up the 0.5% p.a. real interest differential. Assume that

---

[5] We simplify the notation by assuming end-of-year delivery for all forward contracts. In Chapter 7, we utilized a double subscript notation to incorporate different deferred delivery dates. We will adopt that notation when we examine forward premiums later in this chapter.

the current yen-Deutschemark exchange rate is 0.0115. Borrow 10 million yen at the 2.5% p.a. rate and simultaneously lend the proceeds in Germany at 4% p.a. At the current exchange rate, the 10 million yen loan proceeds provide you with 10 million × 0.0115 = DM 115,000. At the end of the year, you must repay the yen-denominated loan with the proceeds of the DM-denominated loan. The yen loan repayment is 10 million × 1.025 = 10.25 million yen. The DM loan repayment is 115,000 × 1.04 = DM 119,600.

Are the proceeds of the DM-denominated investment sufficient to repay the yen-denominated loan? It depends on the exchange rate that will prevail at the end of the year.

If the end-of-year yen-Deutschemark exchange rate is unchanged at 0.0115: Converting DM 119,600 to yen yields $\frac{119,600}{0.0115}$ = 10.4 million yen, for a net gain of 150,000 yen (10.4 minus 10.25 million yen).

If the end-of-year yen-Deutschemark exchange rate increases to 0.012: Converting DM 119,600 to yen yields $\frac{119,600}{0.012}$ = 9.967 million yen for a net loss of 283,333 yen (9.967 minus 10.25 million yen).

If the end-of-year yen-Deutschemark exchange rate decreases to 0.011: Converting DM 119,600 to yen yields $\frac{119,600}{0.011}$ = 10.873 million yen for a net gain of 622,727 yen (10.873 minus 10.25 million yen).

Clearly, this is not a risk free arbitrage opportunity. Your profits are very much at risk. Depending on the exchange rate that will prevail at the end of the year, your investment will be either profitable or unprofitable. But what if you had some way to lock in the end-of-year exchange rate? Then there would not be any exchange rate risk in this transaction. You can see the potential role for a forward contract in eliminating the risk in this transaction. Combining the cross-country borrowing and lending with a forward contract removes the risk from the above transaction and transforms it into a risk free arbitrage opportunity. If no transaction costs were associated with this forward contract, then elimination of this arbitrage opportunity would require the exact balance of cash flows at time period one. That is, for our example, $\frac{119,600}{F}$ = 10.25 million yen, where F is the forward yen-mark exchange rate. Solving for F yields DM0.011668 per yen as the end-of-year yen-mark exchange rate that will eliminate any potential arbitrage profit.

The rate structure that is consistent with the elimination of any risk free arbitrage opportunities conforms with **covered interest rate parity**. Covered interest rate parity equalizes cross-country yields by guaranteeing returns using forward foreign exchange markets. Using the notation of the other three parity relationships, we state covered interest rate parity as

covered interest rate parity: the equalizing of cross-country yields by guaranteeing returns using forward foreign exchange markets.

$$F_t^{JY,US}(1 + r_t^{JY}) = S_t^{JY,US}(1 + r_t^{US})$$

where r_t^{JY}, r_t^{US} are nominal annual interest rates at time t in Japan and the United States, respectively; $F_t^{JY,US}$ is the time t forward exchange rate for end-of-year delivery of currency JY in terms of currency US; and $S_t^{JY,US}$ is the time t spot yen-dollar exchange rate.

Linking the Parity Relationships   For any currency, the differential between forward and spot exchange rates is determined by expectations of exchange rate fluctuations (according to the FEEE). But PPP teaches us that exchange rate fluctuations over time are caused by intertemporal price fluctuations. Cross-country price differentials also drive cross-country interest rate differentials (according to both the IRP and IFR). The glue that links all four parity relationships is each country's rate of domestic inflation. Countries experiencing more rapid inflation than other countries will experience rising nominal interest rates (in both absolute and relative terms), as well as depreciating exchange rates, other things being equal. Figure 8.3 shows how the four parity relationships are linked theoretically.

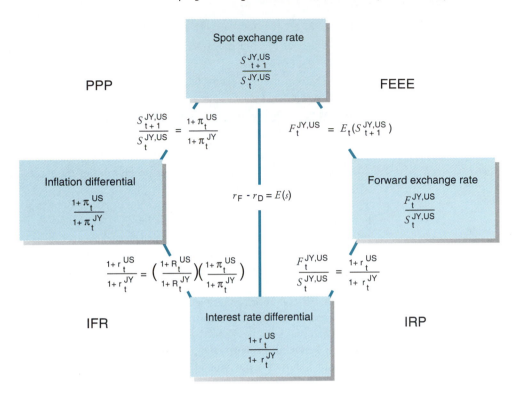

Figure 8.3

In illustrating the linkages among the four parity relationships—PPP, IFR, FEEE, and IRP—suppose that expected inflation rates are 5% p.a. in the United States and only 3% p.a. in Japan. Current spot exchange rates are assumed to be $0.0175 per Japanese yen. Current nominal interest rates in the United States are 4% p.a., and real interest rates are the same across both countries. Let us apply the four parity relationships to determine the nominal and real interest rates and forward yen-dollar exchange rates.

First, utilizing PPP,

$$S_{t+1}^{JY,US} = \left(\frac{1 + \pi_t^{US}}{1 + \pi_t^{JY}} \right) (S_t^{JY,US}) = \frac{1.05}{1.03}(0.0175) = \$0.01784$$

From FEEE, $F_t^{JY,US} = E_t(S_{t+1}^{JY,US}) = \$0.01784$. Forward contracts for end-of-year delivery of Japanese yen in exchange for U.S. dollars will be priced at $0.01784 per yen. Using IRP,

$$1 + r_t^{JY} = \frac{S_t^{JY,US}(1 + r_t^{US})}{F_t^{JY,US}} = \frac{0.0175(1.04)}{0.01784} = 1.02$$

and nominal one year interest rates in Japan will be 2% p.a. Finally, using the IFR, we find that the real interest rates in both countries are −1% p.a. since nominal interest rates (2% p.a. in Japan and 4% p.a. in the United States) minus expected inflation rates (3% p.a. in Japan and 5% p.a. in the United States) equal −1%, a negative real interest rate.

Checkpoint

✓

1.   What are the four parity relationships?

2.   Which of the four parity relationships describes the link between price levels and exchange rates?

3.   Which of the four parity relationships describes the link between today's prices and future prices?

4.   What single factor determines both exchange rates and interest rates?

Do the Parity Relationships Hold?

The Economist puts PPP to the taste test by examining the prices of Big Macs around the world.[6] In 1995 it cost $1.58 to buy a Big Mac in Hungary, $2.32 in the United States, and $4.65 in Japan, thereby violating PPP since the prices of Big Macs were not equalized across borders. Moreover, the Big Mac index for 1986–1995, shown in Table 8.4, shows that these price discrepancies persist over time. Indeed, based on worldwide discrepancies in Big Mac prices, most currencies of industrial countries have been overvalued relative to the U.S. dollar, whereas most currencies of developing countries have been undervalued relative to the U.S. dollar.

The parity conditions present a useful synthesis of some rather complex real-world relationships, but they reflect a deterministic view of the world. If the parity relationships hold, then all rates and prices can be calculated with perfect certainty. It's almost as if you challenged your friend to a billiards game to take place in a complete vacuum. There would be no suspense to the game, since the outcome of every shot could be calculated precisely using the laws of physics. In contrast, real-world trading in foreign exchange has been compared to playing pool "on a cloth untrue with a twisted cue and elliptical billiard balls." You never know what may happen. So it is in foreign currency markets. Empirical studies have documented discrepancies from the theoretical parity relationships. FIs' attempts to exploit these discrepancies fuel financial innovations that have led to the evolution of markets, such as Eurocurrencies and currency swaps. Thus, the discovery of divergences from parity should be viewed not as a failure but as an opportunity.

In Chapter 7, we found that empirical tests of the expectations hypothesis fail to support the conclusion that forward interest rates are equal to expected future spot rates. Unfortunately, the empirical evidence regarding forward exchange rates yields similar results. Figure 8.4 shows that FEEE, which asserts that forward exchange rates equal expected future spot exchange rates, does not hold even for the major world currencies.[7] A risk premium appears to be built into forward rates and behaves in a manner similar to the term premium we saw in Chapter 7. That is, the risk premium varies over time and is largely unobservable.[8]

Meese and Rogoff (1988) present evidence that rejects the IFR for DM-US dollar, dollar-sterling, yen-dollar, DM-yen, DM-sterling, and yen-sterling exchange rates, although Strauss and Terrell (1995), using a slightly different model, find support for the IFR in Canada, France, Italy, Germany, the United Kingdom, and Japan. However, the divergence between the dollar index (the weighted average of all major exchange rates) and the inflation rate shown in Figure 8.5 rejects IFR, which states that exchange rates closely follow inflation rates. Deravi, Gregorowicz, and Hegji (1995) show that the rejection of IFR is a result of contemporaneous

---

[6] The Big Mac index was launched in 1986 by *The Economist* as a lighthearted guide to whether currencies are at their correct level. The "basket" is a McDonald's Big Mac, produced locally in 68 countries.

[7] Fama (1984) and Hodrick and Srivastava (1986) show this more rigorously.

[8] Huang's (1989) estimates the forward exchange rate risk premium for nine major currencies (the Canadian dollar, the British pound, the French franc, the Deutschemark, the Italian lira, the Dutch guilder, the Swiss franc, the Japanese yen, and the Belgian franc) for three month, six month, and twelve month forward maturities only.

Table 8.4

Purchasing Power Parity, 1986–1995

Country	1986	1987	1988	1989	1990	1991	1992	1993	1994	1995
Argentina	NA[a]	NA	NA	NA	NA	NA	152	158	157	129
Australia	67[b]	NA	60	84	79	86	89	77	75	78
Austria	NA	NA	NA	NA	NA	NA	NA	NA	123	173
Belgium	134	144	108	113	127	129	147	147	135	165
Brazil	NA	NA	NA	NA	NA	NA	81	123	69	116
Britain	103	104	92	106	104	133	139	122	116	121
Canada	85	NA	69	89	86	91	106	96	89	86
Chile	NA	NA	NA	NA	NA	NA	NA	NA	100	104
China	NA	NA	NA	NA	NA	NA	53	66	45	45
Czech. Rep.	NA	NA	NA	NA	NA	NA	NA	NA	73	82
Denmark	NA	187	150	167	181	185	197	186	167	212
France	154	173	129	138	143	142	149	152	138	166
Germany	131	136	103	113	116	114	125	128	117	150
Greece	NA	NA	NA	NA	NA	NA	NA	NA	107	NA
Hong Kong	61	NA	41	48	50	51	53	51	52	53
Hungary	NA	NA	NA	NA	NA	68	76	78	71	68
Indonesia	NA	NA	NA	NA	NA	NA	NA	NA	NA	75
Ireland	100	106	82	91	94	100	109	100	NA	NA
Israel	NA	NA	NA	NA	NA	NA	NA	NA	NA	130
Italy	NA	154	112	118	144	129	152	130	121	114
Japan	150	NA	125	138	106	125	130	152	163	200
Malaysia	NA	NA	NA	NA	NA	NA	NA	57	61	65
Mexico	NA	NA	NA	NA	NA	NA	NA	100	105	74
Netherlands	119	132	109	119	127	124	133	135	124	152
New Zealand	NA	NA	NA	NA	NA	NA	NA	NA	NA	84
Poland	NA	NA	NA	NA	NA	NA	NA	NA	60	63
Portugal	NA	NA	NA	NA	NA	NA	NA	NA	110	NA
Russia	NA	NA	NA	NA	284	255	27	50	71	70
Singapore	81	NA	59	71	63	70	131	NA	83	91
Spain	122	NA	107	118	127	151	141	125	109	123
Sweden	150	NA	131	162	179	191	196	151	139	153
Switzerland	NA	NA	NA	NA	NA	NA	NA	172	172	225
S. Korea	NA	NA	NA	178	135	129	135	127	123	129
Taiwan	NA	NA	NA	NA	NA	NA	NA	NA	102	109
Thailand	NA	NA	NA	NA	NA	NA	NA	84	82	84
Venezuela	NA	NA	NA	NA	NA	NA	128	NA	NA	NA
Yugoslavia	NA	NA	69	38	62	94	NA	NA	NA	NA

[a]NA indicates data are not available.

[b]A number less than 100 indicates that the local currency is undervalued relative to the U.S. dollar on a PPP basis. A number greater than 100 indicates that the local currency is overvalued relative to the U.S. dollar on a PPP basis.

Source: Pakko and Pollard (1996), p. 19.

monetary policy feedback, but Johnson (1994) finds the size of the deviation from IFR to be small.

Figure 8.6 shows the evidence supporting the existence of covered interest rate parity (IRP) for short term rates (three month maturities) in the world's major currencies: the U.S. dollar, the Deutschemark, and the Japanese yen. However, during the 1980s French interest rates

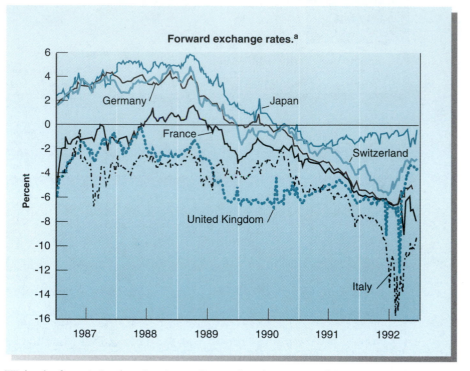

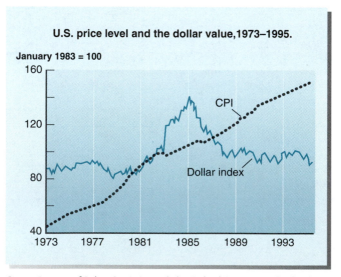

[a]Wednesday figures in London. Premium or discount from the spot rates of the three month forward rates of the currencies shown against the U.S. dollar.

Source: Financial Market Trends, OECD, 1993, vol. 54, p. *i*.

Figure 8.4

Source: Bureau of Labor Statistics and the Federal Reserve Bank of Atlanta. Chang (1995), p. 2.

Figure 8.5

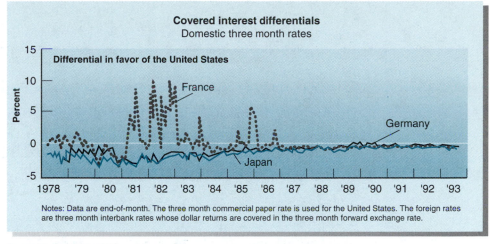

Source: Pigott (1993–1994), p. 29.

Figure 8.6

sometimes diverged from strict covered interest rate parity. Moreover, the evidence for less widely traded currencies and for longer maturities shows considerable divergence from covered interest rate parity, suggesting the existence of potential arbitrage opportunities in these markets.[9] However, for nine major currencies, Gokey (1994) and Abeysekera and Turtle (1995) find that 80% of the deviations from the parity relationships occur because of deviations from PPP, with deviations from IRP relatively minor.

Figure 8.7 investigates the validity of PPP by showing 20 years of exchange rate fluctuations for seven major exchange rates. The ranges of plausible PPP rates are graphed (using an ex ante model of expected inflation rates). Casual observation of the graphs shows considerable deviations from PPP for the U.S. dollar-Swiss franc, U.S. dollar-DM, Australian dollar-DM, and U.S. dollar-yen exchange rates. More consistent with PPP are Australian dollar-Swiss franc, French franc-Swiss franc, and French franc-DM exchange rates. Thus, the parity relationships should be viewed as a rough guide that defines the parameters of currency relationships, and not necessarily as a working trading plan. Lee and Sullivan (1995) show that while PPP does not hold precisely over the period 1976–1993, the deviations from PPP have declined in recent years (since 1987) for the major currencies. Similarly, Michael and Nobay (1994), Phylaktis and Kassimatis (1994), and Cochran and DeFina (1995) find that the deviations from PPP are not sufficient to present either predictable or profitable arbitrage opportunities.[10]

---

[9] However, McCallum (1994) and Brenner and Kroner (1995) show that many of the empirical tests fail to properly estimate the differential between the forward and spot risk premiums. They claim that once taken into account, empirical tests should support covered IRP.

[10] Many empirical tests of the parity relationships are criticized for being joint tests of parity and market efficiency. Empirical results that appear to reject parity may really be rejecting market efficiency. There is some validity to this criticsm. Glassman (1987) finds evidence of inefficiency in the futures markets for the British pound, Canadian dollar, Deutschemark, and Swiss franc in both volatile ("turbulent") and stable time periods. Moreover, Lin and Swanson (1993) find systematic divergences from market efficiency among domestic, Euromarkets, and Asian currency markets for the world's major currencies: the U.S. dollar, British pound, Deutschemark, Swiss franc, and Japanese yen, while Sharma and Obar (1995) obtain some support for PPP when data measurement problems are corrected. The markets for minor currencies would tend to be even less efficient. However, Mahdavi and Zhou (1994) find that PPP is more likely to hold in countries with high rates of inflation.

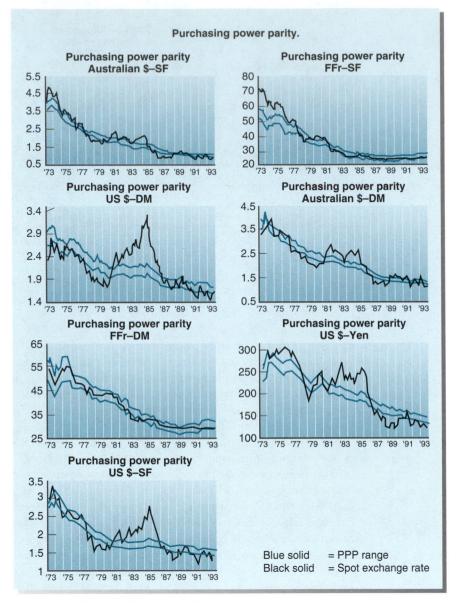

Source: Heri and Rossi (1994), pp. 114, 104.

Figure 8.7

Reasons for Divergence from the Parity Relationships

Although a useful theoretical construct, the parity relationships omit four major real-world factors that may account for empirical deviations from parity. These factors are (1) transaction costs, (2) trade restrictions and capital controls, (3) differences in national tastes and preferences, and (4) regulatory policy regimes.

Transaction Costs   To implement the relatively simple arbitrage trades described above requires the services of broker/dealers to place the loans and investments as well as to undertake the spot and forward currency transactions. Banks may charge US$4.50–$6.50 to clear debit-credit transactions denominated in Deutschemark, whereas the fees increase for less widely traded currencies. Forward transactions denominated in Deutschemark or Swiss francs are typically priced at US$13 per US$1 million, while for French francs the cost is US$20. Another transaction cost, the bid-asked spread, increases with maturity. Thus, Rhee and Chang (1992) found that the bid-asked spread on a one year forward contract was two to three times larger than the spread on spot currency. Consideration of these costs may be sufficient to eliminate apparent arbitrage opportunities in many of the most widely followed currencies.[11]

Transaction costs also include information costs. To take advantage of potential discrepancies in the parity relationships, we must first know that they exist. Currency traders program their computers to continuously examine exchange rates for potentially profitable deviations from parity. Access to real-time information and rapid processing of that information are necessary to participate in these markets.[12] The window of opportunity for trade in the most popular currency markets is in the range of a matter of mere seconds. Without investments in the appropriate informational infrastructure, it is not possible to take advantage of potential arbitrage opportunities.

Trade Restrictions and Capital Controls   Other real-world factors omitted from the parity relationships are import taxes, transportation costs, and trade restrictions such as export subsidies. The completion of the Uruguay Round of the General Agreement on Tariffs and Trade (GATT) in December 1993 after seven years of negotiation commits the signatories (more than 100 countries controlling approximately 90% of world trade) to reduce and eventually remove all barriers to free trade. As beneficial as that was in increasing the world's level of economic activity, we are still far from a world of unfettered international trade. The June 1995 showdown between the United States and Japan regarding restrictions limiting the import of U.S. auto parts into Japan highlights the extent of de facto limitations to the free movement of goods even among friendly trading partners. If goods do not move freely among countries, PPP may not hold. Artificially high prices for apples in Japan may be sustained (even if apples are plentiful and are sold for lower prices in the United States and elsewhere) if the Japanese authorities obstruct the import of apples. Clearly, consumers throughout the world have the most to lose from this abrogation of the equalizing power of PPP.

International trade wars can be viewed as an element of the **political risk** associated with the impact of unanticipated governmental actions on financial market returns. Perhaps even more significant than trade wars in creating political risk is the possibility of **capital controls**, which are limitations on the unrestricted movement of financial flows across countries.[13] Capital controls may prevent arbitrageurs from undertaking transactions that exploit deviations from the parity relationships, thereby removing the equilibrating mechanism that leads to restoration of parity.[14]

political risk: the impact of unanticipated governmental actions on financial market returns.

capital controls: limitations on the unrestricted movement of financial flows across countries.

---

[11] Rhee and Chang (1992) document the elimination of potential arbitrage profits for the pound sterling, the Deutschemark, the Japanese yen, and the Swiss franc when transaction costs are taken into consideration. They confirm the results of the seminal study by Frenkel and Levich (1975), which first verified covered IRP for the U.S. dollar, the pound sterling, and the Canadian dollar once transaction costs are taken into account. They estimate transaction costs for 90 day covered arbitrage transactions to range from 0.14% to 0.18% p.a. Clinton (1988) estimates transaction costs at around 0.08% p.a. for the pound and the Deutschemark and 0.25% p.a. for the French franc.

[12] Automation is a critical part of the foreign exchange market, as indicated by *Business Week*'s estimate that 50% of all currency transactions in 1992 were cleared electronically.

[13] Otani and Tiwari (1981) show the direct impact of Japanese capital controls on transaction costs. The imposition of capital controls raised transaction costs to 0.7% above those in London.

[14] Dooley and Isard (1980) show that the imposition of capital controls in Germany during the 1970s resulted in increases in interest rates of 2% p.a., which were eliminated upon the subsequent removal of the capital controls.

Differences in National Tastes and Preferences   A third factor omitted from the parity relationships is consideration of differences in national tastes and preferences. This is most apparent when discussing cross-country differences in inflation rates. These inflation rate differentials drive much of the exchange rate and interest rate determination and volatility in international currency markets. However, how is inflation measured? Price indexes are constructed utilizing a standardized market basket of goods that is priced at different points in time. To make inflation rates comparable across countries, the same standardized hypothetical market basket of goods must be used in all countries to calculate price inflation. But if tastes vary dramatically from country to country, then the measure of inflation may be skewed. A market basket of consumer goods in the United States may include significant amounts of meat, whereas this may be completely inappropriate for Hindu residents of India who may be vegetarians. If beef prices worldwide increase, this rise will have more impact on the real purchasing power of meat-eating Americans than on the standard of living of vegetarian Indians.[15] Differences in national tastes and preferences across countries lead to divergences between national demands for goods and services, which may undermine PPP. *Practitioner's Primer 8.3* shows how exchange rates may fluctuate randomly if relative prices change across countries with consumers that have different tastes and preferences.

PRACTITIONER'S PRIMER 8.3

CHEERS—FRENCH WINE OR JAPANESE SAKE?

To illustrate the impact of differences in national tastes and preferences, consider the illustration in the following table. At time period 0, the French consumed 9 liters of wine and 1 liter of sake, while the Japanese consumed 9 liters of sake and 1 liter of wine. With a relative price of 1 liter of sake per liter of wine and a yen–French franc exchange rate of 1, the value of each country's liquor bill was 10. Suppose that production problems disturb this equilibrium in time period 1, causing the relative price in Japan to increase to 1.5 liters of sake per liter of wine. This induces a shift in consumption. The French now consume 8 liters of wine and 1.5 liters of sake, while the Japanese, in time period 1, consume 9.5 liters of sake and 0.33 liter of wine.

	France		Japan	
	Time 0	Time 1	Time 0	Time 1
Wine	P = 1, C = 9	P = 1.111, C = 8	P = 1, C = 1	P = 1.5, C = 0.33
Sake	P = 1, C = 1	P = 0.741, C = 1.5	P = 1, C = 9	P = 1, C = 9.5
Basket	1(9) + 1(1) = 10	1.111(8) + 0.741(1.5) = 10	1(1) + 1(9) = 10	1.5(0.33) + 1 (9.5) = 10
Yen –French franc exchange rate at: time 0 = 1 and at time 1 = 0.741				

P = price, relative price in terms of liters of sake per liters of wine; C = consumption, in liters.

Source: B. Solnik, "International Parity Conditions and Exchange Risk," *Journal of Banking and Finance* 2 (1978): 281–93.

If, for simplicity, the rate of inflation is kept equal to zero in both countries, then the cost of the market basket of sake and wine must remain unchanged at 10. The cost of the market basket during time period 1 in Japan is 1.5(0.33) + 1(9.5) = 10 liters of sake.

---

[15] Even the Big Mac is produced in India using nonbeef substitutes, thereby introducing inconsistencies into the Big Mac test of PPP.

What are the relative prices of wine and sake in France? To solve for the French prices, note that the price of wine during time period 1 is 1.5 times the price of sake. These relative prices must hold in France as well as in Japan. Denoting the price of sake as s, we can express the price of wine as $1.5s$. Since there is zero inflation in France, the cost of the liquor basket is unchanged at 10. We now can solve for the price of sake, s, in France, using

$$8(1.5s) + 1.5s = 10$$

where the first component equals the French wine bill and the second component equals the French sake bill. Solving yields the period 1 price of sake in France of $s = 0.741$ and the period 1 price of wine in France of $1.5s = 1.111$. The exchange rate declines to 0.741 French franc per yen since it takes 1 yen to buy a liter of sake, which is valued at 0.741 French francs. In this example, PPP does not hold since exchange rates decline by 35% ($\frac{\Delta P}{P_0} = \frac{0.741-1}{0.741} = -0.35$), but there is no change in inflation rates, which remain zero in both countries. Differences in national tastes for wine versus sake induce different consumption responses to price changes, causing violations of PPP.

Regulatory Policy Regimes   We have seen that exchange rates are simply prices that reflect the purchasing power of a nation's currency. However, if national authorities maintain a religious fervor toward "protection of the value of the currency," then public FIs may intervene to offset (and perhaps delay) the impact of price adjustments that are reflected in exchange rate movements. We need to look no further than our experiences since World War II to examine three major regulatory policy regimes that have impacted exchange rate determination: (1) the Bretton Woods period of fixed exchange rates (1944–1971); (2) the Smithsonian period of freely floating exchange rates (1973–1979); and (3) the European Monetary System (1979–present).

Checkpoint

✓

1. Do empirical tests verify the existence of the parity relationships?

2. Which parity relationships receive more empirical support? less support?

3. What omitted factors might account for deviations from the parity relationships?

➤ Fixed versus Floating Exchange Rates

The primary motive that fueled the Old World's exploration of the New World during the fifteenth and sixteenth centuries was the search for gold. Countries defined their wealth in terms of the size of their gold reserves. As misplaced as this mercantilist attitude toward wealth was, the use of gold as a store of value has survived into the twentieth century. The **gold standard** attaches a value in terms of gold to each currency. Exchange rates under the gold standard are determined indirectly. If each French franc were worth half an ounce of gold bullion and each British pound were worth one-third of an ounce of gold bullion, then each French franc would be worth 1.5 pounds ($\frac{1}{2}$ divided by $\frac{1}{3}$).

gold standard: the fixing of the value of a currency in terms to gold.

Bretton Woods

In 1944 the representatives of 44 Western countries convened in Bretton Woods, New Hampshire, to discuss the postwar monetary order. They agreed on a form of the gold standard called the Bretton Woods system. Each country set a fixed exchange value of its currency redeemable in terms of gold. The fixed exchange rates of Bretton Woods encouraged the growth

currency risk exposure:
the impact of
unanticipated fluctuations
in exchange rates on the
value of real and financial
transactions.

balance of payments: the
difference between the
amount of money flowing
into the country and
money flowing out of the
country.

of international trade by reducing the risk of foreign exchange rate fluctuations. The value of any international transaction was fixed in terms of gold and therefore was not dependent on a changeable currency value. **Currency risk exposure** occurs when unanticipated fluctuations in exchange rates alter the value of real and financial transactions.

The gold content of each nation's currency determined the gold value of the monetary flows in and out of the country. The **balance of payments** is the difference between the amount of money flowing into the country (to pay for exports and purchases of domestic financial securities) and money flowing out of the country (to pay for imports and purchases of foreign financial securities). If one country was running a balance-of-payments deficit with respect to another country, they would settle that difference by transferring gold reserves from the deficit country's central bank to the surplus country's central bank.

Let's calculate a hypothetical balance of payments between the United States and Japan. Suppose that during the course of a year, Japanese importers bought US$125 billion worth of U.S. goods and US$50 billion worth of U.S. securities, whereas U.S. importers bought 17 trillion yen worth of Japanese goods and 5 trillion yen of Japanese securities. If each dollar were pegged at US$35 per ounce of gold and the yen were fixed at 7,000 yen per ounce of gold, then we can calculate the gold value of the two countries' balance of payments. The United States has a money inflow of 3.57 billion ounces of gold from exports (US$125 billion/35) and a money outflow of 2.43 billion ounces of gold from imports (17 trillion yen/7,000). In addition, the United States has a capital inflow of 1.43 billion ounces of gold (US$50 billion/35) and a capital outflow of 714 million ounces of gold (5 trillion yen/7,000). The U.S. balance of payments with Japan is equal to + 3.57 billion – 2.43 billion + 1.43 billion – 0.714 billion ounces of gold bullion, which sums to a balance-of-payments surplus of 1.856 billion ounces of gold. This would be paid by the Bank of Japan to the U.S. Federal Reserve Bank in the form of transfers of gold reserves.[16]

The situation depicted in the previous example was not typical of the U.S. experience during the life of the Bretton Woods system. Indeed, rather than running balance-of-payment surpluses, the United States began running persistent deficits as early as 1950. One way to deal with the gold drain engendered by persistent balance-of-payment deficits is **devaluation**, a situation that occurs when a central bank decreases its currency's exchange rate in terms of gold or other currencies.[17] However, if the Bretton Woods system was to accomplish its goal of encouraging international trade, then exchange rates had to be fixed. Devaluations are disruptive to the international economic order and were supposed to occur only infrequently under the Bretton Woods system when the International Monetary Fund found a particular country to be in "fundamental disequilibrium." During the 27 year history of Bretton Woods, the U.S. dollar was never devalued.[18]

devaluation: a central
bank's decrease of its
currency's exchange rate
in terms of gold or other
currencies.

Floating Rates

By 1971 the U.S. gold stock had fallen below US$10 billion, with no end to the balance-of-payments deficits in sight.[19] As a result of increasing inflationary pressures both at home and abroad, the United States suspended the conversion of dollars into gold on August 15, 1971,

---

[16] Balance-of-payment deficits under Bretton Woods were often paid using combinations of gold reserves and U.S. dollars, the world's reserve currency.

[17] Revaluation would occur if the central bank increased the gold content of its currency.

[18] Indeed, the United States maintained the gold standard from the turn of the twentieth century until the end of the Bretton Woods agreement with only one devaluation. In 1933 the Federal Reserve devalued the dollar from the then prevailing rate of US$21 per ounce of gold to the level of US$35 per ounce that remained in effect until 1971.

[19] The drain on the U.S. gold reserves stemmed from increased international reliance on the U.S. dollar as a reserve currency as well as the persistent U.S. trade deficit. As the volume of international trade expanded without an equivalent increase in the world supply of gold, the United States was increasingly called upon to redeem dollar reserves for gold, thus depleting the U.S. gold supply.

and allowed the value of its currency to fluctuate with market conditions. This marked the end of the Bretton Woods System. In December 1971, an international summit conference was held at the Smithsonian Institute in Washington, D.C., which led to the formal adoption in the spring of 1973 of a new monetary system: the system of floating exchange rates.

The demise of the system of fixed exchange rates terminated the convertibility of currency into fixed amounts of gold. Under floating exchange rates, the value of each currency is freely determined by market forces of supply and demand. Balance-of-payment deficits (surpluses) reduce (increase) the value of a currency because the supply of the currency to pay for imports and investments abroad exceeds (is less than) the demand for the currency to pay for the country's exports and financial securities.

Computing the value of the earlier example of the U.S.–Japanese balance of payments in terms of U.S. dollars, we can calculate the implied yen-dollar exchange rate to be $\frac{US\$35}{7,000yen}$ = US$0.005 per Japanese yen. Based on this exchange rate, the net exports from the U.S. to Japan in our example are US$40 billion (exports of US$125 billion minus imports of US$85, which is 17 trillion yen × US$0.005 per yen). The net capital inflow from Japan to the U.S. is US$25 billion (US$50 billion in purchases of U.S. financial securities minus US$25 billion, which is 5 trillion yen × US$0.005 per yen in purchases of Japanese financial securities). The U.S. dollar balance of payments between the U.S. and Japan in our hypothetical example is a surplus of US$65 billion ($40 billion in goods and $25 billion in financial services). Thus, the demand for U.S. dollars to pay for U.S. exports and financial securities totals US$175 billion (US$125 billion plus US$50 billion), while the supply of U.S. dollars available from the payment for U.S. imports and purchases of foreign securities is only US$110 billion (US$85 billion plus US$25 billion). Demand for U.S. dollars exceeds supply by the amount of the balance-of-payments surplus, US$65 billion. The value of the U.S. dollar is bid up on the world's currency exchanges. Under the Smithsonian system of floating exchange rates, currency values fluctuate with supply and demand.

EMS and the Managed Float

In March 1979 the European Community (EC) initiated a fixed exchange rate system, called the European Monetary System (EMS, also known as the Snake because the narrow bands limiting currency movements resemble a snake). The system was designed to link the exchange rates of the EC countries. Although the currencies subject to the EMS have fixed exchange rates with regard to each other's currency in the EMS, they jointly float against the U.S. dollar and other world currencies. To link the economies of the EC countries, a European Central Bank is planned, with the intent that it will take over the monetary policy functions of each country's central bank in 1999. (See the timetable in Table 8.5.) To be eligible for inclusion in the monetary union, each country must conform to four standards of behavior. For each country: (1) the inflation rate must not exceed the lowest three inflation rates in the EC by more than 1.5% p.a.; (2) the annual government budget must not be more than 3% of GDP; (3) the total outstanding government debt must not be more than 60% of GDP; and (4) the long term interest rates must not exceed average rates by more than 2% p.a. Most of the EC's founding members are still far from compliance with these standards.

The exchange rates of currencies in the EMS must be maintained within preset narrow bands that permit only small fluctuations. The benchmark currency in the EMS is the Deutschemark. The central parity rate is set equal to the prevailing exchange rate between each EMS currency and the Deutschemark. Members of the EMS are required to maintain the values of their exchange rates within a range of 2.25% above and below the central parity rate for their currency; the range is 6% for the British pound sterling and the Spanish peseta. The currency bands for the EMS currencies are shown in Table 8.6. You will note that the entries for the Italian lira and the British pound in the table are blank. This is because these countries

Timetable for European Monetary Union (EMU)

1990	In July, Stage I of EMU begins with free capital movements.
	In October, the U.K. joins the EMS.
1992	The Mastricht Treaty is signed to set the EMU timetable.
	In April, Portugal joins the EMS.
	In September, the U.K. and Italy leave the EMS.
1993	Currency bands are widened in response to the August EMS crisis.
	The Maastricht Treaty takes effect in November.
1994	Stage II of EMU begins.
1995	In January, Austria joins the EMS.
	EMS tensions are created by the devaluation of the peseta and escudo.
1996	Commitment to begin Stage III, a single currency, on January 1, 1999.
1997	Sterling required to rejoin the EMS to qualify for EMU.
	In June, Denmark to hold a referendum on participating in EMU.
1998	Announcement of countries qualifying for EMU.
	Appointment of the board of the European Central Bank.
1999	In January, irrevocable locking in of exchange rates to achieve a single currency.
	European Central Bank to become operational.
2001	Alternative start date for Stage III of EMU.
2002	Introduction of single currency notes and coins.

Source: Euromoney, November 1995, p. 29.

EMS Currencies with Central Parity Levels, Upper and Lower Intervention Boundaries, as of November 1, 1992

EMS Currency	Latest Spot Rate	Central Parity and Intervention Limits vs. DM		
		Upper Limit	Central Parity	Lower Limit
Belgian franc	20.550	21.095	20.626	20.166
Danish krone	3.8332	3.9016	3.8144	3.7300
Dutch guilder	1.1238	1.1524	1.1267	1.1017
French franc	3.3879	3.4305	3.3539	3.2792
Irish punt	2.6109	2.6190	2.6789	2.7400
Italian lira (suspended)	863.26			
Portuguese escudo	89.130	92.340	86.940	81.900
Spanish peseta	70.686	72.622	68.421	64.430
British pound (suspended)	2.4425			

Source: Klopfenstein and Stein (1993), p. 52.

have suspended their participation in the EMS. Current participants in the EMS are the EC countries except Greece, Portugal, Britain, Spain, and Italy. Italy and Great Britain suspended their participation in the EMS in September 1992 during a period of sustained exchange rate pressure. The experience of the pound during this period is typical of the problems associated with maintaining an exchange rate agreement such as the EMS.

From July until September 1992, the pound was trading near its EMS floor of DM 2.80 per pound. The Bundesbank, in keeping with its traditional role as single-minded inflation fighter

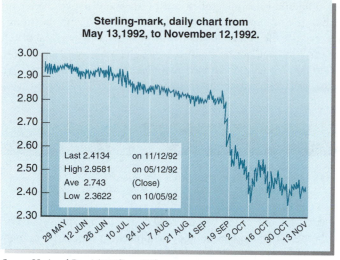

Source: Heri and Rossi (1994), p. 124.

Figure 8.8

(see Chapter 3), was keeping German interest rates high, despite a persistent recession that had gripped most of the EC countries. To keep the pound within the allowable trading band of the EMS, the Bank of England was forced to keep interest rates in line with the high level of German interest rates (constrained by covered IRP). This created political problems for the newly elected Conservative government in England, which had promised pursuit of a stimulative economic policy. The British government was forced to choose between pursuing an independent, expansionary monetary policy or remaining in the EMS. It chose the first alternative. Figure 8.8 shows the response of pound-DM exchange rates to the decoupling of British interest rates from the higher parity levels of German rates. The pound immediately dropped about 15% against the Deutschemark, falling out of the EMS parity bands and suspending British participation in the EMS.

The experience of Great Britain (as well as Spain and Italy) in September 1992 illustrates the pitfalls of maintaining an exchange rate agreement. To prevent the entire system from unraveling, the EMS bands were widened from 2.25% to 15% plus or minus the Deutschemark parity rate, rendering them all but useless. This process, called **realignment**, which is the adjustment of the EMS central parity exchange rate to bring a currency into compliance with its allowable trading band, undermines the discipline that should be imposed by fixed exchange rates. Exchange rate agreements are supposed to reduce the costs of interregional trade by fixing currency values within the region, but realignments cause extreme levels of currency volatility.[20] To maintain fixed currency values, nations must relinquish their sovereignty over

realignment: the adjustment of the EMS central parity exchange rate to bring a currency into compliance with its allowable trading band.

[20] The European Commission estimates the cost savings associated with fixed exchange rates within the EC to be in the range of 0.3 to 0.4% of annual EC gross domestic product. See the European Commission (1990), p. 68. However, Belongia (1988) finds that the greater exchange rate stability of the EMS enhances neither the EC's economic performance, as measured by either the level or volatility of domestic inflation rates, money supplies, and GDP for the EC countries, nor the volume of international trade.

their domestic economic policy and tie their policies to the region leader.[21]   In the case of the EC, the undisputed region leader is Germany, with its strong support for low inflation rates, even at the expense of economic growth. Europe's goal of full monetary unification by the year 2000 will not be attained unless the other countries of the EMS commit themselves to Germany's highly disciplined economic policies.[22]   *Timely Topics 8.2* compares fixed and floating exchange rate arrangements.

TIMELY TOPICS 8.2

FIXED AND FLOATING VOTERS

Every time one of the world's currencies plunges, policymakers start to wonder aloud whether anything can be done to prevent a repeat performance. The recent fall in the dollar has proved no exception. Jacques Santer, the newish president of the European Commission, and various French politicians are among those who have called for a revival of international exchange rate agreements. Such calls have rekindled a long-running debate among economists about the relative merits of fixed and floating exchange rate systems.

The beauty of a floating rate system is that it allows a country to adjust monetary policy without worrying about the exchange rate. . . . There are two snags, however. Floating exchange rates can be highly volatile. This can cause price instability that harms prospects for trade and investment. Under a floating rate system a government may also be tempted to pursue an excessively loose monetary policy, which results in higher inflation. Fixed exchange regimes avoid both of these problems; but at the cost of making it harder for countries to adjust to external shocks. . . .

[M]anaged exchange rate regimes seek to deliver this combination, [but] (1) must be flexible enough to cope with economic shocks; . . . (2) must be robust enough to convince markets that governments are committed to defending their pegged rates in all but the most exceptional circumstances; and (3) must be able to see off speculators who decide to put this commitment to the test.

Some previous managed exchange rate systems have more or less done all this. Under the classic gold standard, for instance, countries suspended convertibility if their economies ran into serious trouble. Under the Bretton Woods system of fixed, but adjustable, exchange rates, which ended in 1971, the International Monetary Fund provided liquidity to help countries maintain their exchange rate peg. In circumstances of "fundamental disequilibrium," however, they were allowed to devalue. The early years of the European exchange rate mechanism (ERM) also passed the tests.

But in the future . . . similar regimes will find it harder [since] politicial pressure to use the exchange rate to cope with economic shocks will undermine a pegged system's credibility, tempting speculators to attack it. [Moreover,] greater capital mobility will make it increasingly difficult for countries to defend target parities against speculators

---

[21] Fixed exchange rate arrangements reduce exchange rate volatility at the expense of greater volatility in economic fundamentals, such as domestic money supply and output levels. However, Flood and Rose (1995) find that fixed exchange rates do not increase macroeconomic volatility.

[22] Whitt (1995) shows that considerable deviations between economic conditions in Germany and those of France, Italy, the Netherlands, and Italy render the countries of the European community unsuitable for monetary union. In his analysis, Canada and the United States are better candidates for monetary consolidation.

.... The success of any [fixed rate] system will depend ... on whether governments will allow the exchange rate to be a big factor in setting domestic policies. [As evidence of the decline in fixed exchange rate arrangements, as of the end of 1994, 32.6% of a total of 178 currencies were freely floating, 18% were managed floating, 39.9% were fixed rate, and 9.5% were classified as other. This represents a decline in the proportion of fixed rate currencies, which comprised 63.5% out of a total of 148 countries as of the end of 1984.]

Source: *The Economist*, April 1, 1993, p. 64.

---

managed float: a system of flexible exchange rates that are monitored by public FIs that may intervene to try to adjust currency rates.

Just because the U.S. dollar is not included in the EMS does not mean that it is a freely floating currency. In February 1985 the U.S. dollar's value peaked against both the yen and the Deutschemark. During the weekend of September 22, 1985, the finance ministers of the G-5 countries (France, Germany, Japan, the United Kingdom, and the United States) met at the Plaza Hotel in New York. The result was the Plaza Accord, which was an agreement to coordinate central bank intervention to reduce the dollar's value. This agreement set in motion a policy of **managed float**—a system of flexible exchange rates that are monitored by public FIs that may intervene to try to adjust currency rates. The non-EMS currencies' exchange rates would fluctuate according to market forces until they reached a level that was perceived to be too high (as in the case of the U.S. dollar against the DM and the yen in 1985) or too low (as in the case of the U.S. dollar against the DM and the yen in 1987 and 1995). The central banks would then coordinate their intervention policies to move exchange rates in the desired direction. That implied selling dollars in 1985 to bring down the value of the U.S. dollar and buying dollars in 1987 and 1995 to raise the dollar-DM and dollar-yen exchange rates.

The effectiveness of central bank intervention in adjusting exchange rates remains unclear. In the heyday following the Plaza Accord, total U.S. interventions amounted to cumulative puchases of US$1.44 billion of yen and US$1.86 billion of DM. Contrast these figures with *daily* volume in the New York market alone, which at that time averaged more than US$100 billion. Thus, it is clear that central bank interventions, no matter how well coordinated, are a miniscule portion of daily foreign exchange activity.[23] Indeed, Table 8.7 shows that total foreign exchange holdings of both the Fed and the Treasury's Exchange Stabilization Fund amount to less than $50 billion. Even including the Fed's **reciprocal currency arrangements**, which permit central banks to borrow currencies from each other up to a predetermined credit limit, the U.S. monetary authorities are provided foreign currency reserves that total less than one day's average daily volume. Despite the small volume, intervention does not act on exchange rates directly but instead alters market expectations of future central bank policies, thereby indirectly inducing exchange rate adjustments.[24] In *Timely Topics 8.3*, Fed Chairman Alan Greenspan discusses the pitfalls and promises of central bank intervention in the context of the Mexican peso crisis of December 1994.

reciprocal currency arrangements: agreements that permit central banks to borrow currencies from each other up to a predetermined credit limit.

---

[23] Moreover, as we saw in Chapter 4, intervention is often "sterilized" so that there is no change in the total monetary base. That is, if the central bank expands the international supply of its domestic currency, it offsets this intervention by reducing the domestic money supply. If foreign and domestic assets are perfect substitutes, then sterilized intervention should have no impact on prices and exchange rates.

[24] Bonser–Neal (1996) and Hung (1995) observe that central bank "stabilization" intervention does not reduce, and may even increase, exchange rate volatility. Belongia (1992) and Dominguez (1990) report that Bundesbank intervention was the most effective agent in moving exchange rates; this suggests that the Bundesbank is the most credible central bank in signaling information about future monetary policies.

Table 8.7

Foreign Exchange Holdings of U.S. Monetary Authorities, December 1994 (US$ million)

	Federal Reserve	Treasury Exchange Stabilization Fund
Deutschemark	13,514.7	6,838.4
Japanese yen	6,872.4	10,088.1
Mexico peso	601.9	11,150.0
Interest and other inflows	110.2	289.9
Total	21,099.2	28,366.4

	Amount of Currency Facility	Amount Outstanding
Austrian National Bank	250	0
National Bank of Belgium	1,000	0
Bank of Canada	2,000	0
National Bank of Denmark	250	0
Bank of England	3,000	0
Bank of France	2,000	0
Deutsche Bundesbank	7,000[a]	0
Bank of Italy	3,000	0
Bank of Japan	5,000	0
Bank of Mexico	9,000[b]	1,300
Netherlands Bank	500	0
Bank of Norway	250	0
Bank of Sweden	300	0
Swiss National Bank	4,000	0
Bank for International Settlements		
Dollars against Swiss francs	600	0
Dollars against other European currencies	1,250	0
Total	39,400	1,300

[a]The German Bundesbank has a $6,000 line with the Fed and a $1,000 currency arrangement with the Treasury Exchange Stabilization Fund.

[b]The Bank of Mexico has a $3,000 regular line, a $3,000 temporary facility with the Fed, and a $3,000 line with the Treasury Exchange Stabilization Fund.

Source: "Treasury and Federal Reserve Foreign Exchange Operations," *Federal Reserve Bulletin* (March 1996): 210–213.

TIMELY TOPICS 8.3

THE MEXICAN PESO CRISIS OF DECEMBER 1994

Mexico's current financial difficulties are best understood in the context of much broader trends in international finance during the last ten to fifteen years—the globalization of finance—in which Mexico has participated and from which it has benefitted.... While there can be little doubt that these extraordinary changes in global finance have on balance been beneficial in facilitating significant improvements in economic structures and living standards throughout the world, they also have some potential negative consequences. In fact, while the speed of transmission of positive economic events has been an important plus for the world in recent years, it is becoming increasingly obvious, and Mexico is the first major case, that significant mistakes in macroeconomic policy also reverberate around the world at a prodigious pace. In any event, progress—and indeed developments affecting the emerging global financial system are truly that—is not reversible. We must learn to live with it. . . .

As part of efforts to accelerate its move toward status as an industrial country, the government of Mexico endeavored to link the peso to the U.S. dollar. It adopted a complex, [fixed] exchange-rate regime through which the Mexican peso was linked to the U.S. dollar via a moving exchange-rate band. Like many nations that have tried to "import" the anti-inflationary policies of another country by locking their exchange rates, to a greater or lesser extent, to the currency of a major trading partner, Mexico hoped to gain quick benefits through significant reductions in inflation. And indeed, Mexico was remarkably successful for several years. The inflation rate fell sharply from almost 160 percent in 1987 to 7 percent by 1994, but at the same time Mexico was losing international competitiveness and its current deficit widened. . . .

Investors' appreciation of the momentum behind Mexico's transformation began to wane in early 1994, at least in substantial part as a consequence of noneconomic events—the Chiapas uprising, political assassination, and the August election. . . . As 1994 progressed, private foreign investment inflows slowed. In their endeavor to support the exchange rate and to finance the very large current account deficit, the Mexican authorities drew down Mexico's foreign exchange reserves. At the same time, Mexico borrowed short term in dollars and in Tesobonos, which are [short term] debt obligations the peso value of which is linked to the peso-dollar exchange rate. Mexican authorities evidently believed or fervently hoped that the reduction in foreign investor interest was temporary. . . . If so, they were tragically mistaken.

Meanwhile, it became increasingly clear to many observers during the autumn that the prevailing level of Mexico's exchange rate could not be sustained short of a significant further tightening of monetary policy. But by then it was by no means clear that the degree of tightening required to support the peso was consistent with economic growth. Mexican authorities apparently were loath to risk a recession. . . . [T]he chosen alternative to dramatically tightened monetary policy, borrowing via Tesobonos and drawing on reserves to intervene in the foreign exchange market [and prop up the peso], had a limit. Indeed, that limit was reached on December 20, and the defense of the peso came to an abrupt end.

Had the adjustment of the peso been made much earlier in the context of a much tighter monetary regime, it is likely to have resulted in a more limited decline rather than the abrupt collapse that Mexico experienced. . . . Looking back, the moving exchange-rate band for the peso apparently failed to compensate fully for the widening differential in prices of tradeable goods denominated in dollars compared to such prices denominated in pesos [that is, the differential in inflation rates between the U.S. and Mexico]. Accordingly, the peso exchange rate at 3.5 to the U.S. dollar was arguably not sustainable indefinitely short of an unrealistically massive increase in domestic saving in Mexico or a continuation of the very large foreign captial inflows of 1992 and 1993 with such inflows being heavily invested in cost-reducing capital formation. . . . [A]s a consequence of the Mexican episode, other developing nations have become sensitized to the problems of depending too heavily on large inflows of foreign portfolio capital.

Source: Testimony by Alan Greenspan before the Committee on Foreign Relations of The U.S. Senate, January 26, 1995.

Checkpoint

✓

1.   Contrast fixed versus floating exchange rate regimes.

2.   What is the Bretton Woods system?

3.   What is the Smithsonian system?

4.   What is the European Monetary System?

5.   What is a managed float?

6.   What is the impact of central bank intervention in foreign currency markets?

➤ Exchange Rate Fluctuations

The value of any currency is determined by the demand for goods, services, and assets denominated in that currency as balanced by the supply of the currency.[25] Fluctuations in the value of the currency will occur when either demand or supply fluctuates. We have seen that the balance of payments is an important determinant of these forces of supply and demand. Unanticipated changes in the balance of payments cause currency fluctuations that create foreign exchange rate risk exposure.

Exchange rate volatility is measured using the standard deviation of currency price changes. Table 8.8 shows that the exchange rate volatilities of all 21 currencies increased dramatically in the post–1972 period. During 1983–1992, the most volatile currencies were those of Australia, Japan, New Zealand, the United States, the United Kingdom, and Greece (Table 8.8). Indeed, the greatly increased exchange rate volatility of the post–Bretton Woods period is obvious in Figure 8.9. Since currency fluctuations are difficult to anticipate, exchange rate risk is unavoidable for participants on international financial markets. We must therefore devise methods to measure currency risk exposure as well as discuss the causes of these exchange rate fluctuations.

Currency Risk Exposure

Our previous balance-of-payments example between the United States and Japan is an oversimplification of the international trade accounts. The balance of payments comprises two accounts: the **current account** and the **capital account**. The current account records all flows associated with international trade in goods and services, whereas the capital account records all international borrowing and lending flows. Capital account transactions can be either autonomous or reactive. Autonomous capital account transactions are generated by international risk return factors affecting the management of portfolios of financial securities. (These are the securities transactions that are enumerated in our hypothetical balance-of-payments example between the United States and Japan.) But since the total supply of each nation's currency is fixed in the short run, any imbalance will be offset by *reactive* capital account transactions.

If the Japanese try to spend more U.S. dollars than they take in, where will they get these dollars? In our example, the Japanese deficit amounted to US$65 billion. To obtain these dollars and avoid default on their international obligations, the Japanese must borrow an *additional* US$65 billion to finance their other lending and trade activities. This borrowing is merely a reaction to the need for U.S. dollars created by the net deficits in the rest of the balance of payments. It is added to the capital account, thereby reducing Japanese net lending to the United States by US$65 billion and bringing the total balance of payments into balance.

current account: record of all flows associated with international trade in goods and services.

capital account: record of all international borrowing and lending flows.

---

[25] Although we speak of the balance of payments as consisting of real goods and services as well as financial assets, less than 10% of the turnover on the foreign exchange market is induced by goods flows, while the bulk of the remainder originates from financial market transactions; see Heri and Rossi (1994).

Table 8.8

Nominal Effective Exchange Rate Volatility, 1963–1992

	Exchange Rate Volatility[a]			Percentage Change	
				1963–72 to 1973–82	1973–82 to 1983–92
Country	1963–72	1973–82	1983–92		
Italy	0.27	1.57	1.12	487.6	−28.5
Australia	0.34	1.96	2.72	469.5	38.8
Sweden	0.32	1.56	1.08	383.7	−30.8
Portugal	0.40	1.91	1.20	379.1	−37.2
Greece	0.38	1.79	1.80	370.0	0.6
United States	0.36	1.65	1.88	352.1	14.3
Japan	0.59	2.44	2.26	311.0	−7.5
Switzerland	0.51	1.82	1.26	255.4	−31.0
Norway	0.34	1.05	0.79	210.2	−25.0
Belgium	0.33	1.01	0.56	207.5	−44.9
Netherlands	0.36	0.94	0.66	157.3	−30.0
Canada	0.44	1.10	1.02	150.1	−7.3
Denmark	0.43	1.05	0.76	142.9	−27.4
Austria	0.33	0.79	0.53	139.7	−33.7
Spain	0.90	2.15	1.05	138.9	−51.1
Germany	0.69	1.44	0.93	107.9	−35.3
United Kingdom	1.02	1.78	1.91	74.4	7.2
Ireland	0.70	1.12	1.06	58.9	−5.3
France	0.89	1.35	0.80	52.2	−40.8
New Zealand	1.72	1.63	2.62	−5.3	61.3
Finland	2.19	1.11	1.12	−49.3	1.0
Geometric average	0.53	1.42	1.15	166.4	−18.8
Median	0.43	1.56	1.08	157.3	−27.4

[a]Standard deviation of percentage changes in monthly average nominal effective exchange rate (BIS 21-country index).

Source: S. Roger, "The Management of Exchange Reserves," BIS Economic Papers No. 38, July 1993.

By definition, then, the total balance of payments for any country cannot be out of balance. Deficits in the current account are *balanced* by reactive surpluses in the capital account. However, these reactive offsetting surpluses in the capital account can be used to forecast exchange rate fluctuations. We know that if a country is running a deficit in its current account and in its autonomous capital account, then interest rates and exchange rates must fluctuate so as to induce an offsetting surplus in its reactive capital account to bring the balance of payments into balance. If we can measure the autonomous components of the balance of trade, then we can predict the resulting exchange rate fluctuations that will be necessary to induce reactive capital movements. In our hypothetical example, from the U.S. perspective the autonomous surplus, in the U.S.-Japanese balance of payments will lead to an increase in demand for U.S. dollar-denominated loans, thereby raising dollar-yen and lowering yen-dollar exchange rates.

The trade-related pressure on exchange rates is reflected in forward exchange rates. Indeed, one of the parity relationships, FEEE, stated that forward exchange rates are estimates of expected future spot rates. Thus, if the market expects exchange rates to increase (decrease), perhaps because of trade imbalances, then we should see forward exchange rates selling at a premium (discount) over spot exchange rates. We can measure the annualized forward premium or discount in exchange rates in order to obtain a measure of the market's expectations of future exchange rate fluctuations. For example, on June 9, 1995 the spot yen-dollar was US$0.0118 per yen. The 180 day forward yen-dollar rate was US$0.01214, suggesting that

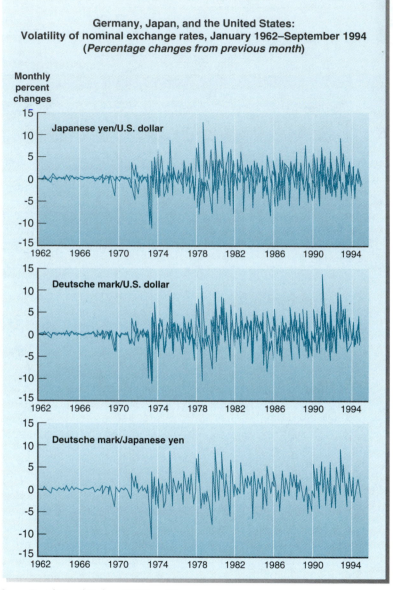

Source: Bartolini and Bodnar (1996), p. 25.

Figure 8.9

the market expected the yen to appreciate against the U.S. dollar over the six month period ending December 1995. We can express this as an annualized forward premium:[26]

$$\text{Annualized Forward Premium/Discount} = \left(\frac{{}_n F_t^{JY,US} - S_t^{JY,US}}{S_t^{JY,US}} \right) \left(\frac{360}{n} \right)$$

where $S_t^{JY,US}$ is the spot yen-dollar exchange rate as of time period t; n is the number of days

---

[26] We annualize using a 360 day year, although a 365 day year could be used.

until delivery on the forward contract; and $_nF_t^{JY,US}$ is the forward yen-dollar exchange rate as of time period t for delivery on date $t + n$.

Applying this to the yen-dollar example of June 9, 1995 yields a forward premium of

$$\left(\frac{0.01214 - 0.0118}{0.0118}\right)\left(\frac{360}{180}\right) = +5.763\% \text{ p.a.}$$

This forward exchange rate premium can be interpreted as an expectation that the yen will appreciate against the U.S. dollar at a rate of 5.763% p.a. From Japan's perspective, this premium reflects the significant surplus in the autonomous balance of payments between the United States and Japan that prevailed in 1995, which, as we have seen, leads to the expectation of rising exchange rates for the currency of the country in surplus. Thus, the market expects the yen to appreciate against the U.S. dollar.

Use of the Forward Rate Premium/Discount to Measure Currency Risk   How can market participants use the information encapsulated in the forward exchange rate premiums and discounts? If the forward rate is an accurate predictor of future spot rates, then the forward premium/discount can be used to measure the currency risk borne by market participants. For example, suppose that a U.S. bank owes 15 million yen on a pure discount loan due to be repaid in June 1996. Using the market expectations embedded in the forward rate in June 1995, the U.S. bank can expect the Japanese yen to appreciate at an annual rate of 5.763% for an expected increase in yen-dollar exchange rates of US$0.0118(1.05763) = US$0.01248 per Japanese yen. If repaid today, the U.S. bank would pay out 15 million yen, which can be changed at spot rates into US$177,000 (= 15 million yen × $0.0118). In June 1996, the expected loan repayment will be US$187,200 (= 15 million yen × $0.01248) for a loss to the U.S. bank of US$10,200, resulting from the exchange rate fluctuation.

We can obtain this estimate of the currency losses by using the formula for the forward premium/discount in currency as opposed to percentage terms. That is, the annualized impact of currency fluctuations denominated in the home currency (the U.S. dollar in this example) is

$$\text{US\$Cash Flows} = \left(_nF_t^{JY,US} - S_t^{JY,US}\right)\left(\frac{360}{n}\right) \text{ (JY Investment)} \qquad (8.1)$$

To apply this, note that the U.S. bank in our example had an investment denominated in yen that provides for the forward delivery of 15 million yen. Since from the perspective of a U.S. bank the Japanese yen is a foreign currency, a way to view this investment is as a choice to pay out Japanese yen instead of U.S. dollars. That is, the U.S. bank will have to sell the U.S. dollars to convert them into yen to repay its loan. A foreign currency trader would state this another way. The trader would say that the U.S. bank was *short* the yen, because the Japanese yen must be paid out on the loan.

long position: an investment that represents an asset or a receipt of funds.

We say that an investment is a **long position** whenever it represents an asset or a receipt of funds. A **short position** is the opposite—an investment that represents a liability or a payment of funds. Throughout this book, we denote short investments by negative signs and long investments by positive signs. Long foreign currency investments profit from increases in exchange rates; short foreign currency investments profit from decreases in exchange rates. Thus, the U.S. bank's 15 million yen loan is denoted as a short position of −15 million yen since the value of the investment *denominated in the investor's home currency* declines as the yen-dollar exchange rate increases. Investments that gain from declines in the yen-dollar exchange rate are short the yen (and long the U.S. dollar). Investments that gain from increases in the yen-dollar exchange rate are long the yen (and short the U.S. dollar). Using our hyphenated exchange rate terminology for two currencies j and k, we see that

short position: an investment that represents a liability or a payment of funds.

1.   If the value of an investment increases when the currency $j - k$ exchange rate increases, then the investment is long currency j and short currency k.

2.   If the value of an investment increases when the currency $j - k$ exchange rate decreases, then the investment is short currency j and long currency k.

We can use the characterization of long and short positions in our formula (8.1) for currency-related cash flows. Applying the formula to determine the impact of a shift in exchange rates on the value of the Japanese bank's short US$15 million investment, we obtain

$$\text{US\$Cash Flows} = (0.01214 - 0.0118) \left(\frac{360}{180} \right) (-\text{JY15m}) = -\text{US\$10,200}$$

Currency Risk for Portfolios of International Financial Investments   The U.S. bank took considerable currency risk when borrowing Japanese yen in the previous example. However, what if the U.S. bank had undertaken another yen-denominated investment? Suppose that this other investment was a Japanese government bill with a face value of 15 million yen maturing on the exact same date as the maturity of the yen-denominated loan. Now there are two exactly offsetting transactions. On the same date, the U.S. bank receives 15 million yen from its government bond investment, which it immediately uses to repay the 15 million yen on its loan obligation. Exchange rate fluctuations are now irrelevant to the cash flows of the U.S. bank because the bank is no longer obligated to exchange U.S. dollars for Japanese yen. The bank's currency risk is zero since it has completely covered one foreign currency transaction with an opposite one. Even though each transaction when considered individually has substantial amounts of currency risk, when combined into a single portfolio, they offset one another and the portfolio has no currency risk.

From this example, we can see that it is myopic to examine the currency risk of individual transactions in isolation from the remainder of the portfolio. Rather, the currency risk of the entire portfolio of international transactions should be examined. This allows us to take into account offsetting transactions that reduce the risk of the portfolio. The mechanism used to measure the currency risk of a portfolio is the **net currency exposure**. The net currency exposure is the sum of all the long and short foreign currency positions in the portfolio. Put differently, for any currency (in this example, the Japanese yen, JY), exchange rate risk exposure can be measured as

net currency exposure: the sum of all the long and short foreign currency positions in the portfolio.

$$JY \text{ Net Currency Exposure } = JY \text{ Assets minus } JY \text{ Liabilities}$$
$$+ JY \text{ currency Purchased minus } JY \text{ currency Sold}$$

The long positions are the assets held plus the amount of currency purchased. The short positions are the liabilities owed plus the amount of currency sold. The net currency exposure is long (short) and therefore positive (negative) if the total long positions exceed (are less than) the total short positions. If the total long positions equal the total short positions, then the net currency exposure is zero and the firm is immunized from the risk of foreign exchange rate fluctuations.

The net currency exposure can be used to calculate the cash flow impact of exchange rate fluctuations on a portfolio of assets and liabilities. Changes in foreign exchange rates cause cash flow effects because of the unmatched currency position represented by the net currency exposure. That is,

$$\text{Cash Flows} = (\Delta FX)(\text{Net Currency Exposure})$$

where ΔFX is the change in foreign exchange rates. To calculate cash flow effects of changes in exchange rates, simply substitute the net currency exposure for the cash investment in equation

(8.1). Thus, the portfolio's currency risk exposure can be measured by

$$\text{US\$Cash Flows} =$$

$$\left({}_nF_t^{JY,US} - S_t^{JY,US}\right)\left(\frac{360}{n}\right)(JY \text{ Net Currency Exposure}) \qquad (8.2)$$

Consider the example of a fictional American portfolio manager named It's a Small World Fund (ISWF). Some of ISWF's portfolio investments, as well as today's spot and forward exchange rates, are shown in Table 8.9. Computing the net currency exposures for the three foreign currencies, note that both the U.K. Treasury bill and Japanese government bond investments are assets, whereas the loans are liabilities; the yen purchased are off-balance sheet assets, and the yen sold are off-balance sheet liabilities. Applying the definition, the pound sterling net currency exposure is £10 million minus £3.5 million plus 0 minus 0 = +£6.5 million. The yen net currency exposure is 125 million yen –0 + 0 – 75 million yen = + 50 million yen. The DM net currency exposure is 0 – DM17 million +0 – 0 = –17 million Deutschemark. ISWF is long the pound sterling and the Japanese yen, and short the Deutschemark.

If the forward rates are accurate predictors of future spot exchange rates, we can use the forward rate premium/discount for each of the currencies to calculate the impact on ISWF's U.S. dollar cash flows. For the dollar-sterling:

$$\left(\frac{1.675 - 1.7}{1.7}\right)\left(\frac{360}{30}\right) = -17.65\% \text{ p.a.}$$

For the yen-dollar:

$$\left(\frac{0.0101 - 0.01}{0.01}\right)\left(\frac{360}{30}\right) = +12.0\% \text{ p.a.}$$

For the DM-dollar:

$$\left(\frac{2.25 - 2.23}{2.23}\right)\left(\frac{360}{30}\right) = +10.762\% \text{ p.a.}$$

These forward rate premiums/discounts suggest that the market expects end-of-year dollar-sterling spot rates to decline by 17.65% to a value of 1.7(1 – 0.1765) = US$1.4 per £; yen-dollar is expected to increase by 12% to 0.01(1 + 0.12) = $0.0112 per yen; and DM-dollar to increase by 10.762% to 2.23(1 + 0.10762) = US$2.47 per DM. Applying these end-of-year expected

Table
8.9

It's A Small World Fund[a]

U.K. Treasury bills: £10 million
Japanese government bonds (pure discount): 125 million yen
£-denominated loan (pure discount): £3.5 million
Deutschemark-denominated loan: DM17 million
Japanese yen sold: 75 million yen

Today's spot rates	Today's 30 day forward rates
Dollar–sterling: US$1.7 per £	Dollar–sterling: US$1.675
Yen–US dollar: US$0.01 per yen	Yen–US dollar: $0.0101 per yen
Deutschemark–US dollar: $2.23 per DM	Deutschemark–US dollar: $2.25 per DM

[a]Recall the reversal in the dollar–sterling rate quotation formats; a dollar–sterling spot exchange rate of 1.7 denotes US$1.7 per pound sterling.

currency rates to the three net currency exposures, using equation (8.2), enables us to solve for the annualized U.S. dollar-denominated cash flow effects on ISWF's portfolio.

The annualized U.S. dollar impact of the dollar-sterling exchange rate fluctuation is

$$\left({}_nF_t^{UK,US} - S_t^{UK,US}\right)\left(\frac{360}{n}\right) \text{(UK Net Currency Exposure)}$$

$$= (1.675 - 1.7)\left(\frac{360}{30}\right)(+£6.5m) = -US\$1.95m$$

The annualized U.S. dollar impact of the yen-dollar exchange rate fluctuation is

$$\left({}_nF_t^{JY,US} - S_t^{JY,US}\right)\left(\frac{360}{n}\right) \text{(JY Net Currency Exposure)} = (0.0101 - 0.01)\left(\frac{360}{30}\right)(+50m)$$

$$= +US\$60,000$$

The annualized U.S. dollar impact of the DM-dollar exchange rate fluctuation is

$$\left({}_nF_t^{DM,US} - S_t^{DM,US}\right)\left(\frac{360}{n}\right) \text{(DM Net Currency Exposure)} =$$

$$(2.25 - 2.23)\left(\frac{360}{30}\right)(-DM\ 17m) = -US\$4.08m$$

The impact of the expected exchange rate fluctuations is an end-of-year cash flow loss to ISWF totaling US\$5.97 million. We ignore currency rate fluctuations at our peril.

Checkpoint

✓

1. Why must the balance of payments between any two countries sum to zero?
2. What is the capital account? What is the current account?
3. Distinguish the two components of the capital account. What are their implications for exchange rate determination?
4. What is the expected impact of surpluses in the autonomous balance of payments on exchange rates? of deficits?
5. What is a long position? a short position?
6. Why is it important to sum up all long and short positions in order to calculate the currency risk exposure? What is this summation called?

The Causes of Exchange Rate Volatility

When investors and observers are faced with recurring episodes of extreme and long-lasting volatility in current exchange rates, they become nostalgic for the "good old Bretton Woods days." Indeed, our graphs of exchange rates show that they appear to fluctuate more or less randomly. Rather than being an indictment of current exchange rate regimes, randomness in exchange rate movements should be viewed as a sign of success. If currency markets are efficient, then exchange rates are determined by new information about fundamentals that generate changes in expectations.

A simple model of exchange rate determination will help pinpoint the central role of expectations in explaining exchange rate volatility. Consider two currencies, the yen and the U.S. dollar, each of which use domestic and foreign markets for real and financial transactions. We know from our discussions of the demand for money in Chapter 4 that increases in both the level of real economic activity and the rate of price inflation increase the demand for money. Similarly, increases in interest rates decrease the demand for money. Expressing this symbolically:

$$m_t^{JY} = a + \pi_t^{JY} + by_t^{JY} - cr_t^{JY}$$
$$m_t^{US} = a + \pi_t^{US} + by_t^{US} - cr_t^{US}$$

where m_t^{JY}, m_t^{US} is the demand for yen, U.S. dollars, respectively at time t; π_t^{JY}, π_t^{US} is the price level in each country; y_t^{JY}, y_t^{US} is the real level of economic activity in each country; r_t^{JY}, r_t^{US} is the level of interest rates in each country; and a, b, and c are parameters.

Invoking the simplified form of PPP, we see that the exchange rate is equal to the differential in prices across countries; we obtain $\Delta S_t^{JY,US} = \pi_t^{JY} - \pi_t^{US}$, whereas $\Delta S_t^{JY,US}$ is the change in spot yen-dollar exchange rates over time. Solving for π_t^{JY}, π_t^{US} and substituting into the PPP relationship yields

$$\Delta S_t^{JY,US} = (m_t^{JY} - m_t^{US}) + b(y_t^{US} - y_t^{JY}) + c(r_t^{JY} - r_t^{US}) \qquad (8.3)$$

Applying the simplified form of IRP, we determine the interest rate differential by obtaining the difference between forward and spot exchange rates, or $r_t^{JY} - r_t^{US} = F_t^{JY,US} - S_t^{JY,US}$. But we know from FEEE that $F_t^{JY,US} = E(S_{t+1}^{JY,US})$, where $E(S_{t+1}^{JY,US})$ is the expected future spot exchange rate. Substituting these two expressions into equation (8.3) yields

$$\Delta S_t^{JY,US} = (m_t^{JY} - m_t^{US}) + b(y_t^{US} - y_t^{JY}) + c[E(S_{t+1}^{JY,US}) - S_t^{JY,US}] \qquad (8.4)$$

What does equation (8.4) tell us? Exchange rate movements are determined by two major factors: (1) shifts in fundamentals (for example, each country's monetary policy, $m_t^{JY} - m_t^{US}$, and real economic activity, $y_t^{US} - y_t^{JY}$); and (2) shifts in expectations of future spot exchange rates. But what determines shifts in expectations of future spot exchange rates? The answer is new information about international fundamental factors.

Now you can understand why international currency markets are so volatile. When new information about, say, a country's monetary policy is released to the public, there is a direct impact on exchange rates resulting from the process depicted in equation (8.4). However, there is also an indirect impact on expectations that may either augment or offset the direct impact of the new fundamental information. The net effect on exchange rates depends on the opinions of the critical market makers in the foreign currency markets who "read the tea leaves" and move markets by placing orders to buy or sell based on their expectations about future spot exchange rates.

Let's suppose that Japan pursues a stimulative monetary policy that increases the growth rate of the Japanese money supply faster than that of the German money supply. Equation (8.4) shows us that the yen-DM exchange rate would rise in proportion to the relative expansiveness of Japan's monetary policy. However, market participants may anticipate that Japan's expansionary monetary policy will increase Japanese imports and lead to a deficit in the Japanese trade balance of payments. This will increase the supply of yen on world markets (to pay for the increased imports) and lead to a downward pressure on yen-DM exchange rates. Which effect will prevail? The direct effect raising yen-DM exchange rates, or the indirect effect lowering yen-DM exchange rates? It depends on the conviction of currency traders' expectations and their willingness to sell the yen in anticipation of a yen decline. If traders are convinced of the yen's decline, they will sell the yen, thereby making their expectations a self-fulfilling prophecy. This is why we observe long term cyclical swings in currency markets. The markets repeatedly reveal considerable and long-lived overshooting of expectations as the market consensus slowly shifts from one expectation to another. The problems associated with disentangling the many factors affecting exchange rate fluctuations are discussed in *Timely Topics 8.4*.

TIMELY TOPICS 8.4

IT'S ONLY MONEY: THE ENDURING MYTH OF "DEVALUATION INFLATION"

The "quality press" is full of wise saws and modern instances about the effects of the many devaluations that we have witnessed over the weeks [after the British pound and the Italian lira dropped out of the EMS]. The most frequent and widely believed allegation is that devaluation (or the free floatation to a lower level) will ignite inflation.... It is surely widely accepted that what causes inflation is too rapid an expansion in the stock of money relative to the flow of output. Inflation is not caused by trade unions, greedy industrialists, pernicious foreigners, etc., who exert little if any control over the quantity of money in circulation.

The same reasoning applies to the exchange rate. By itself, it cannot cause inflation or deflation or disinflation.... Exchange rates between two currencies are determined largely, but not wholly, by the relative monetary growth of those countries per unit of output. The more dollars there are around, compared with say, Deutschemarks, the lower will be the value of the dollar in terms of marks. Simple supply and demand.

In reality, of course, exchange rates are affected by many phenomena that influence, through views of future values, the balance between supply and demand: political swings, commodity price shocks, wars, even the peccadillos of leaders.

But the underlying proposition that relative monetary policies are the main determinant of trends in exchange rates remains the centerpiece of analysis. Free market exchange rates can take long holidays from the trend. Typically, they tend to overshoot on their way to a new equilibrium level. We have seen this in the case of the Deutschemark and Swiss franc in 1978, sterling in 1980/81 and, of course, the great rise of the dollar to its peak in February 1985 [as well as its spectacular fall in 1995]. In terms of purchasing power parity, all were way out of line, but these high exchange rates were performing the task of equilibrating the supply of and demand for financial assets in each currency....

There are many examples of such periods [of falling exchange rates and declining inflation]. In Britain during the period 1980–85, the pound went down from the giddy heights of $2.33 to $1.30. Yet inflation fell from 18 percent to less than 4 percent in 1986. In the United States, the dollar has fallen quite dramatically against the mark and yen over the last three years, yet inflation has come down and is now near zero. The reason for the decline in inflation, in spite of the devaluation of the currency, was that monetary policy—as measured by the growth in the money supply—was tight.... [But, I]t is doubtful that the British, Spanish, and Italian governments have gotten over the macho concern with maintaining the value of their currencies.

Source: "AIG *World Markets Advisory*" by Sir Alan Walters, October 1992

Checkpoint

1. What factors determine exchange rate movements?

2. How has the EMS changed the type of exchange rate volatility for its currencies?

➤ Summary

The four parity relationships are purchasing power parity (PPP), the international Fisherian relation (IFR), the foreign exchange expectation expression (FEEE), and interest rate parity (IRP). Elimination of all arbitrage opportunities keeps exchange rates in line with these four parity relationships. However, in practice, exchange rate determination is more complicated than the four parity relationships. This is because of market imperfections that prevent currency prices from conforming to strict parity. The four factors contributing to these market imperfections are (1) transaction costs; (2) trade restrictions and capital controls; (3) differences in national tastes and preferences; and (4) central bank regulatory policies that create distinct exchange rate policy regimes. During the post–World War II period, there have been three major exchange rate policy regimes: (1) the Bretton Woods system of fixed exchange rates (1944–1971); (2) the floating rate system (1973–1979); and (3) the fixed exchange rates of the European Monetary System and the managed float of non-EC currencies (1979–present).

Since exchange rate fluctuations are a fact of life in either fixed or floating exchange rate policy regimes, we discussed the determinants of currency risk. We can use the forward premium/discount to measure the risk of exchange rate fluctuations. The net currency exposure is used to determine the impact of those fluctuations on portfolio investments.

➤ References

Abeysekera, S. P., and H. J. Turtle. "Long Run Relations in Exchange Markets: A Test of Covered Interest Parity." *Journal of Financial Research* 18, No. 4 (Winter 1995): 431–447.

Bartolini, L., and G. Bodnar. "Are Exchange Rates Excessively Volatile? And What Does 'Excessive Volatility' Mean, Anyway?" Federal Reserve Bank of New York Research Paper 9601 (January 1996).

Belongia, M. "Foreign Exchange Intervention by the United States: A Review and Assessment of 1985–1989." Federal Reserve Bank of St. Louis *Economic Review* (May–June 1992): 32–51.

Belongia, M. "Prospects for International Policy Coordination: Some Lessons from the EMS," Federal Reserve Bank of St. Louis *Economic Review* (July–August 1988): 19–29.

Bessembinder, H. "Bid-Ask Spreads in the Interbank Foreign Exchange Markets." *Journal of Financial Economics* 35 (1994): 317–348.

Bonser-Neal, C. "Does Central Bank Intervention Stabilize Foreign Exchange Rates?" Federal Reserve Bank of New York *Economic Review* 81, No. 1 (First Quarter 1996): 43–58.

Brenner, R., and K. Kroner. "Arbitrage, Cointegration, and Testing the Unbiasedness Hypothesis in Financial Markets." *Journal of Financial and Quantitative Analysis* 30 (March 1995): 23–42.

Chang, R. "Is a Weak Dollar Inflationary?" Federal Reserve Bank of Atlanta *Economic Review* (September–October 1995): 1–14.

Clinton, K. "Transactions Costs and Covered Interest Arbitrage: Theory and Evidence." *Journal of Political Economy* 96, No. 2 (1988): 358–370.

Cochran, S., and R. DeFina. "Predictable Components in Exchange Rates." *Quarterly Review of Economics and Finance* 35, No. 1 (Spring 1995): 1–14.

Deravi, K., P. Gregorowicz, and C. E. Hegji. "Exchange Rates and the Inflation Rate." *Quarterly Journal of Business and Economics* 34, No. 1 (Winter 1995): 42–54.

Dominguez, K. "Market Responses to Coordinated Central Bank Intervention." *Carnegie-Rochester Conference Series on Public Policy* 32 (1990): 121–164.

Dooley, M., and P. Isard. "Capital Controls, Political Risk, and Deviations from Interest-Rate Parity." *Journal of Political Economy* 88, No. 21 (1980): 370–384.

Engel, C., and C. Hakkio. "Exchange Rate Regimes and Volatility." Federal Reserve Bank of Kansas City *Economic Review* (Third Quarter 1993): 43–58.

European Commission. "One Market, One Money: An Evaluation of the Potential Benefits and Costs of Forming an Economic and Monetary Union." *European Economy* 44 (1990).

Fama, E. "Forward and Spot Exchange Rates." *Journal of Monetary Economics* 13 (November 1984): 319–338.

Flood, R. P., and A. K. Rose. "Fixing Exchange Rates: A Virtual Quest for Fundamentals." *Journal of Monetary Economics* 36 (1995): 3–37.

Frenkel, J. and R. Levich. "Covered Interest Arbitrage: Unexploited Profits?" *Journal of Political Economy* 83, No. 2 (1975): 325–338.

Glassman, D. "The Efficiency of Foreign Exchange Futures Markets in Turbulent and Non-Turbulent Periods." *Journal of Futures Markets* 7, No. 3 (1987): 245–267.

Gokey, T. C. "What Explains the Risk Premium in Foreign Exchange Returns?" *Journal of International Money and Finance* 13, No. 6 (1994): 729–738.

Hakkio, C. "The Dollar's International Role." *Contemporary Policy Issues* 11 (April 1993): 62–75.

Heri, E. W., and V. Rossi. *International Financial Market Investment: A Swiss Banker's Guide.* Chichester: John Wiley & Sons, 1994.

Hodrick, R. J., and S. Srivastava. "The Covariation of Risk Premiums and Expected Future Exchange Rates." *Journal of International Money and Finance* (March 1986): 5–21.

Huang, R. "An Analysis of Intertemporal Pricing for Forward Foreign Exchange Controls." *Journal of Finance* 44, No. 1 (March 1989): 183–194.

Hung, J. H. "Intervention Strategies and Exchange Rate Volatility: A Noise Trading Perspective." Federal Reserve Bank of New York Research Paper 9515 (May 1995).

Johnson, P. A. "Estimation of the Specification Error in the Fisher Equation." *Applied Economics* 26 (1994): 519–526.

Klopfenstein, G., and J. Stein. *Trading Currency Cross Rates.* New York: John Wiley & Sons, 1993.

Kumar, V., and J. A. Whitt. "Exchange Rate Variability and International Trade." Federal Reserve Bank of Atlanta *Economic Review* (May–June 1992): 17–32.

Lee, P. M., and W. G. Sullivan. "Considering Exchange Rate Movements in Economic Evaluation of Foreign Direct Investments." *The Engineering Economist* 40, No. 2 (Winter 1995): 171–199.

Lin A., and P. E. Swanson. "Measuring Global Money Market Interrelationships: An Investigation of Five Major World Currencies." *Journal of Banking and Finance* 17 (1993): 609–628.

Mahdavi, S., and S. Zhou. "Purchasing Power Parity in High Inflation Countries: Further Evidence." *Journal of Macroeconomics* 16, No. 3 (1994): 403–422.

McCallum, B. T. "A Reconsideration of the Uncovered Interest Parity Relationship." *Journal of Monetary Economics* 33 (1994): 105–132.

Meese, R., and K. Rogoff. "Was It Real? The Exchange Rate—Interest Differential Relation over the Modern Floating—Rate Period." *Journal of Finance* 43, No. 4 (September 1988): 933–948.

Merrick, J., and A. Saunders, "International Expected Real Interest Rates: New Tests of the Parity Hypothesis and U.S. Fiscal Policy Effects." *Journal of Monetary Economics* 18 (1986): 313–322.

Michael, P., and A. R. Nobay. "Purchasing Power Parity Yet Again: Evidence from Spatially Separated Commodity Markets." *Journal of International Money and Finance* 13 No. 6 (1994): 637–657.

Otani, I., and S. Tiwari. "Capital Controls and Interest Rate Parity: The Japanese Experience, 1978–81." *International Monetary Fund Staff Papers* 28 (1981): 793–815.

Pakko, M. R., and P. S. Pollard. "For Here or to Go? Purchasing Power Parity and the Big Mac." Federal Reserve Bank of St. Louis *Review* (January–February 1996): 3–22.

Phylaktis, K., and Y. Kassimatis. "Does the Real Exchange Rate Follow a Random Walk? The Pacific Basin Perspective." *Journal of International Money and Finance* 13 (1994): 476–495.

Pigott, C. "International Interest Rate Convergence: A Survey of the Issues and Evidence." Federal Reserve Bank of New York *Quarterly Review* (Winter 1993–1994): 24–37.

Rhee, S. G., and R. Chang, "Intra-Day Arbitrage Opportunities in Foreign Exchange and Eurocurrency Markets." *Journal of Finance* 47, No. 1 (March 1992): 363–379.

Sharma, M. K., and R. Obar. "Testing for Purchasing Power Parity: A Data Matching Problem or a Long Run Phenomenon?" *Multinational Business Review* (Spring 1995): 74–81.

Solnik, B. *International Investments.* 2nd ed. Reading, Mass.: Addison–Wesley, 1991.

Strauss, J., and D. Terrell. "Cointegration Tests of the Fisher Hypothesis with Variable Trends in the World Real Interest Rate." *Southern Economic Journal* 61, No. 4 (April 1995): 1047–1056.

Whitt, J. "European Monetary Union: Evidence from Structural VARs." *Federal Reserve Bank of Atlanta Working Paper Series*, March 1995.

➤ Questions

1. Use Table 8.3 to state the following exchange rates:
    a. U.S. dollar-Japanese yen
    b. Japanese yen-U.S. dollar
    c. Swiss franc-Dutch guilder
    d. Dutch guilder-Swiss franc
    e. Mexican peso-Deutschemark
    f. Deutschemark-Mexican peso
    g. Canadian dollar-French franc
    h. French franc-Canadian dollar
    i. Italian lira-Japanese yen
    j. Japanese yen-Italian lira
    k. U.S. dollar-Deutschemark
    l. Deutschemark-U.S. dollar

2. Use the following exchange rate table to determine the following currency cross rates:
    a. sterling-Canadian dollar
    b. sterling-Swiss franc
    c. sterling-Japanese yen
    d. sterling-Deutschemark
    e. Canadian dollar-Swiss franc
    f. Canadian dollar-Japanese yen
    g. Canadian dollar-Deutschemark
    h. Swiss franc-Japanese yen
    i. Swiss franc-Deutschemark
    j. Japanese yen-Deutschemark

Exchange Rate Table

British pound–U.S. dollar	US$1.61 per pound
Canadian dollar–U.S. dollar	US$0.75 per Canadian dollar
Swiss franc–U.S. dollar	US$0.90 per Swiss franc
Japanese yen–U.S. dollar	US$0.01 per Japanese yen
Deutschemark–U.S. dollar	US$0.71 per Deutschemark

3. If the Canadian dollar-Swiss franc exchange rate was 0.78, use your answer to question 2 to demonstrate an arbitrage opportunity.

4. One year (simple) interest rates are 7% p.a. in the Netherlands and 3.5% p.a. in Switzerland, and spot Swiss franc-guilder exchange rates are 1.5.
    a. How can you set up a trade to exploit the interest rate differentials? Is it an arbitrage opportunity?
    b. Calculate the profitability of your trade in part (a) if end-of-year Swiss franc-guilder exchange rates are (i) 1.4; (ii) 1.5; and (iii) 1.6.
    c. What is the forward exchange rate that would eliminate any arbitrage opportunity?
    d. What factors might explain deviations from the forward exchange rate in part (c)?

5. Suppose that expected inflation rates are 10% p.a. in the U.K. but only 5% p.a. in the U.S. If current spot rates are $1.4 per pound, and nominal rates in the U.K. 12.2%, use the four parity relationships to determine forward exchange rates, U.S. nominal interest rates, and real interest rates.

6. Using your answers to question 5, calculate the returns on an international portfolio (with no default risk) consisting of US$100 million in one year maturity British bonds (earning the one year nominal

interest rate in the U.K., r_{UK}) and the issuance of US\$100 million in one year maturity American debt instruments (paying the one year nominal interest rate in the U.S., r_{US}) if end-of-year exchange rates are

a. US\$1.4/£
b. US\$1.47/£
c. US\$1.3/£

7. During the course of a year, German importers have purchased French goods worth 215 million French francs and bought 22 million Ffr. worth of French financial securities. Simultaneously, French importers purchased 375 million Deutschemark of German goods and DM557 million of German securities. The gold content of the French franc is .25 ounces while each ounce is worth 1.25 Deutschemark.

a. What is the gold value of the balance of payments between France and Germany?
b. How would this balance of payments be settled under the Bretton Woods system?
c. What is the Deutschemark-French franc exchange rate?
d. What is the balance of payments in terms of Deutschemarks?
e. How would this balance of payments be settled under the Smithsonian system of freely floating exchange rates?
f. How would this balance of payments be settled under the European Monetary System?

8. Today's dollar-sterling spot rate is US\$1.6 per pound sterling. The 90 day forward rate is US\$1.585 per £.

a. What is the market's expectation about dollar-sterling exchange rates? What might account for these expectations?
b. What is the annualized forward rate premium or discount?
c. If a U.S. investor is obligated to repay £1 million at the end of the year, how would you characterize this position: long or short?
d. Use the annualized forward rate premium/discount to calculate the end-of-year cash flows associated with the investment in part (c).

9. Use the following portfolio for a U.S.-based FI to calculate (a) net currency exposures; (b) expected future spot rates; and (c) the U.S. dollar cash flow impact of the expected exchange rate fluctuations.

Mega Money Manager, Inc.[a]
- -

Swiss government bonds: SwFr 2.5 million
Japanese government bonds: 12 billion yen
German corporate bonds: DM 35 million
£-denominated loan (pure discount): 3.5 million
Deutschemark-denominated loan: DM 75 million
Deutschemark bought: DM 50 million
Japanese yen sold: 6.5 billion yen

Today's spot rates	Today's 60 day forward rates
Dollar–sterling: US\$1.25 per £	Dollar–sterling: US\$1.315
dollar–yen: 95	dollar–yen: 93.5
Deutschemark–dollar: US\$0.75	Deutschemark–dollar: US\$0.725
Swiss franc–dollar: US\$0.86	Swiss franc–dollar US\$0.855

[a]Recall the reversal in the dollar–sterling exchange rate quotation formats. For example, a dollar–sterling spot exchange rate of 1.25 denotes US\$1.25 per pound sterling.
- -

10. Consider the following hypothetical European Monetary System consisting of four countries: Germany, France, Switzerland, and the Netherlands. The benchmark currency is the Deutschemark.

Central parity levels are
    French franc: DM 0.3 per FFr
    Swiss franc: DM 1.2 per SFr
    Dutch guilder: DM 0.9 per guilder

a. If the allowable ranges are 2.25% above and below the central parity levels, what are the EMS currency bands?

b. Current spot rates are French franc–DM 0.28; Swiss franc–DM 1.23; and guilder–DM 0.92. What policy intervention, if any, must be undertaken to bring each country into compliance with the EMS?

c. If interest rate parity holds, what are forward exchange rates if one year interest rates are 10% p.a. in Germany, 11% p.a. in Switzerland, 9% p.a. in the Netherlands, and 7% p.a. in France?

d. If forward rate premiums/discounts are constant at the levels determined in part (c), what is the required interest rate shift that will just bring each currency into compliance with the nearest limit of the EMS bands? (Assume that IRP holds and that German interest rates are unchanged.)

11. Use the following monthly exchange rates to calculate forward rate premiums/discounts. (Assume FEEE holds.)

	DM–US$	yen–US$	Canadian $–US$	Australian $–US$
January	0.72	0.013	0.83	0.75
February	0.721	0.0132	0.82	0.755
March	0.73	0.0135	0.81	0.73
April	0.725	0.0127	0.805	0.719
May	0.74	0.0136	0.80	0.724
June	0.736	0.0142	0.833	0.74
July	0.745	0.015	0.79	0.75
August	0.75	0.015	0.791	0.752
September	0.75	0.0143	0.78	0.75
October	0.759	0.015	0.77	0.74
November	0.76	0.01590	0.767	0.747
December	0.765	0.016	0.77	0.75

CHAPTER 9

MARKET RISK MEASUREMENT

"If there's no money in poetry, neither is there poetry in money."—Robert Graves, speech at London School of Economics, December 6, 1963 in *Mammon and Black Goddess* (1965), p. 3.

Learning Objectives

- To obtain an overall risk measure by bringing together all the risk assessment techniques developed in previous chapters.
- To assess the advantages and disadvantages of standard deviation, beta, and RiskMetrics as yardsticks to measure risk.

➤ Introduction

Whenever you are unsure about the future outcomes of your present actions, you are exposed to risk. Whether you want to reduce or even increase the risk of your activities, chances are that you will use a FI first to measure and then to control that risk exposure. In this chapter, we examine the basic risk factors, their impact on security prices, as well as techniques to measure risk exposure. We have already developed quantitative measures of several types of risk: interest rate risk (Chapter 7), exchange rate risk (Chapter 8), and inflation rate, or price level, risk (Chapter 4). Now it is time to put them all together into a comprehensive measure of total risk.

upside risk: pleasant surprises, or unexpected gains.

Risks are surprises. Pleasant surprises, unexpected gains, are called **upside risk**, whereas unpleasant surprises, unexpected losses, are **downside risk**. But whether upside or downside, all types of risk occur when something unexpected happens. The three sources of risk we examined in earlier chapters—price-level risk, interest rate risk, and exchange rate risk—all emanate from the possibility of unanticipated fluctuations. In this chapter, we first examine these basic risk factors individually and devise a general statistic to measure risk—the standard deviation. Then we consolidate the individual risk factors into an overall risk measure that takes into consideration the interrelationships among the sources of risk.

downside risk: unpleasant surprises, or unexpected losses.

➤ How Do We Measure Risk?

You call your broker and ask her to buy a municipal bond for your investment portfolio. When she asks you what maturity you want to buy, you respond that you want to invest the money for

285

one year, after which time you intend to sell the bond in order to help finance a new business you plan to start. Should you buy a one year bond? It depends on what you expect will happen to interest rates over the next year. If you expect interest rates to decrease, then you would be better off buying a long term bond and selling it at a capital gain after one year. On the other hand, if you expect interest rates to increase, the purchase of a one year bond will lock in your one year holding period yield without exposing you to the possibility of capital loss. The word *expect* should be stressed because you cannot know, with certainty, what will happen to interest rates. The best that you can do is make an educated guess as to the most likely expected value of interest rates on municipal bonds in one year. To make your best guess, you should take into account all possibilities and their likelihoods of occurrence. In other words, you should compute an **expected value**, or **mean value**, of future interest rates. The expected value is simply the weighted average of all possible future outcomes, where the weights are equal to each outcome's likelihood of occurrence. It is your best guess of future values.

expected value, or mean value: the weighted average of all possible future outcomes, where the weights are equal to each outcome's likelihood of occurrence.

If today's one year maturity municipal bond rates are 7% p.a., you might list the following possible scenarios:

Next Year's Scenario	Likelihood of Scenario (%)	Impact on 1 Year Muni Rates (% p.a.)
The Fed tightens monetary policy.	25	+2
German interest rates increase.	10	+1
No change.	30	0
Japanese yen–U.S. dollar exchange rates increase.	10	−1
The Fed eases monetary policy.	25	−2

probability distribution: list of possible future events and their likelihoods of occurrence.

This list of scenarios is a **probability distribution** since it lists all possible future events and their likelihoods of occurrence. You know that you have taken all possible scenarios into account since the probabilities of all outcomes sum to 100% = 25% + 10% + 30% + 10% + 25%.

What is your best guess of expected one year municipal bond rates next year? You have listed five scenarios. There is a 25% chance that rates will increase from 7% to 9% p.a.; a 10% chance that rates will increase to 8% p.a.; a 30% chance that rates will be unchanged at 7% p.a.; a 10% chance that rates will decline by 1% to 6% p.a.; and a 25% chance that rates will decrease from 7% to 5% p.a. You can combine these five scenarios into one estimate of expected interest rates simply by weighting each possible outcome by its likelihood of occurrence. Thus

$$\mu = E(R) = .25(9\%) + .10(8\%) + .30(7\%) + .10(6\%) + .25(5\%) = 7\% \text{ p.a.}$$

where $\mu = E(R)$ is the expected rate of return. Your best guess of the expected value of one year municipal bond rates, using the five scenarios listed, is 7% p.a. This is the mean, or expected, value.

The general formula for the mean, or expected value, is

$$E(R) \equiv \mu \equiv \sum_{i=1}^{N} p_i R_i$$

where there are N possible scenarios, the likelihood of scenario i's occurrence is denoted p_i, and R_i is the return under scenario i. If each potential occurrence is equally likely, then the probability of each scenario is $\frac{1}{N}$.

Your best guess of next year's one year municipal bond rates is 7%, but it is most definitely not a sure thing. Indeed, your own listing of scenarios indicates that there is a very good chance (70% chance) you will be wrong, since there is only a 30% chance that interest rates will remain unchanged at 7%. Rates may go as high as 9% or as low as 5% in your assessment of the possible future scenarios. That means there is a 70% chance that you will be surprised and interest rates will not equal the 7% p.a. level that you expect to prevail. Since surprises equal risk, you might want to evaluate the risk that interest rates will deviate from your expectations. In other words, you want a weighted measure of the possible deviations from expected values under all possible scenarios, where the weights are the likelihood of occurrence for each scenario. That is the **variance** measure, the square root of which is the **standard deviation**.

variance: a weighted measure of the possible deviations from expected values under all possible scenarios, where the weights are the likelihood of occurrence for each scenario.

standard deviation: the square root of variance.

In calculating variance and standard deviation, we take into account both upside and downside risk. Thus, pleasant surprises (interest rates below the mean value of 7% p.a.) must be considered as well as unpleasant surprises (interest rates above the mean value of 7% p.a.).[1] To prevent the negative values of downside risk from offsetting the positive signs of upside risk when we add them together, we square each of the deviations from the mean to change all signs into positive signs. Squaring also gives signficantly greater weight to larger deviations from the mean. We can calculate your risk by taking the squared deviations from the mean for all scenarios and weighting them by their probabilities of occurrence.

$$\sigma^2 = .25(9\% - 7\%)^2 + .10(8\% - 7\%)^2 + .30(7\% - 7\%)^2$$
$$+ .10(6\% - 7\%)^2 + .25(5\% - 7\%)^2 = 2.2$$

This produces the following general formula for variance, denoted σ^2:

$$\sigma^2 \equiv \sum_{i=1}^{N} p_i[R_i - E(R)]^2$$

The standard deviation is simply the square root of variance, and for our example it is

$$\sigma = \sqrt{2.2} = 1.48\%$$

confidence interval: a range of outcomes such that there is a known probability that returns will fall within the given range.

normal probability distribution: bell-shaped probability distribution.

We can use the standard deviation to define a **confidence interval**, which states a range of outcomes such that there is a known probability that returns will fall within the given range. Using a confidence interval of two standard deviations from the mean states that there is a large likelihood (a 95% chance for **normal**, or bell-shaped, **probability distributions**) that returns will be within two standard deviations above or below the mean. For our example, a confidence interval of two standard deviations would range from a low of $7\% - 2(1.48\%) = 4.04\%$ p.a. to a high of $7\% + 2(1.48\%) = 9.96\%$ p.a. That is, you are quite confident that one year municipal bond yields next year will be somewhere in the range of 4.04% to 9.96% p.a., although your best estimate of expected rates is 7% p.a.

Checkpoint

✓

1. What is the expected value? mean?
2. What is the variance? standard deviation?
3. What is a confidence interval? How can it be used to assess risk?

➤ Three Basic Sources of Risk

We can use our two summary statistics—mean and standard deviation—to measure three basic sources of risk in financial markets: interest rate risk, exchange rate risk, and price-

---

[1] Recall from Chapter 7 that if interest rates increase, the price of the bond that you are holding declines, and vice versa.

Table 9.1	Measurement of the Three Basic Risk Factors: Mean and Standard Deviation of Annual Returns, January 1980–December 1992

Risk Factor	Average Annual Return (%)	Standard Deviation (%)
Interest Rate Risk		
U.S. Treasury bills	8.23	0.94
U.S. long term Treasury bonds	13.08	12.64
U.S. corporate bonds	12.72	9.08
U.S. mortgages	12.84	9.94
Foreign bonds	11.76	12.47
Exchange Rate Risk		
European currencies	8.04	10.63
Japanese yen	11.28	12.40
Price-Level Risk		
U.S. real estate	10.56	15.73
U.S. value stocks	15.60	15.14
U.S. growth stocks	15.72	17.42
European stocks	12.48	17.74
Japanese stocks	17.40	25.39
U.S. venture capital	13.20	14.13

Source: Ayman Hindy, "Elements of Quantitative Risk Management," in W. Beaver and G. Parker, *Risk Management: Problems and Solutions* (New York: McGraw–Hill, 1995), p. 107–138.

level risk. Table 9.1 shows the mean and standard deviations of the three basic risk factors, as measured using 13 indexes of security values.[2] Interest rate risk is a function of rate volatility, which is measured using five indexes of interest-sensitive securities: U.S. Treasury bills, U.S. long term Treasury bonds, U.S. corporate bonds, U.S. mortgages, and foreign bonds. Exchange rate volatility is measured using an index of major European currencies and the Japanese yen–U.S. dollar exchange rate. Price-level risk is measured using commodity price volatility as represented by an index of U.S. real estate values, as well as equity price volatility as represented by five indexes of stock price fluctuations: U.S. value stocks, U.S. growth stocks, European stocks, Japanese stocks, and U.S. venture capital firms.

The means and standard deviations in Table 9.1 can be used to calculate confidence intervals. Based on use of two standard deviations, the 95% confidence interval is from 6.35% to 10.11% p.a. for U.S. Treasury bills and from –33.38% to 68.18% for Japanese stocks. Clearly, U.S. Treasury bills fluctuate within a much narrower band than do Japanese stock prices. The basic risk factors are not independent of one another, however. Financial markets often move together. For example, during the stock market crashes of October 1987 and 1989, all financial markets around the world experienced declines, some more and some less. Our measurement of total risk is flawed if we fail to consider these interrelationships.

---

[2] Default, or credit, risk can be measured by the difference between the corporate bond factor and the return on equivalent Treasury securities.

Interrelationships Among Risk Factors

To understand risk interrelationships, let's return to your investment decision. In response to your inquiry about the purchase of a municipal bond, your broker tells you about a hot new 10 year maturity corporate bond issue that is currently yielding 13% p.a. To compare the two investments, you must evaluate the possible interest rate scenarios that might impact the returns on your one year investment in the corporate bond. After some inquiries, you compile the following probability distribution for the corporate bond investment:

Next Year's Scenario	Likelihood of Scenario (%)	Impact on 10 Yr. Corp. Bond (% p.a.)
The Fed tightens monetary policy.	25	+3
German interest rates increase.	10	+2
No change.	30	0
Japanese yen–U.S. dollar exchange rates increase.	10	−2
The Fed eases monetary policy.	25	−3

Summary statistics for the corporate bond rate probability distribution are mean and standard deviation. The mean return is

$$E(R) = .25(16\%) + .10(15\%) + .30(13\%) + .10(11\%) + .25(10\%) = 13\% \text{ p.a.}$$

The variance is

$$\sigma^2 = .25(16\% - 13\%)^2 + .10(15\% - 13\%)^2 + .30(13\% - 13\%)^2$$
$$+ .10(11\% - 13\%)^2 + .25(10\% - 13\%)^2 = 5.3$$

The standard deviation is

$$\sigma = \sqrt{5.3} = 2.3\%$$

Comparing the corporate bond to the municipal bond investment shows that the expected return on the corporate bond is 6% higher (13% versus 7% p.a.), but the risk is significantly higher, as measured by the standard deviation of 2.3% as compared to 1.48%.

Both the municipal and corporate bond yields respond to the same underlying five scenarios. For example, when the Fed tightens monetary policy, the municipal bond yield increases to 9% while the corporate bond yield increases to 16% p.a. We can therefore measure the comovement of the two yields over all the possible future outcomes. The relationship between deviations from the mean for two different probability distributions is called the **covariance**. To calculate the covariance, utilize each distribution's deviation from the mean for each scenario weighted by the likelihood of occurrence. For our example, the covariance between the municipal bond (M) and the corporate bond (C) is

covariance: the relationship between deviations from the mean for two different probability distributions.

$$\text{Cov}(M, C) = .25(9\% - 7\%)(16\% - 13\%) + .10(8\% - 7\%)(15\% - 13\%)$$
$$+ .30(7\% - 7\%)(13\% - 13\%) + .10(6\% - 7\%)(11\% - 13\%)$$
$$+ .25(5\% - 7\%)(10\% - 13\%) = +3.4$$

The general formula for covariance is

$$\sigma_{u,v} \equiv \sum_{i=1}^{N} p_i [R_i^u - E^u(R)][R_i^v - E^v(R)]$$

where $\sigma_{u,v}$ is the covariance between securities u and v; R_i^u, R_i^v is the return on securities u, v if scenario i occurs; and $E^u(R)$, $E^v(R)$ is the expected return on securities u, v. The covariance between the municipal and corporate bond yields is positive because the returns of the two securities move together, always in the same direction. If one security's yield goes up, whereas the other's goes down, then the covariance will be negative. If the two securities are independent of one another, then their covariance will be zero.

The municipal and corporate bond yields move together, but it is difficult to tell from the covariance just how close this comovement is. Do they move together in lockstep—going up and down in complete unison? Casual observation of the probability distribution suggests they do not, since in some scenarios, the municipal bond yields shift in one percentage point increments, while the corporate bond yields shift by two percentage points. The **correlation coefficient** is a measure that tells us how close the interrelationship is. The correlation coefficient is an indexed form of the covariance which ranges from a minimum value of -1 to a maximum value of $+1$. To compute the correlation coefficient, simply divide the covariance by the product of the two securities' standard deviations. That is,

$$\rho_{u,v} \equiv \frac{\sigma_{u,v}}{\sigma_u \sigma_v}$$

For our example, the correlation coefficient is

$$\rho_{M,C} = \frac{3.4}{(1.48)(2.3)} = +.9988$$

Now we have a measure of how closely the two securities' yields follow one another. Since the maximum value of the correlation coefficient is $+1$, $\rho_{M,C} = +.9988$ shows that the two securities' yields are very closely connected. Indeed, if the correlation coefficient was equal to $+1$ (-1), then we would consider the two securities to be perfectly positively (negatively) correlated. The municipal and corporate bond securities are just short of being perfectly positively correlated.

Table 9.2 shows the correlations among the index returns used to measure the three basic risk factors. Long term Treasury bonds, corporate bonds, and mortgages are all highly correlated, although their correlation coefficients are less than one. U.S. Treasury bills are negatively correlated with European currencies, value stocks, growth stocks, and the venture capital index, although they are less than perfectly negatively correlated.

correlation coefficient: an indexed form of the covariance, which ranges from a minimum value of -1 to a maximum value of $+1$.

Checkpoint

✓

1. Use the standard deviations in Table 9.1 to determine which indexes are most risky; least risky.

2. What is the covariance? the correlation coefficient?

3. Use the correlation coefficients in Table 9.2 to determine which indexes are most closely correlated; least correlated.

The Importance of Measuring Correlation Coefficients

The recognition that financial markets move together (see Table 9.2), some more and some less, is hardly a revelation. Indeed, if markets are truly global, then participants will compare yields in different securities markets around the world. This will have the effect of linking the markets, since, for example, if investors in one market are willing to accept lower yields, then downward competitive pressure will be exerted on yields in other markets.

What is to be gained by quantifying these interrelationships among financial markets using covariances and correlation coefficients? To answer this question, let's return to your investment

Table 9.2

Correlations Among the Three Basic Risk Factors, January 1980–December 1992

Risk Factor	Interest Rate Risk				Exchange Rate Risk		
	T-Bills	LT T-Bonds	Corp. Bonds	Mort.	Foreign Bonds	European Currency	Japanese Yen
Treasury bills	1.00	0.16	0.21	0.21	0.01	−0.40	0.00
Long term Treasury bonds		1.00	0.94	0.89	0.43	0.18	0.19
Corporate bonds			1.00	0.95	0.42	0.19	0.20
Mortgages				1.00	0.39	0.20	0.74
Foreign bonds					1.00	0.83	0.85
European curr.						1.00	0.67

Risk Factor	Price-Level Risk					
	Value Stocks	Growth Stocks	European Stocks	Japanese Stocks	Venture Capital	Real Estate
Treasury bills	−0.70	−0.11	0.12	0.00	−0.11	−0.20
Long term Treasury bonds	0.33	0.33	0.24	0.16	0.07	0.27
Corporate bonds	0.35	0.31	0.25	0.15	0.10	0.05
Mortgages	0.29	0.25	0.22	0.11	0.05	0.23
Foreign bonds	0.70	0.60	0.51	0.56	0.10	0.09
European curr.	−0.03	0.01	0.47	0.52	−0.01	−0.09
Value stocks	1.00	0.91	0.60	0.27	0.52	0.74
Growth stocks		1.00	0.58	0.26	0.56	0.68
European stocks			1.00	0.52	0.41	0.54
Japanese stocks				1.00	0.20	0.24
Venture capital					1.00	0.58

Source: Ayman Hindy, "Elements of Quantitative Risk Management," in W. Beaver and G. Parker, eds., *Risk Management: Problems and Solutions* (New York: McGraw–Hill, 1995), pp. 107–138.

problem, but now let's consider a third investment: a venture capital opportunity that is rather risky but tends to do well in low interest rate environments. The venture capital investment offers an expected rate of return of 14% p.a. The same five states of the world are assumed to represent all possible future scenarios over the next year. The following is a probability distribution of yields on the venture capital investment:

Next Year's Scenario	Likelihood of Scenario (%)	Impact on Venture Capital Yield (% p.a.)
The Fed tightens monetary policy.	25	−4
German interest rates increase.	10	−2
No change.	30	0
Japanese yen–U.S. dollar exchange rates increase.	10	+2
The Fed eases monetary policy.	25	+4

The expected return on the venture capital investment is

$$E(R) = .25(10\%) + .10(12\%) + .30(14\%) + .10(16\%) + .25(18\%) = 14\%$$

The variance on the venture capital investment is

$$\sigma^2 = .25(10\% - 14\%)^2 + .10(12\% - 14\%)^2 + .30(14\% - 14\%)^2$$
$$+ .10(16\% - 14\%)^2 + .25(18\% - 14\%)^2 = 8.8$$

The standard deviation of venture capital returns is

$$\sqrt{8.8} = 2.97\%$$

You've certainly come far from the municipal bond investment that you first called your broker about. The risk of the venture capital investment is considerably higher than that of the municipal bond, with a standard deviation of 2.97% p.a. as opposed to only 1.48% p.a. on the municipal bond. Of course, the expected return is double, 14% p.a., on the venture capital investment versus 7% p.a. on the municipal bond. You like the higher expected return, but you don't like the higher risk on the venture capital investment.

Which to choose? The good news is that you don't have to choose one—you can choose both. You can create a portfolio consisting of *both* investments—a portion of your funds invested in the municipal bond and the rest in the venture capital opportunity.[3]

Note that the covariance between the venture capital investment (denoted V) and the municipal bond (denoted M) is

$$\text{Cov}(M, V) = .25(9\% - 7\%)(10\% - 14\%) + .10(8\% - 7\%)(12\% - 14\%)$$
$$+ .30(7\% - 7\%)(14\% - 14\%) + .10(6\% - 7\%)(16\% - 14\%)$$
$$+ .25(5\% - 7\%)(18\% - 14\%) = -4.4$$

The correlation coefficient between V and M is

$$\rho_{M,V} = \frac{-4.4}{(1.48)(2.97)} = -1.00$$

The two investments are perfectly negatively correlated. How can you use this information to make your investment decision? If you combine the two investments into a portfolio, you will usually be able to reduce, and in this case you can *eliminate*, your risk exposure. If you invest two-thirds of your money in the municipal bond and one-third in the venture capital opportunity, you will earn returns equal to 9.33% p.a. *under all possible future scenarios.* In other words, you have transformed two risky investments into one risk free investment—simply by using the magic of negative correlation. Indeed, the combination of risky securities into portfolios so as to reduce the risk of the portfolio is called **diversification** and is a basic tenet of financial risk management.

diversification: the combination of risky securities into portfolios so as to reduce the risk of the portfolio.

Let's see how your portfolio performs in each of the five possible future scenarios. The municipal bond yields represent two-thirds of your portfolio returns, whereas the venture capital yields represent one-third of your yields on the portfolio. Thus, if the Fed tightens monetary policy, the 9% p.a. yield on the municipal bond will be weighted by two-thirds and the 10% p.a. yield on the venture capital investment will be weighted by one-third. If the Fed tightens monetary policy, the portfolio returns will be $\frac{2}{3}(9\%) + \frac{1}{3}(10\%) = 9.33\%$ p.a. Indeed, for all five scenarios, portfolio returns will be the same—9.33% p.a. We have constructed a risk free portfolio using two risky investments that are perfectly negatively correlated with each other. The probability distribution of the portfolio is as follows:

---

[3] To maximize returns, you will want to be fully invested and not leave any of your investment funds idle.

Next Year's Scenario	Likelihood of Scenario (%)	Muni Bond Yield (%)	Venture Capital Yield (%)	Portfolio Yield (%)
The Fed tightens monetary policy.	25	9	10	9.33
German interest rates increase.	10	8	12	9.33
No change.	30	7	14	9.33
Japanese yen–U.S. dollar exchange rates increase.	10	6	16	9.33
The Fed eases monetary policy.	25	5	18	9.33

Not all portfolios can eliminate all risk exposure, and it is truly difficult to find perfectly negatively correlated securities. But even combining a relatively small number of securities permits a considerable amount of risk reduction. To obtain the benefits of diversification, you need not find securities that are perfectly negatively correlated. All you need are securities that are *not* perfectly positively correlated. Fortunately, these are available in abundance, as evidenced in Table 9.2.

As an example of the diversification benefits of combining securities that are not perfectly negatively correlated, consider a portfolio consisting of a 50% investment in the municipal bond of previous examples and the remaining 50% in a new issue of foreign bonds, with the following probability distribution of returns:

Next Year's Scenario	Likelihood of Scenario (%)	Muni Bond Yield (%)	Foreign Bond Yield (%)	Portfolio Yield (%)
The Fed tightens monetary policy.	25	9	12	10.5
German interest rates increase.	10	8	18	13
No change.	30	7	15	11
Japanese yen–U.S. dollar exchange rates increase.	10	6	12	9
The Fed eases monetary policy.	25	5	13	9

The foreign bonds have an expected return of 13.75% p.a. and a variance of

$$\sigma_F^2 = .25(12 - 13.75)^2 + .10(18 - 13.75)^2 + .30(15 - 13.75)^2$$
$$+ .10(12 - 13.75)^2 + .25(13 - 13.75)^2 = 3.5$$

The last column shows the returns on the portfolio under each of the five possible scenarios. The portfolio's expected return is 10.375% p.a., and the variance is

$$\sigma_{M+F}^2 = .25(10.5 - 10.375)^2 + .10(13 - 10.375)^2 + .30(11 - 10.375)^2$$
$$+ .10(9 - 10.375)^2 + .25(9 - 10.375)^2 = 1.47$$

The portfolio, consisting of a municipal security with a variance of 2.2 and a foreign bond with a variance of 3.5 (and a standard deviation of $\sqrt{3.5} = 1.9\%$), has a portfolio variance of only 1.47. The municipal and foreign bonds have a covariance of

$$Cov(M, F) = .25(9\% - 7\%)(12\% - 13.75\%) + .10(8\% - 7\%)(18\% - 13.75\%)$$
$$+ .30(7\% - 7\%)(15\% - 13.75\%) + .10(6\% - 7\%)(12\% - 13.75\%)$$
$$+ .25(5\% - 7\%)(13\% - 13.75\%) = +0.10$$

Thus, the municipal bond and the foreign bond are positively correlated, with a correlation coefficient of

$$\rho_{M,F} = \frac{+0.10}{(1.48)(1.9)} = +0.036$$

As long as the securities are not perfectly positively correlated, diversification offers benefits.

The benefits of diversification are determined by the correlations of the securities included in the portfolio. The less positively (or the more negatively) the securities are correlated, the greater the risk reducing benefits of diversification. This concept is demonstrated by the following formula for the variance of a portfolio of n securities:

$$\sigma_p^2 = \sum_{i=1}^{K} \sum_{j=1}^{K} w_i w_j \sigma_{i,j}$$

where σ_p^2 is the variance of the portfolio's returns; $\sigma_{i,j}$ is the covariance between security i and j's returns (note that if $i = j$, then $\sigma_{i,i} = \sigma_i^2$, which is the variance of security i's returns); and w_i is the weight of security i in the portfolio, where there are K securities in total.[4] Let's work this formula out using two securities (that is, $K = 2$). The general formula is

$$\sigma_p^2 = w_1^2 \sigma_1^2 + w_2^2 \sigma_2^2 + 2 w_1 w_2 \sigma_{1,2} \tag{9.1}$$

But since the covariance between security 1 and security 2 returns ($\sigma_{1,2}$) is equal to $\rho_{1,2}\sigma_1\sigma_2$, we can restate equation (9.1) as

$$\sigma_p^2 = w_1^2 \sigma_1^2 + w_2^2 \sigma_2^2 + 2 w_1 w_2 \rho_{1,2}\sigma_1\sigma_2 \tag{9.2}$$

Applying equation (9.2) to a portfolio consisting of equal parts of the one year municipal bond (security 1) and corporate bonds (security 2), we note that $w_1 = w_2 = .5$. Thus:

$$\sigma_p^2 = .5^2(1.48)^2 + .5^2(2.3)^2 + 2(.5)(.5)(+.9988)(1.48)(2.3) = 3.57$$

$$\sigma_p = \sqrt{3.57} = 1.89\%$$

The portfolio's total risk exposure is 1.89%, somewhere between the municipal bond's standard deviation of 1.48% and the corporate bond's standard deviation of 2.3% p.a. If you look at the last term of equation (9.2), you can see the potential benefits of diversification. The lower the correlation coefficient, $\rho_{1,2}$, the lower the value of the last term, and the lower the risk of the portfolio. Since the lower bound of the correlation coefficient is -1.0, then the benefits of diversification are maximized when securities are perfectly negatively correlated. But diversification reduces the risk of the portfolio whenever portfolios are created using securities that are less than perfectly positively correlated.

Early studies[5] show that as few as 30 stocks traded on the New York Stock Exchange (NYSE), randomly chosen and combined into a portfolio, can reduce average risk exposure by more than 50%.[6] Figure 9.1 shows the benefits of diversification internationally and in four countries: the United States, the United Kingdom, France, and Germany. Just by adding securities to a portfolio, risk exposure can be dramatically reduced even if the securities themselves are not negatively correlated. The average risk of the portfolio (as measured by the portfolio's standard deviation of returns) declines very rapidly at first, as randomly chosen securities are

---

[4] Short sales in any security i are represented as negative values of w_i.

[5] See the classic studies by Wagner and Lau (1971) and Elton and Gruber (1977).

[6] Statman (1987) shows that investors should invest in portfolios consisting of at least 30 to 40 stocks in order to exhaust the benefits of diversification.

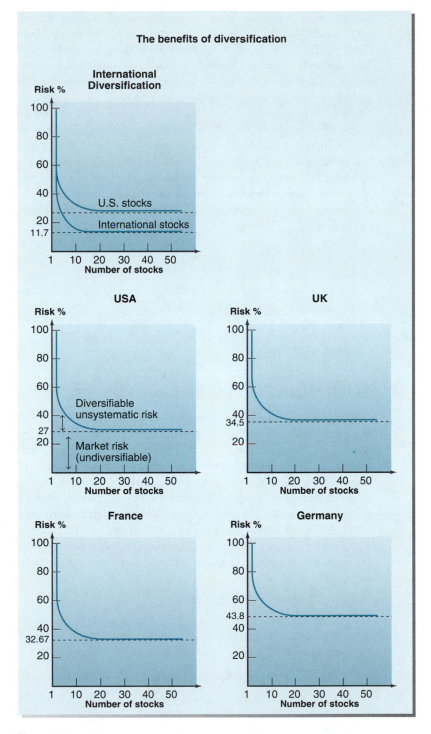

Figure 9.1

added. But the risk reducing effect of adding more securities levels off after the 20 security point. Indeed, a stubborn level of risk remains and cannot be eliminated by adding securities to your portfolio. This "stubborn, leftover" risk is undiversifiable since it reflects the risk of the market in general. If we calculate the correlation coefficient between an index of all NYSE stocks and the portfolio of 20 securities, the correlation coefficient is +.89. They are highly positively correlated, suggesting that the "leftover," undiversifiable risk emanates mostly from market risk factors. Total risk (measured by the standard deviation shown in Figure 9.1) can be divided into two component parts: (1) **unsystematic, or diversifiable, risk**, which is company specific and can be eliminated by combining securities into portfolios; and (2) **systematic, or market, risk**, which is the residual risk left over after all unsystematic risk is diversified away. Undiversifiable market risk, shown in Figure 9.1, is the lowest in the United States (at an average standard deviation of 27%), followed by France (32.67%), the United Kingdom (34.5%), and Germany (43.8%). However, when portfolios are diversified internationally (using international, including U.S., stocks), the market risk falls to 11.7%. How do we measure these two component parts of risk? The answer to that question produced the first, and probably most widely used, asset pricing relationship: the capital asset pricing model (CAPM).

unsystematic, or diversifiable, risk: risk exposure that is company specific and can be eliminated by combining securities into portfolios.

systematic, or market, risk: the residual risk left over after all unsystematic risk is diversified away.

Checkpoint

1.   How does portfolio creation reduce risk?

2.   What security characteristics are required to completely eliminate risk?

3.   What is unsystematic risk? systematic risk?

4.   How can you measure the benefits to diversification?

▶ Asset Pricing Using the Basic Risk Factors

Risk affects security markets directly through security returns. Investors try to avoid risk whenever possible, resulting in a profitable business for FIs managing risk on behalf of their customers. To get investors to accept risk, they must be paid a premium. The **risk premium** is the differential over the risk free rate of return paid to compensate investors for risk exposure. The more risk, the higher the risk premium and the greater the security's expected rate of return. That's why the venture capital investment offers an expected return of 14% p.a. as compared to 7% p.a. for the municipal bond. The doubled expected return is a premium for the doubled risk exposure (a standard deviation of 2.97% as opposed to 1.48% for the two investments). We can measure risk exposure by examining the risk premiums included in security returns. This approach is used in the capital asset pricing model and the arbitrage pricing theory.

risk premium: the differential over the risk free rate of return paid to compensate investors for risk exposure.

The Capital Asset Pricing Model

As we have seen, systematic risk stems from basic market risk, or equivalently, market fluctu-ations can be identified as the most important basic risk factor affecting security returns. We can summarize these conclusions using the following equation:

$$\text{Total Risk} = \text{Systematic Risk} + \text{Unsystematic Risk}$$

We know how to calculate total risk using the standard deviation, but how do we decompose the standard deviation into its two component parts: systematic and unsystematic risk? To answer this question, note that systematic risk is highly correlated with market fluctuations. If we define a **market index** as the return on a diversified portfolio consisting of a subset of securities that are somewhat representative of all securities available in the market, we can calculate any security's market risk exposure by examining the impact of changes in the market index on the security's return. *Practitioner's Primer 9.1* discusses the practical problems in

market index: the return on a diversified portfolio consisting of a subset of securities representative of all securities available in the market.

beta: the correlation coefficient that measures the sensitivity of security returns to fluctuations in market returns, denoted β.

choosing an appropriate market index. However, once an index is chosen, the correlation coefficient that measures the sensitivity of security returns to fluctuations in market returns is called **beta**, denoted β. Restating this in mathematical terms, the β is the $\Delta R_i / \Delta R_m$, which is the change in returns on security i (ΔR_i) for any given change in market returns (ΔR_m). This is simply the slope of a straight line, as shown in Figure 9.2, with the following equation:

$$R_i = \alpha_i + \beta_i R_m + \epsilon_i \tag{9.3}$$

where R_i is the rate of return on any security i; R_m is the rate of return on the market index; α_i is the intercept term; β_i is the slope of the line; and ϵ_i is the error term, which represents deviations between actual returns and the predicted value on the straight line.

So what does this have to do with estimating systematic and unsystematic risk? Figure 9.2 shows a scatter plot of points (A, B, C, D, and E) representing combinations of R_i and R_m, each of which corresponds to a different point in time. A line, equation (9.3), is fitted to the points by reducing the total of the squared deviations between the points and the line. The slope of this fitted, characteristic line, is beta. The deviations from the characteristic line, denoted ϵ_i, take on a different value for each time period. We can use these two statistical concepts to quantify systematic and unsystematic risk. The measure of a security's systematic, or market, risk is

$$\text{Systematic Risk} = \beta_i^2 \sigma_m^2$$

and the measure of a security's unsystematic risk is

$$\text{Unsystematic Risk} = \sigma_\epsilon^2$$

so that security i's risk consists of

$$\text{Total Risk} = \sigma_i^2 = \beta_i^2 \sigma_m^2 + \sigma_{\epsilon_i}^2$$

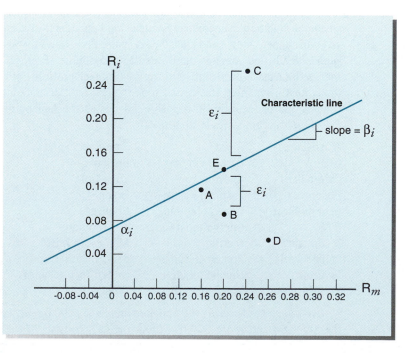

Figure 9.2

Beta is easily interpreted as the relationship between returns on a market portfolio and returns on a security.[7] If the security's beta is 2, then a 10% increase in market returns is consistent with a 20% increase in the security's expected return. If the security's beta is –0.5, then a 10% increase in market returns coincides with a 5% decrease in the security's expected return. The beta of the market portfolio (and any security that is perfectly positively correlated with the market) is 1.0. We can use beta in order to simplify the measurement of the risk of a portfolio. The systematic risk of a portfolio is simply the weighted average of the portfolio securities' betas, or

$$\beta_p = \sum_{i=1}^{K} w_i \beta_i$$

where w_i is the weight of each of the K securities in the portfolio, and β_i is the beta of each security i included in the portfolio.

PRACTITIONER'S PRIMER 9.1

THE CHOICE OF A MARKET INDEX

Beta measures a security's sensitivity to fluctuations in the value of the market portfolio, which consists of *every* financial asset available, in any form, anywhere in the world. Clearly, it is not possible to observe the true market portfolio, and so we rely on empirical proxies, or estimates, of the market portfolio. The securities included in the market index are chosen to be good indicators of the value of the true market portfolio. Two practical matters need to be decided when determining the market index: (1) the identity of securities to be included in the index; and (2) the methodology of combining the securities into an index.

The Dow Jones Industrial Average (DJIA) is the beneficiary of what is arguably the best public relations campaign in financial markets. It is the oldest (introduced in 1896) and most widely known and cited index. Figure PP.1 shows the history of the DJIA, with Figure PP.2 listing some of the Dow's daily highlights. Even so, the DJIA is an index that is the *least* representative of the true market portfolio. It consists of only 30 of the largest companies' stocks traded on the NYSE. At discrete intervals over time, the composition of securities in the DJIA changes as the ranking of companies changes. Currently, the companies in the DJIA are

Allied-Signal	Alcoa	American Express
AT&T	Bethlehem Steel	Boeing
Caterpillar	Chevron	Coca-Cola
DuPont	Eastman Kodak	Exxon
General Electric	General Motors	Goodyear
IBM	International Paper	J. P. Morgan
McDonald's	Merck	Minnesota M&M
Philip Morris	Procter & Gamble	Sears Roebuck
Texaco	Union Carbide	United Technologies
Walt Disney	Westinghouse	Woolworth

Two broader indexes are the Standard and Poor's 100 (fondly known as the OEX) and the Standard and Poor's 500 (the SPX). The OEX consists of the largest 100, and the

---

[7] Beta is not strictly a correlation coefficient since it is calculated as $\Delta R_i / \Delta R_m$, which equals $\text{Cov}(R_m, R_i)/\sigma_m^2$, as opposed to the definition of the correlation coefficient, which is $\text{Cov}(R_m, R_i)/\sigma_m \sigma_i$. Thus, the value of beta can exceed +1 or be lower than –1.

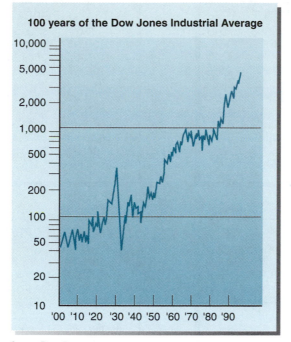

100 years of the Dow Jones Industrial Average

Source: Dow Jones

Figure PP.1

SPX contains the largest 500 stocks on the NYSE, where size is measured by the market value of outstanding shares. A broader market index is the Wilshire 5000 Equity Index, which includes stocks that trade on the NYSE, AMEX, and NASDAQ.

The two basic methodologies used to combine the securities into an index are (1) price weighted and (2) value-weighted. Price-weighted indexes are computed by simply adding the prices of all securities included in the market index portfolio. Therefore, all securities are equally weighted. Price-weighted indexes utilize adjustment factors to control for discrete price changes in the event of stock splits or stock dividends. On the other hand, value-weighted indexes need no adjustment factors. That is because in constructing the value-weighted index, each security's stock price is multiplied by the number of shares outstanding. Thus, the value-weighted index is based on the current value of the total number of shares of the firms included in the index. For price-weighted indexes, the securities with the highest prices have the greatest impact on the value of the index. In contrast, for value-weighted indexes, the firms with the largest **market capitalization** (price per share times number of shares outstanding) have the greatest impact on the value of the index. Since these firms have the largest presence in the financial market, the value-weighted methodology produces a market index that is more indicative of the true market portfolio than does the price-weighted index. The Standard and Poor's indexes and the Wilshire 5000 are all value-weighted.

To illustrate the two methodologies, the DJIA is calculated at each time period t using the following formula:

market capitalization: price per share times number of shares outstanding.

$$\text{DJIA}_t = \frac{\sum_{i=1}^{30} P_{it}}{0.35491922}$$

DAYS WITH GREATEST NET GAIN			
RANK	DATE	CLOSE	NET CHG	% CHG
1	10/21/87	2027.85	186.84	10.15
2	01/17/91	2623.51	114.60	4.57
3	10/20/87	1841.01	102.27	5.88
4	10/29/87	1938.33	91.51	4.96
5	10/16/89	2657.38	88.12	3.43
6	08/21/91	3001.79	88.10	3.02
7	12/23/91	3022.58	88.10	3.00
8	04/05/94	3675.41	82.06	2.28
9	08/27/90	2611.63	78.71	3.11
10	01/04/88	2015.25	76.42	3.94

DAYS WITH GREATEST NET LOSS			
RANK	DATE	CLOSE	NET CHG	% CHG
1	10/19/87	1738.74	−508.00	−22.61
2	10/13/89	2569.26	−190.58	−6.91
3	10/26/87	1793.93	−156.83	−8.04
4	01/08/88	1911.31	−140.58	−6.85
5	11/15/91	2943.20	−120.31	−3.93
6	10/16/87	2246.74	−108.35	−4.60
7	04/14/88	2005.64	−101.46	−4.82
8	02/04/94	3871.42	−96.24	−2.27
9	10/14/87	2412.70	−95.46	−3.81
10	08/06/90	2716.34	−93.31	−3.32

DAYS WITH GREATEST % GAIN			
RANK	DATE	CLOSE	NET CHG	% CHG
1	10/06/31	99.43	12.86	14.87
2	10/30/29	258.47	28.40	12.34
3	09/21/32	75.16	7.67	11.36
4	10/21/87	2027.85	186.84	10.15
5	08/03/32	58.22	5.06	9.52
6	02/11/32	78.60	6.80	9.47
7	11/14/29	217.28	18.59	9.36
8	12/18/31	80.69	6.90	9.35
9	02/13/32	85.82	7.22	9.19
10	05/06/32	59.01	4.91	9.08

DAYS WITH GREATEST % LOSS			
RANK	DATE	CLOSE	NET CHG	% CHG
1	10/19/87	1738.74	−508.00	−22.61
2	10/28/29	260.64	−38.33	−12.82
3	10/29/29	230.07	−30.57	−11.73
4	11/06/29	232.13	−25.55	−9.92
5	12/18/1899	58.27	−5.57	−8.72
6	08/12/32	63.11	−5.79	−8.40
7	03/14/07	76.23	−6.89	−8.29
8	10/26/87	1793.93	−156.83	−8.04
9	07/21/33	88.71	−7.55	−7.84
10	10/18/37	125.73	−10.57	−7.75

Figure PP.2 Biggest moves in the Dow Jones Industrial Average.

where P_{it} is the price per share of security i included in the index at time t and 0.35491922 is the adjustment factor (as of July 31, 1995). When it was first introduced, the DJIA was a simple average with a denominator of 30. Stocks splits and stock dividends over the years have caused that divisor to decline to its current value of 0.35491922.

The SPX, as an example of a value-weighted index, is calculated using the following formula:

$$SPX_t = \frac{\sum_{i=1}^{500} 10(P_{it} N_i)}{\sum_{i=1}^{500} (P_{iB} N_i)}$$

where P_{iB} is the price per share of security i during the base period (chosen to be 1941–1943) and N_i is the total number of shares in firm i outstanding. The multiplicative factor of 10 was originally chosen to make the index roughly comparable to average stock prices, but it is no longer representative. The value-weighted index calculates price changes relative to index stock prices during a benchmark base period.

Despite these differences, all indexes tend to be highly correlated. The market index most commonly used to estimate betas is the SPX. Derivative contracts have been built around many of the indexes to enable FIs to place bets on overall market direction.

country funds:
investment portfolios whose shares are traded on American stock exchanges that are backed by assets in foreign countries.

Just as the DJIA, SPX, OEX (S&P 100), and Wilshire 5000 attempt to replicate the market portfolio of all U.S. stocks, **country funds** can be used as international market indexes. Country funds are investment portfolios whose shares are traded on American stock exchanges that are backed by assets in foreign countries. Unfortunately, the value of these country funds is not always determined solely by the underlying value of the securities in their portfolios, undermining their value as proxies for the market portfolio.[8]

The Risk Factor Used to Price Securities   Systematic risk is the stubborn risk that emanates from unanticipated market fluctuations. Unsystematic risk, on the other hand, is easily eliminated by diversification. Whereas investors can demand compensation in the form of a risk premium for systematic risk, they can make no such demands when it comes to unsystematic risk, since unsystematic risk is easily avoided. Thus, security returns include a premium for systematic risk but not for unsystematic risk. In general, security returns can be characterized by the following formula:

Security Returns = Return for the Time Value of Money
+ Risk Premium for Systematic Risk Only

The return for the time value of money is simply the risk free interest rate. The risk premium for systematic risk is determined by the quantity of systematic risk, measured by β, multiplied by the price of systematic risk. The price of systematic risk is the risk premium offered to holders of the market portfolio, which is simply the difference between the expected return on the market index and the risk free rate. This results in a formula called the capital asset pricing model (CAPM):

$$E(R_i) = R_f + \beta_i [E(R_m) - R_f]$$

where $E(R_i)$ and $E(R_m)$ are the expected returns on security i and the market portfolio, respectively; β_i is security i's beta (the quantity of systematic risk); and R_f is the risk free rate (so that $E(R_m) - R_f$ is the systematic risk premium on the market index). CAPM, our first comprehensive asset pricing model, shows that the market prices systematic risk only, offering higher returns for securities with greater market risk exposure.

Checkpoint

1. How can you measure systematic risk?
2. How can you measure unsystematic risk?
3. Why is systematic risk priced but unsystematic risk unpriced?
4. According to CAPM, what are the two components of security returns? How are they measured?

Criticisms of and Variations in CAPM   CAPM is based on six assumptions:

1. Investors are risk averse and concern themselves with the expected return and standard deviation (as the measure of total risk) of their portfolios.

---

[8] See Hardouvelis, La Porta, and Wizman (1994) for a discussion of the role of market expectations on country fund values.

2. All investors have the same expectations about future returns (that is, we assume homogeneous expectations).

3. Investors can use a risk free asset to take unlimited short (borrowing, represented as $w_i < 0$) and long (lending, represented as $w_i > 0$) positions.

4. All assets are marketable and perfectly divisible.

5. Information is costless and simultaneously available to all investors.

6. There are no market imperfections such as taxes, regulations, and transaction costs.

Although none of these assumptions holds in practice, CAPM is still widely used by practitioners in financial markets. Indeed, several extensions of the basic model have been introduced to improve CAPM's explanatory power. One of these extensions is the International CAPM (ICAPM).[9]

The market index plays a critical role in estimating CAPM. Since the market index is only a proxy for the market portfolio and cannot contain *all* marketable and nonmarketable assets, the true market portfolio is unobservable. Errors in estimating CAPM may emanate from errors in specification of the market index. In attempting to make the market index as complete as possible, early researchers[10] expanded the tests of CAPM by utilizing international market indexes. Indexes that focus only on U.S. assets omit about 60% of the world's bonds and equity. Attempts to correct this problem by including more countries and more assets into the definition of the market index, however, have typically yielded poor results.[11] Figure 9.3 shows the weak relationship between country returns and worldwide market betas. This unsatisfactory performance of ICAPM may be the result of the low correlation among foreign markets. Correlation coefficients across international equity and debt indexes average 0.40.[12] The usefulness of an international market index in estimating CAPM is limited by these low, and erratic, correlations among international financial markets.

Fama and French in their widely cited 1992 study dealt a damaging blow to CAPM's credibility. Using a sample of NYSE, AMEX, and NASDAQ stocks, over the period July 1963 to December 1990, they reported a statistically insignificant relationship between beta and stock returns. Instead, they found that size (as measured by the market value of equity), leverage (as measured by the ratio of book value of equity to the market value of equity), and earnings per share each had significant explanatory power. This finding undermines the basic principle of CAPM that a single basic market risk factor determines expected security returns.

This problem highlights a shortcoming of all variations of CAPM. It is a joint test of two separate hypotheses: (1) the validity of CAPM and (2) the correctness of the market index used to estimate CAPM. Empirical tests of CAPM depend on the assumption that the market index chosen is an appropriate proxy of an efficient market portfolio. It is impossible to disentangle these two aspects of the CAPM, and tests may reject CAPM, even if it is valid, if the market index is inefficient. Thus, CAPM's strength, its identification of a single overall market risk factor, is

---

[9] Other extensions not covered here are the Consumption CAPM—see Breeden (1979); time-varying, intertemporal CAPM—see Fama and Macbeth (1974); and continuous time CAPM—see Merton (1973). Citations for only the seminal papers are listed here, although each of these extensions of CAPM has spawned its own literature of empirical tests and modifications.

[10] See Frankel (1982), Kouri (1976), and Dornbusch (1983).

[11] See Thomas and Wickens (1993) for a discussion.

[12] However, U.S. bear markets appear to be highly contagious. Whenever U.S. stocks fell an average of 3% per month, stocks in Canada fell by an average of 2.33%, in the U.K. by 1.5%, in France by 1.5%, in Singapore by 1.33%, in Germany by 0.58%, in Hong Kong by 0.33%, and in Italy by 0.17%. See Erb, Harvey, and Viskanta (1995). Ziobrowski and Ziobrowski (1995) find that the correlation coefficient between British and Japanese assets is 0.44, the same as the correlation coefficient between U.S. common stocks and U.S. government bonds. However, they report that the correlation is –0.08 between U.S. and British assets and –0.11 between U.S. and Japanese assets.

Source: Ferson and Harvey (1994), p. 792.

Figure 9.3

also its weakness. Its restrictive assumptions led researchers to search for a more general model. In a seminal paper, Professor Steve Ross of Yale University, together with Professor Richard Roll, developed a model that is free of some of CAPM's restrictive assumptions.[13]

Arbitrage Pricing Theory

CAPM relies on the plausible claim that investors can demand a risk premium for systematic risk but not for unsystematic risk, since it is so easily avoidable. Accordingly, if there are two securities with the same expected return, but one has more systematic risk than the other, all investors will buy the less risky security. This situation will cause the price of the riskier security to fall, thereby raising its promised rate of return, while the price of the safer security will rise, thereby lowering its expected return. Equilibrium will occur when the expected return on the riskier security increases by just enough over the expected return on the safer security to compensate investors for the additional systematic risk. Thus, all securities with the same amount of systematic risk have the same expected return.

The innovation of arbitrage pricing is the recognition that equally risky securities can be created using portfolios of other securities. If arbitrage opportunities are not available in financial markets, then all securities must be priced at the same returns as their equally risky "synthetic" cousins. By equating returns on synthetic risk free arbitrage portfolios with the risk free rate, security prices can be calculated for a broad range of financial securities.

Let's take our earlier example of the risk free portfolio consisting of two-thirds investment in the municipal bond and one-third in the venture capital opportunity. Under all five possible scenarios, the rate of return on this investment portfolio is 9.33% p.a. Say that you decided to sell shares in this risk free portfolio by creating a closed-end mutual fund. What would be the price of the mutual fund shares? We can find a replicating investment that, if there are no arbitrage opportunities, has the same return as the mutual fund and can therefore be used to price the mutual fund shares. This is easy enough to do for this example since the mutual fund

---

[13] See Ross (1976) and Roll and Ross (1980).

is itself risk free. Thus, the fund shares must yield a rate of return equal to the risk free rate. If the risk free rate is currently 6% p.a., the mutual fund shares will sell at a premium. For example, consider a $100,000 investment in the mutual fund. With certainty, at the end of the year this investment will yield 9.33% p.a., for a future value of $109,333 = $100,000(1.0933). What is the value of a guaranteed promise of the receipt of $109,333 one year from now worth today? Simply discount the future value at the current risk free rate to find out. Thus, the price of the mutual fund shares is $\frac{109,333}{1.06}$ = $103,144 per $100,000 portfolio face value. The FI that created this risk free mutual fund can earn a fee of $3,144 per $100,000 investment in the portfolio by replicating the risk free investment using the combination of municipal bonds and venture capital investments.[14]

This replication of a risk free portfolio is the basis of the arbitrage pricing theory (APT). This theory, though an asset pricing model, is more general than CAPM. Whereas CAPM concentrates on the market risk of a security, APT permits the consideration of multiple basic risk factors, assuming only that it is possible to construct risk free synthetic securities. APT is therefore not subject to the same criticisms as is CAPM regarding the choice of the market index used to measure systematic risk. Indeed, APT allows for an indeterminate number of risk factors that are not prespecified but instead are estimated from the data. CAPM can be viewed as a special case of APT in which there is only one risk factor—the market risk factor. APT estimates several underlying basic risk factors that together constitute market risk. We can state APT as

$$E(R_i) = R_f + \beta_i^{I1}[E(R_{I1}) - R_f] + \beta_i^{I2}[E(R_{I2}) - R_f] + \cdots + \beta_i^{Ik}[E(R_{Ik}) - R_f]$$

where $E(R_i)$ is the expected return on security i; there are k risk factors, labeled $I1, I2, \ldots, Ik$, each with expected return $E(R_{I1}), E(R_{I2}), \ldots, E(R_{Ik})$; and betas $\beta_i^{I1}, \beta_i^{I2}, \ldots, \beta_i^{Ik}$, which are the sensitivities of security i returns to fluctuations in risk factors $I1, I2, \ldots, Ik$.

A number of studies[15] reveal four significant basic risk factors:[16]

1. Unanticipated changes in industrial production: a measure of the level of macroeconomic activity.

2. Unanticipated changes in the spread between the yield on low risk and high risk bonds: a measure of investor confidence.

3. Unanticipated changes in interest rates and the shape of the yield curve: a measure of interest rate risk.

4. Unanticipated changes in inflation: a measure of price volatility.

The identification of these four basic risk factors is hardly surprising. We have already seen the importance of interest rate fluctuations, inflation expectations, and macroeconomic policy for asset valuation. However, the identity of the basic risk factors using APT is quite idiosyncratic and changes over time. Since the correct number of risk factors is unknown, it has been difficult to define a single set of risk factors that consistently explains asset prices.

Unfortunately, APT cannot be viewed as a new and improved alternative to replace CAPM. Indeed, CAPM is a special case of APT with only one factor, the market index, as opposed to multiple factors. Although empirical evidence has found many deviations from CAPM,

---

[14] Careful readers will note the similarities between this "proof" of the arbitrage pricing theory and the discussion of covered interest rate parity from Chapter 8.

[15] See Gehr (1975), Roll and Ross (1980), Chen, Roll, and Ross (1980), and Reinganum (1981).

[16] Cho, Eun, and Senbet (1986), in their international study using 349 stocks representing 11 different countries (the U.S., Canada, France, Germany, the Netherlands, Switzerland, the U.K., Australia, Hong Kong, Singapore, and Japan), find three or four common worldwide factors, with fewer factors the less integrated the country into the global economy.

APT's track record is not much better because APT can correct only the risk factor omissions of CAPM. However, if the problems are not risk based, but instead emanate from methodological biases, then neither APT nor CAPM will yield reliable results. Some of these methodological biases could be the existence of market frictions, investor irrationality, imperfect capital markets, liquidity effects, and data problems.[17] In the presence of these biases, risk measurement may be reduced to a spreadsheet-type of scenario analysis. That is, a given shock to financial markets is assumed (for instance, interest rates increase by 100 basis points across the board), and the impact of the shock is evaluated individually for each and every financial market.

Timely Topics 9.1 shows that the issue is currently the subject of regulatory and market concern. Concern about risk measurement is not limited to U.S. regulators but is currently being debated around the world—in the Bank of England, the Bank for International Settlements, and the corporate offices of multinational FIs such as J. P. Morgan. Indeed, J. P. Morgan has proposed a new risk yardstick called RiskMetrics, which is the subject of our next section.

TIMELY TOPICS 9.1

RISKY BUSINESS—INFORMING FUND INVESTORS

The subject of the hour at the Securities and Exchange Commission is "risk." Having asked the public whether mutual-fund prospectuses should do a better job of warning investors, the SEC has heard [that] investors want to hear more about risk, and if such a thing is possible, would like to see the risk of each and every fund sized up, summed up, and quantified in a single number, much as oddsmakers put a number on a horse.

One tool getting hot consideration is an arithmetic yardstick beloved to generations of statistics classes, known as "standard deviation." This is a cousin of some measures in favor on Wall Street, such as beta and Morningstar ratings. Each of these algorithms measures historical (usually month-to-month) gyrations of a fund. . . .

Academics are fond of such yardsticks because the underlying data are easily quantifiable. That doesn't mean they are useful. Trading records provide a rear view—not a prospective one. Moreover, as the University of Chicago's Eugene Fama and Kenneth French showed, a fund's prior volatility says nothing about its future returns. . . .

Volatility yardsticks convey only the risk of short term, often transitory, meanderings. Standard deviation, in particular, says nothing about the risk that should truly concern investors: that of a one-time, substantial and sustained loss of capital, such as occurred to bond funds last year. And just as a swimming pool's average depth may be of little comfort to a man drowning in the deep end, a fund that usually varies by only 1% may, on occasion, zigzag wildly.

Indeed, early in 1994, Morningstar assigned the highest, or safest, risk return rating to the Piper Jaffray Institutional Government Income Portfolio. When the bond market crashed, the Piper fund, stocked with high-octane derivatives, plummeted 25%.

Should the SEC then throw up its hands? Not at all. An analyst at the very same Morningstar wrote of the Piper fund, just before the crash: "If interest rates move up again this fund would be hurt far worse than its peers." Donald Phillips, president of Morningstar, draws the obvious conclusion. People willing to do the legwork of studying

---

[17] See MacKinlay (1995) for an empirical study showing that these nonrisk factors are significant determinants of deviations from CAPM, implying that APT alone cannot solve the risk measurement problem.

a fund's holdings can get at its genuine investment risks, which mirror the fundamental risks of the fund's actual assets. The numerical yardstick may provide a quicker fix, but it is sorely superficial.

Source: Roger Lowenstein, *Wall Street Journal*, June 22, 1995, p. C1.

Checkpoint

✓

1. What are the strengths of the capital asset pricing model? the weaknesses?
2. How does the arbitrage pricing theory avoid CAPM's major weakness?
3. What are the risk factors under CAPM? under APT?

RiskMetrics and Value at Risk Models

The risk measures we have examined thus far (standard deviation, correlation coefficient, beta, APT risk index coefficients) all examine how marginal changes in underlying conditions affect security values. This approach neglects consideration of the possibility of discrete, large jumps that lead to drastic, not marginal, changes in portfolio values. Moreover, by employing symmetric statistical measures, which evaluate upside and downside risk equally, the standard measures of risk do not assess the risk of loss from catastrophic occurrences.

In August 1994, the SEC and the Commodity Futures Trading Commission (CFTC) formed a voluntary study group, called the Derivatives Policy Group (DPG), which included top executives of CS First Boston, Goldman Sachs, Morgan Stanley, Merrill Lynch, Salomon, and Lehman, and was chaired by John Heimann and E. Gerald Corrigan (the past president of the New York Federal Reserve Bank). At the same time, J.P. Morgan was at work developing its RiskMetrics program, which was subsequently released in October 1994. The DPG's recommendations, released in March 1995, have some similarities and differences when compared with J.P. Morgan's RiskMetrics,[18] but both models represent attempts to develop common standards of risk measurement for FIs.

Both models calculate total risk by estimating the changes in portfolio values if certain scenarios occur. These scenarios represent two broad categories of fundamental changes in the financial environment: (1) market risk of loss and (2) credit risk factors. **Market risk of loss** is the adverse impact on the portfolio value of unanticipated shifts in interest rates, exchange rates, and prices. RiskMetrics considers only the market risk of loss, whereas the DPG guidelines evaluate both types of risk.

market risk of loss: the adverse impact on portfolio value of unanticipated shifts in interest rates, exchange rates, and prices.

Market Risk of Loss   To calculate the market risk of loss, the DPG recommends computation of core risk factors and capital at risk.[19]

The core risk factors are specified shifts in interest rates, exchange rates, and price levels that affect portfolio values. These factors examine the impact on portfolio value of

1. *Parallel shifts in the yield curve*: Measured as 100 basis point shifts in the yield curve up and down.

2. *Changes in the steepness of the yield curve*: Measured as a 25 basis point steepening and flattening of the difference between the yields on 2 year and 10 year government bonds.

---

[18] The DPG also made recommendations about disclosure which are covered in Chapter 5. Although the DPG focused on evaluating the risk emanating from over-the-counter derivatives, their procedures are generally applicable to an entire portfolio.

[19] RiskMetrics calculates capital at risk without considering core risk factors.

3. *Parallel yield curve shifts combined with changes in steepness of yield curves*: Measured as four permutations consisting of the 100 basis point parallel shift at the same time as the 25 basis point shift in the slope of the yield curve. That is, examine the impact on portfolio value of (i) a 100 basis point increase in all yields and a 25 basis point increase in the slope of the 2 year to 10 year yield differential; (ii) a 100 basis point increase in all yields and a 25 basis point decrease in the slope of the 2 year to 10 year yield differential; (iii) a 100 basis point decrease in all yields and a 25 basis point decrease in the slope of the 2 year to 10 year yield differential; (iv) a 100 basis point decrease in all yields and a 25 basis point increase in the slope of the 2 year to 10 year yield differential.

4. *Changes in yield volatilities*: Measured as increases and decreases in three month yield volatilities by 20% of current prevailing levels.

5. *Changes in the value of equity indexes*: Measured as increases and decreases in equity index values of 10%.

6. *Changes in equity index volatility*: Measured as increases and decreases in equity index volatilities by 20% of prevailing levels.

7. *Changes in the value of key currencies*: Measured as increases and decreases in the exchange rate (relative to the U.S. dollar) of foreign currencies by 6% in the case of major currencies and 20% in the case of other currencies.

8. *Changes in foreign exchange rate volatilities*: Measured as increases and decreases in foreign exchange rate volatilities by 20% of prevailing levels.

9. *Changes in swap spreads in the G-7 countries plus Switzerland*: Measured as increases and decreases in swap spreads by 20 basis points.

Core risk factors 1–4 deal with interest rate risk; factors 5–6 measure equity price-level risk; and 7–9 are exchange rate risk factors. The models we have already developed can be used to evaluate the scenarios under all nine core risk factors. The impact on the value of the portfolio of interest rate risk factors 1–4 can be computed using the duration model of Chapter 7. Exchange rate risk factors 7–9 affect the value of the portfolio according to the net currency exposure model of Chapter 8. The price-level impact, as specified in equity risk factors 5–6, is evaluated using either CAPM or APT.

Suppose that you decided to invest in a portfolio of municipal and corporate bonds with an average yield of 9.5% p.a. and a duration of seven years. To evaluate the first core risk scenario, the 100 basis point change in all rates, simply use Chapter 7's duration model:

$$\frac{\Delta P}{P} \approx -D \frac{\Delta R}{1 + R}$$

$$\frac{\Delta P}{P} \approx -7 \frac{\pm \Delta .01}{1.095} = \mp 6.39\%$$

A 100 basis point increase or decrease in yields will entail a 6.39% decrease or increase in portfolio value.

Both the DPG recommendations and RiskMetrics measure **value at risk**—the maximum loss possible under 99% of the scenarios that may potentially occur over a two week period. If we assume that all financial market returns are normally distributed, then Figure 9.4 shows how value at risk is computed. Since the probability distribution takes into account all possible scenarios, the area under the bell-shaped curve sums to one (100%). One characteristic of the normal probability distribution is that 99% of all possible scenarios occur in the confidence interval range of 2.575 standard deviations around the mean. Since we are only concerned

value at risk: the maximum loss possible under 99% of the scenarios that may potentially occur over a two week period.

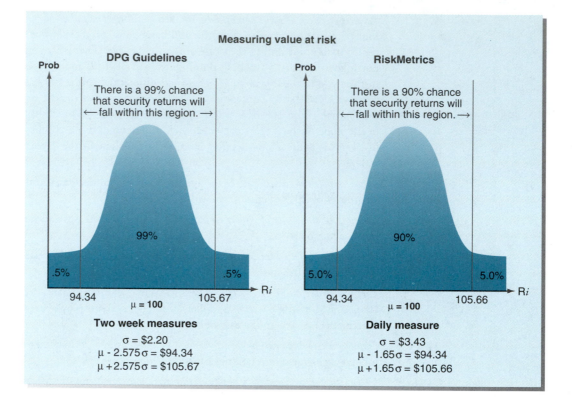

Figure 9.4

with the possibility of loss, we exclude the top 0.5% of potential occurrences and calculate the maximum loss if returns fall to the bottom of the range of the confidence interval: the mean minus 2.575 times standard deviation. Thus, the DPG recommendations calculate the maximum possible losses under all downside risk scenarios except those least likely to occur— that is, eliminating only those downside risk scenarios that have less than a 0.5% probability of occurring.

RiskMetrics calculates value at risk on a daily basis.[20] If each daily return is assumed to be independent, however, then the computation is the same as that recommended by the DPG. Figure 9.4 shows that the daily equivalent of a 2 week (10 business day) period is the maximum *daily* loss that may occur with a probability of at least 5%. The equivalent confidence interval, on a daily basis, is a range of 1.65 standard deviations around the mean. For example, consider the probability distributions of stock prices shown in Figure 9.4, where the expected stock price is assumed to be $100. The biweekly standard deviation of stock prices is assumed to be $2.20, whereas the daily standard deviation of equity prices is assumed to be $3.43.[21] Calculating the confidence intervals, we find a two week confidence interval of $\mu \pm 2.575(2.20)$ = $94.34 to $105.67 and an identical daily confidence interval of $\mu \pm 1.65(3.43)$ = $94.34 to $105.66. To calculate value at risk under both RiskMetrics and DPG guidelines, we evaluate the FI's losses if stock prices fall to the bottom of the range: $94.34. If the FI owned (had a long position in) 10,000 shares, then the value at risk would be $56,600, which is ($100 − $94.34)(10,000).

---

[20] RiskMetrics uses the term *Daily Earnings at Risk*, abbreviated DEaR, to refer to value at risk.

[21] Daily prices are more volatile than are prices over a two week period because if daily stock prices are independently distributed, one day's losses tend to be offset by the next day's gains, thereby dampening the volatility over a two week period.

Suppose that the FI held 10 million yen in a foreign currency account. Today's yen–U.S. dollar exchange rate is US$0.015 per Japanese yen with a daily standard deviation of US$0.002. The FI's net currency exposure is +10 million yen. RiskMetrics calculates the value at risk using the maximum loss if exchange rates decline by 1.65 standard deviations, or in this example, US$0.0033 (1.65 × US$0.002). Thus, following the currency risk model from Chapter 8, the value at risk is

$$\text{US\$ Cash Flows} = (\Delta FX \text{ Rate})(\text{Net Currency Exposure})$$

$$= (-\text{US\$0.0033})(\text{JY10,000,000}) = -\text{US\$33,000}$$

The FI's value at risk from unanticipated declines in the yen–U.S. dollar exchange rate is US$33,000.

Both the core risk factors and the value at risk require that the FI reevaluate the portfolio under various scenarios to calculate potential adverse price movements resulting from interest rate fluctuations, exchange rate fluctuations, and price-level changes. Thus far, however, we have examined each of these adverse price movements in isolation. This overstates risk exposure since we have already seen the risk reducing benefits of portfolio diversification. Thus, the final value of the market risk of loss requires that the portfolio risk be calculated using correlation coefficients among the individual financial markets. This brings us back full circle to the use of the standard deviation of a portfolio. The advantage of the RiskMetrics model is that J.P. Morgan provides a service that calculates these basic risk factors and their correlation coefficients for a broad range of indexes. Table 9.3 shows that this entails 326 volatility estimates and 53,138 correlations updated daily. J.P. Morgan posts updates for these correlations on line at the website WWW.JPMORGAN.COM/MarketDataInd/RiskMetrics/RiskMetrics.HTML.

Consider a FI with a portfolio consisting of the $1 million equity investment described earlier (10,000 shares each priced at $100) and $150,000 in Japanese yen (10 million yen at US$0.015 each). If the correlation coefficient between the distributions of stock prices and yen–U.S. dollar exchange rates is –.05, then we can modify equation (9.2) to calculate the standard deviation of the portfolio. We replace the weighted standard deviations of equation (9.2) with the measures of value at risk (abbreviated VaR_1 for the equity capital at risk and VaR_2 for the foreign exchange risk), to obtain

$$\text{Portfolio } VaR = \sqrt{VaR_1^2 + VaR_2^2 + 2 VaR_1 \, VaR_2 \rho_{1,2}}$$

Based on this portfolio, the value at risk is estimated as

$$\text{Portfolio } VaR = \sqrt{(\$56,600)^2 + (\$33,000)^2 + 2(-.05)(\$56,600)(\$33,000)}$$

$$= \sqrt{4,105,780,000} = \$64,076$$

Table 9.3

RiskMetrics Daily Calculations of Standard Deviations and Correlation Coefficients

Standard Deviations	Number of Markets	Number of Estimates/Market	Total Number
Government bonds	14	7–10	118
Money market and swaps	15	12	180
Foreign exchange	14	1	14
Equities	14	1	14
Total number of standard deviations			326
Total number of correlation coefficients: 0.5(326)(326) =			53,138

Source: J. P. Morgan, RiskMetrics Documentation.

The total value at risk of the FI's portfolio is a potential loss of $64,076. Note that if the individual components of value at risk were simply added together ($56,600 + $33,000 = $89,600), thereby ignoring risk diversification benefits, we would significantly overstate the FI's value at risk.

Credit Risk   The market risk of loss (measured by the core risk factors and the capital at risk) evaluates the impact of unanticipated price fluctuations on portfolio values. However, portfolio values can change, even if prices do not fluctuate, when individual counterparties fail to make their contractually obligated payments. Credit risk occurs whenever there is a failure to meet the terms of financial contracts. Although this failure may be related to market forces (for example, when interest rate increases forced the Orange County, California, municipality into bankruptcy, causing it to default on some of its debt),[22] the DPG guidelines treat credit risk on a case-by-case basis independent of the calculation of market risk of loss.

For each counterparty, default risk is calculated using either historical loss ratios or the values provided by rating services. In all cases, the minimum default ratio to be used is 0.001. The default ratios are then multiplied by **net replacement value**, which is simply the cash flow loss in the event of counterparty default. Thus, if the net replacement value is $100,000, the minimum calculation of credit risk is

$$\text{Credit Risk} = (\text{Default Ratio})(\text{Net Replacement Value})$$
$$\text{Credit Risk} = (.001)(\$100,000) = \$100$$

For estimates of credit risk for several derivative instruments, see Table 9.4.

Shortcomings of RiskMetrics and the DPG Recommendations   RiskMetrics and the DPG guidelines synthesize the standard risk measurements discussed throughout this book. Core risk factors are evaluated using the techniques developed in Chapter 7 for interest rate risk and in Chapter 8 for exchange rate risk. Capital at risk is determined using the standard deviation of the portfolio. Credit risk measurement uses historical loss experiences. Thus, these models are only as good as the underlying concepts that they draw together. They suffer from three major shortcomings: (1) reliance on historical results; (2) violations of model assumptions; and (3) neglect of systemic, catastrophic losses that occur infrequently but periodically.

Both RiskMetrics and the DPG recommendations calculate correlations, standard deviations, and probability distributions based on historical evidence. However, the past is not always a good predictor of the future. Moreover, if any of the models' assumptions are violated, the models' predictive ability may be reduced. For example, both models utilize the assumption that security returns are normally distributed. However, empirical studies reveal that many asset returns, such as interest rates and exchange rates, have "fat tails" because we observe a greater probability of extreme outcomes than would be predicted by the normal probability distribution. If this is true, then models based on the normality assumption will underestimate risk. Hendricks (1996) shows that the accuracy of value at risk models depends on such model parameters as the choice of the confidence level and the number of days in the valuation period.[23]

Finally, by simply extrapolating from recent history, both models ignore the out-of-the-ordinary, dramatic moves in security prices that can decimate the value of a portfolio. These events are difficult to predict, for they occur at infrequent intervals, and their impact on portfolio values is difficult to assess. Despite their contributions, RiskMetrics and the DPG guidelines

net replacement value:
the cash flow loss in the event of counterparty default.

---

[22] See in-depth discussion of the Orange County default in *Timely Topics 11.1*.

[23] To test the accuracy of value at risk models, U.S. regulators proposed (in July 1995) "backtesting" requirements to compare past estimates of risk with actual results. Penalties are assessed if an institution's losses exceeded 1% a total of five times during the backtesting period.

Table 9.4

DPG Guidelines on Credit Risk[a] ($ million)

Financial Security	Net Replacement Value (1)	Default Ratio (2)	Estimated Credit Risk (1) × (2)
Class AA			
Swaps	0.0	0.001	0.000
Foreign exchange forwards	0.0	0.001	0.000
Class A			
Swaps	520.0	0.006	3.12
Foreign exchange forwards	65.0	0.001	0.065
Class BBB			
Swaps	8.0	0.020	0.16
Foreign exchange forwards	0.0	0.002	0.000
Total Estimated Credit Risk			3.345

[a]The net replacement value represents hypothetical investments in each security. The default ratios are taken from bond rating tables of historical averages of defaults for each rating classification (Class AA, A, BBB).

Source: The DPG Guidelines.

are not the last word on risk measurement. FIs seeking managerial information systems to monitor their risk exposure continue to look for ways to improve the analytics of risk.

Checkpoint ✓

1. What is the market risk of loss? How do both RiskMetrics and the DPG guidelines measure it?

2. List the similarities and differences between RiskMetrics and the DPG recommendations.

3. Do RiskMetrics and the DPG guidelines repudiate the statistical models of risk? Why or why not?

4. What are the shortcomings of RiskMetrics and the DPG recommendations?

➤ Summary

With this chapter you now have all of the techniques necessary to analyze the individual financial markets that make up the rest of this book. One of the most important of these techniques is your risk yardstick. Just as a carpenter needs the proper tool designed for each task, we have seen that one risk yardstick is insufficient to measure all types of risk.

An overall measure of risk is standard deviation, which measures the probability-weighted deviation from expected values. This statistical measure aggregates the basic risk factors that we have examined individually in earlier chapters: price-level risk in Chapter 4, interest rate risk in Chapter 7, and foreign exchange rate risk in Chapter 8. However, much of this total risk exposure can be easily eliminated by combining securities into portfolios. Because of these benefits of diversification, security prices contain a risk premium for undiversifiable risk but not for diversifiable risk.

The capital asset pricing model (CAPM) measures diversifiable risk by estimating the correlation of security returns with a market index. The market index should be broadly based so that it accurately reflects the unobservable market of all traded and nontraded securities. The measure of market risk is called beta. It is the slope of the characteristic line, which is a regression line fitted to a scatter plot of points made up of historical security and market returns. Deviations from this line represent unsystematic risk.

The asset pricing theory (APT) is more general than CAPM, for it permits more than one market index. It is estimated by replicating securities using equally risky synthetic security portfolios. The returns are then equalized to eliminate any arbitrage opportunities.

Separating diversifiable and undiversifiable risk is a difficult task. Both CAPM and APT have had limited success in empirical tests of their validity. Two recent additions to the risk toolbox are RiskMetrics and the Derivatives Policy Group recommendations. Both models synthesize existing statistical methods to create a comprehensive measure of downside risk, called value at risk, which quantifies a maximum loss under certain fairly uncommon scenarios. None of the models, however, effectively quantifies the out-of-the-ordinary, catastrophic jolts to financial markets that periodically decimate portfolio values.

References

Beaver, W., and G. Parker, eds., *Risk Management: Problems and Solutions*. New York: McGraw–Hill, 1995.

Breeden, D. T. "An Intertemporal Asset Pricing Model with Stochastic Investment and Consumption Opportunities." *Journal of Financial Economics* (September 1979): 273–296.

Chen, Nai-fu, R. Roll, and S. Ross. "Economic Forces and the Stock Market: Testing the APT and Alternative Asset Pricing Theories." *Journal of Business* (July 1980): 383–403.

Cho, D. C., C. S. Eun, and L. W. Senbet. "International Arbitrage Pricing Theory: An Empirical Investigation." *Journal of Finance* 41, No. 2 (June 1986): 313–329.

Dornbusch, R. "Exchange Risk and Macroeconomics of Exchange Rate Determination." In R. Hawkings, ed., *Research in International Business and Finance*. Greenwich, Conn.: JAI Press, 1983.

Elton, E. J. and M. J. Gruber. *Modern Portfolio Theory and Investment Analysis*. New York: John Wiley & Sons, 1997.

Erb, C. B., C. R. Harvey, and T. E. Viskanta. *Business Week*, July 3, 1995, p. 22.

Fama, E. F., and K. R. French. "The Cross-Section of Expected Stock Returns." *Journal of Finance* 47, No. 2 (June 1992): 427–465.

Fama, E. F., and J. D. Macbeth. "Tests of the Multiperiod Two Period Model." *Journal of Financial Economics* 1 (1974): 43–66.

Ferson, W. E., and W. Harvey. "Sources of Risk and Expected Returns in Global Equity Markets." *Journal of Banking and Finance* 18 (1994): 775–803.

Frankel, J. A. "In Search of the Exchange Risk Premium: A Six Currency Test Assuming Mean-Variance Optimization." *Journal of International Money and Finance* (December 1982): 255–274.

Gehr, A., Jr. "Some Tests of the Arbitrage Pricing Theory." *Journal of the Midwest Finance Association* (1975): 91–105.

Hardouvelis, G., R. La Porta, and T. Wizman. In J. Frankel, ed. *The Internationalisation of Equity Markets*, Chicago: University of Chicago Press, 1994.

Hendricks, D. "Evaluation of Value at Risk Models Using Historical Data" Federal Reserve Bank of NY *Economic Policy Review* (April 1996): 39–69.

Kouri, P. "The Exchange Rate and the Balance of Payments in the Short Run and in the Long Run: A Monetary Approach." *Scandinavian Journal of Economics* 78 (May 1976): 280–308.

MacKinlay, A. C. "Multifactor Models Do Not Explain Deviations from the CAPM." *Journal of Financial Economics* 38 (1995): 3–28.

Merton, R. "An Intertemporal Capital Asset Pricing Model." *Econometrica* (September 1973): 867–888.

Reinganum, M. R. "The Arbitrage Pricing Theory: Some Empirical Results." *Journal of Financial Economics* (May 1981): 313–321.

Roll, R., and S. Ross. "An Empirical Test of the Arbitrage Pricing Theory." *Journal of Finance* (December 1980): 1073–1103.

Ross, S. "The Arbitrage Theory of Capital Asset Pricing." *Journal of Economic Theory* (December 1976): 343–362.

Saunders, A. "Market Risk." *The Financier ACMT* 2, No. 5 (December 1995): 35–45.

Solnik, B. "Why Not Diversify Internationally Rather Than Domestically?" *Financial Analysts Journal* (July/August 1974): 48–54.

Statman, M. "How Many Stocks Make a Diversified Portfolio?" *Journal of Financial and Quantitative Analysis* 22, No. 3 (September 1987): 353–363.

Thomas, S. H. and M. R. Wickens. "An International CAPM for Bonds and Equities." *Journal of International Money and Finance* 12, No. 4 (August 1993): 390–412.

Wagner, W., and S. Lau. "The Effect of Diversification on Risk." *Financial Analysts Journal* (November–December 1971): 2–7.

Ziobrowski, B. J., and A. J. Ziobrowski. "Exchange Rate Risk and Internationally Diversified Portfolios." *Journal of International Money and Finance* 14, No. 1 (1995): 65–81.

Questions

1. Use the following probability distribution for Deutschemark–U.S. dollar exchange rates to calculate (a) the mean; (b) the standard deviation; and (c) the confidence interval using two standard deviations.

Next Year's Scenario	Likelihood of Scenario	DM–US$ exchange rates:
The Fed eases monetary policy.	15%	US$0.77
German interest rates increase.	25	US$0.76
No change.	20	US$0.75
Japanese yen–U.S. dollar exchange rates decrease.	25	US$0.74
The Fed intervenes to support the dollar.	15	US$0.73

2. Use Table 9.1 to calculate two standard deviation confidence intervals for all 13 indexes.

3. Use the following probability distribution for Mexican peso–U.S. dollar exchange rates to calculate (a) the mean; (b) the standard deviation; and (c) the correlation coefficient with the Deutschemark–U.S. dollar exchange rate in question 1:

Next Year's Scenario	Likelihood of Scenario	Mexican peso–US$ Exchange Rates
The Fed eases monetary policy.	15%	US$0.17
German interest rates increase.	25	US$0.18
No change.	20	US$0.20
Japanese yen–U.S. dollar exchange rates decrease.	25	US$0.22
The Fed intervenes to support the dollar.	15	US$0.23

4. Use the following probability distribution for Australian dollar–U.S. dollar exchange rates to calculate (a) the mean; (b) the standard deviation; and (c) the correlation coefficient with the Deutschemark–U.S. dollar exchange rate in question number 1:

Next Year's Scenario	Likelihood of Scenario	Australian $–US$ exchange rates:
The Fed eases monetary policy.	15%	US$0.59
German interest rates increase.	25	US$0.62
No change.	20	US$0.65
Japanese yen–U.S. dollar exchange rates decrease.	25	US$0.68
The Fed intervenes to support the dollar.	15	US$0.71

5. Combine the Deutschemark–U.S. dollar currency investment in question 1 with the Australian dollar–U.S. dollar investment in question 4 to create a risk free (in terms of U.S. dollar exchange rate) currency portfolio.

6. Calculate the risk of a portfolio consisting of a 20% investment in Deutschemark (from question 1) and an 80% investment in the Mexican peso (from question 3).

7a. Calculate betas for the following securities if $\sigma_m^2 = 100$:
   Security 1: $\rho_{1,m} = +.5$; $\sigma_1 = 5\%$.
   Security 2: $\rho_{2,m} = -.5$; $\sigma_2 = 5\%$.
   Security 3: $\rho_{3,m} = +1.0$; $\sigma_3 = 10\%$.
   Security 4: $\rho_{4,m} = +0$; $\sigma_4 = 2.5\%$.
   Security 5: $\rho_{5,m} = +.25$; $\sigma_5 = 3\%$.

7b. What is the systematic risk of a portfolio consisting of equal investments of each of the five securities in part (a)?

7c. Use the capital asset pricing model to calculate the expected returns of the securities in part (a) and the portfolio in part (b). Assume that the risk free rate is 5% p.a. and that the expected return on the market is 11% p.a.

8. Use CAPM to calculate the beta and expected return for the following securities (assuming a variance of the market index, $\sigma_m^2 = 1.65$; a risk free rate of 3% p.a.; and an expected return on the market of 8% p.a.):
   Security 1: Total risk = $\sigma_1^2 = 2.5$; unsystematic risk = $\sigma_\epsilon^2 = 0.5$.
   Security 2: Total risk = $\sigma_2^2 = 1.7$; unsystematic risk = $\sigma_\epsilon^2 = 1.05$.
   Security 3: Total risk = $\sigma_3^2 = 4.2$; unsystematic risk = $\sigma_\epsilon^2 = 3.25$.

9. Use the core risk factors to evaluate the impact on the portfolio in question 6 if it is currently valued at US$1 million. (Assume no change in correlation coefficients.)

10. Use RiskMetrics to calculate the capital at risk for
   a. $1 million investment in a government bond with duration of 5.25 years, currently yielding 8% p.a. with a standard deviation of .5% p.a.
   b. $900,000 investment in Swiss francs currently valued at US$0.90 per Swiss franc with a standard deviation of US$0.05 per SFr.
   c. A portfolio consisting of the investments in parts (a) plus (b) if the correlation coefficient between them is .15.
   d. What would be the portfolio's capital at risk if the two assets in parts (a) and (b) were perfectly positively correlated? Quantify this portfolio's benefits to diversification.

Border Crossing III:
Chapters 7–9

Before proceeding, make sure that you understand the following concepts:

1. The difference between a simple interest yield and a compound interest rate. (Chapter 7, p. 192)

2. The impact of inflation on interest rates. (Chapter 7, p. 217–218)

3. The determinants of the shape of the yield curve. (Chapter 7, p. 210–217)

4. The derivation of forward rates and their role as interest rate forecasts. (Chapter 7, p. 211–213)

5. Calculations involving duration and convexity. (Chapter 7, p. 219–236)

6. Triangular arbitrage and the four parity relationships. (Chapter 8, p. 247–261)

7. Net currency exposure as a measure of exchange rate risk. (Chapter 8, p. 274–277)

8. The forward-spot exchange rate spread as a measure of exchange rate volatility. (Chapter 8, p. 270–274)

9. The derivation of expected return and standard deviation of return. (Chapter 9, p. 286–287)

10. The capital asset pricing model. (Chapter 9, p. 296–301)

11. The basic risk factors and the arbitrage pricing theory. (Chapter 9, p. 301–305)

12. The use of value at risk measures such as RiskMetrics. (Chapter 9, p. 306–311)

Looking Ahead

After each of the market chapters (10 through 21), be sure you can answer the following questions:

1. Describe a brief history of the role of FIs in the origination and the evolution of the financial instrument and market.

2. Who transacts in this market and why?

3. What risk management and intertemporal cash flow services does this financial instrument provide?

4. Describe the specifics of a typical trade including pricing and clearing mechanics.

CHAPTER 10

THE FEDERAL FUNDS MARKET

"What is robbing a bank compared with founding a bank?" Bertolt Brecht, *Threepenny Opera*, 1928, Act 3, Sc. 3.

Learning Objectives

- To learn about a market with the word *federal* in the title that is neither regulated nor controlled by either the *federal* government or the *Federal* Reserve.

- To learn who participates in this important market, why, and how, as well as how the market evolved from the needs of private FIs.

➤ Introduction

Frequent news coverage of Federal Funds may cause you to think that the Federal Funds market has been around forever. It might surprise you to learn that the market was created only in the 1920s by private FIs searching for a novel solution to a financial problem. Neither the federal government nor the Federal Reserve was involved in developing the Federal Funds market; in fact, the Federal Reserve actively discouraged its early development. Thus, the name Federal Funds (abbreviated throughout this chapter as FF) is a misnomer, for the only federal aspect of FF is the source of the funds being traded. This $150 billion market is administered entirely by private FIs.

➤ The Evolution of the Federal Funds Market

Between 1880 and 1910, the Boston Clearing House followed the popular custom of borrowing and lending its customers' balances for repayment later in the day. In this way, the FIs were able to avoid the risky and costly transfer of cash between banks around town. The Boston experience showed the value of a central clearinghouse for cash transfers.

In the summer of 1921, the major New York City banks faced a problem. Some banks were flush with surplus cash (in the form of excess reserves in their Federal Reserve accounts), which they had trouble investing in interest-earning securities, whereas other banks were so short of reserves that they were borrowing significant amounts at the discount window. Although the Federal Reserve Bank of New York did not encourage their efforts, the banks adapted the Boston example to come up with an obvious solution. Those banks with excess reserves arranged to have those reserve balances at the Federal Reserve Bank of New York transferred to banks with deficient reserves. The funds would then be repaid the following day with interest. The surplus funds banks benefited from the opportunity to earn a market interest rate on their idle reserves, while the banks with reserve deficits were able to avoid the transaction costs of pledging collateral for discount window borrowing. By mid-1923, a fairly active market had developed with average daily volume between $40 million and $80 million, still representing less than 1% of average daily volume on the major money markets of the day.

The market grew throughout the 1920s, reaching a daily trading range of $100–$250 million, representing over 1.5% of average daily volume on all money markets. The growth in volume over the decade stemmed from greater acceptance of the practice within the New York City area as well as from interregional expansion. In particular, it became popular to "follow the clock," which in those days was limited to the three-hour time differential between the West and East coasts of the United States. Eastern banks could wait until they calculated their closing balances (as of 3:00 P.M.), so that they had more information about their reserve requirements before transacting in the FF market. The introduction of an electronic payment system, the Fedwire, made these national transactions possible. Clearly, these transactions were early precursors to today's practices of 24 hour global trading.

Along with all other financial markets, the FF market went into hibernation during the Great Depression. It emerged in the post–World War II period substantially changed. Whereas prewar FF trading was driven by the banks' trading of excess reserves, FF market activity in the postwar period became the generally accepted way to clear *all* money market transactions, from commercial paper to bankers' acceptances to U.S. Treasury security sales. This led to the change in the definition of **Federal Funds (FF)** from the lending of excess reserves to simply the lending of any funds in reserve accounts at a Federal Reserve Bank, with the resulting explosion in the volume of activity. By the mid-1960s, average volume ranged between $1.5 billion and $3 billion daily, which was roughly equal to daily trading volume in the entire U.S. Treasury bills market at that time. The FF market had become an integrated national market with banks from around the world as regular participants.

The FF market shifted from bank reserve management to comprehensive portfolio management largely because of the emergence of an international market for U.S. Treasury debt in the 1950s. Postwar budget deficits in the United States fueled the increase in the supply of U.S. Treasury securities, which were allowed to trade at unrestricted free market prices following the Treasury Accord of 1951. Thus, an international market in U.S. Treasury securities was evolving as FIs competed to make markets. The transfer of Treasury securities, sometimes for only short time periods, required the existence of a clearing system to pay for the transactions. Competition among the FIs led to the search for a low-cost, efficient clearing method. FF provided the perfect vehicle, since the funds transferred were immediately available for use by the FIs. Moreover, with the proliferation of interest-bearing, short term money market instruments, FF transfers of immediately available funds reduced the float time between payment and receipt of usable funds.

Federal Funds (FF): the borrowing and lending of any funds in reserve accounts at a Federal Reserve Bank.

Characteristics of the FF Market

Today, banks manage their reserve positions and fund their asset portfolios by trading FF. In keeping with the terminology of a trader, when a bank borrows on the FF market, we say that the bank is a FF buyer; when a bank lends immediately available Federal Reserve account balances, we say that the bank is a FF seller. Most large banks simultaneously buy and sell FF all the time. They act as dealers, making markets in FF by announcing their willingness either to buy or to sell at the current, competitive FF rate. Several prominent FF brokers located in New York City (for example, Fulton Prebon; Garvin GuyButler; Lasser Brothers; and Noonan, Astley, and Pierce) bring together FF buyers and sellers but do not take positions for their own accounts. FF brokers played a more important role as the market's geographic area grew beyond the environs of downtown Manhattan in New York City, attracting the participation of banks around the country as well as foreign banks with U.S. offices. Currently, brokered FF transactions make up approximately 40% of total activity. Brokerage commissions range from one-sixteenth to one-eighth of one percentage point of the size of the transaction.

The FF market is an interbank market, because of the need to transfer immediately usable funds. Currency is expensive and risky to transfer, but central bank balances can be transferred rapidly over electronic payment systems and utilized immediately. Thus, the FF market entails the transfer of ownership of Federal Reserve balances. Since only commercial banks are permitted to hold deposit accounts at Federal Reserve Banks,[1] direct transaction in the FF market is limited to banks. On any given day, however, an average of 10% of volume may be attributed to bank transactions on behalf of nonbank customers, such as government security dealers, other FIs, or nonfinancial companies.

The evolution of the FF market shaped the two major characteristics of FF: (1) the transfer of immediately available funds and (2) the short time horizons. To keep the speed of transfer up and the transaction costs down, the FF transfer of Federal Reserve balances is **unsecured**—that is, it is not backed by any collateral and there is no protection against default by the borrowing bank. The time horizon of FF transactions is as short as it can be—overnight. FF loans must typically be repaid the morning after the transaction. Although overnight FF transactions are by far the most common, comprising about 75% of all FF transactions, **term FF** also exist. Term FF are interbank transfers of immediately available, Federal Reserve funds for a period of time exceeding one day. Seven days is a fairly common time period for a term FF, which rarely exceeds more than 30 days.

Patterns in the FF Market   Large banks in major money markets, though both buying and selling FF, tend to be net buyers, whereas small banks in regional or rural markets tend to be net FF sellers. This creates an upstream, funneling pattern, in which excess funds in small regional banks are channeled to large money center banks, those banks located in the major money centers (for example, New York, Chicago, and San Francisco), which are chronically short of funds to finance their international investment opportunities. This symbiotic relationship is beneficial to both types of banks. Large banks have a low-cost source of funds to finance their asset portfolios, whereas small banks, which lack access to many profitable investment opportunities, can earn interest on their deposit balances. Indeed, large banks in major money centers rely on FF purchases to finance an average of 10.1% of their asset portfolios, while the smallest banks sell FF at an average rate of 10.6% of their assets.[2]

When small banks try to purchase FF, they are often turned away by the large FF bank dealers in New York City because of the unsecured nature of FF. The FF seller takes on a considerable credit risk when FF are lent out. If the borrowing bank does not repay the FF, *on time*, then the FF seller will experience a loss in liquidity. Since FF sellers typically lend out their funds for short time periods, until they are needed for other transactions, even a delay in repayment is considered akin to default in the FF market. Although nonrepayment has never occurred in the history of the FF market, delayed repayment, often resulting from "technical glitches," happens periodically. To avoid potential default, large money center FF traders sell only to other large money center banks that have previously extended lines of credit. These

unsecured: unbacked by any collateral.

term FF: interbank transfers of immediately available, Federal Reserve funds for a period of time exceeding one day.

---

[1] In the 1920s nonbank FIs transacted directly in FF markets because they were allowed to hold Federal Reserve balances. Today, nonbank dealers can transact directly in the market by receiving negotiable Federal Reserve drafts.

[2] See Allen, Peristiani, and Saunders (1989).

lines of credit are not sources of financing, but instead act as limits to the amount of FF that may be sold to any particular bank.

The FF dealer in New York City does not know whether or not the "Rural Bank of Podunk" is a good credit risk, and there is no time in the fast-moving FF market to conduct credit checks for infrequent overnight transactions. Thus, if a smaller bank wants to buy FF, it typically utilizes its **correspondent bank**, which is a larger regional bank that has a history of dealings with the smaller **respondent bank**. The correspondent bank purchases FF from the large FF dealers and then resells them to its smaller respondents that are locked out of direct participation in the market for FF purchases (although they can sell FF directly to the large money center banks). Potential credit risk due to the uncollateralized nature of the FF loan can explain the observed market structure.

correspondent bank: a larger, regional bank that has a history of dealings with the smaller respondent bank.

Intermediate-sized banks tend to be neither net buyers nor net sellers in the FF market,[3] whereas small banks tend to be infrequent buyers and net FF sellers. Since large banks continually transact in the FF market, they develop a reputation for timely repayment of their FF purchases, thus maintaining their ability to buy large amounts of FF regularly.

Checkpoint

✓

1. What led to the development of the FF market?
2. How did the FF market changed from the pre-World War II period to the postwar period?
3. What FIs participate in FF transactions? Why?
4. What distinctive pattern has evolved in the FF market? Why is it mutually beneficial to all FIs?

The Federal Funds Rate   Credit risk in the FF market can also be controlled through the FF rate, which is truly a competitive market rate. It is determined entirely by the supply and demand of banks for FF. Since the market is a closed, interbank system, the aggregate value of all orders to buy FF must equal the supply of FF sales. As Figure 10.1a shows, the FF rate is determined when the supply of FF sales equals the demand for FF purchases. If the demand for FF purchases increases—say, because at the end of the reserve maintenance period[4] many banks find that they have miscalculated their reserve requirements and must buy funds to hit their reserve target—then Figure 10.1a shows the resulting increase in the FF rate.

tiering: a price schedule by which riskier borrowers pay higher rates that contain risk premiums.

Although smaller, less well-known banks are excluded from FF purchases at the widely quoted, competitive FF rate, they can often buy FF at a premium. This **tiering** represents a price schedule through which riskier borrowers pay higher rates that contain risk premiums. Thus, large regional banks and foreign banks may pay up to one-eighth of 1% over the competitive FF rate, whereas less well known foreign banks and intermediate-sized U.S. banks may pay a risk premium of 25 basis points for FF purchases.[5]

The Role of the Fed in Setting the FF Rate   If the market is private, how does the Fed affect the FF rate? Figure 10.1b shows the impact of the Fed's tightened monetary policy. Recall from Chapter 4 that when the Fed tightens, reserves are drained from the system, which means that the banking system as a whole now has a reduced supply of total reserves. Most often the Fed will use open market operations to accomplish this goal by buying up Treasury securities. This bids up Treasury bill rates, making them relatively more lucrative investments than FF sales and

---

[3] Allen, Peristiani, and Saunders (1989) show that the larger regional banks' net FF purchases are 2.6% of their assets, whereas the smaller regional banks' net FF sales are 2.2% of their assets. This is consistent with the role of regional banks as conduit between large money center and small banks for both FF purchase and sale transactions.

[4] See the discussion of reserve requirements in Chapter 4.

[5] See Allen and Saunders (1986) for a discussion of FF rate setting that incorporates a premium for credit risk.

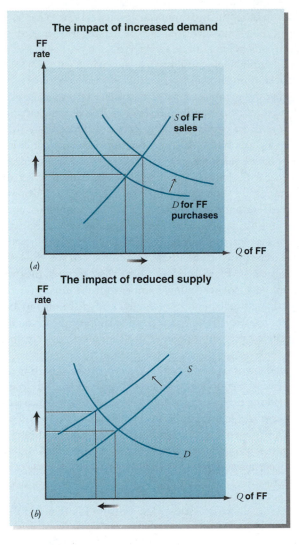

Figure 10.1

shifting some bank investments from the FF market to the Treasury market. As a result, the supply of FF sales declines, as shown in Figure 10.1*b*. The competitive market reaction to this decrease in supply is an increase in the equilibrium FF rate. Thus, the Fed does not set the FF rate as it does the discount rate. It only takes on policies that impact the market-determined FF rate with varying precision. In recent years, the Fed has been quite successful in impacting the FF rate, with an average monthly deviation from intended levels of only 6 basis points.[6]

Disagreement about the FF market's impact on the conduct of monetary policy fueled the Fed's unenthusiastic reaction to the early development of FF. Some viewed the FF market as an efficient mechanism to transmit the Fed's monetary policy. From their perspective, the tightened monetary policy (see Figure 10.1*b*) is facilitated by the increase in the FF rate and the resulting decrease in the number of FF transactions, thereby accomplishing the Fed's goal of reducing the money supply. However, others argued that the existence of a FF market

---

[6] Carlson, McIntire, and Thomson (1995) show that FF futures contracts can be used to predict future monetary policy, since their value is determined by the monthly average overnight FF rate for a $5 million transaction that is hypothetically held for 30 days.

would allow FIs to offset the Fed's monetary policy actions. That is, when the Fed tightens its monetary policy, the FF rate increases, thereby making it more expensive to hold idle balances. This will reduce bank holdings of excess reserves, as more banks seek to sell greater amounts of FF (along the upwardly sloping supply curve shown in Figure 10.1*b*). The Fed may be required to offset this effect by undertaking larger monetary policy actions so as to accomplish its goals. Studies show that the net impact of these two effects is that the existence of the FF market generally enhances, not circumvents, the effectiveness of monetary policy.[7]

Bank holdings of excess reserves have declined dramatically over the postwar period of rapid growth of FF as a result of bank efforts to enhance their efficiency of operation. The development of the FF market is just one aspect of the streamlining of operations that has led banks to mobilize their sources of funds more efficiently in order to maximize their return. Moreover, the availability of a market FF rate that can act as a barometer on financial markets has given the Fed a diagnostic tool that enhances its conduct of monetary policy.[8] Thus, the Fed's early pessimism regarding the FF market appears to be misplaced. In any event, the Fed, as powerful as it was, still was unable to block the FF market's growth.

The most direct impact of the FF market on the Fed was the loss of income. Specifically, when banks utilized the FF market to manage their reserves, they would buy FF rather than borrowing from the discount window in order to make up any reserve shortfalls. In this way, the Fed forfeited significant amounts of interest from discount window loans to the nascent FF market.[9] By 1930, however, the Fed decided to support the FF market by ruling that Federal Funds are not subject to reserve requirements.[10] This decision further encouraged FF market activity.

You may wonder why banks in need of reserves prefer to borrow from the FF market rather than from the Fed at the discount window. The discount rate is always lower than the FF rate because the former is fully collateralized against default; since a FF purchase is unsecured, the FF rate must carry a risk premium for default. The FI will compare rates for similar money market instruments before entering into a FF transaction. Rates are obtained using an electronic quotation system, such as Bloomberg Financial Markets. Figure 10.2 shows the money market composite screen. When observing market rates, you will see that, for similar term transactions:

$$\text{Discount Rate} < \text{U.S. Treasury Bill Rate} < \text{FF Rate}$$

It is difficult to compare these three rates directly in the figure because the FF rate that you see quoted is a simple interest rate based on a 360 day year, whereas the discount rate is a simple interest rate based on a 365 day year and the Treasury bill yield is a rate of discount based on a 360 day year. However, we can use our conversion formulas from Chapter 7 to make the comparisons. The discount rate for an overnight discount window loan highlighted in Figure 10.2 is 5.25% p.a.; the rate of discount on a U.S. Treasury bill maturing in one day is shown

---

[7] For a good overview see, Boughton (1972).

[8] Indeed, Bernanke and Blinder (1992) and Hess and Porter (1993) show that the FF rate is a good indicator of monetary policy and can forecast real macroeconomic variables. Moreover, Thorbecke and Alami (1992) show that the FF rate is a significant risk factor in an arbitrage pricing model and that unexpected increases (decreases) in the FF rate forecast lower (higher) stock prices.

[9] In 1922 the Fed lost an estimated 12% of its income to the newly formed FF market. In 1925 and 1928 estimates of lost Fed income were 48% and 43%, respectively. Indeed, the introduction of the FF market created financial difficulties for the Fed, and in three of the first ten years of the market's existence, the New York Fed was unable to pay dividends without drawing on its surplus. See Boughton (1972), p. 7.

[10] In part, this was the Fed's attempt to induce banks to use FF instead of overnight call loans to stock brokers, which were viewed as a means of financing stock market speculation.

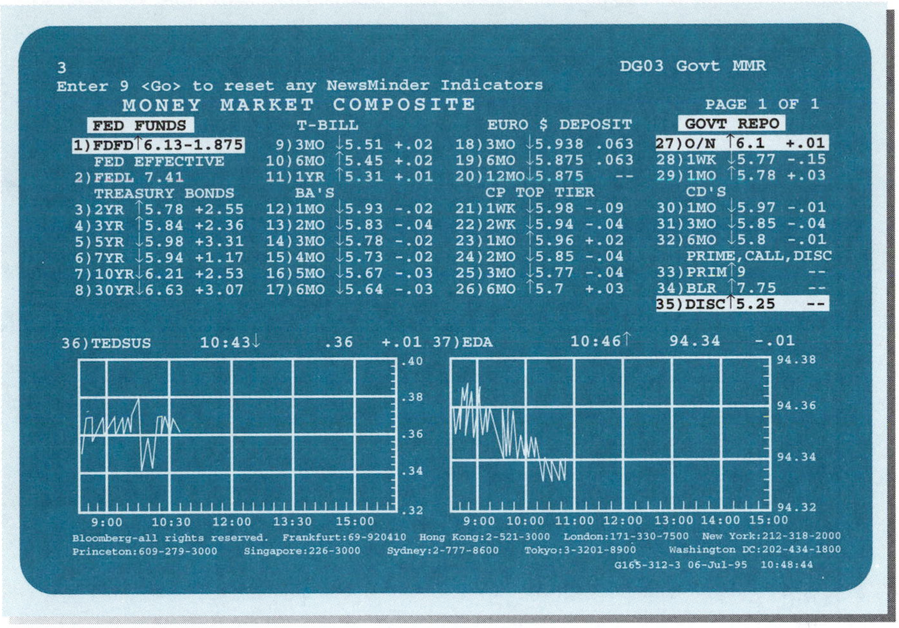
3
DG03 Govt MMR
Enter 9 <Go> to reset any NewsMinder Indicators
MONEY MARKET COMPOSITE
PAGE 1 OF 1
FED FUNDS
T-BILL
EURO $ DEPOSIT
GOVT REPO
1)FDFD↑6.13-1.875
FED EFFECTIVE
2)FEDL 7.41
TREASURY BONDS
3)2YR ↑5.78 +2.55
4)3YR ↑5.84 +2.36
5)5YR ↓5.98 +3.31
6)7YR ↓5.94 +1.17
7)10YR↓6.21 +2.53
8)30YR↓6.63 +3.07
9)3MO ↓5.51 +.02
10)6MO ↑5.45 +.02
11)1YR ↑5.31 +.01
BA'S
12)1MO ↓5.93 -.02
13)2MO ↓5.83 -.04
14)3MO ↓5.78 -.02
15)4MO ↓5.73 -.02
16)5MO ↓5.67 -.03
17)6MO ↓5.64 -.03
18)3MO ↓5.938 .063
19)6MO ↓5.875 .063
20)12MO↓5.875 --
CP TOP TIER
21)1WK ↓5.98 -.09
22)2WK ↓5.94 -.04
23)1MO ↑5.96 +.02
24)2MO ↓5.85 -.04
25)3MO ↓5.77 -.04
26)6MO ↑5.7 +.03
27)O/N ↑6.1 +.01
28)1WK ↓5.77 -.15
29)1MO ↑5.78 +.03
CD'S
30)1MO ↓5.97 -.01
31)3MO ↓5.85 -.04
32)6MO ↓5.8 -.01
PRIME,CALL,DISC
33)PRIM↑9 --
34)BLR ↑7.75 --
35)DISC↑5.25 --
36)TEDSUS 10:43↓ .36 +.01
37)EDA 10:46↑ 94.34 -.01
.40
.38
.36
.34
.32
94.38
94.36
94.34
94.32
9:00 10:30 12:00 13:30 15:00
9:00 10:00 11:00 12:00 13:00 14:00 15:00
Bloomberg-all rights reserved. Frankfurt:69-920410 Hong Kong:2-521-3000 London:171-330-7500 New York:212-318-2000
Princeton:609-279-3000 Singapore:226-3000 Sydney:2-777-8600 Tokyo:3-3201-8900 Washington DC:202-434-1800
G165-312-3 06-Jul-95 10:48:44

Figure 10.2

tick change: the direction of the last rate change, up or down.

as O/N 6.1%; and the FF rate shown in Figure 10.2 is 6.13% p.a. [11] The arrows show the direction of the last rate changes, up or down, called the **tick change**. The number –1.875 next to the FF rate of 6.13% represents the previous day's closing price; that is, the previous day's price was 1.875 basis points below 6.13%, for a closing FF rate on the previous day of 6.11125% p.a.

The rates are not comparable in the forms they appear on the screen in Figure 10.2 because each is quoted in a different format. To convert the 6.1% p.a. U.S. Treasury discount yield to a form comparable to the rate on the discount window loan, which is stated in the form of a simple interest yield on a 365 day basis, we use the following formula for the bond equivalent yield from Chapter 7:

$$i = \frac{365d}{360 - dt} = \frac{365(.061)}{360 - (.061)(1)} = 6.19\% \text{ p.a.}$$

To convert the simple interest FF rate from a 360 day to a 365 day basis, use the conversion factor $\frac{365}{360}$ to obtain

$$365\text{day } FF \text{ rate} = 6.13\% \left(\frac{365}{360}\right) = 6.22\% \text{ p.a.}$$

Comparing the bond equivalent yields for all three overnight instruments results in the correct ordering:

Discount Rate (5.25%) < U.S. Treasury Bill Rate (6.19%) < FF Rate (6.22%)

[11] Although the 30 day U.S. Treasury rate, rather than the overnight Treasury bill rate, is shown on the screen in Figure 10.2, we will see in Chapter 11 that the overnight rate is close to the highlighted overnight repo rate of 6.1% p.a. We therefore use 6.1% p.a. as a proxy for the overnight U.S. Treasury bill rate in the following example.

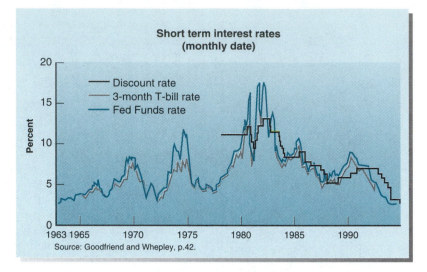

Figure 10.3

Since the discount rate is the lowest interest rate, the question remains: Why do banks prefer to buy FF as opposed to borrowing at a lower discount rate?[12] The answer stems from the implicit costs of borrowing at the discount window. Although the explicit interest expenses are relatively low, the implicit costs of greater central bank scrutiny and the cost of tying up marketable securities as discount window collateral raise the effective cost of discount window borrowing. Moreover, the Fed does not grant discount window loans to all banks at all times. The bank must exhaust its access to all money market sources of funds before it can approach the discount window as a last resort only.

The Fed administers the discount rate and changes it infrequently. But both the Treasury bill rate and the FF rate are competitive rates that adjust instantly to changing market conditions. They therefore tend to be more volatile than the discount rate. Indeed, since the Fed started targeting monetary aggregates in its conduct of monetary policy,[13] the volatility of the FF rate has increased dramatically. Figure 10.3 shows the impact of the change in monetary policy operations on interest rate volatility. Prior to October 1979, the Fed conducted its monetary policy by keeping the FF rate in narrowly proscribed bands. This dampened the fluctuations in the FF rate since whenever the rate increased (declined) too much, the Fed eased (tightened) monetary policy a bit to reduce (increase) the rate. The result was a FF rate that moved gradually to higher and lower levels as monetary policy objectives dictated. In October 1979, the Fed adopted a policy of monetary aggregate targets in which the FF rate was allowed to fluctuate freely according to the supply and demand of FF. The result, clearly visible in Figure 10.3, is a marked increase in both FF rate level and volatility.

Some volatility in FF rates occurs in response to changes in Fed monetary policy activities, but other FF rate fluctuations are the result of changes in FF market supply and demand. A regular pattern that emanates from bank behavior patterns is the end-of-quarter effect. On

---

[12] Indeed, one could even imagine a discount window arbitrage opportunity where the bank would borrow at the lower discount rate to lend at the higher FF rate. This is a serious violation of Fed policy, and the discount window officers presumably scrutinize bank balance sheets for any evidence of this activity. However, Peristiani (1991) finds the FF rate spread over the discount rate to be a significant determinant of the level of individual bank discount window borrowing.

[13] See the discussion of monetary policy targets in Chapter 4.

the last day of the quarter, the FF rate increases an average of 22 basis points and falls on the following day by an average of 17.7 basis points. This pattern can be explained by bank window dressing, in which the banks attempt to increase their asset size on financial reporting dates, which fall on the last day of each quarter.[14] Banks can accomplish this puffery by buying funds on the last day of each quarter to be resold on the next day. The increased demand for FF purchases on the last day of each quarter could account for the increased FF rates on those days.

Another regular pattern in FF rates emanates from the market's role in managing the banks' reserve requirements. If a bank is facing a reserve shortfall, it will offer higher FF rates in order to buy FF to cover its reserve requirement. But Federal Funds are "perishable" since they must be in the bank during the reserve maintenance period. It will not help the bank avoid a deficiency in its reserve requirements if it buys adequate amounts of FF on the Thursday after the last Wednesday in the reserve maintenance period. Those funds must be bought on Wednesday in order to be counted as reserve balances against the bank's reserve requirements. Thus, FF rates will be extremely volatile on the last Tuesday and Wednesday of each reserve maintenance period. How do banks use the FF market to manage their reserve requirements? This is the subject of the next section.

Checkpoint

1. How is the FF rate determined?
2. What is the role of the Federal Reserve Bank in the FF market?
3. How did the development of the FF market influence the effectiveness of monetary policy?
4. How has FF rate volatility changed over the years? What is the major cause of this change?
5. What is the correct ordering of the FF rate, the discount rate, and the U.S. Treasury bill rate?

➤ Typical FF Transactions

Participants in the FF market typically undertake two types of transactions: (1) reserve management transactions and (2) portfolio management transactions.

Reserve Management Transactions

Currently, U.S. banks must comply with contemporaneous reserve requirements. As we saw in Chapter 4, this means that over the two week reserve maintenance period, only on two days (every other Tuesday and Wednesday) does the bank know its reserve requirement exactly. Prior to that time, the bank must estimate its daily deposit balances in order to calculate the reserves required against those deposits.

Another element of uncertainty in reserve maintenance centers on interest rates. Since reserves are noninterest bearing, the cost of the reserve requirement increases as the level of interest rates increases. This is because of the opportunity cost of funds that could have been invested in interest-bearing securities. FF are interest-earning investments that are available to banks on a day-to-day basis.[15] If on any day the bank has excess reserves, these funds can

---

[14] Documented by Allen and Saunders (1992), the incentives for bank window dressing range from managerial risk aversion to the potential for enhanced employment opportunities and possible nonpecuniary benefits from size, such as reputation or "country club bragging rights."

[15] Spindt and Tarhan (1980) find that the FF market and the banking system's supply of short term dealer credit are the primary liquidity shock absorbers.

expeditiously be sold in the FF market, thereby earning a return equal to the daily FF rate. Alternatively, if on any day the bank is deficient in reserves, the shortfall can be bought on the FF market at a cost equal to the daily FF rate. Thus, the measure of the opportunity cost of required reserves is the FF rate.[16]

The FF rate changes each day according to supply and demand. Banks attempt to minimize their overall cost of maintaining reserves by holding excess reserves when the FF rate is relatively low during the 14 day reserve maintenance period. That frees up reserves to be sold when the FF rate is relatively high during the same 14 day period. The bank's FF trading desk therefore forecasts FF rates over the two week period and adjusts the bank's daily reserve balances to minimize the overall cost of meeting the reserve requirement.

Let's consider the example from Chapter 4 where the bank's daily reserve requirement over the period 2/8–2/21 averaged $42 million. In Chapter 4 we considered only the quantity risk of meeting the reserve requirement on average, each and every day of the reserve maintenance period. Considering only the quantity risk, the bank's best strategy is to attempt to meet the same reserve level, equal to the estimated average daily reserve requirement, each day of the maintenance period. However, when we consider the possibility of interest rate risk, the risk of fluctuating FF rates over the reserve maintenance period, we find that it may not be optimal for the bank to hold the same amount of reserves on each day of the reserve maintenance period. Indeed, we can solve for an optimal program of reserve balances based on a forecast of FF rates over the two week period.

Suppose that the bank's FF traders predict that the Fed will tighten its monetary policy on Thursday, 2/15. Since a tightening of monetary policy drains reserves from the system, the FF rate is forecast to increase on 2/15, the eighth day of the reserve maintenance period. Let's suppose that the FF traders expect a FF rate of 4.75% p.a. for the first seven days of the reserve maintenance period, to be followed by a FF rate of 5% p.a. for the remainder of the period. The cost of the reserve requirement is reduced if a greater portion of the reserve requirement is met during the low-rate environment, 2/8–2/14, with fewer reserves held during the time period (2/15–2/21) when the reserves can be invested more lucratively. The relative proportion of reserve balances shifted to the low-rate period depends on how risk averse the FF traders are. If they are willing to take a big gamble, they will hold all reserves during the period 2/8–2/14 and *no* reserves at all during 2/15–2/21. Let's examine the costs of meeting the reserve requirement (assuming it is known with certainty) under the two different scenarios.

The first scenario follows the recommendations of Chapter 4 that the bank attempt to hold the average daily reserve balance on each day of the reserve maintenance period. The average daily reserve balance for this example is $42 million (computed in Chapter 4). The interest cost to the bank of meeting the reserve requirement is

$$\$42m \left(\frac{.0475(7)}{360} \right) + \$42m \left(\frac{.05(7)}{360} \right) = \$79,625$$

where the first term is the interest cost of meeting the reserve requirement during 2/8–2/14 using seven consecutive daily FF purchases at the daily rate of 4.75% and the second term is the interest cost during the remaining seven days.[17] Note that it is immaterial whether the interest cost is an opportunity cost (for reserves that are not sold in the FF market) or a cash expense (for reserves that are bought in the FF market). The cost is the same for both.[18]

---

[16] Brunner and Lown (1993) show that the FF rate is an important determinant of the level of bank excess reserves.

[17] Friday, 2/9, and Friday, 2/16, weekend balances are counted three times each.

[18] This assumes that there is no bid-asked spread—that is, that the bank can buy and sell funds at the same rate. This is true for large money center bank dealers only.

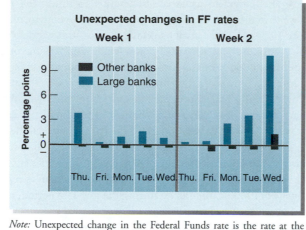

Note: Unexpected change in the Federal Funds rate is the rate at the close less the rate at 11:00 a.m. Large banks are those with total deposits exceeding $10 billion.

Figure 10.4

What is the cost of meeting the reserve requirement by managing the bank's reserve balances to minimize interest costs? Since reserves will be held during the first seven days only, the daily balances must be doubled to enable the bank to meet its reserve requirements. Thus, the bank must hold $84 million in reserves on each of the days during the period 2/8–2/14 and no reserves during 2/15–2/21. The interest cost of meeting the reserve requirement is

$$\$84m \left(\frac{.0475(7)}{360} \right) = \$77,583$$

for a savings of $2,042 (= $79,625 – $77,583). Of course, this second strategy is quite a gamble because, in reality, the bank still faces quantity risk. We ignored consideration of the fact that during the period 2/8–2/19, the bank is not certain of its exact reserve requirement. Moreover, the least cost reserve maintenance program is risky because FF rates become less predictable at the end of the reserve maintenance period.[19] Figure 10.4 shows that the unexpected change in FF rates for large bank borrowers increased an average of more than 10% on the last day of the reserve maintenance period, in contrast to the daily FF rate fluctuations of significantly less than 5% on each of the other days of the two week period. Because of the FF rate's volatility, the second strategy is quite risky; the bank will most likely choose a reserve maintenance program somewhere in between the two extremes. The more certainty the FF traders have about both FF rates and their required reserve levels, the closer their strategy will be to the second, less costly reserve maintenance program. The more uncertainty they face, the more risk averse their reserve maintenance program, thereby resulting in an attempt to even out the daily reserve balances over the two week period.

---

[19] Lasser (1992) shows that FF rate volatility increases significantly on the second Friday, Monday, Tuesday, and Wednesday of the two week reserve maintenance period. Indeed, on the second Tuesday, which is the first day that the bank knows its reserve requirement with certainty, the FF rate volatility increased fourfold over the prior Tuesday, when estimated over the period 1978–1989. Similar results were obtained by Saunders and Urich (1988) and Spindt and Hoffmeister (1988) for contemporaneous reserve accounting, as well as by Dyl and Hoffmeister (1985) for lagged reserve accounting. These studies conclude that FF traders get more aggressive and FF rates move less predictably as the reserve maintenance period draws to a close.

Banks have alternatives to using the FF market to fund their reserve requirements. In Chapter 4, we saw the role of discount window borrowing to meet reserve requirements. Indeed, Figure 10.5 shows that small banks use the discount window more than large banks on a regular basis, with steady amounts of discount window borrowings on each day of the two week reserve maintenance period. But large banks conduct more than 60% of their discount window borrowing on the last day of the borrowing period, when the FF rate's volatility increases, on average, by more than 10%. Moreover, since discount rates will always be less than the FF rate, it appears that the bank can reduce the cost of funding its reserve requirement by using the discount window instead of FF. Indeed, if the spread between the FF rate and the discount rate were 25 basis points (say, a FF rate of 4.75% p.a. and a discount rate of 4.5% p.a.), we could improve on our low-cost strategy by borrowing the bank's entire reserve requirement at the discount window. The lowest cost of maintaining the bank's reserve requirements, using the risky strategy of holding all reserves during the low-rate period, would be

$$\$84m \left(\frac{.045(7)}{365} \right) = \$72,493$$

for an additional savings of \$5,090(= 77,583 − 72,493). Note that this savings derives from the spread between the FF rate and the discount rate. Although this spread is quoted as 25 basis points, we see that it is really more. This is because FF rates are quoted as simple interest rates on a 360 day basis, whereas discount rates are quoted as simple interest rates on a 365 day basis. Recalling our adjustment formula from Chapter 7 (see *Calculation Complications 7.2*), we multiply the 4.5% p.a. discount rate in this example by $\frac{360}{365}$ to obtain a comparable discount rate of 4.438% p.a., resulting in a spread of 31.2 basis points between the FF rate and the discount rate.

Unfortunately, this deal is too good to be true. The Fed states that the discount window is to be utilized only as a last resort. Hence, if the bank has access to the FF market, these funds must be exhausted before the Fed will grant a discount window loan. Any large bank

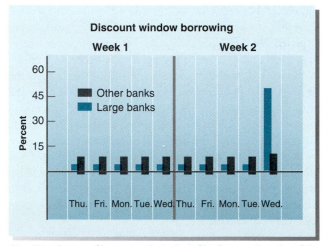

Note: Distribution of borrowings by a class of banks on a given day of the reserve maintenance period is the number of borrowings on that day by banks in that clsass during 1987-93 divided by the total number of borrowings by banks in that class during those years. Large banks are those with total deposits exceeding \$10 billion.

Figure 10.5

will find it difficult to justify discount window loans of this duration (seven consecutive days) and magnitude when Federal funds are readily available. Indeed, during 1980 and 1981, when the spread between the FF rate and the discount rate was unusually large, the Fed imposed a surcharge of 2% to 4% on all discount window borrowings of large banks with deposits of $500 million or more that borrowed too frequently.[20]

Portfolio Management Transactions

FF transactions are useful additions to the FIs' portfolio management tools. The FF market is so liquid and so flexible, with investment time horizons as short as overnight, that transactions can be made rapidly at low transaction costs. These features encourage banks, large banks in particular, to use the FF market to finance the banks' asset portfolio. Indeed, FF purchases appear as bank liabilities (sources of funds), whereas FF sales are bank assets (uses of funds). Suppose that a bank's FF traders contact the bank's Treasury desk with their forecast of impending Fed monetary policy tightening. The prediction of higher rates, if realized, will cause the market value of the bank's securities portfolio to decline. Suppose the bank decides to sell $100 million worth of Treasury securities today, intending to repurchase them tomorrow at the expected lower price. This is another risky strategy, whose return depends entirely on the accuracy of the traders' forecast of rate increases. But let's suppose that this bank truly has earned its name of "Ride 'Em Cowboy Bank."

When the bank sells the Treasuries, it will receive $100 million in immediately available funds that it expects to reinvest the next day. Rather than holding those funds idle for one day, the bank can invest them in the FF market. The prevailing rate is the lower 4.75% p.a. rate (rates are expected to increase tomorrow), but the interest return is still significant at $100m$($\frac{.0475(1)}{360}$) = $13,194$. Of course, the bank is exposed to the risk that rates will decline, causing the bank to repurchase its Treasury portfolio at a loss.[21]

Suppose that on another date Ride 'Em Cowboy Bank decides to raise its reserves by purchasing overnight FF. Given its propensity to take on risk, it will probably not be able to buy FF on the competitive FF market directly. More likely, it will use its correspondent bank as a vehicle to purchase funds. Let's examine the transaction from the viewpoint of the correspondent bank. If the amount of FF purchased is assumed to be $10 million and the competitive FF rate is 6% p.a., suppose that the premium charged to Ride 'Em Cowboy Bank is an exorbitant 50 basis points. Thus, the correspondent bank buys the FF at 6% p.a. and resells them at 6.5%. The profit earned by the correspondent bank is

$$\$10m \left(\frac{.065(1)}{360} \right) - \$10m \left(\frac{.06(1)}{360} \right) = \$139$$

Correspondent banks don't provide this service for high levels of profit. Indeed, FF transactions are simply part of a bundle of transactions that the correspondent bank performs on behalf of its respondent. In total, the relationship is profitable, even if each individual transaction does not appear to be very lucrative.

Checkpoint

✓

1. What major transactions do FIs use in the FF market?
2. Why is the FF rate considered to be the cost of maintaining required reserves?

---

[20] This conclusion is supported by Mitchell and Pearce (1992), who find that the spread between the FF rate and the discount rate has the greatest impact on the discount window borrowing of the smallest banks.

[21] In Chapter 11, we will see how this interest rate risk can be alleviated using repurchase agreements.

3.   What is the primary advantage of using the FF market for portfolio management transactions?

4.   Why are large money center banks more likely than smaller rural banks to use the FF market for portfolio management on a regular basis?

➤ Summary

The Federal Funds market began as a way for banks to manage their reserve requirements more efficiently and has grown into a significant, permanent source of liquidity to fund bank portfolios. The market is an interbank market for unsecured loans of Federal Reserve funds. These funds are immediately available for use by the borrower (FF buyer) and must usually be repaid the next day to the lender (FF seller).

The FF rate is determined by the supply and demand for overnight funds by banks in the market. The Fed impacts, but does not set, the FF rate by affecting the amount of reserves in the system, thereby inducing banks to increase (decrease) their supply of FF sales when monetary policy is eased (tightened), with a resulting decrease (increase) in FF rates.

Banks use the FF market to manage (1) their required reserve balances so as to minimize the cost of meeting their requirement; and (2) their asset portfolios using FF purchases (sales) as a source (use) of financing. Small banks tend to be net FF sellers, whereas large money center banks tend to be net FF buyers. Correspondent banks and FF brokers act as go-betweens, linking banks in this decentralized nationwide market.

➤ References

Allen, L., S. Peristiani, and A. Saunders. "Bank Size, Collateral, and Net Purchase Behavior in the Federal Funds Market: Empirical Evidence." *Journal of Business* 62, No. 4 (1989): 501–515.

Allen, L., and A. Saunders. "Bank Window Dressing: Theory and Evidence." *Journal of Banking and Finance* 16 (1992): 585–623.

Allen, L., and A. Saunders. "The Large-Small Bank Dichotomy in the Federal Funds Market." *Journal of Banking and Finance* 10 (1986): 219–230.

Bernanke, B., and A. Blinder. "The FF Rate and the Channels of Monetary Transmission." *American Economic Review* 82, No. 4 (September 1992): 901–921.

Boughton, J. M. *Monetary Policy and the FF Market.* Durham, N.C.: Duke University Press, 1972.

Brunner, A. D., and C. S. Lown. "The Effects of Lower Reserve Requirements on Money Market Volatility." *AEA Papers and Proceedings* (May 1993): 199–205.

Carlson, J. B., J. M. McIntire, and J. B. Thomson. "Federal Funds Futures as an Indicator of Future Monetary Policy: A Primer." Federal Reserve Bank of Cleveland *Economic Review* 31, No. 1 (1995): 20–30.

Dyl, E. A., and J. R. Hoffmeister. "Efficiency and Volatility in the FF Market." *Journal of Bank Research*, 15 (1985): 234–239.

Goodfriend, M., and W. Whepley. "Federal Funds." In T. Cook and R. LaRoche, eds., *Instruments of the Money Market.* 7th ed., Richmond, VA: Federal Reserve Bank of Richmond (1993): 7–21.

Hess, G. D., and R. D. Porter. "Comparing Interest–Rate Spreads and Money Growth as Predictors of Output Growth: Granger Causality in the Sense Granger Intended." *Journal of Economics and Business* 45 (1993): 247–268.

Lasser, D. J. "The Effect of Contemporaneous Reserve Accounting on the Market for FF." *Journal of Banking and Finance* 16 (1992): 1047–1056.

Mitchell, K., and D. K. Pearce. "Discount Window Borrowing Across Federal Reserve Districts: Evidence Under Contemporaneous Reserve Accounting." *Journal of Banking and Finance* 16, No. 4 (1992): 771–790.

Peristiani, S. "The Model Structure of Discount Window Borrowing." *Journal of Money, Credit, and Banking*, 23, No. 1 (1991): 13–34.

Saunders, A., and T. Urich. "The Effects of Shifts in Monetary Policy and Reserve Accounting Regimes on Bank Reserve Management Behavior in the FF Market." *Journal of Banking and Finance* 11 (1988): 523–536.

Spindt, P. A., and J. R. Hoffmeister. "The Micromechanics of the FF Market: Implications for the Day–of–the–Week Effects in Funds Rate Variability." *Journal of Financial and Quantitative Analysis* 23 (1988): 401–416.

Spindt, P. A., and V. Tarhan. "Liquidity Structure Adjustment Behavior of Large Money Center Banks." *Journal of Money, Credit, and Banking* 12, No. 2 (May 1980): 198–220.

Thorbecke, W., and T. Alami. "The FF Rate and the Arbitrage Pricing Theory: Evidence that Monetary Policy Matters." *Journal of Macroeconomics* 13, No. 4 (Fall 1992): 731–744.

Willis, P. *The Federal Funds Market: Its Origin and Development.* Boston: Federal Reserve Bank of Boston, 1964.

Questions

1a. Calculate the market-clearing FF rate if there are only three banks in the economy and each submits the following orders for FF purchases and sales:

Rate	Small Bank		Medium Bank		Large Bank	
	Sell	Buy	Sell	Buy	Sell	Buy
			($ million)			
5%	375	25	150	50	25	375
5.25%	350	25	125	85	20	385
5.5%	325	40	100	100	0	400
5.75%	300	50	75	125	0	410
6%	275	55	50	150	150	425

1b. What are the net FF market positions of all three banks at the equilibrium FF rate?

2. Using the FF transactions schedule in question 1, determine the impact on FF rates of a tightening of Fed monetary policy operation that drained $115 million in reserves from the system.

3a. Use the following information to compute the bank's required reserves and excess reserves:

Daily Demand Deposit Balances

Date	Mon.2/5	Tues.2/6	Wed.2/7	Thurs.2/8	Fri.2/9
Deposit Amt.($m)	265	300	295	319	211
Date	Mon.2/12	Tues.2/13	Wed.2/14	Thurs.2/15	Fri.2/16
Deposit Amt.($m)	291	304	297	332	276
Date	Mon.2/19	Tues.2/20	Wed.2/21	Thurs.2/22	Fri.2/23
Deposit Amt.($m)	321	296	325	348	402

Daily Balances at the Federal Reserve Bank

Date	Mon.2/5	Tues.2/6	Wed.2/7	Thurs.2/8	Fri.2/9
Deposit Amt.($m)	19	23	19	23	36
Date	Mon.2/12	Tues.2/13	Wed.2/14	Thurs.2/15	Fri.2/16
Deposit Amt.($m)	19	27	35	21	36
Date	Mon.2/19	Tues.2/20	Wed.2/21	Thurs.2/22	Fri.2/23
Deposit Amt.($m)	11	16	29	29	31

Daily Holdings of Vault Cash

Date	Mon.1/22	Tues.1/23	Wed.1/24	Thurs.1/25	Fri.1/26
Deposit Amt.($m)	5	21	5	10	11
Date	Mon.1/29	Tues.1/30	Wed.1/31	Thurs.2/1	Fri.2/2
Deposit Amt.($m)	18	16	18	19	8
Date	Mon.2/5	Tues.2/6	Wed.2/7	Thurs.2/8	Fri.2/9
Deposit Amt.($m)	15	7	8	9	23

3b. If FF rates are forecast to be 6% p.a. on 2/8–2/13, 5.8% on 2/14–2/19, and 5.75% on 2/20–2/21, what is the least cost method of meeting the bank's reserve requirements?

3c. Why is the strategy in part (b) very risky?

3d. If FF rates are forecast to be 6% p.a. on 2/8–2/13, 5.8% on 2/14–2/19, and 5.75% on 2/20–2/21, what is the least risky method of meeting the bank's reserve requirements? What is the cost differential between the least cost and least risky methods?

4. Suppose that a correspondent bank sells $50 million in seven day term FF to its respondent at a premium of 25 basis points over the competitive FF rate of 4.5% p.a. What is the interest cost to the respondent bank? What is the spread earned by the correspondent bank?

5a. What is a bank's net profit if it borrows $10 million in funds on the FF market for 14 days at a rate of 3.55% p.a. to be invested in a 14 day U.S. Treasury bill at a simple interest rate of 3.65% p.a.? (*Hint*: You must calculate the rate of discount on the U.S. Treasury bill using the formula from Chapter 7.)

5b. Do you think that an investment opportunity like the one in part (a) can be found in real-world financial markets? Why or why not?

6a. How could you use the following spot rate schedule to set up a profitable, leveraged transaction with a $10 million face value:

    7 day U.S. Treasury rate of discount: 5% p.a.
    21 day U.S. Treasury rate of discount: 5.35% p.a.
    7 day term FF rate: 5.25% p.a.
    (*Note*: You cannot short the U.S. Treasury bill.)

6b. What is the risk of the transaction in part (a)?

6c. Calculate the cost of unwinding the transaction in part (a). (*Hint*: Calculate the breakeven rate just required to avoid a loss on the transaction.)

7. The discount rate for a five day discount window loan is 4.35% p.a., the rate of discount on a U.S. Treasury bill maturing in five days is 4.3%, and the five day term FF rate is 4.34% p.a. Rank, in order of size, the three interest rates.

8. Demonstrate the impact of an easy money policy on the FF market using supply and demand curves as in Figure 10.1*b*.

9. On the last Tuesday of the reserve maintenance period, a bank discovers that its average daily reserve requirement is $5 million. Up until the last two days, average daily reserve balances equal $7 million.
   a. What are the bank's excess reserves?
   b. How can the bank utilize its excess reserves?
   c. If the bank has total reserves of $5 million on the last Tuesday and Wednesday of the reserve maintenance period, will it be able to utilize all of its excess reserves?

CHAPTER 11

REPURCHASE AGREEMENTS

"Money is better than poverty, if only for financial reasons,"—Woody Allen, *Without Feathers* (1976), "Early Essays."

Learning Objectives

- To see how increases in both the level of interest rates and the volatility of rates have contributed to the development of the markets in repurchase agreements ("repos") and reverse repurchase agreements ("reverses").

- To learn how these participants utilize the market to manage their exposures to credit and interest rate risk as well as to obtain a versatile source of financing.

- To examine the valuation, trading, and clearing of repos and reverses.

➤ Introduction

We have become accustomed to thinking of private FIs as innovators, with public FIs scurrying to catch up with private-sector changes. The markets in repurchase agreements (repos) and reverse repos (reverses) are exceptions to this rule. These vibrant markets, currently averaging about $200–$300 billion in daily transaction volume, were pioneered by a *public* FI: the Federal Reserve System in the United States. Indeed, one of the Fed's mandates, upon its creation in 1913, was to foster exports of U.S. commodities by providing credit to finance these exports. As we will see in Chapter 13, exports are typically financed using **Bankers Acceptances (BAs)**. The BA is a securitized letter of credit guaranteed ("accepted") by the issuing bank. Typically, an exporter receives a BA (or letter of credit) from the importer as payment for a shipment of goods. Payment on the BA is made upon receipt of the goods. If shipment takes, say, three months, then the exporter must wait three months for payment. But the exporter has bills to pay. The exporter can use the BA as collateral on a short term loan (three months in our example) to finance operations.

In 1914 the Fed, in fulfillment of its mandate to support the export sector of the economy, began to make low-rate loans based on BAs as collateral. These were the first **repurchase agreements (repos)**. The repo was a flexible instrument that allowed the Fed to provide financing to private exporters without taking on any credit risk because the repo is a fully collateralized loan in which the collateral consists of marketable securities. Since the BA fully

Bankers Acceptance (BA): a securitized letter of credit guaranteed ("accepted") by the issuing bank.

repurchase agreement (repo): a fully collateralized loan in which the collateral consists of marketable securities.

collateralized the Fed's loan to the private exporter, the Fed retained a marketable security against the possibility of default by the exporter. Use of an artifice (the repo purchase and later resale of the BA) allowed the Fed to inject funds into this sector of the economy without having to worry about collecting loan repayments from private companies. Private FIs and nonfinancial companies realized the versatility of this newly created financial security, and a new financial market was born.

What Are Repos and Reverses?

A repurchase agreement bundles together two separate transactions: the sale of marketable securities and the repurchase (hence the name) of those securities at a prespecified price on a later date. Consider two counterparties participating in a repo transaction. The first, Mr. Owt O'Cash, enters into the transaction in order to borrow short term funds. The second, Ms. Plen T. Doe, has excess cash that she wants to lend for a short time period. As shown in Figure 11.1, Mr. O'Cash sells marketable securities to Ms. Doe at time $t = 0$ with the proviso that at the maturity of the repo (time $t = T$) Ms. Doe will resell these securities back to Mr. O'Cash for a predetermined price. The difference between the sale price at time $t = 0$ and the sale price at time $t = T$ is the interest cost of the repo loan. Note that Mr. O'Cash utilizes the repo to borrow cash and lend securities for a period of T days. For an overnight repo, $T = 1$.

term repo: repo with a maturity of more than one day.

For a **term repo**, $T > 1$. An **open repo** has no set maturity date but is renewed each day upon agreement of both counterparties. Although the repo is structured as a sale and subsequent purchase of securities, in reality it is a loan fully collateralized by the marketable securities.

open repo: a repo with no set maturity date but is renewed each day upon agreement of both counterparties.

Consider the 90 day term repo example in Figure 11.1. Today ($t = 0$) Owt O'Cash sells 270 day Treasury bills with a rate of discount of 5% and a face value equal to $1 million to Plen T. Doe. Using our money market mathematics from Chapter 7, we find that the current market value of these securities is

$$P = \$1\text{m}\left(1 - \frac{.05(270)}{360}\right) = \$962,500$$

Mr. O'Cash borrows cash from Ms. Doe against this collateral. However, since the value of these Treasury bills may fluctuate during the term of the repo (90 days), the amount of the loan is *less than* the current market value of the securities. Ms. Doe charges Mr. O'Cash a *haircut* which, as we saw in Chapter 5, is the margin, or the deduction from current market value of the securities collateral required to do the repo transaction. Note that the haircut protects Ms. Doe (the lender of cash) against any risk of loss resulting from default by Mr. O'Cash.

The haircut is stated in terms of basis points. A 25 basis point haircut is fairly standard. This suggests that the amount of the repo loan will be 25 basis points below the market value of the securities collateral. To compute the amount of the repo loan:

Repo Principal = Securities' Market Value (1 − Haircut)

= $962,500(1 − .0025) = $960,093.75

Mr. Owt O'Cash borrows $960,093.75 from Ms. Plen T. Doe and offers collateral worth $962,500. The repo loan is an *over*collateralized loan in that the amount of the collateral exceeds the loan principal by the amount of the haircut.

After 90 days has passed, the second leg of the repo transaction takes place: Mr. O'Cash repurchases his securities from Ms. Doe by repaying the repo loan principal plus interest. The repo rate is quoted as a simple interest yield on a 360 day basis set upon initiation of the transaction and fixed for the term of the repo. At a 4.75% repo rate, the 90 day term repo loan

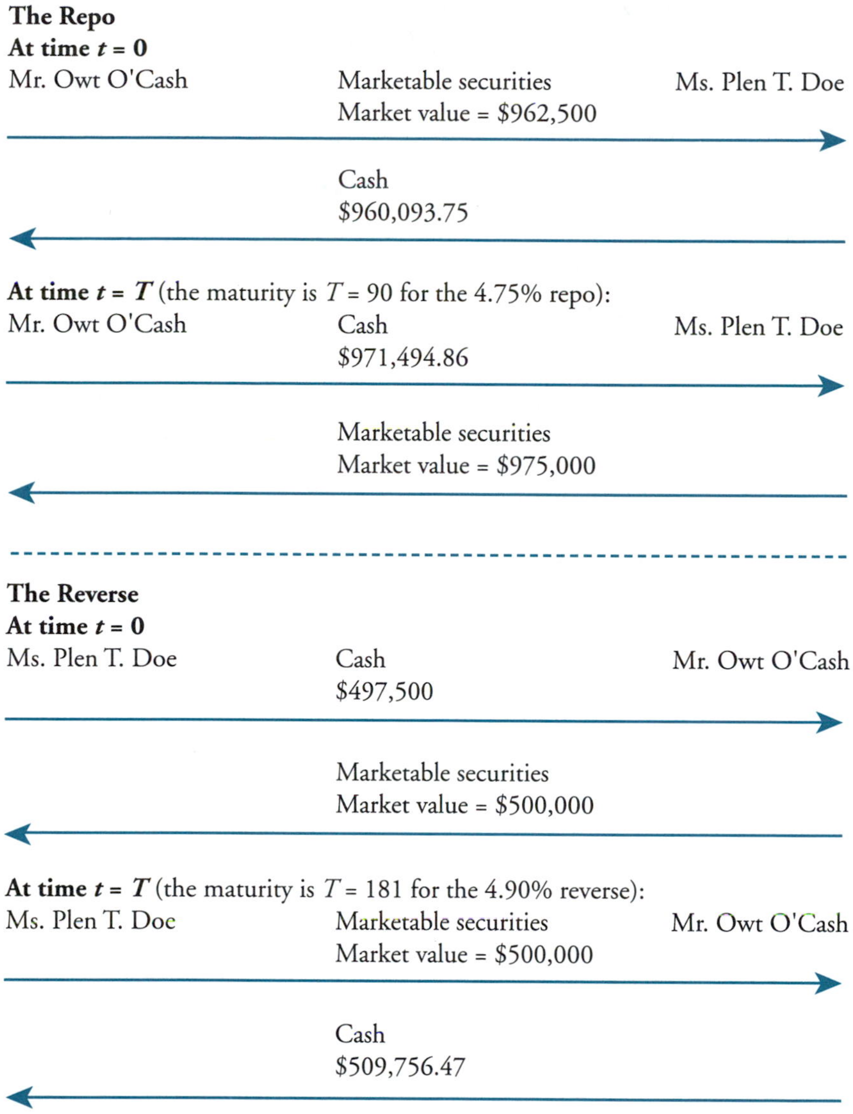

The Repo
At time $t = 0$

Mr. Owt O'Cash   Marketable securities   Ms. Plen T. Doe
                                  Market value = $962,500

                                  Cash
                                  $960,093.75

At time $t = T$ (the maturity is $T = 90$ for the 4.75% repo):
Mr. Owt O'Cash   Cash   Ms. Plen T. Doe
                                  $971,494.86

                                  Marketable securities
                                  Market value = $975,000

- -

The Reverse
At time $t = 0$

Ms. Plen T. Doe   Cash   Mr. Owt O'Cash
                                  $497,500

                                  Marketable securities
                                  Market value = $500,000

At time $t = T$ (the maturity is $T = 181$ for the 4.90% reverse):
Ms. Plen T. Doe   Marketable securities   Mr. Owt O'Cash
                                  Market value = $500,000

                                  Cash
                                  $509,756.47

Figure 11.1   Repos and Reverses

repayment is

$$\text{Repo Principal} + \text{Interest} = \text{Repo Principal}\left(1 + \frac{iT}{360}\right)$$

$$= \$960{,}093.75\left(1 + \frac{.0475(90)}{360}\right)$$

$$= \$971{,}494.86$$

Mr. O'Cash pays Ms. Doe $971,494.86 to repurchase his securities collateral: the $1 million face value of U.S. Treasury bills. However, since 90 days have passed, and these bills originally had 270 days until maturity, the Treasury bill has only 180 days until maturity. If interest rates have not changed over the 90 days, we can use the same 5% rate of discount to determine the market price of the 180 day Treasury bill at time $t = 90$

$$P = \$1m \left(1 - \frac{.05(180)}{360} \right) = \$975,000$$

Mr. O'Cash repurchases $975,000 worth of securities for $971,494.86. Note that the repurchase price is determined by

1. The repo loan principal ($960,093.75).

2. The repo rate of interest (4.75%).

3. The term of the repo (90 days).

The repurchase price of the securities (repo repayment) is completely independent of the market value of the securities on the maturity date of the repo. This reinforces the economic reality that a repo transaction is a collateralized loan.

reverse repurchase
agreement (reverse): the
opposite of the repo used
to borrow securities and
lend cash.

The **reverse repurchase agreement (reverse)**, viewed from the perspective of Plen T. Doe, is the opposite of the repo. Ms. Doe utilizes the reverse to borrow securities and lend cash. That is, at time $t = 0$, Ms. Doe agrees to buy marketable securities from Mr. O'Cash with the proviso that these securities will be resold to Mr. O'Cash at time $t = T$ at a predetermined price. The price differential between times $t = 0$ and $t = T$ comprises Ms. Doe's interest yield on the reverse.

The securities collateral for the reverse in Figure 11.1 is a $500,000 face value Treasury note offering 6% p.a. semiannually priced at par with exactly four years until maturity. Assuming a haircut of 50 basis points results in a reverse principal of $500,000(1 − .0050) = \$497,500$. Upon maturity of the reverse (say, in 181 days), the Treasury note has exactly 3.5 years (four years original maturity less the six months term of the reverse) until maturity. At a repo rate of 4.90%, Ms. Doe receives a reverse repayment of

$$\text{Reverse Principal} + \text{Interest} = \text{Reverse Principal} \left(1 + \frac{iT}{360} \right)$$

$$= \$497,500 \left(1 + \frac{.049(181)}{360} \right)$$

$$= \$509,756.47$$

If the Treasury note is still selling at par on the reverse maturity date, its market value is $500,000.

Clearly, Ms. Plen T. Doe views the repo at the top of Figure 11.1 as a reverse. That is, for the repo transaction, Ms. Doe is borrowing securities and lending cash for T days. Similarly, Owt O'Cash views the reverse at the bottom of Figure 11.1 as a repo since he borrows cash and lends securities. Thus, if one investor views the transaction as a repo, the counterparty always views it as a reverse, and vice versa.

Checkpoint

✓

1. How did the Fed originally use the repo? Why did the Fed have to design a new type of financial transaction to accomplish its goal?

2. What is a repo? What is a reverse? Contrast the two.

3. What is the haircut?

4. What determines the size of the repo principal?

5. What determines the size of the repo repayment?

➤ Market Participants

The repo market has grown exponentially from its humble origins when it was used to finance U.S. exports of commodities. Even the Fed's use of repos has changed over the years. Who are the market participants today, and what are their motivations for transacting in this market?

Central Banks

The repo was originally designed as a tool to funnel credit to specific sectors of the economy. Public FIs, like the Fed, provided financing to the export sector by accepting BAs as collateral on a repo transaction. Today, the Fed's use of the repo is far removed from these beginnings. In fact, the Fed can no longer accept BAs as collateral since, starting in July 1984, eligible collateral was restricted to securities that are either direct obligations of or fully guaranteed by the federal government.

How do central banks utilize repos today? As we saw in Chapter 4, repos are a key tool of monetary policy open market operations. To stimulate the economy, the central bank pursues an easy money policy by injecting additional bank reserves into the system. This can be accomplished either by buying government securities outright or by using repos to temporarily buy government securities. If the central bank wanted to tighten monetary policy, either government securities would be sold outright or the central bank would enter into a reverse repo called a *matched-sale purchase*. As we saw in Chapter 4, the matched-sale purchase is a reverse repo transaction in which the central bank sells securities from its portfolio with the proviso that those securities will be repurchased at a later date, thereby reducing the level of bank reserves.

Note that the terminology of the transaction is determined from Figure 11.1, assuming that the Fed is the counterparty in the transaction. That is, when the Fed wants to buy securities to implement an easy money policy, it does a repo when viewed from the perspective of an investor like Mr. Owt O'Cash, who may be a primary government security dealer preapproved for transactions with the Fed. If, on the other hand, the Fed was pursuing a tight money policy, it might enter into a reverse transaction with Ms. Plen T. Doe.

How does the Fed use the repo to implement an easy money policy to increase the level of bank reserves? The Fed conducts a *go-around* (see Chapter 4) to obtain quotes on repo rates for a certain dollar amount of security purchases. It "hits" (accepts) the highest bid first since this offers the Fed the greatest interest yield on its cash loan. As with outright purchases, the Fed continues accepting bids until the desired amount of repos is reached. The lowest accepted bid rate is the **stop out rate**.

Since the go-around quotes are based on the securities' face values, the Fed does not know the exact level of reserves injected into the banking system until the conclusion of the transaction. Suppose that the Fed wants to do repos totaling $3 million. The following quotes are obtained from the go-around:

Primary Security Dealer	Rate (%)	Face Value
Salomon Brothers	5.26	$500,000
Bankers Trust	5.25	$750,000
Citibank	5.23	$1,500,000
Goldman Sachs	5.22	$800,000
Morgan Guaranty	5.20	$2,000,000

The Fed will hit the bids of Salomon, Bankers Trust, Citibank, and $250,000 of Goldman's bid for a total securities' *face value* of $3 million. However, the Fed does not know the total

stop out rate: the lowest accepted bid rate.

amount of newly created bank reserves until the haircuts are assessed. If, for example, the Fed assesses Salomon and Goldman haircuts of 10 basis points and Citibank and Bankers Trust haircuts of 11 basis points, then the amount of high-powered money created by this stimulative open market operation is as follows:

Primary Security Dealer	Face Value	Repo Principal
Salomon Brothers	$500,000	$500,000(1 − .001) = $499,500
Bankers Trust	$750,000	$750,000(1 − .0011) = $749,175
Citibank	$1,500,000	$1,500,000(1 − .0011) = $1,498,350
Goldman Sachs	$250,000	$250,000(1 − .001) = $249,750
Total		$2,996,775

Rather than the $3 million stimulus to bank reserves, the Fed's repo transactions inject a total of $2,996,775 in additional bank reserves.

Repos and reverses are substitutes for outright purchases and sales of securities used by the Fed to accomplish its monetary policy goals. That is, rather than doing a repo, the Fed could increase the money supply by buying securities. Rather than doing a reverse (matched sale-purchase),[1] the Fed could reduce the size of the money supply by selling securities. Repos and matched sale-purchases are preferable to outright transactions because

1. They do not disrupt the flow of securities in the cash market.

2. They are self-liquidating and therefore allow the Fed greater flexibility to adjust its open market operations as it receives new information about economic conditions.

3. Since less information is required, the go-around process is simpler for repos and matched sale-purchases than it is for outright transactions.

As such, the repo and the matched sale-purchase are the tools of choice for the central bank's conduct of monetary policy.

Nonfinancial Corporations

Private participation in the repo/reverse market began in the 1950s in response to a variety of regulatory and market risk factors. During this period, banks were prohibited from paying interest on demand deposits. Moreover, interest paid on time deposits was strictly limited by a **Regulation Q interest rate cap** that set the maximum allowable deposit rate at 5% for commercial banks and 5.25% for thrift institutions. During this period, creeping inflation and a post–World War II recovery led nonfinancial corporations flush with cash to search for ways to reduce their opportunity costs of holding idle cash. During the 1970s, dramatic increases in the levels of interest rates further increased the opportunity cost of holding idle cash. Nonfinancial corporations sought higher rates of return on their cash investments. However, these companies were unwilling to accept any risk of either default or price fluctuations and thus wanted the safety of a bank deposit but with a higher rate of return.

The reverse was the perfect answer. It allowed the FI (playing the role of Mr. Owt O'Cash in Figure 11.1) to sell securities to the corporate customer (Ms. Plen T. Doe in Figure 11.1) for a short, predetermined term after which they would be repurchased at a fixed, predetermined price.[2] In this way, the corporate customer received an unregulated interest yield equal to

Regulation Q interest rate cap: interest rate ceilings that set maximum allowable rates on bank deposits.

---

[1] Technically, a matched sale-purchase is not precisely the same as a reverse since the Fed actually books the securities sale as an outright sale because the Fed is not permitted to borrow from private sources.

[2] Recall that from the standpoint of the nonfinancial corporation, this transaction is a reverse; from the standpoint of the FI, it is a repo.

the reverse repo rate that was protected from both credit risk and price risk by the securities collateral. The interest yield was higher on reverse repos than on bank deposits because repos were not subject to either Regulation Q interest rate caps or reserve requirements.

Shortly after the first private reverse repo transaction (rumored to be between General Motors Corporation and Discount Corporation, a primary government securities dealer), the potential in the private repo market was realized. Nonfinancial corporations wanted inexpensive forms of financing. The prevalence of book value accounting created an opportunity for the private repo. As interest rates increased during the 1970s–1980s, many companies found that they were locked into financial securities investments that had declined dramatically in price. However, the companies' balance sheet did not reflect this decline in market value since the securities were carried on the books at their higher book values. The companies could not sell these low-priced securities because that would have required them to "book the loss," which was the difference between the securities' book value and the market value. For some companies, booking the loss would have thrown the company into insolvency. For instance, consider the case of Fly-by-Nite Construction Corp. The balance sheet, in book value form, contained:

Fly-by-Nite Construction Corp. ($ million)		
30 year mortgages @6% p.a. $100m	Debt	$90m
	Capital	$10m

If interest rates increase from 6% to 10% p.a., the market value of the $100 million face value portfolio of mortgages will decline to $68.32 million (assuming fixed monthly $599,551 payments that reflect 100% amortization of principal).[3] If these low-priced mortgages were sold, Fly-by-Nite would have to book a loss of $31.68 million, thereby depleting the entire capital of the company.

A repo was the solution to the problem of companies like Fly-by-Nite. The company could avoid booking the loss and still raise cash by using the devalued securities as collateral in a repo transaction. Generally accepted accounting principles permit the continued valuation of the securities at book value, even though they are being repo'd out at market values. Thus, those companies with portfolios of marketable securities found that they could reduce their financing costs by making their securities portfolio work for them in the form of collateral against repo loans. The corporate customer's ability to exploit this market was limited by the size of the company's securities portfolio. However, there is a group of private corporations whose business it is to maintain large portfolios of marketable securities: private FIs. Both the repo and reverse were transactions perfectly suited to the FIs' structure. They became the dominant market participant.

Private FIs

Although nonfinancial corporations view the repo market primarily as a vehicle to earn an almost risk free interest yield on short term investments, private FIs view the market as a source

---

[3] To calculate the fixed monthly payments on the par value 30 year 100% amortized mortgages, solve for $PMT = \$599,551$ using

$$P = \sum_{s=1}^{T} \frac{PMT}{(1 + \frac{y}{n})^s} = \$100m = \sum_{s=1}^{360} \frac{PMT}{(1 + \frac{.06}{12})^s}$$

When interest rates increase to $y = 10\%$ p.a., the price of the mortgage value falls to $P = \$68.32$ million, obtained by solving

$$P = \sum_{s=1}^{360} \frac{599.551}{(1 + \frac{.10}{12})^s} = \$68.32m$$

of funds. Regulatory and structural characteristics in the U.S. market led cash-poor FIs to search out money markets as a means of financing their asset portfolios.

As we saw in Chapter 10, money center banks are chronic net purchasers of funds on international money markets. This hunger for financing stems from the disparity between these banks' deposit sources of funds and their lending or investment opportunities. Since money center banks serve the corporate borrowing needs of an international clientele, they are unable to raise sufficient funds through deposit-taking. This has led the money center banks to a chronic net purchase position in the Federal Funds market. Similarly, they view the repo market as a potential source of inexpensive financing.

Nonmoney center banks tend to be flush with cash from deposit sources. Because of lending regulations that limit any loan size to be under 10% of the bank's capital, these banks tend to have fewer large-loan opportunities than do money center banks. As we noted in Chapter 10, as a result these banks became net suppliers of funds on the Federal Funds market. However, we have seen that the Federal Funds market does not satisfy those regional banks with a net demand for funds (say, those banks situated in a rapidly growing local economic environment). This is because of the unsecured nature of the Federal Funds transaction and the credit risk exposure that results if a small, unknown bank occasionally attempts to buy funds. For these banks, the repo market presents a viable alternative. Because of the collateralization of the repo loan, these smaller, unknown banks can borrow sufficient quantities of funds on the repo market.[4]

Private FIs that often take the other side of the repo market are money market mutual funds. These investment companies hold reverses in their asset portfolios as flexible short term investment vehicles. Individuals who own shares in these mutual funds receive the interest on the reverses. The mutual fund manager can also speculate on interest rate fluctuations using repos and reverses without being subject to limitations placed on speculative derivative transactions.

Securities dealers are the mainstay of the repo market. They make markets by carrying inventories of marketable securities. To fund these inventories, dealers need financing. They can reduce the cost of financing by using their securities inventory as collateral on repo loans. As the repo market matured, the dealers realized that they could utilize repos to take positions on interest rates as well as to finance their securities portfolio. Speculating on future shifts in interest rates became an important part of the FI's activities as interest rate volatility increased in the 1970s and 1980s. Speculative repo and reverse transactions entail the positioning of the FI's portfolio to benefit from expected shifts in interest rates. Typically, dealers simultaneously take on both repo and reverse transactions. Any mismatch between the dealer's repo and reverse portfolios reflects the dealer's views on future interest rate movements. The use of the **repo book**, a portfolio of repo transactions, to place a bet on future interest rates is relatively inexpensive (in terms of transaction costs) when compared to speculative derivative transactions such as options. Suppose that a government security dealer had the following repo/reverse portfolio:

repo book: a portfolio of repo transactions.

Overnight reverse @ 6.8%	$6m	90 day term repo @ 6.99%	$9m
30 day term reverse @ 6.9%	$5m	75 day term repo @ 6.96%	$5m
15 day term reverse @ 6.93%	$3m		

This portion of the government security dealer's portfolio is positioned to benefit from an interest rate increase; that is, the dealer is borrowing longer term (90 and 75 days at fixed rates) in order to lend shorter term ($\leq$ 30 day term reverses). Thus, if interest rates increase, then the dealer's borrowing costs will be locked in, but the reverse returns will increase as the

---

[4] See Allen, Peristiani, and Saunders (1989) for documentation that the smallest banks tended to be the largest net purchasers (relative to their size) of funds on the repo market.

term reverses mature and are replaced with higher yielding transactions. In our discussion of speculative repo transactions, we elaborate on the use of repos and reverses to take interest rate positions.

Municipal Governments

Municipal governments are often required by law to invest their cash reserves in financial securities that have no credit risk. State and local governments typically have cash flows that are uneven and seasonal. For example, property taxes may be received semiannually. Similarly, municipal bond issues may produce large cash balances that are idle until utilized for a particular capital project. The flexibility of the term repo allows the municipality to tailor a reverse transaction that will yield an interest return on cash balances for any desired length of time. The use of government securities to collateralize the repo transaction makes this an eligible investment vehicle for many state and local governments. The municipality can earn a higher interest yield by investing its idle cash reserves in the form of term repos than it can by buying short term Treasury bills since repo rates are usually above Treasury rates for equal maturity dates. In the 1980s state and local governments in the southeastern United States earned the equivalent of 1% of their annual expense budgets from the interest on reverse transactions.[5] Note that repos are viewed as taxable instruments even if the collateral consists of tax-exempt municipal bonds.

Municipalities access the repo market in order to earn a positive yield on idle cash balances that they are required to hold. Central banks also must hold idle balances, usually at other central banks, in order to clear international transactions. Utilizing transactions similar to those of municipalities, public FIs also access the repo market in order to earn an interest return on their central bank balances.

Summary of Market Participants

A broad range of practitioners participate in the repo and reverse markets. Both increased sensitivity to interest rate risk and the opportunity cost of holding idle cash have contributed to the recent explosion in volume of transactions in this market. Nonfinancial companies, municipalities, and private FIs are more likely to utilize reverses to earn an interest yield on their cash balances when interest rate levels are relatively high. Increases in interest rate volatility make speculative repo and reverse transactions more attractive to FIs. More active central bank intervention to manipulate monetary aggregates also leads to greater activity on these markets. Table 11.1 shows the more than fifteenfold increase in overnight repo and reverse volume of activity during the past fifteen years. But even this is an understatement of the volume of activity in the market, because about 10% of all transactions are cleared internally, without use of a transfer payments system. Therefore, they are never revealed to the Fed. Govpx Inc., a bond market pricing service, estimated repos to be a trillion dollar a day market, as of the end of 1995.

Checkpoint

✓

1. How do central banks use the repo market today?
2. Why are repos and matched sale-purchases preferable tools of open market operations in contrast to outright transactions?
3. How do nonfinancial corporations use the repo market today?
4. How do public and private FIs use the repo market today?
5. How do municipalities use the repo market today?

---

[5] See McCrackin, Martin, and Estes (1985).

Table
11.1

Average Daily Balances of Repo and Reverse Transactions, Primary Government Securities Dealers Only, 1981–1996 (*Millions of dollars*)

Year	Repos Overnight[a]	Repos Term	Reverses Overnight[a]	Reverses Term
1981	35,641	29,578	14,667	32,016
1982	51,725	43,495	26,729	48,348
1983	58,029	44,486	29,275	52,650
1984	75,836	57,248	44,200	68,578
1985	103,612	70,149	68,100	80,650
1986	141,943	102,459	99,048	108,628
1987	170,749	121,216	126,700	148,310
1988	172,720	137,046	136,394	177,474
1989	219,115	179,699	157,926	225,184
1990	236,958	185,210	159,272	221,658
1991	282,487	211,566	181,288	235,841
1992	346,359	282,954	209,956	304,620
1993	441,518	368,885	226,529	392,778
1994	446,770	282,076	257,407	300,136
1995	535,088	355,266	240,460	389,626
Jan 1996	553,719	368,819	258,137	405,768

[a]Figures for overnight repos and reverses include open, or continuing, contracts.

Source: Federal Reserve Bulletin, various issues, Table 1.43, and Lumpkin (1993), pp. 73–74.

Ingredients for Developing the Market

Although demand for a market's services is a necessary precondition for the market's development, it is insufficient to ensure that development. In order to make a market viable, we must be able to value the transactions, overcome any regulatory obstacles, and clear the transactions.

Valuation

The terms of the repo (or reverse) are

1. Identification of the marketable securities, including their prices.

2. Specification of the repo rate of interest.

3. The length of the agreement, that is, the date of maturity when the securities are repurchased.

4. The identites of both counterparties.

5. The size of the haircut.

To value any repo transaction, we must be able to price its various components. In this section, we consider the valuation of a repo (or reverse) transaction.

The Repo Rate

Figure 11.2 lists money market rates as quoted on the Bloomberg Financial Market system. The first thing to note is that the interest yields for repos of different terms demonstrate a term structure of interest rates that, as we saw in Chapter 7, reflects the market's consensus interest rate forecast. The overnight repo rate of 6.1% p.a., one week maturity of 5.77% p.a., and one

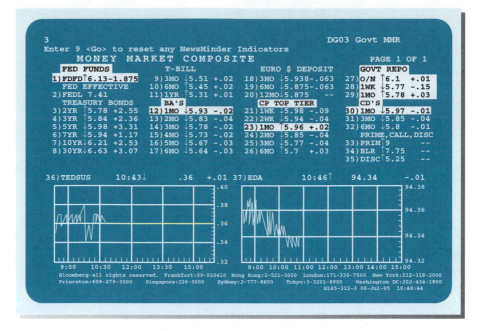

Figure 11.2

month maturity term repo rate of 5.78% p.a. are consistent with expectations of decreasing interest rates over the near term.

There is also a hierarchy of rates that is fairly constant across all terms: one month, three months, and six months. Among the taxable rates, for any given time to maturity:

T-Bill Rates < Repo Rates < BA Rates < CP Rates < CD Rates < Fed Funds Rates

This is illustrated when examining the 1 month maturity rates in Figure 11.2. The 1 month repo rate is 5.78% p.a., the 1 month BA rate is 5.93% p.a., the 1 month CD rate is 5.97% p.a., and the 1 month commercial paper (CP) rate is 5.96% p.a. Moreover, the overnight FF rate of 6.13% is higher than the overnight repo rate of 6.1% p.a. This hierarchy is not accidental; rather, it is the result of the risk characteristics of each money market instrument. The repo rate is significantly lower than other private money market rates because repos are fully collateralized loans, whereas as we saw in Chapter 10, Fed Funds are unsecured loans. The repo rate is higher than the U.S. Treasury rate because all obligations of the U.S. Treasury are completely default risk free, whereas the repo relies on the value of the collateral securities to protect the cash lender against credit risk. Moreover, term repos have no secondary market as do Treasury securities. The repo agreement remains in effect for the entire term, although the investor can offset a repo with an opposing reverse transaction of equal term. Allen and Thurston (1988) find a spread between repo and Treasury bill rates (of equal maturities) that averaged 76 basis points for the period 1982–1986.

The repo rate is maintained by the substitutability among the money market instruments. If the repo rate is too high (exceeding the CD rates or even the Fed Funds rate), then FIs using the repo market as a source of funds will switch out to other, less expensive money market instruments. This will reduce the demand for funds in the repo market. Simultaneously, the unusually high repo rate will attract lenders to the repo market since the reverse transaction offers an exceptionally attractive interest yield. This will increase the supply of funds in the repo market. The combination of reduced demand and increased supply will force the repo rate back down to its correct position in the money rate hierarchy.

Repo rates are higher if nongovernment collateral is offered. A rate spread of 5 to 15 basis points may be charged if the collateral used consists of CDs, BAs, commercial paper, or mortgage-backed securities. Similarly, an unknown counterparty may be required to pay a slight repo rate premium.

Checkpoint

✓

1. What determines repo rates?
2. Order the following rates from lowest to highest: BAs, Federal Funds, CDs, CPs, Treasuries, repos.
3. Why are repo rates higher than same term Treasury rates?
4. Why are repo rates lower than same term Fed Funds rates?

The Haircut

The second major component of repo pricing is the determination of the haircut or margin. The haircut, a critical component of pricing, protects the lender of cash against a loss in value of the collateral. If the haircut is set too low, then the value of the collateral may fall below the repo principal plus interest, thus converting a fully collateralized loan into a partially collateralized loan. If the haircut is set too high, the cost of borrowing on repo will be prohibitive, thereby undermining the viability of the market.

$$\text{Dollar Haircut} \equiv \text{Market Value of Securities} - \text{Repo Principal}$$

Or, alternatively if the haircut is stated as a rate, in terms of basis points:

$$\text{Market Value of Securities} = (\text{Repo Principal})/(1 - \text{Haircut in basis points})$$

Since 1985, the trend has been toward haircut standardization. Standard margins are 25 basis points per month on Treasury securities and agencies; 2% on some repos collateralized by commercial paper; for mortgage-backed securities' collateral, 3% on a one month repo, 4% on a two month repo, and 5% on a three month or longer repo.

The haircut is determined by

1. *The term of the repo transaction.* Because of the greater possibility of price risk, the longer the term, the greater the haircut.

2. *The price volatility of the underlying securities.* The riskier the collateral, the higher the haircut. This depends on
   a. *The identity of the security.* Treasury and federal agency securities have less price volatility than commercial paper, which has less volatility than mortgage-backed securities. The greater the price volatility of the collateral, the higher the haircut.
   b. *Whether the collateral is a coupon or pure discount instrument.* Since, all else being equal, a pure discount instrument has more price risk than does a comparable coupon instrument, then the haircut is higher for zero coupon securities.
   c. *The maturity (duration) of the collateral security.* Since, as we saw in Chapter 7, a longer duration security has more price volatility than a shorter maturity instrument, the haircut increases as duration increases.
   d. *The volume of trading.* Haircuts tend to be larger for securities trading on thin or illiquid markets than for actively traded securities.

3. *The identity of the counterparty.* Haircuts will be smaller for counterparties who are well capitalized or who, over long periods of repetitive dealings in the market, have built up reputations for reliability.

Pricing the Collateral

As we have seen, the securities used as repo collateral are valued at their market price as of the date of initiation of each repo transaction (that is, settlement date). The examples in Figure 11.1 show that this sometimes leads to repo principal amounts that are not nice, round numbers—that is, $960,093.75 instead of $1 million. During the 1980s, market participants became lax and began quoting round prices instead of precise prices. As one dealer noted, "Market practices deteriorated for the sake of convenience."[6] This practice led to several abuses which created a crisis that almost swept away the entire repo market. The case of Drysdale Government Securities illustrates the dangers inherent in deviations from precise valuation. During its three months in existence, Drysdale managed to short $4 billion of bonds and take long positions in another $2.5 billion in bonds—all with only $20 million in capital. The crisis in confidence created by the discovery of the magnitude of Drysdale's losses in May 1982 caused the repo rate to shoot up above the Federal Funds rate and almost shut down trading in the repo market. By October 1982, the New York Fed had issued regulations requiring accurate, full accrual pricing.

The pricing shortcut exploited by Drysdale (and others) was the use of flat pricing rather than full accrual pricing to evaluate coupon bonds. As we saw in Chapter 7, full accrual pricing takes into account the securities' market (flat) price (as of the next coupon payment date) *plus* any interest accrued since the last coupon payment date. Accrued interest (for semiannual coupon instruments) is calculated as

$$\frac{C}{2}\left(\frac{B - t_c}{B}\right)$$

where C is the annual coupon rate; t_c is the number of days from today's settlement date until the next coupon payment date; and B is the total number of days in the basis, which is the current coupon period (from last coupon payment date to next coupon payment date).

Drysdale's scam can be illustrated with the following example. Suppose that a Treasury bond maturing on June 4, 2001, has a 12% p.a. semiannual coupon that is yielding 8% p.a. as of the settlement date, April 28, 1997. Drysdale utilized reverses to borrow high coupon bonds similar to this bond. Since the reverse was priced flat, Drysdale invested cash equal to the flat price of the bond. (Note that this assumes no haircut. With a haircut, Drysdale's investment would be even less.) Drysdale then sold the borrowed bond in the cash market, receiving the full accrual price. This generated a cash inflow equal to the difference between full accrual and the flat price—that is, equal to the accrued interest. Accrued interest is largest for large coupon bonds close to the next coupon date. These were the targets for Drysdale's high-stakes game. In our example, the settlement date (April 28, 1997) is 37 days before the next coupon payment date (June 4, 1997). After the next coupon payment, there are eight remaining coupons until maturity. The coupon payment period from December 4, 1996, until June 4, 1997, contains 182 days. Thus, accrued interest is

$$6\left(\frac{145}{182}\right) = \$4.7802198 \text{ per } \$100 \text{ face value}$$

A Drysdale-type trade would be to borrow on reverse (that is, temporarily buy) the 2001 12% Treasury for a flat price. The price of the Treasury on the morning of the next coupon

---

[6] Stigum (1989), p. 208.

payment date, June 4, 1997, (with nine remaining coupon payments including the June 4, 1997, payment) evaluated at the current yield of 8% p.a. (4% semiannnually) is

$$P_{6/4/97} = \sum_{t=1}^{8} \frac{6}{1.04^t} + \frac{100}{1.04^8} + 6 = \$119.4654897 \text{ per } \$100 \text{ face value}$$

The flat price on April 28, 1997 is the price on June 4, 1997 discounted back 37 days, deducting 145 days of accrued interest:

$$P_{4/28/97} = \frac{119.4654897}{1.04^{\frac{37}{182}}} - 6\left(\frac{145}{182}\right) = \$113.7365063$$

Without a haircut, this is the cash investment Drysdale made in the reverse transaction. Immediately upon completion of the reverse, Drysdale would sell the Treasury bond into the cash market for the full accrual price of

$$\text{Cash } P_{4/28/97} = \frac{119.4654897}{1.04^{\frac{37}{182}}} = \$118.5167261$$

for a net cash inflow (equal to the accrued interest) of $118.5167261 − $113.7365063 = $4.7802198 per $100 face value. This cash amount could be invested at current prevailing interest rates. If the face value of the Treasury bonds is $10 million, then this one transaction alone generates a cash inflow of $478,021.98.

This is not a risk free arbitrage. At the maturity of the reverse, Drysdale must buy back the 2001 Treasury on the cash market for the full accrual price in order to deliver it against the second leg of the reverse transaction. Thus, Drysdale has to pay back all of the accrued interest (plus an additional amount of interest accrued during the term of the reverse) when the bonds are repurchased on the cash market. This transaction could therefore yield a net profit only if (a) Drysdale was able to invest the accrued interest at a return in excess of the settlement date's market yield of 8% p.a. and (b) the price of the Treasury security repurchased at the maturity of the reverse repo did not increase. These requirements for a profitable trade imply that the success of Drysdale's strategy depended on interest rate increases during the reverse period. If interest rates increase after April 28, 1997 (settlement date in our example), a Drysdale-trader would be able to invest the $478,021.98 on a daily basis at higher and higher yields. Moreover, the repurchase price of the 2001 bond (upon the reverse's maturity) would decline. But what happens if interest rates remain the same or even decline during the term of the reverse? Then, the Drysdale-trader's predicament is dire indeed since the decline in interest rates would cause the price of the 2001 Treasury bond to rise, leading Drysdale to experience a loss on its short bond position.

Unfortunately for Drysdale, interest rates began their decline in the early months of 1982, leaving Drysdale unable to make almost $290 million in coupon payments due in May 1982. Other FIs who did business with Drysdale felt the pain. Chase ended up covering $160 million of Drysdale's defaulted interest payments because it had acted as Drysdale's agent. The FIs learned their lesson, and full accrual pricing is now the rule in the repo market.

We have seen why accurate pricing of collateral is necessary on the date of initiation of the repo transaction, but this lesson should apply to every day of the term of the repo. Fluctuations in interest rates lead to fluctuations in the market value of repo collateral. It is conceivable that rate increases may cause prices to fall sufficiently so as to leave the repo position partially uncollateralized. To protect against this possibility, term and open repos include the right to reprice collateral. If the securities' prices fall, then the lender of cash (Ms. Plen T. Doe on the repo transaction) who holds the collateral can demand an additional margin to compensate for the price declines. Marking the collateral to market maintains the ratio between collateral and repo principal. The Government Securities Act of 1986 required that government security dealers' collateral be adjusted daily to reflect price fluctuations.

Checkpoint

✓

1. What are the determinants of the haircut?
2. Why does the haircut increase as the maturity of the collateral increases?
3. Why is the determination of the haircut important?
4. How are securities priced in the repo market?
5. Why was the use of flat pricing hazardous to the health of the repo market?
6. Under what circumstances would Drysdale's reverse transaction earn a positive net profit? a net loss?

Regulatory Treatment

The Drysdale government securities debacle in May 1982 was followed in August 1982 by the bankruptcy of another government securities dealer: Lombard-Wall Securities.[7] Many school districts and nonfinancial companies were holding collateral from Lombard-Wall. When they tried to sell the collateral in order to recoup the repo principal plus interest, they ran into a legal brick wall—a stay in bankruptcy that prohibited all sales of Lombard-Wall assets until the final disposition of bankruptcy hearings. The courts ruled that since the Bankruptcy Act of 1978 made no specific provisions for repos, the securities collateral should be viewed as general assets of the defunct corporation and therefore should be liquidated with all other assets at the end of bankruptcy proceedings. All creditors would then receive partial payment from a common pool of liquidated assets. Repo market participants viewed this ruling with great alarm since it undermined the independence of collateral on each individual repo transaction. The year 1982 was indeed a very bad year in the repo market.

In part to protect the viability of this important market, the bankruptcy code was amended in 1984 to exempt all repos (except those collateralized with commercial paper) from the bankruptcy provision that prohibited the sale of any assets of a company in bankruptcy proceedings. This permits the holder of repo collateral to immediately sell these securities if the counterparty defaults and enters bankruptcy.

The amendment to the bankruptcy code in 1984 resolved the most egregious problems of repo credit risk, but some remain. For instance, it is not applicable to a solvent dealer who defaults on a repo or reverse. Alternatively, if the failed dealer is a custodial agent safekeeping securities for others, the law does not specify whether the collateral is available to the repo counterparties. These questions remain to be resolved by the courts if test cases arise.

As a reaction to the continued legal ambivalence, another response to the events of 1982 was to standardize the repo agreement. Prior to 1982, most repo agreements were in the form of verbal, not written, commitments. They consisted solely of trading confirmations. After 1982, the Public Securities Association (an industry trade group) designed a legal repo contract that specified the inviolability of repo collateral. The most important feature of these legal agreements is the specification of delivery of the collateral. If the repo transaction is cleared as if it were an outright securities purchase, then the courts cannot claim that the securities must be returned to a bankrupt repo cash borrower (say, Mr. Owt O'Cash in the repo transaction

---

[7] Lombard-Wall's problems derived from interest rate risk exposure on a portfolio of flex repos, which set a fixed interest rate but allow the cash borrower to vary collateral and to repay the principal at flexible (hence the name) intervals.

in Figure 11.1). Thus, clearing methods are critical in assuring the accessibility of collateral in the event of default.

Clearing

During the life of any repo or reverse, four transfers take place: the exchange of cash and securities at the initiation of the transaction, and the reverse exchange of securities and cash at the maturity of the transaction. These four transfers take place electronically, using one of the payments systems described in Chapter 6. The payment system of choice is Fedwire. Over Fedwire both securities and cash transfers are made available immediately. Cash payments clear through the banks' reserve accounts at the Fed.

Securities transfers clear through the book-entry system, discussed in Chapter 6. Many securities (such as U.S. Treasuries, federal credit agencies, and many mortgage-backed securities) are issued in book-entry format rather than in physical form as bearer securities. Under the book-entry system, no physical securities are printed. Instead, ownership rights are entered electronically into banks' accounts held at the Fed. These accounts are similar to banks' reserve accounts at the Fed except that instead of consisting of cash, they contain marketable securities.

clearing bank: a bank with direct access to Fedwire that maintains cash and securities accounts at the Fed on behalf of its customers.

Repo transactions are cleared over Fedwire by adjusting the balances in the **clearing bank's** cash and securities accounts at the Fed. A clearing bank is a bank with direct access to Fedwire that maintains cash and securities accounts at the Fed on behalf of its customers. That is, upon initiation of each repo transaction in Figure 11.1, Mr. Owt O'Cash's clearing bank receives a credit to its cash account at the Fed, and Ms. Plen T. Doe's clearing bank receives a credit to its securities account at the Fed. Mr. O'Cash's clearing bank's securities account is debited by the amount of the repo securities collateral, and Ms. Doe's bank's cash account is debited by the repo principal amount.

two-party repo with third-party custody: the safest form of clearing repo transactions since the cash and securities actually change hands as in an outright purchase/sale of securities.

These transactions occur when the repo transaction uses **two-party repo with third-party custody**. This is the safest form of clearing repo transactions since the cash and securities actually change hands as in an outright purchase/sale of securities. The third party is the clearing bank that clears the repo transaction and holds the securities in custody in its securities account on behalf of the counterparties to the transaction. Transaction costs for the two-party repo include securities clearance fees, wire transfer charges (for both cash and securities), custodial fees, and account maintenance fees.

tri-party repo: a repo in which the collateral never changes hands; the clearing bank simply segregates collateral for the term of the repo transaction.

Two-party repos are quite costly to execute, especially for overnight repos, because of the number of wire transfers of cash and securities between the counterparties. To reduce the repo's transaction costs, large investors often utilize the **tri-party repo**. Under this repo, collateral never changes hands. The clearing bank simply segregates collateral for the term of the repo transaction, thereby guaranteeing the completion of the transaction. Because there are no wire transfers of securities, the transaction cost is lower for a tri-party repo than for a two-party repo. However, since there is some risk that the clearing bank will be unable to complete the transaction, tri-party repos are more risky than two-party repos. On average, almost one-third of all repos are tri-party transactions.

letter repo: a repo that uses neither a third-party custodial agent (as in two-party repos) nor a third-party guarantor (as in tri-party repos); often called a "trust me repo."

The least costly to execute, but the most risky in terms of default risk, is the **letter repo**. The letter repo uses neither a third-party custodial agent (as in two-party repos) nor a third-party guarantor (as in tri-party repos). Often called a "trust me repo," the securities lending counterparty promises to hold the collateral in a separated, pledged account. Abuses of the letter repo, in which the dealer pledged the same collateral to multiple repo counterparties, have cost the system dearly: $300 million resulting from the E.S.M. government securities failure in 1985 and $150 million from the Bevill, Bresler and Schulman failure in 1985. The Government Securities Act of 1986 requires dealers to choose the clearing method that is most appropriate to the identity (and risk exposure) of the counterparty. The caution to "know thy counterparty" states that it is acceptable to do letter repos with prime (low default risk) dealers only. Others require more costly clearing operations to act as protective mechanisms to ensure completion of the transaction.

Checkpoint

1. How did the Lombard-Wall court decision undermine the viability of the repo market?
2. How did the 1984 amendment to the bankruptcy code secure the future of the repo market?
3. Why is it important to codify the terms of a repo transaction in the form of a written, legal contract?
4. Contrast the letter repo, the tri-party repo, and the two-party custody repo.

➤ Typical Transactions

Now that we have seen the development and viability of the repo market, how do market participants utilize it today? There are two motives for participation in the repo market.

1. *Liquidity purposes.* Liquidity traders utilize repos as an inexpensive form of financing to borrow either cash (similar to Mr. O'Cash in a repo) or securities (similar to Ms. Doe in a reverse). Some liquidity traders are central banks (to adjust the level of bank reserves), nonfinancial corporations (to earn interest on idle cash balances), FIs (to finance their securities inventories inexpensively), and municipalities (to earn interest on idle cash balances).

2. *Speculative purposes.* In addition to using them as sources of financing, FIs often utilize repos and reverses to place bets on the direction of interest rate shifts. Repos/reverses are relatively inexpensive instruments that can be used to hedge against or speculate on interest rate fluctuations. Therefore, although the repo/reverse is itself a low-risk transaction, it can be used to finance risky speculative activity. Indeed, *Timely Topics 11.1* shows how a municipality, California's Orange County, was thrown into default as a result of interest rate risk arising from speculative repo transactions. How can a trader place a speculative repo transaction?

TIMELY TOPICS 11.1

THE ORANGE COUNTY DEBACLE

Robert Citron was repeatedly reelected Treasurer of Orange County in California despite his Democratic party affiliation in a predominantly Republican community. The reason was his 21 year performance record, which produced average annual returns of 9% p.a. on a fund comprising the reserve money of 187 municipalities (school districts, transportation authorities, and cities) located in Orange County. What his investors didn't know was that he accomplished this feat with a combination of risky investments and leverage. Speculative repo transactions were the centerpiece of his strategy.

A typical transaction: In October 1994, the fund purchased $124.8 million face value of four year 4.75% coupon Treasury notes (maturing in September 1998) with a yield of 4.61% p.a. These were financed using six month repos yielding 3.31% p.a. for a positive carry of 1.3% p.a. As repo rates rose, with the increase in the general level of interest rates, the positive carry declined and ultimately turned negative. In December 1994, when the fund declared bankruptcy, the repo rate had risen to 6.75% p.a., resulting in a negative carry of 2.14% p.a. on this transaction alone.

Unfortunately, this transaction was not alone. Citron, acting as the fund's administrator, parlayed a $7.4 billion investment fund into a $14 billion portfolio primarily using leverage accomplished with speculative repo transactions. As long as interest rates stayed low or even fell, the strategy was profitable. It seemed a sure-fire winning investment strategy. But Citron did not consider the latent interest rate risk exposure inherent in his strategy. When interest rates turned up in February 1994, the losses on the tails of all of the repo transactions started accumulating. By December 1994, it was estimated that the fund would lose approximately $2 billion of its principal.

Upon hearing of Orange County's bankruptcy filing on December 1, 1994, (triggered by a missed $200 million payment on a $2.6 million repo transaction), most counterparties quickly sold collateral, thereby recouping their repo principal plus interest. An exception was Merrill Lynch, which was Orange County's adviser and largest counterparty. Attempting to avoid the excessive losses and depressed prices that result from distress liquidation, Merrill held onto its over $1 billion in repo collateral even as counterparty after counterparty liquidated its holdings.

Merrill's efforts to avoid the unravelling of Orange County's portfolio were to prove futile. On January 12, 1995, Orange County filed a $3 billion lawsuit accusing Merrill of "wantonly and callously" selling highly risky securities to the municipal fund in violation of state and federal laws and contending that Merrill's liability emanated from its "various and conflicting" roles as Citron's "chief financial adviser." The lawsuit demanded the return of over $1 billion in repo collateral to the Orange County fund. The inviolability of repo collateral depends on the court's resolution of this suit. Whatever the outcome, it is clear that repo transactions should most definitely not be considered risk free.

FIs are leveraged investors; they borrow money in order to finance their asset portfolios. A speculative repo or reverse transaction is a leveraged transaction. The FI may borrow money on a repo in order to finance the purchase of a Treasury security. This would be considered a **covered repo transaction** since the repo loan is combined with a securities transaction. Alternatively, the FI may sell a Treasury security in order to lend into the reverse market—that is, a covered reverse transaction. These trades may be profitable if the lending rate exceeds the borrowing rate, or, to say it in another way, if the **carry** is positive. The carry is the difference between the lending rate and the borrowing rate.[8]

covered repo transaction: transaction in which a repo loan is combined with a securities transaction.

carry: the difference between the lending rate and the borrowing rate.

Let's illustrate the covered repo transaction from Mr. Owt O'Cash's viewpoint using Figure 11.3. Suppose that a 90 day Treasury bill has a yield of 5.75%, and a 30 day term repo yields 5.5% p.a. At initiation of the transaction, $t = 0$, O'Cash buys the 90 day Treasury bill and finances it using a 30 day repo. Since the cost of financing is less than the yield on the Treasury bill, the carry is positive. In this example, the carry is 5.75% − 5.5% = .25%, or 25 basis points. The **carry period** is the financing period during which the securities investment is funded using some form of debt. Since the term of the repo is 30 days, whereas the term of the Treasury bill is 90 days, the carry period is 30 days, because that is the period during which both the repo and the Treasury bill investment are held.

carry period: the financing period during which the securities investment is funded using some form of debt.

---

[8] A trade with a negative carry may still be profitable; it's just a lot less likely. We do not consider negative carry trades here.

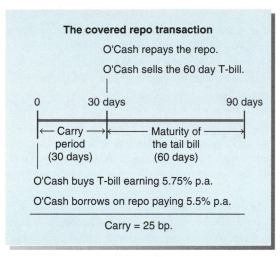

The covered repo transaction

O'Cash repays the repo.

O'Cash sells the 60 day T-bill.

Figure 11.3

Even if you earn a positive carry, you are still not guaranteed a profit on this repo transaction. That is because the transaction is speculative. Embedded in the transaction is a bet on future interest rate shifts. What is that bet? Note that the term repo matures after 30 days. What happens upon maturity of the term repo? The repo investor, Mr. Owt O'Cash, must repay the repo principal plus interest. To raise the cash to repay the repo, the leveraged repo investor O'Cash will have to sell the Treasury bill. At the maturity of the 30 day term repo, the Treasury bill still has 60 days until maturity. The "leftover" Treasury bill that is left uncovered after the period of financing ends is called the **tail bill**. Figure 11.3 shows that the tail bill in this example is the 60 day Treasury bill. The repo transaction will earn a profit only if the tail bill can be sold at a price high enough to repay repo principal plus interest without relinquishing the carry profit. If the tail bill price falls (or equivalently, the rate on the tail bill, called the **tail**, increases), O'Cash can lose his tail (or some money) on this transaction.

Uncertainty about the tail makes this repo transaction speculative. At the initiation of the repo trade, the tail is unknown since it is a forward rate for delivery of the tail security upon the maturity of the term repo. In our example, there is uncertainty about the price of 60 day Treasury bills to be delivered 30 days from today.[9] Why not simply match maturities? That is, the 90 day Treasury bill purchase can be financed with a 90 day repo, as opposed to a 30 day term repo. But if the transaction matches maturities, then the carry will always be negative. This is because, for equal maturities, repo rates are always above Treasury bill rates. To earn a positive carry, there must be some mismatch between maturities of the cash market transaction (the Treasury bill) and the repo transaction. Because the repo transaction utilizes the Treasury bill as collateral, the maturity of the Treasury bill is generally longer than the term of the repo transaction. The choice of cash and repo transactions that will earn a positive carry depends on the slope of the yield curve.

tail bill: the bill that is left uncovered after the period of financing ends.

tail: the rate on the tail bill.

Exploiting the Yield Curve

If the yield curve is upward sloping, then spot rates increase as the time to maturity increases. Transactions that earn a positive carry are those in which longer term bill purchases are financed with shorter term repo funding—as in the previous example, a 30 day repo financing of a 90 day

[9] Forward and futures markets can be utilized to resolve this uncertainty, as we will see in Chapter 18.

Treasury bill, which requires the sale of a 60 day tail bill 30 days after initiation of the transaction. The opposite is true in a downward-sloping yield curve environment. Transactions that earn a positive carry are those in which the proceeds of sales of longer maturity bills are invested in shorter maturity reverses—for example, the sale of a 45 day Treasury bill and investment in a 30 day reverse that requires the purchase of a 15 day maturity Treasury bill 30 days after initiation of the transaction.

The disposition of the tail bill depicts the interest rate gamble. In the case of an upward-sloping yield curve, the tail security must be sold upon maturity of the repo. This short position in the tail security amounts to a bet that interest rates will fall since rate declines cause the tail security's price to increase. Speculative repo trades will be more likely to occur in an upward-sloping yield curve environment if traders believe that rates will fall (or even stay unchanged).

In the case of the downward-sloping yield curve, the tail security must be purchased upon maturity of the reverse. This long position in the tail security amounts to a bet that interest rates will increase, thereby reducing the cost to the buyer of the tail security. The higher rates go, the larger the speculative repo dealer's profit.

How far do rates have to move to justify a speculative repo trade? For example, if the tail bill cannot be sold for a high enough price to repay the repo principal plus interest, the FI will lose money on the speculative repo transaction. Similarly, if the tail bill cannot be bought for a low enough price, the FI will lose money on the speculative reverse transaction. The breakeven rate on the tail is the minimum (maximum) price that must be received (paid) for the tail bill so that the speculative repo (reverse) transaction just breaks even.

Breaking Even on the Tail

Although earning a positive carry is a good way to begin a profitable repo transaction, it does not guarantee success. The positive carry can be lost if the tail moves against your position. Before any trader takes a speculative repo position, he or she will calculate the breakeven rate on the tail. The breakeven rate on the tail in an upward- (downward-) sloping yield curve environment is the maximum (minimum) rate at which the tail bill can be sold (purchased), so that the speculative repo transaction just breaks even.

Take the case of the following spot yield curve:

Fed Funds rate: 5.9% (simple interest yield on a 360 day basis)

90 day Treasury bill rate: 5.75% (rate of discount)

90 day repo/reverse rate: 5.81% (simple interest yield on a 360 day basis)

60 day Treasury bill rate: 5.45% (rate of discount)

30 day Treasury bill rate: 5.25% (rate of discount)

30 day repo/reverse rate: 5.5% (simple interest yield on a 360 day basis)

Plotting the yield curve in Figure 11.4 shows that the yield curve is upward sloping. A positive carry repo transaction would be to finance the purchase of a 90 day Treasury bill earning 5.75%, with a 30 day repo at a cost of 5.5%. The carry is 25 basis points. This can be considered a good trade depending on the dealer's expectations about future interest rates. If interest rates increase, this trade may lose money. How high can interest rates go before the dealer loses the carry profit? Or, equivalently, what is the breakeven rate on the tail?

The answer to this question depends on a number of assumptions about the terms of the repo transaction. We will calculate the breakeven rate on the tail in three different ways: (1) the "quick and dirty" approximation most often used by traders; (2) the exact solution assuming no haircut; and (3) the exact solution assuming a haircut. The breakeven rate on the tail will

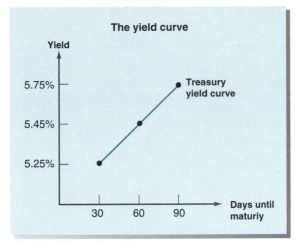

Figure 11.4

depend on the measurement method chosen, thereby affecting the trader's assessment of the advisability of the trade.

Approximation of the Tail   Table 11.2 shows the value of all the cash flows associated with the foregoing speculative repo transaction. The breakeven rate on the tail is the rate of discount on the 60 day tail bill sold at day $t = 30$, which just sets the total dollars received equal to the total dollars paid out; that is, breakeven in terms of total cash flows.[10]

The transactions that take place *simultaneously* on day $t = 0$ appear in Figure 11.5. Mr. Owt O'Cash buys the 90 day $1 million face value Treasury bill from a cash market investor for a price equal to $1 million$(1 - \frac{.0575(90)}{360})$ = $985,625. The money for this purchase comes from a repo loan, with a principal assumed to be equal to $985,625, because the haircut is assumed to be zero. The 90 day Treasury bill is transferred to Ms. Plen T. Doe as collateral on the repo loan. These cash flows are enumerated in Table 11.2.

On day $t = 30$, the repo transaction unwinds. As shown in Figure 11.5, Mr. O'Cash repays the repo principal plus interest, using the proceeds of the sale of the tail bill in the cash market. The tail bill is the 60 day Treasury that Ms. Doe returned to Mr. O'Cash upon the maturity of the repo. Table 11.2 shows that the price received for the tail bill depends on the rate of discount on 60 day Treasury bills at day $t = 30$. Since this is unknown on day $t = 0$, this is the source of risk in the speculative repo transaction. Mr. O'Cash is concerned that he will not receive a high enough price to make the fixed repo repayment. Mr. O'Cash is exposed to an increase in interest rates. That is, if interest rates increase by too much, the price of the tail bill falls, thereby reducing the cash inflow at time $t = 30$ to Mr. O'Cash. The breakeven rate on the tail is the maximum rate on the tail that just causes Mr. O'Cash to break even. As shown in Table 11.2, the breakeven price on the tail bill is $990,208, implying a rate of discount of 5.875% on the 60 day tail bill.

This approximation of the breakeven rate can be stated as

$$d^* = d + (d - r)\frac{t_r}{t_m} \tag{11.1}$$

where d^* is the approximate breakeven rate on the tail, d is the rate of discount of the Treasury bill, r is the repo/reverse rate, t_r is the number of days in the term repo transaction, that is, in

---

[10] Since these transactions are fully leveraged, we utilize dollar cash flows rather than their discounted present values.

Table 11.2

Figuring the Tail: An Approximation

Dollars Out	Dollars In
Day $t = 0$	
Buy a 90 day Treasury @5.75%	Finance using a 30 day term repo @5.5%
$P = \$1\text{m}\left(1 - \frac{.0575(90)}{360}\right) = \$985,625$	$\$985,625$
Day $t = 30$	
Repay repo principal plus interest	Sell tail bill at unknown rate, d^*
Repo interest $= \$1\text{m}\left(\frac{.055(30)}{360}\right) = \$4,583$	$P^* = \$1\text{m}\left(1 - \frac{d^*(60)}{360}\right)$
Repo principal $= \$985,625$	
Total repo repayment $= \$990,208$	
Total cash flows[a] $= \$1,975,833$	Total cash flows[a] $= \$985,625 + P^*$

$$P^* = \$990,208 = \$1\text{m}\left(1 - \frac{d^*(60)}{360}\right)$$

$$d^* = 5.875\%$$

Assumptions

1. $1 million face value.

2. No haircut.

3. Approximation of repo interest since it is calculated as a percentage of face value, not market value, of the collateral.

[a]Total cash flows are the sum of all cash flows received or paid out at times $t = 0$ and $t = 30$, neglecting the time value of money. All cash flows are from Mr. O'Cash's point of view.

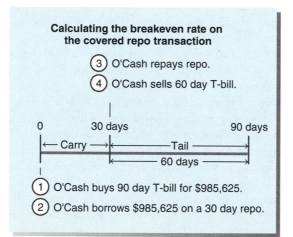

Figure 11.5

the carry period, and t_m is the number of days until maturity of the tail bill. Using our example:

$$d^* = 5.75\% + (5.75\% - 5.5\%)\left(\frac{30}{60}\right) = 5.875\%$$

How do we utilize this solution for the breakeven rate on the tail? Mr. Owt O'Cash will undertake this transaction only if he expects 60 day Treasury bills to be selling at or below 5.875% on day $t = 30$. If the tail is higher than 5.875%, then the trader will lose money. If the tail turns out to be lower than 5.875% on day $t = 30$, then the trader makes money on the transaction. Since spot rates on the 60 day Treasury (on day $t = 0$) are 5.45%, Mr. O'Cash is gambling that interest rates will not increase by more than 42.5 basis points (5.875% minus 5.45%) over the next 30 days. The speculative repo transaction is exposed to interest rate increases and benefits from interest rate declines. For instance, if the tail bill is priced at 5.9% on day $t = 30$, then Mr. O'Cash must purchase the 60 day tail bill at a price equal to $\$1m(1 - \frac{.059(60)}{360}) = \$990,166.67$. Cash inflows over the 30 day life of the transaction total only $\$1,975,791.67$ (= $\$985,625 + \$990,166.67$), whereas the cash outflows total $\$1,975,833$, (= $\$985,625 + \$990,208$), for a net loss of $\$41.33$. Contrast that outcome with the case in which the tail is priced at 5.7%, implying a price equal to $\$1m(1 - \frac{.057(60)}{360}) = \$990,500$. With a lower tail, cash inflows total $\$1,976,125$ (= $\$985,625 + \$990,500$), whereas cash outflows total $\$1,975,833$, for a net gain of $\$292$.

We have referred to the formula for the breakeven rate on the tail as an approximation. Why is this called an approximation? If you were following the example closely, you noted that the calculation of repo interest was incorrect. Interest was computed as if the repo principal was $1 million as opposed to $985,625. This "error" was intentional to correct a fundamental inconsistency in the formula. You will recall that the Treasury yields, d and d^*, are stated in the form of rates of discount. However, the repo rate, r, is stated in the form of a simple interest yield on a 360 day basis. In Chapter 7 we saw that the only difference between these two interest rate specifications is that interest is calculated as a percentage of face value for the rate of discount, while it is calculated as a percentage of price for the simple interest yield. To make the simple interest yield conform with the rate of discount, we calculated the repo interest as if it were paid on the full $1 million face value as opposed to the $985,625 price. Let us examine the practical impact of this approximation.

Exact Solution Without a Haircut   In Table 11.3, we correct the "error" in calculating the repo interest by determining interest on the actual repo principal, rather than the face value. As you can see, the solution for the breakeven rate on the tail is higher—5.91% as compared to

Table 11.3

Figuring the Tail: An Exact Solution Without a Haircut

Dollars Out	Dollars In
Day $t = 0$	
Buy a 90 day Treasury @5.75%	Finance using a 30 day term repo @5.5%
$P = \$1m \left(1 - \frac{.0575(90)}{360}\right) = \$985,625$	$\$985,625$
Day $t = 30$	
Repay repo principal plus interest	Sell tail bill at unknown rate, d^*
Repo interest = $\$985,625 \left(\frac{.055(30)}{360}\right) = \$4,517.45$	$P^* = \$1m \left(1 - \frac{d^*(60)}{360}\right)$
Repo principal = $\$985,625$	
Total repo repayment = $\$990,142.45$	
Total cash flows[a] = $\$1,975,767.45$	Total cash flows[a] = $\$985,625 + P^*$

$$P^* = \$990,142.45 = \$1m\left(1 - \frac{d^*(60)}{360}\right)$$

$$d^* = 5.91\%$$

Assumptions

1. $1 million face value.

2. No haircut.

3. Exact calculation of repo interest using the repo principal amount.

[a]Total cash flows are the sum of all cash flows received or paid out at times $t = 0$ and $t = 30$, neglecting the time value of money. All cash flows are from Mr. O'Cash's point of view.

5.875% for the approximation formula. The approximation therefore reduces the breakeven rate on the tail. This is acceptable to traders since it *under*estimates the returns to the trade. That is, the practical impact of the approximation is that the trader rejects profitable trades when the tail is expected to be between 5.91% and 5.875%. However, these profitable trades are marginal, at best, and use of the approximation on the tail as a cutoff point can be viewed as conservative. Moreover, our calculations thus far have omitted the impact of a haircut, which increases the cost of this transaction to Mr. Owt O'Cash. Let us see the impact of the haircut on the breakeven rate on the tail.

Exact Solution with a Haircut   The haircut protects the lender of cash by reducing the amount of repo principal below the market value of the collateral securities. Assuming a 5 basis point haircut, if the market value of the 90 day Treasury bill is \$985,625 at time $t = 0$, the repo collateral is valued at only \$985,625(1 − .0005) = \$985,132.19, not \$985,625 as in Table 11.3. In order to set up the speculative repo transaction, Mr. O'Cash must add \$492.81 (the Treasury bill price of \$985,625 minus the repo loan of \$985,132.19) of his own money. The cash flows are shown in Table 11.4.

At time $t = 0$, Mr. O'Cash must pay out \$985,625 to buy the Treasury bill, but receives only \$985,132.19 as the principal on the repo loan. This requires an up-front investment of \$492.81, which is the haircut on the repo transaction. The haircut represents an additional cost of the speculative trade, resulting in total cash outflows of \$1,975,272.38 (= \$985,625+\$989,647.38) and total cash inflows of P^* + \$985,132.19, for a breakeven rate on the tail bill of 5.92% p.a.[11] The breakeven price of the tail bill, P^*, is equal to \$990,140.19, which is the repo repayment of \$989,647.38 plus the \$492.81 haircut.

The Speculative Reverse Transaction   We have seen how practitioners utilize the repo market to take speculative positions on future interest rate movements. In a positively sloped

---

Table 11.4

Figuring the Tail: An Exact Solution with a Haircut

Dollars Out	Dollars In
Day $t = 0$	
Buy a 90 day Treasury @5.75%	Finance using a 30 day term repo @5.5%
$P = \$1m \left(1 - \frac{.0575(90)}{360}\right) = \$985,625$	Repo princ. = \$985,625(1 − .0005)
	= \$985,132.19
Day $t = 30$	
Repay repo principal plus interest	Sell tail bill at unknown rate, d^*
Repo interest = $\$985,132.19 \left(\frac{.055(30)}{360}\right) = \$4,515.19$	$P^* = \$1m \left(1 - \frac{d^*(60)}{360}\right)$
Repo principal = \$985,132.19	
Total repo repayment = \$989,647.38	
Total cash flows[a] = \$1,975,272.38	Total cash flows[a] = \$985,132.19 + P^*

$$P^* = \$990,140.19 = \$1m\left(1 - \frac{d^*(60)}{360}\right)$$

$$d^* = 5.92\%$$

Assumptions

1. \$1 million face value.

2. Haircut of 5 basis points.

3. Exact calculation of repo interest using the repo principal amount.

---

[a]Total cash flows are the sum of all cash flows received or paid out at times $t = 0$ and $t = 30$, neglecting the time value of money. All cash flows are from Mr. O'Cash's point of view.

---

[11] This treatment neglects the time value of money, which will be discussed in Table 11.5.

yield curve environment, a covered repo trade will be profitable if interest rates are not expected to increase by much. In a negatively sloped yield curve environment, a covered reverse transaction may be profitable if interest rates are not expected to decrease by much. Let us examine the trade using the following spot yield curve:

> Fed Funds rate: 10.2% (simple interest yield on a 360 day basis)
>
> 90 day Treasury bill rate: 8.5% (rate of discount)
>
> 90 day repo/reverse rate: 8.7% (simple interest yield on a 360 day basis)
>
> 60 day Treasury bill rate: 9.25% (rate of discount)
>
> 30 day Treasury bill rate: 9.5% (rate of discount)
>
> 30 day repo/reverse rate: 10% (simple interest yield on a 360 day basis)

The negatively sloped yield curve implies that the market expects interest rates to fall. The FI can speculate on a limited decline (or an unlimited rise) in interest rates by undertaking a reverse repo transaction. Based on the 30 day repo/reverse rate in the above term structure, a FI could enter into a 30 day reverse to borrow the 90 day Treasury bill and lend cash at a rate of 10% p.a. This could be funded by selling the 90 day Treasury bill in the cash market at a yield of 8.50%. The carry on this transaction is 10% minus 8.5%, or 150 basis points.

Will this transaction offer a guaranteed profit? No, if interest rates fall too low, then the FI will lose the carry profit on the transaction upon buying the tail bill. Whether or not the FI enters into the trade depends on its interest rate forecast. To obtain a cutoff point, below which the FI will reject the trade, we calculate the breakeven rate on the tail. Using our approximation equation (11.1):

$$d^* = d + (d - r)\frac{t_r}{t_m} = 8.50\% + (8.50\% - 10\%)\left(\frac{30}{60}\right) = 7.75\%$$

That is, if the FI expects the 60 day Treasury bill to be selling at a rate *above* 7.75% on day $t = 30$, then it will enter into the trade. This is because the tail bill is the 60 day Treasury that the FI must *buy* at day $t = 30$ in order to deliver against the reverse repayment.

Checkpoint

1. Describe a speculative repo/reverse transaction if the yield curve is upward sloping. What is the interest rate risk exposure of this transaction?
2. Describe a speculative repo/reverse transaction if the yield curve is downward sloping. What is the interest rate risk exposure of this transaction?
3. What is the tail bill? What is the carry?
4. How can you use the tail and the carry to estimate the profitability of a speculative repo/reverse transaction?

The Role of Capital   The haircut serves as a capital cushion against risk. The lender of cash demands an equity contribution from the cash borrower to protect against adverse movements in interest rates that might undermine the market value of collateral in the event of default. In Table 11.4, we have treated the haircut as if the entire amount was lost to the provider of capital (the cash borrower). This is an extremely conservative approach that overstates the cost of the haircut. In actuality, the haircut is returned at the successful conclusion of the repo transaction. Thus, the actual cost of the haircut is the opportunity cost of lost investment income on the $492.81 for the repo period of 30 days. The cost is, therefore, the time value of the capital required to fund the haircut.[12]

---

[12] This is the same logic we will apply to the economic cost of futures margins in Chapter 18.

The opportunity cost of the haircut is the earnings lost because the haircut, $492.81 in our example, cannot be invested in interest-earning assets. To calculate the opportunity cost of funds invested in repo margins, we use the risk adjusted required rate of return on the dealer's equity, as discussed in Chapter 9. Thus, the opportunity cost of the haircut is the foregone interest on the haircut capital. This is sometimes not measured in practice, in part because decentralized decision making often results in traders' treating the cost of capital as zero.

If the risk adjusted required rate of return on Mr. O'Cash's equity (determined using a capital asset pricing model) is assumed to be 15% p.a. (simple interest yield) in this example, we can calculate the opportunity cost of the haircut. The cost of capital to fund the $492.81 haircut for 30 days (the term of the repo) is

$$\frac{Hkt}{365} = \$492.81 \left(\frac{.15(30)}{365} \right) = \$6.08$$

where k is the cost of capital, t is the repo's time to maturity (in days), and H is the dollar value of the haircut. Entering this opportunity cost of the haircut (in place of the 100% cost in Table 11.4) yields the calculation of the breakeven rate on the tail shown in Table 11.5 to be 5.91%. The $989,653.46 breakeven price of the tail bill, P^*, is equal to the repo repayment of $989,647.38 plus the haircut cost of $6.08. The speculative repo transaction is profitable as long as 60 day Treasury bill rates are below 6.21% p.a. The lower the cost of capital to fund the haircut, the more likely the speculative repo trade is to be profitable or, equivalently, the higher (lower) the breakeven rate on the speculative repo (reverse) transaction.

Table 11.5

Figuring the Tail: An Exact Solution with a Haircut Evaluated at the Cost of Capital

Dollars Out	Dollars In
Day $t = 0$	
Buy a 90 day Treasury @5.75%	Finance using a 30 day term repo @5.5%
$P = \$1m \left(1 - \frac{.0575(90)}{360} \right) = \$985,625$	Repo principal = $985,132.19
Opportunity cost of haircut capital =	
$\left(\frac{.015(30)}{365} \right) (\$492.81) = \$6.08$	
Day $t = 30$	
Repay repo principal plus interest	Sell tail bill at unknown rate, d^*
Repo interest = $\$985,132.19 \left(\frac{.055(30)}{360} \right) = \$4,515.19$	$P^* = \$1m \left(1 - \frac{d^*(60)}{360} \right)$
Repo principal = $985,132.19	
Total repo repayment = $989,647.38	Haircut returned = $492.81
Total cash flows[a] = $1,975,771.27	Total cash flows[a] = $985,625 + P^*

$$P^* = \$989,653.46 = \$1m\left(1 - \frac{d^*(60)}{360}\right)$$

$$d^* = 6.21\%$$

Assumptions

1. $1 million face value.

2. Haircut of 5 basis points evaluated at a 15% cost of capital.

3. Exact calculation of repo interest using the repo principal amount.

[a]Total cash flows are the sum of all cash flows received or paid out at times $t = 0$ and $t = 30$, neglecting the time value of money. All cash flows are from Mr. O'Cash's point of view.

Summary

The repurchase agreement originated as an inexpensive source of financing. Its design as a fully collateralized loan emanated from the original users' desire to shield themselves from credit risk exposure. Since its beginnings, the repo market has grown to be an instrument of interest rate speculation. Repo and reverse transactions can be combined with cash market transactions to place speculative bets on the direction of future interest rates.

Upon initiation of the repo, marketable securities are sold (at a discount to allow for a margin requirement called the haircut) with the agreement that they be repurchased at a later date for a prespecified price. Since the repo is overcollateralized (the value of the securities collateral exceeds the principal plus interest repayment on the repo), the counterparties are protected from credit risk but are exposed to interest rate risk. This interest rate risk exposure emanates from the mismatch in maturities between the repo transaction and the underlying collateral security. The returns on a speculative repo/reverse transaction depend on forecasts of future interest rates. The carry period is the financed portion of the speculative repo/reverse transaction. The tail security is the unfinanced security remaining after the maturity of the repo/reverse portion of the speculative repo transaction. The breakeven rate on the tail in an upward- (downward-) sloping yield curve environment is the maximum (minimum) rate at which the tail bill can be sold (purchased), so that the speculative repo transaction just breaks even. The breakeven rate on the tail may be (1) approximated (assuming repo interest is levied on the collateral's face value as opposed to the repo's principal); (2) calculated precisely with the assumption of no haircut; and (3) calculated precisely with the assumption of some cost of the haircut.

References

Allen, L., S. Peristiani, and A. Saunders. "Bank Size, Collateral, and Net Purchase Behavior in the Federal Funds Market: Empirical Evidence." *Journal of Business* (October 1989): 335–361.

Allen, L., and T. Thurston. "Cash-Futures Arbitrage and Forward-Futures Spreads in the Treasury Bill Market." *Journal of Futures Markets*, 8, No. 5 (October 1988): 563–573.

Federal Reserve Bank of Atlanta. "Special Issue on Repurchase Agreements: Taking a Closer Look at Safety." *Economic Review* (September 1985).

Lumpkin, S. "Repurchase and Reverse Agreements." Federal Reserve Bank of Richmond, *Economic Review* (January–February 1987): 15–23.

Lumpkin, S. "Repurchase and Reverse Repurchase Agreements." *Instruments of the Money Market*, 7th ed., Richmond, Va.: Federal Reserve Bank of Richmond (1993): 59–74.

McCrackin, M., M. Martin, and W. B. Estes. "State and Local Governments' Use of Repos: A Southeastern Perspective." in the special issue of the Federal Reserve Bank of Atlanta *Economic Review* (September 1985).

Stigum, M. *The Repo and Reverse Markets*. Homewood, Ill.: Dow-Jones Irwin (1989).

Questions

1. Price the following repo and reverse transactions. Be sure to determine all securities and cash flows at both initiation and maturity of the transaction.
   a. A 30 day term repo with a repo rate of 4.25% based on the following collateral: A $1 million face value Treasury note with a semiannual coupon rate of 6% p.a. and exactly two years until maturity yielding 5.2% p.a. The haircut is 30 basis points.
   b. A 5 day term reverse with a reverse rate of 3.9% based on the following collateral: $5 million face value 90 day Treasury bills with a rate of discount equal to 4.5%. The haircut is 10 basis points.

2.   Suppose that a government security dealer had the following repo/reverse portfolio:

90 day term reverse@4.8%	$16m	Open repo@4.69%	$12m
60 day term reverse@4.79%	$9m	15 day term repo@4.71%	$8m
45 day term reverse@4.73%	$5m	30 day term repo@4.72	$10m

What can you infer about the dealer's interest rate forecast? What change in interest rates will cause the dealer's position to make money? to lose money?

3a. How can you use the following bond to set up a "Drysdale transaction" to exploit the use of flat repo pricing?

A 15% p.a. semiannual coupon Treasury bond yielding 6% on settlement date, January 14, 1998, to mature on March 1, 2002. Utilize a 30 day term reverse transaction (maturing on February 13, 1998) with a reverse rate of 5.5% p.a. (Note that the number of calendar days between September 1, 1997, and March 1, 1998, is 181. Between January 14, 1998, and March 1, 1998, there are 46 days. Assume there is no haircut.)

3b. Assume that current interest rates on January 15, 1998, increase to 8% p.a. and stay there for the term of the repo transaction. Calculate the impact on the profitability of your transaction.

3c. Assume that current interest rates on January 15, 1998, decrease to 4% p.a. and stay there for the term of the repo transaction. Calculate the impact on the profitability of your transaction.

4.   Set up a speculative repo transaction using the following term structure (all Treasury rates are rates of discount; all other rates are simple interest yields on a 360 day basis):

Fed Funds rate: 9.875%
90 day Treasury bill rate: 9.25%
60 day Treasury bill rate: 9.125%
30 day Treasury bill rate: 8.625%
90 day repo/reverse rate: 10.0%
30 day repo/reverse rate: 8.9%

   a. What is the carry on the speculative repo transaction?
   b. Calculate the tail using the approximation. (Be sure both to utilize the formula and to calculate the dollar cash flows.)
   c. Calculate the tail using the exact solution assuming no haircut.
   d. Calculate the tail using a haircut of 25 basis points.
   e. Calculate the tail using a haircut of 25 basis points if the cost of capital is assumed to be 20% p.a. (simple interest yield).
   f. Under what conditions will the speculative repo trade be transacted? Contrast your answer using the three calculations for the breakeven rate on the tail in parts (b), (c), (d), and (e).

5.   Evaluate a 9.25% p.a. semiannual coupon Treasury bond maturing June 12, 2005 on settlement date, May 3, 1998, if yields are 8.5% p.a. Calculate the flat price and the full accrual price. (*Hint:* There are 142 calendar days between December 12, 1997, and May 3, 1998, and 40 calendar days between May 3, 1998, and June 12, 1998. Use $100,000 face value.)

6.   Using the bond in question 5 as collateral for a 15 day term repo with a haircut of 50 basis points and a repo rate of 7.9% p.a., what is the maximum repo principal that can be obtained? Determine the cash and securities flows on the date of initiation of the repo (May 3, 1998) and on the repo's maturity date (May 18, 1998). (Be sure to calculate the market value of the collateral on each date.)

7a. Use the bond in question 5 and the repo in question 6 to set up a speculative repo transaction to exploit an upward-sloping yield curve. What is the interest rate risk of the speculative repo transaction?

7b. *Challenge Question:* Use dollar cash flows to evaluate the breakeven on the tail for the speculative repo transaction in part (a). (*Hint:* Do NOT use the formula.) Under what conditions will the transaction take place?

7c. *Challenge Question:* If the 2005 bond yields 10% on May 18, 1998, what is the net profit/loss on the speculative repo transaction?

7d. *Challenge Question:* If the 2005 bond yields 7.25% on May 18, 1998, what is the net profit/loss on the speculative repo transaction?

7e. *Challenge Question:* Recalculate the breakeven rate on the tail if the cost of capital is assumed to be 18% and the bond's simple interest yield is 8.5% p.a.

8. Set up three "dollars in–dollars out" tables for the speculative reverse transaction in the text.
   a. Showing the approximate break-even rate on the tail of 7.75% p.a.
   b. Solving for the break-even rate's exact solution, assuming no haircut.
   c. Solving for the exact solution with a haircut of 20 basis points.

CHAPTER 12

EUROCURRENCIES

"Letters of thanks, letters from banks, . . .
Receipted bills and invitations
And gossip, gossip for all the nations."—W. H. Auder, *Night Mail* (1936), in *Collected Shorter Poems* (1966).

Learning Objectives

- To explore the what, why, when, and how much of Euromarkets.

- To understand how Euromarkets evolved into a transnational market that crosses national boundaries and transcends regulatory restrictions.

➤ Introduction

Euromarket: financial transactions that involve the issuance of financial securities that are denominated in a currency other than the home currency of the country of issuance.

Nowhere is internationalization more obvious than in the **Euromarket**. Euromarket activity is not synonymous with foreign activity. A financial transaction takes place in the Euromarket if it involves the issuance of a financial security that is denominated in a currency other than the home currency of the country of issuance. In contrast, when a foreign issuer issues a financial security that is denominated in the local currency of the country of issuance, we consider that to be a foreign market transaction. The defining feature of a Euromarket transaction is the mismatch between the country of issuance and the currency of denomination. This mismatch places Euromarket activity outside the jurisdiction of national regulatory authorities and public FIs. The Euromarket transcends national boundaries.

Euromarket financial instruments can be debt (such as bonds), equity-like (such as warrants), or derivatives (such as forward contracts). Since their distinguishing feature is their denomination in a currency other than the currency of the country in which they are issued, Euromarket activity creates a new form of money called Eurocurrency. As mentioned in Chapter 3, a Eurocurrency is a currency on deposit outside its country of origin; for example, U.S. dollars held in banks outside of the United States (or in international banking facilities in the United States) are called Eurodollars.

The terms *Euromarket*, *Eurocurrencies*, and *Eurodollars* are all misnomers, for Eurocurrencies are held throughout the world, not just in Europe. Major Euromarket centers are London, Luxembourg, Paris, New York, Cayman, Nassau, Panama, Singapore, Hong Kong, and Bahrain. However, the market originated predominantly in London, and one of the original banks that pioneered the instrument was Banque Commercial pour l'Europe du Nord, known by its cable code as Eurobank, and the name stuck.

Since Eurocurrency transactions exist outside the authority of any national government or public FI, they are free from regulation or intervention. The Euromarket is truly a free market in which FIs from around the world compete to provide intermediation services to their customers. Such freedom from regulation, coupled with the market's global competitive pressures, has made it the scene for financial market innovation in many spheres. Often, new products are inaugurated in the Euromarket and, if successful, spread to domestic financial markets.

➤ The Evolution of the Eurocurrency Market

An early incarnation of the Euromarket emerged in the 1920s when dollar deposits were made available by the banks of countries, such as Germany, suffering from hyperinflation. But conditions were not yet ripe for the full-fledged development of the Eurocurrency market. The evolution of the market did not begin in earnest until the 1950s. At that time, the U.S. dollar was the unchallenged reserve currency throughout the world, with a value that was fixed by the Bretton Woods price of $35 per troy ounce of gold. (See Chapter 8.) Basic commodity prices (e.g., oil and wheat) were denominated in terms of the U.S. dollar. Indeed, the U.S. dollar was the currency of international trade. This was the backdrop for the development of a Euromarket.

The Role of International Politics

The creation of the world's largest capitalist market, the Euromarket, was largely the work of the world's communist governments. Because the Soviet Union, Eastern European countries, and China had not participated in the Bretton Woods agreement, their currencies were not convertible into U.S. dollars and therefore could not be used in international trade. To support their foreign trade activities, these countries held large reserves of U.S. dollars. Typically, these reserves were held at U.S. banks. Because of the Cold War, the anticommunist fever in the United States as exemplified by the McCarthy hearings, the outbreak of the Korean War, and the uncompensated claims of Americans against communist countries for their nationalized assets, the communist countries began to worry about the possibility that the U.S. government might seize or freeze their U.S. bank deposits.

During the early 1950s, a British FI, S. G. Warburg, advised the communist governments to transfer their U.S. dollar deposits to European banks. The first recipients of large amounts of U.S. dollar deposits from communist governments were two Soviet-owned European banks: the Banque Commercial pour l'Europe du Nord (known as Eurobank) in Paris and the Moscow Narodny Bank in London. These were the first Eurodollars, since they were deposits of U.S. dollars held in banks outside of the United States.

The Arab countries joined in this exodus from U.S. banks when, upon the outbreak of the Suez War of 1956, the United States froze the assets of all the belligerents: Britain, France, Israel, and Egypt. After the war, Arab investors responded by shifting their dollar deposits to banks in Europe. When the oil shocks of the 1970s created an explosion of "petrodollars," much of this money was deposited into the Eurodollar market.

The final political development that led to the birth of the Euromarket was the lifting of foreign currency controls in Western Europe.[1] This move, together with the exchange rate stability provided by Bretton Woods, allowed multinational corporations to shift from currency to currency in order to minimize their borrowing costs and maximize their investment returns.

---

[1] Because France did not lift its capital controls as did other Western European countries, Paris lost out in its battle with London to be the center of the newly emerging Euromarket.

The Role of Financial Regulation

As unbelievable as it may seem, U.S. bank regulations actually contributed to the U.S. banks' declining market share of the world's holdings of dollar-denominated deposits. Five regulatory factors in the United States made the shift to European banks advantageous for foreign depositors and borrowers of U.S. dollars:

1. U.S. reserve requirements on domestic time deposits ranged from 1 to 6%. This reduced the profitability of these deposits for U.S. banks, thereby lowering the interest rate that banks were willing to pay to attract these deposits.

2. All U.S. domestic deposits were federally insured at a cost to the U.S. banks of 8.33 basis points. This insurance premium was charged on all deposit balances, even if some portion of the deposit was not covered by deposit insurance.

3. No interest could be paid on demand deposit balances.

4. All domestic time deposit rates were subject to interest rate ceilings.

5. The legal lending limit constrained the amount of loans a bank could grant to a particular domestic borrower to be less than 10% of the bank's total capital.

The first two factors caused the cost of deposit taking to increase for U.S. banks, since they were subject to additional costs (reserve requirements and deposit insurance premiums) that did not apply to foreign banks. The next two factors limited the interest rates that U.S. banks could offer to attract deposits. Finally, the last factor reduced the competitiveness of U.S. banks in satisfying the loan demand of large, multinational corporations. Together with the high tax rates in the United States (including federal, state, and local taxes), these factors created an environment that was not friendly to U.S. banking. None of these restrictions applied to the newly emerging Euromarkets. The U.S. banks could not compete with the lower cost, more aggressive European FIs. When foreign governments and multinational corporations saw the opportunity to circumvent the expensive and unresponsive U.S. banking industry, they grabbed it. Thus, the Euromarket was born.

Political ineptitude in controlling financial markets solidified the position of the nascent Eurodollar market. To ameliorate its worsening balance-of-payments deficit, the United States passed the Interest Equalization Tax (IET) in mid-1963, which levied a 15% withholding tax on all sales of foreign stocks and bonds. But all this tax accomplished was the acceleration of the transfer of dollar-denominated business out of U.S. financial markets to the newly developing Eurodollar market. As a response to the IET, in July 1963 the **Eurobond** was born. Eurobonds are bonds that are issued outside of their country of origin and are denominated in Eurocurrencies, that is, they are denominated in a currency different from the currency of the country in which they are issued. For example, the first Eurobond was a $15 million, 15 year, U.S. dollar-denominated bond issued by an Italian company, Autostrade, underwritten by London-based S. G. Warburg and co-managed by banks in Belgium, West Germany, the Netherlands, and Luxembourg. By 1964, the Eurodollar bond market had grown to a size of $20 billion.

Eurobonds: bonds that are issued outside of their country of origin and are denominated in Eurocurrencies.

Not leaving bad enough alone, the U.S. government again intervened to try to prevent the surge in capital outflows from the United States. In 1965 both the Voluntary Foreign Credit Restraint Program and the Mandatory Foreign Investment Program were passed, as futile efforts to outlaw the growth of the new market. Since both measures applied only to U.S. companies, their impact was quite the opposite. Financial business that might have gone to U.S. FIs went instead to the unrestricted FIs that pioneered the Eurodollar market.

U.S. regulators were not the only inept challengers of the nascent Euromarket. The Bank of England bungled its original opportunity when, in 1957, in response to a worsening balance of payments, it introduced capital controls on the pound sterling. These controls prohibited sterling financing of multinational operations outside of the United Kingdom. This regulation stymied the development of a Eurosterling market, and it also encouraged British FIs to substitute U.S. dollar financing for outlawed pound sterling financing. Rather than eliminating the business, it only moved out of the reach of the regulations. Because of these regulations, the Eurodollar market dominated the market for all other Eurocurrencies. In 1964, 83% of all Eurocurrency transactions were in terms of Eurodollars.

In another example of the Euromarket's exploitation of governmental policy mistakes, in March 1964 the German government imposed a 25% withholding tax on domestic Deutsche-mark-denominated bonds held by non-German residents (called a coupon tax), thereby inducing issuers to turn to markets outside of Germany in which to sell their bonds. From this original tax avoidance motive sprang the Euro-DM bond market, which in 1993 accounted for 13.3% of the volume on the Eurobond market.

The evolution of the Euromarket illustrates the regulatory dialectic, discussed in Chapter 5. Innovation in financial markets was used to circumvent any regulations that impeded the ability of FIs to offer the intermediation services that their customers wanted. Although the Euromarket may owe its existence to well-intentioned but misplaced regulations, their absence does not imply that the Euromarket will cease to exist. Financial market participants have found the Euromarket to be an extremely valuable addition to their menu of financial choices. Thus, when a 30% withholding tax levied on non-U.S. residents was lifted in 1984, the result was the growth in *both* Euromarket and domestic bond offerings in the United States. For example, in March 1984, Texaco simultaneously issued a record-breaking (for its time) offer of twin $1 billion bond issues: one in the domestic bond market in New York and the other in the Euromarket. The Euromarket does not grow only at the expense of domestic markets; however, it can create an expansion in total financial market activity that increases the liquidity of all financial markets.

Factors Leading to the Explosive Growth of the Euromarket

Political factors and regulatory ineptitude combined to create financial conditions that were conducive to the development of a new *transnational* market that was outside the authority of any national regulatory body. The explosive growth in the Euromarket took place when shifting financial conditions rewarded financial market innovation. The Euromarket's role as an unregulated, perfectly competitive financial market put it in an ideal position to respond to changing financial conditions. It capitalized on that opportunity with a proliferation of new Euromarket financial products.

1. One factor leading to recent growth of the Euromarket was the October 1979 change in the Federal Reserve's conduct of monetary policy. The shift toward the targeting of monetary aggregates, as opposed to Federal Funds rates (see Chapter 4), caused interest rates worldwide to increase drastically. Double-digit inflation in the United States eroded the purchasing power of the U.S. dollar. Dollar depositors demanded higher interest rates to compensate them for the ravages of inflation. Domestic U.S. banks, limited by interest rate ceilings and the other restrictive financial regulations, could not respond to those demands, but Eurobanks could. The exodus of dollar deposits from U.S. banks to foreign banks (and international banking facilities in the United States) provided the funding for the explosive growth of the Eurodollar market. From December 1978 to December 1979, the size of the Eurocurrency deposit market grew from US$835 billion to US$1.111 *trillion*, an annual growth rate of 33%. Within less than five years, the market doubled to a size of US$2.383 trillion in 1983.

2. The second factor was the increased volatility in interest rates, which fueled the inflow of funds into the Euromarket in the form of Eurocurrency deposits. Both the level of interest rates and the size of their day-to-day fluctuations increased. The greater availability of funds led to the growth in the use of funds as well, through the Euroloan and Eurobond markets. One reason for the greater availability of funds on the Euromarket was its pioneering of *floating rate loans*, whose interest rates fluctuated with market interest rates. Since the lending FI did not have to take on interest rate risk exposure, floating rate Euroloans were more readily available to qualified lenders than were fixed rate domestic bank loans. Typical Euroloan rates were priced at the three or six month LIBOR plus a spread of 0.75% to 1% to cover administrative expenses, an amount *lower* than the effective prime rate on bank loans in the United States. Thus, multinational corporations found that they could borrow U.S. dollars more cheaply on the Euromarket than from U.S. banks. Even U.S. banks preferred to lend on the Euromarket, as opposed to domestic markets, because of the lower administrative costs associated with the larger sized Euroloans. Moreover, default risk was lower for Euroloans because of the blue chip status of many of the corporate borrowers that had access to the Euromarket. The result was that the Eurocurrency lending markets grew much more rapidly than their corresponding domestic lending markets.

3. The third factor explaining Euromarket development is the improvement in clearing operations. Euromarket activity received an important boost in October 1981 when CHIPS shifted from next day to same-day settlement. Much of the growth in the volume of electronic transactions on CHIPS emanated from Euromarket transactions. To better compete with the domestic U.S. market, which settled on Fedwire, CHIPS had to approach the Fedwire's immediate availability of funds. Recall from Chapter 6 that CHIPS is a netted electronic payment system, as opposed to the Fedwire gross settlement system, and thus does not make funds available until all transactions have been cleared. Prior to October 1981, this settlement process could take as long as three days (over a weekend) from the initiation of the transaction, exposing the counterparties to considerable amounts of settlement risk. As interest rates increased, the opportunity cost of funds increased, making this time lag unacceptable to market participants. In October 1981 CHIPS responded to these competitive pressures by providing availability of funds at the close of business on the date of the transaction.

International Banking Facilities (IBFs): subsidiaries of U.S. banks that engage only in international banking business.

Japanese Offshore Market (JOM): the Japanese equivalent of an IBF.

4. Another factor contributing to the growth in Eurodollar lending was the introduction, in December 1981, of **International Banking Facilities (IBFs)** in the United States. These are subsidiaries of U.S. banks that engage only in international banking business. In the first four weeks of activity during December 1981, IBF liabilities jumped from zero to $52.4 billion. The inauguration of IBFs enabled U.S. branches of multinational corporations to conduct their Euromarket activity without leaving the United States. The Japanese equivalent of an IBF is the **Japanese Offshore Market (JOM)**. However, because of the tight regulatory environment in Japan until now, JOMs have had limited usefulness and Tokyo has not become a major Euromarket center.

➤ The Euromarket Today

The Euromarket today is truly a global financial market, trading around the clock in all the major financial centers throughout the world. It rivals the U.S. Treasury market in terms of size and liquidity. It is a competitive market, unencumbered by government regulation, and is completely responsive to customers' financial goals. Thus, the Euromarket is quite conducive to financial innovation.

In recent years Euromarkets have evolved to reflect the increased prevalence of institutional rather than retail investors. Formerly, 40 to 60% of all Eurobond issues ultimately ended up in the Swiss bank accounts of retail customers (for example, the proverbial Belgian dentist) who held on to the issue until its maturity.[2] Today, institutional investors are the major category of buyers of Eurobonds, and they actively trade the issues in secondary markets. The institutional Eurobond buyer does not need the FI to analyze the credit on its behalf, since it can do so itself and is willing to evaluate and ultimately buy the security directly. The impact of

---

[2] Fisher (1988), p. 32.

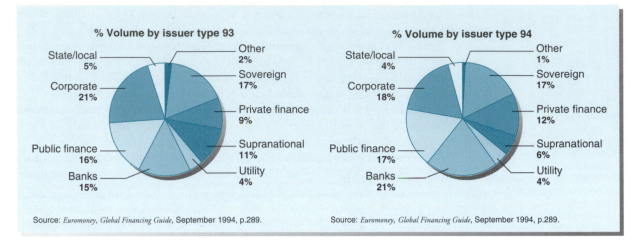

Figure 12.1

the trend toward institutional activity is a shift from unsecuritized to securitized instruments. Figure 12.1 shows the distribution of Eurocurrency issues by type of issuer. The largest category was corporations in 1993 and banks in 1994, each with 21% of the volume of new issues in each year.

A possible exception to the general trend toward greater institutional involvement in Euromarkets is the Euroyen market, in which the retail investor is an important source of funds. Indeed, during the third quarter of 1994, Euroyen activity was so large, and Eurodollar activity so depressed, that the Euroyen overtook the Eurodollar as the most popular currency for fixed rate Euro issues. *Timely Topics 12.1* discusses this issue.

TIMELY TOPICS 12.1

HERE'S TO YOU, MRS. WATANABE

[W]hile the Euroyen sector has boomed, a new and potentially enormous source of funds has opened up—the Japanese retail sector. The Japanese housewife may seem a distant cousin of the Belgian dentist [the prototypical retail investor in Euromarkets]. But Mrs. Watanabe—the mythical housewife who symbolizes Japanese retail investors—is a woman many traditional Euromarket borrowers will want to attract.

The abolition of the lock-up rule for sovereign and supranational issuers in December [1993] has in effect unified the Euroyen and domestic yen markets. (The rule prevented Euroyen issues from being placed with Japanese investors for 90 days after launch.) In doing so, it has put the Euromarkets within the reach of a group of Japanese domestic investors who will not buy foreign-currency bonds.

Retail sector bank deposits in Japan amount to US$5.7 trillion, US$2.4 trillion more than in the U.S. Returns from the equity market and bank debentures have been minimal as Japanese stocks have plummeted and interest rates have reached historic lows. This has encouraged retail investors to shop around for a pick-up in yield. And this year the Japanese securities houses have tried to introduce them to Eurobonds. . . .

The big four securities houses (Daiwa, Nikko, Nomura, and Yamaichi) are understandably keen to expand the retail market, where they have an unbeatable advantage. The U.S. investment banks, which have established a strong presence in Euroyen this year, have no branch network to target retail. And the big Japanese commercial banks, which have set up securities affiliates to compete for mandates, cannot use their bank salesforces to distribute deals because the law bans them from direct involvement in securities business. . . .

Because the lock-up rule still applies to corporate issuers [it was lifted in 1994 for sovereign and supranational government issues only and for all other issues on April 1, 1996], they have been unable to tap retail demand for Euroyen paper. This is particularly galling since the samurai market [sales in Japan of yen-denominated bonds issued by foreign companies] has shown that well-known corporates can attract large sums from Japanese retail.

Earlier this year Nikko brought [to market] issues for two of the world's best known brand names, Walt Disney and PepsiCo. Disney's JY30 billion, three and a half year issue yielded only 3.03%, but still sold to more than 20,000 investors. . . .

Japanese investors by tradition hold bonds to maturity. . . . And for accounting and tax reasons, Japanese investors historically have not been active in the secondary market. . . . [However,] conditions in the yen markets do not entirely favour bonds. Interest rates are so low that they are unlikely to fall any further, even though inflation remains close to or below zero. . . . One treasury official at a leading international borrower fears that the Euroyen sector is in danger of becoming a market apart, like Luxembourg or Swiss francs. But the yen has become such an important reserve currency that every big international investor has to have yen securities in his portfolio.

Source: *Euromoney*, October 1994, pp. 79–86.

The increased importance of the Deutschemark (as the world's second reserve currency), as well as the Japanese yen, has also shifted the focus of the Euromarket. The proportion of Eurodollar deposits in all Eurocurrency transactions fell to 41% in 1994. Figure 12.2 shows the distribution of issues by Eurocurrency for 1993 and 1994.

London and New York are major centers for most Eurocurrencies, whereas Paris leads in Eurosterling, Brussels in Euro-French francs, and Luxemburg in Euro-Deutschemarks and Euro-Belgian francs. Singapore and Hong Kong have also developed active Euromarkets, predominantly because of their time zones, which allow them to trade before Western markets open. Table 12.1 shows the distribution of countries of issue for all public Eurobonds. In 1995

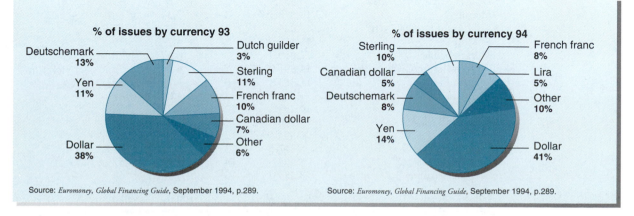

Source: *Euromoney, Global Financing Guide*, September 1994, p.289.   Source: *Euromoney, Global Financing Guide*, September 1994, p.289.

Figure 12.2

Table
12.1

Financial Activity on Euromarkets by Nationality of Borrowers, 1992–1995 (Percent and US$ billions)

Region/Country	1992	1993	1994	1995
OECD area	89.6%	87.2%	88.2%	89.0%
Developing countries	6.1	8.4	8.9	9.6[a]
Central and Eastern Europe	0.2	0.8	0.4	1.4[b]
Others	4.1	3.6	2.5	2.0
Total	100%	100%	100%	100%

By country (in US$ billions)

	1992	1993	1994	1995
United States	$95.0	$124.9	$200.6	$356.0
Germany	28.4	65.0	83.7	127.8
United Kingdom	70.9	51.3	77.4	82.0
Japan	75.5	85.4	74.2	121.4
France	42.5	58.0	62.7	46.1
Canada	30.2	38.7	39.1	36.1
Italy	15.1	31.2	28.0	32.1
Australia	14.7	27.3	23.4	19.6
All other countries	237.4	336.8	378.5	437.2
Total	$609.7	$818.6	$967.6	$1,258.3

[a]For 1995, this figure is reported for all non-OECD countries. Differences due to rounding.

[b] For 1995, this figure is reported for international development institutions.

Source: OECD *Financial Market Trends*, Nos. 61, 63 (June 1995, February 1996): pp. 77, 47.

almost 30% of all Eurobonds were issued in the United States. Table 12.2 shows the top 15 lead managers dominating Eurobond underwriting syndicates, together with their new issue activity in 1995.

Figure 12.3 shows that, in 1994, 47% of all Eurodollar issuance was floating rate, 45% was fixed rate, and 8% was convertible into equity. Figures 12.4, 12.5, and 12.6 show that the

Table
12.2

Top Lead Managers: Eurobond Issues

Manager	January 1, 1995– December 31,1995			
	Amount ($ Millions)	Rank	%	Issues
SBC Warburg	17,961.1	1	6.4	97
Deutsche Morgan Grenfell	15,637.4	2	5.6	69
Merrill	14,820.3	3	5.3	88
ABN Amro Hoare Govett	14,054.3	4	5.0	87
JP Morgan	13,138.7	5	4.7	79
Morgan Stanley	12,059.9	6	4.3	78
CS First Boston/Credit Suisse	11,891.0	7	4.2	59
Lehman Brothers	11,383.3	8	4.1	65
Goldman, Sachs	11,151.4	9	4.0	47
Banque Paribas	10,235.1	10	3.7	57
Dresdner Bank AG	9,756.9	11	3.5	33
UBS	9,353.3	12	3.3	61
Commerzbank AG	8,747.5	13	3.1	31
BZW/Barclays PLC	8,264.6	14	2.9	57
Nomura Securitie	8,235.6	15	2.9	60
Industry Totals	280,399.3	–	100.0	1,840

Source: Investor Dealer's Digest

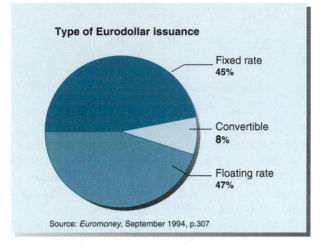

Type of Eurodollar issuance

Fixed rate
45%

Convertible
8%

Floating rate
47%

Source: *Euromoney*, September 1994, p.307

Figure 12.3

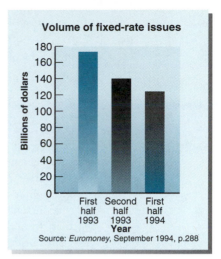

Volume of fixed-rate issues

Source: *Euromoney*, September 1994, p.288

Figure 12.4

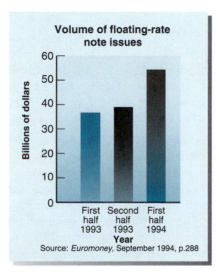

Volume of floating-rate note issues

Source: *Euromoney*, September 1994, p.288

Figure 12.5

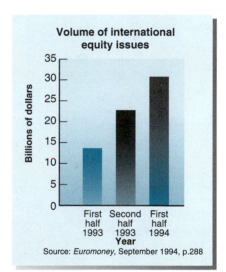

Volume of international equity issues

Source: *Euromoney*, September 1994, p.288

Figure 12.6

volume of fixed rate issues decreased over the years 1993–1994, making way for increases in both the volume of floating rate note issues and international equity issues. The Eurocurrencies tend to be grouped into low-, medium-, and high-interest rate groups. The low-rate group includes the yen, the mark, the Swiss franc, and the guilder; the middle group is the U.S. dollar, the French franc, the Belgian franc, and the Canadian dollar; and the high rate group includes the sterling, the lira, and the Australian dollar.

Checkpoint

1. How is the regulatory dialectic (from Chapter 5) illustrated by the evolution of the Euromarket?

2. How did the political and economic environment of the post–World War II period contribute to the evolution of the Euromarket?

3. Why did the Eurodollar dominate other Eurocurrencies, such as the Eurosterling or Euroyen?

4.   How did the shift in the conduct of U.S. monetary policy in 1979 impact the development of the Euromarket?

5.   Why did the Eurocurrency deposit market develop?

6.   Why did the Eurobond market develop?

➤ Innovation in the Euromarket

The existence of Eurocurrencies in all of the world's major currencies acts as a check on each country's financial market efficiency. If transacting in the domestic market becomes too costly or restrictive, the business will flow to the Euromarket. Similarly, each domestic market acts as a check on its corresponding Euromarket to keep its prices in line with domestic prices. Large deviations will cause arbitrage opportunities that result in large-scale transfers of financial activity from the domestic market to the Euromarket, or vice versa.

The Euromarket offers a "parallel universe" of financial securities that mirrors the securities offered in domestic financial markets. Thus, the same financial services offered in domestic financial markets are also offered in Euromarkets. The two major categories of financial services are (1) intertemporal cash flow transfers and (2) risk shifting services.

Intertemporal Cash Flow Transfers on Euromarkets

Euromarket activity occurs on both the asset and liability side of the FI. In providing cash flow timing services, FIs borrow funds from Funds Surplus Units (thereby creating FI liabilities) and lend them to Funds Deficit Units (creating FI assets). Financial intermediation in the provision of intertemporal cash flow transfers, then, involves both the asset and liability side of the FI's balance sheet. This holds in Euromarkets, just as it holds in domestic financial markets.

time deposits:
nonnegotiable deposits with a fixed time until maturity.

certificates of deposits (CDs): negotiable deposits with a fixed time until maturity.

interbank placements:
short term (often overnight) interbank loans of Eurocurrency time deposits.

call money:
nonnegotiable Eurocurrency deposits without fixed maturity dates that can be withdrawn at any time.

FIs Hold Eurocurrency Liabilities   On the FI's liability side, the FI issues Eurocurrency deposits to Funds Surplus Units and other FIs. Eurocurrency liabilities come in four forms: (1) **time deposits**, nonnegotiable deposits with a fixed time until maturity; (2) **certificates of deposits (CDs)**, negotiable deposits with a fixed time until maturity; (3) **interbank placements**, short term (often overnight) interbank loans of Eurocurrency time deposits; and (4) **call money**, nonnegotiable Eurocurrency deposits without fixed maturity dates that can be withdrawn at any time. Eurocurrency time deposits and CDs are invested for a fixed period of time, most commonly three or six months. Since Eurocurrency time deposits are nonnegotiable and, thus, illiquid, their yields tend to be higher than the yields on equivalent maturity negotiable Eurocurrency CDs. In the secondary market, the typical bid-ask spread in Euro CD rates is $\frac{1}{8}$ = .125%. Euro CDs are usually issued in denominations of $1 million and up, with maturities ranging from overnight to five years. The Euro CD rate is quoted as a simple interest rate (bond equivalent yield), with the assumption that there are 360 days in the year. For example, at maturity, a three month (90 day) Euro CD with par value of $10 million priced at 6.5% p.a. would be worth

$$\$10\text{m}\left(1 + \frac{.065(90)}{360}\right) = \$10,162,500$$

The effective cost to the Eurobank of the Eurocurrency deposit is sometimes less than the effective cost of alternative domestic sources of funds. For example, suppose that, alternatively, the bank could raise $10 million by issuing domestic certificates of deposit that offer a rate of 6.1% p.a., but also carry a 3% reserve requirement[3] and a 0.23% deposit insurance premium.

---

[3] Currently, reserve requirements in the United States on time deposits and Eurocurrency deposits are both set at zero.

The effective cost of funds is

$$c = \frac{i + x}{1 - r}$$

where i is the interest rate on the deposits; x is the cost of deposit insurance (plus other administrative costs); and r is the reserve requirement. Applying this formula, the effective cost of funds, denoted c, for the domestic CD is

$$c = \frac{.0610 + .0023}{1 - .03} = 6.53\%$$

Thus, although the domestic CD carries a lower interest rate (6.5% minus 6.1% equals a spread of 40 basis points), its effective cost is three basis points higher than the cost of the Euro CD (6.53% minus 6.5% equals 3 basis points) since Euro CDs are not subject to either deposit insurance premiums or reserve requirements. Moreover, the bank's transaction costs are lower in the Euromarket than in the domestic market because of the large-size denominations of the accounts, providing the benefits of potential **economies of scale**, which are reductions in average cost as the size of transaction increases. Banks' transaction costs are also reduced by the availability of interbank placements. Marr, Rogowski, and Trimble (1989) show that commercial banks have a cost advantage in Eurobond underwriting.

Interbank placements are the Euromarket equivalent of the Federal Funds market, since they reflect sales or purchases of Eurocurrency time deposits between banks. The existence of interbank placements on Euromarkets permits the transfer of liquidity between banks. Smaller banks can acquire Eurocurrencies without the need for a large, expensive network to attract deposits from multinational corporations. They only have to purchase these funds from the large banks that attract them in quantity. The greatest volume of activity in the Euromarket takes place in the form of interbank placement. Estimates of the volume of interbank liabilities were between US$900 and US$1,335 billion as far back as 1980.

The large volume of interbank placements creates the problem of double counting in the Euromarket statistics. Since interbank placements simply reallocate the existing Eurocurrencies across banks, they do not provide additional sources of funds to finance the activities of Funds Deficit Units. Figure 12.7 shows the distribution of Eurocurrencies and the problem of double counting. Only the last transaction between non-U.S. bank C and the Funds Deficit Unit introduces additional sources of funds into the international financial flow. Inclusion of both of the transactions between Banks A and B and between Banks B and C overstates the volume of Eurodollar activity that represents intermediation between Funds Surplus and Deficit Units. However, this is not to say that this interbank activity is unimportant. The availability of an interbank placement market provides liquidity to the Euromarket, encouraging the fundamental intermediation transactions that take place between the Funds Surplus Unit and Bank A, as

economies of scale: reductions in average cost as the size of transaction increases.

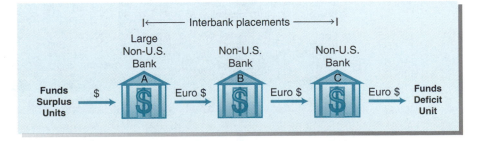

Figure 12.7   Distribution of Eurocurrencies and double counting.

well as between Bank C and the Funds Deficit Unit. Because of the unconcentrated nature of the Euromarket, most interbank placements are facilitated using Eurocurrency brokers.

Now we can add to our earlier definition of LIBOR: **LIBOR** is the average interest rate offered for interbank placements by a sample of eight major Eurobanks in London. The British Bankers' Association's official definition of LIBOR is discussed in *Practitioner's Primer 12.1.* LIBOR can be thought of as the Euromarket analog of the Federal Funds rate. It is a competitive market rate for short-maturity Eurocurrency liabilities. Eurobanks make markets in interbank placements by posting their willingness to buy and sell Eurocurrency time deposits of different maturities.

The rate on call money is tied to the overnight LIBOR and the Fed Funds rate. Call deposits are the Euromarket's version of domestic demand deposits. The rate is lower than that on Euro time deposits, since the money can be obtained, depending on the terms of the call agreement, at any time or on a two day or seven day notice. Thus, the holder of a call Eurodeposit avoids any penalty for early withdrawal if the money is needed prior to the maturity date of the deposit. Call money is likely to equal about 10% of a bank's total Eurodeposits.

PRACTITIONER'S PRIMER 12.1

THE BRITISH BANKERS' ASSOCIATION'S (BBA) OFFICIAL DEFINITION OF LIBOR

BBA interest settlement rates are based on rates quoted by 8 or 16 BBA-designated banks as being, in their view, the offered rate at which deposits are being quoted

```
Page                                                    DG28 M-Mkt B B A L
Screen printed
L I B O R   F I X :   U S D   1   M O N T H
     (Press # <GO> to select an index)                    PAGE 2 OF 13
```

		US	CURRENT		PREVIOUS		
INDEX	TICKER		VALUE	DATE	VALUE	DATE	CHANGE
Fixing							
1) 1 MONTH	US0001M <Indx>		**5.43750**	5/20	5.43750	5/17	.00
Underlying rates							
2) LLOYDS	US0101M <Indx>		**5.40625**	5/20	5.40625	5/17	.00
3) BARCLAYS	US0301M <Indx>		**5.43750**	5/20	5.43750	5/17	.00
4) NATWEST	US0501M <Indx>		**5.43750**	5/20	5.43750	5/17	.00
5) WESTPAC	US1201M <Indx>		**5.43750**	5/20	5.43750	5/17	.00
6) CITIBANK	US1601M <Indx>		**5.43750**	5/20	5.43750	5/17	.00
7) RYL BK SCOTLAND	US1801M <Indx>		**5.43750**	5/20	5.43750	5/17	.00
8) BOT/MITSUBISHI	US2001M <Indx>		**5.46875**	5/20	5.50000	5/17	.00
9) COMMERZ BANK	US2101M <Indx>		**5.40625**	5/20	5.43750	5/17	.00
10) ABBEY NATIONAL	US2201M <Indx>		**5.40625**	5/20	5.40625	5/17	.00
11) CHEMICAL BANK	US2501M <Indx>		**5.43750**	5/20	5.43750	5/17	.00
12) FUJI BANK	US3101M <Indx>		**5.46875**	5/20	5.46875	5/17	.00
13) SUMITOMO TRUST	US3201M <Indx>		**5.46875**	5/20	5.46875	5/17	.00
14) DEUTSCHBANK	US3401M <Indx>		**5.43750**	5/20	5.43750	5/17	.00
15) MERITA	US3501M <Indx>		**5.43750**	5/20	5.43750	5/17	.00
16) HAMBROS	US4501M <Indx>		**5.43750**	5/20	5.43750	5/17	.00
17) SWISS BANK	US4601M <Indx>		**5.43750**	5/20	5.43750	5/17	.00

```
Bloomberg-all rights reserved.   Frankfurt:69-920410  Hong Kong:2-521-3000   London:171-330-7500   New York:212-318-2000
Princeton:609-279-3000    Singapore:226-3000    Sydney:2-777-8600    Tokyo:3-3201-8900    Washington DC:202-434-1800
                                                                  G177-151-0  20-May-96   17:04:41
```

Figure PP.1

to prime banks in the London Interbank market at 11:00 A.M. London time.[4] In the calculation, for 8 contributors, the two highest and two lowest rates are eliminated; for 16 contributors, the four highest and four lowest rates are eliminated. An average of the remaining four or eight is taken. The result (the fixing) is rounded up to five decimal places. Eurosterling rates are simple interest rates calculated on a 365 day basis; U.S. dollar, Deutschemark, Japanese yen, Swiss franc, French franc, Australian dollar, Canadian dollar, Dutch guilder, Italian lira, Spanish peseta, and European currency units rates are simple interest rates quoted on a 360 day basis. The value date for the British pound fixing is the date on which the rates were actually fixed. On all other currencies, the value date is two (London) working days after the fixing.

The 1 month Eurodollar fixing on May 20 is shown on the quote screen in Figure PP.1. The 16 rate quotes range from 5.40625% to 5.46875%. The extremes (the three 5.40625% quotes and the three 5.46875%) are dropped, resulting in the average quote of 5.43750%, which is the 1 month U.S. dollar LIBOR fixing. Thus, the future value of a $1 million 30 day Eurodollar CD is

$$P = F \left(1 + \frac{it}{360}\right) = \$1m \left(1 + \frac{.054375(30)}{360}\right) = \$1,004,531.25$$

The Impact of Eurocurrency Transactions on the Domestic Money Supply   Let's examine how the Eurocurrency deposit liability affects the FI's balance sheet. Suppose that the British office of World Wide Wonka, Inc. (WWW) deposits a check from MMM, Inc. drawn on Citibank New York for $1 million into its account at the London offices of National Westminster (Nat West) Bank. How does this affect the balance sheets of both Citibank and Nat West? Table 12.3 traces the transaction using T-accounts representing the banks' balance sheets.

Citibank New York loses $1 million in reserves, which are deducted from WWW's checking account balance. Those reserves are not transferred to the London offices of Nat West; in fact, the Eurodollars *never* leave the United States. Only the ownership of the dollars leaves the United States, thereby making them Eurodollars. Instead, Citibank's lost $1 million reserves are transferred to Nat West's clearing bank in the United States. Suppose that is Chase New York. Chase's T-account reflects an increase in reserves of $1 million and an increase in liabilities

Table 12.3

Clearing Eurodollar Deposits, Citibank New York

Citibank New York

Reserves	−$1m	MMM demand deposits	−$1m

Chase New York

Reserves	+$1m	Nat West deposits	+$1m

Nat Westminster London

Interbank deposits	+$1m	WWW deposits	+$1m

---

[4] U.S. dollar, Deutschemark, British pound, Japanese yen, Italian lira, and European currency units each have 16 contributor banks.

to Nat West of $1 million. This transaction is recorded on National Westminster's balance sheet as a $1 million increase in both interbank deposit assets and in WWW's deposit balances.

This transaction has *no* impact on the U.S. money supply. Total reserves in the United States are unchanged since Citibank New York loses $1 million in reserves, but Chase New York gains the offsetting $1 million. The only effect of this transaction is to change $1 million in domestic deposits (formerly held by MMM at Citibank New York) into $1 million in Eurodollar deposits (now held by WWW at Nat West London). That may reduce the banking system's reserve requirements (thereby increasing excess reserves), since the reserve requirement on Eurodollar deposits is currently set at zero.[5] However, there is no impact on total reserves available to the banking system in the United States.

Eurocurrency deposit transactions involve the FIs' liabilities. However, Eurocurrency loan and bond transactions take place on the FIs' asset side of the balance sheet. It is hardly surprising that Euromarket activities should involve FIs' assets, since FIs intermediate between Funds Surplus and Deficit Units in providing intertemporal cash flow transfers. The funds transferred to the FIs by the Funds Surplus Units are then passed along to the Funds Deficit Units in the forms of Euroloans, Euronotes, and Eurobonds. The intermediation technology used by most FIs in the Euromarket is asset transformation. Short-maturity, fixed-rate Eurocurrency deposits (such as CDs, interbank placements, or time deposits) are transformed into longer maturity, sometimes floating rate, debt instruments.

Checkpoint

✓

1.   How do FIs intermediate between Funds Deficit and Surplus Units in Euromarkets?
2.   What financial products evolved to offer intertemporal cash flow shifting opportunities?
3.   What is the impact of Eurodollar creation on the size of the U.S. money supply?
4.   Why do U.S. bank reserves remain unchanged when Eurodollars are created?

FIs Hold Eurocurrency Assets   Cross-border lending dates back to the Middle Ages. After expelling the Jews from England in the late thirteenth century, King Edward I was forced to turn to Italian banks to finance his military escapades. These dubious beginnings are the foundation for today's Eurocurrency debt markets.

syndicated Euroloans: bank lending of Eurocurrency deposits to nonfinancial Funds Deficit Units.

The first Eurocurrency assets created by FIs were **syndicated Euroloans**, which originally were short term Eurodollar loans used to finance dollar-denominated foreign trade. As the Euromarket grew, the syndicated loan market broadened to include any bank lending of Eurocurrency deposits to nonfinancial Funds Deficit Units. Syndicated Euroloans were extended to multinational corporations to finance their investments, as well as to sovereign governments to finance their balance-of-payments deficits. Since they were nonnegotiable, banks held the syndicated loans in their portfolios until they matured. Because of their illiquidity, the loans were often made jointly by groups of lending banks called **syndicates**. The goal of syndication is to share the loan's risk among the banks that are members of the syndicate.

syndicates: groups of lending banks.

The heyday for the syndicated loan market was the 1970s and early 1980s. The oil shocks of 1973 and 1979 created a huge inflow of petrodollars into the Eurodollar market, which were recycled predominantly using syndicated loans. Total Eurodollar syndicated loans totaled $181.1 billion in 1981, a record for the time that amounted to 3.4 times the volume of all international bonds. The market collapsed, however, in the face of the less developed

---

[5] There would be no impact on bank reserve requirements in the United States, because current reserve requirements are set at zero for both domestic and Euro time deposits. An impact would be felt on U.S. reserve requirements only if the funds were transferred from a domestic demand deposit to a Eurodollar deposit, thereby eliminating the banking system's 10% reserve requirement on the domestic demand deposit.

countries' (LDC) debt crisis that began with the Mexican government's repudiation of its debt in August 1982. Since then, syndicated loans have been largely replaced by the various Eurocurrency securitized debt markets for negotiable financial assets, such as Eurobonds and Euronotes. However, recent upheavals in Eurobond markets (see *Timely Topics 12.2*) have led to a resurgence of syndicated loans to sovereign governments.

TIMELY TOPICS 12.2

SOMETHING HAS TO GIVE. . .

The primary Eurobond market cannot be profitable, says a syndicate manager at a European bank. "By normal standards, the risk/reward ratio of the business is unacceptable. Many firms regard it as their flagship operation—a useful means to confirm their importance in the capital markets and hopefully win more profitable business in other areas."

That sounds like an extreme view. But many Eurobond bankers suggest their market is approaching some kind of turning point, or even a breaking point. "In the high-profile, high-volume part of the market something has to give," says Walter Henniges, an executive director at Deutsche Bank. The head of capital markets at one leading firm adds: "Never before have so many firms been losing so much money in so many markets for so long. The problem is that surprisingly few people know what they are doing."

Many bankers believe that SG Warburg's recent withdrawal from all but sterling bonds heralds a massive shake-out. Another banker sums things up: 'There must be plenty of European banks asking why on earth they should be throwing away $30 million a year in London. Some of them didn't even make much profit in the easy years.'

There have been signs that institutional investors are also having doubts. In the first two weeks of [1995], the primary market had its usual burst of activity as issuers took advantage of firms eager to establish an early lead in the league tables. Investors were not so quick off the blocks. Instead, says one source, "they stood back and watched the underwriting community go crazy." Some deals have taken weeks to place. By the first week of February [1995], weekly new-issue volume had fallen from $10 billion in the first half of January to just $3 billion. If so many sovereign buyers had not turned to syndicated loans this year, underwriters might have faced real problems. By the end of February, fortunately weekly volume was back to a more healthy $9 billion. . . .

[However, Euromarkets are resilient. In response to the upheaval in the long term Eurobond market, borrowers have shifted their financial activity to the Euro-commercial paper market. For example, in 1995, Latin American companies, most of them affected by the turbulence emanating from the Mexican crisis, arranged for the more than $1.5 billion in commercial paper lending facilities.]

Source: *Euromoney*, March 1995, pp. 32–33.

Euromarket financial instruments can be securitized (for example, Eurocommercial paper, Euronotes, and Eurobonds) or unsecuritized (for example, syndicated loans). Securitized Euromarket instruments are negotiable and can be resold in liquid secondary markets, whereas unsecuritized Euromarket loans are typically nonnegotiable and are held until maturity. Table 12.4 shows a six year breakdown of all Euromarket borrowing activity. Over the years 1990–1995 the volume of international financial activity almost tripled from US$434.9 billion to

Table 12.4

Overall Volume of Euromarket Borrowing, 1990–1995[a]

Instruments	1990	1991	1992	1993	1994	1995
Eurobonds (US$ billion)	229.9	308.7	333.7	481.0	428.6	460.6
% of total	52.9	57.6	54.7	58.8	44.3	36.6
Equities (US$ billion)	7.3	23.4	23.5	40.7	45.0	41.0
% of total	1.7	4.4	3.9	5.0	4.7	3.3
Syndicated Loans (US$ billion)	124.5	116.0	117.9	136.7	236.2	368.4
% of total	28.6	21.6	19.3	16.7	24.4	29.3
Committed Backup Facilities (US$ b)	7.0	7.7	6.7	8.2	4.9	3.1
% of total	1.6	1.4	1.1	1.0	0.5	0.2
Eurocommercial paper (US$ b)	48.3	35.9	28.9	38.4	30.8	44.6
% of total	11.1	6.7	4.8	4.7	3.2	3.5
Euronotes (medium term)(US$ b)	17.9	44.3	99.0	113.6	222.1	340.6
% of total	4.1	8.3	16.2	13.9	23.0	27.1
Total (US$ billion)	434.9	536.0	609.7	818.6	967.6	1,258.3

[a]Because data are unavailable, the totals include a small amount of foreign market activity, which is not part of the Euromarket. However, the proportion of foreign bonds in the totals was only 13.7% in 1994.

Source: Financial Market Trends (Paris: Organization for Economic Cooperation and Development), Nos. 61, 63 (June 1995, February 1996), pp. 3, 5.

annual volume of almost US$1.3 trillion. The proportion of unsecuritized versus securitized financial instruments has been virtually unchanged over the six year period, although there was a dip in syndicated loan activity in 1992 and 1993. Increasingly important are the securitized debt instruments, such as Euronotes.

Eurobonds   Foreign bonds are the debt obligations of foreign companies or governments that are denominated in the currency of the country of issue. In contrast, Eurobonds are denominated in a currency different from the currency of the country in which the bonds are issued. Table 12.5 summarizes the differences between domestic and international bonds and between foreign and Eurobonds. Note that well-known foreign bonds such as Yankee, Samurai, Bulldog, Rembrandt, and Matador bonds are *not* Eurobonds since they are denominated in their home currencies (U.S. dollar, Japanese yen, pound sterling, Dutch guilder, and Spanish peseta, respectively).

We have seen how the Eurobond market evolved to satisfy the demand for a stateless source of funds, unencumbered by either restrictive regulations or taxes. Since Eurobonds are issued in the form of private placements or go to international investors, they are not registered in any particular domestic market and their interest is not subject to withholding tax. Although Table 12.4 shows a decline in the volume of bonds issued in 1995 (the result of interest rate increases in 1994), bonds still represent the largest single category of international financial activity, making up 36.6% of the total. Initially, most Eurobonds were fixed rate, U.S. dollar-denominated straight debt instruments that paid interest annually and repaid principal upon maturity. The first innovation in the Eurobond market was to offer bonds that were denominated in Eurocurrencies other than the Eurodollar. Table 12.6 shows the distribution of bond offerings in terms of Eurocurrency. In 1995, Eurodollar bonds accounted for only 38.9% (= $144.4/$371.2) of the total new issues of international bonds, demonstrating the increasing importance of other Eurocurrencies.

Table 12.5

Bond Markets: Summary of Major Differences

	Domestic	International Foreign[a]	International Euro
Issuer	Public- or private-sector agent of the country in which the market is located	Foreign government or corporation or international institution US: SEC-registered	Any borrower with good credit standing. Explicit ratings rare
Currency	Local currency	Local currency	Any widely used international currency
Amount raised in single issue	U.S. and Japanese governments: US$5,000–25,000 million. Other governments: typically US$50–500 million. Other borrowers: typically US$50–500 million	Typically US$50–500 million	Typically US$50–500 million
Type	Usually registered, except in some European countries (e.g., Germany, Switzerland and the Netherlands)	Bearer except in Bulldog and Yankee markets	Bearer
Tax	Withholding tax is applied in several countries (Japan, United Kingdom, Italy, Switzerland), although foreign holders can usually claim some or all of the tax back	No withholding tax (with the exception of the sterling foreign bond market)	No withholding tax
Interest payments	Annual in some markets in continental Europe; semiannual elsewhere	As in corresponding domestic market	Annual for fixed rate bonds. Semiannual or quarterly for FRNs
Listing	Domestic stock exchange	Domestic stock exchange	Usually London or Luxembourg. For the Deutschemark, a domestic stock exchange
Security covenants	Private-sector issues are often secured	Unsecured	Usually unsecured, but often with a negative pledge
Issuing houses	Largely domestic banks and stock brokers	Largely domestic banks and stock brokers	International syndicate
Investors	Primarily domestic banks and other financial institutions	Domestic and overseas	Wide international profile. Private individuals play a major role
Structure	Government issues: most often bullets with a 5–10 year maturity at issue. Corporate issues: often convertible into equity	Usually bullets	Bullets common, but a wide variety of unusual structures have been employed. FRNs account for 13% of market
Issuing procedures	Public sector: usually sold through auction or syndicate. Private sector: placed by a syndicate or directly by borrower	Placed by a domestic syndicate	Placed by an international syndicate over a period of time
Secondary trading	Often through the domestic stock exchange, although OTC trading is prevalent in some markets (e.g., Deutschemark and Japanese yen). Stamp duty and fixed commissions charged in some markets.	Primarily OTC trading. Stamp duty charge on transactions by residents in Japanese yen and Swiss franc markets	OTC trading organized by issuing banks with settlement by means of book-entry transfer system using one of the standard Euromarket clearing systems

[a]Several currency sectors of the foreign bond market have special names—$ (Yankee), Yen (Samurai), £ (Bulldog), Dutch guilder (Rembrandt), and Spanish peseta (Matador). A distinction in the U.S. financial markets is usually drawn between foreign bonds issued by residents of Canada—termed "Canadians"—and those issued by other foreign agents—termed "Yankee bonds."

FRN = floating rate note. OTC = over the counter. Bullets are non-amortized bonds that pay face value upon maturity.

Source: Benzie (1992), p. 16.

Eurocurrency Bond Issues, 1990–1995 (US$ billions)[a]

Table 12.6

Currency	1990	1991	1992	1993	1994	1995
U.S. dollar	70.0	81.6	103.2	147.7	149.4	144.4
Japanese yen	22.8	36.0	33.7	44.4	67.3	64.5
Deutschemark	18.3	20.5	33.8	54.7	31.6	72.7
Pound sterling	20.9	25.8	23.3	42.7	30.4	21.6
French franc	9.4	17.0	24.3	39.9	27.4	12.7
Italian lira	5.4	9.0	7.7	11.5	17.0	11.7
Canadian dollar	6.4	23.7	15.6	29.3	13.3	2.7
Dutch guilder	0.8	3.3	6.5	11.1	11.9	14.7
Australian dollar	5.2	4.4	4.9	3.5	7.6	10.0
ECU	17.9	32.7	21.3	7.1	7.6	7.1
Swedish kroner	0.3	1.3	0.9	0.5	1.7	0.3
Hong Kong dollar	0	0	0	0.9	1.7	0.8
Danish kroner	0.2	0.3	0.4	1.1	0.7	2.8
Finnish markka	1.2	0.8	0.1	0.1	0.4	0
Other	1.3	1.7	0.4	0.1	0.4	5.2
Total	180.1	258.1	276.1	394.6	368.4	371.2

[a]Totals include a small amount of foreign bonds in addition to Eurobonds.

Source: OECD, *Financial Market Trends*, Nos. 61, 63 (June 1995, February 1996): pp. 120, 88; and Bank of England *Quarterly Bulletin* 35, No. 2 (May 1995): p. 149.

The Eurobond market received a big boost from the introduction of an electronic bond clearing system, Euroclear, in December 1968. Before then, trading in Eurobonds was extremely costly and risky because of the international nature of the transactions. Moreover, since Eurobonds are bearer bonds, they carry no proof of ownership, and, if stolen, they are as good as cash. The electronic clearing, safekeeping, and recordkeeping functions of Euroclear (and as of January 1971, its competitor Cedel) resolved these transactions problems in the Eurobond market.

bought deal: innovation whereby the terms of the bond issue (coupon rate, size, and price) are set prior to the announcement of the issue instead of on the formal offering day, usually two weeks later.

The innovative character of the Eurobond market was again demonstrated with the introduction of the **bought deal** in 1979. In a bought deal, the terms of the bond issue (coupon rate, size, and price) are set prior to the announcement of the issue instead of on the formal offering day, usually two weeks later. This innovation reduced the risk to the Eurobond buyer of unanticipated changes in interest rates that could affect the bond's terms. Other innovations were **convertible Eurobonds** and **warrant Eurobonds**. Convertible Eurobonds are fixed rate Eurobonds that can be exchanged for either shares of common stock or currency. Warrant Eurobonds carry warrants, permitting the bondholder to make subsequent purchases of either common stock or other bonds. They are similar to convertible bonds, except that the warrants may be detached and each piece sold separately, thereby creating a straight Eurobond plus a long term equity call option. The high interest rate environment of the early 1980s led to the inauguration of the **streaker bond**, which was a zero coupon Eurobond, named because it was naked of any coupon. The advantage of a streaker bond, just as for pure discount domestic bonds, is that the yield is guaranteed if the bond is held to maturity. For the issuer of zero coupon bonds, the annual increase in the bond's value as it approaches maturity is tax deductible, although it does not need to be paid out as an actual cash flow. As FIs in the Euromarket engineered novel financial products, the volume of activity grew.

convertible Eurobonds: fixed rate Eurobonds that can be exchanged for either shares of common stock or currency.

warrant Eurobonds: fixed rate Eurobonds that carry warrants, permitting the bondholder to make subsequent purchases of either common stock or other bonds.

streaker bond: a zero coupon Eurobond.

global: a bond that is issued simultaneously in several financial markets throughout the world and settled on Euromarkets.

Another innovation is the **global**, a financial instrument that is a hybrid between a Eurobond and a foreign bond, pioneered in 1989 by the World Bank. The global is a bond that is issued simultaneously in several financial markets throughout the world and settled on Euromarkets. However, it is registered for sale in the country whose currency is the currency of denomination for the issue. For example, the World Bank's 7.625%, 30 year bonds, due in 2023, were issued in U.S. dollars (US$1.25 billion face value); they were registered with the SEC but placed (that is, sold to Funds Surplus Units) throughout the world. Globals share some aspects of Eurobonds because they were U.S. dollar-denominated bonds simultaneously issued in London, Tokyo, and other financial centers. However, they retain some aspects of foreign bonds since they were also issued in the United States for foreign borrowers. Globals have been issued in U.S. dollars, Japanese yen, and Deutschemark. In each case, they are registered with the authority in the currency of denomination of the issue. In 1993 global bond issues totaled US$34.4 billion. In 1994 the World Bank issued the first multicurrency global. Participation in underwriting Eurobonds and globals is a source of prestige for FIs.

The largest category of issuers of Eurobonds is private companies, which seek to raise capital in the most cost-effective manner possible. In recent years, however, the public sector, both national and supranational, has been a more active issuer in the Eurobond market. A **supranational** is a regional or an international public FI that transcends national boundaries. Examples of supranational public FIs are the World Bank, the International Monetary Fund, the Bank for International Settlements, and the European Bank for Reconstruction and Development.

supranational: a regional or international public FI that transcends national boundaries.

The Eurobond's credit quality is determined by the default risk characteristics of the issuer. About 60% of new Eurobond issues are rated by bond rating agencies such as Moody's Investors Services and Standard & Poor's Corporation. The rating standards for both services are:

S & P	Moody's	Definitions
AAA	Aaa	Highest quality; minimum investment risk
AA	Aa	High quality; little investment risk
A	A	Good quality; favorable investment characteristics
BBB	Baa	Medium quality; some speculative characteristics
BB	Ba	Lower medium quality; speculative characteristics
B	B	Low quality; lacking characterics of desirable investments

Below Investment Grade:

S & P	Moody's	Definitions
CCC	Caa	Poor quality; predominantly speculative; default may occur or has occurred.
CC	Ca	Poorer quality; predominantly speculative; default may occur or has occurred.
C	C	Poorest quality; predominantly speculative; default may occur or has occurred.

The Eurobond market has a number of advantages for issuers:

1. The Eurobond market has enough volume to absorb frequent, large-size offerings.
2. Flexibility in the Eurobond market allows issuers to circumvent domestic disclosure, authorization, and listing requirements.
3. The costs of issue are low, ranging up to 2.5% of face value. Moreover, interest costs tend to be lower in the Eurobond market than in the domestic bond market. Kim and Stulz (1988) show that Eurobond rates tend to be lower than rates on comparable domestic bonds.

Investors also have reasons to prefer Eurobonds to similar risk domestic bonds:

1. Interest can be paid free of income tax or witholding taxes. The bearer form of issue of Eurobonds allows investors to maintain anonymity, perhaps to circumvent domestic exchange control regulations or income tax liabilities.
2. Because Eurobond issuers tend to be either well-known companies or sovereign governments, credit quality is excellent.
3. Secondary market trading is efficiently provided at low cost by electronic clearing houses such as Euroclear and Cedel.

Despite these advantages, Table 12.4 describes the 1995 decline in the Eurobond market, with market share declining from 58.8% in 1993 to 36.6% in 1995. The advantages to Eurobond market participation also apply to rapidly growing Euronotes, which appear to be expanding at the expense of the Eurobond market.

Checkpoint

1. Contrast Eurobonds with foreign bonds.
2. How are global bonds similar to Eurobonds? to foreign bonds?
3. Who are the major issuers of Eurobonds?
4. Describe the Eurobond's characteristics.

Euronotes   **Euronotes** are short (often less than one year until maturity) to medium term notes (denoted MTN); unsecured debt instruments that are securitized substitutes for non-negotiable Euroloans. Table 12.7 shows that the outstanding amounts of Euronotes have experienced a spectacular growth rate, almost doubling in size from 1993 to 1995. This growth was largely at the expense of other sectors of the Euromarket. Indeed, the **floating rate note (FRN)** first became an important Euronote product in the aftermath of the LDC debt crisis in the early 1980s, as investors fled the international bond markets. FRNs offer a variable interest rate that is reset periodically (usually semiannually or quarterly) according to some predetermined market interest rate formula.

> **floating rate notes (FRN):** Euronotes that offer a variable interest rate that is reset periodically (usually semiannually or quarterly) according to some predetermined market interest rate formula.

> **Euronotes:** short (often less than one year until maturity) to medium term notes (denoted MTN).

> **LIBID:** the London Interbank bid (as opposed to offer) rate.

The market formula is often set equal to the LIBOR plus a margin that is determined by the issuer's credit risk exposure, as well as by the issue's maturity. If the issuer has a high credit rating, the rate may be set below LIBOR and the FRN rate formula can be tied to the **LIBID**, which is the London Interbank bid (as opposed to offer) rate. Since the LIBID is the bid, or the rate charged for purchases of interbank funds, and LIBOR is the asked, or the rate charged for sales of interbank funds, the difference between them is the bid-asked spread in the interbank market, usually around $\frac{1}{8}$ point (although the spread is less for popular maturities such as three months). That is, a FI that borrows Eurocurrencies by purchasing interbank funds and immediately resells them on the interbank market (without transforming them in any way) can lock in a profit of around 12.5 basis points, since the interest cost on the borrowed funds (LIBID) is less than the interest earned (LIBOR) on the interbank sales.

As an indication of the spreads, the LIBID/LIBOR rates as of February 1994 were:

	LIBID	LIBOR
Overnight	$5\frac{7}{8}$	6
7 days	$5\frac{3}{4}$	$5\frac{7}{8}$
1 month	$5\frac{3}{4}$	$5\frac{13}{16}$
3 months	$5\frac{7}{8}$	$5\frac{31}{32}$
6 months	$5\frac{7}{8}$	6
1 year	$5\frac{31}{32}$	$6\frac{1}{16}$

> **perpetual FRN:** a floating rate Euronote (FRN) that has no fixed maturity date.

> **mini-maxi FRN (collared floater):** a floating rate Euronote with both a cap and a floor on its interest rate.

At their inception, Euronotes were considered to be alternatives to Euroloans for nonfinancial firms and governments. However, as the market evolved, even banks began to issue FRNs to raise funds on the Euromarket. Since **perpetual FRNs**, which have no fixed maturity date, can be used as Tier 1 capital for the purposes of compliance with international risk adjusted capital regulations, they contributed to the market's growing acceptance by the banking industry.

Innovation contributed to the market's growth. A **mini-maxi FRN**, better known as a **collared floater**, (such as Lehman's SURFs, Step-Up Recovery Floaters) is a floating rate

Table 12.7	**Euronote Transactions, 1993–1995[a] (US$ billions)**			
	Transaction	1993	1994	1995 Q1
	Euronotes, amounts outstanding:	255.8	406.1	461.6
	of which are medium term notes (MTN)	146.6	292.0	347.1
	Euronote facilities, announcements:	117.4	193.3	54.9
	of which are commercial paper	24.2	36.4	6.8
	of which are MTN	92.7	157.0	48.1
	of which are NIF/RUF	0.5	0	0

[a]Totals are for those transactions settled through the electronic clearinghouse, Euroclear. 1995 figures are for the first quarter only.

Source: "Financial Market Developments," Bank of England *Quarterly Bulletin* (February and May 1995): pp. 27 and 148, respectively.

Euronote with both a cap and a floor on its interest rate. That is, there is both a maximum and a minimum rate beyond which the rate on the FRN cannot go, whatever happens to LIBOR.

An important innovation in the Euronote market is Eurocommercial paper. The evolution of syndicated Euroloans into Eurocommercial paper is a natural outgrowth of the move toward greater securitization on all financial markets. During 1987–1990, the Eurocommercial paper market dominated the Euronote market; although that trend has reversed in recent years.

Eurocommercial paper: a securitized short term bearer note issued by a major corporation.

Eurocommercial Paper   A separate category of Euronotes is **Eurocommercial paper**, which is a securitized short term bearer note issued by a major corporation. While Euronotes can be medium term or can be issued by sovereign governments, Eurocommercial paper is issued only by private corporations in short maturities. It can be resold in a highly liquid secondary market. Most issues are pure discount zero coupons with maturities that range from 7 to 365 days. Since Eurocommercial paper is an unsecured loan, the issuers are highly rated, blue chip corporations. Direct issuance of Eurocommercial paper is limited to those companies that obtain the highest liquidity credit ratings: P1 in Moody's and A1+ in Standard & Poor's.

revolving underwriting **facility (RUF): a** commitment by a syndicate of banks to buy any notes that cannot be sold to other investors.

Lesser credits can still access the Eurocommercial paper market with the help of banks. The earliest example of a Eurocommercial offering (New Zealand Shipping Corporation in December 1978) was made possible by the introduction of a new financing device: the **revolving underwriting facility (RUF)**. The RUF is a commitment by a syndicate of banks to buy any notes that cannot be sold to other investors. If this sounds a lot like a securitized syndicated Euroloan, then that's because it is. Under a RUF, the issuing company is guaranteed its ability to sell its entire Eurocommercial paper offering. The Eurocommercial paper is issued with either a three month or a six month maturity. Upon maturity, new three month or six month Eurocommercial paper is issued to retire the previously issued paper. The issue continues to roll over for a period of time specified in the RUF, usually around five years. Thus, the banks in the syndicate agree to buy the company's Eurocommercial paper offerings, as needed, during each of the new issues during the life of the RUF.

The growth of Eurocommercial paper offerings using RUFs is a clear example of the replacement of an unsecuritized financial instrument (syndicated Euroloans) with a securitized version (RUFs of Eurocommercial paper). The shift occurred because of the change in the fortunes of the banking system. Before the LDC debt crisis in the early 1980s, the world's largest banks were considered the highest quality credits in the world. The LDC debt crisis began a period of recurring banking crises that affected every banking system in the world. Some examples are the thrift crisis in the United States; the monetary impact of the unification of Germany; and the bursting of the property price bubble in Japan. All of these crises have had an impact on the banking system's credit quality.

How did this deterioration in the condition of the banking system lead to the shift toward securitized financial instruments? If borrowing companies have lower credit risks than their banks, they do not need the bank to borrow on their behalf. Borrowers are better off going to the credit markets directly and borrowing on the basis of their own credit quality. This implies the issuance of debt securities directly to the Funds Surplus Units rather than using the banking system as an intermediary. Issuers found that they could reduce their interest costs if they used a RUF to issue Eurocommercial paper as opposed to a syndicated Euroloan.

In the 1980s Merrill, Credit Suisse, and First Boston were some of the FIs that were developing a brisk business in distributing the Eurocommercial paper that they obtained under RUFs. They, and other FIs, decided that they would like to be able to bid for the Eurocommercial paper offering when they felt that they could resell it profitably. This led to a modification in the RUF, called a **note issuance facility (NIF)**. Under a NIF, the FIs in the RUF-issuing syndicate could bid, along with other potential buyers, for some amount of the Eurocommercial paper offering. Under the straight RUF, the FIs bought the Eurocommercial paper only if there was some left over after it was offered to other investors. Under the NIF, the syndicate could also bid for the new issue in a prespecified, and highly cumbersome, manner called the **tender panel**. The tender panel specified the preset maturities and amounts that the syndicate could bid on. It injected an inflexibility into the market that could delay the transfer of funds by as much as a week. To avoid these restrictions, the NIF has been largely replaced by the **tap offering**, which is a continuous offering of Eurocommercial paper with different rates for different maturities—that is, an unrestricted NIF.

The use of issuance facilities has enabled lower credit quality issuers to enter the Eurocommercial paper market with the backing of bank syndicates. Figure 12.8 shows that only 4% of all Eurocommercial paper is unrated.[6] Eurocommercial paper rates depend on the credit quality of the issuer, 58.9% of which received the highest credit ratings. The dominance of Eurodollar issues in the distribution of Eurocommercial paper currencies is shown in Figure 12.8. Corporations are the largest group of issuers, with 51% of all new issues; banks are second, with 40% of the number of new Eurocommercial paper facilities.

note issuance facility (NIF): a practice that allows the FIs in the RUF-issuing syndicate to bid, along with other potential buyers, for some amount of the Eurocommercial paper offering.

tender panel: a means of specifying the preset maturities and amounts that the syndicate could bid on under a NIF.

tap offering: a continuous offering of Eurocommercial paper with different rates for different maturities; an unrestricted NIF.

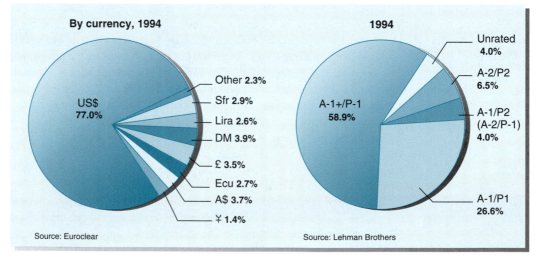

By currency, 1994 (Source: Euroclear):
- US$ 77.0%
- Other 2.3%
- Sfr 2.9%
- Lira 2.6%
- DM 3.9%
- £ 3.5%
- Ecu 2.7%
- A$ 3.7%
- ¥ 1.4%

1994 (Source: Lehman Brothers):
- A-1+/P-1 58.9%
- Unrated 4.0%
- A-2/P2 6.5%
- A-1/P2 (A-2/P-1) 4.0%
- A-1/P1 26.6%

Source: C. Olivier, "US Corporates Ready to Make Euro-CP Debut", *Corporate Finance*, February 1995, p. 36.

Figure 12.8

---

[6] Stigum (1990), p. 1079.

The Euromarkets' freedom from regulation has enabled FIs to innovate and offer Eurocurrency assets that combine cash flow shifting with risk transfer services. In the next section, we will see how Euromarkets have evolved to allow Funds Deficit Units to hedge their currency and interest rate risk exposures while also borrowing to finance capital investment projects.

Checkpoint

1. What are Euronotes?
2. Compare Euronotes to Eurocommercial paper.
3. Contrast RUF, NIF, and tap offerings.
4. How did the Euronote market change over the 1987–1993 period? To what do you attribute this change?

Risk Shifting in Euromarkets

Eurobook: a portfolio of Euromarket assets and liabilities.

FIs make markets in the Euro products on both sides of their balance sheets holding a **Eurobook**, which is a portfolio of Euromarket assets and liabilities. In the Eurobook, the FI holds both Euro deposits and Euro assets, such as Euroloans and Eurobonds. As we have seen, cash flow timing can be altered by transacting on either the asset or liability side of the Euromarket. However, comparisons of the type of transactions on each side of the Eurobook can provide insights into another goal of financial intermediation: risk transfer. Systematic differences between the two sides of the Eurobook demonstrate the FIs' offerings of risk transfer services.

Interest rate risk transfers are accomplished through duration transformation between Euro assets and liabilities, whereas currency risk transfers are accomplished through Eurocurrency transformation between Euro assets and liabilities. Thus, if Funds Surplus Units demand short term, interest-sensitive deposit liabilities for their flexibility in an environment of interest rate increases, whereas Funds Deficit Units demand long term, fixed rate loans as a hedge against interest rate increases, then Eurobanks can provide both with risk sharing services by running a Eurobook with a positive duration gap. That is, the duration of Euro assets exceeds the duration of Euro liabilities. The FI takes on the risk exposure to interest rate increases and provides risk reducing Euro products to both Funds Surplus and Deficit customers. Similarly, if the FI's customers are exposed to exchange rate risk exposure, the Eurobank can transform the currencies used to denominate the Euro assets or liabilities in order to offer risk shifting services.

We can measure the amount of risk that Eurobanks absorb during intermediation by using the risk measurement concepts we have already developed. Interest rate risk shifting services can be measured by the Eurobook's duration gap (from Chapter 7), whereas foreign exchange rate risk shifting services can be measured using the Eurobook's net currency exposure (from Chapter 8). Let's examine the risk shifting services offered by the hypothetical London-based Eurobank, Ltd. shown in Table 12.8.

Table 12.8

Eurobank Ltd.[a] (Restated in £ millions)

1 year Eurodollar loan	£10m	3 mo. Eurodollar CD	£50m
5% annual coupon, priced at par		3% p.a.	
2 year Euroyen note	£60m	6 mo. Euro–DM CD	£45m
7% annual coupon, price = £102/£100 par		2.5% p.a.	
10 year Euro–DM bond	£75m	6 mo. Euroyen CD	£50m
6% annual coupon, price = £95/£100 par		2% p.a.	

[a]The Euro CDs are pure discount instruments since they have no remaining coupon payments until maturity. All Euro assets and liabilities in this Eurobook are fixed rate.

Eurobank's duration[7] of assets is

$$D_A = \sum_{i=1}^{N} \frac{MV_i}{MV_A} D_i = \frac{10}{145}(1) + \frac{60}{145}(1.935) + \frac{75}{145}(7.74) = 4.87 \text{ years}$$

The duration of liabilities is

$$D_L = \sum_{j=1}^{N} \frac{MV_j}{MV_L} D_i = \frac{50}{145}(0.25) + \frac{45}{145}(0.5) + \frac{50}{145}(0.5) = 0.414 \text{ years}$$

The duration gap of the Eurobook is

$$DG = 4.87 - \frac{145}{145}(0.414) = +4.456 \text{ years}$$

The positive duration gap implies that Eurobank, Ltd. is absorbing the risk of interest rate increases from its customers. Essentially, the risk of loss in market value associated with interest rate increases is transferred from the multinational corporations and sovereign governments that are Eurobank's customers to Eurobank itself. Since the FI specializes in risk management, Eurobank, Ltd. can manage this risk exposure better than its customers can.

We can also evaluate the transfer of foreign exchange rate risk between Eurobank, Ltd. and its customers. The net currency exposure, evaluated in terms of pound sterling,[8] is

$$\text{Net Currency Exposure US\$} = \pounds 10m - \pounds 50m = -\pounds 40m$$

$$\text{Net Currency Exposure DM} = \pounds 75m - \pounds 45m = +\pounds 30m$$

$$\text{Net Currency Exposure yen} = \pounds 60m - \pounds 50m = +\pounds 10m$$

Eurobank has positions in all three currencies. In the U.S. dollar, Eurobank is short (exposed to increases in the U.S. dollar-pound sterling exchange rate). Eurobank is long in both the Deutschemark and the Japanese yen, and is thereby exposed to decreases in those exchange rates. Eurobank has provided risk insurance services to its customers by absorbing their currency risk exposure and taking mismatched positions in each of the currencies.

We can utilize these risk measures to estimate the impact of unanticipated interest rate and exchange rate fluctuations on Eurobank's profitability. For example, if all interest rates (across all Eurocurrencies) increase by 1%, then the approximate loss in the market value of Eurobank's equity is

$$\Delta E \approx -DG(A) \left(\frac{\Delta y}{1+y} \right) = -4.456(\pounds 145m)(.01) = -\pounds 6.46m$$

Similarly, the impact of a 1% increase in the value of the U.S. dollar coupled with 1% declines in the Deutschemark and the yen result in a loss to Eurobank, Ltd. of

$$-\pounds 40m(.01) + \pounds 30m(-.01) + \pounds 10m(-.01) = -\pounds 800,000$$

---

[7] To calculate the 1.935 year duration of the Euroyen note, use the yield of 5.91% p.a. implied by the note's premium price. Applying the formula from Chapter 7 to the Euro-DM bond, we find that the yield to maturity is 6.7% p.a. and the duration is 7.74 years.

[8] Since the home currency of the British Eurobank, Ltd. is the pound sterling all foreign exchange rate fluctuations are evaluated with respect to the pound sterling. Thus, exchange rates are stated as the number of units of currency per pound sterling.

The FI's interest rate and exchange rate risk exposures depend on the duration gap and net currency exposure of the Eurobook positions. There are no typical positions for FIs; instead, the Eurobooks' compositions respond to customer demand for risk shifting services.

Checkpoint

1.   What is the Eurobook?
2.   How can you analyze the Eurobook to determine the FI's provision of interest rate risk hedging services?
3.   How can you analyze the Eurobook to determine the FI's provision of exchange rate risk hedging services?

Demand for Risk Shifting in the Euromarket   FIs in the Euromarket offer currency risk hedging services by transforming financial securities denominated in one currency into another currency. Sometimes they do this by intermediating between two customers that have opposite currency requirements—that is, a customer who wants to hold Euro-Deutschemark is paired with another customer who wants to sell Euro-Deutschemark. However, sometimes the FI takes one side of the transaction, acting as a dealer, by injecting the desired currency into the Euromarket. Thus, the FI can supply Eurocurrencies by transforming its domestic transactions into Euromarket transactions. This switch occurs when, say, a German bank uses domestic Deutschemark deposits to buy U.S. dollars and deposits them in a bank in London. This transaction creates a new Eurodollar deposit, which can be used to finance a Eurodollar loan. FIs hedge their customers' exchange rate risk exposure by maintaining a mismatch between the Eurocurrencies of their liabilities and their assets.

In the early years of the Euromarket, there was an overwhelming demand for transformation of local currencies into Eurodollars. Indeed, that was the primary focus of the communist countries that inaugurated the market. Currently, however, the distribution of transactions across Eurocurrencies varies across countries. Demand for Euro-DM and Euroyen is almost equal to, and sometimes exceeds, the demand for Eurodollars. Indeed, Table 12.9 shows

Table 12.9

Currency Distribution of External Bond Offerings By Country, 1995 (US$ billions)

Country	Euro–Dollar	Euro–Swiss Franc	Euroyen	Euro–DM	Euro–Sterling	Other
Australia	2.8	0	3.4	0	0	4.0[a]
Canada	10.5	0	1.9	1.2	0	1.4[b]
France	5.8	2.4	2.2	5.1	0.2	8.9[c]
Germany	14.9	6.5	7.1	28.3	0.8	13.5[d]
Italy	4.3	0	6.8	0.2	0.1	2.2
Japan	11.6	5.3	17.5	2.9	0.8	0.7
Sweden	4.9	0.3	7.8	3.4	0	5.0
United Kingdom	8.1	0.3	0.8	0	14.2	2.2
United States	55.3	2.7	2.8	4.7	1.5	6.5[e]

[a]Other represents $3.8 billion in Euro–Australian dollar bonds.

[b]Other includes $0.7 billion in Euro–Canadian dollar bonds.

[c]Other includes $4.8 billion in Euro–French franc and $0.3 billion in ECU bonds.

[d]Other includes $0.5 billion in Euro–Australian dollar bonds.

[e]Other includes $0.3 billion in ECU; $0.6 billion in Euro–Australian dollar; $0.8 billion in Euro–Canadian dollar bonds.

Source: OECD, *Financial Market Trends*, No. 63 (February 1996): p. 60.

Table
12.10

Average Maturity of Euro credits, 1990–1995 (in years/months)

Region	1990	1991	1992	1993	1994	1995
OECD countries	6/0	5/1	4/8	4/3	5/0	5/3
Central and Eastern Europe	12/11	NA	NA	NA	NA	NA
Developing countries	9/6	7/7	6/8	5/6	6/9	5/7
Other	8/8	3/3	6/11	5/3	5/0	5/1
General average	7/9	5/5	5/9	4/5	5/1	5/3

Source: OECD, *Financial Market Trends*, Nos. 61, 63 (June 1995, February 1996): pp. 111, 80.

that in 1995, Italian Eurobond issuers managed their currency risk by offering $6.8 billion in Euroyen bond issues, which was far more than their bond offerings in any other Eurocurrency.

Similarly, the demand for interest rate risk shifting services differs among Euromarket participants. Analysis of Eurobook duration gaps suggests that Eurobanks provide considerable interest rate risk insurance to nonbanks. British banks tend to be the most aggressive, running large positive duration gaps in their Eurobooks. Therefore, they are absorbing the risks of interest rate increases from their clients. However, the most active risk shifting is done by **consortium banks**, which are owned by a group of other, usually large, banks that are well-established in their own domestic markets. Their ability to diversify their risk across the bank owners of the consortium has given these FIs a comparative advantage in offering interest rate risk transfer services on the Euromarket. In contrast, the interbank market is characterized by matched book transactions, suggesting that the motivation for these transactions is cash flow timing, not interest rate risk shifting.

The positive duration gaps observed in Eurobooks leads us to conclude that FIs hold Eurocurrency assets with longer durations than their Eurocurrency liabilities. That is, Eurocurrency borrowers prefer longer durations than do Eurocurrency lenders. Table 12.10 shows the average maturity of Euroloans by region. Over the period 1990–1995, the average maturity declined from 7 years, 9 months to 5 years, 3 months. As might be expected, the demand for longer maturity credits was greater in developing countries and Central and Eastern Europe than in the industrialized OECD nations.

consortium banks: banks that are owned by a group of other, usually large, banks that are well-established in their own domestic markets.

Checkpoint

1. What are the two motivations for Euromarket activity?
2. How do we observe risk transfer in Euromarkets?
3. What types of interest rate risk shifting services have been offered in Euromarkets over the past decades of rapid expansion?
4. Which Euromarket products offer the greatest number of risk transfer services? the smallest number?
5. How has the demand for exchange rate risk transfer services changed over the years?
6. What is the most widely used Eurocurrency? Why? What does this imply about the currency risk shifting services offered by FIs?

FIs Transfer Risk Using Off-Balance Sheet Positions   The mismatches in the Eurobook summarize the FIs' overall risk taking activities, netted out over all of its customers. However, risk transfer is more efficiently performed using off-balance sheet activity. Rather than using the FI's funds to offer an interest rate risk sensitive customer a FRN, for example, the FI can offer

CME		SIMEX		LIFFE		
7:20 A.M. – 2 P.M.		6:30 P.M. – 2:20 A.M.		2:30 A.M. – 10 A.M.		
Open CME	Close CME	Open SIMEX	Close SIMEX	Open LIFFE	Open U.S.	Close LIFFE
7:20 A.M.	2 P.M.	6:30 P.M.	2:20 A.M.	2:30 A.M.	7:20 A.M.	10 A.M.
Day T					Day T + 1	

Source: T. Schneeweis and J. Yaw, "Financial Futures Markets" in D. Logue, ed., *The WG&L Handbook of Financial Markets,* (Cincinatti: Warren, Gorham, & Lambert, 1995), p. 415.

Figure 12.9 Trading hours of Eurodollar futures markets. (Central Daylight Savings Time)

insurance against interest rate decreases using a forward rate agreement. Because off-balance sheet activities are promises, or contingent claims that require no up-front payments, they are less costly for both the FI and the customer. Three off-balance sheet Euro products permit FIs to transfer interest rate or currency risk exposures: (1) Euro futures; (2) forward rate agreements (FRAs); and (3) Eurocurrency swaps.[9]

Euro Futures   Eurodollar CD futures began trading on the International Monetary Market (IMM) at the Chicago Mercantile Exchange (CME) in December 1981 and now represent the world's most actively traded futures contract. The Euro CD futures contract also trades on the London International Financial Futures Exchange (LIFFE) and on Singapore's SIMEX (Singapore International Monetary Exchange). The three exchanges' staggered trading hours (see Fig. 12.9) allow almost round-the-clock trading in this futures contract, although only the SIMEX and IMM contracts are completely interchangeable.[10] The **Eurodollar CD futures contract** is the obligation to buy/sell a $1 million face value, 91 day Euro CD at a predetermined rate, called the futures rate, on a predetermined date called the delivery date. Although this is the formal definition of the contract, the Euro CD futures contract uses **cash settlement** only. That is, to comply with your obligations under the Euro CD futures contract, you could never deliver an actual $1 million 91 day Euro CD. Upon delivery date, the value of that contract is determined in cash so that only cash, not securities, changes hands between the two parties to the futures contract. Cash settlement takes place on the third Monday of each March, June, September, and December. The minimum price movement, the **tick value**, is approximately $25, or one basis point.[11]

Cash settlement is the secret to the phenomenal success of the Euro CD futures contract. When originally introduced, the LIFFE contract required physical delivery of a Euro CD upon maturity. However, that was soon changed to compete with the less costly IMM cash-settled contract. When the Federal Reserve surprised financial markets in February 1994 with its unanticipated decision to raise short term rates, the volume of activity in Eurodollar CD futures broke all records. It was the first time on any single futures market that volume had exceeded more that one million contracts in one trading session. On February 4, 1994, daily trading volume was an unbelievable $1.5 *trillion.* In contrast, on that same day, a total of around $20 billion worth of equities changed hands on the New York Stock Exchange. **Open interest**, or outstanding contracts, often hits 2.5 million contracts as investors use the market

Eurodollar CD futures contract: the obligation to buy/sell a $1 million face value, 91 day Euro CD at a predetermined rate, called the futures rate, on a predetermined date called the delivery date.

cash settlement: the practice of determining, upon delivery date, the value of the contract determined in cash only, not securities.

tick value: minimum price movement.

open interest: outstanding contracts

---

[9] These off-balance sheet instruments are discussed more generally in Chapters 18 and 20. In Chapter 19, we discuss Eurodollar futures options.

[10] Figure 12.9 shows that there is no trading during the important hours 2:00 P.M. to 6:30 P.M., Central Daylight Savings Time. At least one U.S. banker attributed the bankruptcy of several firms during the market crash of October 1987 to this trading gap.

[11] Recall from Chapter 7 that the dollar value of a 91 day $1 million face value basis point is $0.0001(\frac{91}{360})(\$1m) =$ $25.28.

to hedge the impact of short maturity interest rate fluctuations far into the future. Table 12.11 shows three years of turnover and open interest on the major Euro futures contracts. Although the Eurodollar CD contract on CME has the largest volume, all Eurocurrency interest rate futures experienced rapid growth during the period 1992–1994. By way of comparison, the 1994 annual turnover on the U.S. Treasury bond contract traded on the Chicago Board of Trade in 1994 was $9.996 trillion, which is less than the volume for all Eurocurrency futures contracts except the Eurolira.

Since the Euro CD futures contract trades on organized futures exchanges, all contractual obligations are backed by each exchange's futures clearing corporation. The clearing corporation acts as a third-party guarantor to the agreement between the short and long position in the transaction. If either party reneges on its obligations, the clearing corporation will make the required payment to the counterparty.

The value of the Euro CD futures contract is determined by the difference between the futures rate and LIBOR (as measured using the average three month deposit rate quoted, sometime during the last 80 minutes of trading, by a random selection of 12 of the top 20 banks in the London Eurodollar market). The Euro CD futures contract is priced using the **IMM Index**, which is 100 minus the annualized Eurodollar futures rate in percentage form. The Euro CD futures rate, like the U.S. Treasury bill yield, is stated as a discount yield, based on a 360 day year. Thus, if the Euro CD futures rate was 5.5%, then the IMM Index futures price would be stated as $100 - 5.5 = 94.5$. This would not reflect its dollar price, which would be determined by the discounted value of $1 million to be received in 91 days, that is (from Chapter 7 where F is the face value; d is the discount yield; and t is the time to

IMM Index: 100 minus the annualized Eurodollar futures rate in percentage form.

Table 12.11

Exchange-Traded Eurocurrency Futures Contracts
Three Month Interest Rate Futures[a] (US$ billions)

Contract	Exchange	1992	1993	1994
Eurodollar	CME			
Annual turnover		60,531	64,411	104,823
Open interest at year end		1,325	2,117	2,384
Sterling	LIFFE			
Annual turnover		9,975	9,087	12,713
Open interest at year end		152	294	313
Euromark	LIFFE			
Annual turnover		7,812	12,883	18,080
Open interest at year end		248	405	452
Paris Interbank	MATIF			
Annual turnover		6,045	10,506	11,909
Open interest at year end		91	254	187
Euroyen	TIFFE			
Annual turnover		11,844	21,043	36,631
Open interest at year end		321	894	1,103
Eurolira	LIFFE			
Annual turnover		325	953	2,173
Open interest at year end		7	59	62

[a]CME is the IMM on the Chicago Mercantile Exchange. LIFFE is the London International Financial Futures Exchange. MATIF is the Marché a Terme International de France. TIFFE is the Tokyo International Financial Futures Exchange.

Source: "Statistical Information About Derivatives." Bank of England *Quarterly Bulletin* (May 1995): p. 189.

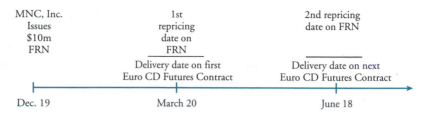

Figure 12.10   Timeline for the FRN transaction.

maturity):

$$P_F = F\left(1 - \frac{dt}{360}\right) = \$1m\left(1 - \frac{.055(91)}{360}\right) = \$986,097$$

If, upon delivery date, LIBOR was 5.75%, then the long position (the counterparty that was obligated to buy the Euro CD upon delivery) would lose, while the short position would gain. This is because the futures contract requires the long position to buy something worth $\$1m(1 - \frac{.0575(91)}{360}) = \$985,465$ for $986,097. The only money that would change hands, however, is the cash difference, that is, $986,097 minus $985,465, or $632. Thus, the sum, π_F, due at settlement of the futures contract, is

$$\pi_F = F\left(1 - \frac{d_m t}{360}\right) - F\left(1 - \frac{d_F t}{360}\right) = F\frac{t}{360}(d_F - d_m)$$

$$= \$1m\left(\frac{91}{360}\right)(.0575 - .055) = \$632$$

where d_m = the LIBOR upon settlement date, d_F = the futures rate; F = the face value, set equal to $1 million; and t = the time to maturity of the Eurodollar CD, set equal to 91 days. Note that the short position earns a positive payoff on the futures contract because interest rates increased from 5.5% (when the futures position was put on) by 25 basis points. Thus, the gain is 25 $1 million face value, 91 day basis points, each of which is worth $25.28, for a total gain of $632 (= 25 × $25.28).

Since the Euro CD futures' payoff is determined by interest rate fluctuations, it can be used to hedge against interest rate risk. Suppose that a multinational corporation named MNC, Inc. has issued a two year FRN, with a face value of $10 million, which is reset quarterly to equal LIBOR (currently standing at 6% p.a. in the example). MNC is worried that if LIBOR increases, its interest costs will also increase. MNC's FI can offer a solution: a short position in a Euro CD futures contract. MNC sells ten $1 million 91 day Euro CD futures at the current futures rate of 6%.[12] This implies an IMM Index price of 94 and a cash price of $10m(1 - \frac{.06(91)}{360}) = \$9,848,333$. The delivery date happens to fall on the first repricing date of the FRN, March 20. Figure 12.10 shows the timeline of events.

Suppose that MNC's worst fears are realized and that in the next three months, LIBOR increases by 30 basis points. If all rates increase by the same amount, on March 20, the Euro CD futures' delivery date, LIBOR is 6.30%. MNC must pay the higher interest rate on the FRN, but as compensation, it receives a positive payoff on its short Euro CD futures hedge of

$$\pi_F = F\frac{t}{360}(r_F - r_m) = -\$10m\frac{91}{360}(.06 - .063) = \$7,583$$

---

[12] A short position is denoted by a negative face value amount.

The payoff on the futures hedge is exactly equal to the additional interest that MNC will pay on its FRN. At an unchanged LIBOR, MNC expected to make quarterly interest payments of $10m($\frac{91}{360}$)(.06) = \$151,667. However, at the higher LIBOR, MNC's quarterly interest payment increases to $10m($\frac{91}{360}$)(.063) = \$159,250, an increase of \$7,583. The futures position negates any impact that unanticipated interest rate changes would have had on its FRN interest costs.

This futures transaction protects MNC from interest rate risk for the first FRN coupon payment only. To fully hedge against the impact of unanticipated interest rates, MNC would have to undertake a series of futures contracts, each with a delivery date that coincided with each one of the FRN repricing dates. Since the Euro CD futures market is very liquid, contracts are traded as far as three years into the future. However, the volume of trading drops off markedly after the first year's contracts.

Luckily for MNC, the quarterly repricing dates happened to coincide with the delivery dates on the Euro CD futures contracts. If this coincidence had not occurred, then MNC would not be able to achieve this "perfect" hedge against the risk of unanticipated interest rate changes. Moreover, if the FRN repriced semiannually rather than quarterly, the standardized Euro CD futures contract would not match MNC's FRN cash flows. Because the Euro CD futures contract is traded on an organized futures exchange, the terms of the contract (face value, delivery date, minimum price movement, etc.) are all fixed. To customize the contract, so as to better match the terms of the FRN, MNC would have to turn to the forward market.

Checkpoint

1. Why are off-balance sheet items useful in providing risk transfer services?
2. What accounted for the enormous success of the Eurodollar CD futures contract?
3. How can the Euro CD futures contract be used to hedge interest rate risk on the Euromarket?

Forward Rate Agreements   The forward rate agreement (FRA) evolved from the British "forward forward" market. The **forward rate agreement (FRA)** is an over the counter Eurodollar CD futures contract, in which all the terms are determined by the two counterparties rather than being standardized by the futures exchange.[13] Thus, if MNC issued its FRN on January 19 instead of December 19, it could arrange a FRA that delivers on its first repricing date, April 20. MNC could not do this in the Euro CD futures market since delivery dates are set by the exchange and cannot be altered. Since using the FRA, MNC would be contracting on January 19 for a forward delivery of a three month Euro CD to be delivered on April 20, we say that MNC is doing "3s against 6s." That is, delivery date is three months from now (on April 20) for a Euro CD that matures six months from now (July 18).

Suppose that the LIBOR on January 19 is 6.10%, increasing to 6.40% on April 20. If the FRA is positioned on April 20, the r_{FRA} is 6.10%. The payoff on April 20, as before, is

$$\pi_F = F\frac{t}{360}(r_{FRA} - r_m) = -\$10\text{m}\frac{91}{360}(.061 - .064) = \$7,583$$

However, there is one difference between the payoff on the futures contract and the FRA. The interest differential of \$7,583 is discounted back to the delivery date using the market rate of

forward rate agreement (FRA): an over the counter Eurodollar CD futures contract, in which all the terms are determined by the two counterparties rather than being standardized by the futures exchange.

---

[13] Although the terms of the FRA are negotiable, the British Banker's Association sets standards. This reduced the cost of writing FRAs and also assured that the FRA would not be subject to the 10% UK tax on gaming threatened because of the speculative cash settlement of the contract.

interest (discounted on an actual 360 day basis for Eurodollars and an actual 365 day basis for Eurosterling). Thus, the payoff on April 20 on the FRA is

$$\pi_{FRA} = \frac{F\dfrac{t}{360}(r_{FRA} - r_m)}{1 + \dfrac{r_m t}{360}}$$

$$= \frac{-\$10m\dfrac{91}{360}(.061 - .064)}{1 + \dfrac{.064(91)}{360}} = \$7,462$$

Since MNC is concerned about interest rate increases, we say that MNC buys the FRA to lock in a fixed rate of interest. The FRA seller obtains a floating rate. When interest rates increase, the FRA buyer gains. When interest rates decrease, the FRA seller gains. The majority of FRAs are denominated in Eurodollars, but other Eurocurrencies are available as well.

The FRA is enforceable only if the counterparties act in good faith. MNC is relying on the reputation of the counterparty to assure that it will honor the FRA's commitments. Indeed, only those regular participants with a reputation for integrity obtained over the course of continual market activity have access to FRAs. It is too risky to do a deal with an unknown counterparty that may or may not be around when the delivery date arrives. Eurocurrency brokers are important to FRA market participants, for they identify potential counterparties.

Checkpoint

1. Compare the Eurodollar CD futures contract to the forward rate agreement.

2. Under what circumstances would you prefer the FRA to the Eurodollar CD futures contract?

3. Under what circumstances would you prefer the Eurodollar CD futures contract to the FRA?

4. Why is the FRA riskier than the Euro CD futures?

Eurocurrency swap: an exchange between two counterparties of either the currency of denomination or the form of interest (fixed versus floating rate) payable on debt instruments.

Eurocurrency Swaps   Whether you call it a "swap," as Americans do, or a "switch," as the British call it, the name fits. A **Eurocurrency swap** is an exchange between two counterparties of either the currency of denomination or the form of interest (fixed versus floating rate) payable debt instruments. By permitting FIs to exploit any price differentials across financial markets, swaps bring prices closer into alignment.

Swaps make financial markets more efficient by crossing over barriers to transactions and connecting once isolated corners of the financial world. In a swap, all parties gain, because they have access to financial markets that they cannot access directly. Whether their access is limited because of lack of information or governmental restrictions and controls, the swap market circumvents these limitations and allows a freer flow of financial transactions.

A swap can be viewed as a portfolio of spot and forward transactions. If a corporate borrower issues floating rate Eurodollar bonds but prefers fixed rate bonds, an interest rate swap can be arranged. On each coupon payment date, the floating rate payment is exchanged for the counterparty's fixed rate payment. This is simply a series of FRAs, each of which has a delivery date corresponding to a consecutive coupon payment date. If interest rates increase, then the FRA seller gains since that counterparty has swapped a floating rate for a fixed rate payment. If interest rates decrease, then the FRA buyer gains since that buyer has swapped a fixed rate payment for a floating rate payment. If you string together enough FRAs with delivery dates that coincide with each coupon payment date, you have constructed an interest rate swap.

Similarly, a Eurocurrency swap is a series of FRAs in which the exchange is in terms of the currency of denomination. Thus, a Eurocurrency swap can enable, for example, the World Bank to extend a Eurodollar-denominated loan using Euroyen. A series of FRAs are linked together that obligate the World Bank to deliver Euroyen against Eurodollars on each coupon payment date. The World Bank agrees to make the Euroyen-denominated payments to its counterparty in exchange for the counterparty's payment of the World Bank's Eurodollar-denominated payments.

Why not simply structure the World Bank's loan in terms of Euroyen? The answer depends on the cost. The World Bank will examine both alternatives and choose the less expensive way to structure the Euroyen loan. Let's illustrate these calculations with a simple example. Suppose that a London-based FI has a customer that wants to borrow 100 million Euroyen for 270 days. The British FI can try to obtain a Euroyen deposit for 270 days to fund the loan, or it can take in Eurodollars and swap them for Euroyen. Today's yen–dollar spot exchange rate is US$0.0105, whereas the nine month forward rate is US$0.0108 per Japanese yen. The forward yen is selling at a premium because the forward rate exceeds the spot rate signalling expectations of a rising yen.

Figure 12.11 shows the two borrowing alternatives. In the top panel, the British FI obtains a 270 day Euroyen deposit of 100 million yen at a rate of 7% p.a. and makes the 100 million yen Euroyen loan earning 8% p.a. All interest rates are simple interest yields based on a 360 day year. In 270 days, the loan repays

$$L = 100m \left(1 + \frac{.08(270)}{360}\right) = JY106m$$

Simultaneously, the FI must repay the Euroyen time deposit:

$$D = 100m \left(1 + \frac{.07(270)}{360}\right) = JY105.25m$$

The profit on the transaction is 750,000 Japanese yen, which when converted into U.S. dollars at the forward rate of US$0.0108 yields a profit of US$8,100.

Consider now the bottom panel in Figure 12.11. At time period 0, the British FI obtains a 270 day Euro*dollar* deposit of US$1.05 million that pays 7.5% interest. The Eurodollars are converted into Euroyen at the spot rate of US$0.0105, yielding JY100 million, which are lent out at a rate of 8% p.a. The British FI sells the proceeds of the Euroyen loan forward, to be converted into Eurodollars at the forward rate of US$0.0108 at the maturity of the Euroloan. What happens on that date? First, the Euroyen loan repays JY106 million. This is converted into US$1.1448 million (= US$0.0108 × JY106 million). Simultaneously, the Eurodollar deposit matures and is repaid at

$$D = US\$1.05m \left(1 + \frac{.075(270)}{360}\right) = US\$1,109,062.50$$

The profit on the transaction is the difference between the loan repayment of US$1.1448 million minus the Eurodollar deposit repayment of US$1,109,062.50, for a gain of US$35,737.50. The transaction is far more profitable using the Eurocurrency swap then using the straight Euroloan/Eurodeposit transaction.

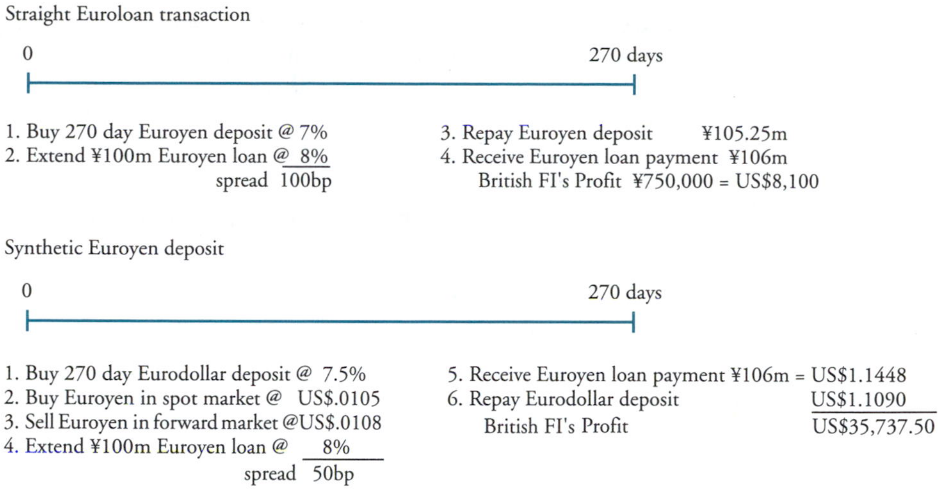

Straight Euroloan transaction

```
0                                              270 days
├──────────────────────────────────────────────┤
```

1. Buy 270 day Euroyen deposit @ 7%
2. Extend ¥100m Euroyen loan @ 8%
   spread 100bp

3. Repay Euroyen deposit   ¥105.25m
4. Receive Euroyen loan payment ¥106m
   British FI's Profit ¥750,000 = US$8,100

Synthetic Euroyen deposit

```
0                                              270 days
├──────────────────────────────────────────────┤
```

1. Buy 270 day Eurodollar deposit @ 7.5%
2. Buy Euroyen in spot market @ US$.0105
3. Sell Euroyen in forward market @US$.0108
4. Extend ¥100m Euroyen loan @ 8%
   spread 50bp

5. Receive Euroyen loan payment ¥106m = US$1.1448
6. Repay Eurodollar deposit   US$1.1090
   British FI's Profit   US$35,737.50

Figure 12.11   Eurocurrency swap arbitrage.

This solution can be obtained using an approximation formula[14] for the effective interest cost of the Euroyen generated using the swap of Eurodollars for Euroyen. The cost of this "synthetic Euroyen deposit," engineered using the Eurodollar deposit and the swap, is

$$i_{JY} = i_{US\$} + \left(\frac{S}{F} - 1\right)\left(\frac{360}{t}\right)$$

where i_{JY} = the effective interest cost of a synthetic Euroyen deposit, $i_{US\$}$ = the interest cost of the Eurodollar deposit, S = the spot exchange rate, F = the forward exchange rate, and t = the time until maturity for the transaction. Substituting in the values of these variables for our example, we obtain

$$i_{JY} = .075 + \left(\frac{US\$.0105}{US\$.0108} - 1\right)\left(\frac{360}{270}\right) = 3.8\% \text{ p.a.}$$

The cost of raising 100 million Japanese yen using a combination of a Eurodollar deposit and a swap is only 3.8% p.a. Compared to the 7% p.a. cost of borrowing by issuing a Euroyen deposit, it is clear why the swap transaction is so much more profitable than the alternative.

If, alternatively, the swap required an exchange of foreign currency into U.S. dollars, the approximation formula for the effective interest cost of the synthetic Eurodollar deposit would be

$$i_{US\$} = i_{FX} + \left(\frac{F}{S} - 1\right)\left(\frac{360}{t}\right)$$

where $i_{US\$}$ = the effective interest cost of the synthetic Eurodollar deposit, i_{FX} = the interest cost of the Eurocurrency deposit, where FX is any Eurocurrency, F = the forward rate, S = the spot rate, and t = the time until maturity. The decision rule is that if the effective interest cost is less than the interest rate on the Eurodollar deposit, then the swap should be undertaken in order to create a less expensive synthetic Eurodollar deposit.

---

[14] The formula is an approximation since it uses the face value of the Euroloan, thereby ignoring the cost of hedging the interest, which is denominated in Euroyen but must be paid out in Eurodollars. The formula is obtained from the approximate covered interest rate parity of Chapter 8.

swap rate: the difference between the spot and forward rates; $S - F$.

The difference between the spot and forward rates, that is, $S - F$, is called the **swap rate**. When the currency is trading at a forward premium, the swap rate is negative. Arbitrageurs will exploit this opportunity in much the same way as the British FI in our example. As they bid for Eurodollar deposits, the rate will increase, thereby increasing the effective interest cost of the synthetic Euroyen deposit. The arbitrage opportunity will be eliminated when the cost of borrowing by issuing a Euroyen deposit is equal to the cost of the synthetic Euroyen deposit constructed using a Eurodollar deposit plus a Eurocurrency swap.

Checkpoint

✓

1. Compare the Eurocurrency swap to the FRA and the Eurodollar CD futures contract.
2. What is the swap rate?
3. Under what conditions is the swap profitable?
4. How do you construct a synthetic Eurocurrency deposit?

TED spread: the difference between the Eurodollar CD futures rate and the U.S. Treasury bill rate.

short the TED spread: a short position in the U.S. Treasury bill futures contract and simultaneously a long position in the equivalent Eurodollar CD futures contract.

long the TED spread: a long Treasury bill futures position and an offsetting short Eurodollar CD futures position.

Arbitrage Between Financial Markets   We have seen how the Euromarket acts as a bridge between foreign and domestic markets. Indeed, Euromarket pricing keeps prices on other financial markets from straying too far out of line, thereby creating the opportunity for arbitrage profits. FIs watch the spreads between the markets for the glimmer of an arbitrage opportunity that can be pounced upon. A popular spread is the **TED spread**, which is the difference between the Eurodollar CD futures rate and the U.S. Treasury bill rate, where "T" stands for Treasury bill rates and "ED" for Eurodollar rates. Since the Euro rate exceeds the default risk free U.S. Treasury bill rate, the spread is always positive. But sometimes the spread widens and sometimes it narrows. If you think that the spread is too wide and you expect it to narrow, you will **short the TED spread**. That is, you will take a short position in the U.S. Treasury bill futures contract and simultaneously a long position in the equivalent Eurodollar CD futures contract. If you expect the spread to widen, you will **long the TED spread**, by buying a long Treasury bill futures position and an offsetting short Eurodollar CD futures position.

If the June Euro futures price is 92.75 and the June U.S. Treasury bill futures price (also quoted on an IMM Index basis) is 93.50, then the Euro futures rate is $100 - 92.75 = 7.25\%$ and the U.S. Treasury bill rate is $100 - 93.50 = 6.5\%$. The TED spread is then $7.25 - 6.5 = 75$ basis points. The TED spread is a measure of the risk premium on Eurobank obligations over equal maturity (91 days) default risk free U.S. Treasury bills. Thus, it is a measure of credit risk exposure in the short term Euromarket.

Suppose that you considered 75 basis points insufficient to compensate for the credit risk exposure in the Euromarket over the next three months. You could then go long the next delivery (say, June) TED spread and lock in the 75 basis point spread. This is a single transaction, referred to as buying the TED spread at 75.

Over the next three months, your expectations are realized. Instability in Euromarkets forces the Euro CD rate up, and a flight to quality pushes the U.S. Treasury bill rate down. The IMM Index prices on delivery date in June are 94.25 for the U.S. Treasury bill and 91.0 for the Euro CD. The TED spread is $(100 - 91.0) - (100 - 94.25) = 9.0 - 5.75 = 325$ basis points. The profit on the TED spread is $325 - 75 = 250$ basis points, or \$6,320 (250 x \$25.28). Of course, this is a speculative trade since the spread could have gone in the opposite direction, resulting in losses. The introduction of a futures contract priced on the TED spread has led to a decrease in the spread's volatility over time although the spread tends to widen as interest rates rise.

The TED spread and other intermarket trades are important links that prevent prices from moving too far out of line. The shifts in the futures prices act as a signal to financial markets. If the market consensus is that the TED spread is too low at 75, many arbitrageurs will buy the TED spread. This will bid up the U.S. Treasury bill futures price and depress the Euro

CD futures price, creating a self-fulfilling price movement. The futures markets are important indicators of market expectations.[15]

Summary

In this chapter, we have traced the evolution of a transnational financial market that is free of regulatory intervention. Indeed, its raison d'etre is its free market flexibility that allows FIs to provide intertemporal cash flow and risk shifting services to their customers. The defining characteristic of a Euromarket transaction is a mismatch between the country and currency of issue. For example, Eurobonds are bonds issued in one country and denominated in the currency of another country. Eurocurrencies are any currencies that are deposited in banks outside of their home country. For example, U.S. dollar deposits into British banks are called Eurodollars. In past years, Eurodollars were the dominant currency for most Euromarket transactions. However, the Eurodollar's dominance is no longer assured, as demand for Euro-DM and Euroyen, as well as other currencies, increases.

FIs maintain Eurobooks of assets and liabilities denominated in Eurocurrencies. Euro assets are syndicated Euroloans, Eurobonds, Euronotes, and Eurocommercial paper. Euro liabilities are Euro CDs, Euro time deposits, interbank placements, and call money. FIs absorb risk in Euromarkets by running gaps in their Eurobooks. They absorb interest rate risk by running a duration gap. If its duration gap is positive, then the FI is taking on the risk of interest rate increases; if its duration gap is negative, then the FI is taking on the risk of interest rate decreases. FIs absorb exchange rate risk by running a nonzero net currency exposure. FIs take on the risk of exchange rate increases when they run a negative net exposure; they take on the risk of exchange rate decreases when they run a positive net exposure.

Off-balance sheet activity is also an important part of Euromarkets. Off-balance sheet items are contingencies that make future commitments but do not require up-front cash flows. They are less expensive than balance sheets for risk hedging purposes. The major off-balance sheet risk hedging devices are Eurodollar CD futures contracts, forward rate agreements (FRAs), and Eurocurrency swaps. Intramarket risk hedging can be performed using the TED spread, the spread between the U.S. Treasury bill rate and the Eurodollar CD futures rate.

References

Abken, P. A. "Using Eurodollar Futures Options: Gauging the Market's View of Interest Rate Movements." Federal Reserve Bank of Atlanta *Economic Review* (March–April 1995): 10–30.

Arshanapalli, B., and J. Doukas. "Common Stochastic Trends in a System of Eurocurrency Rates." *Journal of Banking and Finance* 18 (1994): 1047–1061.

Benzie, R. "The Development of the International Bond Market." BIS Economic Papers, No. 32 (January 1992) .

Bonser-Neal, C., and R. Vance. "Are Japanese Interest Rates Too Stable?" *Journal of International Money and Finance* 13, No. 3 (June 1994): 291–318.

Buckley, A. *The Essence of International Money.* 2nd ed. London: Prentice-Hall, 1996.

Cole, C. S., and W. Reichenstein. "Forecasting Interest Rates with Eurodollar Futures Rates." *Journal of Futures Markets* 14, No. 1 (1994): 37–50.

---

[15] Academic studies of the value of the Eurodollar CD futures rate as an unbiased estimator of expected future spot prices yield mixed results. Futures rates provide accurate predictions for near term forecasts, for example, three months into the future, see Fung and Leung (1993), Cole and Reichenstein (1994), Mougoue and Szakmary (1994), and Bonser–Neal and Vance (1994). However, the futures rate is a poor forecaster farther into the future, and Krehbiel and Adkins (1994) show no forecasting ability. Papazoglou and Turnovsky (1994) and Kawaller, Koch, and Peterson (1994) report that using the volume of activity improves the predictive accuracy of the futures rate. Finally, Arshanapalli and Doukas (1994) observe that all Eurodollar rates, for different maturities, are closely linked.

Fisher, F. G., III. *Eurobonds*. London: Euromoney Publications PLC., 1988.

Fung, H., and W. Leung. "The Pricing Relationship of Eurodollar Futures and Eurodollar Deposit Rates." *Journal of Futures Markets* 13, No. 2 (1993): 115–126.

Gibson, H. *The Eurocurrency Markets, Domestic Financial Policy and International Instability*. New York: St. Martin's Press, 1989.

Johnston, R. B. *The Economics of the Euromarket*. New York: St. Martin's Press, 1982.

Kawaller, I., P. Koch, and J. Peterson. "Assessing the Intraday Relationship Between Implied and Historical Volatility." *Journal of Futures Markets* 14, No. 3 (1994): 323–346.

Kim, Y. C., and R. M. Stulz. "The Eurobond Market and Corporate Financial Policy," *Journal of Financial Economics* 22 (1988): 189–205.

Krehbiel, T., and L. Adkins. "Interest Rate Futures: Evidence on Forecast Power, Expected Premiums, and the Unbiased Expectations Hypothesis." *Journal of Futures Markets* 14, No. 5 (August 1994): 531–543.

Marr, M. W., R. W. Rogowski, and J. L. Trimble. "The Competitive Effects of U.S. and Japanese Commercial Bank Participation in Eurobond Underwriting." *Financial Management* (Winter 1989): 47–54.

Mougoue, M., and A. Szakmary. "The Expectations Hypothesis of the Term Structure in Eurocurrency Markets." *Journal of Business Finance and Accounting* 21, No. 2 (March 1994): 255–269.

Papazoglou, C., and S. Turnovsky. "External Markets, Exchange Rate Dynamics, and the Impact of Monetary Disturbances." *Journal of International Money and Finance* 13, No. 5 (1994): 499–515.

Sarver, E. *The Eurocurrency Market Handbook*. 2nd ed. New York: New York Institute of Finance, Prentice-Hall, 1990.

Stigum, M. *The Money Market*. New York: Business One, Irwin, 1990.

➤ Questions

1. Calculate both the effective costs and the maturity values of the following deposit sources of funds:
   a. A $5 million 5.125% p.a. domestic 180 day CD, with a deposit insurance premium of 23 and a 3% reserve requirement.
   b. A $5 million 5.25% p.a. Euro 180 day CD with no reserve requirements.
   c. What is the spread between the effective costs of the domestic and Euro CD?

2a. Use the following Eurobook to evaluate a British FI's interest rate risk and exchange rate risk exposure.

2b. What do your answers to part (a) suggest about the risk shifting services offered by the Eurobook transactions?

2c. What is the impact on the following British FI's Eurobook's value if there is a 1% increase (across the board) in interest rates? if there is a 1% decline (across the board) in exchange rates?

British FI's Eurobook (£ million)

1 year Eurodollar loan	£55m	3 mo. Euroyen CD	£15m
8% annual coupon, priced at par		5% p.a.	
2 year Euro–DM note	£35m	6 mo. Euro–DM CD	£50m
12% annual coupon, price		6.5% p.a.	
= £105/£100 par			
10 year Euroyen bond	£25m	6 mo. Eurodollar CD	£50m
9% annual coupon, price		7% p.a.	
= £97/£100 par			

[a]The Euro CDs are pure discount instruments since they have no remaining coupon payments until maturity. All Euro assets and liabilities in this Eurobook are fixed rate.

3. Dr. Doris Dentures is planning to open her dental office in six months (182 days) with the proceeds of a $100,000 Eurodollar investment in a 182 day FRN that reprices quarterly. The yield for the first three months is 6.5% p.a.

  a. What will the FRN be worth at maturity if interest rates remain unchanged over the next six months?
  b. To what type of interest rate risk is Dr. Dentures exposed?
  c. How can Dr. Dentures use Eurodollar CD futures to hedge her interest rate risk exposure? How can she use FRAs?
  d. Contrast the characteristics of the hedge using Euro CD futures to the hedge using FRAs.

4a. Suppose that today's Eurodollar CD futures is trading at 94. Using the scenario in question 3, what does this imply about expectations about future spot Eurodollar CD rates?

4b. Use the Eurodollar CD futures contract in part (a) to construct and evaluate a hedge for Dr. Dentures in question 3 if all interest rates decline by 100 basis points for the next six months.

4c. Calculate the cash flows on the 94 Euro CD futures if in the three months that Dr. Dentures holds the position, either: (1) Eurodollar CD futures prices decrease to 92.75; or (2) Eurodollar CD futures prices increase to 95.

5. Construct a hedge for Dr. Dentures using a FRA and the rates in question 4.

6a. Suppose that a London-based FI has a customer that wants to borrow 1 million Euro-DM for 90 days. TheBritish FI can try to obtain a Euro-DM deposit for 90 days to fund the loan, or it can take in Eurodollars and swap them for Euro-DM. Today's DM-dollar spot exchange rate is US$.70 per DM, while the three month forward rate is US$0.67 per Deutschemark. Is the DM selling at a forward discount or premium? How will that affect the profitability of a Eurocurrency swap? What is the swap rate?

6b. If the 90 day Euro-DM CD rate is 2% p.a. and the 90 day Eurodollar CD rate is 5% p.a., calculate the cost of funding the 90 day Euro-DM loan using (1) the Euro-DM CD as financing; and (2) the synthetic Euro-DM CD created by the combination of the 90 day Eurodollar CD and the Eurocurrency swap. The Euroloan rate is 6% p.a. Do you do the swap?

7. Suppose that a German FI has a customer that wants to borrow 5 million Eurodollars for 365 days. Today's sterling-dollar exchange rate is US$1.50 per £, and the one year forward rate is US$1.45 per £. The 365 day Eurodollar CD rate is 8% p.a., while the 1 year Eurosterling CD rate is 6% p.a. The loan rate is 10% p.a. Calculate the cost of funding the 365 day Eurodollar loan using (1) the Eurodollar CD as financing; and (2) the synthetic Eurodollar CD created by the combination of the 1 year Eurosterling CD and the Eurocurrency swap. Do you do the swap?

8a. If the June Euro futures price is 94.05 and the June U.S. Treasury bill futures price (also quoted on an IMM Index basis) is 96.95, what is the TED spread?

8b. How can you take a position that would benefit from a narrowing of the TED spread over the next three months?

8c. The IMM Index prices on delivery date are 96 for the U.S. Treasury bill and 94.75 for the Euro CD. What is the profit/loss on the TED spread position in part (b)?

9a. Calculate LIBOR using the following BBA-designated banks' quotations:

Lloyds	6.8125
Barclays	6.759
Natwest	6.785
Westpac	6.785
Citibank	6.813
Chemical	6.8
Fuji Bank	6.765
Hambros	6.8

9b. What is the face value of a 169 day $10 million Eurodollar CD priced at LIBOR?

10. Clear the following Euromarket transfers determining the impact on monetary reserves:

a. $15 million Eurodollar loan repayment to Nat West London by WWW Inc. by check written on Citibank New York. Nat West's U.S. clearing bank is Chase New York.

b. $25 million Euroyen deposit to Nat West London by MMM Inc. by check written on Sumitomo Trust Tokyo. Nat West's Japanese clearing bank is Fuji Bank Tokyo.

CHAPTER 13

BANKERS ACCEPTANCES, LETTERS OF CREDIT, AND CERTIFICATES OF DEPOSIT

"To be clever enough to get all that money, one must be stupid enough to want it." G. K. Chesterton, *Wisdom of Father Brown* (1914), "Paradise of Thieves."

Learning Objectives

- To learn about two contracting markets: the bankers acceptances (BA) and certificates of deposit (CD).

- To discover how the contraction has been caused by a combination of regulatory and market forces.

- To see how the letter of credit, the standby letter of credit, and the BA offer customers intertemporal cash flow shifting and risk-transfer services.

➤ Introduction

FIs and financial markets follow their customers throughout the world. The earliest global financial activity was designed to facilitate international imports and exports. Exporters want to promote the sale of their products abroad and to receive payment for their goods as soon as possible, whereas importers want to obtain the goods on time, and in good condition, before payment is made. The goals of exporters and importers conflict because of this mismatch in cash flow timing. Exporters want to speed up payment for their goods so that they can pay their workers and other factors of production. In contrast, importers want to delay payment until they can ascertain that the exporter has satisfied the terms of the trade agreement. Whenever a mismatch in the timing of cash flows occurs, FIs have an opportunity to perform financial intermediation. Bankers acceptances and standby letters of credits are financial instruments that provide importers and exporters with intertemporal cash flow shifting services to allow both sides to achieve their goals. They also provide some protection against credit and country risk exposure. What are these versatile instruments?

➤ What Is a Letter of Credit?

International financial transactions can be completed in the blink of an eye using electronic payment systems, but international trade does not move as quickly. Trade of physical goods requires their shipment around the world. Shipment, especially of bulky items, is costly and takes time. While the goods are in transit, both the importer and exporter are short of cash. The exporter must pay its factors of production for their work in creating the goods, but the importer still does not have the goods in possession to be sold. This mismatch in the timing of cash flows lengthens as the shipping period grows.

During this period, the risk also exists that the importer will go bankrupt (and be unable to pay for the goods) or that upheavals in either country will make cash flow transfers impossible. Thus, the exporter may require the importer to guarantee payment, in some way, prior to shipping the goods. The simplest form of a guarantee is the **letter of credit**. The letter of credit is an agreement, by a bank, called the **issuer**, to pay a certain sum of money to an exporter (called the **beneficiary**) on the date that the goods are received at the specified location, with the additional agreement that the importer (called the **account party**) repay the bank so as to take title of the goods. The importer obtains the letter of credit, which authorizes its bank to accept a **time draft** from the exporter, upon receipt of shipping documents that transfer title of the goods to the bank. The time draft is an order to the bank to pay a specified sum of money (set equal to the value of the goods) on a specified date to the bearer (the exporter).[1] It has a fixed term to maturity. That is, if the goods are received any time within the time until maturity, the bank that issues the letter of credit (1) pays the exporter; (2) takes title to the goods; and then (3) releases the goods to the importer in exchange for payment. Thus, the bank first pays the exporter for the goods, upon their receipt at the specified location, and then receives payment from the importer.

The letter of credit does not verify whether or not the goods arrived in good condition. Insurance can be obtained to cover the eventualities of damage or fraud. The letter of credit simply acts as a financial bridge covering the time period between the shipment and receipt of the goods. The letter of credit is an off-balance sheet commitment that requires no cash flows unless it is presented for payment, whereas the time draft is an on-balance sheet liability of the issuing bank.

What role do FIs play in the process of financing international trade? As always, they have two roles: (1) intertemporal cash flow shifting and (2) risk transfer.

letter of credit: an agreement, by a bank (called the **issuer**), to pay a certain sum of money to an exporter (called the **beneficiary**) on the date that the goods are received at the specified location, with the additional agreement that the importer (called the **account party**) repay the bank so as to take title of the goods.

issuer: the account party's bank for purposes of the letter of credit.

beneficiary: the exporter, for purposes of the letter of credit.

account party: the importer, for purposes of the letter of credit.

time draft: an order to the bank to pay a specified sum of money (set equal to the value of the goods) on a specified date to the bearer (the exporter).

Checkpoint

1. Why do importers and exporters demand intertemporal cash flow shifting services?
2. Why do importers and exporters demand risk-transfer services?
3. What is the relationship between the issuer, the account party, and the beneficiary?
4. What is the difference between a letter of credit and a time draft?

Intertemporal Cash Flow Shifting

The letter of credit bridges the time period between the exporter's shipment of goods and the importer's receipt of those goods. This document offers the exporter flexibility to adjust this time period in any way that is desirable. Of course, the letter of credit cannot make the ship move faster so that the goods reach their destination sooner. But it can speed up the payment for the goods so that the exporter can be paid even before the goods reach their destination.

Figure 13.1 shows the timeline of events for a hypothetical example. A $10 million shipment of Japanese televisions leaves the dock bound for the United States on September 15 with

---

[1] Bankers acceptances can originate directly from time drafts issued without letters of credit.

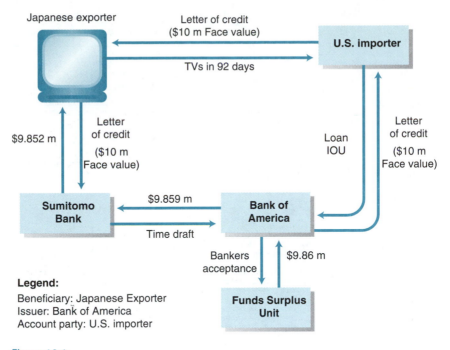

Figure 13.1

expected arrival in Seattle in 92 days on December 17. The 92 days at sea represent a period of cash flow mismatch that is determined by the length of the shipping period. However, if a letter of credit is used, the exporter has the flexibility to alter this period of cash flow mismatch. If desired, the exporter can obtain payment for the goods on the same day that they are shipped. Alternatively, the exporter can wait a week and present the letter of credit for payment on that date. Or payment can be made in 30 days, 60 days, or even 92 days. This is because the letter of credit is an obligation of the issuing bank that must be honored upon presentation by the exporter. When the exporter presents the letter of credit to its local bank, a time draft is issued so that payment for the goods may be made immediately.[2] Figure 13.2 shows a facsimile of a letter of credit.

Suppose that the Japanese exporter presents the time draft on the letter of credit for payment on the date of shipment of the goods. Does the exporter receive $10 million? No. The time draft is discounted to reflect the acceleration of the payment by the number of days until the shipment is to be received. In this case, the Japanese exporter is accelerating the receipt of the $10 million payment by 92 days, and, if the rate of discount on the time draft is, say, 5.78% p.a., the payment received by the exporter is

$$P = FV\left(1 - \frac{dt}{360}\right) = \$10m\left(1 - \frac{.0578(92)}{360}\right) = \$9.852m$$

where P = the immediate payment to the exporter, FV = the face value of the letter of credit (equal to the value of the exported goods), d = the rate of discount, and t = the number of days until the goods are received by the importer. Note that we used this same formula to price the U.S. Treasury bill (and indeed any discount instrument, such as the Eurodollar CD

---

[2] Technically, letters of credit are a contingent liability and are themselves not paid. Instead, the time draft that is transferred upon presentation of both the letter of credit and the shipping documents is paid.

Standard Letter of Credit

Citibank, N.A.
Irrevocable Straight Credit

CABLE ADDRESS "CITIBANK"
Irrevocable Straight Credit

111 WALL STREET, NEW YORK, NY 10015

DATE: May 3,19—

MAIL TO:
A NEW ENGLAND COMPANY
10 WEST STREET
BOSTON, MA 02673

MAIL
All drafts drawn must be marked:
CITIBANK Ref. No.: 30030000
Opener's Reference No.:
317

Dear Sirs:

At the request of:

AN AUSTRALIAN BUYER
SYDNEY, AUSTRALIA

and for the account of AN AUSTRALIAN BUYER we hereby open in your favor our Irrevocable Credit, numbered as indicated above, for a sum or sums not exceeding a total of U.S. $1,214.00 available by your drafts at SIGHT on us subject to the following:

Expiration Date: October 15, 19—
Trans shipment not allowed.
Partial shipment not allowed.
Ship from: U.S.A. PORT
Ship to: SYDNEY, AUSTRALIA

and accompanied by the following documents:

1.ORIGINAL ON BOARD OCEAN BILLS OF LADING ISSUED TO ORDER BLANK ENDORSED.

2.FULL SET NEGOTIABLE MARINE INSURANCE CERTIFICATES INCLUDING WAR RISKS.

3.TRIPLICATE AUSTRALIAN CUSTOMS INVOICE COMBINED WITH CERTIFICATE OF ORIGIN STATING IT COVERS: "SPARE PARTS FOR LOOMS."

This letter is to accompany all draft(s) and documents. When presenting your draft(s) and documents or when communicating with us please make reference to our reference number shown above.
We hereby agree to honor each draft drawn under and in compliance with the terms of this credit, if duly presented (together with the documents specified) at this office on or before the expiration date.
The credit is subject to the Uniform Customs and Practice for Documentary Credits (1974 Revision), International Chamber of Commerce – PUBLICATION 290.

Yours very truly

———————

Beneficiary: A New England Company
Issuer: Citibank
Account Party: An Australian Buyer

Figure 13.2

futures contract) in Chapter 7. The rate of discount on the time draft is higher than the rate of discount on a similar maturity Treasury bill. The spread between the yields is determined by the credit risk exposure of the issuing FI. The greater the FIs credit risk exposure, the higher the rate of discount.

Figure 13.1 shows that the Japanese TV exporter wants immediate payment and presents the letter of credit to its bank, say the Sumitomo Bank. Sumitomo Bank pays the Japanese TV exporter $9.852 million for the goods, as represented by the time draft. Now what can Sumitomo Bank do with the time draft? Just as with the exporter, the bank has a choice either to hold the letter of credit until maturity and receive $10 million from the issuer in 92 days or to cash it in. Suppose that Sumitomo Bank holds the letter of credit for three days (perhaps over a weekend) and decides to cash it in on the fourth day. There are 88 days until the televisions are expected to reach port in Seattle. Therefore, by presenting the letter of credit, Sumitomo Bank receives a time draft that allows it to speed up the payment for the goods by 88 days. Suppose that the issuing bank is Bank of America. Sumitomo Bank presents the time draft to Bank of America for payment. Bank of America discounts the time draft back 88 days and pays Sumitomo Bank. If interest rates have not changed over the past four days, then Bank of America must pay

$$P = FV \left(1 - \frac{dt}{360} \right) = \$10\text{m} \left(1 - \frac{.0578(88)}{360} \right) = \$9.859\text{m}$$

Sumitomo Bank has earned $7,000 ($9.859 million minus $9.852 million) for holding the letter of credit for four days.

By now, the letter of credit has returned to its origin: the issuing bank, the Bank of America. Upon receipt, the Bank of America stamps the letter of credit "accepted" and a **bankers acceptance (BA)** is born, replacing the time draft issued by Bank of America. As described in Chapter 11, a bankers acceptance is a negotiable, securitized time draft that is an unconditional liability of the bank. Since the Bank of America pays Sumitomo Bank $9.859 million for its time draft, how can the Bank of America recoup this payment? The importer does not have to pay Bank of America for another 88 days, until the shipment is received in Seattle. This is where the negotiable nature of the bankers acceptance comes in. The Bank of America can sell the BA on a secondary market to any Funds Surplus Unit that wants a liquid, short term investment. Thus, if the BA is placed the day after it is accepted by the Bank of America from Sumitomo, and interest rates are still unchanged, then its price will be

bankers acceptance (BA): a negotiable, securitized time draft that is an unconditional liability of the bank.

$$P = FV \left(1 - \frac{dt}{360} \right) = \$10\text{m} \left(1 - \frac{.0578(87)}{360} \right) = \$9.86\text{m}$$

Bank of America raises $9.86 million by selling its 87 day BA. Over the next 87 days, the BA can be sold and resold, just as is any other money market instrument, at a price equal to the discounted present value of its $10 million face value. Ultimately, the BA is another form of cash flow shifting between Funds Deficit Units (in this example, the Japanese TV exporter) and Funds Surplus Units (the ultimate investor in the Bank of America BA). Figure 13.3 shows a facsimile of a BA.

Throughout this example, we have used a 5.78% p.a. rate of discount. Where did this rate come from? From the rate quotes on BAs shown in Figure 13.4, we see that the three month BA rate is 5.78% p.a. Although there are quotes for maturities as long as six months, the BA market is most liquid in the range of maturities up until three months. Comparing rates across money market instruments, we see that the one month BA rate of 5.93% p.a. is greater than the one month repo rate of 5.78% p.a., because repos are fully collateralized by marketable securities. Similarly, the three month Treasury bill rate of 5.51% p.a. is less than the three month BA rate of 5.78% p.a., which is less than the three month Eurodollar rate of 5.938% p.a., because of progressively higher credit risk exposures.

BAs originally were used exclusively to finance a country's imports and exports.[3] But during the oil embargoes of the 1970s, when the price of oil skyrocketed, oil-importing nations latched onto the BA to finance their oil imports. However, rather than using the oil as the goods (like the Japanese TVs) to back up the BA, the BA was expanded to finance third country trade. Thus, the goods are neither imports nor exports, but instead are goods stored in or shipped between foreign countries. Table 13.1 shows that in December 1994, $13.417 billion of the

---

[3] Currently about 10% of all BAs stem from domestic shipment and storage acceptances in the United States.

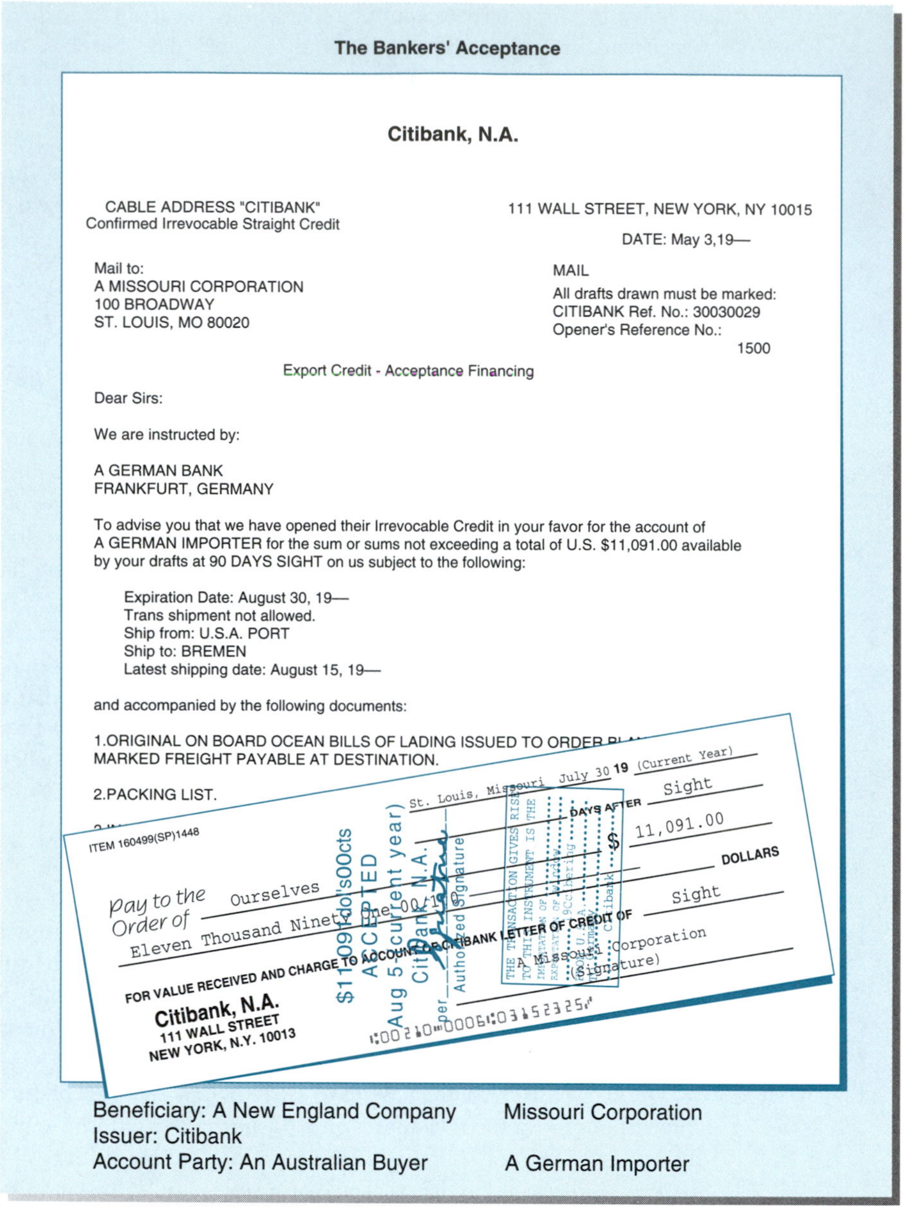

The Bankers' Acceptance

Citibank, N.A.

CABLE ADDRESS "CITIBANK"   111 WALL STREET, NEW YORK, NY 10015
Confirmed Irrevocable Straight Credit
                                                                          DATE: May 3,19—

Mail to: MAIL
A MISSOURI CORPORATION   All drafts drawn must be marked:
100 BROADWAY   CITIBANK Ref. No.: 30030029
ST. LOUIS, MO 80020   Opener's Reference No.:
                                                                                          1500

Export Credit - Acceptance Financing

Dear Sirs:

We are instructed by:

A GERMAN BANK
FRANKFURT, GERMANY

To advise you that we have opened their Irrevocable Credit in your favor for the account of
A GERMAN IMPORTER for the sum or sums not exceeding a total of U.S. $11,091.00 available
by your drafts at 90 DAYS SIGHT on us subject to the following:

    Expiration Date: August 30, 19—
    Trans shipment not allowed.
    Ship from: U.S.A. PORT
    Ship to: BREMEN
    Latest shipping date: August 15, 19—

and accompanied by the following documents:

1. ORIGINAL ON BOARD OCEAN BILLS OF LADING ISSUED TO ORDER BLANK
MARKED FREIGHT PAYABLE AT DESTINATION.

2. PACKING LIST.

ITEM 160499(SP)1448

St. Louis, Missouri   July 30 19 (Current Year)

Pay to the Order of   Ourselves $ 11,091.00   Sight   DOLLARS

Eleven Thousand Ninety One 00/100

FOR VALUE RECEIVED AND CHARGE TO ACCOUNT OF

ACCEPTED Aug 5 (current year) Citibank, N.A.

DAYS AFTER   Sight
LETTER OF CREDIT OF   Sight
A. Missouri Corporation (Signature)

Citibank, N.A.
111 WALL STREET
NEW YORK, N.Y. 10013

Beneficiary: A New England Company   Missouri Corporation
Issuer: Citibank
Account Party: An Australian Buyer   A German Importer

Figure 13.3

total of $29.835 billion (representing 45% of total U.S. volume) of all BAs were backed by third country trade.

Table 13.1 shows how the volume in the BA market has declined considerably in recent years. Alternatives to BA short term financing have proliferated. The exporter can finance the period of time between shipment and receipt of the goods using commercial paper, Euroloans, or bank lines of credit, instead of BAs. The popularity of these substitute sources of financing contributed to the decline in BA volume. A combination of market forces and regulatory changes have determined the evolution of the BA market.

```
3                                                      DG03 Govt MMR
Enter 9 <Go> to reset any NewsMinder Indicators
    MONEY  MARKET  COMPOSITE                           PAGE 1 OF 1
   FED FUNDS           T-BILL          EURO $ DEPOSIT     GOVT REPO
 1)FDFD↑6.13-1.875    9)3MO ↓5.51 +.02  18)3MO ↓5.938 .063  27)O/N ↑6.1  +.01
   FED EFFECTIVE     10)6MO ↑5.45 +.02  19)6MO ↓5.875 .063  28)1WK ↓5.77 -.15
 2)FEDL 7.41         11)1YR ↑5.31 +.01  20)12MO↓5.875  --   29)1MO ↑5.78 +.03
   TREASURY BONDS        BA'S             CP TOP TIER          CD'S
 3)2YR ↑5.78 +2.55   12)1MO ↓5.93 -.02  21)1WK ↓5.98 -.09   30)1MO ↓5.97 -.01
 4)3YR ↑5.84 +2.36   13)2MO ↓5.83 -.04  22)2WK ↓5.94 -.04   31)3MO ↓5.85 -.04
 5)5YR ↓5.98 +3.31   14)3MO ↓5.78 -.02  23)1MO ↑5.96 +.02   32)6MO ↓5.8  -.01
 6)7YR ↓5.94 +1.17   15)4MO ↓5.73 -.02  24)2MO ↓5.85 -.04     PRIME,CALL,DISC
 7)10YR↓6.21 +2.53   16)5MO ↓5.67 -.03  25)3MO ↓5.77 -.04   33)PRIM↑9      --
 8)30YR↓6.63 +3.07   17)6MO ↓5.64 -.03  26)6MO ↑5.7  +.03   34)BLR ↑7.75   --
                                                            35)DISC↑5.25   --

36)TEDSUS    10:43↓     .36   +.01 37)EDA      10:46↑    94.34   -.01

Bloomberg-all rights reserved.  Frankfurt:69-920410  Hong Kong:2-521-3000  London:171-330-7500  New York:212-318-2000
Princeton:609-279-3000    Singapore:226-3000    Sydney:2-777-8600    Tokyo:3-3201-8900    Washington DC:202-434-1800
                                                                    G165-312-3 06-Jul-95 10:48:44
```

Figure 13.4

Bankers Acceptances[a] ($ million)

Holder	1990	1991	1992	1993	1994
Accepting banks (U.S. only)	9,017	11,017	10,555	12,421	11,783
Own BAs	7,930	9,347	9,097	10,707	10,462
Bills bought from other banks	1,087	1,670	1,458	1,714	1,321
Federal Reserve banks					
Foreign central banks	918	1,739	1,276	725	410
Others	44,836	31,014	26,364	19,202	17,642
Total	54,771	43,771	38,195	32,348	29,834
Goods used as collateral					
Imports into the U.S.	13,095	12,843	12,209	10,217	10,062
Exports from the U.S.	12,703	10,351	8,096	7,293	6,355
Third country trade	28,973	20,577	17,890	14,838	13,417

[a]Data on BAs are gathered from approximately 100 U.S. institutions. The reporting group is revised every January. In 1977, the Federal Reserve discontinued operations in BAs for its own account.

Source: Federal Reserve Bulletin, July 1995, Table 1.32.

Checkpoint

1. How does the letter of credit offer cash flow timing services to the exporter? to the importer? to the issuer?

2. How does the BA offer cash flow timing services to the exporter's bank? to the issuer? to Funds Surplus Units?

3. What are alternatives to BA and letters of credit that provide cash flow timing services?

4. How does the letter of credit and time draft become a BA?

> ## The Evolution of the BA Market

Recall from Chapter 11 that one of the first mandates of the newly formed Federal Reserve System was to create a domestic financial market that would encourage the growth of international trade. At the time, the London market was the preeminent financial center in the world, and American exporters felt themselves at the mercy of British FIs. It was the Fed's job to create a domestic analog to the BA market that flourished at that time in London.

To do this, the Fed not only permitted U.S. banks to trade BAs, but at one time was itself an active participant in the market. The Fed bought BAs for its own account, used BAs as collateral for discount window loans, and also employed BAs as collateral for repurchase agreements in open market operations. BAs are *eligible for purchase* by the Fed if they have maturities of up to nine months and arise from the financing of either shipment or storage of goods. The Fed sometimes agrees to pay rates on BAs that are below market rates, particularly during periods of easy money, thereby raising the BA's price and encouraging market activity. During 1916–1931, the Fed held over one-third of all outstanding BAs in its own portfolio. During this peak period, BAs financed about one-half of all U.S. imports and exports.

tenor: time until maturity.

There are some limitations on the Fed's involvement in the market, however. For the Fed to consider a BA *eligible for discount* at the Fed discount rate, it must have a **tenor**, or time until maturity, of no more than six months and must finance a self-liquidating commercial transaction.[4] Only eligible BAs are exempt from reserve requirements when sold by the issuing bank. Note that once the issuing bank accepts the letter of credit, the bank views the BA as a potential source of funds. If the bank decides to hold the BA, then it is added to the bank's loan portfolio, since the importer owes the bank the face value of the BA. If the bank decides to sell the BA, it becomes a liability of the bank that raises funds that can be used to finance loans and other assets in the bank's portfolio. Thus, if the BA is held until maturity, the bank must meet a capital requirement against it. Moreover, the Fed established capital limitations on the amount of BAs that could be sold by any bank. Since the permissible volume of BA activity is tied to the bank's capital levels, declining amounts of bank capital during the early 1990s reduced the banks' ability to issue BAs. These limitations, as well as the Japanese banks' aggressive competition for the market, resulted in the decline in volume of U.S. BAs (see Table 13.1).

The Fed purchases BAs for foreign correspondents, which are foreign central banks and other public FIs with accounts at the Fed. In the course of these transactions, and in order to enhance activity in BAs, the Fed guarantees the BAs against default. In 1974 foreign correspondent holdings of BAs, and equivalently the potential liability to the Fed presented by their guarantee, exceeded $2 billion. Because the market was judged to be mature, and because of the risk implied by the Fed's blanket guarantee, the Fed decided to drop its guarantee in 1974. The Fed ceased buying BAs for its own portfolio in 1977 and stopped accepting BAs as collateral in repos in 1984. The result of the Fed's withdrawal has been a steady decline in volume of activity from the unsustainable levels induced by Fed activity in the 1970s and 1980s.

The Fed's guarantee of BAs injected a moral hazard, risk increasing incentive into the market. Since the Fed guaranteed all BAs, central banks could buy riskier BAs without being concerned about default risk. Indeed, since the riskier the bank issuer of the BA, the higher the yield on the BA, this was a way for a foreign central bank to increase its rate of return—at the expense of the Fed.

With the withdrawal of the Fed's preferential treatment, the BA market had to compete with other rapidly developing money markets. In particular, the markets for repos, commercial

---

[4] A dollar exchange acceptance must have a time to maturity of three months or less. See Stigum (1990), pp. 1002–1003, for a detailed listing of eligibility requirements. However, the Fed has on occasion relaxed many of these requirements in practice.

paper, and Eurodollars can be used as close substitutes to BAs in order to obtain short term financing. The BA market's comparative historical advantage was their exemption from reserve requirements. When in December 1990 the Fed eliminated reserve requirements on Eurocurrency liabilities and certificates of deposit, the BA market became relatively less attractive, further contributing to the decline in the volume of BA activity.

Checkpoint

✓

1. How did the Fed encourage activity in the U.S. BA market?
2. How did the Fed discourage activity in the U.S. BA market?
3. What are eligible BAs?
4. What factors led to the decline in volume in the BA market?

➤ Risk Transfer

BAs offer hedges against both credit risk and country risk exposure. Large, well-known banks headquartered in the world's major money centers create most of the world's BAs. They provide access to international financial markets for smaller FIs and nonfinancial companies that do not have the reputation to directly transact in these markets. BA rates charged for this access are related to the risk of the borrowing institution, with spreads between less well-known foreign bank BAs around five basis points higher than the rates paid on BAs issued by money center banks.

Credit Risk Exposure

The letter of credit acts as an introductory handshake, enabling transactions between importers and exporters who may not have longstanding business relationships. The FI offers its own reputation as guarantee against the commitments undertaken by the commercial counterparties. Since the FI specializes in information production, it is able to ascertain the creditworthiness of its customers and therefore provide this validation service.

Not all international trade requires the use of letters of credit. If the importer and exporter have a long term relationship, they may not need the additional guarantees offered by the letter of credit. This is because the exporter estimates that the importer's credit risk exposure is low. In those cases, international trade proceeds on an **open account** basis, where the exporter ships the goods with the expectation that the importer will pay in good faith. Indeed, studies show that 98.1% of all open account billings on cross-border business under $12,000 are paid within 90 days. The median open account size is $4,200. If the expected loss rate is 1.9%, then the expected loss on the average account is $79.80 (= .019 × $4,200). In contrast, the average transaction costs of the letter of credit is $210.[5] Thus, on small accounts, letters of credit are not economically feasible. The cost ($210) outweighs the benefit (with savings of potential losses expected to be only $79.80). However, on large accounts, letters of credit are a necessity. Not only are expected losses larger for large accounts, but also the transactions cost of the letter of credit (as a percentage of its face value) is lower. On large BAs, the transaction cost ranges from 25 to 30 basis points, whereas the cost of the small letter of credit is 5% ($\frac{\$210}{\$4200}$). This is because large value letters of credit can ultimately be securitized into BAs, while small values cannot.

Letters of credit and the BAs that result from them are used in transactions that carry substantial credit risk exposure. Indeed, in addition to the intertemporal cash flow shifting offered to the exporter by the letter of credit, the exporter also gets protection against default

open account: the shipping of goods by the exporter with the good faith expectation that the importer will pay.

---

[5] Flock (1995), p. 24.

risk. That is, by using the letter of credit, the exporter substitutes the issuing bank's credit risk exposure for the importer's credit risk. The issuing bank is insuring the exporter against a default by the importer. Since the importer is a customer of the issuing bank, it is reasonable to expect that the issuing bank would have more information about the financial condition of the importer than does the exporter. Thus, the issuing bank can use this superior information to absorb the exporter's risk exposure to the possibility of default by the importer.

BAs are equivalent to bank lending financed by deposits. The issuing bank receives a loan IOU from the account party (the importer) and finances the loan by selling its own unconditional liability in the money market. Because the bank must repay its liabilities even if the importer defaults on the loan, the bank absorbs credit risk. The bank can typically borrow at a lower cost than the importer, but the bank earns a positive spread on the BA as compensation for this credit risk exposure.

The risk shifting services available in a letter of credit will be obtained only if the bank's credit risk is less than the importer's credit risk exposure. If the bank is riskier than the importer, then the exporter gains nothing (and indeed loses) in a transaction financed with a letter of credit. Thus, the recent deterioration in banks' financial condition throughout the world has also contributed to a decline in volume in the letter of credit and BA market. Moreover, volume in the market has also been hurt by the removal of an implicit guarantee by national bank regulators to protect all large banks from closure. Formerly, investors were willing to buy the BA of any large bank, expecting that it would always be solvent. Experience has proven otherwise, and now we observe tiering in the BA market. Tiering occurs when rates are risk adjusted so that higher risk issuers must pay a higher interest rate.

If the BA in our example was issued, say, by Bankers Trust, instead of Bank of America, it might carry an additional yield of 10 basis points, if the market was concerned about Bankers Trust's financial condition. Thus, the Bankers Trust BA would sell at a rate of 5.88% p.a. for a price of

$$P = FV \left(1 - \frac{dt}{360}\right) = \$10\text{m} \left(1 - \frac{.0588(87)}{360}\right) = \$9.858\text{m}$$

which is $2,000 less than the lower risk Bank of America BA.

BAs are "two-name" paper because they are obligations of both the accepting bank and the account party (the importer). This reduces their credit risk exposure, since for default to occur, both parties must be unable to pay. On average in 1991, commercial banks held 21% of the BAs outstanding, money market mutual funds held 13%, dealers 3%, and the Fed's foreign correspondents 3%. The remaining 60% were held by investors, including state and local governments, pension funds, and insurance companies.

Checkpoint

✓

1. How does the letter of credit and the BA hedge credit risk exposure?
2. How has the deterioration in the credit quality of the world's banks affected the BA market?

Off-Balance Sheet Risk Hedging

standby letter of credit (SLC): an off-balance sheet, contingent liability that commits the issuing bank to make payments to the exporter only in the event of default by the importer.

We have seen that the BA market has shrunk considerably over the last five years. Another explanation for its decline is the availability of another, less expensive, financial instrument that provides the same credit risk-hedging services as the letter of credit. That instrument is the **standby letter of credit (SLC)**. This document is an off-balance sheet, contingent liability that commits the issuing bank to make payments to the exporter only in the event the importer defaults. The letter of credit performs this same function prior to its transformation into a

BA. Indeed, it is the off-balance sheet nature of both the letter of credit and the SLC that makes them less costly than BAs in providing the introductory handshake required to facilitate international transactions.

The standby letter of credit was a FI innovation designed to circumvent a restrictive regulation. Most U.S. banks were prohibited from issuing guarantees. However, as U.S. companies entered foreign markets after World War II, they were required to post bid bonds and performance bonds as guarantees of their ability to deliver on their contracts. At first, the letter of credit was used. Indeed, *Practitioner's Primer 13.1: The Cuban Letter of Credit Crisis*, shows a novel use of the performance letter of credit in resolving an international crisis. According to a recent survey by *Letter of Credit Update*, U.S. letters of credit currently total $30 billion and SLCs amount to almost $140 billion.[6]

PRACTITIONER'S PRIMER 13.1

THE CUBAN LETTER OF CREDIT CRISIS

The botched Bay of Pigs invasion left U.S. prisoners in Cuban hands. The United States agreed to provide $53 million of food and medical supplies in return for the prisoners' release, but there was a payment problem. How could Cuba be sure that the United States would pay up once the prisoners were released?

[The solution was that] the American Red Cross applied to the Royal Bank of Canada in Montreal to issue a $53 million letter of credit in favor of the Cuban government. If the United States failed to deliver the supplies as agreed, the Cuban government, as beneficiary of the letter of credit, would present a certificate of default to the Royal Bank of Canada, and receive immediate payment in cash, with which it could purchase the supplies.

This arrangement satisfied everyone. The prisoners came home and the Cuban government got its supplies.

Source: Maulella (September 1994), p. 22.

What is the difference between a SLC and a letter of credit? Both letters of credit (also referred to as "commercial" or "trade" letters of credit) and SLCs are obligations of the issuing bank.[7] Both are used to ensure that the contractually obligated payment is made. The difference between the letter of credit and the SLC, then, is simply a matter of degree. The letter of credit will almost certainly be exercised in the course of completing the commercial transaction. As we have seen, the exercise of the letter of credit triggers the transfer of a time draft for payment. In contrast, the SLC is only a backup to ensure payment. It is exercised only in the event of a default by the primary party responsible for payment. Thus, funds will always be drawn against the time draft in a letter of credit, but will be drawn against a SLC only if there is a default. Since letters of credit are short term promissory notes, they are quite complex, stipulating the exact conditions under which the funds will be paid (for example, upon receipt of certain shipping

---

[6] See Maulella (1994), p. 22.

[7] Federal courts have long distinguished letters of credit from SLCs and other guarantees on the ground that a letter of credit is a "direct and primary obligation of the issuer," while under the SLC the "obligation of the issuer is secondary." See *Border National Bank v. American National Bank*, 282 F. 73 (5th Cir. 1922).

Table 13.2

Standby Letters of Credit, 1995 (US$ million)

	All Commercial Banks	< $100m Asset size	$100m—$1b Asset size	≥ $1b Asset size
Financial standby letters of credit & foreign office guarantees	$146,722	$610	$3,620	$142,492
Performance standby letters of credit	43,030	309	1,555	41,165
Amount conveyed to others	20,784	26	393	20,365
Issued to non–US addresses[a]	39,565	0	17	39,548
Commercial letters of credit	31,885	209	1,284	30,392
Total	281,986	1,154	6,870	273,962

[a]Not reported by institutions with less than $1 billion in assets.

Source: FDIC *Statistics on Banking 1995*, April 1996.

documents or upon physical inspection of specified merchandise). The SLC usually requires only one document to cover all purchases from a single party. Since SLCs are simpler with less documentation, their transaction costs are lower than those for letters of credit.

To illustrate the lower costs of the SLC, let's take the case of a letter of credit for a $12 million shipment of merchandise. Suppose that the merchandise is shipped in increments of $1 million per month. A letter of credit is written for each shipment, totaling an annual amount of $12 million. It would cost the buyer and seller a total of approximately $120,000 (1% of total shipment) in fees.[8]

If a SLC were used to guarantee payment, then the amount of the SLC could be considerably lower than $12 million. This is because the SLC is exercised only in the event of default. It is extremely unlikely that a default will occur every month. Thus, the SLC need not cover each month's shipment. If both the importer and exporter agree to cover only 60 days, then the SLC can be written for $2 million (any two monthly $1 million shipments in a year). Using the average cost of the SLC of 2% of the total, we can see that the cost of this SLC is approximately $40,000 (.02 × $2 million), cutting the cost of the guarantee by two-thirds.

In contrast to the BA, the SLC requires no up-front cash payment by the issuing bank. Indeed, the issuing bank makes payments only if the importer defaults on its obligations on maturity date. Thus, the costs of funding the SLC (in terms of capital requirements, reserve requirements, and financing costs) are close to zero for the issuing bank.[9] The SLC is an off-balance sheet contingent liability of the issuer. Moreover, the exporter obtains the same credit enhancement as for the on-balance sheet BA. The full credit quality of the issuing bank is behind the transaction, protecting the exporter from default by the importer. The SLC provides no cash flow shifting services, but offers the full array of risk-transfer services, at a fraction of the cost of a BA.

notional value: the nominal face value that is an upper bound for an off-balance sheet transaction.

Comparing Tables 13.1 and 13.2 shows that the volume of SLCs far exceeds the volume in the U.S. BA market. However, SLC volume is inflated since it is simply **notional value**, the nominal face value that is an upper bound for an off-balance sheet transaction. Experience shows that only 11% of the SLCs, on average, are exercised and must be ultimately funded by the issuing banks.[10] Thus, a notional volume of $166 billion will generate only an expected value of $18.26 billion (.11 × $166 billion) in actual cash flows.

Banks with assets exceeding $1 billion dominate the market for SLCs (see Table 13.2). Since only a small portion of these SLCs are expected to generate actual cash flows, these banks can

---

[8] See Maulella (1994), p. 24.

[9] Following the adoption of risk-based international capital requirements, banks must hold small amounts of capital to back up off-balance sheet items, such as SLCs. Thus, the cost to the bank of issuing an SLC is small but not zero.

[10] See Helmi and Hindi (1995), p. 19.

issue amounts far in excess of their capital levels. That is not to suggest that the high SLC volume creates an added risk of insolvency for the issuing bank. Indeed, Koppenhaver and Stover (1994) suggest that banks with greater volumes of SLC issues have higher capital levels. One reason for this situation may be that if a bank wants to issue SLCs, then it must lower its credit risk exposure so that it can be competitive. One way to lower credit risk is to increase the bank's capital cushion.

The Impact of SLCs on the FI's Credit Risk Exposure   Larger, less risky banks tend to be the most active issuers of SLCs. This is because the bank's ability to issue a SLC depends on its own credit risk exposure. A SLC is not much of a credit enhancement if the issuing bank's financial condition is itself shaky. How does the issuance of SLC affect the risk exposure of the FI itself?

SLC issuance may either increase or decrease the FI's credit risk exposure. Credit risk increases because compliance with the terms of a SLC requires the issuer to extend a loan to a customer in financial distress. Thus, the FI will be forced to extend loans to SLC customers that are poor credit risks. Moreover, if many SLCs must be paid out at any point in time, the issuer may experience a liquidity crisis.

In contrast, the issuance of SLCs may reduce the FI's risk exposure. The FI has the incentive to monitor the activities of the customer on whose behalf the SLC is issued. The FI may have superior information about the riskiness of the customer, and the issuance of the SLC may signal that the customer is not overly risky. By extending SLC and other financial services to less risky customers, the FI may reduce the risk exposure of its own portfolio. Moreover, the SLC may be a vehicle of market discipline. That is, if the FI takes on very risky activities, it will be unable to sell SLCs because potential buyers will be concerned about whether the FI will itself be solvent in the future. Since the SLC provides for a future payment, if certain contingencies occur, then any doubt about the FI's longevity will undermine its ability to issue SLCs.

The question of whether the SLC enhances or reduces the FI's risk exposure is an empirical one. Although Bennett's (1986) results support the risk-enhancing effect of SLC issuance, most other studies find the opposite.[11] Indeed, Hassan (1992), using one of his measures of asset risk, finds that an increase in the SLC volume decreases the FI's asset risk by a statistically significant 1.24%.[12]

Country Risk Exposure

country risk exposure: the risk of a political upheaval that might hamper financial and goods flows.

Foreign transactions always carry the risk of a political upheaval that might hamper financial and goods flows. This **country risk exposure** is particularly important for importers and exporters that specialize in a particular foreign market. Since the FI issues a portfolio of letters of credit, SLCs, and BAs to importers and exporters around the world, some of that country risk is diversified away. Well-diversified FIs can offer their customers protection against country risk exposure by guaranteeing payments.

SLC, BA, and letter of credit activity varied across countries for 1993. Table 13.3 shows the distribution for selected observations in 16 countries. Australia and the United States dominate the market for letters of credit and BAs. All countries, with the exceptions of Japan and Norway, are active participants in the market for standby letters of credit. However, the United States, Finland, and Sweden are dominant in these markets when ranked on the basis of percentage of total assets. The activity of all the Scandinavian countries in standby letters of credit stems from their large volumes of trade with Eastern European countries such as Russia, Ukraine,

---

[11] For example, see Brewer and Koppenhaver (1992) and Koppenhaver and Stover (1994).

[12] The same evidence of market discipline in the market for bank deposits is found by Park (1995) and Flannery and Sorescu (1996). This suggests that the credit risk associated with BA and SLC activity is similar to that of bank lending funded by deposits.

Table 13.3

International BA, Letter of Credit, and Standby Letter of Credit Transactions, 1993[a] (US$ 000)

Country	No. of Banks	BA	Letters of Credit	SLC
Australia	12	33,548	4,197	14,743
% of total assets		11.6	1.5	5.1
Austria	5	42	1,419	4,098
% of total assets		0	1.2	3.5
Canada	46	19,758	2,780	33,515
% of total assets		3.0	0.4	5.2
Switzerland	23	3,941	11,820	56,876
% of total assets		0.4	1.2	5.9
Germany	14	2,838	9,095	67,848
% of total assets		0.2	0.7	5.5
Denmark	6	0	664	7,887
% of total assets		0	0.6	6.8
Spain	11	0	418	14,373
% of total assets		0	0.1	4.4
Finland	10	0	223	13,495
% of total assets		0	0.3	16.2
France	25	0	13	74,600
% of total assets		0	0	6.6
Great Britain	56	0	17,610	105,651
% of total assets		0	1.0	5.8
Hong Kong	8	28	479	2,884
% of total assets		.04	0.7	4.1
Ireland	9	0	136	1,468
% of total assets		0	0.2	2.2
Japan	2	14,934	0	0
% of total assets		4.5	0	0
Norway	6	0	0	0
% of total assets		0	0	0
Sweden	18	0	3,423	13,748
% of total assets		0	1.8	7.1
U.S.	95	10,929	705,599	592,449
% of total assets		0.3	17.5	14.7

[a]Amounts shown are the totals for all available observations. The number of observations varies across countries depending on data availability. Data availability for Japan is low because the fiscal year ends on March 31 (as opposed to December 31), thereby delaying reporting. Acceptances outstanding are unmatured drafts accepted by a bank. Letters of credit are the FI's potential responsibility for payment of all letters of credit it has issued and guaranteed. Standby letters of credit are the FI's potential obligation for payment to a third party when customers fail to perform under the terms of various credit agreements that the FI has guaranteed.

Source: Standard & Poor's GlobalVantage.

and Poland. Because of the political and economic instability of these emerging nations, their country risk exposure is considerable, thereby encouraging the use of country risk-hedging financial instruments such as the SLC.

Checkpoint

1. How do standby letters of credit offer risk-hedging services?
2. Contrast letters of credit, BAs, and SLCs.
3. What is country risk, and how can it be reduced using letters of credit, BAs, and SLCs?

➤ Another Declining Market: The U.S. Certificate of Deposit

BAs facilitate international trade by providing financing to importers for the purchase of goods. The BA links two bank transactions: (1) lending to importers to finance the purchase of goods and (2) borrowing from money markets to fund the loans to the importers. With the decline in the BA market, we have seen how these two transactions are uncoupled using the SLC. Another way to separate the two transactions is the extension of a bank loan to the importer and the separate funding of that loan, along with the bank's other activities, by issuing deposits. A deposit that was dominant in the money markets of the 1970s–early 1980s was the certificate of deposit (CD). The CD is a negotiable time deposit issued by a bank for a fixed rate of interest for a fixed tenor.[13]

Negotiable CDs, also known as jumbo CDs, carry minimum denominations of $100,000, and can be resold in secondary markets.[14] This market developed in response to regulatory incentives created by Regulation Q ceilings on bank interest rates. During the period of high and volatile interest rates in the late 1970s and early 1980s, cash-rich corporations and mutual funds searched for high-yielding, but safe, investments. Banks in the United States could not offer higher yields on their savings accounts because of the limitations of Regulation Q, which limited interest rates to 5% p.a. (5.25% p.a. at thrift institutions). In a world of double-digit inflation, these yields were not very attractive. Citibank invented an instrument that would circumvent this regulatory restriction: the certificate of deposit. CDs were not subject to Regulation Q restrictions, and U.S. banks came to rely on them as their primary source of loan financing.

The same factors that contributed to the explosive growth of the CD market led to its decline. Passage of the Depository Institutions Deregulatory and Monetary Control Act (DIDMCA) of 1980 called for elimination of all interest rate ceilings on time deposits by 1986. This created competition for the CD market, since other instruments could then offer market rates of interest. Moreover, in 1983, the Fed set reserve requirements at 3% for all CDs with maturities less than 18 months and 0% for all CDs with tenors of 18 months or more, thereby increasing the costs of short maturity CDs. By the time the Fed removed all reserve requirements on CDs, in December 1990, the market was already moribund.

Today the CD market is very illiquid. Although CD rate quotes are available, as shown in Figure 13.4, there are few dealers to make markets. This illiquidity is apparent in the spreads between BAs and CDs, both of which are short term obligations of large money center banks (as shown in Figure 13.4 by spreads of 4 basis points in the one month tenor, 7 basis points in the three month tenor, and 16 basis points in the six month tenor). The exception to this rise and fall story is the Eurodollar CD market, which is thriving today, in large part because of its exemption from U.S. regulatory policy. The tradeoff between activity in the two markets is shown in Figure 13.5.

Checkpoint

1. What factors led to the rise in the CD market?
2. What factors led to the decline in the CD market?

---

[13] There are variations on this definition; for example, variable rate CDs were offered in the late 1970s.

[14] Nonnegotiable CDs have face value of less than $100,000 and are therefore eligible for full deposit insurance coverage in the United States. However, they cannot be resold in secondary markets and must be held until maturity, or else an interest penalty for premature withdrawal is paid.

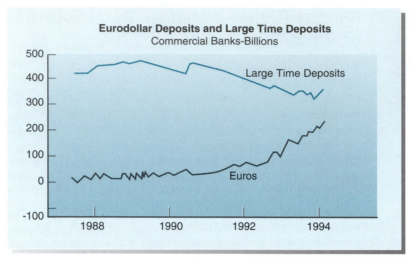

Source: "How bank funding patterns have shifted," A. Smith, III, ABA Banking Journal,Vol. 87, no. 2, p. 21.

Figure 13.5

➤ Summary

Bankers acceptances (BAs), letters of credit (LCs), and standby letters of credit (SLCs) all evolved from the desires of exporters to speed up their cash payments for their exports and importers to delay those payments until the goods are received. The letter of credit and time draft bridge the time gap and allow the exporter to choose the date that she or he will be paid. In addition, the letter of credit and standby letter of credit protect the exporter from the credit risk and country risk exposure of the importer.

The BA evolved to offset the large cash outlay required by the bank that issued the letter of credit upon presentation of the time draft. The BA is a negotiable form of a letter of credit that can be sold in secondary markets. The bank sells the BA to raise funds to recoup its large up-front cash outlay to the exporter's bank.

Another way to offer risk-hedging services is for the FI to use an off-balance sheet item: the standby letter of credit (SLC). The SLC is a contingent letter of credit, that is exercised only if the importer defaults on the contractual payment. Then, and only then, does the issuing bank have to make a payment. Since only a small fraction of SLCs are exercised, at any point in time, the cost to the bank of issuing SLCs is significantly less than issuing either letters of credit or BAs. SLC volume has grown, while BA volume has declined in recent years.

A BA is equivalent to a loan to an importer to finance purchases of goods that are linked to financing by the issuance of a deposit. A deposit market that grew very rapidly in the United States during the late 1970s through the early 1980s was the certificate of deposit, CD. This negotiable instrument was a close substitute for BAs. Its attractiveness waned, however, as regulatory restrictions increased its cost (because of the reserve requirement) and allowed more attractive substitutes (with the lifting of Regulation Q interest rate ceilings).

➤ References

Bennett, B. "Off Balance Sheet Risk in Banking: The Case of Standby Letters of Credit." Federal Reserve Bank of San Francisco, *Economic Review*, No. 1 (Winter 1986): 19–29.

Brewer, E., III, and G. D. Koppenhaver. "The Impact of Standby Letters of Credit on Bank Risk: A Note." *Journal of Banking and Finance* 16 (1992): 1037–1046.

Flannery, M., and S. Sorescu. "Evidence of Bank Market Discipline in Subordinated Debenture Yields: 1983–1991." *Journal of Finance* (September 1996).

Flock, M. "Doing Business Abroad: Open Account or Letter of Credit?" *Business Credit* (March 1995): 23–26.

Harfield, H. "Guaranties, Standby Letters of Credit, and Ugly Ducklings." *Uniform Commercial Code Law Journal* 26, No. 3 (Winter 1994): 195–203.

Hassan, M. K. "An Empirical Analysis of Bank Standby Letters of Credit Risk." *Review of Financial Economics* 2, No. 1 (Fall 1992): 31–44.

Helmi, H., and Hindi, N. "Raining on Banking's Parade: New Rules Promote Fuller Accounting of Liabilities." *National Public Accountant* 40, No. 1 (January 1995): 17–19, 37.

Koppenhaver, G. D. "Standby Letters of Credit." Federal Reserve Bank of Chicago, *Economic Perspectives*. 11, No. 4 (July–August 1987): 28–38.

Koppenhaver, G. D., and R. D. Stover. "Standby Letters of Credit and Bank Capital: Evidence of Market Discipline." *Journal of Banking and Finance* 18 (1994): 553–573.

Koppenhaver, G. D., and R. D. Stover "Standby Letters of Credit and Large Bank Capital: An Empirical Analysis." *Journal of Banking and Finance* 15 (1991): 315–327.

LaRoche, R. K. "Bankers Acceptances." In T. Q. Cook and R. K. LaRoche, eds., *Instruments of the Money Market*. 7th ed., Richmond, VA.: Federal Reserve Bank of Richmond, 1993, pp. 128–138.

Maulella, V. "Standby Letters of Credit Extend Business Drive." *Corporate Cashflow* (September 1994): 21–26.

Park, S. "Market Discipline by Depositors: Evidence from Reduced-Form Equations." *The Quarterly Review of Economics and Finance* 35 (1995): 497–514.

Ryan, R. *Letters of Credit and Bankers Acceptances*. New York: Practising Law Institute, 1983.

Stigum, M. *The Money Market*, 3rd ed., Homewood, IL.: Business One, Irwin, 1990.

Questions

1. Illustrate the regulatory dialectic using (a) the BA market, (b) the CD market.

2. How does information production by FIs play a role in the BA market? in the SLC market?

3. Suppose that the BA rate of discount was 4.5% p.a. Price a BA with $5 million face value:
   a. If there are 183 days until maturity.
   b. If there are 79 days until maturity.
   c. If there are 16 days until maturity.

4. Suppose that the BA in question 3 was issued by a risky FI, so that the BA rate is tiered by 25 basis points. Reprice the BAs in question 3 for the riskier FI. Why are your answers here different from your answers to question 3?

5. Trade between a U.S. shoe retailer and its Italian supplier averages US$10 million per month. Calculate the annual cost to guaranteeing payment to the Italian exporter using
   a. A BA, if the rate of discount is 5.5% p.a. and if payment is accelerated 90 days each month.
   b. A letter of credit.
   c. A standby letter of credit, if 90 days of shipments are covered.

CHAPTER 14

COMMERCIAL PAPER AND LOAN COMMITMENTS

"Man is the only animal that can be skinned more than once."—Jimmy Durante

Learning Objectives

- To examine how commercial paper and loan commitments are used to provide a steady flow of cash to healthy firms.
- To describe takedown risk exposure.

➤ Introduction

commercial and industrial loans: loans to businesses.

Traditionally, when companies wanted to obtain working capital to finance their day-to-day business operations, they turned to banks. Short and medium term **commercial and industrial loans**, or loans to businesses, were the sole realm of the banking sector in the past. This is no longer the case, in part thanks to the growth of the commercial paper market. Figure 14.1 shows that commercial paper accounts for more than 25% of total bank commercial and industrial lending. In 1994 the absolute size of the commercial paper market increased at an annual rate of 10%, reaching a volume of $605.8 billion outstanding as of the end of 1994. Other FIs, such as investment banks and securities brokers, dominate banks in the underwriting of commercial paper, but this does not mean that the banks have been cut out of this business lending. As we will see, the banks issue lines of credit to back up commercial paper offerings.

➤ The Issuers of Commercial Paper

Why did businesses leave the comfort of their local banker for the vagaries of the commercial paper market? We must trace the evolution of the market in the United States, where it is most developed. Indeed, other domestic commercial paper markets (for example, sterling commercial paper), with the possible exceptions of the Canadian and Australian commercial paper markets, are still in their infancies. Although an active commercial paper market existed in the United States during the 1920s, it was decimated by the Great Depression. The early development of the commercial paper market was encouraged by the eligibility of commercial

419

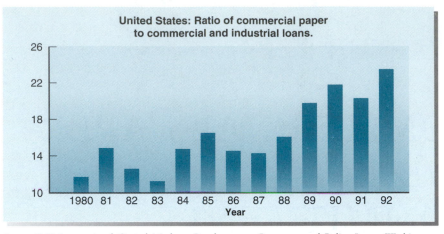

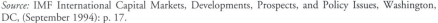

Source: IMF International Capital Markets, Developments, Prospects, and Policy Issues, Washington, DC, (September 1994): p. 17.

Figure 14.1

paper as collateral for discount window loans, as well as the incidence of large-scale defaults on the bond market during the financial panic of 1909. The relative infrequency of default in the commercial paper market led investors to believe that commercial paper was a safe investment. By 1920 more than 4,000 firms were issuing commercial paper, amounting to an annual volume of $1.3 billion.

Following the Great Depression, the domestic U.S. commercial paper market was stagnant until the mid-1960s. Then a combination of a credit crunch (brought on by the Fed's tight money policy of 1966–1967) and a booming economy created ripe conditions for the development of an alternative to bank commercial and industrial loans. The Fed's tight money policy raised interest rates on bank loans. Moreover, restrictions on interest rates that the banks could offer on deposits (see discussion of Regulation Q in Chapter 11) led to an outflow of funds from the banking system, which reduced the availability of bank loans. At the same time, a consumer product boom created an increase in the demand for loans. The **finance company** was in its heyday in the 1960s. A finance company is a FI, often a subsidiary of a manufacturing company, that funds loans to consumers who purchase the manufacturing company's products. For example, GMAC, the General Motors Acceptance Corporation, is a finance company that facilitates auto sales by financing car loans for consumers of GM products. The growing U.S. economy fueled increases in consumer purchases, which were often financed with loans from the finance companies. Thus, the finance companies were "cash guzzlers," always looking for newer, less expensive sources of funds.

Since most of the finance companies were owned by large, blue chip manufacturing companies, they were sufficiently well known to access capital markets directly. Rather than going to the banks for expensive and unreliable lending sources, the finance companies chose to go directly to Funds Surplus Units by selling their own debt securities, one form of which was **commercial paper**. These securities are unsecured, negotiable notes that have maturities of 270 days or less. Why the limitation to maturities of 270 days or less? Because of the regulatory dialectic. To keep down the cost of funds, the finance companies found a loophole in the regulations. Under Section 3(a)(3) of the Securities Act of 1933, all notes whose proceeds are for current transactions and have maturities less than nine months are exempt from

finance company: a FI, often a subsidiary of a manufacturing company, that funds loans to consumers who purchase the manufacturing company's products.

commercial paper: unsecured, negotiable notes that have maturities of 270 days or less.

Table 14.1

Commercial Paper Issues, 1990–1995ᵃ ($ million)

Issuer	1990	1991	1992	1993	1994	1995
Financial companies	414,742	395,462	398,061	399,336	430,739	486,643
Pct. of total	73.7%	74.8%	73.0%	71.9%	72.3%	72.1%
Dealer-directed	214,706	212,999	226,456	218,947	223,038	275,815
Pct. of total	38.1%	40.3%	41.5%	39.4%	37.5%	40.9%
Directly placed	200,036	182,463	171,605	180,389	207,701	210,828
Pct. of total	35.6%	34.5%	31.5%	32.5%	34.9%	31.2%
Nonfinancial companies	147,914	133,370	147,558	155,739	164,643	188,260
Pct. of total	26.3%	25.2%	27.0%	28.1%	27.6%	27.9%
Total	562,656	528,832	545,619	555,075	595,382	674,903

ᵃNonfinancial companies include public utilities and firms engaged primarily in such activities as communications, construction, manufacturing, mining, wholesale and retail trade, transportation, and services. Dealer-directed commercial paper includes all financial company paper sold by dealers in the open market. Directly placed commercial paper is reported by FIs that sell their paper directly.

Source: Federal Reserve Bulletin (May 1996), Table 1.32.

registration requirements with the SEC. Thus, commercial paper could be issued without registration, thereby cutting down the cost of issuance for the finance companies. To avoid costly registration requirements, commercial paper must

1. Have a maturity of less than 270 days. Commercial paper can roll over continuously as long as the rollover is not automatic. In practice, commercial paper maturities range from 5 to 45 days, with an average of 30 days.

2. Be in denominations exceeding $100,000, so that investors tend to be institutions.

3. Be issued to finance "current transactions," such as the funding of operating expenses, receivables, and inventories.

Finance companies were not the only Funds Deficit Units to see the benefits of the commercial paper market. Table 14.1 shows that in 1995 27.9% of all commercial paper issuers were industrial (nonfinancial) firms. At first, the banks looked on the new market with chagrin since it was cutting into their basic lending business. However, during years of tight monetary policy, the banks themselves saw the virtue of the low-cost accessibility of funds offered by the commercial paper market.[1] In 1991 banks issued 4.6% of all commercial paper outstanding, whereas nonbank FIs' issues comprised 61.3%.

Commercial paper financing is a substitute for bond issuance as well as for bank loans. Borrowers in different countries use commercial paper and bonds in varying proportions (see Table 14.2). More than half of the world's commercial paper is issued in the United States, but there is also an active Eurocommercial paper market (see Chapter 12). Eurocommercial paper maturities range from 60 to 180 days and, as opposed to U.S. commercial paper, are traded in active secondary markets. In 1991 foreign FIs constituted 10.5% of all commercial

---

[1] Bank issues of commercial paper became economically feasible when the Fed lifted the reserve requirement on bank commercial paper offerings in August 1970.

Table
14.2

Commercial Paper Markets Throughout the World (US$ billion)

Country	Year of Market Opening	Domestic	Euromarket	Pct. of Bonds Outstanding
United States	pre-1960	$544.9b	$65.3b	12.8%
Japan	end-1987	98.1	0.4	11.5
France	end-1985	31.3	0.3	12.9
Spain	1982	29.3	—	66.8
Canada	pre-1960	24.5	0.1	13.0
Sweden	1983	16.6	—	16.7
Australia	mid-1970s	13.8	4.2	17.9
Germany	early 1991	10.2	3.6	5.4
United Kingdom	1986	6.9	1.7	26.1
Finland	mid-1986	3.8	—	23.0
Norway	end-1984	2.2	—	10.9
Netherlands	1986	2.6	0.4	17.3
Belgium	1990	1.3	—	0.3
Other	—	2.7		
TOTAL		$788.2	$76.0	

Source: Alworth and Borio (1993), pp. 12, 15, 17.

paper issues in the United States, whereas foreign nonfinancial companies issued 4.9% of all outstanding U.S. commercial paper.

The lack of development of domestic commercial paper markets, other than in the United States, is reflected in the activity of foreign issuers in the U.S. domestic commercial paper market, as well as in the Eurocommercial paper market. Foreign issuers account for almost 20% of the total. However, this understates the importance of foreign borrowers in the U.S. commercial paper market. Including issuance by U.S. subsidiaries of foreign companies, the total amount of commercial paper issued on behalf of foreign firms in 1991 was $111.6 billion, or 50.5% of the total.[2] For FIs, Table 14.3 shows that only the U.S. and Swedish FIs issued commercial paper in any volume. Active competition between the Eurodollar commercial paper and the domestic U.S. commercial paper market exists. Since domestic commercial paper rates are lower than Eurodollar commercial paper rates, well-known borrowers and sovereign governments tend to issue in the domestic U.S. market. However, since issues in the domestic market must be rated,[3] while they can be sold unrated on the Euromarket, many firms save the costs of acquiring a credit rating and, instead, meet their short term borrowing needs on the Euromarket. *Timely Topics 14.1: Why CP Stands for Countless Problems* examines the German commercial paper market as a case study of the friction between the domestic and Eurocommercial paper markets.

---

[2] Since many U.S. money market investors are prohibited from foreign investment by their charters, many foreign corporations, financial and nonfinancial, set up U.S. funding subsidiaries in order to tap the U.S. commercial paper market. This accounted for $55.9 billion, or 50.1% of all issues of commercial paper to fund foreign firms in 1991.

[3] There is a small, unrated, "junk" domestic U.S. commercial paper market, but it is illiquid. Nayar and Rozeff (1994) state that poorly rated firms are not able to issue commercial paper in quantity. Crabbe and Post (1994) show that rating downgrades lead to exits from the commercial paper market. Elayan, Maris, and Young (1996) show the negative impacts of credit downgrades of commercial paper issues. In June 1989 Integrated Resources defaulted on an issue of junk commercial paper, creating havoc in the then–$5 billion market.

Table 14.3

Commercial Paper and Loan Commitments by Country, 1993[a] (US$ 000)

Country	No. of FIs	Commercial Paper	Loan Commitments
Australia	12	1,140	44,715
% of total assets		0.4	15.5
Austria	5	0	0
% of total assets		0	0
Canada	46	97	240,349
% of total assets		0	37.0
Switzerland	23	0	55,391
% of total assets		0	5.8
Germany	14	0	50,068
% of total assets		0	4.0
Denmark	6	0	3,357
% of total assets		0	2.9
Spain	11	82	37,194
% of total assets		0.02	11.3
Finland	10	0	438
% of total assets		0	0.5
France	25	0	81,947
% of total assets		0	7.3
Great Britain	56	3,570	198,438
% of total assets		0.2	10.9
Hong Kong	8	0	0
% of total assets		0	0
Ireland	9	88	8,064
% of total assets		0.1	11.8
Japan	2	0	0
% of total assets		0	0
Norway	6	0	5,355
% of total assets		0	8.9
Sweden	18	6,245	7,618
% of total assets		3.2	3.9
U.S.	95	77,655	986,663
% of total assets		1.9	24.5

[a]Amounts shown are the totals for all available observations. The number of observations varies across countries depending on data availability. Data availability for Japan is low because the fiscal year ends on March 31 (as opposed to December 31), thereby delaying reporting.

Source: Standard & Poor's GlobalVantage. Commercial paper, unsecured promissory notes issued in large denominations by FIs, have maturities ranging from a few days to nine months. Loan commitments are legally binding agreements to extend credit to customers. Commitments have fixed expiration dates and generally require the payment of a fee on the unused portion of the commitment.

TIMELY TOPICS 14.1

WHY CP STANDS FOR COUNTLESS PROBLEMS

The Deutschemark commercial paper (CP) market was an immediate success when it opened in 1991. A variety of German issuers rushed to set up and use programmes. By

October 1992, outstandings had reached DM20 billion (US$12 billion), equivalent to 50% utilization of announced programmes.

Since then, the market has lost its momentum [to the EuroDM commercial paper market]. Issuance in Germany's domestic CP market has declined dramatically in the last year, and outstandings have fallen to DM11 billion, or programme usage of only 25%.... The Deutschemark CP market has become stagnant, and significant changes will be required to change this.

As with Deutschemark bonds, there are still clear dividing lines between Deutschemark CP's Euro and domestic sectors—the hallmark of an underdeveloped market.... Although issuance was opened to foreign entities in 1992, foreign financial companies cannot issue paper with maturities of less than two years. The definition of a financial company is very strict and excludes many corporates that fund through finance vehicles, as well as supranationals. "Essentially, only the final user of the funds can borrow in this market," explains one banker. "If your finance company borrows on your behalf, this is considered a transfer of funds and is subject to reserves under German regulations." Confusion as to whether or not this rule applies to holding companies as well as to finance companies has caused concern about some outstanding programmes [and has moved business to the unregulated EuroDM CP market].

Lifting these regulations would boost issuance, not only by letting supranationals into the market, but also by allowing corporates to issue Deutschemarks as an option on multicurrency Euro CP programmes (which most prefer to do).... The consensus seems to be that it is a matter of time before the short term Deutschemark market becomes comparable with those in other currencies. "We have seen borrowers that have issued in dollar Euro CP and swapped into Deutschemarks," says Manfred Schepers, executive director of capital markets and treasury at Swiss Bank Corporation. "Obviously, they would rather issue in Deutschemark direct."

The major obstacle remains the inefficiency resulting from German investors' decisions being driven by name-recognition rather than [creditworthiness]. When Metallgesellschaft stopped servicing its CP last December—the first such crisis to hit the market since its inception—there was much speculation that investors would become more careful about what they bought and would require official ratings and perhaps back-up lines to guarantee outstandings. Although some German companies—such as Thyssen, Volkswagen, and BMW—do have back-up credit facilities, this is not the norm.

The impact has not been nearly so dramatic. This, says one head of CP, was "partly because Metallgesellschaft did not default—it was just a temporary halt in payment. I expect it will take another big problem before credit [risk] is assessed more seriously."...

The high degree of intermediation in the market also constrains its development. The bulk of paper is placed with insurance companies and domestic Luxembourg-based funds (the majority of which are managed or controlled by German banks). In addition, German banks introduced fixed fees for Deutschemark CP from the start, fearing that without these it would quickly become a burdensome and unprofitable business. The cost of arranging a CP programme remains relatively high, and alternatives such as traditional bank loans continue to provide the majority of corporate financing needs.

The fact that domestic banks focus on domestic clients and foreign banks deal with international investors has meant that the full force of international competition has not been felt in this market. Deutsche Bank is the only German bank that is active in both domestic CP and EuroDM CP.... [F]or the full potential of the market to be realized, it must become more efficient through increased involvement of foreign investors—which will not happen until the market reforms. There are calls for increased commitment from domestic banks to make the market more competitive.

Source: *Euromoney Capital Markets Report*, July 1994, pp. 89–90.

Checkpoint

1. To what do you attribute the development of commercial paper as a financial instrument?
2. To what do you attribute the growth of commercial paper as a financial market?
3. What is the role of FIs in the commercial paper market?
4. What are the substitutes for commercial paper?

Pricing, Placing, and Clearing Commercial Paper

The volume of commercial paper offerings is seasonal, reflecting summer declines and holiday peaks in finance company sales. The amount of commercial paper outstanding typically increases in preparation for quarterly corporate tax payments and decreases at year-end.

In contrast to the Eurocommercial paper market (in which 40% of new issues are unrated), most issues in the domestic U.S. commercial paper market are rated by either Standard & Poor's or Moody's. This distinction reveals that the Eurodollar commercial paper market is more speculative (since it is entirely unregulated) than is the domestic U.S. commercial paper market. Figure 14.2 shows the distribution of ratings, using Standard & Poor's liquidity credit ratings A-1 down to A-3 and Moody's ratings P-1 down to P-3. The figure shows that top-rated commercial paper (A-1/P-1 or better) accounted for 75.9% of all new issues, making this market quite safe for investors. Table 14.4 describes the characteristics of industrial issuers of commercial paper by rating.

Since commercial paper is unsecured, the investor is exposed to credit risk, but with the time to maturity so short, the concern is about issuer liquidity rather than outright insolvency. However, in 1970 the market for top-rated commercial paper was shaken up by the bankruptcy of Penn Central, which had $82 million of commercial paper outstanding, and more recently in 1992, when the financially distressed Olympia and York found itself unable to roll over $1.1

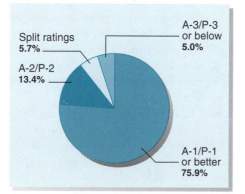

Source: Stigum (1990), p. 1029.

Figure 14.2

Table
14.4

Characteristics of Industrial Commercial Paper Issuers by Rating, Three Year Averages

Standard & Poor's Commercial Paper Rating	Number of Companies	Assets (millions)	Interest Coverage	Debt Coverage	Leverage	Profitability
A-1+	91	$4,547	8x	.7x	27%	18%
A-1	102	$2,924	5x	.5x	35%	16%
A-2	97	$1,866	4x	.4x	36%	14%
A-3	9	$5,252	2x	.2x	52%	10%

Notes: Sample consists of nonfinancial commercial paper issuers required to file with the SEC.

Interest coverage is defined as the ratio of income available for interest to interest expense. Income available for interest is defined as pre-tax income less special income plus interest expense.

Debt coverage is defined as the ratio of cash flow to short and long term debt. Cash flow is income plus preferred dividends plus deferred taxes.

Leverage is defined as the ratio of total debt to invested capital. Invested capital is the sum of short and long term debt, minority interest, preferred and common equity, and deferred taxes.

Profitability is defined as the ratio of income available for interest to invested capital.

Source: Hahn (1993), p. 115.

billion in commercial paper. Interest rates on commercial paper issues reflect the credit ratings of the issuers, with lower rated paper carrying a higher, risk adjusted rate. The commercial paper rate is a discount yield, quoted on a 360 day basis, as is the U.S. Treasury bill. Thus, if the yield is 4.75% p.a. on a 175 day $10 million face value issue, the price (using the discount formula from Chapter 7) is

$$P = FV \left(1 - \frac{dt}{360} \right) = \$10\text{m} \left(1 - \frac{.0475(175)}{360} \right) = \$9.769\text{m}$$

where P = the price of the commercial paper issue, which represents the proceeds (before deducting any commissions or fees) to the issuer, FV = the commercial paper's face value, d = the commercial paper rate, and t = the number of days until maturity.

Commercial paper rates for the highest quality issuers (rated AA or better) have moved closer to the LIBOR over time. Figure 14.3 shows the rate quotes for top-tier commercial paper. Commercial paper rates are higher than rates on securitized repos and Treasury bills, but lower than Eurodollar CD rates. However, commercial paper rates are tiered to reflect the issuer's credit risk exposure. Figure 14.4 shows the spread between prime- and medium-grade commercial paper over the period 1974–1992.

direct-placement: the selling of commercial paper directly to Funds Surplus Units, which hold the paper until maturity.

dealer-directed: a method whereby dealers make markets in commercial paper by buying issues for placement and may redeem notes before maturity.

Because of the large amount of investor interest in the market, many issuers use **direct-placement**; that is, they sell their commercial paper directly to Funds Surplus Units, which hold the paper until maturity. There is no active secondary market in commercial paper in the United States, and so investors try to choose the issue maturity to coincide with their cash timing needs. Table 14.1 shows that 40.9% of all commercial paper offerings in 1995 were **dealer-directed**. Dealers make markets in commercial paper by buying issues for placement and may redeem the notes before maturity, thereby offering some liquidity to the market.[4]

---

[4] The major direct-placement issuers also repurchase their own paper prior to maturity but may charge a penalty rate.

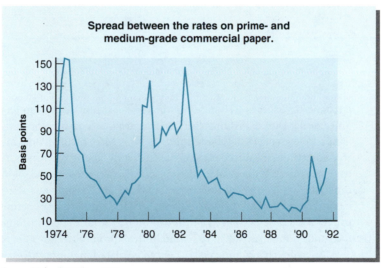

```
3                                                           DG03 Govt MMR
Enter 9 <Go> to reset any NewsMinder Indicators
     MONEY  MARKET  COMPOSITE                              PAGE 1 OF 1
  FED FUNDS              T-BILL         EURO $ DEPOSIT        GOVT REPO
1)FDFD↑6.13-1.875     9)3MO ↓5.51 +.02  18)3MO ↓5.938 .063  27)O/N ↑6.1  +.01
  FED EFFECTIVE       10)6MO ↑5.45 +.02  19)6MO ↓5.875 .063  28)1WK ↓5.77 -.15
2)FEDL 7.41           11)1YR ↑5.31 +.01  20)12MO↓5.875  --   29)1MO ↑5.78 +.03
  TREASURY BONDS         BA'S            CP TOP TIER           CD'S
3)2YR ↑5.78 +2.55    12)1MO ↓5.93 -.02  21)1WK ↓5.98 -.09   30)1MO ↓5.97 -.01
4)3YR ↑5.84 +2.36    13)2MO ↓5.83 -.04  22)2WK ↓5.94 -.04   31)3MO ↓5.85 -.04
5)5YR ↓5.98 +3.31    14)3MO ↓5.78 -.02  23)1MO ↑5.96 +.02   32)6MO ↓5.8  -.01
6)7YR ↓5.94 +1.17    15)4MO ↓5.73 -.02  24)2MO ↓5.85 -.04     PRIME,CALL,DISC
7)10YR↓6.21 +2.53    16)5MO ↓5.67 -.03  25)3MO ↓5.77 -.04   33)PRIM↑9    --
8)30YR↓6.63 +3.07    17)6MO ↓5.64 -.03  26)6MO ↑5.7  +.03   34)BLR ↑7.75 --
                                                            35)DISC↑5.25 --

36)TEDSUS    10:43↓     .36  +.01 37)EDA      10:46↑  94.34  -.01
                                   .40                              94.38

                                   .38                              94.36

                                   .36                              94.34

                                   .34
                                                                   94.32
   9:00   10:30 · 12:00  13:30  15:00 .32  9:00 10:00 11:00 12:00 13:00 14:00 15:00
 Bloomberg-all rights reserved.  Frankfurt:69-920410  Hong Kong:2-521-3000  London:171-330-7500  New York:212-318-2000
 Princeton:609-279-3000  Singapore:226-3000  Sydney:2-777-8600  Tokyo:3-3201-8900  Washington DC:202-434-1800
                                                           G165-312-3 06-Jul-95  10:48:44
```

Figure 14.3

Spread between the rates on prime- and medium-grade commercial paper.

Source: Hahn (1993), p. 119.

Figure 14.4

The difference between the price paid by the dealer and the price received for the commercial paper is the "dealer spread," which averages around 10 basis points annually.

If an issuer is a large and continual borrower in the commercial paper market, maintaining a sales force to directly place its own paper will save on the cost of dealer commissions and underwriting fees. Once annual volumes of commercial paper offerings exceed $500 million, it is economical to set up a direct issuance facility. For large enough volumes—say, average

Table
14.5

Basic Features of the Instrument

	Euro	US	Japan	France	Spain	Canada	Singapore
Bearer	yes	yes	yes	yes[a]	yes	yes	yes
Registered	rare	rare	no	no	rare	rare	no
Discount basis	yes	yes	yes	yes	yes	yes	yes
Interest-bearing basis	no	rare	no	no	no	rare	no
Denomination							
– smallest	500 k	100 k	100 m	1 m	250 k	100 k	1 m
(US$)[b]	(500 k)	(100 k)	(800 k)	(180 k)	(2.2 k)	(80 k)	(140 k)
– typical	5 m	1 m	1–10 b	10–50 m	$1/2$–1 m	$1/2$–1 m	20–50m
(US$)[b]	5 m	(1 m)	(8–80 m)	(1.8–9.1 m)	(5–10 k)	(395–790 k)	(2.8–7.1 m)
Maturity paper (months)							
– range	$1/30$–12	$1/4$–9	$1/2$–9	$1/3$–12	1–18[c]	$1/30$–12	$1/30$–24
– typical	2	$1/2$–$1^{1}/2$	$1/2$–3	<3	3[c]	≤3	3–12
Currency							
– local	US$	yes	yes	yes	yes	yes	yes
– foreign	mainly	no	no	rare	no	yes	no

[a]"Billets de trésorie". By contrast, "Billets à ordre" (promissory notes) are to-the-order instruments, transferable by endorsement without contingent liability for the seller and cleared through the bank acting as a dealer.

[b]Rounded, using end-1992 exchange rates.

---

in funds: an expression meaning that the commercial paper issuer has raised all the funds it presently needs.

firm commitment underwriting: the selling of notes by the issuer outright to the dealer for later resale, so that the dealer hedges the risk of interest rate declines for the issuer.

bought as sold: the marketing of the commercial paper issue by the dealer and transfer of the proceeds of the sale, less commissions, to the issuer, providing no risk hedging services.

outstanding issues of $10 billion—the total cost of issuance can go as low as one basis point. Since dealer-directed issuing costs average around 5 basis points, this amounts to a $4 million annual cost saving ($10 billion times .0004).[5] Most finance companies and several large industrial companies use direct-placement. Currently, about 110 issuers distribute their commercial paper directly. In direct-placement, the issuer sets the rate and allows the buyer to determine the maturity—anywhere from 3 to 270 days. If the company is currently **in funds**—that is, has all the funds it needs—then it will discourage purchases by setting a low interest rate on its paper. Sometimes, however, a firm will borrow from a good customer even if it does not need the funds immediately, just to maintain the customer relationship.

Dealer-directed commercial paper can be placed in one of three ways. One method, called a **firm commitment underwriting**, is to sell the notes outright to the dealer. The issuer receives the face value of the notes less an agreed-upon discount and the commission. The dealer absorbs the risk that the issuer will be unable to place the commercial paper at a given interest rate. This method of dealer-directed placement offers interest rate risk hedging to the issuer.

A second method of dealer-directed placement is **bought as sold**, whereby the dealer markets the commercial paper issue and transfers the proceeds of the sale, less commissions, to the issuer. Because this method of placement does not hedge the issuer's risk, the commission rate is lower than for firm commitment underwriting, which includes risk transfer, as well as placement, services.

---

[5] See Stigum (1990), p. 1061.

Australia	Germany	UK	Finland	Norway	Netherlands	Belgium[a]
yes	yes	yes	yes	yes	yes	yes
yes	yes	yes	yes	no	yes	yes
no	no	no	rare	yes	no	no
100 k	500 k	100 k	1 m	1 m	1 m	10 m
(70 k)	(310 k)	(150 k)	(190 k)	(145 k)	(550 k)	(300 k)
1/2–1 m	500 k	1 m	10–20 m	1 m	1 m	25 m
(345–690 k)	(310 k)	(1.5 m)	(1.9–3.8 m)	(145 k)	(550 k)	(755 k)
1–6	1/4–24	1/4–12	1/30–12	≤12	1/2–24	1–12
≤3	1–3	1–3	1–3	≤3	≤3	≤2
yes	yes	yes	yes	yes	yes	yes
no	rare	no	no	rare	no	yes

[a]In the organized market. May be shorter otherwise.

Source: Alworth and Borio (1993), pp. 20–21.

---

open rate underwriting: a method that does not offer any risk hedging services, although the issuer receives an up-front downpayment equal to some percentage of the face value of the issue.

The **open rate underwriting** method combines the first two methods but does not offer any risk hedging services. The issuer receives a downpayment equal to some percentage of the face value of the issue upon their delivery to the dealer. After the notes are sold, the dealer transfers the proceeds of the sale less commissions and the downpayment. The total proceeds received by the issuer depend on the interest rate at which the commercial paper is sold, which are not guaranteed by the underwriter.

Commercial paper is cleared electronically in most countries, with settlement that ranges from same-day to trade plus two days, as in the foreign exchange market. However, as Table 14.5 shows, most commercial paper is sold in the bearer, as opposed to registered, form. How then can the securities be cleared electronically if they require a physical certificate? In September 1990 the Depository Trust Company (DTC) introduced a service to clear commercial paper in bearer form. Only the ownership is exchanged in book-entry form, although the securities themselves never move from the vaults of the DTC. By May 1992, over 40% of the commercial paper in the United States utilized this form of electronic issuance and clearance. The availability of electronic clearance is necessary to avoid daylight overdrafts (see Chapter 6) that occur when commercial paper issuance occurs at a time different from the time of payment of maturing commercial paper.

asset-backed commercial paper: a commercial paper offering that is securitized by a portfolio of diversified assets, often credit card or trade receivables.

Asset-Backed Commercial Paper

Participation in the U.S. commercial paper market broadened when an innovation expanded the opportunities for existing issuers and increased the number of potential issuers. The innovation was **asset-backed commercial paper**, pioneered by Salomon Brothers in 1985 when it securitized Marine Midland Banks' automobile loans and leases. Asset-backed commercial paper is a commercial paper offering that is securitized by a portfolio of diversified assets, often credit card or trade receivables. Asset-backed commercial paper outstandings increased from $50 to $160 billion during the period 1993–1995.

The collateral behind asset-backed commercial paper protects the issue from default risk. The issuer is a business entity called a **special-purpose vehicle (SPV)**, which is established for the purpose of purchasing pools of receivables from participating companies and funding them with the proceeds from commercial paper issues. Since the assets owned by the SPV are well diversified, the commercial paper issue is highly rated. To further protect investors in the special-purpose vehicle's paper, each company signs an agreement not to file the SPV into bankruptcy for one year plus one day after the last paper matures. Moreover, the SPV is owned by a party unaffiliated with any of the companies doing business with the SPV. Thus, none of the companies can merge the SPV into their own business. Figure 14.5 shows the use of the SPV to structure asset-backed commercial paper. To illustrate the process using the first publicly offered issue of asset-backed commercial paper, Salomon Brothers was the underwriter and sold the issue to investors. A SPV was established to purchase the automobile loans from Marine Midland Banks, the seller in Figure 14.5 that originated the loans. Thus, Marine Midland received cash from the proceeds of the sale of its loans to investors.

special-purpose vehicle (SPV): a business entity established for the purpose of purchasing pools of receivables from participating companies and funding them with the proceeds from commercial paper issues.

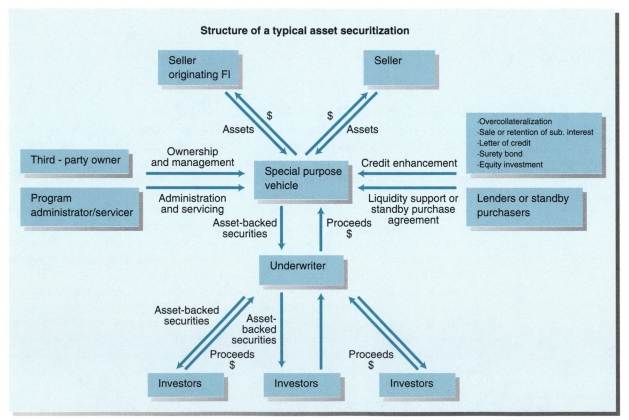

Source: Aidun (1995), p. 21.

Figure 14.5

Collateral takes the form of both marketable and nonmarketable securities. In 1994, 62.4% of asset-backed commercial paper were collateralized with trade receivables, 17.9% used loans, 7.5% used credit card receivables, 8.5% used securities, and 3.7% used leases. Most asset-backed commercial paper was issued by commercial banks (80.5%) and finance companies (11.0%).

To further enhance the credit of the asset-backed commercial paper, the value of the SPV's receivables portfolio exceeds the face value of the commercial paper. Thus, the receivables are collateralized with a haircut, or margin, that further protects the commercial paper investors against credit risk. Average haircuts are approximately 4.5% to 5% for accounts receivables due in 45 days. Finally, the SPV's commercial paper issues are often backed by bank-provided lines of credit.

Asset securitization, as shown in Figure 14.5, is a three-step process:

1. Isolating assets with an ascertainable cash flow into the SPV.
2. Packaging the assets into securities, with specific characteristics and credit enhancements.
3. Selling securities in the capital markets to Funds Surplus Units.

Companies issue asset-backed commercial paper if they are either too small or too poorly rated to access the market directly. However, even highly rated companies issue asset-backed commercial paper if, for example, they want to remove some of their leverage from their balance sheets. For example, bank issuers use asset-backed commercial paper to remove loans from their balance sheet, thereby reducing their capital requirments. FIs encouraged the development of a market for asset-backed commercial paper. Banks, in particular, saw the opportunity to recoup fee income that was formerly earned as interest income on short term bank loans to corporations. The advising FI earns fees for developing the SPV, structuring the SPV's portfolio of receivables, setting the haircut on the issue, and providing a line of credit as a backup credit enhancement.

Liquidity on the Commercial Paper Market

Issuers sell commercial paper to finance their working capital. As inventories and receivables grow, the supply of commercial paper offerings increases. There is also enormous demand for commercial paper by investors. Many of these investors are themselves FIs.

money market mutual funds: funds that sell shares of portfolios of short term money market instruments to Funds Surplus Units.

The largest holders of commercial paper are retail **money market mutual funds** which sell shares of portfolios of short term money market instruments to Funds Surplus Units. In 1994 money market mutual fund assets increased by 17%, or $40 billion, to a total of $277 billion as of January 20, 1995. These funds are always hungry for the commercial paper of highly rated borrowers to fill their portfolios, thereby creating a very liquid market for this paper. Table 14.6 shows that in 1991, money market mutual funds held more than one-third of the commercial paper outstanding. Households and other Funds Surplus Units held another 29.3% of the volume of commercial paper and bankers acceptances, with the remainder distributed among other FIs and nonfinancial corporations (see Table 14.6).[6]

The liquidity in the U.S. domestic commercial paper market increased in December 1993. Prior to that date, money market funds could buy only limited amounts of privately placed, "4(2)" paper. This commercial paper typically was used as bridge financing in mergers and acquisitions. In December 1993 the SEC ruled that the mutual funds could treat these privately placed issues of commercial paper as liquid assets, thereby removing any restrictions on their

---

[6] Bank trust departments accounted for most of the commercial paper held in this sector, amounting to between 15% and 25% of all outstanding commercial paper. See Alworth and Borio (1993).

Table
14.6

Distribution of Investments in Commercial Paper and Bankers Acceptances, 1980–1991 (US$ billions, not seasonally adjusted)

Type of Investor	1980 Amount	Pct.	1985 Amount	Pct.	1991 Amount	Pct.
Money Market Funds	$31.6	19.3	$99.1	27.6	$191.9	33.9
Households, trusts, nonprofits	42.6	26.0	122.1	34.1	165.7	29.3
Nonfinancial corporations	19.4	11.8	45.3	12.6	53.4	9.4
State and local government pension/savings plans	NA	NA	NA	NA	29.4	5.2
Private pension plans	19.5	11.9	19.9	5.6	28.4	5.0
Mutual funds	3.8	2.3	4.1	1.1	21.5	3.8
Life insurance companies	8.3	5.1	20.0	5.6	20.8	3.7
Commercial banks	15.8	9.6	9.7	2.7	10.6	1.9
Other[a]	22.8	13.9	38.3	10.7	44.2	7.8
Total	163.8	100	358.5	100	565.9	100
Commercial paper outstanding	121.6		293.9		528.1	

[a]Includes federally sponsored credit agencies, thrift institutions, and securities brokers and dealers.

Source: Post (1992), p. 882.

holdings. As a result of this ruling, the liquidity in the market increased markedly. Indeed, when American Home Products had to raise $8 billion to finance a merger-related transaction, it was able to access the commercial paper market. The entire sum was raised in only two hours!

High-quality commercial paper offerings are extremely liquid. The number of issuers has increased steadily over the years, so that almost 1,500 companies have active commercial paper programs. Ninety-five percent of all paper issuers (in 1989) received the highest credit ratings from the rating services.[7] But not every company has a top credit rating. If FIs could enhance the credit quality of commercial paper issued by riskier firms, then the overall liquidity of the entire market would increase. That is just what banks accomplished in backing up commercial paper offerings with lines of credit.

Checkpoint

1. How is commercial paper priced?
2. Contrast the various methods of placement of commercial paper.
3. What risk shifting and intertemporal cash flow services are offered in the commercial paper market and to whom?
4. What factors affect the liquidity of the commercial paper market?

▶ Loan Commitments

The demise of the banking industry has been regularly forecast but has not yet been realized. The growth of the commercial paper market presented quite a challenge to the banking industry. When the banks' market share was eroded by commercial paper's incursion into the short term business lending market, how did the banks respond? They developed a new financial product

---

[7] Noninvestment grade or unrated commercial paper is sometimes issued in conjunction with mergers and acquisitions. However, even in its heyday, this market never totaled more than $8 billion.

loan commitment, or line of credit: a preapproved loan, up to a certain amount, in effect for a fixed period of time.

takedown: the borrower's decision to borrow all or some of the balance on the line of credit.

prime rate: a rate set by banks that is used as a reference in pricing many loans.

rollover: repaying maturing paper by issuing new paper.

to meet market demand and reclaim a portion of the market. This new financial product was the **loan commitment**, or **line of credit**. A loan commitment is a preapproved loan, up to a certain amount, in effect for a fixed period of time. The borrower decides whether or not to borrow all or some of the balance on the line of credit, which is called a **takedown** of the loan commitment.

Loan commitments were originated in late 1977 by two banks, Morgan Guaranty and Wells Fargo, to allow selected large customers to borrow funds for short periods of time. They offered "special credit facilities" that carried rates linked to money market rates. This was a novelty in the banking industry, since previously all business lending was based on the **prime rate**. The prime rate is a rate set by banks that is used as a reference in pricing many loans. It is not tied to any particular money market rate, but instead reflects the banking system's cost of funds. The shift from prime-based bank loans to commercial paper offerings and loan commitments can be viewed as a shift from an administered loan price, the prime rate, to competitive loan rates. Competition from nonbanks and foreign banks for commercial lending business led banks such as Morgan and Wells Fargo to innovate and offer commercial loans at market prices. Widespread adoption of this innovation successfully tied commercial loan rates (for large borrowers in particular) to market rates of interest. Thus, commercial borrowers were able to reduce their interest costs as competition limited loan rate charges. Figure 14.6 shows the inverse relationship between bank short term lending and loan commitments.

How do loan commitments satisfy a risk shifting need in the commercial paper market? Active commercial paper issuers typically pay off billions of maturing paper issues each month. Where do they get the money to repay the short maturity commercial paper? From new issues of commercial paper. This **rollover**—repaying maturing paper by issuing new paper—is risky. The issuer is exposed to the risk of interest rate increases (which increase the cost of funds), credit crunches (which may cause funds to temporarily dry up), or the release of unflattering information (which may cause investors to shy away from the company's issue for a short time). Any of these circumstances can create serious problems for an issuing company, initiating severe liquidity problems that could precipitate the bankruptcy of a solvent company. The loan commitment acts as a backup source of liquidity. If, for some reason, the issuer cannot sell sufficient amounts of commercial paper to roll over a maturing issue, the company can repay the issue using the proceeds taken down from a line of credit.

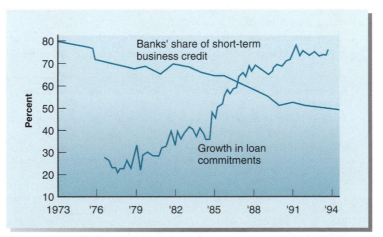

Source: Morris and Sellon, (1995), pp. 61, 62.

Figure 14.6

In response to these competitive pressures and opportunities, banks have altered their delivery of their traditional bank lending products. Indeed, loan commitments are now the dominant way to originate all new commercial and industrial loans of any maturity, not just as as backup for commercial paper.[8] As of 1994, the volume of unused commitments in U.S. banks totaled $1,614.6 billion, more than double the amount of total commercial loans of $701.8 billion. The average U.S. bank, averaged over a total of 11,382 banks reporting in 1994, issued $181,225,000 in loan commitments. In contrast, U.S. banks issued an average of $222,891,000 in *total* loans in that same period. Clearly, loan commitments are an important part of the FI's financial menu of choices.

Backup lines of credit to enhance the credit quality of commercial paper issues have also become a lucrative banking product.[9] Since they are used only in the event of an unsuccessful commercial paper offering, they rarely require the bank to disburse any funds. Risk based capital requirements (see Chapter 5) do not require any capital charge for loan commitments of less than one year. Because all commercial paper offerings have maturities of less than 270 days, their backup lines of credit do not require the bank to hold extra amounts of capital. The fees charged by the banks for these loan commitments make them a lucrative line of business.

Loan commitments are distinguishable from traditional commercial and industrial loans by their distinctive pricing structure. Loan commitments have a multifaceted pricing scheme that typically consists of (1) an up-front loan commitment fee; (2) either a fixed or variable loan rate; and (3) a back-end "usage" fee on any unused portion of the loan commitment. In contrast, the single component of traditional loan prices consists only of the loan rate. The richer nature of loan commitment pricing provides the bank with the opportunity to differentiate borrowers on the basis of their risk characteristics. The different elements of the loan commitment price can be used to sort potential borrowers in order to resolve some of the information asymmetries between lenders and borrowers.[10]

Loan Commitment Pricing and Risk Shifting

Most issuers try to maintain a 100% backing for their commercial paper issues using bank lines of credit. However, large issuers like GMAC would find it too expensive to obtain such a large amount of loan commitments. GMAC has close to 60% backing for its commercial paper. Higher rated issues tend to have a lower line of credit backing than lower rated issues.[11] Nayar and Rozeff (1994) show that for all 132 new issues over the period October 1981–December 1985, 73 were issued without letter of credit backing. Out of the unbacked new issues of commercial paper, 50 were rated A-1+, A-1, or P-1. Only 23 of those new issues without backing were rated A2, P2, or lower.

Loan commitments are an important credit enhancement to commercial paper, but that is not their sole purpose. Table 14.3 shows that even in countries with negligible commercial

---

[8] According to Brady (1985), over 80% of all long term commercial and industrial loans are made under loan commitments.

[9] Standby letters of credit (see Chapter 13) are also used to improve the credit risk of commercial paper offerings.

[10] In recent years, an extensive literature has developed on the information-revealing and risk shifting opportunities made feasible by loan commitment pricing. The more recent contributions focus on the moral hazard problems of asymmetric information. For example, see Shockley (1995), Berkovitch and Greenbaum (1991), Thakor and Udell (1987), Kanatas (1987), Thakor (1982), and Melnik and Plaut (1986a).

The other branch of the literature deals with the risk shifting and insurance aspects of forward lending. Thakor, Hong, and Greenbaum (1981) and Ho and Saunders (1983) evaluate loan commitments as put options. Bartter and Rendleman (1979) examine the use of loan commitments to hedge interest rate risk exposure. Melnik and Plaut (1986b) model the loan commitment as a hedge against default risk. Melnik and Plaut (1987) show that loan commitment pricing may offer a hedge against inflation.

[11] Nayar and Rozeff (1994) state that the highest rated commercial paper issues have bank lines of credit equal to about half the size of the issue.

paper offerings, loan commitments are a significant portion of FIs' assets. That is because small businesses use loan commitments in order to secure bank financing. Table 14.7 describes small business access to lines of credit. Borrowers with longer banking relationships pay lower interest rates, suggesting that banks use information gathered in the course of a customer relationship to better screen potential borrowers. The smallest firms (with assets below $500,000) pay an average premium of 1.73% over the prime rate as compared to the relatively larger firms, which pay an average of 1.32% over prime. The larger firms also have a relationship with the current lender that spans an average of 12.67 years as opposed to only 10.08 years for the smaller firms. Despite the greater liquidity of these smaller firms (higher quick and current ratios as well as lower leverage ratio, defined in Table 14.7), they pay higher rates than the larger, better-known firms.

The cost of bank-provided loan commitments increased in December 1992 upon the full implementation of the Basel risk adjusted capital requirements. Recall from Chapter 5 that these international regulations levy a capital charge for off-balance sheet, as well as on-balance sheet, bank assets. Since loan commitments are a contingent loan, they are considered off-balance sheet assets. They become on-balance sheet assets only if the customer chooses to exercise the commitment and borrow on the line of credit. Currently, the Basel capital requirements levy a 50% risk conversion factor for all loan commitments with an original maturity of more than one year. That is, a $100 million two year loan commitment to a commercial customer increases the bank's risk adjusted asset base by $50 million. With an 8% capital requirement, this implies an increase in the bank's capital requirements of $4 million, even if the loan commitment is ultimately never used.

The capital requirements on loan commitments increase their cost for the providing bank. Thus, if the bank's cost of capital is 10%, a $4 million increase in the capital requirement will cost $400,000 p.a. This cost will be reflected in the up-front loan commitment fee. Moreover, there is evidence that loan commitments do not increase bank risk exposure, and indeed cause

Table 14.7

Bank Lines of Credit

Variable	All Firms	Assets > $500,000	Assets < $500,000
Average assets ($000)	2,331.66	4,442.95	165.84
Premium over prime rate	1.49%	1.32%	1.73%
% Pledging collateral	53%	59%	47%
% Collateralizing with either accounts receivable and/or inventory	36%	46%	25%
% Collateralizing with other securities	18%	14%	22%
Borrower leverage; total debt/assets	60%	60%	59%
Pretax profit margin (% of sales)	12%	8%	16%
Current ratio; current assets/current liabilities	3.51	2.90	4.13
Quick ratio; (current assets minus inventory)/current liabilities	2.52	1.85	3.20
No. of years current owners have owned the firm	14.10	16.49	11.66
Length of relationship with current lender in years	11.39	12.67	10.08
No. of observations	863	437	426

Source: Berger and Udell (1995), p. 361.

risk to decline.[12] Since the justification for increases in bank capital requirements is to provide a cushion for risk enhancing bank activities, it is not clear that loan commitments warrant such treatment.

Loan commitments offer risk shifting services to commercial paper issuers as well as to other corporate borrowers. The bank hedges both the interest rate and the credit risk of the issuer. The loan commitment fees are structured to compensate the bank for provision of risk transfer services.

Credit Risk Exposure   Periodically, the commercial paper market has been roiled by defaults of visible issuers of investment grade paper. In 1982 the Manville Corporation defaulted on its P-2 prime rated commercial paper after filing in bankruptcy court for protection against liabilities connected with its manufacture of asbestos. In February 1990 Drexel Burnham Lambert Group defaulted on its P-3 rated commercial paper, and in March 1990, Mortgage & Realty Trust defaulted on its P-2 rated paper. Since much of this paper was held by money market mutual funds, there was concern that the market value of the funds' portfolios would fall below $1 for each dollar invested, thereby causing fund investors to incur losses. Money market mutual fund managers chose to cover their losses so as to protect the sacrosanct $1 net asset value of their funds. However, the default risk premium on A-2/P-2 rated commercial paper over A-1+/P-1 rated commercial paper spiked up to 100 basis points. In June 1991 the SEC amended its Rule 2a-7 to limit money market mutual funds' holdings of commercial paper below the top two rating classes. In 1989 money market mutual funds held a total of $44.3 billion of second-tier commercial paper, making up 15.9% of their assets. This amount fell to negligible levels in 1991. Large bank direct-issues of commercial paper were particularly affected by the shift to quality. Their issues peaked at $52 billion in January 1990 but fell to $24 billion by year-end 1991. Regulatory intervention and market intolerance for low- and medium-rated paper encouraged commercial paper issuers to search for credit enhancements to improve their credit ratings.

Loan commitments protect commercial paper investors from the impact of a deterioration in the issuer's credit quality. That is, if the issuer experiences liquidity problems, investors may be unwilling to buy its commercial paper. Thus, the borrower may be unable to roll over its commercial paper or may have to pay a very high interest rate to obtain sufficient funds to repay its maturing issues. The loan commitment can provide financing to bridge a period of short term financial difficulties. The loan commitment provides the borrower with a guarantee of credit availability, thereby committing the bank issuing the credit line to repay any backed commercial paper. Indeed, many commercial paper offerings are marketable because they carry 100% backup lines of credit from banks. These are often structured as **revolving credits** with same-day availability of funds. Under a revolving credit, the borrower can borrow or repay funds as desired, up until a maximum allowable credit line.

revolving credit: the practice of borrowing or repaying funds as desired, up to a maximum allowable credit line.

We have seen that commercial paper is a substitute for bank lending and that its primary advantage over the bank loan is its lower cost. However, there is a disadvantage as well. When a bank makes a loan, a customer relationship is created. During the course of the loan, and subsequent loans, the bank obtains information about the credit quality of the borrower. This information is useful because it resolves information asymmetries. Information asymmetries characterize lending markets because borrowers typically have more information about their own credit risk exposure than do lenders. In the course of repeated lending activities, the bank builds up a store of information about its customers that resolves this information asymmetry. Moreover, the bank commits itself to monitor the activities of borrowers in order to gather more information about the borrowers' credit risk. This valuable information is lost when the loan is securitized through the commercial paper market. There is no bank monitor that gathers

---

[12] See Boot and Thakor (1991), Avery and Berger (1991), and Hassan and Sackley (1994).

information about borrower credit quality. Each investor in commercial paper must perform an individual analysis of the issuer's credit quality using publicly available information, such as credit ratings.

The pairing of a loan commitment with commercial paper brings the bank monitor back into the lending relationship. The bank, by extending a letter of credit, builds a customer relationship, just as in the case of traditional bank lending. Moreover, during the life of the loan commitment, the bank must monitor the borrower for any new information about the borrower's financial condition. The loan commitment acts like a bank certification of the issuer's credit quality. Nayar and Rozeff (1994) found that the availability of bank-provided letter of credit backing increased the stock price for 22 companies, as compared to 50 highly rated issues without backing. This suggests that the stock market considers the issuance of bank-backed, highly rated commercial paper as a positive indicator of the firm's value. This increase in firm value stems from the information produced by banks in the course of monitoring their loan commitments.

Monitoring is ongoing, even after the loan commitment has been granted, because of the **material-adverse-change clause** in the line of credit. This clause states that the bank can refuse a loan on the line of credit if the borrower "deteriorates sufficiently so as to jeopardize repayment to the lending institution."[13] This legal escape clause limits the amount of credit risk shifting offered by the loan commitment. Small declines in the borrower's credit quality will be tolerated and the loan commitment honored. But in the face of large-scale increases in the borrower's credit risk exposure, the bank can legally refuse to absorb the greater risk of issuer default.

material-adverse-change clause: the right of a bank to refuse a loan on the line of credit if the borrower "deteriorates sufficiently so as to jeopardize repayment to the lending institution."

Checkpoint

1. Explain how the development of loan commitments can be viewed as a competitive attack on the commercial paper market.
2. Explain how the development of loan commitments can be viewed as support for the commercial paper market.
3. How do loan commitments provide risk shifting services?
4. What is the material-adverse-change clause? What is its impact on the credit risk hedging offered by loan commitments?

Interest Rate Risk Exposure   Under a loan commitment, a borrower pays an up-front fee to secure a preapproved line of credit of a given amount that it can use anytime during a fixed length of time. If the borrower chooses to take down the line of credit, then the interest rate is set according to some predetermined formula. The loan commitment can be either a fixed rate or a variable rate contract. Under a fixed rate contract, the nominal interest rate on the loan commitment takedown is set when the loan commitment is initiated. Under a variable rate contract, the nominal interest rate on the loan commitment takedown is determined at the time of takedown, based on a formula set at the time of the initiation of the loan commitment. Typically, the variable rate loan commitment is tied to a market rate, such as LIBOR or the prime rate. The loan commitment contract specifies a fixed credit risk premium, over the market rate, that the borrower will pay upon takedown of the line of credit. If there is any unused amount in the line of credit upon its maturity, the borrower may be charged a back-end usage fee.

Fixed rate loan commitments offer borrowers interest rate risk protection by locking in the interest rate on the loan at the time of loan commitment. Even variable rate loan commitments offer some interest rate risk protection since the borrower's risk premium is set at the time of the loan commitment. Because of the extra interest rate risk protection provided by fixed rate

---

[13] Post (1992).

loan commitments, they are more expensive than variable rate loan commitments. Most long term loan commitments tend to be variable rate, whereas short term loan commitments are fixed rate. In 1981, 65.5% of short term and 20.2% of long term loan commitments were fixed rate. The Fed's survey of loans made during the week of May 1–5, 1995, indicated that 67.9% and 70.6% of the short (maturity of less than one year) and long term commercial and industrial loans, respectively, were made under commitments. Of these, 80.5% and 82.9% of the short and long term loans, respectively, were variable rate, as opposed to fixed rate. Let's examine the features of these contracts.

Melnik and Plaut (1986a) examined a sample of 101 loan commitments outstanding during 1980–1981. Two-thirds were held by industrial firms, 22% by services firms, and 10% by construction firms, with the average firm holding $46 million in assets and generating $78 million in annual sales. The average commitment size was $7.66 million, with an average length of 29.05 months. The commitment fee averaged 42 basis points, with an average risk premium over the prime rate of 88 basis points. That is, for an average loan commitment, the up-front commitment fee was $32,172 ($7.66 million × .0042), and the loan rate was determined by adding 88 basis points to the prime rate. If the prime rate was 10% p.a., then the loan commitment takedown rate was 10.88% p.a.[14] Out of the total, 20.8% of the loan commitments carried a collateral requirement. The impact of the collateral requirement was to increase the loan commitment size. On average, the inclusion of a collateral clause entitled the borrower to an additional $4.5 million in loan commitments. Large firms (defined as those with sales exceeding $200 million) had loan commitments that were $13 million larger than for smaller firms. Moreover, the large firms were charged a risk premium that was 47 to 50 basis points lower, on average, than the risk premium charged to smaller firms.

A common form of loan commitment pricing used to be "10 + 10" credit lines. In this arrangement, the borrower was required to hold **compensating balances** in the amount of 10% of the line of credit, plus 10% of the amount of the loan commitment taken down. Compensating balances are an indirect form of payment to the bank. The borrower must hold a certain amount in a noninterest bearing account, as a form of collateral for the loan. The cost to the borrower of the compensating balances is the opportunity cost of the funds. This practice has been largely discontinued. Compensating balances were a widely used bank requirement in the days of interest rate ceilings on deposits. Since interest rates were kept artificially low by regulations, banks increased their access to this low-cost source of funds by requiring loan customers to hold compensating balances. With the removal of interest rate ceilings, the cost of these deposits to the bank increased, thereby reducing their desirability.

compensating balances: the requirement that a borrower must hold a certain amount in a noninterest bearing account, as a form of collateral for the loan.

Checkpoint

1. Contrast the fixed rate and variable rate loan contracts with respect to cost, risk hedging services, and availability.

2. How does collateral affect the average loan commitment size? fee schedule? risk premium?

takedown risk: the FI's uncertainty about the loan quantity that will emanate from its loan commitments.

Takedown Risk   The **takedown risk** is the FI's uncertainty about the loan quantity that will emanate from its loan commitments. Thakor, Hong, and Greenbaum (1981) estimated that about 45% of all loan commitments are taken down and ultimately become bank loans. However, Ho and Saunders (1983) show that takedown rates are quite variable over time.

What determines takedown? The borrower will take down the loan commitment if it is advantageous to do so. When will it be advantageous? A loan commitment will be used

---

[14] Melnik and Plaut did not measure back-end usage fees.

when the loan rate in the spot market exceeds the loan rate that could be obtained on the loan commitment. Thus, the borrower's gain is the lender's loss. The loan rate in the spot market may be higher than the loan rate on the line of credit because either the general level of interest rates has gone up or the credit risk of the borrower has deteriorated slightly, thereby causing an increase in the borrower's credit risk premium. Whatever the cause, whenever the rate on the line of credit is attractive when compared to rates in the open market, the line will be used; that is, the loan commitment option will be exercised. The loan commitment is nothing more than a put option, which the borrower can exercise by selling its loan IOU to the FI that wrote the line of credit.

binomial option pricing model: a model assuming that prices can go either up or down, in each period, by a fixed amount, with a set probability.

Because the loan commitment is an option, we can price it using option valuation techniques. For simplicity, we illustrate the pricing of loan commitments using the **binomial option pricing model**, which assumes that prices can go either up or down, in each period, by a fixed amount, with a set probability.

Suppose that the prime rate is currently set at 7.5% p.a. Next month, an industrial company named Realgoods Inc. expects to borrow $15 million to finance its operations over the next three months. The company's credit risk premium is equal to 50 basis points over the prime rate. If a bank offers the company a loan commitment to back up a commercial paper offering, what is the value of that loan commitment? Let's use the binomial option pricing model to compare the value of the variable rate loan commitment with the value of the fixed rate loan commitment. If the loan commitment is variable rate, then the rate will be set equal to the value of the prime rate that prevails next month plus 50 basis points. If the loan commitment is fixed rate, then Realgoods, Inc. knows that its loan rate will be 8% (7.5% plus 50 basis points).

Let's examine two scenarios. In one the prime rate is rather stable; in the other the prime rate is quite volatile (as has been true in our more recent experience). First, we evaluate the loan commitment for the stable rate environment. Suppose that there is a 50–50 chance that the prime rate will go either up or down by 1% over the next month. Thus, if Realgoods' loan rate today is 8% p.a., then next month's rate on the spot market will be either 8.08% or 7.92% p.a., each with a 50% probability. If Realgoods has a fixed rate loan commitment, with the loan rate set at 8% p.a., then the line of credit will be taken down only in the high interest rate environment. That is, if Realgoods' spot market loan rate next month turns out to be 7.92% p.a., the loan commitment will expire unused and Realgoods will borrow in the spot market. However, if Realgoods' spot market loan rate is 8.08% p.a. next month, then the entire $15 million line of credit on the 8% fixed rate loan commitment will be taken down and the annual savings to Realgoods will be 8 basis points. This will result in an interest cost savings of $3,000 ($\frac{.0008}{4} \times$ $15 million). Calculating the expected present value to Realgoods of exercising the loan commitment option in one month is the discounted expected interest savings (.50(3,000) + .50(0) = $1.500) which yields

$$\frac{.50(3,000)}{1 + \frac{.08}{12}} = \$1,490.$$

This amounts to a current fee (option premium) of approximately 0.01%, or one basis point ($\frac{\$1,490}{\$15,000,000}$). Thus, for our example, the fixed rate loan commitment will carry an up-front commitment fee that is one basis point higher than an equivalent variable rate loan commitment.

In contrast, under the volatile rate scenario, let us suppose that there is a 50–50 chance that Realgoods' loan rate will go either up or down by 5% in a month's time. Thus, the loan rate may be either 8.40% p.a. or 7.60% p.a. If the fixed rate loan commitment is still set at 8% p.a., then Realgoods will take down the loan commitment only in the high rate environment, that is, when loan rates are 8.40% p.a. What is the value to Realgoods of receiving a $15 million loan at 8% rather than the prevailing rate of 8.40%? Forty basis points p.a., or simply, $\frac{.0040}{4} \times \$15,000,000 = \$15,000$. The expected present value of the interest savings on the loan commitment is

$$\frac{.50(15,000)}{1 + \frac{.08}{12}} = \$7,450,$$

which amounts to an up-front commitment fee of 5 basis points ($\frac{\$7,450}{\$15,000,000}$) over that of an identical variable rate loan commitment. Comparing the two scenarios, we observe that when interest rates are volatile, the cost of the interest rate risk insurance provided by the fixed rate loan commitment increases, in our example fivefold. Of course, this example is simplified by the one period nature of the loan (three months at a fixed rate), as well as by the use of the binomial option pricing model, which allows only two possible future loan rates. However, it does illustrate the cost of fixed rate loan commitments to the FI. Not only is the cost of interest rate insurance higher, but the takedown risk is higher as well, since there is greater volatility in the amount of loan commitments actually used.

Consumer Loan Commitments: The Home Equity Line of Credit

Thus far, we have been concerned about loan commitments granted to businesses to finance their day-to-day operations. However, consumers also have access to this versatile banking product. This is realized in the form of the **home equity line of credit**, which is a loan commitment collateralized by the residual equity value of a home. Typically, homeowners finance their purchase of a home with a mortgage, which constitutes the first lien on the property. However, as property values increase or principal is repaid on the first mortgage, residual equity value is created. Homeowners cannot use the equity value tied up in their house unless they sell the house. The home equity line of credit enables the homeowner to borrow against the equity value tied up in the value of the home. The homeowner determines when and how much of the loan commitment to take down.

> **home equity line of credit:** a loan commitment collateralized by the residual equity value of a home.

Between 1987 and 1991, home equity lines increased from $25 to $70 billion. Interest rate declines in 1992–1993 sparked a rush to refinancing that cut into the market for home equity lines. Fannie Mae estimated that 55% of the $1 trillion in new mortgages written in 1993 were **mortgage refinancings** that replaced previously issued, higher rate mortgages. However, the market for home equity lines is projected to grow at an annual rate of 7% until 1997.

> **mortgage refinancings:** new mortgages that replace previously issued, higher rate mortgages.

Checkpoint

1. What is takedown risk?
2. Why is the loan commitment like a put option?
3. Why are home equity lines considered loan commitments?

➤ Summary

Commercial paper originated as an alternative to short term bank loans to finance business working capital needs. To exploit a regulatory loophole, commercial paper securities could be issued without registration if their maturities were no more than 270 days. Credit rating agencies and the demand for securities by growing money market mutual funds made it possible for highly rated companies, with low levels of credit risk, to access this market.

To expand access to the commercial paper market and improve its liquidity, credit enhancements were offered. These took the form of bank-provided lines of credit that were backup sources of financing. Asset-backed commercial paper offerings are also backed by a portfolio of diversified receivables.

Loan commitments grew in importance from a mere credit enhancement for commercial paper securities to the major vehicle for origination of all bank lending. Currently, most business loans originate as loan commitments. The flexibility of the loan commitment comes from its risk sharing characteristics. The bank insures the borrower against credit risk exposure resulting from slight changes in the borrower's credit quality. However, if the borrower's condition deteriorates dramatically, the lender can invoke the material-adverse-change clause of the loan commitment contract and deny any loans. The bank can insure the borrower against interest rate risk exposure if the loan commitment is written as a fixed rate contract. Finally, the bank can insure the borrower against credit availability by accepting takedown risk on the loan commitment. That is, the lender does not know whether the borrower will exercise the loan commitment and borrow the full or partial amount of the funds. Moreover, the lender does

not know when the loan commitment will be taken down. By extending a line of credit, the bank agrees to absorb the risk of credit availability for the borrower.

In exchange for these risk sharing services, the loan commitment has a multitiered pricing structure. An up-front commitment fee is paid upon origination of the loan commitment. The loan rate is specified in the loan commitment at either a fixed rate or a markup over a money market rate. Finally, there is an unused commitment fee that is charged at the back end upon maturity of the loan commitment. It is based on the amount of funds in the line of credit that were not taken down over the life of the loan commitment. Consumers have limited access to the loan commitment through the home equity line of credit.

References

Aidun, C.K. "A Primer on Asset Securitization." *Journal of Commercial Lending* (September 1995): 19–32.

Alworth, J. S., and C.E.V. Borio. *Commercial Paper Markets: A Survey.* BIS Economic Papers, No. 37, April 1993.

Asher, J. "The Push Is on for Home Equity Business." *ABA Banking Journal* (April 1995): 56–62.

Avery, R., and A. Berger. "Loan Commitments and Bank Risk Exposure." *Journal of Banking and Finance* 15 (1991): 173–192.

Bartter, B., and R. Rendleman, Jr. "Fee-Based Pricing of Fixed Rate Bank Loan Commitments." *Financial Management* 8, No. 1 (Spring 1979): 13–20.

Berger, A., and G. Udell. "Relationship Lending and Lines of Credit in Small Firm Finance." *Journal of Business* 68, No. 3 (1995): 351–381.

Berkovitch, E., and S. Greenbaum. "The Loan Commitment as an Optimal Financing Contract." *Journal of Financial and Quantitative Analysis* 26, No. 1 (March 1991): 83–95.

Boot, A., and A. Thakor. "Off-Balance Sheet Liabilities, Deposit Insurance, and Capital Regulation." *Journal of Banking and Finance* 15 (1991): 825–846.

Brady, T. "Changes in Loan Pricing and Business Lending at Commercial Banks." *Federal Reserve Bulletin* (January 1985): 1–13.

Crabbe, L., and M. Post. "The Effect of a Rating Downgrade on Outstanding Commercial Paper." *Journal of Finance* (1994).

Cutler, S. "Asset Backed Commercial Paper Poised for Exponential Growth." *Corporate Finance* (August 1994): 17–19.

Deshmukh, S., S. Greenbaum, and G. Kanatas. "Bank Forward Lending in Alternative Funding Environments." *Journal of Finance* (September 1982): 925–940.

Elayan, F. A., B. A. Maris, and P. J. Young. "The Effect of Commercial Paper Rating Changes and Credit-Watch Placement on Common Stock Prices." *The Financial Review* 31, No. 1 (February 1996): 149–167.

Federal Reserve Bank of Cleveland. *Money Market Instruments.* Cleveland: 1970.

Hahn, T. K. "Commercial Paper." In T. Q. Cook and R. K. LaRoche, eds., *Instruments of the Money Market.* 7th ed. Richmond, Va: Federal Reserve Bank of Richmond, 1993.

Hassan, M. K., and W. Sackley. "A Methodological Investigation of Risk Exposure of Bank Off-Balance Sheet Loan Commitment Activities." *Quarterly Review of Economics and Finance* 34, No. 3 (Fall 1994): 283–299.

Ho, T., and A. Saunders. "Fixed Rate Loan Commitments, Takedown Risk, and the Dynamics of Hedging with Futures." *Journal of Financial and Quantitative Analysis* 18 (1983): 499–516.

Johnson, R., and G. Jensen. "Prime Rate Changes and Returns to Industries: Announcement Period Evidence." *Quarterly Review of Economics and Finance* 34 (Spring 1994): 75–93.

Kanatas, G. "Commercial Paper, Bank Reserve Requirements, and the Informational Role of Loan Commitments." *Journal of Banking and Finance* 11 (September 1987): 425–448.

Melnik, A., and S. Plaut. "Loan Commitment Contracts, Terms of Lending, and Credit Allocation." *Journal of Finance* 41, No. 2 (June 1986a): 425–435.

Melnik, A., and S. Plaut. "The Economics of Loan Commitment Contracts: Credit Pricing and Utilization." *Journal of Banking and Finance* 10 (1986b): 267–280.

Melnik, A., and S. Plaut. "Interest Rate Indexation and the Pricing of Loan Commitment Contracts." *Journal of Banking and Finance* 11 (1987): 137–145.

Morris, C. S., and G. H. Sellon, Jr. "Bank Lending and Monetary Policy: Evidence on a Credit Channel." Federal Reserve Bank of Kansas City *Economic Review*, (Second Quarter 1995): 59–75.

Nayar, N., and M. Rozeff. "Ratings, Commercial Paper, and Equity Returns." *Journal of Finance* 49, No. 4 (September 1994): 1431–1449.

Post, M. "The Evolution of the U.S. Commercial Paper Market Since 1980." *Federal Reserve Bulletin* (December 1992): 879–891.

Schockley, R. "Bank Loan Commitments and Corporate Leverage." *Journal of Financial Intermediation* 4, No. 3 (July 1995): 272–301.

Slovin, M., M. Sushka, and E. Waller. "Is There News in the Prime Rate?" *Journal of Financial and Quantitative Analysis* 29 (December 1994): 633–646.

Stigum, M. *Money Markets*. 3rd ed., Homewood, Ill.: Business One Irwin, 1990.

Thakor, A. "Toward a Theory of Bank Loan Commitments." *Journal of Banking and Finance* 6 (March 1982): 55–83.

Thakor, A., H. Hong, and S. Greenbaum. "Bank Loan Commitments and Interest Rate Volatility." *Journal of Banking and Finance* 6 (1981): 55–84.

Thakor, A., and G. Udell. "An Economic Rationale for the Pricing Structure of Bank Loan Commitments." *Journal of Banking and Finance* 11 (1987): 271–289.

➤ Questions

1. Suppose that LIBOR is currently set at 5% p.a. Next month, an industrial company named Realgoods, Inc., expects to borrow $25 million to finance its operations over the next three months. The company's credit risk premium is equal to 25 basis points over LIBOR.

   a. Use the binomial option pricing model to compare the price of a fixed rate (at current rates) loan commitment to the cost of a variable rate loan commitment. Assume that there is a 50–50 chance that LIBOR will go either up or down by 2%.

   b. Use the binomial option pricing model to compare the price of a fixed rate (at current rates) loan commitment to the cost of a variable rate loan commitment. Assume that there is a 50–50 chance that LIBOR will go either up or down by 10%.

   c. When is the fixed rate loan commitment taken down?

2. Suppose that the variable rate loan commitments in question 1 are for six month floating rate loans that roll over every quarter. That is, the loan rate will be determined for the first three months by LIBOR in one month's time (upon the initiation of the loan) and then again in four months' time (upon the completion of the first three months of the loan). Use the binomial model to answer parts (a), (b), and (c) from question 1, using the same assumptions about LIBOR volatility for the next four months. (*Hint:* Assume that LIBOR changes on two discrete dates only: the first one month from today and the second four months from today.)

3. Identify the (i) originating FI, (ii) SPV, (iii) underwriter, and (iv) investor in the following asset-backed commercial paper transactions:

a. Company A's balance sheet contains $150 million in credit card receivables. Company B has neither assets nor liabilities on its balance sheet. Company C has no change in its balance sheet. Company D has $150 million in cash on its balance sheet.

b. Company Z has an extensive network of investment clients. Company Y has an extensive portfolio of nonmarketable assets. Company X is a newly formed entity. Company W is a Funds Surplus Unit.

4. How is takedown risk affected by
   a. Increasing the up-front fee?
   b. Decreasing the loan commitment's fixed interest rate?
   c. Increasing the back-end fee?
   d. Increasing interest rate volatility?
   e. Decreasing the borrower's creditworthiness?

5. Why is the use of a securities depository important in clearing commercial paper? Why was electronic clearance vital for the development of the commercial paper market? How was it accomplished?

CHAPTER 15

GOVERNMENT SECURITIES

"The important thing for Government is not to do things which individuals are doing already, and to do them a little better or a little worse; but to do those things which at present are not done at all." John Maynard Keynes, *End of Laissez-Faire* (1926), pt. 4.

Learning Objectives

- To examine the securities issued by national governments to support their budget deficits.

- To examine the evolution of auction methods used around the world to sell sovereign government debt.

- To compare how federal agencies and municipal governments compete with sovereign governments for financing in world capital markets.

➤ Introduction

Just about everyone worries when the U.S. federal government's budget deficit exceeds $200 billion—everyone, that is, except government securities dealers and other FIs that make markets in U.S. Treasury securities. To finance its deficit, the federal government issues Treasury bills, notes, and bonds. The U.S. Treasury has a total of over $4 trillion in marketable and nonmarketable debt outstanding.[1] This volume makes the U.S. Treasury market the largest and most liquid in the world. FIs and their customers enjoy the benefits of Treasury issues. There is a total of $2.3 trillion of marketable U.S. Treasury securities outstanding. About $175 billion, or 8% of the total, are owned by banks. Insurance companies own $130 billion (6%); state and local governments $339 billion (15%); and pension funds, mutual funds, and other FIs another $700 billion (30%). More than two-thirds of all newly issued Treasury securities are purchased by foreign investors.

U.S. Treasury securities are considered to be default risk free, although the budget deadlock in late 1995 jeopardized that status when Congress refused to pass routine approval to lift the national debt ceiling. Since this prevented the Treasury from issuing new securities to repay

---

[1] In this book, we consider only marketable Treasury securities. We do not discuss nonmarketable Treasury securities, such as series E savings bonds bought by individuals, since there is no secondary market for these nonnegotiable instruments.

Treasury bills: pure discount obligations of the U.S. Treasury that have maturities of one year or less.

Treasury notes: obligations of the U.S. Treasury that are issued with maturities that range from two to seven years and that carry a semiannual coupon payment.

Treasury bonds: obligations of the U.S. Treasury that are issued with maturities that range from 10 to 30 years and that carry a semiannual coupon payment.

maturing Treasury issues, default was avoided only when the Treasury borrowed internally from federal government employees' pension funds. The U.S. Treasury issues three different types of securities: Treasury bills, notes, and bonds. **Treasury bills** are pure discount obligations of the U.S. Treasury that have maturities of one year or less. Treasury bill rates are quoted as discount yields on a 360 day year basis. **Treasury notes** are obligations of the U.S. Treasury that are issued with maturities that range from two to seven years and that carry a semiannual coupon payment. **Treasury bonds** are obligations of the U.S. Treasury that are issued with maturities that range from 10 to 30 years and that carry a semiannual coupon payment. Treasury note and bond yields are quoted as bond equivalent yields, based on a 365 day year.

How does the Treasury issue these new securities? The ongoing goal of the U.S. Treasury is to devise a procedure to issue large volumes of its securities, efficiently, at low cost to the government. Since U.S. Treasury bills were introduced in 1929, the government has sold all new issues using the auction method. However, the type of auction is currently an issue of some controversy.

The U.S. Treasury Auction

Year after year in recent decades, the U.S. federal government's budget has been in deficit. These deficits create a challenge for the Treasury. Large volumes of Treasury securities must be sold each year to cover both the annual deficit and the volume of maturing Treasury securities issued in the past. Figure 15.1 shows the steady growth in new issues of all Treasuries over the past 15 years. In 1994 alone, the U.S. Treasury issued more than $2 trillion of Treasury securities at auctions.

As continually large government deficits became the norm, financial markets found it increasingly difficult to digest the explosion in the volume of new Treasury securities. Since the market did not know which securities would be sold by the Treasury in subsequent auctions, sometimes there was reluctance to bid aggressively. To alleviate the uncertainty about the Treasury's issuing plans, the government adopted the quarterly refunding schedule. Table 15.1 shows the Treasury's auction cycles. Market participants know which issues will be auctioned

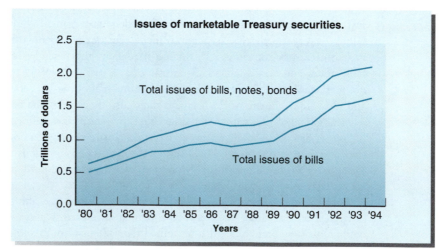

Source: Mester (1995), p. 5.

Figure 15.1

Table 15.1

Treasury Auction Cycles

Issues	Frequency	Announcement Date	Auction Date	Settlement (Issue) Date	Maturity	Comment
Discount Securities						
3 month (91 day) and 6 month (182 dayTreasury bills	Weekly	Each Tuesday	Each Monday	Thursday following auction	Each Thursday	
52 week (364 day) Treasury bills	Every fourth week	Every fourth Friday	Every fourth Thursday	Thursday following auction	Every fourth Thursday	Eventually trade fungibly with 91 day and 182 day Treasury bills
Cash management bills	As needed	Per cash needs	Per cash needs	Per cash needs	Thursday	Usually issued in early April, June, and December to cover temporary cash shortfall
Coupon Securities						
2 year/5 year	Monthly	Wednesday usually the week including the 20th	Tuesday and Wednesday following announcement, respectfully	Last calendar day of month	Last calendar day	
3 year/10 year/30 year/(re-funding cycle)	Quarterly	First Wednesday of midmonth of quarter	Tues., Wed., and Thurs. during first week prior to settlement day.	15th calendar day of Feb/May/Aug/Nov	15th calendar day of Feb/May/Aug/Nov	

[a]Settlement on any holiday or weekend will be postponed until the next business day.

Source: Jones and Fabozzi, (1992), p. 31.

---

reopened auction: the selling of additional shares of an outstanding issue at a later auction.

cash management bills: short term Treasury bills that are issued to fill the Treasury's cash needs just prior to the receipt of tax payments.

and when. The Treasury announces the size of a particular issue about a week before the auction date. The results of the auction set the price of the security. Occasionally, an outstanding issue is **reopened** at an auction so that the new issue is identical to an issue that was previously auctioned.[2] **Cash management bills** are short term Treasury bills that are issued to fill the Treasury's cash needs just prior to the receipt of tax payments. The mix of Treasury offerings

---

[2] In the wake of the Salomon Treasury auction scandal, the Treasury stated a policy of reopening auctions if an "acute, protracted" shortage was detected. For example, in 1992 the Treasury reopened a 10 year note issue in order to prevent a squeeze in supply. Salomon paid $290 million in fines to settle SEC civil charges that it violated rules in nine Treasury auctions. In December 1993 Paul Mozer, who headed Salomon's government securities desk, was sentenced to four months in prison and fined $30,000.

determines the maturity structure of the government's debt. For example, at the end of 1975, the average maturity was 2.5 years since the Treasury issued predominantly shorter maturity debt instruments. Currently, the average maturity is more than double that level. *Timely Topics 15.1: The Treasury's Debt Management Policy* discusses the latest shift (as of May 1993) in the Treasury's debt management policy.

TIMELY TOPICS 15.1

THE TREASURY'S DEBT MANAGEMENT POLICY

In May 1993, the Treasury announced that it would eliminate the seven year Treasury note, reduce the offerings of 30 year Treasury bonds by 40%, and increase its offerings of two and three year notes. Sales of 30 year Treasury bonds were scheduled to be reduced from a high of $45 billion in 1991 to $22 billion in 1993. Then Secretary of the Treasury Lloyd Bentsen justified the move with the statement, "This action to shorten the maturity of Treasury borrowing will produce real savings on interest costs over time" (*New York Times*, May 6, 1993, p. D1). What are the pros and cons of this shift in policy?

There are two arguments in favor of lowering the average maturity of the Treasury's debt. The first is that shorter maturity securities tend to reduce the government's interest costs. That is, since the yield curve is usually upward sloping, shorter maturity instruments tend to have lower interest rates than longer maturity instruments. The government can reduce the cost of financing its deficit by reducing the maturity of its debt securities. The second argument stems from more of a policy issue. Corporations must issue long term debt to finance long-lived real investment projects. The presence of the Treasury as a borrower in the long term debt market increases competition for scarce funds and raises the costs of borrowing, thereby reducing real investment activity in the economy. Shortening the maturity of the Treasury's debt can be viewed as a stimulative macroeconomic policy to induce greater business investment.

Opposing arguments are that the policy of shortening the average maturity of Treasury securities is an imprecise and ineffective way to implement monetary policy. Moreover, shorter maturity debt issues require more and more frequent refinancings as the debt matures and must be rolled over. This increases the costs of debt issuance to the Treasury and makes it more difficult to coordinate the Treasury's auction schedule with issues by other borrowers.

If shortening the Treasury's debt maturity is beneficial, one could ask why the May 1993 proposal was so conservative. If the goal is to minimize borrowing costs, then the entire debt could be funded with short maturity Treasury bills, which almost always have the lowest rates in the market. This would, however, increase the interest rate risk of the federal budgeting process since the Treasury's interest costs would fluctuate in line with short term interest rates. Moreover, the ability of financial market participants to hedge the interest rate risk of long term financial transactions would be hampered by the loss of longer maturity Treasury securities.

Another possibility is that federal debt management has no significant long term impact on Treasury costs. The shift to short term financing increases interest rate sensitivity, thereby eliminating any potential cost savings to the Treasury. This appears to be the case since the adoption of the policy in May 1993.

The most important procedure for the Treasury is to choose a refunding schedule and stick with it. Frequent alternations are disruptive to the marketplace, which plans for a regular and systematic schedule of new issues. It is particularly ironic that the Treasury chose May 1993 to roil financial markets and alter its quarterly refunding schedule. That was a period of record low interest rates. In contrast to the government, corporate borrowers were lengthening their debt maturities so as to lock in historically low interest rates.

- -

tenders: sealed bids.

competitive bidder: a bidder who specifies both the amount of the security that the bidder wants to buy and the price (stated in terms of yield) that the bidder is willing to pay.

noncompetitive bidder: a bidder who specifies only the amount of the security that is desired, without specifying any price.

Upon the Treasury's announcement of the size of an upcoming auction, **tenders**, sealed bids, are solicited. Bidders can submit two different types of bids: **competitive** and **noncompetitive**. A competitive bidder specifies both the amount of the security that the bidder wants to buy and the price (stated in terms of yield) that the bidder is willing to pay. A noncompetitive bidder specifies only the amount of the security that is desired, without specifying any price. This is because noncompetitive bidders automatically pay a price that is calculated by taking an average of all accepted competitive prices. Noncompetitive bidders are generally individuals who purchase small amounts of Treasury securities. Practitioner's Primer 15.1 discusses the procedure for individual purchases of securities directly from the Treasury. Competitive bidders are generally FIs that purchase large quantities of Treasury securities. On average, about 80% of bill auction awards and over 90% of note and bond auction awards are to competitive bidders. However, for any given auction there are only about 75 to 85 competitive bidders. Many of these are the 39 primary government security dealers that deal with the Fed (see Chapter 4). These dealers account for over two-thirds of the awards over $1 million.[3] In contrast, each auction averages 20,000 noncompetitive bidders. Noncompetitive bidders are retail customers who purchase small quantities of the issue and who are not sophisticated enough to submit a price bid. The limit on each noncompetitive tender is $1 million for Treasury bills and $5 million for notes and bonds. Sometimes, foreign public FIs submit noncompetitive bids. If they are replacing maturing issues that they already hold, the securities sold to foreign public FIs are called **add-ons**. The value of the add-ons is added to the announced issue amount, so that if the Treasury has announced a $5 billion auction and there are $1 billion of maturing Treasuries that are being replaced by foreign public FIs, then total auction sales equal $6 billion.

add-ons: noncompetitive bids by foreign public FIs to replace maturing issues that they already hold.

PRACTITIONER'S PRIMER 15.1

DIRECT PURCHASES OF U.S. TREASURY SECURITIES

- -

Individuals may purchase Treasury securities directly, by mail or in person, from any Federal Reserve Bank or from the U.S. Treasury Department in Washington, D.C. The buyer must submit a check (certified for a Treasury bill purchase) for the full face value of the security. If there is any discount on the price of the security, then the Treasury credits the buyer's designated account.

Since all Treasury issues are in book form only, the buyer must set up designated securities and cash accounts. These accounts will hold any securities or cash payments that emanate from the securities' purchase. All interest, principal, and discount pay-

---

[3] Jegadeesh (1993) states that nonbank primary dealers obtain an average 58.78% of the auction issue, whereas commercial banks are allocated 14.60% of the amount that is competitively bid.

ments are made directly into the purchaser's designated cash account. This allows funds to earn interest immediately upon payment date.

No fees or commissions are charged for direct purchase of Treasury securities. Treasury bills are sold in minimum amounts of $10,000, with $5,000 increments above the minimum. Notes with maturities of less than four years are sold in minimum amounts of $5,000, with $5,000 increments. Longer term notes and bonds are sold in minimum amounts of $1,000 with $1,000 increments.

Not all competitive bids that are tendered are accepted. All noncompetitive bids are accepted, with the remainder allocated to competitive bidders. Figure 15.2 compares accepted bids to submitted bids for note and bond auctions during 1989–1994. About 35–45% of the dollar volume of bids submitted in each auction is accepted. Typically, the longer the maturity, the greater the percentage of accepted bids. The percentage of accepted bids is determined by the size of the issue as compared to the amount of bids tendered.

FIs can gauge the activity in a new issue even before the auction results are announced. Upon the announcement of the size of a particular issue, the **when-issued market** begins trading. The when-issued market is a forward market that allows participants to buy and sell the security, with delivery taking place upon its issue date. For example, the weekly 13-week Treasury bill auction size is announced on the Tuesday before the Monday auction. The results of the auction are announced on the day after the auction, the following Tuesday, and the bills are issued the following Thursday, two days after the auction results are announced. Thus, the Treasury bill when-issued market for each issue trades for nine days, from Tuesday until a week from the following Thursday.

when-issued market: a forward market that allows participants to buy and sell the security, with delivery taking place upon its issue date.

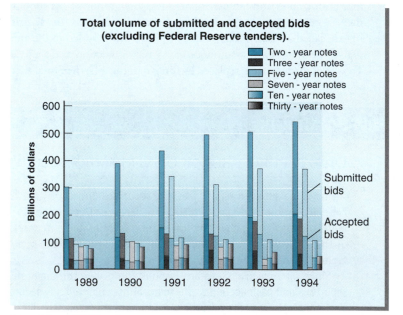

Source: Mester (1995), p. 6.

Figure 15.2

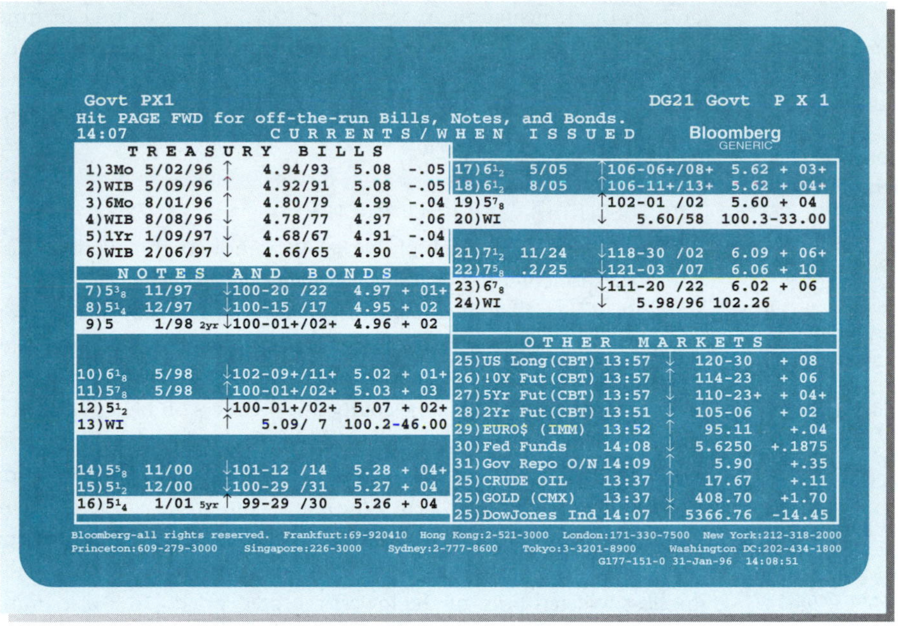

```
Govt PX1                                              DG21 Govt   P X 1
Hit PAGE FWD for off-the-run Bills, Notes, and Bonds.
14:07                     C U R R E N T S / W H E N   I S S U E D    Bloomberg
                                                                       GENERIC
      T R E A S U R Y   B I L L S
 1)3Mo 5/02/96 ↑   4.94/93  5.08  -.05  17)6½   5/05  ↑106-06+/08+ 5.62 + 03+
 2)WIB 5/09/96 ↑   4.92/91  5.08  -.05  18)6½   8/05  ↑106-11+/13+ 5.62 + 04+
 3)6Mo 8/01/96 ↑   4.80/79  4.99  -.04  19)5⅞         ↑102-01 /02  5.60 + 04
 4)WIB 8/08/96 ↓   4.78/77  4.97  -.06  20)WI         ↓    5.60/58 100.3-33.00
 5)1Yr 1/09/97 ↓   4.68/67  4.91  -.04
 6)WIB 2/06/97 ↓   4.66/65  4.90  -.04  21)7½  11/24  ↓118-30 /02  6.09 + 06+
     N O T E S   A N D   B O N D S      22)7⅝  .2/25  ↓121-03 /07  6.06 + 10
 7)5⅜  11/97  ↓100-20 /22  4.97 + 01+  23)6⅞         ↓111-20 /22  6.02 + 06
 8)5¼  12/97  ↓100-15 /17  4.95 + 02   24)WI         ↓    5.98/96 102.26
 9)5   1/98 2yr ↓100-01+/02+ 4.96 + 02
                                            O T H E R   M A R K E T S
                                        25)US Long(CBT) 13:57 ↓  120-30   + 08
10)6⅛  5/98   ↓102-09+/11+ 5.02 + 01+  26)!0Y Fut(CBT) 13:57 ↑  114-23   + 06
11)5⅞  5/98   ↑100-01/02+  5.03 + 03   27)5Yr Fut(CBT) 13:57 ↓  110-23+  + 04+
12)5½         ↓100-01+/02+ 5.07 + 02+  28)2Yr Fut(CBT) 13:51 ↓  105-06   + 02
13)WI         ↑     5.09/ 7 100.2-46.00 29)EURO$ (IMM)  13:52 ↓   95.11    +.04
                                        30)Fed Funds    14:08 ↓  5.6250  +.1875
                                        31)Gov Repo O/N 14:09 ↓   5.90    +.35
14)5⅝  11/00  ↓101-12 /14  5.28 + 04+  25)CRUDE OIL    13:37 ↑  17.67    +.11
15)5½  12/00  ↓100-29 /31  5.27 + 04   25)GOLD (CMX)   13:37 ↓ 408.70   +1.70
16)5¼  1/01 5yr ↑ 99-29 /30  5.26 + 04  25)DowJones Ind 14:07   5366.76  -14.45
Bloomberg-all rights reserved.  Frankfurt:69-920410  Hong Kong:2-521-3000  London:171-330-7500  New York:212-318-2000
Princeton:609-279-3000    Singapore:226-3000   Sydney:2-777-8600   Tokyo:3-3201-8900    Washington DC:202-434-1800
                                                       G177-151-0 31-Jan-96  14:08:51
```

Figure 15.3

Of course, the issue continues to trade after its issue. Secondary market trading in U.S. Treasury securities takes place around the world over the counter. Daily average secondary trading exceeds $120 billion. Particularly liquid securities in this market are **on-the-run** issues. On-the-run issues are the most actively traded issues, usually the issue auctioned most recently. Figure 15.3 shows the rate quotes for on-the-run issues of Treasury bills, notes, and bonds, including the when-issued bond (WIB). On-the-run issues, being more liquid, therefore have narrower bid/ask spreads than older, off-the-run issues. For example, the 30 year on-the-run Treasury bond yielded 8.15% in December 1994, while the previously issued off-the-run issue yielded 8.30%, suggesting a yield differential of 15 basis points.

on–the–run issues: the most actively traded issues, usually the issue auctioned most recently.

In the quotations in Figure 15.3, the first two columns describe the Treasury security. The third column quotes the bid ask spread, where the bid yield exceeds the asked yield since the bid price is below the asked price. For example, the six month (183 day) Treasury bill has a bid yield of 4.80% p.a. and an asked yield of 4.79% p.a. on a discount basis. The bid price per $1 million face value is $975,600 = $1m$(1-\frac{.048(183)}{360})$ and an asked price of $975,651 = 1m$(1-\frac{.0479(183)}{360})$. The next column is the bond equivalent yield, based on the bid price. Using the six month Treasury bill, the bond equivalent yield is 4.99% = $\frac{365(.0480)}{360-(.0480)(183)}$.

Private FIs act as brokers and dealers in secondary markets for U.S. Treasury securities, whereas all primary market transactions occur on auctions conducted by the Federal Reserve. Competitive bidders can submit more than one bid to each auction, with different prices and quantities on each tender. However, no single bidder is allowed to win more than 35% of the total amount of the security offered on any particular auction. This rule is intended to prevent any bidder from cornering the market, thereby squeezing other FIs that have customers for the particular issue. This rule was enforced when, in August 1991, Salomon Brothers admitted to repeated violations in which it obtained 86% of a particular auction of two year Treasury notes. Concerns about the fairness of the Treasury's auction procedure led to Congressional hearings and the implementation, in September 1992, of an auction experiment.[4] The Treasury began selling two and five year notes using a **uniform price auction** as opposed to the **discriminatory price auction** that had prevailed prior to the Salomon scandal. In a uniform price auction, all bidders pay the same price, while in a discriminatory price auction, each bidder pays the bid price. How do these auctions work?

uniform price auction: all bidders pay the same price.

discriminatory price auction: each bidder pays the bid price.

The Discriminatory Price Auction

The Federal Reserve Bank of New York conducts the auctions for U.S. Treasury securities. First, the noncompetitive bids are totaled, and their sum is subtracted from the total issue amount. Thus, all noncompetitive bids are automatically filled. But we still do not know what price the noncompetitive bidders will pay. This is because the prices are determined by the results of the competitive portion of the auction.

stop yield: the lowest rejected bid yield, or equivalently the highest accepted bid yield.

When the Fed receives the competitive tenders on behalf of the U.S. Treasury for a security auction, they are ranked in order of bid yield. Since the Treasury's goal is to minimize the government's borrowing costs, the Fed accepts the lowest competitive bids first. That is, the lowest bid yields, or equivalently the highest bid prices, are accepted until the issue is completely sold. The lowest rejected bid yield, or equivalently the highest accepted bid yield, is called the **stop yield**. The **stop-out price** is the security price implied by the stop yield—that is, the highest rejected price or the lowest accepted price. In a discriminatory price auction, each competitive bidder pays a price for the Treasury security that is determined by the yield that was bid. The **average yield** is the average of all accepted competitive bids, weighted by the amounts allocated at each yield. Noncompetitive bidders all pay the average yield. The **tail** (although not the same term as in Chapter 11) is the difference between the stop yield and the average yield. The **cover** is the ratio of the amount of bids tendered (the total of both competitive and noncompetitive bids) to the amount of bids accepted, that is, the size of the issue. An auction is judged a success if its tail is small and its cover is large. A large cover denotes active market participation in the auction, and a small tail indicates that most competitive bidders evaluate the security's value at around the same level and therefore pay almost the same price for the same issue. The average cover for all Treasury notes and bonds issued between January 1986 and June 1991 was 2.61, with a range between maximum and minimum accepted bid yields averaging three basis points.

stop-out price: the security price implied by the stop yield, that is, the highest rejected price or the lowest accepted price.

average yield: the average of all accepted competitive bids, weighted by the amounts allocated at each yield.

tail: the difference between the stop yield and the average yield.

cover: the ratio of the amount of bids tendered to the amount of bids accepted, that is, the size of the issue.

Consider the following $10 billion auction of 13 week (91 day) Treasury bills. Suppose that noncompetitive bids totaled $2 billion. Thus, $8 billion must be filled from competitive bids. The competitive tenders, ranked in order of yield, are

Amount ($ billion)	Bid Yield (pct.)	Price of $1 million 91 day Bill
$1.5	4.45	$1m$(1 - \frac{.0445(91)}{360})$ = $988,751
$3.0	4.46	$1m$(1 - \frac{.0446(91)}{360})$ = $988,726
$2.5	4.47	$1m$(1 - \frac{.0447(91)}{360})$ = $988,701
$2.0	4.48	$1m$(1 - \frac{.0448(91)}{360})$ = $988,676
$5.5	4.49	$1m$(1 - \frac{.0449(91)}{360})$ = $988,650
$6.1	4.50	$1m$(1 - \frac{.0450(91)}{360})$ = $988,625

---

[4] Jordan and Jordan (1996) estimate that Salomon was able to profit from the squeeze by increasing the price of the cornered two year note by $20–$30 million.

The Treasury is not concerned about whether or not the issue can be sold, since the Fed will simply continue accepting bids until the entire issue is sold out. However, if the Treasury must pay high yields to sell the entire issue and if the spread across accepted yields is high, then the auction is considered unsuccessful, even though the Treasury was able to sell the entire issue. In this example, the Fed will accept the lowest competitive bids up until it has sold $8 billion of the newly issued Treasury bills. To do this, all of the 4.45%, 4.46%, and 4.47% bids are accepted. However, this totals only $7 billion. Thus, the Fed must accept half of the bids at 4.48% to make up the $8 billion total. Each competitive tender at the 4.48% bid is satisfied for only half of their bid amount. The stop yield is 4.48% for this auction. The stop-out price, per $1 million face value, is

$$P = \$1m \left(1 - \frac{.0448(91)}{360} \right) = \$988,676$$

Since total of the first column of all competitive bids is $20.6 billion and there are an additional $2 billion noncompetitive bids, the total amount of tenders for this Treasury bill issue is $22.6 billion. Thus, the cover for this auction is $\frac{\$22.6b}{\$10b} = 2.26$. The average yield is

$$\frac{\$1.5b}{\$8b}(4.45) + \frac{\$3.0b}{\$8b}(4.46) + \frac{\$2.5b}{\$8b}(4.47) + \frac{\$1.0b}{\$8b}(4.48) = 4.46375\%$$

Rounded to two-decimal places, the average yield for this auction is recorded as 4.46% p.a. The average price, per $1 million face value, implied by a 4.46% p.a. discount yield is $988,726, calculated as follows:

$$P = \$1m \left(1 - \frac{.0446(91)}{360} \right) = \$988,726$$

All noncompetitive bidders pay this price for the new issue.

The tail for this auction is 4.48% − 4.46% = 2 basis points. Although the cover is adequate, the relatively large tail (a zero tail is optimal) makes this auction less than fully successful. A tail of more than one basis point is a problem because it causes the auction to violate the law of one price; that is, the same security is sold simultaneously at different prices.[5] This is because the competitive bidders in this discriminatory price auction pay different prices for the same security—the 91 day Treasury bill. The lowest bidders obtain $1.5 billion of the new issue at a price, per $1 million of face value, of

$$P = \$1m \left(1 - \frac{.0445(91)}{360} \right) = \$988,751$$

Thus, depending on whether the bidder was a noncompetitive bidder, a competitive low bidder, or a competitive high bidder, the price paid for the identical security will vary from $988,676 to $988,751. This is what is meant by the discriminatory price auction. The bidder's price is determined by his or her own tender. A low bid (that is, low yield or high price offered) increases the bidder's chance of having the bid accepted. However, it leads to the possibility of the **winner's curse**. The low bidder wins acceptance of the tender but pays a price that is higher than other, lower priced (higher yield) bids. This problem emanates from the discriminatory price auction method. Competitive bidders are therefore reluctant to submit low bids under discriminatory price auctions because that will obligate them to pay high prices for the newly issued securities. In contrast, the uniform price auction, another method currently used by the Fed to auction Treasury securities, is not subject to the winner's curse. It is to this auction method that we now turn.

winner's curse: the low bidder wins acceptance of the tender but pays a price that is higher than other, lower bids.

---

[5] Sundaresan (1994) found that as interest rates became more volatile, the tail increased and the cover decreased, reflecting less successful Treasury auctions.

The Uniform Price Auction

Under the uniform price auction, all procedures except for the final step are the same as those under the discriminatory price auction. Instead of charging each successful competitive bidder a price equal to its bid, all successful competitive bidders under the uniform price auction pay the stop-out price. Thus, all $8 billion in our sample Treasury bill auction would be sold to competitive bidders at a price of $988,676 per $1 million face value. To raise a market value of $8 billion at the auction, the Treasury must sell bills with a total face value of $8.091 billion, or must sell $\frac{\$8b}{\$988,676}$ = 8, 092 $1 million face value Treasury bills. Noncompetitive bidders, paying the stop-out price, buy additional securities with a face value equal to $\frac{\$2b}{\$988,676}$($1m) = $2.023 billion. The face value of all Treasury bills issued in the uniform price auction totals $10.115 billion.

The uniform price auction appears to be more costly for the Treasury. Under the discriminatory price auction, prices paid by competitive bidders ranged from $988,751 to $988,676 per $1 million face value. The face value of the 91 day Treasury bill issued competitively under the discriminatory price auction is

$$\frac{\$1.5b}{\$988,751}(\$1m) + \frac{\$3b}{\$988,726}(\$1m) + \frac{\$2.5b}{\$988,701}(\$1m) + \frac{\$1b}{\$988,676}(\$1m) = \$8.09b$$

Adding the additional $2.023 billion in Treasury bills sold to noncompetitive bidders yields a face value of all Treasury bills issued totaling $10.113 billion. The discriminatory price auction saves the Treasury $2 million ($10.115b − $10.113b) on the cost of the entire 91 day Treasury bill issue. Indeed, the interest cost to the Treasury of the entire $10 billion new issue averages 4.46% p.a. under the discriminatory price auction, but is 4.48% p.a. under the uniform price auction, an increase in the Treasury's interest costs of 2 basis points.

Because of its concerns about the costs of the uniform price auction method, the Treasury has adopted this method for its two and five year notes only. The procedures for the note and bond auctions are the same as for the Treasury bill auctions. However, since Treasury notes and bonds are coupon instruments, as opposed to the pure discount Treasury bills, the pricing procedure is different. Thus, an average yield of 4.46% p.a. for a two year Treasury note issue implies that the notes are priced, on average, to have a simple interest yield of 4.46% p.a. if held to maturity. During the two years until maturity, there are four coupon payments. The auction must set the note's coupon rate as well as its yield to maturity. The coupon is set equal to the average yield, rounded *down* to the nearest eighth of a point. That is, the coupon is set either equal to or lower than the yield to maturity, so that the newly issued Treasury note or bond sells at either par or a slight discount, but never at a premium. The average yield in our example of 4.46% p.a. is between $4\frac{3}{8}$ and $4\frac{1}{2}$. Although the closest eighth point is $4\frac{1}{2}$, the rounding has to be down, and so the coupon is set at $4\frac{3}{8}$ to yield a semiannual coupon payment of $2,187.50 per $100,000 of face value (.021875 × $100,000) and a price of

$$P\sum_{s=1}^{T} \frac{C_s}{\left(1 + \frac{y}{n}\right)^s} = \sum_{s=1}^{4} \frac{\$2,187.50}{(1.0223)^s} + \frac{\$100,000}{(1.0223)^4} = \$99,839$$

This is the price of the notes paid by all noncompetitive bidders, as well as the average of all prices paid by competitive bidders in discriminatory price auctions. Under uniform price auctions, however, all competitive bidders pay the stop-out price. If the stop yield is 4.48% p.a., the stop-out price is

$$P = \sum_{s=1}^{4} \frac{\$2,187.50}{(1.0224)^s} + \frac{\$100,000}{(1.0224)^4} = \$99,801$$

a reduction in Treasury revenue amounting to $38 per $100,000 face value for each of the notes sold to the average competitive bidders under the discriminatory price auction.

Why, then, did the Treasury shift from the discriminatory price auction to the uniform price auction in order to conduct its experiment? Although the direct effect of the move to a uniform price auction appears to increase the cost to the Treasury of the new issue, things are not always what they appear to be. Auctions are not one-shot deals. Market participants know that the Treasury will be in the market week after week, issuing new Treasury securities. If the uniform price auction is judged to be fairer, perhaps because all successful competitive bidders pay the same price, this may induce greater participation in Treasury auctions, making them more successful by increasing the auction's cover. Moreover, the winner's curse is not as significant for bidders under the uniform price auction because they do not pay the price that they bid. Thus, competitive bidders for uniform price auctions will not be afraid to submit low bids. Indeed, they will be more likely to submit low bids since the lower they bid, the greater the likelihood that their bids will be accepted. The result is that all bidders tend to reduce their bids, thereby lowering the average yield on the entire issue. These changes in bidder behavior may offset the direct effect of the uniform price auction that raises the issuer's interest costs.

The Treasury's experiment using the uniform price auction was the result of the Salomon Brothers' scandal. In August 1991 Salomon Brothers, Inc. admitted that their traders placed unauthorized bids so as to gain a larger share of new issues than was permissible. The Treasury's concern was that if bidders (both competitive and noncompetitive) viewed the auction to be rigged in favor of a few large FIs, then participation would decline, thereby undermining the Treasury's ability to place large amounts of securities. But is the uniform price auction fairer than the discriminatory price auction? Because bidders do not pay their tendered price, the uniform price auction may be more subject to manipulation or collusion by informed bidders. Whether or not this is a serious concern must be determined by examination of the evidence generated by the Treasury's experiment.

Table 15.2 shows the evidence gathered to date. Perhaps most interesting is the study by Nyborg and Sundaresan (1994), which finds that the average yield was higher than the average rate in the when-issued market one half hour before the auction only in discriminatory price auctions, but not in uniform price auctions. This suggests that bidders in uniform price auctions were bidding current market prices, whereas bidders in discriminatory price auctions were shading their prices a little (raising their bid yields) so as to reduce their purchase prices. Nyborg and Sundaresan's study concludes that, since bidding under uniform price auctions elicits higher prices and fairer bids, a shift in auction method should *increase* the Treasury's revenues, although this is refuted by Goswami, Noe, and Rebello (1995). A Treasury study finds some evidence that the issues auctioned using the uniform price method are more widely distributed to retail customers and FIs other than the primary government security dealers. But the jury is still out. The Treasury continues to view the uniform price auction method as an experiment for two and five year note auctions only.

Checkpoint

1. Why is the U.S. Treasury market the largest and most liquid in the world?

2. What are the goals of the U.S. Treasury in conducting its auctions?

3. Contrast the discriminatory price auction with the uniform price auction method. Which method better satisfies the Treasury's goals?

4. What is the role of competitive bidders in Treasury auctions? noncompetitive bidders?

5. Contrast Treasury bill auctions with Treasury note and bond auctions.

**Table
15.2**

**Empirical–Study Score Card
The Treasury Auction Experiment**

		Results Favor	
Study		Discriminatory-Price Auction	Uniform-Price Auction
Tsao and Vignola (1977)	16 U.S. Treasury bond auctions, January 1993–August 1976 (data problems subsequently discovered)		x
Simon (1994)	16 U.S. Treasury bond auctions, January 1993–August 1976	x	
Umlauf (1993)	Mexican Treasury bill auctions, 1986–1991		x
Tenorio (1993)	Zambian foreign exchange market auctions, October 1975–January 1987		x
Nyborg and Sundaresan (1994)	U.S. Treasury when-issued market, July 1992–August 1993		x
U.S. Department of Treasury	U.S. Treasury securities, June 1991–May 1994	inconclusive	

Source: L. Mester (1995), p. 14.

➤ U.S. Treasury STRIPS

We have seen how the U.S. Treasury uses auctions to issue bills, notes, and bonds. But there is one obligation of the U.S. Treasury that is not issued at auction. That is the U.S. Treasury STRIPS, or more formally, Separate Trading of Registered Interest and Principal Securities. Recall from Chapter 7 that U.S. Treasury STRIPS are zero coupon debt obligations of the U.S. Treasury with maturities that range from 6 months to 30 years. STRIPS are constructed by separating the coupons and principal payments of Treasury notes and bonds into individual zero coupon instruments. Each STRIPS issue is registered in the book-entry system, with a unique **CUSIP** (Committee on Uniform Securities Identification Procedures) **identification number**. All Treasury securities that were issued after November 1984 with original maturities over 10 years are eligible for stripping. STRIPS originate when a FI informs the Treasury that it wants to strip a particular bond issue. In response to such a request, the Treasury offers the resulting STRIPS segments for sale. Indeed, if a FI wanted to reassemble the STRIPS components of a Treasury bond, the Treasury could do so. This is called **reconstituting** a bond and has been permitted by the Treasury since May 1987. Daves and Ehrhardt (1993) examined 42 bonds and found that while only one could be stripped profitably, 26 could be reconstituted profitably. The average profit from reconstitution was $0.30 per $100 par value, with a maximum profit of $1.10. Table 15.3 shows that the quantities of outstanding STRIPS exceed holdings of reconstituted Treasury securities. There is an active STRIPS market in French and Canadian government bonds. STRIPS of U.K. gilts were first introduced in July 1995.

CUSIP identification number: unique securities identification number assigned by the Committee on Uniform Securities Identification Procedures.

reconstituting a bond: reassembling the STRIPS components of a Treasury bond to recreate the original bond.

Table 15.3

Holdings of Treasury Securities in Stripped Form, April 30, 1996

Security Description	Maturity Date	Principal Amount Outstanding			
		Total	Portion Held in Unstripped Form	Portion Held in Stripped Form	Reconstituted This Month
7-3/8% Note C-1996	05/15/96	$20,085,643	$16,020,043	$4,065,600	$385,600
7-1/4% Note D-1996	11/15/96	20,258,810	16,526,010	3,732,800	90,400
8-1/2% Note A-1997	05/15/97	9,921,237	8,328,837	1,592,400	305,200
8-5/8% Note B-1997	08/15/97	9,362,836	7,084,436	2,278,400	92,800
8-7/8% Note C-1997	11/15/97	9,808,329	6,817,929	2,990,400	158,400
8-1/8% Note A-1998	02/15/98	9,159,068	7,802,268	1,356,800	55,680
9% Note B-1998	05/15/98	9,165,387	7,062,587	2,102,800	50,000
9-1/4% Note C-1998	08/15/98	11,342,646	8,672,246	2,670,400	129,600
8-7/8% Note D-1998	11/15/98	9,902,875	6,789,275	3,113,600	20,800
8-7/8% Note A-1999	02/15/99	9,719,623	8,346,823	1,372,800	104,000
9-1/8% Note B-1999	05/15/99	10,047,103	7,083,903	2,963,200	86,400
8% Note C-1999	08/15/99	10,163,644	7,561,019	2,602,625	14,350
7-7/8% Note D-1999	11/15/99	10,773,960	7,319,560	3,454,400	52,800
8-1/2% Note A-2000	02/15/00	10,673,033	7,967,033	2,706,000	71,600
8-7/8% Note B-2000	05/15/00	10,496,230	5,755,430	4,740,800	0
8-3/4% Note C-2000	08/15/00	11,080,646	7,035,046	4,045,600	152,160
8-1/2% Note D-2000	11/15/00	11,519,682	7,388,882	4,130,800	24,000
7-3/4% Note A-2001	02/15/01	11,312,802	8,026,402	3,286,400	40,800
8% Note B-2001	05/15/01	12,398,083	8,872,508	3,525,575	85,600
7-7/8% Note C-2001	08/15/01	12,339,185	9,705,585	2,633,600	64,000
7-1/2% Note D-2001	11/15/01	24,226,102	21,309,302	2,916,800	286,720
7-1/2% Note A-2002	05/15/02	11,714,397	10,058,397	1,656,000	93,360
6-3/8% Note B-2002	08/15/02	23,859,015	22,780,615	1,078,400	102,400
6-1/4% Note A-2003	02/15/03	23,562,691	23,073,987	488,704	528,576
5-3/4% Note B-2003	08/15/03	28,011,028	27,785,428	225,600	32,000
5-7/8% Note A-2004	02/15/04	12,955,077	12,953,477	1,600	0
7-1/4% Note B-2004	05/15/04	14,440,372	14,435,572	4,800	0
7-1/4% Note C-2004	08/15/04	13,346,467	13,312,867	33,600	0
7-7/8% Note D-2004	11/15/04	14,373,760	14,373,760	0	0
7-1/2% Note A-2005	02/15/05	13,834,754	13,834,354	400	0
6-1/2% Note B-2005	05/15/05	14,739,504	14,739,504	0	0
6-1/2% Note C-2005	08/15/05	15,002,580	15,002,580	0	0
5-7/8% Note D-2005	11/15/05	15,209,920	15,209,920	0	0
5-5/8% Note A-2006	02/15/06	15,513,587	15,513,587	0	0
11-5/8% Bond 2004	11/15/04	8,301,806	4,157,806	4,144,000	176,000
12% Bond 2005	05/15/05	4,260,758	2,208,208	2,052,550	40,000
10-3/4% Bond 2005	08/15/05	9,269,713	7,079,313	2,190,400	64,800
9-3/8% Bond 2006	02/15/06	4,755,916	4,750,604	5,312	0
11-3/4% Bond 2009-14	11/15/14	6,005,584	2,062,384	3,943,200	132,800
11-1/4% Bond 2015	02/15/15	12,667,799	9,313,079	3,354,720	795,200
10-5/8% Bond 2015	08/15/15	7,149,916	2,313,116	4,836,800	200,000
9-7/8% Bond 2015	11/15/15	6,899,859	4,034,259	2,865,600	547,200
9-1/4% Bond 2016	02/15/16	7,266,854	6,666,054	600,800	51,200
7-1/4% Bond 2016	05/15/16	18,823,551	18,584,351	239,200	32,000
7-1/2% Bond 2016	11/15/16	18,864,448	17,974,528	889,920	4,800
8-3/4% Bond 2017	05/15/17	18,194,169	9,770,649	8,423,520	711,520
8-7/8% Bond 2017	08/15/17	14,016,858	9,349,658	4,667,200	864,000
9-1/8% Bond 2018	05/15/18	8,708,639	2,660,639	6,048,000	86,400
9% Bond 2018	11/15/18	9,032,870	3,144,470	5,888,400	211,000
8-7/8% Bond 2019	02/15/19	19,250,798	5,409,198	13,841,600	649,600

Table 15.3

Continued

| Security Description | Maturity Date | Principal Amount Outstanding | | | |
		Total	Portion Held in Unstripped Form	Portion Held in Stripped Form	Reconstituted This Month
8-1/8% Bond 2019	08/15/19	20,213,832	17,073,352	3,140,480	520,000
8-1/2% Bond 2020	02/15/20	10,228,868	6,268,068	3,960,800	502,000
8-3/4% Bond 2020	05/15/20	10,158,883	4,209,923	5,948,960	439,040
8-3/4% Bond 2020	08/15/20	21,418,606	5,247,406	16,171,200	779,360
7-7/8% Bond 2021	02/15/21	11,113,373	10,273,373	840,000	268,800
8-1/8% Bond 2021	05/15/21	11,958,888	5,036,328	6,922,560	206,720
8-1/8% Bond 2021	08/15/21	12,163,482	3,673,242	8,490,240	76,800
8% Bond 2021	11/15/21	32,798,394	6,420,794	26,377,600	667,000
7-1/4% Bond 2022	08/15/22	10,352,790	8,306,390	2,046,400	115,200
7-5/8% Bond 2022	11/15/22	10,699,626	3,594,026	7,105,600	65,600
7-1/8% Bond 2023	02/15/23	18,374,361	14,638,361	3,736,000	340,800
6-1/4% Bond 2023	08/15/23	22,909,044	22,402,164	506,880	244,928
7-1/2% Bond 2024	11/15/24	11,469,662	4,627,982	6,841,680	290,320
7-5/8% Bond 2025	02/15/25	11,725,170	6,920,370	4,804,800	387,200
6-7/8% Bond 2025	08/15/25	12,602,007	12,373,847	228,160	0
6% Bond 2026	02/15/26	12,904,916	12,904,916	0	0
Total		884,881,516	657,998,030	226,883,486	12,497,534

Note: On the 4th workday of each month, this table will be available after 3:00 P.M. eastern time on the Commerce Department's Economic Bulletin Board (EBB). The telephone number for more information about EBB is (202) 482-1986. The balances in this table are subject to audit and subsequent adjustments.

Source: Commerce Department's Economic Bulletin Board.

Why would a FI request the construction of particular STRIPS (or, alternatively, the re-assembling of a STRIPped security)? If the whole is worth less than the sum of its parts, then there is an opportunity to earn more from the sale of the STRIPS segments than from the sale of the assembled security. It was in 1982 that Salomon Brothers, Merrill Lynch, and Lehman Brothers first realized the potential in stripped-down Treasury securities. They constructed private-sector strips (called CATS by Salomon, TIGRs by Merrill, and LIONs by Lehman) by purchasing portfolios of Treasury securities and then selling zero coupon securities backed by the Treasuries' cash flows. Investors flocked to the long term zero coupon Treasury-backed securities that were offering a guaranteed, double-digit yield if held until maturity. These instruments were valuable because the FIs that pioneered the market offered their customers the opportunity to eliminate reinvestment risk exposure. That is, since the CATS, TIGRs, and LIONs have no coupon payments, they have no reinvestment rate risk exposure. Pension funds and individuals holding tax-exempt retirement accounts were large purchasers of the "zoo creatures." As payment for their provision of risk hedging services, the FIs collected the difference between the values of the component parts and the Treasury securities that were backing them.

▶ STRIPS and Spot Rates

To determine whether it is profitable to strip Treasury securities, we must evaluate each of the component parts of the STRIPS using spot rates. Spot rates are the rates for immediate delivery of zero coupon instruments of various maturities. Unfortunately, obtaining these spot rates is *not* always as easy as reading financial quotations. The quoted rates on zero coupon instruments may be inaccurate for specific maturities if the issue is illiquid, say for off-the-run issues, or if there are tax-related distortions. We check quoted spot yields by solving for the theoretical spot yield curve using a method called **bootstrapping**. Bootstrapping uses the rates on more liquid, par value, coupon instruments to construct a spot yield curve.

bootstrapping: a method using the rates on more liquid coupon, par value, instruments to construct a spot yield curve.

Suppose that the following par value, coupon Treasury securities selling in the market were the most liquid for each of the following maturities:

6 month maturity with a semiannual coupon of 10% p.a.

1 year maturity with a semiannual coupon of 10.97% p.a.

1.5 year maturity with a semiannual coupon of 11.73% p.a.

2 year maturity with a semiannual coupon of 12.38% p.a.

Consider the one year security. There are three cash flows: (1) a coupon payment received in six months of $5.485 per $100 face value; (2) a coupon payment received in one year of $5.485 per $100 face value; and (3) a $100 repayment of principal received in one year. The present value of the one year security is $100 since it is selling at par. Thus, the present value of all the cash flows discounted at the yield to maturity of 10.97% p.a. must sum to $100. Since the six month maturity security is a pure discount instrument, its yield to maturity is 10% p.a. Converting this yield to a semiannual yield of 5%, we can use this as the discount factor for the first coupon payment. We then solve for the discount factor for the second coupon payment and the repayment of principal. We then sum to $100, obtaining

$$\$100 = \frac{5.485}{1.05} + \frac{5.485}{\left(1 + \frac{y}{2}\right)^2} + \frac{100}{(1 + \frac{y}{2})^2}$$

Solving for $\frac{y}{2}$ yields a semiannual rate of 5.4984%, or an annual theoretical spot rate of 10.997% p.a. We can do this again using the 18 month, par value coupon 11.73% instrument paying 5.865% semiannually. The present value of the four cash flows is

$$\$100 = \frac{5.865}{1.05} + \frac{5.865}{1.054984^2} + \frac{5.865}{\left(1 + \frac{y}{2}\right)^3} + \frac{100}{\left(1 + \frac{y}{2}\right)^3}$$

Solving for $\frac{y}{2}$ yields a semiannual rate of 5.8975%, or an annual theoretical spot rate of 11.795% p.a. Finally, using the two year, par value 12.38% coupon instrument, the present value of all five cash flows is

$$\$100 = \frac{6.19}{1.05} + \frac{6.19}{1.054984^2} + \frac{6.19}{1.058975^3} + \frac{6.19}{\left(1 + \frac{y}{2}\right)^4} + \frac{100}{\left(1 + \frac{y}{2}\right)^4}$$

Solving for $\frac{y}{2}$ yields a semiannual rate of 6.2477%, or an annual theoretical spot rate of 12.495% p.a. Thus, the theoretical spot yield curve using the bootstrap method for each maturity period is summarized in the following spot yield curves:

Time Until Maturity	Theoretical Spot Rate Obtained Using Bootstrapping
6 months	10% p.a.
1 year	10.997% p.a.
18 months	11.795% p.a.
2 years	12.495% p.a.

Now we can determine whether it is profitable to strip the two year par value Treasury note with, say, a face value of $10 million and a 12.38% p.a. semiannual coupon. The cash flow from this Treasury note consists of four payments of $619,000 to be received every six months and, at the end of two years, a single payment of $10 million. We have two candidates to be used as rates of discount for each of these cash flows: the yield to maturity and the theoretical spot rate obtained using bootstrapping. Using the par value yields to maturity, the sum of present values of each of the Treasury STRIPS is

$$PV_{STRIPS} = \frac{\$619,000}{1.05} + \frac{\$619,000}{1.05485^2} + \frac{\$619,000}{1.05865^3}$$
$$+ \frac{\$619,000}{1.0619^4} + \frac{\$10m}{1.0619^4} = \$10,187,440$$

That is, the first strip of the two year Treasury note is the first coupon payment of $619,000 to be received in six months. The present value of this payment is $\frac{\$619,000}{(1+\frac{.10}{2})^1} = \$571,429$. The second cash flow is the second coupon of $619,000 to be received in one year. The present value of this payment is $\frac{\$619,000}{1.05485^2} = \$539,225$. Continuing for all five cash flows, the present value of the STRIPS of the two year Treasury note is $10,018,744.

If the 2 year Treasury note's cash flows were discounted at the theoretical spot rate, we would obtain a present value equal to par ($10 million) as follows:

$$P = \frac{\$619,000}{1.05} + \frac{\$619,000}{1.054984^2} + \frac{\$619,000}{1.058975^3}$$
$$+ \frac{\$619,000}{1.0624774^4} + \frac{\$10m}{1.0624774^4} = \$10m$$

By stripping the Treasury and selling each piece at a price determined by the security's yield to maturity, the FI can earn a profit of $18,744 (= $10,018,744 − $10 million). The Treasury note can be profitably stripped if the present value of the sum of the parts exceeds the present value of the whole, or if $PV_{STRIPS} > P$.

The profit from the STRIPS is obtained from the divergence between market yields to maturity and theoretical spot rates. For each maturity, if the yield to maturity is equal to the theoretical spot rate, then there is no opportunity to profit from either stripping or reconstituting bonds. If yields to maturity are lower (higher) than theoretical spot yields, then it is profitable to strip (reconstitute) bonds. This occurs when the yield curve is not flat. If the yield curve is upward sloping, each yield to maturity will tend to be lower than the corresponding maturity spot yield, making it profitable to strip bonds. On the other hand, if the yield curve is downward sloping, reconstituting will be profitable. If the yield curve is flat, yields will always equal theoretical spot rates, making it unprofitable to either strip or reconstitute bonds.

As the market grew rapidly,[6] the Treasury realized that the payments that the FIs were earning could instead be directed to the government's coffers. In February 1985 the Treasury created the STRIPS, which officially are obligations of the U.S. Treasury. The Treasury STRIPS were also registered on the book-entry system, so that they could be cleared electronically. It was difficult for the private sector zero coupon instruments to compete with the Treasury STRIPS. The CATS, TIGRs, and LIONs were all obligations of private FIs, although they were backed by a portfolio of Treasury securities. The market was not liquid since each FI refused to trade the zoo creatures created by rival FIs. Moreover, they were not registered in the book-entry system, so clearing was more cumbersome than for the Treasury STRIPS. Thus, the Treasury STRIP has replaced the private Treasury-backed zero coupon security.

Taxation

The Treasury distinguishes between STRIPS constructed from coupon payments and STRIPS constructed from principal payments. This may appear to be odd since the origin of the cash

---

[6] During the first month of their availability, $14 billion of Treasuries were stripped into CATS, TIGRs, and LIONs.

flow on the zero coupon instrument should not matter. Indeed, it does not matter to U.S. investors, who must pay federal taxes on the receipt of all STRIPS cash flows, but at one time it did matter to Japanese investors. Before 1989, Japanese investors were not taxed on STRIPS constructed from principal until their maturity, although they were taxed annually on STRIPS constructed from coupon payments. Japanese investors therefore preferred STRIPS of principal payments so as to reduce their tax liability. The tax laws have changed so that all STRIPS, of coupon or principal payments, are now taxed annually in both the United States and Japan. That is, the interest income on the zero coupon instrument is imputed annually and taxed as if it were paid to the investor. Because no cash flows are made to offset this tax liability, this is costly for the holder of the STRIPS. That is why we see most STRIPS held in tax-exempt structures, such as IRAs or Keogh plans.

Checkpoint

1. How does the shape of the yield curve affect the incentive to create STRIPS?
2. Why did U.S. Treasury STRIPS replace the zeros created by FIs and backed by U.S. Treasury securities?
3. How have tax treatments throughout the world affected the market for Treasury securities?
4. Why does the bootstrap method yield a more accurate measure of spot rates than quoted yields on zero coupon instruments of varying maturities?

➤ Sovereign Government Bonds

sovereign government bonds: bonds issued by a national government.

The U.S. government is not the only government that finances its activities by issuing debt instruments. **Sovereign government bonds** are bonds issued by a national government. Sovereign government obligations, such as U.S. Treasury securities, carry the full faith and credit of the issuing government. The U.S. Treasury market has become the largest market in the world, in large part because the obligations are free of any default risk. The same cannot be said for other sovereign governments' bonds. Indeed, as more governments have sought access to the international bond market, there has been a need for sovereign credit ratings. These ratings analyze the default risk characteristics of a particular country's debt obligations, measuring country, or sovereign, risk exposure. **Sovereign ratings** are the assessment by an independent agency (such as Moody's or Standard & Poor's) of the likelihood that a sovereign government borrower will default on its debt obligations. Sovereign ratings are more difficult to ascertain than corporate bond credit ratings because of the uncertainty of political activities that affect governmental actions. Country risk exposure is more difficult to assess than corporate credit risk because the creditor cannot claim the borrower's assets in the event of default. Instead, sovereign credit ratings assess the governments' power to tax domestic income, as well as to print currency.[7]

sovereign ratings: the assessment of an independent agency (such as Moody's or Standard and Poor's) of the likelihood that a sovereign government borrower will default on its debt obligations.

Yankee bonds: bonds issued in the United States, denominated in United States dollars, that are obligations of foreign issuers.

In the late 1980s and early 1990s, weaker sovereign governments entered the foreign bond market, often in the market for **Yankee bonds**. Yankee bonds are bonds issued in the United States, denominated in U.S. dollars, that are obligations of foreign issuers. Credit ratings are a necessity in the Yankee bond market. Table 15.4 shows that whereas before 1985 most initial sovereign ratings were AAA/Aaa, in the 1990s, the ratings were clustered around the lowest investment grade rating, BBB–/Baa3. More than half (56%) the sovereign bonds issued received a rating below AA/Aa. The market reflects its perception of the greater credit risk of sovereign bond issues by requiring a risk premium. As of December 16, 1994, the difference in

---

[7] Excessive printing of currency to repay outstanding debt obligations will reduce the value of the currency and can be considered a partial default. The rating agencies typically categorize this as market risk rather than credit risk.

Table 15.4

Sovereign Credit Ratings

Year of Initial Rating	No. of Newly Rated Sovereigns	Median Rating (S&P/Moody's)
Pre-1975	3	AAA/Aaa
1975–1979	9	AAA/Aaa
1980–1984	3	AAA/Aaa
1985–1989	19	A/A2
1990–1994	15	BBB-/Baa3

Source: Cantor and Packer (1995), p. 2.

Table 15.5

Size of the Major Government Bond Markets, Year-End 1995 (US$ billions)

Country	Nominal Value of Sovereign Government Bonds Outstanding
United States	2,546.5
Japan	2,002.7
Italy	858.9
Germany	727.1
France	489.9
United Kingdom	361.4
Belgium	225.7
Holland	194.3
Canada	183.0
Spain	160.5
Sweden	111.8
Denmark	106.6
ECU	73.4
Australia	68.3
Austria	54.4
Greece	40.8
Portugal	33.8
Finland	33.3
Switzerland	28.5
Ireland	24.5
Norway	19.5
New Zealand	12.4
Total	8,357.2

Source: Rosario Benevides, "How Big is the World Bond Market?–1994 Update," *Economic and Market Analysis,* New York: Salomon Brothers Inc., (August 1996), Figure 1, p. 1.

yield between comparably rated sovereign and U.S. corporate bonds was an average of 63 basis points. In March 10, 1995, in the wake of the Mexican crisis, this spread stretched to 232 basis points. Table 15.5 shows that the G-7 countries (the United States, Japan, Germany, France, Italy, Canada, and the United Kingdom), Holland, and Belgium have been most successful in tapping the market for their government securities.

Out of 72 governments with outstanding domestic and foreign currency debt, 30 have defaulted at least once since 1970. Indeed, Venezuela defaulted on its foreign currency bank debt, although not on its bonds, in 1982 while obtaining an AA rating on its bonds. A rash of defaults in the early 1980s caused a LDC (less developed country) debt crisis, initiated

Brady bonds: defaulted sovereign debt that is restructured so that it is partially secured by a portfolio of U.S. Treasury bonds, with the remainder of payments paid like equity as a residual.

by Mexico's 1982 repudiation of its bank debt. In the late 1980s, many of these defaulted bonds were exchanged for **Brady bonds** (named after former U.S. Treasury Secretary Nicholas Brady), which are partially secured by a portfolio of U.S. Treasury bonds, with the remainder of payments paid like equity as a residual.

Japanese Government Bonds (JGBs)

After the U.S. Treasuries market, the Japanese bond market is the largest fixed income market in the world. By the end of June 1995, the amount of outstanding Japanese government bonds (JGBs) totaled 209 trillion yen. There are four types of JGBs: (1) short term (maturities up to one year)[8] Treasury bills, first introduced in February 1986 and patterned after U.S. Treasury bills; (2) medium term bonds, both with and without coupons, with maturities of two, three, and four years, usually issued monthly; (3) long term 10 year coupon bearing, noncallable bonds, usually issued monthly; and (4) super long term 20 year coupon bearing, noncallable bonds, issued three times a year. Individual investors tend to dominate the medium term bond markets since they cannot purchase JGB bills. Since Japanese retail investors tend to buy and hold (see our discussion of Mrs. Watanabe in Chapter 12), the medium term market is quite illiquid.

The majority of all JGBs are issued through a public auction, although the auction is dominated by a single underwriting syndicate consisting of 788 FIs. Since 1984, non-Japanese FIs have been permitted to be part of the underwriting syndicate. After consulting with the syndicate, the Ministry of Finance sets the issue size and the coupon rate for all issues JGBs. Then prices are accepted to auction the new issue. The syndicate must purchase any JGBs that remain unsold after the auction.

benchmark bond: a liquid bond issue (usually the most recent issue) chosen by the Big Four Japanese security houses (Yamaichi, Daiwa, Fuji, and Nomura).

Secondary market trading is somewhat illiquid in all issues except the **benchmark bond**. More than 90% of all trading is in the benchmark bond. The benchmark bond, or in U.S. Treasury terminology, the on-the-run issue, is a liquid bond issue (usually the most recent issue) chosen by the Big Four Japanese security houses (Yamaichi, Daiwa, Fuji, and Nomura). Benchmark issues have the following characteristics:

1. A coupon that is near the prevailing market rate.

2. A large outstanding amount (usually 1.5 trillion yen or more).

3. A wide distribution.

4. A remaining maturity as close to 10 years as possible.

The price of the benchmark issue is higher (that is, the yield is lower) than nonbenchmark issues by a benchmark premium, averaging 10 to 30 basis points. Although this premium is observed for U.S. Treasury on-the-run issues as well, the size is higher in Japan than in other countries, sometimes jumping to 100 basis points.

reverse coupon effect: higher coupon JGBs, *ceteris paribus*, carry lower yields (higher prices) than equivalent maturity (duration) JGBs with lower coupons.

Another characteristic of the JGB market that diverges from other financial market practices is the **reverse coupon effect**. Higher coupon JGBs, *ceteris paribus*, carry lower yields (higher prices) than equivalent maturity (duration) JGBs with lower coupons. This is at odds with bond pricing in other markets because it runs counter to the standard response to increases in risk exposure. Since higher coupon bonds have greater reinvestment risk exposure, they should offer a higher risk adjusted yield than equivalent lower coupon bonds. However, Japanese regulations encourage a perverse demand for current income. For example, Japanese insurance companies are unable to pay to their policyholders dividends that exceed their receipts of dividends and interest income. By investing in high-coupon JGBs, the insurance companies can circumvent these regulatory restrictions on their payout policies, so as to compete with other Japanese

---

[8] Before September 1990, the Japanese government did not issue Treasuries with maturities less than six months.

and non-Japanese FIs. This leads to a "clientele effect" in JGBs and other non-Japanese bond markets in which Japanese FIs prefer to invest in high-coupon as opposed to lower-coupon issues.

Over 95% of all JGBs are sold in registered (book-entry) form and are cleared over an electronic payment system operated by the Bank of Japan. The remainder are bearer bonds. Because bearer bond issues are less liquid than registered bonds, they carry a 5 basis point liquidity risk premium in yield. Settlement takes place every fifth day, on the 5th, 10th, 15th, 20th, 25th, and the last calendar day of each month.[9] This noncontinuous settlement produces a lag between the **value date**, the date on which the security is priced, and the settlement date, the date on which the transaction is cleared. Trades are settled on the settlement day that falls approximately two weeks after the value date. This period can last as long as 15 days and leads to considerable speculation within the period.

value date: the date on which the security is priced.

Checkpoint

1. Why are sovereign government bond issues difficult to rate?

2. Contrast the Japanese government bond market to the market for U.S. Treasuries.

3. What do the reverse coupon effect and the benchmark effect imply about the integration of JGBs into international capital markets?

Second-Tier Sovereign Government Bond Markets

The markets for U.S. Treasury securities and JGBs are the most active government bond markets in the world because of their liquidity, resulting from the vast amounts of bond issues. Table 15.5 shows the dominance of the U.S. Treasury and JGB markets in terms of volume outstanding. Other important markets that do not have the level of liquidity seen in the Treasury and JGB markets are the markets for German government bonds (**Bunds**), U.K. government bonds (**Gilts**), French government bonds (**OATs**), and Canadian government bonds. We call these second-tier government bond markets.

Bunds: German government bonds.

Gilts: U.K. government bonds.

OATs: French government bonds.

German Bunds   Bunds have not been issued in large volumes, despite the financial strains of German unification, because of the popularity in Germany of **Schuldscheine**, negotiable private placements of bank loans. The popularity of the latter stems from the market structure of German FIs. Banks are the dominant form of FI in Germany. Indeed, bank activity is a much more important source of financial intermediation than are financial markets. The underdevelopment of German financial markets is reflected in the reliance on bank loans to finance government activities, as opposed to the issuance of financial securities. Banks originated approximately DM4 billion of Schuldscheine *per month* in the years immediately following German reunification.

Schuldscheine: negotiable private placements of bank loans.

Although Bunds have maturities ranging from 6 to 30 years, the most common issue is the 10 year maturity. The Bundesbank intervenes to smooth out rates in the secondary market for Bunds. Bunds are issued using an underwriting syndicate, called the Konsortium, comprising 190 FIs (including some foreign-owned FIs). The Bundesbank sets the terms of the offer and retains 20% of each issue to use in its market intervention activities. The remainder of the issue is allocated to the FIs in the syndicate. They must purchase their specified quota and then resell it to the general public. This exposes the syndicate members to **underwriting risk**, the risk that the FI will be unable to sell the new issue at a price higher than the price it paid. To compensate the syndicate members for underwriting risk, the Bundesbank sets a commission rate of $1\frac{3}{8}\%$. Out of this commission, $\frac{5}{8}\%$ is known as a **reallowance**. A reallowance is a

underwriting risk: the risk that the FI will be unable to sell the new issue at a price higher than the price it paid.

reallowance: a guarantee that will be paid to the syndicate FI if the bond is resold to the Bundesbank within one year at a price less than or equal to its issue price.

---

[9] If any of these dates does not fall on a business day, settlement takes place on the next business day.

guarantee that will be paid to the syndicate FI if the bond is resold to the Bundesbank within one year at a price less than or equal to its issue price.

To enhance the marketability of its government bonds, in July 1990 the German government introduced a uniform price auction to augment the syndicated issuance of Bunds. On the day after the syndicated portion of the new issue is sold, additional Bunds (with the same coupon rate and maturity date) are auctioned, thereby setting a market price for the new issue. Euroclear, CEDEL, and each country's national payment system are used to clear much of the volume on second-tier government bond markets.

British Gilts   There are more types of British gilts (Exchequer, Treasury, Funding, Redemption, Transport, Gas, Conversion, Consols, and War Loan, each named for the specific British government department that issued the bond) than any other government bond markets.[10] There are four categories of gilts: (1) straight gilts, which are obligations of the British government with maturities ranging from less than a year to 15 years; (2) convertible gilts, which have short maturities and give the holder the option to convert into a specified amount of longer maturity gilt; (3) index-linked gilts, with coupons and principal payments tied to the general price index; and (4) irredeemable gilts, perpetuals, without a final maturity, but which can be called by the government after a specified date on three months' notice.

Gilts are issued on primary markets using the uniform price auction method. However, the British government has intermittently experimented with a discriminatory price auction. Typically, one week elapses between the announcement of a new issue and its auction (using either method), although gilts first trade in a when-issued market. In January 1989, the Bank of England conducted a "reverse auction." Because of government budget surpluses, the government repurchased $500,000 of short maturity gilts.

Big Bang: deregulation of British security markets on October 27, 1986.

The secondary market in the United Kingdom changed dramatically on October 27, 1986. This was the date of the **Big Bang** which deregulated British security markets and FIs. The impact of the Big Bang on British gilts was to increase the market's liquidity and reduce bid/ask spreads. Before the Big Bang, gilt transaction costs were inflated by a multilayered system of FIs that limited each to a single function. The old system required stock jobbers to hand off transactions to stockbrokers who were the only FIs empowered to deal directly with customers. The Big Bang allowed FIs to act on a "dual capacity basis," thereby handling the gilt transaction from issuance to ultimate placement. Subsequently, turnover increased as bid/ask spreads were reduced. Another factor increasing gilt market liquidity was the introduction of a gilt repo market in January 1996, causing an increase in average daily turnover in the cash gilt market from £6.2 billion in 1995 to £8.1 billion in the first quarter of 1996. Currently, gilts are cleared using the Bank of England's electronic book-entry system, the Central Gilt Office (CGO).

French OATs   The effects of the Big Bang extended to the market for French government bonds, called Obligation Assimilable du Tresor (OATs). Since the Big Bang broke the monopoly of a few FIs, called the Agents de Change, the liquidity on all French financial markets increased. The monopoly was replaced in 1985 with a deregulated system of 13 primary government securities dealers, called Specialistes en Valeurs du Tresor (SVTs), which became market makers in French government bonds. OATs maturities vary from 3 month discount bills to 30 years. The 10 year OAT is the benchmark, and 60% of all issues have maturities of seven years or more. Coupon bearing instruments can be either fixed or floating rate bonds, where the floating rate OAT securities are repriced quarterly at a rate equal to the weighted average yield of the 13 week OAT Treasury bill auction. All OATs are issued by the French government using a discriminatory price auction method, with new issues offered according to a regular auction

---

[10] Coupon-bearing gilts are called *stocks*, and their coupon payments are called *dividends*.

calendar. The when-issued market trades two to five days before each auction; clearing takes place on Euroclear/CEDEL.

Canadian Government Bonds   Given the close physical proximity of the United States and Canada, the government bond markets of the two countries are closely linked. Thirty percent of Canadian government bonds are held by Americans and other nonresidents of Canada. Indeed, the Canadian government issues **Canadian bills**, which are Canadian Treasury bills denominated in U.S. dollars. This is unique among all the government bond issues that we have covered, all of which are denominated in the local currency.

Canadian bills: Canadian Treasury bills denominated in U.S. dollars.

Only "primary distributors," a group of 60 FIs designated by the Bank of Canada, are permitted to bid on discriminatory price auctions for new issues of Canadian government obligations. In addition, some issues are sold by subscription offering, where the Bank of Canada sets the price and features of the new issues. Each primary distributor receives an allotment, which it can choose to take down in full, or in part, or not at all. Primary distributors receive commission fees that increase with both the maturity of the issue and the portion of the allotment taken down.

inflation-indexed Treasury bonds: debt obligations of sovereign governments that carry regular coupon payments that are fixed in real terms.

U.S. Treasury coupon bearing securities are fixed rate instruments that do not fluctuate with market interest rates. Canada and several other industrialized nations issue **inflation-indexed Treasury bonds**. These bonds carry regular coupon payments that are fixed in real terms. That is, the nominal coupon payment increases when inflation increases (and vice versa) to keep the purchasing power of the coupon payments unchanged over the life of the bond. As of March 31, 1995, Canada had issued US$3.2 billion of inflation-indexed bonds, representing 1.1% of total government debt. The corresponding figures for the United Kingdom are US$37.4 billion (11.8% of the total); for Sweden US$1.6 billion (2.1% of the total); and for Australia US$2.2 billion (3% of the total of Australian government debt). In January 1997, the U.S. Treasury will conduct its first auction of these bonds, so as to provide U.S. dollar investors with an inflation risk hedging vehicle.

We can observe a lot about a country's financial system and the philosophy of its public FIs by observing its government bond market. The tight control over financial market activity wielded by the Bundesbank is exhibited by its reluctance to submit to the uncertainties of freely traded government bond markets. In contrast, the highly entrepreneurial, market-based systems in the United States and Japan are reflected in active government bond markets and innovative sovereign government debt obligations. The relative liquidity of each of the sovereign government debt markets is reflected in the yields, as shown in Figure 15.4 for 10 year government bonds. U.S. Treasury yields are lowest since the market is the most liquid, whereas in the illiquid U.K. gilt market yields are highest.

If each country's sovereign bond returns reflect its own national economic structure, then investors may obtain the risk reducing benefits of diversification. If government bond returns are not highly correlated among countries, then a portfolio consisting of many countries' sovereign debt instruments would reduce investor risk. Table 15.6 shows the considerable potential benefits to diversification made possible by the very low correlation coefficients between countries.

Checkpoint

✓

1. What distinguishes the U.S. Treasury and JGB markets from second-tier government bond markets?
2. What can we learn about each country's financial system and the philosophy of its public FIs by observing its government bond markets?
3. Describe the primary market, secondary market, and clearing procedures for government bonds issued by the governments of Germany, the United Kingdom, France, and Canada.

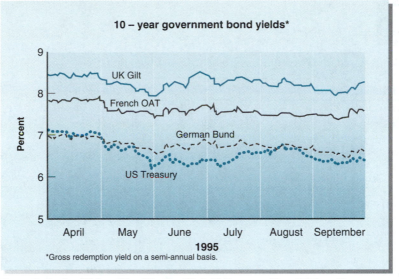

10 – year government bond yields*

*Gross redemption yield on a semi-annual basis.

Source: R. Gordon-Walker, "Can Gilts Get Glitzier?" *Euromoney* (Dec. 1995), p. 60.

Figure 15.4

Table
15.6

Correlation of International Government Bond
Market Returns, January 1978–April 1990

	Germany	Japan	U.K.	U.S.
Germany	1.000			
Japan	0.485	1.000		
U.K.	0.519	0.121	1.000	
U.S.	0.393	0.329	0.100	1.000

Source: Clare, Maras, and Thomas (1995), p. 318.

➤ Risk Shifting

Sovereign government debt obligations may subject investors to (1) interest rate risk exposure; (2) currency risk exposure; or (3) sovereign country risk of default. How can FIs offer risk hedging services to investors in government securities? We have already seen one method: the when-issued market. Since the when-issued market allows forward trading in a particular issue, it can reduce the risk of price fluctuations between the date of announcement of the issue and the settlement date. However, because the when-issued market is narrow in both duration and scope, its risk hedging opportunities are limited.

To expand the opportunities for risk shifting, government bond futures and options have been developed. They trade actively around the world. Table 15.7 lists some examples of exchange-listed futures and options that are based on sovereign government obligations. In addition, liquid, local currency options markets exist for German Bunds and Italian bonds.[11] Since the prices of these derivatives are determined by the prices of the underlying securities, the derivatives can be used to take low-cost, highly leveraged offsetting positions in government securities markets.

---

[11] Liquidity in over-the-counter options on JGBs and OATS is limited to on-the-run issues, with short terms to expiration.

Table 15.7

Futures and Options Based on Sovereign Government Debt Obligations

Underlying Security	Exchange	Quotation	Expiration Dates
U.S. Treasury Securities:			
U.S. T-bond futures $100,000, 20 year, 8% coupon T-bond	CBT	$\frac{1}{32}$ per $100 par	Mar., June, Sept., Dec.
U.S. T-note futures 5 year & 10 year $100,000, 8% coupon T-note 2 year $200,000, 8% coupon T-note	CBT	$\frac{1}{32}$ per $100 par	Mar., June, Sept., Dec.
U.S. T-bill futures $1 million 91 day T-bills	CME	.01% ≈ $25	Mar., June, Sept., Dec.
U.S. T-bond futures options U.S. T-bond futures contract	CBT	$\frac{1}{64}$ per $100 par	Mar., June, Sept., Dec.
U.S. T-note futures options U.S. T-note futures contract	CBT	$\frac{1}{64}$ per $100 par	Mar., June, Sept., Dec.
U.S. T-bill futures options $1 million 91 day T-bill futures contract	CME	.01% ≈ $25	Mar., June, Sept., Dec.
Japanese Government Bonds:			
Long term JGB futures JY100 million, 6% coupon JGB with maturity of 7–11 years	TSE	JY.01 per JY100 par	Mar., June, Sept., Dec.
Super long term JGB futures JY100 million, 6% coupon JGB with maturity of 15–21 years	TSE	JY.01 per JY100 par	Mar., June, Sept., Dec.
Long term JGB futures option JY100 million, 6% coupon JGB with maturity of 7–11 years	TSE	JY.01 per JY100 par	Mar., June, Sept., Dec.
Cash options on JGBs Benchmark JGB	OTC	Negotiable	Negotiable
German Government Bonds:			
Bund futures DM250,000, 6% coupon Bunds with 8.5–10 years to maturity	LIFFE,DTB[a]	DM25 per DM100 par	Mar., June, Sept., Dec.
Option on Bund futures Bund futures contract	DTB	DM25 per DM100	Mar., June, Sept., Dec.
British Government Bonds:			
Long Gilt futures £50,000, 9% coupon gilts with 15–25 years to maturity	LIFFE	£$\frac{1}{32}$ per $100 par	Mar., June, Sept., Dec.
Medium Gilt futures £50,000 gilts, with coupon < 14%, 7–10 years to maturity	LIFFE	£$\frac{1}{32}$ per $100 par	Mar., June, Sept., Dec.
Short Gilt futures £100,000 gilts, with 9% coupon, 3–4.5 years to maturity	LIFFE	£$\frac{1}{64}$ per $100 par	Mar., June, Sept., Dec.
Long Gilt futures options Long gilt futures	LIFFE	£$\frac{1}{64}$ per 100 par	Mar., June, Sept., Dec.

Underlying Security	Exchange	Quotation	Expiration Dates
French Government Bonds:			
Long term OATs futures	MATIF	FFr250	Mar., June, Sept., Dec.
FFr500,000 OATs with 10% coupon, 7–10 years			
Medium term OATs futures	MATIF	FFr200	Mar., June, Sept., Dec.
FFr1 million, 8% coupon, 4 year maturity BTAN (interest bearing French T-note)			
Short term T-bill futures	MATIF	.01% = FFr25	Mar., June, Sept., Dec.
90 day FFr5 million discount Treasury bills			
Long term OATs futures options	MATIF	.01% = FFr50	Month prior to futures contract
Long term OATs futures contract			
Futures options	OTC	Negotiable	Negotiable
Canadian Government Bonds:			
Canadian govt. bond futures	ME	C$10	Mar., June, Sept., Dec.
C$100,000 9% coupon Canadian bond with maturity of 6.5–10 years.			
Canadian bond futures options	ME	C$10	Mar., June, Sept., Dec.
Canadian government futures contract			
Options on Canadian govt. bonds	OTC	.01% of C$100 par	next 3 mos.+ Mar., June, Sept., Dec.
C$25,000 government bonds with specific maturities and coupons			

[a]Although the Bund futures contracts on the LIFFE and the DTB are almost identical, some differences exist: (1) last day of trading, three days before delivery date on LIFFE, and two days before delivery date on DTB; (2) specification of deliverable bonds, limited to those listed on the Frankfurt Stock Exchange for LIFFE, but no limitation for DTB; and (3) trading hours.

CBT = Chicago Board of Trade; CME = Chicago Mercantile Exchange; TSE = Tokyo Stock Exchange; OTC = over the counter; LIFFE = London International Financial Futures Exchange; DTB = Deutsche Termin Borse; MATIF = Marche a Terme d'Instruments Financier, the French Futures Exchange; ME = Montreal Futures Exchange.

To illustrate the risk shifting uses of the contracts in Table 15.7, suppose that the French franc–U.S. dollar exchange rate is currently US$0.20 per French franc. French 90 day Treasury bills offer a discount yield of 6.5% p.a., whereas U.S. 90 day Treasury bills pay only 5% p.a. Financial markets appear to be underpricing the French Treasury bill relative to the U.S. Treasury bill. That is, two risk free securities with the same maturity dates have different yields. If there are no fundamental reasons for this differential, such as differential inflation rates, then this can be viewed as a temporary arbitrage opportunity. If financial markets are efficient, then within a relatively short period of time, the rates will be equalized. Suppose that the investor expects French Treasury bill rates to fall back down to the level of U.S. Treasury bill rates. How can the investor take advantage of this short-lived arbitrage opportunity?

One way for the investor to generate an immediate profit from this mispricing is by selling $1 million U.S. Treasury bills and buying FFr5 million French Treasury bills. The price of the U.S. Treasury bill is $1m$(1 - \frac{.05(90)}{360})$ = $987,500. The price of the French Treasury bill is calculated in the same way, yielding FFr5m$(1 - \frac{.065(90)}{360})$ = FFr4,918,750. Converting the price of the French Treasury bill into dollars, using current spot exchange rates, yields a price of FFr4,918,750 $\times .20$ = US$983,750. Simultaneously buying the French Treasury bill and selling the U.S. Treasury bill yields an immediate profit of US$3,750 ($987,500 - $983,750).

Upon maturity, in 90 days, the French Treasury bill pays its face value of FFr5 million. If exchange rates are unchanged, this can be converted to US$1 million to repay the face value on the short U.S. Treasury bill position. Thus, the French/U.S. Treasury bill position yields a cash flow of US$3,750, paid immediately. The top panel in Table 15.8 shows the cash flows of the transaction. However, this transaction is not risk free. In particular, this transaction is exposed to the risk that the French franc will fall relative to the U.S. dollar. Suppose that the exchange rate does not stay constant at US$0.20 per French franc, but instead declines to US$0.15 per French franc in 90 days. The face value of the French Treasury bill, converted into U.S. dollars, is FFr5 million x US$0.15 = US$750,000. This results in the US$246,250 loss on the transaction shown in the middle panel of Table 15.8.

If the investor did not want to incur the risk of loss, she would have to sell the FFr5 million forward, to be delivered in 90 days, to lock in the exchange rate, using currency risk hedging futures, options, or swaps. However, this hedge can be costly. Is there another way for the investor to exploit the arbitrage opportunity presented by the mispricing between the U.S. and French Treasury bill markets?

Yes, the investor can buy French Treasury bill futures. Suppose that the investor expects the 90 day French Treasury bill rate to fall back to its correct level (5% p.a.) in one day. Rather than taking cash positions in the French and U.S. Treasury bills (with the attendant transactions costs of buying and selling securities), the investor buys a 90 day French Treasury bill that has a delivery date in, say, two months. The French Treasury bill futures contract is quoted in the same way as the Eurodollar CD futures contract (see Chapter 12), on an IMM basis. Thus, if the futures rate is 6.5% p.a., the IMM futures price is 100 – 6.5 = 93.5.

Table 15.8

Cash Flows on an International Government Security Transaction

U.S. Dollars In		U.S. Dollars Out	
Time period 0: French franc–U.S. dollar exchange rate is $0.20			
Sell 90 day $1m U.S. T-bill	$987,500	Buy 90 day FFr5m French T-bill	($983,750)
In 90 days time: French franc–U.S. dollar exchange rate is $0.20			
Receive par value of French T-bill	$1,000,000	Pay par value of U.S. T-bill	($1,000,000)
Total cash flows	$1,987,500		($1,983,750)
Net cash flow	$3,750 (= $1,987,500 – $1,983,750)		
Time period 0: French franc–U.S. dollar exchange rate is $0.20			
Sell 90 day $1m U.S. T-bill	$987,500	Buy 90 day FFr5m French T-bill	($983,750)
In 90 days time: French franc–U.S. dollar exchange rate is $0.15			
Receive par value of French T-bill	$750,000	Pay par value of U.S. T-bill	($1,000,000)
Total cash flows	$1,737,500		($1,983,750)
Net cash flow		($1,737,500 – $1,983,750 =)	($246,250)
Time period 0: French franc–U.S. dollar exchange rate is $0.20			
		Buy French T-bill futures	0
Next day:			
Sell French T-bill futures contract	$3,750		
Net cash flow	$3,750 (= $3,750 – 0)		

The futures contract enables the investor to "buy" the French Treasury bill without paying for it until delivery date.[12] Thus, in the bottom panel of Table 15.8, we show no cash outflow upon the initiation of the futures position today. By tomorrow, the French Treasury bill is corrected to 5% p.a. This implies that the French Treasury bill futures contract price is $100 - 5.0 = 95$. The investor earns 1.50 points on the long futures position, for a cash flow of $(1.5\%)(\text{FFr5m})\frac{90}{360} = \text{FFr18,750}$. Converting this cash flow to U.S. dollars using the current exchange rate of US$0.20 per French franc (assumed to remain constant for one day) yields the cash inflow of US$3,750.

In this stylized example, the investor used futures contracts to speculate on future price movements for foreign government obligations. If, however, the investor had bought long maturity floating rate French OATs with quarterly repricing tied to the 90 day French Treasury bill rate, this futures transaction could be viewed as protection against interest rate risk. That is, the investor is concerned that if the French Treasury bill rate falls (to 5% p.a.), then the coupon on the longer maturity floating rate OATs will decrease, thereby reducing the investor's interest income. The cash inflow from the futures position offsets that loss.

Checkpoint

1. Compare futures options versus cash options as hedging vehicles.
2. What are the types of risks of sovereign government securities?

Federal Agency Securities

In Chapter 5, we discussed the government's credit allocation functions. The government deems certain sectors of the economy to be vulnerable, critical, or merely politically powerful and therefore worthy of governmental aid. The government creates special agencies, which are publicly financed FIs that offer subsidized credit to the sectors designated for special assistance. There are two types of federal agencies: (1) **federally related FIs** and (2) **federally sponsored agencies**. Federally related FIs are branches of the federal government that offer subsidized financing to specified sectors of the economy. All of the funds distributed by federally related FIs are raised by the Federal Financing Bank, which issues securities on each agency's behalf. Federally related FIs are the Commodity Credit Corporation, the Export-Import Bank of the U.S., the Farmers Home Administration, the General Services Administration, the Government National Mortgage Association (known as "Ginnie Mae"), the Maritime Administration, the Private Export Funding Corporation, the Rural Electrification Administration, the Rural Telephone Bank, the Small Business Administration, the Tennessee Valley Authority, and the Washington Metropolitan Area Transit Authority. As of January 1995, the total Federal Financing Bank debt on behalf of all federally related FIs was $101.2 billion.

Federally sponsored agencies are privately owned, publicly chartered FIs that carry only an implicit federal government guarantee. Each federally sponsored agency issues its own securities. In contrast to federally related FIs, whose securities are backed by the full faith and credit of the federal government, the securities of federally sponsored agencies have some credit risk exposure.[13] The credit risk of any federal agency is limited by the implicit federal government backing that should, under all but the most dire circumstances, prevent default.

federally related FIs: branches of the federal government that offer subsidized financing to specified sectors of the economy.

Federally sponsored agencies: privately owned, publicly chartered FIs that carry only an implicit federal government guarantee.

---

[12] Although the futures contract requires an up-front margin payment, this is only a small fraction of the cost of the underlying security. Moreover, the cost to the investor of the futures margin is simply the opportunity cost of the funds, since the margin is refundable to the investor upon completion of all the terms of the futures contract. (See Chapter 18.)

[13] The Private Export Funding Corporation and the Tennessee Valley Authority are the two federally related FIs whose securities do not carry the full credit guarantee of the federal government. In contrast, the Farm Credit Financial Assistance Corporation is a federally sponsored agency that enjoys the full federal government guarantee.

As of January 1995, federally sponsored agencies had a total debt outstanding amounting to $701.3 billion. *Timely Topics 15.2* discusses the value of the implicit government guarantee against default.

TIMELY TOPICS 15.2

FEDERAL AGENCY SUBSIDIES: BOON OR BOONDOGGLE?

A report to Congress raised questions today about whether the Government should continue to provide financial benefits to two private companies established by the Government to make mortgages more readily available to low- and middle-income home buyers.

The report, by the Congressional Budget Office, is certain to intensify a long-running debate over whether the companies, known as Fannie Mae and Freddie Mac, should retain an implicit Government guarantee of the debt securities they issue in their role of purchasing home mortgages from lenders and selling them to investors.

The implied guarantee lowers financing costs for the companies and helps push down rates for the mortgages they acquire—generally on homes costing no more than $207,000—thereby making home ownership more affordable.

But some members of Congress have expressed concern that the financial guarantee provided by the Government, although somewhat hedged, could leave taxpayers financially responsible for a huge-scale bailout if either company ran into a financial crisis.

Lawmakers have also questioned whether the mortgage markets had changed so substantially in recent years that the roles played by Freddie Mac and Fannie Mae could now be fulfilled just as well by other financial institutions that operate without any Government guarantees. . . .

"Improving access to mortgage finance may have been a social benefit worth paying for in the past," the report says. "It is now available without subsidy from fully private firms."

The report valued the implicit guarantees enjoyed by the companies at $6.5 billion last year, although this involved no actual outlay of money. The value of the lower mortgage rates for homeowners as a result of Fannie Mae and Freddie Mac was $4.4 billion, leaving the companies to retain $2.1 billion last year. . . .

David Jeffers, vice president for corporate relations at Fannie Mae said the companies had efficiently passed their financing advantage along to home buyers, citing a quarter-point to a half-point advantage in the interest rates for mortgages, a direct benefit, he said, from participation in the market, compared with loans not backed by Fannie Mae or Freddie Mac.

And he said that more than 70 percent of Fannie Mae's earnings each year were applied to building its capital base—its buffer against possible losses. With capital of $13 billion, he said, Fannie Mae was capable of withstanding immense financial shocks without putting the taxpayer at risk.

Source: R. W. Stevenson, "Report Is Skeptical of U.S.-Backed Home Mortgages." *New York Times*, May 30, 1996, pp. D1, D8.

There are eight federally sponsored agencies: the Federal Farm Credit Bank System (financing the agricultural sector), the Farm Credit Financial Assistance Corporation (formed in

1987 to bail out the Federal Farm Credit Bank System), the Federal Home Loan Bank (formed in 1932 to finance homeownership by backing mortgage-granting thrift institutions), the Financing Corporation (created in 1987 to recapitalize the thrift deposit insurance fund), the Resolution Trust Corporation (created in 1989 to clean up the thrift industry), the Student Loan Marketing Association (established in 1972 and known as "Sallie Mae"), the Federal Home Loan Mortgage Corporation (created in 1970 and known as "Freddie Mac"), and the Federal National Mortgage Association (established in 1938 and known as "Fannie Mae"). Federally sponsored agencies issue either discount notes (with maturities ranging from overnight to one year) or bonds (with maturities exceeding two years). Federally sponsored agency securities trade in the same way as do Treasury securities.

Federally sponsored agency securities are backed by the portfolios of loans issued by each agency. These loans are pooled, and the agency sells securities that offer the investor the right to receive all cash flows emanating from the loans in the pool. These securities are called **pass-throughs**—securities that represent shares in a pool of underlying loans. All cash flows (interest and principal payments) paid on the pool of underlying loans are gathered together and then, on the coupon payment date, are passed through (hence the name) to the security holders. Since the cash flows on the underlying pool can change (if, for instance, there are loan prepayments), the cash flows on the pass-through are not certain. This uncertainty, called **prepayment risk**, creates difficulties in the evaluation of pass-throughs. (This evaluation is discussed at length in Chapter 21.)

pass-throughs: securities that represent shares in a pool of underlying loans.

prepayment risk: uncertainty about the timing of cash flows for a pass-through security.

Checkpoint

1. Contrast the securities issued by federally sponsored agencies to those issued by federally related agency securities with respect to credit risk exposure.

2. What is a pass-through? What are the risk exposures of pass-through securities?

➤ Municipals

general obligation municipal securities: securities used to finance the ongoing operations of the municipality and repaid using the tax receipts and other revenues of the municipal government.

revenue municipal securities: securities issued for a single purpose, such as building a bridge or a power plant, and repaid from the revenue generated by the project.

sinking fund provision: requirement that the municipality make regular contributions, out of the project's net revenues, to be used to repay the revenue municipal bond.

Keeping track of the hundreds of different sovereign government debt issues may seem difficult, but this task is nothing compared to that of a trader in municipal bond markets, where there are 1.5 million separate tax-free bonds. In addition, there are thousands of taxable municipal bonds. The market's complexity comes from the plethora of distinct securities issued by each municipality for different purposes. **General obligation municipal securities** are used to finance the ongoing operations of the municipality. They are repaid using the tax receipts and other revenues of the municipal government. In contrast, **revenue municipal securities** are issued for a single purpose, such as building a bridge or a power plant, and are repaid from the revenue generated by the project. Revenue bonds often carry a **sinking fund provision**, which requires the municipality to make regular contributions out of the project's net revenues, to be used to repay the revenue municipal bond.

Municipal notes are securities with original maturities of less than three years. They take the form of TANs, tax anticipation notes; RANs, revenue anticipation notes; GANs, grant anticipation notes; BANs, bond anticipation notes; FANs, fund anticipation notes; TRANs, a hybrid between TANs and RANs; and tax-exempt commercial paper. All of these securities are temporary borrowings designed to bridge a short time gap prior to the receipt of an expected cash inflow. Tax-exempt commercial paper, for example, is issued for periods of between 30 and 270 days. The short term notes tend to have fixed interest rates. They can be either coupon or pure discount instruments, and they are often sold in minimum denominations of $5,000.

In recent years, partly in response to record low interest rates and high marginal tax rates, FIs have innovated new forms of municipal securities. The opportunity to create pools of municipal securities with novel characteristics came from a 1992 SEC ruling that exempted FIs from a provision of the Investment Company Act of 1940 that limited such activities to certain assets, notably mortgages and credit card debts. The first response to this rule was the introduction of municipal strips in 1993. Patterned after Treasury STRIPS, portfolios of municipal bonds were carved into individual securities consisting of single interest or principal payments. Named Savr-Trs, Cores, and Principal Strip Municipal Tigrs by the FIs, they are reminiscent of the privately offered Treasury STRIPS introduced a decade earlier.

inverse floaters: floating rate securities with coupon payments that are reset periodically to move in the direction opposite to some benchmark rate.

Another novel municipal security is the **inverse floater**. In March 1993 Merrill Lynch sold $15 million of inverse floaters, named TEEMS (Tax Exempt Enhanced Municipal Securities), to individuals as part of an offering by the Puerto Rico Telephone Authority. Before that time, inverse floaters were sold to institutions only, reaching a total volume of $4.8 billion in 1992. Inverse floaters are floating rate securities with coupon payments that are reset periodically to move in the direction opposite to some benchmark rate. Rather than the coupon rate increasing as the benchmark rate increases, as for a standard floating rate security, the inverse floater's coupon rate decreases as market rates increase and increases as market rates decrease. Thus, an inverse floater can hedge the interest rate risk of a portfolio since its coupon rate moves in one direction as market rates move in the opposite direction. This feature increases the inverse floater's price volatility. Prices increase dramatically if interest rates decline (since both the coupon payment increases and the discount factor decreases), but decrease equally dramatically if interest rates increase (since both the coupon payments decrease and the discount factor increases). When interest rates went up in 1994, these inverse floaters declined precipitously in value, and the market virtually disappeared. The 1994 demise of Askin Capital, a large hedge fund, can be traced to losses from inverse floaters.

Compare a 10 year fixed rate municipal bond to a 10 year inverse floater. Both carry an initial annual coupon rate of 6% p.a. and are issued at par. However, the inverse floater's coupon rate is reset annually to decrease by an amount equal to the increase in the market rate on the comparable 10 year fixed rate municipal bond. Thus, if, at the end of the year, the 10 year fixed rate municipal bond (now with nine years until maturity) offers a market yield (the benchmark rate) of 5.5% p.a., then its price will increase to $103.48 per $100 face value, an increase of 3.48%. Since the 5.5% market yield implies a 50 basis point decrease in the benchmark rate, the coupon rate on the inverse floater will *increase* by 50 basis points to 6.5% p.a. Assuming no future rate changes, we see that the inverse floater's price, at the end of the first year, will be

$$P = \sum_{s=1}^{9} \frac{6.5}{(1.055)^s} + \frac{100}{1.055^9} = \$106.95$$

The inverse floater's price increases by 6.95%, double the rate of price increase for the fixed rate, benchmark bond.

If, however, market rates increase to 6.5%, the fixed rate, benchmark bond's price falls by 3.33% to $96.67 per $100 face value. In contrast, the inverse floater's coupon payment declines to 5.5% p.a. for a decrease in price of 6.66%. That is, the price of the inverse floater at the end of its first year is

$$P = \sum_{s=1}^{9} \frac{5.5}{(1.065)^s} + \frac{100}{1.065^9} = \$93.34$$

Taxation and Trading of Municipals

Federal, state, and local governments have a reciprocity agreement with each other. Federal debt obligations are exempt from state and local taxes, whereas municipal obligations are exempt from federal taxes.[14] Tax-free municipals are also exempt from state and local taxes (say, because

---

[14] The Tax Reform Act of 1986 subjected some formerly tax-exempt municipals to possible taxation under the Minimum Alternative Tax.

they were issued by the local municipality), as well as federal income taxation. In 1993 almost 15,000 long term municipal bond issues were sold, raising nearly $300 billion. Out of these, $269 billion were tax exempt, while $42.5 billion out of a total of $46.2 billion of municipal notes issued in 1993 were tax exempt.

Comparing the yield on tax-exempt municipals to the yield on taxable securities requires the computation of the **equivalent taxable yield**. The equivalent taxable yield is the before-tax yield that would, if it were taxed, offer the same after-tax rate of return as the yield on the tax-exempt security. If the marginal tax rate is denoted t and the tax-exempt yield is denoted Y, then the equivalent taxable yield, denoted y, is

$$y = \frac{Y}{1-t}$$

That is, for an investor in a 35% marginal tax bracket, a municipal bond offering 7.5% p.a. pays an equivalent taxable yield of $\frac{7.5}{1-.35}$ = 11.54% p.a. Thus, the higher the investor's marginal tax bracket, the higher the equivalent taxable yield on the tax-exempt security. When the Tax Reform Act of 1990 increased the highest marginal personal income tax rate to 33%, municipal bond prices increased.

More than half of all municipal securities are owned by individuals. Recent events have led to concern about the credit risk exposure of municipals. In 1975 New York City's financial crisis precipitated a default on $100 million in municipal notes and a close brush with bankruptcy. In 1994 California's Orange County declared bankruptcy to escape the obligations of its insolvent investment fund (see Chapter 11). Moody's and Standard & Poor's publish municipal bond ratings. They measure the issuer's ability to repay by examining the municipality's overall debt burden, political discipline, socioeconomic environment, and tax base. For revenue municipals, the projects themselves are evaluated. Although ratings are useful, in 1982 the Washington Public Power Supply System defaulted on $8 billion in long term bonds that had received the highest rating when they were issued.[15] Because of these experiences, some municipal securities are sold with privately provided municipal bond insurance against default offered by companies like MBIA, FGIC, and AMBAC, which offer insurance against default in exchange for a fee.

New issues of municipal securities are either sold privately to large investors or offered publicly by an underwriter. Underwriters are chosen for public offerings by competitive bidding. In 1993, $55.66 billion out of a total of $290.943 billion (19.1%) in new municipal bond issues were sold competitively. Of the total $22.849 billion in municipal note issues in 1993, $9.549 billion (41.8%) were sold competitively, as opposed to privately. The secondary market for municipal securities is an informal over-the-counter market. Each business day, Standard & Poor's publishes a 100-plus-page booklet called *The Blue List* that gives municipal securities offerings and prices. However, because of the sheer number of transactions and the diverse nature of the market, accurate and timely price information is often hard to find, particularly for the smaller and less liquid issues.

Linking the U.S. Treasury Market to Municipal Securities

As for all other financial securities, FIs compare municipal investments to similar risk alternatives when constructing a portfolio. Calculation of equivalent taxable yields makes such comparison possible. Although linking rates across securities increases the efficiency of all financial markets, sometimes it backfires. This is the story of a government-mandated linkage that went astray.

New municipal securities are often issued to refinance previously issued bonds. Often, the municipality receives the proceeds of the new issue before the old issue matures or can be called.

equivalent taxable yield: the before-tax yield that would, if it were taxed, offer the same after-tax rate of return as the yield on the tax-exempt security.

---

[15] To date, the WPPSS default, known as Whoops, remains the largest municipal bond default in history; it took until 1995 to settle all of the resulting lawsuits.

During the waiting period before the old bonds can be repaid, the proceeds of the new issue are placed in an interest-earning escrow account. However, federal law restricts the interest that can be earned on the escrow account to be less than or equal to the interest rate paid on the new bonds. That is, the municipality cannot profit from the new issue. The most it can earn is just enough to make the coupon payments on the newly issued municipal security. This is to prevent the municipality from engaging in a tax arbitrage, where it pays the lower rates on its tax-exempt debt and reinvests the proceeds in higher yielding, taxable securities.

FIs manage the escrow accounts on behalf of the municipalities. However, since tax-exempt municipal bond rates are lower than most other securities' yields, the FI must make sure that the escrow account earns a below-market rate of return. To keep the earnings in the escrow account low, the Treasury issues special low-interest securities called **State and Local Government Series (SLUGS)**. By investing the funds in the escrow accounts in SLUGS and Treasury bills, the interest yield is kept artificially low. Of course, the Treasury benefits from this arrangement since SLUGS provide the federal government with a source of inexpensive funds.

State and Local Government Series (SLUGS): special low-interest Treasury securities issued solely for municipal escrow accounts.

Several FIs have devised another way to keep the yield in the municipal escrow account low. They sell Treasury securities to the escrow account at inflated prices, thereby lowering their yield. Fewer SLUGS are then required to reduce the account's average yield. This shifts some of the Treasury's windfall gain, in the form of the lower interest paid on SLUGS, to the FI, in the form of a higher spread on its Treasury bond sales. This may raise the FI's markup on Treasury bonds from $1 to $2 per $1,000 face value to as high as $8 to $9 per $1,000 face value.

Let's examine a typical transaction. Suppose that a municipality has issued $100 million in new bonds yielding 4% p.a., the proceeds of which must be placed into escrow for six months. Currently, two year Treasury notes are selling at par to yield 5.35% p.a., while SLUGS offer a 1% p.a. yield. To construct a portfolio yielding 4% p.a. using these two securities would require solving

$$4\% = (w)(5.35) + (1 - w)(1)$$

where w is the fraction invested in two year Treasury notes and $1 - w$ is the fraction invested in SLUGS. Solving yields $w = .69$ and $1 - w = .31$.

If, on the other hand, the FI sells the escrow account the two year Treasury notes at a markup of $7 per $1,000, then their yield falls to 4.98%.[16] Solving for the mix of SLUGS in the escrow account's portfolio results in

$$4\% = (w)(4.98) + (1 - w)(1)$$

or $w = .75$ and $1 - w = .25$. On this single $100 million escrow account, the Treasury's sale of low-cost SLUGS declines from $31 million to $25 million. Estimates of the loss to the Treasury total hundreds of millions of dollars.[17]

In March 1995 a federal grand jury was convened to investigate possible illegal activity in the FIs' practices. Predictably, the Treasury and private FIs will argue over who is to receive the windfall gain on the low-yielding municipal escrow accounts. The only parties unable to gain any of the benefit are the municipalities themselves.

---

[16] Solving for the semiannual rate, $\frac{y}{2}$, using

$$1007 = \sum_{s=1}^{4} \frac{26.75}{(1 + \frac{y}{2})^s} + \frac{1000}{(1 + \frac{y}{2})^4}$$

yields $\frac{y}{2} = 2.49$ for an annual yield of 4.98% p.a.

[17] Quint (1995), p. D1.

Checkpoint

✓

1. Contrast general obligation and revenue municipal securities with regard to default risk and liquidity.
2. How have recent innovations in the municipal securities market increased risk exposure?
3. Why are the prices of inverse floaters more volatile than the prices of fixed rate municipal securities?
4. What are SLUGS and what are they used for? Who benefits and who loses in these transactions?

➤ Summary

The market for U.S. Treasury securities is the largest and most liquid debt market in the world. In order to sell huge amounts of Treasury securities in the most efficient manner possible, the Treasury has experimented with several types of competitive auctions. At first glance, the discriminatory price auction appears to yield the highest proceeds for the Treasury, since each bidder pays the maximum price that he or she bid. In contrast, under a uniform price auction, all bidders pay the same, lowest accepted bid price. However, appearances can be deceiving. Studies show that the uniform price auction can yield higher proceeds for the Treasury since it encourages bidders to bid higher prices, knowing that they will not pay those higher prices. The result is that the average level of all price bids increases, thereby increasing the proceeds to the Treasury.

Possible deviations from the expectations hypothesis (see Chapter 7) create the opportunity to strip Treasury and municipal securities into their component parts. That is, each individual interest and principal payment is sold separately as a pure discount instrument. If the security as a whole is worth less (more) than the sum of its parts, it will be profitable to decom-

pose (reconstitute) the security into its component parts.

U.S. Treasury securities of all types have no default risk exposure. The same cannot be said for all government securities. Some sovereign government securities (particularly those issued by less developed countries), some federal agencies, and some municipalities issue securities with varying levels of credit risk exposure. The major credit rating services, Moody's and Standard & Poor's, evaluate these securities' default risks by publishing credit ratings. The credit ratings depend on the tax base of the government entity, its political stability, its socioeconomic condition, and the uses for which the money is being borrowed. Most municipal securities are tax exempt, offering a tax-exempt yield below market yields.

Government securities have been issued with special features such as inflation-indexed bonds, inverse floaters, and various convertibles. Limitations on municipal escrow account earnings have allowed the U.S. Treasury to issue low-interest special securities called SLUGS. FIs aggressively scrutinize the array of possible government security offerings to identify potential arbitrage opportunities.

➤ References

Adams, R. "Debt Management." in Colander and Daane, eds., *The Art of Monetary Policy*. Armonk, New York: M. E. Sharpe, 1994.

Cantor, R., and F. Packer. "Sovereign Credit Ratings." Federal Reserve Bank of New York *Current Issues in Economics and Finance* 1 No. 3 (June 1995).

Clare, A., M. Maras, and S. Thomas. "The Integration and Efficiency of International Bond Markets." *Journal of Business Finance and Accounting* (March 1995): 313–322.

Daves, P., and M. Ehrhardt. "Liquidity, Reconstitution, and the Value of U.S. Treasury Strips." *Journal of Finance* 48, No. 1 (March 1993): 315–329.

Goswami, G., T. Noe, and M. Rebello, "Collision in Uniform Price Auctions: Experimental Evidence and Implications for Treasury Auctions." Federal Reserve Bank of Atlanta Working Paper 95-5, September 1995.

Jegadeesh, N. "Treasury Auction Bids and the Salomon Squeeze." *Journal of Finance* 48, No. 3 (September 1993): 1403–1419.

Jones, F., and F. Fabozzi. *The International Government Bond Markets.* Chicago: Probus, 1992.

Jordan, B. D., and S. D. Jordan. "Salomon Brothers and the May 1991 Treasury Auction: Analysis of a Market Corner." *Journal of Banking and Finance* 20 (1996): 25–40.

Mester, L. "There's More Than One Way to Sell a Security: The Treasury's Auction Experiment." Federal Reserve Bank of Philadelphia *Business Review* (July–August 1995): 3–17.

Nyborg, K., and S. Sundaresan. "Discriminatory vs. Uniform Treasury Auctions: Evidence from When-Issued Transactions." Columbia University working paper (October 1994).

Quint, M. "Accuser in the Muni Bond Industry." *New York Times* (March 3, 1995): D1.

Shen, P. "Benefits and Limitations of Inflation Indexed Treasury Bonds." Federal Reserve Bank of Kansas City *Economic Review* (Third Quarter 1995): 41–56.

Simon, D. "The Treasury's Experiment with Single-Price Auctions in the Mid-1970s: Winner's or Taxpayer's Curse?" *Review of Economics and Statistics* 76 (November 1994): 754–760.

Sundaresan, S. "An Empirical Analysis of U.S. Treasury Auctions: Implications for Auction and Term Structure Theories." *Journal of Fixed Income*, (September 1994): 35–50.

Tenorio, R. "Revenue Equivalence and Bidding Behavior in a Multi-Unit Auction Market: An Empirical Analysis." *Review of Economics and Statistics* 75 (May 1993): 302–314.

Tsao, C. S., and A. Vignola. "Price Discrimination and the Demand for Treasury's Long Term Securities." Unpublished manuscript, U.S. Department of Treasury, 1977.

Umlauf, S. "An Empirical Study of the Mexican Treasury Bill Auction." *Journal of Financial Economics* 33 (1993): 313–340.

U.S. Treasury. "Report to the Secretary of the Treasury from the Treasury Borrowing Advisory Committee of the Public Securities Association." August 3, 1994.

➤ Questions

1a. Consider the following $12 billion discriminatory price auction of 26 week (180 day) Treasury bills. Suppose that noncompetitive bids totaled $3 billion. What portion of the new issue will be sold to competitive bidders? to noncompetitive bidders?

1b. Suppose that the following competitive bids are received:

Amount ($ billion)	Bid Yield
$0.5	5.05%
$1.1	5.06%
$1.9	5.07%
$2.5	5.08%
$2.0	5.09%
$0.5	5.10%
$2.5	5.11%
$0.3	5.12%
$0.2	5.13%
$1.3	5.14%
$1.2	5.15%

What is the stop yield? What is the stop-out price? What portion of bids are accepted at the stop yield? What is the average yield? What is the average price?

1c. Is the auction successful? (Be sure to calculate both the tail and the cover.)

1d. What will noncompetitive bidders pay for the newly issued Treasury bills?

1e. What will each of the competitive bidders pay for the newly issued Treasury bills under the discriminatory price auction method? under the uniform price method?

1f. Assuming no change in the bids, contrast the cost to the Treasury of the discriminatory price versus uniform price auction methods. (Be sure to contrast the interest costs, as well as the face value of the newly issued debt.)

1g. Can you use your answer from part (f) to conclude that one auction method is clearly superior to the other? Why or why not?

2. Answer parts (a) and (b) in question 1 assuming that the security being auctioned is instead a 10 year Treasury bond. (Be sure to determine the bond's coupon yield.)

3. Suppose that the FI examined a two year Treasury note with a 12% p.a. semiannual coupon selling at $9,931,720 per $10 million face value to determine whether it was a candidate for a STRIP. Market yields on par value bonds are as follows:

Time Until Maturity	Spot Rate
6 months	10.2% p.a.
1 year	11.2% p.a.
18 months	12.2% p.a.
2 years	12.7% p.a.

    Can the two year Treasury note be stripped profitably? Why or why not?

4. Calculate the equivalent taxable yields for the following:
    a. An investor in the 25% tax bracket holding a tax-free municipal paying 5.75% p.a.
    b. An investor in the 40% tax bracket holding a tax-free municipal paying 5.75% p.a.
    c. An investor in the 40% tax bracket holding a tax-free municipal paying 8.2% p.a.
    d. Compare the advisability of the investment for each of the investors.

5. Compare the price of a five year maturity inverse floater that has an initial annual coupon rate of 4.25% p.a. with the price of a benchmark 5 year 4.25% p.a. annual coupon, fixed rate bond if the benchmark rate
    a. Increases by 25 basis points.
    b. Decreases by 75 basis points.
    c. Increases by 75 points.

6. Construct a $50 million portfolio for a municipal escrow account that yields 3.5% p.a. using:
    a. A combination of 10 year, par value Treasury bonds yielding 6.25% p.a. and SLUGS yielding 1.75% p.a.
    b. The SLUGS from part (a) and 10 year, 6.25% p.a. semiannual coupon Treasury bonds if they are sold at a premium of $8 per $1,000 face value.

7. Use the bootstrap method to construct spot yields from the following par value, coupon instruments:
    a. 6 month maturity with a semiannual coupon of 7% p.a.
    b. 1 year maturity with a semiannual coupon of 7.5% p.a.
    c. 1.5 year maturity with a semiannual coupon of 8.3% p.a.
    d. 2 year maturity with a semiannual coupon of 8.75% p.a.

8. Compare yields on similar maturity (1) U.S. Treasury securities, (2) Japanese government bonds, (3) German bunds, (4) British gilts, (5) municipals, and (6) federal agency securities with respect to
    a. Market liquidity.
    b. Default risk.
    c. Tax liability.

9. Suppose that the 5% coupon 10 year U.S. Treasury rate is priced at 5.75% p.a. and the 5% coupon 10 year JGB rate is 4.25% p.a. If the yen–U.S. dollar exchange rate is US$0.015 per Japanese yen, how can you profit from the yield discrepancy? Assume that both sovereign government bonds have a semiannual coupon of 5% p.a. (*Hint:* Be sure to price both bonds and calculate

the differential cash flows on coupon payment dates and on maturity date assuming no change in exchange rates.)

10a. What is the risk of the transaction in question 9?

10b. Calculate the cash flows using a yen–U.S. dollar exchange rate of US$0.02 per Japanese yen that takes effect immediately after you undertake the transaction in question 9.

10c. How can you use long term JGB futures to protect against this risk exposure?

CHAPTER 16

CORPORATE BONDS

"A bank is a place that will lend you money if you can prove that you don't need it."—Bob Hope, in Alan Harrington, *Life in the Crystal Palace* (1959), "The Tyranny of Farms."

Learning Objectives

- To survey the wide variety and number of corporate bond issues available in the market.
- To compare bonds with other forms of corporate financing, such as bank debt and private placements.

➤ Introduction

Seventeenth-century Amsterdam was the financial center of the world. To finance trade with the New World, the first bank opened in 1609, and the Amsterdam Bourse opened for business in 1611. To raise money to fund the exploratory activities of companies like the United East India Company and the Dutch West India Company, the market innovated debt instruments such as annuities and perpetual bonds. At the time that Peter Minuit was purchasing Manhattan island for the price of 60 guilders (worth $24), Holland had a perpetual government bond that paid 8% annually. If the proceeds from the sale of Manhattan had been invested in these bonds, some of which are still in existence, they would currently be worth, after 370 years of compounding from 1626 to 1996, a total of $24(1.08)^{370} = \$55,847,110,000,000$! Debt instruments build value like the proverbial tortoise races the hare—slow and steady.

➤ Corporate Bonds Around the World

We have seen how governments issue debt to finance their operations; now we examine the role of debt in business financing. Table 16.1 summarizes the different types of publicly traded debt issues denominated in 22 currencies. The largest type of debt, in terms of quantity, is issued by central governments. Overall, this constitutes 40.8% of all publicly issued debt in the world. In the United States, the Treasury issued $2,546.5 billion of debt obligations in 1995, accounting for 28.8% of all U.S. dollar-denominated publicly issued debt.[1] Federal agency

---

[1] If only U.S. bond markets are considered, we exclude $554.1 billion in Eurodollar bonds to obtain a total size of the U.S. bond market of $8,163 billion in 1995. U.S. Treasury securities made up 31.2% of that total.

482   16.   Corporate Bonds

Table
16.1

Size of Major Bond Markets at Year-End 1995 (Nominal Value Outstanding: Billions of U.S. Dollars or Equivalent)[a]

Bond market	Total publicly issued	As a pct. of public issues in all markets	Central govt.	Central govt. agency & govt. guaranty
U.S. Dollar	$8,837.3	43.1%	$2,546.5	$2,406.1
Japanese Yen	3,807.4	18.6	2,002.7	210.2
Deutschemark	2,282.9	11.1	727.1	67.0
Italian Lira	1,084.4	5.3	858.9	18.6
French Franc	1,024.0	5.0	489.9	234.9
U.K. Sterling	540.9	2.6	361.4	–
Canadian Dollar	424.1	2.1	183.0	–
Belgian Franc	411.6	2.0	225.7	7.4
Dutch Guilder	353.2	1.7	194.3	–
Danish Krone	292.4	1.4	106.6	–
Swiss Franc	279.6	1.4	28.5	–
Swedish Krona	253.6	1.2	111.8	–
Spanish Peseta	219.0	1.1	160.5	–
European Currency Unit	164.4	0.8	73.4	–
Australian Dollar	133.2	0.7	68.3	24.9
Austrian Schilling	132.2	0.6	54.4	2.2
Finnish Markka	55.0	0.3	33.3	–
Portuguese Escudo	51.7	0.3	33.8	–
Norwegian Krone	49.7	0.2	19.5	2.8
Greek Drachma	42.3	0.2	40.8	–
Irish Pound	26.6	0.1	24.5	0.8
New Zealand Dollar	17.6	0.1	12.4	1.1
Total	**$20,483.0**	**100.0%**	**$8,357.2**	**$2,976.0**
Sector as a pct. of public issues in all markets	100.0%		40.8%	14.5%

[a]Exchange rates prevailing as of December 31, 1995: ¥102.83/US$; DM1.4335/US$; Lit1,584.7/US$; Ffr 4.900/US$; £0.6452/US$; C$1.3652/US$; Bfr29.415/US$; Dfl1.6044/US$; Dkr5.546/US$; Sfr1.1505/US$; Skr6.6582/ US$; Pta121.41/US$; Ecu0.7609/US$; A$1.3423/US$; ATS10.088/US$; Fmk4.3586/US$; Esc 149.41/US$; Nkr6.319/US$; Dr237.04/US$; Ir£ 0.6231/US$; and NZ$1.5307/US$.

[b]Includes straight, convertible and floating-rate debt.

[c]In the German bond market, a distinction is not made between Eurobonds and foreign international issues.

debt and bonds backed by the central government comprise the second largest type, amounting to 14.5% of the world's total publicly issued bonds.

Corporate debt represents 12.7% of total publicly issued bonds in the world. In the United States, this fraction is larger than the world average, with corporate debt issues accounting

State & local govt.	Corp. (incl. cvts.)	Other domestic publicly issued	Intl. bonds[b] Foreign bonds		Euro-bonds	Private place. unclass.
$1,029.6	$1,741.9	$283.3	$155.6		$674.3	–
98.8	404.6	745.0	89.9		256.2	$746.6
85.6	1.9	1,120.7	–	$280.6[c]	–	551.2[e]
–	4.3	143.1	1.8		57.8	–
3.3	154.2	–	6.0		135.7	–
0.1	29.9	–	6.1		143.4	–
108.4	54.2	0.7	0.5		77.4	–
–	17.6	125.0	35.1		0.8	–
3.1	91.2	–	3.9		60.7	93.9
–	–	179.6	–		6.3	–
23.2	36.8	77.3	113.9		–	77.4[e]
1.2	8.6	127.9	–		4.1	–
11.8	19.3	15.0	12.4		–	–
–	–	–	–		91.1	–
–	10.4	–	–		29.5	–
0.4	5.0	67.7	2.6		–	6.7
1.6	6.1	12.7	–		1.4	–
1.1	5.5	5.3	5.9		–	–
6.6	3.2	16.7	0.8		0.0	–
–	–	–	1.0		0.5	–
–	0.5	–	0.2		0.6	–
–	2.4	–	0.2		1.6	–
$1,374.8	**$2,597.6**	**$2,919.8**	**$2,257.6[d]**			**$1,475.7[e]**
6.7%	12.7%	14.3%	11.0%			

[d]Includes both foreign and Eurobond totals.

[e]In addition, an unspecified amount of privately placed issues of the private sector exists.

Note: Figures in table may not add up to totals because of rounding.

Source: R. Benavides, "How Big is the World Bond Market?" Salomon Brothers *International Bond Market Analysis*, (August 1996), p.1.

for 19.7% ($1,741.9 billion out of a total of $8,837.3 billion). Table 16.1 shows that some countries have less developed corporate debt markets. For example, corporate bonds issued in Germany amounted to US$1.9 billion in 1995, which was only 0.08% of the total publicly issued German debt. German companies rely on bank debt to finance their operations to a greater extent than do American corporations. In comparison, commercial and industrial bank loans in the United States grew from $404 billion in 1983 to $443 billion in 1993, an annual growth rate of less than 1%. Over the same 1983–1993 period, commercial paper grew at an annual rate of 12%, from $184 billion to $554 billion, and corporate bond issues in the United States increased at an annual rate of 13%, from $643 billion in 1983 to $2,270 billion in 1993.

Bank Debt versus Bonds

What determines whether a company borrows from a bank or issues bonds? In part, the development of the country's capital market determines this choice. Financial markets in the United States and the United Kingdom have evolved more completely than in other countries, where banks and other FIs have more control over financial activity. In Chapter 5, Table 5.10 examined the distinctions between market-based and bank-based economies. These distinctions impact the firm's decision to borrow using either bank debt or by issuing bonds. Table 16.2 shows the history of this tradeoff for U.S. firms over a 15 year period spanning 1979–1994. In this period, nonfarm, nonfinancial corporate debt increased from US$1.58 trillion to US$2.75 trillion in real dollar terms, a 15 year growth rate of 74.1%, or 3.76% p.a., which is greater than the 40.7% real growth in GDP over the period. However, U.S. banks' share of this debt decreased from 19.6% to 14.5% in these years, reflecting a decrease in the importance of bank loans as opposed to bond issues. This decrease is somewhat offset by the fact that foreign banks' share of nonfarm, nonfinancial corporate debt in the United States increased from 5.7% in 1979 to 13.5% (6% onshore plus 7.5% offshore) in 1994.

Table 16.2

U.S. Nonfarm, Nonfinancial Corporate Debt Markets, 1979–1994 (Percent of Total Market)[a]

Year	U.S. Banks	Foreign Banks Onshore	Foreign Banks Offshore	Thrifts	Commer. Paper	Finance Cos.	Corp. Bonds	Revenue Bonds	Mort.	Other Loans	Total ($)
1979	19.6	5.3	0.4	0.1	3.0	8.2	41.2	4.3	15.4	2.5	1.578
1980	20.5	5.5	0.5	0.2	3.2	8.0	41.3	5.2	12.8	2.9	1.557
1981	20.6	5.6	1.6	0.2	4.3	8.0	39.1	5.9	11.6	3.1	1.596
1982	25.9	4.0	2.0	0.3	3.5	7.6	39.6	7.0	7.2	3.0	1.601
1983	25.6	3.5	2.6	0.5	3.1	7.7	38.2	7.2	8.3	3.2	1.694
1984	25.3	3.5	3.1	0.8	4.3	8.1	36.4	7.7	7.8	3.1	1.882
1985	23.7	3.8	3.6	1.0	4.7	8.3	37.6	8.3	6.3	2.8	2.055
1986	22.6	4.3	3.9	1.1	3.6	8.0	40.0	6.7	7.3	2.4	2.291
1987	19.7	4.8	4.4	1.0	3.7	8.7	39.8	5.9	9.7	2.2	2.486
1988	18.8	5.1	5.0	1.1	4.0	9.1	41.0	5.4	8.6	2.0	2.631
1989	18.1	5.4	5.5	1.0	4.5	9.2	40.8	4.9	8.6	2.0	2.739
1990	17.1	5.6	6.7	0.7	4.8	9.6	41.2	4.7	7.9	1.7	2.722
1991	15.2	6.3	6.7	0.4	4.0	9.5	44.0	4.6	7.8	1.5	2.65
1992	14.2	6.3	7.3	0.2	4.2	9.4	45.7	4.5	6.6	1.5	2.632
1993	13.9	5.7	7.8	0.2	4.5	9.0	46.8	4.3	6.2	1.6	2.682
1994	14.5	6.0	7.5	0.2	5.1	9.8	45.6	4.1	5.7	1.5	2.746

[a]Totals are expressed in 1994 dollars ($ trillions) obtained using the GDP implicit price deflator.

Source: Berger, Kashyap, and Scalise (1995), Table A.8.

Table 16.2 distinguishes between bank loans issued by U.S. and foreign banks, showing the increased importance of offshore banking centers in financing American business operations. Indeed, the proportion of offshore lending to U.S. corporations increased from a negligible 0.4% in 1979 to 7.5% in 1994. Much of this growth reflects regulatory avoidance incentives. For example, U.S. offices of foreign banks can avoid all U.S. reserve requirements if they conduct business outside of the United States, either in their home offices or in tax havens such as the Cayman Islands and the Bahamas.[2] Thus, it is less expensive for foreign banks to extend loans using their offshore offices than for U.S.-based banks.

As financial markets mature, we observe a shift away from bank debt toward security financing. Japanese firms are increasingly issuing more securities in their financing packages, reducing the ratio of bank debt to total debt from a high of over 90% in 1975 to less than 50% in 1992. Straight bond financings constituted 79% of the debt structure of AAA-rated companies. For AA- and A-rated companies, the comparable figure was 69%, with only 39% for BBB-rated companies. The development of Japanese securities markets received a boost in July 1994 when the major city (commercial) banks were permitted to open their own securities subsidiaries. As of the end of 1994, 14 of Japan's 22 big banks had chosen to do so, thereby providing additional underwriting, market-making, and trading services to the formerly stunted corporate bond market. This trend was expedited by the U.S.–Japan Financial Services Agreement in January 1995, which opened Japanese pension, mutual fund, and corporate bond markets to greater competition among foreign as well as Japanese FIs. The major features of the agreement were (1) allowing foreign FIs access to public pension fund business; (2) easing restrictions on investment advisers managing private pension money; (3) streamlining the approval process for financial innovations such as derivatives; and (4) loosening restrictions on corporate bond and commercial paper issuance and distribution.

For emerging markets, such as Eastern European countries like the Czech Republic, Poland, and Hungary, most financing is still in the form of short term bank loans. As of 1995, only the Czech Republic had a viable corporate bond market. Most of the issuers have been commercial banks, but the Czech electric company, Ceske Energeticke Zavody, has had two domestic bond offerings and was the first privately held company in Eastern Europe to raise money in the Eurobond market.

Lending When Information Is Asymmetric   We have seen how differences across countries' financial environments impact the borrower's choice between bank debt and bonds. However, differences across borrowers also affect the choice between bank debt and bonds. Some borrowers are unable to access publicly traded bond markets because the borrowers are either too small or too difficult to analyze. These firms may be startup operations that do not yet have enough of a credit history for financial markets to evaluate. They have growth opportunities and other **intangible assets** that are expensive to price. Intangible assets are assets that are not physical and cannot be sold without selling the entire firm. Examples of intangible assets are good will and potential growth opportunities. Before investing, bondholders must assess the bond issuer's ability to repay by evaluating all of the borrower's assets. If the borrower has many intangible assets, these will be very difficult and expensive for the bondholders to evaluate. Indeed, to evaluate these intangibles, bond buyers often have to rely on information provided by the borrower. Borrowers may overstate the value of their intangible assets in order to reduce

intangible assets: assets that are not physical and cannot be sold without selling the entire firm.

[2] McCauley and Seth (1992) show that unreported offshore commercial loans totaled $175 billion. From 1984 to 1990, foreign banks' offshore loans to U.S. firms more than quintupled, whereas U.S. chartered banks' offshore loans increased by only 5%. This is because Regulation D requires U.S.-chartered banks and U.S. subsidiaries of foreign banks to fully report their offshore loans, while this regulation is not applicable to banking institutions not chartered, but doing business, in the United States.

their costs of debt service. This makes the information provided by the borrowers unreliable. Bondholders need an independent source of information about the quality of borrowers. That independent source of information is the FI.

FIs specialize in analyzing and monitoring the activity of borrowers, thereby producing information about a borrower's ability to repay its loans. The most effective way to produce this information is in the course of bank lending. Have you ever wondered why banks offer preferred loan rates and other borrowing inducements to their own customers? Why don't they offer these reduced rates to all good borrowers? One reason is that it is expensive for the bank to differentiate "good" from "bad" borrowers without obtaining information about the borrower's creditworthiness. The bank has a substantial amount of information about its own customers that can be used to analyze a potential borrower's credit quality. When the bank lends to its own customers, it obtains the informational benefits of **relationship lending**. Relationship lending benefits both the lending FI and the borrower since loans can be made at lower cost to long term customers because, over the course of doing business, the FI has gathered a wealth of information about their credit quality. This information can be used to analyze the creditworthiness of borrowers who would otherwise find it difficult to obtain credit. These "informationally handicapped" borrowers often cannot obtain credit ratings and therefore cannot directly access public debt markets. They are limited to borrowing from banks and other FIs.

relationship lending: loans made at lower cost to long term customers because, over the course of doing business, the FI has gathered a wealth of information about their credit quality.

Information produced in the course of bank lending is also used by financial markets. When companies receive bank loans, they are receiving more than just credit. The bank is granting them an imprimatur of creditworthiness that is observed by other FIs and investors in financial markets. Mikkelson and Partch (1986) and James (1987) were the first to find a stock market reaction to bank lending. James found that borrower stock returns increase almost 2% when bank loans are granted, suggesting that the market views the extension of a bank loan as good news. Lummer and McConnell (1989) show that bank loan renewals have an even greater positive response, while Billett, Flannery, and Garfinkel (1995) suggest that the value of the bank's imprimatur is directly related to the bank's credit rating. The extension of bank loans is viewed as good news when the lending bank is highly rated and is therefore regarded by the market as trustworthy. Finally, Hull and Moellenberndt (1994) show that the market views the replacement of bank debt with common stock offerings as bad news, inducing a negative stock price reaction to the announcement of the new issue. These studies all point to the information content of bank loans. Borrowers may be willing to pay the higher costs associated with bank lending in order to communicate good news about their prospects to financial markets. Companies unable to receive bank loans are then doubly handicapped since they are both denied access to credit and unable to use bank debt to communicate positive information signals to financial markets.

A number of studies show that "informationally handicapped" borrowers that must rely on bank loans since they cannot issue publicly traded debt have distinct characteristics.[3] They tend to be smaller and younger, and to invest in higher levels of intangibles, such as research and development (see Table 16.3). The fraction of bank borrowing declines significantly for the largest and oldest firms. Since information about the credit quality of these well established firms is inexpensive to obtain as well as more reliable, these firms are likely to issue public debt instruments, such as bonds. Bond issues are "transaction-driven" as opposed to "relationship-driven" bank loans. Such issues are unlikely to be repetitive and therefore must be evaluated as independent transactions without the additional informational advantages of relationship lending.

---

[3] See Rajan (1992), Petersen and Rajan (1994), Gilchrist and Zakrajsek (1995), Gertler and Gilchrist (1994), and Berger and Udell (1995).

Table 16.3

Concentration of Borrowing: By Size and Age[a]

Book Value Assets ($000)	No. of Firms	Bank Borr. (%)	Nonbank Borr. (%)	Age (yrs.)	No. of Firms	Bank Borr. (%)	Nonbank Borr. (%)
< 15	51	95	93	< 2	150	86	80
15–46	153	93	88	2–5	219	85	77
46–130	359	88	81	5–10	347	85	76
130–488	390	84	79	10–19	426	85	80
488–2,293	296	79	74	19–30	216	82	84
> 2,293	211	76	72	> 30	106	80	78

[a]The top row contains information on the smallest 10% of the firms. The fraction of total borrowing from the largest single lender is reported by type of largest lender.

Source: Petersen and Rajan (1994), p. 11.

Because of these differences among borrowers, "informationally handicapped" firms tend to be disproportionately affected by lending slowdowns. Table 16.4 shows recent U.S. bank corporate lending patterns. When banks restrict credit to small, informationally handicapped firms, such firms are unable to replace bank debt with public debt issues. Thus, reductions in small business lending by banks have a greater impact on small firms than do similar reductions in lending to large firms that have alternative sources of financing. Table 16.4 shows evidence of a recent credit crunch in the United States. As discussed in Chapter 4, a credit crunch occurs when loans are unavailable at any price. As a consequence, interest rates fail to perform their role in rationing credit. Table 16.4 shows that small firms borrowing under $1 million bore the brunt of the credit crunch of the early 1990s in the United States. Megabank loans to small borrowers of less than $1 million declined from $2.6 billion to $2.3 billion from 1992 to 1994. Moreover, in these years small bank loans of less than $1 million declined from $18.8 billion to $17.9 billion, whereas megabanks' loans to large borrowers over $25 million increased from $38.6 billion to $40.8 billion.

Small borrowers are more likely to have difficulty obtaining credit when economic conditions cause credit availability to be reduced. In addition, these borrowers tend to pay higher premiums

Table 16.4

U.S. Bank Commercial and Industrial (C&I) Lending[a] ($US billion)

Year	Total C&I Loans	C&I Loans < $1 million	C&I Loans > $25 million
Megabank Lending			
1989	$40.1	$0.6	$19.2
1992	74.0	2.6	38.6
1994	92.2	2.3	40.8
Small Bank Lending			
1989	30.0	29.2	0.0
1992	23.5	18.8	1.2
1994	21.9	17.9	0.1

[a]Small banks are defined as banks with less than $100 million in real total assets; megabanks are defined as having real assets exceeding $100 billion. All values are real dollar values (in billions) calculated using the GDP implicit price deflator.

Source: Berger, Kashyap, and Scalise (1995).

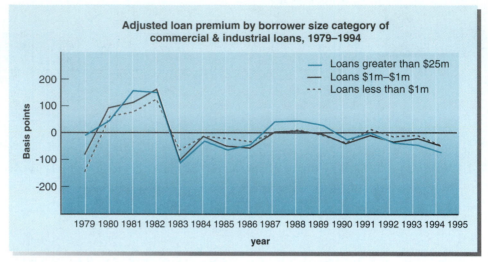

Source: Berger, Kashyap, and Scalise (1995), p. 46.

Figure 16.1

(over the risk free Treasury rate) than do more informationally advantaged, large borrowers. Figure 16.1 shows that small borrowers in 1994 paid an additional 54 basis points in loan premiums over that paid by large borrowers. This gap was only 25 basis points in 1990, suggesting that the increase in costs to small borrowers was more than the increase in costs to large borrowers during a period of tight credit. To reduce their borrowing costs, companies access different types of FIs, not just banks, to construct financing packages consisting of combinations of publicly trade debt and bank loans. FIs compete for this lucrative business. Spreads for the riskier loans range around LIBOR plus 300 basis points, with big up-front fees averaging 2 to 3% of the loan's principal amount.

Checkpoint

✓

1. What factors influence the decision to use bank debt as opposed to issuing bonds?
2. How do FIs influence the choice between bank debt and bonds?
3. What are "informationally handicapped" firms? Describe their characteristics. What are their major sources of debt?

An Interim Case: Private Placements

Up until now we have considered only two polar cases: privately held bank loans versus publicly traded debt.[4] Privately held bank loans are originated by a bank and are never traded. At the opposite extreme, bonds are publicly traded in active secondary markets. Nontraded bank loans are the most closely monitored by the FIs that hold them in their portfolio. In contrast, publicly traded bonds are evaluated only by market participants, who may have little incentive to monitor closely if each bondholder's investment is relatively small. There is an interim case: private placements. **Private placements** are unregistered debt securities that trade in limited secondary markets comprised of large institutional investors. Since private placements are closely held by

private placements:
unregistered debt securities that trade in limited secondary markets comprised of large institutional investors.

---

[4] However, in Chapter 14 we saw that asset-backed commercial paper is a securitized portfolio of loans.

a few large FIs, informational benefits accrue from the FIs' monitoring of borrower activity. However, private placements can be resold, and so under certain circumstances they are more liquid than bank loans. Because the SEC does not require registration, these securities are less costly to issue than are publicly traded bonds. Insurance companies and other nonbank FIs are the primary buyers of private placements.

Private placements jumped 59% in 1993—to $174 billion from $109.5 billion in 1992. Most of this increase comes from *144a securities*, which are private placements that trade in a fairly liquid market made possible by a 1990 exemption in the form of Section 144a of the Securities Law. These 144a securities are the most liquid form of private placements since they have the least amount of restrictions on their transfer. The volume of 144a placements doubled in 1993 to $34.8 billion. Large securities firms and banks are active in the sale of private placements. FIs are important in private placements because of the shortage of supply. The demand for these securities has outstripped supply, thereby making access to distribution lines important for buyers of this debt instrument.

Checkpoint

✓

1. Who invests in private placements? Why?

2. What are the informational characteristics of private placements?

3. Describe why you think private placements would be in demand by investors.

➤ Credit Risk Exposure

Corporate bonds differ from government bonds primarily in their default risk exposure. Although U.S. Treasury securities are considered default risk free, we have seen credit risk exposure in other sovereign government debt instruments. Corporate **debenture bonds** are debt securities that are not secured by a specific pledge of property, but instead represent a general claim on all assets of the firm. **Collateral trust bonds** are backed by specific assets that are pledged as collateral to repay a specific bond issue. The credit risk exposure of a particular bond offering depends on the quality of assets available for repayment.

debenture bonds: debt securities that are not secured by a specific pledge of property, but instead represent a general claim on all assets of the firm.

collateral trust bonds: bonds backed by specific assets that are pledged as collateral to repay a specific bond issue.

Credit Ratings

Banks produce information about their borrowers' creditworthiness in the course of approving or disapproving a loan. However, there is one group of firms whose business it is to disseminate information about other firms' credit risk exposure. These are the rating services that assign credit ratings to all publicly issued debt instruments. The ratings range from highest quality, for which default is a remote possibility, to below investment-grade ratings, which are to be considered quite speculative. The rating classifications, shown in Table 16.5, illustrate this range. In July 1994, Standard & Poor's introduced a rating "highlighter" called "r," which indicates excessive market-related risks. Since the ratings measure credit risk exposure, the "r" highlighter concentrates entirely on potential price risk because of anticipated shifts in financial markets. In practice, the "r" rating is attached to any firm with a significant amount of risk from derivatives.

If ratings are accurate indicators of issuer creditworthiness, higher rated bonds should exhibit better repayment records than do lower rated bonds. Table 16.6 shows this by examining a six year historic default probability for each rating class. Over the first six years of life, Aaa-rated bonds defaulted at a rate of 0.19%, whereas B-rated bonds experienced a 23.66% default rate over the same time period.

Table 16.5

Corporate Bond Ratings

Description	Moody's	S&P
Investment Grade: High Creditworthiness		
Gilt edge, maximum safety	Aaa	AAA
	Aa1	AA+
Very high grade, high quality	Aa2	AA
	Aa3	AA–
	A1	A+
Upper medium grade	A2	A
	A3	A–
	Baa1	BBB+
Lower medium grade	Baa2	BBB
	Baa3	BBB–
Speculative; Low Creditworthiness		
	Ba1	BB+
Low grade, speculative	Ba2	BB
	Ba3	BB–
	B1	B+
Highly speculative	B2	B
	B3	B–
Below Investment Grade; Substantial Risk or in Default		
		CCC+
Substantial risk, in poor standing	Caa	CCC
		CCC–
May be in default, extremely speculative	Ca	CC
Even more speculative	C	C
No interest paid		CI
Default		DDD, DD, D

Source: Fabozzi (1996), p. 143.

Table 16.6

Six Year Historic Default Probabilities[a]

Aaa	0.19%
Aa	0.41%
A	0.73%
Baa	2.50%
Ba	10.99%
B	23.66%

[a]This is the average of six year default rates for all cohorts that have six years of history from Moody's annual default study.

Source: Lucas (1995).

high-yield bonds: "junk" bonds rated BB or lower by Standary & Poor's or Ba or lower by Moody's.

Table 16.7 shows that the market reflects this expectation by levying a higher interest rate premium for lower rated bonds than for higher rated bonds. Indeed, examining the spread over a duration-matched, default risk free U.S. Treasury security, we see that 10 year **high-yield bonds** offer a default risk premium of 198 basis points. High-yield bonds, known as

Table 16.7	**Annualized Return Spreads for Duration–Matched Corporate Bonds versus U.S. Treasuries (Periods ended December 1992)**		
	20 years	10 years	5 years
U.S. Treasuries	9.13%	11.63%	10.85%
All corporates	9.64	12.53	11.46
Spread versus Treasuries (bp)	51	90	61
AAA-rated corporate bonds	9.20	11.89	11.04
Spread versus Treasuries (bp)	7	26	27
AA-rated corporate bonds	9.35	12.18	11.33
Spread versus Treasuries (bp)	22	55	48
A-rated corporate bonds	9.63	12.58	11.54
Spread versus Treasuries (bp)	50	95	69
BBB-rated corporate bonds	10.37	13.45	11.68
Spread versus Treasuries (bp)	124	182	83
High-yield corporate bonds[a]	13.23[b]	13.61	12.38
Spread versus Treasuries[c] (bp)	410[a]	198	153
S&P 500	11.33	16.18	15.88
Spread versus Treasuries (bp)	220	455	503

[a]Rates for all securities except high-yield junk bonds are from Lehman Brothers Government/Corporate Index. Junk bond yields are from the Salomon Brothers Long Term High-Yield Index.

[b]The time to maturity is 13 years.

[c]The spreads comparing junk bond yields to U.S. Treasuries are not duration-matched. The Lehman Brothers Government/Corporate Index duration is 5.36 years as compared to the Salomon Brothers Long Term High-Yield Index, with a duration of 5.8 years as of December 1992.

Source: Bennett, Esser, and Roth (1994), pp. 40, 44.

junk bonds, are rated BB or lower by Standard & Poor's, or Ba or lower by Moody's. In contrast, 10 year AAA-rated corporate bonds offer a default risk premium of only 26 basis points.

Are the risk premiums built into bond yield spreads sufficient to compensate investors for their credit risk exposure? Table 16.8 suggests that the answer is yes. As evidence, Bennett, Esser, and Roth (1994) estimate the default experience for an investor holding an equally weighted portfolio of 10 year corporate bonds.[5] They then estimate the yield spread that would be required to make the corporate bond portfolio break even when compared to a portfolio of U.S. Treasuries of equal duration. The results (see Table 16.8) show that the required yield spread varies from 13 basis points for Aaa-rated corporate bonds to 332 basis points for B-rated bonds. For each rating class, the actual yield spread exceeds the breakeven yield spread, suggesting that investors are adequately compensated for corporate bonds' default risk exposure.

Bond Covenants

Moody's estimates that average recovery rates on defaulted bonds between January 1, 1970, and December 31, 1993, ranked by bond seniority, are as follows: senior secured debt, 64.59%; senior unsecured debt, 48.38%; senior subordinated debt, 39.79%; subordinated debt, 30.0%; and junior subordinated debt, 16.33%. Usually the more senior the debt, the less its risk

---

[5] Bennett, Esser, and Roth (1994) estimate the cost of default by applying the historical 10 year cumulative default rate for each rating classification. They assume a recovery rate of 40% and the complete loss of one semiannual coupon payment. This assumption reflects evidence that the value of defaulted issues falls to 40% of their pre-default value upon announcement of the default.

**Cumulative Default Rates and Breakeven Yield
Spreads, Issues Rated in 1983 and Tracked Through 1992**

Rating	10 Year Cumulative Default Rates	Breakeven Yield Spreads (basis points)
Aaa	2.0%	13
Aa	2.1	13
A	2.9	19
Baa	8.8	58
Ba	22.4	157
B	43.1	332

Source: Bennett, Esser, and Roth (1994), p. 46.

exposure. However, if the subordinated debt is of shorter duration than the senior debt, then the opposite may hold and the senior debt may be riskier than the subordinated debt.

bond covenants:
conditions, requirements, or restrictions that are imposed on bond issuers for the protection of bondholders.

Yet another qualification may affect the bond's repayment record: **bond covenants**. Bond covenants are conditions, requirements, or restrictions that are imposed on bond issuers for the protection of bondholders. These requirements limit the ability of shareholders to undertake activities that might be detrimental to the bondholders. The two major types of covenants are negative (or restrictive) and affirmative. Restrictive covenants limit the operating decisions of the firm. Common restrictions are limitations on the size of dividend payments and other cash distributions; additional debt; liens and leases; loans and other investments; sale of assets; mergers and acquisitions; capital expenditures; and transactions with affiliates. These restrictive covenants prohibit shareholders from paying themselves a liquidating dividend, for example, leaving nothing to repay the bondholders. Restrictive covenants may take the form of financial requirements such as minimum earnings levels, minimum and maximum inventory levels, and cash requirements. Affirmative covenants require the firm to provide information to bondholders in the form of financial reports, cash flow records, and access to books, records, and even, in some cases, physical inventory. Affirmative covenants may require that bondholders receive prior notice of default or impending Chapter 11 filing, as well as impose insurance requirements.

Bond covenants are often necessary to prevent managers from exploiting their positions as corporate insiders in order to pursue policies that are not in the interests of bondholders. This conflict of interest occurs when managers do not bear the full costs of their value-reducing actions, such as purchases of expensive perquisites, because they own little or no corporate stock. Bond covenants can realign incentives between managers and shareholders, as well as between shareholders and bondholders. Bagnani, Milonas, Saunders, and Travlos (1994) consider four specific bond covenants: (1) a lien restriction that prevents the firm from giving other creditors a more senior claim against the firm's assets in the event of bankruptcy; (2) a lease and sale-leaseback covenant that prevents the firm from issuing a liability (a lease) that will have a more senior claim on the firm's assets than the debt issue; (3) limitations on new debt issues unless certain ratio level requirements are met; and (4) dividend restrictions that limit dividends to a specific amount. The goal of each of these restrictions is to protect the bondholders' claims on the firm's assets. Bagnani et al. find that, for a sample of 61 bond issues during 1977–1985, over 11% had all four covenants; almost 13% had no covenants; and over 60% had any two of the covenants.

Financial Distress   The existence of bond covenants can be viewed as an attempt to position the bondholders' claims on the firm's assets in the event of the firm's financial distress. Financial distress is triggered when a required coupon or principal payment is missed. This is considered

default: event triggered when a required coupon or principal payment is missed.

renegotiation: event marked by an optimal deviation from predetermined payout rules.

absolute priority rules: payment in full of all obligations to senior claimants before any cash is paid to junior claimants.

to be **default**. Each party attempts to protect its claim in the event of **renegotiation** triggered by default. Renegotiation occurs when there is an optimal deviation from predetermined payout rules. For example, bankruptcy proceedings are often characterized by deviations from **absolute priority rules**. In absolute priority rules, senior claimants must be paid in full before any cash is paid to junior claimants. Thus, equityholders typically receive no payout in the event of bankruptcy since the firm's assets are insufficient to cover all the claims of the firm's debtholders. Subject to agreement by a majority of the claimants, however, courts may deviate from this rule and pay equityholders and other junior claimants some amount in order to ascertain their cooperation in restructuring the firm's securities. These deviations from absolute priority can be dangerous. For example, many stockholders in bankrupt banks or thrift institutions received full or partial payout when the federal government bailed out all of the creditors, both insured and uninsured. This can lead to a breakdown in market discipline since shareholders and other junior claimants on the firm's assets have less incentive to monitor the firm's activities if they believe that they will receive their money regardless of the firm's financial condition.

Deviations from absolute priority rules are often necessary, however, to avoid two important agency problems of insolvent firms: (1) the underinvestment problem and (2) the risk shifting problem. The underinvestment problem occurs when shareholders refuse to undertake profitable investment projects because all or most of the project's proceeds will accrue to bondholders. The risk shifting problem occurs when shareholders, because they are essentially betting with the bondholders' money, overinvest in risky projects that have extremely high payoffs but very low likelihood of occurrence. If the risky project pays off, the shareholders gain, but if not, the bondholders lose. This sort of risk shifting incentive occurred when banks and thrifts were levied a fixed rate for deposit insurance protection provided by the federal government. These agency problems always exist but are exacerbated by the firm's insolvency during financial distress.

To better define financial distress, John (1993) classifies the financial contracts of a firm as "hard" and "soft" contracts. Hard contracts require specific payments, which if not met, throw the company into default. Examples of hard contracts are bonds and contracts with suppliers and employees. Soft contracts promise expected cash flows that can be postponed if the firm's cash flows are insufficient to meet the claims on its hard contracts. Common and preferred stock are examples of soft contracts. John defines **financial distress** as the condition in which, at a given point in time, the firm's liquid assets are insufficient to meet its obligations under its "hard" contracts. Financial distress can be alleviated by either liquidating "hard" assets so as to increase the firm's liquid assets or "softening" the firm's liabilities so that contractual cash flows are residual rather than obligatory.

financial distress: at a given point in time, the insufficiency of the firm's liquid assets to meet its obligations under its "hard" contracts.

workout: a voluntary restructuring of the firm's assets and debt agreed to by all of the firm's claimholders.

Chapter 11: a formal, legal stage during which the firm obtains protection from its creditors so that it can reorganize and ultimately emerge solvent.

Chapter 7: the court-administered liquidation proceedings for firms that have no hope of recovery.

Asset and debt restructuring generally entail the sale of assets or the renegotiation of debt contracts in order to raise cash and reduce required payouts. This can be accomplished in the context of either a private **workout** or a court-supervised **Chapter 11** or **Chapter 7** liquidation. A workout requires no legal filings since it is a voluntary restructuring of the firm's assets and debt agreed to by all of the firm's claimholders. Chapter 11 is a formal, legal stage during which the firm obtains protection from its creditors so that it can reorganize and ultimately emerge solvent. Chapter 7 is the court-administered liquidation proceedings for firms that have no hope of recovery. Private workouts tend to be less costly than court-administered bankruptcy proceedings. Gilson, John, and Lang (1990) find that private workouts cost about 0.65% of the book value of the firm's assets, whereas the average legal and professional fees reported in Chapter 11 filings range from 2.8% to 7.5% of total assets. Chapter 7 liquidations can cost an average of 41.49% of the firm's assets by the end of the process.[6] Shareholders gain more when the firm returns to solvency using the private workout as opposed to the Chapter 11 route,

---

[6] Ferris, Jayaraman, and Makhija (1993).

realizing an average 41% increase in stock value over the workout period as opposed to a loss of 40% during the Chapter 11 restructuring period. Indeed, the average length of time spent in Chapter 11 is over 20 months as compared to the average workout period of 15 months.

If workouts are less expensive than Chapter 11 filings, why do any firms choose the Chapter 11 route? Private workouts are more likely to be feasible if the distressed company has fewer intangible assets and more tangible ones, more bank debt and less publicly traded debt in its liabilities, or fewer distinct classes of debt outstanding and thus fewer lenders. These characteristics make it possible for claimholders to evaluate the firm's prospects cooperatively as well as to coordinate their claims at less cost. In particular, bank debt permits greater flexibility based on the superior information of bank lenders. Gilson, John, and Lang (1990) find that 49% of bank debt is restructured using an extension of maturity, whereas only 6.7% of public debt can be restructured by extending maturity. The fewer the lenders and the greater their stake in the firm, the more likely they can cooperate to maximize their recovery results. Because of the cooperative nature of a private workout, deviations from absolute priority rules are much more prevalent than under Chapter 11 filings. Deviations from absolute priority payouts are larger when the firm is closer to solvency, banks hold fewer claims, the CEO holds more shares, the firm's original CEO is retained or replaced from inside the firm, or CEO pay is linked to stock performance.[7]

Chapter 11 filings are used for less liquid, less solvent firms with large amounts of public debt issues outstanding. This liquidation form is less dependent on the cooperation of all claimholders since only a majority of all claimants must agree on a plan to allow the firm to emerge from Chapter 11, as opposed to the near unanimity required under private workouts.[8]

debtor-in-possession financing: new debt issued to finance operations that is senior to all other debt issued before the firm entered Chapter 11.

Moreover, the Bankruptcy Code allows firms in Chapter 11 to issue new debt to finance operations. This **debtor-in-possession financing** is senior to all other debt issued before the firm entered Chapter 11. It allows the firm to borrow at relatively low interest rates during the restructuring period.

leveraged buyouts (LBOs): debt-financed acquisition.

Debt securities are designed to reduce the deadweight costs of financial distress. Before the firm is in distress, it chooses securities that minimize the potential costs of insolvency. Thus, firms with relatively illiquid assets may match their obligations to their cash flows by choosing relatively "soft" liabilities. An example is the financing of **leveraged buyouts (LBOs)**, debt-financed acquisitions. Opler (1993) shows that leveraged buyout financing includes innovative techniques to reduce the risk and cost of financial distress. Some of these techniques are:

1. *Specialist sponsors*—FIs, such as Forstmann Little and Kohlberg Kravis and Roberts specialize in LBOs. These **specialist sponsors** are FIs that work on behalf of both bondholders and equityholders to design a private workout in the event of financial distress. Opler (1993) finds that specialist sponsors are used in 49% of all LBOs and reduce financing costs by an average of 61 basis points.

specialist sponsors: FIs that specialize in LBOs.

2. *Strip financing*—in which each owner holds both debt and equity. **Strip financing** serves to align the interests of bondholders and equityholders and therefore make it easier to construct a private workout plan.[9]

strip financing: technique in which each owner holds both debt and equity.

3. *Restrictive covenants*—which require excess cash flows to be paid to debtholders in the event that interest payments are deferred during periods of financial distress.

---

[7] See Betker (1993).

[8] Although the courts can impose a "cram-down" plan for restructuring against the will of a class of claimholders if this group is judged to be recalcitrant.

[9] However, if U.S. banks issue loans to finance LBOs, they cannot—because of Glass-Steagall regulatory restrictions—hold equity, and strip financing cannot be complete.

4. *Payment-in-kind debt*—which gives the issuer the right to meet interest payments by issuing additional debt. **Payment-in-kind debt** effectively gives the firm the ability to do an automatic workout. A similar type of bond is **reset debt**, with interest rates adjusted at fixed dates if the market value of the bonds falls below a certain level. This offers holders of the bonds of financially distressed firms the right to receive additional interest payments.

Sinking Funds   Another bond covenant that reduces credit risk exposure is the sinking fund. As described for municipal bonds in Chapter 15, sinking fund provisions require the issuer to retire a specified portion of principal in each year of the bond issue's life. By the maturity date, all of the bond issue may be liquidated. Alternatively, if a portion of principal is still unpaid on the maturity date, the bond is called a **balloon maturity**. The issuer can satisfy the sinking fund provision either by calling the required number of bonds at par or by purchasing them in the market. Which method is used depends on the level of interest rates. If interest rates are relatively low and bond prices high, then the issuer will call the bonds at par in order to satisfy the sinking fund provision. However, if interest rates are relatively high, then it will be less expensive for the issuer to obtain the required number of bonds by purchasing them at a discount in the open market. Most bonds with sinking fund provisions allow the issuer to designate bonds to meet future sinking fund requirements. Thus, the issuer may purchase bonds in excess of the current year's sinking fund requirement when interest rates are high and designate them to meet future sinking fund requirements. This reduces the issuer's overall cost of borrowing since bonds are repaid during high interest rate environments.

Table 16.9 shows the prevalence of sinking fund provisions for a random sample of 186 bonds. A majority (51.28%) of long term bonds with original maturities exceeding 10 years have sinking fund provisions. Almost 77% of bonds with more than 20 years to maturity have sinking fund provisions, but only 10.14% of bonds with original maturities of 10 years or less have such provisions. Table 16.9 also shows that the lower the bond's credit rating, the greater the likelihood of a sinking fund provision. This provision offers bond issuers charged the highest interest rates (for longest term, highest credit risk debt) the opportunity to manage prepayments so as to minimize borrowing costs.

Sidebar definitions:

payment-in-kind debt: debt that gives the issuer the right to meet interest payments by issuing additional debt.

reset debt: debt whose interest rates are adjusted at fixed dates if the market value of the bonds falls below a certain level.

balloon maturity: a bond issue in which some portion of the principal is still unpaid on the maturity date.

Table 16.9

Sinking Fund Provisions[a]

Original Maturity	No. Bond Issues	No. w/Sinking Fund	Pct. w/Sinking Fund
10 yrs. or less	69	7	10.14%
11–20 yrs.	39	20	51.28%
> 20 yrs.	78	60	76.92%
Rating	**No. Bond Issues**	**No. w/Sinking Fund**	**Pct. w/Sinking Fund**
Aaa	14	1	7.14%
Aa	22	8	36.36%
A	66	28	42.42%
Baa	42	18	42.86%
Ba	17	10	58.82%
B	26	21	80.77%
Caa	2	1	50.00%

[a]Data collected from *Moody's Industrial Manual*, 1990.

Source: Kalotay and Tuckman (1992), pp. 111, 112.

Checkpoint

1. How do credit ratings reveal default risk?

2. What keeps the rating services honest and accurate in their assessments of credit-worthiness? Does historical default evidence demonstrate the value of credit ratings?

3. Contrast the three states of financial distress. Compare them with respect to their cost, feasibility, and desirability.

4. How do bond covenants protect bondholders' rights in the event of financial distress?

5. Describe how financial distress impacts the design of financial securities.

6. What is a sinking fund, and who benefits from its existence in a bond's covenants?

Credit Enhancements

credit enhancements:
third-party guarantees of
financial performance.

Credit risk is reduced by the provision of **credit enhancements**, which are third-party guarantees of financial performance. Commercial banks, insurance companies, and governments all offer guarantees of repayment in exchange for fees. In Chapter 13, we saw the guarantee role provided by commercial banks in the form of letters of credit. As discussed in Chapter 15, specialized insurance agencies, such as AMBAC and Municipal Bond Investors Insurance Corporation, provide credit enhancements for municipal securities. The largest provider of financial guarantees for corporate debt is the U.S. government. In terms of corporate lending, the Small Business Administration has been instrumental in guaranteeing loans to small businesses, without which lending would not occur. The Pension Benefit Guaranty Corporation is another federal agency that guarantees payments on corporate pension plans.

Corporate bonds are not sold with credit guarantees in the United States. Table 16.10 examines the prices of several low-rated corporate bonds *as if* credit enhancements were available. The guarantee's value is the cost required to make the corporate bond default risk free. That is, it is the difference between the corporate bond's price and an equivalent default risk free U.S. Treasury security. As the last two columns of Table 16.10 show, the value of the credit guarantee can be considerable. For example, the extremely high cost of the Pan Am guarantee, 151.1% of the corporate bond price, predicted the company's subsequent bankruptcy.

Table 16.10

Estimates of Loan Guarantee Values Derived from Corporate Bond Prices[a]

Company	Years to Maturity	Corporate Bond Prices With Guarantee	Corporate Bond Prices Without Guarantee	Loan Guarantee Value Price	Loan Guarantee Value Pct. of No Guarantee Price
Continental Air	6	$109.12	$66.00	$43.12	65.3%
MGM/UA	6	118.24	63.38	54.86	86.6
Mesa Capital	9	127.36	95.50	31.86	33.4
Navistar	14	100.00	89.00	11.00	12.4%
Pan Am	14	147.23	58.63	88.60	151.1
RJR Nabisco	11	141.35	76.88	64.47	83.9
Revlon	20	117.25	80.75	36.50	45.2
Union Carbide	9	102.89	92.25	10.64	11.5
Warner	23	124.11	97.00	27.11	27.9

[a]The value of the loan guarantee equals the guaranteed debt price minus the nonguaranteed debt price. The nonguaranteed debt price assumes a flat U.S. Treasury yield curve at 9% and no adjustment for call provisions. The bond prices are closing market prices from the *Wall Street*

Source: Merton and Bodie (1992), p. 99.

Pushing the Envelope: High-Yield Junk Bonds

Below investment-grade corporate borrowers found themselves able to enter the publicly traded debt market for the first time in the 1980s. This was through the debt instrument pioneered by Michael Milken of the brokerage house of Drexel, Burnham, Lambert: high-yield debt, or junk bonds. *Timely Topics 16.1: Junk Bonds—Maligned Breakthrough* shows how the instrument was innovated from its origins as a rescue of **fallen angels**: formerly creditworthy firms that, because of poor performance, have fallen below investment-grade levels.

fallen angels: formerly creditworthy firms that, because of poor performance, have fallen below investment-grade levels.

In 1994 there were only 191 new issues of junk bonds, totaling $34.6 billion. This total was down from the 341 issues in 1993, amounting to $57.2 billion. During the same period, bank loans for mergers and acquisitions quadrupled from $29.6 billion in 1993 to over $116 billion in 1994. Even during a bond rally, junk bond prices are extremely volatile. This may explain the market's continued reluctance to rely on high-yield financing for a significant portion of transactions.

TIMELY TOPICS 16.1

JUNK BONDS—MALIGNED BREAKTHROUGH

Five years ago this week, Drexel Burnham Lambert, the birthplace of the high-yield bond, went bankrupt. It is a good time to voice what has become indisputably clear since then: Far from being a shady tool of fast-talking financiers, the so-called junk bond is an essential generator of economic growth and vitality.

Here are a few of its achievements:

- High-yield bonds democratized business by giving small entrepreneurs access to enough capital to challenge the giants. Many of today's household names—MCI, Viacom, Turner Broadcasting, QVC, and TeleCommunications, Inc. are built on a "junk" foundation.

- High-yield bonds have become a staple of the capital markets and the economy. Three years after Drexel's collapse, there were twice as many high-yield bond offers underwritten on Wall Street as there were at the peak of Drexel's success. . . .

- High-yield bonds globalized American investing. Ten years ago, the U.S. looked outward and realized it was part of a global economy—only to discover that much of the world was less than investment grade. . . . [International o]penness is a direct consequence of the revolution in high-yield bonds. . . .

The junk label was a classic case of putting down a dynamic new concept because it was easier to perpetuate the old one: the assumption that any debt instrument below investment grade was junk. . . . When faced with a debt instrument—a high yield bond—that acts more like equity than debt and requires knowledge, interpretation and analysis, much of the Street turned its back. . . .

[I]n the early 1970's, Drexel saw the potential of something that everyone else considered a problem security: investment-grade bonds that, because of a company disaster, slipped below investment grade. At that time, some shrewd investors had learned to invest in such declining companies, turn them around under original or new management, and through focused financial planning return these fallen angels to investment-grade stature. In developing the financial means to accomplish this task, Drexel acquired skills that no other firm had.

Then came Drexel's great leap forward, in about 1976. Drexel executives, including myself, began wondering if it was possible to create such bonds without having to sit around and wait for disaster to strike the AAA- and AA-rated companies of the world. Wouldn't it be much better, we reasoned, to invest in a young, fresh company with the same creditworthiness of a fallen angel, but with a go-getter entrepreneur at the helm? Wouldn't it be better to back someone with all his personal worth invested in the company, rather than support stodgy, remote managers? By asking such questions, we brought a new factor into credit analysis: the evaluation of human capital. . . .

This thought—that the high-yield bond could be a product rather than an accident—was the vital shot of innovation the financial world desperately needed. In the mid-1980s, for the first time in perhaps 50 years, a small enterprise could actually challenge a Forune 500 company. . . .

[T]he controversy that grew up around Drexel and high-yield bonds was, largely, testimony to the fearful power of our financial innovation. That a small entrepreneur could challenge corporate giants threatened everyone who was big—big business, big labor, and big government—and they responded to protect their interests. . . Junk bonds have brought us. . . the realization that we must respect and encourage, not fear and attack, innovation in business and finance. In today's global economy, our future depends on it.

Source: Chris Andersen, *New York Times*, February 12, 1995.

Checkpoint

✓

1.   Who offers credit enhancements and why?

2.   Why do bondholders sometimes demand credit enhancements?

3.   What innovation did the high-yield bond market discover?

➤ Pricing Risky Corporate Bonds

Corporate bond certificates specify the bond's covenants, maturity dates, face value, and interest rate. The two major forms of interest agreements are fixed rate and floating rate.

bullet bond: a bond that pays only interest during the life of the bond and repays the entire principal in one lump sum at the bond's maturity date.

The type of bond most often used in examples in this book is the fixed rate **bullet bond**. A bullet bond is a bond that pays only interest at a fixed rate during the life of the bond and repays the entire principal in one lump sum at the bond's maturity date. The bond's principal is nonamortized because it is not paid out periodically over the life of the bond.

Pricing Floating Rate Debt   There was a time when creditworthy businesses were proud that they could borrow at the prime rate. The prime rate was considered to be banks' best rate for their best customers. Prime rate lending has now lost this meaning. Indeed, floating rate loans based on the prime rate tend to be more expensive than other floating rate debt instruments. This is because the prime rate is a bank lending rate that reflects the all-in-cost of the bank's funds plus a generous spread. The prime rate does not reflect competitive market conditions. Rather, it is an administered rate, set almost collusively by banks in a follow-the-leader procedure. It is not surprising that when one large bank increases its prime rate, it is invariably followed by prime rate increases at other major banks. Similarly, all banks resist prime rate decreases together, making the rate fairly sensitive to tight market (high rate) conditions and rather insensitive to easy money (low rate) environments.

Prime rate debt is priced as the prime rate plus or minus a spread that reflects the creditworthiness of the borrower. Thus, prime plus $\frac{1}{2}$ carries a coupon rate of the prevailing prime rate plus 50 basis points. Since the prime rate is a sluggish indicator of market movements, a more volatile floating rate loan would be priced against LIBOR. As we saw in Chapter 12, LIBOR is a free market rate, reflecting global financial market conditions around the clock. Typically, a LIBOR based debt instrument will have a lower cost than prime-based lending to the same customer. This reflects the borrower's greater interest rate risk associated with LIBOR pricing because of the greater volatility of the base rate. Moreover, prime-based loans often have more flexible prepayment schedules than LIBOR based debt. Whereas a LIBOR loan may have a prepayment penalty, prime-based lending typically does not. Consequently, business borrowers that have difficulty forecasting either interest rates or their own cash flows accurately over time may prefer prime rate debt.

Using Historical Default Rates to Price Risky Corporate Fixed Rate Debt   In Chapters 7 and 15 we considered the pricing of default risk free government bullet bonds. We set the price equal to the present value of all future coupon and principal cash flows certain to be received at each coupon payment date. How do we price corporate bonds when there is some probability that cash flows will be interrupted by default? One model uses estimated default rates, as tabulated by credit rating classification. For each rating class, a marginal default rate is computed as

$$ d_t(R) = \frac{\displaystyle\sum_{n=1}^{N} m_t^n(R)}{\displaystyle\sum_{n=1}^{N} M_t^n(R)} $$

where $d_t(R)$ = the marginal default rate for bonds originally issued at the R rating (where R = Aaa, Aa,...) as of t years after issue; $m_t^n(R)$ = the number of issuers originally rated R that default in the tth year after issue in each year $n = 1, \ldots, N$; $M_t^n(R)$ = the total number of issuers with original rating R in the tth year after issue in each year $n = 1, \ldots, N$. Thus, if $d_6(\text{Aaa}) = .10\%$, then .10% of all Aaa rated bonds defaulted during the sixth year after issue. That is, 99.9% of all Aaa-rated bonds did not default in their sixth year after issue.

To calculate the percentage of bonds that did not default in any of the first six years of their existence, simply multiply the probabilities of survival in each year (the first, second, third, fourth, fifth, and sixth). The **cumulative survival rate** is $S_t \equiv \Pi_{n=1}^{N}[1 - d_t(R)]$. The **cumulative default rate** is one minus the cumulative survival rate, or the probability that the bond defaults sometime in its first t years. Table 16.11 shows Moody's cumulative default rates for all investment-grade bonds issued during 1970–1993, with maturities of up to 20 years.

We can now use the cumulative survival rate to determine the price of the corporate bond. The expected repayment in any year is the promised cash payment multiplied by the cumulative survival rate up until that year.[10] If the promised coupon or principal payment in period t is denoted C_t, then the expected cash flow in period t is $S_t C_t$. If investors are risk neutral, then they should be indifferent between receiving the expected cash flow $S_t C_t$ and a certain payment of the same amount. We can discount the expected cash flows during the life of the bond at

cumulative survival rate: the probability that the bond did not default in its first t years.

cumulative default rate: one minus the cumulative survival rate, or the probability that the bond defaults sometime in its first t years.

---

[10] This assumes that if the bond issuer defaults, there is no possible recovery of any cash flows. In reality, recovery rates average 15% to 65% (see discussion below). The model can be expanded to incorporate positive expected cash flows in the event of default.

Table
16.11

Weighted–Average Cumulative Default Rates, 1970–1993

Year	Aaa	Aa	A	Baa	Ba	B
1	0.00%	0.02%	0.01%	0.16%	1.79%	8.31%
2	0.00	0.04	0.09	0.51	4.38	14.85
3	0.00	0.08	0.28	0.91	6.92	20.38
4	0.04	0.20	0.46	1.46	9.41	24.78
5	0.12	0.32	0.62	1.97	11.85	28.38
6	0.22	0.43	0.83	2.46	13.78	31.88
7	0.33	0.52	1.06	3.09	15.33	34.32
8	0.45	0.64	1.31	3.75	16.75	36.71
9	0.58	0.76	1.61	4.39	18.14	38.38
10	0.73	0.91	1.96	4.96	19.48	39.96
11	0.90	1.09	2.30	5.56	20.84	41.08
12	1.09	1.29	2.65	6.19	22.22	41.74
13	1.30	1.51	2.99	6.77	23.54	42.45
14	1.55	1.76	3.29	7.44	24.52	43.04
15	1.84	1.76	3.62	8.16	25.46	43.70
16	2.18	1.76	3.95	8.91	26.43	44.43
17	2.38	1.89	4.26	9.69	27.29	45.27
18	2.63	2.05	4.58	10.45	28.06	45.58
19	2.63	2.24	4.96	11.07	28.88	45.58
20	2.63	2.48	5.23	11.70	29.76	45.58

Source: Fons (1994), p. 26.

the risk free rate for each period. Thus, the corporate bond's price is

$$P = \sum_{t=1}^{T} \frac{S_t C_t}{(1 + i_t)^t}$$

where i_t is the risk free spot rate for t year maturity, default risk free government securities.

Consider an A-rated three year, \$100 par value, 6% p.a. annual coupon corporate bond. Suppose that yield to maturity on three year, 6% p.a. annual coupon, risk free government debt is 6% p.a. That is, risk free government bonds sell at par. Using the cumulative default rates in Table 16.11, we can calculate the cumulative survival rates as 99.99% (= 100 – 0.01), 99.91% (= 100 – 0.09), and 99.72% (= 100 – 0.28) for the first three years after the bond's issuance. The price of the A-rated bond is

$$P = \frac{6(0.9999)}{1.06} + \frac{6(0.9991)}{1.06^2} + \frac{106(0.9972)}{1.06^3} = \$99.745$$

If the bond were B-rated instead of A-rated, using the cumulative survival rates in Table 16.11, its price would be

$$P = \frac{6(0.9169)}{1.06} + \frac{6(0.8515)}{1.06^2} + \frac{106(0.7962)}{1.06^3} = \$80.599$$

since the first, second, and third year survival rates are 91.69% (= 100 – 8.31); 85.15% (= 100 – 14.85); and 79.62% (= 100 – 20.38), respectively.

We can use the two bonds' prices to calculate the default risk premiums. The yield to maturity on the A-rated corporate bond is

$$99.745 = \frac{6}{(1+i)} + \frac{6}{(1+i)^2} + \frac{106}{(1+i)^3}$$

or $i = 6.10\%$. The default risk premium on A-rated corporate debt is 10 basis points over the comparable 6% risk free rate. The yield to maturity on the B-rated corporate bond is

$$80.599 = \frac{6}{(1+i)} + \frac{6}{(1+i)^2} + \frac{106}{(1+i)^3}$$

or $i = 14.4\%$. The default risk premium on riskier B-rated corporate debt over Treasury securities is therefore 8.4%.

Some words of caution are in order regarding this model of bond pricing. This model is only as good as historical default and survival rates are. If historical evidence is not a good predictor of future outcomes, perhaps because of a structural shift in credit risk exposure, this model will yield poor results.

CALCULATION COMPLICATIONS 16.1

OPTION PRICING OF RISKY CORPORATE DEBT

Merton (1974) first recognized that risky corporate debt and equity can be valued as options. A debt issue can be viewed as the buying of a call option on the firm's assets by the firm's shareholders. In Figure CC.1 we observe the payoff on a zero coupon issue of corporate debt. Let the face value of the debt be denoted K. If, upon the debt's maturity, the market value of the firm's assets, A, exceeds K, then the firm's shareholders will "buy back" the firm from the bondholders and repay the debt. If, however, the firm is worth less than K on the maturity date of the debt, then the shareholders will be unwilling to pay K for assets that are worth less than K, and it will be optimal for them to default on the debt. The bondholders will be left to liquidate the firm's assets and receive their market value, A. The debtholders' payoff in Figure CC.1 is the same as that of the payoff to the writer of a call option on the firm's assets. Thus, the firm's shareholders can be viewed as holding a call option on the firm's assets, with an exercise price of K equal to the face value of the firm's risky debt. If they exercise their option upon the maturity of the debt, they buy the firm's assets for $\$K$ and repay the bondholders. However, if the firm's assets are worth less than $\$K$, the shareholders will default on the bonds and the option will not be exercised. The firm's assets will fall into the hands of the bondholders.

If asset values fluctuate continuously over time, we can use the Black-Scholes option pricing model to calculate the value of the firm's equity as

$$E = AN(d_1) - Ke^{-rt}N(d_2)$$

where

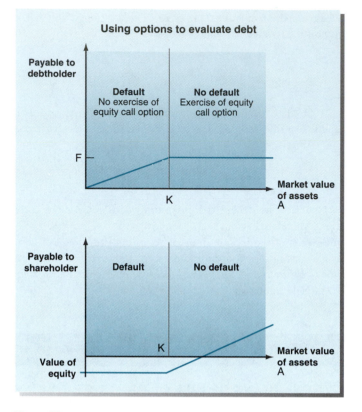

Figure CC.1

E = the present value of the firm's equity

t = the time to maturity of the risky debt

r = the risk free rate

A = the current market value of the firm's assets

K = the face value of the risky, zero coupon bond

$$d_1 = \frac{\ln\left(\dfrac{A}{K}\right) + (r + 0.5\sigma^2)t}{\sigma\sqrt{t}}$$

$$d_2 = d_1 - \sigma\sqrt{t}$$

σ = the riskiness of the firm's assets as measured by the standard deviation of the market value of assets

$N(d)$ = the probability that a value less than or equal to d will be realized using the standard normal probability distribution

E is the value of equity. Since debt plus equity must always equal the value of the firm, the value of the risky debt can be determined by subtracting the value of the call option from the value of the firm's assets, that is, $A - E$. The equity value will be lower and the risky bond's present value will be greater, the lower the credit risk of the borrowing firm—that is, the lower the value of the call option. The bondholders demand a higher credit risk premium if (1) the firm's leverage ratio, d, is higher; (2) the firm's asset risk, σ^2, is higher; (3) the risk free rate, r, is higher; and (4) the time to maturity of the debt, t, is longer.

Suppose that the risk free rate is 10% p.a.; the firm's asset risk $\sigma^2 = 16\%$; $t = 10$ years; the face value of debt, $K = \$80$ million; and the firm's assets, A, are currently valued at \$100 million.[11] The equity call option is valued at

$$E = \$100N \left(\frac{\ln \left(\dfrac{100}{80} \right) + (.10 + .5(.16))10}{(.16)^{.5}(10)^{.5}} \right)$$

$$- \$80 e^{-.10(10)} N \left(1.5994 - (.16)^{.5}(10)^{.5} \right)$$

$$= \$100N(1.5994) - \$80(.36788)N(.3345)$$

$$= \$100(.9451) - \$29.43(.631) = \$75.94$$

The present value of the risky debt is \$100m − \$75.94m = \$24.06m. The yield on the risky debt is: $(\frac{\$80}{24.06})^{1/10} - 1 = 12.77\%$ p.a. The credit risk premium on this risky bond is 2.77% above the risk free Treasury rate of 10% p.a.

This model assumes that capital markets are perfect and frictionless. That is, the model just assumes away real-world wrinkles such as transaction costs, informational asymmetries, and restrictions on capital flows. We have already seen the importance of informational asymmetries, for example, in the corporate debt market. Thus, this assumption may yield misleading results using the option pricing model.[12]

Checkpoint

✓

1. What are the shortcomings of using the marginal default rate to price risky corporate debt?

2. What are the shortcomings of using the option pricing model to price risky corporate debt?

Bonds with Embedded Options

We have used the option pricing model to evaluate bonds as if they were options. Now we consider the case where the bonds have additional options of various types attached to them.

Callable Bonds   Corporate bond returns are sensitive to the interest rate environment. Just as with government bonds, as interest rates increase, bond prices fall. However, when interest rates decrease, corporate bond prices do not rise as much as government bond prices. This is because many corporate bonds are callable.[13] The issuer retains the right, not the obligation, to buy back the bond at some later date at a predetermined price that is higher than the issue price. Callable bonds, then, are straight bonds with an embedded call option retained by the issuer. Prior to 1981, more than 95% of all corporate bond issues were callable. However, that number has dropped to less than 25% in 1991. Most speculative grade corporate bonds are callable, whereas most investment grade bonds are shorter term and noncallable. Figure 16.2 shows the distribution of callable versus noncallable corporate bonds by rating class. The lower the rating, the greater percentage of new issues that are callable. Most 5 year bonds are callable in their third year; most 7 year bonds are callable in their fifth year; and most 30 year bonds are callable in 10 years.

---

[11] This example is taken from Damadoran (1994).

[12] For an option pricing model using more realistic assumptions, see Joon, Ramaswamy, and Sundaresan (1993).

[13] Government bonds may also be callable. Callable bonds were introduced in Chapter 7.

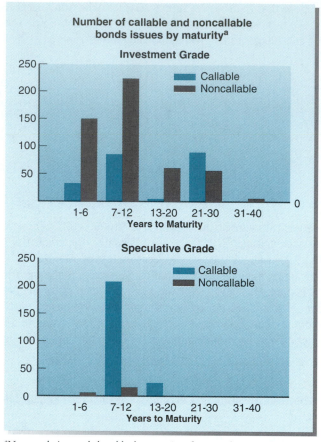

Number of callable and noncallable
bonds issues by maturity[a]

[a]No speculative-grade bond had a maturity of greater than 20 years.
Source: Crabbe and Helwege (1994), p. 8.

Figure 16.2

call premium: the
difference between the
call price and the par
value of the bond.

The callable bond specifies the date of first call and the exercise price, which is the price at which the bond is repurchased if the issuer chooses to buy it back. Typically, the purchase price includes a **call premium**, which is the difference between the call price and the par value of the bond. The call premium on the first call date is often equal to one year's coupon payments and declines throughout the life of the bond according to a prespecified schedule.

The bond issuer can exercise the option and buy back the bond on any date after the first call date. The issuer will call the bond if on the call date interest rates have declined significantly from the bond's coupon rate. This will enable the issuer to refinance its debt at the lower market rates then prevailing. Bondholders are hurt by this practice since they cannot reinvest the proceeds of the bond at the higher rates that were prevailing when the bond was originally issued. Thus, callable bond yields are higher than noncallable bond yields so as to compensate investors for the risk of the call option that can be exercised at any time after the first call date. In order to reduce the cost to the issuer of callable bonds, for example, in July 1994 ABN Amro Bank sold $200 million of 15 year bonds with a 10 year one-time call option. Thus, these bonds could be called on one date only. The added yield on these callable bonds was only about 30 basis points. Indeed, many bond issuers are turning to callable bonds because they are arbitraging the bond and swap market. They "buy" a call option from bondholders when they issue callable bonds, and then they sell back the call option in the swap market at a better price, thereby pocketing the differential.

Why do corporations issue callable bonds? If it were simply to replace high-cost debt with lower cost debt, the issue of callable bonds would represent a net gain to shareholders but a net loss to bondholders, yielding the firm as a whole no net benefit. Three explanations have been advanced to explain the prevalence of callable bonds: (1) to resolve information asymmetries; (2) to align risk taking incentives; and (3) to correct the underinvestment problem. In the first explanation, firms finance projects using callable bonds if they expect to receive information about their project's profitability at some time in the future. They time the call option to coincide with the receipt of the information, so that they have maximum flexibility to react to the new information. Another way of achieving this flexibility is to issue noncallable debt with an original maturity equal to the time until the new information is revealed.

The second explanation hinges on shareholder versus bondholder agency problems. Shareholders have the incentive to switch to riskier projects because they receive payoffs only if there are additional cash flows after the project's returns are used to repay bondholders in full. On the other hand, bondholders prefer safer projects because they do not share in this residual payoff. The issuance of the call option reduces the shareholders' incentives to take on excessive risk because the option's value increases as risk exposure increases. Thus, shareholders are induced to choose an incentive-compatible level of risk that is in the best interests of both shareholders and bondholders alike.

The third explanation stems from the recognition that shareholders will not invest in a project if the project return is merely sufficient to cover the costs of debt financing. This is because when the project returns just cover its interest expenses, there is nothing left over to pay back shareholders. By allowing shareholders to recontract debt on the call date, callable debt removes some of this incentive to underinvest in positive net present value projects.

There is also a tax benefit associated with callable bonds. The call premium is taxed as a capital gain for the bondholder, but it is deductible as ordinary income for the bond issuer. However, Brick and Wallingford (1985) claim that this is insufficient explanation for the prevalence of callable bonds because the same tax advantage can be obtained, with greater flexibility, by repurchasing noncallable debt at market prices.

Valuing Callable Bonds   To the bondholder, the value of a callable bond is equal to the value of an equivalent noncallable bond *minus* the value of the call option retained by the issuer. Consider a noncallable, 10 year 5% p.a. annual coupon bond selling at par. If the first call date is in five years, we can calculate the **yield to call** as the yield earned over the period of time from issue to first call date. Suppose that the call premium is 10%. For a $100 par value bond, the cash flows in the event of a call in five years are five $5 coupon payments plus a principal payment of $110, equal to the bond's face value plus the 10% call premium. Setting the present value of these cash flows equal to the bond's price, we get

yield to call: the yield earned over the period of time from issue to first call date.

$$\$100 = \sum_{t=1}^{5} \frac{5}{(1+y)^t} + \frac{110}{(1+y)^5}$$

or a yield to call of 6.75% p.a. This bond carries a yield premium of 175 basis points to compensate the bondholder for the risk of call.[14]

Because the call option is valuable to the issuer, a callable bond will sell for a lower price than an equivalent noncallable bond. This price differential, equivalent to the call option

---

[14] This assumes that the bond will be called on its first call date. However, the bond may be called at any time after the first call date. Precise valuation would require estimating the likelihood of call on any date from year 5 until maturity in year 10.

premium, is determined by expected future interest rates. We will calculate the price of a callable bond assuming one particular interest rate scenario. Practically, callable bond prices should be evaluated under many alternative interest rate scenarios, with a probability assigned to each possibility. This procedure must therefore be replicated for each interest rate scenario deemed possible.

Consider a three year 5% p.a. annual coupon bond that is callable one year after issue. Assume that the call premium is 1%. Thus, if the bond is called, the issuer repays $101 for each $100 in par value. Since bond cash flows are paid at discrete time intervals, on coupon payment dates, we can use the discrete **binomial interest rate tree** method to depict the possible interest rates that prevail over time. A binomial interest rate tree depicts interest rates over time if, at each discrete time period (called a **node**), there are only two equally likely possibilities: interest rates either increase or decrease by the same amount. In our binomial interest rate tree, we assume that interest rates can either increase or decrease by 100 basis points. If one year yields on comparable noncallable bond currently are 5% p.a., we consider that rate to be the starting point for our binomial interest rate tree. At each node, interest rates can go either up or down by 100 basis points with equal probability.

Figure 16.3 shows all possible interest rates under this scenario for a noncallable bond over the next three years. During the first year, there is a 50% chance that interest rates will increase to 6% p.a. and a 50% chance that they will decrease to 4% p.a. During the second year, there is a 50% chance that interest rates will return to 5% p.a. and a 25% chance for each of the alternatives that interest rates are 7% or 3%. During the third year of the noncallable bond's life, interest rates will either be 8% with a one in six likelihood, or 2% with a one in

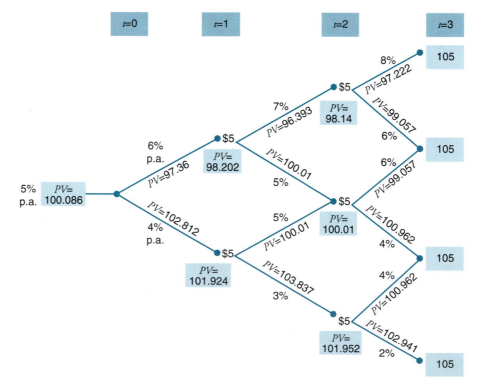

Binomial interest rate tree for a noncallable bond

Figure 16.3

six likelihood, or 6% with a 33% probability, or 4% with a 33% probability. If we consider these to be the only possible interest rates that will prevail over the next three years,[15] we can discount all cash flows to work back to the present price. Thus, to solve the binomial interest rate tree, we work recursively backward.

Valuing the Binomial Interest Rate Tree for a Noncallable Bond. We illustrate the binomial interest rate tree using a three year noncallable bond. We begin evaluating from the last year until maturity; in this case the third year (or tier) of the tree.

Final cash flows are equal to the par value, $100, plus the last coupon payment of $5. We discount $105 back one period by the interest rate noted on each branch of the tree. On the 8% branch, the present value of the last period cash flow is $PV = \frac{105}{1.08} = \$97.222$. For both 6% branches, we obtain $PV = \frac{105}{1.06} = \$99.057$. For both 4% branches, we obtain $PV = \frac{105}{1.04} = \$100.962$. Finally, on the 2% branch, the present value of the last period cash flow is $PV = \frac{105}{1.02} = \$102.941$.

Now that we have evaluated the cash flows on each branch of tier 3, we must do the same for each node at time period $t = 2$. Note that each node has two branches stemming from it. Each of these branches corresponds to a different interest rate scenario. Since each interest rate scenario is equally likely, there is a 50% chance of each branch's cash value. To evaluate the expected present value at each node, simply weight each branch's cash value by its likelihood of occurrence, 50%. At the top node at $t = 2$, there is a 50% chance of receiving $97.222 and a 50% chance of receiving $99.057 for a expected present value of $PV = .5(97.222) + .5(99.057) = \$98.14$, which is shown in the box at the top node. Similarly, for the next node, the present value is $PV = .5(99.057) + .5(100.962) = \$100.01$. For the bottom node, the present value is $PV = .5(100.962) + .5(102.941) = \$101.952$.

We now work backward one year to the second tier of the tree, that is, the cash flows expected in the second year. We repeat the process of evaluating the cash flows on each branch for the second tier of the tree. If interest rates are 7% p.a. in the second year of the life of the bond, the present value of all $t = 2$ cash flows is $PV = \frac{5+98.14}{1.07} = \$96.393$. On the 5% branches of tier 2, the present value of all $t = 2$ cash flows is $PV = \frac{5+100.01}{1.05} = \$100.01$. On the 3% branch of the second tier, the present value of all $t = 2$ cash flows is $PV = \frac{5+101.952}{1.03} = \$103.837$.

Evaluating the expected present value of cash flows at each of the nodes at $t = 1$ yields $.5(96.393) + .5(100.01) = \$98.202$ for the top node and $.5(100.01) + .5(103.837) = \$101.924$ for the bottom node.

Now we can recursively solve back to the present using the present values at the $t = 1$ nodes for first year expected cash flows. Again, we first evaluate the present values on each of the interest rate branches and then take their expected value by weighting each possibility by a 0.5 probability. The 6% p.a. branch is valued at $PV = \frac{5+98.202}{1.06} = \$97.36$. The 4% p.a. branch is valued at $PV = \frac{5+101.924}{1.04} = \$102.812$. The expected present value at the $t = 0$ node is $PV = .5(97.36) + .5(102.812) = \$100.086$. Thus, the noncallable bond sells for a price of $100.086 per $100 face value. This yields 4.97% p.a. until maturity.

Valuing a Binomial Interest Rate Tree for a Callable Bond. Figure 16.4 shows the binomial interest rate tree for a callable bond. It is identical to Figure 16.3 for the noncallable bond with one exception. At each node, a question is asked by the bond issuer. Is the present value of all future cash flows (shown in the box at each node of the figures) greater than the call price (which is equal to the par value plus the call premium)? If the answer to this question is yes, then the bond is immediately called and no future cash flows occur.[16] At the bottom node

---

[15] In reality, many other interest rate scenarios would be considered to price the bonds.

[16] Tax or other considerations may prevent the issuer from calling the bond when it first becomes profitable to do so, but these issues are beyond the scope of this book.

Binomial interest rate tree for a callable bond

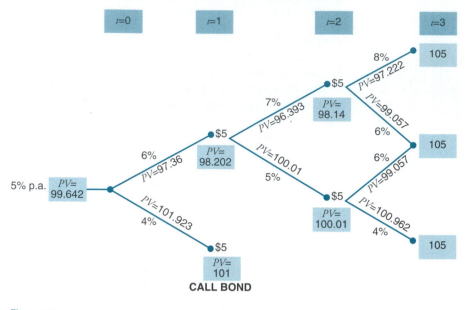

Figure 16.4

at $t = 1$, the present value of all future cash flows in Figure 16.3 is $101.924. Since the call premium is 1%, the call price is $101. The bond is therefore called at that node, and Figure 16.4 replaces the $101.924 cash flow with the lower call price of $101. Now you see why investors dislike callable bonds. If this interest rate scenario prevails, then the bondholder loses $.924 per $100 face value at time $t = 1$.

Bondholders can anticipate this loss, and they will pay less at time period $t = 0$ for the callable bond than for the noncallable bond. We observe this by repeating the last step in the above recursive process for the callable bond in Figure 16.4. The 4% branch in the first tier of the tree is valued at $PV = \frac{5+101}{1.04} = \$101.923$ rather than the $102.812 in Figure 16.3. The expected present value at the node at $t = 0$ is $PV = .5(97.36) + .5(101.923) = \$99.642$. The callable bond's price ($99.642) is therefore below the noncallable bond's price ($100.086). Using the $99.642 price, we see that the yield to maturity for the three year callable bond is 5.13% p.a. The call premium can be expressed as the difference in yields, or 5.13% minus 4.97%, which equals 16 basis points. This premium on the bond's embedded option, expressed in yields, 16 basis points in this example, is called the **option-adjusted spread**.

option-adjusted spread: the premium on the bond's embedded option, expressed in yields.

Puttable Bonds   A response to the disadvantages of callable bonds to the bondholder is the development of a new type of corporate bond: the noncallable, **puttable bond**. The issuer of the puttable bond sells to the bondholder a put option that allows the holder to sell the bond back to the issuer prior to maturity at a predetermined price, usually set equal to par value. The put option offers the bondholder protection against interest rate increases that reduce the bond's market value. The bondholder exercises the put option and sells the bond back to the issuer if either interest rates increase or the issuer's credit quality deteriorates.

puttable bond: a fixed rate bond plus a put option held by the bondholder, which allows the holder to sell the bond back to the issuer prior to maturity at a predetermined price, usually set equal to par value.

The cost of the put option is levied in the form of these bonds' lower yields. In 1995, the average yield sacrifice on a noncallable 30 year A-rated corporate bond that can be put to the issuer at par five years after issue was 20 basis points. The bond puts are almost always European put options, so that they can be exercised on a specific date only. About 900 corporate bonds have a put feature that is triggered only upon a change in corporate ownership or control.

Table 16.12

Some Puttable Bonds as of March 1995

Issuer	Coupon (%)	Maturity	Moody's Rating	Amt. Issued ($mil)	Price ($)	Yield to: Put (%)	Yield to: Mat. (%)	Date of 1st Put	Yield Sacrifice (bp)[a]
Columbia/HCA	8.36	4/15/24	A3	150	101.21	8.16	8.25	4/15/04	41
Corning	7.625	8/1/24	A2	100	99.36	7.72	7.68	8/1/04	62
Eastman Chemical	7.625	6/15/24	Baa1	200	96.90	8.05	7.90	6/15/06	42
Eaton	8.00	8/15/06	A2	100	102.56	6.10	7.66	8/15/96	33
NBD Bank	8.25	11/1/24	Aa3	250	102.20	7.92	8.05	11/1/04	50
New England Tel.	7.875	11/15/29	Aa2	350	102.77	6.11	7.65	11/15/96	91
New Jersey Bell	7.85	11/15/29	Aaa	150	103.66	6.92	7.55	11/15/99	61
Pennsylvania Power & Light	7.70	10/1/09	A2	200	101.86	7.21	7.49	10/1/99	48
RJR Nabisco	6.80	9/1/01	Baa3	100	97.83	7.79	7.23	9/2/97	119
Torchmark	8.25	8/15/09	A3	100	101.27	7.28	8.10	8/15/96	34

[a]Yield forfeited by favoring puttable bond over nonputtable bond of comparable maturity and credit quality.

Source: Hardy (1995), p. 148.

---

poison put covenants: a put feature that is triggered only upon a change in corporate ownership or control.

Referred to as **poison put covenants**, these put options protect management, not the bond investor. This is because they trigger cash outflows (such as immediate repayment of debt at or above par) when hostile takeovers, leveraged buyouts, or other "risk events" take place. Although they also protect bondholders from losses in the event of changes in corporate control, the primary purpose of poison put covenants is to increase the costs of hostile takeovers so as to reduce their likelihood of occurrence, thereby protecting the jobs of existing managers.

Table 16.12 shows 10 puttable corporate bonds that are *not* contingent on changes in corporate control. These bond covenants protect bondholders from the impact of increasing interest rates. In exchange for this protection, bondholders accept yields that are lower than equally risky bonds, with the yield sacrifice for the bonds in Table 16.12 ranging from 33 to 119 basis points. In contrast, Crabbe (1991) estimates that the yield sacrifice on bonds with poison put covenants is only 25 to 30 basis points. Issuers are willing to issue puttable bonds since they can issue their debt more inexpensively. The first puttable bond was a $700 million 30 year bond offering by HydroQuebec in June 1994 which might not have sold without the enhancement of the 12 year put option.[17]

How are puttable bonds valued? Consider the NBD Bank puttable bond in Table 16.12. It has an annual coupon of 8.25% and a put date of 11/1/04. Suppose that today's date is 11/1/94. That means that the bond has 10 years until it can be put, sold back, to NBD at par. If it is not put on this date, then, barring NBD's bankruptcy, the bond continues to exist until its maturity on 11/1/24. To value the bond, we must obtain its values under the two possible maturity dates (1) the exercise date of the put and (2) the maturity date. Using simple bond valuation, we find that the yield to put is the yield, y, that sets the price equal to the present

---

[17] Another form of puttable bonds is the bond with an indexed exercise-price put option. The exercise price is indexed to the interest rate so that the bondholder will exercise the put option when the bond's yield decreases, as opposed to the standard put option case, when exercise is profitable upon an increase in bond yields. See Brick and Palmon (1993) for a discussion of these bonds.

value of the 10 years of cash flows. Since the listed price is $102.20 per $100 face value, that is

$$102.20 = \sum_{t=1}^{10} \frac{8.25}{(1 + y)^t} + \frac{100}{(1 + y)^{10}}$$

The solution is $y = 7.92\%$, which is shown in Table 16.12 as the yield to put. For the yield to maturity, simply substitute 30 years to maturity and solve:

$$102.20 = \sum_{t=1}^{30} \frac{8.25}{(1 + y)^t} + \frac{100}{(1 + y)^{30}}$$

obtaining the yield to maturity $y = 8.05\%$ shown in Table 16.12.

How is the price (in our example, $102.20) of the puttable bond obtained? To obtain this price, we must determine when the put option will be exercised. Since the exercise price is the bond's par value, the put will be exercised on 11/1/04 and the bond resold to NBD Bank, if market yields exceed 8.25% p.a. If market yields are less than or equal to 8.25% p.a., then the investor prefers to hold onto the bond for its remaining 20 years, thereby locking in the higher 8.25% annual yield until maturity on 11/1/24.

If the put option is exercised, then the investor's cash flows are the same as those for a 10 year 8.25% p.a. annual coupon bond that pays its par value of $100 at maturity on 11/1/04. Similar risk, 10 year bonds carry a yield to maturity of 8.42%, obtained from 7.92% (the yield to put) plus the yield sacrifice from Table 16.12 of 50 basis points. The present value of this bond is $98.8806 per $100 face value. But the investor buying the NBD puttable bond obtains something more than a 10 year 8.25% coupon bond yielding 8.42%. The buyer obtains a call option on a 20 year bond that will be "purchased" only if interest yields on 11/1/04 are less than or equal to 8.25%—that is, only if the put option is *not* exercised. What is the price of this option? It depends on the value of the 20 year bond to be "purchased" on 11/1/04 as well as the likelihood that the put option will not be exercised. The put option will be exercised if interest rates on 20 year bonds of equal risk exceed 8.25% p.a. To determine one possible value of the 20 year bond, we calculate an implied yield to maturity. If the 30 year yield to maturity is 8.05% p.a., as shown in Table 16.12, and the first 10 years offer a yield of 8.42% p.a., then we can calculate the yield on the last 20 years as

$$1.0805^{30} = (1.0842)^{10}(1 + y)^{20}$$

convertible bond: a bond that contains a provision that allows the bondholder to convert the bond into a predetermined number of shares of commons stock of the issuer.

Solving yields $y = 7.87\%$ p.a. The present value of a 20 year, 8.25% annual coupon bond yielding 7.87% p.a. to be received on 11/1/04 is $103.462. The call option allows the investor to purchase this bond for only $100, thereby gaining an additional $3.462. Considering other possible interest rate and credit risk scenarios produces a call option value of $3.3194 per $100 for the 20 year 8.25% coupon NBD bond. Thus, the purchase price of $102.20 comprises a $98.8806 straight 10 year bond plus a call option worth $3.3194.

Checkpoint

✓

1. Why are callable bond yields higher than comparable noncallable bond yields? Why are puttable bond yields lower than comparable nonputtable bond yields?

2. What is the option-adjusted spread?

3. What is the difference between bonds with poison put covenants and puttable bonds? What are the similarities?

Convertible Bonds   A **convertible bond** contains a provision that allows the bondholder to convert the bond into a predetermined number of shares of common stock of the issuer.

exchangeable bonds: bonds that allow the bondholder to exchange the bonds for the common stock of a firm other than the issuer of the bond.

conversion ratio: the number of shares that the bondholder receives if the call option is exercised.

conversion price: the par value of the convertible bond divided by the conversion ratio.

conversion value: the market price of the common stock times the bond's conversion ratio.

market conversion price: the market value of the convertible bond divided by the conversion ratio.

market conversion premium per share: the market conversion price minus the current stock price.

The bondholder holds the conversion option. **Exchangeable bonds** allow the bondholder to exchange the bonds for the common stock of a firm other than the issuer of the bond. The number of shares that the bondholder receives if the call option is exercised is the **conversion ratio**. The conversion period is specified on the bond. The conversion ratio may fall over time. The **conversion price** is the par value of the convertible bond divided by the conversion ratio. Thus, if the conversion ratio is 25, the conversion price for a \$100 par value bond is $\frac{\$100}{25}$ = \$4.

The convertible bond will sell at a minimum price equal to the *greater* of the following two values:

1. The bond's **conversion value**, which is the market price of the common stock times the bond's conversion ratio.

2. The bond's straight value, assuming no conversion.

Consider a seven year Aa-rated convertible bond with a 6% p.a. annual coupon. Comparable Aa-rated bonds are currently yielding 7.5% p.a. This bond's straight value is \$92.055 per \$100 face value. If the conversion ratio is 25 and the issuer's stock price is \$4.25, then the bond's conversion value is \$4.25 × 25 = \$106.25. The bond's minimum price is therefore \$106.25 since its conversion value exceeds its straight bond value.[18] However, \$106.25 is only the convertible bond's *minimum price*. Bond buyers will be willing to pay more than the convertible bond's conversion value because of the downside risk protection provided by the bond's straight value. Suppose that this convertible bond sold for \$115. The bond's **market conversion price** is the market value of the convertible bond divided by the conversion ratio. It is a measure of the market price of the stock if purchased using the convertible bond. In this example, the market conversion price is $\frac{\$115}{25}$ = \$4.60. The convertible bondholder pays \$4.60 to acquire shares worth \$4.25. The **market conversion premium per share** is the market conversion price minus the current stock price. In this example, the market conversion premium per share is \$4.60 – \$4.25 = \$0.35. The \$0.35 is a measure of the value of the downside risk protection to the bondholder provided by the straight bond value. The value of the convertible bond will therefore fall by less than the common stock. Alternatively, however, when common stock prices are rising, the value of the convertible bond will increase by less than the common stock price.

Convertible bonds are callable by the issuer. When the stock price rises, the issuer may want to force conversion by calling the bonds. Optimally, the issuer should call the bonds as soon as the conversion value is equal to the call price. If the call price for the convertible bonds in our example were \$110, then the issuer should call the bonds when the stock price reaches \$4.40, which is $\frac{\$110}{25}$. If the issuer calls the bonds when the stock price exceeds \$4.40, that conveys bad information to the market. The issuer is signaling private information that the stock price is expected to decline. Therefore, the issuer is selling stock (by forcing conversion of the bonds at the current high stock price) prior to the expected stock price decline. A number of studies show the negative stock price reaction to conversion-forcing calls when the stock price exceeds the convertible bond's call conversion value.[19]

Measuring Interest Rate Risk for Bonds with Embedded Options

In Chapter 7, we saw how duration could be used to measure a bond's price sensitivity to interest rate fluctuations. This measure was useful since it quantified the bond's price volatility for given interest rate changes. The duration measure was an approximation based on the assumption that the present value of the future cash flows in the duration calculation did not

---

[18] If the bond sold for its straight value of \$92.055, then it could be bought, converted into 25 shares, and sold for \$106.25, yielding an arbitrage profit of \$106.25 minus \$92.055, or \$14.195 per \$100 face value.

[19] See Campbell, Ederington, and Vankudre (1991) and Singh, Cowan, and Nayar (1991).

change much as interest rates fluctuated. This was not a bad approximation as long as interest rate changes were relatively small. But how would this approximation perform if not only the interest rates in the denominator of each present value term changed, but also the cash flows in the numerator changed? Not very well. This is the case of bonds with embedded options. Cash flows are tied to interest rate realizations, and a bond's price fluctuation depends on both interest rate shifts and induced cash flow shifts. We must measure the impact of interest rate changes on both the numerator and denominator of each present value term in order to assess the price volatility of bonds with embedded options.

option–adjusted
duration: the price effect
of cash flow shifts induced
by interest rate changes,
used to measure bond
price sensitivity to interest
rate fluctuations.

The **option-adjusted duration** measures the price effect of cash flow shifts induced by interest rate changes to determine bond price sensitivity to interest rate fluctuations. Using the formula for modified duration, denoted MD, from Chapter 7,

$$\Delta P \approx -MD(P)(\Delta R)$$

we can solve for modified duration as

$$MD \approx -\frac{\Delta P}{P\Delta R}$$

We can now solve for option-adjusted modified duration (denoted OAD) for any given change in interest rates. That is, we value the bond using the binomial interest rate tree method for any two interest rates and then take the difference to get the measure of $OAD = -\Delta P/P\Delta R$.

Using our earlier example of the three year 5% annual coupon callable bond, we can illustrate the calculation of the option-adjusted duration. We found that the price of the callable bond was $99.642 per $100 face value. Consider the impact of a one basis point increase in interest rates.[20] That is, increase all interest rates at each node on the tree by one basis point. Figure 16.5 shows the cash flows on each branch and node on all three tiers. The price of the bond declines to $99.623. Using this measure of price sensitivity, we can calculate a measure of the option-adjusted duration:

$$OAD = -\frac{99.623 - 99.642}{99.642(.0001)} = 1.907$$

The option-adjusted duration of 1.907 years reflects the impact of the potential for a call at the end of the first year. If we use the duration formula from Chapter 7, we see that the duration of the noncallable bond is 2.86 years. The callable bond's option-adjusted duration is therefore below the duration of the noncallable bond.

The duration measure is a linear approximation of bond price sensitivity to interest rate fluctuations. This linear approximation performs quite poorly for bonds with embedded call options. The reason should be clear from the previous example. Even small rate changes cause shifts in both the discount factor (in the denominator of each term) and the cash flows (in the numerator of each term). This undermines the assumption that duration is unaffected by rate changes. To correct this inaccuracy, we saw in Chapter 7 that we could use a measure called convexity. The convexity is a measure of the curvature of the bond's price as a function of its yield.

Figure 16.6 shows the impact of the call option on the bond's convexity. The noncallable bond has the standard convex relationship between price and yields. As yields decrease, prices increase. However, the equivalent callable bond price is bounded from above. If yields decrease

---

[20] Since the solution is sensitive to the assumed interest rates, this calculation would have to be performed for many different interest rate scenarios where each was weighted by its likelihood of occurrence, just as for the binomial interest rate tree method. Such computations are beyond the scope of this book.

**Binomial interest rate tree for a callable bond with
a 1 basis point rate increase across the board**

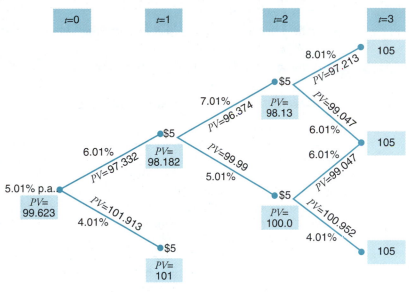

Figure 16.5

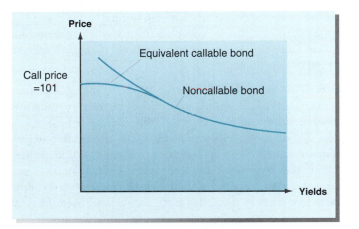

Figure 16.6

so that the noncallable bond price is above the callable bond's call price (in our example, $101),
then the bond will be called. That is, the bond's price can never exceed the call price.[21] At some
rate, further decreases in bond yields no longer increase bond prices for callable bonds. This
creates **negative convexity** in which the price appreciation is less than the price depreciation
for a large change in yields. The callable bond in Figure 16.6 exhibits negative convexity during
the range of interest rates in which the price-yield curve flattens out. Negative convexity is
detrimental to bondholders' returns since the upside price gain potential from interest rate
decreases is limited.

negative convexity:
condition under which the
price appreciation is less
than the price
depreciation for a large
change in yields.

---

[21] This is strictly true only on a coupon payment date, since on any other date, the bond's price is increased by
accrued interest.

1. What determines the price of convertible bonds? When do they trade like equity and when like bonds?

2. Why is the duration approximation particularly ill suited to measuring the price sensitivity of callable bonds?

3. Why do callable bonds have negative convexity?

Other Developments in Corporate Bond Issues

Innovations in corporate bond issues may be a response to cyclical forces. At the height of Japan's 1980s bull market, JY 10 trillion worth of convertible bonds and equity-linked warrants were issued. They carried coupons that were often less than 1% in exchange for the possibility that they would be converted into high-flying equity. These days the high flyers have come back to earth, and fixed rate, bullet bond issues are experiencing a resurgence in Japan.

The Japanese shift toward straight debt issues is particularly dramatic because of the lack of a well-developed secondary bond market in Japan. Indeed, until 1993 issuance of corporate bonds in Japan was hampered by the existence of a rule that limited domestic corporate bonds to twice the value of the company's net worth. In 1994, the ceiling was increased to three times corporate net worth, thereby further encouraging Japanese corporations to issue corporate bonds domestically. At the same time, the Ministry of Finance removed restrictions on debt maturities, allowing the issuance of both fixed and floating corporate bonds with maturities that could range between two and ten years. However, the development of an active secondary market in Japanese corporate debt has been stunted by the absence of a centralized trading and clearing system, as well as by tax policies that levy a transfer tax of 3% on sales and 1% on purchases. This policy encourages a buy and hold strategy, thus making the Japanese corporate bond market quite illiquid.

Medium Term Notes (MTN)   In the 1970s the major U.S. automobile companies sought a way to sell bonds with flexible maturities of between two and five years. Unfortunately, at the time, most debt instruments were either commercial paper securities, with maturities of less than 270 days, or bonds with maturities of 10 years and longer. Borrowers who wanted to maintain maturity flexibility had to commit to one extreme or the other. Particularly in the days before shelf registration, this made it very difficult for bond issuers to time their issues to market movements, since the registration process was so time consuming.

medium term note (MTN) programs, mezzanine financing: a schedule of notes with maturities usually ranging from 1 to 10 years that are offered either continuously or intermittently over time.

Shelf registration, introduced in 1982, coupled with **medium term note (MTN) programs**, also known as **mezzanine financing**, provided a solution to offer corporations debt-financing flexibility. A MTN program of mezzanine financing is a schedule of notes with maturities usually ranging from 1 to 10 years that are offered either continuously or intermittently over time. This plan enables the corporation to register its MTN program and put it on the shelf until financial conditions are ripe for issuance. The issuer posts rates and amounts for various maturity ranges: 9 months to 1 year; 1 year to 18 months; 18 months to 2 years; until 30 years or even longer.[22] Investors choose among the MTN maturities offered. MTN issuance increased from $20 billion in 1985 to $540 billion in 1994. Figure 16.7 shows the phenomenal growth of this flexible instrument. As the yield curve shifted, for example, corporate issuers could take advantage of maturities with relatively low rates by shifting their MTN issues and pricing to reflect market conditions. U.S. banks have availed themselves of the flexibility of MTNs. Although the rate of growth slowed somewhat in 1996, the debt instrument of choice

---

[22] In July 1993, Walt Disney Corporation issued a security with a 100 year maturity using its MTN shelf registration program.

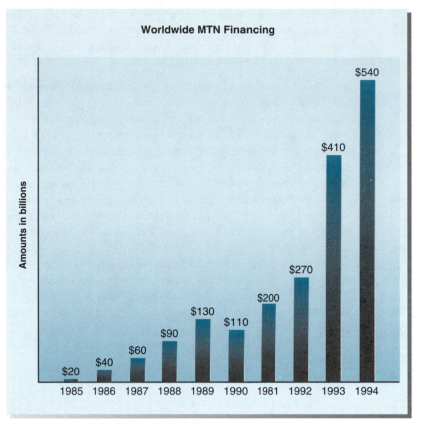

Worldwide MTN Financing

Amounts in billions

$540

$410

$270

$200

$130 $110

$90

$60

$40

$20

1985 1986 1987 1988 1989 1990 1981 1992 1993 1994

Source: Investment Dealers' Digest, May 22, 1995

Figure 16.7

was the MTN, enabling banks to reduce their cost of funds by replacing higher cost liabilities with relatively low-cost MTNs.

MTNs were combined with derivatives in structured note programs to offer investors unusual returns. These **structured notes** account for between 20 and 30% of all new MTN issues. The most common derivative embedded in a structured note is a swap. This instrument allows investors who are required to hold investment-grade vehicles to hedge their risk exposure using previously inaccessible swap vehicles. Investors typically approach the FI that serves as the agent for the MTN issue and request a specific cash flow adjustment—for example, switching currencies, or switching from fixed rate to floating rate or vice versa, or restating the benchmark rate to another fixed rate or to equity or to an index, and so on. The FI then finds the appropriate derivatives transaction to produce the desired cash flows.

Surplus notes are another innovation that stems primarily from regulatory policies. In 1993, in order to encourage insurance companies to increase their capital levels, regulators required the issuance of surplus notes, which were long term bonds with payments subordinated to all other liabilities, including policyholder claims. Indeed, regulators retain the right to approve each principal or interest payment on the surplus notes, thus making surplus notes similar to preferred stock. Since regulators consider these notes to be equity-like, they may block regular payments of interest for marginal insurance companies. For top-rated insurance companies, however, these notes can be considered investment-grade debt, since regulators are unlikely to

structured notes: MTNs combined with derivative transactions.

surplus notes: long term bonds issued by insurance companies with payments subordinated to all other liabilities, including policyholder claims.

block interest payments for sound companies. Since they retain equity characteristics but are priced like debt, surplus notes are an inexpensive source of capital for insurance companies. During the first year of their introduction, from April 1993 to April 1994, insurance companies issued more than $3.5 billion of surplus notes.

Asset-Based Borrowing   Only the most creditworthy firms are able to obtain investment-grade bond ratings that allow them to finance using publicly traded debt. Less creditworthy or "informationally handicapped" firms that are difficult for the market to evaluate are forced to rely on bank debt for financing. However, some corporate borrowers, particularly those with high levels of leverage or depressed earnings, find that even bank debt is unavailable. Indeed, a 1994 Arthur Andersen study showed that 38% of small and midsized businesses had "unfilled working capital needs that prevented them from expanding their businesses." Many of these companies find a solution to their financing problems using **asset-based borrowing**. Asset-based borrowing links financing levels with collateral based on the company's assets and operations. For example, an asset-based loan can be based on a percentage of accounts receivable and inventory.

Most asset-based debt instruments are packages of revolving credit lines secured by receivables and inventory plus term loans secured by real assets (such as real estate or equipment) as collateral. The revolving line of credit acts as an available pool of funds. The lender extends credit based on an agreed percentage, usually 80 to 90% of accounts receivables or 50% of inventory. The borrower can take down the line and borrow the funds, up to the credit limit, as needed. The lender monitors accounts receivables and general business conditions by requiring detailed monthly reports.

asset-based borrowing: loans that link financing levels with collateral based on the company's assets and operations.

Checkpoint

1.   What are medium term notes?

2.   How do financial conditions impact the structure of corporate debt issues?

3.   Why did MTNs grow so rapidly as a financing vehicle?

4.   Why are lenders willing to buy the asset–backed bonds of even the most risky firms?

➤ Issuing, Trading, and Clearing Corporate Bonds

Underwriting

Most corporate debt and private placements are underwritten by investment banks on a firm commitment basis. This guarantees that the issuer receives a certain amount of proceeds from the bond issue. However, MTNs are typically underwritten on a best efforts "bought as sold" basis, reflecting the investor's discretion in choosing among an entire program of maturities and structures. Since the terms of the MTN transaction can change at any time, the FI acts as an agent for the MTN issuer and must get the terms of each transaction approved by the issuer.

Although banks are not well represented in the top 15 underwriters shown in Table 16.13, their market share of U.S. corporate bond issues is growing. This is a result of regulatory changes that make it possible for banks to underwrite limited amounts of debt via their Section 20 subsidiaries. As described in Chapter 5, Section 20 subsidiaries are wholly owned bank holding company affiliates that are allowed to engage in investment banking lines of business such as underwriting. The name "Section 20" comes from the Glass-Steagall Act of 1933, which prohibited banks from affiliating with a company "engaged principally. . . [in the] issue floatation, underwriting, public sale, or distribution at wholesale or retail or through syndicate participation of stocks, bonds, debentures, notes, or other securities." In 1968, Congress

Table
16.13

Underwriting Investment Grade Debt, January 1, 1994–June 30, 1995[a]

Underwriter	Amount ($m)	Rank	Pct. of Issues	No. of Issues	Amount ($m)	Rank	Pct. of Issues	No. of Issues
	January 1, 1995–June 30, 1995				January 1, 1994–June 30, 1994			
Merrill Lynch	60,508.5	1	27.7	366	55,593.7	1	28.1	310
Morgan Stanley	41,790.3	2	19.1	267	39,492.0	4	20.0	217
Goldman Sachs	40,482.8	3	18.5	243	45,974.3	2	23.2	249
Lehman Bros.	37,630.3	4	17.2	248	44,634.0	3	22.6	277
JP Morgan	35,766.6	5	16.4	204	24,711.7	7	12.5	121
Salomon Bros.	34,194.4	6	15.6	252	32,443.6	6	16.4	271
CS First Boston	33,366.2	7	15.3	194	35,285.4	5	17.8	211
Bear Stearns	15,218.5	8	7.0	133	11,902.4	9	6.0	95
First Tennessee	12,349.7	9	5.6	158	6,302.6	14	3.2	59
Smith Barney	11,288.3	10	5.2	107	11,084.3	11	5.6	86
UBS	10,280.6	11	4.7	95	7,226.5	13	3.7	54
Donaldson, Lufkin	10,207.7	12	4.7	79	11,139.7	10	5.6	94
PaineWebber	9,304.4	13	4.3	95	13,183.6	8	6.7	126
Chase Manhattan	6,819.2	14	3.1	101	1,583.3	31	0.8	13
Deutsche Bank	6,749.9	15	3.1	16	3,926.2	20	2.0	10
Total	218,753.4		100	2,416	197,751.4		100	2,094

[a]All issues excluding mortgage and asset-backed securities, convertible debt, and junk bonds, but including taxable municipal securities and federal agency debt. Full credit for each issue is attributed to the lead underwriter in each issue. U.S. domestic and Yankee issues are included.

Source: Investment Dealers' Digest, July 10, 1995.

authorized banks to underwrite municipal revenue bonds used to finance housing, university, and dormitory construction. On April 30, 1987, the Board of Governors of the Federal Reserve authorized Citicorp, JP Morgan, and Bankers Trust to underwrite and sell municipal revenue bonds, mortgage-related securities, consumer receivables, and commercial paper. On January 18, 1989, the Fed added corporate debt and equity underwriting to the list of permissible Section 20 subsidiary activities. As of year end 1996, gross revenues from these activities must not exceed 25% of the bank holding company's total revenue. Most large, money center banks in the United States have Section 20 affiliates. In 1991, they underwrote $16.1 billion in corporate debt issues, for a 9.58% market share (34.2% share of the noninvestment grade market).

Competition for bond underwritings has reached a high pitch even on tightly controlled French financial markets. In October 1993 a cartel agreement was reached among French banks that set strict guidelines for the distribution of underwritings among the leading banks, such that, for instance, Banque Nationale de Paris, Credit Lyonnais, Casisse Nationale du Credit Agricole, CNCA, Banque Paribas, and Societe Generale were all guaranteed 8.5% of any new bond issue over FFr1 billion. The market's response to this restrictive agreement was a flight of new issuers from the cartelized French domestic market to the Euro French franc free market. In March 1995 the agreement (called the *bareme*, or schedule price) was discontinued, and free distribution of all underwritings was permitted in the French domestic bond market.

2 Corp BF

SECURITIES FOUND

PAGE 1 OF 25

SHORT NAME	(TICKER)	COUPON	MATURITY	PRICE BID/ASK	YIELD BID/ASK	DUR	CURR
ITT HARTFORD	(HIG)	8.3	12/1/1	105.031/77	7.17/95	4.53 A1	DOL
BARCLAYS	(BACR)	10.5	12/15/17-97	110.230/230	6.45/45	1.38 AA3	DOL
BARCLAYS 03-S	(BACR)	11 5/8	5/1/3-98	108.125/218	6.96/91	1.74 AA3	DOL
ONT 9 1/2	(ONTSTP)	0	7/13/97	93.953/953	5.80/80	1.09	CD
QUEBEC PROVI	(Q)	9 3/8	12/20/99	111.594/844	5.64/56	3.07	FR
SWEDEN KINGD	(SWED)	FLOAT	2/24/99	100.445/695			DM
DUPONT	(DD)	5.1	2/1/0	95.563/570	6.99/89	4.72 AA3	DOL
UNC INC	(UNC)	9 1/8	7/1/97	96.718/718	9.77/77	5.15 B1	DOL

 05-June-96 14:15:56

Figure 16.8

Secondary Market Trading

Anywhere from 88% to 99% of the trading in corporate bonds in the United States takes place outside an organized exchange such as the New York Stock Exchange. Indeed, in 1990 only 40 of the 1,340 new issues were listed on the NYSE. Although the number of new listings tripled to 96 in 1993, the value of bonds traded on the NYSE totaled $4.63 billion during the first half of 1993, a decline of 12.5% from the year earlier.

Trading in corporate bonds still takes place over the counter using an antiquated paper-based system on which firms post prices on "Axe" sheets. In June 1995 a proprietary trading system called BondNet was introduced, which electronically transmits price bids and offers for market makers. It covers more than 33,000 fixed income securities such as high-grade U.S. corporate bonds, medium term notes, agency securities, and Canadian and Yankee bonds.

Bond price quotations can be obtained in electronic forms (see Figure 16.8). The bonds are identified by their name (note that the "s" in the BARCLAYS 03-5 denotes semiannual coupon payments), the ticker symbol, the coupon payment (note the zero coupon ONTSTP and the floating rate SWED), the maturity date, the duration, the rating, and the currency of denomination. The price is stated both in monetary terms and in yields (using the simple interest yield to maturity). The bid price is usually less than the ask price, so that the bid yield is usually higher than the ask yield, reflecting the profit to the market maker, which consists of the bid-ask spread.

Clearing Corporate Bond Trades

Just as the corporate bond trading system is antiquated, the clearing system is extremely efficient. Corporate bond trades are settled using an electronic system that employs multilateral and multi-issue netting. At the end of each day, each FI obtains a net total of all trades made with each counterparty FI during the course of the day. A single cash flow is exchanged between each pair of FIs to settle the day's transactions. Simultaneously, the net trades of each issue of corporate bonds are calculated and the appropriate amount of securities are transferred between each pair of FIs at the end of the day. This transfer is performed electronically so that the physical securities are never moved.

depository: storage for physical securities so that transfers can be made electronically.

This highly efficient mechanism for settlement is run by two sister corporations: the Depository Trust Company (DTC) and the National Securities Clearing Corporation (NSCC). The DTC was established in the late 1960s by the New York Stock Exchange, the American Stock Exchange, and the National Association of Securities Dealers. The DTC is a **depository** for all corporate bonds and stocks with a CUSIP number. The CUSIP is an identifier code assigned to each issue. The depository institution stores the physical securities so that transfers can be made electronically. The securities never leave the vault, although their ownership is transferred through electronic book entries. By immobilizing approximately 2.5 trillion physical securities, this book-entry settlement process dramatically reduces the cost and risk of transactions.

In 1977 the NSCC was formed to clear interbroker trades. It is equally owned by the NYSE, AMEX, and NASD but is run by a 16-member board consisting of two banks and 14 securities firms. NSCC processes the trades for about 300 FIs, clearing more than 500,000 trades each day, representing about 90% of all trading each day in U.S. securities markets. Each pair of FIs ends up, at the end of the day, with a net position in cash and a net position in each security issue. Once each FI confirms the positions, NSCC guarantees settlement. To self-insure against losses, NSCC has a "defense fund" exceeding $320 million, obtained by requiring each FI to deposit an amount of capital that is proportional to its daily settlement volume. NSCC has a subsidiary that performs international settlement, interfacing with clearinghouses such as Euroclear and Cedel. In addition to NSCC, transactions between FIs are cleared through an institutional delivery system, using a custodial bank as the clearinghouse for each pair of FIs.

In June 1995 securities markets moved to a T + 3 day settlement schedule, which states that trades have three days to be settled from the date on which the transactions are agreed upon. This is a reduction from the previous five day settlement period. In reality, settlement periods across countries vary widely. Germany has a one day settlement period, whereas Italy has T + 51 day settlement. Shorter settlement periods reduce transaction costs and fuel security market activity since there the time between feasible transactions is reduced. However, if the settlement period is too short,[23] then **fails** are more likely to occur. Fails occur if either counterparty fails to deliver on the transaction as agreed. On an average day's activity of 30,000 transactions, Euroclear experiences approximately 70 fails. Although fails represent only a small proportion of total trading volume, they are costly because they must be unwound manually.

> **fails:** the consequence of either counterparty's failure to deliver on the transaction as agreed.

T+3 settlement is required for retail transactions. However, institutional transactions among FIs must be settled on a T+1 basis. In January 1996 the SEC required same-day settlement among FIs. Then transactions can be settled in immediately available funds, such as Federal Funds, by 3 P.M. on the date of the trade. This arrangement requires FIs to invest in highly efficient back-office facilities, suggesting that this will be an important profit center for FIs in the future. This topic is discussed in *Timely Topics 16.2: Squeezed: U.S. Players Have Less Time to Do Business*.

TIMELY TOPICS 16.2

SQUEEZED: U.S. PLAYERS HAVE LESS TIME TO DO BUSINESS

Buyers and sellers of corporate bonds and equities settle their transactions through links to the Depository Trust Company (DTC), an industry utility in New York that keeps accounts for broker/dealers and banks, and facilitates securities deliveries against payments through automation. No cash or certificates need to change hands on the day of the transaction. Many of these deals are payable in next-day money, but by the end of 1995, all payments for institutional securities trades will have to be paid in immediately useable funds when the securities are received on settlement date. . . .

Banks and broker/dealer back offices view the anticipated efficiencies of same-day funds as a boon. But their colleagues in securities lending are furling their brows at the

---

[23] Germany's T+1 settlement reflects a *lengthening* of the settlement period from same-day settlement. The goal is to comply with international T+3 day standards.

move, since with same-day funds processing a honed system for borrowing, lending, and returning securities will have to be scrapped. . . .

All securities practices will have to be re-examined and reorganized. After years of using a clearinghouse fund system, lenders will have to be more creative in investing funds later in the day, and borrowers savvier at accurately determining their needs as early as possible.

Some expect a shake-out in the US lending business. When timing more than ever before will be of the essence, lenders who are ready for the new environment may well muscle in on the business of those who aren't. . . . Under same-day funds, lenders and borrowers will be on either end of a tether, each pulling for more time. Lenders will want to know about new loans or returned ones as early as possible to make their investments for that day. Borrowers meanwhile, may need to hunt around for securities among institutions willing to lend later because they won't know what securities they'll need until then. . . . Large custodians such as State Street Bank & Trust, which uses proprietary links with money managers that trade for their mutual clients, are perhaps best positioned of all. Over these settlement systems, the custodian can receive early notice of trades which they can then match with their clients' securities holdings to see which are loaned. But even these systems are not comprehensive. A custodian like State Street works with numerous investment managers, only some of which are linked to the bank over electronic systems.

Source: G. Wisz, *International Securities Lending*, First Quarter 1995, pp. 26–28.

Checkpoint

✓

1. Contrast the firm commitment and best efforts methods of underwriting. Which is less expensive to the issuer?

2. Describe the clearing and trading systems for corporate debt.

➤ Summary

In this chapter, we described and evaluated corporate debt instruments ranging from publicly traded bullet bonds to nontraded bank debt. The advantages of each form of debt to the business borrower were examined. Publicly traded debt tends to be the least costly to the borrower. However, there are information costs that could be insurmountable to smaller firms with large amounts of intangible assets. To resolve some of the information problems, these firms may turn to private placement debt or they may include bond covenants to position bondholders' claims in the event of financial distress. For the most "informationally handicapped" firms, bank debt or asset-backed debt may be the only feasible source of financing.

Publicly traded debt may be sold as straight debt, at either a fixed or a floating rate. Alternatively, many corporate debt issues are sold with embedded options that alter the bond's cash flows under different interest rate or credit quality scenarios. The most common form of embedded option is the callable bond. Since the call option is exercised by the issuer when interest rates are low enough to make refinancing worthwhile, callable bond yields exceed those of comparable noncallable bonds. In contrast, puttable bonds protect the bondholder and thus carry yields that are lower than the yield on comparable nonputtable bonds. Convertible bonds can be exchanged for equity and provide the bondholder with the possibility of common stock's upside gain potential. Convertible bonds will trade like equity when their conversion value is very high relative to their straight bond value. In contrast, convertible bond values will approach a minimum value equal to their straight debt value when stock prices are low.

References

Bagnani, E., N. Milonas, A. Saunders, and N. Travlos. "Managers, Owners, and the Pricing of Risky Debt: An Empirical Analysis." *Journal of Finance* 49, No. 2 (June 1994): 453–477.

Bennett, T., S. Esser, and C. Roth. "Corporate Credit Risk and Reward." *Journal of Portfolio Management* 20, No. 3 (Spring 1994): 39–47.

Berger, A., A. Kashyap, and J. Scalise. "The Transformation of the U.S. Banking Industry: What a Long, Strange Trip It's Been." *Brookings Papers on Economic Activity* 2 (1995).

Berger, A. and G. Udell. "Relationship Lending and Lines of Credit in Small Firm Finance." *Journal of Business* 68 (July 1995): 351–382.

Betker, B. "Equity's Bargaining Power and Deviations from Absolute Priority in Chapter 11 Bankruptcies." Working Paper, Ohio State University, 1993.

Billett, M., M. Flannery, and J. Garfinkel. "The Effect of Lender Identity on a Borrowing Firm's Equity Return." *Journal of Finance* (June 1995): 699–718.

Brick, I., and O. Palmon. "The Tax Advantages of Refunding Debt by Calling, Repurchasing, and Putting." *Financial Management* (Winter 1993): 96–105.

Brick, I., and B. Wallingford. "The Relative Tax Benefits of Alternative Call Features in Corporate Debt." *Journal of Financial and Quantitative Analysis* (March 1985): 95–105.

Campbell, C. J., L. H. Ederington, and P. Vankudre. "Tax Shields, Sample-Selection Bias, and the Information Content of Conversion-Forcing Bond Calls." *Journal of Finance* (September 1991): 1291–1324.

Crabbe, L. "An Analysis of Losses to Bondholders and 'Super Poison Put' Bond Covenants." *Journal of Finance* 46 (1991): 689–706.

Crabbe, L., and J. Helwege. "Alternative Tests of Agency Theories of Callable Corporate Bonds." *Financial Management* (Winter 1994): 3–20.

Damodaran, A. *Damodaran on Valuation*, New York: John Wiley & Sons, 1994.

Fabozzi, F. *Bond Markets, Analysis and Strategies*. 3rd ed. Upper Saddle River, N.J.: Prentice Hall, 1996.

Ferris, S. P., N. Jayaraman, and A. K. Makhija. "Direct Costs of Bankruptcy: Evidence from Filings of Liquidations and Reorganizations by Small Firms." Working Paper, Georgia Institute of Technology, 1993.

Fons, J. "Using Default Rates to Model the Term Structure of Credit Risk." *Financial Analysts Journal* (September–October 1994): 25–32.

Gertler, M., and S. Gilchrist. "Monetary Policy, Business Cycles, and the Behavior of Small Manufacturing Firms." *Quarterly Journal of Economics* 109 (1994): 309–340.

Gilchrist, S., and E. Zakrajsek. "The Importance of Credit for Macroeconomic Activity: Identification Through Heterogeneity." Working Paper, June 1995.

Gilson, S., K. John, and L. Lang. "Troubled Debt Restructurings: An Empirical Study of Private Reorganization of Firms in Default." *Journal of Financial Economics* (October 1990): 355–388.

Hardy, T. "Power to the Creditors." *Forbes*, March 27, 1995, p. 148.

Helwege, J., and P. Kleiman. "Understanding Aggregate Default Rates of High Yield Bonds." Federal Reserve Bank of New York *Current Issues* 2, No. 6 (May 1996).

Hull, R., and R. Moellenberndt. "Bank Debt Reduction Announcements and Negative Signaling." *Financial Management* 23, No. 2 (Summer 1994): 21–30.

James, C. "Some Evidence of the Uniqueness of Bank Loans." *Journal of Financial Economics* 19 (1987): 217–235.

John, K. "Financial Distress." *Financial Management* (Autumn 1993): 60–77.

Joon, I. K., K. Ramaswamy, and S. Sundaresan. "Does Default Risk in Coupons Affect the Valuation of Corporate Bonds?: A Contingent Claims Model." *Financial Management* (Winter 1993): 117–131.

Kahn, S. "Buying Discounted Debt." *Global Finance* 5, No. 11 (November 1991): 58.

Kalotay, A., and B. Tuckman. "Sinking Fund Prepurchases and the Designation Option." *Financial Management* (Winter 1992): 110–118.

Lucas, D. "Default Correlation and Credit Analysis." *Journal of Fixed Income* (March 1995): 76–87.

Lummer, S., and J. McConnell. "Further Evidence on the Bank Lending Process and the Capital Market Response to Bank Loan Agreements." *Journal of Financial Economics* 25 (1989): 99–122.

McCauley, R., and R. Seth. "Foreign Bank Credit to U.S. Corporations: The Implications of Offshore Loans." Federal Reserve Bank of New York *Quarterly Review* (Spring 1992): 52–65.

Merton, R. "On the Pricing of Corporate Debt: The Risk Structure of Interest Rates." *Journal of Finance* 29, (1974): 449–470.

Merton, R., and Z. Bodie. "On the Management of Financial Guarantees." *Financial Management* (Winter 1992): 87–109.

Mikkelson, W., and M. Partch. "Valuation Effects of Securities Offerings and the Issuance Process." *Journal of Financial Economics* 15, (1986): 31–60.

Opler, T. "Controlling Financial Distress Costs in Leveraged Buyouts with Financial Innovations." *Financial Management* (Winter 1993): 79–90.

Petersen, M., and R. Rajan. "The Benefits of Lending Relationships: Evidence from Small Business Data." *Journal of Finance* 49 (March 1994): 3–38.

Rajan, R. G. "Insiders and Outsiders: The Choice Between Informed and Arm's-Length Debt." *Journal of Finance* 43, No. 2 (1992): 1367–1400.

Sharp, R. *The Lore and the Legends of Wall Street.* Homewood, Ill.: Dow Jones-Irwin, 1989.

Singh, A. K., A. R. Cowan, and N. Nayar. "Underwritten Calls of Convertible Bonds." *Journal of Financial Economics* (March 1991): 173–196.

▶ Questions

1. Use the cumulative default rates in Table 16.11 to calculate the price, yield, and default risk premium for each of the following bonds:
    a. Five year risk free government bond with an annual coupon rate of 7.5% p.a. with a yield to maturity of 7.5% p.a.
    b. Five year A-rated corporate bond with an annual coupon rate of 7.5%.
    c. Five year B-rated corporate bond with an annual coupon rate of 7.5%.

2. Use a binomial interest rate tree where 100 basis point increases and decreases in interest rates are equally probable at each node to value:
    a. A noncallable three year bond with a 7% annual coupon if current one year yields are 8% p.a.
    b. A callable three year bond with a 7% annual coupon with one year until first call date if current one year yields are 8% p.a. (Assume that the bond is callable at par.)
    c. What is the call premium expressed in basis points?

3. Decompose the puttable bond prices (as of the issue date in 1995) in Table 16.12 into their straight bond values and the embedded option value.

4. Use the Black-Scholes model to price risky, noncallable debt if the risk free rate is 10% p.a.; the firm's asset risk $\sigma^2 = 20\%$; $t = 10$ years; the face value of debt, $K = \$50$ million; and the firm's assets, A, are currently valued at $100 million.

5. State the bid-ask quotations for the following bonds:
    a. A five year, 8% p.a. semiannual coupon bond with a bid price of $95.75 per $100 face value and a bid-ask spread of $0.25.
    b. A 25 year, 12% p.a. quarterly coupon bond with an ask price of $107.50 per $100 face value and a bid-ask spread of $1.05.
    c. A two year, 6.75% p.a. annual coupon bond with an ask yield of 4.90% p.a. and a bid-ask spread of three basis points.
    d. A six year, 10% p.a. semiannual coupon bond with a bid yield of 5.75% p.a. and a bid-ask spread of five basis points.

6. Use the schedule of rate differentials on the following page, together with a risk free rate of 7% p.a. to price the following corporate bonds:

Bond Type	Basis Points	Bond Covenant	Basis Points
AAA-rating	9	Specialist sponsors	61
AA-rating	18	Strip financing	15
A-rating	22	Payment-in-kind debt	10
BBB-rating	37	Third-party guarantee	75
BB-rating	42	Sinking fund	50
B-rating	65	Lien restrictions	25
2 yr. duration	15	Lease covenants	18
3 yr. duration	27	New debt limits	25
4 yr. duration	41	Dividend restrictions	22

a. AA-rated bonds with a duration of three years, a sinking fund, dividend restrictions, and a credit enhancement consisting of a third-party guarantee.

b. B-rated bonds with a duration of two years, lien restrictions, specialist sponsors, and limitations on new debt.

c. BBB-rated bonds with a duration of four years, lease and sale-leaseback covenants, strip financing, payment-in-kind debt, and specialist sponsors.

7. Suppose that a corporation can issue one year 10% p.a. annual coupon bonds that generate proceeds of $25 million to be invested in a project that guarantees a 25% p.a. yield at the end of the year.

   a. Would shareholders invest in the project if the corporation's current market value balance sheet (before the investment) consisted of the market value of assets equal to $99 million and the market value of liabilities equal to $100 million?

   b. Would shareholders invest in the project if the corporation's current market value balance sheet (before the investment) consisted of the market value of assets equal to $90 million and the market value of liabilities equal to $100 million?

   c. Why are your answers to parts (a) and (b) different?

8. Calculate the conversion price for the following convertible bonds:

   a. $100,000 par value bonds with a conversion ratio of 750.

   b. $100 par value bonds with a conversion ratio of 5.

   c. $1,000 par value bonds with a conversion ratio of 35.

9a. Use the binomial tree method to calculate the price of the noncallable bond in question 2a if all interest rates increase by 1% at each point in time.

9b. Use the duration formula of Chapter 7 to calculate the duration of the noncallable bond.

10a. Calculate the price of the callable bond in question 2b if all interest rates increase by 1% at each point in time.

10b. Use your answer to part (a) to calculate the option-adjusted duration of the callable bond.

10c. Compare the durations of the callable and noncallable bonds.

CHAPTER 17

EQUITY

"Wall Street is a street that begins in a graveyard and ends in a river."—Anonymous

- To examine the issuance and trading of common and preferred stock.

- To understand the role of FIs in innovating financial securities with equity components, particularly for preferred stocks.

- To learn about recent changes in equity markets in the wake of the market crashes of 1987 and 1989, as well as several trading scandals on the Nasdaq and other markets.

➤ Introduction

The dullest day in recorded U.S. stock market history was March 16, 1830, when 26 shares of the U.S. Bank traded for $119 and five shares of the Morris Canal and Banking Company sold for $75.25. The total volume of trades on that day was $3,470.25.[1] Contrast that with the record daily volume of trading on the New York Stock Exchange which took place on July 16, 1996. A total of 680.3 million shares changed hands on that day, utilizing just over half of the exchange's volume capacity.

The current specialist system of trading on the New York Stock Exchange developed because a broker named Boyd broke his leg in 1875. Until that time, prices were determined using a method called the **call through**, which is a noncontinuous auction during which all issues are called once or twice a day. Bids are accepted during those times only.[2] The most popular stocks were traded continuously in pits adjacent to the auction room. Brokers had to rush back and forth between the auction room and the pits to execute their trades. Sometimes they missed the best prices because they were in the wrong place at the wrong time.

When he broke his leg, Boyd placed a chair on the floor of the exchange and announced that he would trade only shares of Western Union, one of the most actively traded stocks of

call through: a noncontinuous auction during which all issues are called once or twice a day.

---

[1] Sharp (1989), p. 93.

[2] For example, the *itayose* on the Japanese stock market is a call auction used to set opening and sometimes closing prices. The call through is also used on the Tel Aviv stock exchange.

the time. Brokers would tell Boyd the price at which they were willing to trade, and he would fill the order when the market moved to the stated price (or limit price in today's jargon). He guaranteed other brokers good execution of their orders and charged a fee for each trade. Boyd's broken leg therefore resulted in the evolution of both the limit price and the specialist system. Today all stocks on the NYSE and AMEX trade through a specialist, and 45% of all trades on the NYSE originate from limit prices.

▶ World Equity Markets

World stock market capitalization, the market value of equity outstanding (price per share times number of shares outstanding), for developed countries exceeded $13 trillion in 1994, quadruple the nominal level of 10 years earlier. Equity markets are also characterized by greater global integration than in the past. U.S. investor holdings of foreign stocks in 1993 totaled $210 billion, more than double the level of 1990. Moreover, foreign companies on London's International Stock Exchange represent more than 50% of market capitalization, although U.K. securities dominate trading, with 80% of the turnover. Both measures of activity, market capitalization and stock turnover, are shown in Table 17.1 for selected equity markets throughout the world. In 1989 the total value of stock traded in Japan exceeded that of the U.S. stock market for the first time, although in 1994 the size of U.S. equity markets (measured using

Table 17.1

Equity Markets Around the World, End of 1994[a]

Country	Market Capitalization ($m)	Stock Turnover ($m)	Number of Listed Domestic Cos.
Australia	219,188	94,726	1,144
Belgium	84,103	12,820	155
Brazil	189,281	109,498	544
Canada	451,263	161,058	1,185
France	451,263	615,371	459
Germany	470,519	460,617	317
Greece	14,921	5,145	216
Hong Kong	269,508	147,158	529
Italy	180,135	117,894	223
Japan	3,719,914	1,121,438	2,205
Korea	191,778	286,056	699
Malaysia	199,276	126,458	478
Mexico	130,246	82,964	206
Netherlands	283,251	170,596	317
South Africa	225,718	15,974	640
Singapore	134,516	81,054	240
Spain	154,858	61,452	379
Sweden	130,939	85,407	114
Switzerland	284,092	226,723	237
Taiwan	247,325	711,346	313
Thailand	131,479	80,188	389
United Kingdom	1,210,245	928,171	2,070
United States	5,081,810	3,592,668	7,770

[a]Market capitalization based on end of 1994 market values of listed domestic companies. Value of trading based on end of 1994 total value traded of listed domestic companies.

Source: 1995 Factbook: Emerging Markets Database.

either market capitalization or stock turnover shown in Table 17.1) again exceeded levels in Japan.[3]

German equity markets are far less developed than those of the United States, the United Kingdom, or Japan. German businesses rely on bank lending to finance their operations, as opposed to equity issues.[4] In the United States, financial markets are much more important in financing business activity, whereas in Germany banks represent a much larger portion of the economy (189% of GDP in Germany as opposed to only 87% of GDP in the United States in 1989). Market capitalization on all German equity markets represented only 28% of GDP as of the end of 1989.[5] In contrast, stock market capitalization represented 51% of GDP in the United States and 132% of GDP in Japan in 1989.[6]

U.S. equity market activity, as measured in Table 17.1, is larger than in any other country in the world. Around 50% of external funds raised by nonfinancial firms in the United States has been obtained through the sale of securities. In contrast, nonfinancial businesses in most other countries use financial markets to raise only about 10% of their financings. Figure 17.1 shows the distribution of equity market capitalization across the world in 1994. The share of developed markets was 87%, whereas emerging markets represented 13% of the value of global equities.

Equity activity in developing countries has been increasing in recent years. Total equity flows to emerging countries were $13.2 billion in 1993, almost quadruple the level in 1989 (see Table 17.2). Latin America received about 60% of all equity flows to developing countries in 1993. More than 55% of equity sales by firms in developing countries were in the form of **American and global depository receipts (ADRs and GDRs)**. ADRs and GDRs are negotiable receipts issued by FIs in developed countries against shares in foreign companies, with the shares held in custody for investors. ADRs are issued in the United States and are denominated in U.S. dollars. Often, GDRs are simultaneously issued in Europe. In 1994, the first GDR was listed on the London Stock Exchange for East India Hotels. The FI collects and distributes the dividends paid by the foreign firm to the ADR or GDR investor. FIs facilitate access to world equity markets by intermediating between world investors and firms in developing countries. ADRs and GDRs accomplish this by reducing both transaction costs and risk for investors. The FI prices and pays out dividends in U.S. dollars for ADRs, even though the underlying security's cash flows are denominated in terms of the foreign issuer's home currency.[7] As of December 1995, there

American depository receipts (ADRs): negotiable receipts issued by U.S. FIs against shares in foreign companies, with the shares held in custody for investors.

global depository receipts (GDRs): receipts issued by FIs in developed countries other than the U.S. against shares in foreign companies that are held in custody for investors.

---

[3] In nominal value terms, Japanese stock market capitalization first exceeded U.S. stock market capitalization in 1988. When the values are adjusted for Japanese cross holdings, Japanese market capitalization declines, thereby making 1989 the first year in which Japanese stock market volume exceeded U.S. equity market volumes. Subsequently, U.S. stock market volume regained its lead in the wake of the bursting of the Japanese equity price bubble.

[4] Allen and Gale (1995) show that the financial system based on German banks tends to be more efficient at smoothing variations in economic activity over time, reducing the likelihood of boom and bust business cycles, whereas the U.S. system of financial markets is more efficient at allocating resources at any point in time. In a population of heterogeneous individuals with different risk preferences, such as in the United States, cross-sectional allocation is more important than the intertemporal risk allocation of the German system, which is composed of more homogeneous individuals.

[5] The German equity market comprises eight regional stock exchanges which are grouped together under the umbrella of the Federation of the German Stock Exchanges. The Frankfurt (Dusseldorf) Stock Exchange represented 50% (25%) of all equity turnover in Germany during 1989.

[6] This extraordinarily high ratio of stock market capitalization to GDP in Japan reflects the unsustainably high levels of equity prices in Japan at the time. Subsequently, this speculative price bubble burst, resulting in a 60% decline in stock prices as of 1995, from its peak in 1989.

[7] ADRs differ in terms of their reporting requirements. An "unsponsored" ADR, created without the foreign company's involvement, is traded over the counter and, since it is not registered by the SEC, has no reporting requirements. "Sponsored level I" ADRs are initiated by the foreign company but can be traded only in the OTC "Pink Sheet" market; in addition, they have only limited registration and reporting requirements. "Sponsored level II" ADRs are listed on Nasdaq or some other United States stock exchange, but there is no public offering in the United States. The most information-intensive are "sponsored level III" ADRs, which require a full filing using U.S. Generally Accepted Accounting Principles (GAAP) and registration with the SEC.

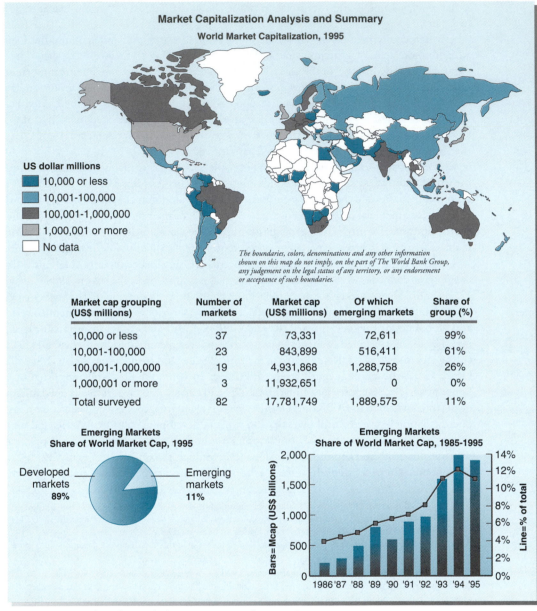

Market Capitalization Analysis and Summary

World Market Capitalization, 1995

US dollar millions
- 10,000 or less
- 10,001-100,000
- 100,001-1,000,000
- 1,000,001 or more
- No data

The boundaries, colors, denominations and any other information shown on this map do not imply, on the part of The World Bank Group, any judgement on the legal status of any territory, or any endorsement or acceptance of such boundaries.

Market cap grouping (US$ millions)	Number of markets	Market cap (US$ millions)	Of which emerging markets	Share of group (%)
10,000 or less	37	73,331	72,611	99%
10,001-100,000	23	843,899	516,411	61%
100,001-1,000,000	19	4,931,868	1,288,758	26%
1,000,001 or more	3	11,932,651	0	0%
Total surveyed	82	17,781,749	1,889,575	11%

Emerging Markets Share of World Market Cap, 1995

Developed markets 89%   Emerging markets 11%

Emerging Markets Share of World Market Cap, 1985-1995

Bars=Mcap (US$ billions) — Line=% of total
1986 '87 '88 '89 '90 '91 '92 '93 '94 '95

Source: Emerging Stock Markets Factbook, 1996, International Finance Corp.

Figure 17.1

Table 17.2

Equity Flows to Developing Countries, 1989–1993 (millions of U.S. dollars)

Type of Flow	1989	1990	1991	1992	1993	Total 1989–1993
Country funds[a]	2.2	2.9	1.2	1.3	2.7	10.3
ADRs and GDRs	—	0.1	4.9	5.9	7.3	18.2
Direct equity	1.3	0.8	1.5	5.8	3.2	12.6
Total	3.5	3.8	7.6	13.0	13.2	41.1

[a]Country funds are closed-end mutual funds that invest in a portfolio of a particular country's stock.

Source: Claessens and Rhee (1994), p. 232.

were 1,800 ADRs, representing over $50 billion of equity in companies from 58 countries. However, equity represented only about 7% of the aggregate net financing (as of 1993) for developing countries. Debt represented a more important source of financing for businesses in these emerging countries.

Checkpoint

1. How have equity flows to developing equity markets changed in recent years?
2. What is market capitalization? Contrast the market capitalization of the largest equity markets in the world.

The Decision to Issue Equity versus Debt

There is a long history of debate about the relevance of the amount of debt versus equity in the capital structure of the firm. Logic and empirical evidence suggest that an optimal financing policy includes both debt and equity. The relative amounts of each depend on the attributes of the firm. For example, Smith and Watts (1992) show that firms with more intangible assets, such as growth opportunities, tend to have lower leverage and lower dividend yields, with greater use of stock option plans in executive compensation packages. Some of the considerations that determine the firm's optimal capital structure are agency conflicts, tax incentives, signaling benefits, and the costs of financial distress.

Agency Conflicts   As we saw in Chapter 16, when a corporation finances a substantial portion of its operations using risky debt, an inherent conflict arises between bondholders and stockholders. Stockholders may refuse to undertake profitable projects because the bondholders' senior claim status entitles them to receive the project's proceeds. Moreover, stockholders have the incentive to take on riskier activities in the hope of receiving the payoffs if extreme positive outcomes occur.

A simple example illustrates this problem. Suppose that the firm's market value is $100 million and that it is financed with $50 million of debt and $50 million of equity. The firm suffers financial losses, and the market value of its assets falls to $30 million. During this time, a risk free opportunity is made available to the firm. It can borrow an additional $10 million to invest in an asset that has a present value of $12 million. Investing in the asset would yield a net present value of $2 million, thereby increasing the value of the firm to $32 million. The shareholders must decide whether to accept the risk free opportunity.[8] Although the asset has a positive net present value, the shareholders reject the opportunity. The increase in the firm value is insufficient to fully repay the bondholders, and thus the stockholders realize no gain from the investment.

Suppose that stockholders were offered an alternative, risky investment that also required an initial investment of $10 million. This asset has a 90% chance of losing 100% of the investment (a loss of $10 million) and a 10% chance of quadrupling in value (a gain of $40 million). The expected value of this asset is .90(−$10 million) + .10($40 million) = −$5 million. This asset has a negative net present value of −$15 million, but stockholders prefer it to the risk free asset. This is because they evaluate the projects from the viewpoint of their own cash flows. Because the risk free project can never yield any value to shareholders, the expected return to shareholders is zero. The expected value of the risky project to shareholders is .90(0) + .10($30m − $10m − $50m + $40 million) = + $1 million.[9] The risky investment has a positive

---

[8] Although the firm is technically insolvent with a net worth of −$20 million ($30 minus $50 million), assume that there have been no contractually mandated debt payments yet to trigger default. Thus, the stockholders are still in charge of the firm.

[9] The shareholders receive a payoff only if the risky project is successful, a probability of 10%. In that event, the $30 million in assets less $10 million paid to invest in the risky project less $50 million paid to bondholders plus the $40 million return on the risky investment yield the net payoff to shareholders of $10 million.

net present value *for stockholders* since they are investing the bondholders' money, not their own. Stockholders are willing to take on the risky project because they have **limited liability**; that is, they cannot lose more than the initial value of their stock investment. As a result, the stockholders may pass up value-enhancing opportunities and take on value-reducing, risk enhancing investments. Realizing this conflict, bondholders may be reluctant to lend (or will impose restrictive covenants, discussed in Chapter 16), forcing firms to rely on equity as their primary source of financing.

limited liability: common stockholders cannot lose more than the initial value of their stock investment.

Tax Incentives   The tax deductibility of interest payments, but not dividends, provides firms with a strong incentive to finance their operations using debt as opposed to equity. The higher the tax rate of the firm, the greater the value of the tax shield of debt. In our discussion of preferred stock, we will see that the search for tax deductibility has motivated important financial security innovations.

pecking order hypothesis: expectation that firms will use the least costly methods of financing first, moving to higher cost capital sources only after the others are exhausted.

Signaling Benefits   The Myers-Majluf (1984) **pecking order hypothesis** states that firms will use the least costly methods of financing first, moving to higher cost capital sources only after the others are exhausted. Thus, firms would choose to finance using debt before equity. Indeed, firms that issue equity to finance their investments are signaling the market that the firm's insiders believe that their equity is overvalued since they are willing to sell at the current price. Accordingly, shareholders issue debt to signal their confidence in the firm's ability to meet fixed interest payments. Kalay and Shimrat (1987) find that a randomly selected unregulated firm examined during the period 1964–1983 issued equity, on average, once every 50 years. Mikkelson and Parch (1986) examined a sample of 360 firms and found only 80 equity issues over a period of 10 years. Empirical evidence also shows that firms financing with equity are of a lower quality than firms financing with debt.

Costs of Financial Distress   The tax incentives and signaling benefits of debt imply that we should observe firms with high amounts of leverage: mostly debt and very little equity. In reality, with the exception of highly leveraged FIs, the opposite is true—most firms have more equity than debt in their capital structure. An explanation for this statement is the deadweight costs of financial distress. Since debt, but not equity, can trigger financial distress, increases in the firm's leverage increase the risk of insolvency. Since default and bankruptcy are costly experiences, firms seek to minimize their credit risk by including more equity in their capital structure.

The Case of FIs   To determine an optimal capital structure, each firm must weigh the four consequences of debt/equity issuance. Those firms that have the largest agency conflicts, the lowest income tax bracket, the least undervalued stock price, or the highest costs of financial distress will tend to issue more equity to finance their activities. Hybrid securities bridge the gap between debt and equity. For example, convertible debt is often viewed as delayed equity, since the issuance of common stock is delayed until the bond's conversion date.

Most of this standard theory of capital budgeting does not apply to FIs. That is because FIs, by their very nature, are highly leveraged firms. Does that mean that there are no costs of financial distress for FIs? Of course not. FIs must also control their risk of insolvency by limiting their leverage. That is the justification behind capital requirements. Capital requirements specify the maximum leverage allowable for FIs. Indeed, the United States has two forms of capital requirements for banks: (1) the Basel risk adjusted international capital requirements (see Chapter 5); and (2) leverage requirements that take the form of a minimum required capital-to-total assets ratio. Currently, the regulations for U.S. banks are that the Basel risk adjusted capital ratio must not be lower than 8% and the leverage ratio must attain a minimum value of 3%.[10]

---

[10] That is, the ratio of Tier 1 capital to average (on-balance sheet) assets must be greater than or equal to 3%, allowing the bank to have a maximum leverage ratio of 97%.

Do these requirements mean that FIs have no discretion over the level of capital they hold? The answer is no. Capital regulations are minimum requirements. FIs can always hold levels above the capital requirement. However, since capital is the FI's most expensive source of financing, excessive capital levels may subject the FI to a competitive disadvantage vis-à-vis other FIs that are just at the regulatory minimum. How then can the FI exercise control over its capital position? The FI's primary control mechanism is its discretion over the composition of its capital. As we saw in Chapter 5, the three levels of capital are Tier 1, Tier 2, and Tier 3. The FI has some leeway in the allocation of capital both across tiers as well as in using different securities within each tier. Indeed, this discretion spawned some of the recent innovation in the design of equity securities. Regulators include in their definition of the FI's capital any security issued by the FI that bears an appreciable amount of risk and therefore provides a cushion to senior claimants on the FI's assets.

Checkpoint

1. Why does high leverage exacerbate the agency conflicts of interest between shareholders and bondholders?

2. Why does financial distress exacerbate the agency conflicts of interest between shareholders and bondholders?

3. Why is the optimal capital level of FIs different from that for comparable nonfinancial firms?

The Role of Preferred Stock in Meeting Capital Requirements

Preferred stock is a hybrid between debt and equity.[11] It offers investors a stream of dividend payments but no voting rights. Preferred stock is junior to debt but senior to common stock. Preferred stock dividends can therefore be paid out only if all debtholders are first paid in full, just as common stock dividends can be paid only if all preferred stock dividends are first paid in full. As described in Chapter 5, preferred stock can be either cumulative or noncumulative. All cumulative preferred stock dividend payments missed in the past must be paid in full prior to paying common stock dividends. Noncumulative preferred stock issues do not require the firm to make up past unpaid preferred stock dividends.

The United States has the most developed market for preferred stocks in the world. In the past, utilities were the primary issuers because they issued preferred stock in order to finance construction projects without increasing their leverage. Since the introduction of the Basel risk adjusted capital requirements, however, banks and other FIs have been the largest issuers of preferred stocks. This is because it is the least expensive source of Tier 1 capital. FIs can, therefore, increase their core capital levels by issuing preferred at a lower cost of capital than if they issued common stock. This is particularly true for U.S. and Japanese banks, since their share prices were depressed during the early 1990s.[12]

Banks and other FIs throughout the world were forced to raise capital during the early 1990s. The goal was to issue the combination of equity-like securities that minimized the FI's total cost of capital. This can be viewed as an optimization problem in which FIs try to balance the equity-like nature of their securities against the cost of capital. The more equity-like the security is, the greater its cost. The FIs issued just enough securities to satisfy their regulatory capital requirement while trying to minimize their costs by reducing these securities' equity-like

---

[11] Kimmel and Warfield (1995) show that the risk characteristics of preferred stock are different from those of both debt and equity, thus qualifying it for classification as a hybrid.

[12] Cornett and Tehranian (1994) and Laderman (1994) show that U.S. banks that issued common stock between 1989 and 1992 experienced decreases in their stock returns.

Table 17.3

Costly Securities Features

All else being equal, the issuer's cost of issuing innovative securities
INCREASES (in terms of rates of return required by security investors)
as more of the following features are included:
* Subordinated cash flow (lack of seniority)
* Unsecured by the assets of the issuer
* Longer maturity (infinite maturity versus term securities)
* Noncumulative dividends
* Convertibility and security redemption (if at option of issuer)
* Fixed rate with respect to
  * Issuer's credit standing
  * Market interest rates

----

characteristics. Table 17.3 shows that costly securities features can be mixed and matched to construct securities to fill the FI's capital requirement.

FIs have innovated new securities to satisfy their capital requirements by engineering the least costly securities to fill each capital tier. Tier 1 is the highest form of capital and thus carries the highest cost. The securities in Tier 1 are therefore the most equity-like and have most of the features listed in Table 17.3. Tier 2 is the next highest form of capital and carries a higher cost than Tier 3, but lower than Tier 1 capital. In Table 17.4, we see how securities are designed to meet Tier 1 and 2 requirements using the least number of costly features.

Preferred stock can be considered either Tier 1 or Tier 2 capital, depending on the security's features. Perpetual fixed rate preferred stock has the highest cost of capital of all perferred stock issues because it has no maturity date and therefore is exposed to both market and interest rate risk. It is considered to be Tier 1 capital. Fixed rate preferred with a sinking fund is also considered Tier 1 capital. It generally has a fixed maturity date and a repurchasing schedule that stipulates a fixed number of shares to be retired each year.

Preferred stock is an attractive source of financing for all highly leveraged companies, not just FIs. For example, RJR Nabisco regularly issues substantial amounts of preferred stock, in part because doing so does not increase the firm's debt-to-equity ratio, which was already high because of the leveraged buyout of 1989. The first shift from bank common stock issues to newly innovated preferred stock issues in 1982 is shown in Table 17.5. U.S. banks were able to supplement their capital levels while also controlling interest rate risk using newly developed preferred stock and hybrid securities designed to minimize the cost of capital.

Adjustable rate issues of preferred stock were introduced in 1982 and are particularly attractive in increasing interest rate environments. If the dividend is reset each quarter according to a preestablished formula based on the U.S. Treasury rate, these issues are considered to be Tier 1 capital. However, there is a type of adjustable rate preferred called an **auction rate preferred stock (ARPS)**, which resets the dividend rate periodically using a Dutch auction method.[13] The reset date can be as frequent as every 49 days. However, since the auction method allows the rate to adjust to reflect changes in the issuer's credit standing, ARPS are considered Tier 2 capital. It also has significantly lower yields, often as low as 2% to 3%, because of the characteristics it shares with money market instruments. With such an inexpensive source of financing, why don't nonfinancial firms issue ARPS instead of debt? Although the government considers ARPS to be capital (albeit of Tier 2 level), the rating services are not as lenient. An issue of ARPS therefore increases the issuer's leverage ratio, which increases the firm's cost of capital. Because of this factor as well as a declining interest rate environment in recent years, there has been a dwindling supply of ARPS issues by nonfinancial corporations.

auction rate preferred stock (ARPS): preferred stock that resets the dividend rate periodically using a Dutch auction method.

----

[13] This security is also known as Single Point Adjustable Rate Stock (SPARS).

Table
17.4

Classification of Securities Innovations into Capital Tiers[a]

TIER 1

* Common stock
* Warrants
    - Can be converted into common stock at the option of the investor.
    - Can be either sold for cash, or separated from the security with which they were originally issued.
* Preferred stock: perpetual, noncumulative, nonconvertible
    - Fixed rate perpetual preferred.
    - Adjustable rate perpetual preferred (e.g., Arps, Spars): rate change formula based on market interest rates only.
    - Fixed-adjustable preferred: fixed rate for some period, after which rates are adjusted using a market interest rate formula.
* Preferred stock: perpetual, noncumulative, convertible
    - Percs (Yes, Mandatory Conversion Premium Dividend Preferred Stock): issuer cannot retain an option to redeem for cash prior to maturity.

TIER 2: UPPER

* Floating rate perpetual preferred stock (e.g., money market preferred, remarketed preferred): rate reset by Dutch auction incorporates changes in issuer's credit standing.
* Fixed rate term preferred stock (e.g., Mips, Epics, Toprs): dividends can be deferred for as long as five years, but are cumulative.[b]
* Perpetual subordinated debt (e.g., convertible capital notes): convertible (at issuer's option) into noncumulative preferred stock.
* Mandatory convertible debt (e.g., equity contract notes, equity commitment notes): issuer must convert debt into either perpetual preferred or common stock.

TIER 2: LOWER

* Intermediate term preferred stock
* Nonmandatory convertible term subordinated debt
* Term subordinated debt with terms > five years at issue
    - Nonconvertible debt: fixed rate (most popular) or floating rate (interest rate formula or Dutch auction).
    - Lyons—Liquid yield option notes: zero coupon; holder can exercise put to convert into common stock at least five years after issuance.
    - ISFDs—Indexed sinking fund debentures: contains interest rate contingent sinking fund.
    - YCNs—Yield curve notes or inverse floaters: coupon rate is inversely related to benchmark interest rate.

[a]Some of the trademarked names of securities with the listed features are included in parentheses.

[b]In October 1996, the Federal Reserve Board approved the use of certain cumulative preferred stock instruments as Tier 1 capital for bank holding companies.

Preferred stock investments have a tax advantage to institutional investors. Dividends paid to any incorporated investor are 70% tax exempt. Insurance companies are the biggest institutional buyers of preferred stocks; this is because of regulatory reasons as well as because of the tax exemption. Preferred stock is carried on the insurance company's balance sheet at cost rather than at market value. The insurance company therefore does not have to mark to market its preferred stockholdings, thereby reducing the risk of loss that might trigger the need for an offsetting capital infusion.

In 1991 Morgan Stanley introduced a new security called **preferred equity redemption cumulative stocks (Percs)**.[14] Percs pay dividends (and are thus 70% tax exempt for corporate investors) and automatically are converted into common stock at a conversion price and date

preferred equity redemption cumulative stocks (Percs): stocks that pay dividends and automatically are converted into common stock at a conversion price and date.

---

[14] Morgan Stanley invented Percs. Goldman Sachs calls its version of the security Yield Enhanced Stock (Yes), and Merrill Lynch calls its version Mandatory Conversion Premium Dividend Preferred Stock.

Table
17.5

**Sources of Externally Raised Primary Capital for Banks and Bank Holding Companies,[a]
1979–1985 (in millions of dollars)**

	1979	1980	1981	1982	1983	1984	1985
Common stock	0	144	133	12	424	425	631
Convertible preferred stock	25	60	0	0	150	48	0
Fixed rate preferred stock	0	150	0	0	25	0	0
Debt–equity swaps			191	204	97	29	0
Mandatory convertibles[b]							
Equity contract notes[c]				250	0	4,325	2,468
Equity commitment notes[c]				1,025	575	1,285	1,485
Variable rate preferred stock							
Adjustable rate preferred stock[c]				1,847	2,342	445	45
Dutch auction rate preferred stock[c]							1,163

[a]Includes all public issues of $10 million or more.

[b]All mandatory convertibles must be fully converted to equity within 12 years.

[c]Securities developed after 1981.

Source: Ingram and Eiseman (1990), p. 25.

(usually three years after issue). Percs are also callable at any time after issuance for a price that is usually set at 40% above the issue price and gradually declines as the conversion date approaches. The convertibility of Percs gives the investor the opportunity to benefit from an increase in the common stock price of the issuer (up to 40% above issue price) and obtain a higher dividend payout than is paid to common stockholders. If, on the other hand, the issuer's common stock price declines below the conversion price, the Percs offer downside risk protection because the investor is guaranteed a minimum number of shares. Sears Percs in December 1994 had a conversion price of $59 and a maximum conversion value of 1.3525 shares. At the conversion price, this places a floor value under the Percs of $43.623 ($\frac{\$59}{1.3525}$) per share. In addition, the investor receives higher preferred stock dividends during the period of time prior to conversion. In October 1992, Citicorp issued $1.003 billion of Percs. Since Percs are noncumulative convertible preferred stocks that must convert into common stock at some future date, regulators classify these securities as Tier 1 capital.

In 1993 Salomon Brothers introduced a new and improved version of Percs called Decs (Dividend Enhanced Convertible Stock). Decs have higher dividend yields than Percs, but in exchange they give up the first 20% of potential stock price appreciation upon conversion into common stock. It was not long, however, before Goldman improved on this innovation by introducing **Monthly Income Preferred Securities (Mips)**, structured so that the dividend payouts are tax deductible to the issuer. **Exchangeable Preferred Income Cumulative Shares (Epics)** are a type of Mips, invented by Bear, Stearns & Company, that allows the security holder to redeem Mips for the parent company's preferred stock. If the investor decides to convert Mips into shares of preferred stock, proceeds from the sale of the parent's preferred stock are used to retire the loan to the Mips subsidiary. These innovations became so popular that, between the first issue in October 1993 and February 1995, $6.5 billion of Mips and "Mips clones" had been offered, representing more than half of all preferred stock issues. Mips issues exploded in one year after their introduction, increasing from 3.7% in 1993 to 52.0% of all preferred issues in 1994.[15] *Timely Topics 17.1: Innovation in the Preferred Stock Market* traces the evolution of the innovations in the preferred stock market.

Monthly Income Preferred Securities (Mips): a preferred stock innovation structured so that the dividend payouts are tax deductible to the issuer.

Exchangeable Preferred Income Cumulative Shares (Epics): a type of Mips that allows the security holder to redeem the Mips for the parent company's preferred stock.

---

[15] In November 1994 Grand Metropolitan issued Quips, quarterly income preferred stock, and in January 1995 Arizona Public Service Company issued $50 million of subordinated debt called Mids (Monthly Income Debt Securities).

TIMELY TOPICS 17.1

INNOVATION IN THE PREFERRED STOCK MARKET

Until the early 1980s, the preferred stock sector was little more than a sleepy outpost of the capital markets. With a plain vanilla, fixed-rate product that hadn't changed for decades and an issuer base comprised almost entirely of utilities—who found preferreds attractive for regulatory reasons—there wasn't much to get excited about.

But over the past decade, the preferred sector has become one of the most innovative on Wall Street. "Suddenly, it's the area where—pound for pound—there's more innovation than any other," says Chris Hogg, VP and head of preferred marketing and product development at Goldman, Sachs and Company.

First, in the early 1980s came adjustable-rate preferreds, offering a quarterly yield reset based on a spread to the highest of the yields on three month, 10 year, or 30 year Treasury securities.

Although the adjustable-rate product protected investors against interest rate risk, it didn't allow for the possible changes in credit quality or tax policy that can affect the value of a preferred.

Then in 1984 came the introduction of money-market preferreds, in which new, market-clearing dividend rates are determined periodically by either an auction or a remarketing process. While those mechanisms gave investors even greater protection, corporate America has largely given up on the product in recent years; because of the repricing risk and the possibility of a failed auction, companies can't get equity credit for such products from the rating agencies.

The original fixed-rate market got a shot in the arm in the late 1980s when Federal bank regulators agreed to count perpetual preferreds as Tier 1 capital—a change that spurred many major banks to tap the market.

Later still, an assortment of foreign companies used offshore vehicles to issue preferred, the proceeds of which were then loaned back to the parent companies resulting in a form of tax-deductible equity.

In 1993, Goldman, Sachs & Co. adapted that basic idea for U.S. issuers creating the "Holy Grail" of this hybrid market. Goldman's "Mips" or Monthly Income Preferred Securities, have the tax-deductibility of debt combined with at least some equity credit from the rating agencies.

Mips were originally issued from an offshore limited life company, but the technology has since evolved to allow issuance through domestic limited liability companies, limited partnerships, or trusts. In any case, the subsidiary issues preferred interest to U.S. investors, then loans the proceeds to its parent. The loan typically is deeply subordinated, with a long (usually 30 year) maturity and, most importantly, a five year interest deferral option.

The structure apparently fits Internal Revenue Service requirements for a debt obligation so the parent gets to take tax deductions on the related interest payments. But the transaction shows up on the issuer's balance sheet as a "minority interest."

Netting out a number of positives and negatives, rating agencies view the product as similar to ordinary preferred stock. "The principal breakthrough is a rating agency breakthrough," says Robert Kantowitz, managing director in global structured products at UBS Securities. "What Mips achieves for the corporation is a package of benefits similar to preferred stock, but at a lower after-tax cost, so to a large degree it represents the demise of preferred stock."

Several variations on the basic fixed rate Mips product have already been created: adjustable-rate Mips, convertible Mips, and Mips-type debt issued directly by the parent company. "What's happened here is that we've transformed a market," says Goldman's Hogg.

Kantowitz says there will continue to be certain issuers who will continue to use the regular preferred market. But for the majority of potential issuers, Mips are simply a better choice."

Source: T. Pratt, "Wall Street's Engineers Find Preferred Stock's 'Holy Grail': A Sleepy Backwater Turns into a Hotbed of Innovation," *Investment Dealers' Digest*, May 22, 1995, p. 44.

In April 1995 the SEC ruled that separately incorporated trusts could be used to structure Mips transactions.[16] This substantially reduces the costs of such deals since, prior to the SEC ruling, offshore subsidiaries had to be created to handle the transactions. Mips are structured so that a specially created subsidiary issues preferred stock to investors. The subsidiary then loans the proceeds of the preferred stock issue to the parent company. Although the earliest Mips issues had maturities of 100 years, most deals currently have maturities of 50 years. The parent company's interest payments are sufficient to cover the dividend payout on the subsidiary's preferred stock. However, the interest payments are tax deductible for the parent. The parent pays what is in effect the preferred stock dividend but can gain the advantages of the tax deductibility of debt.[17]

Because the ratings agencies treat Mips as equity, a Mips issue does not increase the firm's leverage ratio. Figure 17.2 contrasts the cash flows associated with a standard preferred stock issue with those associated with a Mips issue. The dividend streams from preferred stock are not tax deductible from the standpoint of the issuer, but the interest payments to the Mips subsidiary from the parent company are. Mips, therefore, transform a nondeductible dividend

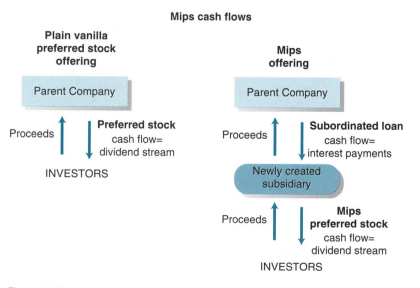

Figure 17.2

[16] In April 1995 Merrill Lynch was the first to use trusts to issue Mips. It named the product TOPrS (Trust Originated Preferred Securities).

[17] A shadow was cast on this market by the Clinton administration's proposal at the end of 1995 (as yet unadopted) to treat these "abusive" securities as nondeductible equity.

stream into an equivalent, tax-deductible series of interest payments. Investors receive the dividend stream. This also has tax advantages for corporate investors since they can claim a 70% dividends-received deduction. The issuer is able to deduct the interest payments, and the corporate investor is able to deduct the dividends received. To better align the cash flows, Mips permit the issuer to defer interest and dividend payments for up to five years. The parent guarantees that any accumulated dividends will eventually be paid. Fixed rate dividends are payable on the last day of each month.

Debt and preferred stock innovations proliferated during the 1980s. During the period 1974–1990, issuance of 43 innovative securities[18] accounted for 11.6% of all public offerings. The mid-1980s were the most active years for financial market innovations, with six or more securities pioneered in each of the years 1983, 1985, and 1986. During this period, Merrill Lynch was the most innovative FI, engineering 12 new securities; Drexel Burnham Lambert and First Boston Corporation each designed 6 new financial securities during this period. Table 17.6 compares the structure of several of these innovative securities.

Checkpoint

✓

1. Why does the cost of capital increase with the inclusion of each feature in Table 17.3?
2. How have preferred stocks evolved in recent years?
3. Why are Mips superior to standard preferred stock offerings for issuers? for investors?

Failed Securities Innovations

From the proliferation of securities with snappy acronyms, one could get the impression that any new security will be profitable for the innovator. Nothing could be further from the truth. Indeed, more than 50% of all new financial instruments cease trading only a few months after they are first listed in financial newspapers. Since each new security may cost the innovators more than $1 million to design and market, this represents a considerable cost to FIs. Here are three case studies of financial innovations gone awry.

CASE STUDY 17.1

trusts: closed-end mutual funds.

Prescribed Right Income and Maximum Equity Securities (Primes): securities that entitled the investor to receive cash dividends plus voting rights.

Special Claims on Residual Equity Securities (Scores): long term call options on the Score holders that allowed the trust to purchase the shares from the trust at a predetermined price.

PRIMES AND SCORES

Introduced during 1985–1987, Primes and Scores were actually shares in **trusts**, closed-end mutual funds comprising shares of common stock for 26 companies trading on the American Stock Exchange. Each trust purchased the common stock of one company. The goal of this financial innovation was to separate the common stock dividend from its capital gain component. Each unit of each trust, representing one share of common stock, was divided into one Prime and one Score. The **Prescribed Right Income and Maximum Equity Securities (Primes)** entitled the investor to receive cash dividends as well as voting rights. The **Special Claims on Residual Equity Securities (Scores)** were long term call options on the score holders that allowed the trust to purchase the shares from the trust at a predetermined price. If the stock price increased, the Score holders received the capital gain in the form of the differential between the market stock price and the exercise price of the call option, and the Prime holders received the Score's exercise price. If there were no capital gains, then the Score investors received

---

[18] This listing of securities innovations includes only debt and preferred stock products, excluding mortgage-backed securities, asset-backed debt, and common stock.

Table 17.6

Comparison of Structures for Recently Innovated Securities

	Dividends-Received Deduction: Preferred Stock	Trust Structure: TOPrS* Trust Quips	Domestic Partnership Structure: Mips
Legal form of issuer	US corporation	Delaware business trust	US or offshore limited partnership
US tax characterization of issuer	Corporation	Grantor trust	Partnership
Security offered	Preferred stock	Preferred security representing undivided beneficial interest in trust	Preferred security representing limited partnership interest
Payment frequency	Quarterly	Quarterly	Monthly
Par amount/liquidation preference	Most recently $25	$25	$25
Investor tax reporting	Form 1099	Form 1099	Schedule K-1
Cumulative	Yes, may also be non-cumulative	Yes	Yes
Maturity	Perpetual	30 to 49 years	Generally, 30 to 49 years
Call features	Non-call five or 10 years	Generally, non-call five years	Generally, non-call five years
Special tax call	No	Yes	Yes
Ability to defer payments	Indefinite	Up to 20 consecutive quarters	Up to 60 months
Accrual of interest income	No accrual of interest income; entire amount of dividend income payable is recognized on payment date	Holders taxed on interest accrued for days that security is owned	Holders at the *end of each month* are taxed on all accrued interest for that month
Tax on investors on deferred payments and interest	No	Yes	Yes
Rank in capital structure (actual rank on dissolution, not parent guarantee)	Subordinated to senior debt; *pari passu* with company preferred stock or preference shares; senior to common stock	Subordinated to senior debt; *pari passu* with other issuance of junior subordinated debt and trade creditors; senior to preferred and common stock	Subordinated to senior debt; *pari passu* with other issuance of junior subordinated debt and trade creditors; senior to preferred and common stock
Parent guarantee	N/A	Yes, under certain conditions	Yes, under certain conditions
Voting rights on non-payment of dividends or interest	Voting rights	Enforcement of debenture guarantee	Enforcement of debenture guarantee
Company exchange option to debt	No	Generally, yes	Generally, yes
Withholding tax for US investors	No	No	No
Withholding tax for non-US investors	Yes	No	No
DRD-eligible*	Yes	No	No

*Trust-originated Preferred Securities and TOPrS are service marks of Merrill Lynch & Co. DRD-eligible is eligible for the corporate dividends received deduction.

Junior Subordinated Deferrable Interest Debentures: Mids Qids/Quids Quics	Foreign Partnership Structures: UK Mips UK Quips	Taxable Foreign Preferred Stock: All-Cash Structures or ADS Foreign Offshore
US corporation	Delaware limited partnership	Offshore company
Corporation	Limited partnership	Corporation
Junior subordinated debt	Preferred security	Preference share
Quarterly (or monthly)	Quarterly	Quarterly
$25	$25	$25
Form 1099	Schedule K-1	Form 1099
Yes	Yes, except for banks	Yes, except for banks
30 to 49 years	Perpetual	Perpetual
Generally, non-call five or 10 years	Generally, non-call seven or 10 years	Non-call five or 10 years
Yes	Yes	Yes
Up to 20 consecutive quarters (or 60 months)	Indefinite	Indefinite
Holders taxed on interest accrued for days that security is owned	No accrual of interest income; entire amount of dividend income payable is recognized on payment date	No accrual of interest income; entire amount of dividend income payable is recognized on payment date
Yes	No	No
Subordinated to senior debt; *pari passu* with other issuance of junior subordinated debt and trade creditors; senior to preferred and common stock	Subordinated to senior debt; *pari passu* with preferred stock; senior to common stock	Subordinated to senior debt; *pari passu* with preferred stock; senior to common stock
N/A	Yes	Yes, under certain conditions
No	Voting rights	Voting rights
No	No	No
No	No	No
No	No	No
No	No	No

Source: *Euromoney* (November 1995), p. 64.

nothing and the Prime holders received the value of the common stock. The trust operator received 5 cents per share from the dividend payout to administer the securities.

To see how the Prime plus the Score equals the common stock, consider the case of a company with a current price of $50 and a quarterly dividend payout of 4% p.a. Under current prices, each quarter a $0.50 (1% of $50) dividend payment was paid to the trust. The trust distributed the $0.50 per share by giving $0.45 to each Prime share and retaining the remaining $0.05 per share to cover its administrative expenses.

Suppose that the trust was established to expire after five years. At the end of five years, the trust sold all of its shares of common stock and was dissolved. Also, suppose that the Score exercise price was set at $50. If the price of the common stock, at the end of five years, was $75, then the Score investors received $25 ($75 minus $50), whereas the Prime holders received a terminating payment of $50 per share. If, on the other hand, the price of the common stock at the end of the five years was $30, then the Score investors received nothing and the Prime holders received a terminating payment of $30 per share.

The IRS proved to be the undoing of the Prime/Score securities when it classified these trusts as corporations and thus made them subject to federal income tax. This subjected the investors to double taxation since their cash flows would be taxed at both the trust and the personal levels. The original 26 trusts were grandfathered into a status that exempted them from double taxation, but no new trusts were established.

CASE STUDY 17.2

Index Participation Shares (IPSs): "ownership shares" in an index of common stocks.

Toronto Index Participation Shares (Tips): IPSs based on the Toronto Stock Exchange index.

Standard & Poor's Index Depository Receipts (SPDRs): IPSs based on the S&P 500.

INDEX PARTICIPATION SHARES

Index Participation Shares (IPSs) are "ownership shares" in an index of common stocks. Each IPS unit represents 1/100th of the value of the stocks that make up the index. Thus, IPS investors are entitled to receipt of 1/100th of both the value of the index and any dividend payout. The IPSs are perpetual securities with no fixed maturity date. The investor can choose to liquidate her position at any time.[19] IPSs make it easier to trade a stock index, such as the S&P 500. The innovation is valuable to investors who want to trade a basket of stocks but want to avoid the costs of trading index futures or options.

Because the innovation was a competitive threat to their lucrative index futures and options products, the Chicago futures exchanges sued the SEC, claiming that IPSs are futures contracts and, under the Commodity Exchange Act, must be traded only on markets regulated by the Commodity Futures Trading Corporation (the CFTC). The courts agreed with that argument and ruled that the SEC had no jurisdiction over the new securities. That left the instrument to the futures exchanges. To date, only two IPS securities are trading. The first, the **Toronto Index Participation Shares (Tips)**, are based on the Toronto Stock Exchange index. In 1992, 6 million shares of Tips, totaling over $60 billion, were traded on the Toronto Stock Exchange. In February 1993 the AMEX introduced **Standard & Poor's Index Depository Receipts (SPDRs)**, which are IPSs based on the S&P 500.

---

[19] There are some limitations on cash-out dates. Liquidation can occur only on selected Thursdays before the quarterly expiration of the S&P 500 futures contract.

CASE STUDY 17.3

targeted stock (alphabet or letter stock): common stock that pays its holders an added dividend if a specified division performs well.

TARGETED STOCK

This financial innovation was killed not by regulators nor by the IRS, but by its own design. In criticizing the instrument, Professor Bruce Greenwald of Columbia University stated, "It is absolutely the purest form of financial engineering, and it yields no benefit at all."[20] **Targeted stock**, also known as **alphabet** or **letter stock**, is common stock that pays its holders an added dividend if a specified division performs well.

In 1984 General Motors was the first company to issue targeted stock: Class E shares linked to the performance of H. Ross Perot's Electronic Data Systems. The idea was to distribute shares in subsidiaries without incurring the cost of a formal spinoff. However, the holder of targeted stock does not get first claim on the targeted subsidiary's earnings. The subsidiary's earnings can be diverted to satisfy the parent company's liabilities, thereby undermining the targeted shareholders' rights to a dividend premium. Thus, the instrument is subject to extreme moral hazard and is very difficult to evaluate. In 1994 Kmart's shareholders rejected a plan to issue targeted stocks tied to individual store revenues.

Checkpoint

✓

1. Explain why some financial innovations fail.

2. What were the original goals of Primes and Scores? What were the shortcomings of the instrument?

3. What were the original goals of Index Participation Shares? What were the shortcomings of the instrument?

4. What were the original goals of targeted stock? What were the shortcomings of the instrument?

➤ New Equity Issues

spinoff: the divestiture of assets by distributing shares to existing shareholders with few disclosure requirements.

carveout: a divestiture of assets that is used to raise additional funds for the firm's operations by selling equity to a new group of shareholders and is subject to strict disclosure requirements by the SEC.

Firms issue new equity in order to finance their operations. Figure 17.3 delineates the distribution of new U.S. equity offerings between 1987 and 1994 (first quarter). New equity issues increased by 46% from 1992 to 1993. Since a firm is simply a portfolio of investment opportunities, sometimes it is profitable to separate one investment opportunity from the others in the firm's portfolio. Ownership shares, or equity, in this segmented investment opportunity can be sold. This is desirable if the risk/reward characteristics of the segmented investment opportunity are different from those of other investment opportunities in the firm's portfolio. In divesting itself of assets, the firm can choose between a **spinoff** and a **carveout** divestiture. In a spinoff, shares are distributed to existing shareholders, and since the transfer does not yield the firm any immediate cash flows, there are few disclosure requirements. A carveout is used to raise additional funds for the firm's operations by selling equity to a new group of shareholders and is subject to strict disclosure requirements by the SEC. Michaely and Shaw (1995) show that carveouts tend to significantly outperform spinoffs since firms tend to place undervalued assets in the spinoff.

---

[20] Strom (1994), p. D1.

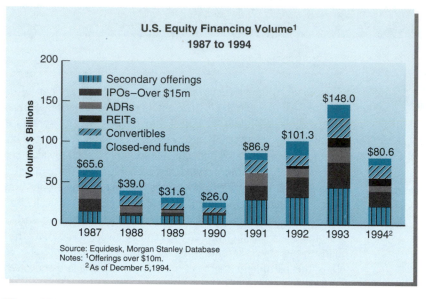

U.S. Equity Financing Volume[1]
1987 to 1994

Legend:
- Secondary offerings
- IPOs—Over $15m
- ADRs
- REITs
- Convertibles
- Closed-end funds

Source: Equidesk, Morgan Stanley Database
Notes: [1]Offerings over $10m.
[2]As of Decmber 5,1994.

Figure 17.3

Initial Public Offerings

We have seen that the FI specializes in producing information about the future cash flows of financial securities. Nowhere is this more apparent than in the area of **initial public offerings (IPOs)**. In an IPO, the underwriting FI is called upon to value a firm that has never traded before in any public market. What is being priced is the firm's growth prospects—an intangible that is very difficult to value. FIs with superior information about the firm's financial performance can use this information to better forecast future outcomes. This is important because the FI must satisfy both sides of the transaction. The IPO must be priced high enough to raise enough for the issuer to be willing to sell the shares. Moreover, the FI prefers to set the **offer price** (the opening price for the newly issued shares) higher because the FI's commissions are generally a percentage of issue price. Bae and Levy (1990) show that average underwriting spreads for firm commitments contracts is 4.37% of offer price, with 3.05% for utility companies and 4.76% for industrial companies. Total fees for equity IPOs in 1995 were $4.02 billion, up 23% from $3.26 billion in 1994. The average fee paid in 1995 was 4.98%, although there was concern about underwriter price cutting, as exemplified by Merrill Lynch's fee of only 1.9% to privatize Brazil's Companhia Vale do Rio Doce. However, the IPO must not be priced so high that it will not sell to investors, who must take the risk of buying a potentially illiquid and risky security.

From 1960 to 1993, over 10,000 firms in the United States went public. The IPO process must be handled efficiently, since newly public firms tend to be the most rapidly growing and dynamic of all businesses in the economy. In recent years, IPO volume has hit new records. Annual volume of new offerings in 1995 totaled more than $29 billion. IPOs tend to occur in waves (Figure 17.4): in the United States, hot IPO cycles have occurred during 1960–1962, 1968–1972, 1980–1986, and 1990–1993. During the hot IPO cycles, first-day returns tend to be extremely high. The initial IPO returns can spike as high as 130% per month (see Figure 17.5). This means that some IPOs are **underpriced** because their closing price on the first day of trading significantly exceeds the offer price. However, according to Rock (1986) and Beatty and Ritter (1986), IPOs are underpriced in order to overcome an information asymmetry that would prevent uninformed investors from participating in the new issue. If the IPO is

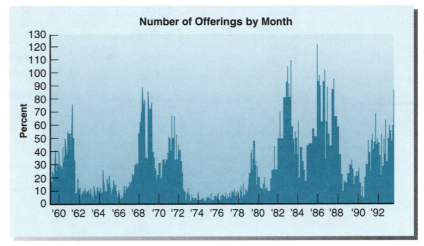

Source: Katz (1995), p. 19.

Figure 17.4

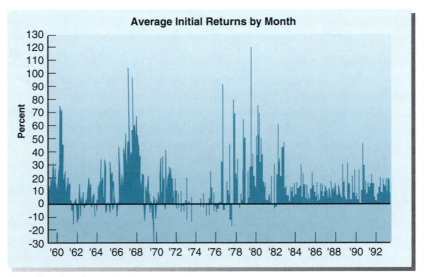

Source: Katz (1995), p. 19.

Figure 17.5

priced above its true value, then informed investors will not participate. If the IPO is priced below its true value, then informed investors will buy up all of the shares issued. Uninformed investors will know that if they are successful in obtaining shares of an IPO, chances are that they are overpaying. Called a *winner's curse* (see Chapter 15), overpricing will discourage participation by the general public in IPOs. To attract uninformed investors into the IPO market, underwriters price them at a considerable discount. The more uncertainty about the value of a new issue, the greater the amount of underpricing.

puttable common stock:
a stock issue that allows the investor to sell the stock back to the issuer at a predetermined exercise price at a prespecified date.

Puttable common stock can resolve the underpricing problem for IPOs. Similar to puttable bonds (see Chapter 16), the puttable stock is a stock issue that allows the investor to sell the stock back to the issuer at a predetermined exercise price at a prespecified date. If the common stock price is below the put option exercise price, then the issuer can make up the difference by

Figure 17.6

granting the investor additional shares in the company. The puttable stock places a floor under the possible price of the common stock, while still allowing the investor to gain from any stock price appreciation. The puttable stock protects the investor from overpricing the new issue. From the issuer's standpoint, the puttable stock is comparable to a convertible bond. However, since it is classified as equity, puttable stock issues do not increase the firm's leverage ratio.

The underwriter's job begins long before the offer date (Figure 17.6). The underwriter analyzes the company's prospects to set a range for the offer price. A **red herring prospectus** describes the offering, subject to SEC approval and usually without specifying an offer price.[21] During this pre-offer time period, the underwriter gathers information about demand among investors for the issue. This will help the underwriter set the offer price. Typically, the offer price is not set until the day before the sale of the IPO.

The underwriter's job does not end on the offer date. The underwriter is required to use its distribution network to place the new issue as well as to make a market in the security after the completion of the IPO. How do IPOs perform over the long run? As shown in Figure 17.7, IPOs tend to underperform established firms of equal size for as long as five years after going public. This supports the contention that newly public firms with large amounts of intangible assets are risky and difficult to value properly. The success of specific IPOs and the economy in general hinge on the FIs' abilities to facilitate the financing of innovative businesses in the IPO market.

red herring prospectus: description of an offering without specifying an offer price.

Universal Banking and Possible Conflicts of Interest

The Pecora Committee investigations of the U.S. Senate during 1933–1934 laid the foundations for passage of the Glass–Steagall Act, which would shape the structure of FIs in the United States over the following 50 years. The contention was that it was improper for commercial banks to engage in underwriting because of the potential conflicts of interest. To quote from *Congressional Record*, Senator Glass accused commercial banks of "chok[ing] the portfolios of their correspondent banks from Maine to California with utterly worthless investment

---

[21] The preliminary prospectus is called a red herring because a warning that the issue has not yet received approval from the SEC is printed in red vertically across the front page.

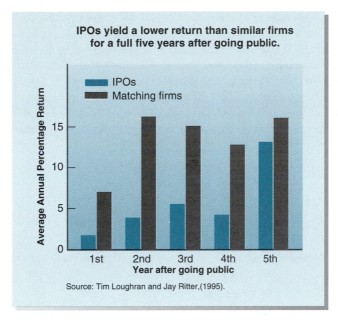

IPOs yield a lower return than similar firms for a full five years after going public.

Source: Tim Loughran and Jay Ritter,(1995).

Figure 17.7

securities" that were sold to an unsuspecting public and used to retire bank debt in danger of default. Leaving aside the question of how unsuspecting the public truly is, the potential for conflicts of interest is exacerbated when the bank simultaneously lends to and underwrites the publicly issued securities of its customers.

The Pecora hearings are filled with innuendo regarding security underwritings gone bad. For example, Chase National Bank made a $15 million loan to General Theaters and Entertainment (GTE) in 1929. In 1930 Chase Securities, an affiliate of the bank, underwrote $23 million of common stock and a total of $60 million of bonds for GTE, using the proceeds to repay the bank loan from Chase. Two years later, GTE went into bankruptcy. The Pecora Committee used this incident to illustrate the conflict of interest between commercial banking and underwriting. However, Benston (1990) shows that these were more likely cases of bad business judgment rather than conflicts of interest, particularly since in the GTE example Chase ended up owning most of the new issue and ultimately lost over $70 million.

This matter might simply be one for economic historians to ponder, except that the conflict of interest argument has resurfaced during recent legislative attempts to reintroduce de jure universal banking to the United States. One way either to confirm or to refute the conflict of interest assertion once and for all is to compare the quality of the securities underwritten by commercial banks to those underwritten by investment banks, as done by Kroszner and Rajan (1994), Ang and Richardson (1994), and Puri (1996). They find that the securities underwritten by commercial banks were less likely to default than those underwritten by investment banks. In addition, yields tended to be lower and the credit quality higher for commercial bank-underwritten issues than for issues underwritten by investment banks. As of 1939, 39.8% of the bonds underwritten by commercial banking affiliates had defaulted, in contrast to 48.4% of bonds underwritten by investment banks. Moreover, there is no significant difference in the performance of the stock underwritten by investment banks as opposed to commercial bank affiliates.[22] This refutes the conflict of interest argument. Indeed, Puri

---

[22] However, those stocks underwritten by Chase tended to perform somewhat more poorly than the others, a result that is consistent with Benston's bad business judgment explanation.

(1996) finds evidence of a certification role for commercial banks, where bank underwriters communicate their private information about the issuer's creditworthiness in the course of underwriting. Thus, combining commercial banking and underwriting appears to *improve* the availability of information about issuer quality provided to the public.

Universal banks provide all equity services in Germany. They are the only FIs entitled to stock exchange membership. As of 1989, there were 131 member banks on the Frankfurt Stock Exchange, 61 of which were subsidiaries of foreign banks or securities firms. There is less concern about the conflict of interest problem in Germany, since most banks are long term investors in the equity that they underwrite.

Checkpoint

1. Contrast spinoffs and carveouts.
2. Why are IPOs often underpriced?
3. Why is there a potential conflict of interest between commercial banking and under-writing?
4. What role do commercial bank underwriters play in certifying new issues?

Equity Trading in Emerging Countries

Equity markets have been opening throughout the world, but despite their promise, the volume of trading is often quite small. In 1994 the average value of trades on the NYSE was $30,707,692 each minute. Figure 17.8 shows how long it would take to trade that same value in Malaysia, Chile, Morocco, Hungary, and the Ivory Coast. It would take two years, 204 days, and 37 minutes in the Ivory Coast to accomplish what the NYSE does in one minute.

Although many developing countries have removed restrictions on foreign purchases of direct equity, barriers to entry still exist. Emerging countries in Europe and Latin America have been most progressive in removing restrictions on foreign ownership and improving accounting standards so as to improve access to foreign investors. However, many countries still have barriers to trade for foreign equity investors (Table 17.7). Claessens and Rhee (1994) show that stock price earnings ratios increase in countries that allow greater access to their markets.

privatization: sale of state-owned enterprises to private owners.

Privatization, the sale of state-owned enterprises to private owners, has increased the op-portunity to invest in the equity of companies in emerging countries. By 1990, the value of

Volume of trading on selected equity markets

| Malaysia | Chile | Morrocco | Hungary | Ivory Coast |
| 2 hours, 8 minutes | 2 days, 3 hours 7 minutes | 14 days, 5 hours 22 minutes | 41 days, 12 hours 18 minutes | 2 years, 204 days, 37 minutes |

Source: New York Times, November 11, 1995, p.37.

Figure 17.8

Table 17.7

Restrictions on Foreign Investors in Selected Countries

Argentina

The market is considered 100% investable, although some corporate statute limitations apply.

Brazil

The market is considered generally investable. Since May 1991 foreign institutions may own up to 49% of voting common stock and 100% of nonvoting preferred stock. Some corporate statute limitations (e.g., Petrobras common) apply.

Chile

Foreign capital investment funds are limited to 25% of a listed company's shares.

Colombia

The market has been 100% investable since February 1, 1991.

Greece

The market is generally 100% investable.

India

As of September 14, 1992, foreign FIs could invest in all listed securities if registered with the Board of India before making any investment. Investments are subject to a ceiling of 24% of issued share capital for the total holdings of all registered foreign FIs and 5% for the holding of a single foreign FI in any one company. Ceiling includes full conversion of convertible securities.

Indonesia

In December 1987 the government introduced deregulation measures to allow limited foreign investment. On September 16, 1989, foreigners were allowed to purchase up to 49% of all companies' listed shares, including foreign joint ventures but excluding banks. On October 30, 1992, foreigners were allowed to invest in up to 49% of listed shares of all banks except private national banks.

Jordan

The market is considered 49% investable.

Korea

Since January 1, 1992, authorized foreign investors have been allowed to acquire up to 10% of capital of listed companies, subject to some corporate statute limitations. In July 1992 Korean companies could apply to temporarily increase their limits to 25%.

Malyasia

The central bank limits ownership of banks and FIs by foreigners to 30%, although these limits are not strictly enforced. The approval of the Foreign Investment Committee is required for acquiring 15% or more of the voting power of a company by any one foreign interest and for acquiring the assets of a company when they exceed M$5 million, whether by Malaysian or foreign interests.

Mexico

Foreign portfolio investment is permitted in designated classes of shares and since May 1989 in most other shares through a trust arrangement. The market is now considered generally 100% investable, except for banks, where foreign ownership is restricted to 30%.

Nigeria

The market is closed to foreign investment.

Pakistan

The market has been considered 100% investable since February 22, 1991.

Table
17.7

Continued

Philippines

A minimum of 60% of issued shares of domestic companies should be owned by Philippine nationals. Two classes of stock are issued: A shares, which may be traded only among Philippine nationals, and B shares, which may be traded to either Philippine nationals or foreign investors. Mass media, retail trade, and rural banking companies are closed to foreign investors.

Portugal

The market is generally 100% investable, subject to some corporate statute limitations, especially regarding shares in privatizations.

Taiwan

The market was opened to foreigners on January 1, 1991, although foreign investors must meet high registration requirements and total cash inflows from abroad cannot currently exceed an official ceiling of $2.5 billion. There is a 10% limit on aggregate foreign ownership of capital. The domestic transportation industry is closed to foreigners.

Thailand

Laws restrict foreign shareholdings in Thai companies: banks are limited to 49%. The Alien Business Law restricts foreign ownership to stocks in specified sectors to 49%. Company bylaws also restrict foreign investors to ownership stakes between 15% and 65%. The Foreign Board was established in 1988 to facilitate trading in shares registered in foreign names.

Turkey

The market has been considered 100% investable since August 1989.

Venezuela

Nonfinancial stocks have been considered 100% investable since January 1, 1990, but some restricted classes do exist. Bank stocks are currently not available.

Zimbabwe

The market is closed to foreign investment because of severe exchange controls.

Source: Claessens and Rhee (1994), pp. 266–269.

---

privatized enterprises exceeded $185 billion. If privatization is to be successful, the emerging companies should operate more efficiently since they are monitored by private owners. Megginson, Nash, and van Randenborgh (1994) examine 57 companies privatized in the following countries: Austria, Canada, Chile, France, Germany, Italy, Jamaica, Japan, Korea, Mexico, New Zealand, Oman, Singapore, Spain, Sweden, and the United States. They find that after privatization, on average, return on sales increases by 2.49%, net income by 25.08%, real sales by 24.1%, employment by 2,346 employees per year, and dividend payout by 22.55%.

Country Funds   Because of the transaction costs of investing in developing countries' equity markets, the role of FIs is critical. FIs have long facilitated trading by offering ADRs and GDRs in foreign stocks. However, since ADRs and GDRs must be registered in the country in which they are sold, they have high transaction costs. Many equity issues in emerging countries do not qualify for ADR status because of deficiencies in their country's accounting standards that make compliance with U.S. disclosure requirements prohibitively expensive.

A way around this limitation is the country fund. To expand on the definition given in Chapter 9, we can now say that a **country fund** is a closed-end mutual fund that trades as shares on the equity market at a price that may be greater than, equal to, or less than the net asset value of the fund's portfolio of a particular country's stocks. In December 1992 there was

country fund: (expanded definition) a closed-end mutual fund that trades as shares on the equity market at a price that may be greater than, equal to, or less than the net asset value of the fund's portfolio of a particular country's stocks.

41 funds, each specializing in one of 26 countries and representing a total of $4.3 billion in equity value. Since closed-end funds invest in a fixed portfolio, shares can be liquidated by sales of the fund's shares in secondary markets.[23]

Country funds' prices *on issue* typically trade at a premium, which is eroded by about 20% over the 24 weeks following the IPO, after which they are usually priced at a discount from their portfolio's net asset value. The discount can vary considerably over time. Indeed, in the case of Germany, the discount became a substantial premium during the euphoria in the period surrounding the fall of the Berlin Wall in 1989. Country fund prices reflect investor sentiment about the emerging country's economic prospects. However, Hardouvelis, La Porta, and Wizman (1994) find that country fund price fluctuations do not reflect fundamental country-specific information or barriers to entry, but rather appear to be basically irrational. *Timely Topics 17.2: South Sea Style* shows the dangers of following the herd into the latest emerging country fund. Note that the article came out in September 1994, just prior to the December 1994 crash in the Mexican stock market.

The country funds adopted an activist stance during the Mexican crisis. Rather than acting as passive investors, the managers of the country funds advised the Mexican government and even made offers to pour an additional $17 billion into Mexico if certain reforms were enacted. Indeed, the country funds took on a monitoring role similar to that of public FIs, like the IMF, and private FIs, like banks.

TIMELY TOPICS 17.2

SOUTH SEA STYLE

Emerging stock markets around the world attained a total capitalization of over $1 trillion in 1993—which the International Finance Corporation (IFC) says proves that these markets have "come into their own" as places to invest and to raise capital. But some believe it could just as easily point to a new South Sea Bubble in the making.

It is not just capitalizations, equity valuations and turnover levels are soaring under the impact of unprecedented inflows of foreign and domestic funds. . . .

One investment banker notes that this is reminiscent of the 1970s, when venture capitalism proved to be "the biggest mousetrap of the decade." Investors eagerly financed venture capitalists who were often no more than mad inventors or pure charlatans—until the trap sprang shut. Now the trap may be baited again, this time in emerging markets.

Emerging markets enable developing countries to attract inflows of foreign equity that help insure against the over-dependence on foreign banking flows which led to the Third World debt crisis in the 1980s. And they help to mobilize domestic savings to finance needed investments.

But the rapid emergence of so many new stock markets around the world since the late 1980s—the IFC lists 47 of them in Latin America, Asia, the Middle East and elsewhere—coincided with a period of unprecedented liquidity among US FIs in particular, though also in Europe and Japan.

These trends reached a crescendo in 1993 when, according to Baring Securities, the global net inflow into emerging markets reached around $37 billion—double the amount in 1992. Mexico alone received inflows of some $10.7 billion, South Korea $5.7 billion, Brazil $5.5 billion, India $1.5 bilion, and Peru received $1.2 billion.

---

[23] In an open-end mutual fund, shares are redeemed by the mutual fund at their net asset value, which is the market value of the fund's portfolio.

The really big spenders were Americans. . . . U.S. mutual funds targeting emerging markets received net inflows of $20 billion in 1993. . . . The IFC's Asian emerging markets index rose by 94% last year, the Latin American index rose 56%. (And even this was tame compared with the 718% rise in the Polish stock market.)

The scramble for emerging stocks also pushed secondary market turnover ratios (the number of times a market turns over its capitalization in one year) well above what is usually regarded as a healthy 50–75%. In Taiwan, the ratio reached 235% and in South Korea 172% while even China's embryonic markets achieved a turnover ratio of 164% and Poland's reached 129%. . . .

But some investment bankers suggest that normal underwriting prudence is being sacrificed on the altar of emerging market mania as US and other international investors—not to mention (often sophisticated) local investors—clamor to get a slice of the action. And listing standards are being compromised in the rush to bring ever more new companies to market, analysts say.

A good example is privatization stocks. Privatization issues comprised a significant portion of the $38 billion total new issues last year, with Argentine companies alone raising almost $9.5 billion for this purpose and Indian companies a further $7.4 billion.

Emerging stock markets, says the IFC's 1994 report on emerging markets, "fill critical niches by providing mechanisms for the sale of state-owned enterprises and by linking capital markets to broader international markets." All well and good if the state entities have first been corporatized, so as to teach them commercial ways and to allow them to establish a track record of profitability and dividend paying.

But in the case of many Latin American and some Asian countries, cash-strapped governments caught up with the obsession to privatize do not have the resources or the patience to go through the corporatization phase first. As a result, portfolio investors are shouldering risks normally associated with direct investors and commercial lenders.

Thailand is going even further and proposing to list so-called "greenfield" infrastructure ventures on the Bangkok stock exchange. This means that concerns possessing the franchise, though not yet the capital and assets, to operate anything from toll roads and mass-transit systems to telecommunications and transport facilities, will be able to list stocks on the exchange. . . .

All this promises yet more liquidity to help fuel what looks suspiciously like a growing bubble in emerging primary and secondary markets. If assets and returns prove to be illusory in the case of at least some developing country stocks, then emerging markets as a whole could get a bad name. Emerging markets could become the "mousetrap" of the 1990s.

Source: A. Rowley, *The Banker*, September 1994, 54–55.

Checkpoint

✓

1. What factors prevent equity markets in emerging countries from pricing efficiently?
2. What are country funds and how are they priced?
3. What explains the recent growth in country funds?

➤ Trading in Secondary Markets

If economies are to grow, financial markets must handle new issues effectively and efficiently. New issues inject the lifeblood of investment capital into the economy. But no new issues can succeed without an efficient and fair secondary market. No one would invest in a financial security if there was no way to realize the value of that investment through liquidation in a secondary market. This explains the dual role of underwriters as initiators of new issues and market makers for these issues as they trade in secondary markets.

Whereas Table 17.1 describes total equity transactions in each country, Figure 17.9 deals with cross-border equity transfers. The decade from 1980 to 1990 saw an increase in international transactions in equities from US$73 billion to over US$1,500 billion. The United States and the United Kingdom attracted considerable amounts of investment from abroad. However, net foreign investment in the United States fluctuates over time in response to exchange rate risk exposure. As seen in Figure 17.9, there were periods of significant *dis*investment in U.S. stocks during 1987, 1990, 1992, and 1994–1995. In contrast, Japanese and German investors are consistent net exporters of equity capital.

Pricing Equities

price earnings (P/E) ratio: the stock price divided by earnings per share.

In Chapter 7, we used the constant dividend growth model to price common stock. Up-to-date quotations on stock prices are available on electronic screens such as the one shown in Figure 17.10. The current price for DEC shown in Figure 17.10 is 72 $\frac{7}{8}$, or US$72.875. The volume of shares trading (574,100), opening price (72), high price (73), low price (71 $\frac{5}{8}$), and previous quote (72 $\frac{3}{8}$) are all shown. Moreover, the **price earnings (P/E) ratio**, the stock price (72 $\frac{7}{8}$) divided by earnings per share (3.55), is displayed (20.53). The screen showns a measure of risk, beta (1.09), as well as information about competitors' stocks. Electronic quotations allow traders to obtain current information on stock prices so necessary in today's volatile markets. Table 17.8 compares stock market returns and volatilities around the world. Italian stock markets are the most volatile (with a 10.41 variance) and equity markets in Belgium least volatile (3.82 variance).

The Equity Premium Puzzle   Over the last one hundred years, the average real return to stocks in the United States has been about 6% higher than that on Treasury bills, which has averaged only about 1% p.a.[24] The difference between the return on stocks and the risk free

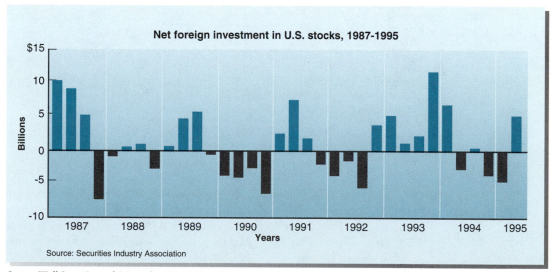

Source: Wall Street Journal, November 25, 1995, p. C1.

Figure 17.9

---

[24] Roy (1994) also finds evidence of this relationship in post-World War II Germany and Japan. Kocherlakota (1995) asserts that the inexplicably high rate of return on equities is a feature of all organized asset markets.

DEC US$ 72 7/8 +1/2 M /MADF   Equity BQ
DELAY   Vol 574,100 Op 72 m Hi 73 N Lo 71 5/8 N Prev 72 5/8
DES   DIGITAL EQUIP   DVD EX-Date   EE Est 6/96   11) BETA Beta 1.09
2)   52Hi 73 7/8 1/25   3) REG CASH   8) P/E 20.53 12) GE   P/E 27.81
       52Lo 31 1/2 3/20   Div Yld n.a.   EPS 3.55   9) HDS Holdings

GPO   GIP
5)   6)
                               2MIL   10:00 12:00 14:00 16:00 10:00 12:00 14:00 16:00
                               2MIL   JAN 30   JAN 31
       5JAN96   12   19   26

       VOL-WGHT AVG:72.636   COMPUTERS   5Day Chg P/E   GrIndYld 1 Yr Ret
       1/30 424   72 5/8 N   DEC 72 7/8 +1/2   -.34 27.81   .00 +115.13
       13:26 230 ↑ 73   N   IBM 109   +3/8   +1.87 15.10   .92 +52.78
AQR   1/30 200 ↓ 72 3/8 T   AQR   CPQ 46 3/4 -5/8 -2.09 16.18   .00 +30.77
4)   1/30 424 ↑ 72 5/8 T   4)   SGI 28   +3/8   +3.70 21.05   .00 -10.40
       12:41 184 ↓ 72 1/2 M   AAPL 27 3/4 +7/16 -13.95 20.56   1.73 -30.49
       9:30 177 ↓ 72   N   EMC 19 1/4 unch   unch 15.04   .00 +3.36
       1/30 150 ↑ 72 3/4 N   COMS 45 1/4 +13/16 +1.12 40.95   .00 +97.54
       1/30 141   72 3/8 N   SUNW 45 5/8 -1/16 +4.89 20.28   .00 +178.63
CN   NEL 14:14 Morgan Stanley "Guess who came to dinner"
10)   NEL 14:14 Morgan Stanley "Solid quarter"
       NEL 14:13 Chicago Corp "Downgrading Digital Equipment rating from Buy to"
Bloomberg-all rights reserved. Frankfurt:69-920410 Hong Kong:2-521-3000 London:171-330-7500 New York:212-318-2000
Princeton:609-279-3000   Singapore:226-3000   Sydney:2-777-8600   Tokyo:3-3201-8900   Washington DC:202-434-1800
                                                                G165-312-3 31-Jan-96 10:48:44

Figure 17.10

Stock Market Returns and Volatility

Country	Weekly Returns (means)	Return Volatility (variance)	Volatility Persistence (in weeks)
Australia	0.32%	4.66	0.58
Belgium	0.23	3.82	7.02
Canada	0.16	4.56	13.8
France	0.29	5.07	10.5
Germany	0.08	5.286	35.9
Italy	0.11	10.41	7.6
Japan	0.25	5.449	15.1
Switzerland	0.15	5.98	14.8
United Kingdom	0.25	6.75	13.1
United States	0.20	4.28	6.8

Source: Theodossiou (1994), pp. 9–11.

rate is a measure of the risk premium on equities. However, the size of this risk premium is not justified by the stock market's risk exposure, unless investors are assumed to be unreasonably averse to risk. Indeed, Mehra and Prescott (1985) could justify an equity premium of only 0.35% as a risk premium. They called the persistent overpricing of the risk premium on stocks an **equity premium puzzle**.

If the equity premium puzzle is the result of security mispricing, there is an arbitrage opportunity. That is, an investor can gain by borrowing at the Treasury bill rate and investing in stocks. Borrowing limitations and transaction costs may reduce this arbitrage profit, but not eliminate it. Researchers continue to be puzzled by an explanation for this persistent relationship.

equity premium puzzle: the persistent overpricing of the risk premium on stocks.

Figure 17.11

Brokerage Commissions

The most active stock markets in the world are in the United States and Japan; activity on the British and German equity markets pales in comparison (see Table 17.1). FIs facilitate the turnover volume by providing brokerage services. Equity brokerage is fiercely competitive in the United States and the United Kingdom, but less so in Japan and Germany. Since 1975 in the U.S. and 1986 in the U.K., brokerage commissions have been determined competitively, in contrast to the fixed fees still levied in Germany and Japan. Competitive fee-setting allows FIs in the U.S. and the U.K. to pass along to their customers the cost savings realized from economies of scale in brokerage.[25] Commissions, as a fraction of broker–dealer revenues, declined precipitously in May 1975 after the abolition of fixed commissions in the U.S.

Figure 17.11 compares global trading costs in 10 of the largest equity markets throughout the world. Transaction costs, including commissions, fees, and taxes, are smallest in the United States and largest in Australia. Average direct costs total about 30 basis points in the U.S., 76 basis points in Japan, and 96 basis points in the U.K. Because of the prohibition against price competition in providing brokerage services, the big four investment banks in Japan (Nomura, Nikko, Daiwa, and Yamaichi) controlled 41% of stock trading and 55% of convertible bond trading in 1988. However, to reduce their dominance, in 1988 the Ministry of Finance imposed a regulation that no FI could account for more than 30% of any stock's monthly turnover. Foreign FIs' market share of volume on the Tokyo Stock Exchange increased from 1.5% in 1986 to 7.3% in 1990.

The Interbank Information System (IBIS), inaugurated in December 1989, is a pricing and trading system for the shares of large, blue chip corporations that operates both during and after exchange trading hours. In 1993 IBIS accounted for about 40% of total volume on these stocks. Trading in secondary equity markets is characterized by a pronounced shift from

---

[25] Although commissions are fixed in Germany, there is some discount for volume. As of July 1995, commissions were set at a uniform 0.04% for the 30 blue chip stocks in the DAX (the German stock exchange) Index, and 0.08% for all other stocks.

retail, small-sized trades to institutional, block trades. Stock is widely held in the United States, although the fraction of shares held by households has decreased steadily over time. Indeed, the fraction decreased from 62.1% in 1980 to 47.9% in 1994, reflecting greater institutional equityholdings.[26] In 1989 block trading represented 51% of all trading on the NYSE, up from 27% in 1979. This shift reflects the explosion in growth of mutual funds during this period. The vehicle for individual investing has shifted from retail purchases of stock to purchases of shares in diversified stock portfolios in the form of mutual funds.

World equity markets are highly integrated by electronic trading systems that transmit prices around the globe in an instant. The experience after the stock market crashes of October 1987 and 1989 suggests that there is contagion in equity prices. A high degree of correlation exists between world equity market returns, particularly for the United States and Japan. Roll (1988) and Remolona (1991) find evidence of a contagious overreaction to stock market fluctuations that is passed from one market to another around the world over a 20 year period. This experience fueled reforms in equity markets. Huth (1994) shows that U.S. stock market returns significantly impact returns on the Canadian, German, French, Japanese, and British stock markets on the following day.

Because of the volatility of today's global financial markets, FIs are finding it increasingly necessary to police themselves against abuses of the public trust. In recent years, there has been a spate of well-publicized "rogue traders," pictured in Figure 17.12, who allegedly undertook unauthorized trades that ultimately resulted in substantial losses for the FI. We saw the impact of Robert Citron's risk taking in the repo market (see Chapter 11) and Paul Mozer's Treasury auction violations (see Chapter 15). In 1994, Joseph Jett of Kidder Peabody was accused of faking $350 million in government bond trading profits to hide trading losses of $85 million, leading to Kidder Peabody's loss of its independence when it was absorbed by PaineWebber Group, Inc. Nicholas Leeson pleaded guilty in November 1995 to fraud in futures and options on the Japanese stock market, costing Barings PLC $950 million and its independence, as it was acquired by ING Bank. In July 1995, Toshihide Iguchi admitted to 11 years of bond-trading losses to Daiwa Bank totaling over $1 billion. In June 1996, a decade of unauthorized copper trades by Yasuo Hamanaka of Sumitomo was revealed to have generated losses of exceeding $2 billion. FIs have responded by instituting automatic technological red flags to detect traders that violate rules.

Checkpoint

1. Which countries have fixed brokerage commissions? Which countries allow competitively determined commissions?

2. How would you describe the FI's costs of providing brokerage services?

Circuit Breakers and Reforms in the Wake of the 1987 Stock Market Crash

October 19, 1987, is known as Black Monday: on this day the Dow Jones Industrial Average plunged 22.61%. With market makers swamped by sell orders, prices could not reflect value and went into a freefall. The market experienced a liquidity crisis of previously unknown proportions. To a certain extent, the liquidity crisis fed a panic that exacerbated the price decline.[27] As a result of this experience, in order to provide time for market participants to regroup and obtain backup sources of liquidity, a series of **circuit breakers** were put into

circuit breakers:
automatic halts or limitations in trading that are triggered upon the attainment of certain stipulated price moves.

---

[26] However, when households' indirect holdings of stock, say through their pension funds, are included, this percentage increases to 64%.

[27] The Fed was able to contain the liquidity crisis by issuing a statement at 8:15 A.M. on Tuesday, October 20, 1987, that read: "The Federal Reserve System, consistent with its responsibilities as the nation's central banker, affirmed today its readiness to serve as a source of liquidity to support the economic and financial system." This statement extended lender of last resort privileges to nonbank FIs.

Robert L. Citron   Yasuo Hamanaka   Joseph Jett

Nicholas W. Leeson   Paul L. Mozer

Figure 17.12   Rogue's Gallery

50 point collar: provision that prohibits computer-assisted trading if the Dow rises or falls by 50 points.

250 point rule: provision that halts all trading for one hour if the Dow falls by 250 points in a day.

effect. Circuit breakers are automatic halts or limitations in trading that are triggered upon the attainment of certain stipulated price moves. For example, under the **50 point collar** provision, if the Dow rises or falls by 50 points, computer-assisted trading is prohibited. The **250 point rule** halts all trading for a half hour if the Dow falls by 250 points in a day, and for one hour if prices fall 400 points.[28]

Since the circuit breakers are stated in terms of point movements, they are sensitive to the Dow's level. In October 1988, when this method was adopted, a 250 point movement in the Dow represented a 12% move. In 1996, as the Dow exceeded 5,700, the same 250 point movement represented only a 4% move. Thus, a 250 point movement and the triggering of the circuit breaker become much more likely as the Dow increases in value. The SEC has still not responded to calls to restate the circuit breakers in terms of percentage changes as opposed to absolute point movements.

---

[28] The original circuit breakers called for trading halts of 1 hour and 2 hours if prices fall 250 points and 400 points, respectively. The duration of trading halts was halved in July 1996.

portfolio insurance: a
program that
automatically rebalances a
portfolio in response to
market shifts.

Portfolio Insurance and Market Volatility   One of the culprits widely blamed for the volume of sell orders on October 19 was **portfolio insurance**, which is a program that automatically rebalances a portfolio in response to market shifts. When the stock market declines, portfolio insurance automatically sells stocks so as to lower the proportion invested in the stock market and raise the proportion invested in bonds and held in cash. When the stock market increases, the program automatically purchases stock. Portfolio insurance is a form of dynamic hedging, which alters the risk level of the portfolio in response to market conditions, shifting to safer portfolios in declining markets and riskier portfolios in rising markets.

Portfolio insurance programs buy and sell stocks in response to market movements. On October 19, sales of stock by portfolio insurers accounted for 15 to 20% of daily volume. The 50 point collar restrictions on computer-assisted trading is directed toward eliminating portfolio insurer's trades during volatile periods, because such trades exacerbate stock price movements. However, to reduce transaction costs, program trading mostly uses futures and options to rebalance the portfolio. Stock sales (purchases) in declining (rising) markets are accomplished via futures sales (purchases) and purchases of put (call) options on stock indices. Portfolio insurers sold stock on October 19 because the futures markets were out of sync with cash markets. Furbush (1989) provides evidence that portfolio insurers' transactions in both the cash and derivatives markets actually reduced the price discrepancies that arose because of the unprecedented volatility and illiquidity in the markets.

Bid-Ask Spreads on the Nasdaq

For years, the second largest equity market in the world was the electronic Nasdaq. In 1994 average daily volume on the Nasdaq edged past that of the NYSE. Nasdaq had 49% of all 1994 share volume in the United States, while NYSE had 48% and AMEX 3%. In 1995 average daily volume on the Nasdaq was 372 million shares in contrast to the average daily volume on the NYSE of 337 million shares, although dollar volume was higher on the NYSE at $11.5 billion versus $8.4 billion a day on Nasdaq.[29] As of 1994, there were 4,861 domestic and foreign companies trading on Nasdaq, with an annual rate of IPOs of about 450. Membership in the National Association of Securities Dealers (NASD) totals 5,200 FIs, with 427,000 registered representatives.

FIs that make markets in particular securities receive payment for their liquidity services in the form of the bid-ask spread. The bid-ask spread is wider (1) the higher the FIs' order processing costs; (2) the greater the FIs' inventory holding costs; or (3) the greater the adverse information costs (that is, the more uncertainty about the security's fundamental value). If there are large information asymmetries between corporate insiders and market makers, then this uncertainty increases, thereby increasing the bid-ask spread. The information costs of the third component represent an estimated 8 to 40% of the total bid-ask spread.[30]

The minimum bid-ask spread on Nasdaq is usually 1/8th of a point. This is equal to the minimum acceptable price movement, or tick value, on Nasdaq. However, in April 1994, Nasdaq moved to a tick value of 1/64th, or from 12.5 cents per dollar to 1.5625 cents per dollar. This refinement in the minimum acceptable price fluctuation was insufficient to address a critique that was to cause quite a bit of grief for the Nasdaq.

A study by Christie and Schultz (1994a, 1994b) showed that bid-ask spreads on Nasdaq were wider than they should be, in part because market makers "tacitly colluded" to keep their profit margins wide. Christie and Schultz found that traders were reluctant to trade on "odd-eighths," thus making the minimum bid-ask spread effectively 1/4 point, or 25 cents per dollar. Thus, if the last bid price quotation is $13.25, the next ask price is unlikely to be $13.375, but instead will be $13.50, keeping the bid-ask spread at 25 cents ($13.50 minus $13.25). Table

---

[29] Some observers contend that Nasdaq share volume is inflated because it contains multiple dealer-to-dealer trades.

[30] See Glosten and Harris (1988), Stoll (1989), and George, Kaul, and Nimalendran (1991).

| | **Table 17.9** | **Bid–Ask Spreads on Some Popular Nasdaq Stocks (Percentage Distribution)**[a] |

Bid–Ask Spreads on Some Popular Nasdaq Stocks (Percentage Distribution)[a]

| | Dollar Spread | | | |
Stock Name	1/8	1/4	3/8	1/2
Apple Computer	1.2%	49.3%	1.8%	47.7%
Lotus Development	1.3	49.3	2.0	47.3
MCI Communications	50.3	48.7	1.0	0

[a]The percentages reflect the fraction of closing price quotes at a particular quotation (in terms of eighths).

Source: Christie and Schultz (1994a), pp. 1813–1840.

17.9 shows the suspicious spreads. With the exception of MCI, stocks were significantly more likely to trade at even-eighths than at odd-eighths.

Some analysts contend that this phenomenon represents an "under-the-table" (as opposed to "over-the-counter") payment for **order flow**, or the right to execute customers' trades, and therefore abuses small investors who do not receive the best price for their trades. On the other hand, others maintain that these are just the posted quotations while actual trades occur continuously between the even-eighths. Indeed, Christie and Schultz themselves acknowledge that odd-eighths trading increased after the appearance of their study.

order flow: the right to execute customers' trades.

To address the criticism and assure small investors of the best possible price execution, Nasdaq introduced a new trading system called Aqcess in March 1995. The system allows a small trader to place a limit order "inside the spread," presumably at odd-eighths. Thus, if the bid-ask were $13.25–$13.50, an Aqcess trader could place an order at $13.375.

Aqcess was to replace another system, introduced after the market crash of 1987, called the Small Order Execution System (SOES). This system gave small investors instantaneous priority trading rights. That created an opportunity for "SOES bandits" to exploit the system. Small FIs, like Datek Securities, exploit SOES for their own account by entering a bid 20% above the highest price market makers are quoting. The high bid moves the bandit to the head of potential buyers. But since the SOES system is used, the orders (up to 1,000 shares) are automatically executed at the market maker's ask price. Thus, the SOES bandit does not have to pay the outrageously high price that he bids and instead uses that bid simply to get immediate execution. SOES trading had become so profitable that, as of 1995, volume approached 8% of all Nasdaq share volume. SOES bandits claim that they make pricing more efficient on Nasdaq. But because of nimble SOES bandits trading for their own accounts, many of the small investors who were to be the original beneficiaries of the system are locked out of preferential SOES pricing.

Checkpoint ✓

1. How do circuit breakers reduce stock price volatility?
2. When might circuit breakers provide a destabilizing influence on financial markets?
3. How does market maker reluctance to trade in odd-eighths affect small investors?
4. Contrast the SOES and the Aqcess systems. What are their goals? How are they achieved?

Mutual Funds

Mutual fund assets in the United States, as of the end of 1995, totaled more than $3 trillion in over 3,000 funds, although about *half* of those assets are controlled by the 10 top funds. Outside of the United States, mutual fund assets grew from $141 billion in 1983 to over

$2 trillion in 1993. Mutual funds offer small investors the diversification benefits and low transaction costs that they could not obtain if they were investing on their own. Because mutual funds are valued at the net asset value of their portfolio, investors can reduce their liquidity risk by investing in mutual funds. The entire portfolio is not liquidated when one investor liquidates its holdings, and thus the cost of liquidation is minimized. Indeed, fund purchases may exceed fund redemptions, thereby eliminating the need for any liquidation of the fund's portfolio. However, large-scale redemptions by many of the investors after an unfavorable event, such as the stock market crash of October 1987, may require liquidation of a portion of the fund's portfolio at a capital loss for an open-end mutual fund.

Open-End Versus Closed-End Mutual Funds   We have seen that country funds are closed-end mutual funds. The fund's manager invests in a portfolio that is fixed, or closed; and then shares in that fixed portfolio are sold to the public. Liquidating an investment in a closed-end fund requires the sale of shares to another investor since the fund's total number of shares is always fixed. In contrast, the portfolio of an open-end mutual fund is never fixed. As more money pours in, or as money is redeemed, the fund's portfolio either expands or contracts.

Open-end mutual funds attempt to discourage redemptions via a series of fees. **Load charges** are sales commissions that can be charged either as front-end (upon the investor's initial purchase of the mutual fund shares) or back-end (upon the investor's sale of the mutual fund shares). Other fees are management, advisory, exchange, and **12b-1 fees**, which are distribution fees paid to selling agents. To minimize costs and improve distribution, *Timely Topics 17.3: Fund Company's Size Is Seen as Essential to Survival* shows that bigger funds, with more assets under management, have an important competitive advantage. This explains the proliferation of families of funds that allow investors to shift between funds at low transaction costs. To compete with the bigger funds, smaller funds have employed wholesalers who sell funds to brokers who, in turn, sell them to investors.

load charges: sales commissions that can be charged either as front-end, upon the investor's initial purchase of the mutual fund shares, or back-end, upon the investor's sale of the mutual fund shares.

12b-1 fees: distribution fees paid to selling agents.

TIMELY TOPICS 17.3

FUND COMPANY'S SIZE IS SEEN AS ESSENTIAL TO SURVIVAL

Big is better than good if you're in the mutual-fund business.

At least that's the conclusion of a report by Goldman, Sachs & Co. that argues buyers of mutual-fund companies are more interested in the size of a company's sales system than whether its funds outperform the S&P500.

"Growth in the mutual-fund industry has been driven by distribution far more than investment performance," concludes the report. So, unless a fund company has a large distribution mechanism it should merge with a bigger company before it's too late, Goldman concludes.

Of course, Goldman will be there to help. The more mutual-fund companies that go on the auction block, the more investment-banking fees Goldman and other investment banks can earn.

But the report isn't entirely self-serving.... "We are going to have to be big to be cost-efficient." The reason is simple. After a decade of torrid growth, the mutual-fund industry appears to be settling onto a plateau, making competition tougher and profits harder to achieve. The only way for a fund company to maintain market share these days is to spend more money on advertising and customer service, and to pay more money to brokers and others who sell mutual funds.... [F]unds with less than $10 billion under management will have a tough time surviving....

Goldman's recommendations for small mutual fund companies:

- Sell the company
- Form strategic alliances
- Create niche products that generate high fees
- Buy distribution channels to help accumulate new assets
- Innovate aggressive marketing strategies

Source: G. Steimetz and S. Calian, *Wall Street Journal*, May 26, 1994.

Money Market Mutual Funds   Over 27% of all mutual fund assets are held in money market mutual funds which invest in a portfolio of short term, highly liquid money market instruments. Figure 17.13 shows the breakdown of mutual fund assets across money market funds, bond and income funds, and equity funds. Over the three years shown in the figure, the amount of assets invested by money market mutual funds have been quite stable. Because of the high liquidity of their portfolios, money market mutual funds offer limited transaction services such as check-writing privileges. The $1 net asset value is sacrosanct to the money market fund. That is, the fund's portfolio is managed so as to ensure that each share repays its full face value. Any income earned on the fund's assets is distributed in the form of interest paid on the fund's $1 net asset value.

In September 1994 the Community Bankers U.S. Government Money Market Fund was the first to "break the buck" and pay less than $1 net asset value. The fund was liquidated at 94 cents for each dollar invested. Other money market mutual funds experiencing losses in the face value of their portfolios have gone to great lengths to avoid breaking the buck. Although

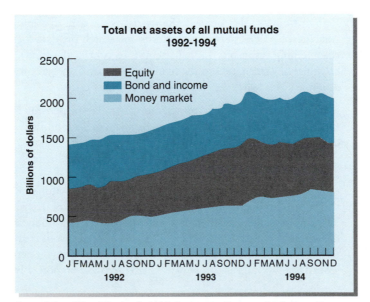

Source: Mutual Fund Factbook, 1995, Investment Company Institute, p. 7.

Figure 17.13

not legally required to do so, Bank of America injected $67.9 million into its Pacific Horizon money funds to maintain its $1 net asset value.

Hedge Funds   A type of mutual fund that has suffered from market reversals in recent years is the **hedge fund**. Although there is no universally accepted definition, during congressional testimony in 1994, John LaWare, member of the Board of Governors of the Federal Reserve System, defined hedge funds as those having some, but not all, of the following characteristics:

- An investment partnership or mutual fund that is unregulated.
- A fund that seeks high rates of return by investing or trading in virtually any form of financial instrument.
- An entity that may take long and short positions and invests in many markets.
- An entity that uses leverage.
- An entity whose manager's compensation is based on its financial performance.

LaWare also detailed the participation requirements of the hedge funds: "so that managers of hedge funds can be free to use various trading strategies, and free to change those strategies quickly, the funds are structured in order to avoid the regulatory limitations on permissible assets, leverage, and concentration of assets that apply to other managed funds that are offered to the public. . . . The number of investors in hedge funds is also limited by their high minimum investments, typically from $250,000 to $1,000,000 or more. Participation in some funds is further restricted to professional traders or persons with specialized knowledge of particular markets, regardless of their wealth."[31] Hedge funds are usually organized as closed-end funds because of the volatility of the value of the assets in the fund's portfolio. Indeed, many of these hedge funds periodically experience liquidity crises when trading dries up in the assets they hold, thereby making it difficult to evaluate the fund's net asset value.

Hedge funds are not the only types of mutual funds that may be difficult to evaluate. In June 1994, the largest mutual fund family, Fidelity Investments, admitted that it had knowingly reported day-old net asset values for 166 funds instead of their true closing prices. Every afternoon, funds send their data to the NASD in time to meet a reporting deadline of 5:30 P.M. Eastern time. At that time, NASD transfers the data to a mutual fund analysis firm, Lipper Analytical Services, to calculate returns and search the data for extreme price moves. If there is something suspicious, Lipper attempts to contact the fund's managers. However, the final list must be transmitted to the financial press by 6:15 P.M. in order to meet the publication deadline. This leaves very little leeway to correct errors.

Pension Funds   Another form of mutual fund is the **pension fund**, a structured, tax-deferred fund that provides either a lump-sum payment or an annuity upon retirement. A pension fund can be either **defined contribution** or **defined benefit**. Under a defined contribution plan, the payout to any employee upon retirement is determined entirely by the balance in the pension fund. Both the employee and the employer make tax-deferred contributions to the fund over the years, and these contributions are invested in a portfolio of financial securities. Whatever the value of the portfolio upon an employee's retirement determines the payout to the retiree. The employee takes on all investment risk. In contrast, under a defined benefit pension fund, the employer takes on the investment risk, since the payout is determined by a formula that is a function of the employee's salary history, not the investment performance of the fund assets. A federal agency, the Pension Benefit Guarantee Corporation (PBGC), guarantees the promised

hedge fund: fund that has an unregulated investment partnership; seeks high rates of return; takes long and short positions; uses leverage; and compensates management based on its financial performance.

pension fund: a structured, tax-deferred fund that provides either a lump-sum payment or an annuity upon retirement.

defined contribution pension plan: pension plan in which the payout upon retirement, is determined entirely by the balance in the pension fund.

defined benefit pension plan: pension plan in which the payout is determined by a formula that is a function of the employee's salary history, not the investment performance of the fund.

---

[31] Statement by John P. LaWare before the Committee on Banking, Finance, and Urban Affairs of the U.S. House of Representatives, April 13, 1994.

pension benefits up to a certain amount. The assets in the pension fund serve as collateral for the fund's benefit liabilities to employees.

Legal and tax regulations affect the portfolio choices of defined benefit pension funds. The Employee Retirement Income Security Act (ERISA) of 1974 and asymmetric tax treatment of overfunded versus underfunded defined benefit plans have led to a demand for long term, fixed-duration debt instruments. This is in contrast to defined contribution plans, which, by definition, are fully funded and offer investors a choice among equity, debt, and money market investments. Defined benefit plans are characterized by their extreme aversion to risk taking in the form of their choice of investment assets. Defined benefit plans are important forces behind the proliferation of innovative risk management techniques using debt, equity, and derivatives. This is because the corporate employer must guarantee the benefits to its employees, but retains the rights to only a portion of any **surplus value** of the fund's assets—that is, the difference between the fund's asset value and the present value of benefits owed to employees under the benefits formula. To reduce the cost of the guarantee, the employer invests the funds in assets that will generate cash flows sufficient to meet *minimum* levels of defined benefits. This is not the investment strategy that is desired by the pension fund holders, since they prefer the goal of *maximizing* retirement benefits. Both ERISA and the tax treatment of defined benefit plans encourage employers to increase their demand for financial products to hedge their investment risk.

More than 32% of 1995 mutual fund assets, or $687 billion out of a total of $2,162 billion, was in retirement plans of one kind or another. Moreover, this fraction has been increasing in recent years. Mutual fund managers are quite happy about this development because "retirement money behaves like an oil tanker. It doesn't turn quickly, moves steadily, and is hard to stop. In contrast, regular fund accounts behave more like a mix of sailboats tacking into the wind and powerboats whizzing around at random."[32]

Index Funds   Mutual funds offer investors the opportunity to diversify even if their investment stake is rather small. There is no limit to the degree of diversification possible. **Index funds** offer investors a well-diversified, passively managed portfolio with returns that mirror the returns of a large, broad-based portfolio. Index funds can be tied to indexes that range from the Dow Jones Industrial Average to the Wilshire Large Capitalization Value Index to bond indices.[33] The number of index funds increased from 17 at the end of the 1980s to 86 as of 1994. Index funds have very low transaction costs since the portfolio has very little turnover. The fund manager invests in the securities that make up the index and does virtually nothing else. Average expense ratios for index funds are 0.18% as compared to 1.40% for actively managed funds.

surplus value: the difference between the fund's asset value and the present value of benefits owed to employees under the benefits formula.

Index funds: well-diversified, passively-managed portfolio with returns that mirror the returns of a large, broad-based portfolio.

Checkpoint

✓

1. Contrast closed-end and open-end mutual funds.

2. Why are hedge funds closed-end and money market mutual funds open-end?

3. Why do you think that Bank of America went to such great lengths to avoid "breaking the buck" on its money market mutual fund?

4. Contrast the defined contribution and defined benefit pension plans. Who bears investment risk in each?

---

[32] E. Schultz, "Tidal Wave of Retirement Cash Anchors Mutual Funds," *Wall Street Journal*, September 27, 1995, p. C1.

[33] For a discussion of the construction of indexes, see Chapter 9.

Summary

Companies issue equity despite the tax advantages and signaling benefits of debt. To assist them in equity issues, they use FIs to innovate, advise, underwrite, and distribute their shares. In recent years, the market in preferred stocks has been the scene of much financial innovation. Banks and other FIs have become the dominant issuers of preferred stock issues because of regulatory advantages that encourage the issuance of preferred stock instruments that qualify as Tier 1 capital. To minimize the cost of capital for these issuers, preferred stock innovations have

- Allowed for convertibility into common stock.

- Offered variable rate dividend payments.

- Subordinated payments to senior debtholders' claims.

- Structured dividend payments so that they are tax deductible.

Some financial innovations fail if they do not obtain regulatory and tax approvals or if their information requirements are too difficult to satisfy. Examples of failed financial innovations are Primes and Scores, Index Participation Shares, and targeted stock.

New issues are especially information intensive if they are initial public offerings (IPOs). IPOs are often underpriced upon issue, so that their first day's returns are usually positive and can be quite high for "hot" issues. However, IPOs tend to underperform other securities over time.

Secondary market trading must be liquid and efficient to enable new issues to be successful. To promote market efficiency, the SEC introduced circuit breakers on the NYSE. To promote fairness in pricing, the NASD introduced small-order processing systems such as SOES and Aqcess on the Nasdaq. These initiatives have met with limited success.

Equity markets in emerging markets are growing rapidly, but they are still subject to frictions and barriers to entry. ADRs, GDRs, and country funds expand access to stock markets in developing countries.

Mutual funds expand access to financial markets for small investors. By reducing transaction costs and offering diversification benefits, mutual funds are used to structure retirement benefits (pension funds), offer transactions services (money market mutual funds), and provide investment services (index funds).

References

Allen, F., and D. Gale. "Financial Markets, Intermediaries, and Intertemporal Smoothing." Rodney White Center for Financial Research Working Paper, The Wharton School, 1995.

Allen, F., and D. Gale. "Welfare Comparisons of the German and U.S. Financial System." The Wharton Financial Institutions Center Working Paper No. 94–12, 1994.

Ang, J., and T. Richardson. "The Underwriting Experience of Commercial Bank Affiliates Prior to the Glass–Steagall Act: A Reexamination of Evidence for the Passage of the Act." *Journal of Banking and Finance* 18 (1994): 351–395.

Bae, S. C., and H. Levy. "The Valuation of Firm Commitment Underwriting Contracts for Seasoned New Equity Issues: Theory and Evidence." *Financial Management* 19, No. 2 (Summer 1990): 48–59.

Beatty, R. P., and J. R. Ritter. "Investment Banking, Reputation, and the Underpricing of Initial Public Offerings" *Journal of Financial Economics* 15, No. 1/2 (January–February 1986): 213–232.

Benston, G. *The Separation of Commercial and Investment Banking*, New York: Macmillan, 1990.

Brennan, M. J. "The Individual Investor." *Journal of Financial Review* 48, No. 1 (April 1995):

Chordia, T. "The Structure of Mutual Fund Charges." *The Wharton Financial Institutions Center Working Paper* No. 94–20, 1994.

Christie, W., and P. Schultz. "Why Do Nasdaq Market Makers Avoid Odd-Eighth Quotes?" *Journal of Finance* 49 (1994a): 1813–1840.

Christie, W., and P. Schultz. "Why Did Nasdaq Market Makers Stop Avoiding Odd-Eighth Quotes?" *Journal of Finance* 49 (1994b): 1841–1860.

Claessens, S., and M. W. Rhee. "The Effect of Barriers to Equity Investment in Developing Countries." In J. Frankel, ed., *The Internationalization of Equity Markets*. Chicago: University of Chicago Press, 1994, pp. 231–270.

Cornett, M. M., and H. Tehranian. "An Examination of Voluntary versus Involuntary Security Issuances By Commercial Banks." *Journal of Financial Economics* 35 (1994): 99–122.

Francis, J. C. "Why Do Financial Instruments Fail or Succeed?" Mimeo, April 1993.

Frankel, J. *The Internationalization of Equity Markets* Chicago: University of Chicago Press, 1994.

Furbush, D. "Program Trading and Price Movement: Evidence from the October 1987 Market Crash." *Financial Management* (Autumn 1989): 68–83.

George, T. J., G. Kaul, and M. Nimalendran. "Estimation of the Bid-Ask Spread and Its Components: A New Approach." *Review of Financial Studies* 14 (1991): 217–252.

Glosten, L., and L. E. Harris. "Estimating the Components of the Bid-Ask Spread." *Journal of Financial Economics* 21 (1988): 123–142.

Hardouvelis, G., R. La Porta, and T. Wizman. "What Moves the Discount on Country Equity Funds?" In J. Frankel, ed., *The Internationalization of Equity Markets*. Chicago: University of Chicago Press, 1994, pp. 345–397.

Huth, W. "International Equity Market Integration." *Managerial Finance* 20, No. 4 (1994): 3–7.

Ingram, V., and P. Eisemann. "An Empirical Study of the Regulatory Dialectic: Bank Holding Company Issuance of Variable Rate Preferred Stock." Working Paper, September 1990.

Kalay, A., and A. Shimrat. "Firm Value and Seasoned Equity Issues." *Journal of Financial Economics* 19 (1987): 109–126.

Katz, J. "Going Public." Federal Reserve Bank of Boston *Regional Review* 5, No. 1 (Winter 1995): 18–24.

Kimmel, P., and T. D. Warfield. "The Usefulness of Hybrid Security Classifications: Evidence from Redeemable Preferred Stock." *The Accounting Review* 70, No. 1 (January 1995): 151–167.

Kocherlakota, N. R. "The Equity Premium: It's Still a Puzzle." Institute for Empirical Macroeconomics Federal Reserve Bank of Minneapolis *Discussion Paper* No. 102, August 1995.

Kroszner, R. S., and R. G. Rajan. "Is the Glass-Steagall Act Justified? A Study of the U.S. Experience with Universal Banking Before 1933." *American Economic Review* 84, No. 4 (1994): 810–831.

Laderman, E. S. "Wealth Effects of Bank Holding Company Securities Issuance and Loan Growth under the Risk-Based Capital Requirements." Federal Reserve Bank of San Francisco *Economic Review* No. 2 (1994): 30–41.

Loughran, T., and J. Ritter. "The New Issues Puzzle." *Journal of Finance* 50, No. 1 (March 1995): 23–51.

Megginson, W. L., R. C. Nash, and M. van Randenborgh. "The Financial and Operating Performance of Newly Privatized Firms: An International Empirical Analysis." *Journal of Finance* 49, No. 2 (June 1994): 403–452.

Mehra, R., and Prescott, E. "The Equity Premium: A Puzzle." *Journal of Monetary Economics* 15, No. 2 (March 1985): 145–161.

Michaely, R., and W. Shaw. "The Choice of Going Public: Spin-offs vs. Carve-outs." *Financial Management* 24, No. 3 (Autumn 1995): 5–21.

Mikkelson, W., and M. Parch. "Valuation Effects of Security Offerings and the Issuance Process." *Journal of Financial Economics* 15 (1986): 31–60.

Myers, S., and N. S. Majluf. "Corporate Financing and Investment Decisions When Firms Have Information that Investors Do Not Have." *Journal of Financial Economics* (June 1984): 187–221.

Puri, M. "Commercial Banks in Investment Banking: Conflict of Interest or Certification Role?" *Journal of Financial Economics* 40 (March 1996): 373–401.

Remolona, E. M. "Do International Reactions of Stock and Bond Markets Reflect Macroeconomic Fundamentals?" Federal Reserve Bank of New York *Quarterly Review* (Autumn 1991): 1–13.

Rock, K. "Why New Issues Are Underpriced." *Journal of Financial Economics* 15, No. 1/2 (January–February 1986): 187–213.

Roll, R. "The International Crash of October 1987." In R. Kamphius, R. Kormendi, and J. W. H. Watson, eds., *Black Monday and the Future of Financial Markets*, Homewood, Ill.: Irwin, 1988.

Roy, A. "Multicountry Comparisons of Consumption-Based Capital Asset Pricing Model: Germany, Japan, and U.S.A." Working Paper, University of London, 1994.

Sharp, R. *The Lore and Legends of Wall Street*. Homewood, Ill.: Dow Jones-Irwin, 1989.

Smith, C. W. and R. L. Watts. "The Investment Opportunity Set and Corporate Financing, Dividend, and Compensation Policies." *Journal of Financial Economics* 32 (1992): 263–292.

Stoll, H. "Inferring the Components of the Bid-Ask Spread: Theory and Empirical Tests." *Journal of Finance* 44 (1989): 115–134.

Strom, S. "It's Called Targeted Stock; Shun It, Some Experts Say." *The New York Times*, July 12, 1994, p. D1.

Theodossiou, P. "Models for Predicting Prices and Volatility Patterns in Major International Stock Markets." *Managerial Finance* 20, No. 5/6 (1994): 5–13.

Turner, P. *Capital Flows in the 1980s: A Survey of Major Trends.* Basel, Switzerland: Bank for International Settlements, 1991.

➤ Questions

1. Design a Prime and Score using the following securities. (Be sure to state all of the cash flows. Assume that the call exercise price is equal to the current stock price.)
    a. Common stock priced at $35 that sells at $105 in five years and pays quarterly dividends at a rate of 8% p.a.
    b. Common stock priced at $35 that sells at $15 in five years and pays quarterly dividends at a rate of 8% p.a.

2. Use the constant dividend growth model of Chapter 7 to derive the price of DEC's common stock shown in Figure 17.10.
    a. Assume that last year's dividend per share is $2.65, DEC's cost of capital is 14% p.a., and the growth rate is 10% p.a.
    b. Assume that last year's dividend per share is $2.65, DEC's cost of capital is 10% p.a., and the growth rate is 2% p.a.
    c. Assume that last year's dividend per share is $2.65, DEC's cost of capital is 20% p.a., and the growth rate is 18% p.a.
    d. Compare the assumptions in parts (a)–(c). What do these assumptions imply about the type of company DEC is?

3. Calculate the bid-ask spread for 10,000 shares of the following:
    a. Bid price $65 \frac{3}{8}$, ask price $65 \frac{1}{2}$.
    b. Bid price $14 \frac{7}{8}$, ask price $15 \frac{1}{4}$.
    c. Bid price $23 \frac{1}{4}$, ask price $23 \frac{17}{64}$.
    d. What determines the size of the bid-ask spread?

4. Consider a technically insolvent firm, with assets valued at $5 million and liabilities valued at $15 million. Which of the following investment projects is preferred by stockholders and which is preferred by bondholders? Why?
    a. Invest $7 million in a project that will be worth $10 million with a probability of 60% and $6 million with a probability of 40%.
    b. Invest $7 million in a project that will be worth $25 million with a probability of 5% and $5 million with a 95% probability.

5. Explain how the following resolve the investment problems in question 4:
    a. Deviations from absolute priority.
    b. Elimination of equity's limited liability.

6. Use the following price list of securities features to calculate the cost of capital for
    a. Fixed rate, noncumulative, perpetual preferred stock.
    b. Perpetual, noncumulative, convertible preferred stock.
    c. Mandatory convertible debt (e.g., equity contract notes, equity commitment notes): issuer must convert debt into either perpetual preferred or common stock.
    d. Fixed rate term preferred stock (e.g., Mips, Epics, TOPrS): dividends can be deferred for as long as five years but are cumulative.

Securities Features Price List

- Subordinated cash flow (lack of seniority) = 0.75% for each level (from debt to preferred, and from preferred to common).
- Unsecured by the assets of the issuer = 0.38%.
- Longer maturity (infinite maturity versus term securities) = 0.30%.
- Noncumulative dividends = 0.22%.
- Convertibility and security redemption (if at option of issuer) = 0.15%.
- Fixed rate debt = 12% p.a.

7. When are the 50 point collar, the 250 point and the 400 point rules triggered in the following scenarios? What is the percentage change in each scenario?
   a. The Dow decreases from 5735 to 5680.
   b. The Dow decreases from 1550 to 1535.
   c. The Dow decreases from 2685 to 2405.
   d. The Dow increases from 3677 to 3740.

8. A money market fund is started up with assets consisting of 75 day zero coupon instruments with a face value of $175 million earning a simple interest yield $i = 4.9\%$.
   a. What is the value of the fund's liabilities sold to shareholders?
   b. If interest rates immediately increase by 100 basis points, what is the impact on the value of the mutual fund's assets?
   c. If the fund is liquidated immediately upon the increase in rates, what is the net asset value paid out to each fund shareholder?

9. What is the impact on retirement benefits if a $5.5 billion pension fund experiences a 2% default rate on its assets if
   a. It is a defined benefit fund that pays retirees 35% of the average of their last three years of salary.
   b. It is a defined contribution fund that obligates the firm to contribute matching funds equal to 50% of the employees' contributions.
   c. It is a defined contribution fund with no matching funds contributed by the employer.

10. Calculate the net asset values and share prices of the following mutual funds:
    a. 400 million shares of an open-end money market mutual fund with assets consisting of 91 day Eurodollars CDs with face value of $270 million earning 6.25% p.a. and 250 day prime-rated commercial paper with face value of $230 million earning 6.1% p.a. (All yields are simple interest yields on a 365 day basis.)
    b. Closed-end country fund with assets consisting of 20 year 6.7% p.a. annual coupon bonds, yielding 15.5% p.a., with a face value of $15 million and perpetual preferred stock with a cumulative annual dividend of 7% p.a., face value of $27 million, and a yield of 12.4% p.a.

BORDER CROSSING IV:
HEDGING AND THE ROLE OF DERIVATIVES

Many misconceptions surrounding derivatives emanate from our own explanations of these instruments. That is because academics and practitioners, in their rush to show off their knowledge about new and sometimes exotic instruments, describe these instruments as if they were separate and distinct from other business activities. It is misleading and inaccurate to consider, say, a futures or options position in isolation from other, perhaps offsetting positions in other markets. Indeed, the attempt to counterbalance cash flows generated by other investments is the primary objective of most derivatives trades. Thus, we will examine all derivatives trading from the standpoint of a portfolio of both derivatives and nonderivatives transactions. In the financial vernacular, this is known as *hedging* since the cash flows on one transaction typically offset cash flows on other transactions. However, this is a misleading term since all derivatives transactions, even the speculative ones, must be understood in this context.

Participants in derivatives markets own portfolios of financial securities that must be taken into consideration when understanding the impact of any particular derivatives transaction. This is true whether the ultimate impact of the transaction is to dampen risk exposure (which is commonly referred to as hedging) or to exacerbate risk exposure (which is commonly referred to as speculating). Our approach treats both hedging and speculating as points on a continuum of derivatives transactions whereby the derivatives' cash flows are more or less opposite the cash flows generated by other securities in the portfolio. When the two sets of cash flows move in opposite directions, we have a hedge. When the two sets of cash flows move in the same direction, we have a *speculative position*. This is why speculative trades increase risk exposure, whereas hedging reduces risk exposure. Hedging offers counterbalancing cash flows that reduce the dispersion of possible outcomes, thereby reducing risk. By adding more cash flows that all move in the same direction, speculating increases the good news when the outcomes are favorable, but it also increases the bad news when outcomes are unfavorable, thereby increasing risk.

In either extreme, pure hedging or pure speculating, we cannot understand either transaction without first examining the *underlying cash position*. The underlying cash position is the twin transaction that is undertaken simultaneously with the derivatives trade. The underlying cash position motivates the hedge transaction.

microhedge: derivatives transaction with the underlying cash position consisting of a single financial security.

macrohedge: derivatives transaction with the underlying cash position consisting of a portfolio of financial securities.

The underlying cash position may consist of a single financial security. In that case, we have a **microhedge**. If the underlying cash position consists of a portfolio of securities, then the offsetting derivatives trade is considered a **macrohedge**. Since FIs specialize in holding portfolios of financial assets, macrohedging is much more prevalent for FIs than for nonfinancial firms, which may be hedging only a single financial security on their balance sheets. The Commodity Futures Trading Commission (CFTC) finds that up to 85% of all futures trades are explicitly linked to other transactions. The bulk of all derivatives trades occur in combination with, and indeed are motivated by, other financial transactions. The material in the derivatives chapters in this book is linked to the other financial instruments presented in the earlier chapters since portfolio decisions, described earlier in the book, motivate derivatives trades. Indeed, the transactions described in Chapters 10–17 constitute the securities that constitute what we call the underlying cash position.

To clarify the link between the derivatives chapters and the rest of this book, we present a step-by-step hedging procedure. This procedure can be used to analyze futures, options, swaps, and any other derivatives that may be designed sometime in the future. It proceeds from an initial analysis of the business of the hedger. There is no "one size fits all" hedge; the hedge must be tailored to the hedger's underlying cash position. No FI can dictate a hedge to its customer. The FI is dependent on the customer to provide information about the hedger's cash flows. These cash flows, as well as the hedger's goals, will determine the configuration of the derivatives transaction. It is the FI's responsibility to choose the derivatives trade that will appropriately and efficiently implement those goals. *Timely Topics BC.1: Bank on It—Upheaval Breeds Derivatives* describes how FIs design derivatives to assist their clients in coping with volatile economic conditions. Far from being new, Space Age instruments, these derivatives have been around as long as there has been economic activity.

TIMELY TOPICS BC.1

BANK ON IT: UPHEAVAL BREEDS DERIVATIVES

On the wall of Charles Smithson's office in Princeton, N.J., is a Confederate bond that he likes to call a "dual-currency commodity convertible with optional delivery"—a Civil War-era financial derivative.

In explaining the modern variety of these products for Chase Manhattan, a major derivatives issuer, manager director Smithson of the bank's risk management research unit likes to employ history. It's a technique he used as a Texas A&M economics professor in the 1970s when he wrote a book ("The Doomsday Myth") to dispel the idea that the world was running out of oil.

Now there is a minipanic over derivatives, whose unwinding is blamed for dragging down the markets. Mr. Smithson points out that conceptually they're little different from what the Japanese rice traders or the Dutch explorers were doing in the 17th century with crude options. The principle is to spread risk and reward so that uncertainty doesn't inhibit commerce. Even in Aristotle's time, he says, olive presses were optioned because of crop volatility.

Over the ages, hedging has diminished when conditions settled down. No such luck today, after 25 years of international economic upheaval. Demand is up for products that mitigate risks—and can be used to capitalize on them.

Banks and other FIs that design these hedges are now at the center of controversy. At currencies zigged and interest rates zagged. . . . unexpectedly big losses have been felt in derivatives. Instead of risk being controlled, it seems to have exploded.

Has theory been turned on its head? Is this, as House Banking Committee Chairman, Henry Gonzalez called it this month, "a giant, global, electronic Ponzi possibility"?

The theory behind derivatives is that by allowing any exposure to be hedged with economic sidebets, stress will be taken off those institutions most exposed to a turn in the economy. Case in point: the 1980s thrift crisis. Although the S&L story had many sidebars, the industry was basically ravaged by an unhedged mismatch of long term mortgages at low rates and interest-bearing deposits at rising rates.

Lesser extremes of that clash exist throughout the marketplace, and the task of creative finance—banking at its best, really—is to resolve them. Some fuddy-duddies cavil that derivatives have disrupted good old stocks and bonds, but given the unsteadiness of today's economy, anyone who prefers to have markets allocate resources (as opposed to administrative fiat) ought to welcome the notion of high-tech hedging. Without it, businesses would have to "avoid the elements" in much more cumbersome ways, such as moving plants around as currencies fluctuate.

Instead, we have analysts playing multidimensional chess, swapping risks to match and cover while requiring the least deadweight loss (capital cushions) to the economy. For example: It's better for a corporation to have paid $5,000 for an arcane option than to keep liquid $500,000 to cover an exigency; the half million can be invested. In trying to model for untold circumstances, or simply being short-run greedy, the designers (or the buyers) of derivatives have made errors, and these have made news. But usually these things work. . . .

[S]ome politicians and other worrywarts say the situation is out of control. It bothers them when the action is off balance sheets (and out of regulatory sights). Where regulation exists, it is carved into competing jurisdictions. But some scholars, such as Harvard business Professor Robert Merton, think diversified (though more rationally structured) regulation can, like dispersed risk, promote stability.

The control crowd wants to impose financial restraints. To "settle the fever," Representative Gonzales suggested a tax on derivative use. Others want caps on bank activity in this area. The Basle Committee in Switzerland, on behalf of international banking regulators, is at work on refining capital reserve requirements (a form of tax) for derivative exposure.

Those who want to rein in a "dislocative" influence in the markets need to understand that every tax or trading limit discourages marginal capital from entering. Owners of wealth don't want to have their escape routes blocked or their yields diminished. And when they stay out, liquidity (the capacity to trade at some realistic price) is reduced and risk for everyone is increased.

Back when Mr. Smithson's Confederate bond was issued, textile mills in London and Paris wanted not only to guard against devaluation but to hedge the possibility that a long Civil War would deplete cotton supplies and send prices skyward. The note entitled them to the goods if they could bust a blockade. After defeat at Vicksburg sealed the South's fate, the paper lost worth. But the idea has been spun into the threads of a useful if leaky canopy for a grander yet still gun-shy global economy.

Source: T. Ferguson, *The Wall Street Journal*, April 26, 1994.

Timely Topics BC.1 shows a "derivative" dating back to 1863. Risk sharing contracts have been valuable tools over the years, and their value is enhanced when the economic environment is more volatile. It would be a shame to abandon this valuable financial tool just when it is most useful. To set the stage for consideration of these useful tools, we now consider a step-by-step approach to hedging that will be used to motivate transactions in each of the derivatives markets described in Chapters 18–21.

Step 1: Risk Analysis of the Underlying Cash Position

Derivatives transactions cannot be understood in isolation from all of the hedger's other transactions. Throughout the rest of this book, we will consider *perfect hedges*. Perfect hedges are constructed so that the cash flows on the derivatives hedge exactly offset the cash flows generated by some underlying cash position. If, for example, the hedger is holding a long term fixed income bond as an asset, then this underlying cash position will experience negative cash flows when interest rates increase (that is, the price of the long term bond will decrease). A perfect hedge will generate an equal-sized, opposite-signed cash flow (that is, a positive cash flow under the same circumstances that the bond investment loses value). Thus, when the cash flows on the perfect hedge and the underlying cash position are added together, the sum is zero.

To construct a perfect hedge, then, fluctuations in the value of the underlying cash position must be calculated. That is, the underlying cash position's risk exposure must be measured. Derivatives markets have been most successful in manipulating two types of risk: interest rate risk and exchange rate risk. Here we will limit our attention to these two sources of risk, thereby inducing us to focus on derivatives transactions that manipulate only the interest rate and exchange rate risk exposures of underlying cash positions. To measure the interest rate and exchange rate risk exposures of the underlying cash position, we use the duration measure of Chapter 7 and the net currency exposure of Chapter 8. Table BC.1 summarizes the conclusions from these risk measurement models. The signs of the duration gap and the net currency exposure determine the direction of the risk exposure of a portfolio of underlying cash instruments. If the duration of assets exceeds the duration of liabilities (a positive duration gap) the portfolio will decline in market value if interest rates increase. Alternatively, if the net currency exposure to a particular foreign currency is positive, then the portfolio's value will decline if the exchange rate, denominated in the home currency, declines.

Step 2: Quantification of the Impact on the Cash Position of Interest Rate and Exchange Rate Shifts

In Step 1, we examined the sign of the cash flow impact of interest rate and exchange rate shifts. In Step 2, we quantify the impact by examining the size of the effect of interest rate and exchange rate shifts on the value of an underlying cash position. Again we use models from Chapters 7 and 8.

From Chapter 7, for any exogenously determined interest rate shock, the impact on the market value of equity is calculated as $\Delta E \approx -DG(A)(\frac{\Delta y}{1+y})$, where ΔE is the impact on the

Table BC.1

Step-by-Step Hedging

Step 1	Step 2	Step 3	Step 4
Interest rate risk	Cash flows < 0 when:	Hedge cash flows > 0 when:	Examples of hedge:
Duration gap > 0	Interest rates ↑	Interest rates ↑: Short hedge	Sell futures/buy puts
Duration gap < 0	Interest rates ↓	Interest rates ↓: Long hedge	Buy futures/buy calls
Exchange rate risk	Cash flows < 0 when:	Hedge cash flows < 0 when:	Examples of hedge:
Net exposure > 0	Exchange rates ↓	Exchange rates ↓: Short hedge	Sell forwards/buy puts
Net exposure < 0	Exchange rates ↑	Exchange rates ↑: Long hedge	Buy forwards/buy calls

market value of equity of the underlying cash position; A is the assets in the underlying cash position; and $\Delta y, y$ denote the change in interest rates and the level of interest rates, respectively.

From Chapter 8, for any exogenously determined exchange rate shock, the impact on the underlying cash position is calculated as Δ Cash Flow $= (NCE)(\Delta FX_i)$, where NCE is the net currency exposure and ΔFX_i is the exogenous shift in the exchange rate of currency i vis-á-vis the home currency.

Step 3: Stating the Goal of a Hedge

This part is easy. The goal of a hedge is to make money when the underlying cash position is losing money. A perfect currency hedge would generate positive cash flows that, under the same exchange rate shifts, exactly offset the negative cash flows of the underlying cash position. An *imperfect hedge* would generate some positive cash flows to offset the negative cash flows of the underlying cash position, but the offset would not be complete. A *speculative position* would generate negative cash flows under the same circumstances that the underlying cash position generated negative cash flows. In this book, we always solve for the perfect hedge position since this is free of any subjective risk valuation. The imperfect hedge and the speculative position depend on the hedger's attitudes toward risk. The less risk averse the hedger, the more speculative and the less perfect the chosen hedge. The perfect hedge, however, is not a function of the hedger's risk aversion. It is simply the derivatives trade needed to generate cash flows that exactly offset the cash flows generated by the underlying cash position.

This is not to say that the FI will recommend that the perfect hedge be implemented. In general, the perfect hedge is a benchmark used to delineate the extreme hedge position. As shown in Figure BC.1, the actual hedge will depend on the hedger's attitudes toward risk. The more risk averse, the closer to the perfect hedge transaction; the less risk averse, the closer to the no hedge or even speculative transaction.

The hedging spectrum

Speculative position	No hedge	Perfect hedge

The hedger's attitude towards risk is:

	Risk neutral	Risk averse
Less risk averse/risk taker		

If the cash flows on the underlying cash position are negative, then the cash flows on the derivatives transaction are:

Negative	Zero	Positive

Figure BC.1   The hedging spectrum.

Step 4: Implementing the Hedge

The final step is where most discussions of derivatives begin. This is the point at which we examine the derivatives instruments themselves and fashion a transaction that has the required cash flow characteristics. That is, if we are interested in a short hedge, we want a transaction that will have a positive cash flow when prices are decreasing (or equivalently interest rates increasing). Moreover, a long hedge will generate a positive cash flow when prices are decreasing (interest rates increasing). The remaining chapters in this book are devoted to describing how the desired cash flow characteristics can be obtained using the major derivatives instruments: futures/forward contracts; options; swaps; and pass-throughs.

As we get into the specifics of hedging, as outlined in Step 4, a word of caution is in order. To reduce the cost of hedging, derivatives typically employ a significant amount of leverage. That is, a little expenditure goes a long way. Future cash flows may be many times the initial expenditure for the derivatives contract. This means that the derivatives themselves can be risk enhancing if not used properly. *Timely Topics BC.2* examines this issue. The cautions about proper derivatives use can be applied to all business activities. If not handled prudently, the firm can flounder on debt, expenses, inventories, or a host of other decision items. Just because you don't have a doctoral degree in mathematics does not mean that you cannot understand derivatives. You can, and you must, if your business is to prosper.

TIMELY TOPICS BC.2

DIRECTORS, CONTROL YOUR DERIVATIVES

In recent years there has been a crescendo of discussion about the need to regulate the activities of financial institutions in the burgeoning market for over-the-counter derivatives of all types. Central bankers in the U.S. and around the world, among others, have persistently suggested they may need a stronger regulatory role.

Despite some legitimate supervisory issues, the public-policy debate too often sounds like a case of regulation in search of a problem rather than the other way around. The greatest threat from derivatives is not to the financial system as a whole, but rather to the earnings of particular companies, notably companies using derivatives.

Yes, these markets are complex, but the competing firms are already subject to market disciplines that are far stronger than bureaucratic do's and don'ts. The proliferation of triple-A rated derivatives subsidiaries is a sign of the healthy functioning of these market disciplines.

More important than regulators, the people who should be looking most closely at derivatives activities are the senior executives and directors (especially members of audit committees) of any company with significant levels of participation in derivatives. This is the crucial group for preventing unnecessary losses through the failure of companies to follow sensible management practices in addressing both risk taking and risk controls. . . .

Losses in these markets can strike an individual company with hurricane force. Within any company active in the markets, managers or traders can turn valuable tools for risk management into potent tools for risk creation.

What is needed are strong internal controls, not one-size-fits-all regulation. Designing such controls is something that must be done in a manner highly specific to each company's organization, culture, and objectives. Even so, a few general principles apply. In looking at a firm's policies and practices, every director or chief executive of a company with a significant derivatives position would do well to ask the following questions:

1. Do we know who is betting our company's future? (If the answer is yes, "on what?" and "how often?" also may usefully be asked.)

2. Do we know what our positions are, right now? Many companies use weekly or even monthly financial reports, yet positions in most financial markets can change radically in a matter of hours.

3. Do we know what our risks are, and what variables will affect profit and loss in each operational area? It should be axiomatic that you can't control risk, much less manage it, if you don't know exactly where it is created within the organization. Management should have a rigorous and comprehensive "risk map" to evaluate both the types and degrees of risk the company incurs.

4. Do we know how our positions were valued? The Group of 30 [international regulatory body] and others have said that FIs should mark their derivatives to market at least daily. However, this is easier said than done because many over-the-counter derivatives markets are illiquid. The "value" of positions in such illiquid markets often can be determined only by mathematical models, since there are not any reported trading market prices on equivalent transactions. Even assuming a firm's model is correct, the computation of "value" that results is only as good as the assumptions about yield curves, volatilities and other inputs that are fed into the model. Put differently, companies will be accruing profits today that in the real world will be realized only over many years.

5. Just exactly how, where, for how long, and against what are we hedged? "Don't worry, we are hedging the risk" should not be considered an acceptable answer to the question of how a company is making offsetting provisions for the specific risks it incurs. All hedges are not created equal, and it is important to understand exactly what interest rate risk, volatility risk, etc. is being hedged, and how the hedge is being implemented. Even within a particular type of risk, such as interest rate risk, it may not be possible to hedge more than a portion of the yield curve, and the duration of risks and available hedges may not match.

6. How much does our compensation system encourage perverse behavior? Awarding bonuses solely on the basis of "accrued" profits without regard to the amount of the firm's capital put at risk, or how long the company will be at risk before profits are actually realized, may encourage undue risk taking.

7. How effective are our controls? When companies lose large sums through unauthorized trading or speculation, it often occurs due to the actions of senior personnel. Junior personnel in a treasurer's office may not feel comfortable calling the CEO if their own boss takes abnormally large or risky positions. Therefore, written risk limits, automated exception reporting, strong internal auditing, and other steps are vital to make sure that risk control policies are always followed.

8. Who is responsible for making sure we know what we're doing? Both the CEO and the members of the board share direct responsibility for overseeing the company's internal financial controls. Where large exposures are being incurred in derivatives, the board (or at least the audit committee) should look hard at all the issues discussed above.

Members of the board may not know how to create or trade derivatives, but they should know how to ask the right questions and to demand the right answers. Used with care, derivatives are terrific products that can enhance profitability and reduce volatility. Used in a wild or uncontrolled manner, they can be a one-way ticket to financial disaster.

The board and senior managers shouldn't wait for regulators to make sure their company is following a well-controlled and prudent path.

Source: R. Breeden, *The Wall Street Journal*, March 7, 1994.

CHAPTER 18

FINANCIAL FUTURES AND FORWARD CONTRACTS

"My interest is in the future because I am going to spend the rest of my life there."—Charles F. Kettering.

- To learn about the development of futures and forward contracts based on financial securities.

- To understand interest rate risk hedging using Eurodollar futures and U.S. Treasury bond futures contracts, as well as forward rate agreements (FRAs).

- To learn how to construct perfect hedges against foreign exchange rate risk using currency futures and forwards.

- To understand hedging against market risk exposure using the S&P 500 and IBEX-35 futures contracts.

➤ The Evolution of Futures and Forward Contracts

The concept of a forward contract originated in sixteenth-century Japan when landowners raised money by selling rice in advance of delivery to rice merchants. A more formal, exchange-based contract, the precursor to the modern futures contract, originated in the U.S. Midwest during the early nineteenth century. In 1848, some 82 merchants met above a flour store on Chicago's South Water Street and formed the Chicago Board of Trade to

- Maintain a commercial exchange.
- Promote uniformity in the customs and usages of merchants.
- Inculcate principles of justice and equity to trade.
- Facilitate the speedy adjustment of business disputes.
- Acquire and disseminate valuable commercial and economic information.
- Secure for its members the benefits of cooperation in the furtherance of their legitimate pursuits.[1]

---

[1] Chandler (1994), p. 4.

The most popular contract exchanged on the newly formed exchange was the "to arrive" contract, which specified delivery of a particular commodity at a predetermined deferred date at a prespecified price. This contract would evolve into today's commodity futures contract. It allowed farmers to escape the erratic shifts in prices caused by supply fluctuations. No longer was it true that farmers had to accept the very low prices generally prevailing at harvest time, only to watch helplessly as the price jumped up at times of scarce supply. The use of the futures contracts allowed them to smooth out price fluctuations over the agricultural calendar, thereby shielding their incomes from the effects of short term shifts in supply that corresponded to harvesting schedules.

Futures markets evolved to reduce the farmers' transaction costs of exchanging "to arrive" contracts. Today's futures markets are an extension of the informal clearing arrangements designed by **rings** of participants. Rings were informal groups of traders who dealt in the same commodity and held counterbalancing positions. "Ringing up" reduced the need for costly delivery, allowing only the differences to be transferred. Consequently, if trader 1 owes 100 bushels of wheat to trader 2 and trader 2 owes 300 bushels of wheat to trader 1, then only the difference, 200 bushels, is ultimately transferred from trader 2 to trader 1.

Figure 18.1 shows how traders join up to complete a ring. If trader 1 owes 100 bushels of wheat to trader 2, trader 2 owes 100 bushels to trader 3, and trader 3 owes 100 bushels to trader 1, then the ring is complete. There is no need for any wheat to change hands. Only monetary differences must be cleared. Suppose that trader 1 sells its wheat to trader 2 for $400; trader 2 sells to trader 3 for $350; and trader 3 sells for $375. Trader 1 will receive $400 from trader 2 and pay $375 to trader 3. Trader 2 will pay $400 to trader 1 and receive $350 from trader 3. Trader 3 will receive $375 from trader 1 and pay $350 to trader 2. The development of rings allowed participants to save on the costs of transferring physical commodities by substituting monetary payments.

Rings quickly evolved to reduce transaction costs even further. In the ring in Figure 18.1, each trader has two cash flows—one outflow and one inflow. It would be preferable to replace those two cash flows with one net cash flow that is equal to the difference between the cash inflow and the cash outflow. That is, rather than simultaneously paying out $375 and receiving $400, trader 1 would reduce transaction costs by simply receiving the net amount of $25. The net cash flows are noted in parentheses under each trader's number. Note that, because of the counterbalancing cash flows in the ring, all net cash flows in the ring sum to zero. Rings therefore evolved to permit centralized clearing using a clearinghouse. The bottom panel of the figure shows the monetary transfers. Trader 2 pays $50 into the ring clearinghouse. Trader 1 and trader 3 each receive $25 from the ring clearinghouse. Comparing the earliest form of the ring, without centralized clearing, to the ring with centralized clearing, we find that the required number of transfers is reduced from six (three commodity transfers and three monetary transfers) to three (one monetary transfer for each trader with the clearinghouse). This ring-based form of settlement is simply the multilateral, gross netting procedures we discussed in Chapter 6.

Multilateral netting offers agents cost-saving benefits, since all trades are settled using the clearinghouse as the counterparty. Each futures exchange currently operates its own clearinghouse to process all cash flows and commodity transfers for all futures trades on the exchange. The clearinghouse, in effect, forms a "giant ring" of all members of the exchange so that the required number of monetary and commodity transfers is minimized. This protects the traders from the risk that their counterparties will fail to comply with the terms of the contract. Since the exchange clearinghouse acts as a counterparty to all trades on the exchange, it must ensure that *all* members of the exchange fully comply with the terms of their contracts. For example, if trader 2 in Figure 18.1 defaulted on its futures obligation, then the clearinghouse would still have to pay traders 1 and 3.

rings: informal groups of traders who dealt in the same commodity and held counterbalancing positions.

How traders complete a ring

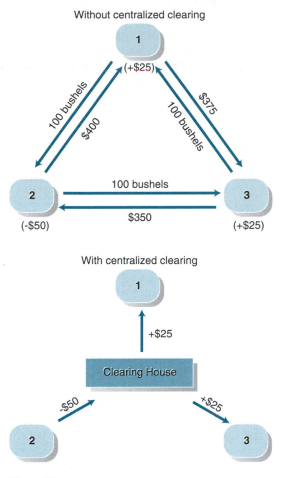

Figure 18.1

To protect itself from the credit risk of trading with all members of the exchange, the clearinghouse developed the concept of margin, which the Chicago Board of Trade *voluntarily* adopted 40 years after the institution of the clearinghouse. The institution of margins is an example of a private market, not governmental, response to the problem of credit risk. The **futures margin** is a good-faith performance bond designed to guarantee the trader's compliance with the terms of the contract; it is *not* a downpayment. Both the buyer and seller of the futures contract are required to post margin with a futures commission merchant (FCM).[2] Margin can be deposited as cash, U.S. Treasury bills, or other short term, low-risk securities. Since the margin is refunded when the futures position is closed out (either by delivery or by undertaking an offsetting contract), the cost of the margin is merely the opportunity cost of lost use of the funds restricted by margin requirements. Thus, the economic cost of margins is far less than the absolute size of the margin.

futures margin: a good-faith performance bond designed to guarantee the trader's compliance with the terms of the contract; it is *not* a down payment.

---

[2] The FCM must also post margin with the clearinghouse to execute trades on behalf of its customers. However, brokers can use offsetting customer positions to limit the margin they must place to cover their net exposure. If, for example, a broker has one customer with a long March Eurodollar futures position and another with a short March Eurodollar futures position of equal size, the two offset one another, and the FCM does not have to post any margin with the clearinghouse. However, each customer will still have to post margin with the FCM.

initial margin: the amount that must be posted upon the origination of the futures position.

maintenance margin: the minimum required margin that must be maintained in order to retain the futures position.

margin call: requirement that the holder of the futures contract restore the value of the margin account to the initial margin level.

The **initial margin** is the amount that must be posted upon the origination of the futures position. The **maintenance margin** is the minimum required margin that must be maintained in order to retain the futures position. If the balance in the margin account falls below the maintenance margin, the trader receives a **margin call**, requiring the holder of the futures position to restore the value of the margin account to the initial margin level. If the trader does not meet the margin call in a timely manner, the clearinghouse has the legal right to sell out the position. The value of the margin account fluctuates daily because the futures position is **marked to market**. That is, each day's trading gains (losses) are credited to (debited from) the margin account. The day's closing price is the settlement price used to mark the futures position to market. The procedure of marking to market evolved in order to limit the clearinghouse's credit risk exposure, since each day's gains and losses are collected at the end of each trading day. From the perspective of clearinghouse credit risk, the maximum value at risk at any given time is one day's trading losses.

Checkpoint

1. Trace the role of the futures exchange in the evolution of futures clearing mechanisms.
2. What is the role of the margin? What is the cost of the margin?
3. What is the role of the futures commission merchant (FCM)?
4. List two reasons why the development of a clearinghouse was necessary for the proliferation in futures trading.

➤ Financial Futures

marked to market: crediting (debiting) of each day's trading gains (losses) to (from) the margin account.

financial futures: obligations to make or take delivery of some underlying financial asset at a predetermined price on a prespecified date.

futures price: the predetermined price on a futures contract.

delivery date: the prespecified maturity date of the futures contract.

spot price: the cash market price of the underlying deliverable asset for a futures/forward contract.

Financial futures are obligations to make or take delivery of some underlying financial asset at a predetermined price (called the **futures price**) on a prespecified date (called the **delivery date**). The counterparty that buys the futures contract agrees to buy the underlying financial asset and holds a long position. The counterparty that sells the futures contract is obligated to sell the underlying financial asset and holds a short position. The three identifying features of the financial futures contract are:

1. The identity of the underlying financial asset.
2. The futures price.
3. The delivery date.

The value of the futures contract is *derived* from the value of the underlying deliverable asset—hence, the term *derivatives*. The holder of the long futures position is obligated to buy the underlying asset at the predetermined futures price, denoted P_F. If the cash market **spot price** of the underlying deliverable asset, denoted P_S, is above P_F, then the long futures position profits from the futures contract. The long futures position can purchase an asset for P_F although it costs more, P_S, in the open market. However, if the spot price P_S is lower than P_F, then the corresponding short position gains from the futures contract. That is because the short futures position can sell the asset at a price P_F that is higher than the price available in the open market, P_S. The value of the futures contract on any date t is simply the difference between the spot and futures price: $P_S^t - P_F$. If this is multiplied by the size of the futures position, denoted F, then we can value any futures transaction at any point in time t. The value of any futures position of size F is therefore $F(P_S^t - P_F)$. Note that since long positions are denoted by positive quantities ($F > 0$) and short positions are expressed as negative quantities ($F < 0$), the long position value is positive if $P_S^t > P_F$ and the short position value is positive if $P_F > P_S^t$. Figure 18.2 shows the values of both long and short futures positions as a function of the spot price of the contract's underlying asset.

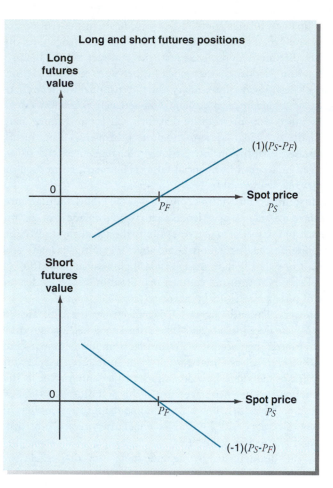

Figure 18.2

A simple illustration demonstrates this basic concept. Suppose that on January 1 your employer agrees to sell you the company car for $10,000 at the end of the year. The predetermined price, the futures price, in this example is P_F = $10,000. The underlying deliverable asset is one company car, and the delivery date is in one year. You have the long position, and your employer is short. If the car is worth $12,000 on the delivery date, then the long position in the "futures contract" is valued at $(1)(\$12{,}000-\$10{,}000)$ = +$2,000, or a profit of $2,000 for you. Your employer, the short, evaluates the contract as $(-1)(\$12{,}000-\$10{,}000)$ = −$2,000, a loss of $2,000.

The three features characterizing any futures contract are standardized and are determined by the futures exchange sponsoring the contract. Although the definition specifies "delivery," this most often takes the form of cash settlement. That is, the value of the contract is paid in cash rather than in terms of **physical delivery** (actual sale/purchase) of the underlying financial asset. Some contracts, for example, the most popular futures contract in the world—the Eurodollar futures—do not permit physical delivery and settle only by exchanging cash flows on "delivery date." In practice, more than 98% of all financial futures contracts are cash settled, whether or not they allow physical delivery.

The innovation most relevant to FIs was the introduction, in the 1970s, of financial futures contracts. Not long after their inception, activity in financial futures far exceeded commodity futures' trading volume. However, the innovation was not an instantaneous success. In 1970

physical delivery: the actual sale/purchase of the underlying financial security in order to settle the futures contract.

the first financial futures contract was introduced in the United States in order to serve as a currency risk hedging vehicle. In that era of fixed exchange rates during the waning, but still prevailing, Bretton Woods agreement, this contract failed. It was not until 1972, after the fall of Bretton Woods, that currency futures were reintroduced on the Chicago Mercantile Exchange's newly formed subsidiary, the International Monetary Market (IMM). Volatility in the price of a fundamental economic value (such as interest rates, exchange rates, or stock prices) is a necessary prerequisite that fuels activity on futures markets. As markets become more volatile, participants attempt to protect themselves from the impact of unexpected shifts. The increased volatility in interest rates, exchange rates, and stock prices during the 1970s encouraged innovation of financial futures contracts. From then on, the success of financial futures trading was assured.

The first interest rate futures contract was the GNMA futures introduced in October 1975. It was geared toward mortgage lenders who typically made loan commitments to their customers anywhere from six weeks to one year prior to the actual granting of the loan. During this period of time, interest rate fluctuations could affect the mortgage loan's profitability to the point that an increase of only 1% in mortgage rates might reduce the market value of the mortgage by 5 to 6%. The GNMA futures contract permitted mortgage lenders to protect themselves from the risk of unexpected shifts in mortgage rates.

In January 1976 and August 1977, respectively, the U.S. Treasury bill and U.S. Treasury bond contracts were introduced. The primary market was government security dealers who sought to protect their securities inventories from loss because of interest rate fluctuations. In spring 1982, the Kansas City Board of Trade introduced a stock index futures contract based on the value of the Value Line Stock Index. The bull market in stocks and the rapid growth of stock mutual funds encouraged use of this and other stock index futures to hedge market risk exposure. Table 18.1 shows the most popular futures contracts in the world. The financial futures contracts are divided into three broad categories: (1) interest rate futures; (2) currency futures; and (3) stock index futures.[3]

Futures are distinguished by the underlying assets deliverable against the contract. *Interest rate futures* have underlying financial securities that are sensitive to interest rate fluctuations; *currency futures* have underlying securities that are sensitive to exchange rate fluctuations; and *stock index futures* have underlying financial securities that consist of specific stock indexes. The value of each futures contract is determined by fluctuations in the price of the contract's deliverable asset. Interest rate futures comprise the biggest category of futures contracts, with 41 distinct contracts accounting for 52% of global trading. In 1994 the most actively traded futures contract in the world was the three month Eurodollar, with average daily volume of 414,321 contracts. This was the first year that average daily volume in the Eurodollar overtook the longstanding top-traded futures market, the U.S. Treasury bond futures contract. Table 18.1 shows that in 1994 average daily volume on the U.S. Treasury bond futures market was 395,098 contracts. Kapner and Marshall (1992) show that the increase in Eurodollar futures trading volume can be attributed to the growth of the swap market, fueling the use of Eurodollar futures to hedge FIs' swap portfolios. The table also presents daily volume for the world's largest futures contracts. Seven out of the ten most active contracts were traded on non-U.S. futures exchanges.

Futures exchanges have proliferated around the world. From a virtual monopoly in its earliest days, trading on U.S. futures exchanges has fallen to represent about 45% of world-wide activity. Although turnover on established exchanges increased gradually (and even

---

[3] We do not consider commodity futures in this book, and therefore we will not discuss futures on precious metals, energy, and grains and other agricultural products.

Table
18.1

The Most Popular Futures Contracts in the World, 1994

Contract	Exchange	Contract Months	Contract Size	Tick Size & Value	Daily Volume	Options Volume[a]
Long Term Interest Rates						
U.S. Treasury bond	CBOT	Mar, Jun, Sep, Dec	US$100,000	1/32 pt = US$31.25	395,098	111,235
French notional	MATIF	Mar, Jun, Sep, Dec	FF500,000	0.02 pt = FF100	200,613	72,098
German bund	LIFFE	Mar, Jun, Sep, Dec	DM250,000	0.01 pt = DM25	148,156	34,024
10 year U.S. Treasury note	CBOT	Mar, Jun, Sep, Dec	US$100,000	1/32 pt = US$31.25	95,169	25,444
Long gilt	LIFFE	Mar, Jun, Sep, Dec	£50,000	1/32 pt = £15.625	75,588	9,355
German bund	DTB	Mar, Jun, Sep, Dec	DM250,000	0.01 pt = DM25	56,192	1,036
10 year Spanish government bond	MEFF-F	Mar, Jun, Sep, Dec	Pta10 million	0.01 pt = Pta1,000	53,408	8,224
10 year Japanese government bond	TSE	Mar, Jun, Sep, Dec	¥100 million	0.01 pt = ¥10,000	52,630	6,850
Italian government bond	LIFFE	Mar, Jun, Sep, Dec	L200 million	0.01 pt = L20,000	46,920	4,090
10 year Australian Treasury bond	SFE	Mar, Jun, Sep, Dec	A$100,000	0.005% = A$44	27,043	3,176
10 year Canadian government bond	ME	Mar, Jun, Sep, Dec	C$100,000	0.01 pt = C$10	5,962	25
U.S. Treasury bond	MidAm	Mar, Jun, Sep, Dec	US$50,000	1/32 pt = US$15.625	5,478	12
10 year Swedish government bond	OM	Mar, Jun, Sep, Dec	SKr1 million	0.01 pt = SKr100	4,534	—
Swiss government bond	SOFFEX	Next 4 months of Mar, Jun, Sep, Dec cycle	SFr100,000	0.01 pt = SFr10	3,754	214
Short Term Interest Rates						
3 month Eurodollar	CME	Mar, Jun, Sep, Dec + spot month	US$1 million	0.01 pt = US$25	414,321	111,249
3 month Euroyen	TIFFE	Mar, Jun, Sep, Dec	¥100 million	0.01 pt = ¥2,500	151,522	2,309
3 month Euromark	LIFFE	Mar, Jun, Sep, Dec	DM1 million	0.01 pt = DM25	116,318	11,682
1 day interbank deposits	BM&F	All months	Cr50,000	0.1 pt = Cr0.05	116,223	1
3 month sterling	LIFFE	Mar, Jun, Sep, Dec	£500,000	0.01 pt = £12.50	65,886	16,103
3 month PIBOR	MATIF	Mar, Jun, Sep, Dec	FF5 million	0.01 pt = FF125	52,705	13,445
90 day Australian bank bill	SFE	Mar, Jun, Sep, Dec	A$1 million	0.01 pt = A$25	37,179	3,745
3 month Eurodollar	SIMEX	Mar, Jun, Sep, Dec	US$1 million	0.01 pt = US$25	33,647	53
3 month Euroyen	SIMEX	Mar, Jun, Sep, Dec	¥100 million	0.01 pt = ¥2,500	26,335	488
3 month forward rate agreement	OM	Mar, Jun, Sep, Dec	SKr1 million	0.01 pt = SKr25	19,037	
90 day MIBOR	MEFF-F	8 months in Mar, Jun, Sep, Dec cycle	Pta10 million	0.01 pt = Pta250	15,101	1,235
180 day notional T-bill	OM	Mar, Jun, Sep, Dec	SKr1 million	0.01 pt = SKr50	14,609	—
3 month Eurolira	LIFFE	Mar, Jun, Sep, Dec	L1 billion	0.01 pt = L25,000	13,716	—
1 month LIBOR	CME	All months	US$3 million	0.01 pt = US$25	7,554	313
3 month Canadian bankers' acceptance	ME	Mar, Jun, Sep, Dec	C$1 million	0.01 pt = C$25	7,645	161
3 month Euroswiss	LIFFE	Mar, Jun, Sep, Dec	SFr1 million	0.01 pt = SFr25	6,741	76
90 day U.S. Treasury bill	CME	Mar, Jun, Sep, Dec	US$1 million	0.01 pt = US$25	4,034	21

Table 18.1

Continued

Contract	Exchange	Contract Months	Contract Size	Tick Size & Value	Daily Volume	Options Volume[a]
Medium Term Interest Rates						
5 year U.S. Treasury note	CBOT	Mar, Jun, Sep, Dec	US$100,000	1/64 pt = US$15.625	49,260	10,574
3 year Australian Treasury bond	SFE	Mar, Jun, Sep, Dec	A$100,000	0.01 pt = A$28	38,531	2,013
German note	DTB	Mar, Jun, Sep, Dec	DM250,000	0.01 pt = DM25	22,412	183
2 year Swedish government bond	OM	Mar, Jun, Sep, Dec	SKr1 million	0.01 pt = SKr100	6,795	—
5 year Swedish government bond	OM	Mar, Jun, Sep, Dec	SKr1 million	0.01 pt = SKr100	6,781	342
2 year U.S. Treasury note	CBOT	Mar, Jun, Sep, Dec	US$200,000	1/4 of 1/32 pt = US$15.625	3,712	51
Other Interest Rates						
Interest rate swap	BM&F	Min. 2 days, max. 730 days	Min. Cr40,000	N/A	24,500	—
Interest rate swap x exchange rate swap	BM&F	Min. 2 days, max. 730 days	Min. Cr40,000	N/A	14,964	—
Municipal bond index	CBOT	Mar, Jun, Sep, Dec	US$1,000 x index	1/32 pt = US$31.25	6,326	98
Stock Indexes (Futures)						
IBEX-35	MEFF-V	All months	Pta100 x index	1 pt = Pta100	111,932	—
S&P 500	CME	Mar, Jun, Sep, Dec	US$500 x index	0.05 pt = US$25	73,947	15,102
IBOVESPA	BM&F	Feb, Apr, Jun, Aug, Oct, Dec	Cr0.20 x index	5 pts = Cr1	43,198	54
CAC-40	MATIF	Mar, Jun, Sep, Dec & next 2 months	FF200 x index	0.5 pt = FF100	29,858	—
Nikkei 225	OSE	Mar, Jun, Sep, Dec	¥1,000 x index	10 pts = ¥10,000	25,137	17,302
Nikkei 225	SIMEX	Mar, Jun, Sep, Dec	¥500 x index	5 pts = ¥2,500	23,582	6,085
DAX	DTB	Mar, Jun, Sep, Dec	DM100 x index	0.5 pt = DM50	20,400	197

[a]We discuss options on futures contracts in chapter 19.

Source: Futures (March 1995): p.55.

decreased in some years), volume on the new exchanges exploded. In 1994 trading volume on U.S. futures exchanges increased 32%, as compared to a 74% increase in trading volume on non-U.S. exchanges (for example, 1994 volume on the French MATIF alone increased almost 75%). Turnover on Far Eastern exchanges increased at an annual rate of 29% in recent years.

The London International Financial Futures and Options Exchange (LIFFE) grew rapidly during 1989–1994, in terms of both trading volume and number of traders. In 1995 LIFFE accounted for 15% of global futures volume, with a 1994 growth rate in volume of almost 100%. About 70% of the members live outside of the United Kingdom. Adding to its international flavor, two-thirds of the contracts traded on LIFFE are non-British products.

Table 18.2

Futures Exchanges Around the World, 1994

Exchange	Country	Volume Traded[a] (No. of contracts)
Chicago Board of Trade (CBOT)	United States	175,697,680
Chicago Mercantile Exchange (CME)	United States	162,696,029
London International Financial Futures Exchange (LIFFE)	United Kingdom	148,726,421
Marche a Terme International de France (MATIF)	France	93,438,671
New York Mercantile Exchange (NYMEX)	United States	68,010,380
Bolsa Mercadorias and de Futuros (BM&F)	Brazil	102,981,783
London Metal Exchange (LME)	United Kingdom	47,687,717
Osaka Securities Exchange	Japan	14,935,942
Sydney Futures Exchange (SFE)	Australia	31,556,584
Tokyo International Financial Futures Exchange (TIFFE)	Japan	38,034,953

[a]Volume includes futures and futures options.

Source: Commodity Research Bureau, *Commodity Yearbook*, 1995.

The Singapore International Monetary Exchange (SIMEX) has grown in recent years because of the country's favorable tax and banking laws, instituted in order to encourage financial market activity. Moreover, because of its strategic geographic location, it acts as a bridge between the time zones of the Far East and Europe. Table 18.2 describes the most active futures exchanges in the world as of 1994.

Checkpoint

1. Why did financial futures become popular in the 1970s?

2. Explain why long futures positions gain when prices increase and short futures positions gain when prices decrease.

3. What are the three identifying characteristics of any futures contract? Who sets these characteristics?

4. What are the three categories of financial futures contracts?

5. What is the most actively traded futures contract in the world?

Futures Contracts

As futures exchanges expand around the world, the volume of futures market activity also grows. Volume in established contracts increases as futures find increased acceptance among FIs and nonfinancial end-users. Moreover, new contracts proliferate as futures exchanges innovate to meet the demands of potential customers.

Four broad developments give rise to these demands: (1) Increased volatility in interest rates, exchange rates, and market prices exposes everyone to greater risk, thereby feeding the demand for risk management services; (2) the growth in the volume of activity in spot markets (for example, government bond markets) generates increased liquidity that expands the range of deliverable assets on which futures contracts can be based; (3) financial engineering and innovations in cash instruments induce demand for innovative ways to manage risk efficiently and inexpensively; and (4) global financial markets are less tolerant of individual countries' regulatory impediments to free capital flows. Often, derivatives are used to create synthetic instruments that bypass restrictive conditions in spot markets.

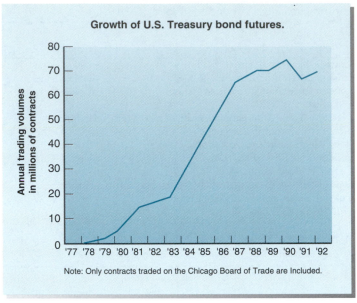

Growth of U.S. Treasury bond futures.

Note: Only contracts traded on the Chicago Board of Trade are Included.

Source: Remolona (1994), p. 34.

Figure 18.3

When futures contracts satisfy these demands, they are successful and their trading volume increases. Figure 18.3 shows the life cycle of one of the most successful of all futures contracts: the U.S. Treasury bond futures contract. About 10 years after its introduction, the rapid growth rate in the Treasury bond futures trading volume leveled off as other financial futures gained popularity.

To illustrate the basic characteristics of each category of futures contract shown in Table 18.1, we examine the most popular contracts only. These contracts are successful because they have low transaction costs and are highly liquid, thereby enabling traders to participate anonymously. In the section on interest rate futures, we describe the particulars of the Eurodollar and U.S. Treasury bond futures contracts. For stock index futures, we consider Spanish stock index futures (IBEX-35) and the S&P 500 futures contracts. For currencies, we consider the Deutschemark futures contract. Table 18.3 shows the basic characteristics of these five contracts.

Interest Rate Futures   The Eurodollar futures is traded on the Chicago Mercantile Exchange, with delivery dates on the third Monday of each of the following delivery months: March, June, September, December, plus the spot month.[4] The underlying security is a $1 million face value, 91 day maturity, pure discount instrument.[5] The price is quoted using the IMM price index, which is constructed as $100 - $ (rate of discount, d). Figure 18.4 shows the Bloomberg quotation of 96.64 on the March 1994 Eurodollar futures contract. This quotation reflects a rate of discount of 3.36% p.a., since the IMM Index price is $100 - d = 100 - 3.36 = 96.64$.

---

[4] Although we refer to "delivery dates," the Eurodollar futures contract is cash settled with a transfer of the contract's cash value on delivery date. Physical delivery is not allowed.

[5] The Eurodollar futures contract has an embedded option since the underlying asset could be either a 90, 91, or 92 day maturity, pure discount instrument. The price is adjusted to reflect the number of days until maturity.

Table
18.3

Characteristics of Five Representative Futures Contracts[a]

	Eurodollar	U.S. T-bond	IBEX-35	S&P 500	Deutschemark
Exchange	CME	CBOT	MEFF-V	CME	CME
Face value	$1 million	$100,000	Pta100 x IBEX–35	$500 x S&P500	DM125,000
Tick size	1bp = $25	$\frac{1}{32}(1,000) = \$31.25$	Pta100 = US$0.75	.05pt = $25	$12.50
Daily Limit Move	None	$3,000		$2,500	$1,875
Last trading day	2nd London bus. day before 3rd Wed. contract mo.	7 days before last bus. day of contract mo.		Bus. day before 3rd Friday of contract mo.	2 days before 3rd Wed. of contract mo.
Delivery date	Last trading day	Any day during delivery month			3rd Wed. of contract mo.
Initial margin[b]	$540	$3,000	$400	$6,000	$1,500
Maintenance margin[b]	$400	$2,000	$250	$3,000	$1,000

[a]"Pta" denotes the Spanish peseta; "bp" denotes basis points. Whenever not stated otherwise, $ denotes US$. CME = the Chicago Mercantile Exchange. CBOT = the Chicago Board of Trade. MEFF-V = the Spanish Mercado de Opciones y Futuros Financieros - Renta Variable.

[b]Margin requirements are subject to change upon regular review by the futures exchanges.

```
/SWPCO Corp FYH                                                      Corp FYH
   FUTURES              YIELD-SHIFT        (DURATION)               HEDGING
PAY                   Settlement   1/31/94   TRADE   1/27/94
FIXED       1000.(M)  Maturity:   12/15/98   Fixed: 6.12500%  ($)    Pay Reset
Ccy:US                Effective: 12/15/93   Float: 3.25000% + 0.0 bp (Q)/(Q)
   Market Value:         -41.37 All-in-cost: 5.238   Risk:   4.23   EEquiv/Conv
   BUY                   Yld Beta 1.00
FUTURES              Futures   HEDGE NUMBER   Proxy Security for Futures Valuation
Size Contract        Price     OF FUTURES     Issue       Yield    Risk   Factor
1MM CME Euro$ 3Mo TD
EDH4        Mar94     96.64       16.9         EURO$ 3Mo T  3.36     .25    n.a.
EDM4        Jun94     96.35       16.9         EURO$ 3Mo T  3.65     .25    n.a.
PS 100M CBT US 10yr 8%
TYH4        Mar94     114-00       7.0         T 8 1/2 11/00  5.34    6.23   1.0250
TYM4        Jun94     113-05       6.7         T 7 3/4 2/01   5.40    6.27    .9875
PV 100M CBT US 5yr 8%
FVH4        Mar94     111-284      9.6         T 5 1/8 6/98   4.91    3.95    .8980
FVM4        Jun94     111-07       8.9         T 5 1/8 11/98  5.02    4.25    .8947
PU 200M CBT US 2yr 8%
TUH4        Mar94     106-15      10.9         T 4 1/4 12/95  4.06    1.83    .9398
TUM4        Jun94     Y105-27      9.8         T 7 3/4 9/96   4.16    2.14    .9958
→ CHOICES: US TY FV FD TH TU TH MR  AUME    GI    MN MP    J JB JL    <help>
FX rates:      $=1.00         DM 1.737  £ 3.501  Ff 5.905   ¥ 108.8   A$ .7096
Bloomberg-all rights protected.  London:71-330-7500  New York:212-318-2000  Princeton:609-497-3500  Singapore:226-3000
Sydney:2-241-1133   Tokyo:3-3578-1625   Washington DC:202-434-1800   G104-37-14   27-Jan-94  14:18:48
```

Figure 18.4

This rate corresponds to a price, using the discount formula from Chapter 7, of

$$P = FV \left(1 - \frac{dt}{360} \right) = \$1\text{m} \left(1 - \frac{.0336(91)}{360} \right) = \$991,506.67$$

where P = the price; FV = the face value, standardized for the Eurodollar futures at $1 million;

d = the rate of discount, in this example 3.36% p.a.; and t = the number of days until maturity, standardized for the Eurodollar futures at 91 days. Each 91 day basis point is worth $25.28 (= $.0001 \times \$1m \times \frac{91}{360}$). A 1% rate shift, say from 96.64 to 97.64, represents a 91 day basis point shift of 100, which is valued at $25.28.

The U.S. Treasury bond futures contract, on the CBOT, is based on a benchmark U.S. Treasury bond that has at least 15 years (beyond the futures delivery date) until either maturity or call, face value of $100,000, and a semiannual coupon rate of 8% p.a. Many U.S. Treasury bonds, of varying maturities, would satisfy these conditions. The Treasury bond futures contract contains an embedded **delivery option** that allows the short position to choose to deliver any one of several bonds against physical delivery on the contract. This can potentially have value since the short can choose the least expensive bond to deliver against the contract.[6]

The U.S. Treasury bond futures price is quoted in terms of 32nds. That is, the tick value, the minimum allowable price change, is $\frac{1}{32}(\$1,000)$ = $31.25. Thus, a price of 101-3 denotes $101\frac{3}{32}$ per $100 face value, or a total of $101,093.75 for the $100,000 of the standardized Treasury bond futures contract. The price is quoted for a hypothetical 20 year 8% p.a. semiannual coupon U.S. Treasury bond. The actual delivery price depends on which of any of about two dozen U.S. Treasury bonds are delivered against the contract. The CBOT publishes **conversion factors** that convert any deliverable bond's price into the price it would be if it yielded 8% p.a. during the delivery month. Conversion factors are fixed for the life of the futures contract. This gives rise to potentially profitable trades based on a divergence between the fixed futures delivery price and the actual spot price. For example, the **wild card play** allows the short to give notice of intent to sell the Treasury bond even after the futures market has closed and the price has been set. This will be profitable for the seller if spot prices have been falling during the time period after the close of the futures market because the seller receives the higher closing price.

Stock Index Futures   The CME introduced the S&P 500 futures contract in April 1982. The contract cash settles on the third Friday of each delivery month: March, June, September, and December. The value of the index at the opening on the delivery Friday is used to determine the futures cash value upon delivery. The Bloomberg quotation screen for S&P 500 futures, showing 12 days of futures prices, is presented in Figure 18.5. The price on February 18, 1994 of 468.15 implies a value of $234,075 (= 468.15 × the multiple of $500). We can also see how volatile S&P 500 prices have been over various periods ranging from a 10 day (7.18%) through a 90 day (8.07%) period.

The high trading volume on the Spanish stock index futures contract, the IBEX-35 introduced in 1992, stems from the contract's small size of $2,500, which is 1/100th the size of the S&P 500 contract. Both contracts have cash values that are set to equal the index value times a multiple ($500 for the S&P 500 and 100 pesetas (Pta) for the IBEX-35). The IBEX-35 is a market value weighted index, calculated using the prices of the 35 most liquid stocks on four Spanish stock exchanges. Nonresidents of Spain constitute over 50% of the daily futures volume of IBEX-35 futures contracts. The contracts expire in March, June, September, and December, with contracts extending 12 months into the future.

Currency Futures   For foreign currency transactions, there is a forward market that dominates the futures market in terms of volume of trade. However, the two markets coexist, although their contracts are quite similar, because they serve two different clienteles. Forward traders tend

---

[6] Kane and Marcus (1986) estimate that the three month delivery option may be worth from $1,390 to $4,690 per $100,000 face value of the futures contract. Ritchken and Sankarasubramanian (1995) estimate an upper bound for the option's value at 5% of contract price.

---

delivery option: option that allows the short position to choose to deliver any one of several bonds against physical delivery on the U.S. Treasury bond futures contract.

conversion factors: numerical values published by CBOT used to convert any deliverable bond's price into the price it would be if it yielded 8% p.a. during the delivery month.

wild card play: trade that allows the short to give notice of intent to sell the Treasury bond even after the futures market has closed and the price has been set; the seller can profit if spot prices have been falling during the time period after the close of the futures market.

```
HVT3                                                                    Index HVT
    ENTER ALL VALUES AND HIT <GO>
    14:14                    HISTORICAL PRICE VOLATILITY
    Mon 2/21
                     S P H 4     S & P   500   FUTURE    Mar94
                                   N-DAY VOLATILITY
                              of Historical Closing Prices
                    PRICE     N=10-DAY    30        60        90
    2/18/94        468.15      7.18%     9.63%     8.16%     8.07%
    2/17/94        470.40      7.77     10.04      8.09      8.30
    2/16/94        473.15     14.98     10.10      8.00      8.23
    2/15/94        473.60     15.04     10.10      8.05      8.23
    2/14/94        471.30     15.06     10.01      8.07      8.19
    2/11/94        470.00     14.79     10.02      8.10      8.20
    2/10/94        469.45     15.46     10.04      8.11      8.24
    2/9/94         473.30     15.17      9.89      8.02      8.11
    2/8/94         471.90     15.77      9.94      8.09      8.10
    2/7/94         472.05     16.03      9.94      8.14      8.10
    2/4/94         468.95     15.56      9.73      8.18      8.11
    2/3/94         480.20      7.50      6.69      6.44      7.00
                              260 Annualization Factor
    Bloomberg-all rights protected.  London:71-330-7500  New York:212-318-2000  Princeton:609-279-3000  Singapore:226-3000
    Sydney:2-241-1133    Tokyo:3-3578-1625    Washington DC:202-434-1800    G104-33-10    21-Feb-94  14:15:06
```

Figure 18.5

to be large FIs that use the forward market to hedge foreign exchange rate risk for themselves and their commercial customers. Futures currency traders tend to be smaller commercial users and speculators.

The Deutschemark futures contract is priced in terms of US$ per DM with a contract size of DM125,000. Delivery months are March, June, September, and December. Delivery is by wire transfer, usually CHIPS, two days after the last day of trading.

Dual Trading

dual trading system: members' execution of trades for their own accounts, as well as on behalf of customers.

front running: the broker's purchases of shares ahead of large customer orders in expectation of ensuing price increases.

Only members of the futures exchange can trade futures. Members, in their role as broker/dealers, execute trades for their own accounts as well as on behalf of customers. This **dual trading system** enhances market liquidity. The CFTC estimates that over 50% of trading volume is executed by dual traders.[7] However, dual trading may lead to a conflict of interest between broker and customer. One such conflict is called **front running** in which the broker buys shares ahead of large customer orders in expectation of ensuing price increases. In this way, the broker exploits for personal profit the private information provided by customer trading orders.

Although front running is illegal in the United States, it is very difficult to distinguish from legal dual trading. Thus, in May 1991 the CME passed Rule 552, which prohibited all dual trading in contracts with an average daily volume of 10,000 contracts or more.[8] Chakravarty (1994) suggests that this prohibition is likely to do more harm than good. Potential front-running damages are alleviated in competitive markets, where brokers compete for customers' orders. Indeed, dual trading increases the number of market makers by giving them two potential sources of income: brokering and dealing. This reduces the bid-ask spread, as well as the cost of trading to all participants.

Fishman and Longstaff (1992) show that dual traders earn a median daily value of $763.02 more than nondual traders. They find a mixed impact on customers' trading profits. Some

---

[7] Smith and Whaley (1994), p. 216.

[8] In 1987 the CME enacted the "top step rule," which prohibits dual trading by members on the top step of the S&P 500 futures trading pit.

customers benefit from better price execution by their dual trading brokers, thereby increasing customer trading profits. Other customers lose because their dual trader brokers front-run their orders. Despite these potential costs, prohibitions against dual trading cannot completely prevent front running. This is because market makers can collude to exploit the information contained in each other's customer orders. Thus, the benefits of dual trading restrictions are elusive, whereas the costs are real. Indeed, British, German, and Swiss FIs make no attempt to disclose their trading profits, as distinct from brokerage commissions, and they appear unconcerned about the problem of dual trading.

Marking to Market

settlement price: either the closing price or an average of several of the last trading prices of the day (computed following some predetermined formula).

At the close of each trading day, all futures contracts are marked to market based on the day's **settlement price**. The settlement price is either the closing price or an average of several of the last trading prices of the day (computed following some predetermined formula). On each day t, the value of the futures position F, is calculated as $F(P_S^t - P_F)$, where P_S^t is the settlement (closing) price on day t and P_F is the futures price. The day's gains or losses are either added to or subtracted from the balance in the futures margin account.

Suppose that you initiated a long futures position in U.S. Treasury bond futures, with June delivery, at a price of 101-3. The next day, day 1, the Treasury bond futures price increases to a settlement price of 101-18. The following day, day 2, the futures price closes at 101-7. The third day's settlement price is 100-30. What are the margin cash flows at the end of each trading day?

Upon initiation of the long futures position, you placed an initial margin of $3,000 (see initial margin requirements in Table 18.3) and obtained a futures contract that obligates you to buy a U.S. Treasury bond at a price of $101,093.75. On day 1, the futures price increases to 101-18, or $101,562.50—an increase of 15 ticks,[9] or $\frac{15}{32}(\$1,000) = \$468.75$. The long position gains from this price movement since the futures contract allows the purchase of a security worth $101,562.50 for only $101,093.75; that is, the futures value of one long futures position, where $F = +1$, is $(+1)(\$101,562.50 - \$101,093.75) = \$468.75$. The trader holding the corresponding short position would lose $468.75. These cash flows are marked to market at the end of the trading day. Thus, the margin balance in your long futures position increases to $3,468.75, while the margin balance of the holder of the short position would decline by $468.75.

The news on day 2 of the futures transaction is not as good for you. The futures price closes at 101-7, or $101,218.75—a decline of 11 ticks, or $343.75. This is debited from your margin account, bringing the total to $3,125. That is, to mark to market the futures position, simply calculate the *change* in the value of the futures position from yesterday's settlement price, P_S^{t-1}, to today's settlement price, P_S^t or $F(P_S^t - P_S^{t-1})$. Using our example, we find that the change in the long futures value is $(+1)(\$101,218.75 - \$101,562.50) = -\$343.75$. This daily change in the value of the futures position is added to day 1's closing balance, $\$3,468.75 - \$343.75 = \$3,125$, which is the balance at the end of day 2.

The bad news continues on day 3, since the price moves down 9 ticks ($281.25) further to 100-30, or $100,937.50. Now the long position is losing money. The cumulative loss is $F(P_S^t - P_F) = (+1)(\$100,937.50 - \$101,093.75) = -\$156.25$, or 5 ticks, which is the change from the initial margin value of $3,000. The balance in your margin account falls to $2,843.75 at the end of day 3. This is still not sufficient to warrant a margin call since the balance exceeds the maintenance margin of $2,000.

---

[9] A trader would calculate the futures price appreciation by multiplying the number of ticks by each tick value; that is, for this example, $15 \times \$31.25 = \$468.75$.

Suppose that on day 4, the price falls 64 ticks or $2,000. Settlement price is 98-30 (100-30 minus 2), and the day 4 balance in your margin account declines by $2,000 to $843.75. Note that on any given day, the balance in the margin account minus the initial margin reflects the cumulative gains or losses on the futures position to that date. On day 4, the long futures position is worth $98,937.50 − $101,093.75 = −$2,156.25. The long position has cumulative losses of $2,156.25, which are deducted from the initial margin deposit of $3,000 to obtain the balance of $843.75. Since this balance is below the maintenance margin, you will receive a margin call to return the balance to the *initial* margin of $3,000. Thus, you will have to pay off your cumulative losses to date in order to maintain your long futures position. If you do not meet the margin call, then your position is immediately sold out by the futures clearing corporation.

Note that the clearinghouse protects itself from credit risk by using *two* requirements that it controls. It is the juxtaposition of the margin requirement and the daily limit move that protects the clearinghouse from trader defaults on their obligations. The maintenance margin is set equal to either one day's maximum trading losses or maximum expected losses based on past price volatility.[10] Even the unluckiest trader, then, will always have enough margin on hand to cover one day's maximum losses. If any account does not meet its maintenance margin by the start of trading the next day, it is immediately terminated, and the losses are paid out of the balance in the margin account to date. The combination of the margin requirement and the daily limit move then requires each trader to *insure* the clearinghouse against losses by putting up a cash amount that equals the maximum possible loss that could be incurred.

Reversing a Futures Position

Futures represent contractual obligations to make or take delivery of some underlying asset. The trader gets out of this obligation by undertaking a reverse futures position. In our example of the long Treasury bond futures investment, the trader would reverse the position by selling an equivalent Treasury bond futures contract. Let's see how this works.

Suppose that the trader decides to call it quits after four days of losses on the 101-3 June delivery Treasury bond futures contract in the previous example. But the trader is obligated to buy the Treasury bonds at a price of 101-3 ($101,093.75), although the current spot price (on day 4 after initiation of the futures position) is $98,937.50, or a futures price of 98-30. If the trader wants to get out of the long futures position on day 5, she will initiate a short futures position with the same delivery date as the original futures contract. Thus, in June, the trader is obligated to both sell and buy one Treasury bond, and the two transactions cancel one another out, thereby eliminating the delivery date obligation. What is the cost of this reversal? The two contracts together obligate the trader to buy at 101-3 and sell at 98-30, for a loss of $98,937.50 − $101,093.75 = −$2,156.25. The offsetting transaction therefore limits the losses at the cumulative losses to date.

To see how the two contracts cancel one another, examine the value of both the long and short futures positions on delivery date. Suppose that the spot price on delivery date is 98-3. The value of the long futures contract is $(1)(\$98,093.75 - \$101,093.75) = -\$3,000$, a loss of $3,000. However, the offsetting short futures contract has a positive value of $(-1)(\$98,093.75 - \$98,937.50) = \$843.75$. The net cash flow on both the long and short positions is −$3,000 + 843.75 = −$2,156.25, a net loss of $2,156.25. No matter what happens to Treasury bond prices after day 4, the offsetting short contract locks in the cash flows on the long futures position.

---

[10] Exchanges often set margin below daily limit movements in popular, highly liquid contracts such as Treasury bond futures, for competitive reasons.

Checkpoint

✓

1. Describe the major interest rate futures contracts. What determines the contract value?
2. Describe the major stock index futures contracts. What determines the contract value?
3. Describe the major currency futures contract. What determines the contract value?
4. How does the margin adjust daily to reflect the cumulative futures trading gains or losses?
5. How is a futures position reversed?

The Role of Futures Contracts in the Economy

We have seen how futures originated to smooth the income of farmers from the impact of fluctuations in the prices of their crops. If this were all that futures contracts had to offer, then it would be hard to explain the existence, let alone the success, of financial futures. Futures contracts offer important services to economic players in addition to income smoothing: (1) price discovery; (2) implicit money markets; and (3) risk shifting.

carrying charges: the relevant interest expenses, storage costs, and depreciation charges that affect the asset underlying the futures contract.

Price Discovery   Futures prices create a pattern of financial security prices that must be consistent with spot prices. If a trader takes immediate delivery of some underlying financial instrument in a spot market transaction and simultaneously sells that instrument forward in a futures contract, then the spread between the prices should reflect the **carrying charges**. The carrying charges are the relevant interest expenses, storage costs, and depreciation charges that affect the asset underlying the futures contract.

We can solve for the carrying charges using the price spreads between contracts with different delivery dates. Suppose that a five year $100,000 note with semiannual coupons of 8% p.a. sells in the spot market for $98,500 and in the futures market with delivery in three months at $98,750.[11] The annualized yield to maturity on the spot transaction is 8.37% p.a. In contrast, the yield to maturity on the note deliverable in three months against the futures contract is 8.31% p.a. The three month carrying charge is six basis points. The price spread between the two notes is $98,750 minus $98,500, or $250. If carrying charges are constant over time, we can solve for any futures price. For example, the contract delivering in another three months would be priced another $250 above the price of the previous contract. The five year note would consequently sell at a price of $99,000 ($98,750 + $250) for a yield to maturity of 8.25% p.a., for a three month carrying charge of six basis points (8.31% − 8.25%).

If carrying charges were always constant, then futures markets would not offer any new information because you could calculate any futures price by simply marking up the spot price once you knew the spot price and the carrying charge. But, in general, carrying charges are *not* observable and *not* constant. Futures markets thus provide us with valuable price discovery information that reflects volatility in interest rates as well as the other factors included in carrying charges. The volatility in spreads that is observed in all futures markets reflects fluctuations in the underlying asset's carrying costs. We can therefore utilize the information embedded in futures spreads to obtain timely information about costs.

---

[11] The value of y equal to 8.37% p.a. is from:

$$\$98,500 = \sum_{t=1}^{10} \frac{4,000}{\left(1 + \frac{y}{2}\right)^t} + \frac{100,000}{\left(1 + \frac{y}{2}\right)^{10}}$$

Adapting Our Notation   Chapter 7 introduced a double subscript notation that is particularly useful for futures or forward transactions. To review, we expressed any interest rate[12] as $_nR_t$, where $n \equiv$ number of periods until delivery, $R \equiv$ choice of interest format (i, i^*, y, y^*), and $t \equiv$ the number of periods between delivery and maturity. Implied in this rate notation was a superscript, call it s, which denoted the date on which the rate was quoted. The full notation would therefore be $_n^s R_t$, which states the rate on date s for a t period security to be delivered on date n.

If $n = 0$ and $s = 0$, then we are discussing a spot market transaction. That is, $_0^0 R_5 = 7.5\%$ denotes that today's rate on a five year note, for immediate delivery, is 7.5%. Whenever $n > 0$, we have a deferred delivery transaction, such as for a forward or futures contract. If $n > 0$ and $s = 0$, today's futures rates are referenced. That is, $_1^0 R_5 = 7.75\%$ denotes that today's rate on a five year note to be delivered in one year is 7.75%. Comparing the spot rate to this forward rate, one might conclude that the market expects yields for five year notes to increase over the next year.

We can consider an entire sequence of futures rates over the period of time from $s = 0, \ldots, n$. That is, each day until delivery date, there will be another rate that is quoted. Thus, $_2^0 R_5$ is today's rate on the five year note to be delivered in two years, whereas $_2^1 R_5$ is the expected rate, as of the end of next year, on the five year note to be delivered two years from today. Similarly, we can represent different deferred delivery contracts using different values of n in this notation. Suppose that the near term delivery contract delivers in three months (0.25 year), say, in September, and a new contract delivers every three months for the following year. Today's sequence of rates on the futures contract based on the 5 year note is $_0^0 R_5, _{.25}^0 R_5, _{.5}^0 R_5, _{.75}^0 R_5, _1^0 R_5$, where the first rate represents the spot rate, the second delivers in September, the next in December, the next in March, and the last rate delivers the five year note next September. The **calendar spread** is the difference between the rates on two identical futures contracts with different delivery dates, for example, $_{.75}^0 R_5 - _1^0 R_5$.

On the delivery date, $s = n = 0$ and the forward rate equals the spot rate. When $n = s > 0$ then we are referring to the future spot price upon delivery date. That is, $_1^1 R_5$ is the rate expected to prevail in one year on a five year note to be delivered in one year. This expected rate is revealed in futures prices.

Implicit Money Markets   The spread between futures contracts with different delivery dates can be viewed as the cost of borrowing the underlying commodity. If a trader buys the five year note in the spot market and simultaneously sells a futures contract on that note with delivery in three months, then the trader has arranged to borrow the note for a period of three months. This should be reminiscent of a money market transaction that we covered in Chapter 11—the repo market. The spread between futures and spot markets can be viewed as a repo rate.

Let us construct a reverse repo transaction using the futures and spot markets. Recall from Chapter 11 that from the viewpoint of the counterparty in the reverse repo, the transaction consists of simultaneously lending cash and borrowing securities. At the maturity of the reverse repo, the cash is repaid by the resale of the securities. Simultaneous transactions in the spot and futures markets are called **cash and carry transactions**. These transactions can be used to create synthetic loans that (a) determine the relationship between futures and spot prices and (b) also perform the role of price discovery in futures markets. The interest rate on these synthetic repo loans, called the **implied repo rate**, must be equal to spot rates.

Figure 18.6 shows the timing of each leg of a generic reverse repo and a cash and carry transaction. At time period $s = 0$, the reverse repo holder receives an $n + t$ period asset and lends out cash for a period of n days. On the cash and carry transaction, there is also the receipt of an $n + t$ period asset, paid for with a cash outflow in the spot market. In n days, under both

calendar spread: the difference between the rates on two identical futures contracts with different delivery dates.

cash and carry transactions: simultaneous transactions in the spot and futures markets.

implied repo rate: the interest rate on synthetic repo loans created by cash and carry transactions.

---

[12] We discuss the notation in terms of interest rates, but the same notation could be used to express prices by simply substituting P for R.

Reverse Repo Cash Flows

Borrow $(n + t)$ period asset
Lend cash over n days

Return t period asset
Receive cash payment on reverse repo

$0 = s$
Current date

n = delivery date

$n + t$ = maturity of
underlying asset

Cash and carry transaction:

Borrow $(n + t)$ period asset on spot market
Sell futures contract on t period asset for
   delivery at time n

Deliver t period asset
   on short futures position

$0 = s$
Current date

n = delivery date

$n + t$ = maturity of
underlying asset

Example Cash Flows

−$968,069.44

+$977,250
91 days

$0 = s$

30 days

121 days

Buy 121 day 9.5% Eurodollar CD on spot market
$968,069.44

Sell 91 day 9% Eurodollar futures contract
$977,250

$ 9,180.56

"Deliver" 91 day Eurodollar
   CD on futures position

Figure 18.6   Cash and Carry Transaction

transactions, the t period asset is returned (sold) and payment received. In *Practitioner's Primer 18.1*, we show how futures prices can be used to determine an implied repo rate, which must be consistent with the repo rate discussed in Chapter 11.

PRACTITIONER'S PRIMER 18.1

THE IMPLIED REPO RATE

We can solve for the relationship between spot and futures prices as[13]

$$ {}_n^s P_t = {}_0^s P_{n+t} \left(1 + {}_0^s r_n \frac{n}{360} \right) \tag{18.1} $$

where ${}_n^s P_t$ = the futures price, quoted on date s, for delivery n periods from now, of a t period underlying asset; ${}_0^s P_{n+t}$ = the spot price, at period s, of an $n + t$ period underlying asset; and ${}_0^s r_n$ = the implied repo rate, which must equal the spot interest rate for an n period loan as of date s.

   As a specific example of the cash and carry transaction, shown in the bottom panel of Figure 18.6, suppose that on day $s = 0$ you purchased a $1 million 121 day Eurodollar CD on the spot market at a rate of discount of 9.5% p.a. Using the pricing formula for

---

[13] For simplicity, in considering synthetic money market transactions, we use pure discount instruments only. If there were coupon payments during the three months' maturity of this transaction, the cash flows would have to be adjusted. We therefore limit our attention to transactions without interim cash flows.

a pure discount instrument, we see that the Euro's spot price is $\$1m(1 - \frac{.095(121)}{360}) =$ $\$968,069.44$. If today's Eurodollar futures price is 91.00 for delivery in 30 days, this implies a rate of discount of 9% p.a. and a Euro futures price of $\$1m(1 - \frac{.09(91)}{360}) =$ $\$977,250$. Assuming no haircut, on date $s = 0$, you lend out $\$968,069.44$ to receive $\$977,250$ in 30 days. These cash flows are akin to a synthetic 30 day Treasury bill with a dollar discount of $\$9,180.56$ (= $\$977,250 - \$968,069.44$). Rearranging terms in equation (18.1), we can solve for the implied repo rate ${}_0^s r_n$:

$$ {}_0^s r_n = \frac{{}_n^s P_t - {}_0^s P_{n+t}}{{}_0^s P_{n+t}} \left(\frac{360}{n}\right) $$

Substituting the values from our example, where ${}_n^s P_t = {}_{30}^0 P_{91} = \$977,250$ and ${}_0^s P_{n+t} = {}_0^0 P_{121} = \$968,069.44$, we obtain

$$ {}_0^0 r_{30} = \frac{\$977,250 - \$968,069.44}{\$968,069.44} \left(\frac{360}{30}\right) = 11.38\% \text{ p.a.} $$

The cash and carry transaction comprising a short futures transaction and a long spot transaction constitutes the cash flows of a 30 day pure discount instrument with a 11.38% annual yield.

If the actual spot rate on 30 day Treasury bills is 11.20% p.a., then an arbitrage opportunity exists. Figure PP.1 shows the cash flows on the arbitrage opportunity. The synthetic 30 day Treasury bill requires a cash outflow, on date 0, of $\$968,069.44$. The arbitrageur would simultaneously sell $\$968,069.44$ worth of 30 day Treasury bills at the spot rate of 11.20% p.a. After 30 days, the synthetic Treasury bill yields $\$977,250$ since the short futures contract locks in the sale price of 91.00 (9% p.a.) on the 91 day Euro. However, the actual 30 day Treasury bill will have a face value FV, that we can calculate from the equation $\$968,069.44 = FV(1 - \frac{.112(30)}{360})$. Solving this expression for FV, we get a cash outflow of $FV = \$977,189.88$. The arbitrageur has no net cash flows at time period 0 since both transactions' cash flows cancel each other out. In 30 days, the arbitrageur receives $\$977,250$ and pays out $\$977,189.88$ for an arbitrage

Buy Synthetic 30 day Treasury bill @ 11.38% p.a.
    −$968,069.44   +$977,250
    t = 0   30 days

Buy 121 day 9.5% Euro   Sell 91 day Euro at 9%
                                on short futures

Plus

+$968,069.44   −$977,189.88
t = 0   30 days

Sell actual 30 day Treasury bill @ 11.20% p.a.   Pay out face value of 30 day Treasury bill

= Net Cash Flows on Cash and Carry Arbitrage

t =0   30 days

$0 (= −$968,069.44 + $968,069.44)   +$60.12 arbitrage profit per contract
                                      (= $977,250 − $977,189.88)

Figure PP.1

profit, without risk and without investment of $60.12 per contract. If there are no limitations on short sales of spot Treasury bills, the arbitrageur can perform this magic 100,000 times for a total profit of $6,012,000 at no initial cost! Exploitation of this arbitrage opportunity will bid up the rates on 30 day spot Treasury bills and lower Euro futures prices until equilibrium is reached when the implied repo rate on the cash and carry transaction equals the actual spot rate.

If futures prices are high relative to spot prices, the long cash–short futures arbitrage may be profitable. That is, the implied repo rate on a cash and carry transaction consisting of long spot and short futures transactions will be less than the spot financing rate. The cash and carry transaction simulates a money market loan. The impact of both directions of cash and carry arbitrages is to equate the implied repo rate on any synthetic transaction to its comparable spot money market rate.

Risk Shifting We have seen how unanticipated fluctuations in fundamental prices create risk exposure. In the step-by-step hedging procedure outlined in Border Crossing IV, we described how offsetting cash flows on derivatives transactions can alter that risk exposure. In particular, when the derivatives transaction tends to generate cash flows that are opposite the cash flows in an underlying cash position, then we call the derivatives transaction a risk reducing hedge. On the other hand, if all the cash flows move in the same direction when fundamental prices fluctuate, then we consider the derivatives transaction to be a risk enhancing speculative trade.

A Wharton survey of derivatives usage by U.S. non-financial firms, see Bodnar et al. (1995), found that 67% of the firms used derivatives to minimize fluctuations in cash flows, with an additional 28% choosing minimization in fluctuations of accounting earnings as their "most important" objective for derivatives transactions. Almost 50% of firms using derivatives used OTC forwards to hedge foreign exchange rate risk exposure. In the rest of this chapter, we will see how futures and forward contracts can be used to hedge interest rate risk, exchange rate risk, and market risk. Indeed, we will consider many of the financial futures/forwards to have evolved in response to the increased volatility of interest rates, exchange rates, and stock prices—hence, the growth of interest rate futures, currency forwards, and stock index futures. These will be the primary instruments used to demonstrate the risk shifting capacity of these versatile derivatives.

Checkpoint

✓

1. What are the three major roles of futures markets in the economy?

2. How do futures markets perform these roles?

3. What is the cash and carry arbitrage? Explain why a combination of short spot and long futures transactions is profitable if the implied repo rate is less than the spot repo lending rate.

4. Explain why the absence of cash and carry arbitrage opportunities is necessary to enable futures markets to perform their price discovery function.

Contrasts Between Futures and Forward Contracts

Thus far, we have considered only futures contracts as possible hedging instruments. However, a closely related contract, the **forward contract**, can also be used to hedge interest rate, currency, and market risk exposure. The forward contract, or forwards, can be viewed as an over-the-counter futures contract that is not traded on an organized exchange. However, just like futures, forwards are obligations either to make or to take delivery of some underlying

forward contract: an over-the-counter futures contract that is not traded on an organized exchange.

Table 18.4	Contrasts Between Futures and Forward Contracts

Futures Contracts	Forward Contracts
Traded on organized exchange	Traded electronically OTC
Open outcry auction system	Quotes displayed electronically
Standardized contracts	Negotiated contracts
Futures Clearing Corp. protects counterparties against credit risk	Considerable credit risk
	Only trade between FIs
Margin deposit upon initiation of contract	No up-front cash flows
Marked to market daily	Marked to market on delivery date only

asset at some predetermined price on some prearranged delivery date. This definition should look familiar since it is identical to that of the futures contract. What then are the differences between futures and forwards?

Table 18.4 contrasts the characteristics of futures and forward contracts. Whereas futures are traded in designated trading pits on futures exchanges, forward transactions are consummated electronically by mutual agreement between two FIs. The counterparties agree to the terms of the contract; they set the underlying deliverable asset, the price, and the delivery date. Whereas these terms are standardized for futures by the futures exchange on which trading takes place, for forwards these characteristics can take on any values that are mutually agreeable to the counterparties. As a result, forwards are negotiated contracts as opposed to the standardized futures contract.

Since there is so much discretion in the terms of the forward contract, the counterparties in the forward market tend to be FIs that are themselves active market makers. This consideration becomes even more important when one realizes that there is no protection against counterparty default on the forward market. There is no clearinghouse that acts as a third-party guarantor as on the futures market. The two counterparties are induced to fulfill their obligations because they know that if they default, they will lose access to this important market. Thus, the reputation of the counterparty is critical in assessing the credit risk of the forward transaction. If the counterparty is an active participant in the market, with a reputation for integrity, the chances of default are slim. However, if the counterparty is an unknown without active participation in the market, there will be grave concerns about the credit risk of the forward transaction, no matter how highly rated the counterparty is in other markets. The forward market often performs like a closed club in which access is limited to active market makers. Since these counterparties know one another, and need one another, the incentives to default, even in the face of large losses, are very low. Defaults are therefore quite rare in the forward market.

In contrast, futures markets are anything but closed clubs. They are open to anyone with the price of a seat on the exchange. Paying that price entitles you not to an actual seat, but rather to a standing spot only about 13 inches wide in a rough and tumble futures trading pit. Futures contracts trade on an **open outcry auction** method. All traders gather at a designated spot, called the **trading pit**, and place orders using hand signals, shouts, shoves, garish jackets, and any other means they might devise to get attention. *Timely Topics 18.1: Pit Presence* describes some of the more outlandish methods.

The "honors system" that prevails on forward markets is apparent in the way cash flows are handled. Cash flows on forward transactions are not transferred—marked to market—until delivery date. Accordingly, no money changes hands upon initiation of the transaction or on any date until the contract expires. This is in sharp contrast to the futures contract, in which cash flows are exchanged on a daily basis, reflecting the day's gains or losses. The impact of these distinctions between the contracts is that the transaction costs of trading futures are higher than those of forwards.

open outcry auction: the gathering of all traders at a designated spot to place their orders.

trading pit: designated spot for futures auction.

PIT PRESENCE

Traders in the CME's Mexican peso futures trading pit have adopted a uniform consisting of multicolored jackets emblazoned with cacti and sombreros. Said a veteran trader, "I wanted a jacket that would be easy to pick out in the crowd. Runners get orders to me more quickly and clerks find me faster when I'm trying to do trades."

Increasingly in places such as the CBOT's bond pit, where hundreds of people cram into a space only slightly larger than a tennis court, garb is being used to grab attention.... Traders choose from a subdued Harvard University crest on a crimson background to a slinky leopard skin pattern or turquoise frogs cavorting on a neon-pink background.... It's important to have what veterans of the mayhem describe as "pit presence" to make money in the crowded and noisy trading pits of the Merc and the CBOT. That elusive quality, they say, involves such stratagems as finding the best spot in the pit from which to communicate with clerks and other traders, maintaining good posture and using a loud, well-projected voice and forceful hand signals to attract attention.

Source: "Loud Jackets Add to Clamor of Chicago Pits," *The Wall Street Journal*, July 31, 1995, pp. C1, C14.

➤ Forward Contracts

Everything that has been said, or remains to be said, about the role of futures in the economy applies equally to forward contracts. Forwards perform price discovery, money market, and risk shifting functions; indeed, forward markets are active competitors to futures markets, competing for the business of FIs. Because forward currency markets are so well developed, we tend to discuss exchange rate risk hedging using forward hedges. In contrast, interest rate risk hedging and market risk hedging are, by and large, the domain of the futures markets. There is one exception to this generalization: the forward rate agreement (FRA).

Forward Rate Agreements

Most exchange rate risk is hedged using currency forwards, as opposed to futures contracts. In September 1994 the CME introduced exchange-listed "forwards" to try to wrest some of the currency trading from the over-the-counter forward market. That effort was unsuccessful as 1995 volume on currency contracts fell even below 1994 levels. Futures markets cannot compete with the 24-hour trading desks available in the forward currency market.

When it comes to interest rate futures, however, the futures markets dominate the forward market. The most active futures contracts in the world, the Eurodollar and U.S. Treasury bond futures contracts, are interest rate futures. However, there is one forward contract that, since 1984, has proven quite popular as an interest rate risk hedging instrument. This contract is the forward rate agreement (FRA). The FRA is an over-the-counter version of the Eurodollar futures contract with one difference. For the Eurodollar futures, the underlying deliverable asset is the 91 day Eurodollar CD; for the FRA, the deliverable can be a Eurodollar CD of any maturity. The most common are the 3, 6, 9, and 12 month maturities. However, because the FRA is a negotiated contract, a nonstandard date, or **broken date**, can be used if both parties agree. FRAs can be traded in any currency; sterling FRAs and Deutschemark FRAs are both actively traded. The delivery dates are flexible and allow the counterparties to better match the

broken date: nonstandard (other than the 3, 6, 9, and 12 month) maturities.

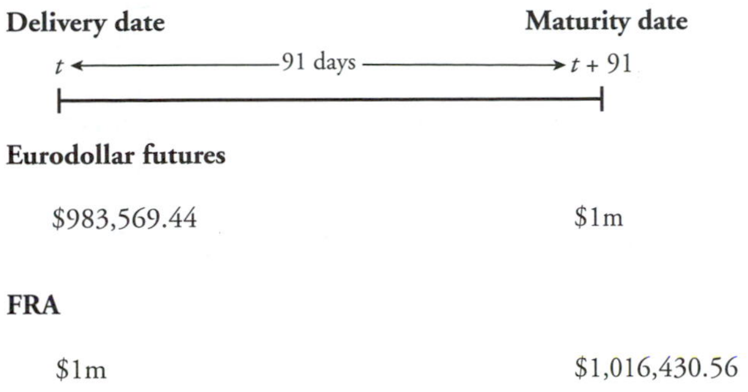

Delivery date   **Maturity date**

$t \longleftarrow\!\!\!\!\!\!\!\!\!\!\!\!\text{91 days}\!\!\!\!\!\!\!\!\!\!\!\!\longrightarrow t + 91$

Eurodollar futures

$983,569.44 $1m

FRA

$1m $1,016,430.56

Figure 18.7

cash flows on any underlying cash position that they might be hedging. The FRA is cash settled so that the only cash flows that change hands, upon delivery date, are the net gains/losses on each pair of long/short contracts.

The maturity is not the only difference between the underlying deliverable assets on the futures versus the FRA. We have seen that the Eurodollar futures contract is based on a 91 day maturity, pure discount instrument. The FRA is based on a Eurodollar CD that accrues interest on an add-on, simple interest basis. For example, a FRA based on a $1 million 91 day Eurodollar CD yielding 6.5% p.a.[14] would pay, upon maturity, $1m$(1 + \frac{.065(91)}{360})$ = $1,016,430.56. In contrast, the 91 day Eurodollar futures priced at 93.5 would have a rate of discount of 6.5% p.a. and a price of $1m$(1 - \frac{.065(91)}{360})$ = $983,569.44. Figure 18.7 compares the cash flows on each of the 91 day Eurodollar contracts. As we saw in Chapter 7, although both Euros offer a 6.5% annual yield, the actual yields differ because of the different ways in which they are accrued. The Eurodollar futures contract uses the discount method, whereas the FRA contract uses the equivalent bond yield approach.

This distinction creates a wrinkle in evaluating the value of the FRA on delivery date. Suppose that a FI took a short position in the FRA that obligated the FI to pay 6.5% p.a. for the $1 million 91 day Eurodollar CD. The FRA would be profitable if, upon delivery date, market rates exceeded 6.5% p.a. Then the FI would be able to borrow at a lower rate than was available in the spot market. Suppose that the spot rate on Eurodollar CDs was 6.7% p.a. The market cost of borrowing $1 million would be 6.7% p.a., requiring a repayment, 91 days after the delivery date, of $1m$(1 + \frac{.067(91)}{360})$ = $1,016,936.11. The FRA saves the FI $505.55 ($1,016,936.11 – $1,016,430.56) in borrowing costs since it can borrow on the FRA at 6.5% p.a. However, that savings is not realized until the CD's maturity date, which is 91 days after the delivery date. But, the FRA is cash settled on the delivery date. We must therefore discount the $505.55 savings over the 91 days. That is, the FRA's cash value upon delivery date is:

$$\frac{\$505.55}{1 + \dfrac{.067(91)}{360}} = \$497.13$$

We can obtain a general formula for the settlement value of the FRA by observing that the future value of the add-on, simple interest contract is $F(1 + \frac{r_s t}{360})$, where F is the principal; r_s is the spot rate on the CD; and t is the number of days until maturity. The value of the FRA is the difference between the CD's future value using the spot rate as opposed to the FRA-rate, denoted r_f. This difference is

---

[14] FRAs based on Eurosterling CDs use a 365 day year to calculate cash flows. All formulas are the same as for Eurodollar FRAs, except that 360 is replaced by 365.

$$F\left(1 + \frac{r_f t}{360}\right) - F\left(1 + \frac{r_s t}{360}\right)$$

This difference must be discounted at the spot rate, r_S, to obtain the value of the FRA:

$$\frac{F\left(1 + \frac{r_f t}{360}\right) - F\left(1 + \frac{r_s t}{360}\right)}{1 + \frac{r_s t}{360}}$$

Simplifying the first two terms yields the settlement value on the FRA of[15]

$$\frac{F(r_f - r_s)\frac{t}{360}}{1 + \frac{r_s t}{360}}$$

In the example of the short FRA used above, $r_s = 6.7\%$, $r_f = 6.5\%$, $F = -\$1$ million, and $t = 91$. The FRA therefore settles at: $\frac{(-1m)(.065-.067)91/360}{1+.067(91)/360} = +\$497.13$. Note that the short position gains when interest rates increase. The corresponding long position in the FRA is represented as $F = +\$1$ million and valued at $-\$497.13$.

Forward Prices as Forecasts

Forward markets provide valuable sources of information to all other financial markets. Forward prices are often used as forecasts of expected future spot prices. In this way, the FRA may be viewed as a predictor of the three month LIBOR that is expected to prevail in, say, 60 days. This forecast is used in structuring an array of financial transactions that vary from repurchase agreements to swaps.

Is the forward price a good predictor of expected future spot prices? Unfortunately, it is a biased predictor. As we saw in our discussion of the forward yield curve in Chapter 7, the forward rate contains a liquidity premium that biases it upward as a predictor of expected future spot prices. Indeed, Figure 18.8 shows the error in the predictor. The figure shows that forward rates tend to be higher than actual future spot rates by an amount that varies over time.[16] Thus, although we know the direction of the bias (positive), we cannot control for it exactly since the size of the premium shifts over time. Despite this shortcoming, we will use forward rates and prices as a forecast in pricing other financial instruments.

Checkpoint

✓

1. What are the differences between futures and forward contracts?

2. What are the similarities between futures and forward contracts?

3. Describe the forward rate agreement. Distinguish between FRAs and the Eurodollar futures contract.

4. Explain how forward prices can be used as forecasts of expected future spot prices. What are their shortcomings when used in this way?

---

[15] The valuation formula of the FRA is $F(r_f - r_s)$, which is the reverse of the futures contract valuation, $F(P_s - P_f)$, because the FRA is quoted in terms of interest rates, not prices.

[16] See Mankiw and Summers (1984), Fried (1994), and Cole and Reichenstein (1994) for estimates of the positive bias in forward interest rate forecasting. Jabbour (1994) finds that currency futures have little forecasting value in predicting foreign exchange rates.

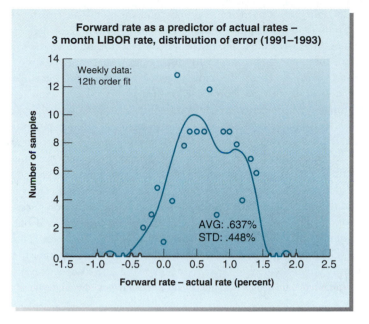

Figure 18.8

Hedging Using Futures/Forward Contracts

The success of any particular futures or forward contract depends on its efficacy as a hedging vehicle. Although we have focused on the successful contracts, more than half of all new futures contracts fail.[17] Four conditions are required for contract success:

1. *Hedging effectiveness*: The contract must respond to underlying risk factors (interest and exchange rate fluctuations and market movements) so as to generate offsetting cash flows.

2. *Liquidity*: In order for the contract to be viable, its transaction costs must be reasonable, enabling hedgers to adjust their positions frequently to reflect changes in their portfolios and market conditions.

3. *Price volatility in the underlying cash market*: We have seen that futures and forward contracts derive their value from fluctuations in the price of each contract's underlying security. Without volatility in this price, the contract would have little or no value since there would be relatively little need for hedging.

4. *Size of cash market*: There must be enough activity in the cash market to generate demand for hedging vehicles.

The step-by-step hedging procedure in Border Crossing IV will guide us through interest rate, currency, and market risk hedging using futures and forward contracts. The procedure solves for the perfect hedge, which eliminates all risk exposure from shifts in interest rates, exchange rates, or market prices. The perfect hedge acts as a benchmark to delineate the risk minimizing solution. However, only the most risk averse investors will choose this solution.

---

[17] For example, the mortgage-backed futures contract, auspiciously introduced on June 16, 1989, on the CBOT, was the first that was simultaneously introduced in both futures and options form. Because of a decrease in interest rate volatility and subsequent market illiquidity, the last contract matured on March 13, 1992. See Nothaft, Lekkas, and Wang (1995).

crosshedges: imperfect hedges because the asset underlying the hedge contract (e.g., the futures or forward contract) is not the same as the underlying cash position that motivates the hedge.

In reality, most participants cannot, and will not, utilize perfect hedges. Indeed, many of our transactions will utilize **crosshedges**. By definition, crosshedges cannot be perfect hedges because the asset underlying the hedge contract (for example, the futures or forward contract) is not the same as the underlying cash position that motivates the hedge. Crosshedges may have asset mismatches if the underlying cash position is not the same as the asset that underlies the futures or forward contract. Crosshedges may also contain maturity mismatches if the maturity dates of the futures/forward contract and the underlying cash position are not the same. Crosshedges are necessary since there is not enough potential volume of transactions to trade a derivatives contract based on every possible underlying cash position. Moreover, by definition, a macrohedge must be a crosshedge because the underlying cash position is a portfolio that cannot be matched exactly by the hedge contract.

The goal of the perfect hedge is to generate cash flows that exactly offset the cash flows on the underlying cash position resulting from shifts in either interest rates, exchange rates, or market prices.[18] The starting point, and indeed the first three steps of our four-step procedure, are devoted to utilizing our risk measurement tools from Chapters 7, 8, and 9 in order to analyze the underlying cash position. It is not until Step 4 that we enter the futures/forward markets to implement the hedge. Let's use the following case studies to examine this process using the simplest types of hedge: the microhedge that targets one underlying spot transaction.

CASE STUDY 18.1

INTEREST RATE MICROHEDGE

Consider the case of a corporation called Upnaway, Inc. that intends to sell its Treasury bond portfolio in 60 days in order to underwrite an $11.168 million investment project. The bond portfolio consists of 15 year U.S. Treasury benchmark bonds (8% p.a. semi-annual coupons), with face value of $10 million and yield to maturity of 6.75% p.a. Upnaway is concerned that during the next 60 days bond prices will drop, thereby reducing the proceeds of the bond sale. The FI handling the bond sale can protect Upnaway from the impact of bond price fluctuations by hedging its interest rate risk exposure.

Step 1.   Analyze the risk of the underlying cash position.
The value of Upnaway's bonds will decrease if interest rates increase. We use the duration measurement of price sensitivity to interest rate changes, from Chapter 7, to evaluate the impact of an unanticipated rate increase. At a yield of 6.75% p.a., the 15 year 8% p.a. semiannual coupon Treasury bond is priced at $111.68 per $100 face value with a duration of $D = 9.33$ years. Assume that U.S. Treasury bond rates increase 50 basis points over the next 60 days.[19] The duration model can be used to calculate the impact of a 50 basis point rate increase (i.e., $\Delta y = .005$) on Treasury bond prices, denoted P:

$$\Delta P \approx -DP\frac{\Delta y}{1 + .5y}$$

$$= -(9.33)(\$111.68)\frac{.0050}{1.03375} = -\$5.04$$

---

[18] If the transaction is identified as a hedge, then U.S. tax law treats any gains or losses as ordinary income, as opposed to capital gains.

[19] In each of these examples, we arbitrarily choose an exogenous rate or price change to calculate the impact on both the underlying cash and the hedge positions. The perfect hedge solutions would be the same whatever rates were chosen. Specific rate or price changes are chosen just to provide specific examples.

for a Treasury bond price of $106.64 per $100 face value (= $111.68 – $5.04) if Treasury bond rates increase 50 basis points.

Step 2. State the impact of the unanticipated rate change on the value of the underlying cash position.

The unanticipated increase in interest rates increases Upnaway's interest costs. Upnaway expected to raise $11.168 million by selling bonds with a face value of $10 million. However, if the price of the bonds falls to $106.64 per $100 face value, then Upnaway will raise only $10.664 million from the sale of bonds with $10 million face value, incurring a loss of $504,000.

Step 3. State the goal of a perfect hedge.

The goal of the perfect hedge is to generate positive cash flows to exactly offset the negative cash flows earned by the underlying cash position. Thus, the goal of the hedge would be to earn $504,000 when Treasury bond rates increase by 50 basis points. Since the goal of the hedge is to generate positive cash flows when interest rates increase, a *short hedge* is required. A short hedge is implemented by selling either futures or forward contracts.

Step 4. Implement the hedge using futures/forward contracts.

Since the source of the risk exposure is unanticipated fluctuations in U.S. Treasury bond rates, the closest hedge instrument is the Treasury bond futures contract. Thus, the hedge consists of selling Treasury bond futures. Suppose that on the day that the hedge is implemented, the Treasury bond futures price is 111–22, which is $111,687.50.

The change in the value of the futures contract is determined by the change in the spot Treasury bond price. If Treasury bond rates increase by 50 basis points, the Treasury bond price falls approximately $5.04 per $100 face value to $106,640. Accordingly, the change in the futures contract value, ΔF, is $\Delta F = F(P_S - P_F)$, where $P_S = \$106,640$ is the Treasury bond spot price if interest rates increase by 50 basis points (calculated in Step 1). To obtain a perfect hedge, we must set $\Delta F = +\$504,000$, the cash inflow required to offset the losses in the cash position. The size of the futures position required to implement the perfect hedge is

$$F = \frac{\Delta F}{P_S - P_F} = \frac{\$504,000}{\$106,640 - \$111,687.50} = -99.85$$

The negative sign supports the conclusion of Step 3 that the short hedge be implemented by selling futures. The perfect hedge is implemented by selling approximately 100 U.S. Treasury bond futures contracts at a futures price of 111–22.

CASE STUDY 18.2

EXCHANGE RATE MICROHEDGE

Step 1. Analyze the risk of the underlying cash position.

Consider the case of Global Goodies, Inc., a U.S. company that is expecting delivery of consumer electronics worth 125 million Japanese yen in 45 days. Today's yen–U.S. dollar exchange rate is US$0.00985 per Japanese yen. Global Goodies is concerned that its cost of imported goods will increase if the yen appreciates against the dollar. Since the company knows that it will have to purchase 125 million yen in 45 days, it approaches a FI for assistance in locking in today's exchange rate. Global Goodies' net currency exposure, a measurement of exchange rate risk discussed in Chapter 8, is negative since it has a yen-denominated liability that is not balanced by any other yen-denominated transactions, either off or on the balance sheet. If the yen appreciates by US\$0.00015, for example, to US\$0.01 per yen (that is, the $\Delta FX = 0.00015$), the dollar cost to Global Goodies is

$$\$\text{Cash Flow} = \text{Net Currency Exposure}(\Delta FX)$$

$$= -\text{JY}125m(0.01 - 0.00985) = -\text{US}\$18,750$$

Step 2. State the impact of the unanticipated rate change on the value of the underlying cash position.

Whenever the yen–dollar exchange rate increases, the cost of purchasing the yen increases, thereby increasing the dollar cost of the imported goods. Using the arbitrarily chosen exchange rate shock of US\$0.00015 per yen, we find that the impact is a loss of US\$18,750.

Step 3. State the goal of a perfect hedge.

The hedge must generate a positive cash flow when yen–dollar exchange rates increase. A long hedge can be implemented by buying futures or forward contracts with Japanese yen as the underlying asset.

Step 4. Implement the hedge using futures/forward contracts.

Suppose that a forward contract can be written today for delivery of JY125 million in 45 days at a price of US\$0.00985. This is a perfect hedge. If the yen appreciates against the U.S. dollar, then the long hedge will generate an exactly offsetting positive cash flow. Consider the impact of a \$0.00015 increase in yen–dollar exchange rates to US\$0.01 per yen on delivery date. The long forward position has a value at delivery of $F(P_S - P_F) = +\text{JY}125m(0.01 - 0.00985) = \text{US}\$18,750$, exactly offsetting the US\$18,750 loss in the underlying cash position. To perfectly hedge the exchange rate risk exposure, Global Goodies, Inc. must buy 125 million yen forward at US\$0.00985.

CASE STUDY 18.3

MARKET RISK MICROHEDGE

Step 1. Analyze the risk of the underlying cash position.

A balanced mutual fund invests in a broad portfolio of stocks similar to the S&P 500. The fund manager is taking a 14 day trip to Tahiti and is concerned about being out of touch in the event of a drastic market decline. She decides to hedge the fund's market risk exposure. Suppose that the fund's net asset value currently equals \$60 and that there are 5,000 fund shares outstanding, for a fund portfolio valued at \$300,000 (= \$60 × 5000). If the fund's net asset value declines by \$1, the fund's portfolio declines \$5,000 to \$295,000, a loss in value of $1\frac{2}{3}\%$.

Step 2. State the impact of the unanticipated rate change on the value of the underlying cash position.

The value of the underlying cash position, the fund's portfolio, declines as stock prices fall. Since the S&P 500 is a broadly based, value-weighted index, declines in the value of the index will result in declines in the mutual fund's portfolio value.

Step 3. State the goal of a perfect hedge.

The perfect hedge should generate positive cash flows when market prices, that is, the S&P 500, are declining. A short hedge can be implemented by selling S&P 500 futures contracts.

Step 4. Implement the hedge using futures/forward contracts.

To perfectly offset the losses in the underlying cash position, the futures hedge must generate a cash inflow of $5,000 when the S&P 500 declines by one point. Suppose that the current value of the S&P 500 index is 600, with a futures contract priced at 600. Each point on the S&P 500 futures contract is valued at $500, and so the futures price is $300,000 $(= 600 \times \$500)$. The assumed one point decline in the index value (to $299,500) generates a change in the futures position of $\Delta F = F(P_S - P_F)$, where to set up the perfect hedge, $\Delta F = +\$5,000$. Solving for the futures position required to generate sufficient cash flows to perfectly hedge the losses in the underlying cash position, we get

$$ F = \frac{\Delta F}{P_S - P_F} = \frac{+\$5,000}{\$299,500 - \$300,000} = -10 $$

To perfectly hedge the market risk of the mutual fund, the manager must sell ten S&P 500 futures contracts at a futures price of 600.

These three simple case studies illustrate how a perfect hedge can be constructed to generate positive cash flows to offset losses in other areas of the balance sheet. However, because of the symmetry of cash flows for futures and forward contracts, when the other parts of the balance sheet are generating profits, the perfect hedge will generate offsetting losses. Thus, the perfect hedge is a particularly sharp double-edged sword. It will protect the hedger against unanticipated losses, but it will also "protect" the hedger against unanticipated gains.

Checkpoint

1. Evaluate the cash flows on Upnaway's interest rate microhedge if, at bond issuance, the U.S. Treasury bond rate declines 25 basis points.

2. Evaluate Global Goodies' cash flows if yen–dollar exchange rates decline by US$0.00010 per yen.

3. Evaluate the mutual fund's portfolio and hedge values if the S&P 500 increases by 2 points.

CALCULATION COMPLICATIONS 18.1

CROSSHEDGING

Rarely does the real world work out as perfectly as did the simple microhedges in the case studies just described. One reason for this was mentioned in our definition of crosshedging: most underlying cash positions cannot be matched to a futures or forward contract. That may be because liquidity may be limited in a forward contract on, say, the Malaysian currency (the ringgit). Another reason for a mismatch between the hedge and the underlying cash position is the prevalence of macrohedging. With a macrohedge, the underlying cash position is a portfolio that is idiosyncratic to the hedger. It would be impossible to construct futures or forward contracts with underlying assets that are exactly analogous to the hedger's balance sheet. Thus, a crosshedge is necessarily imperfect. The goal is to choose the futures/forward contract that is most similar to the underlying cash position.

As an example, consider the case of a FI hedging the interest rate risk of its balance sheet. Since the FI has both interest-sensitive assets and interest-sensitive liabilities, the hedge will be geared toward the unmatched portion of the portfolio.

Step 1. Analyze the risk of the underlying cash position.
Suppose that the FI has assets with a weighted average duration of seven years and liabilites with a weighted average duration of five and a half years. If total assets are $150 million and total liabilities $120 million, the FI's duration gap is $DG = D_A - \frac{L}{A}D_L = 7 - \frac{120}{150}(5.5) = +2.6$ years.

Using the duration model from Chapter 7, we see that ΔE, the impact of a 10 basis point increase in rates $\left(\frac{\Delta y}{1+y}\right)$ on the market value of equity is

$$\Delta E \approx -DG(A)\frac{\Delta y}{1+y} = -2.6(\$150m)(.0010) = -\$390,000$$

Step 2. State the impact of the unanticipated rate change on the value of the underlying cash position.
Since the FI has a positive duration gap, the market value of equity declines when interest rates increase.

Step 3. State the goal of a perfect hedge.
The hedge must generate positive cash flows when interest rates increase to offset the impact of the FI's positive duration gap. When interest rates increase only 10 basis points, the market value of equity declines $390,000. To offset that loss, a short hedge can be implemented by selling interest rate futures/forward contracts.

Unfortunately, there is no actively traded contract that exactly matches the duration of 2.6 years. The most actively traded interest rate futures are at opposite ends of the maturity spectrum: 91 days and 15 years. The FRAs range from 3 to 12 months. This is the dilemma of the crosshedge. Since there is no perfectly matching hedge instrument, we use the 12 month FRA.

Step 4. Implement the hedge using futures/forward contracts.
To implement the hedge, sell 12 month (365 day) FRAs. Suppose that the FRA rate, r_f, upon the initiation of the hedge is 7.3% p.a. If all interest rates increase by 10 basis points, the spot rate, upon delivery, is $r_s = 7.4\%$ p.a. Setting the change in the FRA value upon delivery, ΔF, equal to the desired cash inflow of $390,000, we obtain

$$\Delta F = \frac{\left(F(r_f - r_s)\frac{t}{360}\right)}{\left(1 + \frac{r_s t}{360}\right)}$$

$$+\$390,000 = F(.073 - .074)\frac{\left(\frac{365}{360}\right)}{\left(1 + \frac{.074(365)}{360}\right)}$$

Solving this expression for F yields $F = -\$413,517,534$. Thus, a perfect crosshedge would require the sale of $413,517,534 worth of 12 month FRAs. The mismatch between the maturities of the FRAs' underlying asset and the duration gap requires an exorbitant, and extremely costly, adjustment in the number of hedge contracts.

CALCULATION COMPLICATIONS 18.2

BASIS RISK

Consideration of crosshedging creates another calculation complication. If the underlying assets consist of various types of securities rather than one type only, then their price volatilities may be different as well. In our last example, the 10 basis point increase in interest rates on the securities in the FI's portfolio may not be matched by a 10 basis point increase in the 12 month Eurodollar rate. If the two rates are unrelated, then the crosshedge is useless. This is because when interest rates increase on the FI's portfolio, thereby reducing the value of the FI's equity, there may be no corresponding increase in the FRA rate that is necessary to generate an offsetting gain on the hedge. This is called **basis risk**.

Basis risk is unanticipated deviation between futures and spot price fluctuations. The **basis** is defined as the difference between the spot and futures price[20]; that is, on date t, the basis is $P_S^t - P_F$. Accordingly, basis risk can be defined as unanticipated shifts in the basis. If the basis is constant, then the spread between the spot and futures prices is always the same. To keep the basis constant, whenever the spot price increases, say, 15 points, the futures price must also increase 15 points. Or whenever the futures price declines 75 points, the spot price declines 75 points. If there is a one-to-one relationship between the two fluctuations, the basis is constant, and there is no basis risk.

Another way to state this concept is that no basis risk will arise if the change in the spot price always equals any change in the futures price. If the change in the spot price is denoted ΔP_S and the change in the futures price is denoted ΔP_F, there is no basis risk if $\Delta P_S/\Delta P_F = 1$. The **hedge ratio** is defined as $\Delta P_S/\Delta P_F$, or (change in the spot price)/(change in futures price). Thus, if there is no basis risk, the hedge ratio is one, the ratio of futures contracts to underlying cash position value is one, and all solutions to our earlier hedging examples are correct.

In general, most futures/forward contracts are exposed to basis risk as the difference between the futures price and the spot price of the deliverable security fluctuates. Figure CC.1 shows the history of basis fluctuations over the life of a Eurodollar futures contract. If the spot price exceeds (is less than) the futures price, then the basis is positive (negative). Over the life of the contract, the basis may shift from positive to negative or vice versa, exposing the hedger to a great deal of basis risk. When spot prices exceed futures prices, that is, when the basis is positive, we say that the futures market is in **backwardation**. When futures prices exceed spot prices, the basis is negative and the futures market is in **contango**.

If there is basis risk, then our earlier solutions must be adjusted to reflect the appropriate hedge ratio. For example, if spot prices are twice as volatile as futures prices, then the number of hedge contracts needed to implement a perfect hedge must be doubled. This is because to achieve a hedge cash flow of sufficient size to offset the cash flow on the spot position, twice as many contracts are required. In contrast, if the futures prices are three times as volatile as spot prices, then the number of futures contracts required to achieve a perfect hedge is only a third of the no-basis-risk solution.

To adjust for basis risk, simply multiply the solution in Step 4 of the hedging procedure by the hedge ratio, $\Delta P_S/\Delta P_F$. But how do we determine the hedge ratio? That's not so

basis risk: unanticipated deviation between futures and spot price fluctuations.

basis: the difference between the spot and futures price.

hedge ratio: $\Delta P_S/\Delta P_F$, or (Change in the spot price)/(Change in the futures price).

backwardation: condition whereby spot prices exceed futures prices; the basis is positive.

contango: condition whereby futures prices exceed spot prices; the basis is negative.

---

[20] This definition is unrelated to the use of the term basis as the number of days in the coupon payment period, described in Chapter 7

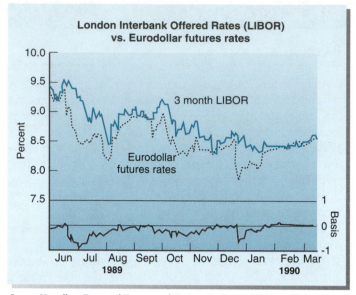

Source: Kawaller, *Financial Futures and Options,* Probus Publishing, Chicago, 1992.

Figure CC.1

simple. The most common method used is a statistical technique called the regression method. This method fits a linear function to a history of past futures and spot prices to determine the factor of proportionality. The factor of proportionality, or the β, is the hedge ratio. Thus, the estimated regression equation is

$$P_S^t = \alpha + \beta P_F^t + \epsilon$$

where P_S^t represents a time series of spot prices; α and β are regression coefficients; and P_F^t represents a time series of futures prices.[21] The hedge ratio, or β, that minimizes the risk of the hedged position is

$$\beta = \frac{\sigma_{S,F}}{\sigma_F^2} = \frac{\Delta P_S}{\Delta P_F}$$

where $\sigma_{S,F}$ is the covariance between the spot and futures prices and σ_F^2 is the variance of futures prices. If the spot and futures prices move together in lockstep—that is, the correlation coefficient between P_S and P_F is equal to +1—then $\sigma_{S,F} = \sigma_F^2$ and the hedge ratio is equal to one. In the regression equation, $\beta = 1$, and $\alpha = \epsilon = 0$. This is the case of zero basis risk since the difference between spot and futures prices is always constant.

Table CC.1 shows optimal hedge ratios using the regression model as obtained by Herbst, Kare, and Caples (1989) for currency futures.[22] Although they are very close to one, all of the hedge ratios are below one, suggesting that hedgers can reduce risk with fewer futures contracts.

---

[21] This expression should be reminiscent of the market risk measure β discussed in Chapter 9. The hedge ratio is derived using the same statistical technique and also reflects the correlation between the dependent variable on the left-hand side of the regression equation and the independent variable on the right-hand side. In the market model, the variables were individual security returns and returns on a market index. In this model of the hedge ratio, the variables are the spot and futures prices.

[22] The study by Herbst, Kare, and Caples (1989) actually improves the estimate of the hedge ratio by using an ARIMA regression model that controls for lags in the adjustment of futures prices to spot price changes. The ARIMA model obtains lower estimates of optimal hedge ratios than those reproduced here.

Table CC.1	Optimal Hedge Ratios for Foreign Currency Futures

Optimal Hedge Ratios for Foreign Currency Futures

Currency	Hedge Ratio Obtained from Regression Model
British pound	0.9893
Canadian dollar	0.9622
German mark	0.9800
Swiss franc	0.9627
Japanese yen	0.9812

Source: Herbst, Kare, and Caples (1989), p. 190.

The existence of basis risk further undermines the perfection of even the most carefully chosen "perfect hedge." Since basis risk is not perfectly predictable, even a risk minimizing hedge ratio cannot accommodate shifts in the volatility of either spot or futures prices. Hedging using futures or forward contracts cannot eliminate residual basis risk. The risk shifting role of the futures/forward hedge, then, is to exchange price risk for the smaller exposure to basis risk. So risk can be reduced, not eliminated.

Checkpoint

✓

1. Evaluate Upnaway's interest rate microhedge if the futures hedge price is twice as volatile as the U.S. Treasury bond spot rate.

2. Evaluate Global Goodies' currency microhedge if spot yen–dollar exchange rates are half as volatile as forwards rates.

3. Evaluate the mutual fund's portfolio market risk microhedge if the S&P 500 spot index is three times more volatile than the futures hedge.

CALCULATION COMPLICATIONS 18.3

convergence: movement of the futures price to equal the spot price upon delivery date.

HEDGES LIFTED BEFORE DELIVERY DATE

In each of our previous hedging examples, it was assumed that the hedge was held until the delivery date. On delivery date, the forward/futures contract becomes a spot transaction, since delivery takes place immediately, as in a spot transaction. This is called **convergence** because the futures price converges to the spot price upon delivery date. Because of convergence, the cumulative gains/losses on the futures position are just enough to assure the hedger that he or she has locked in the futures price. Thus, for example, Global Goodies, Inc. locked in the US$0.00985 per Japanese yen exchange rate by holding the long forward hedge until delivery date. However, sometimes the hedge is not held until delivery date. We have seen how the hedger can reverse the hedge at any time by taking an offsetting futures or forward position.[23]

When the hedge is lifted prior to delivery date, it is no longer assured that the futures price is locked in. This is because the futures price is not equal to the spot

---

[23] This may be more difficult to accomplish with nonstandardized forward contracts that may have limited liquidity. Moreover, since the delivery date is set at the discretion of the counterparties, it can be chosen to coincide with the desired length of the hedge period. Thus, forward hedges are more likely to be held until the delivery date than are futures hedges. According to Siegel and Siegel (1994), 90% of the forward currency contracts and fewer than 1% of the futures currency contracts are settled on delivery date.

Futures Hedges Lifted on and Before Delivery Date[a]

| Spot Price (1) | Held Until Delivery Date | | | Lifted Before Delivery | |
	Futures (2)	Cash Position (3)	Futures + Cash (4) = (2 + 3)	Futures (5)	Futures + Cash (6) = (3 + 5)
$0.60/DM	$12,500	$75,000	$87,500	$10,000	$85,000
$0.65/DM	$6,250	$81,250	$87,500	$3,750	$85,000
$0.70/DM	0	$87,500	$87,500	($2,500)	$85,000
$0.75/DM	($6,250)	$93,750	$87,500	($8,750)	$85,000
$0.80/DM	($12,500)	$100,000	$87,500	($15,000)	$85,000

[a]The short DM futures hedge has a price of $0.70 per DM with a face value of DM125,000.

price on any given date. The cash flows on the futures contract may therefore not be sufficient to exactly offset the cash flows on the underlying spot transaction, and the effective price may not equal the "locked in" futures price. This is illustrated by the valuation expression for the futures/forward contract, $F(P_S^t - P_F)$. On delivery date T, that is, when $t = T$, by convergence, P_S^T = the current spot price. Thus, if there is an underlying cash position, denoted S, that is priced at the current spot price, P_S^T, then the total cash flows on the unhedged position (SP_S^T) minus the hedge position cash flows are

$$SP_S^T - F(P_S^T - P_F)$$

If $S = F$, then the spot cash flows cancel out, leaving FP_F, the locked in futures price.

When $t < T$, before delivery date, then the futures contract is valued using $F(P_S^t - P_F)$, where P_S^t is the settlement price, not the spot price. The settlement price is the closing futures price. If the basis is nonzero, the settlement price will not be equal to the day's spot price. The cash flows on the futures contract may therefore not cancel out the spot cash flows, and the total hedged position may not obtain the locked in futures price.

As an illustration, consider the case of an American investor who will receive a cash payment of DM125,000 in 15 days. The investor wants to convert that payment into U.S. dollars but is concerned that the Deutschemark will depreciate against the U.S. dollar. To "lock in" today's spot rate, say $0.70 per DM, the investor sells one Deutschemark futures contract at $0.70 per DM. However, the next DM futures delivery date is set to occur in 60 days, and the investor needs the hedge for only 15 days. Thus, the hedge will be lifted prior to delivery date.

Table CC.2 examines the investor's cash flows both if the futures hedge is held until delivery and if it is lifted prior to delivery date. The first column lists five possible exchange rate scenarios that might prevail on the date that the hedge is lifted, and the second column shows the value of the short DM futures position if the futures price is $0.70 per DM. Thus, if the spot exchange rate upon delivery is $0.60 per DM, then the short futures position is worth $(-DM125,000)($0.60 - $0.70) = $12,500$. Simultaneously, the spot value of the DM125,000 is only $75,000 (= $0.60 \times 125,000$). The total cash flows from both futures and cash positions are shown in column (4) to be equal to $87,500.

Indeed, if the futures hedge is held until delivery date, then no matter what the spot exchange rate, $0.70 per DM is locked in and the investor yields a total of $87,500 on the sale of the DM125,000. However, this is not the case if the investor lifts the hedge prior to delivery date. The futures settlement price is not necessarily equal to the spot price in column (1). To obtain the futures values prior to delivery date, shown in column (5), we assume a constant basis of –$0.02. That is, the futures settlement price is always $0.02 higher than the spot price on each date except delivery date.[24] Thus, if the spot exchange rate on the date that the hedge is lifted is $0.60, the futures settlement price is $0.62 (using the definition of basis, $0.60 – (–$0.02) = $0.62), and the value of the short futures position is (–DM125,000)($0.62 – $0.70) = $10,000, rather than the $12,500 value upon delivery date. The total value of the spot and futures position is $85,000, thus yielding the investor an exchange rate of only $0.68 per DM.

The effective exchange rate earned by the investor in this example depends on the size of the basis only if the hedge is to be lifted prior to the delivery date. Thus, the effective exchange rate can fluctuate if the basis shifts. In other words, all hedges that are lifted prior to delivery date are subject to basis risk. Conversely, all hedges that are guaranteed held until delivery date are free of any basis risk, no matter how volatile the basis. The only way to truly eliminate basis risk is to design a hedge that must be held until its delivery date. Because of their flexibility, forward hedges are useful in implementing hedges for spot transactions with high amounts of basis risk.

Checkpoint

1. Why is a hedge that is held until delivery date free of any basis risk?
2. Why is a hedge that is lifted prior to delivery date exposed to basis risk?

➤ Hedging Effectiveness

There is no perfection in a perfect hedge because of basis risk, but it is not clear that perfection is the goal. That is because a risk free position may not be as desirable as it sounds. Risk reduction is not a free good. The lower the risk, the lower the expected return. There is a tradeoff between risk reducing hedging and cost, in terms of both reduced returns and outright transaction costs. *Timely Topics 18.2: Words to the Wise About Achieving Perfection* illustrates the futility of attempting to completely eliminate risk via hedging.

TIMELY TOPICS 18.2

WORDS TO THE WISE ABOUT ACHIEVING PERFECTION

Portfolio Insurance and the October 1987 Market Break

Academic proponents of hedging effectiveness encouraged a flirtation with a risk elimination technique that performed about as well as the wings of Icarus.[25] This technique was called portfolio insurance. It consisted of selling stock index futures when the stock market began to fall in order to protect the value of a portfolio of stocks. Although

---

[24] The assumption of a constant basis simplifies the problem since it eliminates basis risk. If there were basis risk, then the value of the futures position on any day prior to delivery date would fluctuate as the basis fluctuated, and the values in column (6) would not be constant.

[25] In Greek mythology, Icarus was the youth who attempted to escape from Crete using wings made of wax. Since he flew too close to the sun, his wings melted and he fell into the sea to his death.

the cash value of the stock portfolio would fall, the profit on the short futures position would offset that loss. Hence, investors could lock in, or insure, any gains they had already earned on their stock portfolios.

The sun that burned the wings of the proponents of portfolio insurance was the market break of October 1987. In Chapter 17, we discussed the impact of the 22% plunge in the Dow Jones Industrial Average on October 19, 1987. This was just the event that the portfolio insurers sought to insure their portfolios against. The record is not kind to them. During those few days, the S&P 500 futures contract traded at a steep discount to the value of the S&P 500 index. Furthermore, the chaos in the markets made execution impossible, just at the time that it was most needed. Moreover, on October 20, 1987, the NYSE effectively barred index arbitrage by requesting that members not use the computerized DOT clearing system to implement portfolio insurance strategies. Despite their claims, the purveyors of portfolio insurance were unable to protect their clients from the ravages of a general decline in stock prices.

The Oil-Futures Bloodbath: Is the Bank the Culprit?

It's a classic mystery twist: No sooner do the police arrest the obvious suspect than a brainy private eye comes on the scene and says that they've got the wrong guy—the real villain is innocent-looking Mr. X.

That's more or less the latest turn in a real life financial whodunit involving a $1.3 billion loss from trading in oil futures, Germany's most powerful bank, and the New York subsidiary of one of Germany's largest industrial concerns.

Last winter, when Deutsche Bank whisked Metallgesellschaft, a sprawling metals and oil conglomerate, from the brink of ruin, most observers accepted the bank's version of events: A bunch of financial cowboys at Metallgesellschaft's Amercian subsidiary, MG Refining and Marketing, were making hugely risky bets with oil futures. When an unexpected plunge in oil prices threatened staggering losses, Deutsche Bank, Metallgesellschaft's biggest shareholder and creditor and the power behind the company's supervisory board, did what it had to do: It fired the old management, brought in a SWAT team to liquidate the bets, installed a new management and lent the company money to cover the losses.

[But, it now appears that] far from being the good guy, Deutsche Bank is the culprit. It misunderstood a prudent, fully hedged oil marketing strategy...and in a blind panic, sold off the hedges with catastrophic consequences.

"They thought it was an oil bet that had gone sour," said Professor Merton Miller, [Nobel prize-winning economist on the] faculty of the University of Chicago's business school. "But that's not what happened. They cut the hedge off too soon. If they had done things right, they wouldn't have lost $1.3 billion."...

MG Refining and Marketing seemed to have been engaged in a hedging strategy rather than simple speculation. "I could understand how you can lose $1.3 billion by speculation," said Professor Miller. "But I couldn't see how you could lose $1.3 billion hedging."

Complicated as hedging strategies often are, they all boil down to the same thing. Hedging is a technique for offsetting the price risk inherent in any cash market position by taking an opposite position in the futures or options market. . . .

To break into the American market, in 1991, [MG Refining] began offering small retail customers—gas stations and fuel oil dealers—fixed-price contracts for 5 to 10 years for heating oil and gasoline. Oil prices had just dived in the wake of the Gulf War and lots of customers were keen to lock in cheap supplies. By mid-1993, MG Refining had entered into contracts to deliver some 160 million barrels over the next 10 years.

To protect itself against the possibility that oil prices would rise above the selling price minus some margin to cover costs and profits, MG Refining bought futures contracts. These were bets that oil prices would rise. If they did rise, MG Refining would reap large short term profits to offset looming losses on its long term delivery contracts. Because futures contracts typically are purchased to cover deliveries just three to six months down the line, MG Refining had to keep rolling them over to hedge its long term commitment to deliver the 160 million barrels.

If oil prices fell, MG Refining would lose money on its futures contracts, since it had agreed to pay a higher amount for the oil involved in those deals. But those would be paper losses as long as the futures contracts were rolled over. The losses would be offset, over time, by bigger profits on MG Refining's long term supply contracts because in that case the company would be buying oil at a substantially lower price than its customers had agreed to pay for it. . . .

MG Refining's hedging strategy had huge cash flow requirements once paper losses grew, since that forced the company to ante up bigger cash deposits, or margins, to back up its investments. The parent company's $1.5 billion standby line of credit was supposed to finance that effort.

But last December, as MG Refining's paper losses grew, Metallgesellschaft's supervisory board refused to let it use the credit line. After dismissing virtually the entire management of Metallgesellschaft and MG Refining, Mr. Schmitz and other Deutschebank supervisors ordered the futures contracts liquidated. That not only turned paper losses into real ones, . . . but it left MG Refining exposed to the risk that oil prices would rise, which they did, causing losses on the long term delivery contracts, a classic double whammy. . . .

Mr. Schmitz's basic point is that the hedges were too expensive to keep in this case, and some traders think he is partly right. . . Still there is little sympathy for Mr. Schmitz, who was already under heavy criticism for not spotting the problems at Metallgesellschaft sooner. . . . The hedging strategy "might have been considered aggressive, but it wasn't outrageous or even unusual," said a senior executive at another European bank. In any case, "you would expect group management to be aware of it. The notion that they were bamboozled is absolute hogwash."

Source: S. Nasar, *The New York Times*, October 16, 1994, p. 5.

The Last Word: To Hedge or Not to Hedge?

Should a company protect itself from fluctuating interest rates or foreign exchange rates? The decision can be just as difficult as the more technical question of figuring which financial institution will best accomplish the job, say Kenneth Froot of the Harvard Business School and David Scharfstein and Jeremy Stein of MIT. They believe creating corporate value requires investments in new products, efficient facilities, and a well-trained workforce. But the firm's ability to fund investments can be disrupted when volatile exchange rates or interest rates threaten its flow of cash. So if internal funds are cheaper than debt or equity, firms will want to consider hedging. And the goal is not merely to smooth earnings, but also to allow the firm to make the investments that will top the competition. When deciding how much to hedge, firms should consider not only their own strategic plans, but also those of rivals: the risks to their own cash flow, whether they are hedged, and what they would do (would they raise prices?) if foreign exchange rate or interest rate changes threatened earnings. You can raise prices in foreign markets if the dollar strengthens, but that also leaves room for competitiors to undercut you.

Harvard Business School Professor Peter Tufano suggests that, in practice, some companies may hedge to protect the interests of their risk averse managers. In a study of the gold mining industry, Tufano found that firms in which managers own a large amount of stock are more willing to reduce risk. This suggests that some firms may hedge to protect managers' wealth rather than to maximize the value of the company.

Source: J. Katz, "Cashing Out: The Treasurer's Evolving Role," Federal Reserve Bank of Boston, *Regional Review*, Fall 1995, p. 16.

➤ Summary

Financial futures contracts are obligations to make or take delivery of some underlying financial security on a predetermined delivery date at a predetermined price (called the futures price). Financial forward contracts are over-the-counter versions of futures contracts. Although the futures contracts' defining characteristics are standardized by futures exchanges, contract characteristics are negotiated by the counterparties in forward market transactions.

Futures and forwards provide (1) price discovery; (2) implicit money markets; and (3) risk shifting services. Cash and carry trades, combining futures/forwards with spot transactions, determine arbitrage-free prices and synthetic repo transactions.

Financial futures/forwards can be used to hedge interest rate, exchange rate, and market risk exposures. A perfect hedge is constructed by determining futures/forward cash flows that are just sufficient to offset the cash flows on an underlying cash position. Unfortunately, several complications prevent the matching of cash flows on the futures/forwards with the spot transaction:

1. *Crosshedging*: By definition, crosshedges entail a mismatch between either the assets or maturities of the futures/forward contract and the underlying cash position. Macrohedges are crosshedges.
2. *Basis risk*: The basis is defined as the spot price minus the futures price.

If spot price fluctuations are not exactly equal to fluctuations in futures prices, then the cash flows on the futures/forward hedge may not offset cash flows on the spot transactions. If the relationship between spot and futures/forward prices is predictable, then the hedge can be adjusted using a hedge ratio. However, there is always some element of basis risk that is unpredictable. That is, there are unanticipated fluctuations in the basis. This will undermine the perfection of any hedge. In effect, risk hedging in futures/forward markets can be viewed as the substitution of interest rate, exchange rate, or market risk exposures for a lower quantity of basis risk. Risk cannot be eliminated, only reduced.

3. *Lifting the hedge prior to delivery date*: If the hedge is lifted prior to delivery date, then the basis on the day the hedge is lifted is unknown. These transactions are most exposed to basis risk. If the hedge is maintained until delivery date, there is no basis risk.

4. *Throwing out the baby with the bathwater*: Risk elimination is not necessarily desirable because of its costs, in terms of both transaction costs and reduced expected returns.

➤ References

Bodnar, G., G. Hayt, R. Marston, and C. Smithson. "Wharton Survey of Derivatives Usage by U.S. Non-Financial Firms." *Financial Management*, vol. 24, no. 2 (Summer 1995): 104–114.

Chakravarty, S. "Should Actively Traded Futures Contracts Come Under the Dual-Trading Ban?" *Journal of Futures Markets* 14, No. 6 (1994): 661–684.

Chandler, B. *Managed Futures: An Investor's Guide.* Chichester: John Wiley & Sons, 1994.

Cole, C. S., and W. Reichenstein. "Forecasting Interest Rates with Eurodollar Futures Rates." *Journal of Futures Markets* 14, No. 1 (1994): 37–50.

Fishman, M., and F. Longstaff. "Dual Trading in Futures Markets." *Journal of Finance* 47 (June 1992): 643–671.

Fried, J. "U.S. Treasury Bill Forward and Futures Prices." *Journal of Money, Credit, and Banking* 26, No. 1 (February 1994): 55–71.

Herbst, A. F., D. D. Kare, and S. C. Caples. "Hedging Effectiveness and Minimum Risk Hedge Ratios in the Presence of Autocorrelation: Foreign Currency Futures." *Journal of Futures Markets* 9, No. 3 (1989): 185–197.

Jabbour, G. M. "Prediction of Future Currency Exchange Rates from Current Currency Futures Prices: The Case of GM and JY." *Journal of Futures Markets* 14, No. 1 (1994): 25–36.

Kane, A., and A. Marcus. "The Quality Option in the Treasury Bond Futures Market: An Empirical Assessment." *Journal of Futures Markets* 6 (1986): 231–248.

Kapner, K. R., and J. F. Marshall. "1991–1992 Market Update." *The Swaps Handbook: 1991–92 Supplement.* New York: New York Institute of Finance, 1992.

Mankiw, N., and L. H. Summers. "Do Long Term Interest Rates Overreact to Short Term Interest Rates?" *Brookings Papers on Economic Activity* I (1984): 223–242.

Nothaft, F., V. Lekkas, and G. Wang. "The Failure of the Mortgage-Backed Futures Contract." *Journal of Futures Market* 15, No. 5 (1995): 585–603.

Pitts, M. and F. J. Fabozzi. *Interest Rate Futures and Options,* Chicago: Probus Publishing Co., 1990.

Remolona, E. "The Recent Growth of Derivative Markets." Federal Reserve Bank of New York *Quarterly Review* (Winter 1992–1993): 28–43.

Ritchken, P., and L. Sankarasubramanian. "A Multifactor Model of the Quality Option in Treasury Futures Contracts." *Journal of Financial Research* 18, No. 3 (Fall 1995): 261–279.

Siegel, D. and D. Siegel. *The Futures Markets: The Professional Trader's Guide to Portfolio Strategies, Risk Management and Arbitrage,* Chicago: Probus Publishing, 1994.

Smith, T. and R. Whaley. "Assessing the Costs of Regulation: The Case of Dual Trading." *Journal of Law and Economics* (April 1994): 215–246.

http://www.cftc.gov

➤ Questions

1. Calculate the cash flows upon delivery date for a 180 day Eurodollar FRA with a face value of $5 million and a rate of 7.5% if spot rates on the delivery date are 7.35% p.a. Calculate the cash flows of both the long and short positions.

2. Mark to market a short Eurodollar futures position with March delivery at 93.25 if daily settlement prices are

   Day 1:   93.90
   Day 2:   93.55
   Day 3:   93.10
   Day 4:   92.75

   Be sure to specify whether an additional margin is required on any given day.

3. If, on day 4 after the initiation of the futures position in question 2, the trader bought a Eurodollar futures with March delivery at the settlement price, would this reverse the initial futures trade? Calculate the value of both futures positions if the Eurodollar futures price on delivery date is 94.05.

4a. Set up a cash and carry transaction using the following quotation (be sure to compute the implied repo rate and use a $1 million face value):
   181 day spot Euro rates are 5.25% p.a.
   Euro futures, with delivery in 90 days, have IMM Index prices of 95.00.

4b. If the 90 day Treasury bill has a spot rate of 5% p.a., is there an arbitrage opportunity? If so, what is the arbitrage profit?

5. Construct a *reverse* cash and carry arbitrage using the following information:
   a. Spot Treasury bill rates are 6.5% p.a. for 151 day maturity and 4.75% p.a. for 60 day maturity.
   b. Today's Euro futures IMM Index price is 92.00.
   Be sure to calculate the implied repo rate and the arbitrage profit opportunity. (*Hint*: The cash and carry transaction will be used to borrow money for 60 days.)

6. Consider the case of a FI called Upnaway, Inc. that is holding a portfolio of 15 year 8% p.a. semiannual coupon fixed rate corporate bonds with a face value of $5 million, priced at the 15 year U.S. Treasury benchmark bond rate plus a 300 basis point credit risk premium. Currently, the U.S. Treasury benchmark bond rate is 5.5% p.a., and the Treasury bond futures price is 120-3. Construct a perfect hedge for Upnaway's interest rate risk exposure, assuming a 50 basis point increase in Treasury bond rates.

7. Consider the case of Global Goodies, Inc., a U.S. company that is making delivery of consumer electronics worth 80 million Japanese yen in 15 days. Today's yen–U.S. dollar exchange rate is US$0.0095 per Japanese yen. Construct a perfect hedge against Global Goodies' exchange rate risk if the yen–dollar futures price is US$0.009 per yen. (Assume depreciation in the yen of US$0.0005.)

8. A bank offers an account with an interest rate that is tied to the value of the S&P 500, with one twist. For every point *decrease* in the S&P 500, there is an equal point *increase* in the value of the bank account and vice versa. Construct a perfect hedge for the bank account holder's market risk, assuming that the current value of the S&P 500 futures contract is 705. (Assume a 5 point increase in the S&P 500 index.)

9. Suppose that a FI has assets with a market value of $525 million and a weighted average duration of 12.2 years and liabilites with a market value of $425 million and a weighted average duration of 6.75 years. Construct a perfect hedge using an 18 month (547 day) FRA if FRA rates are 5.80% p.a. (Assume 10 basis point increase in all interest rates, that is, $\frac{\Delta y}{1+y}$ = .0010.) How feasible is this hedge?

10. Restate the perfect hedges in questions 6–9 assuming that you obtain the following regression results:

$$P_S^t = 0.45 + 0.89 P_F^t + \epsilon$$

CHAPTER 19

FINANCIAL OPTIONS

"It is the ability to foretell what is going to happen tomorrow, next week, next month, and next year. And to have the ability afterwards to explain why it didn't happen."—Sir Winston Churchill, in B. Adler, *Churchill Wit* (1965), p. 4.

Learning Objectives

- To learn how options can be used to hedge interest rate, exchange rate, and market risk.
- To compare futures and cash options; simple and compound options; and futures/forward hedges to options hedges.

➤ Introduction

Options have traded over the counter for centuries. Indeed, 2,600 years ago, Aristotle told of Thales' speculation on the price of olives by originating an "over the counter call option" (in Aristotle's terminology, "giving deposits") on olives. But it was not until 1973 and the introduction of an exchange-traded option that these versatile instruments entered into our collective consciousness. It took several academic researchers to set the stage for this feat. Black and Scholes published their pioneering article on pricing options in the spring of 1973, and the floodgates opened. Before this breakthrough, FIs were reluctant to make markets in options since they did not know how to price them. The Black-Scholes pricing algorithm made it possible to trade options by stating the option value in terms of several easy-to-understand variables. This reduced the cost of making markets. It is no coincidence that the first options exchange, the Chicago Board Options Exchange (CBOE), opened for trading in 1973, after the publication of the seminal Black-Scholes article.

➤ What Is an Option?

To understand what options are, we first state what they are not. Recall the payoff function for futures and forward contracts shown in Figure 18.2, which shows the value, upon delivery date, of both a long and short futures/forward position. The picture shows both good news and bad news. The good news is that the long (short) futures/forwards have positive cash flows when spot prices exceed (are less than) futures/forward prices. The bad news is that a long (short) futures/forward has *negative* cash flows when spot prices are less than (exceed) futures/forward prices. Wouldn't it be great if we could keep the positive cash flows and jettison the negative cash flows? That's the concept behind the options contract.

The top panel of Figure 19.1 reproduces the long futures/forward cash flows, with the negative region replaced by a floor of zero. That is, if the spot price exceeds the futures/forward price, denoted P_F, then the value of the payoff per contract is $(P_S - P_F) > 0$, where P_S is the spot price of the underlying asset. If, however, the futures/forward price exceeds the spot price, that is, $(P_S - P_F) < 0$, then the negative cash flows are replaced by a lower limit of zero. This is the payoff function for a **call option**. A call option is the right, not the obligation, to buy some underlying asset at some predetermined price (called the **exercise** or **strike price**) at or before some predetermined date (called the **expiration date**).[1] In Figure 19.1 the strike price is set equal to the futures/forward price, P_F, and the expiration date is set equal to the futures/forward delivery date. Since the option represents a *right*, not an obligation, the holder of the option will choose to exercise it only if it has value. Since the call option has value only if, upon its expiration date the spot price exceeds the strike price, it will be exercised only when $(P_S - P_F) > 0$.

call option: the right, not the obligation, to buy some underlying asset at some predetermined price at or before some predetermined date.

exercise or **strike price:** predetermined price on option contract.

expiration date: predetermined maturity date of an option contract.

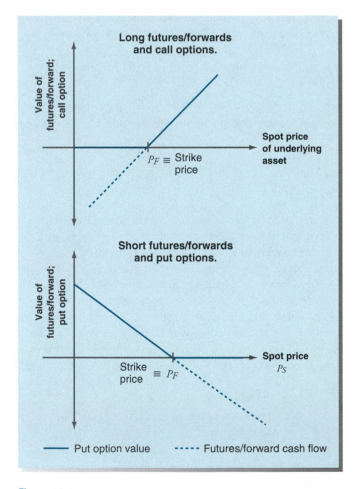

Figure 19.1

---

[1] An American option can be exercised at any time on or before the exercise date, whereas a European option can only be exercised on the expiration date.

intrinsic value: the value of the option upon expiration.

in the money: an option with a strictly positive, that is, greater than zero, intrinsic value.

out of the money: an option with an intrinsic value that would be negative, if not for the lower boundary.

at the money: the option's intrinsic value exactly equals zero.

put option: the right, not the obligation, to sell some underlying asset at some predetermined price at or before some predetermined expiration date.

Figure 19.1 shows the option's **intrinsic value**, which is the value of the option upon expiration. The intrinsic value of the call option is $\max(0, P_S - P_E)$, where P_E is defined as the exercise price. We say that the call option is **in the money** when the spot price exceeds the exercise price, or equivalently, when the option's intrinsic value is positive. If on the expiration date the exercise price exceeds the spot price, the call option is **out of the money** and will expire unexercised, with an intrinsic value of zero. If the spot price equals the exercise price upon the expiration date, the option is **at the money** and also has a zero intrinsic value.

We can engineer the same transformation of the short futures/forward contract shown in the bottom panel of Figure 19.1. Keeping the positive cash flows yields a **put option** that is in the money when the spot price is less than the futures/forward price, that is, $(P_S - P_F) < 0$. A put option is the right, not the obligation, to sell some underlying asset at some predetermined exercise price at or before some predetermined expiration date. The intrinsic value of the put option upon expiration is $\max(0, P_E - P_S)$, where the exercise price P_E is set equal to P_F in Figure 19.1. A put option is in the money when its intrinsic value is strictly positive, that is, when $\max(0, P_E - P_S) > 0$. It is out of the money when the intrinsic value would be negative, if not for the lower boundary, which occurs when $P_E - P_S < 0$. The put is at the money if its intrinsic value exactly equals zero, that is, when $P_E - P_S = 0$.

The identity of put and call options is determined by the three characteristics of the contract:

1. The identity of the underlying asset.

2. The strike price.

3. The expiration date.

Flex options: exchange-listed options that can be customized with respect to strike price, expiration date, and settlement time.

For exchange-listed options, these three features are standardized by the options exchange. Over-the-counter options are negotiated options in which the three identifying characteristics are determined by agreement of the two counterparties to the transaction. In February 1993, the CBOE introduced **Flex options**. These are exchange-listed options that can be customized with respect to strike price, expiration date, and settlement time. Flex options help realize the benefits of the credit enhancement of the exchange's clearing corporation while preserving the flexibility of over-the-counter options. As of the end of 1994, trading volume in Flex options had grown to over 5,000 contracts per day, with an equivalent of over $200 million in underlying stock value.

In this book, we consider only financial options that use financial securities as the option's underlying asset. We limit our attention to interest rate options, currency options, and stock index options in order to construct interest rate, exchange rate, and market risk hedges.

The transformation of good news–bad news futures/forwards into good-news-only options is not accomplished without cost. Indeed, the option writer (seller) agrees to buy the negative futures/forward cash flows from option buyers. But option writers charge option buyers for

premium: the price of an option contract.

that service. The price of an option contract is the **premium**. It can be viewed as the cost of insuring the option buyer from negative cash flows. The option premium is very different from the futures margin. Recall that the futures margin is a good faith deposit, paid by both futures buyers and sellers, which is refundable upon completion of each counterparty's contractual obligations. In contrast, the option premium is a nonrefundable payment by the option buyer to the option seller for the insurance against negative cash flows in the event that the option expires out of the money. Thus, the premium is the cost of lopping off the negative cash flow portion of the futures/forward payoffs in Figure 19.1. It was not until Black and Scholes formulated their model to determine options premiums that exchange-listed options became feasible. Table 19.1 shows the volume of activity in the most active derivative contracts in the world.

Table 19.1

World Activity in Exchange-Listed Contracts

Market risk factor	All instruments		Futures	Options	Over the Counter Derivatives[b]	
					Notional amounts outstanding	
	In billions of U.S. dollars	Percentage shares	Percentage shares		In billions of U.S. dollars	Percentage shares
Foreign exchange[a]	120	1	33	67	13,095	100
DM–US$	49	41	26	74	2,102	16
JY–US$	37	31	42	58	3,565	27
US$/currencies other than DM and JY	29	24	32	68	5,072	39
JY–DM	0	0	22	78	223	2
DM/ currencies other than US$ and JY	3	2	23	77	972	7
JY/currencies other than US$ and DM	0	0	100	0	424	3
All other pairs of currencies	1	1	51	49	737	6
Interest Rates[c]	15,669	96	79	21	26,645	100
US Dollar	7,702	49	75	25	9,307	35
Deutschemark	1,548	10	82	18	3,376	13
Japanese Yen	3,748	24	92	8	5,562	21
Other interest rates	2,671	17	74	26	8,400	31
Equity and stock indices	442	3	35	65	579	100
US	131	30	34	66	123	21
Japanese	166	38	36	64	100	17
European	105	24	36	64	278	48
Other	39	9	30	70	74	13
Commodities	142	1	65	35	318	100
of which: Gold[d]	34	24	35	65	147	46
Total	16,373	100	78	22	40,637	–

[a]The data refer to exchange-traded transactions reported by survey participants in the reporting countries, and not to the notional amounts outstanding of all contracts traded on exchanges in the reporting countries. The data are not adjusted for double-counting and are not directly comparable with outstandings reported by exchange organizations.

[b]Data on amounts outstanding of OTC contracts are incomplete because they do not include outstanding forwards and foreign exchange swaps positions of market participants in the United Kingdom. The percentage shares have been calculated on data that exclude figures for currency swaps and options reported by dealers in the United Kingdom.

[c]Currency breakdown of OTC gross market values partly estimated.

[d]Adjustment for OTC local and cross-border double-counting estimated.

Source: Bank for International Settlements, "Central Bank Survey of Foreign Exchange and Derivatives Market Activity 1995," (May 1996), Basle.

➤ Simple Options Transactions

Options trade on exchanges throughout the world, as well as over the counter. Exchange-listed options are guaranteed by the exchange Options Clearing Corporation. Over-the-counter

Table 19.2

S&P 500 Index Options Quotations[a]

Expiration	Strike	Volume	Premium	Net Chg.	Open Interest
Calls					
Jan.	600	104	$15\frac{1}{4}$	$-2\frac{1}{2}$	12,401
Feb.	600	20	$21\frac{1}{2}$	$+\frac{1}{2}$	403
Mar.	600	NA	NA	NA	NA
Jan.	605	708	$9\frac{7}{8}$	$-4\frac{3}{8}$	3,629
Feb.	605	NA	NA	NA	NA
Mar.	605	2	22	$+3$	176
Jan.	610	1,138	7	-3	5,199
Feb.	610	105	$10\frac{5}{8}$	-4	119
Mar.	610	1	16	$+\frac{1}{8}$	1,502
Puts					
Jan.	600	7,564	$4\frac{1}{4}$	$+1\frac{1}{4}$	32,960
Feb.	600	111	$4\frac{3}{4}$	$\frac{3}{4}$	6,934
Mar.	600	377	$8\frac{1}{2}$	$1\frac{1}{8}$	12,020
Jan.	605	927	$5\frac{5}{8}$	$+1\frac{3}{8}$	14,374
Feb.	605	5,249	$6\frac{3}{4}$	...	1,206
Mar.	605	1,340	$8\frac{1}{2}$	$-\frac{1}{2}$	5,925
Jan.	610	2,685	$7\frac{3}{4}$	$+2$	9,935
Feb.	610	322	10	$+1\frac{1}{4}$	5,443
Mar.	610	152	$10\frac{3}{8}$	$-1\frac{7}{8}$	8,132

[a]Prices are as reproduced from *The Wall Street Journal*, December 21, 1995. The spot price of the S&P 500 Index on that date was 605.94.

warrants: over the counter options issued by companies, usually in conjunction with debt or equity issues.

LEAPS: Long term Equity AnticiPation Securities—options with two to three years until expiration.

options, however, are subject to credit risk since repayment depends on the creditworthiness of the option writer. **Warrants** are over-the-counter options issued by companies, usually in conjunction with debt or equity issues. When separated from the debt or equity, these warrants trade like options.

Typically, options are short term instruments with expiration periods of up to nine months. One exception is the category of options called **LEAPS**. LEAPS, a trademarked acronym for Long term Equity AnticiPation Securities, were introduced in October 1990 on the Chicago Board of Options Exchange (CBOE). They are options with two to three years until expiration. Because of their longer time period, LEAPS have a 25% margin requirement to act as collateral for the uncovered option position. LEAPS gains are taxed as capital gains if the option is held long enough, whereas all option cash flows are taxed as ordinary income.

SPX is the trading symbol of a very popular options contract that is based on the value of the S&P 500 index and trades on the Chicago Mercantile Exchange (CME).[2] Table 19.2 shows a sample quotation from the December 21, 1995, *Wall Street Journal*. The spot price of the S&P 500 index on that date was 605.94. The January 600 call gives the holder the right to "buy" the

---

[2] Innovations such as PENs and SPINs contribute to the volume of trading on the S&P 500 index option. PENs (Protected Equity Notes) are intermediate term bonds with a small coupon and a payment at maturity that is equal to the principal times the greater of either one, or one plus the rate of growth in an underlying index. SPINs (S&P 500 Indexed Notes) are Salomon innovations that link the notes' principal repayment to the value of the S&P 500 on the notes' maturity date. Issuers of these instruments use S&P 500 index options to hedge their market risk exposure. Babbel (1989) also shows how banks can use S&P 500 index options to hedge their systematic credit risk exposure resulting from changes in economic fundamentals that precipitate large-scale defaults. Schlesinger and Crause (1996) find that volatility on the S&P 500 index averaged 10.44% over the period January 1994 to January 1996.

S&P 500 for 600. The S&P 500 option is cash settled by valuing the contract's intrinsic value multiplied by a factor of $100. Since the current spot price is 605.94, the intrinsic value of the January 600 call is $\max(0, P_S - P_E) = (605.94 - 600)(\$100) = \$594$. However, the premium listed in Table 19.2 is $15\frac{1}{4}$, or $1,525. Why is the option selling for a premium that is greater than its intrinsic value? The reason is that the option still has one month until expiration. During that time, the S&P 500 index could increase even further. The high call premium reflects an expectation of increases in the S&P 500. The difference between the premium and the option's premium value is determined by the time value of the option. The longer the time until expiration, the greater the time value of the option and the higher the option premium. This is apparent in the call with a 600 strike price since the option expiring in February has a premium of $21\frac{1}{2}$, or $2,150.

Figure 19.2 shows the payoff function, upon expiration, if the January 600 call option is purchased on December 21. The call expires in the money as long as the spot index value exceeds 600. However, that does not mean that the holder of the call will definitely make money. The premium of $1,525 is deducted from the call option value. Thus, the first $1,525 in call value goes toward recouping the option premium. Not until the index rises above 615.25 does the holder of the January 600 call make a profit. For example, if the S&P 500

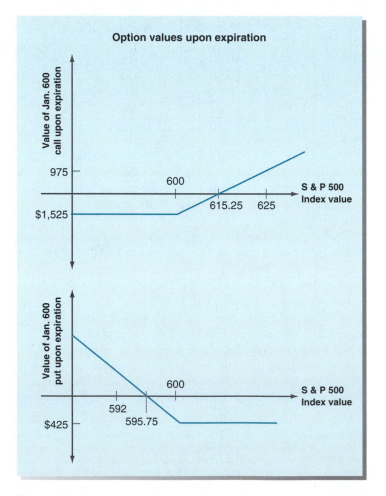

Figure 19.2

index value upon expiration is 625, the option's intrinsic value is max(0, [625 − 600]$100) = $2,500. Deducting the premium cost yields an options profit of $975 (= $2,500 − $1,525).

Figure 19.2 also shows the payoff function, upon expiration, for the January 600 put option on the S&P 500 index. The put is in the money if the S&P 500 falls below 600. However, the put holder does not break even until the S&P 500 falls below 595.75, which is the 600 exercise price minus the put premium of $4\frac{1}{4}$ = $425. If the value of the S&P 500 upon expiration is 592, then the put's intrinsic value is max(0, [600 − 592]$100) = $800. Deducting the $425 put premium yields an options profit of $375.

The premiums in Table 19.2 reveal some basic options characteristics:

1. *Both call and put option premiums increase as the time to expiration increases.* For example, comparing the January 600, February 600, and March 600 put premiums, we observe $4\frac{1}{4} < 4\frac{3}{4} < 8\frac{1}{2}$.

2. *Call premiums decrease as the strike price increases.* This is because the call is more likely to be in the money the lower the strike price. For example, comparing the January 600, January 605, and January 610 call premiums, we see $15\frac{1}{4} > 9\frac{7}{8} > 7$.

3. *Put premiums increase as the exercise price increases.* This is because the put is more likely to be in the money the higher the exercise price. For example, comparing the January 600, January 605, and January 610 put premiums, we see $4\frac{1}{4} < 5\frac{5}{8} < 7\frac{3}{4}$.

From these basic characteristics we can derive a general formula to determine any option premium. This is the Black-Scholes model that is so critical to the operation of options markets.

Checkpoint

✓

1. What are the distinguishing characteristics of options as opposed to futures/forwards?
2. What determines the options premium?
3. Why do over-the-counter options have more credit risk than exchange-listed options?
4. What are Leaps?

Using Black-Scholes to Evaluate Option Premiums

In Chapter 16, we used one form of the Black-Scholes model to value risky debt. Here we consider the simplest form of the model applicable for European call options on underlying assets that have no cash flows prior to expiration. A **European option** cannot be exercised prior to the expiration date, in contrast to the **American option**, which can be exercised at any time. However, if the underlying asset has no cash flows (such as dividends or coupon payments) prior to expiration, the American option will never be exercised prior to expiration. This is because the option will always have more value "alive," with additional time value, than "dead," already exercised. Evaluation of American options without interim cash flows is equivalent to the evaluation of European options.[3]

The Black-Scholes model is built on the construction of a risk free arbitrage. The call option's cash flows can be replicated by a combination of a purchase of the underlying spot instrument plus a risk free loan. The Black-Scholes formula simply calculates the present value of expected cash flows upon expiration of both sets of transactions. If no arbitrage opportunities exist, (an assumption of the Black-Scholes model), then the cash flows on the call option must always equal the cash flows on the spot plus loan combination transaction.

A simple example illustrates this arbitrage solution. Suppose that the current exchange rate is $0.50 per Deutschemark. You know that in exactly one year the exchange rate will be either

European option: option that cannot be exercised prior to the expiration date.

American option: option that can be exercised at any time.

---

[3] Closed-form solutions for option premiums that are alternatives to the Black-Scholes formula have been presented by Ho and Lee (1990), among others.

Table 19.3a

A Call Option Replicating Arbitrage

Transaction	$t = 0$: $0.50/DM	$t = 1$: $0.40/DM	$t = 1$: $0.60/DM
Spot DM and Loan Combination Transaction			
Buy DM 200 at $0.50	−$100	DM200($0.40) = $80	DM200($0.60) = $120
Borrow at 5% p.a.	$\frac{80}{1.05}$ = $76.19	−$80	−$80
Sell 2 Calls			
Exercise price = $0.50	Premium	0	−2(DM200)($0.60 − $0.50) = −$40
Net cash flows	Premium −$23.81	0	0 (= $120 −$80 −$40)

$0.40 or $0.60 per DM.[4] Table 19.3a shows the cash flows today, at $t = 0$, and in one year, at expiration $t = 1$. The combination transaction consists of the spot purchase of DM 200 at $0.50 per DM, for a cost of $100. Offsetting that cost is a pure discount loan with a face value of $80 discounted at the risk free rate, assumed to be 5% p.a. The present value of the one year loan is $\frac{80}{1.05}$ = $76.19. The net cash outflow, at $t = 0$, on the combination transaction, is −$23.81 (= $76.19 − $100).

Simultaneously, at $t = 0$, you sell two DM $0.50 calls that expire in exactly one year.[5] The calls are in the money only if the exchange rate, in one year, exceeds $0.50 per DM. Since there are only two possible scenarios, by assumption, this occurs when the exchange rate is $0.60 per DM. Since you sold the calls, you are obligated to pay the holder of the calls their intrinsic value, which is (DM200)(−2)($0.60 − $0.50) = −$40 if the DM sells for $0.60 at $t = 1$.

Examining the cash flows at $t = 1$ from both sets of transactions in Table 19.3a, we see that no matter what the exchange rate, the net cash flows are zero. If you know that this combination of trades is guaranteed to have zero value, you will be willing to pay at most zero for it. That is, the cash flows at $t = 0$ must also equal zero, or else there will be arbitrage profit opportunities. If the net cash flows at $t = 0$ were positive, then the calls would be overvalued with respect to the combination transaction. You could earn a risk free arbitrage profit by writing additional calls, buying more Deutschemark, and borrowing greater amounts at the risk free rate. But exploitation of this arbitrage opportunity will bid down the call premium, bid up the spot exchange rate, and bid up the risk free rate until the arbitrage profit is eliminated and the net cash flows at $t = 0$ equal zero. Since the net cash flows at $t = 0$ sum to the call premium minus $23.81, you can set this equal to zero and obtain the arbitrage-free call option premium. In this example, the two call options will sell for a total of $23.81, or $11.905 each.

The Black-Scholes model sets up this arbitrage combination of transactions and then solves for the premium that will set the net cash flows at $t = 0$ equal to zero. The only complication arises because, rather than considering only two possible scenarios for future prices (in our example, $0.40 and $0.60), the Black-Scholes model incorporates an infinite number of possible

---

[4] This assumption is made only to simplify our example. The Black-Scholes model assumes that future exchange rates can take on any of an entire continuous spectrum of values where the probability distribution of exchange rates is assumed to be normal—hence, the use of the normal probability distribution in the Black-Scholes formula presented later in this section. In this example, we use the binomial probability distribution for simplicity.

[5] In this example, to set up a risk free arbitrage, the ratio of calls to spot DM is 2. The derivation of this *hedge ratio* is discussed later in this chapter in the section on delta hedging.

scenarios. The Black-Scholes formula is

$$\text{Call Premium} = P_S N(d_1) - e^{-rT} P_E N(d_2)$$

$$d_1 \equiv \frac{\ln(P_S/P_E) + (r + .5\sigma^2)T}{\sigma\sqrt{T}}$$

$$d_2 \equiv d_1 - \sigma\sqrt{T}$$

where P_S = the spot price of the option's underlying asset; $N(d_1)$, $N(d_2)$ = the cumulative probability of d_1, d_2 assuming the standard normal distribution function (reproduced in Appendix A of this book); r = the risk free rate; σ^2 = the volatility of the spot price of the option's underlying asset; and T = the time until expiration.

Despite its apparent complexity, the Black-Scholes call option premium is a function of only five variables: P_S, P_E, T, r, and σ^2.

To use the Black-Scholes model to price a DM call option, we need to specify the values of the five input variables. Now assume that the spot price, P_S = \$0.55/DM; the exercise price, P_E = \$0.50/DM; the DM spot price volatility, σ = .20; the risk free rate, r = 8% p.a.; and the time to expiration is three months, T = .25 years. Substituting into the Black-Scholes formula, we get

$$\text{Call Premium} = 0.55N\left(\frac{\ln(\frac{0.55}{0.50}) + (.08 + .5(.20)^2).25}{.2\sqrt{.25}}\right) - e^{-(.08)(.25)}(.50)N(d_1 - .2\sqrt{.25})$$

$$= 0.55N(1.2031) - 0.4901N(1.1031)$$

Using the standard normal probability tables, we see that $N(1.2031)$ = .885 and $N(1.1031)$ = .8645, so the call option premium is \$0.06305 per DM. For a 200 DM call, the call option premium[6] is \$12.61 (= 200 × \$0.06305).

Call option premiums increase as (1) P_S increases, (2) P_E decreases, (3) T increases, (4) r increases, and (5) σ^2 increases. We can demonstrate each of these five causes of call option premium increases using our simple example. We have already made the first three observations by simply examining the premiums listed in the *Wall Street Journal*. To illustrate the last two, we amend the example in Table 19.3a. First, the impact of an increase in the risk free rate, r, to 6% p.a. is shown in Table 19.3b. The call option premium increases to \$12.265 (= $\frac{\$24.53}{2}$). Table 19.3c illustrates the impact of an increase in volatility (as demonstrated by the wider range of DM fluctuation, \$0.30–\$0.70, as opposed to \$0.40–\$0.60). The call premium increases to \$21.43 (= $\frac{\$42.86}{2}$).

Checkpoint ✓

1. Use the simple DM example of Table 19.3a to show that the call option premium increases if the spot price increases to \$0.55 per DM.

2. Use the simple DM example of Table 19.3a to show that the call option premium increases if the exercise price decreases to \$0.45 per DM.

3. Use the simple DM example of Table 19.3a to show that the call option premium increases if the time to expiration increases to two years.

Implied Volatility The Black-Scholes formula requires five input variables: the spot price, the exercise price, the time until expiration, the risk free rate, and the spot price volatility. The

---

[6] The value of the call option premium obtained using the Black-Scholes formula is different from the simplified solution shown in Table 19.3a because the parameters are different. (For example, the spot price changes from \$0.50 to \$0.55.) Also recall that e = 2.71828.

Table 19.3b

A Call Option Replicating Arbitrage—The Impact of an Increase in the Risk Free Rate

Transaction	$t = 0$: \$0.50/DM	$t = 1$: \$0.40/DM	$t = 1$: \$0.60/DM
Spot DM and Loan Combination Transaction			
Buy 200 DM at \$0.50	−\$100	DM200(\$0.40) = \$80	DM200(\$0.60) = \$120
Borrow at 6% p.a.	$\frac{80}{1.06}$ = \$75.47	−\$80	−\$80
Sell Two Calls			
Exercise price = \$0.50	Premium	0	−2(DM200)(\$0.60 − \$0.50) = −\$40
Net cash flows	Premium − \$24.53	0	0 (= \$120 −\$80 −\$40)

Table 19.3c

The Impact of an Increase in Spot Price Volatility

Transaction	$t = 0$: \$0.50/DM	$t = 1$: \$0.30/DM	$t = 1$: \$0.70/DM
Spot DM and Loan Combination Transaction			
Buy 200 DM at \$0.50	−100	DM200(\$0.30) = \$60	DM200(\$0.70) = \$140
Borrow at 5% p.a.	$\frac{60}{1.05}$ = \$57.14	−\$60	−\$60
Sell Two calls			
Exercise price = \$0.50	Premium	0	−2(DM200)(\$0.70 − \$0.50) = −80
Net cash flows	Premium − \$42.86	0	0 (= \$120 −\$80 −\$40)

first four of these variables are easily observable; the last is not. We could use historical prices to estimate the volatility of past prices. However, the past is not necessarily predictive of the future. The value that should be used is the expected volatility of spot prices over the time period until expiration. Since this is not observable, we cannot estimate it directly.

If we use the posted call option premium, we can solve for the **implied volatility**. The implied volatility is the value of σ^2 that sets the Black-Scholes formula value equal to the observed call option premium. We can use the Black-Scholes formula to solve for the spot price volatility instead of the call option premium.

implied volatility: the value of spot price volatility (σ^2) that sets the Black-Scholes formula value equal to the observed call option premium.

Put-Call Parity   If the Black-Scholes formula is used to price call options, how are premiums on put options determined? The answer is that once the call option is valued, we can use an arbitrage condition to value the put option. The arbitrage condition is **put-call parity**, which is obtained by combining a long spot, a long put, and a short call to obtain a risk free cash flow. The long put and short call portion of the portfolio is obtained by buying a put and selling a call with the same exercise price and the same expiration date.

put-call parity: arbitrage condition stating that combining a long spot, a long put, and a short call yields a risk free cash flow.

To see put-call parity, examine the investment in the spot, put, and call contracts shown in Table 19.4. The spot contract is the purchase of 200 Deutschemark at the spot exchange rate. Both the long put and the short call have exercise prices of \$0.50 per DM. Five possible spot exchange rate scenarios are shown in Table 19.4. No matter what the exchange rate is, the

Table
19.4

Put-Call Parity: An Illustration

Spot Price	Long Spot	Long Put	Short Call	Total Cash Flow
$0.30/DM	DM200($0.30) = $60	DM200($0.50 – $0.30) = $40	0	$100
$0.40/DM	DM200($0.40) = $80	DM200($0.50 – $0.40) = $20	0	$100
$0.50/DM	DM200($0.50) = $100	0	0	$100
$0.60/DM	DM200($0.60) = $120	0	–DM200($0.60 – $0.50) = –$20	$100
$0.70/DM	DM200($0.70) = $140	0	–DM200($0.70 – $0.50) = –$40	$100

[a]All values are received upon expiration, in three months.

portfolio has a value of $100, which is just the exercise value of the option (= DM200 × $0.50). A risk free asset has been created that must have the same value as a risk free Treasury security with maturity equal to the options' time to expiration.

Suppose that the options expire in three months (one quarter) and that the spot exchange rate at t = 0 is $0.55 per DM. Then purchase of a put plus sale of a call plus purchase of DM200 yields a risk free return of $100, the exercise price of the option, to be received in three months. If the risk free rate is 8% p.a., the present value of this riskless cash flow is $100/(1 + \frac{.08}{4})$ = $98.039. This is the cost of obtaining the $100 riskless cash flow in three months. This riskless cash flow is equal to the option's strike price (in this example P_E = $0.50), multiplied by the number of shares (in this example DM200), for an exercise value of $0.50(DM200) = $100. But we have already seen how to obtain that riskless cash flow: buy DM200 on the spot market, sell one call, and buy one put. On any given date, we can observe the spot price for the Deutschemark; in this example, $0.55. We can use that in the Black-Scholes model to solve for the call premium. With three out of the four prices determined, we can solve for the put premium.

In general terms, the put-call parity formula is

Present Value of the Option's Exercise Value = Cost of Long Spot
$$+ \text{Put Premium} - \text{Call Premium}$$

If the call is valued, using the Black-Scholes formula, at $12.61 and the spot exchange rate at t = 0 is $0.55 for a cost of the long spot position of $110, the put premium can be derived from

$$\$98.039 = \$110 + \text{Put Premium} - \$12.61$$
$$\text{Put Premium} = \$0.649$$

If the underlying spot transaction pays interim cash flows, such as dividends or coupon payments, both the Black-Scholes formula and the put-call parity relationship must be adjusted to reflect the present value of the cash flows.

Checkpoint

✓

1. List the two ways to solve for an underlying asset's price volatility.

2. Explain how arbitrage profit opportunities can be generated if put-call parity is violated.

3. Explain how selling a call and buying a put with the same exercise price generates the same payoff function at expiration as a short futures position.

Delta Hedging   Because of their asymmetric cash flows limiting downside losses, options are natural hedges. Indeed, options can be used as a form of insurance against unanticipated shifts in interest rates, exchange rates, and market prices. Accordingly, we will use our step-by-step hedging procedure to fashion risk minimizing hedges. To determine the perfect hedge in the simplest case of a microhedge where the option's underlying asset and the underlying cash position are identical, the optimal number of options must be determined. Thus, an options hedge ratio must be determined.

As in the case of futures hedges, the relationship between derivatives prices and the prices of the underlying assets must be determined in order to derive the appropriate hedge ratio. For options, the hedge ratio is determined by the option's delta. The **delta** of an option is the rate of change of the option premium with respect to the price of the underlying asset. That is,

$$\delta \equiv \frac{\Delta P_O}{\Delta P_S},$$

where δ is the option's delta; ΔP_O is the change in the option's premium; and ΔP_S is the change in the underlying asset's spot price.[7] The delta of a call is always positive, while the delta of a put is always negative because the call (put) is in (out of) the money and increases (decreases) in value when the price of the underlying asset increases. If the option is in the money, its $|\delta|$ is between 0.5 and 1.0. If it is out of the money, the $|\delta|$ is between 0 and 0.5. If the option is at the money, the $|\delta|$ is approximately 0.5. This is because changes in the prices of underlying assets cause an immediate, almost dollar for dollar change in the option premium if the option is in the money (delta is around one), but almost no change in the option premium if the option is out of the money (delta is around zero).

A perfect hedge, such that the option premium adjusts to exactly offset price changes in the underlying cash instrument, can be constructed using a **delta neutral hedge ratio**. The delta neutral hedge ratio is the reciprocal of the option's delta. It states the number of options contracts that must be held to create a perfect hedge.[8]

To calculate the option's delta, let's use the example of the DM 200 call with exercise price of \$0.50 introduced earlier and the same parameter values (r = 8% p.a.; σ = .20; T = .25 years). If the spot price decreases from \$0.55 to \$0.53, using the Black-Scholes model, the call option premium decreases from \$0.06305 per DM when P_S = \$0.55 to \$0.04616 per DM when P_S = \$0.53. The option's delta is

$$\delta = \frac{\Delta P_O}{\Delta P_S} = \frac{0.06305 - 0.04616}{0.55 - 0.53} = .8445$$

The delta of .8445 is close to one since the call option is in the money. It means that when the DM–U.S. dollar exchange rate increases by \$1, the price of the option increases by \$.8445.[9]

How can this information be used to construct a perfect hedge? As with futures hedges, we must begin with analysis of the underlying cash position following the step-by-step hedging procedure.

> ***Step 1.*** Suppose that the hedger has a Deutschemark-denominated liability of DM200. If this is the only DM-denominated transaction on the balance sheet, the hedger's net

margin notes:

delta: the rate of change of the option premium with respect to the price of the underlying asset.

delta neutral hedge ratio: the reciprocal of the option's delta.

---

[7] The delta is the first derivative of the option's price with respect to the price of the underlying spot instrument.

[8] The hedge ratio that is used in our example in Table 19.3a to create the no arbitrage, risk free portfolio is the delta neutral hedge ratio.

[9] This is an approximation since the delta represents the change in the option value for infinitesimally small changes in the price of the underlying asset.

currency exposure is –DM200. That is, the hedger has a short DM spot position that is exposed to exchange rate fluctuations. For example, if the spot exchange rate increases by $0.02 from $0.53 up to $0.55, the value of the underlying cash position declines from $(-DM200)(\$0.53) = -\$106$ to $(-DM200)(\$0.55) = -\$110$, $-\$110 - (-\$106) = -\$4$, or a loss of $4. The loss represents an increase in the value of the hedger's liabilities.

Step 2. Since the underlying spot transaction is a short Deutschemark-denominated liability, the value of the underlying cash position declines if exchange rates increase.

Step 3. The hedge should generate a positive cash flow to offset the negative cash flows of the underlying spot transaction. The hedge must therefore make money when exchange rates increase; that is, a long hedge is required. A long hedge can be constructed by buying call options.

Step 4. How many call options should be bought to construct a perfect hedge? To answer that question, compute the delta neutral hedge ratio. In this example, the call option's delta neutral hedge ratio is $\frac{1}{.8445} = 1.18$. This suggests that, to perfectly offset any cash flow resulting from changes in spot exchange rates, the hedger must buy 1.18 DM of calls for every Deutschemark in the underlying cash position. If the underlying cash position contains –DM 200, then the perfect hedge will require the purchase of call options on DM 236 (= 200 × 1.18).

When exchange rates increase $0.02, the underlying cash position loses $4. When exchange rates increase $0.02, the value of the call options on DM236 increases by the difference in the call option premiums: $-DM236(\$0.04616) - [-DM236(0.06305)] = +\$3.99$. Hence, the cash inflow on the options position (+$3.99) just offsets the cash outflow on the underlying cash position (–$4) resulting from exchange rate fluctuations.

Protective Puts   Individual options can be used to construct perfect hedges. An example of a common option hedge is the **protective put**. The protective put consists of a long spot combined with a long put position. Thus, the value of the underlying cash position is protected against declines resulting from price decreases. Protective puts can, therefore, be viewed as a form of insurance against price declines. The protective put places a floor under the value of the underlying cash position.

> **protective put:**
> combination of a long spot and a long put position.

To illustrate the protective put, consider an underlying cash position consisting of the S&P 500, evaluated at the spot value of the index. If the spot index value is 600, the value of the underlying cash position is $60,000 (= 600 × $100). As Table 19.5 shows, the value of the underlying cash position declines as the spot price of the index falls.

We consider the implementation of a protective put using an at the money option, which has an exercise price equal to the spot index value. Therefore, if the spot index value is 600, then the put's exercise price is also set at 600. The put will have value only if, upon expiration, the S&P 500 index falls below 600. The third column in Table 19.5 shows the put option's intrinsic value at each possible spot price.

The option will be priced at its intrinsic value only upon its expiration. At any date prior to expiration, the option premium will exceed the option's intrinsic value. That is because of the remaining time value of the option. Column 4 in Table 19.5 shows the option premiums three months prior to expiration date for each possible spot price. The put option's delta can be calculated for each possible change in spot prices. If the spot price drops from 595 to 590, a change in value of $500, the put premium increases from $520 to $1,015, which is a change in put value of $495. The ratio of put premium change to change in the value of the underlying

Table 19.5

Hedging with an At-the-Money Protective Put

Underlying Cash Position		Protective Put with P_E = 600					Cash & Put
Spot Price (1)	Spot Value (2)	Intrinsic Value (3)	Put Premium (4)	Delta (absolute value) (5)	Hedge Ratio (6)	Option Value (7)	Total Value at Expir.[a] (8)
590	$59,000	$1,000	$1,015	1	1		$60,460
595	$59,500	$500	$520	$\frac{495}{500}$ = .99	1.01	1.01(1,015 − 520) = +$500	$59,960
600	$60,000	0	$270	$\frac{250}{500}$ = .5	2	2(520 − 270) = +$500	$59,460
605	$60,500	0	$94	$\frac{176}{500}$ = .352	2.84	2.84(270 − 94) = +$500	$59,960
610	$61,000	0	$32	$\frac{62}{500}$ = .124	8.065	8.065(94 − 32) = +$500	$60,460

[a]The option value upon expiration is calculated for each of the spot prices in column (1), assuming that the spot price equals the closing price upon price upon expiration date. The protective put position consists of the underlying S&P 500 plus two puts, with P_E = 600, purchased at a cost of $270 each.

cash position is $\frac{\$495}{\$500}$, giving a delta with an absolute value of .99. The δ is solved for each of the price changes in column 5 of Table 19.5. The delta neutral hedge ratio is simply the reciprocal of the delta and is shown in column 6. The seventh column shows the change in the put option value prior to expiration, as the spot price changes. For example, if the spot price decreases from 595 to 590, the option premium increases from $520 to $1,015. If the delta neutral hedge ratio was used, that would generate a positive cash flow equal to 1.01($1,015 − $520) = +$500, just sufficient to offset the $500 loss on the underlying cash position.

The delta neutral hedge ratio is a function of the spot price. As the spot price increases, the number of put options needed to construct a perfect hedge also increases. Thus, the hedge must be continually adjusted as spot prices change to reflect any changes in the delta neutral hedge ratio. The hedge placed when spot prices were 595 is no longer sufficient to protect the portfolio when spot prices are 605. Figure 19.3 shows the impact of changes in the underlying spot price on the Black-Scholes delta.

If the hedge is not adjusted as spot prices change, it will cease to be a perfect hedge. If spot prices move to 605, for example, the delta neutral hedge ratio increases to 2.84. If the hedge is not updated, and remains at 2 puts, and spot prices fall back to 600, the option cash flows will be insufficient to offset the losses on the underlying cash position. That is, the spot position loses $500(= $60,000 − $60,500) when the spot price falls from 605 to 600. However, the change in the 2 put options' value prior to expiration is only (2)($270 − $94) = +$352, for a net cash outflow on the total portfolio of $148 (= −$500 + $352). This is called **slippage** since the hedge position must be rebalanced to reflect changes in the delta neutral hedge ratio.

slippage: changes in the delta neutral hedge ratio as the spot price changes.

gamma: the impact of a change in the price of the underlying asset on the option's delta.

The measurement of the impact of a change in the price of the underlying asset on the option's delta is called the **gamma**.[10] The gamma is $\gamma = \frac{\Delta\delta}{\Delta P_S}$, where δ is the option's delta and P_S is the spot price of the underlying asset. The gamma is the slope of the curve shown in Figure 19.3. The gamma curve is shown in the lower panel of the figure. The option's gamma measures the sensitivity of delta to changes in (1) spot prices; (2) time to expiration; (3) the

---

[10] The gamma is the second derivative of the option price with respect to the spot price of the underlying asset.

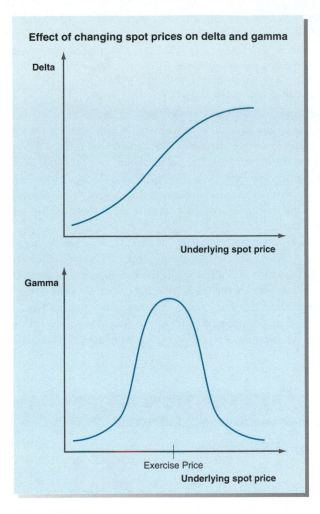

Figure 19.3

option's exercise price; and (4) the volatility of spot prices. Gamma is also a measure of the adjustment in the delta neutral hedge ratio to any one of these four fundamental shifts. Large values of gamma suggest that the delta neutral hedge is stable since even large changes in the four fundamental factors cause relatively small changes in the delta neutral hedge ratio, which is the reciprocal of the delta.

Up to this point in this example, we have evaluated the put option prior to expiration date; that is, when its value exceeds its intrinsic value. In the last column of Table 19.5, we show the value of the cash and option position upon expiration date if the delta neutral hedge had been implemented when the spot price was 600 and was held unaltered until expiration, as opposed to a dynamically adjusted hedge. In this case, two 600 put options were bought three months prior to expiration for a total premium of $540 (= $270 × 2). If the spot price upon the expiration date is 590, the value of the underlying cash position is $59,000. The put options are worth $1,000 each (= $60,000 − $59,000) for a total put value, upon expiration, of $2,000. Deducting the options' premium of $540 (= 2 × $270) yields a total cash flow of $60,460

(= \$59,000 + \$2,000 − \$540). If instead the spot price is 595, the total cash flow is \$59,960 (= \$59,500 + \$1,000 − \$540). If the spot price of the S&P 500, upon expiration, is 600, the total cash flow is \$59,460 (= \$60,000 + 0 − \$540) since the put options expire unexercised. Similarly, if the spot prices are 605 or 610, the cash flows are \$59,960 or \$60,460, respectively (= \$60,500 + 0 − \$540) or (= \$61,000 + 0 − \$540).

The protective put hedge places a floor under the value of the underlying cash position. The minimum value of the entire portfolio is \$59,460, the value of the portfolio at the "locked in" spot price of 600 (the put exercise price) less the premium cost of the options hedge. An alternative protective put hedge could be constructed using out of the money put options as opposed to at the money puts. The advantage of out of the money puts is that their premiums are lower, thereby lowering the cost of the options hedge. However, their disadvantage is that they offer less insurance against declines in the value of the underlying cash position. The floor under the value of the underlying cash position is therefore lower than the minimum value using at the money puts.

time decay: the decline in the value of an option as it approaches its expiration date.

theta: the change in the option price as the time to expiration decreases.

As the option approaches its expiration date, its value declines, ceteris paribus, since its time value declines. This is called **time decay**. The rate of time decay is measured by the option's **theta**, which is the change in the option price as the time to expiration decreases. Even if the spot price of the underlying asset does not change during the life of the option hedge, the delta neutral hedge ratio will change over time. Thus, the perfect option hedge must be continually rebalanced to adjust the hedge ratio to reflect the changing value of delta. *Calculation Complications 19.1: Hedging Volatility* discusses hedging volatility.

CALCULATION COMPLICATIONS 19.1

HEDGING VOLATILITY

Delta neutral hedges are not risk free. Table CC.1 shows that the risk of the delta hedged portfolio is lower than that of an unhedged portfolio, but it is not zero. Why does some risk remain? The risk of the delta neutral hedge is determined by the volatility of option prices with respect to underlying asset prices. It was assumed that these volatility measures follow a lognormal distribution. However, if there is a discrete jump in volatility, then the delta neutral hedge ratio will be incorrect. Thus, the impact of delta hedging is to trade exposure to the volatility in underlying asset prices for the volatility in the options premium. Neuberger (1994) proposes an innovative "Log Contract" that could theoretically be used to hedge option volatility. *Timely Topics 19.1: Delta Hedging* describes the problems associated with "risk free" delta neutral hedges.

Table CC.1

Profit on Writing Currency Call Options as a Proportion of the Option Premium Distribution of Monthly Outcomes, 1987–1992:\$/£

	Unhedged	Delta Hedged
Mean	−29%	2%
Standard deviation	171%	32%
Range	−200%—+100%	−23%—+24%

Source: Neuberger (1994), p. 75.

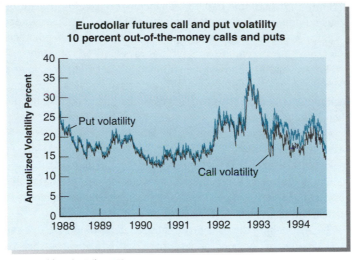

Source: Abken (1995), p. 19.

Figure CC.1

Figure CC.1 shows that, for Eurodollar futures options, historical volatility is not constant. Volatility shifts over time, wreaking havoc with a delta neutral hedge position.

Volatility is also a function of the option's strike price. The **volatility smile** is an unexplained empirical anomaly that has been observed. As the option strike price moves away from the at the money price (either in or out of the money), the option's volatility increases. This is contrary to the Black-Scholes model's assumption of a constant volatility across all strike prices for a given expiration date. The Black-Scholes option premium is mispriced for options with large volatility smiles, thereby further complicating the construction of a delta neutral hedge.

volatility smile: the increase in the volatility of the option as the option's strike price moves away from the at the money price (either in or out of the money).

TIMELY TOPICS 19.1

DELTA HEDGING: THE NEW NAME IN PORTFOLIO INSURANCE

Banks, securities firms and other big traders rely heavily on portfolio insurance to contain their potential losses when they buy and sell options. But since portfolio insurance got a bad name after it backfired on investors in 1987 [see *Timely Topics 18.3*], it goes by an alias these days—the sexier, Star Trek moniker of "delta hedging."

Whatever you call it, the recent turmoil in European bond markets taught some practitioners—including banks and securities firms that were hedging options sales to hedge funds and other investors—the same painful lesson of earlier portfolio insurers: Delta hedging can break down in volatile markets, just when it is needed most.

What's more, at such times, it can actually feed volatility. The complexities of hedging certain hot-selling "exotic" options may only compound such glitches.

"The tried-and-true strategies for hedging [these products] work fine when the markets aren't subject to sharp moves or large shocks," says Victor S. Filatov, president of Smith Barney Global Capital Management in London. But turbulent times can start "causing problems for people who normally have these risks under control."...

In theory, delta hedging takes place with computer-timed precision, and there aren't any snags. But in real life, it doesn't always work so smoothly.

"When volatility ends up being much greater than anticipated, you can't get your delta trades off at the right points," says an executive at one big derivatives dealer. "In a choppy market like we saw [recently in European bonds], people can end up chasing their tails."

And when delta hedges go awry, "dealers suddenly may not want to do the business because the risk management tools aren't in place," says Mr. Filatov. "The market-making process for complicated products can break down."...

Earlier this year, when bond bulls were raging, international banks and securities firms aggressively sold call options to investors, including highly leveraged hedge-fund traders, traders say.

Because selling the calls made those dealers vulnerable to a rally, they delta hedged by buying bonds. As bond prices turned south, the dealers shed their hedges by selling bonds, adding to the selling orgy. The plunging markets forced them to sell at lower prices than expected, causing unexpected losses on their hedges.

Making things worse was another group of options players. These were speculators who bought calls early in the year and paid for them by selling bearish put options to other investors.... So when the crunch came in Europe, these traders, too, began hedging their bets by frantically selling into the rout....

"People sold in the [bond] market until prices got pushed too far, then in the bond futures markets, then the swap market. And then they started trying to hedge in other instruments—like selling German bonds to hedge losses in Italian bonds—until all the markets were rolling along in the same black hole," says a dealer at one European bank.... While experts may agree that delta hedging doesn't actually cause crashes, in some cases it can speed the decline once prices slip.

By the same token, delta hedging also tends to buoy prices once they turn up—which may be one reason why markets correct so suddenly these days.

Source: B. D. Granito, *Wall Street Journal*, March 17, 1994.

Checkpoint

✓

1. What is the option's delta? the gamma? What is the delta neutral hedge ratio? How are these measures used to implement a perfect hedge?

2. Why must a hedge be continually adjusted?

3. What determines the value of gamma?

4. Why do options suffer from time decay?

Options on Financial Futures

To this point, we have considered options on underlying cash instruments which are options on "physicals" such as foreign currency or stock indexes. Indeed, the most popular cash options contracts are the stock index options. However, for FIs a much more important category of financial options is options on financial futures, or **futures options**. Futures options are option contracts in which the underlying asset is a financial futures contract. If the option expiration date falls on the futures delivery date, then the futures option

futures options: option contracts in which the underlying asset is a financial futures contract.

is essentially identical to a cash option. That is because on delivery date the futures contract is identical to a spot contract. However, if the options expiration date occurs prior to the futures delivery date, the underlying asset will be an obligation to buy or sell another underlying asset in the futures market. Exercising a call option on a futures contract entitles the option holder to buy a futures and ultimately take delivery of the underlying financial security. Exercising a put option on a futures contract entitles the option holder to sell a futures and ultimately make delivery of the underlying financial security.

Futures options often trade side by side with options on physicals. Thus, the Philadelphia Stock Exchange trades options on foreign currencies, whereas the CME trades options on foreign currency futures. Similarly, five year Treasury cash options are sold on the Chicago Board of Options Exchange (CBOE), whereas five year Treasury futures options are sold on the Chicago Board of Trade (CBOT). Although options in physicals are popular for currency and stock index underlying assets, interest rate options are almost exclusively based on interest rate futures. Why have interest rate futures options outsold interest rate cash options?

One reason deals with regulation or, more precisely, regulators. The interest rate cash options are under the auspices of the SEC, whereas the interest rate futures options are regulated by the Commodities Futures Trading Corporation (CFTC). If FIs perceive the CFTC to be a more lenient regulatory body, they will direct their business to the market of least resistance.

A more important reason accounting for the success of interest rate futures options deals with the costs of writing the two different types of options. FIs, in providing risk shifting services to their clients, often make markets in these instruments and will write (sell) options to their customers to manage customer interest rate, exchange rate, or market risk exposures. The FIs can manage their own risk exposure by covering their own short option position with a long spot market investment in the option's underlying assets. This approach will be less costly to implement using futures options as opposed to cash options. For example, to cover a short options position in U.S. Treasury bond calls would require the cash purchase of the bond. For a Treasury bond futures option, the cost would be only the margin cost of buying the Treasury bond futures contract. Thus, the transaction costs of writing options are lower for futures options than for options on physicals.

Finally, the futures option is easier to price and utilize in hedging. This is because, all other things being equal, the delta of a futures option is always less than the delta of an equivalent cash option.[11] This is useful, since a lower delta implies a higher gamma and a more stable hedge ratio. The delta neutral hedge ratio is less subject to changes when fundamental factors shift.

Everything we have discussed with regard to hedging using cash options applies to futures options with one exception. The delta neutral hedge ratio must be adjusted for futures options. The delta neutral hedge ratio for a futures option is the delta neutral hedge ratio for the cash option, δ, multiplied by the futures hedge ratio, denoted β in Chapter 18. This is reasonable since if the goal is to perfectly hedge some underlying cash position, first the sensitivity of futures prices to shifts in spot prices must be measured, by the futures β, and then the sensitivity of options values to shifts in futures prices must be measured, by the futures options δ.

To derive this adjusted hedge ratio, note that if ΔP_O, ΔP_F, and ΔP_S represent changes in the option price, the futures price, and the spot price, respectively, then

$$\frac{\Delta P_O}{\Delta P_S} = \left(\frac{\Delta P_O}{\Delta P_F}\right)\left(\frac{\Delta P_F}{\Delta P_S}\right)$$

---

[11] Black (1975) shows that the delta of the futures option is equal to the discounted present value of the delta of the cash option.

where $\frac{\Delta P_O}{\Delta P_F}$ is the futures option delta value, δ, and $\frac{\Delta P_F}{\Delta P_S}$ is the reciprocal of the futures hedge ratio, $\beta = \frac{\Delta P_S}{\Delta P_F}$. Since the delta neutral options hedge ratio is $\frac{1}{\delta}$, the delta neutral futures option hedge ratio, denoted $\frac{1}{\delta_F}$, is

$$\frac{1}{\delta_F} = \frac{1}{\delta}\beta$$

If the futures hedge ratio, β, is .7 and the at the money futures options delta, δ, is .5, then the delta neutral futures option hedge ratio, $\frac{1}{\delta_F}$, is $\frac{.7}{.5} = 1.4$. That is, every \$1 worth of the underlying cash position requires \$1.40 in futures options hedges. If the cash options delta is $\frac{\Delta P_O}{\Delta P_S} = .6$ (which is greater than the futures options delta of .5), then the cash options hedge ratio is $\frac{1}{.6} = 1.67$—requiring \$1.67 in cash options hedges for every \$1 worth of the underlying cash position.

Checkpoint

✓

1. Contrast options on physicals to options on futures with regard to liquidity, regulation, and transaction costs.

2. Compare the delta and gamma on a cash option to those on a futures option.

3. How do you calculate the delta neutral hedge ratio for a futures option?

4. Calculate the delta neutral hedge ratios for both the futures and cash options if $\frac{\Delta P_O}{\Delta P_F} = .77$, $\frac{\Delta P_O}{P_S} = .83$, and $\frac{\Delta P_F}{\Delta P_S} = 1.05$.

Hedging Using Interest Rate Futures Options   Interest rate risk hedging can be accomplished using futures, options on physicals, or futures options. To illustrate the contrasts between futures and futures options hedges, reconsider several case studies from Chapter 18.

CASE STUDY 19.1

UPNAWAY AND THE SHORT HEDGE

Consider the case of a corporation called Upnaway, Inc., from Case Study 18.1, which is in the process of selling its \$11.168 million 15 year U.S. Treasury bond portfolio. The U.S. Treasury bond yield is 6.75% p.a. and the semiannual coupon rate is 8% p.a. Because Upnaway's bond portfolio will decline in value if interest rates increase, we chose a short futures hedge, which was implemented by selling Treasury bond futures. As an alternative to hedging Upnaway's interest rate risk exposure using Treasury bond futures, the FI could hedge using Treasury bond futures options. Recall that Treasury bond futures options are quoted in 64ths, whereas U.S. Treasury bond futures are quoted in 32nds. Steps 1, 2, and 3 are identical to those in Case Study 18.1, and so we begin the analysis at Step 4.

Step 4. Implement the short options hedge by buying futures put options.
Since the source of the risk exposure is unanticipated fluctuations in U.S. Treasury bond rates, the closest hedge instrument is based on the Treasury bond futures contract. The short options hedge therefore consists of buying Treasury bond futures put options. Suppose that on the day that the hedge is implemented, the Treasury bond futures price is 111-22, which is \$111,687.50. Upnaway's FI uses an at the money put option to hedge the risk of increasing interest rates. The hedge would be to buy Treasury bond

futures put options with a strike price of 111-44, which is $111\frac{44}{64}$, or 111.6875 per $100. Assume that the put premium is 4 ticks, worth $\frac{1}{64}(\$1,000) = \$15.625$ each, for a put premium of $62.50 (= 4 \times \$15.625$) per $100,000 face value.

The change in the put option premium is determined by the change in the value of the Treasury bond futures contract. But the change in the value of the futures contract is determined by the change in the spot Treasury bond price. If Treasury bond rates increase by 50 basis points, the duration analysis performed in Case Study 18.1 shows that the Treasury bond price falls approximately $5.04 per $100 face value to $106,640 per $100,000 face value. Suppose that the futures price upon the date of the option's expiration is 106-20, which in 32nds is $106\frac{20}{32}$, or $106,625. The put option is deep in the money, since it gives the holder the right to sell U.S. Treasury bonds at a price of 111-22 when their market price is only 106-20. The intrinsic value of the put option, upon expiration, is 324 futures options ticks, stated in 64ths, which is $111\frac{44}{64} - 106\frac{40}{64}$, or $5,062.50. The delta neutral hedge ratio for a futures option can be expressed as

$$\left(\frac{\Delta P_F}{\Delta P_O}\right)\left(\frac{\Delta P_S}{\Delta P_F}\right)$$

When Treasury bond rates increase by 50 basis points, then the values for these variables per $100,000 face value are $\Delta P_S \approx -\$5,040$; $\Delta P_F = -\$5,062.50$; and $\Delta P_O = +\$5,000$ (= $5,062.50 intrinsic value upon expiration minus the $62.50 put premium). Thus, the delta neutral hedge ratio is

$$\left(\frac{-\$5,062.50}{\$5,000}\right)\left(\frac{-\$5,040}{-\$5,062.50}\right) = -1.008$$

The delta neutral hedge ratio for the futures option is approximately −1, denoting a short hedge consisting of the purchase of $1 worth of puts per $1 bond face value. Since Upnaway intends to sell $11.168 million in Treasury bonds with a face value of $10 million, a perfect options hedge would require the purchase of 100 put options, each with a face value of $100,000, at 111-44. The negative sign in the delta neutral hedge ratio reflects the short options hedge, which is implemented by buying puts.

If interest rates increase by 50 basis points, the Treasury bond spot prices fall to $106.72 and the futures price decreases to 106-20 upon the put option's expiration date, then the values of the unhedged and hedged positions are shown in the first row of Table CS.1. The value of the underlying cash position declines by $504,000. However, the futures hedge offsets that with a profit of 162 ticks, or $506,250, for a negligible loss of $2,250, shown in the column labelled Δ(Cash + Futures). The put options hedge has an intrinsic value, upon expiration, of $506,250 (111-44, $111\frac{44}{64}$ exercise price minus the futures price, upon expiration, of 106-40, $106\frac{40}{64}$ or 324 ticks). However, the put premium is $62.50 for a total cost of $6,250, or an options hedge value of $500,000. The cash plus the options position therefore loses a net amount of $4,000, shown in the column labelled Δ(Cash + Put).

Table CS.1

Comparing the Futures and Options Short Hedges

Spot Price	ΔCash Value	Futures Price	ΔFutures Value	Δ(Cash +Futures)	ΔPut Value	Δ(Cash +Put)
106.72	−$504,000	106–20	+$506,250	−$2,250	+$500,000	−$4,000
111.68	0	111–22	0	0	−$6,250	−$6,250
112.285	+$60,500	112–9	−$59,375	+$1,125	−$6,250	+$54,250

On the other hand, if interest rates do not increase, but instead decrease, the major difference between the futures and options hedges becomes apparent. When interest rates decrease, Upnaway benefits from an increase in the value of its bond portfolio. However, the futures hedge loses those benefits because the short futures position loses value when interest rates decrease. The last row in Table CS.1 shows this by assuming an interest rate decrease of 6 basis points, which results in an increase in the value of the cash position of Upnaway's bonds of

$$\Delta P \approx -(9.33)(111.68)\frac{-.0006}{1.03375} = +\$.605$$

The value of Upnaway's cash position *increases* because the price of each Treasury bond increases by +\$.605 × \$100,000 = +\$60,500.

If interest rates decrease by 6 basis points, the Treasury bond futures price will increase. Suppose that the Treasury bond futures price increases to 112-9. As shown in Table 19.7, the short futures position loses value such that

$$F(P_S - P_F) = (-\$100,000)\left(112\frac{9}{32} - 111\frac{22}{32}\right) = -\$59,375$$

The net change in the cash plus futures position is +\$60,500 − \$59,375 = +\$1,125. The futures position, therefore, protects Upnaway from losses when interest rates increase, but it also "protects" Upnaway from gains when interest rates decrease.

The put options hedge, on the other hand, expires worthless when interest rates decline, and the gains on Upnaway's underlying cash position are preserved. These asymmetric cash flows for the options hedge are the primary advantage over an equivalent futures hedge. In the example shown in Table CS.1 then, the value of the put option is simply the loss of the put premium, \$6,250 (= 100 puts × \$62.50 premium each), for a cash plus option position gain of +\$54,250 (= \$60,500 − \$6,250).

CASE STUDY 19.2

THE GIC-HOLDER AND THE LONG HEDGE

As another example, consider the case of an investor in \$150 million worth of pure discount Guaranteed Investment Contracts (GICs) that have maturities of 91 days and are priced at 91 day LIBOR. The investor intends to roll over the GICs each quarter, at the then prevailing rate. Interest rate declines create losses in interest income for the "GIC-flipper."

Step 1. Analyze the risk of the underlying cash position.
Suppose that the current LIBOR is 9% p.a. for a GIC price of \$977,250, or $\$1m(1-\frac{.09(91)}{360})$. If the LIBOR falls, say, 100 basis points to 8% p.a., the GIC price increases to \$979,778, or $\$1m(1-\frac{.08(91)}{360})$, an increase in the cost to the investor buying the GIC amounting to \$2,528 per \$1 million face value. For \$150 million, the total loss to the GIC investor is \$379,200 (= \$2,528 × 150).

Step 2. State the impact of the unanticipated rate change on the value of the underlying cash position.

Since the investor loses money when the price of the GIC increases, the underlying cash position decreases in value when interest rates decrease.

Step 3. State the goal of a perfect hedge.

The hedge must generate positive cash flows when interest rates decrease to offset the impact of the losses in the underlying cash position. When interest rates decrease 100 basis points, the cost of the GIC increases by $379,200. To offset that loss, a long hedge can be implemented by buying interest rate futures call options.

Step 4. Implement the long hedge by buying futures call options.

On the date of implementation of the hedge, suppose that the Eurodollar futures IMM Index price is 91, for a rate of discount of 9% p.a., which is equal to the spot LIBOR, implying a price of $977,250 $[= \$1m(1 - \frac{.09(91)}{360})]$. There are three call options with three different strike prices for sale on that date. The Eurodollar futures call with a strike price of 90.5 is in the money and selling at a premium of 60 basis points, or $1,516.80 (= $25.28 × 60). The Eurodollar futures call with a strike price of 91 is at the money and selling at a premium of 10 basis points ($252.80), whereas the out of the money call option has a strike price of 91.5 and a premium of 2 basis points ($50.56).

Consider the cash flows on the at the money call option in Table CS.2 if interest rates decline by 100 basis points to 8% p.a., on the expiration date of the calls. Thus, the Eurodollar futures price upon expiration of the calls is an IMM Index price of 92.00, for a cash price of $1m(1 - \frac{.08(91)}{360})$ = $979,778. If the perfect long hedge was implemented by buying at the money calls, the investor bought 150 ($150 million worth) Eurodollar futures call options with an exercise price of 91.00, or $977,250, prior to their expiration date. The loss on the cash position ($379,200) is exactly offset by the intrinsic value of the call options upon expiration—that is, 150($979,778 – $977,250) = +$379,200, or 150 calls × 100 basis points worth $2,528 per call. However, the call option premium must be deducted. Using the at the money call, we find that the cost of the call options is $37,920 (= 150 calls × $252.80 premium each). The net value of the call option position upon expiration is therefore $341,280 (= $379,200 – $37,920), leaving the hedged position with a net loss of only $37,920 (= –$379,200 + $341,280).

If the out of the money call option was used to hedge the investor's interest rate risk exposure, the cost of the options premiums would be significantly lower at $7,584 (= 150 calls × $50.56 premium each). However, the amount of insurance that is purchased is also lower, since the option will have a positive intrinsic value at expiration date only

Table CS.2

The Long Interest Rate Hedge Using At the Money and Out of the Money Call Options

Underlying Cash Position			At the Money Call			Out of the Money Call		
ΔR (bp) (1)	ΔCash Value ($) (2)	Futures Price (IMM P) (3)	ΔOption Value ($) (4)	Premium ($) (5)	OptionValue +Option ($) (6) = (2+4+5)	ΔCash ($) (7)	Premium ($) (8)	Cash +Option ($) (9) = (2+7+8)
−100	−379,200	92.00	+379,200	−37,920	−37,920	+189,600	−7,584	−197,184
−25	−632	91.25	+632	−37,920	−37,920	0	−7,584	−8,216
0	0	91.00	0	−37,920	−37,920	0	−7,584	−7,584
+50	+189,600	90.50	0	−37,920	+151,680	0	−7,584	+182,016

if interest rates decrease more than 50 basis points. Examining the cash flows on the out of the money option hedge if interest rates decrease 100 basis points (the first row in Table CS.2), we find that the intrinsic value of the out of the money call options is $150(\$979{,}778 - \$978{,}514) = \$189{,}600$ since the options' exercise price is 91.50, or $\$1m\left(1 - \frac{.085(91)}{360}\right) = \$978{,}514$. Deducting the cost of the premiums yields a net option value for the out of the money hedge of $182,016 (= $189,600 − $7,584), which represents a net loss of −$197,184 (= −$379,200 + $182,016) if the out of the money calls are used to hedge the GIC interest rate risk exposure.

Table CS.2 also shows the value of the hedged position upon the options' expiration date, if interest rates decline 25 basis points, increase 50 basis points, or remain unchanged. When interest rates increase, or do not decrease by much, then the out of the money option hedge is less costly and results in a larger net cash value. However, if interest rates decrease by a large amount, the at the money hedge offers the most protection against losses in the underlying cash position. The choice of which option hedge to use depends on the hedger's attitude toward risk, as well as interest rate expectations.

Comparing Options to Futures/Forward Hedges

Options and futures/forwards can all be used to hedge interest rate, exchange rate, and market risk exposure. A well-rounded hedge program will tend to include all of these versatile instruments. When should one be used as opposed to the others? The answer to this question depends on the hedger's goals. The hedger must answer the question by examining the pros and cons of the options versus those of the futures/forward hedge. Table 19.6 summarizes the basic attributes of each hedging instrument.

The forward and the OTC options contracts have the greatest amount of credit risk exposure because they represent private agreements between two counterparties. Exchange traded futures and options have the guarantee of the clearinghouse to assure compliance with the terms of the contract. Forwards have the lowest transaction costs, whereas options (both OTC and exchange listed) have the highest: the options premium. The transaction cost of the futures is the opportunity cost of the futures margin. The forward contract is marked to market; that is, credited with its cumulative value, only upon delivery date. In contrast, futures are marked to market upon the market's close each day. An option is marked to market continuously since the option premium includes its intrinsic value.

The primary advantage of the options hedge over the futures hedge is the former's asymmetric cash flows, which provide insurance against losses in the value of the underlying cash position without sacrificing possible gains. The major disadvantage of the options hedge is its cost. The premium is an out of pocket, nonrefundable expense that significantly increases the transaction costs of the options hedge. One way to reduce options premiums is to use out of the money options in constructing hedges. However, the out of the money option offers less insurance against losses than does the at the money option hedge.

Table 19.6

Comparing Options, Futures, and Forwards

Instrument	Credit Risk Exposure	Transaction Costs	Marked to Market
Forwards	Considerable	Negligible	Upon delivery date
Futures	Negligible	Cost of margin	Market close daily
OTC options	Considerable	Premium	Continuously
Exchange options	Negligible	Premium	Continuously

knock-out, or barrier, option: a standard option that is rendered worthless if the price of the underlying asset reaches a prespecified price barrier.

compound option positions: portfolios made up of different options.

Much of the recent innovation in compound option positions has been spurred by attempts to reduce the cost of the options hedge. The **knock-out**, or **barrier, option** is an example of a cost-reducing option innovation. The knock-out option is a standard option that is rendered worthless if the price of the underlying asset reaches a prespecified price barrier. Since this feature reduces the option's potential cash payouts, the knock-out option carries a lower premium than a standard option. **Compound option positions** are another way to reduce the costs of option hedging. Compound options are portfolios made up of different options.

Checkpoint

1. How can a long (short) hedge be implemented using a simple options strategy?

2. Contrast options on physicals with options on futures.

3. Contrast futures, forwards, and options instruments with respect to transaction costs, credit risk exposure, and cash flows.

➤ Compound Options Transactions

Combinations of options can be used to design customized risk/return characteristics for options positions. Compound options can be used both for fashioning speculative transactions and for hedging. Typically, compound option positions that reduce the cost of options hedging take the form of buying an option together with selling another option. Thus, the premium received from the option sale offsets the cost of the option purchase. *Practitioner's Primer 19.1, 19.2, 19.3, and 19.4* demonstrate examples of compound options positions.

PRACTITIONER'S PRIMER 19.1

bull spread: a compound options strategy implemented by buying at the money calls while simultaneously selling out of the money calls in order to implement a less expensive long hedge.

THE BULL SPREAD

Bull spread: Buy at the money calls while simultaneously selling out of the money calls in order to implement a less expensive long hedge.

Type of Hedge: Long.

Goal of Hedge: Generate positive cash flows when the price of the underlying asset increases above a certain level.

Comparison with Simple Options Hedge: Sacrifice upside gain potential when prices increase significantly.

How to Implement the Bull Spread:

a. Buy at the money calls. For example, buy 100 March calls on Treasury bond futures at an exercise price of 96 with a premium of 1-34.

b. Sell out of the money calls. Sell 100 March calls on Treasury bond futures at an exercise price of 98 with a premium of 0-32.

The cost of each 96 call is $1\frac{34}{64}$ = $1,531.25, or $153,125 for 100 calls. Simultaneously, the 98 calls are sold, generating a cash inflow of $\frac{32}{64}$ = $500 per call, or $50,000 for 100 calls. The net cost of the bull spread is $103,125.

If the futures price, upon the options' expiration date, is below the exercise price of either call, then both options expire unexercised. If the futures price falls between the spread in exercise prices, then the option bought has a positive cash flow while the option sold expires worthless. If, however, the futures price, upon option expiration date, is above both call prices, then both options expire in the money. For the option bought, this produces a positive cash inflow. However, the option sold will generate a negative cash outflow since the option writer must pay the call holder the intrinsic value of the option. Since the exercise price of the option sold is greater than the exercise price of the option bought, the cash inflow will always exceed the cash outflow, generating a constant cash flow, as shown in Figure PP.1.

Table PP.1 shows the cash flows upon expiration of the bull spread. If the futures price upon expiration is 96-00 or less, then both options expire unexercised and the cost of the bull spread is –$103,125. If the futures price upon expiration is 97-1($= 97\frac{1}{32}$), then each 96 call has an intrinsic value of $1,031.25 (= 97.03125 – 96), or +$103,125 for 100 calls. The intrinsic value of the 98 calls is zero. The net proceeds (adding columns 2, 3, and 4 in Table PP.1) are zero. This is the breakeven price on the bull spread. If futures prices upon expiration exceed 98, then both options have intrinsic value. For example, if the futures price is 98-16, $98\frac{16}{32}$, then each 96 call's intrinsic value is $2,500 (= 98.5 – 96), or +$250,000 for 100 calls. This cash inflow is offset by a loss on the 98 call written. Each 98 call has an intrinsic value of $500 (= 98.5 – 98), or $50,000 for 100 calls. The call writer must pay this amount—hence, the negative cash flow of –$50,000 in Table PP.1. The net proceeds of the bull spread, if futures prices upon expiration are 98-16, are +$96,875. Indeed, no matter how high futures prices go, this is the maximum gain on the bull spread.

The bull spread sacrifices some of the potential gain from increases in futures prices (above 98) for a reduction in the cost of the hedge. If a simple 96 call were used to implement the long hedge, the maximum loss on the simple options hedge if futures prices remain below 96 would be –$153,125 (equal to the premium on 100 calls), as compared to the maximum loss of –$103,125 on the bull spread. In contrast, if futures prices rise above 98, the bull spread earns at most $96,875, while there is no limit to the potential cash inflows on the simple call option hedge.

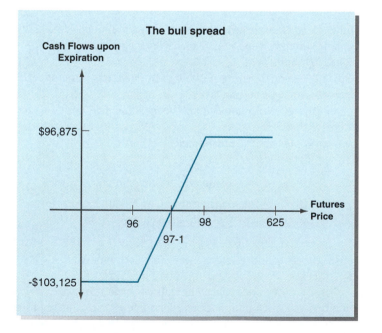

Figure PP.1

Table PP.1

Bull Spread Using Treasury Bond Futures Options[a]

Futures Price (1)	96 Call Intrinsic Value (2)	98 Call Intrinsic Value (3)	Premium (4)	Net Proceeds (5) = (2+3+4)
95-3	0	0	−$103,125	−$103,125
96-00	0	0	−$103,125	−$103,125
97-1	+$103,125	0	−$103,125	0
98-16	+$250,000	−$50,000	−$103,125	+$96,875
100-00	+$400,000	−$200,000	−$103,125	+$96,875

[a]Cash flows are upon option expiration date, calculated for various futures price scenarios.

The cost of the bull spread can be adjusted by altering the spread between the call exercise prices. The wider the spread, the higher the cost of the bull spread and the less the sacrifice of upside gain potential. In contrast, a **bear spread** is implemented by buying the out of the money call and simultaneously selling the at the money call. The bear spread is a short hedge since it generates a positive cash flow if prices fall below the lowest of the two exercise prices. Since the out of the money call is less expensive than the at the money call, the premium on the bear spread generates a positive cash inflow rather than a cost.

bear spread: a compound option strategy implemented by buying the out of the money call and simultaneously selling the at the money call; the bear spread is a short hedge.

PRACTITIONER'S PRIMER 19.2

THE SHORT BUTTERFLY SPREAD WITH CALLS

Butterfly spread: Sell one call with a low exercise price (in the money), sell one call with a high exercise price (out of the money), while simultaneously buying two calls with an intermediate exercise price (at the money) in order to implement a hedge against extreme price movements (up or down).

Type of Hedge: Against extreme price movements (either up or down).

Goal of Hedge: Generate positive cash flows when the price of the underlying asset either increases above or decreases below a certain level.

Comparison with Simple Options Hedge: If prices do not fluctuate much from current spot prices, the butterfly spread generates losses.

How to Implement the Short Butterfly Spread with Calls: Suppose that the Eurodollar futures contract currently sells at an IMM Index price of 95. To implement the short butterfly spread, buy two June at the money calls with an exercise price of 95. Sell one out of the money June call with an exercise price of, say, 96, and sell another June in the money call with an exercise price of 94. Assume that the 96 call option premium is 15 basis points (where each 90 day $1 million basis point is worth $25 using 90 days for simplicity); the premium for the 95 call is 50 basis points; and the premium for the 94 call is 155 basis points. Using a 90 day Eurodollar futures call option, we see that the proceeds from the sale of the 96 call are $375 (= 15 × $25) plus $3,875 (= 155 × $25) for the 94 call, minus the cost of buying two 95 calls priced at $1,250 (= 50 × $25) each. The short butterfly spread's premium cash inflow is +$1,750 (= $375 + $3,875 − $2,500). This compound option premium is not a cost but a source of income.

Butterfly spread: a compound option strategy implemented by selling one call with a low exercise price (in the money), selling one call with a high exercise price (out of the money), while simultaneously buying two calls with an intermediate exercise price (at the money) in order to implement a hedge against extreme price movements (up or down).

Table PP.2

Cash Flows on a Short Butterfly Spread upon Expiration

Futures Price (1)	Sell One 96 Call: Value (2)	Buy Two 95 Calls: Value (3)	Sell One 94 Call: Value (4)	Premium (5)	Net Proceeds (6) = (2+3+4+5)
93.50	0	0	0	+$1,750	+$1,750
94.00	0	0	0	+$1,750	+$1,750
94.70	0	0	−$1,750	+$1,750	0
95.00	0	0	−$2,500	+$1,750	−$750
95.30	0	+$1,500	−$3,250	+$1,750	0
95.70	0	+$3,500	−$4,250	+$1,750	+$1,000
96.00	0	+$5,000	−$5,000	+$1,750	+$1,750
97.00	−$2,500	+$10,000	−$7,500	+$1,750	+$1,750

Table PP.2 shows the short butterfly spread's cash flows upon expiration for several possible futures prices. At the futures price of 94.70, only the 94 call expires in the money with an intrinsic value of $1,750 (= 70 × $25). Since the 94 call is sold by the holder of the short butterfly spread, this represents a cash outflow. Together with the option premium of +$1,750, this represents one breakeven point for the short butterfly spread. In contrast, if the futures price upon expiration is 95.70, then the two 95 calls bought have an intrinsic value of +$3,500 (= 70 × $25 × 2), while the 94 call sold loses $4,250 (= 170 × $25) for a net intrinsic value of −$750. Adding the butterfly spread premium of +$1,750 yields the net proceeds of +$1,000 when the futures price upon expiration is 95.70.

The cash flows upon expiration for the short butterfly spread are shown in Figure PP.2. The compound options position yields its maximum positive cash flow of $1,750 when Eurodollar futures are either below 94 or above 96 upon expiration date. The

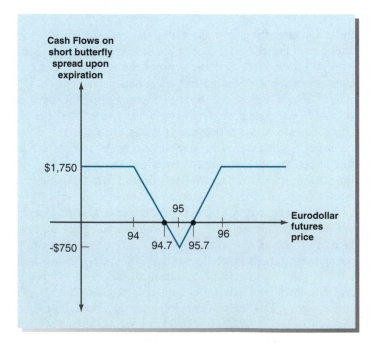

Figure PP.2

butterfly spread yields negative cash flows if Eurodollar futures prices move little from the futures price upon initiation of the options position (in this case the at the money value of 95). Indeed, the maximum losses occur if there is no change in the Eurodollar futures price over the life of the options position.

PRACTITIONER'S PRIMER 19.3

long condor: a compound option strategy implemented by buying one put with the lowest exercise price, selling one put with a higher exercise price, selling a put with an even higher exercise price, and buying a put with the highest exercise price in order to implement a hedge against small price changes (up or down).

THE LONG CONDOR WITH PUTS

Long Condor: The long condor consists of four options. Buy one put with the lowest exercise price, sell one put with a higher exercise price, sell a put with an even higher exercise price, and buy a put with the highest exercise price, in order to implement a hedge against small price changes (up or down).

Type of Hedge: Against small price changes (either up or down).

Goal of Hedge: Generate positive cash flows when the price of the underlying asset remains around the price of the underlying asset upon initiation of the compound options position.

Comparison with Simple Options Hedge: If prices fluctuate a lot from current spot prices (that is, if spot prices are volatile), then the long condor position generates losses.

How to Implement the Long Condor with Puts: The Deutschemark futures option on the CME is sold in denominations of DM125,000. Consider a condor constructed by buying one put with an exercise price of $0.50 per DM; selling one put with exercise price of $0.55; selling another put with $0.60 strike price; and buying a put with a strike price of $0.65.

The long condor consists of four put options. Suppose that the put option premiums are $0.01 for the $0.50 strike price; $0.15 for the $0.55 strike price; $0.25 for the $0.60 strike price; and $0.43 for the $0.65 strike price. The condor premium costs $0.04 per DM, since it consists of −$0.01 + $0.15 + $0.25 − $0.43 = −$0.04 per DM, or $5,000 per contract (DM125,000 × $0.04).

Table PP.3 and Figure PP.3 show the cash flows on the long condor at the expiration date. If the Deutschemark futures contract is priced at $0.45 upon the options' expiration date, the $0.50 put bought yields a positive cash inflow of $6,250 (= $0.05 × DM125,000); the $0.55 put sold yields a negative cash outflow of $12,500 (= $0.10 × DM125,000); the $0.60 put sold yields a negative cash outflow of $18,750 (= $0.15 × DM125,000); and the $0.65 put bought yields a positive cash inflow of $25,000 (= $0.20 × DM125,000) for a total condor intrinsic value of $0 (= +$6,250 − $12,500 − $18,750 + $25,000). The net proceeds, including the premium, are −$5,000 (= 0 − $5,000).The condor breaks even when the DM futures price is $0.54 upon expiration date. The $0.50 put expires worthless; the $0.55 sold generates a cash outflow of $1,250 (= $0.01 × DM125,000); the $0.60 put sold generates a cash outflow of $7,500 (= $0.06 × DM125,000); and the $0.65 put bought generates a cash inflow of $13,750 (= $0.11 × DM125,000). The intrinsic value of the condor is $5,000 (= +$0 − $1,250 − $7,500 + $13,750). Subtracting the premium of $5,000 yields the net proceeds of zero when the DM futures price is $0.54 upon condor expiration date.

Table PP.3

The Cash Flows on the Long Condor upon Expiration

Futures Price (1)	Buy $0.50 Put: Value (2)	Sell $0.55 Put: Value (3)	Sell $0.60 Put: Value (4)	Buy $0.65 Put: Value (5)	Premium (6)	Net Proceeds (7) = (2+3+4+5+6)
$0.45	+$6,250	−$12,500	−$18,750	+$25,000	−$5,000	−$5,000
$0.50	0	−$6,250	−$12,500	+$18,750	−$5,000	−$5,000
$0.52	0	−$3,750	−$10,000	+$16,250	−$5,000	−$2,500
$0.54	0	−$1,250	−$7,500	+$13,750	−$5,000	0
$0.55	0	0	−$6,250	+$12,500	−$5,000	+$1,250
$0.60	0	0	0	+$6,250	−$5,000	+$1,250
$0.61	0	0	0	+$5,000	−$5,000	0
$0.66	0	0	0	0	−$5,000	−$5,000

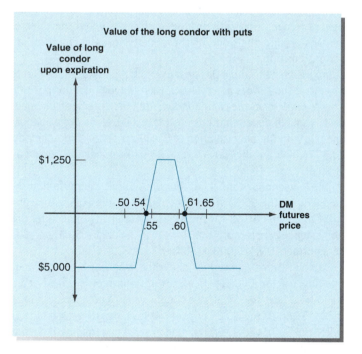

Figure PP.3

PRACTITIONER'S PRIMER 19.4

THE COLLAR

Collar: Buy an out of the money put and sell an out of the money call in order to implement a less expensive short hedge.
Type of Hedge: Short.

collar: a compound option strategy implemented by buying an out of the money put and selling an out of the money call in order to implement a less expensive short hedge.

cap: a multiperiod interest rate put that acts as a short hedge against interest rate increases.

floor: a multiperiod interest rate call that offers the holder a long hedge against interest rate decreases.

Goal of Hedge: Generate positive cash flows when the price of the underlying asset decreases below a certain level.

Comparison with Simple Options Hedge: Sacrifices limitation on downside losses when prices increase significantly.

How to Implement the Collar: The collar is constructed by buying a put and selling a call. The interest rate put portion of the collar is called a **cap**, which is a multiperiod put since it acts as a short hedge against interest rate increases over the life of a floating rate debt instrument. The other portion of the collar is a multiperiod interest rate call that is called a **floor**, since it offers the holder a long hedge against interest rate decreases over the life of a floating rate debt instrument. Caps and floors can be viewed as strips of options with expiration dates corresponding to each coupon payment date in the underlying debt instrument.

As an example, suppose that current 90 day Eurodollar futures prices are 95.00. To implement the collar, buy a September put with an exercise price of 94.00 and sell a September call with an exercise price of 96.00. Assume that the 94 put premium is 25 basis points and the 96 call premium is 15 basis points. The collar's premium is a cost of 10 basis points, or $250 (= 10 × $25).

Table PP.4a shows the cash flows upon expiration of the short collar. The collar breaks even at a Eurodollar futures price, upon expiration, of 93.90. The 94 put has an intrinsic value of $250 (= 10 × $25) that just offsets the collar premium of $250. The collar generates positive cash flows when Eurodollar futures prices are below 93.90 and negative cash flows when Eurodollar futures prices are above 93.90. These cash flows offset the gains/losses on an underlying cash position that are held against the short hedge.

Innovations that led to the design of collars and other compound options were originally motivated by attempts to achieve options hedges at lower transaction costs. It soon became apparent, however, that if the exercise prices were adjusted properly the collar could generate income for FIs. In Table PP.4b we consider the income-generating collar. The only difference between the collars in Tables PP.4a and PP.4b is the exercise price on the put option. The put in the income-generating collar is further out of the money than the put in the collar in Table PP.4a. This reduces the put premium, say to 9 basis points for the example in Table PP.4b, and thereby reduces the cost of the collar. Indeed, the collar in Table PP.4b has a negative cost; that is, it generates a positive cash inflow of 6 basis points (−9 put premium + 15 basis point call premium), or $150 (= $25 × 6). This collar does not have negative net proceeds until the Eurodollar futures price increases above 96.06. Of course, the holder of the income-generating collar sacrifices positive cash flows when Eurodollar futures prices decrease. That is,

Table PP.4a

Cash Flows on a Short Collar upon Expiration

Futures Price (1)	Buy 94 Put: Intrinsic Value (2)	Sell 96 Call: Intrinsic Value (3)	Premium (4)	Net Proceeds (5) = (2+3+4)
92.00	+$5,000	0	−$250	+$4,750
93.00	+$2,500	0	−$250	+$2,250
93.50	+$1,250	0	−$250	+$1,000
93.90	+$250	0	−$250	0
94.00	0	0	−$250	−$250
95.00	0	0	−$250	−$250
96.25	0	−$625	−$250	−$875
97.00	0	−$2,500	−$250	−$2,750

Table
PP.4b

Cash Flows on an Income Generating Short Collar upon Expiration

Futures Price (1)	Buy 93 Put: Intrinsic Value (2)	Sell 96 Call: Intrinsic Value (3)	Premium (4)	Net Proceeds (5) = (2+3+4)
92.00	+$2,500	0	+$150	+$2,650
93.00	0	0	+$150	+$150
93.50	0	0	+$150	+$150
93.90	0	0	+$150	+$150
94.00	0	0	+$150	+$150
95.00	0	−$150	+$150	0
96.25	0	−$625	+$150	−$475
97.00	0	−$2,500	+$150	−$2,350

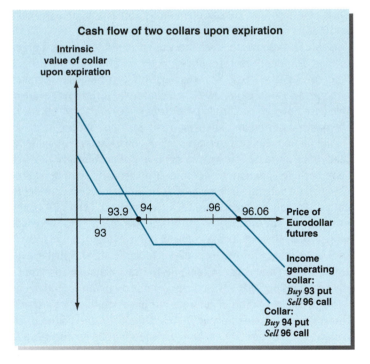

Figure PP.4

the income-generating collar is less of a short hedge than the collar in Table PP.4a. Figure PP.4 compares the cash flows, upon expiration, of the two collars.

Checkpoint

1. What are the advantages of compound option hedges as compared to simple option hedges?

2. Compare the cash flows on the protective put, the bull spread, and the collar.

3. Compare the cash flows on the short collar and the short futures hedge. How can you construct a short futures hedge using a collar?

➤ Summary

Options are derivatives with asymmetric cash flows. This feature stems from their definition as rights, not obligations, to buy (call options) or sell (put options) some underlying asset at a predetermined price (exercise or strike price) at or before some predetermined date (expiration date). These asymmetric cash flows are quite valuable. Thus, the cost of options exceeds the cost of comparable futures/forward contracts. The cost of an option is its premium. The option premium is determined using the Black-Scholes model, which is a function of (1) the exercise price; (2) the spot price of the underlying asset; (3) the volatility of the price of the underlying asset; (4) the risk free rate; and (5) the time to expiration.

Options can be written on physicals (cash options) or on futures contracts. Exchange-listed futures options are generally more liquid than cash option contracts. A long hedge can be implemented by buying a call option on either a futures or a physical underlying asset. A short hedge can be implemented by buying a put option.

Options are marked to market continuously, as opposed to futures contracts, which are marked to market only at the end of each trading day, and forwards, which are marked to market only on the delivery date. Exchange-listed options have little credit risk because of the guarantee of the clearinghouse, as well as the value of the option premium. Writers of futures options must place the premium in margin accounts to protect futures options buyers against possible noncompliance with the terms of the options contract.

The primary disadvantage of options versus futures/forward contracts is the high premium cost of the former. Compound options are portfolios of options undertaken to reduce their premium costs and design desirable risk/return characteristics. Compound options have evolved to the point that they are important profit centers for FIs.

➤ References

Abken, P. "Using Eurodollar Futures Options, Gauging the Market's View of Interest Rate Movements." Federal Reserve Bank of Atlanta *Economic Review* (March–April 1995): 10–30.

Babbel, D. "Insuring Banks Against Systematic Credit Risk." *Journal of Futures Markets* 9, No. 6 (1989): 487–505.

Black, F. "Fact and Fantasy in the Use of Options in Corporate Liabilities." *Financial Analysts Journal* 31 (July–August 1975): 36–41, 61–72.

Black, F., and M. Scholes. "The Pricing of Options and Corporate Liabilities." *Journal of Political Economy* 81 (May–June 1973): 637–659.

Blank, S., C. Carter, and B. Schmiesing. *Futures and Options Markets: Trading in Financials and Commodities,* Englewood Cliffs, N.J.: Prentice Hall, 1991.

Ho, T., and S. Lee. "Interest Rate Futures Options and Interest Rate Options." *Financial Review* 25, No. 3 (August 1990): 345–366.

Kolb, R. W. *Understanding Options.* New York: John Wiley & Sons, 1995.

Merton, R. "Theory of Rational Option Pricing." *Bell Journal of Economics and Management Science* 4 (Spring 1973): 141–183.

Neuberger, A. "The Log Contract." *Journal of Portfolio Management* (Winter 1994): 74–80.

Pitts, M., and F. Fabozzi. *Interest Rate Futures and Options.* Chicago: Probus Publishing, 1990.

Roth, H. *Leaps: What They Are and How to Use Them for Profit and Protection.* Burr Ridge, Ill.: Irwin Professional Publishing, 1994.

Schlesinger, D., and R. Crause. "Volatility Cones Come in Many Flavors." *Futures* 25, No. 5 (April 1996): 42–43.

Siegel, D., and D. Siegel. *The Futures Markets: The Professional Trader's Guide to Portfolio Strategies, Risk Management, and Arbitrage.* Chicago: Probus Publishing, 1994.

➤ Questions

1. Use the Black-Scholes model to price a DM 200 call option if the spot price is P_S = $0.65/DM; the exercise price is P_E = $0.50/DM; the DM spot price volatility is σ = .20; the risk free rate is r = 8% p.a.; and the time to expiration is three months is T = .25 year.

2. Use the Black-Scholes model to price a DM 200 call option if the spot price is P_S = $0.55/DM; the exercise price is P_E = $0.53/DM; the DM spot price volatility is σ = .20; the risk free rate is r = 8% p.a.; and the time to expiration is three months is T = .25 year.

3. Use the Black-Scholes model to price a DM 200 call option if the spot price is P_S = $0.55/DM; the exercise price is P_E = $0.50/DM; the DM spot price volatility is σ = .10; the risk free rate is r = 8% p.a.; and the time to expiration is three months is T = .25 year.

4. Use the Black-Scholes model to price a DM 200 call option if the spot price is P_S = $0.55/DM; the exercise price is P_E = $0.50/DM; the DM spot price volatility is σ = .20; the risk free rate is r = 4% p.a.; and the time to expiration is three months is T = .25 year.

5. Use the Black-Scholes model to price a DM 200 call option if the spot price is P_S = $0.55/DM; the exercise price is P_E = $0.50/DM; the DM spot price volatility is σ = .20; the risk free rate is r = 8% p.a.; and the time to expiration is six months is T = .5 year.

6a. Use your answer to question 1 to calculate the delta of the DM 200 $0.50 call option if the spot price increases from $0.55 to $0.65. Explain your answer. (Assume the same parameter values as in the text and in question 1.)

6b. Construct a delta neutral options hedge.

6c. Show how the delta neutral options hedge is a perfect hedge if the spot exchange rate increases from $.55 to $.65 and the underlying cash position consists of a DM 200 liability.

7. Construct a protective hedge using a put with an exercise price of 595. The put premiums, at each possible spot price, are shown in the table below.

Underlying Cash Position		Protective Put				
Spot Price	Spot Value	Intrinsic Value	Put Premium	Delta	Hedge Ratio	Option Value
590	$59,000	$1,000	$2,050			
595	$59,500	870	$1,300			
600	$60,000	620	$420			
605	$60,500	410	$110			
610	$61,000	330	$30			

a. Calculate the delta values at each spot price.

b. Calculate the delta neutral hedge ratios at each spot price.

c. Calculate the cash flows, prior to expiration, on the options at each possible spot price.

d. Calculate the value of the total portfolio, upon expiration, at each possible spot price, if the protective put was initiated when the spot price of the S&P500 Index was 600 and left unchanged.

e. State the advantages and disadvantages of the out of the money put as compared to the at the money protective put with an exercise price of 600. Assume that the schedule of put premiums for each put with a 600 exercise price is $100 more than the premium of a put with an exercise price of 595. (Be sure to calculate the cash flows upon expiration under all five spot price scenarios.)

8. Construct a short collar and evaluate the cash flows upon expiration date if

   - Current 90 day Eurodollar futures prices are 96.00.

   - The premium on a December Eurodollar futures call with an exercise price of 96.50 is 35 basis points.

   - The premium on a December Eurodollar futures put with an exercise price of 95.75 is 55 basis points.

   Evaluate the cash flows upon expiration if the futures price on expiration date varies from 92 to 97.

9. Use the information in question 8 to construct an income generating collar if

   - The premium on the December Eurodollar futures call with an exercise price of 97 is 5 basis points, and the December Eurodollar futures call with an exercise price of 96.50 is priced at 35 basis points.

   - The premium on a December Eurodollar futures put with an exercise price of 94 is 10 basis points.

   Evaluate the cash flows upon expiration if the futures price on expiration date varies from 92 to 98.

10. How could you construct a collar that has the same cash flows as a short futures contract?

11. Fill in the blanks in the following table for a protective put based on a long position in a five year U.S. Treasury bond with a face value of $100,000. What is the lower bound under the Treasury bond price, upon expiration, guaranteed by the protective put if the put's exercise price is $100?

Underlying Cash Position		Protective Put					
Spot Price (1)	Spot Value (2)	Intrinsic Value (3)	Put Premium (4)	Delta (5)	Hedge Ratio (6)	Option Value (7)	Total (8)
95	$95,000		$5,075	1	1	–	
97.5	$97,500		$2,600				
100	$100,000		$1,350				
102.5	$102,500		$470				
105	$105,000		$160				

12. Use put-call parity to solve for the put premiums in questions 1–5.

13. Use the Black-Scholes model to calculate the implied volatility on a DM200 call option if the spot price is $P_S = \$0.65/DM$; the exercise price is $P_E = \$0.50/DM$; the option premium is $32; the risk free rate is $r = 8\%$ p.a.; and the time to expiration is three months, $T = .25$ year.

CHAPTER 20
SWAPS

"One can no more ban derivatives than the Luddites could ban power looms in the early nineteenth century."—R. Bliss, "Risk Based Bank Capital: Issues and Solutions," Federal Reserve Bank of Atlanta *Economic Review* (September–October 1995): 33.

Learning Objectives

- To obtain an in-depth analysis of swaps.
- To learn why the swap market is the success story of the 1990s.
- To understand the role of FIs in the swap market, in terms of both innovation and implementation of the transactions.

➤ Introduction

It was August 1981. The U.S. dollar was entering a period of strength against European currencies. In 1979 IBM had issued debt denominated in Swiss francs and Deutschemark, in the course of its regular financing program. With the increase in the dollar, the dollar cost of IBM's liabilities declined significantly. IBM could realize a significant cash inflow if only the liabilities could be repurchased and converted into U.S. dollars. But the retirement of debt at a discount would expose IBM to a considerable tax liability. Moreover, in the European bearer bond market, it would have been difficult for IBM to find the bonds for repurchase. It seemed that the opportunity would pass IBM by.

Enter the World Bank. The World Bank typically borrows in all major currencies to finance its activities. Because of the upheaval in the European currencies, the World Bank was concerned that further borrowing would soak up the credit available in those markets. How could the World Bank borrow Swiss francs and Deutschemark without competing with other borrowers?

Enter Salomon Brothers, who saw the opportunity to match the needs of IBM and the World Bank. IBM wanted to replace DM and Swiss franc borrowings with U.S. dollar borrowings. The World Bank wanted those DM and Swiss franc borrowings and was willing to borrow U.S. dollars in order to avoid disrupting the European debt markets. The synergies were obvious, at least once someone pointed them out, and a new financial instrument was born.

The World Bank issued $290 million of Eurobonds denominated in U.S. dollars and swapped this liability into DM and Swiss francs directly with IBM. IBM agreed to pay the U.S. dollar-denominated interest payments over the life of the World Bank bonds, creating a regular stream of cash flows between the World Bank and IBM. Salomon collected its match-maker's fee and administered the regular cash flows. Because of the credit quality of the two counterparties, Salomon was able to guarantee payments by each counterparty to the other. The credibility of the participants in this early swap attracted attention and set the market well on the way to its ultimate success. The new instrument was christened a "swap."[1]

➤ What Is a Swap?

cross currency swaps: agreements between two counterparties to periodically exchange a given amount of one currency for another, at a given exchange rate and interest rate for a specific period of time.

interest rate swaps: agreements between two counterparties to periodically exchange two given stream of cash flows (for example, fixed for floating rate coupon payments) for each other.

fixed–for–floating currency swap: combination of an interest rate and currency swap.

reset dates: the coupon payment dates on which cash flows are exchanged between the counterparties.

Soon after the IBM–World Bank deal was consummated, an active market in **cross currency swaps** developed. Cross currency, or just currency swaps, are agreements between two counterparties to periodically exchange a given amount of one currency for another, at a given exchange rate and interest rate for a specific period of time. Shortly after the earliest currency swap deals were initiated, **interest rate swaps** were innovated.[2] Interest rate swaps are agreements between two counterparties to periodically exchange two given stream of cash flows (for instance, fixed for floating rate coupon payments). The two types of swaps can be combined in a **fixed-for-floating currency swap**.

The essential ingredients of a swap are

1. *The identity of the counterparties and the swap intermediary.* Because of the relatively long term commitments, the creditworthiness of the counterparties is an important consideration in a swap. The swap intermediary acts as the third party guarantor. Generally, only FIs with AAA credit ratings can intermediate swaps.

2. *The swap prices (interest rates and exchange rates).* For currency swaps, both an exchange rate and an interest rate must be specified. For interest rate swaps, typically trading fixed for floating rate payments, the terms of the swap trade must be determined.

3. *The term or time to maturity of the swap.* The life of the swap agreement, which is usually equal to the tenor of the securities underlying the swap.

4. *The **reset dates**.* The coupon payment dates on which cash flows are exchanged between the counterparties.

5. *The swap notional value.* Typically, the notional value (the principal value of the securities underlying the swap) is not swapped; that is, only the interest payments based on the notional value are exchanged. The notional value is used to calculate the cash flows but does not itself represent a cash flow—hence, the connotation of notional as hypothetical values.[3]

To illustrate, consider the following standard interest rate swap. Each of two companies decides to issue $10 million in five year debt instruments on the same date. One company, RocknRoll (RR), is quoted a market rate of 16% p.a. for fixed rate debt and LIBOR plus 200 basis points for floating rate debt. RockSteady (RS) is a less risky company and can issue the notes at either a fixed rate of 14% p.a. or a floating rate of LIBOR plus 100 basis points.

There does not appear to be any basis for a swap between RR and RS since RR is riskier than RS and must pay a higher risk adjusted rate for its debt in both the fixed and floating rate debt markets. Why would the safer RS ever agree to swap interest payments with the

---

[1] Unfortunately, this was hardly original terminology. In the foreign exchange markets, a "swap" is a currency repo. As far as central bankers are concerned, "swap lines" are lines of credit between public FIs for the borrowing of foreign currencies. Again, the lack of originality in financial etymology leads to the reusing of the same words to reflect different meanings. In the United Kingdom, a "swap" is called a "switch."

[2] Beckstrom (1986) discusses the first interest rate swap, which originated in London.

[3] However, in most currency swaps, notional principal values are exchanged.

riskier RR? To answer that question, let us analyze the risk premiums in both the fixed and floating rate market. Since RR must pay 16% p.a. on its fixed rate debt as opposed to RS's fixed rate payment of 14% p.a., RR's credit risk premium, in the fixed rate market, is 200 basis points (16% minus 14% p.a.). However, the floating rate debt market charges RR a different credit risk premium. In the floating rate debt market, RR must pay only 100 basis points more than RS (LIBOR + 200 minus LIBOR + 100). This suggests that the credit risk premium is mispriced. RR's credit risk premium is 100 basis points in the floating rate market and 200 basis points in the fixed rate market.

Mispricing anomalies create an opportunity for profitable swaps. Indeed, potential profit of 100 basis points can be earned by swapping RS's and RR's interest payments. This potential profit is equal to the mispricing of RR's credit risk premium between the two markets. Let us examine how this potential profit can be earned and allocated among the counterparties.

Although RR pays a higher interest rate than RS in both markets, RR's coupon rate is *relatively* higher in the fixed rate market than in the floating rate market. Although RS has an *absolute* advantage in both markets, RR has a *comparative* advantage in issuing floating rate debt, whereas RS has a *comparative* advantage in issuing fixed rate debt. It is relatively cheaper for RS to borrow in the fixed rate market since it saves 200 basis points from RR's borrowing costs, while in the floating rate market RS saves only 100 basis points. This 100 basis points is called the **quality spread differential**. The quality spread differential is the premium that a lower quality borrower must pay over a higher rated borrower for funds of the same denomination and maturity.

quality spread differential: the premium that a lower quality borrower must pay over a higher rated borrower for funds of the same denomination and maturity.

Suppose that each firm exploits its comparative advantages. RS would issue fixed rate debt in the cash market at an interest cost of 14% p.a. RR would issue floating rate debt in the cash market at an interest cost of LIBOR plus 200 basis points. Together, their annual coupon payments total 16% plus LIBOR (14% plus LIBOR + 2% p.a.). Table 20.1 shows their annual coupon payments in each of the five years for a notional value of $10 million at the expected LIBOR for each year.[4]

It still does not appear that RR can do anything for RS. But suppose RR agrees to pay a fixed rate of 15.55% p.a. RR saves 45 basis points on its fixed rate debt, since the coupon rate on its fixed rate debt would have been 16% p.a. Suppose also that RS agrees to pay LIBOR plus

Table 20.1

Interest Rate Swap Cash Flows ($ millions)

Year (1)	Expected LIBOR (2)	Total Coupons (3)	RR Owes (4)	RS Owes (5)	Total Swap Payments (6) = (4+5)	Swap Net Cash Flows to		
						RS (7)	RR (8)	Intermediary (9) = (6−3)
1	10%	$2.6	$1.555	$1.055	$2.61	$+.345	−$.355	+$.01
2	12	2.8	1.555	1.255	2.81	+.145	−.155	+$.01
3	14	3.0	1.555	1.455	3.01	−.055	+.045	+$.01
4	16	3.2	1.555	1.655	3.21	−.255	+.245	+$.01
5	18	3.4	1.555	1.855	3.41	−.455	+.445	+$.01

---

[4] In this example, we assume that all yields are bond equivalent yields based on a 365 day year. However, if floating rate payments are based on money market yields, assuming a 360 day year, the adjustment factor $\frac{365}{360}$ must be applied. See *Calculation Complications 7.2*.

55 basis points. RS saves 45 basis points on its floating rate debt, since the coupon rate on its floating rate debt would have been LIBOR plus 100 basis points. Together, RS and RR pay a total of 16.10% plus LIBOR (15.55% plus LIBOR + .55% p.a.). That is more than enough to make their combined coupon payments of 16% plus LIBOR. Indeed, there are 10 basis points to spare, and they can be paid to the swap intermediary for constructing this interest rate swap.

Figure 20.1 shows the transactions in both the cash and swap markets. In the cash market, RS issues $10 million of fixed rate debt with an annual coupon of 14% p.a., and RR issues $10 million of floating rate debt with an annual coupon of LIBOR plus 2% p.a. In the swap market, RS pays the intermediary LIBOR, which is passed on to RR to be used to pay its floating rate coupons. RR pays 13.55% p.a. to the swap intermediary. Out of this amount, 13.45% is passed on to RS, to pay most of the fixed rate payment of 14%, leaving only .55% p.a. that RS pays in addition to its payment of LIBOR. Thus, RS's total financing costs are LIBOR plus 55 basis points. RR incurs total financing costs on the swap amounting to 15.55% p.a. (= 13.55% – LIBOR + LIBOR + 2%). The remaining 10 basis points are retained by the swap intermediary as a fee.

Table 20.1 shows the annual cash flows between the two counterparties. Since RR has swapped in fixed rate payments, its annual interest payment on $10 million worth of debt is $1.555 million (= .1555 × $10 million). The swap's notional value is $10 million, which is simply the principal of the underlying debt issues. The notional value never changes hands. It is used just to calculate the value of the annual cash flows.

RS has swapped in floating rate payments tied to LIBOR. Therefore, if LIBOR is equal to 10% at the end of the first year, RS's annual coupon payment is $1.055 million (= [.10 + .0055] × $10 million). In each year, RS pays the prevailing LIBOR plus 55 basis points. The swap intermediary collects the coupon payments made by both RS and RR. At the end of the first year, RR pays $1.555 million and RS pays $1.055 million, for total payments of $2.61 million. Out of this total, $2.6 million must be paid to the holders of RS's and RR's debt. That leaves $10,000 left over for the swap intermediary's annual fee of 10 basis points (.001 × $10 million). Note that no matter what the level of LIBOR, the FI earns the $10,000 fee.

The total swap gain to the counterparties (in this example, 100 basis points minus the 10 basis point intermediary fee, or 90 basis points) is determined by the borrowing rate differential.[5] We have seen how the two counterparties, RS and RR, share this total gain equally. This is not

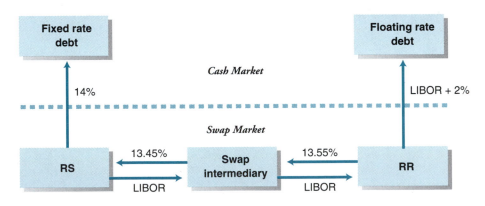

Figure 20.1   Transactions in cash and swap markets.

---

[5] To be complete, the borrowing costs should be all-in-costs, which include any transaction costs associated with the debt issues in each market. See Bansal, Bicksler, Chen, and Marshall (1993).

the only swap possible under these circumstances. Indeed, an array of possible swap prices is possible where the gains from the swap can be shared by the counterparties in any way. Figure 20.2 shows how the gains to the swap can be allocated entirely to RS or entirely to RR or anywhere in between.

What determines the spot on the spectrum in Figure 20.2 at which the swap is priced? In part, the relative bargaining position of the counterparties determines their gains to the swap trade. Swaps do not exist in a vacuum, and there are alternatives to the swap market for each of the counterparties. The more alternatives either of the counterparties has, the more aggressively it can bargain for a larger share of the swap gains.

In practice, the total cash flows shown in columns (4) and (5) of Table 20.1 are not exchanged. Swaps are cleared using net cash flows based on interest differentials. Thus, rather than RR paying $1.555 million and RS paying $1.055 million at the end of the first year, only the net cash flows on the swap are exchanged. Examining Figure 20.1, we see that the swap cash flows are those shown below the dotted line. RS pays out LIBOR and receives 13.45% of the $10 million notional value, whereas RR receives LIBOR and pays out 13.55% of $10 million. The swap cash flows to RS are calculated as (.1345 – LIBOR)($10m) and the swap cash flows to RR are (LIBOR – .1355)($10m). Columns (7) and (8) of Table 20.1 show these net swap cash flows for the different values of LIBOR expected to prevail in each year. In the first year, RS receives (.1345 – .10)($10m) = $345,000 and RR pays out, or receives the negative cash flow of (.10 – .1355)($10m) = –$355,000. The difference between these cash flows is the swap intermediary's fee of $10,000. In contrast, in the fifth year, when LIBOR is 18% p.a., RS receives (.1345 – .18)($10m) = –$455,000 and RR receives (.18 – .1355)($10m) = +$445,000, with the difference of $10,000 going to the swap intermediary.

Examining the eighth column of Table 20.1, we can observe RR's net cash flows on the swap. When LIBOR is 10%, RR pays $355,000; when LIBOR is 12%, RR pays $155,000; when LIBOR is 14%, RR receives $45,000; when LIBOR is 16%, RR receives $245,000; and when LIBOR is 18%, RR receives $445,000. These cash flows have familiar characteristics. They look a lot like futures/forward cash flows based on an interest differential. Indeed, if we construct an "IMM Index-like" price by subtracting LIBOR from 100, and plot the cash flows, as is done in Figure 20.3, we have the classic case of a short futures/forward position. This should be obvious from our calculation of RR's net swap cash flows as (LIBOR–.1355)($10m). This is equivalent to a forward price of 86.45 (= 100–13.55) and a short forward position of $10 million. RR can replicate the swap cash flows by selling five $10 million forward contracts, each with forward prices of 86.45 and with delivery dates on each of the annual coupon payment dates of its five year fixed rate debt. The swap is simply a portfolio of forward contracts. Accordingly, the

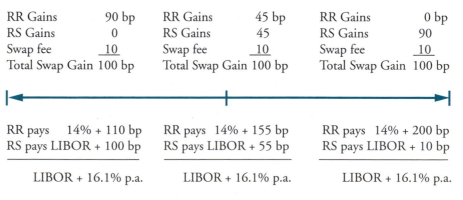

RR Gains	90 bp	RR Gains	45 bp	RR Gains	0 bp
RS Gains	0	RS Gains	45	RS Gains	90
Swap fee	10	Swap fee	10	Swap fee	10
Total Swap Gain	100 bp	Total Swap Gain	100 bp	Total Swap Gain	100 bp

RR pays 14% + 110 bp	RR pays 14% + 155 bp	RR pays 14% + 200 bp
RS pays LIBOR + 100 bp	RS pays LIBOR + 55 bp	RS pays LIBOR + 10 bp
LIBOR + 16.1% p.a.	LIBOR + 16.1% p.a.	LIBOR + 16.1% p.a.

Figure 20.2 Distributing the swap gains.

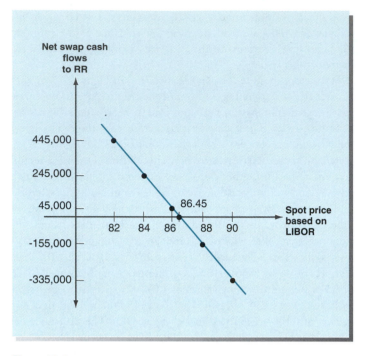

Figure 20.3 Viewing a swap as a short forward.

cash flows on the short forward transaction would be $F(P_S - P_F)$, where F = the amount of the forward contract, P_S = the spot price (100 minus the current LIBOR on delivery date), and P_F = the forward price, set equal to 86.45 for this transaction. When LIBOR is 10%, the spot price is P_S = 90, and the forward cash flow is $-\$10\text{m}(.90 - .8645) = -\$355,000$. This corresponds to RR's first cash flow on the swap. The other swap cash flows can be replicated by solving for the value of the other short forwards, using the spot prices implied by the end of year values of LIBOR (that is, P_S = .88, .86, .84, .82 as LIBOR = 12%, 14%, 16%, and 18%, respectively).

To calculate the forward price, P_F, for the swap from the perspective of the short hedge (that is, the fixed rate payer on the swap—in this example, RR), deduct the fixed portion of the cash floating rate debt payment from the fixed swap rate. In this example, RR's floating rate debt is priced at LIBOR plus 2%, so that the fixed portion of the RR's cash floating rate debt payment is 2%. Deducting 2% from the fixed swap rate of 15.55% yields the 13.55% p.a. forward rate corresponding to 86.45 for RR, the short hedger.

This exercise demonstrates that swaps are simply portfolios of forward contracts, with the delivery dates chosen to coincide with coupon payment dates. RR views the interest rate swap in our example as equivalent to a series of short forward contracts with delivery dates at the end of each of the next five years. From RR's perspective, then, the swap is a short hedge extending over five years. The short hedge generates positive cash flows when interest rates increase, as is the case when LIBOR increases.

From RS's perspective, the swap is a long hedge, since RS receives cash inflows when interest rates decrease. RS could replicate the cash flows of the swap using a portfolio of long forward contracts. To calculate the forward price, P_F, for the swap from the perspective of the long hedge (that is, the floating rate payer on the swap—in this example, RS), deduct the fixed portion of the swap floating rate debt payment from the fixed rate on the cash market debt. In this example, RS swaps in floating rate debt priced at LIBOR plus 0.55%, so that the fixed portion of the RS's swap floating rate debt payment is 0.55%. Deducting 0.55% from the cash fixed rate of 14% yields the 13.45% p.a. forward rate corresponding to 86.55 for RS, the long hedger. The cash flows in column (7) of Table 20.1 are obtained using the valuation of the forward contract, $F(P_S - P_F) = (+\$10m)(P_S - .8655)$. For example, when LIBOR = 10%, $P_S = .90$, and RS's swap net cash flows are $(\$10m)(.90 - .8655) = +\$345,000$.

Checkpoint

✓

1. What forces led to the evolution of swaps?
2. What determines the gains to a swap?
3. Compare the characteristics of interest rate and currency swaps.
4. Describe why a swap is like a portfolio of forward contracts.

Why Swap?

To understand why the counterparties in our example would be willing to swap, we must again appeal to the step-by-step hedging procedure presented in Border Crossing IV. The first steps in the procedure require analysis of an underlying cash position. In the case of RR and RS, in the interest rate swap example, we can surmise their underlying cash positions by observing their transactions in the swap. RS prefers to issue floating rate debt as opposed to fixed rate debt. However, because of its comparative advantage in the fixed rate market, it is "forced" into borrowing in the fixed rate market. Why would RS prefer floating rate liabilities to fixed rate liabilities? If RS's assets are floating rate, then RS's interest rate risk exposure would be reduced by issuing floating rate debt, thereby reducing the duration gap of its balance sheet. The swap can be viewed as a vehicle that allows RS to issue the least cost form of debt (fixed rate), while still obtaining a liability that minimizes its risk exposure (floating rate). Similarly, RR prefers fixed rate debt payments so as to balance its fixed rate asset payments. The swap allows RR to match its book at lower interest cost.

Swaps can be viewed as cost effective, long term hedges. They are cost effective because they exploit any mispricing anomalies in the cash market to reduce borrowing costs. They have longer terms than options or futures/forward hedges, because they can be constructed for the life of the underlying debt instrument.[6]

Swaps obtain their value by exploiting mispricing anomalies in financial markets. Indeed, they are the great harmonizers of global finance. If there are any inconsistencies between different financial markets, swaps take advantage of the differentials and bring prices into line across markets. Why do these anomalies exist?

One explanation is information costs. Domestic companies may be better known, and easier for the market to evaluate, than foreign companies. Accordingly, foreign companies attempting to access domestic capital markets may find their borrowing costs higher than warranted by their credit risk exposure.

Another explanation is regulation. Capital restrictions and barriers to entry create limitations to access that may allow anomalies to develop and persist. Although the markets may not be accessed directly, they may be accessed indirectly via swaps. Swaps are also motivated by tax considerations, such as IBM's concerns about the tax involved in repurchasing its bonds at a discount from par value. Moreover, FASB 115 does not require FIs to mark swaps to market (see Chapter 5).

Just like other derivatives, swaps are affected by financial market volatility. When volatility increases, so does the demand for swaps, as does the demand for all other hedging instruments.

---

[6] Swaps can be constructed on assets as well as liabilities. Thus, the swap could exchange interest income on fixed rate securities for interest income on floating rate securities.

In particular, if financial markets are tight in one country, perhaps because of a restrictive monetary policy, the swap can be used to circumvent financial limitations.

Finally, transaction costs may explain the existence of differential pricing across markets. Loeys (1985) estimates that the transaction costs of issuing debt in the United States add an average of 80 basis points over the costs of a comparable Eurodollar issue. Borrowers can save on these transaction costs by issuing in the floating rate, Eurodollar market and swapping into the fixed rate market. Transaction costs may also stem from the exchange rate risk that is encountered whenever crossing country boundaries to access foreign markets. Although this currency risk can be hedged, it is not costless. The cost of hedging may therefore create a mispricing anomaly across financial markets. As the swap market has developed, the extent of mispricing anomalies has been reduced, as reflected in reductions in potential swap gains. However, evidence on deviations from the basic parity relationships (see Chapter 8) suggests that mispricing anomalies have not yet been eliminated, thereby allowing room for continuing swap market activity.

These explanations of why swaps are transacted are based on the exploitation of comparative advantage resulting from various mispricing anomalies. However, this is only part of the story. Indeed, the exploitation of mispricing anomalies by the swap market should reduce their incidence, thereby leading to a *reduction* in swap volume as arbitrage opportunities disappear. The explosive growth of the swap market suggests that there are other, more basic, justifications for swap transactions that do not rely on the existence of arbitrage opportunities.

1. *Effective risk shifting:* Swaps allow counterparties to separate interest rate risk from credit risk. Fixed borrowing rates consist of (a) the risk free rate; (b) an interest rate risk premium determined by the volatility of risk free rates; (c) a credit risk premium determined by the risk of borrower bankruptcy; and (d) a premium for possible future fluctuations in borrower credit risk. Swaps permit decomposition of these components of fixed, long term rates so that counterparties can benefit from their own expectations about risk free rates, interest rate risk, and borrower credit quality. Thus, in the presence of information asymmetries, swaps offer counterparties more effective risk shifting opportunities.

2. *Agency costs:* Long term, fixed rates on debt tend to be higher than short term, floating rates because of moral hazard agency conflicts between borrowers and lenders. Borrowers' incentives to increase their risk exposure, at the expense of lenders, are exacerbated for long term debt. Lenders therefore impose a substantial risk premium into fixed rate debt, which can be avoided using swaps.

3. *Flexibility:* In a world of volatile interest and exchange rates, swaps offer counterparties the ability to adjust their debt's repricing frequency, notional value, linked rate, and so on. However, the volume of activity in the swap market cannot be justified by simply referring to the risk of borrower's debt issues. Figure 20.4 shows that the volume of swap issuance far outstrips bond and note issuance over the period 1987–1991. These swaps cannot be motivated simply by the desire to reduce financing costs. The major role of a swap is as a hedging instrument. Swaps are used just like options, futures, and forwards to hedge the balance sheet's interest rate, exchange rate, and market risk. Swaps have been in demand in recent years since price volatility feeds the demand for all hedging vehicles. As an example, interest rate swaps have been a particularly effective hedge against the interest rate risk in fixed rate loan commitments.

parallel, or back-to-back loans: private agreements between two firms in different countries, such that each company borrows in its domestic market and then lends those borrowed funds to the other firm.

The Evolution of Swaps   Swaps evolved from **parallel,** or **back-to-back loans**, an instrument that originated in the United Kingdom to circumvent foreign exchange controls. Parallel, or back-to-back loans are private agreements between two firms in different countries. Rather

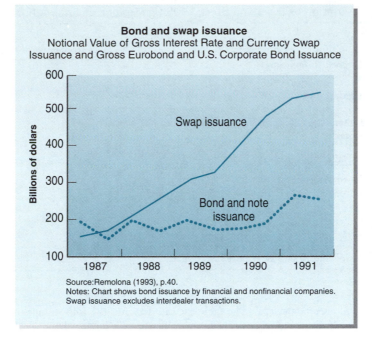

Bond and swap issuance
Notional Value of Gross Interest Rate and Currency Swap
Issuance and Gross Eurobond and U.S. Corporate Bond Issuance

Source:Remolona (1993), p.40.
Notes: Chart shows bond issuance by financial and nonfinancial companies.
Swap issuance excludes interdealer transactions.

Figure 20.4

than borrowing in a foreign country, each company borrows in its domestic market and then lends those borrowed funds to the other firm. This approach avoids the cost of accessing foreign capital markets for both firms. However, parallel loans exposed both firms to considerable credit risk. That is because both principal and interest payments change hands. Moreover, since each loan agreement is independent of the other, there is no netting of cash flows. Both firms are required to pay the full amount to the other, and if one defaults, that does not release the other from the obligation to repay. Finally, it is quite costly to locate another firm, in another country, with exactly matching borrowing requirements. The search costs for parallel loans are considerable.

Swaps responded to all the shortcomings of parallel loans. Only coupon payments, not notional principal values, exchange hands in an interest rate swap. Moreover, only net cash flows are paid out in the swap. And the swap intermediary reduces search costs by maintaining an inventory of swaps, as well as utilizing its extensive network of clients as an information base for swap brokerage. Swaps are structured as a single contractual agreement. Thus, if one counterparty defaults, the nondefaulting counterparty or the swap intermediary can seek damages even if the swap is terminated. All parties to the swap have greater legal recourse than in the case of back-to-back loans.

Who uses swaps? Table 20.2 shows the distribution of end users. Nonfinancial corporations use swaps to hedge the risk exposure of their debt, comprising 21% of all interest rate swaps and 30% of all currency swaps in 1995. Remolona (1993) shows that nonfinancial swap users tend to have more leverage than average, suggesting that they are using swaps to hedge the risk exposure of their liabilities. Indeed, most nonfinancial fixed rate swap payers appear to be hedging the interest rate risk associated with bank loans, as opposed to floating rate notes. Although nonfinancial swap end users are important sources of swap market activity, most of swap counterparties are FIs located in either the United States or Europe. Table 20.2 shows that in 1995 FIs (banks plus nonbank FIs) accounted for 61% of all interest rate swaps and 47%

Table 20.2

Description of Swap End Users, 1995 (Percentage of total notional principal)

Location	Corporate	Banks	Nonbank FIs	Government	Other	Total
Interest Rate Swaps						
North America	8	16	4	4	4	36
Europe	6	31	3	2	5	46
Asia	6	6	0	0	0	13
Other	1	1	2	0	1	5
Total	21	53	8	6	11	100
Currency Swaps						
North America	7	4	3	4	1	19
Europe	13	28	2	9	4	56
Asia	8	6	2	2	0	19
Other	1	2	1	1	1	6
Total	30	40	7	16	6	100

Source: International Swap Dealers Association.

of all currency swaps. The table even understates the importance of FIs in the swap market, since it omits swaps exclusively between intermediaries. Who are these swap intermediaries, and what functions do they serve?

Checkpoint

1.   How did swaps improve back-to-back loans?
2.   Describe the benefits of participating in a swap.

The Role of the Swap Intermediary

Swaps trade over the counter. The role of the FI is critical in intermediating a swap. More than 150 swap dealers are members of the International Swap Dealers Association. Without an organized exchange, the swap intermediary plays the role of broker, market maker, and clearinghouse. As broker, the swap intermediary simply brings the counterparties together. Sometimes the swap intermediary cannot find a counterparty that can be matched to a specific swap. The swap intermediary can still make the deal by taking on one leg of the transaction. In its role as market maker, the swap intermediary builds an inventory of swaps.

The swap intermediary also plays the role of clearinghouse. This entails the mundane matters of managing the transfer of cash flows upon reset dates. It also requires that the swap intermediary provide a third party guarantee to the swap counterparties. Since the swap intermediary substitutes its own guarantee for the counterparties' credit risks, the creditworthiness of the swap dealer must be exemplary. Only FIs with AAA credit ratings can make swap markets. Some FIs—for example, Salomon—have created specially capitalized swap subsidiaries that are distinct from the parent company and that specialize in swap intermediation. These subsidiaries are fully capitalized with U.S. Treasury securities, so as to obtain the AAA credit rating necessary to play an active role in this market.

The swap intermediary's guarantee limits credit risk to the counterparties. Some swaps have a **walkaway,** or **two-way payment clause**. This legal clause in a swap agreement allows a solvent counterparty to terminate the swap if the swap counterparty becomes bankrupt. The impact is to allow the solvent counterparty to withhold swap payments to bankrupt counterparties, on the grounds that the bankrupt counterparty would not be able to fulfill its obligations under

walkaway, or two-way payment clause: a legal clause in a swap agreement that allows a solvent counterparty to terminate the swap if the swap counterparty becomes bankrupt.

the swap. This regulation offers counterparties, and the swap intermediary, legal recourse in the event of counterparty insolvency that threatens the viability of the swap. This is a standard provision in the 1992 International Swaps and Derivatives Association Master Agreement used in many swap transactions.

current exposure, or replacement cost: the marked to market value of the swap's cash flows.

The swap intermediary's credit risk exposure is measured by the swap's **current exposure, or replacement cost**. Replacement cost is the marked to market value of the swap's cash flows. Figure 20.5 shows current exposure for commercial bank swap dealers. Combined replacement costs are less than 10% of the book value of assets. However, this figure overstates the dealers' swap credit risk exposure, since many of these swaps have offsetting cash flows that could be netted out to reduce the dealers' current exposure. Swap credit risk exposure exceeded 100% of equity capital for ten of 13 major swap dealers in 1992. This is less of a cause for concern when we realize that commercial loan exposures for bank dealers, range from 350% to 1200% of the bank's equity capital.

The swap intermediary's credit risk exposure is exacerbated by inconsistencies across the legal systems of different countries in this international market. Swap intermediaries learned this painful lesson in 1991 when the British House of Lords invalidated all of the swap contracts undertaken by the London municipality of Hammersmith and Fulham on the grounds that the transactions were "beyond its capacity." This decision voided contracts between 130 government entities and 75 FIs. Over half of the credit losses on swaps during 1991 were the result of the Hammersmith and Fulham decision. Because of concerns about how the swap will be treated in the event of bankruptcy, FIs are reluctant to enter into swaps with sovereign governments and certain types of trust companies.

The swap intermediary's fee is determined by the level of services provided by the intermediary. If the cost of the guarantee is high, perhaps because of the poor credit quality of the counterparties, the swap intermediary fee will be relatively high. Swap intermediary fees range from as low as 5 basis points to as high as 37.5 basis points times the swap's notional value.[7] Derivatives trading in general is quite profitable. In ten years of derivatives trading, total trading revenues amounted to $35.9 billion, whereas cumulative trading losses totaled

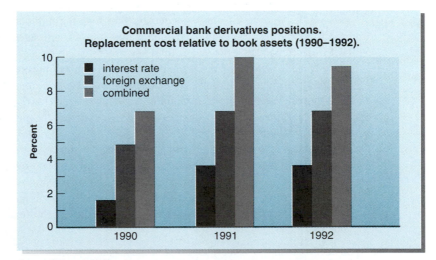

Source: Abken, (1994), p. 7.

Figure 20.5

---

[7] Mason, Merton, Perold, and Tufano (1995), p. 503.

only $19 million. *Timely Topics 20.1: Swaps as the Building Blocks* shows the evolution of the role of the swap intermediary in this growing market.

TIMELY TOPICS 20.1

SWAPS AS THE BUILDING BLOCKS

Sit down with the swaps chiefs of the leading players and the conversation will soon turn to the intensity of competition within the market. Some eight years on from the first public currency swaps, half a dozen banks regularly fill the top positions in *Euromoney's* [annual] swap polls. One in particular is regularly placed first in the overall tables—Citicorp.

The successful banks in the field all share one key capability: they have proved themselves able to adapt quickly to changing market conditions.

The swaps market developed in three clearly defined phases, each of which required different skills. In the earliest days, success rested on the origination and sourcing of deals, and then finding counterparties. Citicorp's huge network, and in particular its relationships with the US and European names likely to use the new instrument, enabled the bank to build up a name for itself as the premier swap arranger.

As the demand for swaps boomed on the back of an explosion of Eurobond issuance and active interest rate and currency management by corporations, the simple arranger function gave way to the warehousing of swaps and the creation of market makers. Says Mike Smith, head of options/swaps: "The counterparty arrangement was basically like barter. Market makers performed the same service to the swaps market as cash does to barter—bridging the timing gap." In this phase, intermediaries had to be able to evaluate and take on the risk of holding swaps on their books. They had to understand swap portfolio movements and what to do when they occurred. "It was also important," says Smith, "to have a senior management that took these things on board."

Although transaction volumes for individual banks are never released, it is accepted that Citicorp handles more swaps than any other institution.

Continued success for the leading houses will depend on technology and financial engineering. Improvements in technology will enable banks to monitor their positions even more accurately and to formulate hedging strategies for their own books.

This will enable the leading houses to offer swaps faster, cheaper, and more efficiently than the smaller players.

Swaps are now part of an overall set of basic risk management products which are the building blocks of financial engineering. Simply offering a swap capability is no longer enough. Says Mike Smith: "In the 1990s, we will see the withdrawal of marginal players—those who do not have the size coupled with the other specializations. The market making operation will continue to be refined in the context of overall customer business."

Source: Euromoney, January 1990, Special Supplement, p. 15.

The Swap Market Today

Figure 20.6 shows that the swap market is one of the world's fastest growing financial markets. As of the end of 1995, there was a total of $14 trillion interest rate and currency swaps outstanding.

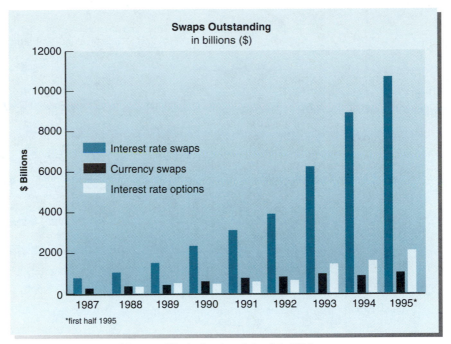

Source: ISDA International Swaps and Derivatives Association, July 1996.

Figure 20.6

Annual growth rates often exceed 30%, sometimes spiking to 100% a year. As of 1992, interest rate and currency swaps accounted for 15% of global financial activity, at a total notional value of $4 trillion. This is two and a half times the size of all futures and options trading combined. The average swap contract size has a notional value 127 times larger than the average futures and options contract. However, turnover on futures and options markets is much higher, in part because of the longer maturities of swaps. The average maturity of futures and options contracts is less than one year, with most trading taking place in contracts with maturities of one month or less. In contrast, about 60% of interest rate swaps have maturities between one and three years and about 30% have maturities of three to seven years, with the remaining 10% maturing in more than seven years. Figure 20.7 shows the distribution of maturities for interest rate swaps from 1993 to 1995. Currency swaps tend to be skewed toward even longer maturities.

   Despite its later start, activity in interest rate swaps far exceeds currency swap activity. Table 20.3 ("Pct. change" columns) shows that activity in currency swaps has not expanded as rapidly as activity in interest rate swaps.[8] In 1986 Chase Manhattan Bank introduced a **commodity swap**, followed in 1989 by Bankers Trust's introduction of an **equity swap**. A commodity swap converts a floating price tied to a specific commodity to a fixed price. An equity swap converts a fixed rate to a floating rate pegged to some equity index at predetermined dates. However, volumes of transactions in these markets are still small, and we will focus on currency and interest rate swaps.[9]

commodity swap: a swap that converts a floating price tied to a specific commodity to a fixed price.

equity swap: a swap that converts a fixed rate to a floating rate pegged to some equity index at predetermined dates.

---

[8] An exception is the large increase in French franc-denominated swaps, which reversed a dramatic decline in 1994. The decline in French franc-denominated derivatives was triggered by a sudden increase in interest rates in 1994. For a discussion, see Kochan (1995).

[9] One reason for the slow start of commodity swaps was the CFTC's challenge to the contract's legality, which initially drove the market abroad. In 1989 the CFTC dropped its legal challenge.

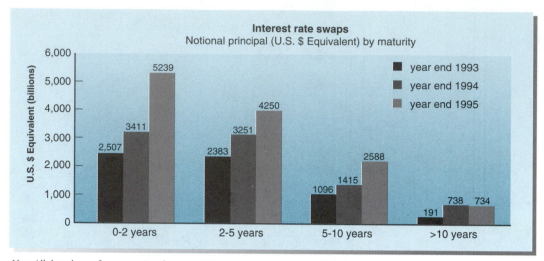

Note: All data shown for transactions between ISDA members has been divided by two to eliminate double counting.

Source: ISDA International Swaps and Derivatives Association, Inc., July 1996.

Figure 20.7

Table 20.3

Interest Rate and Currency Swaps, 1995[a] (US$ billions)

	1995 Activity			Amount Outstanding		
Currency	US$ Equiv.	Pct. Change	Pct. of Total	US$ Equiv.	Pct. Change	Pct. of Total
Interest Rate Swaps						
U.S. dollar	$2,856.5	29.0%	32.8%	$4,371.7	35.3%	34.1%
Japanese yen	2,259.3	89.5	26.0	2,895.9	45.7	22.6
Deutschemark	984.5	59.0	11.3	1,438.9	57.8	11.2
British sterling	433.4	8.9	5.0	854.0	26.7	6.7
French franc	1,110.5	48.2	12.8	1,219.9	164.2	9.5
Other currencies	1,054.6	0.0	12.1	2,030.3	30.9	15.8
Total Interest Rate	8,698.8	39.4		12,810.7	45.3	
Currency Swaps						
U.S. dollar	154.0	8.9	33.8	418.9	30.3	35.0
Japanese yen	82.2	25.5	18.1	200.0	17.7	16.7
Deutschemark	39.0	12.8	8.6	119.0	54.7	9.9
British sterling	11.7	−21.0	2.6	45.7	6.4	3.8
French franc	20.8	42.4	4.6	40.7	66.1	3.4
Other currencies	148.4	37.8	32.6	373.1	33.7	31.2
Total Currency	456.1	20.0		1,197.4	30.9	

[a]Percent change is calculated from the second half of 1994 until the first half of 1995. Currency swap totals have been divided by two to avoid double counting of both sides. Outstanding amounts include swaps that have not yet yet reached maturity or been terminated.

Source: International Swaps and Derivatives Association News Release, December 4, 1995.

An informal equity swap that has been growing in popularity in recent years is one used by corporate executives. These "equity swaps" are not tied to any equity index value, but instead are used by corporate insiders to realize capital gains without paying taxes, as well as to retain their voting rights in their companies. The executive "sells" a large block of the company's stock to a FI, who agrees to pay the executive income on a floating rate investment purchased with the proceeds of the stock sale. However, since the shares are not actually sold, they are registered to the executive and the executive continues to vote the shares. The executive agrees to repurchase the shares from the FI at a specified time. If the stock price decreases during that time period, the FI pays the executive that amount. If the stock price appreciates, then the executive pays the FI that amount. The advantages are as follows.

1. *Tax advantages.* Since the "sale" is not registered, the executive does not have to pay capital gains taxes on the shares.

2. *Voting rights.* The executive can diversify risk by reducing exposure to the company's returns without relinquishing voting power. Moreover, since the sale is not registered, it does not signal the same negative information to the market as would a large block sale of stock by a corporate insider. However, in September 1994 the SEC ruled that insiders have to report equity swaps to the SEC. This might lead the IRS to require that these transactions be treated as taxable events.

3. *Income stream.* The investment of the proceeds from the "sale" of stock generates a regular series of cash flows. Thus, the executive can transform the unrealized appreciation in the corporation's equity value into a realizable, steady stream of (taxable) income.

About two-thirds of all swaps are generic and easily standardized. They are denominated in U.S. dollars and have maturities of less than five years. Nevertheless, as yet there is no developed secondary market in swaps. To trade swaps, documentation must be further standardized, and the swaps must be written with a right of assignment that allows them to be transferable. A swap is reversed by negotiating cancellation of the agreement directly with the counterparty. However, in December 1994 both the Chicago Mercantile Exchange (CME) and the Chicago Board of Trade (CBOT) announced plans to set up systems to monitor and price over the counter swaps. The CBOT established a clearinghouse to guarantee swaps and mark them to market on a daily basis. The CME established a margin system that values swap positions and adjusts collateral values daily based on updated swap pricing.[10] Even if traders do not utilize the margin or clearinghouse systems, they will benefit from the improved price discovery. Swaps are currently unregulated, but dealers are concerned that standardization could expose them to CFTC or SEC regulation. *Timely Topics 20.2: Commodities Boss Forswears Future in Swaps* discusses the issue.

swaptions: options on swaps.

monetizing: the process of stripping the call from a callable bond, to be sold separately.

Swaptions—options on swaps—are a rapidly growing over the counter derivative of swaps. As of the end of 1992, the volume of swaptions was $108 billion. Swaptions are commonly used to strip the call from a callable bond, a practice called **monetizing** the bond's call. The issuer of callable bonds simultaneously sells the bonds and a swaption with the same cash flows as the bond's embedded call option. If investors have overvalued the call and thus underpriced the callable bonds, the issuer can recapture the value of the call by selling the call separately from the bond.

TIMELY TOPICS 20.2

COMMODITIES BOSS FORSWEARS FUTURE IN SWAPS

A squeeze play by the "swaps" industry (a part of the largely unregulated derivatives market) sent the [SEC and the CFTC] . . . to fashion consent decrees that wouldn't be seen as attempts to encroach on honest trade in these high-tech financial tools. . . .

---

[10] In 1994 Arthur Anderson's survey of dealers found that counterparty collateral, pledged to reduce credit risk exposure, totaled $6.9 billion, or 8.9% of net swap replacement value of $77.9 billion.

"We did not say that swaps are futures"—and thus subject to control by [the CFTC] "or use a statutory provision that says swaps are futures," [said Mary Schapiro, the chair of the CFTC at the time]. . . .

Dealers of derivatives don't want them subject to the same rules that apply to what's sold on exchanges. This would prove cumbersome to a business thriving on customized innovation to shift currency and interest rate risks—usually for hedging but sometimes for speculative profit. It could suffer higher transaction costs, which matters a lot in a field that shuffles trillions of dollars of paper obligation for relatively piddling real expenditure.

The bank-dominated industry says its customers are savvy to risks posed by the leverage often built into these gizmos and therefore should be regarded as big borrowers— that is, protected by their own sophistication. But the recent raft of large losses has inspired notions of rampant dishonesty and recklessness in the trade. . . .

Ms. Schapiro said, in terms of appropriate behavior, that "a big part of this is an understanding" in advance between parties in a trading relationship. "Regulations can't define" a standard for different levels of awareness. In some cases, she said "caveat emptor" should apply. "The obligation in the first instance is not to buy what you don't understand." But in all situations, she warned dealers, "you can't lie."

That Bankers Trust did that to Gibson [Greeting Cards Company, a big loser in derivatives transactions] and moreover did so as an adviser and not just a dealer is what sets its case apart, she argued. It is "always a risk" that CFTC or SEC sanctions will provide a smoke screen for other buyers attempting to get out of losing trades. . . . It is cause to define fraud precisely.

The Gibson affair wasn't pretty, and nobody wants to defend liars. However, it might be relevant to ask, for the sake of future applications, what the effect of any deception is. That is, could Gibson have acted on accurate information, or was the harm simply an inability to properly account for the loss at a given point? If the latter, were investors much misled, given that many other parts of a corporate balance sheet aren't marked to market?

Indeed, the linkages of private and public markets make it difficult to say how much of the disclosure provisions that apply to traded financial instruments need attach to a derivatives deal. And the SEC may pack the real regulatory punch here. . . .

Much customized finance moved offshore the last time the CFTC tried to muscle in [see footnote 9 on commodity swaps]. Might the volume of domestic business— booming again until lately—be watched as an indicator of whether regulation is getting too tight? Ms. Schapiro was skeptical, noting that the overseas share of futures has grown because many "risk management vehicles" are developed locally in emerging markets.

Here's another viewpoint from chairman of Continental Bank Corporation, Thomas Theobald, in the *Wall Street Journal,* **May 23, 1994:**

As a nation, we've compromised lots of free market principles in recent years. But, even so, it is hard to imagine Congress passing a law forbidding businesses to borrow once interest rates rose past an arbitrary point, mandating a specific capital structure, or outlawing fixed rate loans. Until last week, it would have been harder still to conceive of federal regulations that forced companies to assume identifiable risks—such as exposures to sudden shifts in exchange rates or unforseen swings in commodities prices—that they would prefer not to take, and that might even put them out of business. . . .

The General Accounting Office's report. . .asserts that "there ought to be a law" regulating derivatives, citing the 1987 stock market crash, the savings and loan debacle, and the breakdown of the European monetary system. In none of these cases, however, were derivatives the problem. Indeed, a reasoned retrospective view may question whether any of these three events would have been prevented by any conceivable kind of legislation.

For all the talk about the complexities of the derivatives markets, the basic function of these tools is simple: Whether traded on an exchange or structured in the over the counter market to manage a specific financial exposure, derivatives allow business users, ranging from farmers to major corporations and government agencies, to achieve certainty about future costs and revenue streams in an uncertain world, and to do so with remarkable efficiency.

Of course, derivatives—like cash instruments—also allow business users to take a view on the direction of interest rates, exchange rates, or commodities prices: that is, to speculate. If the users' views happen to be right, derivatives can be efficient money makers. If the users' views happen to be wrong, however, derivatives can erase earnings just as efficiently, as a few companies have recently and unfortunately found.

Certainly, those losses are regrettable. No one likes to see respected companies take earnings hits. But those losses are inherently no more regrettable than if they had resulted from a major marketing miscue, the expenditure of millions of research and development dollars on a product that bombed, or a substantial operating blunder. Congress would be unlikely to consider legislative or regulatory controls on marketing or manufacturing strategies to protect the minority that make poor or "speculative" marketing or operating decisions. So why should it consider writing laws to insulate the small percentage of firms that make risk management mistakes?

The answer to put it bluntly, is that it shouldn't.

Extensive SEC and Federal Reserve studies of the issues—and research from the academic community—agree that, far from a serious, or even a significant, threat to the nation's financial system, derivatives have been an important stabilizing factor. The use of derivatives by banks and other FIs in managing their balance sheets is actively encouraged by regulators to prevent the sort of asset/liability mismatches that produced the savings and loan debacle.

Rumblings of legislation to control the purchase or sale of derivatives threaten not only to put certain dealers, like U.S. commercial banks, at a disadvantage vis-a-vis other providers, but also threaten to undermine the efforts of companies using derivatives to their shareholders' benefit.... Risk management is an integral part of running a successful business, and investors have the right to expect companies that use derivatives to state their risk management policies clearly and stick to them.

But the responsibility for setting financial policies and implementing financing strategies—including the use of derivatives—should belong to owners, managers, and boards of directors. Managers who make informed decisions and have appropriate internal controls in place to ensure that their derivatives activities support their financial and business objectives will emerge as winners in the marketplace. Those that don't will be losers, subject to the discipline of the market.

That discipline may be harsh at times, but in the long run free markets are far more effective than a roster of prohibitive laws and regulations. All companies should have the ability to make informed, intelligent decisions to manage existing, identifiable—and avoidable—risks.

Source: T. Ferguson, *The Wall Street Journal*, January 3, 1995, p. 9.

Checkpoint

✓

1.   What is the role of the FI in a swap?
2.   What determines the size of the swap intermediary's fee?
3.   Which types of swaps make up the largest portion of the market?
4.   Why has it been difficult to organize a secondary market in swaps?

Currency Swaps

Currency swaps are similar to interest rate swaps, with one major exception. In an interest rate swap, the principal value of the underlying cash market debt is notional only and does not change hands. In a currency swap, the principals are exchanged, both at the inception of the swap and at its maturity. The re-exchange of principal value at the maturity of the swap takes place at the exchange rate prevailing at the inception of the swap.

In the simplest, "pure" currency swap, only currencies are exchanged. That is, the interest rate on both currency legs of the swap is of the same type: either fixed or floating rate. In this example, we consider a standard fixed-for-fixed rate currency swap. Suppose that an American Company (known as AC) can borrow in the United States in the fixed rate market at an annual coupon rate of 9% p.a. for a seven year maturity. The up-front borrowing costs are 1.5%, so that for every $100 of bonds sold AC's net proceeds are $98.50. Calculating the all-in-cost of the debt, you discover that AC's financing costs are 9.3% p.a.[11] You consider this rate rather high. But AC is well known abroad, in particular in Japan, where the cost of a fixed rate, yen-denominated seven year debt issue would be only 5% p.a. paid annually. Because borrowing transaction costs are higher in Japan than in the United States, the up-front costs are 5%, resulting in a cost of yen-denominated financing of 5.89% p.a.[12] You would like to access the low cost Japanese capital market but must raise U.S. dollars to finance AC's operations. A currency swap is the solution to your quandary.

A swap intermediary calls AC's attention to a U.S. affiliate of a Japanese company. This company, known as JC, can borrow in the United States at a rate of 8.5% p.a. for a seven year debt, with an up-front charge of 1.5%, for an all-in-cost of debt of 8.80% p.a. The only problem for JC is that the company wants to raise Japanese yen, not U.S. dollars. For JC to borrow in Japan, it must pay the rates charged to its troubled parent company, 5.25% p.a. with a 5% up-front fee for an all-in-cost of financing of 6.15% p.a.

To recap, AC wants to borrow U.S. dollars but must pay 9.30% p.a., while the cost of borrowing yen is only 5.89%. JC wants to borrow Japanese yen but must pay 6.15% p.a., while the cost of borrowing dollars is 8.80% p.a. The swap intermediary has an opportunity to make both companies, and itself, happy. It offers AC a swap financing of U.S. dollars at the cost of 9% p.a. and JC a swap financing of Japanese yen at the cost of 5.95% p.a. AC benefits because it obtains U.S. dollar financing at a cost of 9%, as opposed to 9.30%, a cost savings of 30 basis points. JC benefits because it obtains Japanese yen financing at a cost of 5.95%, as opposed to 6.15%, a cost savings of 20 basis points. Together AC and JC enjoy total swap

---

[11] That is, the yield $y = 9.3\%$ such that

$$98.50 = \sum_{s=1}^{7} \frac{9}{(1+y)^s} + \frac{100}{(1+y)^7}$$

[12] That is, the yield $y = 5.89\%$ such that

$$95.00 = \sum_{s=1}^{7} \frac{5}{(1+y)^s} + \frac{100}{(1+y)^7}$$

gains of 50 basis points. The intermediary earns an annual swap fee of 6 JY basis points, from the Japanese yen debt transactions (5.95% – 5.89%), plus 20 US$ basis points, from the U.S. dollar debt transactions (9% – 8.8%). Since AC's swap position is long the Japanese yen and JC's swap position is short the Japanese yen, AC (JC) receives positive net swap cash inflows when the yen-U.S. dollar exchange rate increases (decreases).

Figure 20.8 shows the transaction. In the cash market, AC issues seven year, 5% p.a. annual coupon bonds in Japan with a face value of JY100 million, yielding 5.89% p.a. at a price of JY95 million.[13] Simultaneously, JC issues $1 million worth of seven year, 8.5% p.a. annual coupon debt in the United States, for a cost of 8.80% p.a.[14] Columns (3) and (4) of Table 20.4 show the annual cash flows in the cash market for AC's and JC's debt. Rather than making the payments shown in these columns, however, AC and JC enter into a currency swap.[15] AC swaps its yen-denominated debt for a seven year U.S.$-denominated swap loan with a face value of $1 million, an annual coupon rate of 8.702% p.a., yielding 9% p.a.,[16] resulting in AC's swap cash flows shown in column (2) of Table 20.4. Similarly, JC swaps in the JY100

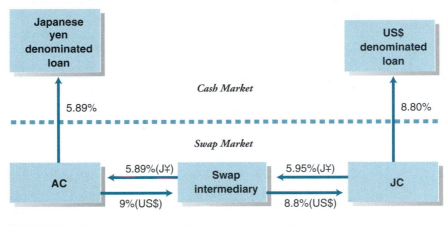

Figure 20.8   A currency swap example

---

[13] The present value of the seven year bonds issued in the Japanese cash market is

$$P = \sum_{s=1}^{7} \frac{JY5m}{1.0589^s} + \frac{JY100m}{1.0589^7} = JY95m$$

[14] The present value of the seven year bonds issued in the U.S. cash market is

$$P = \sum_{s=1}^{7} \frac{85,000}{1.088^s} + \frac{\$1m}{1.088^7} = \$985,000$$

[15] We structure the swap so as to eliminate any up-front payments. Thus, the coupon rates are adjusted so as to keep the present values of the swap and cash debt issues equal. (See calculations in footnotes 13, 14, 16, and 17.) This is just one example; if the terms of the swap were adjusted, the cash flows would change.

[16] The present value of the seven year swap loan is

$$P = \sum_{s=1}^{7} \frac{87,020}{1.09^s} + \frac{\$1m}{1.09^7} = \$985,000$$

Table
20.4

Currency Swap Cash Flows

| | AC | | JC | | Swap Intermediary | |
Year (1)	US$ Swap (2)	Japanese Yen Cash Market (3)	US$ Transactions (4)	Yen Swap (5)	US$ (6)	Yen (7)
Yield	9% p.a.	5.89% p.a.	8.8% p.a.	5.95% p.a.	20 bp	6 bp
0	+$985,000	−JY95m	−$985,000	+JY95m	0	0
1	−87,020	+5m	+85,000	−5.056m	+2,020	+56,000
2	−87,020	+5m	+85,000	−5.056m	+2,020	+56,000
3	−87,020	+5m	+85,000	−5.056m	+2,020	+56,000
4	−87,020	+5m	+85,000	−5.056m	+2,020	+56,000
5	−87,020	+5m	+85,000	−5.056m	+2,020	+56,000
6	−87,020	+5m	+85,000	−5.056m	+2,020	+56,000
7	−1,087,020	+105m	+1,085,000	−105.056m	+2,020	+56,000

million seven year yen loan with an annual coupon rate of 5.056% p.a. and a yield of 5.95% p.a.[17]

What happens on each coupon payment date? First, in time period 0, AC receives JY95 million from its issuance of cash market debt in Japan, which is immediately transferred to the swap intermediary in exchange for a payment of US$985,000. The swap intermediary receives the US$985,000 from JC's issuance of debt in the U.S. cash market in exchange for the JY95 million payment. This enables AC to raise US$985,000 and JC to raise JY95 million at time period 0. At time period 0, there is no payment to the swap intermediary, since the US$985,000 it receives from JC is immediately paid to AC, and the JY95 million it receives from AC is immediately paid to JC.

On each coupon payment date in years 1–7, AC pays the swap intermediary US$87,020 (the coupon payment on the seven year swap loan yielding 9% p.a.) and receives a payment of JY5 million, which is paid to AC's Japanese bondholders (holding AC's seven year Japanese bonds yielding 5.89% p.a.). Simultaneously, JC pays the swap intermediary JY5.056 million (the coupon payment on the seven year swap loan yielding 5.95% p.a.) and receives a payment of US$85,000, which is paid to JC's U.S. bondholders (holding JC's seven year U.S. bonds yielding 8.8% p.a.). The swap intermediary keeps any cash flows that are not paid out to the swap counterparties. AC pays the swap intermediary US$87,020 and receives JY5 million. JC pays the swap intermediary JY5.056 million and receives US$85,000. In each period 1–7, the swap intermediary keeps US$2,020 (= US$87,020 − US$85,000) and JY56,000 (= JY5.056m – JY5 m). The swap intermediary cash flows are shown in columns (6) and (7) of Table 20.4.

In the seventh year, the principal also changes hands. Therefore, AC pays the swap intermediary US$1,087,020 and receives JY105 million to be transferred to AC's Japanese bondholders. Simultaneously, JC pays the swap intermediary JY105.056 million and receives US$1,085,000 to be transferred to JC's U.S. bondholders. At the end of year seven, the swap intermediary keeps US$2,020 (= US$1,087,020 − US$1,085,000) and JY56,000 (= JY105.056m – JY105m). For each of the seven years of the life of the swap, the swap intermediary receives US$87,020 from AC and pays out US$85,000 to JC, for net proceeds of

---

[17] The present value of the seven year swap loan is

$$P = \sum_{s=1}^{7} \frac{JY5.056m}{1.0595^s} + \frac{JY100m}{1.0595^7} = JY95m$$

US$2,020, or 20 basis points on $1 million face value U.S. debt. In addition, for each of the seven years, the swap intermediary pays AC JY5 million and receives JY5.056 million from JC, for net proceeds of JY56,000, or approximately 6 basis points on JY100 million face value. These are the swap intermediary fees from the currency swap.

From AC's perspective, the swap is equivalent to a portfolio of long currency forward contracts, each with a yen-dollar forward exchange rate of US$0.0174 = US$87,020/JY5m. AC benefits, therefore, from increases in the yen-dollar exchange rate. For example, if the spot exchange rate on coupon payment date increases to US$0.02 per yen, the U.S. dollar value of AC's cash inflows is US$100,000 (= $0.02 × JY5m), whereas the cost of the swap payment is only US$87,020, for a new swap cash inflow of US$12,980. This is equivalent to the value of a long forward contract where P_S = $0.02, P_F = $0.0174, and F = +JY5 million; that is, $F(P_S - P_F)$ = JY5m($0.02 - 0.0174$) = +$13,000 (with differences due to rounding).

Simultaneously, when yen-dollar exchange rates are $0.02, JC loses on the swap, since JC's position is equivalent to a short yen forward contract, with a forward rate of US$0.0168 = US$85,000/JY5.056m. At the $0.02 exchange rate, JC makes a swap payment of US$101,120 (= $0.02 × JY5.056m) as opposed to the $85,000 cash payment, for a net swap cash outflow of –$16,120(= –$101,120 + $85,000). This is equivalent to the value of a short forward contact where P_S = $0.02, P_F = $0.0168, and F = –JY5.056 million; that is, $F(P_S - P_F)$ = –JY5.056m($0.02 - 0.0168$) = –$16,180, with differences due to rounding. The $3,140 difference between JC's $16,120 net swap outflow less AC's $12,980 net swap inflow is the swap intermediary's fee, consisting of $2,020 plus $1,120 (= JY56,000 × $0.02).

In contrast, if the yen-dollar exchange rate on the coupon payment date decreases to, say, $0.009, AC has a net swap cash outflow of –$42,020 (which is $0.009(JY5m) = $45,000 minus $87,020) whereas JC receives a net swap cash inflow of +$39,496 (which is +$85,000 minus $0.009(JY5.056m) = $45,504). Stated in another way, AC's equivalent long forward contract is valued at +JY5($0.009 - $0.0174) = –$42,000 and JC's equivalent short forward contact is valued at –JY5.056($0.009 - $0.0168) = +$39,440. The $2,524 difference between AC's and JC's net swap cash flows (= $42,020 – $39,496) is the swap intermediary's fee of $2,020 plus $504 (= JY56,000 × $0.009).

AC's $0.0174 and JC's $0.0168 forward rates implied by the currency swap are the breakeven rates required to set the up front cost of the swap to zero. If instead AC entered into a long forward contract at a US$0.01 forward exchange rate, AC would have to pay an up-front cost of the swap, since the guaranteed forward rate ($0.01) is below the breakeven forward rate on AC's leg of the swap ($0.0174). Table 20.5 evaluates the up front cost of a long forward position with a $0.01 forward exchange rate.

Table 20.5

AC's Japanese Yen–Denominated Loan Plus Forward Currency Hedges as Alternatives to Currency Swaps

Year (1)	Expected Spot FX (2)	Yen Cash Flow (3)	Value of Long Forwards (4)	Unhedged JY Coupon (5)	Hedged US$ Coupon Cost (6)
1	$.0102	–JY5m	$1,000	–$51,000	–$50,000
2	$.0105	–JY5m	$2,500	–$52,500	–$50,000
3	$.0108	–JY5m	$4,000	–$54,000	–$50,000
4	$.0109	–JY5m	$4,500	–$54,500	–$50,000
5	$.0111	–JY5m	$5,500	–$55,500	–$50,000
6	$.0118	–JY5m	$9,000	–$59,000	–$50,000
7	$.0122	–JY105m	$281,000	–$1,281,000	–$1,000,000

Column (2) in Table 20.5 shows the consensus forecast of expected future spot foreign exchange rates at the end of each of the next seven years. Column (5) shows AC's U.S. dollar cost of making the JY5 million coupon payments on its Japanese yen-denominated loan if it is not hedged. For example, if the exchange rate is US$0.0109 per yen at the end of year 4, the US$ cost of JY5 million is US$54,500 (= JY5m × US$0.0109). AC's costs increase as the yen appreciates against the U.S. dollar. AC can hedge this currency risk exposure by putting on a long hedge and buying yen-dollar forwards. Assuming a forward price of $0.01 per yen, column (4) in the table shows the value of the long hedge. That is, at the end of the first year, if the exchange rate is $0.0102 per yen, the value of the long forward hedge is $F(P_S - P_F) = \text{JY5m}(\$0.0102 - \$0.01) = \$1,000$. Adding the value of the long forward hedge to the unhedged cost of the Japanese yen coupon in column (5) yields the constant coupon of $50,000 annually, with a principal repayment at the end of seven years of $1 million.

The long forward hedge is not free, however. If the expected futures spot exchange rates shown in column (2) of Table 20.5 are truly consensus forecasts, then no counterparty will be willing to lock in the series of losses shown in column (4).[18] If the counterparty's cost of capital is 5% p.a., the present value of the losses is

$$\frac{1,000}{1.05} + \frac{2,500}{1.05^2} + \frac{4,000}{1.05^3} + \frac{4,500}{1.05^4}$$
$$+ \frac{5,500}{1.05^5} + \frac{9,000}{1.05^6} + \frac{231,000}{1.05^7} = \$185,570.18$$

This amount must be paid by AC as an up-front fee to the counterparty on the forwards transaction. The present value of the Japanese yen loan is JY95 million, or US$950,000. If the cost of the forward hedge is set equal to its present value, AC's initial proceeds from the yen debt will fall to $764,429.82 (= US$950,000 – US$185,570.18). With a coupon payment of US$50,000 (locked in using the long forwards), a face value of US$1 million, and a seven year maturity, this loan will yield 9.81% p.a.[19] Compared to the cost of the swap loan, 9% p.a., AC reduces its financing costs by using the swap as opposed to the forward hedge.

If instead the FI has a cost of capital of 10% p.a., then the cost of the forward hedge is

$$\frac{1,000}{1.10} + \frac{2,500}{1.10^2} + \frac{4,000}{1.10^3} + \frac{4,500}{1.10^4}$$
$$+ \frac{5,500}{1.10^5} + \frac{9,000}{1.10^6} + \frac{231,000}{1.10^7} = \$136,088.88$$

and AC's cost of the loan with the forward hedge is only 8.65% p.a.[20] Thus, the determination of whether to swap or to hedge the currency risk exposure will depend on the costs of the alternatives.

This method of calculating the "cost" of the forward hedge is what is done to calculate the up-front cost of the swap. It should be clear that the swap is merely a series of forward contracts

---

[18] Recall that if AC is long the yen-dollar forwards, a counterparty must be short.

[19] The yield $y = 9.81\%$ is obtained from

$$P = \sum_{s=1}^{7} \frac{\text{US}\$50,000}{(1+y)^s} + \frac{\text{US}\$1\text{m}}{(1+y)^7} = \text{US}\$764,429.82$$

[20] AC's proceeds from the Japanese debt issue are US$813,911.12 (= US$950,000 – US$136,088.88). The yield $y = 8.65\%$ is obtained from

$$P = \sum_{s=1}^{7} \frac{\text{US}\$50,000}{(1+y)^s} + \frac{\text{US}\$1\text{m}}{(1+y)^7} = \text{US}\$813,911.12$$

with delivery dates that correspond to each annual coupon payment date. On each delivery date, shown in Figure 20.9, AC receives the U.S. dollar equivalent of JY5 million and pays out US$87,020 for a forward exchange rate of $0.0174, whereas JC's forward exchange rate is $0.0168. These are the breakeven forward rates that set the up-front cost of the swap to zero.

Checkpoint

1. What is notional value? Contrast the treatment of notional value on an interest rate swap and a currency swap.

2. The terms of the swap are determined by prices in other derivative markets. Discuss and illustrate using the previous example.

Fixed-for-Floating Currency Swaps

The interest rate swap and the currency swap are combined in the fixed-for-floating currency swap. In this swap, the counterparties exchange both currencies and interest rate risk exposure. In the following example, one company (call it AR for "American Risky") has a comparative advantage in borrowing floating rate, U.S. dollar debt, while another company (call it GS for "German Safe") has a comparative advantage in borrowing fixed rate, DM debt. However, because of the companies' respective balance sheet positions, they would reduce their risk exposure if AR obtained fixed rate DM-denominated debt, whereas GS wants floating rate, U.S. dollar-denominated debt. The two companies have matched interests and can be paired profitably in a swap.

The prices in the cash debt markets are:

Cash Market 3 Year Debt	AR	GS	Differential Rate (AR – GS)
Fixed rate, DM debt	12.5%p.a.	10%p.a.	+2.5%
Floating rate, DM debt	LIBOR + 4%	LIBOR + 2%	+2%
Fixed rate, US$ debt	12%	11.5%	+0.50%
Floating rate, US$ debt	LIBOR + 3%	LIBOR + 4%	−1%

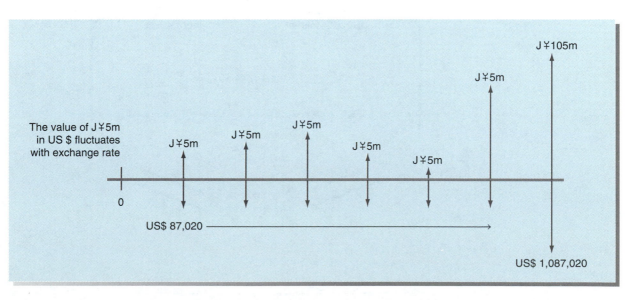

Figure 20.9   Currency swap cash flows from AC's perspective.

In the cash market, AR has a comparative advantage in issuing floating rate U.S. dollar debt, because its costs are 100 basis points lower than GS's: LIBOR + 3% versus LIBOR + 4%. On the other hand, GS has a comparative advantage in issuing fixed rate DM debt, because its costs are 2.5% below AR's: 12.5% versus 10%. The top of Figure 20.10 shows how each firm pursues its own comparative advantage in the cash market. AR issues US$50 million of floating rate three year notes at LIBOR plus 3%, whereas GS issues DM100 million of fixed rate three year notes at 10% p.a. Assume that the spot exchange rate is US$0.50 per DM and that there are no up-front charges in either cash debt market.

How can a swap intermediary enable the firms to achieve their preferable debt choices? The intermediary offers AR a fixed rate DM-denominated loan at a rate of 8.5% p.a. and offers GS a floating rate, dollar-denominated loan at a rate of LIBOR. Out of these loan payments, the swap intermediary transfers 8.4% in fixed rate DM payments to GS and US$LIBOR to AR. Thus, AR's total cost of financing is 8.5% fixed rate DM plus 3% fixed rate US$ (= 11.5% p.a. = LIBOR + 3% + 8.5% − LIBOR), for a cost savings of 100 basis points from the 12.5% fixed rate, DM cash debt rate.[21] GS's cost of financing is US$LIBOR plus 1.6% fixed rate DM (= 10% + LIBOR − 8.4%) for a cost savings of 240 basis points from GS's floating rate, US cash debt rate of LIBOR + 4%. The swap intermediary's fee is 10 basis points, since it takes in payments totaling DM8.5% plus US$LIBOR and pays out 8.4% plus US$LIBOR.

The top portion of Table 20.6 shows cash flows on the fixed-for-floating currency swap for a given interest rate scenario; that is, LIBOR is 8% at the end of year 1, 9% in year 2, and 10% in year 3. In this example, it is assumed that principals are exchanged, although the fixed-for-floating currency swap can be constructed with notional principals only. At time period 0, AR receives US$50 million from its cash market floating rate U.S. debt issue. This cash flow is immediately transferred to the swap intermediary (shown as −US$50 million in column (4) in the top panel of Table 20.6), in exchange for a cash inflow of DM100 million (column (3) in the top panel of Table 20.6), which GS pays to the swap intermediary out of the proceeds of its cash market fixed rate DM debt issue (column (5) in the top panel of Table 20.6). The swap

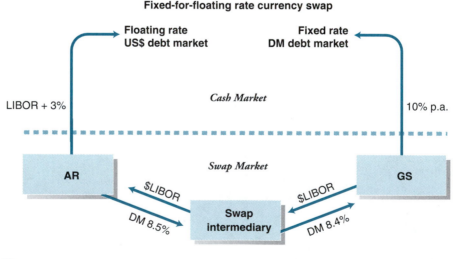

Figure 20.10

---

[21] The cost savings ignore differentials in the DM and U.S. dollar rates and are thus only first approximations. Adjustments to make interest rates in different countries directly comparable are beyond the scope of this book.

Table 20.6

Fixed–for–Floating Currency Swap Cash Flows (US$ Million and DM Million)

Period (1)	LIBOR (2)	AR Swap (3)	GS Cash Market Transactions (4)	GS Cash Market Transactions (5)	GS Swap (6)	Intermediary (3+6) – (4+5)
0		+DM100m	–$50m	–DM100m	+$50m	0
1	8%	DM8.5m+$1.5m	$5.5m	DM10m	DM1.6m+$4m	DM100,000
2	9%	DM8.5m+$1.5m	$6m	DM10m	DM1.6m+$4.5m	DM100,000
3	10%	DM108.5m+$1.5m	$56.5m	DM110m	DM1.6m+$55m	DM100,000

U.S. Dollar Swap Cash Flows

(1)	AR Swap Outflow (2)	AR Swap Inflow (3)	AR Net Cash Flow (4)	GS Swap Outflow (5)	GS Swap Inflow (6)	GS Net Cash Flow (7)
Yr 1 cash flows	DM8.5m	$4m	$4–DM8.5m	$4m	DM8.4m	DM8.4m–$4m
Yr 1 $0.45/DM	$3.825	$4	+$0.175	$4	$3.78	–$0.22
Yr 1 $0.55/DM	$4.675	$4	–$0.675	$4	$4.62	+$0.62
Yr 2 cash flows	DM8.5	$4.5	$4.5m–DM8.5m	$4.5	DM8.4	DM8.4m–$4.5m
Yr 2 $0.45/DM	$3.825	$4.5	+$0.675	$4.5	$3.78	–$0.72
Yr 2 $0.55/DM	$4.675	$4.5	–$0.175	$4.5	$4.62	+$0.12
Yr 3 cash flows	DM108.5	$55	$55m–DM108.5m	$55	DM108.4	DM108.4m–$55m
Yr 3 $0.45/DM	$48.825	$55	+$6.175	$55	$48.78	–$6.22
Yr 3 $0.55/DM	$59.675	$55	–$4.675	$55	$59.62	+$4.62

intermediary pays GS US$50 million (column (6) in the top panel of Table 20.6), so that the intermediary retains no up-front cash inflows. (That is, the swap intermediary receives US$50 million from AR and pays it to GS and receives DM100 million from GS and pays it to AR.)

At the end of year 1, AR pays the swap intermediary DM8.5 million (8.5% of DM100 million fixed rate swap loan) plus US$1.5 million, which is 3% on its U.S. dollar fixed rate $50 million loan that is not paid by GS (column (3) of the top panel of Table 20.6).[22] GS pays the swap intermediary $4 million, which is 8% LIBOR on the $50 million U.S. dollar loan, plus DM1.6 million, which represents the portion of its fixed rate, DM debt not paid by AR (= 10% – 8.4%) where the cash flows are shown in column (6) of the top panel of Table 20.6. The swap intermediary pays the cash debtholders out of these proceeds: Table 20.6, column (4) cash flows of $5.5 million to AR's floating rate debtholders at a rate of 11% (= LIBOR + 3 bp) plus column (5) cash flows of DM10 million to GS's fixed rate debtholders. This leaves the swap intermediary with net cash inflows of DM100,000 (= DM8.5m + US$1.5m + US$4m +DM1.6 – US$5.5m – DM10m).

Transferring these large cash flows would be cumbersome and costly. The top panel of Table 20.6 shows all cash flows on annual reset dates in both the cash and swap markets for both AR and GS. In practice, the only cash flows that are handled by the swap intermediary are the swap cash flows. Suppose that at the end of the first year, the spot exchange rate was US$0.45 per DM. Then, GS owes a payment of LIBOR, which amounts to $4 million (= 8% × $50 million), and receives a payment of DM8.4 million, which amounts to $3.78 million (= DM8.4m × $0.45). At the same time, AR owes a payment of DM8.5 million, which amounts to $3.825 million (= DM8.5 × $0.45) and receives a LIBOR payment of $4 million. Netting these cash

---

[22] The swap intermediary is assumed to collect all cash flows and pay out cash debtholders. In reality, only net cash flows exchange hands.

flows, GS will pay the swap intermediary US$220,000 (= −$4m + $3.78m), and the swap intermediary will pay AR $175,000 (= +$4m − $3.825). The swap intermediary keeps the difference, $45,000 (= $220,000 − $175,000) as its fee (equivalent to DM100,000 at the US$0.45 DM-dollar exchange rate). These cash flows are shown in the bottom panel of Table 20.6

If the exchange rate at the end of the first year were instead $0.55 per DM, then AR would pay GS the difference between the net cash flows. The bottom panel of Table 20.6 shows that AR owes a payment of DM8.5 million, which amounts to $4.675 million (= DM8.5m × $0.55), while AR receives $4 million LIBOR (= 8% × $50m), for a net cash outflow of $675,000, shown in column (4) of the bottom panel of Table 20.6. At the same time, GS receives DM8.4 million worth $4.62 million (= DM8.4m × $0.55) and pays out $4 million for a net cash inflow of $620,000 shown in column (7) of the bottom panel of Table 20.6. The swap intermediary keeps the difference of $55,000 for a fee of DM100,000 (= $55,000/$0.55).

If LIBOR increases, then AR gains at GS's expense. Thus, even if the Deutschemark increases to $0.55, if LIBOR increases to 10%, then AR receives a net cash flow from GS, via the swap intermediary. That is, AR owes a fixed rate payment of DM8.5m, or $4.675 million (= DM8.5 × $0.55), but receives a LIBOR payment of $5 million (= 10% × $50m), for a net cash inflow of $325,000. At the same time, GS receives DM8.4m worth $4.62 million (= DM8.4 × $0.55) and pays out $5 million (= LIBOR of 10% × $50m), for a net cash outflow of $380,000. Thus, GS pays out $380,000 to the swap intermediary, who keeps $55,000 as a fee and transfers the balance of $325,000 to AR.

In this fixed-for-floating currency swap, AR gains when interest rates (LIBOR) increase or the Deutschemark declines against the U.S. dollar. From AR's perspective, this swap is a short interest rate hedge and a short DM currency hedge, for it generates positive cash flows when interest rates increase and the Deutschemark decreases. The swap can be viewed as an alternative to other hedging vehicles. Alternatively, the short interest rate hedge could be implemented by buying interest rate put options or selling interest rate futures/forwards. Similarly, the short currency hedge could be implemented by buying currency put options or selling currency futures/forwards.

From GS's perspective, this fixed-for-floating currency swap is a long interest rate hedge and a long DM currency hedge, for GS earns positive cash flows when rates (LIBOR) fall and the Deutschemark appreciates against the U.S. dollar. Alternatives to this swap, as hedging vehicles, are the purchase of interest rate call options or interest rate futures/forwards for the long interest rate hedge, and the purchase of currency call options or currency futures/forwards for the long currency hedge portions of the swap.

Comparing the Swap Hedge to Options and Futures/Forward Hedges

Although we have motivated swaps by appealing to cost savings associated with exploitation of mispricing anomalies, our last example should make clear that swaps would exist even in perfect financial markets in which all parity relationships held. That is because the swap can be viewed as another hedging instrument that can be used to manage interest rate or currency risk exposure.

How does the swap compare with our other major hedging vehicles? Comparing swaps to the instruments in Table 19.9, we can examine the swap's transaction costs, credit risk exposure, and frequency of marking to market. The swap intermediary fee is an out of pocket expense, similar to the options premium. As a result, the transaction costs of the swap are higher than the cost of a futures/forwards hedge. Because of its longer term, the swap intermediary fee may even be larger than the call option premium, making it the most expensive hedging instrument.

However, as swap markets have become more efficient, these fees declined, thereby reducing the cost of a swap below that of a comparable option.[23]

The credit risk exposure of a swap depends on the guarantee provided by the swap intermediary. Although not backed by a clearinghouse, as in exchange-listed options and futures, such a guarantee reduces the swap's credit risk exposure. The swap has less credit risk exposure than unbacked forwards and over the counter options but more credit risk exposure than exchange-listed futures and options.

Marking to market takes place upon reset, coupon payment dates for the swap, because net cash flows are exchanged on these dates. This is in contrast to forwards, which mark to market only upon maturity; futures, which mark to market daily; and options, which mark to market continuously.

Swaps extend the terms of financial instruments available for hedging. Thus, their primary advantage is their long time to maturity, a feature unmatched in any of the alternative, short term hedging instruments. Swaps are, therefore, a useful addition to the FIs' stable of hedging instruments.

Checkpoint

1. What is the fixed-for-floating currency swap?
2. Compare options, futures, forwards, and swaps with regard to (a) credit risk exposure; (b) transaction costs; and (c) marking to market frequency.
3. How can swaps be used to hedge interest rate, exchange rate, and market risk?
4. What is the primary advantage of the swap as a hedging vehicle?

Hedging with Swaps: Some Case Studies

CASE STUDY 20.1

HEDGING CURRENCY RISK WITH SWAPS[24]

Step 1: Analysis of the Underlying Cash Position

A Swiss FI sells retirement annuity contracts worldwide. In the United States, the FI offers a 15 year fully amortizing annuity paying a quarterly fixed rate coupon of 9% p.a., with no lump-sum payment of principal at maturity. The annuity offering is very successful and raises $50 million in new policy revenues.

When investing the proceeds of the annuity offering, the Swiss FI discovers an opportunity to lend a German firm DM100 million at a fixed rate of 10% p.a., paid quarterly for 15 years. The German loan is fully amortizing, and with a spot exchange rate of $0.50 per DM, the $50 million raised in the new annuity offering is sufficient to make the loan.

---

[23] Because option terms are generally less than one year, there are no simple options comparable in time to maturity to the swap. To extend the term of the options hedge, the options position would have to be rolled over periodically, at a high transaction cost. Thus, the cost of the long term options hedge generally exceeds the cost of a comparable swap hedge.

[24] This case study is adapted from Marshall and Kapner (1993), pp. 96–99.

What is the Swiss FI's risk exposure? Since both securities offer fixed rates with equal durations, there is no interest rate risk exposure. However, there is considerable currency risk exposure. From the point of view of the Swiss FI, the German loan is a DM-denominated asset, whereas the U.S. annuities are US dollar-denominated liabilities. The Swiss FI has a positive net currency exposure of DM100 million (= DM100m – 0) and is exposed to decreases in the Deutschemark with respect to the U.S. dollar.

Step 2: Impact on the Underlying Cash Position

Table CS.1 shows the impact of changes in the DM-dollar exchange rate on the Swiss FI's net cash flows. Each quarter, the German loan pays a fully amortized annuity PMT of DM3.235 million, obtained from the following annuity formula (see Chapter 7):

$$\text{DM100m} = \sum_{s=1}^{60} \frac{PMT}{\left(1 + \dfrac{.10}{4}\right)^s}$$

where the quarterly annuity rate is 2.5% ($\frac{.10}{4}$) and the number of quarterly periods is 60 (= 15 years × 4). Using the same formula, the fully amortized retirement annuities, yielding 9% p.a., has a quarterly annuity value of PMT = US$1.527 million, that is

$$\$50m = \sum_{s=1}^{60} \frac{PMT}{\left(1 + \dfrac{.09}{4}\right)^s}$$

When the Deutschemark appreciates against the U.S. dollar, then the Swiss FI's net cash flows increase, for example, to $155,200 when the exchange rate is $0.52 per DM.[25]

In contrast, when the Deutschemark depreciates against the U.S. dollar, the Swiss FI's net cash flows decrease, even becoming losses when the exchange rate falls to $0.465 per DM, as shown in Table CS.1.

Table CS.1

Cash Flows on the Swiss FI's Unhedged and Hedged Positions
(US$ million and DM million)

	Exchange Rates ($ per DM)			
	$0.52	$0.50	$0.4825	$0.465
Underlying Cash Position: The Swiss FIs Net Cash Flows				
Quarterly German loan payments:				
DM3.235	$1.682	$1.618	$1.561	$1.504
Quarterly annuity payments: $1.527	$1.527	$1.527	$1.527	$1.527
Net US$ cash flows	$.155	$.091	$.034	–$.023
Swap Hedge Cash Flows				
Swap intermediary pays Swiss FI	$1.604	$1.604	$1.604	$1.604
Swiss FI pays swap intermediary	$1.682	$1.618	$1.561	$1.504
Net swap payments to Swiss FI	–$.078	–$.014	+$.043	+$.1
Hedged Cash Flows				
Net cash flows	$.077	$.077	$.077	$.077

---

[25] We calculate the Swiss FI's net cash flows in terms of U.S. dollars, but we would get the same results if the net cash flows were repatriated into DM or Swiss francs after paying out the cash flows on the U.S. retirement annuities. Thus, at a $0.52 per DM exchange rate, the Swiss FI's net cash flows are (DM3.235m × $0.52) – $1.527m = $155,200, shown in Table CS.1.

Step 3: The Goal of the Hedge

The goal of the hedge is to generate positive cash inflows when the DM declines against the U.S. dollar. That is, the Swiss FI seeks a short DM currency hedge. This can be accomplished by swapping out its DM-denominated cash flow on the German loan in exchange for a U.S. dollar-denominated cash inflow.[26]

Step 4: Implementing the Hedge Using a Currency Swap

A swap intermediary offers to pay 9.85% quarterly for the 10% quarterly coupon German loan DM payments. Thus, the swap intermediary's fee is 15 basis points, and the Swiss FI foregoes some profit for a net currency risk free profit of 85 basis points (9.85% – 9%). This is the cost of hedging currency risk using the swap.

The Swiss FI agrees to transfer quarterly payments of DM3.235 million to the swap intermediary. In exchange for the receipt of the DM, on each payment date the swap intermediary pays the Swiss FI US$1.604 million, which is the value of the fully amortizing US$50 million 15 year quarterly annuity yielding 9.85% p.a., that is

$$\$50m = \sum_{s=1}^{60} \frac{PMT}{\left(1 + \dfrac{.0985}{4}\right)^s}$$

In practice, only net cash flows change hands. If the exchange rate on the quarterly coupon payment date is $.52 per DM, then the Swiss FI pays the swap intermediary $78,000, which is shown in Table CS.1 as the U.S. dollar value of the DM3.235 million payment of $1.682 million (= DM3.235 × $.52) minus the swap intermediary's payment of $1.604 million. On the other hand, if the exchange rate on the reset date is $.465, then the swap intermediary pays the Swiss FI a net cash amount of $100,000, which is $1.504 million (= DM3.235m × $.465) minus $1.604 million.

The swap cash flows shown in Table CS.1 for selected exchange rates are sufficient to exactly offset the losses in the Swiss FI's unhedged underlying cash position resulting from currency risk. Adding the net cash flows on the underlying cash position in the top section of Table CS.1 to the net swap cash flows in the middle section of Table CS.1 yields a constant cash inflow of $77,000 for the Swiss FI. Thus, the Swiss FI uses the currency swap to lock in its profit on its cross-currency cash position.

CASE STUDY 20.2

HEDGING INTEREST RATE, EXCHANGE RATE, AND MARKET RISK USING SWAPS

This is the story of a Japanese mutual fund that invests in a $75 million portfolio that consists of $50 million in an S&P 500 index and $25 million in a six month LIBOR yielding instrument. In this way, the portfolio is exposed to both market and interest rate risk. If either the S&P 500 or LIBOR declines, the underlying cash position, the mutual fund's portfolio value, will decline. Moreover, since the mutual fund is a Japanese FI, it is exposed to currency risk, for its portfolio yield is denominated in U.S. dollars. If the yen appreciates against the dollar, the yen value of the mutual fund's portfolio will decline.

---

[26] Since the debt instrument underlying the swap is the German loan, which is an asset from the perspective of the Swiss FI, this is an example of a swap of assets.

Thus, this is an underlying cash position that is subject to interest rate, exchange rate, and market risk exposures. If undertaken separately, perfectly hedging the Japanese mutual fund's risk exposure would require a short market risk hedge (generating positive cash flows when equity values decrease), a long interest rate hedge (generating positive cash flows when interest rates decline), and a long currency hedge (generating positive cash flows when yen-dollar exchange rates increase).

The Japanese mutual fund can use the swap market to hedge all three sources of risk exposure. The hedge is structured as three swaps: an equity swap, a currency swap, and a fixed-for-floating currency swap. Table CS.2 shows the cash flows assuming five possible scenarios at reset date. Scenario A corresponds to a return on the S&P 500 of –15% p.a., a LIBOR of 4%, and so on.[27]

Figure CS.1 shows the three swaps. The US$50 million equity swap exchanges the return on the S&P 500 for a fixed U.S. dollar rate of 7% p.a. The currency swap

Table CS.2

Hedging Interest Rate, Exchange Rate, and Market Risk Using Swaps

(1)	A S&P500↓15% LIBOR = 4% (2)	B S&P500↓10% LIBOR = 5% (3)	C No S&P 500 change LIBOR = 6% (4)	D S&P500↑5% LIBOR = 7% (5)	E S&P500↑20% LIBOR = 8% (6)
$50 Million Equity Portfolio Earning the Yield on the S&P 500					
ΔUnderlying Cash Position	–$7.5m	-$5m	0	+$5m	+$20m
Equity Swap					
Outflow: US$50m S&P500 Leg	+$7.5m	+$5m	0	–$5m	–$20m
Inflow: US$50m 7% Fixed Leg	+$3.5m	+$3.5m	+$3.5m	+$3.5m	+$3.5m
Currency Swap					
Outflow: US$50m 7% Fixed Leg	–$3.5m	–$3.5m	–$3.5m	–$3.5m	–$3.5m
Inflow: JY5b 5% Fixed Leg	+JY250m	+JY250m	+JY250m	+JY250m	+JY250m
Sum of Δ Underlying Cash Position Value + Equity Swap Cash Flows + Currency Swap Cash Flows	+JY250m	+JY250m	+JY250m	+JY250m	+JY250m
$25 Million LIBOR–Linked Portfolio					
ΔUnderlying Cash Position	$1m	$1.25m	$1.5m	$1.75	$2m
Fixed-for-Floating Currency Swap					
Outflow: US$25m LIBOR Leg	–$1m	–$1.25m	–$1.5m	–$1.75	–$2m
Inflow: JY2.5b 4.5% Fixed Leg	+JY112.5m	+JY112.5m	+JY112.5m	+JY112.5m	+JY112.5m
Sum of ΔUnderlying Cash Position Value + Fixed-for-Floating Currency Swap Cash Flows	+JY112.5m	+JY112.5m	+JY112.5m	+JY112.5m	+JY112.5m
Sum All Cash Flows	+JY362.5m	+JY362.5m	+JY362.5m	+JY362.5m	+JY362.5m

[27] These scenarios are presented simply to demonstrate the impact of risk on cash flows. The hedge is not in any way dependent on these scenarios or their likelihoods of occurrence, although that might affect the costs of the swaps.

Hedging interest rate risk, exchange rate risk, and market risk using swaps

Figure CS.1

exchanges an annual fixed rate U.S. dollar payment of 7% of US$50 million for a fixed rate Japanese yen payment of 5% p.a. of JY5 billion. The US$25 million fixed-for-floating currency swap exchanges a U.S. dollar LIBOR payment for a 4.5% p.a. fixed Japanese yen payment, based on a notional value of JY2.5 billion. The notional principal of the equity and currency swaps is US$50 million, or JY5 billion. The notional value of the fixed-for-floating currency swap is US$25 million, or JY2.5 billion. In none of these swaps does the notional principal change hands.

All cash flows cancel out, with the exception of the fixed rate Japanese yen swap cash inflows. The S&P 500 dollar cash inflows are offset by the equity swap cash outflows. For example, if the S&P500 falls by 15% and LIBOR is 4% (Scenario A), the value of the S&P500-linked cash portion of the portfolio falls by $7.5 million (= $-.15 \times \$50$ million), which is passed along to the equity swap intermediary in exchange for a cash inflow of $3.5 million on the US$50 million 7% fixed leg of the equity swap (.07 $\times$ US$50m = US$3.5 million).

The equity swap cash inflows are in turn offset by the currency swap cash outflows. For example, in Scenario A, US$3.5 million is paid out against the US$50m 7% fixed leg of the currency swap, in exchange for a cash inflow of JY250 million from the JY5 billion 5% fixed leg (.05 $\times$ JY5 billion = JY250 million), thereby locking in a $0.014 per JY exchange rate. Thus far, the net cash flows of the S&P500 cash position plus the equity and currency swaps yield a constant cash inflow of JY250 million under all possible scenarios.

The U.S. dollar LIBOR cash inflows are offset by the fixed-for-floating currency swap cash outflows. For example, the value of the LIBOR cash position under Scenario A is US$1 million (= .04 $\times$ US$25 million). This is paid out on the US$25 million LIBOR leg of the fixed-for-floating currency swap in exchange for a JY112.5 million cash inflow on the JY2.5 billion 4.5% fixed leg (.045 $\times$ JY2.5 billion = JY112.5 million). All that is left when all cash flows are summed up is a fixed cash inflow of JY362.5 million. Using swaps, the Japanese mutual fund has been able to convert its risky portfolio cash flows into a stream of fixed, yen-denominated cash flows.

> ## Pricing Swaps

When swaps were still in their infancy, swap intermediaries generally required up-front fees to arrange a swap. As the market matured, and the costs of documenting and designing standard swaps declined, these fees disappeared. Now up-front fees are required only if the swap is exotic, requiring special design features. Swap pricing then typically takes the form of the swap intermediary fee built into the terms of the swap.

If swaps are alternatives to options and futures/forwards hedging vehicles, the values of these instruments must be roughly comparable. That is, if the swap hedge was priced out of line with the alternative hedging vehicles, either it would price the others out of the market or they would price the swap out of the market. Swap prices must therefore be consistent with options, futures, and in particular, forwards price. Because the swap is simply a series of forward contracts, it can be priced as forwards. Moreover, swap intermediaries make markets in swaps by announcing prices that they would be willing to accept on either leg of the swap transaction. To hedge the risk exposure of taking on one leg of a swap, the intermediary will use other hedging instruments. Thus, the swap intermediary's breakeven price, on which all swap prices are based, is determined by the cost of hedging using alternative hedging vehicles.

Swap dealers make markets in swaps by posting quotes for generic swaps on electronic trading systems. A **swap bid** is the price of a swap to pay out fixed rate payments and receive floating rate payments. A **swap offer** or **swap ask** is the price of a swap to receive fixed rate and pay out floating rate payments. The standard floating rate used in swaps is the three month or six month LIBOR. The bidder for a swap, seeking to pay fixed rate payments, is said to *buy* or go *long* the swap, thereby benefiting when interest rates increase. Since the long swap position generates cash inflows when interest rates increase (or prices fall), it is a *short hedge*. Unfortunately, intuition does not drive terminology in this market; the way to put on a short hedge in the swap market is to buy, go long, the swap. Alternatively, the *seller* of the swap benefits from interest rate declines, since the *short* swap pays floating rate payments and receives fixed rate payments. Hence, the short swap position benefits from declining rates (increasing prices)—the profile of a long interest rate hedge. Table 20.7 shows average bid-ask spreads on swaps of various maturities.

The **swap curve** is a series of fixed rate, par value bids for swaps of various maturities against the standard swap floating rate; the six month LIBOR. Figure 20.11 shows a swap curve as quoted on the Bloomberg electronic quotation system. In the screen, the term lists the swap maturities, and bid-ask rates are the par value coupon rates for the fixed rate leg of each swap. Using the quotes in the figure, this swap dealer is willing to pay out three years of 6.5% p.a. fixed rate semiannual coupon payments in exchange for the receipt of three years of floating rate payments tied to six month LIBOR and reset every six months. This is the bid swap rate of 6.5% for three year maturities. In contrast, the swap dealer offers to receive three years of 6.53% semiannual coupon payments in exchange for paying out three years of six month LIBOR floating rate payments. The difference between the swap bid and the swap ask rates is the **swap spread**. The dealer will pay out fixed rate at 6.5% and receive 6.53% fixed rate over the three year maturity for a swap spread of 3 basis points. Bloomberg also shows the spreads as compared to a benchmark Treasury yield. The benchmark yield is the yield for the on the

swap bid: the price of a swap to pay out fixed rate payments and receive floating rate payments.

swap offer or **swap ask:** the price of a swap to receive fixed rate and pay out floating rate payments.

swap curve: a series of fixed rate bids for swaps of various maturities against the standard swap floating rate, six month LIBOR.

swap spread: difference between the swap bid and swap ask rates.

Table 20.7

Bid-Ask Spreads on U.S. Dollar Interest Rate Swaps (basis points)

Maturity of Swap	Average Spread	Standard Deviation	Range[a]
2 years	4.9	1.8	23.0
5 years	4.6	1.4	16.0
7 years	4.8	1.5	19.0
10 years	4.9	1.5	13.0

[a]Maximum minus minimum bid-ask rate of swap spread against U.S. Treasury securities of similar maturity.

Source: Alworth (1993), p. 32.

```
ENTER ALL VALUES AND HIT <GO>                               Corp S W Y C
LAST UPDATE:              US DOLLARS SWAP CURVE              Page 2 of 11

           Source:  X BGN        User Rates        User Spreads
              DAY    CMPND    SWAP RATE       BENCHMARK      SPREAD
     TERM    TYPE    FREQ    BID      ASK      YIELD      BID      ASK
     1 WK   ACT/360    1   4.3750% / 4.3750%   4.3149%    6.0bp  /  6.0bp
     1 MO   ACT/360    1   4.4375% / 4.4375%   4.3149%   12.3bp  / 12.3bp
     2 MO   ACT/360    1   4.5000% / 4.5000%   4.3149%   18.5bp  / 18.5bp
     3 MO   ACT/360    1   4.6875% / 4.6875%   4.3149%   37.3bp  / 37.3bp
     4 MO   ACT/360    1   4.7500% / 4.7500%   4.4683%   28.2bp  / 28.2bp
     5 MO   ACT/360    1   4.9375% / 4.9375%   4.6218%   31.6bp  / 31.6bp
     6 MO   ACT/360    1   5.0000% / 5.0000%   4.7752%   22.5bp  / 22.5bp
     9 MO   ACT/360    1   5.3750% / 5.3750%   5.0245%   35.1bp  / 35.1bp
     1 YR   ACT/360    1   5.6250% / 5.6250%   5.2737%   35.1bp  / 35.1bp
     2 YR   ACT/ACT    2   6.1400% / 6.1700%   5.8680%   27.2bp  / 30.2bp
     3 YR   ACT/ACT    2   6.5000% / 6.5300%   6.2386%   26.1bp  / 29.1bp
     4 YR   ACT/ACT    2   6.8000% / 6.8300%   6.4421%   35.8bp  / 38.8bp
     5 YR   ACT/ACT    2   6.9700% / 7.0000%   6.6456%   32.4bp  / 35.4bp
     7 YR   ACT/ACT    2   7.2300% / 7.2600%   6.8088%   42.1bp  / 45.1bp
    10 YR   ACT/ACT    2   7.4700% / 7.5000%   7.0536%   41.6bp  / 44.6bp
    30 YR   ACT/ACT    2   7.4700% / 7.5000%   7.2620%   20.8bp  / 23.8bp

Bloomberg-all rights protected.  London:71-330-7500  New York:212-318-2000  Princeton:609-279-3000  Singapore:226-3000
Sydney:2-241-1133   Tokyo:3-3578-1625   Washington DC:202-434-1800   G146-73-15   17-May-94  15:09:08
```

Figure 20.11

run par value Treasury security (see discussion in Chapter 16). Thus, the three year swap bid rate is 26.1 basis points higher than the benchmark yield (6.5% – 6.2386%), and the three year swap ask rate is 29.1 (6.53% – 6.2386%) basis points higher.

To commit to four years of floating rate payments, the swap dealer must receive an additional 30 basis points, or a fixed bid rate of 6.8%, as shown on the swap curve. The four year swap spread is still 3 basis points, for an ask swap rate of 6.83% p.a. The swap dealer is willing to receive 6.83% p.a. and to pay out six month LIBOR semiannually for the next four years.

How does the dealer arrive at the prices in the swap curve? Interest rate swap prices are obtained from two sources of financial market prices: spot prices for par value U.S. Treasury securities and forward/futures prices. Many shorter term swap prices are based entirely on Eurodollar futures prices. Because Eurodollars futures exist for maturities extending up to five years, with good liquidity for the first three years of maturities, they provide pricing for swaps of maturities up to five years. Beyond that maturity, the forwards yield curve is obtained using the bootstrapping method discussed in Chapter 15. Thus, the basic building block for swap pricing is a series of expected future spot rates as expressed in the forward yield curve. The forwards yield curve is important for interest rate swaps that exchange fixed for floating rate payments for two reasons: (1) the floating rate payments are expected to equal the notional value times the expected future spot rate (the forward yield), upon reset date, for all reset dates during the life of the swap; and (2) the present value of all payments, fixed and floating, is discounted using the series of forward rates expected to prevail during each of the coupon payment periods.

An **at market,** or **par, swap** is a swap that is priced so that the present value of all fixed payments equals the present value of all expected floating payments over the life of the swap. An at market swap has no up-front payment since the present values of the two sides are already equal. An **off market swap** is a swap with an inequality between the present values of cumulative fixed and expected floating payments, which requires an up-front cash payment to balance the values of the two sides. In the following example, we price an at market interest rate swap with quarterly reset dates that correspond to Eurodollar futures delivery dates.[28]

at market, or par, swap: a swap that is priced so that the present value of all fixed payments equals the present value of all expected floating payments over the life of the swap.

off market swap: a swap with an inequality between the present values of cumulative fixed and expected floating payments, which requires an up-front cash payment to balance the values of the two sides.

---

[28] This example is adapted from Dattatreya, Venkatesh, and Venkatesh (1994), pp. 167–177.

Table 20.8

The IMM Swap—Market Data, Cash Flows, and Pricing

	IMM Date (A)	Day Count (B)	Futures Price (C)	Convexity Adjustment (bp) (D)	Forward Rate (%) (E)	Discount Factor (F)
1	07/08				3.20	
2	09/15	69	96.65	0.0	3.35	0.99390406
3	12/15	91	96.31	0.0	3.69	0.98555829
4	03/16	91	96.24	0.0	3.76	0.97645045
5	06/15	91	95.95	0.0	4.05	0.96725721
6	09/21	98	95.66	(1.0)	4.33	0.95670949
7	12/21	91	95.24	(1.0)	4.75	0.94635141
8	03/15	84	95.13	(1.0)	4.86	0.93597766
9	06/21	98	94.89	(1.0)	5.10	0.92375636
10	09/20	91	94.69	(1.0)	5.30	0.91199917
11	12/20	91	94.39	(1.0)	5.60	0.89994244
12	03/20	91	94.35	(1.0)	5.64	0.88738107
13	06/19	91	94.20	(1.0)	5.79	0.87490780

Swap Rate: 4.46127920%

The three year, fixed-for-three month LIBOR interest rate swap is priced effective July 8, with a notional value of $100 million. Table 20.8, column (A), shows the swap's 12 reset dates, occurring at three month intervals.[29] Column (B), shows the actual number of days in each period between the swap's reset dates.

Column (C) in Table 20.8 shows today's Eurodollar futures IMM Index prices for each of the delivery dates corresponding to a reset date on the swap. The forward rate is assumed to be equal to the Eurodollar futures rate embedded in the IMM Index price, that is, 100 − Eurodollar futures price (see Chapter 18). For example, the forward rate, shown in column (E), for the 12/15 payment is 100 − 96.31 = 3.69%.

There is one wrinkle in the direct use of the forward yield curve to price swaps. In Chapter 18, we saw that a major difference between forwards and futures is the futures' margin requirement, which is marked to market daily. The swap dealer who agrees to receive fixed rate payments and pay floating rates will hedge the swap's risk by selling futures, since the swap exposes the dealer to the risk of interest rate increases. But when interest rates increase, then the short futures position will increase in value, and the margin balance will increase and be reinvested at the higher prevailing rates. Similarly, if interest rates fall, the short futures position will decrease in value, reducing the value of the margin just at the time that it is less costly to borrow funds to meet any margin call. Thus, the short futures position has more convexity than an equivalent forward position since the futures value increases by more than the linear amount when interest rates increase and decreases by less when interest rates decrease. The convexity is passed on to the swap end user in the form of a lower fixed rate. Column (D) in Table 20.8 shows the convexity adjustment for the swap. The convexity adjustment is larger (1) the more volatile the interest rates; (2) the longer the time to delivery for the futures contract; and (3) the larger the number of futures contracts needed to hedge a swap position. The forward rate for the period from 3/15 to 6/21 is 4.86%, which is 100 − 95.13 − .01%, or the Eurodollar futures rate of 4.87% minus the 1 basis point deduction for futures convexity.

The forward rates in column (E) of Table 20.8 are converted into the discount factors shown in column (F) using the expectations model of yield curve decomposition discussed in Chapter 7. That is, we can iterate forward from current spot rates to derive the implied discount rate

---

[29] The first period, from the effective date to the swap's first reset date, is not a full period. It is called a stub period.

Floating Leg Cash Flow ($) (G)	Floating Leg Present Value ($) (H)	Fixed Leg Cash Flow ($) (I)	Fixed Leg Present Value ($) (J)	Net Payment (G)–(I) (K)
613,333.33	609,594.49	855,078.51	849,866.00	–241,745.18
846,805.56	834,576.24	1,127,712.24	1,111,426.15	–280,906.68
932,750.00	910,784.16	1,127,712.24	1,101,155.13	–194,962.24
950,444.44	919,324.24	1,127,712.24	1,090,787.80	–177,267.80
1,102,500.00	1,054,772.21	1,214,459.34	1,161,884.77	–111,959.34
1,094,527.78	1,035,807.90	1,127,712.24	1,067,212.07	–33,184.46
1,108,333.33	1,037,375.23	1,040,965.15	974,320.12	+67,368.18
1,323,000.00	1,222,129.66	1,214,459.34	1,121,864.54	+108,540.66
1,289,166.67	1,175,718.93	1,127,712.24	1,028,472.63	+161,454.43
1,339,722.22	1,205,672.89	1,127,712.24	1,014,876.11	+212,009.98
1,415,555.56	1,256,137.20	1,127,712.24	1,000,710.49	+287,843.32
1,425,666.67	1,247,326.89	1,127,712.24	986,644.24	+297,954.43
13,441,805.56	**12,509,220.04**	13,346,660.28	**12,509,220.04**	

for any forward period. This process is illustrated in Figure 20.12. The spot rate of 3.2% p.a. applies to a 69 day pure discount instrument. The discount factor for the first swap payment on 9/15 is: $\frac{1}{1+.032(69)/360}$ = .99390406.

The second swap reset date is 12/15. To discount that second swap payment to the present, the forward rate of 3.35% p.a. is used for the 91 day period from 9/15 to 12/15, and the spot rate of 3.2% p.a. is used for the 69 day period from 7/8 to 9/15. That is, the discount factor for the second swap payment on 12/15 is

$$\frac{1}{\left(1+\frac{.032(69)}{360}\right)\left(1+\frac{.0335(91)}{360}\right)} = .98555829$$

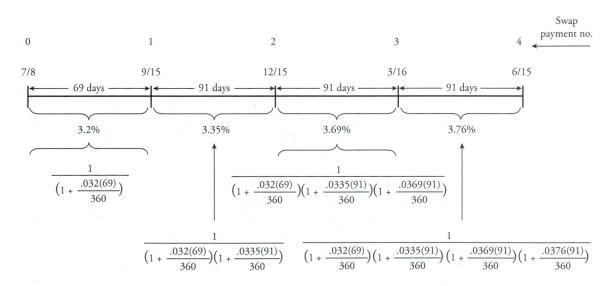

Figure 20.12

The general formula for the forward discount factor, from Chapter 7, is

$$\frac{1}{\left(1 + \frac{f_1 t_1}{360}\right)\left(1 + \frac{f_2 t_2}{360}\right) \cdots \left(1 + \frac{f_n t_n}{360}\right)}$$

where $f_1, \ldots, f_n$ = the series of forward yields from the forward yield curve shown in column (E) of Table 20.8, where all yields are stated as simple interest yields on a 360 day p.a. basis; and $t_1, \ldots, t_n$ is the number of days in each forward period.

The discount factor for each of the 12 swap payment dates is shown in column (F) of Table 20.8. The floating rate payments on the swap are shown in column (G). They are calculated using the expected future spot rate, assumed to be the forward yield in column (E), adjusted for the number of days in each payment period. Thus, the swap's first floating payment is the payment for the first 69 days on the notional value of \$100 million of $\$100m(\frac{.032(69)}{360})$ = \$613,333.33. The second floating payment on the swap is $\$100m(\frac{.0335(91)}{360})$ = \$846,805.56. In general, the nth floating rate payment on the swap is calculated as $F(\frac{f_n t_n}{360})$, where F is the swap's notional value; f_n is the nth forward rate from column (E); and t_n is the number of days in the nth swap payment period shown in column (B).

Applying the discount factor in column (F) to the floating leg cash flow in column (G) yields the present value of the floating rate payment on the swap. The cumulative expected present value of all floating rate payments on this swap is \$12,509,220.04. If the swap is at market, then the present value of all fixed rate payments must equal this amount. The fixed rate that sets the two payments equal to one another is obtained by trial and error. In this case, the fixed rate of 4.4612792% p.a. generates fixed rate payments with a cumulative present value just equal to \$12,509,220.04. At that annual rate, the first fixed rate coupon payment on the swap is $\$100m(\frac{.044612792(69)}{360})$ = \$855,078.51. The second fixed rate coupon payment on the swap is $\$100m(\frac{.044612792(91)}{360})$ = \$1,127,712.24.

The cash flows shown in columns (G) and (I) do not change hands during the life of the swap. Column (K) shows the actual net cash flows that will be exchanged if the forward rates shown in column (E) prevail on each reset date of the swap. The cash flows are denoted from the point of view of the fixed rate payor. Thus, on 12/21 the fixed rate payor pays \$33,184.46 to the floating rate payor (= \$1,094,527.78 – \$1,127,712.24). In contrast, on 3/20, the floating rate payor pays \$287,843.32 to the fixed rate payor (= \$1,415,555.56 – \$1,127,712.24).

The swap dealer prices this swap at a fixed rate of 4.4613% p.a. The swap price is expressed as the fixed rate usually quoted on a 360 day basis. The floating rate is understood as a particular market rate—in this case the three month LIBOR underlying the Eurodollar futures contract.

midrate swap price: the cost of the swap to the swap dealer.

This price is the cost to the swap dealer of the swap, or the **midrate swap price**. When the swap intermediary makes a market in this swap, it quotes a price slightly above or below the midrate price. The difference between the midrate price and the quoted price is the swap intermediary's fee. Figure 20.13 presents a Bloomberg swap quote screen. The swap shown is at market because the present value of all cash flows is expected to be zero. In the swap example in Table 20.8, if the swap intermediary sells this swap to a customer that wants a short hedge, then the swap price might be set at 4.5%. This would give the swap intermediary a fee of 3.9 basis points (4.5% minus the swap midrate of 4.4613%).

The size of the swap intermediary's fee is determined by the risk exposure of the transaction. This is a function of (1) the counterparties' credit risk exposure; (2) the duration of the swap; and (3) the volatility of interest and exchange rates. The longer the duration of the swap or the greater volatility of interest rates, the greater the price risk of the swap. Because the swap intermediary provides a credit guarantee for each of the counterparties, their credit risk exposure directly impacts the size of the swap fee. In general, currency swaps have more credit

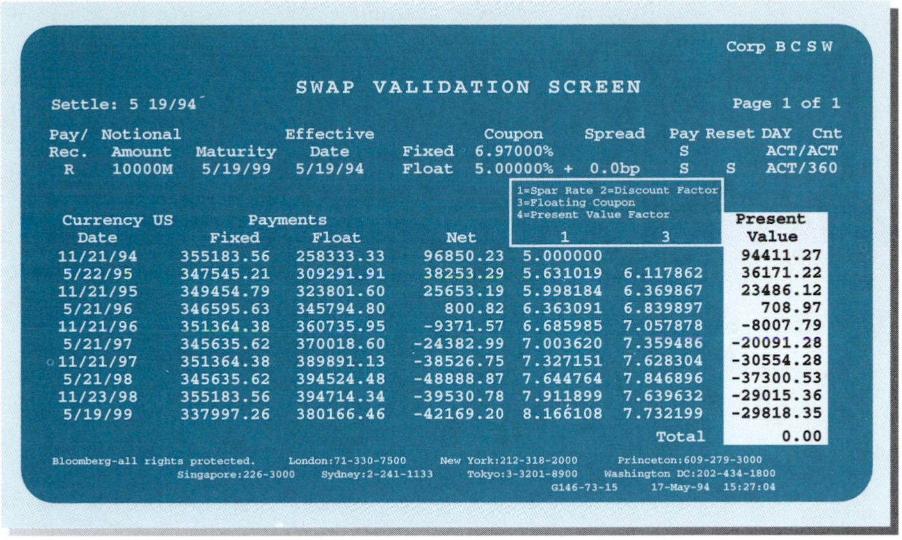

Date	Payments Fixed	Payments Float	Net	1	3	Present Value
11/21/94	355183.56	258333.33	96850.23	5.000000		94411.27
5/22/95	347545.21	309291.91	38253.29	5.631019	6.117862	36171.22
11/21/95	349454.79	323801.60	25653.19	5.998184	6.369867	23486.12
5/21/96	346595.63	345794.80	800.82	6.363091	6.839897	708.97
11/21/96	351364.38	360735.95	-9371.57	6.685985	7.057878	-8007.79
5/21/97	345635.62	370018.60	-24382.99	7.003620	7.359486	-20091.28
11/21/97	351364.38	389891.13	-38526.75	7.327151	7.628304	-30554.28
5/21/98	345635.62	394524.48	-48888.87	7.644764	7.846896	-37300.53
11/23/98	355183.56	394714.34	-39530.78	7.911899	7.639632	-29015.36
5/19/99	337997.26	380166.46	-42169.20	8.166108	7.732199	-29818.35
					Total	0.00

Figure 20.13

risk than interest rate swaps because (a) currency swaps include principal as well as interest payments, whereas interest rate swaps do not transfer notional value; and (b) exchange rate changes impact the swap price more than interest rate changes. This is reflected in the wider bid-ask spread in the currency swap market as compared to interest rate swaps.

This difference between currency and interest rate swaps is illustrated in the Basel international capital requirements' treatment of the credit risk of swaps.[30] The Basel requirements assess three components of swap credit risk:

1. Replacement cost, which is the marked to market present value of the swap. The Basel capital requirements stipulate that only positive values are considered. Thus, if the swap is currently losing money, its replacement cost is set at zero.
2. **Potential exposure**, possible future changes in credit risk exposure, which is calculated by multiplying the swap's notional value by a risk factor that is obtained from the capital requirement for off-balance sheet items presented in Table 5.3. Current exposure tends to be more significant than add-on, potential exposure. However, both measurements represent gross credit risk exposure, rather than **net exposure**. Net exposure reduces credit risk exposure because offsetting contracts' values reduce the sum notional value at risk. Net exposure is the more appropriate measure if there are closeout clauses in the swap agreements.
3. Counterparty credit risk exposure, which as determined by the Basel standards is 0% for OECD (developed countries') central governments and central banks, 20% for FIs in OECD nations and public institutions, 50% for municipalities and consumers, and 100% for commercial and industrial firms.[31]

potential exposure: possible future changes in credit risk exposure.

net exposure: the measure of credit risk exposure obtained by adding offsetting contracts' values.

Although swap pricing has been illustrated using the standard case, without complications of date mismatches or hedge unavailability, the concept is the same for all swap prices. The swap intermediary estimates the cash flows expected on both legs of the swap during its entire

[30] See discussion in Chapter 5.

[31] These factors are the risk weights from the Basel capital requirements discussed in Chapter 5.

life. Applying the proper discount factors, we see that the at market swap is priced so that the present values of the two legs are equal, thereby setting the swap's net present value to zero. Indeed, the same is true of all financial innovations, no matter how complex their structure.

Checkpoint

1. What determines swap prices?
2. What is the swap bid? the swap offer? the swap curve?
3. Why is the long swap (swap bidder) implementing a short interest rate hedge? Why is the short swap (swap offer) implementing a long interest rate hedge?
4. What determines the risk of a swap?
5. Why are currency swap fees generally higher than interest rate swap fees?

Variations and Innovations

zero coupon swap: an off market swap in which one of the counterparties makes a lump–sum payment instead of periodic payments over the life of the swap.

basis swap: an interest rate swap between two floating rates indexes.

diff swap: a basis swap with one floating rate leg pegged to a domestic rate and the other leg to a foreign floating rate.

quanto swap: a basis swap with one floating rate leg and the other leg pegged to a foreign equity index, such as the Nikkei index.

The primary selling point of swaps is their versatility. A swap can be structured so that it produces a customized series of cash flows. The cash flows may be linked perfectly to an underlying cash position, so that the swap hedge creates a perfectly offsetting security. This makes the swap a popular vehicle for financial innovation. FIs have engineered swaps tied to different underlying market prices, with different maturities and with unique timing of cash flow features.

A **zero coupon swap** is an off market swap in which one of the counterparties makes a lump sum payment instead of periodic payments over the life of the swap. The credit risk of a zero coupon swap is extremely high because one counterparty makes regular payments, whereas the other defers all payments until the maturity date of the swap. A **basis swap** is an interest rate swap between two floating rate indexes. If one floating rate leg is pegged to a domestic rate and the other leg to a foreign floating rate, then the swap is called a **diff swap**. If the other leg is pegged to a foreign equity index, such as the Nikkei index, it is called a **quanto swap**. These products are swaps of spreads and are designed to eliminate basis risk if the underlying cash position and the hedge are pegged to different market interest rates. A basis swap is particularly useful for FIs that lend at rates pegged to the prime rate but obtain their funding from sources pegged to LIBOR. The basis swap can be used to hedge the risk that the rates will not fluctuate in lockstep with one another. Although diff swaps were innovated as recently as 1991, their notional principal amount, as of 1995, was $50 billion.[32] *Timely Topics 20.3: A Swap Innovation* examines another such innovation in the area of insurance.

TIMELY TOPICS 20.3

A SWAP INNOVATION

- -

The New York Insurance Department said yesterday that it had approved the creation of an exchange that would allow insurance companies to reduce their exposure to huge losses by swapping blocks of policies in different parts of the country.

If the exchange, called the Catastrophe Risk Exchange, is accepted by insurance companies, it could solve the biggest problem facing many property insurers: how to protect against huge losses that could arise if a severe hurricane or earthquake hit a heavily developed area.

---

[32] Mahoney (1995), p. 9.

Using the exchange, a company with too much exposure to loss from a hurricane in southern Florida, for example, might arrange to swap some of its business with another company that was overly exposed to loss from a Los Angeles earthquake. Or a company with too much risk from insuring oil rigs might swap with another company with too much exposure to aircraft damage.

The individuals or businesses whose policies might be swapped would not be affected by the change, since the original company would still control the policies and would be responsible for paying claims. . . . [The Exchange] will operate over electronic mail with no central trading floor. . . .

Insurance companies' vulnerability to major catastrophes was highlighted by the more than $28 billion of combined losses from Hurricane Andrew in 1992 and the Northridge, California earthquake. . . . Reinsurance companies, which sell policies to insurers, are too expensive for some companies and are not large enough to provide all the coverage needed by some large companies. And state regulators will not allow insurers to simply pull up stakes and abandon risky areas.

The problem has led some Wall Street houses like Salomon Brothers and JP Morgan to develop securities where outside investors might share the risk of major catastrophes with insurance companies. In another approach, the Chicago Board of Options recently announced changes to its catastrophe futures and options contracts to make them more attractive to insurance companies and other investors.

Although insurance companies could swap blocks of insurance policies without an exchange, those attempts have generally failed.

Source: M. Quint, "New York Lets Insurers Swap Huge Risks," *New York Times*, July 26, 1995, p. D2.

---

interest amortizing rate swap: a fixed-for-floating interest rate swap with a condition that the notional principal declines over the life of the swap if short term interest rates fluctuate according to a predetermined schedule.

knock-out swap: a swap with an embedded knock-out option such that the swap is canceled if prices fall below a prespecified level.

A swap that serves as a useful hedging vehicle for collateralized mortgage obligations (see Chapter 21) is the **interest amortizing rate swap**, which is a fixed-for-floating interest rate swap with a twist. The twist is that the notional principal declines over the life of the swap if short term interest rates fluctuate according to a predetermined schedule. That is, if short term floating rates (say, three month LIBOR) decrease, then the rate of amortization of principal increases. This has the impact of canceling, or calling, the swap, if interest rates fall below a certain level. A related innovation is the **knock-out swap**, which has an embedded knock-out option such that the swap is canceled if prices fall below a prespecified level. These innovations help adjust the swap's cash flow profile. For the interest amortizing swap, the long swap position (fixed rate payor) is less at risk than for a standard interest rate swap, which may lose substantial amounts when interest rates decline. The downside of adding special features to the swap in order to customize its cash flows is the loss of liquidity. Only a limited number of dealers have the market depth to participate in transactions involving nonstandard swaps.

Structured Notes

The versatility of swaps makes them ideal for financial engineering. They can be used as building blocks in designing a stream of cash flows with the desired risk characteristics. The initiative for the design of the customized security may come from either the Funds Deficit or Funds Surplus Unit—that is, from either the borrower or the lender.

A popular form of customized security is the structured note, which as noted in chapter 16, is a debt issue combined with a swap. The first example in this chapter, that of the deal between RocknRoll (RR) and RockSteady, illustrates a structured note, since the swap and the debt were issued simultaneously. Indeed, for a structured note transaction, the swap is part of the terms of the initial transaction. Without the swap portion, the deal would not be possible.[33] Banks and thrift institutions used structured notes to improve the yield on their CDs, so as to increase their liability funding. However, in July 1994 the U.S. Comptroller of the Currency issued an advisory letter (number 94-2) stating that some types of structured notes are inappropriate for national banks.[34]

FIs respond to market conditions and design securities for specific customers. Often the structured note transaction is designed to achieve the goals of the Funds Surplus Unit (the investor) as opposed to those of the borrower. The investor presents a desirable set of cash flow characteristics to the FI, which customizes a security using debt and swaps. During the early 1990s, when interest rates were declining, many structured notes were issued with inverse floaters. Recall from Chapter 15 that an inverse floater is a floating rate debt issue where the coupon payment declines as interest rates increase. An inverse floater is a structured note because it is typically engineered using a combination of a fixed rate note and a swap. For example, an inverse floater, paying a coupon rate equal to 12% minus LIBOR p.a., for example, can be constructed by combining a 7% fixed rate note with a swap of LIBOR for 5%. Figure 20.14 shows the cash flows. The note issuer sells a three year note with a fixed rate annual coupon of 7% p.a. Simultaneously, the issuer buys an interest rate swap of LIBOR for 5% fixed. That is, the issuer agrees to pay 5% p.a. in exchange for the receipt of the payment of LIBOR. The total interest costs to the note issuer are 12% (= 7% plus 5%) minus LIBOR. Thus, the coupon payments decline as LIBOR increases. If LIBOR is 4%, the coupon payment is 8%, whereas if LIBOR is 10%, the coupon is 2% p.a.

Checkpoint

1. Why are swaps particularly useful in financial engineering?
2. What is a basis swap? How could it be used?
3. What is a zero coupon swap? What is its risk exposure?
4. What is a structured note? How does it combine the cash market and the derivatives market to create a unique set of risk/reward characteristics?

Structured note

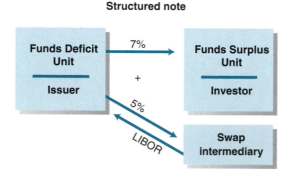

Figure 20.14

---

[33] Structured notes can also be constructed by combining debt issues with caps or floors.

[34] See Betzold and Berg (1994) for a case study of a structured note, using caps, that was a bad deal.

Summary

Swaps are agreements between two counterparties to exchange a series of cash flows over an extended period of time. Swaps can be viewed as a string of forward contracts, where on each payment date, called the reset date, a specified payment, tied to some underlying market price, is made. The first swaps arose out of the desire to exploit the arbitrage opportunities available in mispricing anomalies between financial markets. The first swaps typically were initiated across country boundaries to take advantage of capital price inefficiencies between national financial markets. The role of the swap intermediary, a FI that makes a market in swaps, was crucial given the international nature of the swap. The swap intermediary must have international networks of potential clients and information about their financing desires, as well as financial market expertise, so as to customize an exchange of cash flows that is mutually beneficial to both counterparties. Even relatively standard swaps require a great deal of customization by the swap intermediary.

As the swap market matured, the pricing anomalies that motivated the earliest swaps all but disappeared. However, the market continued to grow exponentially because of its versatility as a hedging vehicle. Interest rate swaps are fixed-for-floating rate exchanges that can be used to hedge interest rate risk exposure. The buyer (seller) of the interest rate swap agrees to pay fixed (floating) rate payments in exchange for the receipt of floating (fixed) rate payments. Thus, the long (short) swap position can be viewed as a short (long) hedge, since it benefits when interest rates increase (decrease).

Currency swaps are exchanges of payments that are denominated in different currencies. Since all swaps are priced at expected values using forward prices, the currency swap holder will benefit if the currency bought appreciates in value against the currency sold. Currency swaps can be combined with interest rate swaps to create a fixed-for-floating currency swap. Market risk exposure can be hedged using an equity swap.

Swaps are priced by swap dealers using forward rates obtained either from market prices (in futures or FRA markets) or by decomposing spot yield curves using bootstrapping methods (seen in earlier applications to Treasury security stripping). The at market swap is priced so that the present values of all cash flows on the two legs of the swap are equal. The swap dealer will then add on a premium for the swap's credit risk and price risk exposure. This premium is the swap intermediary's fee. The swap fee is determined by the credit risk of the counterparties, the duration of the swap, and the volatility of underlying market prices.

References

Abken, P. A. "Over-the-Counter Financial Derivatives: Risky Business?" Federal Reserve Bank of Atlanta *Economic Review* (March–April 1994): 1–22.

Alworth, J. S. *The Valuation of U.S. Dollar Interest Rate Swaps*. BIS Economic Papers, No. 35, January 1993.

Arak, M., A. Estrella, L. Goodman, and A. Silver. "Interest Rate Swaps: An Alternative Explanation." *Financial Management* (Summer 1988): 12–18.

Bansal, V. K., J. L. Bicksler, A. H. Chen, and J. F. Marshall. "The Gains from Interest Rate Swaps: Fact or Fancy?" *Journal of Applied Corporate Finance*, 1993.

Beckstrom, R. "The Development of the Swap Market." In Boris Antl, ed., *Swap Finance* London: Euromoney Publications, 1986.

Betzold, N., and R. Berg. "Conservative's Structured Notes Can Hurt You." *ABA Banking Journal* (September 1994): 75–78.

Dattatreya, R. E., R. E. S. Venkatesh, and V. E. Venkatesh. *Interest Rate and Currency Swaps*. Chicago: Probus Publishing, 1994.

Fernald, J. "The Pricing and Hedging of Index Amortizing Rate Swaps." Federal Reserve Bank of New York. *Quarterly Review* (Winter 1994): 71–74.

Galaif, L. "Index Amortizing Rate Swaps." Federal Reserve Bank of New York *Quarterly Review* (Winter 1994): 63–70.

Hendricks, D. "Netting Agreements and the Credit Exposures of OTC Derivatives Portfolios." Federal Reserve Bank of New York. *Quarterly Review* (Spring 1994): 7–18.

Kochan, N. "Better the Devil You Know." *Euromoney* (September 1995): 480–486.

Loeys, J. G. "Interest Rate Swaps: A New Tool for Managing Risk." *Business Review* (May–June 1985): 17–25.

Mahoney, J. M. "Correlation Products and Risk Management Issues." Federal Reserve Bank of New York *Economic Policy Review* (October 1995): 7–20.

Marshall, J. F., and K. R. Kapner. *Understanding Swaps.* New York: John Wiley & Sons, 1993.

Mason, S. P., R. C. Merton, A. F. Perold, and P. Tufano. *Cases in Financial Engineering: Applied Studies of Financial Innovation.* Englewood Cliffs N.J.: Prentice Hall, 1995.

Remolona, E. M. "The Recent Growth of Financial Derivative Markets." Federal Reserve Bank of New York *Quarterly Review* (Winter 1993): 28–43.

Wall, L. D. "Interest Rate Swaps in an Agency Theoretic Model with Uncertain Interest Rates." *Journal of Banking and Finance* 13 (1989): 261–270.

Wall, L. D., and J. J. Pringle. "Alternative Explanations of Interest Rate Swaps: A Theoretical and Empirical Analysis." *Financial Management* (Summer 1989): 59–73.

➤ Questions

1. Clear the swap in Table 20.1 and Figure 20.1 assuming that LIBOR is 11%, 13%, 15%, 14%, and 12% at the end of each of the next five years, respectively.

2. Suppose that an American Company (known as AC) can borrow in the United States in the fixed rate market at an annual coupon rate of 11% p.a. for seven year maturity. The up-front borrowing costs are 1.5%. AC can also borrow in Japan at a cost of 6% p.a. with up-front costs of 5%.

   A Japanese Company (known as JC) can borrow in the United States at a rate of 9.25% p.a. for seven year debt, with an up-front charge of 1.5% and in Japan at a cost of 6.5% p.a. with an up-front charge of 5%. Calculate

   a. The all-in-cost of all sources of debt financing.

   b. The potential swap gains.

   c. The range of possible terms of the currency swap if the swap intermediary fee of 48 basis points is reallocated between AC and JC.

   d. AC's and JC's swap gains if the terms of the swap are a U.S. dollar-denominated swap loan for 9.95% p.a. and a Japanese yen-denominated swap loan for 7.01% p.a.

   e. AC's, JC's, and the intermediary's cash flows for the swap in part (d) if the notional principal is JY100 million and US$1 million and the loans' values are JY95 million and US$985,000, respectively.

3. Consider the following standard interest rate swap. Each of two companies decides to issue $100 million in two year debt instruments on the same date. One company, RocknRoll (RR), is quoted market rate of 12.5% p.a. (paid annually) for fixed rate debt and LIBOR plus 150 basis points (paid annually) for floating rate debt. RockSteady (RS) is a less risky company and can issue the notes at a fixed rate of 11% p.a. or a floating rate of LIBOR plus 75 basis points.

   a. Is there any possibility of constructing an interest rate swap? Why or why not?

   b. What are the total possible swap gains?

   c. How does each firm exploit its comparative advantage in the cash market?

   d. Suppose that RS has a negative duration gap and RR has a positive duration gap. What is the impact of the positions undertaken in part (c) on each firm's interest rate risk exposure?

   e. Suppose that the swap intermediary's fee is 5 basis points. How can RR and RS enter into an interest rate swap that evenly splits the remaining gains?

   f. Calculate the end of year cash flows if LIBOR is expected to be 10% on the first coupon payment date and 12% on the second coupon payment date.

g. How does the swap perform as an interest rate risk hedge? Express the swap as portfolios of forward contracts from the perspectives of both RS and RR.

h. Using a 7% discount factor, what is the present value of the swap, assuming the interest rate scenario in part (f). How would this affect the pricing of the swap?

4. Using the scenario in question 3, solve for the fixed rate in the interest rate swap such that the present value of the swap is zero; that is, there is no up-front fee. (*Hint*: Calculate the price of the "IMM Index-like forward" required to make the present value of all cash flows to RS equal to zero.)

a. What are each firm's swap gains? Will the swap be undertaken by both firms? Why or why not?

b. Calculate the end of year cash flows on the swap if it takes place.

5. Find the breakeven fixed rate on the interest rate swap in question 4 using a discount factor of 30% p.a.

a. What are each firm's swap gains? Will the swap be undertaken by both firms? Why or why not?

b. Calculate the end of year cash flows on the swap, if the swap takes place.

6. Price, as of May 3, 1998, the following 18 month interest rate swap with a notional value of $100 million, priced at LIBOR. (Be sure to include the expected cash flows on the swap on each reset date.):

Reset Date	Day Count	EuroFutures Price	Convexity Adjustment
May 3, 1998		97.05	0
June 18, 1998	46	96.99	0
Sept. 17, 1998	91	96.84	0
Dec. 31, 1998	91	96.70	1
March 18, 1999	91	96.55	1
June 17, 1999	91	96.45	1
Sept. 16, 1999	91	96.22	1

7. Consider the following information on $100 million face value 3 year, annual coupon cash market debt for two companies, RR and RS.

Co.	Fixed rate	Floating rate	Swap fee
RR	10.5%	LIBOR + 100	5 bp
RS	10%	LIBOR + 75	

a. Is there any possibility of constructing an interest rate swap? Why or why not?

b. What are the total possible swap gains?

c. How does each firm exploit its comparative advantage in the cash market?

d. What are the terms of the swap if RR and RS split the swap gains evenly?

e. Calculate the swap cash flows, using the swap terms in part (d), if LIBOR is 8%, 10%, and 12% p.a. at the end of each of the next three years.

f. Describe the forward contracts that offer the same interest rate hedge as the swap in part (d).

g. If RR obtains all of the gains to the swap, what are the swap terms? Will the swap be undertaken?

h. Answer parts (e) and (f) for the swap in part (g).

i. If RS obtains all of the gains to the swap, what are the swap terms? Will the swap be undertaken?

j. Answer parts (e) and (f) for the swap in part (i).

8. Consider the following information on $100 million face value 3 year, annual coupon cash market debt for two companies, RR and RS:

Co.	Fixed rate	Floating rate	Swap fee
RR	10.5%	LIBOR + 100	10 bp
RS	10%	LIBOR	

a. Is there any possibility of constructing an interest rate swap? Why or why not?

b. What are the total possible swap gains?

c. How does each firm exploit its comparative advantage in the cash market?

d. What are the terms of the swap if RR and RS split the swap gains evenly?

e. Calculate the swap cash flows, using the swap terms in part (d), if LIBOR is 8%, 10%, and 12% p.a. at the end of each of the next three years.

f. Describe the forward contracts that offer the same interest rate hedge as the swap in part (d).

g. If RR obtains all of the gains to the swap, what are the swap terms? Will the swap be undertaken?

h. Answer parts (e) and (f) for the swap in part (g).

i. If RS obtains all of the gains to the swap, what are the swap terms? Will the swap be undertaken?

j. Answer parts (e) and (f) for the swap in part (i).

9. For two companies, AR and GS, use the following prices in the cash debt markets to construct a fixed-for-floating currency swap.

Cash Market 2 Year Debt	AR	GS	Differential Rate (AR – GS)
Fixed rate, DM debt	18%p.a.	17.5%p.a.	+.5%
Floating rate, DM debt	LIBOR + 4%	LIBOR + 2%	+2%
Fixed rate, US$ debt	15%	13.5%	+1.5%
Floating rate, US$ debt	LIBOR + 3%	LIBOR%	+3%

a. Describe each company's comparative advantage in the cash market.

b. If AR prefers issuing fixed rate, U.S. dollar-denominated debt and GS prefers issuing floating rate DM-denominated debt, how can a swap be constructed? Assume that the current DM-dollar exchange rate is US$.50 and that the principal is DM100 million.

c. In the swap, AR pays US dollar LIBOR and receives 17% on a fixed rate DM loan and GS pays 17.2% on a fixed rate DM loan and receives US dollar LIBOR. What is the swap intermediary's fee? What are each party's gains for the swap?

d. What are the swap cash flows if LIBOR is 17% at the end of the first year and 18% at the end of the second year? (Assume that principal *are* exchanged.)

e. Calculate the net swap cash flows if the DM-dollar exchange rates are $0.45 at the end of the first year and $0.55 at the end of the second year.

10. Construct forwards hedges to replicate the swaps in questions 2(d) and 9.

CHAPTER 21

MORTGAGE-BACKED SECURITIES

"The Stately Homes of England,
How beautiful they stand...
Though the fact that they have to be rebuilt
And frequently mortgaged to the hilt..."
—*The Stately Homes of England* (1938 song). *Oxford Dictionary of Quotations* (1979), 244:21.

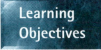

Learning Objectives

- To understand a financial instrument that contains elements of debt and derivatives.

- To examine how mortgage-backed securities (MBSs) and collateralized mortgage obligations (CMOs) are priced.

- To be able to analyze the risk characteristics of the securities and define new risk measurements.

- To understand methods of hedging MBS and CMO risk exposure.

➤ Introduction

It is particularly fitting that we cover mortgage-backed securities (MBSs) in the last chapter of this book. Nowhere are the concepts of financial innovation better summarized and illustrated. We have seen how successful innovation by FIs led to the creation of Federal Funds, repos, commercial paper, loan commitments, medium term notes, strips of government securities, equity and equity-like securities, forward rate agreements (FRAs), futures, options, and swaps. Their success in all of these markets simply primed the FIs for the financial fight of their lives.

During the 1970s, banks and other FIs experienced a series of shocks that threatened their very existence. Increases in interest rate and exchange rate volatility made all financial market participants more concerned about their risk exposure. FIs were squeezed both on the asset side and on the liability side. Funds Deficit Units demanded more cost effective, lower yielding financial assets, whereas Funds Surplus Units, on the FIs' liability side, demanded higher returns. At first, FIs responded to the pressure by reducing their capital levels, thereby making assets work harder, through the magic of leverage, in order to earn a profit. But the FIs soon found that they too were exposed to greater risk. Public FIs, observing the dangerous mix of higher risk and lower capital, intervened to impose higher capital standards.

The FIs were caught in a vise. Hemmed in by strict capital requirements, by hungry FSUs, and by hard-bargaining FDUs, the FIs were forced by their financial distress to become true mothers of invention. The only way they could survive was to earn additional income without simultaneously booking assets. Securitization was the rabbit that the FIs pulled out of the hat. As described in Chapter 2, securitization is the creation of marketable financial securities out of packages of individually nonmarketable assets. In this way, firms can pledge the cash flows on their assets to directly obtain financing. Securitization enabled FIs to originate financial assets such as mortgage loans, thereby earning fee income, without keeping those assets on their balance sheets, where they would have to be financed with costly liabilities and nonexistent capital. Securitized loans are called pass-through securities because the cash flows on the underlying pool of loans are passed through to the ultimate FSU investor on a pro rata basis, after deduction of fees. **Mortgage-backed securities (MBSs)** are pass-throughs based on underlying pools of mortgage loans.

Securitization proved to be a feasible solution to the squeeze play threat to the FIs' existence. FIs had developed large distribution networks so that they were able to sell the newly created pass-throughs. Advances in information technology gave the FIs techniques to price the new securities. A newly acquired history of successful financial innovation encouraged the FIs to experiment with different structural forms. The success of the securitization experiment led the SEC to comment in 1992 that asset securitization was becoming "one of the dominant means of capital formation in the United States."[1] In 1992 the volume of new MBSs issued surpassed $550 billion. In the United States, nearly half of all U.S. home mortgages are funded by the issuance of MBSs. The total value of MBSs outstanding as of June 1994 was $1.2 trillion, compared with $1.3 trillion in mortgage loans held on FIs' books. Figure 21.1 shows

mortgage–backed securities (MBSs):
pass-throughs based on underlying pools of mortgage loans.

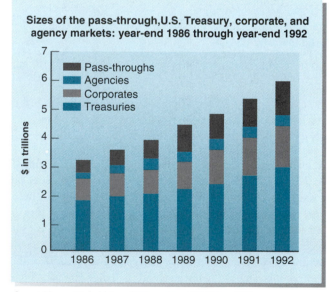

Sizes of the pass-through, U.S. Treasury, corporate, and agency markets: year-end 1986 through year-end 1992

Legend:
- Pass-throughs
- Agencies
- Corporates
- Treasuries

Y-axis: $ in trillions

X-axis: 1986 1987 1988 1989 1990 1991 1992

Source: Hayre, Mohebbi, and Zimmerman (1995), p. 507.

Figure 21.1

---

[1] Investment Company Act Release No. 19105 [1992 Transfer Binder] Fed. Sec. L. Rep. (CCH) paragraph 85,062, at 83,500 (November 19, 1992).

the growth of pass-throughs in both absolute and relative terms during the years 1986–1992. As Schwarcz (1994) writes, "securitization is an alchemy that really works."[2]

➤ ## Mortgage-Backed and Other Asset-Backed Securities

mortgages: loans secured by real estate as collateral.

It was not accidental that the first asset-backed securities were based on home mortgages. Residential **mortgages** (loans secured by real estate as collateral) had all of the necessary prerequisites for successful securitization. There were ample supplies of mortgages to provide the assets on which to base the pass-through securities. By definition, mortgages are diversified by lender, borrower, and geographic region. Finally, mortgages are easy to evaluate because their cash flows are standardized and highly predictable.

Real Estate Mortgage Investment Conduits (REMICs): pass-through tax entities that pool mortgages and issue ownership interests to multiple classes of investors, primarily in the form of MBSs.

The United States government has long encouraged home ownership by creating subsidies for mortgage lenders. Indeed, thrifts were granted preferred access to a low-cost pool of deposits in exchange for their dedication to financing home mortgages. Tax treatment is also favorable to home mortgage lending. The Tax Law of 1986 provided for **Real Estate Mortgage Investment Conduits (REMICs)**, which are pass-through tax entities that pool mortgages and issue ownership interests to multiple classes of investors, primarily in the form of MBSs. If structured properly, REMICs are not taxable, thereby eliminating the double taxation of the cash flow from pass-through pools.

To improve the liquidity in the secondary mortgage market, in 1938 the federal government created the Federal National Mortgage Association (FNMA, or Fannie Mae) to buy up federally insured mortgages. In 1968 Fannie Mae was split into FNMA and the Government National Mortgage Association (GNMA or Ginnie Mae), and in 1970 the Federal Home Loan Mortgage Corporation (FHLMC or Freddie Mac) was created. Currently, GNMA is a federally related FI, whereas FNMA and FHLMC are federally sponsored agencies.[3] These agencies encouraged thrifts and other mortgage originators to increase the availability of home mortgages by offering the FIs a liquid secondary market. Thus, the original focus of these FIs was to service FIs, which, in turn, serviced the general public.

collateralized mortgage obligations (CMOs): mortgage pass-throughs that divide the pool of underlying mortgages into different maturity classes with different risk/return characteristics.

In 1970 this focus was shifted to include broader financial markets with GNMA's public offering of the first pass-throughs. The market grew steadily with the issuance of pass-throughs by FNMA, FHLMC, and private issuers, thereby broadening the MBS market from FIs to general investors. But the market did not truly take off until 1983 when Freddie Mac issued $1 billion in **collateralized mortgage obligations (CMOs)**, and the market entered a new wave of innovation. CMOs are mortgage pass-throughs that divide the pool of underlying mortgages into different maturity classes, called **tranches**,[4] with different risk/return characteristics.

tranches: different maturity classes of a CMO.

tilt problem: a condition in which the real cost of a mortgage is highest during the early years of the mortgage.

The most familiar type of mortgage (and the one that is used in the examples in this chapter) is the fixed rate, level payment mortgage. In these mortgages, the borrower repays the loan in equal installments over a specified time until maturity. These mortgages suffer from a **tilt problem**. That is, the real cost of the mortgage is highest in its earliest years, when both family income and the general price level tend to be at their lowest during the life of the mortgage. To alleviate the tilt problem, the **graduated payment mortgage (GPM)** was introduced to allow monthly mortgage payments to increase gradually over the life of the mortgage, when presumably the borrower would be better able to afford to pay higher nominal amounts. GPMs suffer from negative amortization, since in the early years of the mortgage, the payments are not

graduated payment mortgage (GPM): a fixed rate mortgage that allows monthly mortgage payments to increase gradually over the life of the mortgage.

---

[2] Schwarcz (1994), p. 53.

[3] See Chapter 15 for a discussion of the distinction between federally related and federally sponsored agencies.

[4] The word *tranche* stems from a French word meaning "to cut."

balloon mortgage: a fixed rate mortgage that schedules a lump-sum payment of principal at the end of a predetermined period of time.

adjustable rate mortgage (ARM): a floating rate loan pegged to some reference market interest rate, such as the Federal Home Loan Bank Board Index.

price level adjusted mortgage (PLAM): constant mortgage payments for the life of the mortgage, in *real dollar* terms.

sufficient to cover the interest due. They have been largely replaced by the **balloon mortgage**, a mortgage that addresses the tilt problem by scheduling a lump-sum payment of principal at the end of a predetermined period of time, say seven years.

All of these mortgage types are fixed rate, locking in a fixed interest rate for the life of the mortgage. Another type of mortgage is the **adjustable rate mortgage (ARM)**, which is a floating rate loan pegged to some reference market interest rate. The ARM specifies the loan's reset dates as well as the formula to determine the floating rate. A commonly used formula is to set the rate on the ARM equal to the Federal Home Loan Bank Board Index of costs for thrifts plus some fixed premium (say 50 basis points).

A cross between fixed and floating rate mortgages is the **price level adjusted mortgage (PLAM).** The mortgage payments on a PLAM are constant for the life of the mortgage, in *real dollar* terms. These mortgages solve the tilt problem for the borrower, thereby increasing the affordability of the payments during the life of the mortgage. For mortgage investors and lenders, PLAMs offer an attractive inflation-proof, fixed real rate of return. This mortgage is fully amortizing, with monthly payments adjusted in each payment period by some inflation index. Although the borrower accepts inflation risk on the mortgage (mortgage payments increase as inflation increases), the house value and income levels provide a natural hedge since their values also increase when inflation increases. However, Leeds (1993) and Peek and Wilcox (1991) find that the lender's prepayment and default risks of PLAMs exceed those of conventional mortgages.

The phenomenal success of CMOs encouraged further experimentation. Table 21.1 shows the introduction of pass-throughs based on pools of loans other than mortgages. Although the volume of activity on the MBS market far exceeds that of any other categories of pass-throughs, there is considerable volume of credit card and automobile loan receivables. In 1995, 47.9% of all asset-backed securities were based on credit card receivables, whereas 18.5% were auto loans and 14% home equity loans.

The advantages of asset-backed securities (ABS) are

1. *Access to debt markets for borrowers:* Securitization enables borrowers (home buyers, credit card users, etc.) to obtain funding from financial markets that they could not access as individuals.

2. *Efficient pricing of debt:* Since asset-backed securities are constructed by combining similar quality loans into a single portfolio, the credit risk of the loans in the pool can be evaluated more accurately.

3. *Reduction of the issuer's leverage:* Since the sale of asset-backed securities is viewed as a sale of assets, the FI issuing the ABS does not show an increase in debt outstanding.

4. *Lower capital costs for the issuer:* The issuing FI does not need to hold capital against the ABS since the sale of ABSs reduces the FI's assets.

5. *Generating fee income:* The FI issuing the ABS transforms risky net interest income earned from lending (the difference between income received on fixed rate loans and the income paid on the source of funds to finance the loans, which fluctuates as the cost of funds fluctuates) into a steady stream of servicing fees.

6. *Risk reduction:* The issuing FI's risk exposure is reduced as assets are transferred off the FI's books and credit enhancements are utilized.

7. *Reduced cost of financing:* The portfolio risk diversification and liquidity benefits of the pool of assets are passed along in the form of reduced risk adjusted required rates of return paid by borrowers.

Table 21.1

Asset–Backed Securities, Excluding Mortgage–Backed Securities
Chronology by Collateral Type Through 1992

Collateral Type	Date of First Issue	Principal Amount ($m)
Computer leases	March 1985	$1,847.8
Retail auto loans	May 1985	76,363.6
Affiliate notes	July 1986	638.0
Light truck loans	July 1986	187.4
Credit card receivables	Jan. 1987	80,238.4
Standard truck loans	June 1987	478.6
Trade receivables	Sept. 1987	311.5
Automobile leases	Oct. 1987	470.0
Consumer loans	Nov. 1987	1,092.5
Boat loans	Sept. 1988	1,202.5
Manufactured housing loans	Sept. 1988	7,653.7
Equipment leases	Oct. 1988	214.6
RV loans	Dec. 1988	1,525.8
Home equity loans	Jan. 1989	24,718.0
Harley Davidson motorcycle loans[a]	July 1989	86.1
Timeshare receivables	Aug. 1989	111.5
Wholesale dealer vehicle loans	Aug. 1990	5,900.0
Wholesale dealer truck loans	Dec. 1990	300.0
Small business loans	Jan. 1992	349.8
Railroad car leases	May 1992	998.4
Prefabricated home loans	June 1992	249.9
Agricultural equipment loans	Sept. 1992	1,052.4
Total		$205,904.3

[a]Private placement transactions. Not included in total.

Source: Hudson van Eck (1995), p. 586.

8. *Increased balance sheet liquidity:* By packaging individually illiquid loans into marketable securities, the FI increases the liquidity of its assets.

Offsetting these benefits are the following costs of issuing asset-backed securities:

1. *Increased fees for services:* Issuing ABSs requires the services of many intermediaries (issuing FIs, underwriters, credit guarantors, legal counsel, etc.) not required in the underlying debt transactions.

2. *Assets marked to market upon the ABS issue:* Assets that are valued at their book value must be revalued at market value upon their sale as part of a pool of ABSs.

3. *Borrower sophistication:* If borrowers are unfamiliar with securitization, they may be unable to evaluate its applicability to their financing needs.

Those loans that are securitized are those for which the benefits exceed the costs. This is most obvious for the largest form of ABSs—the MBSs.

Checkpoint

✓

1. Describe the financial conditions leading to the innovation of MBSs.
2. Why was it so important for FIs to find a way to earn income off their balance sheets?
3. What are pass-through securities? Why are mortgages particularly well suited for pass-throughs?
4. Describe the different types of mortgages.
5. Contrast the pros and cons of issuing ABSs.

MBS Credit Risk Exposures

The cash flows on the MBS stem from the interest and principal payments on the underlying pool of mortgages. So to understand MBSs, we have to begin with mortgages. The lending FI is the **mortgage originator**, or **mortgagee**, to the borrower, the **mortgagor**. The initiating FI typically receives an up-front **origination fee** that is stated in terms of **points**, with each point representing 1% of the mortgage principal.

The FI that gathers the mortgages into a pool and issues the MBS is called a **conduit**. REMICs are examples of specially created entities that serve as mortgage conduits, as are GNMA, FNMA, and FHLMC. Mortgage-backed securities issued by GNMA, FNMA, and FHLMC constitute 98% of all of the MBSs in the market. GNMA, FNMA, and FHLMC purchase only **conforming mortgages** for their pools. Conforming mortgages are mortgages that meet certain underwriting standards with respect to (1) a maximum acceptable ratio of monthly mortgage payment to mortgagor's income; (2) a maximum acceptable mortgage loan to property value ratio; and (3) a maximum loan amount.

GNMA pass-throughs are guaranteed directly by the federal government against default. FNMA and FHLMC pass-throughs carry federal agency guarantees only, although default is highly unlikely. Both GNMA and FNMA guarantee all interest and principal when due, whereas FHLMC guarantees the timely payment of interest but allows a delay of up to one year for principal payments, in the event of borrower default.

The fixed rate, level payment mortgage is repaid in equal monthly installments consisting of interest and principal. It is 100% amortizing because all principal is repaid during the course of the monthly payments. Using standard present value techniques from Chapter 7 to value fixed rate mortgage payments, we obtain

$$P = \sum_{s=1}^{T} \frac{C_t}{\left(1 + \frac{y}{n}\right)^s}$$

where C_t = the tth monthly mortgage payment; P = the original mortgage balance; T = the number of monthly mortgage payments; $\frac{y}{n}$ = the monthly mortgage rate, where n = 12. For example, if y = 10% p.a., T = 30 years, and P = \$250,000, then the monthly mortgage payment, C_t, is

$$\$250,000 = \sum_{s=1}^{360} \frac{C_t}{\left(1 + \frac{.10}{12}\right)^s}$$

such that C_t = \$2,193.93.

Although each monthly mortgage payment is equal during the life of the mortgage, the proportion of interest and principal repaid each month varies. Table 21.2a shows an amortization schedule for the fully amortizing, fixed rate mortgage in the previous example. The monthly interest rate is $\frac{10\%}{12}$ = .833%. Each monthly mortgage payment can be divided into two component parts. The first part, \$2,083.33, is the interest payment, calculated as $\frac{.10}{12}(\$250,000)$ for the first month's payment. The second component of each payment is the principal payment, defined to be the remainder of the monthly mortgage payment after the interest is paid. Thus, the first month's principal payment is \$2,193.93 − \$2,083.33 = \$110.60. This leaves a balance on the mortgage, after the first month, of \$249,889.40, or \$250,000 − \$110.60.

The second month's interest portion of the mortgage payment is calculated on the basis of the remaining balance on the mortgage as of the end of the first month. Thus, the interest portion is \$2,082.41, or $\frac{.10}{12}(\$249,889.40)$, and the principal repaid is \$111.52, or \$2,193.93 − \$2,082.41. That leaves a mortgage balance as of the end of the second month of \$249,889.40 −

---

mortgage originator: the lending FI that initiates the mortgage loan.

mortgagee: holder of the mortgage, that is, the lender.

mortgagor: the mortgage borrower.

origination fee: up-front fee paid to mortgage originator.

point: 1% of the mortgage principal.

conduit: the FI that gathers the mortgages into a pool and issues the MBS.

conforming mortgages: mortgages that meet the underwriting standards set by GNMA, FNMA, and FHLMC.

**Table
21.2a**

Amortization Schedule for a Fixed Rate, Level Payment Mortgage

Month	Beginning Balance	Monthly Payment	Monthly Interest	Principal Repayment	Ending Balance
1	$250,000	$2,193.93	$2,083.33	$110.60	$249,889.40
2	249,889.40	2,193.93	2,082.41	111.52	249,777.88
3	249,777.88	2,193.93	2,081.48	112.45	249,665.43
4	249,665.43	2,193.93	2,080.55	113.38	249,552.05
5	249,552.05	2,193.93	2,079.60	114.33	249,437.72
6	249,437.72	2,193.93	2,078.65	115.28	249,322.44
7	249,322.44	2,193.93	2,077.69	116.24	249,206.20
8	249,206.20	2,193.93	2,076.72	117.21	249,088.99
9	249,088.99	2,193.93	2,075.74	118.19	249,970.80
10	248,970.80	2,193.93	2,074.76	119.17	248,851.63
11	248,851.63	2,193.93	2,073.76	120.17	248,731.46
12	248,731.46	2,193.93	2,072.76	121.17	248,610.29
...					
350	22,966.69	2,193.93	191.39	2,002.54	20,964.14
351	20,964.14	2,193.93	174.70	2,019.23	18,944.92
352	18,944.92	2,193.93	157.87	2,036.06	16,908.86
353	16,908.86	2,193.93	140.91	2,053.02	14,855.84
354	14,855.84	2,193.93	123.80	2,070.13	12,785.71
355	12,785.71	2,193.93	106.55	2,087.38	10,698.32
356	10,698.32	2,193.93	89.15	2,104.78	8,593.55
357	8,593.55	2,193.93	71.61	2,122.32	6,471.23
358	6,471.23	2,193.93	53.93	2,140.00	4,331.23
359	4,331.23	2,193.93	36.09	2,157.84	2,173.39
360	2,173.39	2,173.39[a]	18.11	2,173.39	0

[a]Difference due to rounding. The mortgage value is $250,000, the mortgage rate 10% p.a. paid monthly, and the term is 30 years (360 months).

$111.52 = $249,777.88, and so on for the entire 360 months of the life of the mortgage. As the mortgage continues, the interest payments get progressively smaller and the principal repayments get larger.

Suppose that 100 of these mortgages are assembled into a pool to back a mortgage pass-through. In practice, not all of the mortgages in the pool need be identical as in this example. The face value of the mortgages in the pool totals $25 million. The originating banks receive origination fees, and, if there are any credit enhancements, there will be a premium for the guarantee. Credit enhancements may take the form of third party guarantees, letters of credit, mortgage pool insurance, reserve funds, and other types of collateral. The greater the protection against credit risk, the higher the credit enhancement fee.

Assume that the originating fee is 44 basis points and the premium for the credit guarantee is 6 basis points, for a total monthly servicing fee of 50 basis points. The cash flows on the underlying mortgages are unchanged. But now instead of the entire $2,193.93 monthly payment from each mortgage paid to the holders of the MBS (for a total of $219,393 = 100 × $2,193.93, for the $25 million MBS), a 50 basis point servicing fee must be deducted. Since the servicing fee is taken out before the cash flows are distributed to the MBS investors, the monthly yield on the pass-through securities is $\frac{.10 - .0050}{12}$ = .7917%. If the mortgages in the pool are not identical, then the MBS coupon is the **weighted average coupon (WAC)** of all coupons in the pool, where each mortgage's payment is weighted by its value in the pool.

Table 21.2b shows the cash flow for the MBS with a 50 basis point servicing fee. The servicing fee is calculated by multiplying the beginning mortgage balance each month by

weighted average coupon (WAC): the MBS coupon payment, where each mortgage's payment is weighted by its value in the pool.

Amortization Schedule for a Fixed Rate MBS with a Servicing Fee, No Prepayment

Month	Beginning Balance	Monthly Payment	Monthly Interest	Servicing Fee	Principal Repayment	Ending Balance
1	$250,000	$2,193.93	$1,979.17	$104.17	$110.59	$249,889.40
2	249,889.40	2,193.93	1,978.29	104.12	111.52	249,777.88
3	249,777.88	2,193.93	1,977.41	104.07	112.45	249,665.43
4	249,665.43	2,193.93	1,976.52	104.03	113.38	249,552.05
5	249,552.05	2,193.93	1,975.62	103.98	114.33	249,437.72
6	249,437.72	2,193.93	1,974.72	103.93	115.28	249,322.44
7	249,322.44	2,193.93	1,973.80	103.88	116.24	249,206.20
8	249,206.20	2,193.93	1,972.88	103.84	117.21	249,088.99
9	249,088.99	2,193.93	1,971.95	103.79	118.19	249,970.80
10	248,970.80	2,193.93	1,971.02	103.74	119.17	248,851.63
11	248,851.63	2,193.93	1,970.08	103.69	120.17	248,731.46
12	248,731.46	2,193.93	1,969.12	103.64	121.17	248,610.29
...						
350	22,966.69	2,193.93	181.82	9.57	2,002.54	20,964.14
351	20,964.14	2,193.93	165.96	8.73	2,019.23	18,944.92
352	18,944.92	2,193.93	149.98	7.89	2,036.06	16,908.86
353	16,908.86	2,193.93	133.86	7.05	2,053.02	14,855.84
354	14,855.84	2,193.93	117.61	6.19	2,070.13	12,785.71
355	12,785.71	2,193.93	101.22	5.33	2,087.38	10,698.32
356	10,698.32	2,193.93	84.69	4.46	2,104.78	8,593.55
357	8,593.55	2,193.93	68.03	3.58	2,122.32	6,471.23
358	6,471.23	2,193.93	51.23	2.70	2,140.00	4,331.23
359	4,331.23	2,193.93	34.29	1.80	2,157.84	2,173.39
360	2,173.39	2,173.39[a]	17.20	0.91	2,173.39	0

[a]Difference due to rounding. The mortgage value is $250,000, the mortgage rate is 10% p.a. paid monthly, the term is 30 years (360 months), and the servicing fee is 50 basis points per month.

$\frac{.0050}{12}$ = .0417%. The first month's servicing fee, for example, is $\frac{.0050}{12}$($250,000) = $104.17, and so on for the entire 360 months of the mortgage.

There is a delay between the date the mortgage payments are received by the servicing FIs and the pass-throughs' payment date. For GNMAs (FNMAs), each month's interest is paid on the fifteenth (twenty-fifth) of the next month. For FHLMC, the interest is paid on the fifteenth of the month after. Thus, May's mortgage payments are paid on June 15 for GNMAs, on June 25 for FNMAs, and on July 15 for FHLMCs. These payment delays are built into the pricing of each type of MBS.

Checkpoint

1. Do MBSs have credit risk? How does this risk differ across MBSs?

2. What is the role of the mortgagor? the mortgage originator? the mortgage conduit?

3. What determines the interest and principal portions in each fixed rate, level mortgage payment? What happens to the relative size of these components as the mortgage ages?

MBS Interest Rate and Prepayment Risk Exposures

The MBS cash flows shown in Table 21.2b are based on the assumption that all the 30 year mortgages in the pool make their regular payments each month for the entire 360 months. In reality, this rarely happens. If any of the mortgagors in the pool default, then the cash flows are altered. However, if there are credit enhancements, then these defaults may not affect the holder of the MBS.

prepayment risk: the likelihood that mortgagors will decide to pay the balances on their mortgages before their maturity dates, thereby terminating the mortgages.

Far more important from the standpoint of the pass-through investor is **prepayment risk**. Prepayment risk is the likelihood that mortgagors will decide to pay the balances on their mortgages before their maturity dates, thereby terminating the mortgages. Prepayment is essentially a call option on the mortgage, held by the mortgagor. The borrower will exercise the prepayment call option for one of two reasons:

1. *Lifestyle reasons:* For example, one may relocate to a new home because of a new job or a step up in home quality. Both require that the old mortgage be terminated upon the sale of the home. Lifestyle reasons for mortgage prepayment explain the seasonality in mortgage payments, as homes tend to turn over with greater frequency in the spring and summer than in the fall and winter. Moreover, the general level of economic activity affects prepayments because of worker migration in response to employment opportunities.

2. *Financial reasons:* Interest rate decreases make it worthwhile for mortgagors to refinance their mortgages at lower mortgage rates. The critical factor is the spread between the mortgage rate and prevailing mortgage rates. If the mortgage rate is high enough above prevailing mortgage rates to cover origination fees, legal expenses, and all other costs of initiating a mortgage, then the mortgagor refinances the mortgage by prepaying the higher priced mortgage in full.

Prepayment risk is a function of interest rates as well as the age of the mortgage. Prepayments are costly for MBS investors because they receive lump-sum distributions of principal just at a time when interest rates are low and their reinvestment rate opportunities unattractive. Thus, the prepayment call option is valuable for mortgagors and costly for mortgage lenders such as MBS investors. Correctly pricing MBSs then requires the pricing of this embedded option.

Measuring Prepayment Risk   Over the years, several prepayment risk models have been tried. At one time, the standard approach was to assume a 12 year prepaid life. That is, the mortgage experienced no prepayments during its first 12 years and then prepaid in full at the end of the twelfth year. This method ignores the impact of interest rates on the prepayment rate.

Another model that has fallen into disfavor is one based on the Federal Housing Administration's (FHA) experience. This model uses the historical prepayment and default history for all 30 year FHA mortgages. Since the FHA prepayment rate changes periodically, it is not clear that it has any predictive power at any point in time for a broad pool of mortgages.

constant prepayment rate (CPR): index that expresses prepayments, over the regular contractually determined principal payments, as a fraction of the prior month's outstanding principal balance.

A simpler and widely used model is the **constant prepayment rate (CPR)** method, which assumes that a certain fraction of a pool of mortgages prepays each month. The CPR is an index that expresses prepayments, over the regular contractually determined principal payments, as a fraction of the prior month's outstanding principal balance. The advantage of this method is its simplicity. However, it ignores the fact that newer mortgages prepay at slower rates than mortgages that are closer to their maturity dates.

Public Securities Association (PSA) prepayment model: a model that combines the information in FHA prepayment history with the simplicity of the CPR method by assuming that the constant prepayment rate increases by a fixed amount each month (0.2% for 100% PSA) until it reaches its maximum after 30 months.

The current industry standard is the **Public Securities Association (PSA) prepayment model**. The PSA model combines the information in FHA prepayment history with the simplicity of the CPR method. The PSA benchmark is set at 100% PSA. This benchmark assumes a series of CPRs that begin at 0.2% p.a. in the first month and increase by 0.2% p.a. in each month thereafter, until the CPR reaches 6% p.a. 30 months after the mortgage origination date. Thereafter, the prepayment rate is assumed to remain unchanged until the maturity of the mortgage pool is reached. Multiples of PSA are easy to use. That is, 200% PSA denotes a prepayment rate that is double that of 100% PSA. Therefore, the first month's prepayment rate is 0.4%, the second month's 0.8%, and the prepayment rate goes up by 0.4% each month until it reaches its maximum at 12% in 30 months. A 50% PSA has a prepayment rate that is half that of the 100% PSA. Figure 21.2 shows the annual prepayment rates for 50% PSA,

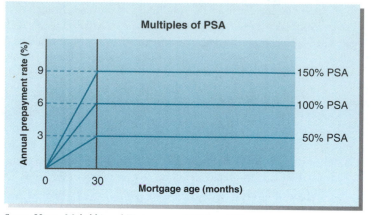

Source: Hayre, Mohebbi, and Zimmerman (1995), p. 507.

Figure 21.2

100% PSA, and 150% PSA. Table 21.3 shows the average time to full repayment for different PSA levels.

Although actual prepayment experience deviates from PSA averages, the PSA prepayment rates are useful, and widely used, as rules of thumb. Indeed, MBS market makers typically use sophisticated econometric models to incorporate macroeconomic factors, demographics, seasonality, geographical characteristics, and interest rate forecasts into their analysis of prepayment risk. The estimates derived from these models are then converted into PSA factors for quotation purposes. MBS quotes on Bloomberg screens shown in Figure 21.3 quote consensus PSA values.

Monthly prepayments are assumed to occur at the rate implied by the CPR specified in the PSA model. To use annual CPRs to calculate the size of monthly prepayments, we define the **single-monthly mortality rate (SMM)** as a monthly prepayment rate. The SMM is

single-monthly mortality rate (SMM): a monthly prepayment rate.

$$SMM = 1 - (1 - CPR)^{1/12}$$

Thus, a CPR of 6% implies a SMM of $1 - (1 - .06)^{1/12} = .005143$. This means that there is a repayment of .5143% of the remaining mortgage balance in addition to the scheduled principal repayment. That is:

> Prepayment in month t = SMM (Beginning Mortgage Balance − Scheduled Principal Payment in month t)

Average Time to Full Repayment by PSA (years)

Mortgage Age (mos.)	PSA (%)									
	75%	100%	125%	150%	175%	200%	225%	250%	275%	300%
0	22.9	17.4	14.1	11.8	10.3	9.1	8.1	7.4	6.8	6.3
6	22.5	17.0	13.6	11.4	9.8	8.6	7.7	7.0	6.4	5.6
12	22.2	16.6	13.3	11.1	9.5	8.3	7.4	6.6	6.0	5.5
24	21.8	16.2	12.8	10.7	9.1	7.9	7.0	6.2	5.8	5.1

Source: Wagner and Firestone (1995), Exhibit 2.

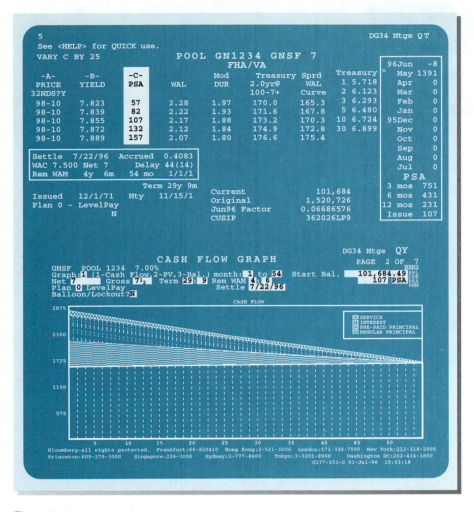

Figure 21.3

Table 21.4, column (7), shows each month's SMM for a mortgage of 100% PSA.[5] For example, the sixth month's SMM is calculated as $1 - (1 - 6(.002))^{1/12} = .001006$; the twelfth month's SMM is the maximum value of $1 - (1 - 12(.002))^{1/12} = .002022$. If the mortgage was 200% PSA, these values of CPR would be doubled, and the sixth month's SMM would be $1 - (1 - 6(.002)(2))^{1/12} = .002022$, whereas the twelfth month's SMM would be $1 - (1 - 12(.002)(2))^{1/12} = .004091$.

The cash flows on the MBS in Table 21.2b were calculated using 0% PSA. Table 21.4 recalculates the cash flows using 100% PSA. The mortgage is completely paid off in 156 months at that prepayment rate.[6] A column-by-column description of Table 21.4 is as follows:

---

[5] In practice, the mortgages in this MBS would be considered "seasoned" because the time to maturity is less than 30 years, and the PSA schedule would be accelerated, perhaps by 204 months (360 minus 156 expected full repayment month). In Table 21.4, we use the standard 100% PSA for illustrative purposes.

[6] The mortgages could be structured to reduce the fixed mortgage payment as the mortgage balance is drawn down by prepayments. Then the mortgage would not be repaid as rapidly as in the example shown in Table 21.4.

**Table
21.4**

Amortization Schedule for a Fixed Rate MBS with a Servicing Fee and 100% PSA

Month (1)	Beginning Balance (2)	Monthly Payment (3)	Monthly Interest (4)	Servicing Fee (5)	Principal Payment (6)	SMM (7)	Principal Prepayment (8)	Ending Balance (9)
1	$250,000	$2,193.93	$1,979.17	$104.17	$110.59	.000167	$41.69	$249,847.74
2	249,847.74	2,193.93	1,977.96	104.10	111.87	.000334	83.40	249,652.40
3	249,652.40	2,193.93	1,976.42	104.02	113.49	.000501	125.11	249,413.80
4	249,413.80	2,193.93	1,974.53	103.92	115.48	.000669	166.81	249,131.50
5	249,131.50	2,193.93	1,972.29	103.81	117.83	.000837	208.47	248,805.30
6	248,805.30	2,193.93	1,969.71	103.67	120.55	.001006	250.06	248,434.60
7	248,434.60	2,193.93	1,966.77	103.51	123.64	.001174	291.57	248,019.40
8	248,019.40	2,193.93	1,963.49	103.34	127.10	.001343	332.97	247,559.40
9	247,559.40	2,193.93	1,959.84	103.15	130.94	.001513	374.24	247,054.22
10	247,054.22	2,193.93	1,955.85	102.94	135.15	.001682	415.35	246,503.70
11	246,503.70	2,193.93	1,951.49	102.71	139.73	.001852	456.29	245,907.70
12	245,907.70	2,193.93	1,946.77	102.46	144.70	.002022	497.02	245,265.90
...								
155	3,021.41	2,193.93	23.92	1.26	2,168.75	.005143	4.39	848.27
156	848.27	855.34[a]	6.72	0.35	848.27	.005143	0	0

[a]Difference due to rounding. The mortgage value is $250,000, the mortgage rate is 10% p.a. paid monthly, the term is 30 years (360 months), and the servicing fee is 50 basis points per month. The prepayment rate is assumed to be 100% PSA.

Table 21.4, Col. (1): The month number, ranges from 1 to 360 for a 30 year mortgage.

Col. (2): The principal balance on the mortgage as of the beginning of the month. The first month's beginning balance is the mortgage face value of $250,000. All values would be multiplied by 100 to obtain the cash flows on the $25 million MBS.

Col. (3): The fixed monthly mortgage payment, assumed to be level for the life of the mortgage.

Col. (4): Interest on the MBS pass-throughs, calculated at the rate of 9.5% p.a., which is 10% p.a. on the underlying mortgage pool minus the 50 basis point monthly servicing fee. The monthly interest payment is calculated as $\frac{.095}{12}$ (mortgage balance at the beginning of each month). For example, the tenth month's interest payment is calculated as $\frac{.095}{12}$($247,054.22) = $1,955.85.

Col. (5): The servicing fee, calculated as $\frac{.005}{12}$ (mortgage balance at the beginning of each month). For example, the fifth month's servicing fee is $\frac{.005}{12}$($249,131.50) = $103.81.

Col. (6): The regular principal payment, which is the total monthly payment minus the interest and servicing fees. That is, for the third month, the regular principal payment is
$2,193.93 − 1,976.42 − $104.02 = $113.49.

Col. (7): The SMM calculation as discussed above.

Col. (8): The principal prepayment assuming a 100% PSA. The principal prepayment is calculated by multiplying the month's SMM by the beginning balance less the regular principal payment. Thus, the fourth month's principal prepayment is[7] .000669($249,413.80 − $115.48) = $166.78.

---

[7] Differences (entry in Table 21.4 is $166.81) are due to rounding.

Current-coupon GNMA cash flows at various prepayment rates

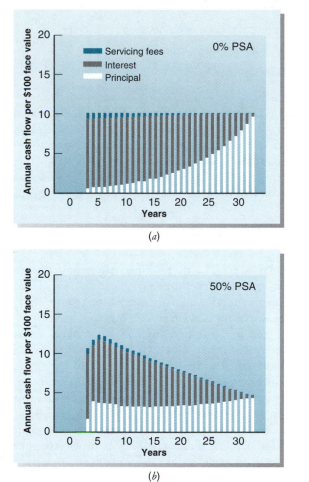

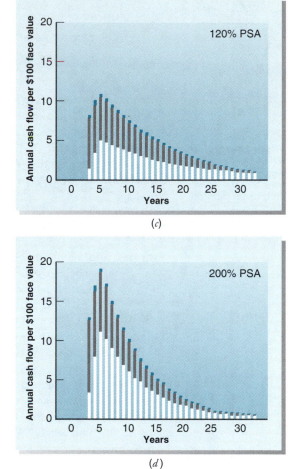

Source: Hayre, Mohebbi, and Zimmerman (1995), p. 515.

Figure 21.4

Col. (9):   The month's ending balance, which is the beginning balance minus the month's regular and prepaid principal repayments. Thus, the ninth month's ending balance is $247,559.40 - 130.94 - 374.24 = $247,054.22.

How is the PSA used to denote the interest sensitivity of mortgage prepayment? The choice of the PSA percentage depends on the fixed rate on the mortgage as compared to current mortgage yields. Thus, for 10%, 30 year, fixed rate mortgages, prevailing PSA rates might realistically be 228% if market mortgage rates are 9%; 178% if market rates are 9.5%; 152% if market rates are 10%; 123% if market rates are 10.5%; and 93% if market rates are 11% p.a. Figure 21.4 shows the impact of higher PSA percentages on the monthly payments of principal, interest, and servicing fees. As the market mortgage rate falls and the PSA increases, the monthly principal prepayment increases and the monthly interest and servicing fees decrease. This illustrates the impact of prepayment risk on both the MBS investor and the mortgage originator. Both lose, the faster the prepayment rate.

Checkpoint

1. Why are mortgages prepaid? Why is the rate of prepayment important to the MBS investor?
2. Discuss and compare the four prepayment models described in this section.
3. What are the advantages and disadvantages of the PSA model?
4. Define CPR and SMM.

Measuring Interest Rate Risk in the Presence of Prepayment Risk   We have seen how prepayment risk can alter the maturity of the mortgage security. Thus, the mortgage's original term is not a good measure of the life span of the instrument. An alternative measure is the **weighted average life (WAL)**, also known as the **weighted average maturity (WAM)**. WAL is the weighted average time to the return of each dollar of principal. The WAL is calculated by weighting each principal payment by the date it is received and dividing by the total principal, so that

> weighted average life (WAL), or weighted average maturity (WAM): weighted average time to the return of each dollar of principal.

$$WAL = \sum_{t=1}^{T} \frac{tP_t}{P}$$

where T = the number of periods until maturity; P_t = the principal repayment in any period t; and P is the mortgage's initial face value. Table 21.5a shows a sample calculation of WAL for a two year, quarterly payment, fully amortizing, 5% p.a. fixed rate mortgage with a face value of $75,000. Each quarterly principal repayment is weighted by the period, in terms of years. The WAL is $\frac{85,597.61}{75,000}$ = 1.14 years. If there were prepayments, the WAL would be shorter, for more principal payments would be received sooner.

The calculation of WAL should look vaguely familiar. It is a simplified version of the duration calculation. Duration weights the present value of each cash flow by its time period in order to determine a more accurate measure of the timing of cash flows. Duration uses the entire cash flow, rather than just the principal payment of WAL, thereby obtaining a value that is greater than WAL. But offsetting this is the impact of discounting, which reduces duration below WAL. Whether duration is above or below WAL depends on the mortgage's prepayment schedule. The faster the prepayment, the shorter both duration and WAL.

Table 21.5a

Calculation of Weighted Average Life: 0% PSA[a]

Period	Beginning Balance	Quarterly Payment	Quarterly Interest	Principal Repayment	Ending Balance	Period × Principal
0.25 yr	$75,000	$9,909.99	$937.50	$8,972.49	$66,027.51	$2,243.12
0.50	66,027.51	9,909.99	825.34	9,084.65	56,942.86	4,542.33
0.75	56,942.86	9,909.99	711.79	9,198.20	47,744.66	6,898.65
1	47,744.66	9,909.99	596.81	9,313.18	38,431.48	9,313.18
1.25	38,431.48	9,909.99	480.39	9,429.60	29,001.88	11,787.00
1.5	29,001.88	9,909.99	362.52	9,547.47	19,454.41	14,321.21
1.75	19,454.41	9,909.99	243.18	9,666.81	9,787.60	16,916.92
2	9,787.60	9,909.99	122.35	9,787.60	0	19,575.10
Totals				$75,000.00		$85,597.61

[a]The WAL is $\frac{85,597.61}{75,000}$ = 1.14 years for the two year $75,000 5% p.a. mortgage face value paid in quarterly installments of $9,909.99.

Table 21.5b

Calculation of Mortgage Duration: 0% PSA[a]

Period	Quarterly Payment	PV of Cash Flow	Period × PV of Quarterly Payment
0.25 yr	$9,909.99	$9,787.64	2,446.91
0.50	9,909.99	9,666.81	4,833.40
0.75	9,909.99	9,547.47	7,160.60
1	9,909.99	9,429.60	9,429.60
1.25	9,909.99	9,313.18	11,641.48
1.5	9,909.99	9,198.20	13,797.31
1.75	9,909.99	9,084.65	15,898.13
2	9,909.99	8,972.49	17,944.98
Totals		$75,000.00	$83,152.41

[a]The duration is $\frac{83,152.41}{75,000}$ = 1.11 years for the two year $75,000 5% p.a. mortgage face value paid in quarterly installments of $9,909.99. Quarterly yield is 1.25%.

Table 21.5c

Calculation of Mortgage Duration with 150% PSA[a]

Period (1)	Beginning Balance (2)	Interest Payment (3)	Principal Repayment (4)	SMM 100% PSA (5)	Pre–payment (6)	Total Payments (7)	PV of Total (8)	Period × PV (9)
0.25	$75,000	$937.50	$8,972.49	.001503	$148.90	$10,058.89	$9,934.70	2,483.68
0.50	65,878.61	823.48	9,086.51	.003014	256.72	10,166.71	9,917.23	4,958.62
0.75	56,535.38	706.69	9,203.30	.004531	321.67	10,231.66	9,857.37	7,393.03
1	47,010.41	587.63	9,322.36	.006055	342.29	10,252.28	9,755.29	9,755.29
1.25	37,345.76	466.82	9,443.17	.007586	317.50	10,227.49	9,611.56	12,014.45
1.5	27,585.09	344.81	9,565.18	.009124	246.62	10,156.61	9,427.11	14,140.67
1.75	17,773.29	222.17	9,687.82	.010670	129.40	10,039.39	9,203.27	16,105.72
2	7,956.07	99.45	7,956.07	.012222	0	8,055.52	7,293.45	14,586.90
Totals							$75,000.00	$81,438.36

[a]The duration is $\frac{81,438.36}{75,000}$ =1.09 years for the two year $75,000 5% p.a. mortgage face value paid in quarterly installments of $9,909.99 with 150% PSA.

Table 21.5b calculates the duration for the mortgage in Table 21.5a. The mortgage's duration is 1.11 years, which is less than the WAL of 1.14 years.[8]

Table 21.5c shows the calculation for the mortgage in Table 21.5a assuming a 150% PSA.[9] The effect of the prepayments is to reduce the mortgage's duration to 1.09 years. In contrast, the 100% PSA mortgage's WAL decreases to 1.12 years.

Here is a column-by-column explanation of Table 21.5c:

[8] The mortgage is assumed to be selling at par so that the yield remains at 5% p.a. paid quarterly.

[9] The PSA standards are calculated for 30 year mortgages and would, in practice, not be directly applicable to this two year mortgage.

Table 21.5c, Col. (1):   The payment period in terms of a fraction of a year.

Col. (2):   The beginning balance on the mortgage, which is the same as the previous quarter's ending balance (not shown separately). The ending balance for each quarter is calculated by deducting all principal payments from the beginning balance.

Col. (3):   Interest on the underlying mortgages accrues at a rate of 5% p.a. paid quarterly, based on the mortgage's beginning balance. For example, the second quarter's interest is $\frac{.05}{4}(\$65,878.61) = \$823.48$.

Col. (4):   The regular quarterly principal repayment, obtained by deducting the interest payment in column (3) from the fixed monthly payment of $9,909.99. The fixed monthly payment is the value of *PMT* that solves

$$75,000 = \sum_{s=1}^{8} \frac{PMT}{(1 + \frac{.05}{4})^s}$$

The fourth quarter's regular principal payment is: $9,909.99 - 587.63 = \$9,322.36$.

Col. (5):   The SMM under the assumption of 100% PSA. The prepayment rate is assumed to increase at a steady rate of .2%, even though mortgage payments are made quarterly. Thus, each quarter's CPR increases by $3 \times .002$, or .006. The first quarter's SMM is $1 - (1 - .006)^{1/4} = .001503$; the second quarter's SMM is $1 - (1 - .012)^{1/4} = .003014$; and so on.[10]

Col. (6):   The quarterly prepayment is 1.5 times the 100% PSA prepayment. That is, $1.5 \times SMM \times$ (beginning balance – regular quarterly principal payment). For the fifth quarter, this is $1.5(.007586)(\$37,345.76 - \$9,443.17) = \$317.50$.

Col. (7):   The total quarterly payment is the sum of the interest payment, the regular principal repayment, and the principal prepayment, or for the second quarter $823.48 + \$9,086.51 + \$256.72 = \$10,166.71$. We calculate the total payment for the duration calculation, rather than just the total principal repayment used for the WAL calculation.

Col. (8):   The total payment is discounted at a quarterly rate of 1.25%. For example, the present value of the third quarter's total payment is $\$10,231.66/(1 + \frac{.05}{4})^3 = \$9,857.37$.

Col. (9):   The last column is the present value of the quarterly payment multiplied by the period in which it is received, to be summed up for the duration calculation. For example, the weighted present value of the last quarterly payment is $2(\$7,293.45) = \$14,586.90$.

Duration is important because it is a measure of the security's exposure to interest rate risk. The longer the duration, the greater the price risk associated with interest rate fluctuations. Prepayments, by reducing duration, reduce the mortgage's interest rate risk exposure.

Checkpoint

✓

1. What is the weighted average life?
2. Show that the WAL of the 150% PSA mortgage in Table 21.5c is 1.12 years.
3. What is the relationship between WAL and interest rate risk exposure?

---

[10] This assumes that the CPR is a constant .6% for the entire first quarter, 1.2% for the second quarter, and so on.

Shortcomings of Using Duration to Measure Interest Rate Risk In Chapter 7, we discussed the shortcomings of duration in measuring interest rate risk. We saw that it is a linear approximation because the duration measure is assumed to be constant even as interest rates fluctuate. This problem is exacerbated for MBSs in the presence of prepayment risk. The duration calculations in Tables 21.5b and 21.5c assume that the mortgage payments are unaffected by the level of interest rates. Once the assumption of a particular PSA model is made, either 0% or 100% or any other possibility, prepayment rates are fixed. But we know that as interest rates decline, prepayment rates increase. If we use duration to measure the impact of interest rate fluctuations on security prices, we will be omitting this important effect.

The impact of interest rates on the mortgage's prepayments exacerbates the security's interest rate risk exposure. When interest rates decline, our standard duration equation dictates that security prices increase in proportion to the security's duration. That is:

$$\frac{\Delta P}{P} \approx -D \frac{\Delta y}{1 + y}$$

where P = the security's initial price and y = the security's yield. However, if rate decreases cause mortgagors to speed up their prepayments, then the duration of the mortgage will start to fall. This will offset the price increase, thereby causing the security's price to increase by less than would be predicted by the duration equation.

Similarly, if interest rates increase, the duration equation predicts that security prices will decrease in proportion to the security's fixed duration. However, as interest rates increase, prepayments decrease, thereby lengthening the mortgage's duration. This exacerbates the price decrease, causing the mortgage's price to decline by more than would be predicted by the duration equation. This is because of the prepayment option embedded in the mortgage security. Correctly measuring the interest rate risk of mortgage securities requires the derivation of an option-adjusted duration, such as used in Chapter 16 for callable bonds.

In short, the duration equation underestimates the price decreases and overstates price increases for mortgages subject to prepayment risk. The impact of prepayment risk is to exaggerate the mortgage's price swings resulting from interest rate fluctuations, that is, to increase interest rate risk. To accurately measure interest rate risk, we must account for the impact of interest rate fluctuations on payments. To derive a better measure of MBS price sensitivity, we must return to the basics of security pricing.

Determination of MBS Prices

If MBSs had no prepayment risk, then their pricing would be simply another example of discounting future cash flows at a risk adjusted yield. Unfortunately, MBS cash flows are not known in advance since prepayment options can be exercised at any time. Thus, MBS yields are made up of three components:

1. *Risk free rates:* MBS yields are based on the yields on similar U.S. Treasury securities. MBSs are typically paired with Treasuries by matching their maturities to the MBS WAL.[11]

2. *Default risk premiums:* MBSs are rated by the major credit rating agencies. Their rating depends on the credit enhancement offered by the issuing conduit. The credit enhancement may be external (that is, government guarantees, letters of credit, or

---

[11] This is not unambiguous since the MBS WAL depends on the cash flows from principal payments, regular plus prepayments. For the choice of the risk free rate, the MBS WAL is calculated assuming no prepayments.

bond insurance) or internal (that is, built into the pricing structure so that the MBSs are overcollateralized and generate excess cash flow as reserves).

3. *Interest rate option values:* This last component is the source of difficulty for our standard pricing measures. The problem with duration is that it does not take into consideration the embedded option in a mortgage security. The prepayment option enables the mortgagor to call portions of the mortgage security on any regular payment date. In Chapter 16, we saw how the option adjusted spread (OAS) was used to evaluate the implicit call option in a callable bond. The OAS measures the difference between two similar securities, one with the embedded option and the other without it. An options pricing model, such as the Black-Scholes model from Chapter 19, can be used to evaluate the MBSs' embedded call option.

To evaluate the risk exposure of MBSs and illustrate the shortcomings of relying on duration as a risk measure, we evaluate three MBSs using back-to-basics pricing methods. That is, we discount all cash flows on each of the MBSs under an assumed interest rate shift. To simplify the example, we assume a flat yield curve and only a parallel shift in the yield curve when interest rates fluctuate. In practice, FIs use this methodology but reestimate MBS prices assuming complex interest rate processes and incorporating forward yields. This iterative process, called **Monte Carlo simulation**, is performed for many different interest rate scenarios until the observed security price is determined. The MBS price is obtained by multiplying the price implied by each interest rate scenario by its likelihood of occurrence.

Monte Carlo simulation: an iterative process of security price evaluation based on the solution of security prices under different interest rate scenarios.

Consider the case of the $250,000 mortgage underlying a $25 million MBS.[12] To simplify the calculations, assume that there is no servicing fee. The mortgages in the pool comprising the MBS are all fully paid off, assuming a level monthly payment of $2,193.93 and 100% PSA, in 13 years (156 months). The MBS duration is 5.005 years.

At an interest rate of 10% p.a., the MBS is priced at $100 par. The present value of each cash flow is shown in Table 21.6a. If interest rates decrease instantaneously upon issuance of the MBS by a full 100 basis points and remain at that level for the life of the MBS, security prices will increase. What will be the impact on the MBS price? If we use our duration equation, the answer will be

$$\Delta P \approx -D(P)\frac{\Delta y}{1+y} = -5.005(\$100)\frac{-.01}{(1+\frac{.10}{12})} = +\$4.964$$

That is, the security price increases $4.964 per $100 face value if interest rates decline by 100 basis points. Let's see if this answer is correct by evaluating the MBS.

Table 21.6b lists the MBS cash flows discounted at a rate of 9% p.a. compounded monthly. However, when interest rates decrease, the cash flows on the MBS do not remain unchanged. We have seen that lower rates encourage mortgage prepayments. Assume that when interest rates decline by 100 basis points, the rate of prepayment on this MBS increases from 100% PSA to 200% PSA. Thus, the mortgages are fully paid off, and the MBSs are retired, in 118 months, or less than 10 years. This is disadvantageous to the MBS investor since the MBS principal is called when reinvestment rates are low. Indeed, the sum of the present values of all cash flows in Table 21.6b shows that the security's price increases to $104.024 per $100 face value. This is an increase of only $4.024 from the $100 par value at a rate of 10% p.a. The duration equation overestimates the increase in MBS prices, when interest rates decrease by 100 basis points, estimating a price increase of $4.964 rather than the accurate (assuming our prepayment scenario is correct) $4.024. This pricing error becomes even more significant when we remember that duration is a *pessimistic* estimator, understating security price increases

---

[12] We perform the analysis using the cash flows on the prototypical mortgage, but the totals for the entire MBS issue are simply obtained by multiplying by 100.

Table 21.6a

Amortization Schedule for a Fixed Rate MBS, 100% PSA

Month	Beginning Balance	Month Payment	Interest Payment 10% p.a.	Principal Repayment	100% PSA Prepayment	Total Principal Repayment	Ending Balance	PV of CF @10%
1	$250,000.00	$2,193.93	$2,083.33	$110.60	$41.67	$152.29	$249,847.70	$2,217.14
2	249,847.70	2,193.93	2,082.06	111.87	83.40	195.27	249,652.40	2,239.84
3	249,652.40	2,193.93	2,080.44	113.49	125.11	238.60	249,413.80	2,262.02
4	249,413.80	2,193.93	2,078.45	115.48	166.81	282.29	249,131.50	2,283.66
5	249,131.50	2,193.93	2,076.10	117.83	208.47	326.30	248,805.30	2,304.75
6	248,805.30	2,193.93	2,073.38	120.55	250.06	370.61	248,434.60	2,325.28
7	248,434.60	2,193.93	2,070.29	123.64	291.57	415.21	248,019.40	2,345.23
8	248,019.40	2,193.93	2,066.83	127.10	332.97	460.07	247,559.40	2,364.59
9	247,559.40	2,193.93	2,062.99	130.94	374.24	505.18	247,054.20	2,383.34
10	247,054.20	2,193.93	2,058.78	135.15	415.35	550.50	246,503.70	2,401.49
11	246,503.70	2,193.93	2,054.20	139.73	456.29	596.02	245,907.70	2,419.00
12	245,907.70	2,193.93	2,049.23	144.70	497.02	641.72	245,265.90	2,435.88
...								
151	11,645.98	2,193.93	97.05	2,096.88	49.11	2,145.99	9,499.99	640.64
152	9,499.98	2,193.93	79.17	2,114.76	37.98	2,152.74	7,347.25	632.19
153	7,347.24	2,193.93	61.23	2,132.70	26.82	2,159.52	5,187.73	623.83
154	5,187.72	2,193.93	43.23	2,150.70	15.62	2,166.32	3,021.41	615.56
155	3,021.40	2,193.93	25.18	2,168.75	4.39	2,173.14	848.27	607.37
156	848.27	855.34	7.07	848.27	0.00	848.27	0.00	234.37
								250,000.00
								100.00

when rates decrease. Thus, a convexity adjusted price change would overstate the price impact of the rate decline even more.

When interest rates increase, the duration measure's performance is even worse. Table 21.6c shows the MBS cash flows if interest rates increase by 100 basis points immediately after the MBS issue and remain at the 11% level for the life of the mortgage. Since higher rates discourage prepayments, we assume a shift to a 50% PSA prepayment schedule.[13] This is disadvantageous to investors in MBSs, for they are left holding lower yielding MBSs for longer periods of time. Under these assumptions, the MBS is fully paid in 199 months, almost 17 years. When rates increase to 11% p.a., Table 21.6c shows that the MBS price declines to $94.27876 per $100 face value. This is a decline of –$5.72124, as compared to the duration approximation's estimate of a decline of –$4.964 per $100 face value.

We can use these prices to solve for the duration of the MBS, assuming this prepayment process. Recall from Chapter 7 that modified duration is defined as $\frac{D}{1+y}$, where y is the original interest rate prevailing. The duration equation can therefore be expressed as

$$\frac{\Delta P}{P} = -MD\Delta y$$

where ΔP = the security's price change; P = the original price of the security; MD = the security's modified duration = $\frac{D}{1+y}$; and Δy = the interest rate change. Rearranging terms, we can solve for modified duration, using observed price and rate changes. In the case of the MBS

---

[13] As noted earlier, the expected shifts in the prepayment schedule induced by rate changes would be obtained using econometric models.

Table 21.6b

Amortization Schedule for a Fixed Rate MBS, 200% PSA

Month	Beginning Balance	Month Payment	Interest Payment 10% p.a.	Principal Repayment	200% PSA Prepayment	Total Principal Repayment	Ending Balance	PV of CF @9%
1	$250,000.00	$2,193.93	$2,083.33	$110.60	$83.37	$193.97	$249,806.00	$2,260.35
2	249,806.00	2,193.93	2,081.72	112.21	166.77	278.98	249,527.00	2,325.68
3	249,527.00	2,193.93	2,079.39	114.54	250.10	364.64	249,162.40	2,389.86
4	249,162.40	2,193.93	2,076.35	117.58	333.28	450.86	248,711.50	2,452.80
5	248,711.50	2,193.93	2,072.60	121.33	416.23	537.56	248,174.00	2,514.44
6	248,174.00	2,193.93	2,068.12	125.81	498.85	624.66	247,549.30	2,574.72
7	247,549.30	2,193.93	2,062.91	131.02	581.05	712.07	246,837.30	2,633.57
8	246,837.30	2,193.93	2,056.98	136.95	662.74	799.69	246,037.60	2,690.92
9	246,037.60	2,193.93	2,050.31	143.62	743.84	887.46	245,150.10	2,746.71
10	245,150.10	2,193.93	2,042.92	151.01	824.25	975.26	244,174.90	2,800.88
11	244,174.90	2,193.93	2,034.79	159.14	903.88	1,063.02	243,111.80	2,853.37
12	243,111.80	2,193.93	2,025.93	168.00	982.63	1,150.63	241,961.20	2,904.13
...								
113	10,971.11	2,193.93	91.43	2,102.50	91.22	2,193.72	8,777.39	982.25
114	8,777.38	2,193.93	73.14	2,120.79	68.47	2,189.26	6,588.13	965.24
115	6,588.12	2,193.93	54.90	2,139.03	45.76	2,184.79	4,403.34	948.43
116	4,403.33	2,193.93	36.69	2,157.24	23.10	2,180.34	2,222.99	931.85
117	2,222.99	2,193.93	18.52	2,175.41	0.49	2,175.90	47.09	915.48
118	47.09	47.48	0.39	47.09	0.00	47.09	0.00	19.66

Total = 260,059.19

$$\text{MBS Price} = \frac{260,059.19}{250.000} = 104.02$$

in our example, a 100 basis point decrease in rates caused an increase in MBS price of $4.024 per $100 face value since the MBS originally sold at par, $P = 100$. Thus, the estimate of modified duration for the MBS is

$$MD = -\frac{4.024}{(-.01)(100)} = 4.024 \text{ years}$$

However, when rates increase 100 basis points, we observe a decrease in prices of $5.72124. This implies a modified duration of

$$MD = -\frac{-5.72124}{(.01)(100)} = 5.72124 \text{ years}$$

The standard modified duration measure of 4.964 years is incorrect in both interest rate scenarios. Duration *over*estimates the MBS's price increases when interest rates decline and *under*estimates the MBS's price decrease when interest rate increase. The standard duration measure is inaccurate because it does not account for the MBS's embedded option value. We can correct that by calculating duration using the construction of a synthetic pass-through.

Checkpoint

✓

1. What are the shortcomings of using duration to measure the interest rate risk exposure of a MBS?

2. Derive the cash flows in Tables 21.6a, 21.6b, and 21.6c.

Table 21.6c

Amortization Schedule for a Fixed Rate MBS, 50% PSA

Month	Beginning Balance	Month Payment	Interest Payment 10% p.a.	Principal Repayment	50% PSA Prepayment	Total Principal Repayment	Ending Balance	PV of CF @11%
1	$250,000.00	$2,193.93	$2,083.33	$110.60	$20.84	$131.44	$249,868.60	$2,194.66
2	249,868.60	2,193.93	2,082.24	111.69	41.70	153.39	249,715.20	2,195.20
3	249,715.20	2,193.93	2,080.96	112.97	62.57	175.54	249,539.60	2,195.57
4	249,539.60	2,193.93	2,079.50	114.43	83.45	197.88	249,341.70	2,195.75
5	249,341.70	2,193.93	2,077.85	116.08	104.32	220.40	249,121.30	2,195.75
6	249,121.30	2,193.93	2,076.01	117.92	125.19	243.11	248,878.20	2,195.56
7	248,878.20	2,193.93	2,073.99	119.94	146.05	265.99	248,612.20	2,195.19
8	248,612.20	2,193.93	2,071.77	122.16	166.89	289.05	248,323.20	2,194.62
9	248,323.20	2,193.93	2,069.36	124.57	187.70	312.27	248,010.90	2,193.86
10	248,010.90	2,193.93	2,066.76	127.17	208.49	335.66	247,675.30	2,192.90
11	247,675.30	2,193.93	2,063.96	129.97	229.24	359.21	247,316.10	2,191.75
12	247,316.10	2,193.93	2,060.97	132.96	249.94	382.90	246,933.20	2,190.40
...								
189	22,097.33	2,193.93	184.14	2,009.79	51.66	2,061.45	20,035.89	400.26
190	20,035.89	2,193.93	166.97	2,026.96	46.31	2,073.27	17,962.62	395.68
191	17,962.62	2,193.93	149.69	2,044.24	40.93	2,085.17	15,877.44	391.15
192	15,877.44	2,193.93	132.31	2,061.62	35.53	2,097.15	13,780.30	386.65
193	13,780.30	2,193.93	114.84	2,079.09	30.09	2,109.18	11,671.12	382.21
194	11,671.12	2,193.93	97.26	2,096.67	24.62	2,121.29	9,549.83	377.80
195	9,549.82	2,193.93	79.58	2,114.35	19.12	2,133.47	7,416.36	373.44
196	7,416.35	2,193.93	61.80	2,132.13	13.59	2,145.72	5,270.64	369.13
197	5,270.63	2,193.93	43.92	2,150.01	8.02	2,158.04	3,112.60	364.85
198	3,112.60	2,193.93	25.94	2,167.99	2.43	2,170.42	942.18	360.62
199	942.18	950.03	7.85	942.18	0.00	942.18	0.00	154.57

Total = 235,696.90

MBS Price = $\dfrac{235,696.90}{250.000}$ = 94.28

---

synthetic pass-through: a security that is constructed to replicate the cash flows on the actual pass-through security.

Synthetic Pass-Throughs   A **synthetic pass-through** is a security constructed to replicate the cash flows on the actual pass-through security. In the case of a MBS issued by a federal agency, the synthetic version can be constructed by combining a noncallable agency debt instrument with interest rate call options sold by the issuer that allows the mortgagor to prepay the mortgage when interest rates fall. If the agency debt instrument is chosen to match the duration and WAL of the MBS, then the yield includes both the risk free rate and credit risk premium components of MBS yields. The issuer of the MBS simultaneously issues interest rate call options to mortgagors, who can exercise these options by prepaying their mortgages. The value of the pass-throughs as compared to the value of equivalent noncallable securities is decreased by the value of the call options granted to the mortgagors. The actual pass-through value must be equal to the synthetic pass-through price, which can be expressed as

> Synthetic Pass-Through Price
> = Price of Noncallable Agency Debt Security − α (Call Option Price)

The value of α is the number of call options embedded in the MBS. It depends on the prepayment process that underlies the MBS cash flows. In practice, α is obtained using Monte Carlo simulation techniques. To understand this, note that MBSs are traded in the secondary market and quoted in terms of 32nds per $100 face value. Thus, the MBS price is observable. Prices of agency debt securities and call options (usually for Treasury call options) are also observable. Thus, α is solved from the expression

Observed MBS Price = Synthetic MBS Price
= Observed Price of Agency – α(Observed Call Option Price)

For example, suppose that the MBS with a WAL of 13 years is priced at 100-16 ($100.50 per $100 face value), the noncallable agency note is priced at 102, and each Treasury bond call option premium is $2.50. Then, α is solved as .60 using

$$100.5 = 102 - \alpha(2.50)$$

This suggests that each $100 face value of the MBS has a $60 embedded short position in an interest rate call. The greater the α, the greater the option component in the MBS and the greater the MBS prepayment risk.

Another way to express this is as an option adjusted spread (OAS). The OAS can be calculated as the extra discount yield required to set the price of the MBS equal to the present value of the projected cash flows. The OAS is calculated by solving

$$P_{MBS} = \sum_{s=1}^{T} \frac{PMT}{\left(1 + \frac{y}{n} + \frac{OAS}{n}\right)^s}$$

where y = the spot rate on equivalent, noncallable securities (for example, the noncallable agency note with the same duration and WAL as the MBS); n = the number of payments per year; PMT = the expected cash flow; and P_{MBS} = the MBS price. The OAS is the yield differential between the noncallable agency security and the callable MBS with identical cash flows.

Suppose that the agency note with a WAL of 13 years (156 months) has a yield of 7.35% p.a. The monthly payment is $1.017 for the $100 note.[14] Using the same monthly payment, we find[15] that the yield that sets the present value of the MBS cash flows equal to 100.5 is 7.62% p.a., for an OAS of 27 basis points (= 7.62 – 7.35).

Effective Duration   Once α is determined for the synthetic pass-through, then the MBS's effective duration can be calculated. **Effective duration** is the duration of the debt instrument adjusted to include the duration of any embedded options. The duration of the MBS can be expressed as

$$D_{MBS} = D_A - \alpha D_C$$

effective duration: the duration of the debt instrument adjusted to include the duration of any imbedded options.

---

[14] Obtained solving for PMT = $1.017 using

$$102 = \sum_{s=1}^{156} \frac{PMT}{\left(1 + \frac{.0735}{12}\right)^s}$$

[15] Solve for OAS = .27% p.a. using

$$100.5 = \sum_{s=1}^{156} \frac{1.017}{\left(1 + \frac{.0735}{12} + \frac{OAS}{12}\right)^s}$$

This solution for the OAS depends on the realization of the assumed cash flows, which may not occur since interest rate fluctuations affect prepayments. In practice, Monte Carlo simulation is used to calculate the OAS under different interest rate and prepayment scenarios.

where D_{MBS} = the effective duration of the MBS; D_A = the duration of the agency security; α = the ratio of calls to face value embedded in the MBS; and D_C = the duration of the call option. Since duration is simply the factor of price volatility, the duration of the call option is simply equal to the option's δ times the duration of the underlying cash instrument, in this case a U.S. Treasury bond, denoted D_T.[16] For a Treasury call option, the duration is δD_T. Thus, the MBS effective duration is

$$D_{MBS} = D_A - \alpha \delta D_T$$

All terms on the right-hand side can be calculated using market data. Thus, suppose that the duration of the agency security is 12.3 years, the duration of the Treasury bond is 9.75 years, and the option δ is .82. Using the α of .60 solved in the last section yields a MBS duration of

$$D_{MBS} = 12.3 - .6(.82)(9.75) = 7.5 \text{ years}$$

This value of effective duration for the MBS can be used to obtain estimates of MBS price fluctuations when interest rates fluctuate.[17]

effective convexity: the value of convexity adjusted to include the convexity of any embedded options.

Effective Convexity   The option adjusted **effective convexity** can be determined as the value of convexity adjusted to include the convexity of any embedded options. Thus:

$$CV_{MBS} = CV_A - \alpha \delta CV_T$$

where CV_A = the convexity of the agency debt instrument; α = the ratio of calls embedded in the MBS; δ = the U.S. Treasury bond call option hedge ratio; and CV_T = the convexity of the U.S. Treasury bond underlying the call. For example, if CV_A = 155 and CV_T = 97, then the convexity of the MBS in our previous example is

$$CV_{MBS} = 155 - .6(.82)(97) = 107.3$$

As a note of caution, however, the values of both effective duration and effective convexity are highly sensitive to the assumptions about interest rate scenarios and prepayment responses. Kish and Greenleaf (1993) illustrate how small changes in interest rate scenarios cause large shifts in α, δ, and the duration and convexity parameters used in the model.

The option adjustment for the short call position embedded into the MBS reduces both the duration and the convexity of the MBS. This increases the likelihood that the MBS will have negative duration or negative convexity. What does this mean? Negative duration implies that as interest rates decrease (increase), prices decrease (increase)—a reversal of a fundamental of finance. This occurs because when rates decrease, prepayments increase on the MBS. If the size of prepayments increases at a fast enough rate, the amount of interest paid will decrease rapidly as the principal is paid down. Moreover, this will occur when reinvestment rates are low. The impact is to reduce the present value of MBS cash flows.

Similarly, negative convexity (first discussed in Chapter 16) results in price compression on the upside. That is, when interest rates decrease, prices increase, but at a slower rate than they decrease as rates increase. The top panel in Figure 21.5 illustrates the price/yield relationship for a bond with negative duration. The bottom panel illustrates bonds with both positive duration and convexity and negative duration and convexity below a certain rate level i^*. When rates fall below i^*, the bond's price declines at an increasing rate. This is the worst of both worlds.

---

[16] Recall from Chapter 19 that the option δ is the sensitivity of the option's premium to changes in the price of the underlying cash instrument. It is equal to the option hedge ratio for δ neutral hedges.

[17] Of course, the effective duration will perform poorly for large changes in rates, because options premiums and delta neutral hedge ratios change as prices change. See Chapter 19 for a discussion of shifting δ and γ.

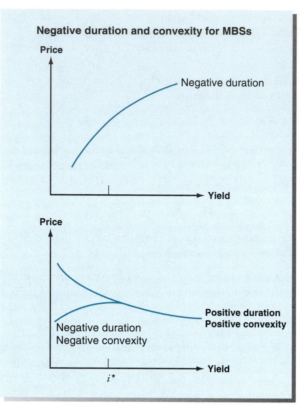

Figure 21.5

1. What is a synthetic pass-through?

2. Define effective duration and effective convexity.

3. Why are the effective duration and convexity results highly sensitive to the interest rate scenarios assumed?

4. What is the impact of negative duration? negative convexity?

Collateralized Mortgage Obligations

The MBS revolution began to falter because of prepayment risk and negative effective duration and convexity. Investors found the risk characteristics undesirable, and growth slowed. This effect is seen in the leveling off in volume during the mid-1980s, shown in Figure 21.6. To rescue their innovation, FIs had to pull another rabbit out of the hat. They did so through the collateralized mortgage obligation (CMO). The issuing FI can use CMOs to alter the prepayment risk of MBSs. By allocating the cash flows on the underlying mortgage pool in a sequential fashion, each resulting CMO tranche has a different maturity date, cash flow features, and risk exposure. Thus, relatively low risk tranches can be marketed to more risk averse investors, and the riskier tranches can be retained by the FI or sold to less risk averse investors. By more finely allocating risk among the securities, the CMO began a new revolution in risk distribution using the pass-through technology.

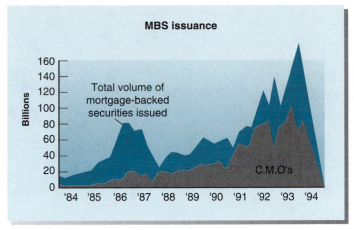

MBS issuance

Source: New York Times, Sept. 20, 1994, p. D1.

Figure 21.6

Sequential payment structure

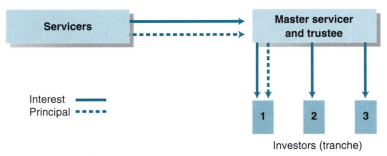

Source: Canon (1994), p. 251.

Figure 21.7

The primary difference between a mortgage pass-through and a CMO is the way in which the cash flows from the underlying mortgage pool are distributed. In a pass-through, each investor receives a pro rata share of all cash flows, consisting of principal and interest payments. The CMO is more flexible because it allows other distribution rules. The entire pool is divided into separate tranches, each of which has a different payment priority. A commonly used distribution rule is sequential payment, where principal cash flows are distributed to the highest priority tranches first. Only after the priority tranches are retired are principal cash flows paid to more junior tranches. This payment structure is shown in Figure 21.7 for a CMO with three tranches. All principal payments are paid to tranche 1 until it is fully repaid. Then all principal payments are paid to tranche 2 until it is fully repaid. Only then do tranche 3 investors receive principal payments. This payment structure considerably shortens the maturity of the earliest tranches. The impact is to stratify the prepayment risk by allocating it differentially across the different tranches.

The CMO trustee is almost always a REMIC because of its favorable tax treatment. Figure 21.8 shows the composition of this $750 billion market. All CMOs based on pools of conforming mortgages are issued by either FHLMC or FNMA, accounting for two-thirds of the

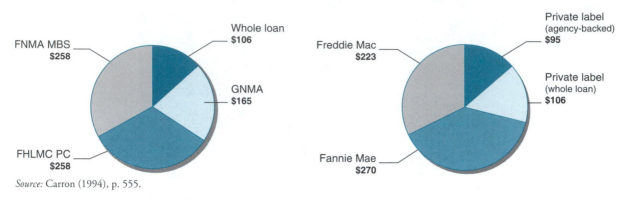

Composition of CMO market ($ billion)

Source: Carron (1994), p. 555.

Figure 21.8

market. Private REMICs, issued by FIs without government backing, construct CMOs using portfolios of "whole loans," which are the mortgages that collateralize the debt.

CMO structure is the subject of continuing innovation. Any combination of risk/cash flow characteristics can be constructed by stratifying the mortgage pool into tranches with different features. CMOs have either fixed or floating rates. The **Z tranche**, or accrual class, of the CMO is a "pay in kind" bond. The interest earned by Z tranche holders is transferred to the tranche currently receiving principal payments, in exchange for more bonds. Thus, the principal amount of the Z tranche increases at the rate of interest of other tranches. Only when all other tranches have been paid does the Z tranche receive interest and principal payments in cash. This is the riskiest tranche of bonds because of the residual nature of their cash flows.

Another innovation was the introduction of **planned amortization class (PAC)** CMOs. A PAC specifies a predetermined principal payment schedule. This is followed, using a sinking fund structure, as long as the PSA of the underlying mortgage pool is within a predetermined acceptable range. The REMIC offers the CMO investor greater cash flow certainty by guaranteeing principal payments in all except the most unexpected circumstances. This guarantee is not free, and PAC tranches have higher prices and lower yields than equivalent non-PAC tranches.

> **Z tranche:** a "pay in kind" CMO accrual class, such that the interest earned by Z tranche holders is transferred to the tranche currently receiving principal payments, in exchange for more bonds.

> **planned amortization class (PAC):** a CMO that specifies a predetermined principal payment schedule.

Cash Flows on CMOs

CMOs are structured to segment cash flows into separate securities so that investors can choose the stream that is most desirable. This increases the marketability of CMOs, since investors can achieve securities that are more customized to their needs. Figure 21.9 shows the principal payments for a four tranche, sequential pay CMO under different prepayment assumptions. If the underlying mortgage pool prepays at 100% PSA, then tranche A is fully repaid in 64 months. However, if the prepayment rate is 300% PSA, then tranche A is retired in only 31 months. The WAL of each tranche depends on its seniority and on the prepayment process in the underlying pool. Table 21.7 shows the impact of prepayment on the WAL of each tranche for a CMO based on $1 billion of 10% p.a. 30 year mortgages.

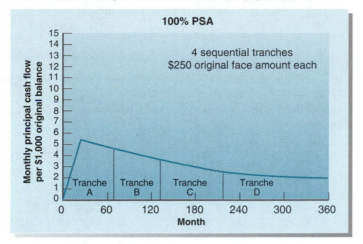

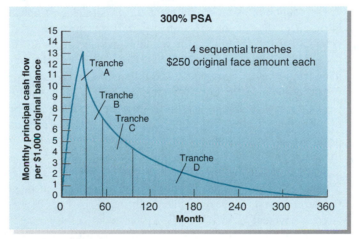

Source: Carron, (1995), p. 557.

Figure 21.9

Table 21.7

CMO Average Life Sensitivity to Prepayments

Tranche	Face Value ($million)	Average Life: 100% PSA (years)	Average Life: 300% PSA (years)
A	$250	3.1	1.6
B	250	7.8	3.6
C	250	14.3	6.1
D	250	23.8	12.4
Pool	1,000	12.3	6.0

Source: Carron (1995), p. 558.

CASE STUDY 21.1

CMOs

Let's construct a three tranche sequential pay CMO using an underlying pool of mortgages worth $250 million. Consider these mortgages to have two years until maturity, with a fixed rate of 5% p.a. paid quarterly and a 100% PSA. The cash flow on this underlying pool of mortgages is divided into the following three tranches:

Tranche	Face Value	Coupon Rate (pd. quarterly)
A	$100 million	4% p.a.
B	$100	4.75%
C	$50	5.5%

All three tranches receive interest payments based on their coupon rate, but principal payments are distributed in order of seniority: A first, B second, and C last. Thus, tranche A has a shorter maturity than tranche B, which has a shorter maturity than tranche C. The coupon rates on the different tranches reflect an upward-sloping yield curve. In practice, the coupon rates on the CMO tranches are determined by comparison with similar risk securities. The weighted average of the CMO coupon rates is 4.6% ($= \frac{\$100}{\$250} 4\% + \frac{\$100}{\$250} 4.75\% + \frac{\$50}{\$250} 5.5\%$). This is less than the 5% p.a. generated by the underlying pool of mortgages. The differential is the servicing fee retained by the REMIC originating the CMO. Investors are willing to pay higher prices (accept lower yields) in order to obtain securities with more attractive risk characteristics. The sum of the values of each of the CMO tranches therefore exceeds the value of the single pass-through security and CMOs create value. The FI that originates the CMO retains that value.

Table CS.1a shows the cash flows on the mortgages underlying the CMO if the prepayment rate is assumed to be 100% PSA. The WAL of the pool is 1.125 years, and the duration is 1.093 years. Table CS.1b shows the cash flows on tranche A. The first interest payment is $1 million ($= \$100m \times \frac{.04}{4}$). The entire first quarterly principal payment is paid to the holders of tranche A CMOs. That is, they receive a regular principal payment of $29.91 million plus an expected prepayment of $330,880 for a total quarterly principal payment of $30,240,880. The balance remaining at the start of the second quarter is $69,759,120(= $100 million minus $30,240,880). Interest is paid on this balance at a rate of 4% p.a. for an interest payment in the second quarter of $697,591 ($= \$69,759,120 \times \frac{.04}{4}$). In the second quarter, the entire principal payment of $30,860,983 (regular principal payment of $30.29 million plus expected prepayments of $570,983) is paid to tranche A investors, reducing the ending balance on tranche A to $38,898,137 (beginning balance of $69,759,120 minus the principal payment of $30,860,983). Continuing this way each quarter, tranche A is completely repaid by the end of the fourth quarter. Tranche A's WAL is only .54 years.

After tranche A is completely paid off in quarter 4, there are $24,314,381 in principal payments still undistributed. This is because tranche A uses only $7,511,252 of the fourth quarter's principal payments to retire all principal. But during the fourth quarter the underlying mortgages generate total principal payments of $31,825,633 (regular principal payments of $31.06 million plus prepayments of $765,633). The difference is paid to investors in tranche B. Table CS.1c shows the cash flows on tranche B. Tranche B's interest payments are calculated on the basis of the beginning balance each quarter.

Table
CS.1a

Cash Flows on the Pool of Underlying Mortgages ($million)[a]

Period (1)	Beginning Balance (2)	Total Quarterly Payment (3)	Interest Payment 5% p.a. (4)	Quarterly Principal Repayment (5) = (3−4)	Quarterly Principal Prepayment (6)	Total Quarterly Payment (7) = (3+6)	PV of Quarterly Payment (8)	PV × Period (9)
.25 year	250.00	33.0333	3.125	29.91	0.33088	33.36418	32.95228	8.238069
.50	219.7591	33.0333	2.746989	30.29	0.570983	33.60428	32.77967	16.38983
.75	188.8981	33.0333	2.361227	30.67	0.716884	33.75018	32.51555	24.38666
1.00	157.5113	33.0333	1.968891	31.06	0.765633	33.79893	32.16051	32.16051
1.25	125.6856	33.0333	1.57107	31.46	0.714784	33.74808	31.71568	39.64459
1.50	93.51083	33.0333	1.168885	31.86	0.562509	33.59581	31.18279	46.77418
1.75	61.08833	33.0333	0.763604	32.27	0.307478	33.34078	30.56402	53.48704
2.00	28.51085	28.87	0.356386	28.51	0	28.86723	26.13635	52.2727
							250.0000	273.3536

$$\text{Duration} = \frac{273.3536}{250} = 1.0934 \text{ years}$$

[a]The underlying mortgage pool consists of $250 million of 2 year, 5% p.a. quarterly, 100% amortizing mortgages, with 100% PSA.

Table
CS.1b

Cash Flows on Tranche A: $100 million @ 4% p.a. ($million)

Period	Beginning Balance	Interest Payment	Regular Principal	Principal Prepayment	Total Principal	Ending Balance	WAL (years)
.25 years	100.00	1.00	29.91	0.33088	30.24088	69.75912	7.56
.50	69.75912	0.6967591	30.29	0.570983	30.86098	38.89814	15.43
.75	38.89814	0.388981	30.67	0.716884	31.38688	7.511252	23.54
1.00	7.511252	0.075113	7.511252	0	7.511252	0	7.51
					100.00		

$$\text{WAL} = \frac{54.04}{100} = .54 \text{ years}$$

Thus, at the start of the fifth quarter, there is a balance of $75,685,619 ($100 million face value minus fourth quarter principal repayments totaling $24,314,381). Interest on this balance is $898,767, or $75,685,619(\frac{.0475}{4})$.

Cash flows continue to be distributed in this way until the seventh quarter when tranche B is completely paid off. The WAL of tranche B is 1.33 years. Only after tranche B is retired can tranche C investors receive any principal payments, although they have received interest payments of $687,500 (= $50m$\frac{.055}{4}$) on the entire face value since the beginning of the CMO. During the seventh quarter, tranche C receives the $21,489,148 in principal payments remaining after tranche B is retired (pool principal payments of $32,577,478 less tranche B's last principal payment of $11,088,330). Tranche C's WAL is 1.893 years.

The CMO has transformed a single MBS with a WAL of 1.125 years for the pool of underlying mortgages into three choices for investors: one CMO with a WAL of around six months, another with a WAL of just under 16 months, and another with

Table CS.1c

Tranche B: $100 million @ 4.75% p.a. ($million)

Period	Beginning Balance	Interest Payment	Principal Repayment	Principal Prepayment	Total Principal	Ending Balance	WAL (years)
1	100.00	1.1875	0	0	0	100	0
2	100.00	1.1875	0	0	0	100	0
3	100.00	1.1875	0	0	0	100	0
4	100.00	1.1875	23.54875	0.765633	24.31438	75.68562	24.31
5	75.68562	0.898767	31.46	0.714784	32.17478	43.51083	40.22
6	43.51083	0.516691	31.86	0.562509	32.42251	11.08833	48.63
7	11.08833	0.131674	11.08833	0	11.08833	0	19.40
					100.00		132.56

$$WAL = \frac{132.56}{100} = 1.33 \text{ years}$$

Table CS.1d

Total Payments on Tranches A, B, and C ($million)

Period	Total Interest on Underlying Mortgage[a]	Interest Tranches A, B, & C[b]	Regular Principal	Prepayment	Interest Differential[c]
.25 years	3.125	2.875	29.91	0.33088	0.25
.50	2.746989	2.572597	30.29	0.570983	0.174398
.75	2.361227	2.263981	30.67	0.716884	0.097245
1.00	1.968891	1.950113	31.06	0.765633	0.018778
1.25	1.57107	1.586267	31.46	0.714784	−0.0152
1.50	1.168885	1.204191	31.86	0.562509	−0.03531
1.75	0.763604	0.819174	32.27	0.307478	−0.05557
2.00	0.356386	0.392024	28.51085	0	−0.03564
Totals		13.66334	246.0308	3.969153	0.398701

[a]Column (4) of Table 21.8a.

[b]Sum of column (3) of Table 21.8b plus column (3) of Table 21.8c plus interest payments on Tranche C (not shown separately).

[c]The difference between the total interest payments on the underlying mortgages (column (2) of Table 21.8d) minus the interest on Tranches A, B, and C (column (3) of Table 21.8d).

a WAL of almost two years. Table CS.1d shows the total disbursements on all three tranches of the CMO. By construction, the sum of all CMO principal payments is exactly equal to the principal payments on the underlying mortgages. But the last column of Table CS.1d shows the difference between the interest received by the issuing REMIC from the underlying pool of mortgages and the CMO interest paid out by the REMIC. During the first quarter, the REMIC collects $250,000 more in interest than it pays to the three tranches ($3.125 million minus $1 million paid on tranche A minus $1.1875 million paid on interest to tranche B minus $687,500 paid on interest to tranche C). This is because the weighted average yield on the CMO is less than the yield on the underlying mortgages. This differential is the fee earned by the FI that creates value by issuing the CMO. It also compensates the CMO for the later periods in which the interest earned on the underlying mortgage pool is insufficient to cover the CMO interest payouts. This is because as principal is paid down, the interest paid on the underlying mortgage pool is reduced at a rate of 5% p.a. However, the first tranches to be paid are the lowest yielding tranches. Thus, the REMIC's obligations are reduced at the rate of 4% and 4.75% p.a., while the cash inflows from the underlying pool are reduced at a rate of 5% p.a. The CMO is structured to yield enough extra cash flows in early periods to cover shortfalls in later periods. The net cash inflow to the REMIC issuing the CMO is $398,711. Evaluating the present value of the interest differentials (at the CMO's average yield of 4.6% p.a. compounded quarterly) yields an up-front fee for the REMIC originating the CMO of $398,373.

Checkpoint

1. What motivated the innovation of CMOs?

2. How do CMOs create value?

3. How are cash flows distributed on a sequential pay CMO? on a Z tranche? on a PAC?

Strips of MBS

principal only (PO): MBSs that generate cash flows equal to the principal amount on the underlying pool of mortgages.

interest only (IO): MBSs that strip off the coupon, interest payments from the underlying pool of mortgages.

In 1986 Fannie Mae issued the first stripped MBS. In Chapter 15, we saw the versatility of U.S. Treasury stripping to create zero coupon securities. The same opportunities exist for MBSs, although the outcome is not a zero coupon bond. **Principal only (PO)** securities generate cash flows equal to the principal amount on the underlying pool of mortgages. There is no fixed coupon payment. Payments are made only as principal payments (regular as well as prepayments) are received on the underlying mortgage pool. **Interest only (IO)** securities strip off the coupon, interest payments from the underlying pool of mortgages.

Both the PO and IO securities are sensitive to prepayment rates. When interest rates decrease, the price of PO securities increases dramatically because the principal cash flows increase. However, the price of IO securities may decrease (or not increase as much) because as prepayments cause the mortgage balance to decline, the interest payment declines. The disastrous impact of interest rate declines on the value of some of these MBSs led to a crisis in the market during 1994, which is the subject of the articles in *Timely Topics 21.1: Déjà Vu All Over Again?*

TIMELY TOPICS 21.1

DÉJÀ VU ALL OVER AGAIN?

It is truly amazing. I never thought that we would ever again see mortgages being made at the rates that are now [in 1993] available.... A generation has grown up since we last saw interest rates at levels to which they have now declined.... Back then, mortgage lending was dominated by thrift institutions, and the types of loans they made, and the process of funding them, were regulated by government fiat. Now many commercial banks have started making mortgages in a big way. And the secondary mortgage market has become so dominant that the tone of most mortgage lending is set by conditions in the capital markets both domestic and international.

Source: J. Noel Fahey, *Measuring and Pricing Mortgage Risk: A Guide to Safe and Profitable Lending*, Financial Managers Society, 1994.

The impact of the inevitable increase in interest rates during 1994 was to wreak havoc in the mortgage-backed securities market. The next article describes the impact of this on FIs.

Behind much of Wall Street's year of distress, which is forcing the first round of retrenchment and layoffs since 1990, is the collapse of the market for bonds backed by home mortgages.

The bonds, known as MBS, make up some $1.5 trillion or 30 percent, of the total American bond market, and in recent years they accounted for half or more of the earnings of some firms. The business had grown because of a boom in mortgage refinancings and a willingness among many investors looking for a high yield to bet that interest rates would not rise. When rates shot up unexpectedly last winter, mortgage refinancings fell and the firms lost money on their mortgage-bond holdings. They also had more trouble creating and selling new securities.

Watching profits plummet—or losses emerge—Wall Street firms are dismissing traders, slashing the bonuses of others, and dumping their mortgage-bond holdings.... "We've been in bear markets before," said Brian Zipp, who oversees MBS trading at Lehman Brothers. "But we've never had a bear market for rates, and a bear market in terms of new mortgage porduction and a bear market in terms of investor attitude toward the product."...

Last year two thirds of all mortgage pass-throughs were transformed into CMOs. Overall the initial profit on the $324 billion in CMOs created last year produced revenue for Wall Street to as much as $1.5 billion. In addition, the CMO business also created the opportunity for firms to earn money trading them in the secondary market and by holding certain bonds in inventory and selling them later.

But as is typical of the markets with the biggest booms, the MBS business was hardest hit when the bond market crashed this spring. Like all bonds, mortgage securities lost value as interest rates went up. But many of the more complex CMOs designed for high yield fell further and faster than anybody expected.

This set off a chain reaction: Disgruntled investors sold the mortgage bonds they owned and refused to buy new ones. At the same time, mortgage bond dealers were trying to get rid of the billions in MBSs they owned—and had hoped they would be able to sell at good profits....

Source: S. Hansell, "Wall Street Mourns its Mortgage Profits," *New York Times*, September 20, 1994, p. D1.

The downturn was not soon reversed. On September 18, 1995, J.P. Morgan announced that it was drastically shrinking its MBS business after incurring a $120 million loss, resulting in a downturn in the volume of CMO activity. The list of losers in MBSs reads like a "who's who" of FIs: Kidder, Peabody, & Co.; Askin Capital Management; ITT; SunAmerica; Security Benefit Life Insurance Company; to name a few. MBS turned out to be the cause of the demise of Kidder, Peabody and Askin Capital.

SEC regulations, adopted in 1991, to control the risks of CMOs were soon found to be inadequate. The rules require that individual CMOs have WAL of ten years or less and that the average return of principal not stretch out more than six years if interest rates increase three percentage points or shorten by more than four years if interest rates fall 3%. The price of the bond may not change by more than 17% if all rates move up or down 3%. But, as predicted by the regulatory dialectic, the market was one step ahead of these regulations, asthe next article shows.

Wall Street 1, banking regulators 0.

That's the score 17 months after federal banking regulators imposed tight limits on certain investments by banks.

The new rules were meant to keep banks from overexposing themselves.... But it didn't take long for Wall Street to figure out how to sell certain types of CMOs that normally would have flunked the regulators' tests. How? By creating a prettier package for the affected CMOs so that they would pass muster under the new regulations.

"It's actually a good day when we are only one day behind Wall Street," conceded one rueful senior regulator from the Office of the Comptroller of the Currency, among the drafters of the new rules.

Now regulators fear that these new MBS dubbed "extend-o-matics," will expose banks to undue risks. That is because these bonds won't fit regulators' strict criteria after the first year. So banks that hold extend-o-matics will be at the mercy of an examiner who can force them to sell the bonds immediately, perhaps at a loss, or mark them to market, which means the daily price changes will jostle the bank's balance sheet.

Source: L. Jereski, "Extend-o-matics Keep Wall Street Ahead of Regulators," *Wall Street Journal*, July 12, 1993.

CASE STUDY 21.2

MBS STRIPS

Suppose that the mortgages in the $250 million pool used in Case Study 21.1 were divided up in another way. Instead of three tranches, another structure could be to sell the interest and principal payments independently. IO and PO strips can be created from the mortgage pool. Suppose that the IO and PO strips are derived directly from the underlying pool of mortgages, with no discount for the FI's fee. Table CS.2 shows the cash flows under various interest rate and prepayment scenarios. If interest rates decline to 3% p.a., the prepayment rate is assumed to speed up to 300% PSA. If interest rates fall further to 2% p.a., the prepayment rate is 500% PSA. If, on the other hand, interest rates increase to 7% p.a., the expected prepayment is 25% PSA.

IO and PO strips are fixed rate instruments because the coupon rate does not change as interest rates fluctuate. However, that does not mean that their cash flows are fixed. IO and PO cash flows are affected by prepayments. Thus, if prepayments increase, PO cash flows increase, in earlier periods, and IO cash flows decrease in all periods. That is, the total value of PO payments does not change over the life of the strip. It is just reallocated across time. As the prepayment rate increases (decreases), earlier period cash flows increase (decrease), while later period cash flows decrease (increase).

That is not the case for the IO. As prepayment rates increase (decrease), the outstanding mortgage balance decreases (increases), thereby decreasing (increasing) the total amount of interest payments. Thus, for the IOs in Table CS.2, as the prepayment rate increases, the absolute amount of cash flows over the life of the security decreases. This injects an element of instability into IO pricing. How are IOs and POs priced? Table

Table CS.2

IO and PO MBSs ($million)

Period (1)	Yield 5% 100% PSA		Yield 7% 25% PSA		Yield 3% 300% PSA		Yield 2% 500% PSA	
	CF ($m) (2)	PV(CF) ($m) (3)	CF ($m) (4)	PV(CF) ($m) (5)	CF ($m) (6)	PV(CF) ($m) (7)	CF ($m) (8)	PV(CF) ($m) (9)
Valuing the IO								
1 qtr.	3.125000	3.086420	3.125000	3.071253	3.125000	3.101737	3.125000	3.109453
2	2.746989	2.679581	2.750091	2.656307	2.738717	2.698094	2.730445	2.703344
3	2.361227	2.274849	2.369804	2.249620	2.338755	2.286912	2.316260	2.281860
4	1.968891	1.873447	1.984304	1.851273	1.928556	1.871768	1.888487	1.851185
5	1.571070	1.476456	1.593763	1.461341	1.511836	1.456396	1.453850	1.418042
6	1.168885	1.084930	1.198486	1.080007	1.092397	1.044504	1.018929	.988889
7	.763604	.700008	.798785	.707439	.674174	.639818	.590573	.570311
8	.356386	.322671	.394854	.343685	.261042	.245895	.175200	.168347
Totals		13.498360		13.420930		13.345120		13.091430
Valuing the PO								
1 qtr.	30.24088	29.867540	29.99272	29.47687	30.90264	30.67260	31.56440	31.40737
2	30.86098	30.103680	30.42294	29.38545	31.99697	31.52236	33.13482	32.80594
3	31.38688	30.238695	30.84001	29.27597	32.81594	32.08852	34.22179	33.71356
4	31.82563	30.282860	31.24329	29.14869	33.33756	32.35591	34.77101	34.08420
5	32.17478	30.237120	31.62218	28.99477	33.55515	32.32465	34.79368	33.93674
6	32.42251	30.093759	31.97610	28.81502	33.45784	31.99099	34.26841	33.25812
7	32.57748	29.864295	32.31448	28.61912	33.05055	31.36630	33.22986	32.08973
8	28.51000	25.8129097	31.59000	27.49630	20.88000	19.66845	14.02000	13.47161
Totals	250.00000	236.5008587	250.00000	231.21220	250.00000	241.98980	250.00000	244.76730

CS.2 shows that the prices are just the expected present value of all cash flows under prevailing interest rate and prepayment scenarios. Thus, at an assumed 5% p.a. yield and a 100% PSA, the IO is priced at $13.49836 million (obtained by discounting the cash flows in column (4) of Table CS.1a, reproduced in column (2) of the top panel of Table CS.2) and the PO at $236.5008587 million (obtained by discounting the cash flows in column (5) plus (6) of Table CS.1a, reproduced in column (2) of the bottom panel of Table CS.2), for a total par value of $250 million.[18]

On the PO, as interest rates increase, the cash flows in earlier periods decrease because prepayments slow. The impact is to reduce the present value of all cash flows on the PO since cash flows are received further into the future. Together with the impact of a higher discount factor, the two effects cause the PO's price to decline rapidly when interest rates increase. In the PO in Table 21.9, the PO's price declines from $236,500,858.70 to $231,212,200, a decline of 2.236% (= $\frac{231.2122m - 236.5009m}{236.5009m}$) when interest rates increase from 5% to 7% p.a. and PSA decreases from 100% to 25%. However, when interest rates decrease, the PO's price increases just as rapidly. This is because cash flows are received sooner as the prepayment rate speeds up and the discount factor is smaller. Thus, when interest yields are 3% p.a. (2% p.a.), the PO's

---

[18] The cash flows in columns (4), (6), and (8) of Table CS.2 are obtained by replicating Table CS.1a, using each of the yield and PSA scenario assumptions (see end of chapter question number 7).

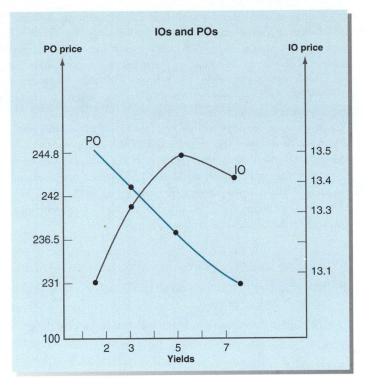

Figure CS.1

price increases to \$241.9898 (\$244.7673) million, an increase of 2.32% (3.50%). The rate of PO price increase when interest rates decline is slightly higher than the rate of price decrease when interest rates go up. The PO valuation curve in Figure CS.1 is therefore slightly more steep on the upside than on the downside.

The interest rate risk exposure of the IO strip can be seen in Table CS.2 and Figure CS.1. When interest rates increase, both the absolute amount of interest payments and the discount factor increase, thereby causing the IO's price to fall. For example, at a 7% yield, the IO's price falls to \$13.42093 million, a decline of .574% ($\frac{13.42093m - 13.49836m}{13.49836m}$). But when interest rates decrease, the story is quite unusual. The interest rate decrease and rapid prepayment reduce the total amount of IO cash flows, although the earlier payments are worth more because of the lower discount factor. If the impact of the premature prepayment outweighs the impact of the lower discount factor, then reductions in interest rates will cause reductions in IO prices. This is the case for the IOs in Table CS.2. At a rate of 3% p.a. and a 300% PSA, the IO price declines to \$13.34512 million, a decrease of 1.135%. When rates fall further to 2% p.a. with a 500% PSA, the IO price falls precipitously to \$13.09143 million, a decline of 3.015%. The IOs in Figure CS.1 display both negative convexity and negative duration. Negative duration is seen when interest rates fall below 5%, and prices decline. Negative convexity is apparent because the rate of price increases is lower than the rate of price decreases.

Hedging MBS Risk Exposure

MBSs allow the FI to calibrate risk exposure. MBSs can be constructed with very small amounts of risk or with extreme risk exposures, or anything in between. FIs, either as investors or as originators of MBSs, control their risk exposure by hedging. Fortunately, there are several choices of instruments that are very good hedges for MBSs. These are over-the-counter options on mortgages and forwards in MBS; exchange-traded futures and options on Treasury securities are also acceptable hedging instruments. Interest amortizing swaps are designed to hedge CMOs' prepayment risk. The primary advantage of the exchange-traded derivatives is their liquidity. Although the over-the-counter instruments are better matches for MBS cash flows, they are less liquid.

When utilizing Treasury futures or options to hedge MBS interest rate risk exposure, it is important to monitor the effectiveness of the hedge continually. That is because shifts in interest rates affect the perfect hedge ratio for MBS even more than for other underlying cash instruments. MBS prices are affected by interest rate shifts in two ways: the standard discounting effect and the impact of interest rate fluctuations on prepayments. We have already seen how prepayment risk can disturb the best laid investment plans. As in all other cases, there are no free lunches in financial markets.

Checkpoint

1. What are MBS strips? Distinguish between IOs and POs.

2. How do interest rate increases affect PO and IO prices? How do interest rate decreases affect PO and IO prices?

3. Compare the various derivatives that can be used to hedge MBS.

➤ Summary

MBSs are created using pools of mortgage loans as collateral. The cash payouts on the MBSs emanate from the mortgage pool. Cash payouts are simply passed along to the MBS investor for mortgage pass-through securities. CMOs alter the distribution of the cash flows from the mortgage pool to the CMO investor in order to increase the CMO's marketability. By designing different risk/cash flow characteristics for different tranches of the CMO issue, the originating FI can create value.

The major sources of risk on MBSs are credit risk, interest rate risk, and prepayment risk. Credit risk is resolved using credit enhancements, either provided by the government or offered privately using overcollateralization or backup lines of credit. Interest rate risk for MBSs is exacerbated by prepayment risk. That is, the cash flows on a MBS are not known at the initiation of the security, because the cash flows depend on interest rates. Although many mortgages are originated as 30 year loans, they rarely last that long. Lifestyle reasons induce mortgagors to sell their homes, requiring that the mortgage be retired before its maturity date. More important, perhaps, as interest rates decrease, mortgagors choose to refinance their mortgages, replacing high-cost loans with rela-

tively cheaper ones. Thus, interest rate fluctuations affect MBS values in two ways: (1) the standard manner through the discount factor and (2) the impact of interest rate fluctuations on prepayments.

Prepayments are measured using a standard model based on the Public Securities Association (PSA) tabulation of assumed prepayment rates. Although many FIs use sophisticated econometric models to estimate prepayment risk, their results are stated in terms of this widely used standard. Fluctuations in PSA levels induced by interest rate changes can cause unexpected fluctuations in MBS prices. One possible outcome is negative duration and negative convexity. Negative duration occurs when MBS prices decrease, rather than increase, as interest rates decrease. Negative convexity occurs when the rate of price decrease for MBSs is greater than the rate of price increase.

CMOs can be split into tranches on the basis of payment priority. Sequential pay CMOs allocate all principal payments to more senior tranches first. Junior tranches do not receive any principal cash flows, other than their regular interest payments, until the higher priority tranches are paid in full. MBS payouts can also be separated along the lines of interest only (IO) and principal only (PO) securities. IOs have a great deal of interest rate and prepayment risk exposure.

MBSs can be hedged using over-the-counter options on mortgages, forwards on mortgages, or exchanged-listed Treasury futures and options. Exchange-listed derivatives are more liquid hedging instruments, but the mortgage derivatives are closer matches to the cash flow characteristics of the MBS.

▶ References

Baek, H., B. Lancaster, and A. Kimura. "Commercial Mortgage-Backed Securities: A Market Overview." *The Financier: ACMT* 2, No. 3 (August 1995): 14–32.

Becketti, S., and C. S. Morris. "The Prepayment Experience of FNMA Mortgage-backed Securities." *Monograph Series in Finance and Economics*, Monograph 1990-3, New York University, 1990.

Carron, A. S. "Collateralized Mortgage Obligations." In F. J. Fabozzi and D. Fabozzi (eds.), *The Handbook of Fixed Income Securities*, pp. 549–82. Burr Ridge, Ill.: Irwin Professional Publishing, 1995.

Fabozzi, F. J. *Bond Markets, Analysis and Strategies*. 3rd ed. Upper Saddle River, N. J.: Prentice Hall, 1996.

Gilkeson, J. H., P. Jacob, and S. D. Smith. "Buy Sell or Hold? Valuing Cash Flows from Mortgage Lending." Federal Reserve Bank of Atlanta *Economic Review* 79, No. 6 (November–December 1994): 1–16.

Hayre, L. S., C. Mohebbi, and T. A. Zimmerman. "Mortgage Pass-Through Securities." In F. J. Fabozzi and D. Fabozzi (eds.), *The Handbook of Fixed Income Securities*, pp. 502–48. Burr Ridge, Ill.: Irwin Professional Publishing, 1995.

Hudson van Eck, T. "Asset-Backed Securities." In F. J. Fabozzi and D. Fabozzi (eds.), *The Handbook of Fixed Income Securities*, pp. 583–601. Burr Ridge, Ill.: Irwin Professional Publishing, 1995.

Johnson, D., and E. Eldridge. "Asset Securitization as a Corporate Finance Tool." *The Financier: ACMT* 2, No. 3 (August 1995): 7–13.

Kish, R. J., and J. Greenleaf. "Teaching How Mortgage Pass-Through Securities Are Priced." *Financial Practice and Education* (Spring–Summer 1993): 85–94.

Leeds, E. M. "The Riskiness of Price-Level Adjusted Mortgages." *Review of Business* 15, No. 1 (Summer–Fall 1993): 42–45.

Peek, J., and J. A. Wilcox. "A Real Affordable Mortgage." Federal Reserve Bank of Boston *New England Economic Review* (January–February 1991): 51–66.

Schwarcz, S. "The Alchemy of Asset Securitization." *The Financier* 1, No. 5 (December 1994): 53–64.

Wagner, K., and E. B. Firestone. "Homeowner Mobility and Mortgage Prepayment Forecasting." In F. J. Fabozzi (ed.), *Handbook of Mortgage-Backed Securities*. Chicago: Probus Publishing, 1995.

William, S., and A. Houston. "Inflation Risk, Payment Tilt, and the Design of Partially Indexed Affordable Mortgages." *Journal of the American Real Estate and Urban Economics Association* 21, No. 1 (1993): 1–9.

▶ Questions

1. Evaluate the following mortgages:
   a. The present value of a 30 year, 7% p.a. fixed rate mortgage, 100% amortizing, with a monthly payment of $1,500.
   b. The monthly payment on a $350,000 15 year mortgage, 5.5% p.a. fixed rate, 100% amortizing.
   c. The yield on a $175,000 20 year 100% amortizing mortgage with a monthly payment of $2,050.
   d. The time until maturity for a $550,000 100% amortizing mortgage, with a monthly payment of $6,745 and a fixed rate of 8.25% p.a.

2. Consider a 36 month $50,000 mortgage paying a fixed rate of 6% p.a. in fully amortized monthly installments. Calculate

a. The monthly mortgage payment.

b. The amortization schedule for each of the 36 months of the life of the mortgage, assuming 0% PSA.

c. The MBS's amortization schedule if there is a 50 basis point monthly servicing fee.

d. The amortization schedule assuming 100% PSA for the mortgage in part (c).

3. Construct a MBS using the following mortgages. All mortgages are 100% amortizing, with fixed monthly payments.

T	P	y
20 yrs.	$10m	9.375% p.a.
30 yrs.	$15m	10.5% p.a.
15 yrs.	$30m	8.75% p.a.

a. Calculate the payment on each mortgage in the pool.

b. Calculate the MBS's WAC.

c. If there is an annual 50 basis point fee for servicing and credit enhancement, calculate the payment on the MBS.

d. How does the MBS's WAC change if there is a servicing fee?

4. Using the mortgage in Table 21.5c with a 100% PSA, calculate the WAL and the duration.

5. Calculate the CPR and SMM for

a. The 7th month of a 100% PSA mortgage.

b. The 30th month of a 200% PSA mortgage.

c. The 150th month of a 300% PSA mortgage.

d. The 2nd month of a 50% PSA mortgage.

e. The 5th month of a 150% PSA mortgage.

6. Use the pool of mortgages in Table CS.1a to construct a three tranche CMO if the mortgages prepay at a rate of 300% PSA. Assume that the CMO is structured in the same way as the tranches in Tables CS.1b, CS.1c, and CS.1d. Be sure to calculate the cash flows on the underlying mortgage pool, the cash flows on the three tranches, the WAL of each security, and the up-front fee to the REMIC issuing the CMO.

7. Derive the cash flows the WAL, and the duration on the mortgages in Table CS.2 for 100% PSA, 300% PSA, 500% PSA, and 25% PSA, replicating Table CS.1a for each of the yield and PSA scenarios.

8. Calculate α, effective duration, and effective convexity for the following:

a. MBS with a 7 year WAL priced at 104-7; an agency note with a WAL of 7 years priced at 101-1, a duration of 5.3 years, and convexity of 47; and a Treasury bond call option with a premium of $3.10, a δ of .75, a duration of 8.6 years, and convexity of 86.

b. MBS with a 12.5 year WAL priced at 98-12; an agency note with a WAL of 12.5 years priced at 96-17, a duration of 8.2 years, and convexity of 120; and a Treasury bond call option with a premium of $1.90, a δ of .35, a duration of 7.56 years, and convexity of 55.

c. Contrast your answers to parts (a) and (b).

9. Evaluate the IO in Table CS.2 assuming the following yield and PSA scenarios: (a) yield = 4% p.a. PSA = 100%; (b) yield = 6%, PSA = 25%; (c) yield = 2%, PSA = 300%; (d) yield = 1% p.a., PSA 500%. What is the price change if the scenario changes from (a) to (b) to (c) to (d)?

10. Evaluate the PO in Table CS.2 assuming the scenarios in question 9. For each scenario, what is the total of the IO and PO strips of the MBS? What is the price change if the scenario changes from (a) to (b) to (c) to (d)?

BORDER CROSSING V:
THE FRONTIER

Alger "Duke" Chapman, the chairman and CEO of the Chicago Board of Options Exchange, remarked at the 1994 Financial Management Association meetings:

> Financial markets have experienced a large amount of innovation and change in recent years. As a practitioner in the derivative's marketplace, I have seen tremendous growth in the development of markets for derivatives on financial assets.... Looking back 37 years, my business lifetime, there have been unbelievable changes. Who would have thought that the 1950s investment matrix, "shall I (buy, sell, or hold) (stocks, bonds, or cash)," would have developed the complexities of [today].
>
> In 1960, who could have imagined that the 3.5 million shares average daily volume on the New York Stock Exchange would have grown to the 290 million per day of 1994,; or that the 1993 earnings for one investment firm, Goldman Sachs, would be four times the total equity capitalization of all the NYSE members in 1960; or that mutual fund holdings of $7.8 billion in 1955 would be $2.1 trillion by 1993; or that pension fund holdings of under $50 billion in 1955 would be $3 trillion by 1993.
>
> For reference, during the 1955–1993 period, the consumer price index went from 26.8 to 144.5 and the Dow Jones Industrial Average went from 488.40 to 3,875.15.

Sitting here in 1994, how far can we let our imaginations run as we look ahead for the next 25 or 30 years. The cold war is over, and capitalism is breaking out around the world. Eastern Europe, the Pacific Rim, and Africa all promise great global expansion potential. Communication technology is exploding and the needs of investors world wide have become very complex.

My guess is that we will see more change in the next 30 years than in the past 30.

That's where you come in. In this book, we have examined the *process* of innovation as practiced by FIs. The outputs of this process are financial securities that offer novel approaches to risk sharing and cash flow management. Throughout this book we have described selected financial innovations, their characteristics, and their goals. There are many more, with catchy names like Buy–write Option Unitary Derivatives (BOUNDS), Unbundled Stock Units (USUs), Structured Upside Participating Equity Receipt (SUPERs), Pharmaceutical Exchange Notes (PENs) at Goldman Sachs, while PENs are Protected Equity Notes at Bankers Trust, Heaven & Hell Bonds, and Switch (As you like) Options.[1] And the list grows every day. There are still a multitude of opportunities to innovate in today's fast–moving financial markets. There are still many securities for FIs to design, market, standardize, and distribute.

A wise philosopher once said, "Fish for me, and I'll eat for a time. Teach me to fish, and I'll eat my entire life." You have been taught to fish in today's financial markets. Now, go out and catch a whopper!

---

[1] This list was compiled by Professor Jack C. Francis of Baruch College, CUNY.

GLOSSARY

Absolute priority rules The requirement that senior claimants must be paid in full before any cash is paid to junior claimants.

Account party The importer, for purposes of the letter of credit.

Accrued interest Interest due from issue date or last coupon payment date until *settlement date.*

Add-ons Noncompetitive bids by foreign public FIs to replace maturing issues that they already hold.

Adjustable rate mortgage (ARM) A floating rate loan pegged to some reference market interest rate, such as the Federal Home Loan Bank Board Index.

Adjustment credit Short term, often overnight loans from the central bank, available to banks experiencing unanticipated or seasonal *liquidity* problems.

Aggregate level of economic activity The economy's use of scarce resources to produce goods and services.

American depository receipts (ADRs) Negotiable receipts issued by U.S. FIs against shares in foreign companies that are held in custody for investors.

American option Option that can be exercised at any time.

Announcement time The time period between the beginning of the *go-around* and the execution of the orders for open market operations.

Arbitrage An opportunity to earn profit that does not require either risk or investment.

Asked yield Price offered by market makers to sell securities.

Asset-backed commercial paper A *commercial paper* offering that is securitized by a *portfolio* of diversified assets, often credit card or trade receivables.

Asset-based borrowing Loans that link financing levels with collateral based on the company's assets and operations.

Asset transformation The FI's creation of new financial securities by selling financial securities that are different from the financial securities it buys.

At market, or par, swap A swap that is priced so that the present value of all fixed payments equals the present value of all expected floating rate payments over the life of the swap.

At the money The option's intrinsic value when it exactly equals zero.

Auction rate preferred stock (ARPS) *Preferred stock* that resets the dividend rate periodically, using a Dutch auction method.

Automated clearing house (ACH) A national network to process small-value payments.

Automatic teller machines (ATMs) Systems that allow the electronic transfer of funds both within and between banks after normal banking hours.

Average yield The average of all accepted competitive *bids,* weighted by the amounts allocated at each yield for U.S. Treasury auctions.

Backwardation Condition whereby *spot prices* exceed *futures prices;* that is, the *basis* is positive.

Balance of payments The difference between the amount of money flowing into the country and the amount of money flowing out of the country.

Balloon maturity The portion of principal still unpaid on the maturity date.

Balloon mortgage A fixed rate *mortgage* that schedules a lump sum payment of principal at the end of a predetermined period of time.

Bank examination An on-site auditing of a *depository* FI to ascertain its financial condition and future prospects.

Bank holding companies Parent companies that own a controlling interest in at least one subsidiary bank.

Bank reserves The sum of vault cash and demand deposits at the Fed, the bankers' bank.

Bank run Behavior that occurs when depositors rush to withdraw their funds when they suspect the bank has a liquidity problem.

Bankers acceptance Short term liabilities issued by banks, often in conjunction with letters of credit supporting international trade.

Banknotes Domestic currency.

Barrior option A standard option that is rendered worthless if the price of the underlying asset reaches a prespecified price barrier.

Basis (*ch. 7*)   The number of days in a coupon payment period.

Basis (*ch. 18*)   The difference between the *spot* and *futures price*.

Basis point   One hundredth of one percentage point.

Basis risk   Unanticipated deviations between *futures* and *spot price* fluctuations; that is, unanticipated shifts in the *basis*.

Basis swap   An interest rate swap between two floating rate indexes.

Bear spread   A *compound option* strategy implemented by buying the *out of the money* call and simultaneously selling the *at the money* call; a short hedge.

Bearer bonds   Bonds on which periodic interest payments are made upon presentation of coupon clipped from the bond by the bearer.

Bearer securities   Securities that are not registered to any owner upon issuance.

Benchmark bond   A liquid Japanese government bond issue (usually the most recent issue) chosen by the Big Four Japanese security houses (Yamaichi, Daiwa, Fuji, and Nomura).

Beneficiary   The exporter, for the purposes of the *letter of credit*.

Beta   The *correlation coefficient* that measures the sensitivity of security returns to fluctuations in market returns; denoted β.

Bid   Price offered by *market maker* to buy securities.

Big Bang   Deregulation of British security markets on October 27, 1986.

Bilateral net credit limit   A cap on exposure vis-à-vis each other FI on the network.

Bilateral netting   A *settlement* method that requires a single end-of-day net settlement of the entire day's transactions in each currency between each pair of *counterparties*.

Binomial interest rate tree   Valuation method that depicts interest rates over time if, at each discrete time period (called a node) there are only two equally likely possibilities: increase or decrease by the same amount.

Binomial option pricing model   A model assuming that prices can go either up or down, in each period, by a fixed amount, with a set probability.

Blue Sky laws   Laws that prohibit the FI from making misleading or false claims.

Bond covenants   Conditions, requirements, or restrictions that are imposed on bond issuers for the protection of bondholders.

Book-entry bonds   Bonds registered to a specific owner so that ownership and any payments can be automatically transferred electronically.

Book-entry depository   A specialized FI that accepts securities for safekeeping and maintains transferable accounts of those securities.

Book-entry securities   The names of all security owners recorded in a computerized database.

Book value accounting methods   Methods that value assets and liabilities on the basis of historical acquisition costs.

Bootstrapping   A method using the rates on more liquid coupon, par value instruments to construct a spot yield curve.

Bought as sold   The marketing of the *commercial paper* issue by the dealer and transfer of the proceeds of the sale, less commissions, to the issuer, providing no risk hedging services.

Bought deal   Innovation whereby the terms of the bond issue (coupon rate, size, and price) are set prior to the announcement of the issue instead of on the formal offering day, usually two weeks later.

Brady bonds   Defaulted sovereign debt that is restructured so that it is partially secured by a *portfolio* of U.S. *Treasury bonds,* with the remainder of payments paid like equity as a residual.

Bridge loans   Short maturity loans offered by FIs as a stopgap measure until permanent financing can be arranged.

Broken date   Nonstandard date for Forward Rate Agreements; that is, other than 3, 6, 9, and 12 month maturities.

Broker   A FI that brings together buyers and sellers without acting as a principal in the transaction.

Budget line   A line showing all possible combinations of current and future cash flows.

Bull spread   A *compound option* strategy implemented by buying *at the money* calls, while simultaneously selling *out of the money* calls in order to implement a less expensive long hedge.

Bullet bond   A bond that pays interest only during the life of the bond and repays the entire principal in one lump sum at the bond's maturity date.

Bunds   German government bonds.

Butterfly spread   A *compound option* strategy implemented by selling one call with a low *exercise price* (*in the money*), while simultaneously buying two calls with an intermediate exercise price (*at the money*) in order to implement a *hedge* against extreme price movements, up or down.

Calendar spread   The difference between the rates on two identical futures contracts with different delivery dates.

Call money   Nonnegotiable Eurocurrency deposits without fixed maturity dates that can be withdrawn at any time.

Call option   The right, not the obligation, to buy some underlying asset at some predetermined price at or before some predetermined date.

Call premium   The difference between the call price and the par value of the bond.

Call reports   Quarterly balance sheet and income statements that must be submitted to federal regulators of all *depository* FIs in the United States.

Call through   A noncontinuous auction during which all issues are called once or twice a day.

Callable bonds   Straight bonds with an embedded call option retained by the issuer.

CAMEL rating   A bank rating scheme based on a scale of 1 (best) to 5.

Canadian bills   Canadian Treasury bills denominated in U.S. dollars.

Cap   A multiperiod interest rate put (portion of the collar) that acts as a short hedge against interest rate increases.

Capital   The investment made by shareholders and other long-term stockholders in the FI.

Capital account   Record of all international borrowing and lending flows.

Capital–asset ratio   The minimum acceptable percentage of total assets that must be held in the form of equity capital.

Capital controls   Limitations on the unrestricted movement of financial flows across countries.

Carry   The difference between the lending rate and the borrowing rate.

Carry period   The financing period during which the securities investment is funded using some form of debt.

Carrying charges   The relevant interest expenses, storage costs, and depreciation charges that affect the asset underlying the futures contract.

Carveout divestiture   A divestiture of assets that is used to raise additional funds for the firm's operations by selling equity to a new group of *shareholders,* subject to strict disclosure requirements by the SEC.

Cash and carry transactions   Simultaneous transactions in the *spot* and *futures market.*

Cash management bills   Short term *Treasury bills* that are issued to fill the Treasury's cash needs just before the receipt of tax payments.

Cash settlement   The practice of determining upon delivery date, the value of the contract determined in cash only, not securities.

Certificate of deposit (CDs)   Negotiable *deposits* with a fixed time until maturity.

Chapter 11   A formal, legal stage during which the firm obtains protection from its creditors so that it can reorganize and ultimately emerge solvent.

Chapter 7   The court-administered liquidation proceedings for firms that have no hope of recovery.

Check truncation   Technological advance that allows a digital image of a check to be transmitted from the payee's bank to payor's bank, thereby eliminating the need to transport the physical check.

Circuit breakers   Automatic halts or limitations in trading that are triggered upon the attainment of certain stipulated price moves.

Classified assets   Nonperforming assets that are not yielding the contractually obligated cash flows.

Cleared transactions   Transactions that have been settled.

Clearing bank   A bank with direct access to *Fedwire* or other electronic payment systems that maintains cash and securities accounts at the Fed on behalf of its customers.

Collar   A *compound option* strategy implemented by buying an *out of the money* put and selling an *out of the money* call in order to implement a less expensive short hedge.

Collateral trust bonds   Bonds backed by specific assets that are pledged as collateral to repay a specific bond issue.

Collateralized mortgage obligations (CMOs)   Mortgage *pass-throughs* that divide the pool of underlying *mortgages* into different maturity classes with different risk/return characteristics.

Commercial and industrial loans   Loans to businesses.

Commercial paper   Short term (fewer than 270 days to maturity when issued) unsecured debt instruments.

Commitments   Promises that are exercised when the party who made the promise is required to carry out the promised activities.

Commodity swap   A swap that converts a floating price tied to a specific commodity to a fixed price.

Common stock   An equity share that does not have a fixed dividend yield.

Compensating balances   The requirement that a borrower must hold a certain amount in a noninterest bearing account as a form of collateral for a loan.

Competitive bidder   A bidder in a U.S. Treasury auction who specifies both the amount of the security that the bidder wants to buy and the price (stated in terms of yield) that the bidder is willing to pay.

Compound interest   The rate of interest earned on principal, assuming periodic compounding—that is, reinvestment of previously earned interest.

Compound option positions   *Portfolios* comprised of different options.

Condor   A *compound option* strategy implemented by buying one put with the lowest *exercise price,* selling one put with a higher exercise price, selling a put with an even higher exercise price, and buying a put with the highest exercise price in order to implement a hedge against small price changes, up or down.

Conduit   The FI that gathers the *mortgages* into a pool and issues the *mortgaged-backed securities* (*MBS*).

Confidence interval   A range of outcomes such that there is a known probability that returns will fall within the given range.

Conforming mortgages   *Mortgages* that meet the *underwriting* standards set by the GNMA, FNMA, and FHLMC.

Conservatorship   The condition of a FI over whom a conservator has been appointed to manage or liquidate the incompetently managed, though not necessarily, insolvent FI.

Consortium banks   Banks that are owned by a group of other, usually large banks, that are well-established in their own domestic markets.

Constant prepayment rate (CPR)   Index that expresses payments over the regular contractually determined payments as a fraction of the prior month's outstanding principal balance.

Contagion   A condition that develops if a troubled bank's illiquidity could bring about subsequent financial distress at other FIs.

Contango   Condition whereby *futures prices* exceed *spot prices;* that is, the *basis* is negative.

Convertible Eurobonds   Fixed rate *Eurobonds* that can be exchanged either for shares of *common stock* or currency.

Convexity   The degree of curvature of the price-yield relationship around some interest level.

Copayment   The amount of loss that is uninsured.

Core risk factors   The impact of systemic shifts in market conditions on the value of a *portfolio.*

Correlation coefficient   An indexed form of the *covariance* which ranges from a minimum value of -1 to a maximum of $+1$.

Correspondent bank   A large, regional bank that has a history of dealings with a smaller respondent bank.

Counterparties   The participants who agree to enter into a *financial transaction.*

Country funds   Investment *portfolios* whose shares are traded on American stock exchanges, but are backed by assets in foreign countries.

Country fund (*expanded definition*)   A closed-end mutual fund (see also *Trusts*) that trades as shares on the equity market at a price that may be greater than, equal to, or less than the *net asset value* of the fund's *portfolio* of a particular country's stocks.

Country risk exposure   The risk of a political upheaval that might hamper financial and goods flows.

Convergence   Movement of the *futures price* to the *spot price* upon delivery date.

Conversion factors   Numerical values published by the Chicago Board of Trade (CBOT) used to convert any deliverable bond's price into the price it would be if it yielded 8% p.a. during the delivery month.

Conversion price   The par value of the *convertible bond* divided by the *conversion ratio.*

Conversion ratio   The number of shares that the bondholder receives if the *call option* is exercised.

Conversion value   The market price of the *common stock* times the bond's *conversion ratio.*

Convertible bond   A bond that contains a provision that allows the bondholder to convert the bond into a predetermined number of shares of *common stock* of the issuer.

Covariance   The relationship between deviations from the mean for two different *probability distributions.*

Cover   The ratio between the amount of *bids* tendered to the amount of bids accepted; that is, the size of the issue.

Covered interest rate parity   The equalizing of cross-country yields by guaranteeing returns using forward foreign exchange markets.

Covered repo transaction   The combination of a *repo* loan with a securities transaction.

Credit crunch   Reduction in the overall availability of credit even for prudent investment.

Credit enhancement   Third-party guarantees of financial performance.

Credit risk   The extent to which unanticipated *defaults* on assets affect a FI's market value and profitability.

Critically undercapitalized banks   Technically solvent banks with equity less than 2% of total assets.

Cross currency swaps   Agreements between two *counterparties* to periodically exchange a given amount of one currency for another, at a given *exchange rate* and interest rate for a specific period of time.

Crosshedges   *Imperfect hedges* because the asset underlying the hedge contract is not the same as the underlying cash position that motivates the hedge and may have asset or maturity mismatches.

Cumulative default rate   One minus the *cumulative survival rate.*

Cumulative perpetual preferred stock   *Preferred stock* with dividends that are deferred and accumulated to be paid at some later date, if they cannot be paid on their due date.

Cumulative preferred stock   Stock requiring that any *preferred stock* dividend missed in the past must be paid in full prior to paying *common stock* dividends.

Cumulative survival rate   The mathematical expression of the probability that a bond did not default in its first year.

Currency cross rate   An *exchange rate* when both of the currencies are nondomestic.

Currency risk exposure   The impact of unanticipated fluctuations in *exchange rates* on the value of real and *financial transactions.*

Current account   Record of all flows associated with international trade in goods and services.

Current exposure or **replacement cost**   The marked to market value of the swap's cash flow.

CUSIP Identification number   Unique securities identification numbers assigned by the Committee on Uniform Securities Identification Procedures.

Customer MSPs   A *matched sale purchase* (*MSP*) that usually matures the next business day and is of smaller magnitude than the system RP (repurchase agreement).

Customer RP   A repurchase agreement (RP) that usually matures the next business day and is of smaller magnitude than the system RP.

Daylight overdrafts   Negative balances during the day, but a nonnegative balance at day's end.

Dealer   A FI that makes a market in a financial security, thereby participating as a principal in the *financial transaction.*

Dealer-directed   A method by which dealers make markets in *commercial paper* by buying issues for placement and may redeem notes before maturity.

Debenture bonds   Debt securities that are not secured by a specific pledge of property, but instead represent a general claim on all assets of the firm.

Debtor-in-possession financing   New debt issued to finance operations that is senior to all other debt issued before the firm entered *Chapter 11.*

Deductible or copayment   The amount of loss that is uninsured.

Default   Event triggered when a required coupon or principal payment is missed.

Defined benefit pension plan   The employer's assumption of the investment risk, since the payout is determined by a formula that is the function of the employee's salary history, not the investment performance of the fund's assets.

Defined contribution pension plan   The payout upon retirement determined entirely by the balance in the pension fund.

Delivery date   The prespecified maturity date of the futures contract.

Delivery option   An option that allows the *short position* to choose to deliver any one of several bonds against physical delivery on the U.S. *Treasury bond* futures contract.

Delivery versus payment   The settlement method in which securities and cash change hands simultaneously.

Delta   The rate of change of the option premium with respect to the price of the underlying asset.

Delta neutral hedge ratio   The reciprocal of the option's *delta.*

Demand deposits   Checking accounts.

Deposit insurance   A program that compensates depositors (either fully or partially) for losses in the event that the bank fails.

Deposit insurance fund   The government funds available to compensate depositors of insured banks that fail.

Depository   Storage for physical securities so that transfers can be made electronically.

Derivatives   Securities whose value is derived from the value of other financial securities.

Devaluation   The central bank's decrease of its currency's *exchange rate* in terms of gold or other currencies.

Diff swap A *basis swap* with one floating rate pegged to a domestic rate and the other leg to a foreign floating rate.

Direct placement The selling of *commercial paper* directly to *Funds Surplus Units,* which hold the paper until maturity.

Discount rate The interest rate charged to banks for borrowing from the central bank.

Discount window loans Loans by the central bank to depository institutions.

Discriminatory price auction Auction in which each bidder pays the *bid* price.

Diversification The combination of risky securities into *portfolios* so as to reduce the risk of that portfolio.

Dollar-denominated deposits Deposit of U.S. dollars in either a U.S. bank or a foreign bank in the United States.

Downside risks Unpleasant surprises, unexpected losses.

Dual trading system Members' execution of trades for their own accounts, as well on behalf of customers.

Duration gap A measure of the duration of equity computed as the difference between the durations of assets and liabilities.

Earned surplus Past retained earnings (net profits after taxes) that are not paid out as dividends.

Earnings credits Bank *reserves* that can be used to pay for Fed services but cannot be used to satisfy reserve requirements.

Easy money policy Monetary policy transaction to stimulate the economy by increasing the level of bank *reserves* through (1) decreasing the *discount rate;* (2) decreasing reserve requirements; or (3) buying securities (RPs) on *open market operations.*

Economies of scale Reductions in average cost as the size of transactions increases.

Edge Act corporations Separately incorporated bank subsidiaries that specialize in international transactions.

Effective convexity The value of *convexity* adjusted to include the convexity of any embedded options.

Effective duration The duration of the debt instrument adjusted to include the duration of any embedded options.

Efficient frontier The set of all *portfolios* that are not dominated by any other feasible portfolio.

Electronic Benefit Transfer (EBT) An *electronic payment system* that allows recipients of government programs to access cash benefits from special accounts established by the government at designated FIs or retail establishments.

Electronic funds transfer network A computerized system of payments for transactions.

Electronic payment systems Systems that require no physical delivery and instead use accounts held at central banks to settle transactions.

Endowment A financial starting point.

Equity capital Funds raised though the FI's sale of both *common* and *preferred stock.*

Equity margin requirements The percentage of stock price that must be paid for in cash as opposed to borrowings using the stock as collateral.

Equity premium puzzle The persistent overpricing of the risk premium on stocks.

Equity swap A swap that converts a fixed rate to a floating rate pegged to some equity index at predetermined dates.

Equivalent bond yield The simple interest yield on a *zero coupon* bond restated as a simple interest yield on a coupon bearing security.

Equivalent taxable yield The before-tax yield that would, if taxed, offer the same after-tax rate of return as the yield on the tax-exempt security.

Eurobonds Bonds issued outside of their country of origin that are denominated in *Eurocurrencies.*

Eurobook A *portfolio* of *Euromarket* assets and liabilities.

Eurocommercial paper A securitized short-term bearer note issued by a major corporation.

Eurocurrencies Currency deposits held in banks outside the country of the currency's origin.

Eurocurrency swap An exchange between two *counterparties* of either the currency of denomination or the form of interest (fixed versus floating rate) payable on debt instruments.

Eurodollars U.S. dollars held in banks outside of the U.S. or in international banking facilities in the U.S.

Eurodollar CD futures contract The obligation to buy/sell $1 million face value, 91 day Euro CDs at a predetermined rate called the futures rate on a predetermined date called the delivery date.

Euromarket *Financial transactions* that involve the issuance of financial securities denominated in a currency other than the home currency of the country of issuance.

Euronotes Short (often less than one year until maturity) to *medium term notes (denoted MTNs).*

European option Option that cannot be exercised prior to the expiration date.

Excess reserves or **free reserves**   *Reserves* over the reserve requirement.

Exchange rate   The price of one currency in terms of another.

Exchange rate intervention   The Fed's intervention in currency markets to adjust *exchange rates.*

Exchangeable bonds   Bonds that allow the bondholder the right to exchange the bonds for the *common stock* of a firm other than the *issuer* of the bond.

Exchangeable preferred income cumulative shares (Epics)   A type of *monthly income preferred securities (Mips)* that allows the security holder to redeem the Mips for the parent company's *preferred stock.*

Exercise or **strike price**   Predetermined price on an option contract.

Expectations hypothesis   The per period yield is the same across securities for all possible holding periods.

Expected (mean) value   The weighted average of all possible future outcomes, where the weights are equal to each outcome's likelihood of occurrence.

Expiration date   Predetermined maturity date of an option contract.

Extended credit   Credit granted to banks experiencing prolonged *liquidity* and solvency problems.

Fails   The consequence of either *counterparty's* failure to deliver on the transaction as agreed.

Fallen angels   Formerly creditworthy firms that, because of poor performance, have fallen below investment grade level.

Federal funds (FF)   Unsecured interbank loans of immediately available funds.

Federal Reserve float   The value of checks written, credited to the payee bank, but not yet collected from the payer bank.

Federally related FIs   Branches of the federal government that offer subsidized financing to specified sectors of the economy.

Federally sponsored agencies   Privately owned, publicly chartered FIs that carry only an implicit federal government guarantee.

Fedwatching   A preoccupation of market participants as each one tries to guess the upcoming Fed positions.

Fedwire   An *electronic payment* network that allows the transfer of cash and securities.

Fees   Distribution fees paid to the selling agents.

50 point collar   Provision that prohibits computer-assisted trading if the Dow rises or falls by 50 points.

Finance company   A FI, often a subsidiary of a manufacturing company, that funds loans to consumers who purchase the manufacturing company's products.

Financial distress   At a given point in time, the insufficiency of the firm's liquid assets to meet its obligations under its "hard" contracts.

Financial futures   Obligations to make or take delivery of some underlying financial asset at a predetermined price on a prespecified date.

Financial leverage   Firm indebtedness as measured by the ratio of either total debt to total assets or total debt to total equity.

Financial transactions   Agreements that entail the transfer of financial securities or cash from one party to another.

Firm commitment underwriting   The selling of notes by the issuer outright to the dealer for later resale, so that the dealer hedges the risk of interest rate declines for the issuer.

Fixed-for-floating currency swap   Combination of an interest rate and currency swap.

Flat price   The "clean price," the quoted price of a coupon bearing security excluding accrued interest.

Flex options   Exchange-listed options that can be customized with respect to *exercise price, expiration date,* and *settlement time.*

Float   The increase in bank *reserves* resulting from delays in check clearing.

Floating rate instruments   Debt instruments with coupon payments that vary with variations in some prespecified market interest rate.

Floating rate note (FRN)   *Euronotes* that offer a variable interest rate that is reset periodically (usually semiannually or quarterly) according to some predetermined market interest rate formula.

Floor   A multiperiod interest rate call that offers the holder a long hedge against interest rate decreases.

Forbearance   Laxity in monitoring the activities of troubled banks.

Foreign exchange expectation expression (FEEE)   The statement that foreign *exchange rates* are equal to the expected future spot rates.

Foreign exchange rate   The price of one currency in terms of another.

Foreign exchange rate risk   The impact of unanticipated *exchange rate* fluctuations on the FI's market value and profitability.

Forward contract   An over-the-counter futures contract that is not traded on an organized exchange.

Forward market   Deferred *settlement* transactions.

Forward rate agreement (FRA)   An over-the-counter Eurodollar CD futures contract, in which all the terms are determined by the two counterparties rather than being standardized by the futures exchange.

Forward yield curve   A graph that depicts the implied forward rates for different maturities on a specific date in the future.

Fractional reserve system of banking   The requirement that banks need hold only a small fraction of their deposit liabilities in the form of liquid assets available to meet the withdrawal demands of depositors.

Front running   The broker's purchase of shares ahead of large customer orders in expectation of ensuing price increases.

Full accrual price   The sum of the *flat price* and any *accrued interest,* "the dirty price."

Funds Deficit Units   Individuals, corporations, and governments that spend more than they currently earn.

Funds Surplus Units   Entities that spend less than they currently earn.

Futures commission merchant   A FI that executes or clears any futures contract approved for trading on an organized exchange.

Futures margin   A good-faith performance bond designed to guarantee the trader's compliance with the terms of the contract; *not* a downpayment.

Futures options   Option contracts in which the underlying asset is a *financial futures* contract.

Futures price   The predetermined price on a futures contract.

G-5 countries   The United States, Germany, Japan, France, and England.

G-7 countries   Germany, France, Japan, the United Kingdom, Italy, Canada, and the United States.

Gamma   The measurement of the impact of a change in the price of the underlying asset on the option's *delta.*

Generally accepted accounting principles (GAAP)   The rules of financial reporting required of all companies.

General obligation municipal securities   Securities used to finance the ongoing operations of the municipality, repaid using the tax receipts and other revenues of the municipal government.

Gilts   British government bonds.

Global   A bond that is issued simultaneously in several financial markets throughout the world and settled on *Euromarkets.*

Global depository receipts (GDRs)   Receipts issued by FIs in developed countries other than the U.S. against shares in foreign companies that are held in custody for investors.

Go-around   The process of obtaining market quotations for *open market transactions* to implement the Fed's daily program.

Gold standard   The fixing of the value of a currency in terms of gold.

Goodwill   The difference between the purchase price and the book value of acquired assets.

Graduated payment mortgage (GPM)   A fixed rate *mortgage* that allows monthly mortgage payments to increase gradually over the life of the mortgage.

Gross domestic product (GDP)   The sum total of the economy's production of goods and services.

Haircut   The function of a broker/dealer's securities portfolio that cannot be traded but must instead be held as capital to act as a cushion against loss.

Hausbank   A single bank used to satisfy most business deposit and investment needs.

Hedge fund   Fund that has an unregulated investment partnership; seeks high rate of return; takes *long* and *short positions;* uses leverage; and compensates management based on its financial performance.

Hedge ratio $\Delta P_S / \Delta P_F$, or the change in the *spot price* divided by change in the *futures price.*

Hedging   The process of investing in two sets of securities whose values move in opposite directions, thereby reducing the overall risk of the *portfolio.*

Herstatt risk   The risk associated with the fact that payment in one currency is finalized before the offsetting payment in another currency becomes final.

Hidden reserves   Capital *reserves* held by FIs in Germany, Switzerland, the Netherlands, and the United Kingdom, whose value is not revealed.

High-powered money   Bank *reserves.*

High-yield bonds   "Junk" bonds rated BB or lower by Standard and Poor's or Ba or lower by Moody's.

Holding period yield   The annualized rate of return over the expected investment time horizon.

Home equity line of credit   A loan commitment collateralized by the residual equity value of a home.

Human capital   Knowledge and expertise that makes a person a more productive worker.

Hyperinflation   A very rapid and extreme increase in the general level of prices.

IMM Index   100 minus the annualized *Eurodollar* futures rate in percentage form.

Immediately available funds   Funds in reserve accounts at Federal Reserve Banks that are available for immediate transfer.

Immunization   The balancing of the duration of assets and liabilities to eliminate any interest rate risk exposure.

Imperfect hedge   *Derivatives* transactions that would generate cash flows to offset the negative cash flows of the underlying cash position, but the offset would not be complete.

Implied repo rate   The interest rate on synthetic *repo* loans created by *cash and carry transactions.*

Implied volatility   The value of *spot price* volatility (σ^2) that sets the Black-Scholes formula value equal to the observed call option premium.

In funds   An expression meaning that the *commercial paper* issuer has raised all the funds it presently needs.

Index funds   Well diversified, passively managed portfolio with returns that mirror the returns of a large, broad-based portfolio.

Index participation shares (IPSs)   "Ownership shares" in an index of *common stocks.*

Indifference curve   A curve depicting the income combinations that maintain a constant level of satisfaction.

Inflation-indexed Treasury bonds   Debt obligations of sovereign governments that carry regular coupon payments that are fixed in real terms.

Information asymmetries   A situation in which one side is more informed than the other.

Initial margin   The amount that must be posted upon the origination of the futures position.

Initial margin payment   Upfront good faith deposit on a futures contract.

Initial public offerings (IPOs)   Equity issued by a firm that has never traded before in any public market.

Intangible assets   Assets that are not physical and cannot be sold without selling an entire firm.

Interbank placements   Short term (often overnight) interbank loans of *Eurocurrency* time deposits.

Interest amortizing rate swap   A fixed-for-floating interest rate swap with a condition that the notional principal declines over the life of the swap if short-term interest rates fluctuate according to a predetermined schedule.

Interest only (IO) MBSs   *Mortgage-backed securities* (*MBSs*) that strip off the coupon interest payments from the underlying pool of *mortgages.*

Interest rate parity (IRP)   Relationship that equates risk adjusted nominal rates of return on financial securities for different countries.

Interest rate risk   Impact of unanticipated changes in interest rates on the FI's market value and profitability.

Interest rate swaps   Agreements between two *counterparties* to periodically exchange two given streams of cash flows (for example, fixed-for-floating rate coupon payments) for each other.

International Banking Facilities (IBFs)   Subsidiaries of U.S. banks that only engage in international banking banking business.

International Fisherian relation (IFR)   Relationship that dictates the association between nominal and real interest rates across countries.

Intertemporal cash flow shifting   Cash flow transfers across time.

In the money   An option with a strictly positive, that is, greater than zero, intrinsic value.

Intrinsic value   The value of the option upon expiration.

Inverse floaters   Floating rate securities with coupon payments that are reset periodically to move in the opposite direction as a benchmark rate.

Issuer   The account party's bank for purposes of the *letter of credit.*

Japanese offshore market (JOM)   The Japanese equivalent of an *International Banking Facility* (*IBF*).

Knock-out, or barrier, option   A standard option that is rendered worthless if the price of the underlying asset reaches a prespecified price barrier.

Knock-out swap   A swap with an embedded knock-out option such that the swap is canceled if prices fall below a prespecified level.

Law of diminishing returns   The principle that the more you invest the less each additional investment dollar earns.

LEAPS   Long term Equity Anticipation Securities—options with two or three years until expiration.

Lender of last resort   The role of a central bank when it lends to private FIs that cannot borrow on private capital markets.

Less developed countries (LDCs)   Nonindustrialized countries in Africa, Asia, and Latin America.

Letter of credit   An agreement, by a bank (called the *issuer*), to pay a certain sum of money to an exporter (called the *beneficiary*) on the date that the goods are received at the specified location, with the additional agreement that the importer (called the *account party*) repay the bank so as to take title of the goods.

Letter repo   A *repo* that uses neither a third-party custodial agent, as in *two-party repos,* nor a third-party guarantor (as in *tri-party repos*); often called a "trust me repo."

Leverage ratio   The proportion of debt to equity.

Leveraged buyouts (LBOs)   Debt-financed acquisitions.

LIBID   The London InterBank Bid (as opposed to offer) rate.

LIBOR   London InterBank Offer Rate, which is an international money market interest rate.

LIBOR (*expanded definition*)   The average interest rate offered by a sample of eight Eurobanker or interbank placements of Eurodollars.

Liquidity   The ability to sell a financial security at its fair market value at any point in time.

Liquidity preference   The fact that, other things being equal, investors prefer securities with shorter maturities.

Limited liability   A condition in which common stockholders cannot lose more than the value of their stock investment.

Line of credit   A preapproved loan, up to a certain amount, in effect for a fixed period of time.

Load charges   Sales commissions charged either as front-end, upon the investor's initial purchase of mutual fund shares, or back-end, upon the investor's sale of the mutual fund shares.

Loan commitment, or **line of credit**   A preapproved loan, up to a certain amount, in effect for a fixed period of time.

Loan writeoffs   Losses resulting from defaults on loans that the bank does not expect to collect from borrowers.

London gold fixing   The official gold price setting.

Long position   An investment that represents an asset or a receipt of funds.

Long condor   A *compound option* strategy implemented by buying one put with the lowest exercise price, selling one put with a higher exercise price, selling a put with an even higher exercise price, and buying a put with the highest exercise price in order to implement a hedge against small price changes.

Long the TED spread   A long *Treasury bill* futures position and an offsetting short *Eurodollars CD futures* position.

Macaulay duration   The factor of proportionality that relates a given change in interest rates to an induced security price change.

Macrohedge   *Derivatives* transaction with the underlying cash position consisting of a *portfolio* of financial securities.

Main bank system   A relationship form of banking whereby close bank–firm ties are fostered by interlocking directorates and cross holdings of shares.

Maintenance margin   The minimum required margin that must be maintained in order to retain the futures position.

Managed float   A system of flexible *exchange rates* that are monitored by public FIs that may intervene to try to adjust currency rates.

Mandatory convertible debt   A debt issue that obligates the issuer to exchange the debt for either *common* or *preferred stock.*

Margin call   The requirement that the holder of the futures contract restore the value of the margin account to the initial margin level.

Marked to market   Crediting or debiting of each day's trading gains or losses to or from a margin account.

Market capitalization   Price per share times the number of shares outstanding.

Market conversion premium per share   The *market conversion price* minus the current stock price.

Market conversion price   The market value of the convertible bond divided by the conversion ratio.

Market discipline   Scrutiny by stockholders and other stakeholders based on financial information disclosed about the FI.

Market index   The return on a diversified *portfolio* consisting of a subset of securities representative of all securities available in the market.

Market maker   A FI who stands ready to buy and sell securities upon demand.

Market risk of loss   The adverse impact of *portfolio* value of unanticipated shifts in interest rates, *exchange rates,* and prices.

Market segmentation   Discontinuities in securities' prices that cause yields to be unequal across all holding periods.

Market value accounting methods   Methods that evaluate assets and liabilities at their current market prices.

Matched sale purchase (MSP)   The Fed's sale of securities to dealers who agree to sell them back at a later date.

Material-adverse-change clause   The right of a bank to refuse a loan on a *line of credit* if the borrower deteriorates sufficiently so as to jeopardize repayment to the lending institution.

Medium term note (MTN)   A schedule of notes with maturities usually ranging from one to ten years that are offered either continuously or intermittently over time.

Mezzanine financing   Intermediate term *medium term note* (*MTN*) programs.

Microhedge   *Derivatives* transaction with the underlying cash position consisting of a single financial security.

Midrate swap price   The cost of the swap to the swap dealer.

Mini-maxi FRN (collared floater)   A floating rate *Euronote* with both a cap and a floor on its interest rate.

Modified duration   Macaulay duration divided by 1 plus the interest rate; that is $D \equiv D/(1 + y/n)$.

Monetary aggregates   The supply of money.

Monetary base (high-powered money)   The sum of all bank *reserves* in the system.

Monetary policy   Manipulation of *monetary aggregates* or interest rates so as to achieve the macroeconomic policy objectives of full employment and stable prices.

Monetizing   The process of *stripping* the call from a *callable bond* to be sold separately.

Money center banks   Banks located in major money centers; for example, New York, Chicago, and San Francisco.

Money market mutual funds   Funds that sell shares of *portfolios* of short term money market instruments to Funds Surplus Units.

Money multiplier   The inverse of the *reserve ratio*, $1/RR$, that tells us the upper bound on the money creation powers of the banking system.

Money supply   The amount of money in circulation.

Monte Carlo simulation   An iterative process of security price evaluation based on the solution of security prices under different interest rate scenarios.

Monthly income preferred securities (Mips)   A *preferred stock* innovation structured so that the dividend payouts are tax deductible.

Moral hazard   A problem that occurs when one party has an incentive to shift risk onto an uninformed other party.

Moral suasion   Informal discussions used by central banks and other public FIs to convince private FIs to follow certain policies.

Mortgage-backed securities (MBSs)   *Pass-throughs* based on the underlying pools of *mortgage* loans.

Mortgage originator   The lending FI that initiates the *mortgage* loan.

Mortgage refinancings   New *mortgages* that replace previously issued, higher rate mortgages.

Mortgagee   Holder of the *mortgage;* that is, the lender.

Mortgages   Loans secured by real estate as collateral.

Mortgagor   The *mortgage* borrower.

Multilateral net credit limit   A cap on aggregate exposure to all other FIs on a network.

Multilateral netting   A *settlement* method that requires only a single end-of-day settlement in each currency for each FI, consisting of the FI's net transactions with the rest of the network.

Negative convexity   Condition under which the price appreciation is less than the price depreciation for a large change in yields.

Negative externalities   Result whereby individual actions impose costs on society not paid for by the person initiating the action.

Net asset value   The market value of the fund's *portfolio* divided by the number of shares outstanding.

Net currency exposure   The sum of all the *long* and *short* foreign currency positions in the *portfolio*.

Net exposure   The measure of swap credit risk exposure obtained by adding offsetting contracts' values.

Net replacement value   The cash flow loss in the event of *counterparty default*.

Netted settlement method   Method whereby the parties take advantage of offsetting transactions by waiting until the end of the day to settle the entire day's payments.

Netting by novation   Legal replacement of one net obligation for many individual transactions transferred over the network.

Newly industrialized countries (NICs)   Also known as the Asian Tigers such as Taiwan, South Korea, and Singapore.

Node   A discrete time period on a *binomial interest rate tree.*

Noncompetitive bidder   A bidder who specifies only the amount of the security that is desired, without specifying any price in a U.S. Treasury auction.

Noncumulative perpetual preferred stock   The same as *cumulative perpetual preferred stock,* but the dividends do not accumulate.

Noncumulative preferred stock   Stock that does not require the firm to make up past unpaid *preferred stock* dividends.

Nonelectronic payment systems   Systems that require the physical transfer of assets (either cash, checks, or securities) to settle transactions.

Non-Federal Reserve float   The value of checks written but not yet credited from the payee bank.

Normal probability distribution   A bell-shaped *probability distribution.*

Note issuance facility   A practice that allows the FIs in the RUF (*revolving underwriting facility*) issuing syndicate to bid, along with other potential buyers, for some amount of the *Eurocommercial paper* offering.

Notional value   The nominal face value of a swap, usually connoting hypothetical values, since these cash flows are often not exchanged.

OATs   French government bonds.

Off-balance sheet items   Contingencies that, under certain circumstances, may eventually become balance sheet items, but since they require no current cash flows, they do not appear on the balance sheet.

Off market swap   A swap with an inequality between the present values of cumulative fixed and expected floating payments that requires an up-front cash payment to balance the values of the two sides.

Offer price   Opening price for the newly issued shares in an IPO.

On-the-run issues   The most actively traded issues, usually the issue auctioned most recently.

Open account   The shipping of goods by the exporter with the good faith expectation that the importer will pay.

Open interest   Outstanding contracts.

Open market operations   The central bank's buying and selling of government securities to implement monetary policy.

Open outcry auction   The gathering of all traders at a designated spot to place their orders.

Open rate underwriting   A method that does not offer any risk hedging services, although the issuer re-ceives an up-front downpayment equal to some percentage of the face value of the issue.

Open repo   A repo with no maturity date, but which is renewed each day upon agreement of both *counterparties.*

Opportunity cost   The foregone return on alternative investments.

Option-adjusted duration   The price effect of cash flow shifts induced by interest rate changes to measure bond price sensitivity to interest rate fluctuations.

Option-adjusted spread   The premium on the bond's embedded option, expressed in yields.

Order flow   The right to execute customers' trades.

Origination fee   Up-front fee paid to *mortgage* originator.

Out of the money   An option with an intrinsic value that would be negative, if not for the lower boundary of zero.

Paid-in surplus   The funds received in excess of par value when a firm sells stock; often generated by stock dividends.

Parallel, or **back-to-back, loans**   Agreements between two firms in different countries, such that each company borrows in its domestic market and then lends those borrowed funds to the other firm.

Pass-through securities   Securities that represent shares in a pool of underlying loans.

Payment-in-kind debt   Debt that gives the issuer the right to meet interest payments by issuing additional debt.

Payments system   The means of making payment for transactions.

Pecking order hypothesis   Expectation that firms will use the least costly methods of financing first, moving to higher cost capital sources only after the others are exhausted.

Pension fund   A structured, tax-deferred fund that provides either a lump sum payment or an annuity upon retirement.

Perfect hedges   *Derivatives* transaction that is constructed so that the cash flows on the derivatives hedge exactly offset the cash flows generated by the underlying cash position.

Perpetual FRN   A floating rate *Euronote* (FRN) that has no fixed maturity date.

Perpetual preferred stock   Preferred stock with an infinite time to maturity.

Physical delivery   Settlement of a futures contract via actual sale/purchase of the underlying financial security.

Planned amortization class (PAC)   A *collateralized mortgage obligation* (*CMO*) that specifies a predetermined principle payment schedule.

Point   1% of the *mortgage* amount.

Point of sale   Systems installed at retail establishments that directly debit the amount of the purchase from an electronically accessed bank account.

Poison put covenants   A put feature that is triggered only upon a change in corporate ownership or control.

Political risk   The impact of unanticipated governmental actions on financial market returns.

Portfolio   A combination of investments in individual securities.

Portfolio insurance   A program that automatically rebalances a *portfolio* in response to market shifts.

Positive externality   Result whereby individuals whose actions benefit society are not compensated for them.

Potential exposure   Possible future changes in credit risk exposure, calculated by multiplying the swap's *notional value* by a risk factor.

Preferred equity redemption cumulative stocks (Percs)   Preferred stocks that pay dividends and automatically are converted into *common stock* at a conversion price and date.

Preferred stock   An equity security that carries a predetermined constant dividend payment.

Premium   The price of an option contract.

Prepayment risk   Uncertainty about the timing of cash flows for a *pass-through security;* the likelihood that *mortgagors* will decide to pay the balance on their *mortgages* before their maturity dates, thereby terminating their mortgages.

Prescribed right income and maximum equity securities (Primes)   Securities that entitle the investor to receive cash dividends plus voting rights.

Price bubble   Speculative excess that drives prices far above their fundamental values.

Price earnings (P/E) ratio   The stock price divided by earnings per share.

Price level adjusted mortgage (PLAM)   Constant *mortgage* payments for the life of the mortgage in real dollar terms.

Primary government security dealers   37 firms preapproved for trading with the Fed.

Prime rate   A rate set by banks that is used as a reference in pricing many loans.

Principal only (PO)   *Mortgage-backed securities* (*MBSs*) that generate cash flows equal to the principal amount on the underlying pool of *mortgages*.

Private FIs   Profit-seeking firms whose assets are predominantly financial.

Private placements   Unregistered debt securities that trade in limited secondary markets comprised of large institutional investors.

Privatization   Sale of state-owned enterprises to private owners.

Probability distribution   List of all possible future events and their likelihood of occurrence.

Production possibilities frontier   A concave schedule of investment returns that are subject to the *law of diminishing returns.*

Prospectus   A sales document that must be prepared before any financial security can be publicly sold.

Protective put   The combination of a long spot with a long put position.

Public companies   Companies with stocks traded on the New York Stock Exchange, American Stock Exchange, Nasdaq, or over the counter.

Public disclosure   The release of publicly available information about FI performance and risk exposure.

Public Securities Association (PSA) prepayment model   A model that combines the information in FHA prepayment history with the simplicity of the *constant prepayment rate* (*CPR*) method by assuming that the constant prepayment rate increases by a fixed amount each month (0.2% for 100% PSA), until it reaches its maximum after 30 months.

Publicly held corporations   Firms that issue stock that is publicly traded on an organized exchange or over-the-counter.

Purchasing power parity (PPP)   Sale of identical physical goods and services for the same price, whatever the currency of denomination.

Put-call parity   The combination of a long spot with a long put and a short call that obtains a *risk free* cash flow.

Put option   The right, not the obligation, to sell some underlying asset, at some predetermined price at or before the predetermined expiration date.

Puttable bond   A fixed rate bond plus a *put option* held by a bondholder that allows the investor to sell the bond back to the issuer prior to maturity at a predetermined price, usually set equal to par value.

Puttable common stock   A stock issue that allows the investor to sell the stock back to the issuer at a predetermined exercise price at a predetermined date.

Qualified Thrift Lender Test   Restrictions on thrifts to hold at least 65% of their assets in *mortgage-*related securities.

Quality spread differential   The premium that a lower quality borrower must pay over that paid by a higher rated borrower for funds of the same denomination and maturity.

Quanto swap   A *basis swap* with one floating rate leg and the other leg pegged to a foreign equity index, such as the Nikkei rate index.

Rate of time preference   The value, in terms of individual satisfaction, of accelerating the timing of future cash flows.

Real Estate mortgage investment conduits (REM-ICs)   *Pass-through* tax entities that pool *mortgages* and issue ownership interests to multiple classes of investors, primarily in the form of *mortgage-backed securities* (MBSs).

Real-time gross settlement   Final *settlement* of transactions as soon as they are received.

Realignment   The adjustment of the European Monetary System central parity *exchange rate* to bring a currency into compliance with its allowable trading bond.

Reallowance   A guarantee that will be paid to the *syndicate* FI if the bond was resold to the Bundesbank within one year at a price less than or equal to its issue price.

Receivership   The condition of an insolvent FI over whom a receiver has been appointed for protection of its assets and for ultimate sale and distribution to its creditors.

Reciprocal currency arrangements   Agreements that permit central banks to borrow currencies from each other up to a predetermined credit limit.

Reconstituting a bond   Reassembling the *STRIPS* (*Separate Trading of Registered Interest and Principal Securities*) components of a *Treasury bond* to re-create the original bond.

Red herring prospectus   A description of the offering without specifying an *offer price* for an IPO.

Regulation Q interest rate cap   Interest rate ceilings that set maximum allowable rates on bank deposits.

Regulatory accounting principles (RAP)   Financial reporting methods required of regulated firms such as thrifts and banks.

Regulatory arbitrage   The search of private FIs for the least restrictive regulatory environments in which to introduce their new products.

Regulatory dialectic   A cyclical process of regulatory and market evolution.

Relationship lending   Loans made at a lower cost to long term customers because, over the course of do-

ing business, the FI has gathered a wealth of information about their credit quality.

Renegotiation   Event marked by an optimal deviation from predetermined payout rules.

Reopened auction   The selling of additional shares of an outstanding issue at a later auction.

Replacement cost   The marked to market value of the swap's cash flow.

Repo book   A *portfolio* of *repo* transactions.

Repricing date, or roll date   The day on which interest rates on *floating rate instruments* are recalculated, using some specified current interest rate.

Repurchase agreements (Repo)   Fully collateralized loan where the collateral consists of marketable securities.

Reserve computation period   Period over which *reserves* are calculated.

Reserve currency   Currency used throughout the world as the basis for international trade and *settlement* of accounts.

Reserve maintenance period   Period over which actual *reserves* have to meet or exceed the required reserve target.

Reserve ratio   The minimum required fraction of *reserves* for each type of bank deposit.

Reserve requirement   The minimum level of *reserves* required as a cushion against the liquidation of bank deposits.

Reserve tranche   International Monetary Fund (IMF) lending tied to members' quotas.

Reserves   Bank holdings of vault cash and demand deposits at the central bank.

Reset date   The coupon payment dates on which cash flows are exchanged between the *counterparties*.

Reset debt   A debt whose interest rates are adjusted at fixed dates if the market value of the bonds falls below a certain level.

Residual claims   Capital securities that receive cash flows only after all other claimants (creditors and FIs) are fully paid.

Revenue municipal securities   Securities issued for a single purpose, such as building a bridge or power plant, and repaid from the revenue generated by the project.

Reverse coupon effect   Higher coupon Japanese government bonds that carry lower yields (higher prices) than equivalent maturity (duration) JGBs with lower coupons.

Reverse repurchase agreement (reverse)   The opposite of the *repo* used to borrow securities and lend cash.

Revolving credit   The practice of borrowing or repaying funds as desired, up to a maximum allowable credit line.

Revolving underwriting facility (RUF)   A commitment by a *syndicate* of banks to buy any notes that cannot be sold to other investors.

Rings   Informal groups of traders who deal in the same commodity and hold counterbalancing positions.

Risk free   An investment that contains no risk at all.

Risk premium   The differential over the *risk free* rate of return paid to compensate investors for risk exposure.

Rollover   Repaying maturing paper by issuing new paper.

Safety and soundness   The maximum allowed risk taking behavior permitted for regulated private FIs.

Safety net   Government benefits provided directly to private FIs to guarantee their financial viability.

Same-day settlement   *Settlement* that enables the payee's bank to present local checks to the payor's bank directly for payment in same-day funds.

Schuldscheine   Negotiable private placement of bank loans.

Section 20 subsidiaries   Investment banking subsidiaries of bank holding companies that can deal directly in "ineligible activities."

Securitization   The packaging of nontraded financial securities into a newly created tradeable financial security.

Seignorage   The profit earned on currency because the sum of the production costs and the intrinsic value (cost) of materials in the *bank notes* is less than their transaction value.

Sell short   The sale of assets that the investor does not own.

Seniority   Status whereby holders of securities are the first to receive payment according to the securities' contractual obligations.

Separate Trading of Registered Interest and Principal Securities (STRIPS)   Pure discount instruments constructed by detaching each individual coupon or principal payment from a *Treasury note* or *bond*.

Settlement or clearing   The *counterparties'* compliance with the terms of their financial agreement.

Settlement date   The date on which the transaction is cleared by completing the specified funds/securities transfer.

Settlement price   Either the closing price or an average of several of the last trading prices of the day,

computed by following some predetermined formula for futures contracts.

Settlement risk   The risk that a *counterparty* may be unable to make final payment.

Shareholders   Owners of *common stock;* the owners of the corporation.

Shelf registration   The SEC's preapproval of a security for later sale.

Short position   An investment that represents a liability or a payment of funds.

Short the TED spread   A *short position* in the U.S. *Treasury bill* futures contract and simultaneously a *long position* in the equivalent *Eurodollars CD futures contract.*

Simple interest   The rate of interest earned on principal, assuming no compounding.

Single-monthly mortality rate (SMM)   A monthly prepayment rate.

Sinking fund provision   The requirement that the issuer retire a specified portion of the principal in each year of the life of the bond issue's life.

Slippage   Failure to rebalance the hedge position to reflect changes in the *delta neutral hedge ratio* as the spot price changes.

Solvent   Having nonnegative net worth—the value of assets minus liabilities.

Sovereign government bonds   Bonds issued by a national government.

Sovereign ratings   The assessment of an independent agency (such as Moody's or Standard and Poor's) of the likelihood that a sovereign government borrower will default on its debt obligations.

Special claims on residual equity securities (Scores)   Long term call options on the Score holders that allowed the trust to purchase the shares from the trust at a predetermined price.

Special drawing rights (SDRs)   International Monetary Fund (IMF) reserve assets consisting of a basket of five international currencies that act as the IMF's unit of account.

Special-purpose vehicle (SPV)   A business entity established for the purpose of purchasing pools of receivables from participating companies and funding them with the proceeds from *commercial paper* issues.

Specialist sponsors   FIs, such as Forstmann Little and Kohlberg, Kravis and Roberts, that specialize in *leveraged buyouts* (LBOs).

Speculative position   Movement of the cash flows on the *derivatives* transaction in the same direction as the cash flows on the underlying cash position.

Spinoff   The divestiture of assets by distributing shares to existing *shareholders* with few disclosure requirements.

Spot markets   Transactions that are settled immediately upon arrangement of the financial agreement.

Spot price   The cash market price of the underlying deliverable asset for a futures/forward contract.

Stakeholders   Any party who benefits from the success of the company, for example, *shareholders,* bondholders, creditors, managers, and employees.

Standard & Poor's 500 Index Depository Receipts (SPDRs)   Index Participation Shares (IPSs) based on the S&P 500.

Standard deviation   The square root of the variance.

Standby letter of credit (SLC)   An *off-balance sheet,* contingent liability that commits the issuing bank to make payments to the exporter only in the event of *default* by the importer.

State and local government series (SLUGS)   Special low interest Treasury securities issued solely for municipal escrow accounts.

Stock index   A basket of stocks.

Stop-out price   The security price implied by the *stop yield,* that is, the highest rejected price, or the lowest accepted price.

Stop yield   The lowest rejected *bid* yield or equivalently the highest accepted bid yield.

Streaker bond   A *zero coupon Eurobond.*

Strike price   Predetermined price on an option contract.

Strip financing   Technique in which each owner holds both debt and equity.

Stripping   Separating the whole (the fixed coupon bond) into the sum of its parts.

Structured notes   *Medium term notes* (*MTNs*) combined with *derivatives* transactions.

Subordinated   Status whereby holders of securities receive their contractually obligated payments only after all senior claims are fully paid.

Supranational   A regional or international FI that transcends national boundaries.

Surplus notes   Long term notes issued by insurance companies with payments subordinated to all other liabilities, including policyholder claims.

Surplus value   The difference between a pension fund's asset value minus the present value of benefits owed to employees under the benefits formula.

Swap bid   The price of a swap to pay out fixed rate payments and receive floating rate payments.

Swap curve   A series of fixed rate *bids* for swaps of various maturities against the standard swap floating rate, six month *London Interbank Offer Rate* (*LIBOR*).

Swap offer or **Swap rate**   The price of a swap to receive fixed rate and pay out floating rate payments.

Swap spread   Difference between the *swap bid* and the *swap offer* rates.

Swaptions   Options on swaps.

Syndicated Euroloans   Bank lending of Eurocurrency deposits to nonfinancial *Funds Deficit Units.*

Syndicates   Groups of lending banks.

Synthetic pass-through   A security that is constructed to replicate the cash flows on the actual *pass-through security.*

System MSPs   A *matched sale purchase* (*MSP*) with a term of up to 15 days.

System repurchase agreement (RP)   A *repurchase agreement* with a term of between 1 day and 15 days.

Systematic risk   Market risk; the residual risk left over after all *unsystematic risk* is diversified away.

Systemic risk   The risk of *default* resulting from a breakdown in the global payments mechanism.

Systemic risk exposure   The risk that the failure of one participant may trigger a chain reaction that may lead to the collapse of the entire system.

T plus 3   "Trade plus three days," the time limitation allowed to settle securities transactions.

Tail (*ch. 11*)   The rate on the *tail bill.*

Tail (*ch. 15*)   The difference between the *stop yield* and the *average yield.*

Tail bill   The bill that is left uncovered after the period of financing ends.

Take down   The borrower's decision to borrow all or some of the balance on the *line of credit.*

Takedown risk   The FI's uncertainty about the loan quantity that will emanate from its loan commitments.

Tap offering   A continuous offering of *Eurocommercial paper* with different rates for different maturities, that is, an unrestricted *note issuance facility* (*NIF*).

Target variables   Empirical measures of macroeconomic conditions that are used as *monetary policy* goals.

Targeted stock (**alphabet** or **letter stock**)   *Common stock* that pays its holders an added dividend if a specified division performs well.

TED spread   The difference between the *Eurodollar CD futures* minus the U.S. *Treasury bill* rate.

Tender panel   A means of specifying the preset maturities and amounts that the *syndicate* could bid on under a *note issuance facility* (*NIF*).

Tenders   Sealed *bids*.

Tenor   Time until maturity.

Term   Time to maturity of the swap.

Term FF   Interbank transfers of immediately available Federal Reserve funds for a period of time exceeding one day.

Term premium   The extra yield necessary to compensate investors for a greater price risk upon liquidation.

Term repo   A *repo* with a maturity of more than one day.

Term structure of interest rates   The range of yields for securities with varying maturities.

Theta   The change in the option price as the time to expiration decreases.

Tick change   The direction of the last rate change, up or down.

Tick value   Minimum price movement.

Tiering   A price schedule by which riskier borrowers pay higher rates that contain *risk premiums*.

Tight money policy   *Monetary policy* transactions to cool off an overheated economy by decreasing the level of bank *reserves* by one or more of the following acts: (1) increasing *discount rate;* (2) increasing reserve requirements; (3) selling securities (*matched sale price*) on *open market operations*.

Tilt problem   A condition in which payments are higher in both relative and real dollar terms during the early years of the *mortgage*.

Time decay   The decline in the value of an option as it approaches its *expiration date* as its time value declines.

Time deposits   Nonnegotiable deposits with a fixed time until maturity.

Time draft   An order to the bank to pay a specified sum of money (set equal to the value of a shipment of goods) on a specified date to the bearer (the exporter).

Toronto Index Participation Shares (Tips)   Index Participation Shares (IPSs) based on the Toronto Stock Exchange Index

Trading pit   Designated spot for futures auction.

Tranches   Different maturity classes of *collateralized mortgage obligations* (*CMOs*).

Transaction account   A deposit against which the account holder is permitted to make an unlimited number of withdrawals using negotiable or transferable instruments such as checks.

Treasury bills   Pure discount obligations of the U.S. Treasury that have maturities less than or equal to one year.

Treasury bonds   Obligations of the U.S. Treasury that are issued with maturities that range from 10 to 30 years and that carry a semiannual coupon payment.

Treasury notes   Obligations of the U.S. Treasury that are issued with maturities that range from two to seven years and that carry a semiannual coupon payment.

Treasury tax and loan note accounts (TT & L)   Interest-bearing deposits issued to the Treasury by private banks.

Tri-party repo   A *repo* in which the collateral never changes hands, and the *clearing bank* simply segregates collateral for the term of the repo transaction.

Trusts   Closed-end mutual funds.

12b–1 fees   Distribution fees paid to selling agents.

Two-party repo with third-party custody   The safest form of clearing *repo* transactions, since the cash and securities actually change hands as in an outright purchase/sale of securities.

Two-way payment clause   A legal clause in a swap agreement that allows a solvent *counterparty* to terminate the swap if the other swap counterparty becomes bankrupt.

250 point rule   Provision that halts all trading for one hour if the Dow falls by 250 points in a day.

Undercapitalized   FIs with insufficient amounts of equity capital.

Underlying cash position   The cash market transaction that is undertaken simultaneously with the *derivatives* trade.

Underpriced IPOs   Initial public offering with a closing price on the first day of trading that significantly exceeds the issue price.

Underwriting   The process whereby the FI brings to market a newly issued financial security.

Underwriting risk   The risk that the FI will be unable to sell the new issue at a price higher than the price it paid.

Uniform price auction   An auction at which all bidders pay the same price.

Universal banking   The offering of a wide range of financial services, such as banking, insurance, securities trading, and *underwriting,* in one financial supermarket.

Unsecured   Unbacked by any collateral.

Unsystematic risk   Diversifiable risk; risk exposure that is company specific and can be eliminated by combining securities into *portfolios.*

Upside risks   Pleasant surprises, unexpected gains.

Value at risk   Maximum loss possible under 99% of the scenarios that may potentially occur over a two week period.

Value date   The date on which the security is priced.

Variance   A weighted measure of the possible deviations from *expected values* under all possible scenarios where the weights are the likelihood of occurrence of each scenario.

Velocity of money   The measure of the rate of monetary turnover; the number of times that the average dollar is spent in the course of the year.

Volatility smile   The increase in the volatility of the option as the option's strike price moves away from the money price, either *in* or *out of the money.*

Walkaway, or two-way, payment clause   A legal clause in a swap agreement that allows a solvent *counterparty* to terminate the swap if the other swap counterparty becomes bankrupt.

Warrant Eurobonds   Fixed rate *Eurobonds* that carry *warrants* permitting the bondholder to make subsequent purchases of either *common stock* or other bonds.

Warrants   Over-the-counter options issued by companies, usually in conjunction with debt or equity issues.

Weighted average coupon (WAC)   The *mortgage-backed security* coupon payment in which each *mortgage's* payment is weighted by its value in the pool.

Weighted average life (WAL) or **weighted average maturity (WAM)**   Weighted average time until the return of each dollar of principal.

When-issued market   A forward market that allows participants to buy and sell the security, with delivery taking place upon its issue date.

Wild card play   Trade that allows the short to give notice to sell the *Treasury bond* even after the futures market has closed and the price set; the seller can profit if *spot prices* have been falling during the time period after the close of the futures market.

Winner's curse   The low bidder wins acceptance of the *tender,* but pays a price that is higher than other lower *bids.*

Workout   A voluntary restructuring of the firm's assets and debt agreed to by all the firm's claimholders.

Yankee bonds   Bonds issued in the United States, denominated in U.S. dollars, that are the obligations of foreign *issuers.*

Yield curve   A graphical depiction of the current relationship between interest rates and time to maturity, holding all other factors (such as *credit risk*) constant.

Yield to call   The yield earned over the period of time from issue to first call date.

Zero coupon swap   An *off market swap* in which one of the *counterparties* makes a lump sum payment instead of periodic payments over the life of the swap.

Z tranche   A "pay in kind" collateralized mortgage obligation (CMO) accrual class, such that the interest earned by the Z tranche holders is transferred to a tranche currently receiving principal payments in exchange for more bonds.

APPENDIX A

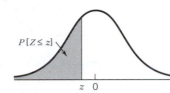

$P[Z \leq z]$

Standard Normal Probabilities

z	.00	.01	.02	.03	.04	.05	.06	.07	.08	.09
−3.5	.0002	.0002	.0002	.0002	.0002	.0002	.0002	.0002	.0002	.0002
−3.4	.0003	.0003	.0003	.0003	.0003	.0003	.0003	.0003	.0003	.0002
−3.3	.0005	.0005	.0005	.0004	.0004	.0004	.0004	.0004	.0004	.0003
−3.2	.0007	.0007	.0006	.0006	.0006	.0006	.0006	.0005	.0005	.0005
−3.1	.0010	.0009	.0009	.0009	.0008	.0008	.0008	.0008	.0007	.0007
−3.0	.0013	.0013	.0013	.0012	.0012	.0011	.0011	.0011	.0010	.0010
−2.9	.0019	.0018	.0018	.0017	.0016	.0016	.0015	.0015	.0014	.0014
−2.8	.0026	.0025	.0024	.0023	.0023	.0022	.0021	.0021	.0020	.0019
−2.7	.0035	.0034	.0033	.0032	.0031	.0030	.0029	.0028	.0027	.0026
−2.6	.0047	.0045	.0044	.0043	.0041	.0040	.0039	.0038	.0037	.0036
−2.5	.0062	.0060	.0059	.0057	.0055	.0054	.0052	.0051	.0049	.0048
−2.4	.0082	.0080	.0078	.0075	.0073	.0071	.0069	.0068	.0066	.0064
−2.3	.0107	.0104	.0102	.0099	.0096	.0094	.0091	.0089	.0087	.0084
−2.2	.0139	.0136	.0132	.0129	.0125	.0122	.0119	.0116	.0113	.0110
−2.1	.0179	.0174	.0170	.0166	.0162	.0158	.0154	.0150	.0146	.0143
−2.0	.0228	.0222	.0217	.0212	.0207	.0202	.0197	.0192	.0188	.0183
−1.9	.0287	.0281	.0274	.0268	.0262	.0256	.0250	.0244	.0239	.0233
−1.8	.0359	.0351	.0344	.0336	.0329	.0322	.0314	.0307	.0301	.0294
−1.7	.0446	.0436	.0427	.0418	.0409	.0401	.0392	.0384	.0375	.0367
−1.6	.0548	.0537	.0526	.0516	.0505	.0495	.0485	.0475	.0465	.0455
−1.5	.0668	.0655	.0643	.0630	.0618	.0606	.0594	.0582	.0571	.0559
−1.4	.0808	.0793	.0778	.0764	.0749	.0735	.0721	.0708	.0694	.0681
−1.3	.0968	.0951	.0934	.0918	.0901	.0885	.0869	.0853	.0838	.0823
−1.2	.1151	.1131	.1112	.1093	.1075	.1056	.1038	.1020	.1003	.0985
−1.1	.1357	.1335	.1314	.1292	.1271	.1251	.1230	.1210	.1190	.1170
−1.0	.1587	.1562	.1539	.1515	.1492	.1469	.1446	.1423	.1401	.1379
−.9	.1841	.1814	.1788	.1762	.1736	.1711	.1685	.1660	.1635	.1611
−.8	.2119	.2090	.2061	.2033	.2005	.1977	.1949	.1922	.1894	.1867
−.7	.2420	.2389	.2358	.2327	.2297	.2266	.2236	.2206	.2177	.2148
−.6	.2743	.2709	.2676	.2643	.2611	.2578	.2546	.2514	.2483	.2451
−.5	.3085	.3050	.3015	.2981	.2946	.2912	.2877	.2843	.2810	.2776
−.4	.3446	.3409	.3372	.3336	.3300	.3264	.3228	.3192	.3156	.3121
−.3	.3821	.3783	.3745	.3707	.3669	.3632	.3594	.3557	.3520	.3483
−.2	.4207	.4168	.4129	.4090	.4052	.4013	.3974	.3936	.3897	.3859
−.1	.4602	.4562	.4522	.4483	.4443	.4404	.4364	.4325	.4286	.4247
−.0	.5000	.4960	.4920	.4880	.4840	.4801	.4761	.4721	.4681	.4641

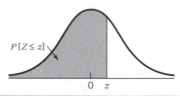

$P[Z \le z]$

Standard Normal Probabilities (Continued)

z	.00	.01	.02	.03	.04	.05	.06	.07	.08	.09
.0	.5000	.5040	.5080	.5120	.5160	.5199	.5239	.5279	.5319	.5359
.1	.5398	.5438	.5478	.5517	.5557	.5596	.5636	.5675	.5714	.5753
.2	.5793	.5832	.5871	.5910	.5948	.5987	.6026	.6064	.6103	.6141
.3	.6179	.6217	.6255	.6293	.6331	.6368	.6406	.6443	.6480	.6517
.4	.6554	.6591	.6628	.6664	.6700	.6736	.6772	.6808	.6844	.6879
.5	.6915	.6950	.6985	.7019	.7054	.7088	.7123	.7157	.7190	.7224
.6	.7257	.7291	.7324	.7357	.7389	.7422	.7454	.7486	.7517	.7549
.7	.7580	.7611	.7642	.7673	.7703	.7734	.7764	.7794	.7823	.7852
.8	.7881	.7910	.7939	.7967	.7995	.8023	.8051	.8078	.8106	.8133
.9	.8159	.8186	.8212	.8238	.8264	.8289	.8315	.8340	.8365	.8389
1.0	.8413	.8438	.8461	.8485	.8508	.8531	.8554	.8577	.8599	.8621
1.1	.8643	.8665	.8686	.8708	.8729	.8749	.8770	.8790	.8810	.8830
1.2	.8849	.8869	.8888	.8907	.8925	.8944	.8962	.8980	.8997	.9015
1.3	.9032	.9049	.9066	.9082	.9099	.9115	.9131	.9147	.9162	.9177
1.4	.9192	.9207	.9222	.9236	.9251	.9265	.9279	.9292	.9306	.9319
1.5	.9332	.9345	.9357	.9370	.9382	.9394	.9406	.9418	.9429	.9441
1.6	.9452	.9463	.9474	.9484	.9495	.9505	.9515	.9525	.9535	.9545
1.7	.9554	.9564	.9573	.9582	.9591	.9599	.9608	.9616	.9625	.9633
1.8	.9641	.9649	.9656	.9664	.9671	.9678	.9686	.9693	.9699	.9706
1.9	.9713	.9719	.9726	.9732	.9738	.9744	.9750	.9756	.9761	.9767
2.0	.9772	.9778	.9783	.9788	.9793	.9798	.9803	.9808	.9812	.9817
2.1	.9821	.9826	.9830	.9834	.9838	.9842	.9846	.9850	.9854	.9857
2.2	.9861	.9864	.9868	.9871	.9875	.9878	.9881	.9884	.9887	.9890
2.3	.9893	.9896	.9898	.9901	.9904	.9906	.9909	.9911	.9913	.9916
2.4	.9918	.9920	.9922	.9925	.9927	.9929	.9931	.9932	.9934	.9936
2.5	.9938	.9940	.9941	.9943	.9945	.9946	.9948	.9949	.9951	.9952
2.6	.9953	.9955	.9956	.9957	.9959	.9960	.9961	.9962	.9963	.9964
2.7	.9965	.9966	.9967	.9968	.9969	.9970	.9971	.9972	.9973	.9974
2.8	.9974	.9975	.9976	.9977	.9977	.9978	.9979	.9979	.9980	.9981
2.9	.9981	.9982	.9982	.9983	.9984	.9984	.9985	.9985	.9986	.9986
3.0	.9987	.9987	.9987	.9988	.9988	.9989	.9989	.9989	.9990	.9990
3.1	.9990	.9991	.9991	.9991	.9992	.9992	.9992	.9992	.9993	.9993
3.2	.9993	.9993	.9994	.9994	.9994	.9994	.9994	.9995	.9995	.9995
3.3	.9995	.9995	.9995	.9996	.9996	.9996	.9996	.9996	.9996	.9997
3.4	.9997	.9997	.9997	.9997	.9997	.9997	.9997	.9997	.9997	.9998
3.5	.9998	.9998	.9998	.9998	.9998	.9998	.9998	.9998	.9998	.9998

INDEX